Treat this book with care and r

*It should become part of your personal
and professional library. It will
serve you well at any number
of points during your
professional career.*

Sixth Edition

Intermediate Accounting

comprehensive volume

Sixth Edition Revised By:

JAY M. SMITH, JR., PhD, CPA

Professor of Accounting

Brigham Young University

K. FRED SKOUSEN, PhD, CPA

Professor of Accounting

Brigham Young University

Published by

A56 **SOUTH-WESTERN PUBLISHING CO.**

CINCINNATI   WEST CHICAGO, ILL.   DALLAS   PELHAM MANOR, N.Y.   PALO ALTO, CALIF.

ISBN: 0-538-01560-8

Library of Congress Catalog Card Number: 76-21455

1 2 3 4 5 6 K 2 1 0 9 8 7

Printed in the United States of America

Preface

The sixth edition of *Intermediate Accounting — Comprehensive Volume*, revised by Smith and Skousen, is a significant revision of this textbook. Designed for a full-year course to follow the introductory study of accounting, it seeks to serve the needs of two groups: (1) economics, business, or management students who do not plan to go beyond the intermediate course and (2) accounting students who expect to continue their study on an advanced level. Each group must be familiar with the objectives of accounting and the principles that have evolved in response to the objectives. They must also possess a full understanding of the nature of the basic accounting statements and the limitations involved in their preparation. With such a background, the student who does not specialize in accounting can properly interpret the statements and reports that emerge from the accounting process. Likewise, the accounting major can make important progress in the study of accounting and can look forward to achieving a full accounting competence and ultimate admission into the accounting profession.

Important advances have taken place in both the theory and the practice of accounting since the publication of the fifth edition of *Intermediate Accounting*. Accordingly, the current edition has been totally updated. It contains all statements of the Financial Accounting Standards Board issued through December, 1976, including the extensive changes in accounting for leases described in Statement No. 13; the requirements for reporting financial information on a less than total company or segment basis presented in Statement No. 14; and reference to the FASB discussion memorandum, "Conceptual Framework for Financial Accounting and Reporting: Elements of Financial Statements and Their Measurement." Text discussion highlights current developments and focuses particularly on the challenges to currently accepted principles and practices and on the responses made to these challenges.

Special reference is made to the significant contributions to accounting theory and practice rendered in the last decade by professional and research groups. Prominence is given to the FASB's current developments and its interaction with the Securities and Exchange Commission and other regulatory agencies. Reference is made to the many publications of the American Institute of Certified Public Accountants, including the series of Accounting Research Studies and the statements and opinions of the Accounting Principles Board. The special studies and committee reports of the American Accounting Association also receive prominent attention. In addition, discussions include references to the latest tax laws and other legislation affecting current practice. Terminology, statements, and forms currently found in practice are used in the illustrations.

In the sixth edition, emphasis is placed on a blending of theory and current practice. For each topic in the text, the currently accepted position of the profession is clearly presented with numerous examples to help students grasp the essentials of the topic. Alternative views to the generally accepted position are explored and evaluated, and the dynamic nature of the accounting profession is emphasized throughout the text. As accounting has become more complex, the authors — having extensive teaching experience — have distilled the essential features of new pronouncements and have presented them with the clarity which has always been characteristic of this textbook.

Specific changes in the sixth edition are described in the following paragraphs.

● Two new chapters have been included. Chapter 16, "Accounting for Income Tax," combines in one chapter the discussion of intraperiod tax allocation, interperiod tax allocation, and operating loss carryback and carryforward under 1976 income tax law. This integrated presentation makes possible the introduction of such advanced topics as intraperiod tax allocation when tax rates change due to crossing over rate breaks and the alternative uses of the gross and net methods of accounting for interperiod tax allocation.

The second new chapter, Chapter 17, "Accounting for Leases and Pension Costs," provides proper emphasis for these two increasingly important topics. With the adoption of FASB Statement No. 13, accounting for leases was extensively altered. The essential provisions of this complex new statement are presented in a highly readable and understandable fashion. The accounting for leases by lessees and lessors under alternative lease terms is presented, including explanations for handling such complexities as unguaranteed residual values, implicit interest, and sale-leaseback arrangements. Updated and expanded coverage of pension accounting is included with consideration given to the implications of the Pension Reform Act of 1974. Present value concepts are used to clearly illustrate the differences between funding and accruing pension costs.

● Three new appendixes have been provided. With the inclusion of Appendix A, the authors recognize the importance of present value concepts in financial accounting. This self-contained, clearly written appendix presents both the concepts and applications of present and future value analysis. Applications of concepts are illustrated by accounting examples and sample problems, and they are reinforced by student exercises. The concepts of this appendix are incorporated throughout the text and end-of-chapter material. In Appendix B, selected specimen financial statements are reproduced; and in Appendix C, all official pronouncements, such as FASB statements and APB opinions, are listed. The contents of both Appendixes B and C are cross-referenced to text material.

● To assist students in their review and study of certain topics, selected chapter materials have been rearranged. For example, the review of basic accounting procedures has been condensed from two chapters in the fifth edition to one chapter in the sixth, and it is presented earlier in the text as Chapter 2. The accounting process from the recording phase to the summarizing phase is fully explained and illustrated. Changes in the form and content of the basic financial statements receive special emphasis. The use of this chapter is optional, depending upon students' needs. Students with a strong accounting background will find this chapter useful as a review for expanding their understanding of the basic accounting processes and for adding to their security in applying accounting fundamentals. Students without such a background will be able to acquire a firm foundation in basic theory and important experience in the application of such theory.

Furthermore, previous editions have separated accounting for bonds as an investment from accounting for bonds as a liability; but these two areas have been carefully integrated into one chapter, Chapter 15, in this edition. Similarities and differences in accounting for the two ends of the same transaction are highlighted.

Finally, treatment of accounting changes, including error correction, has been integrated into one substantive chapter, Chapter 22.

● Chapter 1, "Framework of Accounting: Basic Concepts and Principles," has been updated to include a discussion of the current organizations which influence accounting principles, such as the FASB, CASB, and SEC; material from the Trueblood report; and reference to the FASB "Conceptual Framework" study. The changing nature of accounting principles development is explored and evaluated. Full recognition is given to the development of the conceptual structure of accounting and those groups who have contributed importantly to this development.

● The inventory chapters, 7 through 9, have been carefully revised. There is a significantly expanded discussion of lifo inventory, including a description of the impact of lifo layers on specific goods and descriptions of the dollar-value-lifo and retail-lifo methods. Also included is an explanation of how to compute company indexes using either the double-extension or the link-chain method.

● The chapter on book value and earnings per share, Chapter 21, contains expanded explanations and examples to clarify the computation of primary and fully diluted earnings per share under varying conditions.

● Chapter 24, "The Statement of Changes in Financial Position," has been completely revised. A simplified work sheet approach to funds presentation is utilized.

● In Chapter 25, dealing with financial statements reporting price changes, the discussion of accounting for inflation has been amplified to cover all price changes, both specific and general. Discussions are presented on current value accounting and on recent proposals in the United Kingdom and by the SEC — proposals which are likely to have significant impact on the accounting model and the accounting profession.

Obviously, the preceding description of changes is not exhaustive. Modifications have been made throughout the text to make this revision as up-to-date as possible. Similarly, all end-of-chapter materials have been extensively revised. Each chapter concludes with a broad selection of new and revised questions, exercises, and problems. The questions provide a review of theory, while the exercises and problems offer practice in the application of theory to business-like situations. The exercises are relatively brief and require the application of the theory presented in the chapter, whereas the problems are comprehensive and require the application of the theory presented to date. Almost all of the chapters conclude with problems adapted from the CPA examination. Such problems have been selected because they represent a strong challenge to students and at the same time contribute importantly to their accounting growth and maturity. Carefully presented solutions highlight the steps students must take to solve the problems.

Those familiar with the earlier editions of this textbook will recognize that the time-tested, positive elements of previous editions have been preserved. The form, nature, and accuracy of presentations have been maintained. Changes have been incorporated only where needed to improve the usefulness of the text and to reflect that the accounting process is viewed not as a static process but as one that must respond to changes in the economic, political, and social environment.

The authors wish to thank the Financial Accounting Standards Board, the American Institute of Certified Public Accountants, the Securities and Exchange Commission, and the American Accounting Association for permission to quote from their various publications and pronouncements.

For the Sixth Edition,

Jay M. Smith, Jr.

K. Fred Skousen

Contents

1

Framework of Accounting: Basic Concepts and Principles

The basic economic problem facing each individual or business entity is the allocation of scarce resources among competing alternative uses. Because resources are limited and because there is uncertainty as to which alternative use of resources is best, each business entity is required to make decisions which have important economic consequences. As indicated in the following quotation, accounting assists in providing information which can be used in the decision process.

> Accounting is a service activity. Its function is to provide quantitative information, primarily financial in nature, about economic entities that is intended to be useful in making economic decisions — in making reasoned choices among alternative courses of action.[1]

Several important concepts are included in this definition of accounting. Accounting is a *service activity*. It is intended to fulfill a *useful function* in our society by offering to provide service to various segments of the economic community involved directly or indirectly with business entities. It is primarily concerned with *quantitative financial information* describing the activities of a business, rather than qualitative, judgmental evaluations of those activities. The output of the accounting system is intended to serve as an aid to users who must make *decisions* between alternative actions available to them. To the extent accounting information fulfills these goals, the accounting system is fulfilling its major purpose. Accounting is *utilitarian in nature*. It has developed to meet the needs of society. Accounting is also *dynamic*. As the needs of society and environmental conditions change, the techniques, concepts, and to some extent even the basic objectives of accounting must also change.

To insure that changes are orderly and in the right direction, it is important to consider questions such as the following: What is the nature and purpose of accounting? Who are the primary users of accounting information and what are their needs? What should be the reporting

---

[1] *Statements of the Accounting Principles Board, No. 4,* "Basic Concepts and Accounting Principles Underlying Financial Statements of Business Enterprises" (New York: American Institute of Certified Public Accountants, 1970), par. 40.

1

objectives underlying financial statement presentation? What is the essential nature of assets, liabilities, and equities? What valuation and measurement bases should be used in accounting? To what extent should the accounting model reflect current price changes?

The impression should not be left that these and similar questions have not been considered in the past nor that the traditional accounting model is without merit. Overall, accounting has served society well. However, continual modification and improvement of accounting is needed to keep pace with a changing business world.

This chapter provides an overview of the basic elements of accounting. The remaining chapters in the book not only consider how to apply the basic accounting concepts and principles, but also explain the theoretical issues relating to the concepts, although some of the issues are not fully resolved.

USERS OF ACCOUNTING INFORMATION

Users of accounting information may be divided into two major categories: external users and internal users. *External users* are those groups or individuals who are not directly concerned with the day-to-day operations of the business, but who are indirectly related to the business. They include absentee owners, creditors, potential owners and creditors, labor union representatives, and governmental agency employees. *Internal users* include all levels of management personnel within an entity who are responsible for the planning and control of operations.

Several branches of accounting have evolved to meet the needs of these groups. Two of the most important branches have been identified as financial accounting and managerial accounting. *Financial accounting* systems are primarily designed to provide financial statements to external users for their decision processes, although internal users also have access to the statements and use them in many of their decisions. *Managerial accounting* systems are primarily designed to supplement the financial accounting information for internal users, thus assisting them in reaching certain operating decisions. As businesses have become more complex, the availability of relevant information provided on a timely basis has become highly important to both classes of users. In order to meet these informational needs, companies have found it necessary to establish improved information systems. The increasing availability and use of business computers have resulted in vastly improved information systems that can provide more relevant and timely data than was possible heretofore.

This book is primarily concerned with financial accounting and thus places particular emphasis on the needs of external users.

GENERAL OBJECTIVES OF FINANCIAL ACCOUNTING

Financial accounting has been described as a system providing "a continual history quantified in money terms of economic resources and obligations of a business enterprise and of economic activities that change these resources and obligations."[1] This history has become increasingly important to the external user as the complexities of organizations and operations have made it more difficult to determine the position of a company and the results of its operations. The corporate form of business organization has contributed to this difficulty.

By its very nature the corporate form calls for extended and accurate accounting. It has permitted the accumulation of large amounts of resources by a single entity. In large corporations the investment and management groups are separated. Ownership interests are liquid and readily transferable. The number of investors having any first-hand knowledge of the activities of the companies in which they have an interest is small. Accounting becomes a major source of information concerning corporate financial status and progress for the investor. Accounting also becomes an indispensable source of information for a variety of purposes, including a report of stewardship accountability, for other absentee groups interested in an entity's activities.

If important economic decisions must be made by absentee owners, creditors, and other external users from statements produced by the financial accounting system, these statements should meet several general objectives. They should:

1. Provide information useful for making economic decisions.
2. Serve primarily those users who have limited authority, ability, or resources to obtain information and who rely on financial statements as their principal source of information about an enterprise's economic activities.
3. Provide information useful to investors and creditors for predicting, comparing, and evaluating potential cash flows in terms of amount, timing, and related uncertainty.
4. Provide users with information for predicting, comparing, and evaluating enterprise earning power.
5. Supply information useful in judging management's ability to utilize enterprise resources effectively in achieving primary enterprise goals.
6. Provide factual and interpretive information about transactions and other events which is useful for predicting, comparing, and evaluating enterprise earning power. Basic underlying assumptions with respect to matters subject to interpretation, evaluation, prediction, or estimation should be disclosed.[2]

Satisfying these objectives requires continual study of the needs of external users. Financial statements designed to meet the needs of the external user and the objectives listed above are frequently referred to as *general purpose statements*. They include statements disclosing financial position, the balance sheet; results of operations, the income statement; and changes in financial position, the funds statement.

---

[1]*Ibid.*, par. 41.

[2]Adapted from *Objectives of Financial Statements, Report of the Study Group on the Objectives of Financial Statements* (New York: American Institute of Certified Public Accountants, 1973), pp. 61–63; see also *Tentative Conclusions on Objectives of Financial Statements of Business Enterprises* (Stamford, Conn.: Financial Accounting Standards Board, 1976).

ACCOUNTING AND THE ATTEST FUNCTION

A special responsibility of some accountants is to attest to the reliability and fairness of accounting statements prepared for external users by other accountants. Some persons regard this as the most important role accountants can assume, a role giving them professional status. Accountants performing this role are called *auditors*. [1] They examine and review the statements prepared under the direction of management and issue an opinion as to how fairly the data in the statements are presented. The auditor thus adds some greater degree of confidence to the various segments of the business community which utilize and rely on such statements.

THE NEED FOR ACCOUNTING PRINCIPLES

If accounting data were used only within a company, management could prescribe the rules and procedures to be followed. If the rules and procedures were consistently and accurately applied, the resulting information could be used in the decision process without change. But many external users of financial statements use accounting reports in a comparative way. Company A is compared with Company B; Industry X is compared with Industry Y. As a result of this use, standards and guidelines are necessary so that accounting information can be compiled and reported in a manner that will enable comparisons to be made. These standards and guidelines are referred to most commonly as "generally accepted accounting principles."

Accounting principles are not static or unchanging. Many of them do not have universal acceptance, and there are frequently alternative procedures for recording identical events. Before accountants can either prepare financial statements for external use or engage in audits of management's external statements, they must have a working knowledge of these generally accepted accounting principles. Persons who rely on the financial statements in making decisions also need to understand these principles so they can better understand the nature of the statements as well as their limitations.

ORGANIZATIONS INFLUENCING ACCOUNTING PRINCIPLES

There have been numerous attempts by individuals and by professional and governmental organizations to establish fundamental accounting concepts and principles. These efforts have met with varying degrees of success. Before discussing some of the more important of these attempts, reference to the different accounting bodies who share the responsibility in developing principles is essential.

---

[1] In late 1974, the American Institute of Certified Public Accountants established a Commission on Auditor's Responsibilities to examine the present and future role of the auditor. The results of this study are expected to have significant impact on financial reporting and auditing.

**American
Institute of
Certified
Public
Accountants
(AICPA)**

The American Institute of Certified Public Accountants is the professional organization of practicing certified public accountants in the United States. The organization was formed in 1887 and was originally named the American Institute of Accountants. A monthly publication, the *Journal of Accountancy*, was first issued by the Institute in 1905, providing a means of communication concerning the problems of accounting and the challenges and responsibilities faced by the profession.

Certified public accountants (CPAs) are licensed by the various states. Although a uniform examination is prepared by the AICPA and administered twice each year throughout all of the states and territories, the individual states still set the educational and experience requirements for certification. Some states issue a CPA certificate upon passing the examination without any required experience; others require one to four years of experience before a certificate is issued. A number of states now require a bachelor's degree in business with an emphasis in accounting as a requirement for taking the examination. Some have proposed a five-year accounting educational requirement. Still other states have lesser requirements. For some time, the AICPA has exerted considerable pressure among the states for standardizing educational and experience requirements. The Institute has recommended that the states require a college program that includes a "common body of knowledge" specified by a special AICPA committee and eliminate the experience requirements for certification. More recently, the AICPA has suggested that Schools of Accounting, similar in concept to those of Law or Medicine, may be a desirable means of training professional accountants.

There are two groups within the states that assume responsibility for the professional activities of certified public accountants: (1) state boards and (2) state societies. The members of a *state board of accountancy* are normally appointed by the governor of the state. The state board is responsible for determining and regulating the admission requirements of new members into the profession. This responsibility includes administering the examination and evaluating the candidate's education and experience prior to the issuance of a certificate. Once a state board has approved issuance of a certificate, it must further determine that the appropriate regulations governing the use of the certificate are followed by those who are recognized as CPAs. These boards, therefore, have the power to issue and to revoke the CPA certificate.

The *state societies of certified public accountants* are responsible for meeting the professional organizational needs of the members in each state. State societies are presently independent organizations; however, they maintain close relationships with the staff of the AICPA. National committee assignments of the Institute, for example, are generally initiated by the state societies. Several state societies are also instituting continuing education requirements, often utilizing AICPA course offerings as one means of satisfying these requirements. While not all states have adopted mandatory continuing education requirements, there is a definite trend in that direction.

Neither the Institute nor the state societies can issue or revoke a certificate. They may admit and suspend members from their respective organizations based upon their own rules and regulations; however, they cannot prevent one from using the "CPA" designation.

Financial Accounting Standards Board (FASB)

The Financial Accounting Standards Board is completely independent from the AICPA. It is an organization representing not only accountants but also other members of the business community, such as financial analysts and business executives. The FASB is comprised of seven persons who serve as full-time, paid members of the Board. The Board members are assisted by an Advisory Council, by various members of task forces selected for each major project undertaken, and by a full-time staff of approximately 100 people.

The FASB is charged with the responsibility of establishing and improving financial accounting standards and reporting practices. It held its first official meeting in March, 1973, replacing the *Accounting Principles Board* (APB) as the chief accounting standard-setting body in the private sector. The history of how the FASB came into existence and a discussion of the procedures followed by the FASB in determining accounting standards is presented in a later section of this chapter.

American Accounting Association (AAA)

The American Accounting Association was known as the American Association of University Instructors in Accounting from 1918 until 1935, when its name was changed to its present designation. The AAA is primarily an organization for accounting educators, although others are admitted to membership. A quarterly journal, the *Accounting Review*, is sponsored by the AAA. Articles in the *Accounting Review* generally discuss matters of accounting theory as compared with articles in the *Journal of Accountancy* that are primarily concerned with matters of accounting practice. AAA committee reports and discussions of these reports are communicated to AAA members through the *Accounting Review Supplement*. Selected research projects are published by the AAA in the accounting research monograph series.

Although the AAA has a permanent executive secretary, its officers and committees rotate each year among the members. The AAA does not claim to serve as a majority voice for accounting educators. Its major role is to serve as a forum within which individual educators can express their views either individually or in specially appointed committees. Another important objective is to encourage and support research activity to add new understanding in the field of accounting.

Securities and Exchange Commission (SEC)

The Securities and Exchange Commission was created by an act of Congress in 1934. Its primary role is to regulate the issuance and trading of securities by corporations to the general public. The Commission's intent is not to prevent the trading of speculative securities, but to insist that investors have adequate information. Thus, the SEC's objective is to insure *full and fair* disclosure of all material facts concerning securities offered for public investment. The SEC may use its statutory authority to prescribe accounting and reporting requirements for all companies falling under its jurisdiction. This includes most major companies in the United States.

The regulations of the SEC require independent audits of annual financial statements. The SEC reviews both the reports and the supporting verification to ascertain compliance with the law. The principal governing acts of the SEC are the Securities Act of 1933 and the Securities Exchange Act of 1934. Although the SEC has the power to issue regulations declaring how corporations should report financial affairs to shareholders, it has, for the most part, relied upon the accounting profession, through the AICPA and FASB, to perform this function. In recent years, the SEC has taken some actions that have motivated the profession to accelerate its efforts to improve accounting practices and to achieve greater uniformity in reporting.[1]

Other Organizations　　Although the four organizations discussed here have traditionally exercised considerable influence upon the establishment of accounting principles, the influence of other groups has also been felt. The *Financial Executives Institute* (FEI), formerly the Controllers' Institute, is a national organization composed of financial executives employed by large corporations. The FEI membership includes treasurers, controllers, and financial vice-presidents. The FEI publishes a monthly journal, *The Financial Executive*, and has sponsored several research projects relating to financial reporting problems. These research projects have covered a variety of topics including the manner in which a company operating in a number of industries should report the financial progress attained by different company segments, the effect of price-level adjustments upon managerial decisions, the concept of materiality in financial reporting, and the accounting problems of multinational companies.

The *Cost Accounting Standards Board* (CASB) is another important standard-setting body. The CASB was established in 1970 by act of Congress and charged with the responsibility of setting cost accounting standards to be followed by contractors in negotiated defense contracts. The CASB has issued several standards; however, because of their restricted focus, to date these standards have had limited impact upon financial accounting in general.

Another influential group is the *National Association of Accountants* (NAA). This organization is more concerned with the use of accounting information within the enterprise than with external reporting, and thus has directed its research primarily toward cost accounting and information systems. Its monthly publication, *Management Accounting*, has traditionally dealt mainly with problems involving information systems and the use of accounting data within the business organization. Because a

---

[1]For additional information on the nature and workings of the SEC, see K. Fred Skousen, *An Introduction to the SEC* (Cincinnati: South-Western Publishing Co., 1976).

firm's information system can provide information for both internal and external users, the NAA is concerned about the relationship of accounting principles for internal reporting to those for external reporting.

Several societies of financial analysts have been formed. The most prominent of these groups is the *Financial Analysts Federation*. Admittance to this group is based upon a qualifying examination. Because financial analysts are a major user of external accounting reports, they are very much concerned with the present status of financial reporting. Members of this group have often been quite critical of corporate financial reporting practices and have continued to request increased disclosure of pertinent financial data.

DEVELOPMENT OF ACCOUNTING PRINCIPLES

Accounting was originally defined by the Committee on Terminology of the AICPA as follows:

> Accounting is the art of recording, classifying, and summarizing in a significant manner and in terms of money, transactions and events which are, in part at least, of a financial character, and interpreting the results thereof.[1]

The reference to accounting as an art does not rule out the fact that an accountant's work is practiced within a framework of fundamental doctrine. This body of doctrine consists of certain concepts, principles, and practices that have won acceptance within the profession because of both their logic and their proved usefulness. These principles in effect represent the response of the accounting profession to the needs and expectations of the various user groups requiring financial information. Again it should be emphasized that when reference is made to accounting principles, the term is not used to suggest natural laws of universal applicability but rather the body of standards that as of the time are considered to be good accounting practice. This concept is well described in APB Statement No. 4 as follows:

> Present generally accepted accounting principles are the result of an evolutionary process that can be expected to continue in the future. Changes may occur at any level of generally accepted accounting principles. . . . Generally accepted accounting principles change in response to changes in economic and social conditions, to new knowledge and technology, and to demands of users for more serviceable financial information. The dynamic nature of financial accounting — its ability to change in response to changed conditions — enables it to maintain and increase the usefulness of the information it provides.[2]

The evolutionary process followed and the primary groups involved in the development of accounting principles are described in the following sections.

---

[1]*Accounting Research and Terminology Bulletins — Final Edition*, "Accounting Terminology Bulletins, No. 1, Review and Résumé" (New York: American Institute of Certified Public Accountants, 1961), par. 9.

[2]*Statements of the Accounting Principles Board, No. 4, op. cit.*, pars. 208 and 209.

Development of Principles by the AICPA

The AICPA began to play a significant role in the development of financial accounting principles in the early 1930's. From 1932 to 1934, an Institute committee worked with the New York Stock Exchange in an attempt to establish some basic standards. From this committee came a short list of "accepted accounting principles" designed to improve financial reporting. The Institute continued to study financial reporting through various committees, and in the late thirties formed the Committee on Accounting Procedure. The primary responsibility of this committee was to prepare Accounting Research Bulletins (ARBs) establishing more detailed guidelines for reporting corporate financial activity. Between 1939 and 1958, fifty-one bulletins were issued. These bulletins covered a variety of matters. In some instances, the conclusions of newly-released bulletins were not consistent with those issued in the past. Furthermore, no serious attempt was made to relate the various topics studied into an integrated theory of accounting, although a consolidation of the first 42 bulletins was issued in 1953 as Bulletin No. 43.

During this same time period, a subcommittee of the Committee on Accounting Procedure continued to examine the terminology used in financial statements. The first terminology committee had been formed in 1920 by the Institute. Several of the ARBs issued between 1939 and 1952 dealt primarily with terminology. When the Accounting Research Bulletins were consolidated in 1953, the terminology bulletins were also consolidated into Terminology Bulletin No. 1. Between 1953 and 1958, three additional terminology bulletins were issued.

The progress of the AICPA in improving reporting practices through almost 20 years of publishing bulletins was not regarded by all parties as entirely satisfactory. Critics, both inside and outside of the profession, have felt there was a lack of sufficient research and documentation in the study and deliberations of the committees leading to the publication of the bulletins. Many of the bulletins, it was claimed, were either overly permissive or overly vague, which permitted the accountant wide discretion in applying the position taken in the bulletins. Some members of the profession preferred this flexibility; in fact, some felt it was absolutely necessary. Other members were of the opinion that the lack of a strong theoretical foundation and the resulting large number of alternative principles regarded as equally acceptable tended to undermine seriously the potential usefulness of financial statements.

The critics' voices became more influential, and a new organization was initiated by the AICPA in 1959. In place of the Committee on Accounting Procedure, the Institute adopted a dual approach in the development of accounting principles. One part of the program created the Accounting Research Division with a full-time director of accounting research. Research projects were developed by the staff and others who were asked to assist the staff. The results of the research projects were published in a series of *Accounting Research Studies* (ARS). The second part of the program provided that these studies were to be used by the profession as a whole and more specifically by a special board of the

AICPA referred to earlier as the Accounting Principles Board. The APB consisted primarily of practicing accountants who reviewed all evidence available on a given subject and were authorized to issue Opinions that served to replace or supplement preceding recommendations. Initially, the Board was composed of 21 members. However, the number of members and the composition of the membership varied after its creation.

Before an APB opinion was issued in final form, an exposure draft was made available to a wide variety of interested parties. This procedure has resulted in extensive discussion within the profession of proposed opinions, and in some cases opinions were substantially revised after comments on the exposure draft had been reviewed by the Board. However, some problems were not fully understood until after the issuance of an opinion. In some instances, this made it necessary for the Board to issue opinions that rescinded or amended all or parts of an opinion that had been released earlier.

The influence of the Accounting Principles Board was greatly enhanced in 1964 when the Council of the Institute unanimously adopted a set of recommendations which stated in effect that departures from the APB Opinions must be disclosed either in the notes to the financial statements or in the audit reports prepared by members of the AICPA. In 1972, this recommendation was effectively incorporated in the rules of conduct of the AICPA's Code of Professional Ethics.[1] As a result, official pronouncements are applied almost universally to financial reporting.

The Board, in some situations, authorized the issuance of Statements. These statements do not carry the authority of an Opinion. Statements were considered necessary when the Board felt it did not have sufficient evidence to recommend specific action but believed certain analyses or observations on accounting matters should be brought to the attention of its membership. For example, Statement No. 4 was a statement on the "Basic Concepts and Accounting Principles Underlying Financial Statements of Business Enterprises." The objectives of this statement were (1) "to provide a basis for enhanced understanding of the broad fundamentals of financial accounting," and (2) "to provide a basis for guiding the future development of financial accounting."[2]

Statement No. 4 was the first publication of the Board that established a general framework for the development of generally accepted accounting principles. In this statement the APB defined the environment of accounting as faced by the profession, and divided the basic concepts of accounting into (1) objectives, (2) basic features, (3) basic elements, (4) pervasive principles, (5) modifying conventions, (6) broad operating principles, and (7) detailed accounting principles. Members of the Board who prepared the statement benefited from earlier research studies of the Accounting Research Division and from publications of the

---

[1]See Rule 203, Restatement of the *Code of Professional Ethics* (New York: American Institute of Certified Public Accountants, 1972).

[2]*Statements of the Accounting Principles Board, No. 4, op. cit.*, par. 2.

American Accounting Association.[1] Many of the definitions, terms, and concepts contained in Statement No. 4 are incorporated into the material presented in the remainder of this book.

During the Spring of 1971, the president of the AICPA appointed two important committees. The first is referred to as the Wheat Committee and was charged with examining the process of establishing accounting principles. The committee was specifically directed to examine how the organization and operation of the APB might be improved or whether a new approach was needed. The recommendations of this Committee resulted in the replacement of the APB by the FASB.

The second committee was chaired by the late Robert M. Trueblood and was charged to refine the objectives of financial statements. The study group considered such questions as: Who needs financial statements? What information is needed? How much of the information can be provided by accounting? The basic objectives of financial statements presented on page 3 are adapted from The Trueblood Report.

With the dissolution of the APB and the establishment of the FASB, the AICPA formed its *Accounting Standards Executive Committee* (AcSEC). This is the Institute's senior technical committee authorized to speak for the AICPA in the area of financial reporting.[2] AcSEC is comprised of 15 CPAs. It issues Statements of Position (SOPs) which are more advisory than authoritative. Whatever support these statements receive is attained from general acceptance by the profession. They have no official status like FASB statements.

Recently, AcSEC has devoted most of its attention to emerging problems. In effect, AcSEC serves as a screening device for the FASB. As a problem emerges, AcSEC considers it and makes a recommendation as to whether the FASB should add the project to its agenda. If the FASB does not add it to its agenda, AcSEC has the option to issue a SOP on the topic.

Development of Principles by the FASB

As indicated, the FASB is now the official advocate for the accounting profession in the private sector. The FASB issues "Statements of Financial Accounting Standards" and "Interpretations" of those statements. The statements establish new standards or modify existing ones; the interpretations provide explanations and clarification for previously issued pronouncements, including those of the FASB's predecessors.

The FASB's standard-setting process usually involves: (1) the distribution of a *discussion memorandum* which analyzes the issues involved in a particular project; (2) the holding of a *public hearing* on the subject; (3) the issuance of an *exposure draft* of a proposed statement; and (4) the

---

[1]Special credit was given by the Accounting Principles Board to ARS No. 1, *The Basic Postulates of Accounting* by Moonitz, ARS No. 3, *A Tentative Set of Broad Accounting Principles* by Sprouse and Moonitz, and ARS No. 7, *Inventory of Generally Accepted Accounting Principles for Business Enterprises* by Grady.

[2]The Auditing Standards Executive Committee (AudSEC) is the AICPA's senior technical committee in terms of auditing standards.

adoption of a final *statement of financial accounting standard*. FASB Statements, APB Opinions, and ARBs which have not been superceded are among those authoritative pronouncements forming the basis for generally accepted accounting principles and reporting practices in the United States. Appendix C provides a summary of the statements, opinions, and ARBs currently in force, cross-referenced to the appropriate chapters where cited in this book.

In a relatively short period of time, the FASB has issued over 20 standards and interpretations, and has a full agenda of important topics under consideration. Many feel the leadership to be given by the FASB during the next few years is critical to the maintenance of a standard-setting body in the private sector.

Development of Principles by the AAA

The American Accounting Association has also had as one of its major objectives the development of accounting principles. The general approach of the executive committee of the Association has been to establish broad basic principles upon which financial reporting should be based. Five basic statements under a variety of titles have been issued by special committees appointed by the AAA. These statements have not attempted to cover all possible aspects of accounting theory. Rather, these statements have directed attention to areas where the committees have felt serious objections could be raised to existing practices. The statements were issued in 1936, 1941, 1948, 1957, and 1966. A number of statements of a supplementary nature were issued relative to both the 1948 and 1957 statements. Although each of the AAA statements made some impact upon the profession, frequently their conclusions were regarded by many accountants as too theoretical for practical use.

The 1966 statement, *A Statement of Basic Accounting Theory*, broke tradition from the earlier statements. Not only was it much longer and broader in scope, but it purported to develop a more cohesive framework underlying accounting data. The members of the committee preparing the statement attempted to specify what constituted accounting data. They established four standards that, in their opinion, should be found in all accounting information: (1) relevance; (2) verifiability; (3) freedom from bias; and (4) quantifiability.[1] Using these standards as a foundation, they also proposed certain communication guidelines and indicated how accounting information for both internal and external use could be developed in terms of these standards. A number of the concepts introduced in this statement were incorporated in Statement No. 4 of the Accounting Principles Board.

Development of Principles by the SEC

The Securities and Exchange Commission has made extensive contributions to the development and the expression of accounting doctrine by issuing rules and regulations relating to the reports to be filed by registrants and by rendering opinions on matters of theory and practice

---

[1] *A Statement of Basic Accounting Theory* (Evanston, Illinois: American Accounting Association, 1966), p. 8.

in its official decisions, reports, and its Accounting Series Releases (ASRs). The issuance of Accounting Series Releases by the Commission is intended to provide opinions on accounting principles for the purpose of contributing to the development of uniform standards and practices in major accounting questions.

To date there have been about two hundred Accounting Series Releases issued. Their major role has been to point out problems requiring some action by the accounting profession and to encourage research in establishing more universally acceptable accounting principles. In late 1975, the SEC began the practice of issuing staff accounting bulletins (SABs). The purpose of the staff bulletins is to provide unofficial interpretations of SEC releases and to describe practices followed in administering SEC disclosure requirements.

Summary of Developments of Accounting Principles   The progress made in defining the body of doctrine applicable to contemporary reporting has been highly important both to the accounting profession and to those who use the services offered by the profession. Practitioners, aware of standards having general support, are afforded guidance as well as a sense of security in their performance. The product of accounting is improved and at the same time tends to achieve greater uniformity and comparability. The reader of the financial report, familiar with the standards applied in its preparation, can view it with added confidence and compare it with other reports prepared within a common framework.

GENERALLY ACCEPTED ACCOUNTING CONCEPTS AND PRINCIPLES

Major objectives of this book are to present the theory underlying current accounting practice, to explain the alternative methods presently acceptable for recording transactions, and to develop the analytical ability required for one to evaluate the strengths and weaknesses of both present and proposed accounting alternatives. The theory in support of specific accounting procedures is discussed in the appropriate sections of the text. However, there are a number of basic concepts and principles that should be understood before the different classes and types of transactions are reviewed. These basic concepts and principles have had alternative terms applied to them: assumptions, standards, conventions, basic features, objectives, postulates, and axioms. Many frameworks of theory have been prepared attempting to classify concepts and principles into various categories. The first serious attempt by the Accounting Principles Board to do this resulted in the publication of Statement No. 4. In several of these frameworks, some concepts and principles are identified as being more basic than others. The APB referred to the primary factors that financial accounting should possess as *qualitative objectives*.[1] Other

---

[1]Similar concepts were labeled "standards" by the special committee of the American Accounting Association in *A Statement of Basic Accounting Theory*.

accounting concepts and principles are descriptive of conventions developed over time and partly dictated by the environment in which accounting functions.

In the remaining pages of this chapter, the reasoning forming the basis for several of the more important concepts and principles will be presented. The discussion is divided into: (1) *basic qualitative objectives* as outlined in Statement No. 4; and (2) *other basic concepts and principles*. The concepts and principles discussed in the second category are presented in alphabetical sequence to avoid any implication of priority in the theoretical framework. The set of principles included in this chapter is not intended to be an exhaustive one. Additional concepts and principles considered less general will be discussed in subsequent chapters.

Basic Qualitative Objectives

In order for accounting information to be useful, it must have certain qualities or characteristics. Seven qualities were identified by the APB in Statement No. 4 as being basic if financial accounting is to fulfill its service objectives. These qualities are:

1. Relevance
2. Understandability
3. Verifiability
4. Neutrality
5. Timeliness
6. Comparability
7. Completeness

The objectives listed are related to the broad ethical goals of society, goals of truth, justice, and fairness. These objectives must be achieved in financial reporting if the statements generated by the accounting system are to achieve maximum usefulness.[1]

Relevance. The Accounting Principles Board identified relevance as the primary qualitative objective. Information must be relevant to its intended use. If it is not relevant, it is useless regardless of how well it meets the other objectives. The objective of relevance is to select methods of measuring and reporting that will aid those individuals who rely upon financial statements to make decisions. Many critics of financial statements have argued that traditionally prepared statements are irrelevant to many decisions that must be made. An increasing amount of research is being conducted to evaluate this criticism. What information is required by those who must make a decision? How can current practice be changed to improve the relevance, and thus the usefulness, of accounting information?

In its statement in 1966, the American Accounting Association commented on the importance of the concept of relevance as follows:

> The accounting function should, under many circumstances, provide information with a high degree of relevance to a specific intended use although it may have little relevance to any other. When this is done, care

---

[1]*Statements of the Accounting Principles Board, No. 4, op. cit.*, pars. 85 and 86.

must be taken to disclose the limitations of the information to prevent the possible assumption of universal relevance. To have information used for purposes for which it has no relevance is likely to be worse than having no information at all. Not only may decisions be influenced wrongly, but the user may be diverted from an effort to acquire relevant information.[1]

Understandability. In order for financial information to be useful in a decision process, it must be expressed in terminology that is understandable to the user. Business transactions and activities have become increasingly complex. It is not always possible to describe complex transactions in simple terms; therefore, the user of the statements must attain a minimum level of competence in understanding the terminology used in accounting statements. However, the accountant has a basic responsibility to describe business transactions clearly and concisely.

Verifiability. Accountants seek to base their findings on facts that are determined objectively and that can be verified by other trained accountants. The APB in listing verifiability as an objective stated, "verifiable financial accounting information provides results that would be substantially duplicated by independent measurers using the same measurement methods."[2]

All accounting measurements, however, cannot be completely free from subjective opinions and judgments. Cash receipts and disbursements can be adequately supported by vouchers, and cash on hand is determined by count; full support and verification for this element and its changes are available. Findings here can be readily verified. Purchases of goods and services, as well as sales, are also generally well supported by evidence and subject to verification. There are a number of areas in accounting, however, where determinations must be based in part upon judgment, estimate, and other subjective factors. The recognition of depreciation is an example of the latter. But the degree of estimate can be minimized by the attempt to develop evidence lending objective support to conclusions. Verifiable determinations are encouraged as a means of reducing possible error, bias, or intentional distortion, and achieving an accounting that can be accepted with confidence.

Neutrality. Financial statements should not be biased in favor of one group to the detriment of another. This objective may conflict with the basic objective of relevance; however, the presumption of the Accounting Principles Board was that external financial reports are general purpose statements meeting the common needs of a wide variety of users. Specialized needs must be met in other ways. The qualitative objective of neutrality is similar in concept to the American Accounting Association standard "freedom from bias" and to the all-encompassing principle of "fairness."

---

[1]*A Statement of Basic Accounting Theory, op. cit.*, p. 9.
[2]*Statements of the Accounting Principles Board, No. 4, op. cit.*, par. 90.

The following observations were made concerning freedom from bias in the AAA statement:

> The standard of freedom from bias is advocated because of the many users accounting serves and the many uses to which it may be put. . . . It is conceivable that biased information could properly be introduced if it would aid one group without injuring the position of any other, but this conclusion cannot be reached with certainty in external reporting, where all potential users must be considered. Thus, bias should be avoided in external general purpose reports.[1]

Neutrality, freedom from bias, and fairness to all parties are terms that together describe an important qualitative objective of financial accounting information.

Timeliness. The meaning of the qualitative objective of timeliness is almost self-evident. However, it is so vital to the concept of usefulness that it must be explicitly included. Information furnished after a decision has been made is of no value. All accounting systems should be established to provide information to all users in a timely manner. In meeting this objective, financial statements must be prepared prior to the time an accountant can be absolutely certain as to the results of an entity's operations. The entity is an ongoing enterprise with many interacting activities. Thus, any attempt to measure the success of an entity at some point in time before its dissolution must rely heavily on estimates. Unless such estimates are made and reported, it is not possible for users to judge the success or failure of the entity during a given period. Decisions by investors, creditors, governmental authorities, managements, and others rely on these estimates. By convention, the year has been established as the normal period for reporting. Annual statements, as well as statements covering shorter intervals, such as quarters, have been provided by entities to satisfy the needs of those requiring financial information.[2]

Comparability. Comparability may be regarded as intra-comparability, or comparability within a single enterprise, and inter-comparability, or comparability between enterprises.

Consistency is an important ingredient of intra-comparability. In view of variations, such as the different procedures for cost allocation in measuring depreciation, the different approaches for pricing inventories in developing cost of goods sold, and the different forms and classifications for the presentation of operating and financial data, methods adopted should be consistently employed if there is to be continuity and comparability in the accounting presentations. In analyzing statements one constantly seeks to identify and evaluate the changes and trends within the enterprise. Conclusions concerning financial position and operations may be materially in error if, for example, accelerated depreciation is applied against the revenue of one year and straight-line depreciation

---

[1]*A Statement of Basic Accounting Theory, op. cit.*, p. 11.

[2]There is a definite trend toward increased disclosure of information in interim reports. See, for example, Securities and Exchange Commission, *Accounting Series Release No. 177*, "Adoption of Article 11A of Regulation S-X" (Washington: U.S. Government Printing Office, 1975).

against the revenue of the next year, or if securities are reported under long-term investments in one year and under current assets in the following year. Consistency in the application of accounting procedures is also recognized as a means of insuring integrity in financial reporting; the use of alternate procedures in succeeding periods opens the doors to manipulation of net income and asset and equity measurements.

This is not to suggest that methods once adopted should not be changed. A continuing analysis of the business activities, as well as changing conditions, may suggest changes in accounting methods and presentations leading to more informative statements. These changes should be incorporated in the accounting system and statements. But the financial statements should be accompanied by a clear explanation of the nature of the changes and their effects, where they are material, so current reporting can be properly interpreted and related to past reporting.

Inter-comparability, or comparability between enterprises, is more difficult to achieve than comparability within a single enterprise. A primary objective of external financial accounting reports is to provide information permitting a comparison of one company with another. This concept of comparability requires that like things be accounted for in the same manner on the financial statements. Basic similarities and differences in the activities of companies should be clearly apparent from the financial statements. They should not be influenced by selection and use of different accounting methods.

One of the greatest unsolved problems in accounting is the present acceptance of alternative accounting methods under situations that do not appear to be sufficiently different to warrant different practices. Much current research in accounting is directed toward identifying circumstances justifying the use of a given method of accounting. If this research is successful, alternative methods can be eliminated where circumstances are found to be the same. In the meantime, current practice requires disclosure of the accounting methods used, as well as the impact of changes in methods used when a change can be justified. Although this disclosure does not generally provide enough information for a user to convert the published financial information from one accounting method to another, it does provide information that will assist the user to determine the degree of inter-company comparability. The Accounting Principles Board recognized the importance of comparability and its related concept of consistency, and in Statement No. 4 declared:

> The Board ranks comparability among the most important of the objectives of financial accounting, . . . and is attempting to narrow areas of difference in accounting practices that are not justified by differences in circumstances.[1]

Completeness. The last qualitative objective enumerated by the Accounting Principles Board was completeness. This requires all financial accounting data meeting the other six qualitative objectives to be reported.

---

[1]*Statements of the Accounting Principles Board, No. 4, op. cit.*, par. 105.

This objective is frequently referred to in accounting literature as *full disclosure*. Completeness, however, does not mean disclosure of just any data. Too much data may be valueless to users if it does not meet the basic requirements of relevance, understandability, verifiability, neutrality, timeliness, and comparability. Excessive detail, descriptions, and qualifications may actually serve to obscure certain significant facts and relationships and thus impair financial presentations. A better term for full disclosure is *adequate disclosure* — disclosure meeting the needs and purposes of the users.

The importance attached to adequate disclosure is underlined in the Code of Professional Ethics of the AICPA. Rule No. 2.02a of this code provides in part:

> In expressing an opinion on representations in financial statements which he has examined, a member or associate may be held guilty of an act discreditable to the profession if he fails to disclose a material fact known to him which is not disclosed in the financial statements but disclosure of which is necessary to make the financial statements not misleading . . .

The objective of completeness calls not only for disclosure of all financial facts but also for the presentation of such facts in a manner leading to their proper interpretation. Care should be taken in developing data classifications, arrangements, and summaries, and in employing exhibits and supporting and supplementary schedules.

It may be possible to provide all significant financial information within the body of the financial statements through the use of descriptive account titles and supporting data developed in parenthetical form. Frequently, however, certain matters can better be handled by means of (1) special notes to accompany the statements, or (2) explanations in the auditor's report accompanying the statements. Whenever the data are not included in the statements, the statements should refer to such supporting material as representing an integral part of financial reporting.

Other Concepts and Principles of Accounting

A number of other concepts and principles of accounting have become widely accepted. These have not been regarded as being as basic as the qualitative objectives just discussed. They are frequently found to be the result of a combination of both theory and practice. As further knowledge is gained concerning the purposes and uses of accounting statements, new concepts and principles may become accepted. This is the evolving process characterizing the art of accounting.

The following accounting concepts and principles are discussed in the remaining pages of this chapter:

1. Conservatism
2. Continuity of life — the going concern
3. Entity
4. Historical cost
5. Income determination
6. Materiality
7. Quantifiability
8. Stable monetary measure

Conservatism. Alternative approaches may frequently be indicated in resolving certain problems relative to the measurement of financial position and progress. Generally accountants have felt they can serve business best by adopting a conservative approach — choosing the alternative with the least favorable effect upon owners' equity.

The doctrine of conservatism is illustrated in the application of practices such as the following: increases in the values of assets and anticipated gains are normally ignored until realized by means of sale; declines in asset values and anticipated losses, however, are normally recognized before a sale occurs. Inventories, for example, are normally valued at cost or market, whichever is lower. A market value in excess of cost is ignored or shown only parenthetically, recognition of the gain awaiting realization through sale; a decrease in market value, however, although not yet incurred through sale, is recognized. Again, certain expenditures are charged in full against current revenue despite the possibility of future benefits. For example, a large-scale advertising campaign may contribute to future revenues; however, in view of the indeterminate character of the contribution, conservatism would suggest no deferral but rather the recognition of the entire amount as expense.

A conservative approach in the measurement process may be desirable. However, the deliberate and arbitrary understatement of asset values or overstatement of liabilities simply to achieve conservatism on the balance sheet is hardly the appropriate application of this concept. There are instances when, as a means of arriving at conservative appraisals of business worth or business debt-paying ability, inventories have been deliberately understated, property and intangible assets have been reported at nominal amounts, and allowances for possible losses and future contingencies have been established and reported among the liabilities. Conservatism expressed in this manner results in financial statements that no longer serve to report a revenue-expense matching process. The understatement of inventories to achieve a conservative working capital position carries with it an understatement of current income; the current understatement of inventories results further in the understatement of cost of goods sold and the overstatement of net income in the next period. The arbitrary reduction of property items to report a conservative asset position results in the understatement of depreciation charges and in the overstatement of net incomes in subsequent periods; balance sheet conservatism here has been accompanied by a contrary effect on subsequent income statements. The recognition of fictitious liabilities to achieve a conservative owners' equity results in the misrepresentation of financial position until such balances are canceled; if payment of expenses in the future is applied against such liability balances, net incomes of these periods will be overstated. Departures from sound measurement procedures to accomplish balance sheet conservatism serve to distort net income and net asset and owners' equity measurements. Conservatism should be accepted only as a moderating and refining influence to be applied carefully to the matching process as a whole.

Continuity of Life — the Going Concern. When the future is unpredictable, one can only assume a continuity of existence and a business environment to follow similar to that in which the enterprise finds itself currently. The business unit thus is viewed as a *going concern* in the absence of evidence to the contrary. The continuity assumption is support for the preparation of a balance sheet reporting costs assignable to future activities rather than realizable values that would attach to properties in the event of voluntary liquidation or forced sale. The continuity assumption calls for the preparation of an income statement reporting only such portions of costs as are allocable to current activities. Obviously, the assumption of a going concern may be invalidated by future experience. Financial statements, then, should be regarded as of a provisional nature, with support for their conclusions still to be found in the events of the future. If business termination were anticipated, a *quitting concern* or *liquidation* assumption would be called for; the implications of such change of status would then require recognition.

In applying the assumption of continuity, the intent of management must frequently be recognized in problems of valuation and presentation. For example, if it is the policy of management to trade in automotive equipment at three-year intervals even though such equipment may have a materially longer life, the intent of management governs the allocation of cost. Or if management has taken steps to replace a currently maturing bond issue with a new issue, the maturing issue continues to be reported as noncurrent since it will make no claim upon current assets.

Entity. Accountants normally view the business enterprise as a specific entity separate and distinct from its owners and any other business unit. It is the entity and its activities that assume the focus of attention. The unit owns resources contributed by creditors and by its owners, whether sole proprietor, partners, or stockholders. The boundaries of the accounting entity may not be the same as the legal boundaries. The entity concept is most directly in conflict with the proprietorship concept under which the individual owner receives the focus of attention, and the owner's personal assets are not legally separated from the assets invested in the business venture.

Historical Cost. Accounting, as it is practiced today, is founded upon the *cost valuation principle*. The amount of money actually exchanged in a transaction is the amount used as a basis for the recognition of goods or services acquired. Cost represents a value regarded as definite and immediately determinable, and thus also satisfies the objectives of verifiability and neutrality. Its use is supported as a means of closing the doors to possible error, bias, or even intentional misstatement, and achieving an accounting that can be accepted with confidence.

The exclusive use of cost as opposed to alternative current value measurements has been questioned with increasing frequency in recent years. Several committees of the American Accounting Association have suggested that supplementary statements be provided to reflect current values for items such as inventory and long-term assets. In its 1966 statement, the AAA recommended that multivalued reports be adopted providing both historical cost data that had been verified by market transactions and current values that went beyond completed transactions to reflect the effects of the environment and possessed a high degree of relevance.[1] Advocacy of the current value approach has not been limited to committees of the American Accounting Association. The SEC in its recent ASR No. 190 adopted requirements for supplementary disclosure of selected current replacement cost information. In the United Kingdom, there are current proposals for an even more extensive departure from historical cost to a current value basis for accounting and reporting. Individual practitioners and some of the large public accounting firms have also recently become more vocal in maintaining adequate disclosures cannot be made unless current value information is presented.[2]

It is conceivable that in the relatively near future, the accounting profession will forsake the historical cost valuation principle in favor of some form of current value reporting. Before that happens, however, several important issues will have to be carefully thought through and many implementation problems resolved.

Income Determination. As has been previously emphasized, one of the chief functions of financial statements is to provide information that will aid users in evaluating the effectiveness of an entity in meeting its objectives. The income statement has been increasingly used to provide information assisting in this evaluation. The income statement is divided into two main categories: net inflows of resources from the profit-directed activities of an enterprise, referred to as *revenues*; and net outflows of resources from the profit-directed activities of an enterprise, referred to as *expenses. Net income* is the difference between these two categories.

The revenue for a period is generally determined independently from expense by application of the concept of *revenue realization*. Essentially, the realization of revenue is a timing problem. Revenue could be recognized at a number of points during the production and sales cycle of a product. The realization principle, however, provides that before revenue is realized (1) the earning process must be complete or virtually complete, and (2) an arms-length market exchange must have taken place.[3] Based upon these criteria, revenue is generally recognized at *the point of sale*, that is, at the point when an arms-length transaction between two willing and competent parties has been completed. Other points in the cycle are sometimes used because of the special nature of the transactions.

---

[1]*A Statement of Basic Accounting Theory, op. cit.*, pp. 30 and 31.

[2]For example, Howard Ross, a practitioner and partner in Touche, Ross, & Co., published a book in 1969 entitled *Financial Statements — A Crusade for Current Values*. In this book, Mr. Ross is in agreement with the multivalued statement approach advocated by the 1966 AAA Statement. More recently, Touche, Ross, & Co. has published a booklet entitled "Economic Reality in Financial Reporting" which provides a program for experimenting with a current value accounting model.

[3]*Statements of the Accounting Principles Board, No. 4, op. cit.*, par. 150.

Expenses for a period are determined by their recognition either directly against revenue or indirectly against revenue by association with the time period involved. This process has frequently been referred to as *the matching process.* Many allocations of cost are arbitrary because of the artificiality of attaching a cost to each unit of revenue and because of the uncertainty that remaining unallocated costs will contribute to the realization of future revenue.

It should be emphasized that since the point in time for the recognition of revenue and expense is identical with the point in time that changes in assets and liabilities are recognized, income determination is directly interrelated with asset valuation. Because of the importance attached to net income, a more detailed discussion of income determination is included in Chapter 4.

Materiality. Financial reporting is concerned only with information affecting the decisions to be made by users of the financial statements. Contrary to the belief of many readers of financial statements, the amounts reported in the statements are often not exact. For many decisions such exactness is not required. There is, of course, a point at which information that is incomplete or inexact does affect a decision. This point defines the boundary between information that is material and information that is immaterial. At the present time, there are few guidelines to assist the accountant in applying the concept of materiality. The accountant must exercise judgment as to whether a failure to disclose inexact amounts or certain incomplete data will affect the decisions of the users of financial statements.

The American Accounting Association Committee on Concepts and Standards Underlying Corporate Financial Statements comments on materiality and offers a criterion for judging materiality in the following statement:

> In the selection of classifications, in planning the extent of summarization, in giving emphasis to or omitting information, and in determining periodic net income, materiality is often a deciding factor. Materiality, as used in accounting, may be described as a state of relative importance. The materiality of an item may depend on its size, its nature, or a combination of both. An item should be regarded as material if there is reason to believe that knowledge of it would influence the decisions of an informed investor.[1]

Additional research is presently being conducted by the FASB to assist in defining and applying the materiality concept to situations encountered by accountants in their practice.[2]

Quantifiability. There are many kinds of information of interest to a person who wishes to be fully informed about a business. This information includes not only matters that can be readily measured, such as the number of machines in operation, the wages paid to employees, and the

---

[1]*Accounting and Reporting Standards for Corporate Financial Statements and Preceding Statements and Supplements* (Madison, Wisconsin: American Accounting Association, 1957), p. 8.

[2]See the FASB Discussion Memorandum, "Criteria for Determining Materiality" (Stamford, Conn.: Financial Accounting Standards Board, 1975).

amount of raw materials used, but also more subjective facts, such as the attitudes of the employees about their employer and their work, the motivation of management to achieve previously stated objectives, and the effectiveness of the research department. What types of information, or parts thereof, should be measured and presented by accountants if they are to fulfill their responsibility?

Generally, accounting attempts to reduce information to a common denominator so facts may be conveniently summarized. The monetary measure has traditionally been accepted as that common unit and is generally used in most financial reporting. The statement by the American Accounting Association in 1966 urged the money concept be broadened to include nonmonetary information that could be quantified. Measurements in terms of pounds, yards, and months could also be included as accounting information if they meet the other prescribed standards. However, if the information is to be included in the body of the financial statements, the data must be converted to monetary terms to permit aggregation. Parenthetical remarks and notes, however, may contain data measured in nonmonetary units and, indeed, must be provided if the principle of full disclosure is to be realized.

Stable Monetary Measure. The dollar is the common money denominator of financial accounting in the United States. Value changes in the dollar have traditionally been assumed to be unimportant. Accounting systems are designed to account for the use of given units of money, that is, their inflow and their outflow. Thus, the accounting systems tend to produce statements that summarize stewardship functions of management. Changes in the value of the monetary unit fail to assume importance when a historical cost principle is adopted that regards only the accounting for original dollars as important. However, many accountants have felt uncomfortable about the relevance of accounting information that is insensitive to changes in the value of the measuring unit. Although all accounts shown on the balance sheet are labeled dollars, they are not dollars of equal purchasing power. Accountants add these various dollars together as though the monetary units were stable. But when the value of the dollar fluctuates greatly over time, the stable monetary unit assumption obviously loses its validity.

Some countries, recognizing the need for reporting a stable unit, have adopted some form of *price-level accounting*. Although price-level accounting has been proposed from time to time by accountants in the United States, a strong movement to require price-level adjusted data has not materialized. In 1969, the Accounting Principles Board issued Statement No. 3 in which it concluded that statements adjusted for changes in the purchasing power of the dollar should be provided as supplements to the conventional financial statements. However, this recommendation has not been followed in practice. As indicated earlier, there is a current movement toward current value accounting which may or may not be coupled with general price-level adjustments. The nature of the problems involved are presented in Chapter 25.

CHALLENGES FOR THE FUTURE

The accounting profession has been criticized because of the weaknesses of current financial statements and the lack of a conceptual accounting framework. Among the major deficiencies attributed to financial statements are the following:

1. The balance sheet presents only historical costs; it does not reflect the current financial position or worth of a business.
2. The income statement tends to match current revenues and historical costs (expenses) rather than current costs.
3. The income statement does not reflect those increases in net asset values that are not considered realized, e.g., increases in securities or land values held as investments.
4. Financial statements do not show the impact of inflation.
5. Because alternative accounting procedures are often equally acceptable, financial statements do not always present comparable data for similar reporting entities.

Some accountants argue that most, if not all, of the above deficiencies of financial statements are the result of not having an established conceptual framework which is accepted by the accounting and business community. Such a framework should define: (1) the objectives of financial statements, i.e., their purpose and to whom they are directed; (2) the various accounting elements, i.e., assets, liabilities, capital, revenue, and expense; (3) the accounting valuation basis, i.e., historical entry value, market value, present value of future cash flows, or expected exit value; and (4) the extent and comparability of disclosures required by reporting entities. The framework should provide a basis for resolving many of the issues facing accountants today and should help strengthen the usefulness of financial information presented by business enterprises.[1]

Establishing a generally accepted accounting framework will not be easy nor necessarily provide a panacea for all accounting problems. Meeting user needs for financial information in an increasingly complex environment will continue to be a major problem for accounting professionals. Increasing governmental control and regulation of business and accounting is another challenge to be faced. Furthermore, accountants are being asked to assume additional responsibilities, e.g., the detection of fraud or the reporting of the social impact of enterprise activity. And these responsibilities must be performed in a manner which will maintain high professional standards and thus avoid legal difficulties.

The challenges facing the accounting profession are significant. They provide an exciting opportunity for future accountants to make important contributions to their profession and to society. Resolution of problems may not be easy, but it will be rewarding and it will certainly make a career in accounting interesting.

---

[1]For an analysis of the issues, see the FASB Discussion Memorandum, *Conceptual Framework for Financial Accounting and Reporting: Elements of Financial Statements and Their Measurement*, (Stamford, Conn.: Financial Accounting Standards Board, 1976).

QUESTIONS

1. How may accounting help in solving the basic economic problem of allocating scarce resources among alternative uses?

2. For whom should the general purpose external financial statements be prepared? What kinds of decisions are made on the basis of financial statements?

3. Describe the nature of information that general-purpose financial statements should provide.

4. Why is an attest function necessary in our economic environment?

5. The owner of a business is planning to sell and has requested a CPA to prepare statements for the information of prospective buyers. "Don't use your regular statements," the owner instructs the CPA, "because I want to get as much as I can. Make the business look as good as possible." Would it be proper for the CPA to prepare statements that are different from those ordinarily prepared for the client at the end of the year? If so, what form would they take?

6. M. Lowe, president of Lowe Enterprises, Inc., has read much in the business literature about the controversies over accounting principles. Lowe does not understand why the development of principles is important. Explain why it is important for the accounting profession to have a set of principles.

7. "Prescribed principles are hindrances to creative and flexible financial reporting. More misleading information is likely to be communicated as the rules of accounting become more rigid." Comment upon these thoughts.

8. Summarize the essential differences between the methods used by each of the following organizations in formulating accounting principles: (a) the AAA, (b) the AICPA, (c) the FASB, (d) the SEC.

9. Why is relevance considered the most basic of the qualitative objectives?

10. How can the quality of verifiability be measured?

11. What is the difference between consistency and comparability?

12. Some accountants have suggested that budgets and profit plans should be reported to external users. Evaluate this type of forecast statement in terms of each of the seven qualitative objectives.

13. Which of the qualitative objectives is most likely violated by each of the following situations? (Briefly support your answers.)

(a) A prospective purchaser of a company receives only the conventional financial statements.

(b) An investor examines the published annual reports of all companies in the steel industry for the purpose of investing in the most profitable one.

(c) A company uses the prefix "reserve" for a contra asset, a liability, and a retained earnings appropriation.

(d) A company reports all of its land, buildings, and equipment on the basis of a recent appraisal.

(e) Management elects to change its method of inventory valuation in order to overcome an unprofitable year from operations. This change enables the company to report a gradual growth in earnings.

14. Why is the concept of conservatism considered to have both favorable and unfavorable connotations?

15. If the entity concept were not applied, how would financial reporting differ for a sole proprietorship?

16. The historical cost concept has been seriously challenged. What deficiencies does it have, and what alternative measurement methods have been proposed to overcome these weaknesses?

17. What conditions must exist before revenue is recognized as having been earned?

18. Why is the materiality concept a difficult one to apply?

19. Identify the accounting principle or principles that are applied in each situation:

(a) A company uses the lower of cost or market for valuation of its physical inventory.

(b) An inventory delivery on the last day of the year was omitted from the physical inventory. No adjustment was made on the books for the omission.

(c) During the year, inflation of 5% took place. No adjustment for this change is made on the books.

(d) Product development costs are deferred as assets to be written off against future income.

(e) Albert Haws owns a laundry, a restaurant, and a bookstore. He has separate financial statements prepared for each business.

(f) The Metropolitan Construction Company prepares an annual statement reflecting the profitability of its contracts in process.

20. What is needed to give direction to the development of accounting principles and practices?

EXERCISES

1. Mr. Fence, a sole proprietor of a small store and an equipment rental shop, prepared the following income statement for 1977:

Sales	$40,000
Expenses	30,000
Net income	$10,000

An examination of the records of both operations showed that store sales were $30,000 and rent revenues were $10,000. Expenses consisted of the following:

Cost of goods sold (store)	$15,000
Other expenses (store)	2,000
Expenses (rental operations)	8,000
Living expenses of the Fence family	5,000
Total expenses	$30,000

(a) Indicate what changes, if any, you would make in reporting income for 1977.
(b) Give theoretical support for your conclusions.

2. Jane Roxey is impressed with her accountant's defense of conservatism in accounting and therefore suggests that the accountant currently make the adjustments indicated below. State your position on each item and give theoretical support for your position.

(a) Inventories are reported at a cost of $56,000. Roxey would report these at the lower of cost or market, $52,500.
(b) Goods that have been unsaleable for a five-year period have been excluded from the inventory and have been set aside in the warehouse with the hope that someone might buy them. They are carried at $5,000 and Roxey would write them off.
(c) An account receivable for $1,080 is carried with a customer that Roxey has not seen for more than a year. Roxey would write this balance off.
(d) Leasehold improvements of $15,000 were made by Roxey. However, these improvements will ultimately revert to the owner of the property on termination of the lease, and Roxey would write off the full cost currently.
(e) Cash surrender value on life insurance with a balance of $4,930 is reported among the assets. Since Roxey does not expect to make any claim on the policy until the maturity, she believes this balance should be written off.
(f) Goodwill of $45,000 had been recorded on the books currently when Roxey acquired a branch unit and paid this amount in excess of tangible assets acquired because of exceptionally high earnings of the branch unit. Roxey believes this asset is one that cannot be sold and therefore should be written off.
(g) Roxey is being sued for breach of contract in the amount of $8,500. No liability has yet been established on the books for this item. Although the court has not yet rendered a final decision, Roxey believes that the statements should reflect this potential liability. Roxey's attorney is uncertain as to the outcome of the suit.
(h) All goods are sold with a warranty for repairs and replacements for a six-month period. In the past, expenses for repairs and replacements were recorded at the time they were incurred. Roxey estimates that expenses for repairs and replacements still to be incurred on goods sold during the last half of the year will total $5,000 and believes that a liability for this amount should be reported.

3. The following items were reported in the machinery account on the books of the Barns Company in 1977. What position would you take on each item? Give theoretical support for your conclusions.

Date	Description	Debit	Credit
January 3	Costs of dismantling and removing old machine	$ 1,000	
January 5	Proceeds from disposal of old machine		$4,500
January 10	Invoice price of new machine	40,000	
January 16	Freight charges paid on delivery of new machine	1,200	
February 12	Costs of installing new machine	8,500	
February 12	Costs of labor, spoilage, etc., in test runs prior to actual use of machine	1,500	

PROBLEMS

1-1. For each of the circumstances enumerated below, give the letter item indicating the accounting objective attained or the principle applied.

(a) Understandability
(b) Verifiability
(c) Timeliness
(d) Comparability
(e) Completeness
(f) Conservatism

(g) Continuity of life — the going concern
(h) Entity
(i) Historical cost
(j) Income determination
(k) Quantifiability
(l) Materiality

   (1) Goodwill is only recorded in the accounts when it arises from the purchase of another entity at a price higher than the fair market value of the purchased entity's tangible assets.
   (2) A note describing the company's possible liability in a lawsuit is included with the financial statements even though no formal liability exists at the balance sheet date.
   (3) All payments out of petty cash are debited to Miscellaneous Expense.
   (4) Fixed assets are classified separately as land and buildings, with an accumulated depreciation account for buildings.
   (5) A retail store uses estimates rather than a complete physical count of its inventory for purposes of preparing monthly financial statements.
   (6) Marketable securities are valued at the lower of cost or market.
   (7) Marketable securities are valued at cost.
   (8) An advance payment of insurance premiums is reported as an asset.
   (9) A system of vouchers is used to account for all cash disbursements.
  (10) Small tools used by a large manufacturing firm are recorded as an expense when purchased.
  (11) Periodic payments of $1,000 per month for services of J. Roy, who owns all of the stock of the company, are reported as salary; additional amounts paid to Roy are reported as dividends.

1-2. J. L. Lode opened a retail store at the beginning of 1976. From informal records maintained, a comparative income statement for 1977 and 1976 was prepared as shown below.

	Year Ended	
	Dec. 31, 1977	Dec. 31, 1976
Sales	$ 81,200	$ 65,000
Cost of goods sold	46,500	52,500
Gross profit	$ 34,700	$ 12,500
Selling and general expenses	26,500	24,000
Net income (loss)	$ 8,200	$ (11,500)

You are called in to review Lode's records, and in the course of the review you find the following:

   (a) Lode has included in sales only amounts collected from customers. Receivables from customers on December 31, 1976, were $1,650 and on December 31, 1977, $2,600.
   (b) Lode has reported all purchases of goods for resale each year as cost of goods sold. No inventory was taken at year-end since the amounts would be approximately the same. You determine that the inventories had a cost of approximately $18,000 at the end of 1976 and at the end of 1977.
   (c) Advertising charges were assigned to the year in which the specific charges were incurred. Advertising charges totaled $6,000 of which $4,500 was incurred in the first year in view of the heavy promotion to inform the public of the store opening.
   (d) Acquisitions of furniture and fixtures were recognized as debits to general expense each year, since Lode believed that acquisitions would be more or less continuous during the life of the business. Furniture and fixtures acquisitions were $4,500 in 1976 and $3,600 in 1977. Furniture and fixtures had an estimated life of 10 years.
   (e) Lode withdrew $400 per month in 1976 and $500 per month in 1977 and debited general expenses for such drawings. Lode insisted that the time and effort spent in the business were worth double the amounts withdrawn and that such charges were very conservative.

(f) Lode contributed certain supplies to the business that had been salvaged from a previous operation. These supplies had an original acquisition cost of approximately $800, had a replacement cost as of the beginning of 1976 of $1,200, but since the expenditure had been made prior to 1976, Lode had recognized no charge on the transfer to the new business. The supplies had been fully consumed in approximately equal amounts in 1976 and 1977.

Instructions: Prepare a corrected comparative income statement. In supporting schedules for each balance, indicate any changes made and the accounting concept or principle you would use to support such changes.

1-3. The Farber Company does not maintain a formal set of accounting records. However, a description of all transactions is kept in chronological order. For the month of June the following summary of transactions was provided by management to their public accountant:

(a) Total sales on account, $75,000.
(b) Cash receipts totaled $82,500, including $58,000 from customers, $6,000 from rent received in advance (July–October) on a warehouse owned by the company, and the balance from a loan from the Mid-Central Bank on a six-month note.
(c) Purchases of merchandise on account, $70,000.
(d) A physical inventory of merchandise at June 30 disclosed a value of $23,000, an increase of $6,000 from the beginning of the month.
(e) Cash disbursements for the month were listed as follows:
  (1) Payments for purchases of merchandise on account, $45,000.
  (2) Payment of a one-year fire insurance policy dated June 1, $2,400.
  (3) Payments for supplies, $6,200 (60% of these supplies are on hand on June 30).
  (4) Payments for salaries, $1,850. An additional $300 is owed at June 30.

Instructions:
  (1) Prepare an income statement from the above list of transactions. What accounting concepts and principles are illustrated by the preparation of this statement?
  (2) What additional information would be necessary to more completely apply the income determination principle?

1-4. G. M. Money has drawn up a financial statement on December 31, 1977, employing valuation procedures as follows:

Cash..................................	$20,000	(includes cash in the bank, $15,000, and customers' checks that could not be cashed but that Money feels will ultimately be recoverable, $5,000.)
Marketable securities......	$45,000	(represents the value on December 31 of securities reported at the beginning of 1977 at a cost of $34,500.)
Value of insurance policy	$15,000	(the sum of the payments made on a life insurance policy that requires further payments through 1987. The cash surrender value of the policy at the end of 1977 is $5,000.)
Furniture and fixtures......	$45,000	
Less accumulated depreciation..................	45,000	
Book value.......................	$ 0	(represents furniture and fixtures acquired in 1970 that have been fully depreciated although they are still in use.)
Intangible assets..............	$40,000	(recorded in 1977 when a competitor offered to pay Money this amount for the lease entered into when the company was formed and which still has 5 years to run at a rental that is 5% of net sales.)
Sundry payables	$1	(recorded as a result of a suit of $50,000 against Money for breach of contract; the attorney for Money has offered to pay $15,000 in settlement of the suit but this has been rejected; it is the opinion of the attorney that the suit can be settled by payment of $25,000.)

Instructions: Indicate what change, if any, you would make in reporting each of the items listed above. In each case disclose any theoretical failure indicated in the present reporting and the theoretical support for the suggested change.

2

Overview of the Accounting Process

Certain procedures must be established by every business unit to provide the data to be reported on the financial statements. These procedures are frequently referred to as the *accounting process*.

The accounting process consists of two interrelated parts: (1) the *recording phase* and (2) the *summarizing phase*. During the fiscal period it is necessary to engage in a continuing activity — the recording of transactions in the various books of record. At the end of the fiscal period, the recorded data are brought up to date through adjustments, are summarized, and the financial statements are prepared. The recording and summarizing phases of the accounting process are reviewed and illustrated in this chapter. Data from a hypothetical manufacturing company, the Jensen Corporation, are used to illustrate the various procedures involved. The form and content of the basic financial statements are discussed and illustrated in Chapters 3 and 4.[1]

The accounting process generally includes the following steps, in well-defined sequence:

Recording Phase
1. *Appropriate business documents are prepared or received.* This documentation provides the basis for making an initial record of each transaction.
2. *Transactions are recorded.* Based upon the supporting documents from Step 1, each transaction is recorded in chronological order in books of original entry (journals).
3. *Transactions are posted.* Each transaction, as classified and recorded in the journals, is posted to the appropriate accounts in the general and subsidiary ledgers.

Summarizing Phase
4. *A trial balance of the accounts in the general ledger is taken.* The trial balance, usually prepared on a work sheet (Step 6), offers a summary of the information as classified in the ledger, as well as a general check on the accuracy of recording and posting.
5. *The data required to bring the accounts up to date are compiled.* Before financial statements can be prepared, all of the accountable information that has not been recorded must be determined. Often adjustments are first

---

[1]Appendix B provides an illustrated set of financial statements from the 1976 annual report of General Mills, Inc.

made on a work sheet (Step 6), then they are formally recorded and post-ed (Step 8).

6. *A work sheet is prepared.* By means of the work sheet, data in Steps 4 and 5 are summarized and classified. This step is not essential, but it facilitates statement preparation.

7. *Financial statements are prepared.* Statements summarizing operations and showing the financial condition are prepared from the information supplied on the work sheet.

8. *Accounts are adjusted and closed.* Accounts in the ledger are brought up to date by journalizing and posting adjusting entries. Balances in the inventory and *nominal* (temporary) *accounts* are then closed into appropriate summary accounts.[1] As determined in summary accounts, the results of operations are transferred to the appropriate owners' equity accounts.

9. *A post-closing trial balance is taken.* A trial balance is taken to determine the equality of the debits and credits after posting the adjusting and closing entries.

10. *Accounts are reversed.* Accrued and prepaid balances that were established by adjusting entries are returned to the nominal accounts that are to be used in recording and summarizing activities involving these items in the new period. This last step is not required but is often desirable as a means of facilitating recording and adjusting routines in the succeeding period.

RECORDING PHASE

Accurate statements can be prepared only if transactions have been properly recorded. A *transaction* is an action resulting in a change in the assets, the liabilities, or the owners' equity of a business. There are two general classes of transactions requiring accounting recognition: (1) *business transactions*, or transactions entered into with outsiders; and (2) *internal transactions*, or accountable transfers of costs within the business. For example, among the latter in manufacturing activities are the transfers of materials, labor, and manufacturing overhead costs to goods in process and transfers of goods in process to finished goods.

Accounting Records

The accounting records of a business consist of: (1) the original source materials evidencing the transactions, called *business documents*; (2) the records for classifying and recording the transactions, known as the *books of original entry* or *journals*; and (3) the records for summarizing the effects of transactions upon individual asset, liability, and owners' equity accounts, known as the *ledgers*.

The manner in which the accounting records are organized and employed within a business is referred to as its *accounting system*. The exact form the accounting records take depends on the complexity and degree of mechanization of the system. The various recording routines in each system are developed to meet the special needs of the business unit. Recording processes must be designed to provide accurate information

---

[1]The process of recording the proper inventory account balance may be treated as part of the adjusting process or as part of the closing process. This text will illustrate it as part of the closing process.

on a timely and efficient basis, while they must also serve as effective controls in preventing mistakes and guarding against dishonesty.

Business Documents. Normally a business document prepared or received is the first record of each transaction. Such a document offers detailed information concerning the transaction and also fixes responsibility by naming the parties involved. The business documents provide support for the data to be recorded in the books of original entry. Copies of *sales invoices* or *cash register tapes*, for example, are the evidence in support of the sales record; *purchase invoices* support the purchase or invoice record; *debit* and *credit memorandums* support adjustments in debtor and creditor balances; *check stubs* or *duplicate checks* provide data concerning cash disbursements; the corporation *minutes book* supports entries authorized by action of the board of directors; *journal vouchers* prepared and approved by appropriate officers are a source of data for adjustments or corrections that are to be reported in the accounts. Documents underlying each recorded transaction provide a means of verifying the accounting records and thus form a vital part of the information and control system.

Books of Original Entry. Transactions are analyzed from the information provided on business documents. They are then recorded in chronological order in the appropriate books of original entry. Transactions are analyzed in terms of accounts to be maintained for (1) assets, (2) liabilities, (3) owners' equity, (4) revenues, and (5) expenses. Classes (4) and (5) are nominal or temporary owners' equity accounts summarizing income data for the current period. The analysis is expressed in terms of *debit* and *credit*. Asset and expense accounts have left-hand or debit balances and are decreased by entries on the right-hand or credit side. Liabilities, owners' equity, and revenue accounts have credit balances and are decreased by entries on the debit side.

Although it would be possible to record every transaction in a single book of original entry, this is rarely done. Whenever a number of transactions of the same character take place, special journals may be designed in which the transactions can be conveniently entered and summarized. Special journals eliminate much of the repetitive work involved in recording routine transactions. In addition, they permit the recording function to be divided among accounting personnel, each individual being responsible for a separate record. This specialization often results in greater efficiency as well as a higher degree of control.

Some examples of special journals are the *sales journal*, the *purchases journal*, the *cash receipts journal*, the *cash disbursements journal*, the *payroll register*, and the *voucher register*. Some of these journals are used by the Jensen Corporation and are illustrated later in this chapter. Regardless of the number and nature of special journals, certain transactions cannot appropriately be recorded in the special journals and are recorded in the *general journal*.

Sales on account are recorded in the sales journal. The subsequent collections on account, as well as other transactions involving the receipt of cash, are recorded in the cash receipts journal. Merchandise purchases on account are entered in the purchases journal. Subsequent payments on account, as well as other transactions involving the payment of cash, are recorded in the cash disbursements journal or in the *check register*. A *payroll record* may be employed to accumulate payroll information, including special payroll withholdings for taxes and other purposes.

Column headings in the various journals specify the accounts to be debited or credited; account titles and explanations may therefore be omitted in recording routine transactions. A Sundry column is usually provided for transactions that are relatively infrequent and account titles are specially designated in recording such transactions.

The use of special columns facilitates recording and also serves to summarize the effects of a number of transactions upon individual account balances. The subsequent transfer of information from the books of original entry is thus simplified as this process is performed with the aggregates of many transactions rather than with separate data for each transaction. Certain data must be transferred individually — data affecting individual accounts receivable and accounts payable and data reported in the Sundry columns — but the volume of transcription is substantially reduced.

Transactions not occurring frequently enough to justify a special journal are recorded in the general journal. The general journal provides debit and credit columns and space for designating account titles; thus, it can be used in recording any transaction. A particular business unit may not need certain special journals, but it must have a general journal.

The Voucher System. A relatively large organization ordinarily provides for the control of purchases and cash disbursements through adoption of some form of a *voucher system*. With the use of a voucher system, checks may be drawn only upon a written authorization in the form of a *voucher* approved by some responsible official.

A voucher is prepared, not only in support of each payment to be made for goods and services purchased on account, but also for all other transactions calling for payment by check, including cash purchases, retirement of debt, replenishment of petty cash funds, payrolls, and dividends. The voucher identifies the person authorizing the expenditure, explains the nature of the transaction, and names the accounts affected by the transaction. Vouchers related to purchase invoices should be compared with receiving reports. Upon verification, the voucher and the related business documents are submitted to the appropriate official for final approval. Upon approval, the voucher is numbered and recorded in a *voucher register*. The voucher register is a book of original entry and takes the place of a purchases journal. Charges on each voucher are classified and summarized in appropriate Debit columns and the amount to be paid is listed in an Accounts Payable or Vouchers Payable column.

After a voucher is entered in the register, it is placed in an unpaid vouchers file together with its supporting documents.

Checks are written in payment of individual vouchers. The checks are recorded in a check register as debits to Accounts Payable or Vouchers Payable and credits to Cash. Charges to the various asset, liability, or expense accounts, having been recognized when the payable was recorded in the voucher register, need not be listed in the payments record. When a check is issued, payment of the voucher is reported in the voucher register by entering the check number and the payment date. Paid vouchers and invoices are removed from the unpaid vouchers file, marked "paid," and placed in a separate paid vouchers file. The balance of the payable account, after the credit for total vouchers issued and the debit for total vouchers paid, should be equal to the sum of the unpaid vouchers as reported in the voucher register and as found in the unpaid vouchers file. The voucher register, while representing a book of original entry, also provides the detail in support of the accounts or vouchers payable total. Thus, the need for a separate record reporting the individual payable accounts is eliminated.

Posting to the Ledger Accounts. Information as reported on a business document and analyzed, classified, and summarized in terms of debits and credits in the books of original entry is transferred to accounts in the ledger. This transfer is referred to as *posting*. The accounts then summarize the full effects of the transactions upon assets, liabilities, and owners' equity and are used for preparing the financial statements.

Accounts are sometimes referred to as *real* (or *permanent*) accounts and *nominal* (or *temporary*) accounts. The balance sheet accounts are referred to as real accounts; the income statement accounts are referred to as nominal accounts. If during the course of the accounting period a balance sheet or an income statement account balance represents both real and nominal elements, it may be described as a *mixed account*. For example, the store supplies account before adjustment is composed of two elements: (1) the store supplies used, and (2) the store supplies still on hand. There is no need to analyze mixed accounts until financial statements are prepared. At this time the real and nominal portions of each mixed account must be determined.

When accounts are set up to record subtractions from related accounts reporting positive balances, such accounts are termed *offset* or *contra accounts*. Allowance for Doubtful Accounts is a contra account to Accounts Receivable. Sales Returns and Allowances is a contra account to Sales. Certain accounts relate to others and when added to them on the statements are referred to as *adjunct accounts*. Examples of these are Freight In that is added to the Purchases balance and Paid-In Capital from Sale of Capital Stock at More Than Stated Value that is added to the Capital Stock balance.

The real and nominal accounts required by a business unit vary depending upon the nature of the business, its properties and activities, the information to be provided on the financial statements, and the controls to be employed in carrying out the accounting functions. The accounts to be maintained by a particular business are usually expressed in the form of a *chart of accounts*. This chart lists in systematic form the accounts with identifying numbers or symbols that are to form the framework for summarizing business operations.

It is often desirable to establish separate ledgers for detailed information in support of balance sheet or income statement items. The *general ledger* carries summaries of all of the accounts appearing on the financial statements, while separate *subsidiary ledgers* afford additional detail in support of general ledger balances. For example, a single accounts receivable account is usually carried in the general ledger, and individual customers' accounts are shown in a subsidiary *accounts receivable ledger*; the capital stock account in the general ledger is normally supported by individual stockholders' accounts in a subsidiary *stockholders ledger*; selling and general and administrative expenses may be summarized in a single general ledger account, individual expenses being carried in a subsidiary *expense ledger*. The general ledger account that summarizes the detailed information reported elsewhere is known as a *control account*. The accounts receivable account from a general ledger and excerpts from the corresponding accounts receivable subsidiary ledger are shown below.

GENERAL LEDGER

ACCOUNT   Accounts Receivable   **ACCOUNT NO.**   113

DATE		ITEM	POST. REF.	DEBIT	CREDIT	BALANCE	
						DEBIT	CREDIT
1977 Oct.	1	Balance	✓			5,260	
	13		J18		25	5,235	
	28		J18		65	5,170	

ACCOUNTS RECEIVABLE LEDGER

NAME   Allen Company
ADDRESS   436 Monroe St., Danville, California 94526

DATE		ITEM	POST. REF.	DEBIT	CREDIT	BALANCE
1977 Oct.	10		S35	750		750
	13		J18		25	725

NAME   King & Co.
ADDRESS   48 Converse Rd., Los Angeles, California 90036

DATE		ITEM	POST. REF.	DEBIT	CREDIT	BALANCE
1977 Oct.	24		S35	1,502		1,502
	28		J18		65	1,437

Whenever possible, individual postings to subsidiary accounts are made directly from the business document evidencing the transaction.

This practice saves time and avoids errors that might arise in summarizing and transferring this information. A business document also provides the basis for the journal entry authorizing the postings to the control account in the general ledger. In many instances business documents themselves are used to represent a book of original entry. When this is done, business documents are assembled and summarized, and the summaries are transferred directly to the appropriate control accounts as well as to the other accounts affected in the general ledger. Whatever the procedure may be, if postings to the subsidiary records and to the control accounts are made accurately, the sum of the detail in a subsidiary record will agree with the balance in the control account. A reconciliation of each subsidiary record with its related control account should be made periodically, and any discrepancies found should be investigated and corrected.

The use of subsidiary records results in a number of advantages: (1) the number of accounts in the general ledger is reduced, thus making the general ledger more useful as a basis for preparing reports; (2) errors in the general ledger are minimized because of fewer accounts and fewer postings; (3) the accuracy of the posting to a large number of subsidiary accounts may be tested by comparing the total of the balances of the accounts with the balance of one account in the general ledger; (4) totals relating to various items are readily obtained; (5) specialization of accounting duties and individual accounting responsibilities is made possible; and (6) daily posting is facilitated for accounts that must be kept up to date, such as customer and creditor accounts.

Illustration of Journals and Posting. The Jensen Corporation maintains the following books of original entry: sales journal, cash receipts journal, voucher register, cash disbursements journal, and general journal.[1]

Sales Journal. The sales journal as summarized at the end of the month appears as follows:

SALES JOURNAL

CASH SALES DR.	ACCOUNTS RECEIVABLE DR.	DATE	DESCRIPTION	SALES CR.
	2,100	31	Sales on account for day..................	2,100
2,250		31	Cash sales for day............................	2,250
9,800	40,150	31	Total...	49,950
(√)	(116)			(41)

One entry is made to record the sales on account for each day. Accounts Receivable is debited; Sales is credited. Debits are posted to the individual customer's account in the accounts receivable ledger directly from the sales invoices.

---

[1]The format of a particular journal must satisfy the needs of the individual business unit. Those presented here are illustrative only. For example, a one-column sales journal is used by some companies instead of a multi-column sales journal like the one illustrated.

One entry is also made for the cash sales for each day. Cash Sales is debited and Sales is credited. The Cash Sales column is used so that all sales transactions are included in the sales journal. An entry crediting Cash Sales is also made in the cash receipts journal.

The numbers in parentheses at the bottom of the journal refer to the accounts to which the totals are posted. The ($\sqrt{}$) under the Cash Sales column will be explained later in the chapter.

Cash Receipts Journal. The cash receipts journal appears as follows:

CASH RECEIPTS JOURNAL

CASH DR.	SALES DISCOUNTS DR.	DATE	DESCRIPTION	POST. REF.	SUNDRY CR.	CASH SALES CR.	ACCOUNTS RECEIVABLE CR.
8,565		31	Notes Receivable..................	113	8,500		
			Interest Revenue...................	72	65		
1,960	40	31	Collection on accounts........	$\sqrt{}$			2,000
2,250		31	Cash Sales............................	$\sqrt{}$		2,250	
151,550	395	31	Total.................................		106,245	9,800	35,900
(111)	(42)				($\sqrt{}$)	($\sqrt{}$)	(116)

One entry is made each day for the total amount collected on accounts receivable. In this entry Cash and Sales Discounts are debited and Accounts Receivable is credited. Credits are posted to the individual customer's account in the accounts receivable subsidiary ledger from a separate list of receipts on account maintained by the cashier.

In order to maintain the cash receipts journal as a complete record of all cash received, an entry crediting Cash Sales is made each day. An entry debiting Cash Sales is also made in the sales journal as explained earlier. To avoid double posting of the transaction, the total of the Cash Sales Dr. column in the sales journal and the total of the Cash Sales Cr. column in the cash receipts journal are checked ($\sqrt{}$) and are not posted. As a result, the debit to Cash for cash sales is posted from the cash receipts journal as a part of the total of the Cash Dr. column, and the credit to Sales for cash sales is posted from the sales journal as a part of the total of the Sales Cr. column. A ($\sqrt{}$) under the Sundry column indicates that the amounts in this column are posted individually and not in total. In the illustration, $8,500 was posted to Notes Receivable (account number 113), and $65 was posted to Interest Revenue (account number 72).

Voucher Register. The voucher register takes the place of a purchase journal, providing a record of all authorized payments to be made by check. The voucher register appears on page 37. For illustrative purposes, separate debit columns are provided for two accounts — raw materials purchases and payroll. Other items are recorded in the Sundry Dr. column. Additional separate columns could be added for other items, such as advertising, if desired. The total amount of each column is posted to the corresponding account, with the exception of the Sundry Dr. and Cr. columns which are posted individually.

VOUCHER REGISTER

DATE	VOU. NO.	PAYEE	PAID DATE	PAID CK. NO.	ACCOUNTS PAYABLE CR.	RAW MATERIALS PURCHASES DR.	PAYROLL DR.	SUNDRY ACCOUNT	SUNDRY POST. REF.	AMOUNT DR.	AMOUNT CR.
31	7132	Security National Bank....	12/31	3106	9,120			Notes Payable	211	9,120	
31	7133	Payroll.............................	12/31	3107	1,640		2,130	FICA Taxes Payable......	215		90
								Income Tax Payable......	214		400
31	7134	Far Fabrications...............			3,290	3,290					
31	7135	Midland Mining................			1,500	1,500					
31	7136	Nyland Supply Co.			5,550	5,550					
31		Total................			55,375	24,930	2,130			33,645	5,330
					(213)	(51)	(620)			(√)	(√)

Cash Disbursements Journal. The cash disbursements journal is illustrated below. It accounts for all of the checks issued during the period. Checks are issued only in payment of properly approved vouchers. The payee is designated together with the number of the voucher authorizing the payment. The cash disbursements record when prepared in this form is frequently called a *check register*.

CASH DISBURSEMENTS JOURNAL

DATE	CHECK NO.	ACCOUNT DEBITED	VOU. NO.	ACCOUNTS PAYABLE DR.	PURCHASE DISCOUNTS CR.	CASH CR.
31	3106	Security National Bank	7132	9,120		9,120
31	3107	Payroll	7133	1,640		1,640
31	3108	Pat Bunnell	7005	1,500	30	1,470
31		Total		61,160	275	60,885
				(213)	(52)	(111)

General Journal. The general journal, with illustrative entries for the month of December, is given below. This general journal is prepared in three-column form. A pair of columns is provided for the entries that are to be made to the general ledger accounts. A "detail" column is provided for the individual debits and credits to subsidiary records that accompany entries affecting general ledger control accounts.

GENERAL JOURNAL

DATE		DESCRIPTION	POST. REF.	DETAIL	DEBIT	CREDIT
1977 Dec.	1	Notes Receivable...........................	113		8,000	
		Accounts Receivable	116			8,000
		M. E. Scott....................................	AR	8,000		
		Received note from customer.				
	13	Allowance for Doubtful Accounts	117		1,270	
		Accounts Receivable	116			1,270
		W. G. Haag....................................	AR	1,270		
		To write off uncollectible account.				
	31	Payroll Taxes Expense..................	625		250	
		FICA Tax Payable........................	215			250
		To record employer's FICA tax for month.				

From Manual Operations to Electronic Data Processing

As a business grows in size and complexity, the recording process becomes more involved and means are sought for improving efficiency and reducing costs. Some business units may find that a system involving primarily manual operations is adequate in meeting their needs. Others may find that recording requirements can be handled effectively only through mechanical devices, elaborate electronic data processing equipment, or computer systems.

In a manual accounting system all operations are performed by hand. Original source materials — invoices, checks, and other business documents are written out, and the data they contain are transferred by hand to the journals, the ledgers, and the trial balance. Many small businesses rely solely on manual methods of processing accounting data.

As the volume of record keeping expands, machines may be added to the system. Machines to supplement manual operations often include posting machines, accounting machines, and billing machines. By using special papers, these machines are able to prepare original documents and journal and ledger records at one time, thus saving the work of transferring data. They also can perform a few routine arithmetic operations, such as adding journal columns and computing ledger balances.

Companies requiring great speed and accuracy in processing large amounts of accounting data may utilize an electronic computer system capable of storing and recalling vast quantities of data, performing many mathematical functions, and making certain routine decisions based on mathematical comparisons. These systems normally include various other machines that can "read" data from magnetic tapes or punched cards and print information in a variety of forms, all under the control of the computer.

Despite their tremendous capabilities, electronic systems cannot replace skilled accountants. In fact, their presence places increased demands on the accountant in directing the operations of the system to assure the use of appropriate procedures. Although all arithmetical operations can be assumed to be done accurately by the computer, the validity of the output data depends upon the adequacy of the instructions given it. Unlike a human accountant, a computer cannot think for itself but must be given explicit instructions in performing each operation. This has certain advantages in that the accountant can be sure every direction will be carried out precisely. On the other hand, this places a great responsibility on the accountant to anticipate any unusual situations requiring special consideration or judgment. Particular techniques must also be developed for checking and verifying data recorded in electronic form.

The remainder of this chapter is concerned with the summarizing activities required in preparing periodic financial statements. The exact manner in which these activities are carried out may vary somewhat, depending upon the degree of mechanization of the particular accounting system. The underlying objectives of these procedures are the same, however, whether the operations are performed manually or with a high-speed computer.

SUMMARIZING PHASE

The accounting routine at the close of the fiscal period is frequently referred to as the *periodic summary*. The steps in the process were outlined earlier, and they are described in more detail in the following sections.

Preparing a Trial Balance

After all transactions for the period have been posted to the ledger accounts, the balance for each account is determined. Every account will have either a debit, credit, or zero balance. A trial balance is a list of each account balance and it, therefore, indicates whether the debits equal the credits. Thus, a trial balance helps provide a check on the accuracy of the recording and posting.

Compiling Adjusting Data

Division of the life of a business into periods of arbitrary length creates many problems for the accountant who must summarize the financial operations for the designated period and report on the financial position at the end of that period. Transactions during the period have been recorded in real and nominal accounts. At the end of the period, accounts with mixed balances require adjustment. At this time, too, other financial data, not recognized currently, must be entered in the accounts to bring the books up to date. This is done by analyzing individual accounts and various source documents.

In order to illustrate this part of the accounting process, the adjusting data from Jensen Corporation are presented in the following sections. The data are classified according to the typical areas requiring updating at the end of a designated time period, in this case the year 1977. The adjusting data must be combined with the information on the trial balance in bringing the accounts up-to-date. The trial balance data for Jensen Corporation are listed in the first two amount columns of the work sheet on pages 44 to 45. It is found that the accounts of Jensen Corporation do not reflect the following information.[1]

Asset Depreciation and Cost Amortization
(a) Buildings and equipment depreciation, 5% a year.
(b) Office furniture and fixtures depreciation, 10% a year.
(c) Patent amortization for the year, $2,900.

Doubtful Accounts
(d) The allowance for doubtful accounts is to be increased by $1,100.

Accrued Expenses
(e) Salaries and wages:
    Direct labor, $1,700.
    Indirect labor, $450.
(f) Interest on bonds payable, $5,000.

Accrued Revenues
(g) Interest on notes receivable, $250.

---

[1] The adjusting data are coded to correspond to the letters given on the work sheet on pages 44 to 45.

Prepaid Expenses
(h) Prepaid insurance, $3,800.

Deferred Revenues
(i) Royalties received in advance, $475.

Provision for Income Tax
(j) Provision of $8,000 to be made for federal and state income taxes.

The expenses associated with buildings and equipment, insurance, and taxes (exclusive of income tax) are to be distributed 85% to manufacturing operations and 15% to general and administrative operations. Ending inventory balances are: raw materials, $22,350; goods in process, $26,500; and finished goods, $51,000.

Asset Depreciation and Cost Amortization. Charges to operations for the use of buildings and equipment and intangible assets must be recorded at the end of the period. In recording asset depreciation or amortization, operations are charged with a portion of the asset cost and the carrying value of the asset is reduced by that amount. A reduction in an asset for depreciation is usually recorded by a credit to a contra account. Adjustments at the end of the year for depreciation and amortization for Jensen Corporation are as follows:

(a) Depreciation Expense — Buildings and Equipment................. 7,800
         Accumulated Depreciation — Buildings and Equipment   7,800
            To record depreciation on buildings and equipment.

(b) Depreciation Expense — Office Furniture and Fixtures............. 1,900
         Accumulated Depreciation — Office Furniture and Fixtures.   1,900
            To record depreciation on office furniture and fixtures.

(c) Amortization of Patents.. 2,900
         Patents   2,900
            To record amortization of patents.

Doubtful Accounts. Provision is ordinarily made for the probable expense resulting from failure to collect receivables. In recognizing the probable expense arising from the policy of granting credit to customers, operations are charged with the estimated expense, and receivables are reduced by means of a contra account. When there is positive evidence that receivables are uncollectible, receivables are written off against the contra account. To illustrate, the adjustment for Jensen Corporation at the end of the year assumes the allowance account is to be increased by $1,100. The adjustment is as follows:

(d) Doubtful Accounts Expense 1,100
         Allowance for Doubtful Accounts   1,100
            To provide for doubtful accounts.

Accrued Expenses. During the period, certain expenses may have been incurred although payment is not to be made until a subsequent period. At the end of the period, it is necessary to determine and record the expenses not yet recognized. In recording an accrued expense, an expense account is debited and a liability account is credited. The adjusting entries to record accrued expenses for Jensen Corporation are:

```
(e)  Direct Labor..............................................................................  1,700
     Indirect Labor...........................................................................    450
         Salaries and Wages Payable ....................................................          2,150
             To record accrued salaries and wages.

(f)  Interest Expense .........................................................................  5,000
     Interest Payable...........................................................................          5,000
         To record accrued interest on bonds.
```

At the beginning of the new period, adjustments for accrued expenses may be reversed to make it possible to record expense payments during the new period in the usual manner. The nature of reversing entries is explained more fully later in the chapter.

Accrued Revenues. During the period, certain amounts may have been earned although collection is not to be made until a subsequent period. At the end of the period, it is necessary to determine and record the earnings not yet recognized. In recording accrued revenue, an asset account is debited and a revenue account is credited. The illustrative entry recognizing the accrued revenues for the year for Jensen Corporation is shown below:

```
(g)  Interest Receivable ......................................................................   250
     Interest Revenue..........................................................................          250
         To record accrued interest on notes receivable.
```

Prepaid Expenses. During the period, charges may have been recorded on the books for commodities or services that are not to be received or used up currently. At the end of the period it is necessary to determine the portions of such charges that are applicable to subsequent periods and hence require recognition as assets.

The method of adjusting for prepaid expenses depends upon how the expenditures were originally entered in the accounts. The charges for the commodities or services may have been recorded as debits to (1) an expense account or (2) an asset account.

Original Debit to an Expense Account. If an expense account was originally debited, the adjusting entry requires that an asset account be debited for the expense applicable to the future period and the expense account be credited. The expense account then remains with a debit balance representing the amount applicable to the current period. The adjusting entry may be reversed at the beginning of the new period as is explained later in the chapter.

Original Debit to an Asset Account. If an asset account was originally debited, the adjusting entry requires that an expense account be debited for the amount applicable to the current period and the asset account be credited. The asset account remains with a debit balance that shows the amount applicable to future periods. In this instance, no reversing entry is needed. An adjusting entry for prepaid insurance for Jensen Corporation illustrates this situation as follows:

(h) Insurance Expense 4,200
        Prepaid Insurance   4,200
            To record expired insurance ($8,000 − $3,800 = $4,200).

Since the asset account Prepaid Insurance was originally debited, the amount of the prepayment must be reduced to reflect only the $3,800 that remains unexpired.

Deferred Revenues. During the period, cash or other assets may have been received from customers in advance of fulfillment of the company's obligation to deliver goods or services. In recording these transactions, assets are debited and accounts reporting such receipts are credited. The latter balances must be analyzed at the end of the period to determine the portions that are applicable to future periods and hence require recognition as liabilities.

The method of adjusting for deferred revenues depends upon how the receipts for undelivered goods or services were originally entered in the accounts. The receipts may have been recorded as credits to (1) a revenue account or (2) a liability account.

Original Credit to a Revenue Account. If a revenue account was originally credited, this account is debited and a liability account is credited for the revenue applicable to a future period. The revenue account remains with a credit balance representing the earnings applicable to the current period. Again, this adjustment may be reversed as is explained later.

Assuming the credit was made originally to the revenue account, the entry to record royalties received in advance for Jensen Corporation is as follows:

(i) Royalty Revenue 475
        Royalties Received in Advance   475
            To record royalties received in advance.

Original Credit to a Liability Account. If a liability account was originally credited, this account is debited and a revenue account is credited for the amount applicable to the current period. The liability account remains with a credit balance that shows the amount applicable to future periods. In this instance, no reversing entry is needed.

Provision for Income Tax. When a corporation reports earnings, provision must be made for federal and state income taxes. Income Tax is debited and Income Tax Payable is credited. The entry to record estimated tax payable for Jensen Corporation is as follows:

(j) Income Tax 8,000
        Income Tax Payable   8,000
            To record estimated income tax payable.

Preparing a Work Sheet

The adjusting data must be combined with the information on the trial balance to bring the accounts up to date. This may be done and the financial statements developed through the preparation of a work sheet. In the construction of a work sheet, trial balance data are listed in the first two amount columns. The adjusting entries are listed in the second pair of columns. Sometimes a third pair of columns is included to show the trial balance after adjustment. Account balances as adjusted are carried to the appropriate statement columns. A work sheet for a manufacturing enterprise usually includes a pair of columns for (1) manufacturing schedule accounts, (2) income statement accounts, and (3) balance sheet accounts. Two columns for retained earnings may be placed between the Income Statement and Balance Sheet columns if sufficient transactions to this account warrant it. A similar work sheet form may be used for a merchandising enterprise except for the absence of Manufacturing Schedule columns. There are no columns for the statement of changes in financial position because this statement contains a rearrangement of information included in the balance sheet and income statement. A discussion of the preparation of the statement of changes in financial position is deferred to Chapter 24.

The work sheet for Jensen Corporation is shown on pages 44 to 45. All adjustments previously illustrated are included. The simple procedure for reporting the ending inventory balances should be noted. Beginning balances are transferred as debits to the Manufacturing Schedule or Income Statement columns, while ending balances are entered directly as credits in the Manufacturing Schedule or Income Statement columns and as debits in the Balance Sheet columns.[1]

It was indicated earlier that expenses associated with buildings and equipment, insurance, and taxes (exclusive of income tax) are allocated 85% to manufacturing activities and 15% to general and administrative activities. These percentages were developed by analyzing the expenses during the period. The percentages are then applied to the appropriate items on the work sheet.

Preparing Financial Statements

The financial statements are prepared using the work sheet as the basic source of data for the presentations. The basic financial statements are illustrated in the next two chapters. They include the balance sheet, the income statement, and the statement of changes in financial position.

Adjusting and Closing the Inventory Accounts

When perpetual or book inventory records are not maintained, physical inventories must be taken at the end of the period to determine the inventory to be reported on the balance sheet and the cost of goods sold to be reported on the income statement. When perpetual or book inventories are maintained, the ending inventory and the cost of goods sold

---

[1]An alternative procedure is to adjust the inventory balances in the Adjustments column by crediting the beginning balance and debiting the ending balance. Corresponding amounts are closed through Cost of Goods Sold or Income Summary to the Income Statement columns and the ending inventory balances transferred to the Balance Sheet.

Jensen
Work
For Year Ended

#	ACCOUNT TITLE	TRIAL BALANCE DEBIT	TRIAL BALANCE CREDIT	ADJUSTMENTS DEBIT	ADJUSTMENTS CREDIT	#
1	Cash	83,110				1
2	Notes Receivable	28,000				2
3	Accounts Receivable	106,500				3
4	Allowance for Doubtful Accounts		1,610		(d) 1,100	4
5	Raw Materials	21,350				5
6	Goods in Process	29,400				6
7	Finished Goods	45,000				7
8	Prepaid Insurance	8,000			(h) 4,200	8
9	Land	114,000				9
10	Buildings and Equipment	156,000				10
11	Accumulated Depreciation—Buildings and					11
12	Equipment		19,300		(a) 7,800	12
13	Office Furniture and Fixtures	19,000				13
14	Accumulated Depreciation—Office Furniture					14
15	and Fixtures		1,600		(b) 1,900	15
16	Patents	55,400			(c) 2,900	16
17	Accounts Payable		37,910			17
18	Payroll Taxes Payable		5,130			18
19	Dividends Payable		3,400			19
20	8% First-Mortgage Bonds		250,000			20
21	Common Stock, $20 par		150,000			21
22	Additional Paid-In Capital		50,000			22
23	Retained Earnings		113,610			23
24	Dividends	13,600				24
25	Sales		533,000			25
26	Sales Discounts	3,500				26
27	Raw Materials Purchases	107,500				27
28	Purchase Discounts		3,290			28
29	Freight In	5,100				29
30	Direct Labor	95,150		(e) 1,700		30
31	Indirect Labor	67,300		(e) 450		31
32	Factory Heat, Light, and Power	27,480				32
33	Payroll Taxes Expense	13,300				33
34	Miscellaneous Factory Overhead	12,610				34
35	Sales Salaries and Commissions	31,000				35
36	Advertising Expense	13,200				36
37	Administrative Salaries	87,300				37
38	Miscellaneous General Expense	14,700				38
39	Interest Revenue		1,100		(g) 250	39
40	Royalty Revenue		2,550	(i) 475		40
41	Interest Expense	15,000		(f) 5,000		41
42	Doubtful Accounts Expense			(d) 1,100		42
43	Depreciation Expense—Buildings and Equipment			(a) 7,800		43
44	Depreciation Expense—Office Furniture					44
45	and Fixtures			(b) 1,900		45
46	Amortization of Patents			(c) 2,900		46
47	Salaries and Wages Payable				(e) 2,150	47
48	Interest Payable				(f) 5,000	48
49	Insurance Expense			(h) 4,200		49
50	Interest Receivable			(g) 250		50
51	Royalties Received in Advance				(i) 475	51
52	Income Tax			(j) 8,000		52
53	Income Tax Payable				(j) 8,000	53
54		1,172,500	1,172,500	33,775	33,775	54
55	Cost of Goods Manufactured					55
56						56
57	Net Income					57
58						58
59						59

Corporation
Sheet
December 31, 1977

	MANUFACTURING SCHEDULE		INCOME STATEMENT		BALANCE SHEET		
	DEBIT	CREDIT	DEBIT	CREDIT	DEBIT	CREDIT	
1					83,110		1
2					28,000		2
3					106,500		3
4						2,710	4
5	21,350	22,350			22,350		5
6	29,400	26,500			26,500		6
7			45,000	51,000	51,000		7
8					3,800		8
9					114,000		9
10					156,000		10
11							11
12						27,100	12
13					19,000		13
14							14
15						3,500	15
16					52,500		16
17						37,910	17
18						5,130	18
19						3,400	19
20						250,000	20
21						150,000	21
22						50,000	22
23						113,610	23
24					13,600		24
25				533,000			25
26			3,500				26
27	107,500						27
28		3,290					28
29	5,100						29
30	96,850						30
31	67,750						31
32	27,480						32
33	11,305		1,995				33
34	12,610						34
35			31,000				35
36			13,200				36
37			87,300				37
38			14,700				38
39				1,350			39
40				2,075			40
41			20,000				41
42			1,100				42
43	6,630		1,170				43
44							44
45			1,900				45
46	2,900						46
47						2,150	47
48						5,000	48
49	3,570		630				49
50					250		50
51						475	51
52			8,000				52
53						8,000	53
54	392,445	52,140					54
55		340,305	340,305				55
56	392,445	392,445	569,800	587,425	676,610	658,985	56
57			17,625			17,625	57
58			587,425	587,425	676,610	676,610	58
59							59

balances appear in the ledger and an adjustment is not required. The closing procedures are described in the following paragraphs.

Physical Inventories — The Merchandising Enterprise. In a merchandising enterprise, the beginning inventory and the purchases account may be closed into the income summary account. The ending inventory is then recorded by a debit to the inventory account and a credit to the income summary account. The asset account now reports the inventory balance at the end of the period; the income summary account shows the cost of goods sold.

Physical Inventories — The Manufacturing Enterprise. In a manufacturing enterprise, three inventories are recognized: raw materials, goods in process, and finished goods. If cost of goods manufactured is to be summarized separately, beginning and ending raw materials and goods in process inventories are recorded in the manufacturing summary account, and beginning and ending finished goods inventories are recorded in the income summary account. To illustrate, assume the following data from Jensen Corporation:

Inventories, January 1, 1977: Raw materials, $21,350; Goods in process, $29,400; Finished goods, $45,000.

Charges incurred during 1977: Raw materials purchases, $107,500; Direct labor, $96,850; Manufacturing overhead, $134,055.[1]

Inventories, December 31, 1977: Raw materials, $22,350; Goods in process, $26,500; Finished goods, $51,000.

The entries to close the beginning inventories and to record the ending inventories follow:

To close the beginning inventories:	Manufacturing Summary	21,350	
	Raw Materials		21,350
	Manufacturing Summary	29,400	
	Goods in Process		29,400
	Income Summary	45,000	
	Finished Goods		45,000
To record the ending inventories:	Raw Materials	22,350	
	Manufacturing Summary		22,350
	Goods in Process	26,500	
	Manufacturing Summary		26,500
	Finished Goods	51,000	
	Income Summary		51,000

After manufacturing costs are closed into the manufacturing summary account, the balance in this account summarizes the cost of goods manufactured. The cost of goods manufactured is transferred to the income summary account and the latter then reports cost of goods sold. Inventory and summary accounts will appear as shown on page 47.

---

[1]For purposes of this illustration, manufacturing overhead includes all amounts shown on the Manufacturing Schedule of the Jensen Corporation work sheet, except net purchases and direct labor.

Raw Materials

Beginning inventory	21,350	To Manufacturing Summary	21,350
Ending inventory	22,350		

Goods in Process

Beginning inventory	29,400	To Manufacturing Summary	29,400
Ending inventory	26,500		

Finished Goods

Beginning inventory	45,000	To Income Summary	45,000
Ending inventory	51,000		

Manufacturing Summary

Beginning Raw Materials Inventory	21,350	Ending Raw Materials Inventory	22,350
Beginning Goods in Process Inventory	29,400	Ending Goods in Process Inventory	26,500
Raw Materials Purchases	107,500	Cost of Goods Manufactured to Income Summary	340,305
Direct Labor	96,850		
Manufacturing Overhead	134,055		
	389,155		389,155

Income Summary

Beginning Finished Goods Inventory	45,000	Ending Finished Goods Inventory	51,000
Cost of Goods Manufactured	340,305		

(Balance: Cost of goods sold, $334,305)

Perpetual Inventories — The Merchandising Enterprise. When a perpetual inventory is maintained, a separate purchases account is not used. The inventory account is charged whenever goods are acquired. When a sale takes place, two entries are required: (1) the sale is recorded in the usual manner, and (2) the merchandise sold is recorded by a debit to Cost of Goods Sold and a credit to the inventory account. Subsidiary records for inventory items are normally maintained. Detailed increases and decreases in the various inventory items are reported in the subsidiary accounts, and the costs of goods purchased and sold are summarized in the inventory control account. At the end of the period, the inventory account reflects the inventory on hand; the cost of goods sold account is closed into Income Summary.

Perpetual Inventories — The Manufacturing Enterprise. When perpetual inventories are maintained by a manufacturing enterprise, materials purchases are recorded by a debit to Raw Materials. Materials removed from stores for processing are recorded by debits to Goods in Process and credits to Raw Materials. Labor and manufacturing overhead costs, also, are debited to Goods in Process. Finished Goods is debited and Goods in Process is credited for the cost of goods completed and transferred into the finished goods stock. The entry to record a sale is accompanied by an entry to record the cost of goods sold, Cost of Goods Sold being debited and Finished Goods being credited. At the end of the period, inventory accounts report the balance of goods on hand; Cost of Goods Sold is closed into Income Summary. Normally raw materials, goods in process, and finished goods inventory accounts are control accounts, individual changes in the various inventory items being reported in the respective subsidiary ledgers. Frequently such procedures are maintained as a part of a system designed to offer detailed information concerning costs.

Even if the perpetual inventory system is not used, a closing procedure similar to the foregoing may be preferred. The raw materials purchases account can be closed into the raw materials inventory account. The inventory account would then be reduced to the ending inventory balance, and Goods in Process would be debited. Direct labor and manufacturing overhead accounts are closed into Goods in Process. Goods in Process is then reduced to the ending inventory figure and Finished Goods is debited. Finished Goods is finally reduced to its ending balance and a cost of goods sold account is opened and debited for the inventory decrease. Cost of Goods Sold is closed into Income Summary.

Closing the Nominal Accounts

Upon completing the work sheet and statements, entries are made in the general journal to bring all accounts up to date and to close the accounts. The procedures for closing the inventory accounts were just described. Before closing the inventory and the nominal accounts, any correcting and adjusting entries are recorded. Although such entries usually have been prepared on the work sheet, these are now entered formally in the general journal. Closing entries may be conveniently prepared by using as a basis for the entries the balances as shown in the Manufacturing Schedule and Income Statement columns of the work sheet. The following entries, including those needed to adjust and close inventories, are required for Jensen Corporation.

Closing Entries
December 31, 1977

Manufacturing Summary	340,305	
Raw Materials	22,350	
Goods in Process	26,500	
Purchase Discounts	3,290	
Raw Materials		21,350
Goods in Process		29,400
Raw Materials Purchases		107,500
Freight In		5,100
Direct Labor		96,850
Indirect Labor		67,750
Factory Heat, Light, and Power		27,480
Payroll Taxes Expense		11,305
Miscellaneous Factory Overhead		12,610
Depreciation Expense — Buildings and Equipment		6,630
Amortization of Patents		2,900
Insurance Expense		3,570
To close manufacturing accounts into Manufacturing Summary.		

Sales..	533,000	
Interest Revenue..	1,350	
Royalty Revenue..	2,075	
Income Summary...		536,425
To close revenue accounts into Income Summary.		
Income Summary	518,800	
Finished Goods	51,000	
Finished Goods..		45,000
Manufacturing Summary		340,305
Sales Discounts		3,500
Payroll Taxes Expense..		1,995
Sales Salaries and Commissions		31,000
Advertising Expense..		13,200
Administrative Salaries..		87,300
Miscellaneous General Expense		14,700
Interest Expense		20,000
Doubtful Accounts Expense		1,100
Depreciation Expense — Buildings and Equipment		1,170
Depreciation Expense — Office Furniture and Fixtures		1,900
Insurance Expense		630
Income Tax..		8,000
To close expense accounts into Income Summary.		
Income Summary	17,625	
Retained Earnings		17,625
To transfer the balance in Income Summary to Retained Earnings.		
Retained Earnings...	13,600	
Dividends...		13,600
To close Dividends into Retained Earnings.		

Preparing a Post-Closing Trial Balance

After the adjusting and closing entries are posted, a post-closing trial balance is prepared to verify the equality of the debits and credits. The post-closing trial balance for Jensen Corporation is given below:

Jensen Corporation
Post-Closing Trial Balance
December 31, 1977

Cash	83,110	
Notes Receivable..	28,000	
Accounts Receivable	106,500	
Allowance for Doubtful Accounts..		2,710
Interest Receivable...	250	
Raw Materials	22,350	
Goods in Process..	26,500	
Finished Goods	51,000	
Prepaid Insurance	3,800	
Land	114,000	
Buildings and Equipment...	156,000	
Accumulated Depreciation — Buildings and Equipment..................		27,100
Office Furniture and Fixtures...	19,000	
Accumulated Depreciation — Office Furniture and Fixtures.............		3,500
Patents..	52,500	
Accounts Payable..		37,910
Income Tax Payable..		8,000
Payroll Taxes Payable...		5,130
Salaries and Wages Payable		2,150
Interest Payable..		5,000
Dividends Payable...		3,400
8% First-Mortgage Bonds...		250,000
Royalties Received in Advance		475
Common Stock, $20 par..		150,000
Additional Paid-In Capital...		50,000
Retained Earnings...		117,635
	663,010	663,010

Reversing the Accounts   At the beginning of a new period, the adjusting entries for accrued expenses, accrued revenues, prepaid expenses when the original debit was to an expense account, and deferred revenues when the original credit was to a revenue account may be reversed. Reversing entries are not necessary, but they make it possible to record the expense payments or revenue receipts in the new period in the usual manner. If a reversing entry is not made, for example, for accrued expenses, the expense payments would have to be analyzed as to (1) the amount representing payment of the accrued liability, and (2) the amount representing the expense of the current period. Alternatively, the accrued and deferred accounts could be left unadjusted until the close of the subsequent reporting period when they would be adjusted to their correct balances.

To illustrate accounting for an accrued expense when (1) reversing entries are made and (2) reversing entries are not made, assume that accrued salaries on December 31, 1977, are $350 and on December 31, 1978, are $500. Payment of salaries for the period ending January 4, 1978, is $1,000. Adjustments are made and the books are closed annually on December 31. The possible entries are shown below:

	(1) ASSUMING LIABILITY ACCOUNT IS REVERSED	(2) ASSUMING LIABILITY ACCOUNT IS NOT REVERSED	
		(a) Transaction in Next Period is Analyzed.	(b) Transaction in Next Period is Not Analyzed. Adjustment at Close of Next Reporting Period.
December 31, 1977 Adjusting entry to record accrued salaries.	Salaries....... 350 Salaries Payable.... 350	Salaries....... 350 Salaries Payable.... 350	Salaries....... 350 Salaries Payable.... 350
December 31, 1977 Closing entry to transfer expense to the income summary account.	Income Summary .... xxx Salaries ... xxx	Income Summary .... xxx Salaries ... xxx	Income Summary .... xxx Salaries ... xxx
January 1, 1978 Reversing entry to transfer balance to the account that will be charged when payment is made.	Salaries Payable....... 350 Salaries ... 350	No entry	No entry
January 4, 1978 Payment of salaries for period ending Jan. 4, 1978.	Salaries....... 1,000 Cash 1,000	Salaries Payable .... 350 Salaries....... 650 Cash 1,000	Salaries....... 1,000 Cash 1,000
December 31, 1978 Adjusting entry to record accrued salaries.	Salaries....... 500 Salaries Payable.... 500	Salaries....... 500 Salaries Payable.... 500	Salaries....... 150 Salaries Payable.... 150

The adjustments establishing accrued and prepaid balances for Jensen Corporation were illustrated earlier in the chapter. The appropriate reversing entries are shown on page 51.

Reversing Entries
January 1, 1978

Salaries and Wages Payable	2,150	
Direct Labor		1,700
Indirect Labor		450
Interest Payable	5,000	
Interest Expense		5,000
Interest Revenue	250	
Interest Receivable		250
Royalties Received in Advance	475	
Royalty Revenue		475

FROM TRANSACTION TO STATEMENTS

The preceding chapter discussed the accounting concepts and principles underlying the financial statements and stressed the importance of financial reports in a modern economic society. The usual procedures for recording transactions and the sequence of events incident to the preparation of such reports have been briefly reviewed in this chapter. The treatment applied to these transactions and events was referred to as the accounting process.

The accounting process includes the entire field of analyzing, classifying, recording, summarizing, and reporting. It includes the successive steps that constitute the accounting cycle. It starts with the first written record of the transactions of the business unit and concludes with the final summarized financial statements.

The significance of the accounting process and its applicability to every business unit, regardless of size, in our economic society must be appreciated. Although the procedures may be modified to meet special conditions, the process reviewed here is basic in accounting for every business unit.

QUESTIONS

1. Distinguish between the recording phase and the summarizing phase of the accounting process.

2. List and describe the procedures in the accounting process. Why is each step necessary?

3. What is the accounting function of: (a) the business document, (b) a book of original entry, (c) the ledger?

4. Distinguish between: (a) real and nominal accounts, (b) general journal and special journals, (c) general ledger and subsidiary ledgers.

5. What advantages are provided through the use of: (a) special journals, (b) subsidiary ledgers, and (c) the voucher system?

6. The Isom Co. maintains a sales journal, a voucher register, a cash receipts journal, a cash disbursements journal, and a general journal. For each account listed below and on page 52 indicate the most common journal sources of debits and credits.

    Cash
    Marketable Securities
    Notes Receivable
    Accounts Receivable
    Allowance for Doubtful Accounts
    Merchandise Inventory
    Land and Buildings
    Accumulated Depreciation
    Notes Payable
    Vouchers Payable
    Capital Stock
    Retained Earnings

Sales
Sales Discounts
Purchases
Freight In
Purchase Returns and Allowances
Purchase Discounts
Salaries
Depreciation

7. As Robinson Company's independent certified public accountant, you find that the company accountant posts adjusting and closing entries directly to the ledger without formal entries in the general journal. How would you evaluate this procedure in your report to management?

8. Define a mixed account. Should any accounts remain mixed after the adjusting entries have been posted? Explain.

9. Explain the nature and the purpose of (a) adjusting entries, (b) closing entries, and (c) reversing entries.

10. Give three common examples of contra accounts; explain why contra accounts are used.

11. What are the major advantages of electronic data processing as compared with manual processing of accounting data?

12. One of your clients overheard a computer manufacturer sales representative saying the computer will make the accountant obsolete. How would you respond to this comment?

13. What are the implications of electronic data processing for the accountant?

14. Payment of insurance in advance may be recorded in either (a) an expense account or (b) an asset account. Which method would you recommend? What periodic entries are required under each method?

15. The receipt of rentals in advance may be recorded in either (a) a revenue account or (b) a liability account. Which method would you recommend? What periodic entries would be required under each of these methods?

16. The bookkeeper for the Florence Co. does not reverse accrued and prepaid balances at the beginning of the period. At the end of the period debits or credits are made to these accounts to bring them to the appropriate balances as of the end of the fiscal period, and the offsetting debits and credits are made to the related revenue and expense accounts. Revenue and expense accounts at the end of the year thus report receipts and disbursements and the adjustments resulting from variations in the accrued and prepaid balances. Evaluate this procedure.

17. The bookkeeper for the Sterling Corporation does not adjust the revenue and expense accounts at the end of the period but makes closing entries in the usual manner, leaving certain revenue accounts with debit balances and certain expense accounts with credit balances. The bookkeeper claims this saves the effort required in adjusting and reversing accounts, adjusting, closing, and reversing being accomplished at the same time. Do you agree?

18. What columns might be used on a work sheet for: (a) a merchandising company; (b) a manufacturing company; (c) a departmentalized business, the gross profit to be ascertained for each department; (d) a manufacturing organization with retail sales departments, an operating income to be determined for each department?

19. When would work sheets with columns reporting an adjusted trial balance be recommended?

20. The accountant for the Slater Co. in adjusting the accounts on the work sheet debits or credits the beginning inventory to adjust it to the ending balance, with an offsetting credit or debit to an inventory variation balance. The inventory as adjusted is carried to the Balance Sheet column and the variation balance is carried to the appropriate Income Statement column. Appraise this procedure.

21. Distinguish between closing the inventory account for a merchandising enterprise using a physical inventory system and one using a perpetual inventory system.

22. The accountant for the D. A. Anderton Store, after completing all adjustments except for the merchandise inventory, makes the entry reported below to close the beginning inventory, to set up the ending inventory, to close all nominal accounts, and to report the net result of operations in the capital account.

Mdse. Inv., Dec. 31, 1977	22,500	
Sales	250,000	
Purchase Discounts	2,500	
Mdse. Inv., Jan. 1, 1977		25,000
Purchases		175,000
Selling Expense		25,000
General and Admin. Expense		18,750
Interest Expense		1,875
D. A. Anderton, Capital		29,375

(a) Would you regard this procedure as being acceptable?
(b) What alternate procedure could you have followed in adjusting and closing the accounts?

EXERCISES

1. The Commercial Refining Corporation, a manufacturer, engaged in the following transactions during April, 1977. Commercial Refining Corporation records inventory on the perpetual system.

1977

Apr. 1 Purchased a factory building and land for $100,000 in cash and a 30-year mortgage payable for $500,000. The land was appraised at $200,000 and the buildings at $600,000.

4 Sold finished goods to the Arnaud Company for $9,000; terms 2/10, n/30, FOB shipping point. Arnaud paid $150 freight on the goods. Finished goods cost $5,580.

5 Received raw materials worth $15,000; terms, n/30.

7 Received payment from Arnaud for goods shipped April 4.

15 The payroll for the first half of April was $16,000.

18 Traded in a truck that cost $6,000 with a net book value of $1,000 for a machine with a fair market value of $8,700. A trade-in allowance of $800 is allowed on the truck.

22 Declared a dividend at $1.15 per share on the common stock. Common stock outstanding is 45,500 shares.

Record the above transactions in general journal form.

2. Using sales and cash receipts journals, as illustrated previously in the text, record the following transactions:

(a) A sale on account is made to J. A. Wells for $900.

(b) A check for $882 is received from Wells representing payment of the invoice less a sales discount of $18.

(c) Cash sales for the day are $1,315.

(d) Cash of $1,200 is received on a 60-day, 8% note for this amount issued to the bank.

(e) A dividend check for $80 is received on shares of stock owned.

3. In analyzing the accounts of Gerry Garner, the adjusting data listed below are determined on December 31, the end of an annual fiscal period. (1) Give the adjusting entry for each item. (2) What reversing entries would be appropriate? (3) What sources would provide the information for each adjustment?

(a) The prepaid insurance account shows a debit of $900, representing the cost of a 3-year fire insurance policy dated July 1.

(b) On October 1, Rental Revenue was credited for $1,200, representing revenue from subrental for a 4-month period beginning on that date.

(c) Purchase of advertising materials for $800 during the year was recorded in the advertising expense account. On December 31 advertising materials of $175 are on hand.

(d) On November 1, $750 was paid as rent for a 6-month period beginning on that date. The expense account, Rent, was debited.

(e) Miscellaneous Office Expense was debited for office supplies of $450 purchased during the year. On December 31 office supplies of $95 are on hand.

(f) Interest of $65 is accrued on notes payable.

4. The following information is taken from the records of the Basil Company:

	Balance January 1, 1977	Balance December 31, 1977	Transactions During 1977
Accruals:			
Interest receivable	$270	$325	
Wages payable...	550	575	
Interest payable	400	225	
Cash receipts and payments:			
Interest on notes receivable			$ 620
Wages...			32,000
Interest on notes payable			465

Compute the interest revenue, the wages expense, and the interest expense for the year.

5. Upon inspecting the books and records for the Bombay Manufacturing Co. for the year ended December 31, 1977, you find the following data. What entries are required to bring the accounts up to date?

(a) A receivable of $450 from R. W. Brown is determined to be uncollectible. The company maintains no allowance for such losses.

(b) A creditor, the Arne Co., has just been awarded damages of $3,200 as a result of breach of contract during the current year by Bombay Manufacturing Co. Nothing appears on the books in connection with this matter.

(c) A fire destroyed part of a branch office. Furniture and fixtures that cost $17,000 and had a book value of $13,000 at the time of the fire were completely destroyed. The insurance company has agreed to pay $10,000 under the provision of the fire insurance policy.

(d) Advances of $2,000 to salespersons have been recorded as Sales Salaries.

(e) Machinery at the end of the year shows a balance of $34,500. It is discovered that additions to this account during the year totaled $8,000, but of this amount $4,500 should have been recorded as repairs. Depreciation is to be recorded at 10% on machinery owned throughout the year, but at one half this rate on machinery purchased or sold during the year.

6. Accounts of Modern Products Co. at the end of the first year of operations show the following balances:

Cash	$ 13,600	
Investments	16,000	
Machinery	40,000	
Factory Buildings	64,000	
Land	32,000	
Accounts Payable		$ 24,000
Common Stock		160,000
Premium on Common Stock		32,000
Sales		240,000
Raw Materials Purchases	112,000	
Direct Labor	80,000	
Manufacturing Overhead	58,000	
Operating Expenses	41,600	
Investment Revenue		1,200
	$457,200	$457,200

At the end of the year physical inventories are: raw materials, $32,000; goods in process, $24,000; finished goods, $24,000. Prepaid operating expenses are $1,200 and manufacturing overhead payable is $400. Investment revenue receivable is $240. Depreciation for the year on buildings is $1,600, apportioned $1,200 to the factory and $400 to general operations. Depreciation of machinery is $2,000. Federal and state income taxes for the year are estimated at $8,000. Give the entries to adjust and close the books.

7. Account balances before and after adjustment on December 31 follow. Give the adjustment that was made for each account.

	Before Adjustment		After Adjustment	
Account Title	Debit	Credit	Debit	Credit
(a) Merchandise Inventory	$33,500		$38,000	
(b) Allowance for Doubtful Accounts	1,750			$ 7,000
(c) Accumulated Depreciation		$18,000		21,500
(d) Sales Salaries	32,200		32,950	
(e) Income Tax	5,500		6,350	
(f) Royalty Revenue		9,000		11,500
(g) Interest Revenue		650		875

8. On May 16, 1977, Susan Young paid insurance for a three-year period beginning June 1. She recorded the payment as follows:

Prepaid Insurance	1,512	
Cash		1,512

(a) What adjustment is required on December 31? What reversing entry, if any, would you make?

(b) What nominal account could be debited instead of Prepaid Insurance? What adjustment would then be necessary? What reversing entry, if any, would you make?

9. Ed Warnick received $14,400 for rent of an office suite for one year beginning May 1. He recorded the receipt as a deferred revenue.

(a) What adjustment is required on December 31? If a reversing entry is appropriate, what is the entry?
(b) If he had credited a nominal account, what adjustment would now be necessary? If a reversing entry is appropriate, what is the entry?

10. The data listed below were obtained from an analysis of the accounts of Bradford Publishing Company as of March 31, 1977, in preparation of the annual report. Bradford records current transactions in nominal accounts and does not reverse adjusting entries. What are the appropriate adjusting entries?

(a) Prepaid Insurance has a balance of $9,400. Bradford has the following policies in force.

Policy	Date	Term	Cost	Coverage
A	1/1/77	2 years	$2,400	Shop equipment
B	12/1/76	6 months	1,200	Delivery equipment
C	7/1/76	3 years	8,000	Office and factory buildings

(b) Subscriptions Received in Advance has a balance of $37,500. The following subscriptions were included in the balance.

Inception	Amount	Term
July 1, 1976	$18,000	1 year
October 1, 1976	14,800	1 year
January 1, 1977	19,200	1 year
April 1, 1977	13,800	1 year

(c) Interest Payable has a balance of $550. Bradford owes an 8%, 90-day note for $30,000 dated March 1, 1977.
(d) Supplies has a balance of $1,460. An inventory of supplies revealed a total of $940.
(e) Salaries Payable has a balance of $6,500. The payroll for the 5-day workweek ended April 3, totaled $7,500.

11. Some of the accounts appearing in the ledger of the Thorn Manufacturing Co. on November 30, the end of a fiscal year, follow:

Finished Goods	$84,000	Sales	$1,080,000
Goods in Process	48,000	Operating Expense	180,000
Raw Materials	72,000		

(a) Prepare closing entries given the following information. Physical inventories on November 30 are: raw materials, $70,000; goods in process, $40,000; finished goods, $45,000. Raw materials purchases are $340,000; direct labor is $156,000; and manufacturing overhead is $120,000.
(b) Assuming that on a perpetual basis, cost of goods sold totals $665,000, close the accounts.

12. An accountant for the Sandell Stamping Co., a manufacturing enterprise, has just finished posting all the year-end adjusting entries to the ledger accounts and now wishes to close the ledger balances in preparation for the new period.

For each of the accounts listed below indicate whether the year-end balance should be: (1) carried forward to the new period, (2) closed by debiting the account, or (3) closed by crediting the account. If the account is to be closed, identify into which summary account it will be closed.

(a) Cash
(b) Sales
(c) Dividends
(d) Finished Goods—Beginning Inventory
(e) Selling Expense
(f) Capital Stock
(g) Income Summary
(h) Direct Labor
(i) Dividends Payable
(j) Raw Materials Purchases
(k) Manufacturing Summary
(l) Accounts Receivable
(m) Prepaid Insurance
(n) Interest Receivable
(o) Raw Materials—Beginning Inventory
(p) Freight In
(q) Interest Revenue
(r) Factory Supervision
(s) Retained Earnings
(t) Accumulated Depreciation

13. The Oster Sales Co. shows a credit balance in the income summary account of $32,400 after the revenue and expense items have been transferred to this account at the end of a fiscal year. Give the remaining entries to close the books, assuming:

    (a) The business is a sole proprietorship: the owner, P. B. Oster, has made withdrawals of $9,000 during the year and this is reported in a drawing account.

    (b) The business is a partnership: the owners, P. B. Oster and T. Z. Oster, share profits 5:3; they have made withdrawals of $12,000 and $9,600 respectively, and these amounts are reported in drawing accounts.

    (c) The business is a corporation: the ledger reports additional paid-in capital, $200,000, and retained earnings, $50,000; dividends during the year of $14,000 were charged to a dividends account.

PROBLEMS

2-1. J. Ellis, a fruit wholesaler, records his business transactions in the following books of original entry: general journal (GJ); voucher register (VR); check register (CKR); sales journal (SJ); and cash receipts journal (CRJ). Ellis uses a voucher system. At the close of business on April 18, Ellis recorded and filed the following business documents:

    (a) Sales invoices for sales on account totaling $2,300.

    (b) The day's cash register tape showing receipts for cash sales at $350.

    (c) A list of cash received on various customer accounts totaling $1,465. Sales discounts taken were $15.

    (d) The telephone bill for $30 payable in one week.

    (e) Vendor's invoices for $2,500 worth of fruit received.

    (f) Check stub for payment of last week's purchases from All-Growers Farms, $2,970. Terms of 1/10, net 30 were taken.

    (g) Check stub for repayment of a $5,000, 90-day note to Mercantile Bank, $5,100.

    (h) A letter notifying Ellis that Littex Markets, a customer, has declared bankruptcy. All creditors will receive 10 cents on every dollar due. Littex owes Ellis $650.

Instructions:

    (1) Indicate the books of original entry in which Ellis recorded each of the business documents. (Use the designated abbreviations.)

    (2) Record the debits and credits for each entry as though only a general journal were used. Use account titles implied by the voucher system.

2-2. A fire destroyed Rodriquez Company's journals. However, the general ledger and accounts receivable subsidiary ledger were saved. An inspection of the ledgers reveals the information shown below and at the top of the next page.

General Ledger

	Cash (11)			Sales (41)	
May 1 Bal.	15,000			May 31	17,850
31	14,330				

	Sales Discounts (42)			Accounts Receivable (12)	
May 3	50		May 1 Bal.	5,850	May 31	8,850
			31	12,320		

Accounts Receivable Ledger

	A			B	
May 1 Bal.	550		May 1 Bal.	2,400	May 13	2,400
5	3,000		5	750		

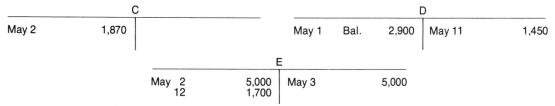

		C						D		
May 2		1,870			May 1	Bal.	2,900	May 11		1,450

		E		
May 2	5,000	May 3		5,000
12	1,700			

Rodriquez's credit policy is 1/10, n/30.

> **Instructions:** Reconstruct the sales and cash receipts journals from the information given above. Assume a Cash Sales column is used in the journals.

2-3. The trial balance of Dennis, Inc., shows, among other items, the following balances on December 31, 1977, the end of a fiscal year:

Accounts Receivable	90,000	
9% Century City Bonds	60,000	
Buildings	120,000	
Accumulated Depreciation — Buildings		34,650
Land	110,000	
8% First-Mortgage Bonds Payable		120,000
Rental Revenue		28,600
Office Expense	3,000	

The following facts are ascertained on this date upon inspection of the company's records.

(a) It is estimated that approximately 2% of accounts receivable may prove uncollectible.
(b) Interest is receivable semiannually on the Century City bonds on March 1 and September 1.
(c) Buildings are depreciated at 2½% a year; however, there were building additions of $20,000 during the year. The company computes depreciation on asset acquisitions during the year at one half the annual rate.
(d) Interest on the first-mortgage bonds is payable semiannually on February 1 and August 1.
(e) Rental revenue includes $1,500 that was received on November 1, representing rent on part of the buildings for the period November 1, 1977, to October 31, 1978.
(f) Office supplies of $800 are on hand on December 31. Purchases of office supplies were debited to the office expense account.

Instructions:
(1) Prepare the journal entries to adjust the books on December 31, 1977.
(2) Give the reversing entries that may appropriately be made at the beginning of 1978.

2-4. The bookkeeper for the Boyer Co. is preparing an income statement for the year ended December 31, 1977, reporting income from operations as $110,900. Accounts have not yet been closed, and a review of the books disclosed the need for the following adjustments:

(a) The account, Office Expense, shows the cost of all purchases of office supplies for the year. At the end of 1977 there are supplies of $600 on hand.
(b) The allowance for doubtful accounts shows a debit balance of $200. It is estimated that 3% of the accounts receivable as of December 31 will prove uncollectible. The accounts receivable balance on this date is $29,100.
(c) The ledger shows a balance for accrued salaries and wages of $1,800 as of December 31, 1976, which was left unchanged during 1977. No recognition was made in the accounts at the end of 1977 for accrued salaries and wages which amounted to $1,950.
(d) The ledger shows a balance for interest receivable of $375 as of December 31, 1976, which was left unchanged during 1977. No recognition was made in the accounts at the end of 1977 for accrued interest which amounted to $440.
(e) The prepaid insurance account was debited during the year for amounts paid for insurance and shows a balance of $1,200 at the end of 1977. The unexpired portions of the policies on December 31, 1977, total $560.
(f) A portion of a building was subleased for three months, November 1, 1977, to February 1, 1978. Unearned Rental Revenue was credited for $1,200 and no adjustment was made in this account at the end of 1977.

(g) The interest expense account was debited for all interest charges incurred during the year and shows a balance of $1,900. However, of this amount, $250 represents debits applicable to notes due in 1978.

(h) Provision for income tax for 1977 is to be computed at a 45% rate.

Instructions: Give the entries that are required on December 31, 1977, to bring the books up to date. (In recording income tax, provide a schedule to show how the corrected income subject to tax was determined.)

2-5. The bookkeeper for the Barry Co. prepares no reversing entries and records all revenue and expense items in nominal accounts during the period. The following balances, among others, are listed on the trial balance at the end of the fiscal period, December 31, 1977, before accounts have been adjusted:

Accounts Receivable	38,000
Allowance for Doubtful Accounts	250
Interest Receivable	700
Discount on Notes Payable	75
Prepaid Real Estate and Personal Property Taxes	450
Salaries and Wages Payable	1,000
Discount on Notes Receivable	700
Unearned Rental Revenue	375

Inspection of the company's records reveals the following as of December 31, 1977:

(a) Uncollectible accounts are estimated at 3% of the accounts receivable balance.

(b) The accrued interest on investments totals $600.

(c) The company borrows cash by discounting its own notes at the bank. Discount on notes payable at the end of 1977 is $400.

(d) Prepaid real estate and personal property taxes are $450, the same as at the end of 1976.

(e) Accrued salaries and wages are $1,075.

(f) The company accepts notes from the customers giving its customers credit for the face of the note less a charge for interest. At the end of each period any interest applicable to the succeeding period is reported as a discount. Discount on notes receivable at the end of 1977 is $375.

(g) Part of the company's properties had been sublet on September 15, 1976, at a rental of $750 per month. The arrangement was terminated at the end of one year.

Instructions: Give the adjusting entries required to bring the books up to date.

2-6. The income statement for the Marble Electric Co. for the year ended December 31, 1977, was as follows:

Marble Electric Co.
Income Statement
For Year Ended December 31, 1977

Sales			$1,200,000
Cost of goods sold:			
Materials purchased	$360,000		
Add decrease in materials inventory	20,000	$380,000	
Direct labor		110,000	
Manufacturing overhead		140,000	
		$630,000	
Add decrease in goods in process inventory		20,000	
		$650,000	
Deduct increase in finished goods inventory		15,000	635,000
Gross profit on sales			$ 565,000
Selling and general expenses			205,000
Income before income tax			$ 360,000
Deduct income tax (income tax, $165,000 plus credit applicable to extraordinary loss, $25,000)			190,000
Income before extraordinary items			$ 170,000
Less loss on early bond retirement (net of $25,000 income tax credit)			25,000
Net income			$ 145,000

Instructions: Give the journal entries to close the accounts at the end of 1977.

2-7. Account balances taken from the ledger of the Jones Supply Corporation on December 31, 1977, follow:

Accounts Payable	$ 36,000	Land	$ 69,600
Accounts Receivable	67,200	Long-Term Investments	12,600
Advertising	4,800	Mortgage Payable	48,000
Accumulated Depreciation —		Notes Payable — Short Term	15,000
Buildings	19,800	Office Expense	16,080
Allowance for Doubtful Ac-		Purchases	138,480
counts	1,380	Purchase Discounts	1,140
Buildings	72,000	Retained Earnings, Dec. 31,	
Capital Stock, $10 par	180,000	1976	14,040
Cash	24,000	Sales	246,000
Dividends	14,400	Sales Discounts	5,400
Freight In	3,600	Sales Returns	3,360
Insurance Expense	1,440	Selling Expense	49,440
Interest Expense	2,640	Supplies Expense	4,200
Interest Revenue	660	Taxes — Real Estate, Payroll,	
Inventory, Dec. 31, 1976	64,800	and Other	7,980

Adjustments on December 31 are required as follows:

(a) The inventory on hand is $90,720.
(b) The allowance for doubtful accounts is to be increased to a balance of $3,000.
(c) Buildings are depreciated at the rate of 3⅓% per year.
(d) Accrued selling expenses are $3,840.
(e) There are supplies of $780 on hand.
(f) Prepaid insurance relating to 1978 and 1979 totals $720.
(g) Accrued interest on long-term investments is $240.
(h) Accrued real estate, payroll and other taxes are $900.
(i) Accrued interest on the mortgage is $480.
(j) Income tax is estimated to be 45% of the income before income tax.

Instructions:
(1) Prepare an eight-column work sheet.
(2) Prepare adjusting, closing, and reversing entries.

2-8. The following account balances are taken from the books of the Hales Manufacturing Co. on December 31, 1977.

Cash	$ 30,875	Retained Earnings	$ 15,850
Accounts Receivable	92,800	Sales	590,000
Allowance for Doubtful Ac-		Raw Materials Purchases	245,700
counts	650	Freight In	7,000
Raw Materials	30,000	Direct Labor	105,000
Goods in Process	12,000	Indirect Labor	25,500
Finished Goods	28,000	Heat, Light, and Power	10,500
Factory Supplies	1,200	Factory Insurance Expense	1,000
Office Supplies	700	Factory Supplies Expense	1,200
Prepaid Rent	2,000	Maintenance and Repairs	7,200
Prepaid Factory Insurance	2,500	Miscellaneous Factory Over-	
Land	50,000	head	3,500
Buildings and Equipment	205,000	Office Rent	15,000
Accumulated Depreciation —		Sales Salaries and Commis-	
Buildings and Equipment	25,000	sions	24,000
Accounts Payable	86,000	Advertising	18,000
Wages and Salaries Payable	7,000	Office Salaries	19,500
Interest Payable	4,500	Office Supplies Expense	700
9% Bonds Payable	150,000	Miscellaneous Selling and Ad-	
Common Stock, $20 par	100,000	ministrative Expense	26,625
		Interest Expense	13,500

The following information was supplied by management:

(a) Inventories, Dec. 31, 1977:

Raw Materials	$22,000	Finished goods	$26,000
Goods in Process	14,000	Factory supplies	500
		Office supplies	250

(b) Provision for doubtful accounts, 1% of annual sales of finished product.
(c) Depreciation, 8%, applied to manufacturing operations.

(d) Accrued wages and salaries:

	12/31/77		12/31/76
Direct labor	$4,200	Direct labor	$5,400
Indirect labor	500	Indirect labor	900
Sales salaries	300	Sales salaries	700

(e) A dividend of $1 per share had been declared December 28, 1977, and is payable January 10, 1978.
(f) Bond interest payment dates are March 1 and September 1.
(g) Rent paid, applicable to 1978, is $1,800.
(h) Insurance paid, applicable to 1978, is $500.
(i) Income tax for 1977 is estimated at $13,000.

Instructions:
(1) Prepare a ten-column work sheet.
(2) Prepare the adjusting and closing entries.

2-9. The account balances taken from the ledger of Frank Arnold and Vern Bradshaw at the end of the first year's operations on December 31, 1977, and the data for adjustments are given below:

Accounts Payable	$12,600	Drawing—Frank Arnold (debit)	$ 2,400
Accounts Receivable	3,100	Drawing—Vern Bradshaw (debit)	900
Capital—Frank Arnold	10,000	Purchases	82,000
Capital—Vern Bradshaw	8,150	Purchase Discounts	2,300
Cash	9,650	Purchase Ret. and Allow.	1,650
Interest Expense	500	Sales	85,000
Interest Revenue	350	Sales Salaries	8,000
Miscellaneous General Expense	12,600	Store Furniture	3,700
Notes Payable	6,000	Store Supplies	600
Notes Receivable	2,000	Taxes	600

Data for adjustments, year ended December 31, 1977:

(a) Inventories: merchandise, $24,100; store supplies, $280.
(b) Depreciation of store furniture, 10% a year. Additions to store furniture were recorded on March 1 costing $900.
(c) Accrued advertising, $95.
(d) Taxes paid in advance, $200.
(e) Accrued taxes, $215.
(f) Accrued interest on notes payable, $75.
(g) Accrued interest on notes receivable, $105.
(h) 5% of the accounts receivable are expected to prove uncollectible.
(i) Arnold and Bradshaw divide earnings in the ratio 3:2.

Instructions:
(1) Prepare an eight-column work sheet.
(2) Prepare adjusting, closing, and reversing entries.

2-10. The following account balances are taken from the general ledger of the James Manufacturing Co. on December 31, 1977, the end of its fiscal year. The corporation was organized January 2, 1971:

Cash on Hand and in Banks	$ 36,125	Buildings	$125,000
Notes Receivable	18,500	Accumulated Depreciation —	
Accounts Receivable	56,000	Buildings	18,000
Allowance for Doubtful Accounts	650	Machinery and Equipment	160,000
Finished Goods — January 1, 1977	40,500	Accumulated Depreciation — Machinery and Equipment	30,000
Goods in Process — January 1, 1977	42,000	Office Furniture and Fixtures	15,000
Raw Materials — January 1, 1977	24,000	Accumulated Depreciation — Office Furniture and Fixtures	9,000
Factory Supplies	17,000	Shipping Department Equipment	12,000
Shipping Supplies	8,500	Accumulated Depreciation — Shipping Department Equipment	7,200
Office Supplies	6,200	Patterns and Dies	30,000
Land	20,000		

Tools	$ 20,000	Maintenance and Repairs of	
Patents	27,500	Machinery	$ 7,000
Notes Payable	20,000	Heat, Light, and Power (Facto-	
Accounts Payable	45,700	ry)	11,000
9% First-Mortgage Bonds	100,000	Taxes	10,200
6% Preferred Stock, $100 par	100,000	Miscellaneous Factory Over-	
Common Stock, $100 par	100,000	head	3,600
Additional Paid-in Capital	10,000	Sales Salaries	35,000
Retained Earnings	125,000	Sales Commissions	12,300
Sales	560,000	Traveling Expense	8,500
Sales Returns and Allowances	10,000	Advertising Expense	23,125
Sales Discounts	7,000	Shipping Department Salaries	6,000
Raw Materials Purchases	107,950	Miscellaneous Shipping De-	
Freight In	8,800	partment Expense	1,000
Purchase Returns and Allow-		Officers Salaries	25,000
ances	3,000	Office Salaries	14,000
Purchase Discounts	3,400	Insurance Expense	8,500
Direct Labor	108,000	Postage, Telephone, and Tele-	
Indirect Labor	32,000	graph	1,400
Plant Superintendence	20,000	Miscellaneous Office Expense	1,500
Maintenance and Repairs of		Interest Revenue	800
Buildings	6,300	Interest Expense — Bonds	5,250
		Interest Expense — Other	1,000

Data for adjustments at December 31, 1977, are as follows:

(a) Inventories:

Finished goods, $49,500; goods in process, $60,200; raw materials, $36,600; factory supplies, $2,700; shipping supplies, $2,500; office supplies, $1,000.

(b) Depreciation and amortization (to nearest month for additions):

Shipping department equipment, 12½%.

Office furniture and fixtures, 10%.

Machinery and equipment, 5%. New machinery and equipment costing $60,000 was installed on March 1, 1977.

Buildings, 4%. Additions to the buildings costing $50,000 were completed June 30, 1977.

Patents were acquired on January 2, 1971. A charge for patent amortization for 1977 is to be made at $1/17$ of the original patents cost.

A charge for patterns and dies amortization for 1977 is to be made at 15% of the balance in the patterns and dies account.

A charge for tools used during the year is to be made at 25% of the balance in the tools account.

(c) The allowance for doubtful accounts is to be increased to a balance of $3,200.

(d) Accrued expenses:

Salaries and wages: direct labor, $1,400; indirect labor, $300; sales salaries, $400; shipping department salaries, $200.

Interest on bonds is payable semiannually on February 1 and August 1.

Interest on notes payable, $50.

Property tax, $2,000.

(e) Prepaid expenses: insurance, $2,500.

(f) Accrued revenue: interest on notes receivable, $500.

(g) The following information is also to be recorded:

(1) It is discovered that sales commissions of $1,200 were charged in error to the account Shipping Department Salaries.

(2) On December 30 the board of directors declared a quarterly dividend on preferred stock and a dividend of $1.50 on common stock, payable January 25, 1978, to stockholders of record January 15, 1978.

(3) Income tax for 1977 is estimated at $30,000.

Taxes, expired insurance, and building expenses are to be distributed as follows: manufacturing operations, 60%; selling operations, 25%; general operations, 15%.

The only charges to retained earnings during the year resulted from the declaration of the regular quarterly dividends on preferred stock.

Instructions:

(1) Prepare a ten-column work sheet. There should be a pair of columns for trial balance, adjustments, manufacturing schedule, income statement, and balance sheet.

(continued)

(2) Prepare all of the journal entries necessary to give effect to the foregoing information and to adjust and close the books of the corporation.

(3) Prepare the reversing entries that may appropriately be made.

2-11. The Forbes Company commenced operations on July 1, 1977. The following shows the gross debits and credits in each account of the ledger as of December 31, 1977, except for goods in process and finished goods inventory accounts. The company uses a cost system for its manufacturing operations.

	Transactions		Trial Balance December 31, 1977	
	Debit	Credit	Debit	Credit
Cash	464,000	370,000	94,000	
Notes Receivable	20,000	12,000	8,000	
Accounts Receivable	340,000	302,000	38,0000	
Finished Goods	compute	compute	30,000	
Goods in Process	compute	compute	14,000	
Raw Materials	125,000	118,000	7,000	
Supplies	18,000	14,000	4,000	
Prepaid Insurance	1,900	1,500	400	
Land, Buildings, and Equipment	95,000	0	95,000	
Mortgage Payable	0	50,000		50,000
Interest Payable	0	750		750
Wages Payable	145,100	147,000		1,900
Vouchers Payable	325,000	365,500		40,500
Capital Stock	0	150,000		150,000
Sales	0	360,000		360,000
Cost of Goods Sold	250,000	0	250,000	
Selling Expense	27,500	0	27,500	
Administrative Expense	29,000	0	29,000	
Financial Expense	6,250	0	6,250	
			603,150	603,150

You are also given the following information:

(a) The ending goods in process inventory consists of the following: materials, $6,000; direct labor, $4,500; and manufacturing overhead, $3,500.

(b) Insurance premiums apply two thirds to the factory and one third to the office.

(c) The cost of the finished product is made up of: materials, 40%; labor, 40%; and manufacturing overhead, 20%.

Instructions: Set up skeleton ledger "T" accounts. Show therein the entries making up the transactions included in the figures shown on the trial balance. Key each entry (debit and offsetting credit) by use of a number, and on a separate sheet give an explanation and support for each entry. (AICPA adapted)

Financial Statements — The Balance Sheet

The principles and techniques applied in the preparation of financial statements have been presented in the preceding chapters. Accounting systems are established to provide the various reports and analyses for internal and external use. Traditionally, however, only one set of statements has been made available externally. This set normally consists of (1) a *balance sheet* reporting the financial position of a business at a certain date; (2) an *income statement* presenting the results of operations of an entity for a reporting period, i.e., the changes in owners' equity arising from operations since the position of the enterprise was last stated; and (3) a *statement of changes in financial position* describing the changes in the financial resources that have occurred during the last reporting period of an enterprise. When the change in owners' equity is not fully explained by the income statement, a supplemental statement referred to as the *statement of changes in owners' equity*, or for a corporation, the *retained earnings statement*, is usually provided to offer a full reconciliation of the difference.

This set of financial statements has become accepted as general purpose statements. They are intended to be relevant to a broad variety of external users. Although there has been some discussion about the need to prepare special purpose statements directed to specific external users, there has been no significant movement toward this in practice.

The balance sheet is discussed in this chapter. The essential nature of the statement of changes in financial position is also introduced in this chapter, but is explained in more detail in Chapter 24. The income statement will be discussed in Chapter 4. Items relating to these primary financial statements, as well as a number of supplementary analytical statements, are described in later chapters.

CONTENT OF THE BALANCE SHEET

The *balance sheet*, also called the *statement of financial position*, reports the assets, liabilities, and owners' equity of a business unit at a given date. The *financial position* is the cumulative result of all transactions of a business from its beginning. Since the balance sheet is basically histori-cal, reporting the position growing out of a series of recorded transac-tions, only a thorough understanding of the principles and practices fol-lowed in the recording process offers an appreciation of the nature of the statement. Some of the basic concepts of balance sheet content, form, and presentation are considered in this chapter. Discussions of the indi-vidual asset, liability, and owners' equity items in later chapters will serve to develop more fully the nature of the balance sheet.

The balance sheet is an expansion of the basic accounting equation, Assets = Liabilities + Owners' Equity. The character and the amount of the assets are exhibited. The liabilities and owners' equity normally bear no relationship to specific assets and hence are presented as balances related to the assets as a whole.

For accounting purposes, assets include those costs that have not been applied to revenues in the past and are considered to afford eco-nomic utility in the production of revenues in the future. Assets, then, include both monetary assets, such as cash, certain marketable securities, and receivables, and those costs recognized as recoverable and hence properly assignable to revenues of future periods, such as inventories, prepaid insurance, equipment, and patents.[1]

Liabilities measure the economic obligations of the enterprise to the creditor group. The method for settlement of liabilities varies. Liabilities may call for settlement by cash payment or settlement through goods to be delivered or services to be performed.[2]

Owners' equity measures the interest of the ownership group in the total resources of the enterprise. This interest arises from investments by owners, and the equity increase or decrease from the change in net assets resulting from operations. An ownership equity does not call for settle-ment on a certain date; in the event of business dissolution, it represents a claim on assets only after creditors have been paid in full. The method of reporting the owners' equity varies with the form of the business unit. Business units are typically divided into three categories: (1) *proprietor-ships*, (2) *partnerships*, and (3) *corporations*.

Balance sheet items are generally classified in a manner to facilitate analysis and interpretation of financial data. Information of primary con-cern to all parties is the business unit's liquidity and solvency — its abil-ity to meet current and long-term obligations. Accordingly, assets and

---

[1]The authors of Accounting Research Study No. 3 define assets as ". . . expected future eco-nomic benefits, rights to which have been acquired by the enterprise as a result of some current or past transaction." Robert T. Sprouse and Maurice Moonitz, *A Tentative Set of Broad Accounting Principles for Business Enterprises*, Accounting Research Study No. 3 (New York: American Institute of Certified Public Accountants, 1962), p. 8. The Accounting Principles Board defined assets as ". . . economic resources of an enterprise that are recognized and measured in conformity with generally accepted accounting principles." *Statements of the Accounting Principles Board, No. 4*, "Basic Con-cepts and Accounting Principles Underlying Financial Statements of Business Enterprises" (New York: American Institute of Certified Public Accountants, 1970), par. 132.

[2]Liabilities are defined by Sprouse and Moonitz in ARS No. 3 as ". . . obligations to convey assets or perform services, such obligations resulting from past or current transactions and requiring settlement in the future." *loc. cit.* The Accounting Principles Board defined liabilities as ". . . econom-ic obligations of an enterprise that are recognized and measured in conformity with generally accept-ed accounting principles." *Statements of the Accounting Principles Board, No. 4, loc. cit.*

liabilities are classified as (1) *current* or *short-term* items and (2) *noncurrent, long-term,* or *fixed* items. When assets and liabilities are classified, the difference between current assets and current liabilities may be determined. This is referred to as the company's *working capital* — the liquid buffer available in meeting financial demands and contingencies of the future.[1]

Current Assets and Current Liabilities

The position of the American Institute of Certified Public Accountants' Committee on Accounting Procedure on current assets follows:

> For accounting purposes, the term *current assets* is used to designate cash and other assets or resources commonly identified as those which are reasonably expected to be realized in cash or sold or consumed during the normal operating cycle of the business. Thus the term comprehends in general such resources as (a) cash available for current operations and items which are the equivalent of cash; (b) inventories of merchandise, raw materials, goods in process, finished goods, operating supplies, and ordinary maintenance material and parts; (c) trade accounts, notes, and acceptances receivable; (d) receivables from officers, employees, affiliates, and others, if collectible in the ordinary course of business within a year; (e) installment or deferred accounts and notes receivable if they conform generally to normal trade practices and terms within the business; (f) marketable securities representing the investment of cash available for current operations; and (g) prepaid expenses such as insurance, interest, rents, taxes, unused royalties, current paid advertising service not yet received, and operating supplies. Prepaid expenses are not current assets in the sense that they will be converted into cash but in the sense that, if not paid in advance, they would require the use of current assets during the operating cycle.[2]

The *normal operating cycle* referred to is the time required for cash to be converted into inventories, inventories into receivables, and receivables ultimately into cash. The Committee further suggested a one-year period be used as a basis for current assets classification in those instances when the average operating cycle is less than twelve months. When the operating cycle exceeds twelve months, as in the case of tobacco, distillery, and lumber industries, the Committee suggested the longer period be used.

In accordance with the foregoing concept of current assets, the Committee lists the following items as noncurrent:

1. Cash and cash claims restricted to use for other than current operations, designated for the acquisition of noncurrent assets, or segregated for the liquidation of noncurrent debts.

2. Advances or investments in securities, whether marketable or not, made for the purposes of control, affiliation, or other continuing business advantage.

---

[1]"Working Capital" is used in this text to denote the excess of current assets over current liabilities. Sometimes this excess is referred to as "net working capital," the term "working capital" then being used to denote total current assets.

[2]*Accounting Research and Terminology Bulletins — Final Edition*, "No. 43, Restatement and Revision of Accounting Research Bulletins" (New York: American Institute of Certified Public Accountants, 1961), Ch. 3, Sec. A, par. 4. The American Accounting Association Committee on Concepts and Standards Underlying Corporate Financial Statements supports the Institute's conclusions on working capital in its Supplementary Statement No. 3, "Current Assets and Current Liabilities," 1951.

3. Receivables not expected to be collected within twelve months arising from unusual transactions such as the sale of capital assets or advances to affiliates, officers, or employees.
4. Cash surrender value of life insurance policies.
5. Land and other natural resources.
6. Depreciable assets.
7. Long-term prepayments fairly chargeable to the operations of several years.[1]

Current liabilities are described as follows:

> The term *current liabilities* is used principally to designate obligations whose liquidation is reasonably expected to require the use of existing resources properly classifiable as current assets, or the creation of other current liabilities. As a balance sheet category, the classification is intended to include obligations for items which have entered into the operating cycle, such as payables incurred in the acquisition of materials and supplies to be used in the production of goods or in providing services to be offered for sale; collections received in advance of the delivery of goods or performance of services; and debts which arise from operations directly related to the operating cycle, such as accruals for wages, salaries, commissions, rentals, royalties, and income and other taxes. Other liabilities whose regular and ordinary liquidation is expected to occur within a relatively short period of time, usually twelve months, are also intended for inclusion, such as short-term debts arising from the acquisition of capital assets, serial maturities of long-term obligations, amounts required to be expended within one year under sinking fund provisions, and agency obligations arising from the collection or acceptance of cash or other assets for the account of third persons.[2]

The current liability classification, however, generally does not include the following items, since these do not require the use of resources classified as current.

1. Short-term obligations expected to be refinanced.[3]
2. Debts to be liquidated from funds that have been accumulated and are reported as noncurrent assets.
3. Loans on life insurance policies made with the intent that these will not be paid but will be liquidated by deduction from the proceeds of the policies upon their maturity or cancellation.
4. Obligations for advance collections that involve long-term deferment of the delivery of goods or services.[4]

With respect to short-term obligations which normally would come due within the operating cycle but which are expected to be refinanced, i.e., discharged by means of the issuance of new obligations in their place, the Financial Accounting Standards Board (FASB) has concluded such obligations should be excluded from current liabilities if the following conditions are met:

1. The intent of the company is to refinance the obligations on a long-term basis, and

---

[1]*Ibid.*, par. 6.

[2]*Ibid.*, par. 7.

[3]*Statement of Financial Accounting Standards No. 6*, "Classification of Short-Term Obligations Expected to Be Refinanced" (Stamford, Conn.: Financial Accounting Standards Board, 1975), par. 16.

[4]*Accounting Research and Terminology Bulletins — Final Edition, op. cit.*, par. 8, and footnotes 2 and 3.

2. The company's intent is supported by an ability to consummate the refinancing as evidenced by a post-balance-sheet-date issuance of long-term obligations or equity securities or an explicit financing agreement.[1]

In effect, the FASB is recognizing that certain short-term obligations will not require the use of working capital during a period even though they are scheduled to mature during that period. Thus, they should not be classified as current liabilities.

Current assets are normally listed on the balance sheet in the order of their liquidity. These assets, with the exception of marketable securities and inventories, are usually reported at their estimated realizable values. Thus, current receivable balances are reduced by allowances for estimated doubtful accounts. Marketable equity securities should be reported at the lower of aggregate cost or market.[2] Inventories may be reported at cost or on the basis of "cost or market, whichever is lower."

Few problems are generally found in the valuation of current liabilities. Payables can usually be determined accurately, even though some items may require estimates as to the amounts ultimately to be paid. These claims, however determined, if payable currently, must be included under the current heading.

The importance of an adequate working capital position cannot be minimized. A business may not be able to survive in the absence of a satisfactory relationship between current assets and current liabilities. Furthermore, its ability to prosper is largely determined by the composition of the current asset pool. There must be a proper balance between liquid assets in the form of cash and temporary investments, and receivables and inventories. Activities of the business center around these assets. Cash and temporary investments, representing immediate purchasing power, are used to meet current claims and purchasing, payroll, and expense requirements; receivables are the outgrowth of sales effort and provide cash in the course of operations; merchandise is also a source of cash as well as the means of achieving a profit. Management, in setting policies with respect to selling, purchasing, financing, expansion, and dividends, must work within the limitations set by the company's working capital position.

Noncurrent Assets and Noncurrent Liabilities   Assets and liabilities not qualifying for presentation under the current headings are classified under a number of noncurrent headings. Noncurrent assets, often referred to as *fixed assets*, may be listed under separate headings, such as "Long-term investments," "Land, buildings, and equipment," "Intangible assets," and "Other long-term assets." Noncurrent liabilities are generally listed under separate headings, such as "Long-term liabilities," "Deferred revenues," and "Other long-term liabilities."

---

[1]*Statement of Financial Accounting Standards No. 6, op. cit.*, par. 9–11.

[2]*Statement of Financial Accounting Standards No. 12*, "Accounting for Certain Marketable Securities" (Stamford, Conn.: Financial Accounting Standards Board, 1975), par. 8.

Long-Term Investments. Investments held for such long-term purposes as regular income, appreciation, or ownership control are reported under the heading "Long-term investments." Examples of items properly reported under this heading are long-term stock, bond, and mortgage holdings; securities of affiliated companies as well as advances to such companies; sinking fund assets consisting of cash and securities held for the redemption of bonds or stock, the replacement of buildings, or the payment of pensions; land held for future use or sale; the cash surrender value of life insurance; and other miscellaneous investments not used directly in the operations of the business. Although many long-term investments are reported at cost, there are modifications to the valuation of some investments which will be discussed in later chapters.

Land, Buildings, and Equipment. Properties of a tangible and relatively permanent character that are used in the normal business operations are reported under the heading "Land, buildings, and equipment." Land, buildings, equipment, machinery, tools, furniture, fixtures, and vehicles are included under this heading. Buildings and equipment items are normally reported at cost less accumulated depreciation.

Intangible Assets. The long-term rights and privileges of a nonphysical character acquired for use in business operations are reported under the heading "Intangible assets." Included in this class are such items as goodwill, patents, trademarks, franchises, copyrights, formulas, leaseholds, and organization costs. Intangible assets are normally reported at cost less amounts previously amortized.

Other Long-Term Assets. Those noncurrent or fixed assets not suitably reported under any of the previous classifications may be listed under the general heading "Other long-term assets" or may be listed separately under special descriptive headings. Such assets include cash funds representing deposits received from customers on returnable containers, deposits made with vendors to secure contracts, and long-term advances to officers.

Prepayments for services or benefits to be received over a number of periods are properly regarded as noncurrent. Among these are such items as plant rearrangement costs and developmental and improvement costs. These long-term prepayments are frequently reported under a "Deferred costs" or "Deferred charges" heading. However, objection can be raised to a deferred costs category since this designation could be applied to all costs assignable to future periods including inventories, buildings and equipment, and intangible assets. The deferred costs heading may be avoided by reporting long-term prepayments within the other long-term assets section or under separate descriptive headings.

A debit balance in the deferred income tax account may be shown under "Other long-term assets" or may be reported separately. Income tax is considered to be prepaid when paid on a computed income that is more than the income reported on the financial statements. The tax difference may be a temporary one caused by a *timing* difference — a difference in the period in which revenue or expense is recognized on the tax return and on the books. Under these circumstances, matching of income tax expense with revenue requires that the tax paid on taxable income in excess of the book income be deferred and recognized as an addition to tax paid in the period when the income is ultimately recognized on the books.

Contingent Assets. Circumstances at the balance sheet date may indicate the existence of certain rights or claims that could materialize as valuable assets depending upon the favorable outcome of certain events. In the absence of a legal right to the properties at that time, these can be viewed only as *contingent assets.* Contingencies that might result in gains are not usually recorded in the accounts; they may be disclosed by a special note or by appropriate comment under a separate "Contingent assets" heading following the "Other asset" classifications. Care should be exercised not to present misleading implications with respect to possible realization.[1] Tax claims, insurance claims, and claims against merchandise creditors may warrant such treatment. Reference to contingent assets in the balance sheet is rare in practice.

Long-Term Liabilities. Long-term notes, bonds, mortgages, and similar obligations not requiring the use of current funds for their retirement are generally reported on the balance sheet under the heading "Long-term liabilities."

When an amount borrowed is not the same as the amount ultimately required in settlement of the debt, and the debt is stated in the accounts at its maturity amount, a debt discount or premium is reported. The discount or premium should be related to the debt item: a discount, then, should be subtracted from the amount reported for the debt, and a premium should be added to the amount reported for the debt. The debt is thus reported at its present value as measured by the proceeds from its issuance. Amortization of the discount or premium brings the obligation to the maturity amount by the end of its normal term. When a note, a bond issue, or a mortgage formerly classified as a long-term obligation becomes payable within a year, it should be reclassified and presented as a current liability, except when the obligation is expected to be refinanced as discussed earlier or is to be paid out of a sinking fund.

Deferred Revenues. Cash may be received or other assets recognized for goods and services to be supplied in future periods. Such transactions are recognized in the accounts by debits to assets and credits to liability accounts reporting the advance payments. The latter balance is properly

---

[1]*Statement of Financial Accounting Standards No. 5,* "Accounting for Contingencies" (Stamford, Conn.: Financial Accounting Standards Board, 1975), par. 17.

carried forward until the company meets its responsibilities through the delivery of goods or the performance of services. If, in subsequent periods, the expenses of providing the goods and services are less than the obligations that are discharged thereby, earnings will be recognized; on the other hand, if expenses are greater than the obligations that are discharged, losses will be incurred. Examples of transactions that call for revenue deferral and recognition as long-term obligations include fees received in advance on long-term service contracts, and long-term leasehold and rental prepayments. These prepayments are normally reported on the balance sheet under the heading of "Deferred revenues."

All revenues received in advance for goods and services are frequently reported under the "Deferred revenues" heading, including those calling for settlement in the near future. However, the noncurrent classification is appropriate only when an item represents no significant claim upon current assets. When significant costs are involved in satisfying a claim and these costs will be met from the company's current assets, the prepayment should be recognized as a current liability. The obligation arising from the receipt of cash in advance on magazine subscriptions, for example, is properly recognized as a current liability in view of the claim it makes upon current assets.

Other Long-Term Liabilities. Those noncurrent liabilities not suitably reported under the "Long-term liabilities" or "Deferred revenues" headings may be listed under the general heading "Other long-term liabilities" or may be listed separately under special descriptive headings. Such liabilities include obligations to customers in the form of long-term refundable deposits or returnable containers, long-term obligations to company officers or affiliated companies, matured but unclaimed bond principal and interest obligations, and long-term liabilities under pension plans.

A credit balance in the deferred income tax account may be shown under "Other long-term liabilities" or may be reported separately. Income tax is considered to have accrued when tax is paid on a computed income that is less than the income reported on the financial statements. The difference, as in the case of the deferred income tax expense previously mentioned, may be a temporary one caused by a timing difference. In this case, however, the timing difference has resulted in postponing income tax until a later period. Timing differences may occur, for example, in recognizing a different amount of depreciation on the tax return and on the books, and also in recognizing revenue on installment sales and on long-term construction contracts. A matching of income tax expense with revenue requires that postponed income tax be accrued and recognized as a subtraction from tax paid in the period when the revenue is ultimately recognized on the tax return.

Contingent Liabilities. Past activities or circumstances may have given rise to possible future liabilities, although legal obligations do not exist on the date of the balance sheet. These possible claims are known as *contingent liabilities*. They are potential obligations involving uncertainty as to possible losses. As future events occur or fail to occur, this uncertainty will be resolved. Thus, a contingent liability is distinguishable from an *estimated liability*. The latter is a definite obligation with only the amount of the obligation in question and subject to estimation at the balance sheet date. There may not be any doubt as to the amount of a contingent liability, for example, a pending lawsuit, but there is considerable uncertainty as to whether the obligation will actually materialize.

In the past, contingent liabilities have not been recorded in the accounts and presented on the balance sheet. When they have been disclosed, it has been in the notes to the financial statements. Now, with the issuance of *Statement of Financial Accounting Standards No. 5* by the FASB, if certain criteria are met, a contingent liability should be recorded by a debit to a loss account and a credit to a contingent liability.[1] Examples of contingent liabilities and further discussion of their treatment is presented in Chapter 16.

Owners' Equity

In the case of a proprietorship, the owner's equity in assets is reported by means of a single capital account. The balance in this account is the cumulative result of the owner's investments and withdrawals as well as past earnings and losses. In a partnership, capital accounts are established for each partner. Capital account balances summarize the investments and withdrawals and shares of past earnings and losses of each partner, and thus measure the partners' individual equities in the partnership assets.

In a corporation, the difference between assets and liabilities is referred to as *stockholders' equity, shareholders' equity*, or simply, *capital*. In presenting the stockholders' equity on the balance sheet, a distinction is made between the equity originating from the stockholders' investment, referred to as *paid-in capital*, and the equity originating from earnings, referred to as *retained earnings*. Sometimes the term *surplus* is applied to all corporate capital balances other than capital stock. Thus, paid-in capital other than that portion representing capital stock may be designated *paid-in surplus* or *capital surplus*, and retained earnings may be designated *earned surplus*. The use of the term surplus is not recommended as will be discussed later in this chapter.

Paid-In Capital. Paid-in capital is generally reported in two parts: (1) *capital stock* representing that portion of the contribution by stockholders assignable to the shares of stock issued; (2) *additional paid-in capital* representing investments by stockholders in excess of the amounts assignable to capital stock as well as invested capital from other sources.

Capital stock outstanding having a par value is shown on the balance sheet at par. Capital stock having no par value is stated at the amount received on its original sale or at some other value as stipulated by law or

---

[1] *Ibid.*, par. 8–13.

as assigned by action of the board of directors of the corporation. When more than a single class of stock has been issued and is outstanding, the stock of each class is reported separately. *Treasury stock*, which is stock issued but subsequently reacquired by the corporation, is subtracted from the total stock issued or from the sum of paid-in capital and retained earnings balances. The capital stock balance is viewed as the *legal capital* or *permanent capital* of the corporation.

A premium received on the sale of par-value stock or the amount received in excess of the value assigned to no-par stock is recognized as additional paid-in capital. Additional paid-in capital may also arise from transactions other than the sale of stock, such as from the acquisition of property as a result of a donation or from the sale of treasury stock at more than cost. The additional paid-in capital balances are normally added to capital stock so the full amount of the paid-in capital may be reported. When stock is sold at less than par, capital stock is shown at par and the discount is reported as a subtraction item in arriving at paid-in capital.

Retained Earnings. The amount of undistributed earnings of past periods is reported as *retained earnings*. The amount thus shown may not represent cash available for payment as dividends since retained earnings of past years have probably already been reinvested in other assets. An excess of dividends and losses over earnings results in a negative retained earnings balance called a *deficit*. The balance of retained earnings is added to the paid-in capital total in summarizing the stockholders' equity; a deficit is subtracted from paid-in capital.

Portions of retained earnings are sometimes reported as restricted and unavailable as a basis for dividends. Restricted earnings may be designated as *appropriations*. Appropriations are frequently made for such purposes as sinking funds, plant expansion, loss contingencies, and the reacquisition of capital stock. When appropriations have been made, retained earnings on the balance sheet consists of an amount designated as *Appropriated* and a balance designated as *Unappropriated* or *Free*.

Offsets on the Balance Sheet

A number of balance sheet items are frequently reported at gross amounts calling for the recognition of offset balances in arriving at proper valuations. Such offset balances are found in contra asset, liability, and owners' equity categories. In the case of assets, for example, an allowance for doubtful accounts is subtracted from the sum of the customers' accounts in reporting the net amount estimated collectible; accumulated depreciation is subtracted from the related buildings and equipment balances in reporting the costs of the assets still assignable to future revenues. In the case of liabilities, bonds reacquired, or *treasury bonds*, are subtracted from bonds issued in reporting the amount of bonds outstanding; a bond discount is subtracted from the face value of bonds outstanding in reporting the net amount of the debt. In the case of stockholders' equity in the corporation, a discount on capital stock is subtracted from the par value of capital stock in reporting paid-in capital; a deficit is subtracted from paid-in capital.

The types of offsets described above, utilizing contra accounts, are required for proper reporting of particular balance sheet items. Offsets are improper, however, if applied to different asset and liability balances or to asset and owners' equity balances even when there is some relationship between the items. For example, a company may accumulate cash in a special fund to discharge certain tax liabilities; but as long as control of the cash is retained and the liabilities are still outstanding, the company should continue to report both the asset and the liabilities separately. Or a company may accumulate cash in a special fund for the redemption of preferred stock outstanding; but until the cash is applied to the reacquisition of the stock, the company must continue to report the asset as well as the owners' equity item. A company may have made advances to certain salespersons while at the same time reporting accrued amounts payable to others; but a net figure cannot be justified here, just as a net figure cannot be justified for the offset of trade receivables against trade payables.

Balance Sheet Terminology

The accounting profession has engaged in a continuing effort to define appropriate terms for use in accounting. It has also directed attention to those terms that have been subject to misinterpretation and inappropriate use. Such efforts have been accompanied by a movement to modify terminology where modification might contribute to a better understanding of accounting.

Net Worth and Surplus. The use of *net worth* to designate stockholders' equity has been challenged on the grounds that a balance sheet does not purport to reflect and could not usefully reflect the value of the enterprise or of equity interests therein. The need for designations emphasizing *investment* rather than *value* is recognized. The use of the term *surplus* is also objectionable because its popular use to indicate excess, residue, or that which remains when use or need has been satisfied, is hardly in agreement with its accounting use. As indicated earlier, *surplus*, as employed in an accounting sense, has been used to suggest investment by owners or earned surplus as in paid-in surplus and accumulated earnings. To clarify reporting, the AICPA has recommended the discontinuance of the term *surplus* in the balance sheet presentation of stockholders' equity, and the substitution of terms clearly indicating the sources from which capital was derived.[1]

---

[1]See *Accounting Research and Terminology Bulletins — Final Edition*, "Accounting Terminology Bulletins, No. 1, Review and Résumé" (New York: American Institute of Certified Public Accountants, 1961), par. 65–70. However, the Institute has continued to use the term *surplus* in some of its pronouncements. The committee on Accounting Procedure states in its preface to "Accounting Research Bulletin No. 43," "Although the committee has approved the objective of finding a better term than the word *surplus* for use in published financial statements, it has used *surplus* herein as being a technical term well understood among accountants, to whom its pronouncements are primarily directed."

Reserves. The term *reserve* has been employed in the following conflicting ways on the balance sheet.

1. As a contra account — Reserve for Bad Debts, for example, to reduce a receivable balance to the estimated amount collectible, or Inventory Reserve, for example, to reflect an adjustment for lifo inventory changes.
2. As a liability whose amount is uncertain — Reserve for Federal Income Tax, for example, to indicate the amount of income tax estimated to be payable.
3. As an appropriation of retained earnings — Reserve for Bond Retirement Fund, for example, to represent an appropriation of retained earnings corresponding to the assets that have been segregated and that are to be used for bond retirement.

Since the generally accepted meaning of the term *reserve* relates only to appropriations of retained earnings, the AICPA Committee on Terminology recommended its use be limited to items within this class.[1] Contra asset accounts should be referred to by more descriptive titles, such as Allowance for Doubtful Accounts and Accumulated Depreciation. Liabilities involving estimates should be reported as estimated liabilities.

Use of reserve as a contra asset, liability, or owners' equity account should be discouraged. Even more objectionable is the practice of listing such diverse reserve elements under a common heading "Reserves," usually reported between the liabilities and owners' equity sections on the balance sheet. This practice results in a distortion of asset, liability, and owners' equity balances, making necessary a full analysis of the reserves and their identification with the appropriate balance sheet section in arriving at a summary of assets and related equities. Further, the use of such titles as Miscellaneous Reserves, General Reserves, and Contingency Reserves within a reserves section frequently makes accurate identification of the reserve item impossible.

The term *net worth* is rarely found in modern practice. However, the terms *surplus* and *reserve* are still used, although not as extensively.[2] Most of the illustrations in the text employ the statement forms and terminology recommended by leading accounting authorities. However, alternate forms and terms are used in some text questions, exercises, and problems, since these are still encountered in practice. It must be pointed out that in communicating the business story, movement toward more readily understood terminology is only one phase of the problem. The person who uses the statement must be educated to understand the na-

[1]*Ibid*., par. 57–64.

[2]*Accounting Trends & Techniques* published annually by the American Institute of Certified Public Accountants, summarizes and analyzes the accounting practices that are found in the financial reports released each year by 600 industrial companies. In the AICPA list of 600 survey companies, the number using the term "surplus" in reporting paid-in capital ("capital surplus," for example), was 104 in 1975 as compared with 375 in 1948; the number using the term "surplus" in reporting accumulated earnings ("earned surplus," for example) was 11 in 1975 as compared with 501 in 1948. The term "reserve" was used in reporting accumulated depreciation by 15 companies in 1975 as compared with 118 companies in 1960. *Accounting Trends & Techniques* (30th ed.; New York: American Institute of Certified Public Accountants, 1976), pp. 176, 177, 167.

ture of accounting, the service it can legitimately perform, the limitations to which it is subject, and the kind of analysis and interpretation appropriate under these circumstances.

Form of the Balance Sheet

The form of the balance sheet varies in practice. Its form may be influenced by the nature and size of the business, by the character of the business properties, and, in some instances, by requirements set by regulatory bodies. The balance sheet is generally prepared in *account form*, assets being reported on the left-hand side and liabilities and owners' equity on the right-hand side. It may also be prepared in *report form*, with assets, liabilities, and owners' equity sections appearing in vertical arrangement.

The order of asset and liability classifications may vary, but usually emphasis is placed upon a company's working capital position and liquidity, with asset and liability groups, as well as the items within such groups, presented in the order of liquidity. A balance sheet in account form with financial data reported in the order of liquidity is illustrated on pages 76 and 77.

When the report form is used, liability and owners' equity totals may be added together to constitute an amount equal to the asset total. In other instances, total liabilities are subtracted from total assets, and owners' equity is reported as the difference. A variation of the report form referred to as the *financial position form* has found some favor. This form emphasizes the current position and reports a working capital balance. The financial position form is illustrated at the top of page 78. (Individual assets and liabilities are omitted in the example.)[1]

Related balance sheet items are frequently combined so the balance sheet may be prepared in condensed form. For example, land, buildings, and equipment may be reported as a single item; raw materials, goods in process, and finished goods inventories may be combined; and long-term investments may be reported in total. Consolidation of similar items within reasonable limits may actually serve to clarify the business position and data relationships. Supporting detail for individual items, when considered of particular significance or when required by law, may be supplied by means of special summaries referred to as *supplementary schedules*.

Balance sheet data are generally presented in comparative form. With comparative reports for two or more dates, information is made available concerning the nature and trend of financial changes taking place within the periods between balance sheet dates. When a statement is presented in a special form, the heading should designate the nature of the form that is provided, as for example, "Condensed Balance Sheet," or "Comparative Balance Sheet."

---

[1]Analysis of the reports of the AICPA list of survey companies with fiscal years ending within the calendar year 1974 showed that 13 companies used the financial position form. This was down from the total of 79 companies that used this form in 1959. *Ibid.*, p. 95.

Andersen
Balance
December

Assets

Current assets:

Cash in bank and on hand		$ 36,500	
Marketable securities (reported at cost; market value, $71,500)		70,000	
Notes receivable, trade debtors (Note 2)............................	$ 15,000		
Accounts receivable..	50,000		
	$ 65,000		
Less allowance for doubtful accounts............................	5,000	60,000	
Claim for income tax refund		9,000	
Creditors' accounts with debit balances...........................		750	
Advances to employees..		1,250	
Interest receivable...		250	
Inventories (Note 1a)...		125,000	
Prepaid expenses:			
Supply inventories..	$ 3,000		
Insurance..	4,250	7,250	$310,000
Long-term investments:			
Investment in land and unused facilities (Note 1d)...............		$ 22,500	
Cash surrender value of officers' life insurance policies		9,000	31,500

Land, buildings, and equipment (Note 1b):

	Cost	Accumulated Depreciation	Book Value	
Land	$ 80,000		$ 80,000	
Buildings...	150,000	$ 35,000	115,000	
Equipment	100,000	45,000	55,000	
	$330,000	$ 80,000		250,000

Intangible assets (Note 1c):

Patents		$ 70,000	
Goodwill...		18,500	88,500
Other long-term assets:			
Advances to officers		$ 15,000	
Customer deposits on returnable containers		5,000	20,000
Total assets			$700,000

See accompanying notes to financial statements.

Account Form

Notes to the Financial Statements

Along with the movement toward more descriptive terminology have come attempts to improve the manner of presentation and the extent of disclosure of financial data. Notes to the financial statements are now considered an integral part of any formal financial statement presentation. They are essential in explaining the basic financial data and should be prepared and read with care.[1]

---

[1]The required disclosures for each balance sheet item are of such detail that they cannot be completely discussed in Chapters 3 and 4. Therefore, the notes to the financial statements illustrated in this chapter and in the end-of-chapter material do not provide complete disclosure, but are only illustrative of the general nature and content of the notes which are included in financial statements. Notes to financial statements in end-of-chapter material need only be prepared when specifically required by the problem.

Corporation
Sheet
31, 1977

Liabilities

Current liabilities:

Notes payable, trade creditors		$ 14,250	
Accounts payable		12,500	
Dividends payable		5,000	
Advances from customers		5,750	
Income tax payable		27,000	
Other liabilities:			
Salaries and wages payable	$ 1,000		
Taxes payable	1,500	2,500	$ 67,000
Long-term liabilities:			
8% First-mortgage bonds due December 31, 1997 (Note 3)		$100,000	
Less unamortized bond discount		5,000	95,000
Deferred revenues:			
Unearned lease revenue (Note 1d)			20,000
Other long-term liabilities:			
Deferred income tax		$ 3,000	
Liability under pension plan (Note 4)		65,000	68,000
Total liabilities			$250,000

Stockholders' Equity

Paid-in capital:

Common stock, $5 stated value, 100,000 shares authorized, 50,000 shares issued and outstanding	$250,000	
Paid-in capital from sale of common stock at more than stated value	45,000	$295,000
Retained earnings		155,000
Total stockholders' equity		450,000
Total liabilities and stockholders' equity		$700,000

Balance Sheet

Summary of Significant Accounting Policies Followed

In addition to the other notes, a summary of the significant accounting policies followed should be presented with the financial statements. In this regard, the Accounting Principles Board concluded in APB Opinion No. 22:

> . . . When financial statements are issued purporting to present fairly financial position, changes in financial position, and results of operation in accordance with generally accepted accounting principles, a description of all significant accounting policies of the reporting entity should be included as an integral part of the financial statements.[1]

---

[1]*Opinions of the Accounting Principles Board, No. 22,* "Disclosure of Accounting Policies" (New York: American Institute of Certified Public Accountants, 1972), par. 8.

Andersen Corporation
Statement of Financial Position
December 31, 1977

Current assets		$310,000
Less current liabilities...		67,000
Working capital		$243,000
Add:		
Long-term investments...		31,500
Land, buildings, and equipment...		250,000
Intangible assets		88,500
Other long-term assets		20,000
Total assets less current liabilities..		$633,000
Deduct:		
Long-term liabilities less unamortized bond discount	$95,000	
Deferred revenues...	20,000	
Deferred income tax	3,000	
Liability under pension plan..	65,000	183,000
Net assets..		$450,000
Stockholders' equity:		
Paid-in capital..		$295,000
Retained earnings		155,000
Total stockholders' equity...		$450,000

Financial Position Form of Balance Sheet

The Board further stated:

> . . . In general, the disclosure should encompass important judgments as to appropriateness of principles relating to recognition of revenue and allocation of asset costs to current and future periods; in particular it should encompass those principles and methods that involve any of the following: (a) A selection from existing acceptable alternatives; (b) Principles and methods peculiar to the industry in which the reporting entity operates, even if such principles and methods are predominantly followed in that industry; (c) Unusual or innovative applications of generally accepted accounting principles (and, as applicable, of principles and methods peculiar to the industry in which the reporting entity operates.)[1]

Examples of disclosure of accounting policies required by this opinion would include, among others, those relating to depreciation methods, amortization of intangible assets, inventory pricing methods, the recognition of profit on long-term construction-type contracts, and the recognition of revenue from leasing operations.[2]

The exact format for reporting the summary of accounting policies was not specified by the Board. However, the Board recommended such disclosure be included as the initial note or as a separate summary preceding the notes to the financial statements. As an illustration, the notes to the financial statements for the Andersen Corporation, including a summary of accounting policies followed, are shown at the top of the following page.

Careful classification of items under descriptive headings, appropriate explanatory notes, and the presentation of data in comparative form provides more meaningful statements. Presentations in condensed

---

[1]*Ibid.*, par. 12.
[2]*Ibid.*, par. 13.

ANDERSEN CORPORATION
NOTES TO FINANCIAL STATEMENTS — YEAR ENDED DECEMBER 31, 1977

1. Summary of Significant Accounting Policies:

   (a) Inventories are valued at cost or market, whichever is lower. Cost is calculated by the first-in, first-out method.

   (b) Depreciation is computed for both the books and tax return by the double-declining balance method.

   (c) Intangible assets are being amortized over the period of their estimated useful lives: patents, 10 years, and goodwill, 20 years.

   (d) The company leased Market Street properties for a 15-year period ending January 1, 1984. Leasehold payment received in advance is being recognized as revenue over the life of the lease.

2. The company is contingently liable on guaranteed notes and accounts totaling $40,000. Also, various suits are pending on which the ultimate payment cannot be determined. In the opinion of counsel and management, such liability, if any, will not be material.

3. Bonds may be called at the option of the board of directors at 105 plus accrued interest on or before December 31, 1979, and at gradually reduced amounts but at not less than $102\frac{1}{2}$ plus accrued interest after January 1, 1985.

4. The pension plan covers all employees. The company funds all pension costs accrued. The liability under the company pension plan has been calculated on the basis of actuarial studies.

---

forms and the rounding of numbers to the nearest dollar, hundred or thousands of dollars clarify relationships and facilitate analysis. A variety of different balance sheet forms are found in practice.[1]

OVERVIEW OF THE STATEMENT OF CHANGES IN FINANCIAL POSITION

The statement of changes in financial position, also commonly referred to as the *funds statement,* may be characterized as a condensed report of how the activities of a business have been financed and how the financial resources have been used. It is a flow statement, emphasizing the inflows and outflows of resources related to the significant financial events of an enterprise during a reporting period.

Although based on the same data as the balance sheet and the income statement, the statement of changes in financial position helps to answer questions not readily apparent from cursory examination of either or both of the other two statements. For example, the funds statement helps the reader answer questions, such as Where did the profits go? Why were dividends not larger? How can dividends be distributed in excess of current earnings or when there was a reported net loss? Why are current assets decreasing when the results of operations are positive? How was the plant expansion financed? and What use was made of the proceeds from the sale of stock?

---

[1]An illustrative set of financial statements, complete with applicable notes, is provided in Appendix B of this textbook. Included is a balance sheet illustrating one approach taken in the development of a statement summarizing financial status.

By helping to answer questions such as the above, the statement of changes in financial position serves an important function. Its purposes and the techniques used in its preparation are discussed more fully in Chapter 24. An illustration of a simple funds statement, presented on a working capital basis, is provided below:

Andersen Corporation
Statement of Changes in Financial Position — Working Capital Basis
For Year Ended December 31, 1977

Working capital was provided by:			
Operations:			
Income before extraordinary items...............................		$25,000	
Add items not requiring working capital:			
Depreciation...	$10,000		
Amortization of patents and goodwill........................	10,600	20,600	
Working capital provided by operations...........................		$45,600	
Issuance of bonds		95,000	
Issuance of common stock to acquire land		70,000	$210,600
Working capital was applied to:			
Dividends..		$20,000	
Retirement of long-term debt....................................		80,000	
Acquisition of land by issuance of common stock...........		70,000	170,000
Increase in working capital*...................................			$ 40,600

*Details of increase in working capital are not given. The above figures are illustrative only. They cannot be derived from the financial statements presented because comparative statements are not provided.

QUESTIONS

1. Which accounting statements are considered general purpose financial statements?

2. What is the composition of the balance sheet? How is it related to the income statement and the statement of changes in financial position?

3. What is the balance sheet equation? Define each of the elements of that equation.

4. Why is the distinction between current and noncurrent assets and liabilities so important?

5. What criteria would you use (a) in classifying assets as current or noncurrent? (b) in classifying liabilities as current or noncurrent?

6. (a) Give examples of expense prepayments properly reported as (1) current items and (2) noncurrent items. What factors govern in the determination of the appropriate classification? (b) Give examples of unearned revenues properly reported as (1) current items and (2) noncurrent items. What factors govern here?

7. Farnley's Inc., reports the cash surrender value of life insurance on company officials as a current asset in view of its immediate convertibility into cash. Do you support this treatment?

8. Indicate under what circumstances each of the following can be considered noncurrent: (a) cash, (b) receivables, (c) inventories, (d) collections received in advance of the delivery of goods.

9. Under what circumstances may bonds payable due in six months be reported as a long-term liability, even though they will not be liquidated from accumulated noncurrent funds?

10. What objections can be made to the use of the heading "Deferred costs"?

11. What justification is there for treating intangible items as assets on the balance sheet?

12. Explain how a credit balance in the deferred income tax account meets the commonly accepted definition of liabilities.

13. Why is a premium or discount on bonded indebtedness reported as an addition to or subtraction from the face value of the bond liability?

14. Give an example of (a) a contingent asset, (b) a contingent liability, and (c) a contingent owners' equity item.

15. Distinguish between the following: (a) contingent liabilities and estimated liabilities, (b) appropriated retained earnings and free retained earnings.

16. What are the major classifications of (a) assets, (b) liabilities, and (c) owners' equity items? Indicate the nature of the items reported within each major classification.

17. Under what circumstances may offset balances be properly recognized on the balance sheet?

18. (a) What objections are raised to the use of the terms (1) reserve, (2) net worth, and (3)

surplus? (b) What suggestions have been made with respect to these terms in attempts to improve financial reporting?

19. What information is emphasized by use of the financial position form of the balance sheet?

20. Indicate those balance sheet items that may require the disclosure of significant accounting policies or other parenthetical remarks or notes if the reader of the statement is to be adequately informed.

21. What is the basic purpose of the statement of changes in financial position? What kind of information does this statement provide that is not readily available from the other general purpose statements?

EXERCISES

1. A balance sheet contains the following classifications:

(a) Current assets
(b) Long-term investments
(c) Land, buildings, and equipment
(d) Intangible assets
(e) Other long-term assets
(f) Current liabilities

(g) Long-term liabilities
(h) Deferred revenues
(i) Capital stock
(j) Additional paid-in capital
(k) Retained earnings

Indicate by letter how each of the following accounts would be classified. Place a minus sign (−) after all accounts representing offset or contra balances.

____ (1) Discount on Bonds Payable
____ (2) Stock of Subsidiary Corporation
____ (3) 7% Bonds Payable (due in six months)
____ (4) U.S. Treasury Notes
____ (5) Income Tax Payable
____ (6) Sales Tax Payable
____ (7) Estimated Claims Under Guarantees for Service and Replacements
____ (8) Accounts Payable (debit balance)
____ (9) Unearned Rental Revenue (three years in advance)

____(10) Accumulated Depletion
____(11) Interest Receivable
____(12) Preferred Stock Retirement Fund
____(13) Trademarks
____(14) Allowance for Doubtful Accounts
____(15) Dividends Payable
____(16) Accumulated Depreciation
____(17) Petty Cash Fund
____(18) Prepaid Rent
____(19) Prepaid Interest
____(20) Organization Costs

2. State how each of the following accounts should be classified on the balance sheet.

(a) Accumulated Patent Amortization
(b) Retained Earnings
(c) Vacation Pay
(d) Retained Earnings Appropriated for Loss Contingencies
(e) Allowance for Doubtful Accounts
(f) Liability for Pension Payments
(g) Marketable Securities
(h) Paid-In Capital from Sale of Stock at More Than Stated Value
(i) Unamortized Bond Issue Costs
(j) Goodwill
(k) Receivables — U.S. Government Contracts
(l) Advances to Salespersons
(m) Customers Accounts with Credit Balances

(n) Raw Materials
(o) Cash Representing Refundable Deposits on Returnable Containers
(p) Unclaimed Payroll Checks
(q) Employees Income Tax Payable
(r) Subscription Revenue Received in Advance
(s) Interest Payable
(t) Deferred Income Tax (debit balance)
(u) Tools
(v) Deferred Income Tax (credit balance)
(w) Loans to Officers
(x) Leasehold Improvements
(y) Patents

3. Indicate how each of the following items should be classified on the balance sheet:

    (a) Cash surrender value of life insurance.
    (b) Sinking fund cash for retirement of bonds.
    (c) Bonds payable in six months out of sinking fund cash.
    (d) Note receivable that will be collected in 10 annual installments.
    (e) Cash deposited with broker on option to buy real estate.
    (f) Land held as future plant site.
    (g) Warehouse in process of construction.
    (h) Cash fund representing customers' deposits on returnable containers.
    (i) Cash fund representing sales tax collections.
    (j) Goods in process that will require more than one year for completion.

4. The bookkeeper for Can-Co, Inc., submitted the following balance sheet as of June 30, 1977.

Can-Co, Inc.
Balance Sheet
December 31, 1977

Cash	$ 15,000	Accounts payable — trade	$ 25,000
Accounts receivable — trade	25,000	Salaries payable	10,000
Inventories	40,000	Stockholders' equity	70,000
Machinery	10,000		
Goodwill	15,000		
	$105,000		$105,000

Reference to the records of the company indicated the following:

    (a) Cash included:

Petty cash	$ 500
Payroll account	5,000
Savings account for cash to be used for building re-modeling	5,000
General account	4,500
	$15,000

    (b) State and local taxes of $1,200 were accrued on December 31. However, $1,200 had been deposited in a special cash account to be used to pay these and neither cash nor the accrued taxes were reported on the balance sheet.

    (c) Twenty-five percent of Can-Co, Inc.'s inventory is rapidly becoming obsolete. The obsolete portion of the inventory as of the balance sheet date was worth only one-half of what Can-Co, Inc., paid for it.

    (d) Goods costing $1,500 were shipped to customers on December 30 and 31, at a sales price of $2,200. Goods shipped were not included in the inventory as of December 31. However, receivables were not recognized for the shipment since invoices were not sent out until January 3.

    (e) One of Can-Co, Inc.'s machines costing $4,000 is located on the Autonomous Island Republic, Tropicana. The dictator of Tropicana nationalized several foreign business-es during 1977 and is threatening to expropriate Can-Co, Inc.'s machinery for per-sonal use. All machinery was acquired in July of 1977 and will not be depreciated this year.

    (f) The corporation had been organized on January 1, 1977, by exchanging 5,500 shares of no-par stock with stated value of $10 per share for the net assets of the part-nership Canfield and Collins.

Prepare a corrected balance sheet as of December 31, 1977.

5. From the following chart of accounts, prepare a balance sheet in account form showing all balance sheet items properly classified. (No monetary amounts are to be recognized.)

Accounts Payable	Allowance for Doubtful Accounts
Accounts Receivable	Bond Fund
Accumulated Depreciation — Building	Bonds Payable
Accumulated Depreciation — Equipment	Buildings
Advertising Expense	Cash in Bank
Allowance for Decline in Value of Market-able Securities	Cash on Hand
	Common Stock

Cost of Goods Sold	Miscellaneous General Expense
Deferred Income Tax (debit balance)	Notes Payable
Depreciation Expense — Buildings	Notes Receivable
Dividends	Notes Receivable Discounted
Dividends Payable	Paid-In Capital from Sale of Common
Doubtful Accounts Expense	Stock at More Than Stated Value
Equipment	Paid-In Capital from Sale of Treasury
Estimated Warranty Expense Payable	Stock
FICA Tax Payable	Patents
Gain on Sale of Land	Pension Fund
Gain on Sale of Marketable Securities	Petty Cash
Goodwill	Premium on Bonds Payable
Income Summary	Prepaid Insurance
Income Tax	Prepaid Taxes
Income Tax Payable	Property Tax
Interest Receivable	Purchases
Interest Revenue	Purchase Discounts
Inventory	Retained Earnings
Investment in Bonds	Retained Earnings Appropriated for Loss
Land	Contingencies
Land Improvements	Salaries Payable
Leasehold Improvements	Sales
Loss on Purchase Commitments	Sales Salaries
Marketable Securities	Travel Expense

PROBLEMS

3-1. Kalish Realty, Inc., a dealer in land, is searching for funds for a long-term expansion program. Kalish must maintain a working capital balance of $4,000,000 to be in a favorable position for borrowing. The post-closing trial balance as of December 31, 1977, is as follows:

Accounts Payable — Trade		1,226,000
Accounts Receivable	5,232,000	
Accumulated Depreciation — Office Buildings		8,000,000
Additional Paid-In Capital		7,500,000
Advances to Affiliates	550,000	
Allowance for Doubtful Accounts		63,000
Bonds (payable in installments of $500,000 on June 1 of each year)		7,500,000
Cash Surrender Value of Life Insurance	15,000	
Common Stock, $10 par		5,000,000
Deferred Income Tax		750,000
First National Bank Fund for Construction of Office Building	800,000	
First National Bank — General Account	622,000	
Income Tax Payable		485,000
Land	14,000,000	
Loans on Life Insurance Policies		10,000
Marketable Securities	3,000,000	
Notes Payable to Bank		2,000,000
Office Building	12,000,000	
Office Supplies	75,000	
Organization Costs	2,000	
Prepaid Insurance	25,000	
Retained Earnings		2,087,000
Retained Earnings Appropriated for Loss Contingencies		500,000
Salaries and Wages Payable		150,000
Unearned Lease Revenue		50,000

Additional investigation revealed:

      (a) Accounts receivable consists of:

Due in six months from vice-president of finance	$ 232,000
Employee advances — long-term	500,000
Due in 1979 from sale of old office building	1,250,000
Installment notes receivable — trade	2,500,000
Accounts receivable — trade	650,000
Dividends receivable	100,000
	$5,232,000

(b) Land includes several parcels purchased for $5,000,000, which have become subject to severe flooding, thus lowering the value to $250,000. All the land is for sale except the $5,300,000 site for Kalish's new office building.
(c) Kalish purchased 25% of the voting stock of a savings and loan company for $2,500,000 and included the acquisition in marketable securities.
(d) Kalish received $50,000 in advance for next year's lease payments by tenants of Kalish's office building.
(e) The loans on the life insurance policies come due in 18 months; the bank notes fall due in 8 months.

Instructions: Show whether Kalish Realty, Inc., is in a favorable position for borrowing money by preparing the first portion of a balance sheet in financial position form: current assets less current liabilities equal working capital. Because of the nature of the business, land for sale is considered inventory.

3-2. Below is a list of account titles and balances for the Compiano Sales Corp. as of January 31, 1977.

Accounts Payable	$ 42,900	Investment in Stock of Subsidiary Company	$125,000
Accounts Receivable	53,000	Investment in Undeveloped Properties	106,000
Accumulated Depreciation — Buildings	70,000	Land	65,000
Accumulated Depreciation — Machinery and Equipment	20,000	Machinery and Equipment	72,000
Advances from Customers on Contracts in Progress	6,500	Misc. Supplies Inventories	3,100
Allowance for Doubtful Notes and Accounts	2,100	Notes Payable (current)	34,630
		Notes Payable (due 1982)	25,000
Buildings	150,000	Notes Receivable	11,200
Cash in Banks	53,650	Preferred Stock, $6 par	150,000
Cash on Hand	4,440	Premium on Common Stock	30,000
Cash Surrender Value of Life Insurance	8,500	Prepaid Insurance	2,250
		Property Tax Payable	2,100
Claim for Income Tax Refund	2,500	Raw Materials	16,900
Common Stock, $20 par	300,000	Retained Earnings (debit balance)	63,470
Employees Income Tax Payable	1,820	Salaries and Wages Payable	3,700
Finished Goods	21,000	8% Serial Bonds Payable (due March 1, 1978)	50,000
Franchises	21,000		
Goods in Process	39,400	8% Serial Bonds Payable (due in 1979 and thereafter)	150,000
Income Tax Payable	12,300	Temporary Investments in Marketable Securities	78,440
Interest Payable	1,000		
Interest Receivable	200	Tools	5,000

Instructions: Prepare a properly classified balance sheet.

3-3. Account balances and supplemental information for the Padden Corporation, as of December 31, 1977, are given below:

Accounts Payable	$ 32,160	Furniture, Fixtures, and Store Equipment	$769,000
Accounts Receivable — Trade	57,731	Inventory	201,620
Accumulated Depreciation — Leasehold Improvements and Equipment	579,472	Investment in Unconsolidated Subsidiary	80,000
Additional Paid-In Capital	100,000	Insurance Claims Receivable	120,000
Allowance for Doubtful Accounts	1,731	Land	6,000
		Leasehold Improvements	65,800
Automotive Equipment	132,800	5½–10% Mortgage Notes	200,000
Cash	30,600	Notes Payable — Banks	17,000
Cash Surrender Value of Life Insurance	3,600	Notes Payable — Trade	63,540
		Patent Licenses	57,402
Common Stock	200,000	Prepaid Insurance	5,500
Deferred Income Tax (credit balance)	45,000	Profit Sharing, Payroll, and Vacation Payable	40,000
Dividends Payable	37,500	Retained Earnings	225,800
Franchises	12,150	Tax Receivable — In Litigation	13,000

Supplemental information:

(a) Depreciation is provided by the straight-line method over the estimated useful lives of the assets.

(b) Common stock is $5 par, and 40,000 of the 100,000 authorized shares were issued and are outstanding.

(c) The cost of an exclusive franchise to import a foreign company's ball bearings and a related patent license are being amortized on the straight-line method over their remaining lives: franchise, 10 years; patents, 15 years.

(d) Inventories are stated at the lower of cost or market: cost was determined by the specific identification method.

(e) Insurance claims based upon the opinion of an independent insurance adjustor are for property damages at the central warehouse. These claims are estimated to be one-half collectible in the following year and one-half collectible thereafter.

(f) The company leases all of its buildings from various lessors. Estimated fixed lease obligations are $50,000 per year for the next ten years. The leases do not meet the criteria for capitalization.

(g) The company is currently in litigation over a claimed overpayment of income tax of $13,000. In the opinion of counsel, the claim is valid. The company is contingently liable on guaranteed notes worth $17,000.

Instructions: Prepare a properly classified balance sheet in account form. Include all notes and parenthetical notations necessary to properly disclose the essential financial data.

3-4. The following balance sheet was prepared by the accountant for Norvell Fabrics, Inc.

Norvell Fabrics, Inc.
Balance Sheet
June 30, 1977

Assets

Cash	$ 25,500
Marketable securities (includes 25% ownership in stock of Town Textiles, Inc., at cost of $250,000)	332,000
Inventories (net of amount still due suppliers of $75,980)	624,600
Prepaid expenses (includes a deposit of $10,000 made on inventories to be delivered in 18 months)	32,100
Fixed assets (excluding $50,000 of equipment still in use, but fully depreciated)	220,000
Goodwill (based upon estimate of President of Norvell Fabrics, Inc.)	50,000
Total assets	$1,284,200

Liabilities and Stockholders' Equity

Notes payable ($75,000 due in 1979)	$ 135,000
Accounts payable (not including amount due to suppliers of inventory — see above)	142,000
Long-term liability under pension plan	80,000
Reserve for building expansion	75,000
Reserve for depreciation — fixed assets	73,000
Taxes payable	44,500
Bonds payable (net of discount of $30,000)	270,000
Reserve for deferred income tax	83,000
Common stock (20,000 shares @ $10 par)	200,000
Premium on common stock	50,500
Reserve for loss contingencies	15,000
Retained earnings — unappropriated	116,200
Total liabilities and stockholders' equity	$1,284,200

Instructions: Prepare a corrected statement in good form using account titles that meet the recommendations of the AICPA.

3-5. The Rist Ranch summarizes its financial position in the following letter to their accountant.

January 20, 1978

Dear Harold:

The following information should be of value to you in preparing the balance sheet for Rist Ranch as of December 31, 1977. The balance of cash as of December 31 as reported on the bank statement was $43,825. There were still outstanding checks of $9,320 that had not cleared the bank and cash on hand of $3,640 was not deposited until January 4, 1978.

Customers owed the company $40,500 at December 31. We estimated 5% of this amount will never be collected. We owe suppliers $32,000 for poultry feed purchased in November and December. About 80% of this feed was used before December 31.

Because we think the price of grain will rise in 1978, we are holding 10,000 bushels of wheat and 5,000 bushels of oats until spring. The market value at December 31 was $3.50 per bushel of wheat and $1.50 per bushel of oats. We estimate that both prices will increase 10% by selling time. We are not able to estimate the cost of raising this product.

Rist Ranch owns 1,850 acres of land. Two separate purchases of land were made as follows: 1,250 acres at $200 per acre in 1959, and 600 acres at $400 per acre in 1965. Similar land is currently selling for $800 per acre. The balance of the mortgage on the two parcels of land is $270,000 at December 31; 10% of this mortgage must be paid in 1978.

Our farm buildings and equipment cost us $176,400 and on the average are 50% depreciated. If we were to replace these buildings and equipment at today's prices, we believe we would be conservative in estimating a cost of $300,000.

We have not paid property tax of $5,500 for 1978 billed us in late November. Our estimated income tax for 1977 is $18,500. A refund claim for $2,800 has been filed relative to the 1975 income tax return. The claim arose because of an error made on the 1975 return.

The operator of the ranch will receive a bonus of $7,000 for 1977 operations. It will be paid when the entire grain crop has been sold.

As you will recall, we issued 14,000 shares of $10 par stock upon incorporation. The ranch received $255,000 as net proceeds from the stock issue. Dividends of $45,000 were declared last month and will be paid on February 1, 1978.

The new year appears to hold great promise. Thanks for your help in preparing this statement.

Sincerely

Alice Mahle
President — Rist Ranch

Instructions: Based upon this information, prepare a properly classified balance sheet as of December 31, 1977.

3-6. The bookkeeper for the Tonai Corporation prepares the following condensed balance sheet.

Tonai Corporation
Balance Sheet
December 31, 1977

Current assets	$106,830
Less current liabilities	58,000
Working capital	$ 48,830
Add other assets	120,880
	$169,710
Deduct other liabilities	7,200
Investment in business	$162,510

A review of the account balances disclosed the data listed below:

(a) An analysis of the current asset grouping revealed the following:

Cash	$ 9,200
Trade accounts receivable (fully collectible)	25,000
Notes receivable (notes of customer who has been declared bankrupt and is unable to pay anything on the obligations)	2,000
Marketable securities, at cost (market value, $5,150)	8,500
Inventory	57,930
Cash surrender value of insurance on officers' lives...................................	4,200
Total current assets	$106,830

The inventory account was found to include the cost of supplies of $850, a delivery truck acquired at the end of 1977 at a cost of $4,200, and fixtures at a depreciated value of $20,800. The fixtures had been acquired in 1974 at a cost of $25,000.

(b) The total for other assets was determined as follows:

Land and buildings, at cost of acquisition on July 1, 1975	$154,000
Less balance due on mortgage, $32,000, and accrued interest on mortgage, $1,120 (mortgage is payable in annual installments of $8,000 on July 1 of each year together with interest for the year at that time at 7%)	33,120
Total other assets..	$120,880

It was estimated that the land, at the time of purchase, was worth $60,000. Buildings as of December 31, 1977 were estimated to have a remaining life of 17½ years.

(c) Current liabilities represented balances that were payable to trade creditors. Other liabilities consisted of withholding, payroll, real estate and other taxes payable to the federal, state, and local governments. However, no recognition was given the accrued salaries, utilities, and other miscellaneous items totaling $700.

(d) The company was originally organized in 1973 when 10,000 shares of no par stock with a stated value of $5 per share were issued in exchange for business assets that were recognized on the books at their fair market value of $110,000.

Instructions: Prepare a corrected balance sheet in financial position form with the items properly classified.

3-7. The bookkeeper for the Marcot Corporation submits the following condensed balance sheet.

Marcot Corporation
Balance Sheet
June 30, 1977

Current assets	$252,150	Current liabilities........................	$136,550
Other assets................................	638,400	Other liabilities	90,000
		Capital..	664,000
	$890,550		$890,550

A review of the account balances reveals the data listed below and on page 88:

(a) An analysis of current assets discloses the following:

Cash	$ 49,250
Marketable securities held as temporary investment	60,000
Trade accounts receivable	57,400
Inventories, including advertising supplies of $2,500...................................	85,500
	$252,150

(b) Other assets include:

Land, buildings, and equipment, cost $665,000, depreciated value.............	$549,000
Deposit with a supplier for merchandise ordered for August delivery..........	2,000
Goodwill recorded on the books to cancel losses incurred by the company in prior years	87,400
	$638,400

(c) Current liabilities include:

Payroll payable	$ 7,650
Taxes payable..	4,000
Rent payable..	12,000
Trade accounts payable, $90,400, less a $1,500 debit balance reported in the account of a vendor to whom merchandise had been returned after the account had been paid in full	88,900
Notes payable	24,000
	$136,550

(d) Other liabilities include:

9% mortgage on land, buildings and equipment, payable in semiannual installments of $9,000 through June 30, 1982...	$ 90,000

(e) Capital includes:

20,000 shares of preferred stock, $20 par...	$400,000
160,000 shares of common stock at stated value..	264,000
	$664,000

(f) Common shares were originally issued for a total consideration of $400,000, but the losses of the company for past years were charged against the common stock balance.

Instructions: Using the balance sheet and the related data, prepare a corrected balance sheet in report form showing individual asset, liability, and capital balances properly classified.

3-8. The balance sheet below is submitted to you for inspection and review.

Raynor Corporation
Balance Sheet
December 31, 1977

Assets		Liabilities and Stockholders' Equity	
Cash	$ 50,000	Miscellaneous liabilities	$ 2,500
Accounts receivable	180,000	Loan payable................................	56,250
Inventories	220,000	Accounts payable.........................	146,250
Prepaid insurance........................	12,500	Capital stock................................	250,000
Land, buildings, and		Paid-in capital	332,500
equipment...............................	325,000		
	$787,500		$787,500

In the course of the review you find the data listed below:

(a) The possibility of uncollectible accounts on accounts receivable has not been considered. It is estimated that uncollectible accounts will total $5,000.

(b) $50,000 representing the cost of a large-scale newspaper advertising campaign completed in 1977 has been added to the inventories, since it is believed that this campaign will benefit sales of 1978. It is also found that inventories include merchandise of $16,250 received on December 31 that has not yet been recorded as a purchase.

(c) Prepaid insurance consists of $1,000, the cost of fire insurance for 1978, and $11,500, the cash surrender value on officers' life insurance policies.

(d) The books show that land, buildings, and equipment have a cost of $525,000 with depreciation of $200,000 recognized in prior years. However, these balances include fully depreciated equipment of $75,000 that has been scrapped and is no longer on hand.

(e) Miscellaneous liabilities of $2,500 represent salaries payable of $7,500, less noncurrent advances of $5,000 made to company officials.

(f) Loan payable represents a loan from the bank that is payable in regular quarterly installments of $6,250.

(g) Tax liabilities not shown are estimated at $11,250.

(h) Deferred income tax (credit balance) arising from timing differences in recognizing income totals $23,750. This tax was not included in the balance sheet.
(i) Capital stock consists of 6,250 shares of preferred 6% stock, par $20, and 12,500 shares of common stock, stated value $10.
(j) Capital stock had been issued for a total consideration of $312,500, the amount received in excess of the par and stated values of the stock being reported as surplus.

Instructions: Prepare a corrected balance sheet in report form with accounts properly classified.

3-9. George Jenkins incorporated his concrete manufacturing operations on January 1, 1977, by issuing 10,000 shares of $10 par common stock to himself. The following balance sheet for the new corporation was prepared.

Concrete Corporation
Balance Sheet
January 1, 1977

Cash	$ 10,000	Accounts payable—suppliers	$ 45,000
Accounts receivable	45,000	Capital stock, $10 par	100,000
Inventory	75,000	Premium on capital stock	100,000
Equipment	115,000		
	$245,000		$245,000

During 1977, Concrete Corporation engaged in the following transactions:

(a) Concrete Corporation produced concrete costing $270,000. Concrete costs consisted of $200,000, raw materials purchases; $25,000, labor; and $45,000, overhead. Concrete Corporation paid the $45,000 owed to suppliers as of January 1, and $130,000 on the $200,000 of raw materials purchased during the year. All labor, except for $1,500, and recorded overhead were paid for in cash during the year. Other operating expenses of $15,000 were incurred and paid in 1977.
(b) Concrete costing $300,000 was sold during 1977 for $425,000. All sales were made on credit, and collections on receivables were $365,000.
(c) Concrete Corporation purchased machinery (fair market value = $190,000) by trading in old equipment costing $50,000 and paying $140,000 in cash. There is no accumulated depreciation on the old equipment as it was revalued when the new corporation was formed.
(d) Concrete Corporation issued an additional 4,000 share of common stock for $25 per share and declared a dividend of $4 per share to all stockholders of record as of December 31, 1977, payable on January 15, 1978.
(e) Depreciation expense for 1977 was $27,000. The allowance for doubtful accounts after year-end adjustments is $2,500.

Instructions: Prepare a properly classified balance sheet in report form for the Concrete Corporation as of December 31, 1977.

4

Financial Statements —
The Income Statement

The *income statement*, also variously called the *earnings statement*, the *statement of profit and loss*, and the *statement of operations*, summarizes business activities for a given period and reports the net income or loss resulting from operations and from certain other defined activities. The close relationship between the income statement, balance sheet, and statement of changes in financial position should be recognized. For example, a change in valuation of marketable securities on the balance sheet will alter reported net income, and the amount of income from operations is a major item on the statement of changes in financial position. The importance of measuring and reporting income, as well as the nature and the content of the income statement, is described in the following sections.

IMPORTANCE OF MEASURING AND REPORTING INCOME

The measuring and reporting of business income has acquired steadily increasing importance and, at present, accountants generally regard this as one of their most important responsibilities.[1] Reference is made to the income statement by many different groups who need to evaluate the results of business activities. Reference is also made to this statement by those who desire to determine the worth of a business, for it is business earnings that ultimately validate asset values. Proper measurement of income helps capital flow to the most profitable and presumably the most efficient enterprises, providing for optimal allocation of scarce economic resources.

The measurement of income has presented many problems to accountants because of the absence of a precise definition for *income*, and

---

[1]For example, APB Statement No. 4 states: "The information presented in an income statement is usually considered the most important information provided by financial accounting because profitability is a paramount concern to those interested in the economic activities of the enterprise." *Statements of the Accounting Principles Board, No. 4*, "Basic Concepts and Accounting Principles Underlying Financial Statements of Business Enterprises" (New York: American Institute of Certified Public Accountants, 1970), par. 12.

because of the need to exercise judgment on a great many matters in arriving at such measurement. Thus, considerable research has been directed toward the matter of *income determination*.

A number of factors have contributed to the importance of the income statement. Primary factors have been the income tax laws, the absentee ownership of corporations, and the increased internal use of accounting information.

Income Tax Laws

Since 1913 when the 16th Amendment to the Constitution was passed, taxes on income at both national and state levels have become very significant. This has created a need for every business entity to establish some system for the measurement of income. Various tax regulations have become increasingly specific as to what constitutes income for tax purposes. In the majority of cases these regulations follow practices currently being applied by accountants in preparing general financial statements. However, some troublesome areas arise because the objective of income measurement for the government is related to its regulatory and financial responsibilities. These may not always coincide with procedures considered appropriate in measuring the profitability of a specific enterprise over a limited time span. Serious questions can often be raised when certain tax regulations become the accepted procedures for financial accounting.

Absentee Ownership of Corporations

The growth of the corporate form of ownership has created a large group of absentee owners. There are millions of stockholders of American corporations, most of whom have very little contact with the operations of the companies in which they have holdings except through the published reports they receive periodically. Although they can attend annual stockholders meetings, very few of them actually do. The stockholders regard their involvement as a financial one and evaluate their investment in comparison with other financial alternatives. Because of these conditions, the average stockholder requires financial data to assist in the evaluation of the investment. The net income figure, as well as related income or earnings per share data, is widely reported in newspapers and financial services. Although there is much theorizing among observers of the stock market as to the degree to which the market value of stock is affected by periodic reports of earnings, it is clear that the stockholder is interested and does pay close attention to this measure of profitability. Stockbrokers often refer to the relationship between stock prices and current earnings (price/earnings ratio) and use the measurement of price times earnings to reflect the profitability of an entity.

Increased Internal Use of Accounting Information

Not only has there been increased interest in the income statement by outside users, but the same can also be said for the primary internal user — management. Years ago, proprietors often could acquire an intuitive feel as to how well things were going in an enterprise; but, today, in most situations, the complexity of modern business makes this impossible. Managements of large and growing corporate enterprises, dealing in many different product areas, need to have profitability information to answer questions relating to past, present, and projected programs. Questions arise such as: How effective was our past advertising policy? Should we make or buy certain component parts for our end-line products? Should we add to our product lines? Information systems within the enterprise must be prepared to answer these and related questions and often do so in the context of some version of an income report.

NATURE OF INCOME

With the increasing attention being given to reporting the results of operations, it is only natural that certain questions have been raised: What purpose should the measurement of income serve in our economy? How can it best serve this purpose? Is our function limited to that of an historian reporting on the past? Or are we trying to provide the best guide for estimating future earning power?[1] All of these questions are appropriate ones; however, all of the answers may not be provided by the same income statement. Some of the purposes, perhaps, are being satisfied better by present accounting methods than others. Before examining the concepts underlying present income measurement and reporting, some of the other concepts suggested by accounting and economic literature deserve attention.

The Valuation (Indirect) Method of Income Determination

As suggested earlier, a business entity commences activities in the attempt to increase its net assets through profitable operations. This increase in net assets is referred to by many economists as a change in the *well-offness* of the entity, alternately referred to as the *income* of the firm. This is indeed an appealing concept. Income normally connotes something desirable in our economy and thus is reasonably represented by such net asset increase. This suggests that one way to determine income is to value the net assets of an entity at two different times and compute the change that has occurred. If the change is positive after adjustment for any investment or withdrawal of assets by the owners, there has been *income*. If the change is negative, there has been a *loss*. Because income is determined by comparing net assets at two different times, this method is referred to as the *valuation method*, or *indirect method*.

The valuation method is most commonly used by economists in their discussion of income. One of the most quoted economists in accounting literature, J. R. Hicks, defined income as the maximum value which an entity can distribute during a period and still expect to be as well-off.[2]

---

[1] As indicated in Chapter 1, the general objectives of financial accounting that were enumerated by the APB in Statement No. 4 include both of these general concepts. Objective 2 emphasizes the provision of reliable information about changes in net resources that result from profit-directed activities, and objective 3 emphasizes the provision of financial information that assists in estimating the earning potential of the enterprise. *Ibid*., par. 78 and 79. More recently, the *Report of the Study Group on the Objectives of Financial Statements* has been published by the AICPA. It states "an objective of financial statements is to provide users with information for predicting, comparing, and evaluating enterprise earning power." *Report of the Study Group on the Objectives of Financial Statements* (New York: American Institute of Certified Public Accountants, October, 1973).

[2] J. R. Hicks, *Value and Capital* (2d ed.; Oxford University Press, 1946).

Although net assets is accepted as the indicator of importance, it is necessary to arrive at a precise definition of the meaning of *value of net assets*. Is it the historical cost of the net assets reduced by some amount for their use? Is it the current value of the net assets determined by replacement or market values? Is it the historical cost of the net assets adjusted for the change in price levels since original acquisitions? All of these, as well as other concepts, may be regarded as satisfying the general term, value of net assets. Another question that must be resolved is what is to be included in net assets. Should intangible items, such as goodwill, patents, and leaseholds be included in assets? Should the net worth of employees be reported as an asset? Should estimated payments relating to warranties and pensions be included in liabilities?

For many years economists, and recently some accountants, have approached these difficult questions by attempting to define net assets in terms of the present value of the cash benefits that net assets are expected to provide. These parties maintain that we should arrive at *future cash flows* in amount and time, and with the use of appropriate discount rates determine the present worth of these streams of future benefits. Net assets, as thus computed, can be compared as of different time intervals in arriving at income.

Although this concept has some theoretical merit, it has had minor influence upon practice primarily because of the measurement problems involved. We live in an uncertain world with limited knowledge of future cash flows. Expectations as to these future flows vary among those individuals with interest in the company. Also, with limited knowledge of the future, what should be accepted as the appropriate discount rates to apply to cash flows in arriving at asset values? Because of these uncertainties, the accountant has turned to more direct ways of defining income.

The Matching (Direct) Method of Income Determination

The method of income determination that has proved most acceptable to the accountant has been the *matching method*, or *direct method*. The matching method involves the determination of the amount of revenue earned by an entity during a given period and the amount of expired costs applicable to that revenue. The difference between these two items is recognized as *net income*. If users were willing to wait until the end of the life of a business unit for the full results of its operations, it would be an easy matter to compute the total revenues and total expenses of the business and the resulting net income or net loss. However, users of income statements, seeking to judge the progress of an entity, need periodic measurements of business profitability. In fact, users seem increasingly interested in receiving financial statements more frequently than at the traditional annual intervals. To satisfy this need, interim statements are also provided by most large companies. Thus, the element of timing, both for revenue and expense, becomes ever more significant. Rather than concentrating on asset valuations, the center of attention is thus transferred to a discussion of *revenue realization* and *expense recognition*.

It should be recognized, however, that because the financial statements are fundamentally interrelated, the point in time at which revenues and expenses are recognized is also the time when changes in amounts of net assets are recognized.[1]

Nature of Revenues

The Accounting Principles Board in Statement No. 4 defined *revenues* as:

> . . . gross increases in assets or gross decreases in liabilities recognized and measured in conformity with generally accepted accounting principles that result from those types of profit-directed activities of an enterprise that can change owners' equity.[2]

Generally, revenues are derived from three main activities:

1. Selling products.
2. Rendering services and permitting others to use enterprise resources, which result in interest, rent, royalties, fees, and the like.
3. Disposing of resources other than products — for example, plant and equipment or investments in other entities.[3]

Revenues do not include assets acquired by purchase, proceeds from borrowing, investments by owners, or adjustments of revenue of prior periods.

Although the above description of revenue defines the activities that produce revenue, it does not specify the time period in which revenue should be recorded and recognized in the income statement. A general realization rule has evolved stating that revenue should be recorded when two conditions are met: (1) the earnings process is complete or virtually so; and (2) an exchange has taken place. These criteria have led to the conventional recognition of revenue at a specific point in the earnings process — when assets are sold or services are rendered.[4] However, some accountants would argue that an exchange does not necessarily have to occur for recognition of revenue. What is critical is that objective measurement is possible, whether or not an exchange has taken place, in addition to the earning process being substantially complete. There are sufficient deviations from the general rule to justify a closer look into the nature of revenue.

The first type of activity described as producing revenue is the sale of products. The cycle of revenue-producing goods as it passes through an entity can be a long one. The beginning point is not well defined, but assume it begins with the development of proposals for a certain product by an individual or by the research and development department of a business unit. From the idea stage, the future product is carefully described in plans and engineering specifications. Bills of material are prepared, a production schedule is agreed upon, and raw materials are ordered, delivered, and placed into production. Labor and factory

---

[1]This interrelatedness is recognized and described in *Statements of the Accounting Principles Board, No. 4, op. cit.*, par. 136 and 147.

[2]*Ibid.*, par. 134.

[3]*Ibid.*, par. 134 and 148.

[4]*Ibid.*, par. 150 and 151.

overhead are added to the raw materials as the product proceeds through the manufacturing process. Once completed, the product is transferred to the finished goods warehouse. The product is listed in company catalogs, it is promoted in advertising campaigns, and it moves through the company's distribution system to the final sale. Frequently sales are on a credit basis, and, after a period of time, collections are made on the accounts. The product may be sold with a warranty for necessary repairs or replacements. The cycle thus extends from the original idea to the end of the warranty period. All these steps are involved in the realization of the sales revenue. If there is a failure at any step, revenue may be seriously curtailed or possibly completely eliminated. And yet, there is only one aggregate revenue amount for the entire cycle, the sale price of the goods. The question then is: When should revenue be recognized?

Answers to the question of when revenue should be recognized can be divided into two broad categories: (1) at one specific point in the cycle, or (2) at two or more points in the cycle.[1] The prevailing practice provides for recognition of revenue at one specific point in the cycle. Of course, determining the specific point presents a problem. Applying the previously mentioned guidelines, revenue from sale of products is recognized at the *point of sale*, usually interpreted to mean the time of delivery to customers. It is felt that prior to the sale, there has not been an arm's-length determination of the market value of the goods. This makes any objective measure of revenue subject to dispute. In addition, most accountants feel that the critical event is the sale of an item, and that the earning process is not complete until the sales commitment has been substantially fulfilled. The same guidelines dictate that revenue from services is recognized *when services have been performed and are billable*, and that revenue from permitting others to use enterprise resources is recognized *as resources are used* or *as time passes*.

There are two notable exceptions to the general rule. One exception to the rule of recognition of revenue at the point of sale is found, for example, when market values are firmly established and the marketability of a given product is assured. Revenue in such instances is recognized at the *point of completed production*. Farm products with assured sales prices meet these criteria. In other instances, when uncertainty exists as to the collectibility of a receivable arising from the sale of goods or services, recognition of revenue may be deferred to the *point of actual cash collection*. The *installment sales method* of accounting is an example of the application of this practice. Although the installment sales method of deferring revenue beyond the point of sale is accepted as an alternate method for purposes of income taxation, it is not generally accepted for financial statement purposes "unless the circumstances are such that the collection of the sale price is not reasonably assured."[2]

---

[1]This subject was considered by a special AAA Committee on Realization which was established in 1964 and published its conclusions in 1966. Some of their comments on the point of revenue realization are included in this section. *Accounting Review* (Evanston, Illinois: American Accounting Association, April 1965), pp. 312–322.

[2]*Opinions of the Accounting Principles Board, No. 10* , "Omnibus Opinion — 1966" (New York: American Institute of Certified Public Accountants, 1966), par. 12.

The second exception is found when revenue is recognized at two or more points in the cycle. Although conceptually one can maintain that revenue is being earned continuously throughout the cycle, the measurement of revenue under this concept may become impractical. It also raises special questions, such as: Should revenue of an equal amount be assigned to each phase of the cycle? Or should revenue be recognized in proportion to the costs incurred in each phase of the cycle? In certain cases, however, the production phase of the cycle extends over more than one accounting period and some allocation of revenue over the periods involved is considered essential to meaningful statements. Construction contracts for buildings, roads, and dams requiring several periods to complete are often of this nature. The *percentage-of-completion* method of accounting is used to meet these special conditions. This method requires a firm contract for sale prior to construction and an ability to estimate with reasonable accuracy the costs remaining to be incurred on the project. Portions of the total estimated revenue are recognized as the project progresses.

Thus, revenue recognition occurs at certain specifically defined points in the revenue-producing cycle. Prior to these points, valuations are stated in terms of cost. After these points, use is made of *estimated* or *actual realizable values.* Discussion will certainly continue within the accounting profession as to the validity and acceptability of alternative points of revenue recognition. However, regardless of the point of revenue recognition selected, the relationship that has been defined between revenues and expenses will still hold.

Nature of Expenses

In Statement No. 4, the Accounting Principles Board defined *expenses* as:

> . . . gross decreases in assets or gross increases in liabilities recognized and measured in conformity with generally accepted accounting principles that result from those types of profit-directed activities of an enterprise that can change owners' equity.[1]

The APB stated further that expenses are:

> . . . costs that are associated with the revenue of the period, often directly but frequently indirectly through association with the period to which the revenue has been assigned.[2]

Some costs are not charged currently to the income statement because they relate to future revenues and, therefore, are shown as assets on the balance sheet. If the future service potential has expired, the costs are associated with current revenues and reported as expenses. Expenses are classified in Statement No. 4 as follows:

1. Costs directly associated with the revenue of the period.
2. Costs associated with the period on some basis other than a direct relationship with revenue (such as time, for example).

---

[1]*Statements of the Accounting Principles Board, No. 4, op. cit.*, par. 134.
[2]*Ibid.*, par. 155.

> 3. Costs that cannot, as a practical matter, be associated with any other period. [1]

The Accounting Principles Board used the terminology of *gains* and *losses* to refer to the results of transactions involving revenues and expenses from other than sales of product, merchandise, or service. Expenses, as defined by the APB, do not include repayments of borrowing, expenditures to acquire assets, distributions to owners (including the acquisition of treasury stock), or corrections of expenses of prior periods. The terms revenue and expense will be used in this text in the manner in which they are defined by the APB, inasmuch as these definitions have not yet been changed by the Financial Accounting Standards Board.

A primary difficulty in income determination is the decision as to how various expenses are, in fact, to be associated with revenues. It has not been possible to prescribe exact rules for *association* or *matching*. [2] Certain guidelines for the matching of expenses with revenues in arriving at net income or loss have evolved through time. When an accountant is faced with an absence of guidelines, judgment must be exercised. Three expense recognition principles have been noted as being of special significance: (1) *associating cause and effect*; (2) *systematic and rational allocation*; and (3) *immediate recognition*. [3]

Associating Cause and Effect. Some costs can be associated directly with specific revenues. When this association is possible, the cost is recognized as an expense of the period in which the revenue is recognized. Thus, if an inventory item on hand at the end of a period represents a source of future revenue under the point of sale principle, the cost of producing the item is deferred to a future period and it is reported as an asset. Certain costs, such as labor and materials, usually can be directly related to the cost of producing the inventory item. Other costs, such as manufacturing overhead, may be assumed to be associated with an inventory item on some logical basis such as the number of labor hours or the number of machine hours required to produce the item. Judgment plays an increasingly more important part as the association becomes less direct.

Care must be taken to assure that proper recognition is made of all costs already incurred, as well as those yet to be incurred relative to any revenue currently recognized.

Systematic and Rational Allocation. In the absence of a direct cause and effect relationship, a different basis for expense recognition is commonly used. Here the attempt is made to associate costs in a systematic and

---

[1]*Ibid.*

[2]Recent accounting pronouncements have been more specific in establishing guidelines for making these associations. Critics of this trend have stated their fear that accounting may become a set of rigid rules if such a trend continues.

[3]*Statements of the Accounting Principles Board, No. 4, op. cit.*, par. 157–160.

rational manner with the products or the periods benefitted. In arriving at period expense recognition, estimates must be made of the timing pattern of the benefits received from the individual costs and systematic allocation methods developed. The methods adopted should appear reasonable to an unbiased observer and should be followed consistently.

Some of the costs allocated to a period become expenses immediately and are associated with current revenue. Other costs *attach* to inventories and other similar assets on some logical basis, and thus are associated with future revenue by being deferred as assets. Examples of costs that are associated with periods in a systematic way include costs of buildings and equipment, insurance, and taxes.

Immediate Recognition. Those costs that cannot be related to revenue either by associating cause and effect or by systematic and rational allocation, must be recognized as expenses of the current period or in some instances written off as prior period adjustments. Because of specific restrictions on the items that qualify as prior period adjustments, most of the asset balances or costs currently incurred are recognized as expenses in the period when no discernible future revenues can be associated with them, and their deferral cannot be supported.[1]

EFFECTS OF CHANGING PRICE LEVELS

Thus far, reference has been made to the use of historical cost association. There is nothing in income determination requiring use of historical costs. When the current costs of replacing the goods and services of an entity differ from historical transaction-based costs, such current costs could be matched against currently generated revenues. This approach was suggested by Sprouse and Moonitz in Accounting Research Study No. 3 and was also implicit in the recommendations of the American Accounting Association in their *Statement of Basic Accounting Theory*. In the latter publication, the study committee advocated the use of multivalued statements: both the balance sheet and the income statement would show in one column historical costs, and in a second column, current values. When it is maintained that the primary purpose of the income statement is to enable the user to predict future income, it would follow that current values will more closely suggest the costs expected to be experienced in the future.

There has been increasing discussion of the use of current values. Accountants generally do not appear ready to move completely away from the more traditional and objective historical cost structure, but requests for supplementary disclosure of current values are becoming more numerous.

---

[1]Previously, some development stage companies deferred many costs without regard to recoverability or matching on the basis that they were not yet a fully operating enterprise. In Statement No. 7, the FASB indicates this practice is no longer acceptable. Development stage enterprises must follow the same generally acceptable accounting principles that apply to established operating enterprises. *Statement of Financial Accounting Standards No. 7*, "Accounting and Reporting by Development Stage Enterprises" (Stamford, Conn.: Financial Accounting Standards Board, 1975), par. 10.

One of the principal causes of deviation between historical costs and current values in the United States is the steady decline in the value of the dollar. As indicated in Chapter 1, accountants operate on the *as if* assumption. They account for activities as if the value of the dollar were stable. To the extent this assumption is not valid, effects will be far-reaching on all financial statements. Particular care is necessary in interpreting comparative statements. With changing price levels, income statements comparing operations for several years may lead to inaccurate conclusions: reported sales increases may, in real terms, represent decreases.

In some countries general price-level adjustments are regularly made on the financial statements to reflect changes in the *general price index*.[1] Such adjustments are applied to historical costs, and, therefore, are not usually measures of current value.

SPECIAL PROBLEMS IN THE PREPARATION OF THE INCOME STATEMENT

The importance of the revenue-expense relationships and the significance attached to the earnings and earning power of the entity for the user of the income statement have been described in the first part of this chapter. In view of the importance attached to these matters, the question continually arises: How can these matters be expressed on the income statement in the most informative and useful form?

Reporting Results of Operations on an All-Inclusive Basis

Historically, there have been two generally accepted forms that could be used for income statement presentation, and the selection of the form determined the manner in which the business unit preferred to recognize extraordinary items. One form, referred to as the *current operating performance income statement*, provided for reporting only normal and recurring operating items; extraordinary items and prior period adjustments were recorded directly in retained earnings and reported on an accompanying statement that summarized all of the changes in the retained earnings for the period. An alternative form, known as the *all-inclusive income statement*, provided for the presentation of extraordinary items on the face of the income statement after reporting normal operating items. In employing the first form, the final amount was generally designated as net income; in the second form the final amount was designated by some as net income and by others as net income after extraordinary items. Because both of these income statement forms were being used in practice, there was a lack of consistency in the reporting by enterprises and thus a real danger of misinterpretation of the results of operations by statement users.

With the issuance of Accounting Principles Board Opinion No. 9, a modified all-inclusive concept of income presentation was adopted. Ordinary operations as well as extraordinary items are to be presented on

---

[1] Chapter 25 discusses in some detail the concepts involved in price-level adjustments.

the income statement, but as separate and distinct categories, with the nature and amounts of extraordinary items being disclosed net of tax. In effect, all items of income are to be recognized on the income statement with the exception of certain prior period adjustments.

The Accounting Principles Board recognized that the distinction between ordinary operating items and extraordinary items will require the use of judgment by an accountant. To assist the accountant in making the distinction, the Board established certain criteria which must be met before an item should be classified as extraordinary. In Accounting Principles Board Opinion No. 30, the APB provided more definitive criteria for extraordinary items and clarified and modified to some extent the existing criteria originally established in APB Opinion No. 9.

Extraordinary items, according to APB Opinion No. 30, are "events and transactions that are distinguished by their unusual nature *and* by the infrequence of their occurrence."[1] Thus, to qualify as extraordinary, an item must "possess a high degree of abnormality and be of a type clearly unrelated to or only incidentally related to the ordinary and typical activities of the entity . . . [and] be of a type that would not reasonably be expected to reoccur in the forseeable future."[2] In addition, the item must be material in amount.

The overall effect of APB Opinion No. 30 is to restrict the items that can be classified as extraordinary. The Board offers certain examples of gains and losses that should *not* be reported as extraordinary items. They include: (1) the write-down or write-off of receivables, inventories, equipment leased to others, or intangible assets; (2) the gains or losses from exchanges or translation of foreign currencies, including those relating to major devaluations and revaluations; (3) the gains or losses on disposal of a segment of a business; (4) other gains or losses from sale or abandonment of property, plant, or equipment used in the business; (5) the effects of a strike; (6) the adjustment of accruals on long-term contracts.[3]

On the other hand, according to the FASB, at least one item — gains or losses from extinguishment of debt — is to be reported as an extraordinary item regardless of the criteria stated in APB Opinion 30.[4] This is discussed in more detail in a later chapter.

Items which are either unusual in nature or occur infrequently, but do not meet both criteria and, therefore, should not be classified as extraordinary items, should be reported as items of ordinary income under "Other revenue and expense items." However, if these items are material, separate disclosure should be made either in a note to the statement or by reporting them as separate components of income in the operating section of the income statement as the last items below "Other revenue and expense items."

---

[1]*Opinions of the Accounting Principles Board, No. 30*, "Reporting the Results of Operations" (New York: American Institute of Certified Public Accountants, 1973), par. 20.

[2]*Ibid.*

[3]*Ibid.*, par. 23.

[4]*Statement of Financial Accounting Standards No. 4*, "Reporting Gains and Losses from Extinguishment of Debt" (Stamford, Conn.: Financial Accounting Standards Board, 1975).

Prior period adjustments have also been the subject of much discussion in connection with the current operating performance and all-inclusive approaches. Prior period adjustments were usually handled in the same manner as extraordinary items and reported either in the retained earnings statement or in the income statement. In Opinion No. 9 the Board set up specific criteria for the recognition of items as prior period adjustments and provided that only adjustments meeting these criteria may be excluded from the determination of net income and reported as direct changes in owners' equity accounts. More recently, the Financial Accounting Standards Board has proposed a standard which is even more restrictive with respect to prior period adjustments. The FASB has proposed that all items of profit and loss recognized during a period should be included in the determination of net income with only two exceptions. The two items that would still qualify as prior period adjustments, and which therefore would be excluded from the determination of current period income, are: (1) corrections of errors in financial statements of prior periods, and (2) adjustments resulting from realization of income tax benefits of pre-acquisition operating loss carry forwards of purchased subsidiaries.[1]

This policy is in harmony with APB Opinion No. 20 where the APB recognized there would be occasions when account balances would require correction as a result of the discovery of errors made in previously issued statements. These errors may arise from mathematical mistakes, the misuse or omission of certain data, mistakes in the application of accounting principles, as well as failures to apply generally accepted accounting principles. When a correction of an error made in the past is required, the Board specified that the effect of such a change be reported as a prior period adjustment. Assets and liabilities, as of the beginning of the period, are to be restated to corrected balances; the accompanying debit or credit, recognizing the cumulative effect of the error on past earnings, is to be reported directly in the owners' equity.[2]

Disposal of Business Segment

In APB Opinion No. 30, the Board added another major category to the income statement. It concluded "that the results of normal or continuing operation should be reported separately from discontinued operations and that any gain or loss from disposal of a segment of a business . . . should be reported in conjunction with the related results of discontinued operations and not as an extraordinary item."[3] The Board further indicated that the results of operating a business segment that has been or is expected to be discontinued should be reported as a separate component of income before extraordinary items. A format similar to the one shown at the top of the next page is considered appropriate.[4]

---

[1]*Proposed Statement of Financial Accounting Standards*, "Prior Period Adjustments" (Stamford, Conn.: Financial Accounting Standards Board, 1976), par. 11.

[2]*Opinions of the Accounting Principles Board, No. 20*, "Accounting Changes" (New York: American Institute of Certified Public Accountants, 1971), par. 36–37.

[3]*Opinions of the Accounting Principles Board, No. 30, op. cit.*, par. 8.

[4]The captions and earnings per share disclosure would need to be modified appropriately when also reporting extraordinary items and/or the cumulative effect of a change in accounting principle in accordance with APB Opinion No. 20.

Income from continuing operations before income tax......................	$ xxx	
Provision for income tax	xx	
Income from continuing operations...		$ xxx
Discontinued operations (Note __):		
Income (loss) from operations of discontinued business segment (less applicable income tax of $xx)...	$ xxx	
Loss on disposal of business segment (less applicable income tax of $xx)..	xx	xxx
Net income		$ xxx[1]

Accounting Changes

In Opinion No. 9, the Board did not answer certain questions concerning the manner of reporting a change in accounting principle or accounting estimate or the manner of reporting the correction of an error in previously issued financial statements. A key question involved in reporting changes is whether the effects of the change should be applied retroactively, currently, or prospectively. If retroactive treatment is followed, the change may be reported either by restating financial statements of prior periods or by reporting the full effect of the change as a special cumulative item in the current income statement. The restatement of prior period financial statements for some changes is frequently difficult, if not impossible, because of the unavailability of data. In addition, a policy of restating prior period statements may confuse the reader and may also erode confidence in financial statements. On the other hand, if the effects of the change are reported currently and prospectively, trend summaries of operations and other analytical computations could be misleading to statement users.

In Opinion No. 20 on accounting changes, the Board gave a full statement of its position on these matters and provided guidelines for the reporting procedures to be employed in each instance. The Opinion specifically provides for a new, separate category on the income statement for the cumulative effect of a change in accounting principle.[2]

Change in Accounting Principle. There will be occasions when a company will adopt a generally accepted accounting principle that is different from the one used previously. The term *accounting principle* includes not only principles and practices but also the methods of applying them. The following are specifically named as examples of such changes: a change in the method of inventory pricing, such as from the last-in, first-out method to the first-in, first-out method; a change in the method of depreciation for previously recorded assets, such as from the double-declining-balance method to the straight-line method; a change in the method of accounting for long-term construction contracts, such as from the completed-contract method to the percentage-of-completion method.

There is the presumption that an accounting principle once adopted should not be changed in recording events and transactions of a similar type. Consistent application of accounting principles is important to the

---

[1]*Opinions of the Accounting Principles Board, No. 30, loc. cit.*
[2]*Opinions of the Accounting Principles Board, No. 20, op. cit.*, par. 20.

user of financial statements in the satisfactory analysis and evaluation of comparative data. The presumption of use of the same principle may be overcome, however, if the use of an alternate principle can be supported as preferable. The Board comments:

> . . . The issuance of an Opinion of the Accounting Principles Board that creates a new accounting principle, that expresses a preference for an accounting principle, or that rejects a specific accounting principle is sufficient support for a change in accounting principle. The burden of justifying other changes rests with the entity proposing the change.[1]

When a change in principle can be supported, the Board generally takes the position that the effect of the change should be included in net income of the period in which the change is made. Assets and liabilities as of the beginning of the period would be recomputed to find the balances that would be found if the new principle had been applied in past periods; the accompanying debit or credit recognizing the cumulative effect of such change in principle upon past earnings would be recorded separately and reported on the income statement for the current period following "Extraordinary items." Other revenue and expense balances for the period would be reported on the basis of the newly adopted principle. The balance sheet as of the end of the period would then report the asset and liability balances that would be found if the new principle had been applied in past periods as well as in the current period.

Change in Accounting Estimate. Accounting Principles Board Opinion No. 20 recognizes that changes in accounting estimates are necessary consequences of the periodic financial presentations. Judgments relative to future events and their effects may require modification as additional experience or more information is gained. Changes in estimates, as previously concluded in APB Opinion No. 9, should be recognized in the current and subsequent periods. A change in the method of depreciation of an asset, for example, would be treated as a change in accounting principle; a change in the estimated remaining life of an asset would require a change in current and subsequent charges for depreciation. Although a change in an estimate does not require the restatement of the account balances, a description on the income statement of the change and its effect upon income and earnings per share should generally be provided.[2]

OVERVIEW OF CONTENT OF THE INCOME STATEMENT

The income statement generally consists of a series of sections developing the net income for the period. As mentioned earlier, all elements of income, except for prior period adjustments, are to be included. However, a distinction should be made between the results of normal operations and other elements affecting net income. Major categories included

---

[1]*Ibid.*, par. 16.
[2]*Ibid.*, par. 31–33; Chapter 22 discusses accounting changes more completely.

within the normal operations section are: (1) revenues from the sale of goods and service; (2) cost of goods sold and expenses of providing services; (3) operating expenses; (4) other revenue and expense items; and (5) income tax relative to income from normal operations. Depending upon individual circumstances, additional sections in the income statement may include: (1) disposal of a business segment; (2) extraordinary items; and (3) cumulative effect on prior years due to change in accounting principle, all shown net of their tax effect. Illustrative statements are presented on pages 107 and 108.

On the income statement for a corporation, the summary of net income is followed by a special presentation of earnings per share for the period. Earnings per share is computed by dividing income from normal operations, and any other major category of income subsequently disclosed, by the weighted average number of shares of common stock outstanding. For example, the Andersen Corporation income statement illustrated on page 107 shows earnings per share of 50¢ for income before extraordinary items and 20¢ for extraordinary items. These figures are derived by dividing the respective amounts in the income categories by 50,000 shares of common stock outstanding during the period.

Sales

Revenue from sales reports the total sales to customers for the period. This total should not include additions to billings for sales and excise taxes that the business is required to collect on behalf of the government. These billing increases are properly recognized as current liabilities. Sales returns and allowances and sales discounts should be subtracted from gross sales in arriving at net sales revenue. When the sales price is increased to cover the cost of freight to the customer and the customer is billed accordingly, freight charges paid by the company should also be subtracted from sales in arriving at net sales. Freight charges not absorbed by the buyer are recognized as selling expenses.

Cost of Goods Sold

When merchandise is acquired from outsiders, the cost of goods relating to sales of the period must be determined. *Cost of merchandise available for sale* is first determined. This is the sum of the beginning inventory, purchases, and all other buying, freight, and storage costs relating to the acquisition of goods. A net purchases balance is developed by subtracting purchase returns and allowances and purchase discounts from gross purchases. *Cost of goods sold* is calculated by subtracting the ending inventory from the cost of merchandise available for sale.

When the goods are manufactured by the seller, the *cost of goods manufactured* must first be calculated. Cost of goods manufactured replaces purchases in the summary just described. The determination of cost of goods manufactured begins with the cost of goods in process at the beginning of the period. To this is added the cost of materials put into production, the cost of labor applied to material conversions, and all of the other costs for services and facilities utilized in manufacturing, including factory superintendence, indirect labor, depreciation and other costs relating to factory buildings and equipment, factory supplies used, patent amortization, and factory light, heat, and power. The total thus obtained represents the cost of goods completed and goods still in production. The goods in process inventory at the end of the period is subtracted from this total in arriving at the cost of the goods finished and made available for sale.

Operating Expenses

Operating expenses are generally reported in two categories: (1) selling expenses and (2) general and administrative expenses. Selling expenses include such items as sales salaries and commissions and related payroll taxes, advertising and store displays, store supplies used, depreciation of store furniture and equipment, and delivery expenses. General and administrative expenses include officers and office salaries and related payroll taxes, office supplies used, depreciation of office furniture and fixtures, telephone, postage, business licenses and fees, legal and accounting services, contributions, and similar items. Charges related to the use of buildings, such as rent, depreciation, taxes, insurance, light, heat, and power, should be allocated in some equitable manner to manufacturing activities and to selling and general and administrative activities. In the case of the merchandising concern, charges relating to buildings are generally reported in full in the general and administrative category.

Other Revenue and Expense Items

Other revenue and expense items include items identified with financial management and other miscellaneous recurring items not related to the central operations. Other revenue includes earnings in the form of interest and dividends, and miscellaneous earnings from rentals, royalties, and service fees. Other expense includes interest expense and other expenses related to the miscellaneous revenue items reported. Items not qualifying as extraordinary, i.e., which are unusual or occur infrequently, but not both, may be shown in this section or as separate items following this section if material. They are not presented net of tax effects.

Income Tax Relative to Income from Normal Operations

The income tax expense should report the tax on revenue and expense transactions included in pretax ordinary income from normal operations. This will require application of income tax allocation procedures described in Chapter 16. In reporting the tax, the components included in its determination should be disclosed. Parenthetical remarks or notes in the income statement may be considered appropriate in defining the nature and purpose of the allocations.

Other Categories

Special sections for reporting the disposal of a business segment, any items qualifying as extraordinary gains and losses, and the cumulative effect of changing an accounting principle should be provided for if applicable. These items are to be adjusted for related income tax effects.

FORM OF THE INCOME STATEMENT

The income statement traditionally has been prepared in either multiple-step or single-step form. An example of an income statement in multiple-step form is presented on page 107 and in condensed single-step form on page 108. In each example, the presentation is made in accordance with the recommendations in the APB opinions and FASB statements discussed earlier, although only one special category, extraordinary items, is shown.

In the *multiple-step* form, the ordinary operations are first summarized and designated as "Income before income tax." The income tax related to ordinary operations is computed and deducted. The title of the remaining figure varies depending upon the company circumstances. For example, if a disposal of a business segment were to be shown, the above mentioned figure would be designated "Income from continuing operations." The gain or loss on the disposal of the business segment would be added or deducted from this figure. Any extraordinary gains or losses and any cumulative effect of a change in accounting principle would then be added or deducted to arrive at the final figure of net income. These last three items are each shown net of their tax effect.

Revenue and expense items are grouped to provide different income measurements as follows:

1. *Gross profit on sales* (or *gross margin*) — the difference between sales and the costs directly related to such sales.
2. *Operating income* — gross profit on sales less operating expenses.
3. *Income before income tax* — operating income increased by other revenue items and decreased by other expense items.
4. *Income after tax* (or *Income before extraordinary items*) — income less the income tax applicable to ordinary income.
5. *Net income* — income from normal operations plus or minus any special items net of applicable income tax.
6. *Earnings per common share* — the presentation of earnings per common share in terms of income by major category.[1]

The *single-step form* is in reality a modified single-step form because of the required separation of ordinary and extraordinary items. However, as illustrated, all ordinary revenue and expense items are listed and summarized without separate headings for cost of goods sold, gross profit, and other revenue and expense items.

Many accountants have raised objections to the multiple-step income statement form. They point out that the various income designations have no universal meaning and may prove a source of confusion to the reader. Quoting such designations in the absence of a complete income statement may prove ambiguous or actually misleading. They further maintain that multiple-step presentation implies certain cost priorities

---

[1]APB Opinion No. 15 calls for the presentation of earnings per common share data on the face of the income statement. If dilution of earnings is possible because of the existence of convertible securities or stock options or warrants, separate earnings figures disclosing potential dilution must also be shown. This subject is discussed in detail in Chapter 21.

and an order for cost recoveries. But there is no such order and there can be no earnings unless all costs are recovered. These persons support the single-step form that minimizes sectional labeling. However, the recent

Andersen Corporation
Income Statement
For Year Ended December 31, 1977

Revenue from sales:			
Sales		$510,000	
Less: Sales returns and allowances	$ 7,500		
Sales discounts	2,500	10,000	$500,000
Cost of goods sold:			
Merchandise inventory, January 1, 1977		$ 95,000	
Purchases	$320,000		
Freight in	15,000		
Delivered cost of purchases	$335,000		
Less: Purchase returns and allowances $1,000			
Purchase discounts 4,000	5,000	330,000	
Merchandise available for sale		$425,000	
Less merchandise inventory, December 31, 1977		125,000	300,000
Gross profit on sales			$200,000
Operating expenses:			
Selling expenses:			
Sales salaries	$ 30,000		
Advertising expense	15,000		
Depreciation expense — selling and delivery equipment	5,000		
Miscellaneous selling expense	10,000	$ 60,000	
General and administrative expenses:			
Officers and office salaries	$ 48,000		
Taxes and insurance	20,000		
Miscellaneous supplies expense	5,000		
Depreciation expense — office furniture and fixtures	5,000		
Doubtful accounts expense	2,500		
Amortization expense	10,600		
Miscellaneous general expense	4,400	95,500	155,500
Operating income			$ 44,500
Other revenue and expense items:			
Interest revenue	$ 3,000		
Dividend revenue	5,000		
Gain on sale of investment	5,000	$ 13,000	
Interest expense		(7,500)	5,500
Income before income tax			$ 50,000
Income tax:			
Current tax charge, $27,000 less $5,000 applicable to gain on extinguishment of debt reported below		$ 22,000	
Tax charge arising from timing difference in computing depreciation		3,000	25,000
Income before extraordinary items			$ 25,000
Extraordinary items:			
Gain on extinguishment of debt		$ 20,000	
Less applicable income tax		10,000	10,000
Net income			$ 35,000
Earnings per common share:[1]			
Income before extraordinary items			$ .50
Extraordinary items			.20
Net income			$ .70

[1]$25,000 ÷ 50,000 shares = $.50; $10,000 ÷ 50,000 shares = $.20.

Multiple-Step Income Statement

Andersen Corporation
Income Statement
For Year Ended December 31, 1977

Revenues:		
Net sales	$500,000	
Other revenue — interest and dividends	13,000	$513,000
Expenses:		
Cost of goods sold	$300,000	
Selling expense	60,000	
General and administrative expense	95,500	
Interest expense	7,500	
Income tax (including deferred tax of $3,000)	25,000	488,000
Income before extraordinary items		$ 25,000
Extraordinary gain on extinguishment of debt (net of income tax of $10,000)		10,000
Net income		$ 35,000
Earnings per common share:[1]		
Income before extraordinary items		$ .50
Extraordinary income		.20
Net income		$ .70

[1]$25,000 ÷ 50,000 shares = $.50; $10,000 ÷ 50,000 shares = $.20.

Condensed Single-Step Income Statement

accounting pronouncements seem to be requiring greater sectionalization of the income statement.

The income statement is frequently prepared in condensed form and simply reports totals for certain classes of items, such as cost of goods sold, selling expenses, general expenses, other revenue and expense, and extraordinary items. Additional detail may be provided by the use of supporting schedules.

It may be observed that the use of condensed income statements by large units engaged in a number of diversified activities has been severely criticized. There have been many mergers of companies with a large diversity of products and services provided by each unit. Income statements prepared in condensed form may tend to disguise the important trends operating within the individual segments of a diversified company. Because of this, the FASB, in Statement No. 14, and the Securities and Exchange Commission both require disclosure of sales and profit information by major segments of a company.

When goods are manufactured by the seller, the cost of the goods manufactured must be determined before the cost of goods sold can be computed. If a summary of cost of goods manufactured is to accompany the financial statements, it should be presented as a schedule in support of the amount reported on the income statement. Assuming the merchandise available for sale in the example on page 107 was obtained by manufacture rather than by purchase, cost of goods sold on the income statement would be presented as shown at the top of the next page. The supporting schedule immediately follows the presentation.

Cost of goods sold:

Finished goods inventory, January 1, 1977	$ 40,000	
Add cost of goods manufactured per manufacturing schedule	310,000	
Merchandise available for sale	$350,000	
Less finished goods inventory, December 31, 1977	50,000	$300,000

Andersen Corporation
Manufacturing Schedule
For Year Ended December 31, 1977

Goods in process inventory, January 1, 1977				$ 25,000
Raw materials:				
Inventory, January 1, 1977			$ 30,000	
Purchases		$105,000		
Freight in		10,000		
Delivered cost of raw materials		$115,000		
Less: Purchase returns and allowances	$1,000			
Purchase discounts	4,000	5,000	110,000	
Total cost of raw materials available for use			$140,000	
Less inventory, December 31, 1977			40,000	100,000
Direct labor				140,000
Manufacturing overhead:				
Indirect labor			$ 20,000	
Factory superintendence			14,500	
Depreciation expense — factory buildings and equipment			12,000	
Light, heat, and power			10,000	
Factory supplies expense			8,500	
Miscellaneous factory overhead			15,000	80,000
Total goods in process during 1977				$345,000
Less goods in process inventory, December 31, 1977				35,000
Cost of goods manufactured				$310,000

Manufacturing Schedule

Frequently, only the cost of goods sold is reported on the income statement. If a schedule of the cost of goods sold is to be provided, it should summarize the cost of goods manufactured as well as the change in finished goods inventories. Instead of reporting beginning and ending inventories, it is possible simply to report inventory variations for the period in arriving at the cost of materials used, cost of goods manufactured, or cost of goods sold. For example, an increase in the finished goods inventory would be subtracted from the cost of goods manufactured in arriving at the cost of goods sold; a decrease in the finished goods inventory would be added to the cost of goods manufactured in arriving at the cost of goods sold.

THE STATEMENT OF CHANGES IN OWNERS' EQUITY

When the only change in the owners' equity arises from earnings for the period, the balance sheet prepared at the end of the period may report in the owners' equity section the balance of the equity at the beginning of the period, the change arising from earnings for the period, and the resulting balance at the end of the period. Normally, however, more than the earnings must be recognized in explaining the change in equity, and a *statement of changes in the owners' equity* may be prepared to accompany the financial statements. In the case of a corporation, if transactions affecting the stockholders' equity have been limited to changes in retained earnings, a *retained earnings statement* is prepared. This statement reports the beginning balance for retained earnings, any prior period adjustments shown net of tax to arrive at the adjusted retained earnings at the beginning of the period, earnings for the period, and dividend declarations. A retained earnings statement to accompany the income statement prepared on page 107 is shown below.

Andersen Corporation
Retained Earnings Statement
For Year Ended December 31, 1977

Retained earnings, January 1, 1977	$149,000
Deduct prior period adjustment — correction of inventory overstatement, net of income tax refund of $9,000	9,000
Adjusted retained earnings, January 1, 1977..	$140,000
Add net income per income statement..	35,000
	$175,000
Deduct dividends declared	20,000
Retained earnings, December 31, 1977	$155,000

Retained Earnings Statement

The income statement and retained earnings statement may be prepared in *combined* form. In preparing the combined statement, net income data are first listed and summarized. The net earnings for the period is then combined with the retained earnings balance at the beginning of the period or the adjusted balance due to prior period adjustments. This total is adjusted for dividend declarations in arriving at the retained earnings balance at the end of the period. Data can be presented in either multiple-step or single-step form. The combined statement listing data in single-step form can be prepared in the following form (details for revenues and expenses have been omitted).

Andersen Corporation
Income and Retained Earnings Statement
For Year Ended December 31, 1977

Revenues		$513,000
Expenses..		488,000
Income before extraordinary item		$ 25,000
Extraordinary gain on extinguishment of debt (net of income tax of $10,000)..		10,000
Net income..		$ 35,000
Adjusted retained earnings, January 1, 1977:		
Retained earnings, January 1, 1977................................	$149,000	
Deduct prior period adjustment — correction of inventory overstatement, net of income tax refund of $9,000.............................	9,000	140,000
		$175,000
Deduct dividends declared		20,000
Retained earnings, December 31, 1977..		$155,000

Combined Income and Retained Earnings Statement

Prior to the issuance of APB Opinion No. 9, the combined income and retained earnings statement was frequently prepared because it offered a means of reporting both ordinary operations and extraordinary items on the same statement while still offering a clear distinction between the two classes of data. Now that the extraordinary items are clearly set forth on the income statement, the popularity of this form may decline. However, the combined statement may still be preferable when prior period adjustments are reported.

Some companies depart from the conventional forms of income reporting in the attempt to display revenue and expense data in simplified or more popular and readable form. Data may be presented in narrative or graphic form to help the reader grasp significant relationships. An illustration of an income statement and a related retained earnings statement is provided in Appendix B of this textbook.

QUESTIONS

1. An article in a financial journal was titled "What are Earnings? The Growing Creditability Gap." What do you think was meant by this title?

2. What reasons can you offer for the increased importance of the income statement?

3. What are the major differences between the valuation and matching methods of income determination?

4. What concepts of the "value of net assets" might be applied in the valuation method of income determination? Which do you prefer and why?

5. What factors determine the timing of revenue recognition?

6. A manufacturer of farm implements sells its products to dealers who in turn sell them to farmers. To induce dealers to carry an adequate stock, the dealer is not required to pay for merchandise received until 30 days after sale to the customer. In addition, dealers are permitted to return unsold merchandise at any time within nine months from the time it is received. Dealers hold title to the merchandise while it is in their hands. In some years, the returns were low; in others years they have amounted to 25% of the shipments. Bad debts are low. No interest is charged dealers on the balances in their accounts. At what point should the manufacturer recognize revenue?

7. At harvest time, a wheat producer moves the wheat to a grain elevator and receives a warehouse receipt for it. The decision to sell wheat is based on the need for cash and on the forecast of the market. At what point should the producer recognize revenue?

8. Why is the process of matching costs with revenues in income determination so difficult?

9. Do you think matching expenses with revenues is more difficult to apply in a machine assembly plant than in a CPA firm? Why?

10. What guidelines are used to match costs with revenues in determining income?

11. Small loan companies often experience operating losses in the operation of newly opened branch loan offices. Such results can usually be anticipated by management prior to making a decision on expansion. It has been recommended that the operating losses of newly opened branches should be reported as deferred charges during the first twelve months of operation or until the first profitable month occurs. Such deferred charges would then be amortized over a five-year period. Would you support this recommendation?

12. A construction contractor classifies all revenues and expenses by project, each project being considered a separate venture. All revenue from uncompleted projects are treated as unearned revenue and all expenses applicable to each uncompleted project as "work in process" inventory. The income statement for the year includes only the revenues and expenses related to the projects completed during the year. (a) Evaluate the practice described. (b) What alternative approach can you suggest for the above described practice?

13. What items on the income statement are most significantly affected by price-level changes?

14. How does the all-inclusive form of the income statement differ from the current operating performance form?

15. How would you distinguish between ordinary items and extraordinary items for income statement presentation? Where should extraordinary items be presented on the income statement?

16. How would you distinguish between a change in an accounting estimate and a correction of an accounting error? What difference would your distinction make for income statement purposes?

17. (a) What objections can be made to the multiple-step income statement? (b) What objections can be made to the single-step statement?

18. What information not found in the income statement or the balance sheet is disclosed in the retained earnings statement?

EXERCISES

1. Changes in account balances for the Sanchez Sales Co. during 1977 were as follows:

	Increase (Decrease)
Cash	$ 45,000
Accounts Receivable	5,000
Merchandise Inventory	40,000
Buildings and Equipment (net)	120,000
Accounts Payable	(35,000)
Bonds Payable	100,000
Capital Stock	75,000
Additional Paid-In Capital	15,000

Dividends paid during 1977 were $25,000. Calculate the net income for the year assuming there were no transactions affecting retained earnings other than the dividend payment.

2. Indicate which of the following items involves the realization of revenue or gain. Give the reasons for your answer.

(a) Land acquired in 1952 at $15,000 is now conservatively appraised at $100,000.

(b) Timberlands show a growth in timber valued at $40,000 for the year.

(c) An addition to a building was self-constructed at a cost of $3,600 after two offers from private contractors for the work at $4,650 and $5,000.

(d) Certain valuable franchise rights were received from a city for payment of annual licensing fees.

(e) A customer owing $4,600, which was delinquent for one year, gave securities valued at $5,000 in settlement of the obligation.

(f) Merchandise, cost $1,000, is sold for $1,600 with a 50% down payment on a conditional sales contract, title to the merchandise being retained by the seller until the full contract price is collected.

(g) Cash is received on the sale of gift certificates redeemable in merchandise in the following period.

3. How would you report each of the following items on the financial statements?

(a) Plant shut-down and start-up costs due to a strike.

(b) Loss on sale of the fertilizer production division of a lawn supplies manufacturer.

(c) Material penalties arising from early payment of a mortgage.

(d) Gain resulting from changing asset balances to adjust for the effect of excessive depreciation charged in error in prior years.

(e) Loss resulting from excessive accrual in prior years of estimated revenues from long-term contracts.

(f) Costs incurred to purchase a valuable patent.

(g) Net income from the discontinued dune buggy operations of a custom car designer.

(h) Costs of rearranging plant machinery into a more efficient order.

(i) Error made in capitalizing advertising expense.

(j) Gain on sale of land to the government.

(k) Loss from destruction of crops by a hail storm.

(l) Purchase and retirement of bonds outstanding at a price in excess of book value.

(m) Additional depreciation resulting from a change in the estimated useful life of the asset.

(n) Gain on sale of long-term investments.

(o) Loss from spring flooding.

(p) Sale of obsolete inventory at less than book value.

(q) Additional federal income tax assessment for prior years.

4. Where in the income or retained earnings statement would each item be reported?

(a) Gain on sale of land.

(b) Purchase discounts.

(c) Charge for doubtful accounts in anticipation of failure to collect receivables.

(d) Loss from long-term investments written off as worthless.

(e) Loss from a strike.

(f) Error in prior period of recording revenue.

(g) Loss from inventory price decline.

(h) Depletion.

(i) Sales discounts.

(j) Dividends received on long-term investments.

(k) Income tax for current period.

(l) Charge for omission of depreciation in prior periods.

(m) Collection of life insurance policy upon death of officer.

(n) Vacation pay of employees.

(o) Payment in settlement of damage suit for breach of contract arising in current period.

5. Using proper headings, prepare a manufacturing schedule in good form selecting the proper accounts from the following:

Purchases	$100,000	Beginning Inventory — Goods in Process	$13,000
Purchase Returns and Allowances	10,000	Beginning Inventory — Finished Goods	20,000
Beginning Inventory — Raw Materials	15,000	Factory Labor	26,000
Accounts Receivable	85,000	Factory Overhead	15,000
Equipment	26,000	Ending Inventory — Raw Materials	18,000
Depreciation of Factory Equipment	2,500	Ending Inventory — Goods in Process	12,000
Depreciation of Factory Building	2,000	Ending Inventory — Finished Goods	16,000
Selling Expenses	18,000	Cash	11,000

6. The selling expenses of Colvin, Inc., for 1977 are 10% of sales. General expenses, excluding doubtful accounts, are 25% of cost of goods sold but only 15% of sales. Doubtful accounts are 2% of sales. The beginning merchandise inventory was $62,000 and it decreased 25% during the year. Income for the year before income tax of 45% is $52,000. Prepare an income statement, including earnings per share data, giving supporting computations. Colvin, Inc., has 104,000 shares of common stock outstanding.

7. From the chart of accounts presented below and at the top of the next page, prepare a multiple-step income statement in good form showing all appropriate items properly classified, including disclosure of earnings per share data. Assume a supporting manufacturing statement has been prepared. (No monetary amounts are to be recognized.)

Accounts Payable
Accumulated Depreciation — Buildings
Accumulated Depreciation — Delivery Equipment
Accumulated Depreciation — Office Furniture and Fixtures
Advertising Expense
Allowance for Doubtful Accounts
Amortization of Patents
Cash
Common Stock, $20 par (10,000 shares outstanding)
Delivery Salaries

Depreciation Expense — Buildings
Depreciation Expense — Delivery Equipment
Depreciation Expense — Office Furniture and Fixtures
Depreciation Expense — Tools
Direct Labor
Dividend Revenue
Dividends Payable
Dividends Receivable
Doubtful Accounts Expense
Extraordinary Loss (net of tax savings)
Factory Heat, Light, and Power

Factory Superintendence	Miscellaneous Selling Expense
Factory Supplies	Office Salaries
Factory Supplies Used	Office Supplies
Finished Goods	Office Supplies Used
Freight In	Officers' Salaries
Federal Unemployment Tax Payable	Patents
Goods in Process	Purchase Discounts
Goodwill	Raw Materials
Income Tax	Raw Materials Purchases
Income Tax Payable	Raw Materials Returns and Allowances
Insurance Expense	Retained Earnings
Interest Expense — Bonds	Royalties Received in Advance
Interest Expense — Other	Royalty Revenue
Interest Payable	Salaries and Wages Payable
Interest Receivable	Sales
Interest Revenue	Sales Discounts
Loss on Disposal of Discontinued Operations (net of tax)	Sales Returns and Allowances
	Sales Salaries and Commissions
Miscellaneous Delivery Expense	Sales Tax Payable
Miscellaneous Factory Overhead	Taxes
Miscellaneous General Expense	Tools

8. R. A. Curtis, Inc., shows a retained earnings balance on January 1, 1977, of $230,000. For 1977, the income from continuing operations was $75,000 before income tax. Following is a list of special items:

Income from operations of a discontinued cosmetics division	$ 9,000
Loss on the sale of the cosmetics division	25,000
Gain on extinguishment of long-term debt	12,500
Correction of sales understatement in 1975	14,000
Omission of depreciation charges of prior years (A claim has been filed for an income tax refund of $4,000.)	10,000

Income tax paid during 1977 was $20,200, which consisted of the tax on continuing operations, plus $4,000 resulting from operations of the discontinued cosmetics divisions and $6,000 from the gain from extinguishment of debt, less a tax credit of $12,300 for loss on the sale of the cosmetics division. Dividends of $15,000 were declared by the company during the year (50,000 shares of common stock are outstanding). Prepare the income statement for R. A. Curtis, Inc., beginning with "Income from continuing operations before income tax." Include an accompanying retained earnings statement.

PROBLEMS

4-1. Selected account balances of the Jason Company along with additional information as of December 31, 1977, are as follows:

Contribution to Employees Pension Fund	$290,000	Loss on Sale of Marketable Securities	$ 50,000
Delivery Expense	425,000	Loss from Write-Down of Obsolete Inventory	125,000
Depreciation Expense — Delivery Trucks	29,000	Merchandise Inventory, Jan. 1, 1977	900,000
Depreciation Expense — Office Buildings and Equipment	35,000	Miscellaneous General Expense	45,000
Depreciation Expense — Store Equipment	25,000	Miscellaneous Selling Expense	50,000
Dividends	150,000	Officers and Office Salaries	950,000
Dividend Revenue	5,000	Purchase Discounts	47,700
Doubtful Accounts Expense	22,000	Purchases	4,633,200
Federal Income Tax, 1977 (applicable to continuing operations)	315,000	Retained Earnings, Jan. 1, 1977	550,000
		Sales	8,350,000
Freight In	145,000	Sales Discounts	55,000
Gain on Sale of Office Equipment	10,000	Sales Returns and Allowances	95,000
		Sales Salaries	601,000
Interest Revenue	1,500	State and Local Taxes	100,000
		Store Supplies Expense	50,000

(a) Inventory at year-end was valued at $750,000 — $875,000 cost less the $125,000 write-down of obsolete inventory.

(b) On April 15, 1977, management committed itself to a formal plan for selling by December 1, 1977, its import-export division. Gain from sale of the discontinued division was $200,000 less income tax of $60,000. Income from operations of the division was $77,000 less income tax of $37,000.

(c) Jason Company made an error by understating depreciation expense in 1975 by $125,000. (Ignore any tax implications.)

(d) Jason Company has 100,000 shares of common stock outstanding.

Instructions: Prepare a combined statement of income and retained earnings for the year ended December 31, 1977. (Use a multiple-step form.)

4-2. The Lane Co. on July 1, 1976, reported a retained earnings balance of $762,500. The books of the company showed the following account balances on June 30, 1977:

Sales	$1,250,000
Inventory: July 1, 1976	80,000
June 30, 1977	82,500
Sales Returns and Allowances	15,000
Purchases	768,000
Purchase Discounts	12,000
Gain from Extinguishment of Debt	40,000
Dividends	130,000
Selling and General Expenses	125,000
Income Tax: Applicable to ordinary income	99,750
Applicable to gain from extinguishment of debt	20,000
Overstatement of depreciation erroneously recorded in prior years (Ignore tax implications)	26,000

Instructions: Prepare a single-step income statement accompanied by a retained earnings statement. The Lane Co. has 200,000 shares of common stock outstanding.

4-3. Fidelity Investment Company purchased 100 shares of Dorsey, Inc., and 100 shares of Hoyt Stores, Inc., on January 1, 1977. Data on these investments on a per share basis are as follows:

	Dorsey	Hoyt
Cost	$60.50	$82.25
Net income reported — 1977	7.00	7.50
Dividend paid — 1977	6.00	5.00
Market value — December 31, 1977	54.25	79.75

Fundamental Investment Company and American Shares, Inc., each purchased 100 shares of Hume Manufacturing Co. and 100 shares of Kovar Electronics, Inc., on January 1, 1977. Data on these investments, also on a per share basis, are as follows:

	Hume	Kovar
Cost	$50.75	$90.25
Net income reported — 1977	4.00	6.00
Dividend paid — 1977	3.00	none
Market value — December 31, 1977	56.25	94.00

American Shares, Inc., sold its shares of Kovar Electronics, Inc., on December 31, 1977, at the market value shown above. At the same time it purchased 200 shares of Magnatronics, Inc., for $9,350. The other companies continued to hold their original investment.

Instructions:

(1) Compute the revenues for the three companies, using each of the following approaches to revenue recognition for each company (no expenses are to be recognized in computing your answers):

(a) Dividends received (plus gain on sales, if any).

(b) Net income reported by company whose stock is owned.

(c) Dividends received adjusted by any change in the market value of the stock.

(2) Evaluate each of the approaches as to its informational value to investors.

4-4. The Emerson Company has released the following condensed financial statements for 1975 and 1976 and has prepared the following proposed statements for 1977.

Emerson Company
Comparative Balance Sheet
December 31

	1977	1976	1975
Assets			
Current assets	$ 83,000	$ 73,000	$ 55,000
Land	20,000	15,000	10,000
Equipment	50,000	50,000	50,000
Accumulated depreciation — equipment	(15,000)	(10,000)	(5,000)
Total assets	$138,000	$128,000	$110,000
Liabilities and Stockholders' Equity			
Current liabilities	$ 59,000	$ 59,000	$ 49,000
Common stock	20,000	20,000	20,000
Retained earnings	59,000	49,000	41,000
Total liabilities and stockholders' equity	$138,000	$128,000	$110,000

Emerson Company
Comparative Income Statement
For Years Ended December 31

	1977	1976	1975
Sales	$105,000	$100,000	$ 85,000
Cost of goods sold	$ 80,000	$ 75,000	$ 63,000
Other expenses except depreciation	10,000	12,000	11,000
Depreciation expense — equipment	5,000	5,000	5,000
Total costs	$ 95,000	$ 92,000	$ 79,000
Net income	$ 10,000	$ 8,000	$ 6,000

The Emerson Company acquired the equipment for $50,000 on January 1, 1975, and began depreciating the equipment over a ten-year estimated useful life with no salvage value, using the straight-line method of depreciation. The double-declining balance method of depreciation, under the same assumptions, would have required the following depreciation expense:

$$1975 = 20\% \times \$50,000 = \$10,000$$
$$1976 = 20\% \times \$40,000 = \$ 8,000$$
$$1977 = 20\% \times \$32,000 = \$ 6,400$$

Instructions: In comparative format, prepare a balance sheet and a combined statement of income and retained earnings (including earnings per share data) for 1977, giving effect to the following changes. Ignore any income tax effect. Emerson Company has 10,000 shares of common stock outstanding. The following situations are independent of each other.

(1) For justifiable reasons, Emerson Company changed to the double-declining balance method of depreciation in 1977. The effect of the change should be included in the net income of the period in which the change was made.
(2) During 1977, Emerson Company found the equipment was fast becoming obsolete and decided to change the estimated useful life from ten years to five years. The books for 1977 had not yet been closed.
(3) During 1977, Emerson Company found additional equipment, also acquired on January 1, 1975, costing $8,000, had been recorded in the land account and had not been depreciated. This error should be corrected using straight-line depreciation over a 10-year period.

4-5. The Norway Supply Co. prepares a multiple-step income statement. The statement is supported by (1) a manufacturing schedule, (2) a selling expense schedule, and (3) a general and administrative expense schedule. You are supplied the data shown at the top of the next page.

Income tax for the current year was as follows:

Applicable to ordinary income	$18,925
Applicable to extraordinary items...	5,000
Total income tax	$23,925

Inventory balances at the end of the fiscal period as compared with balances at the beginning of the fiscal period were as follows:

Finished goods	$20,000 decrease
Goods in process..	4,500 increase
Raw materials...	10,000 decrease

Other account balances include the following:

Advertising Expense..................	$ 15,000	Interest Expense	$ 10,200
Delivery Expense	23,000	Miscellaneous Factory Costs.....	10,500
Depreciation Exp. — Mach.	5,600	Miscellaneous General Ex-	
Direct Labor	184,000	pense..	3,200
Dividend Revenue......................	300	Miscellaneous Selling Expense.	2,150
Dividends...................................	30,000	Officers Salaries.........................	116,200
Doubtful Accounts Expense	1,600	Office Salaries............................	70,000
Extraordinary Gain	10,400	Office Supplies Expense............	3,200
Factory Heat, Light, and Power.	26,990	Raw Materials Purchases...........	196,900
Factory Maintenance..................	15,000	Raw Materials Returns...............	2,000
Factory Superintendence...........	60,000	Royalty Revenue	2,700
Factory Supplies Expense	14,000	Sales	989,800
Factory Taxes............................	14,000	Sales Discounts	8,000
Freight In on Raw Materials.......	10,000	Sales Returns and Allowances ..	6,500
Gain on Sale of Land.................	8,000	Sales Salaries............................	65,000
Indirect Labor............................	74,000		

Norway Supply Co. has 50,000 shares of common stock outstanding.

Instructions: Prepare an income statement with supporting schedules using the data for the year ended April 30, 1977, listed above.

4-6. The Ellis Corporation was organized on March 21, 1977, 15,000 shares of no-par stock being issued in exchange for land, buildings and equipment valued at $60,000 and cash of $15,000. Data below summarize activities for the initial fiscal period ending December 31, 1977:

(a) Net income for the period ending December 31, 1977, was $15,000.
(b) Raw materials on hand on December 31 were equal to 25% of raw materials purchased in 1977.
(c) Manufacturing costs in 1977 were distributed as follows:

Materials used...................50%
Direct labor 30%
Manufacturing overhead...20% (includes depreciation of building, $2,500)

(d) Goods in process remaining in the factory on December 31 were equal to 33⅓% of the goods finished and transferred to stock.
(e) Finished goods remaining in stock were equal to 25% of the cost of goods sold.
(f) Operating expenses were 30% of sales.
(g) Cost of goods sold was 150% of the operating expenses total.
(h) Ninety percent of sales were collected in 1977; the balance was considered collectible in 1978.
(i) Seventy-five percent of the raw materials purchased were paid for; there were no expense accruals or prepayments at the end of the year.

Instructions:

(1) Prepare a balance sheet, an income statement, and a supporting manufacturing schedule. (Disregard income tax.)
(2) Prepare a summary of cash receipts and disbursements to support the cash balance reported on the balance sheet.

4-7. Kwik-Bild Corporation sells and erects shell houses. These are frame structures completely finished on the outside but unfinished on the inside except for flooring, partition studding and ceiling joists. Shell houses are sold chiefly to customers who are handy with tools and who have time to do the interior wiring, plumbing, wall completion and finishing, and other work necessary to make the shell houses livable dwellings.

Kwik-Bild buys shell houses from a manufacturer in unassembled packages consisting of all lumber, roofing, doors, windows and similar materials necessary to complete a shell house. Upon commencing operations in a new area, Kwik-Bild buys or leases land as a site for its local warehouse, field office and display houses. Sample display houses are erected at a total cost of from $3,000 to $7,000 including the cost of the unassembled packages. The chief element of cost of the display houses is the unassembled packages, since erection is a short low-cost operation. Old sample models are torn down or altered into new models every three to seven years. Sample display houses have little salvage value because dismantling and moving costs amount to nearly as much as the cost of an unassembled package.

Instructions:

    (1) A choice must be made between (a) expensing the costs of sample display houses in the period in which the expenditure is made, and (b) spreading the costs over more than one period. Discuss the advantages of each method.

    (2) Would it be preferable to amortize the cost of display houses on the basis of (a) the passage of time or (b) the number of shell houses sold? Explain. (AICPA adapted)

5

Cash and Temporary Investments

The first part of this book has established a foundation for a careful analysis of the specific balance sheet classifications. The order of presentation begins with the most liquid assets, cash and temporary investments, and proceeds with the other current assets, long-term assets, current liability items, long-term liabilities, and owners' equity.

CASH

Cash is the most active item on the accounting statement. It is involved in most business transactions. This is due to the nature of business transactions which include a price and conditions calling for settlement in terms of a medium of exchange. For example, the movement of cash completes almost all purchases and sales transactions. Purchases of goods and services normally result in cash payments; sales normally result in cash receipts.

In striking contrast to the activity of cash is its unproductive nature. Since cash is the measure of value, it cannot expand or grow unless it is converted into other properties. Excessive balances of cash on hand are often referred to as *idle cash*. Efficient cash management requires available cash to be continuously working in one of several ways — e.g., as part of the operating cycle or as a short-term or long-term investment.

Composition of Cash

Cash is represented by those monetary as well as nonmonetary items immediately available to management for business purposes. Cash includes commercial and savings deposits in banks and elsewhere, available upon demand, and money items on hand that can be used as a medium of exchange or that are acceptable for deposit at face value by a bank. Cash on hand would include petty cash funds, change funds, and other regularly used and unexpended monetary funds, together with nonmonetary items consisting of personal checks, travelers' checks, cashiers' checks, bank drafts, and money orders.

"Acceptance at face value on deposit" is a satisfactory test in classifying as cash the items found in the cash drawer. It is assumed that deposits in a bank are made regularly and that deposits become the basis for disbursements by the depositor. Although postage stamps may in some instances pass for mail payments of small amounts, they are not accepted for deposit and should be classified as office supplies. Post-dated checks are in effect notes receivable and should not be recognized as cash until the time they can be deposited. Checks deposited but returned by the bank because of insufficient funds in the debtor's account are receivables. Cash-due memorandums for money advanced to officers and employees are receivable items, in some instances less satisfactory receivables than those of trade customers. Paper left at a bank for collection represents a receivable until collection is made and the amount is added to the depositor's account. Stocks, bonds, and United States securities, although immediately convertible into cash, generally are not used as a means for making payments, hence do not constitute cash but should be recognized as temporary or long-term investments.

Deposits in foreign banks subject to immediate and unrestricted withdrawal qualify as cash. Such balances should be converted into their U.S. dollar equivalents as of the date of the balance sheet. However, cash in foreign banks blocked or otherwise restricted as to use or withdrawal and cash in closed banks should be designated as claims or receivables of a current or noncurrent character and should be reported subject to allowances for losses on their realization.

Cash balances having been specifically designated by management for special purposes may be separately reported. Those cash balances to be applied to some current purpose or current obligation are properly reported in the current section on the balance sheet. For example, cash funds for employees' travel, payment of current interest and dividends, or payment of taxes or other obligations included in the current liabilities may be separately reported but are still classified as current.

Cash restricted as to use by agreement should be separately designated and reported. Restricted cash should be reported as a current item only if it is to be applied to some current purpose or obligation. Classification of the cash balance as current or noncurrent should parallel the classification applied to the liability.

Cash balances not available for current purposes require separate designation and classification under a noncurrent heading on the balance sheet. The noncurrent classification applies to items such as the following: time deposits not currently available as a result of withdrawal restrictions; cash deposits on bids or options that may be applied to the acquisition of noncurrent assets; and cash funds held by trustees for plant acquisitions, bond retirement, and pension payments.

Since the concept of cash embodies the standard of value, no valuation problem is encountered in reporting those items qualifying as cash.

A credit balance in the cash account resulting from the issuance of checks in excess of the amount on deposit is known as a *cash overdraft* and should be reported as a current liability. An overdraft may not necessarily embarrass a company if a number of checks are outstanding and deposits are made to cover the checks before clearance. When a company has two balances with a single bank, there can be no objection to the offsetting of the overdraft against an account with a positive balance; failure by the depositor to meet the overdraft will actually result in bank action to effect such an offset. However, when a company has accounts with two different banks and there is a positive balance in one account and an overdraft in the other, both an asset balance and a liability balance should be recognized in view of the claim against one bank and an obligation to the other; if recognition of an overdraft is to be avoided, cash should actually be transferred to cover the deficiency.

Control of Cash

The term *internal control* has been broadly defined as ". . . the plan of organization and all of the coordinate methods and measures adopted within a business to safeguard its assets, check the accuracy and reliability of its accounting data, promote operational efficiency, and encourage adherence to prescribed managerial policies."[1] This definition may be considered to embrace both *accounting controls* and *administrative controls.* Accounting controls dealing with the safeguarding of assets and the reliability of records are expressed in the form of systems of authorization and approval, separation of duties concerned with record keeping and reporting from those concerned with operations and asset custody, physical controls over assets, and internal auditing. Administrative controls dealing with operational efficiency and adherence to managerial policies are expressed in the form of statistical analyses, time and motion studies, performance reports, employee training programs, and quality controls.[2]

Obviously, the system of internal control must be developed with appropriate regard to the size and nature of the particular unit to be served. Its design should provide the maxium contributions practicable considering the special risks faced as well as the costs of providing controls. The increased use of data processing equipment for processing accounting transactions has not eliminated the need for carefully designed control systems; on the contrary, it may have increased the need. As new equipment is acquired and introduced into a system, the establishment or modification of controls should be considered.

In any system of internal accounting control, special emphasis must be placed on the procedures for handling and accounting for cash.

[1]*Statement on Auditing Standards No. 1*, "Codification of Auditing Standards and Procedures" (New York: American Institute of Certified Public Accountants, 1973), par. 320.09.
[2]*Ibid.*, par. 320.10.

Problems in Cash Control. Because of the characteristics of cash — its small bulk, its lack of owner identification, and its immediate transferability — it is the asset most subject to misappropriation, intentional or otherwise. Losses can be avoided only by careful control of cash from the time it is received until the time it is spent.

Control over business cash normally requires as a minimum the separation of cash custodial functions and cash recording functions. When the same persons have access to cash and also to cash records, the business becomes vulnerable to the misappropriation of cash and to the manipulation or falsification of cash records. The following are representative of practices found under these circumstances: (1) cash receipts from sales, from recoveries of accounts previously written off, from refunds on invoice overpayments, and from other sources are understated, the unrecorded cash being pocketed; (2) receivables are not entered on the books and cash collected on these receivables is withheld; (3) customers' accounts are credited for remittances but Sales Returns or Doubtful Accounts Expense is debited and the cash is withheld; (4) checks for personal purposes are debited to business expense; (5) invoices, vouchers, receipts, payroll records, or vouchers once approved and paid are used in support of fictitious charges, and endorsements on checks issued in payment of these charges are subsequently forged; (6) the cash balance is misstated by erroneous footings in the cash receipts and disbursement records, cash equivalent to the misstatement being withheld.

Two additional practices, check kiting and lapping, may be found when those who handle cash also maintain the cash records of the business.

Check kiting occurs when at the end of a month a transfer of funds is made by check from one bank to another to cover a cash shortage, and the entry to record the issue of the check is held over until the beginning of the new period. A cash increase in the customer's balance is recognized by the second bank in the current month as a result of the receipt of the check, but a corresponding decrease in the customer's balance is not recognized by the first bank because the check has not yet been presented for payment. When the bank statements are received, the balance in the bank in which the check was deposited shows an increase. At the same time, the balance shown in the bank on which the check was drawn remains unchanged. A cash shortage is thus temporarily concealed.

Lapping occurs when a customer's remittance is misappropriated, the customer's account being credited when cash is collected from another customer at a later date. This process may be continued with further misappropriations and increasing delays in postings. To illustrate lapping, assume that on successive days cash is received from customers A, B, and C in amounts of $75, $125, and $120. A's payment is misappropriated. A is subsequently credited with $75 out of B's payment and the difference, $50, is misappropriated. B is credited for $125 upon C's $120 payment and $5 is returned on the amounts originally *borrowed*. The shortage at this point is $120, the unrecorded credit to C's account. This procedure can be continued with but slight delay in recording any customer's payment. The embezzler usually intends to return the money and avoid the strain of lapping after a profit has been made on the investments. Unable to make restitution, the embezzler may resort to a fictitious entry debiting Doubtful Accounts Expense or some other expense account and crediting the customers' balances to bring these up to date.

When, during the course of the day, cash records and summaries report a cash total differing from the amount available for deposit and it is assumed that cash has been lost or errors have been made in making change, an adjustment is made to a cash short and over account. The balance in this account may be reported as a financial management item in summarizing net income. However, a cash shortage resulting from employee defalcation should be charged to an employee account or the bonding company liable for such losses. Failure to recover the shortage requires the recognition of a loss from this source.

Attributes of Cash Control Systems. A system of accounting control over cash funds should serve to disclose cash discrepancies as well as to fix responsibility for any possible misappropriations or mistakes in handling and recording cash. When misuse of funds or errors are indicated, it is only fair to members of an organization to determine the causes and to fix the responsibility so that innocent parties may be spared any embarrassment. Responsibilities for the handling and recording functions should be specifically defined and scrupulously observed and carried out.

The system for the control of cash must be adapted to a particular business. It is not feasible to attempt to describe all of the features and techniques employed in businesses of various kinds and sizes. In general, however, systems of cash control deny access to the records to those who handle cash. This reduces the possibility of improper entries to conceal the misuse of cash receipts and cash payments. The misappropriation of cash is greatly reduced if two or more employees must conspire in the embezzlement. Further, systems normally provide for separation of the receiving and paying functions. The basic characteristics of a control system of cash control are listed below:

1. Specifically assigned responsibility for handling cash receipts.
2. Separation of handling and recording cash receipts.
3. Daily deposit of all cash received.
4. Voucher system to control cash payments.
5. Internal audit at irregular intervals.

Specifically Assigned Responsibility for Handling Cash Receipts. A fundamental principle in controlling any asset is that the responsibility be specifically assigned to one person. This principle is especially vital in the area of cash. If more than one person must have access to the same cash fund at different times, a reconciliation of the cash on hand should be made each time the responsibility is shifted. Any shortage or questionable transaction can then be identified with a particular person.

Separation of Handling and Recording Cash Receipts. An adequate control system normally requires cash from sales and cash remittances from customers be made available directly to the treasurer or the cashier for deposit, while records related to these transactions, as well as records related to bank deposits, be made available directly to the bookkeeping division. It is also desirable that comparisons of bank deposits with the book records of cash be made regularly by a third party who is engaged neither in the cash handling nor in the cash recording functions. Frequently, for example, a clerk opens the mail, prepares lists of remittances in duplicate, and then sends the cash and one copy of the list of remittances to the cashier and the second copy of the list to the bookkeeping division. Readings of cash registers are made by some responsible individual other than the cashier at the end of the day. The cash, together with a summary of the receipts, is sent to the cashier; a summary of the receipts is also sent to the bookkeeping division. Although deposits in the bank are made by the cashier or treasurer, entries on the books are made from lists of remittances and register readings prepared by individuals not otherwise involved in handling or recording cash. Members of the accounting or auditing staff compare periodic bank statements with related data on the books to determine whether the data are in agreement. If customers' remittances are not listed and the cash is misused, statements to customers will report excessive amounts and protests will lead to sources of the discrepancies; if cash receipts listed are not deposited properly, the bank record will not agree with cash records.

Daily Deposit of All Cash Received. The daily deposit of all cash received prevents sums of cash from lying around the office and being used for other than business purposes. Officers and employees have less opportunity to borrow on IOU's. Both the temptation for misappropriation of cash and the risk of theft of cash are avoided. The bank now protects company funds and releases these only upon proper company authorization. When the full receipts are deposited daily, the bank's record of deposits must agree with the depositor's record of cash receipts. This double record provides an automatic check over cash receipts.

Voucher System to Control Cash Payments. The use of a voucher system to control cash payments is a desirable feature of cash control. Vouchers authorizing disbursements of cash by check are made at the time goods or services are received and found acceptable. Entries in the voucher register recording the expenditures and the authorizations for payment are made by the bookkeeping division. Checks are also prepared and are sent, together with documents supporting the disbursements, to the person specifically authorized to make payment, normally the official designated as treasurer. This person signs and issues checks only after careful inspection of the vouchers supporting and authorizing payments. The bookkeeping department, upon notification of the issuance of checks, makes appropriate records of this fact. Receiving and paying functions of the business are maintained as two separate systems.

In each instance, custodial and recording activities are exercised by different parties.

Internal Audit at Irregular Intervals. Internal audits at irregular and unannounced intervals may be made a part of the system of cash control. A member of the internal auditing staff verifies the records and checks on the activities of those employees handling cash to make sure the provisions of the system are being carried out. Such control is particularly desirable over petty cash and other cash funds where cash handling and bookkeeping are generally combined.

Double Record of Cash. The preceding section listed the daily deposit of all cash received as an important factor in the control of cash. If all cash receipts are deposited daily, then the bank record of deposits will agree with the depositor's record of cash receipts. As a complementary device, all cash payments should be made by check; the bank's record for checks should agree with the depositor's record of cash payments. Two complete cash summaries are thus available, one in the cash account and the other on the monthly bank statement. In addition to the advantages resulting from organized and consistent routines applied to cash receipts and disbursements, a duplicate record of cash maintained by an outside agency is made available as a check upon the accuracy of the records kept by the company.

Maintenance of the double record of cash involves two special business and accounting procedures described in the following sections: (1) the adoption of a system of cash disbursements from a petty cash fund, and (2) reconciliation of the bank balance with the cash account balance at regular intervals.

Imprest System of Cash Funds. Immediate cash payments and payments too small to be made by check may be made from a petty cash fund. Under the *imprest system*, the petty cash fund is created by drawing a check to Petty Cash for the amount of the fund. In recording the establishment of the fund, Petty Cash Fund is debited and Cash is credited. The cash is then turned over to a cashier or some person who is solely responsible for payments made out of the fund. The cashier should require a signed receipt for all payments made. These receipts may be printed in prenumbered form. Frequently, a bill or other memorandum is submitted when a payment is requested. A record of petty cash payments may be kept in a *petty cash journal*.

Whenever the amount of cash in the fund runs low and also at the end of each fiscal period, the fund is replenished by writing a check equal to the payments made. In recording replenishment, expenses and other appropriate accounts are debited for petty cash disbursements and Cash is credited. Replenishment is necessary whenever statements are to be prepared since petty cash disbursements are recognized on the books only when the fund is replenished.

The request for cash to replenish the fund is supported by a summary and analysis of the signed receipts required at the time of the disbursement from the fund. This analysis is the basis for the debits recognized on the books when the replenishing check is issued. The signed receipts, together with appropriate documents, are filed as evidence supporting petty cash disbursements.

The cashier of the petty cash fund is held accountable for the total amount of the fund. The person responsible must have on hand at all times cash and signed receipts equal in amount to the original balance of the fund. The cashier should be discouraged from cashing employees' checks from petty cash or otherwise engaging in a banking function. If a banking function is to be undertaken, it should represent a separate activity with a fund established for this purpose.

The imprest system may be employed not only for petty cash but for other cash funds in a large organization. For example, a branch office or agency may be allowed a fund subsequently replenished for amounts equal to disbursements out of the fund. Evidence concerning payments out of the fund is submitted with the request for replenishment, and fund disbursements are recorded on the books at the time of fund replenishment.

The petty cash operation should be maintained apart from other cash funds employed for particular business purposes. For example, a business may require funds for making change. Certain sums of coins and currency are withheld from deposit at the end of each day to be carried forward as the change funds for the beginning of business on the next day. A separate account should be established to report a cash supply always on hand. Also, special funds or bank accounts may be established for payrolls, dividend distributions, and bond interest payments. Each fund requires a separate accounting.

Reconciliation of Bank Balances. When daily receipts are deposited and payments other than those from petty cash are made by check, the bank's statement of its transactions with the depositor can be compared with the record of cash as reported on the depositor's books. A comparison of the bank balance with the balance reported on the books is usually made monthly by means of a summary known as a *bank reconciliation statement.* The bank reconciliation statement is prepared to disclose any errors or irregularities existing in either the records of the bank or the records of the business unit. It is developed in a form that points out the reasons for discrepancies in the two balances. It should be prepared by an individual who neither handles nor records cash. Any discrepancies should be brought to the immediate attention of appropriate company officials.

An understanding of the reciprocal relationship existing between the records of the depositor and of the bank is necessary in the preparation of the reconciliation statement. All debits to the bank on the books of the depositor should be matched by credits to the depositor on the books of the bank; all credits to the bank on the books of the depositor should be matched by debits to the depositor on the books of the bank. To illustrate, cash from sales is recorded on the books of the depositor by a debit to the account with the bank, for example, Cash — State First National Bank, and a credit to Sales; the bank upon receiving the deposit debits Cash and credits the account with the depositor. A check in payment of an account is recorded on the books of the depositor by a debit to Accounts Payable, and a credit to the account with the bank; the bank upon clearing the check debits the account with the depositor and credits Cash.

When the two records are compared, certain items may appear on one record and not on the other, resulting in a difference in the two balances. Most of these differences result from timing lags, and are thus normal. The differences in depositor and bank balances may be classified as follows:

1. *Debits on the depositor's records without corresponding credits on the bank records.* For example, a deposit recognized on the depositor's records on the last day of the month may have been mailed, put into an after-hours depository, or held for transfer to the bank on the next day, and does not appear on the bank statement. This item is referred to as a *deposit in-transit.*
2. *Credits on the depositor's records without corresponding debits on the bank records.* For example, checks drawn and recognized on the depositor's records may not have cleared and do not appear on the bank statement. This item is referred to as an *outstanding check.*
3. *Debits on the bank records without corresponding credits on depositor's records.* For example, the bank may have charged the depositor's account for bank services, checkbooks, interest, returned customers' checks, and other items, but the depositor has not been notified of these charges before receiving his or her bank statement and these do not appear on the depositor's books.
4. *Credits on the bank records without corresponding debits on the depositor's records.* For example, the bank may have credited the depositor's account for amounts collected on his or her behalf, but the depositor has not been notified of these before receiving a bank statement and these do not appear on his or her books.

If, after considering the items mentioned, the bank statement and the book balances cannot be reconciled, a detailed analysis of both the bank's records and the depositor's books may be necessary to determine whether errors or other irregularities exist on the records of either party.

There are two common forms of the bank reconciliation statement. One form is prepared in two sections, the bank statement balance being adjusted to the corrected cash balance in the first section, and the book balance being adjusted to the same corrected cash balance in the second section. The first section, then, contains items the bank has not recognized as well as any corrections for errors made by the bank; the second section contains items the depositor has not yet recognized and any corrections for errors made on the depositor's books.

The other form begins with the bank statement balance and reports the adjustments that must be applied to this balance to obtain the cash balance on the depositor's books. The second form, then, simply reports the items accounting for the discrepancy between the bank and book balances. The first form is illustrated below; the second is shown at the top of page 129.

Caughman, Inc.
Bank Reconciliation Statement
November 30, 1977

Balance per bank statement, November 30, 1977..		$2,979.72
Add: Receipts for November 30 not yet deposited.........................	$658.50	
Charge for interest made to depositor's account by bank in error	12.50	671.00
		$3,650.72
Deduct outstanding checks:		
No. 1125..	$ 58.16	
No. 1138..	100.00	
No. 1152..	98.60	
No. 1154..	255.00	
No. 1155..	192.07	703.83
Corrected bank balance..		$2,946.89
Balance per books, November 30, 1977..		$2,552.49
Add: Proceeds of draft collected by bank November 30 ($500 face less $1.50 bank charges)......................................	$498.50	
Check No. 1116 for $46 recorded by depositor as $64 in error	18.00	516.50
		$3,068.99
Deduct: Bank service charges..	$ 3.16	
Customer's check deposited November 25 and returned marked uncollectible...	118.94	122.10
Corrected book balance..		$2,946.89

Reconciliation of Bank and Book Balances to Corrected Balance

Although the first form of bank reconciliation may be considered preferable because it develops a corrected cash figure and shows separately all of the items requiring adjustment on the depositor's books, some accountants prefer to use the second form, which is consistent with the nature of the reconciliation required for many other accounts.

After preparing the reconciliation, the depositor should record any items appearing on the bank statement and requiring recognition on the company's books as well as any corrections for errors discovered on its own books. The bank should be notified immediately of any bank errors. The following entries are required on the books of Caughman, Inc., as a result of the reconciliation just made:

Cash	498.50	
Miscellaneous General Expense..	1.50	
Notes Receivable		500.00
To record collection of a $500 time draft by the bank on which bank charges were $1.50.		
Cash	18.00	
Advertising		18.00
To record correction for check in payment of advertising recorded as $64 instead of the actual amount, $46.		
Accounts Receivable	118.94	
Miscellaneous General Expense..	3.16	
Cash..		122.10
To record customer's uncollectible check and bank charges for November.		

Caughman, Inc.
Bank Reconciliation Statement
November 30, 1977

Balance per bank statement, November 30, 1977			$2,979.72
Add: Receipts for November 30 not yet deposited		$658.50	
Charge for interest made to depositor's account by bank in error		12.50	
Bank service charges		3.16	
Customer's check deposited November 25 and returned marked uncollectible		118.94	793.10
			$3,772.82
Deduct: Outstanding checks:			
No. 1125	$ 58.16		
No. 1138	100.00		
No. 1152	98.60		
No. 1154	255.00		
No. 1155	192.07	$703.83	
Check No. 1116 for $46 recorded by depositor at $64 in error		18.00	
Proceeds of draft collected by bank on November 30		498.50	1,220.33
Balance per books, November 30, 1977			$2,552.49

Reconciliation of Bank Balance to Book Balance

After these entries are posted, the cash account will show a balance of $2,946.89. This is the amount to be reported on the balance sheet. These adjustments are clearly distinguishable when using the first form of bank reconciliation. They are shown separately as adjustments on the books. If the second form is used, adjustments can be determined only after careful analysis of all reconciling items.[1]

The bank reconciliation is frequently expanded to incorporate a proof of both receipts and disbursements as separate steps in the reconciliation process. This is often referred to as a *four-column reconciliation* or a *proof of cash*. Two reconciliation forms may be employed here as in earlier examples. One form develops corrected balances for both receipts and disbursements of the bank and the depositor, as illustrated at the top of page 130. The other form, as illustrated at the bottom of page 130, reports the items accounting for the discrepancies in receipts and disbursement balances on the two sets of records.

Opening balances, increases, decreases, and closing balances as reported on both the bank statement and the depositor's books are first listed. A reconciliation as of the end of the preceding period is then provided in the first column. Receipts are reconciled in the second column and disbursements in the third column. With proof of receipt and disbursement data, adjustments relating to ending balances may now be reported in the final column and the closing bank and book balances proved.

---

[1]A customer's check returned by the bank when it cannot be cashed may be redeposited when it is assumed that a deposit has been made by the customer to cover the check. When a charge is made to the customer's account upon the return of a check, the redeposit would be recorded as a normal collection of a receivable. When a check is returned by the bank and redeposited in the same period, some systems provide for no entry to be made; the omission does not affect the cash balances but it does affect the total receipts and disbursements reported by the bank.

Caughman, Inc.
Reconciliation of Receipts, Disbursements, and Bank Balance
November 30, 1977

	Beginning Reconciliation October 31	Receipts	Disbursements	Ending Reconciliation November 30
Balance per bank statement	$5,895.42	$21,212.40	$24,128.10	$2,979.72
Receipts not deposited:				
October 31	515.40	(515.40)		
November 30		658.50		658.50
Outstanding checks:				
October 31	(810.50)		(810.50)	
November 30			703.83	(703.83)
Charge for interest made by bank in error			(12.50)	12.50
Corrected bank balance	$5,600.32	$21,355.50	$24,008.93	$2,946.89
Balance per books	$5,406.22	$21,057.00	$23,910.73	$2,552.49
Bank service charges:				
October	(5.90)		(5.90)	
November			3.16	(3.16)
Customer's check deposited November 25 found to be uncollectible			118.94	(118.94)
Drafts collected by bank:				
October	200.00	(200.00)		
November		498.50		498.50
Check No. 1116 for $46 recorded by depositor at $64 in error			(18.00)	18.00
Corrected book balance	$5,600.32	$21,355.50	$24,008.93	$2,946.89

Reconciliation of Bank and Book Balances to Corrected Balance

Caughman, Inc.
Reconciliation of Receipts, Disbursements, and Bank Balance
November 30, 1977

	Beginning Reconciliation October 31	Receipts	Disbursements	Ending Reconciliation November 30
Balance per bank statement	$5,895.42	$21,212.40	$24,128.10	$2,979.72
Receipts not deposited:				
October 31	515.40	(515.40)		
November 30		658.50		658.50
Outstanding checks:				
October 31	(810.50)		(810.50)	
November 30			703.83	(703.83)
Bank service charges:				
October	5.90		5.90	
November			(3.16)	3.16
Customer's check deposited November 25 found to be uncollectible			(118.94)	118.94
Drafts collected by bank:				
October	(200.00)	200.00		
November		(498.50)		(498.50)
Charge for interest made by bank in error			(12.50)	12.50
Check No. 1116 for $46 recorded by depositor at $64 in error			18.00	(18.00)
Balance per books	$5,406.22	$21,057.00	$23,910.73	$2,552.49

Reconciliation of Bank Balance to Book Balance

In order to complete this type of reconciliation, each adjustment must be carefully analyzed. Two columns are always affected for each adjustment. For example, receipts of $515.40 on October 31, 1977, were received by the bank in November and are therefore included in the total bank receipts of $21,212.40 for November. However, the deposit was recorded on the books as a receipt in October and is not included in the book receipts of $21,057 for November. The reconciliation accounts for this by deducting the in-transit receipt from the total bank receipts.

The two previous illustrations assume adjustments of the book amounts are made in the month subsequent to their discovery. If the adjustments were made in the same month, as might be true at year-end, there would be no adjustments in the first column for adjusting the book amounts.

Often the parentheses in the disbursements column are reversed, and the total disbursement is shown with parentheses to indicate a deduction when adding horizontally. Using this reverse procedure requires a careful analysis of the reconciling items because whenever an item is to be added vertically to the disbursement total it must be enclosed in parentheses, while an item to be deducted is not enclosed in parentheses.

The expanded reconciliation procedure normally reduces the time and effort required to find errors made by either the bank or the depositor. In developing comparisons of both receipts and disbursements, the areas in which errors have been made, as well as the amounts of the discrepancies within each area, are immediately identified and checking procedures can be directed and narrowed accordingly. This procedure is frequently used by auditors when there is any question of possible discrepancies in the handling of cash.

Misrepresentation of Current Condition. Although a system of internal control may provide for the effective safeguarding of cash, careful examination of the records is still necessary at the end of an accounting period to determine whether transactions have been satisfactorily recorded and cash and the current position of the business are properly presented. Certain practices designed to present a more favorable financial condition than is actually the case may be encountered. Such practices are sometimes referred to as *window dressing*. For example, cash records may be held open for a few days after the close of a fiscal period and cash received from customers during this period reported as receipts of the preceding period. An improved cash position is thus reported. If this balance is then used as a basis for drawing predated checks in payment of accounts payable, the ratio of current assets to current liabilities is improved. For example, if current assets are $30,000 and current liabilities are $20,000 providing a current ratio of 1.5 to 1, recording payment to creditors of $10,000 will produce balances of $20,000 and $10,000, a current ratio of 2 to 1. The current ratio is also improved by writing checks in payment of obligations and entering these on the books even though checks are not to be mailed until the following period. Or the current position, as well as earnings and owners' equity, is overstated by predating sales made at the beginning of the new period. A careful review of the records will disclose whether improper practices have been employed. If such practices are discovered, the accounts should be corrected.

Cash Planning

Cash planning within a company does not take place without management effort. Many companies which are basically sound in organization and product control frequently have financial problems because managements do not understand the basic importance of cash planning. A full knowledge of the techniques of budgeting and forecasting is essential to sound financial control. These topics are considered in detail in managerial accounting texts and will not be covered here.

TEMPORARY INVESTMENTS

A company with excess cash temporarily available may deposit these funds as a time deposit, a certificate of deposit at a bank, or it may purchase securities. As a result, revenue will be produced that would not otherwise be available if cash were left idle. Investments made during seasonal periods of low activity can be converted into cash in periods of expanding operations. Asset items arising from temporary conversions of cash are commonly reported in the "Current assets" section of the balance sheet as "Temporary investments."

Criteria for Reporting Securities as Temporary Investments

Investments in securities qualify for reporting as temporary investments as long as (1) there is a ready market for converting such securities into cash, and (2) it is management's intention to sell them if the need for cash arises.

Securities are considered marketable when a day-to-day market exists and when they can be sold on short notice. The volume of trading in the securities should be sufficient to absorb a company's holdings without materially affecting the market price. Generally, marketable securities include such items as listed stocks, high-grade bonds, and first-mortgage notes. United States government securities, despite their relatively low yield, are also a highly favored form of marketable security because of their stable prices and wide market. Securities having a limited market and which fluctuate widely in price are not suitable for temporary investments.

Marketable securities may be converted into cash shortly after being acquired or they may be held for some time. In either case, however, they are properly classified as temporary investments as long as management intends to sell them if the need for cash arises. The deciding factor is management's intent, not the length of time the securities are held. Therefore, the following types of investments do not qualify as temporary investments even though the securities may be marketable: (1) reacquired shares of the company's own stock; (2) securities acquired for control of a company; (3) securities held for maintenance of business relations; and (4) any other securities that cannot be used or are not intended to be used as a ready source of cash.

Recording Purchase and Sale of Marketable Securities

Stocks and bonds acquired as temporary investments are recorded at cost, which includes brokers' fees, taxes, and other charges incurred in their acquisition. Shares are normally quoted at a price per single share; bonds are quoted at a price per $100 face value although they are normally issued in $1,000 denominations. The purchase of 100 shares of stock at 5⅛, then, would indicate a purchase price of $512.50; the purchase of a $1,000 bond at 104¼ would indicate a purchase price of $1,042.50.

When bonds are acquired between interest payment dates, the bond price is increased by a charge for accrued interest to the date of purchase. This charge should not be reported as part of investment cost. Two assets have been acquired — bonds and accrued interest — and the purchase price should be reported in two separate asset accounts. Upon the receipt of bond interest, the accrued interest account is closed and Interest Revenue is credited for the excess. Instead of recording the interest as an asset, Interest Revenue may be debited for the accrued interest paid. The subsequent collection of interest would then be credited in full to Interest Revenue. The latter procedure is usually more convenient.

To illustrate the entries for the acquisition of securities, assume that $100,000 in United States Treasury bonds are purchased at 104¼ on April 1. Interest is 8% payable semiannually on January 1 and July 1. Accrued interest of $2,000 would thus be added to the purchase price. The entries to record the purchase of the bonds and the subsequent collection of interest under the alternate procedures would be as follows:

Asset Approach:

Apr. 1	Marketable Securities — 8% U.S. Treasury Bonds......	104,250	
	Interest Receivable..	2,000	
	Cash		106,250
July 1	Cash...	4,000	
	Interest Receivable		2,000
	Interest Revenue		2,000

Revenue Approach:

Apr. 1	Marketable Securities — 8% U.S. Treasury Bonds......	104,250	
	Interest Revenue...	2,000	
	Cash		106,250
July 1	Cash...	4,000	
	Interest Revenue		4,000

When bonds are acquired at a higher or lower price than their maturity value and it is expected that they will be held until maturity, periodic amortization of the premium or accumulation of the discount with corresponding adjustments to interest revenue is appropriate. However, when bonds are acquired as a temporary investment and it is not likely the bonds will be held until maturity, such procedures are normally not necessary. Accounting and reporting for long-term investments is treated in Chapters 14 and 15.

When a temporary investment is sold, the difference between the sales proceeds and the cost is reported as a gain or loss on the sale.

Valuation of Marketable Securities

Three different methods for the valuation of marketable securities have been advanced: (1) cost, (2) cost or market, whichever is lower, and (3) market.

Cost. Valuation of marketable securities at cost refers to the original acquisition price of a marketable security including all related fees, unless there has been recognition previously of a permanent impairment of value and a new cost basis has been assigned to the marketable security. Cost is to be used unless circumstances require another method as is the case with marketable equity securities, to be explained later. The recognition of either gain or loss is deferred until the asset is sold, at which time investment cost is matched against investment proceeds. The cost basis is consistent with income tax procedures, recognizing neither gain nor loss until there is a sale or exchange.

Cost or Market, Whichever is Lower. When using the lower of cost or market method, if market is lower than cost, security values are written down to the lower value; if market is higher than cost, securities are maintained at cost, gains awaiting confirmation through sale.

Traditionally, the lower of cost or market method has been used only under special conditions when market was considered substantially lower than cost, and the decline was not considered temporary. Because of the difficulty in defining substantial and nontemporary declines, this method has not been widely used in practice.[1]

Significant fluctuations of the stock market in recent years have created many more situations where market values are lower than cost. After due consideration of the issues involved, the FASB, in December of 1975, issued Statement No. 12 concerning accounting for certain marketable securities. This statement requires that marketable equity securities (primarily common stocks) be carried at the lower of aggregate cost or market value.[2] Other marketable securities, such as bonds, still may be carried at cost unless there is a decline that is substantial in amount and is not due to temporary conditions.[3]

---

[1]In the AICPA trends and techniques survey, only 25 out of 291 companies reported marketable securities at the lower of cost or market. *Accounting Trends & Techniques* (30th ed.; New York: American Institute of Certified Public Accountants, 1976), p. 80.

[2]*Statement of Financial Accounting Standards No. 12*, "Accounting for Certain Marketable Securities" (Stamford, Conn.: Financial Accounting Standards Board, 1975), par. 8.

[3]While FASB Statement No. 12 deals only with marketable equity securities and does not require the lower of aggregate cost or market for other marketable securities, it seems logical to treat all short-term marketable securities similarly. In the illustrations and end-of-chapter material for this chapter, the lower of cost or market rule is used for all marketable securities, whether stocks or bonds.

The lower of cost or market method may be employed in two ways: (1) it may be applied to securities in the aggregate; or (2) it may be applied to individual items. To illustrate, assume marketable securities with cost and market values on December 31, 1977, as follows:

	Cost	Market	Lower of Cost or Market on Individual Basis
1,000 shares of Carter Co. common..........	$20,000	$16,000	$16,000
$25,000 Emerson Co. 7% bonds................	25,000	26,500	25,000
$10,000 Gardner Co. 8% bonds	10,000	7,500	7,500
	$55,000	$50,000	$48,500

The lower of cost or market value on an aggregate basis is $50,000; on an individual basis, $48,500.

In accounting for marketable equity securities, it should be noted that FASB Statement No. 12 requires the use of the aggregate method. An important factor in choosing the aggregate basis is that many companies consider their marketable securities portfolios as collective assets. Further, the Board felt that applying the lower of cost or market procedure on an individual security basis would be unduly conservative.

However, the FASB did recognize that many companies classify separately their current and noncurrent securities portfolios. Therefore, when a classified balance sheet is presented, the lower of aggregate cost or market is to be applied to the separate current and noncurrent portfolios. When an unclassified balance sheet is presented, the entire marketable equity securities portfolio is to be considered a noncurrent asset.

In adopting the lower of aggregate cost or market method for marketable equity securities, the FASB chose to recognize declines in the realizable value of marketable equity securities portfolios as a charge against the current period. The possibility of a future recovery in the market value was not considered sufficient reason to maintain the carrying value at cost.

Recognition of a decline in value on the books calls for a reduction of the asset and a debit to a loss account; however, the loss is not recognized for income tax purposes and the basis of the securities for measurement of gain or loss for final disposition continues to be cost. Cost can be preserved on the books by the use of a valuation account to reduce the securities to market. The following entry may be made to illustrate this procedure.

Unrealized Loss on Marketable Securities.....................................	5,000	
Allowance for Decline in Value of Marketable Securities..........		5,000

The balance sheet would show:

Marketable securities (at cost)	$55,000	
Less allowance for decline in value of marketable securities...	5,000	
Marketable securities (at market, December 31, 1977)		$50,000

This information could also be reported:

Marketable securities (reported at market; cost, $55,000)............................ $50,000

The $5,000 loss must be reported on the current income statement, probably as a charge related to financial management. If in the future, there is an increase in the market value of the equity securities portfolio, the write-down should be reversed to the extent that the resulting carrying value does not exceed original cost. The original write-down is to be viewed as a valuation allowance, representing an estimated decrease in the realizable value of the portfolio. Any subsequent market increase reduces or eliminates this valuation allowance.[1]

In subsequent years, the portfolio of temporary investments will change through purchases and sales of individual securities. Because cost remains the accepted basis for income tax purposes, it is preferable to record sales as though no valuation account existed; i.e., on a cost basis. At the end of the accounting period, an analysis can then be made of cost and aggregated market values for the securities held, and the allowance account adjusted to reflect the new difference between cost and market. If market exceeds cost at a subsequent valuation date, the allowance account would be eliminated, and the securities would be valued at cost, the lower of the two values. The offsetting revenue account for the adjustment is Unrealized Gain on Marketable Securities.

To illustrate accounting for subsequent years' transactions, assume in the preceding example that in 1978 the Carter Co. stock is sold for $17,000 and $25,000 of 7% U.S. Treasury bonds are purchased for $24,500. The following entries are made:

Cash..	17,000	
Loss on Sale of Marketable Securities	3,000	
Marketable Securities —— Carter Co. Common........................		20,000
Marketable Securities — 7% U.S. Treasury Bonds........................	24,500	
Cash		24,500

Assuming the market value of the remaining securities remains unchanged and the market value of the U.S. Treasury bonds remains at cost, the aggregate market value of the temporary investments is $58,500. When comparing the aggregate market value to the aggregate cost value of $59,500, the following adjusting entry would be made at the end of 1978:

Allowance for Decline in Value of Marketable Securities..............	4,000	
Unrealized Gain on Marketable Securities		4,000

This entry leaves the valuation account with a balance of $1,000 which, when subtracted from cost of $59,500, will report the marketable securities at their aggregate market value of $58,500.

---

[1] The reversal of a write-down is, therefore, considered a change in accounting estimate of an unrealized loss. (See FASB Statement No. 5, paragraph 2 and APB Opinion No. 20, paragraph 10.)

If the aggregate market value of the securities portfolio had fallen during 1978 to $53,000, the adjusting entry would be:

Unrealized Loss on Marketable Securities	1,500	
Allowance for Decline in Value of Marketable Securities		1,500

The entry increases the allowance account to $6,500 which, when subtracted from cost of $59,500, will report marketable securities at their aggregate market value of $53,000.

On the other hand, if the aggregate market value of the securities portfolio had risen to $60,000, the adjusting entry at year end would be:

Allowance for Decline in Value of Marketable Securities	5,000	
Unrealized Gain on Marketable Securities		5,000

This entry cancels the allowance account since the $59,500 original cost of securities is lower than their $60,000 aggregate market value.

Market. Market value refers to the current market price of the marketable security. Current market prices are recognized as affording an objective basis for the valuation of marketable securities. Securities on the balance sheet are reported at their current values whether higher or lower than cost. As with the lower of cost or market method, asset increases and decreases may be reported in a special valuation account.[1]

In applying market, it would be possible to recognize changes in security values by reporting the gain or the loss on the income statement. However, if it is felt that any increase in income, caused by market values in excess of cost, should await the sale of securities, a separate capital account, such as Unrealized Appreciation in Valuation of Marketable Securities, may be credited.

To illustrate the procedure that may be followed, assume at the end of 1977 securities costing $50,000 have quoted values of $60,000. The securities are sold in 1978 for $62,000. An unrealized gain is reported at the end of 1977. This is canceled when the securities are sold in 1978 and the effect of the sale is reported in the income statement. The entries are:

December 31, 1977

Marketable Securities — Increase to Current Market Value	10,000	
Unrealized Appreciation in Valuation of Marketable Securities		10,000

March 5, 1978

Cash	62,000	
Unrealized Appreciation in Valuation of Marketable Securities	10,000	
Marketable Securities (at cost)		50,000
Marketable Securities — Increase to Current Market Value		10,000
Gain on Sale of Marketable Securities		12,000

---

[1]The valuation account is normally considered the same as an offset account. In adjusting for market, the amount in the valuation account is often added to instead of subtracted from the asset account, making the valuation account an adjunct account, rather than an offset account in some instances.

In the previous illustration, instead of just recording the valuation change in the balance sheet, it is possible to reflect the change in the income statement by crediting Unrealized Gain on Marketable Securities instead of the unrealized appreciation account.

Although changes in market values must be disregarded for general income tax purposes, regulations do permit recognized dealers in securities to value periodic security inventories at cost; cost or market, whichever is lower; or market. The valuation procedure adopted must be applied consistently in successive tax reportings.

Evaluation of Methods

Valuation at cost finds support on the grounds that it is an extension of the cost principle; the asset is carried at cost until a sale or exchange provides an alternative asset and confirms a gain or loss. The cost method offers valuation on a consistent basis from period to period. It is the simplest method to apply and adheres to income tax requirements. However, certain objections to cost can be raised. The use of cost means investments may be carried at amounts differing from values objectively determinable at the balance sheet date, and the integrity of both balance sheet and income statement measurements can be challenged. The use of cost also means identical securities may be reported at different values because of purchases at different prices. A further objection is that management, in controlling the sale of securities, can determine the periods in which gains or losses are to be recognized even though these changes may have accrued over a number of periods.

The use of market value is advocated on the basis that there is evidence of the net realizable value of the marketable securities held at the balance sheet date and any changes from previous carrying values should be recognized as gains or losses in the current period. Assuming marketable securities are defined as having a readily available sales price or bid and ask price from one of the national securities exchanges or over-the-counter markets, this method is objective and relatively simple to apply. The major drawback of this method is that gains or losses may be recognized prior to realization, i.e., prior to the actual sale of the securities. In addition, market values fluctuate, often significantly, which would require continual changing of the carrying value of marketable securities on the balance sheet. Market is also challenged as a departure from the cost principle and as lacking in conservatism. Furthermore, market is not acceptable for general income tax purposes.

The lower of cost or market procedure provides for recognizing market declines and serves to prevent potential mistakes arising in analyzing statements when these declines are not reported. The lower of cost or market is supported as a conservative procedure. This approach may be challenged on the basis that it may be the most complicated method to apply, and it fails to provide consistency in valuation — cost at the end of one period may be replaced by a lower market at the end of the next. Furthermore, if applied to individual securities, the lower of cost or market procedure may be overly conservative, providing valuations less than the aggregate lower market. Also, the lower of cost or market does not conform with income tax requirements. Thus, timing differences in the recognition of losses on the books versus on the tax returns will create a need for interperiod tax adjustments.

CASH AND TEMPORARY INVESTMENTS ON THE BALANCE SHEET

For statement purposes, cash may be reported as a single item or it may be summarized under several descriptive headings, such as cash on hand, commercial deposits, and savings deposits. Since current assets are normally reported in the order of their liquidity, cash is listed first, followed by temporary investments, receivables, and inventories. When temporary investments are pledged for some particular purpose, the nature and the purpose of the pledge should be disclosed parenthetically or by note.

Cash and temporary investments may be reported on the balance sheet in the following manner:[1]

Current assets:			
Cash on hand and demand deposits in banks..			$ 46,000
Special cash deposits (to pay interest and dividends)			24,000
Temporary investments:			
Certificates of deposit		$100,000	
Marketable securities:			
U.S. Government obligations (reported at cost; market, $158,500; $50,000 in bonds has been pledged as security on short-term bank loan)...	$150,000		
Other stocks and bonds (reported at cost; market, $44,200)...	35,000	185,000	285,000

QUESTIONS

1. Why is cash on hand both necessary and yet potentially unproductive?

2. State how each of the following items should be reported on the balance sheet: (a) demand deposits with bank, (b) restricted cash deposits in foreign banks, (c) payroll fund to pay accrued salaries, (d) change funds on hand, (e) cash on deposit in escrow on purchase of property, (f) cash in a special cash account to be used currently for the construction of a new building.

3. The following items were included as Cash on the balance sheet for the Lawrence Co. How should each of the items have been reported?

(a) Customers' checks returned by the bank marked "Not Sufficient Funds."
(b) Customers' postdated checks.

(c) Cashier's note with no due date.
(d) Postage stamps received in the mail for merchandise.
(e) Postal money orders from customers awaiting deposit.
(f) Receipts for expense advances to buyers.
(g) Change funds.
(h) Notes receivable in the hands of the bank for collection.
(i) Special bank account in which sales tax collections are deposited.
(j) Customers' checks not yet deposited.

4. (a) Explain check kiting and lapping. (b) Mention at least six other practices resulting in misappropriations of cash in the absence of an adequate system of internal control. (c) What is the basic principle of cash control making fraudulent practices extremely difficult?

---

[1]FASB Statement No. 12 requires extensive disclosure of information with respect to marketable equity securities, including aggregate cost and market values, gross unrealized gains and losses, and the amount of net realized gain or loss included in net income. *Statement of Financial Accounting Standards No. 12, op. cit.*, par. 12.

5. As an auditor, what basic features would you hope to find in your client's system of cash control?

6. (a) What are the major advantages in using imprest petty cash funds? (b) What dangers must be guarded against when petty cash funds are used?

7. The Riverside Country Club maintained a $1,500 change fund. It was used to cash members' checks and to pay miscellaneous bills under $50. The fund was used by any of four persons in the office (including the book-keeper), depending upon which one was free when a need arose. At the close of each day, all cash collected from the cash registers in the club was merged with the fund and with collections on account received from members. All checks and sufficient cash to equal daily receipts were deposited, and the remainder was returned to the fund. (a) What system weaknesses do you observe? (b) How would you correct them?

8. How may the differences between depositor and bank balances be classified? Give an example of each type of difference.

9. (a) What two methods may be employed in reconciling the bank and the cash balances? (b) Which would you recommend? Why?

10. (a) What purposes are served by preparing a four-column reconciliation of receipts and disbursements? (b) Why would this form be used by auditors?

11. The Phelps Co. engaged in the following practices at the end of a fiscal year:

    (a) Sales on account from January 1–January 5 were predated as of the month of December.

    (b) Checks in payment of accounts were prepared on December 31 and were entered on the books, but they were placed in the safe awaiting instructions for mailing.

    (c) Customers' checks returned by the bank and marked "Not Sufficient Funds" were ignored for statement purposes.

    (d) Amounts owed company officers were paid off on December 31 and reborrowed on January 2.

Explain what is wrong with each of the practices mentioned and give the entries that are required to correct the accounts.

12. Define *temporary investments*. What criteria must be met for a security to be considered a temporary investment?

13. What two methods may be used to record the payment for accrued interest on bond investments? Which method is preferable?

14. (a) What positions are held with respect to the valuation of marketable securities? (b) What arguments can be advanced in support of each and which position do you feel has greatest merit?

15. The Canning Co. reports marketable securities on the balance sheet at the lower of cost or market. What adjustments are required on the books at the end of the year in each situation below:

    (a) Securities are purchased early in 1975 and at the end of 1975 their market value is more than cost.

    (b) At the end of 1976 the market value of the securities is less than cost.

    (c) At the end of 1977 the market value of the securities is greater than at the end of 1976 but is still less than cost.

    (d) At the end of 1978 the market value of the securities is more than the amount originally paid.

16. One of the arguments advanced for using market as the valuation procedure for temporary investments is that it assists in a "proper evaluation of managerial decisions and activities relative to purchases, sales, and holdings of marketable securities." Give an example supporting this statement.

17. On reconciling the cash account with the bank statement, it is found the general cash fund is overdrawn $436 but the bond redemption account has a balance of $5,400. The treasurer wishes to show cash as a current asset at $4,964. Discuss.

18. The Eazy Co. shows in its accounts a cash balance of $66,500 with Bank A, and an overdraft of $1,500 with Bank B on December 31. Bank B regards the overdraft as in effect a loan to the Eazy Co. and charges interest on the overdraft balance. How would you report the balances with Banks A and B? Would your answer be any different if the overdraft arose as a result of certain checks deposited and proved to be uncollectible and the overdraft was cleared promptly by the Eazy Co. at the beginning of January?

19. Under certain conditions it is proper to offset either assets against liabilities or liabilities against assets. Comment upon the following practices of the Weber Company.

    (a) An overdraft of $300 in the payroll fund kept with Farmers and Mechanics Bank is offset against a restricted savings account balance kept with the same bank.

    (b) A mortgage of $130,000 is offset against the buildings account of $180,000 to reflect a net equity in the buildings of $50,000.

    (c) Advances to employees of $500 are offset against Salaries Payable of $1,100.

EXERCISES

1. Mr. Richardson, proprietor of the Hillcrest Golf Course, would like to know how much cash may be reported on Hillcrest's balance sheet. Hillcrest has the following bank accounts and balances:

Overdrawn checking account	$(10)
United States savings bonds	200
Payroll account	50
Sales tax account	75

In addition to the bank accounts, Hillcrest has the following items in the office:

Postage stamps	$10
Employee's postdated check	15
IOU from Richardson's brother	50
A wristwatch (reported at market value; surrendered as security by a customer who forgot his wallet)	15
Credit memo from a vendor for a purchase return	32
Traveler's check	20
Insufficient funds check	9
Ten cases of empty soft drink bottles (returnable value)	12
Petty cash fund ($8 in currency and expense receipts for $42)	50
Money order	18

How much may be reported as cash on Hillcrest's balance sheet?

2. In auditing the books of Modiano, Inc., for 1977, you find a petty cash fund of $200 is maintained on the imprest basis, but the company has failed to replenish the fund on December 31. Replenishment was made and recorded on January 15, 1978, when a check for $185 was drawn to petty cash for expenses paid. Your analysis discloses $150 of petty cash was spent in 1977. What entry would be made in correcting the records, assuming the books for 1977 have been closed?

3. An examination on the morning of January 2 by the auditor for the Valley Hardware Company discloses the following items in the petty cash drawer:

Currency and coin		$ 35.22
IOU's from members of the office staff		45.00
An envelope containing collections for a football pool, with office staff names attached		15.00
Petty cash vouchers for:		
Typewriter repairs	$ 8.00	
Stamps	15.00	
Telegram charges	9.50	32.50
Employee's check postdated January 15		50.00
Employee's check marked "N.S.F."		70.00
Check drawn by Valley Hardware Company to Petty Cash		115.00
		$362.72

The ledger account discloses a $350 balance for Petty Cash. (a) What adjustments should be made on the auditor's working papers so petty cash may be correctly stated on the balance sheet? (b) What is the correct amount of petty cash for the balance sheet? (c) How could the practice of borrowing by employees from the fund be discouraged?

4. The following data are assembled in the course of reconciling the bank balance as of December 31, 1977, for Hinton Tool Co. What cash balance will be found on the company books, assuming no errors on the part of the bank and the depositor?

Balance per bank statement	$1,215.60
Checks outstanding	1,760.00
December 31 receipts recorded but not deposited	350.00
Bank charges for December not recognized on books	7.50
Draft collected by bank but not recognized on books	550.00

5. The Sterling Mining Co. receives its bank statement for the month ending June 30 on July 2. The bank statement indicates a balance of $230. The cash account as of the close of business on June 30 has a balance of $45. In reconciling the balances, the auditor discovers the information found below and at the top of the next page.

        (a) Receipts on June 30, $1,750, were not deposited until July 1.
        (b) Checks outstanding on June 30 were $2,215.

(c) The bank has charged the depositor for overdrafts, $10.

(d) A canceled check to H. M. Ship for $1,528 was entered in cash payments in error as $1,258.

Prepare a bank reconciliation statement. (Use the form reconciling bank and depositor figures to corrected cash balance.)

6. The following information was included in the bank reconciliation for Farr Corporation for June. What was the total of the outstanding checks at the beginning of June? Assume all other reconciling items are listed below:

Checks and charges returned by bank in June, including a June service charge of $15	$32,869
Service charge made by bank in May and recorded on books in June	10
Total of credits to Cash in all journals during June	38,583
Customer's N.S.F. check returned as a bank charge in June (no entry made on books)	200
Customer's N.S.F. check returned in May and redeposited in June (no entry made on books in either May or June)	500
Outstanding checks at June 30	16,119
Deposit in transit at June 30	1,200

7. Give the entries necessary to record these transactions of the Greely Corporation in 1977:

(a) Purchased $25,000 U.S. Treasury 8% bonds, paying 102½ plus accrued interest of $750. Broker's fees were $185. Greely Corporation uses the revenue approach to record accrued interest on purchased bonds.

(b) Purchased 1,000 shares of Fails Co. common stock at 64 plus brokerage fees of $300.

(c) Received semiannual interest on the U.S. Treasury bonds.

(d) Sold 300 shares of Fails Co. common at 65¼.

(e) Sold $15,000 of U.S. Treasury bonds at 103 plus accrued interest of $200.

(f) Purchased a $5,000, six-month certificate of deposit.

8. During 1977, the Monroe Company purchased the following marketable securities:

	Cost	Year-end Market
Arnold Co. common	$6,000	$7,000
Bench Co. 8% bonds	9,000	5,500

Marketable securities are to be reported on the balance sheet at the lower of aggregate cost or market. (a) What entry would be made at year-end assuming the above values? (b) What entry would be made during 1978 assuming one-half of the Arnold Co. common stock is sold for $3,500? (c) What entry would be made at the end of 1978 assuming: (1) the market value of remaining securities is $9,000? (2) The market value of remaining securities is $10,500? (3) The market value of remaining securities is $14,000?

9. Grotto Corp. acquires marketable securities in 1976 at a cost of $75,000. Market values of the securities at the end of each year are as follows: 1976, $70,000; 1977, $73,000; 1978, $80,000. Give the entries at the end of 1976, 1977, and 1978 indicating how the securities would be reported on the balance sheet at the end of each year under each of the following assumptions:

(a) Securities are reported at cost.

(b) Securities are reported at the lower of cost or market on an aggregate basis.

(c) Securities are reported at market.

10. At the end of 1977, The Turbo Company reports account balances relating to cash and temporary investments as follows:

Petty Cash	$ 300
Cash in City Bank — General	54,652
Cash in City Bank — Payroll	(2,300)
Cash in First Security Bank	25,362
Cash on Deposit with Union Utilities	300
Cash in Central Bank	(2,100)
Marketable Securities	135,600

Show the account balances as they would appear within the "Current assets" and "Current liabilities" sections of the balance sheet.

PROBLEMS

5-1. The balance of $49,000 in the cash account of the Hunter Company consists of these items:

Petty cash fund	$ 200
Receivable from an employee	100
Cash in bond sinking fund	4,500
Cash in a foreign bank unavailable for withdrawal	10,000
Cash in Central Bank	30,000
Currency on hand	4,200

The balance in the marketable securities account consists of:

U.S. Treasury bonds	$ 10,420
Voting stock of a subsidiary company (70% interest)	122,000
Advances to a subsidiary company (no maturity date specified)	30,000
A note receivable from a customer	10,000
The company's own shares held as treasury stock	5,000
Stock of Western Telephone Co.	14,000

Instructions: Calculate the correct Cash and Marketable Securities balances and state in what accounts and in what sections of the balance sheet the other items would be properly reported.

5-2. The cash account of Lathrop Co. disclosed a balance of $6,595.73 on October 31, 1977. The bank statement as of October 31 showed a balance of $8,483.78. Upon comparing the statement with the cash records, the following facts were developed:

(a) The Lathrop Co.'s account had been charged for a customer's uncollectible check amounting to $457.20 on October 26.
(b) A two-month, 9%, $1,200 customer's note dated August 25, discounted on October 12, had been protested October 26, and the bank had charged the Lathrop Co. for $1,220.33, which included a protest fee of $2.33.
(c) A customer's check for $290 had been entered as $190 both by the depositor and the bank but was later corrected by the bank.
(d) Check No. 661 for $497 had been entered in the cashbook as $479, and check No. 652 for $32.90 had been entered as $329. The company uses the voucher system.
(e) There were bank service charges for September of $15.77.
(f) A bank memo stated that M. Stum's note for $1,000 and interest of $25 had been collected on October 29, and the bank had made a charge of $5 on the collection. (No entry had been made on the books when the note was sent to the bank for collection.)
(g) Receipts of October 29 for $2,740 were deposited November 1.

The following checks were outstanding on October 31:

No. 620	$ 500.00		No. 671	$293.00
621	1,379.29		673	75.16
632	962.10		675	110.29
670	710.15		676	893.26

Instructions:
(1) Construct a bank reconciliation statement, using the form where both bank and book balances are brought to a corrected cash balance.
(2) Give the journal entries required as a result of the information given above. (Assume the company makes use of the voucher system.)

5-3. Analysis of the December bank statement for Trost Tractors, Inc., discloses the following information:

(a) Statement balance at December 31, 1977, was $16,675.
(b) Check issued by Transpo-Matic, Inc., for $315 was charged to Trost Tractors, Inc., in error.
(c) December bank charges were $30.
(d) Deposit of $700 was erroneously credited to Trost Tractors, Inc., account by the bank.
(e) Outstanding checks at December 31, 1977, were $5,280. They included a $300 check outstanding for 8 months to Amco Products which was canceled in December and a new check issued. No entry was made for the cancellation.

(f) Receipts on December 31 were $4,500. Receipts were deposited on January 2.

(g) An error in addition was made on the December 23 deposit slip. This slip showed a total of $2,120. The correct balance as credited to the account by the bank was $2,020. A count of cash on hand showed an overage of $100 as of December 31.

(h) The Cash in Bank balance in the general ledger as of December 31, 1977, was $15,640.

Instructions:

(1) Prepare a bank reconciliation statement which reconciles the bank balance with the balance per books.

(2) Give all entries required on the books at December 31, 1977.

5-4. The following data are applicable to the RTB Corporation:

(a) The July 31 bank statement balance of $14,975 included a bank service charge of $47 not previously reported to the company but recorded on the company's books in August.

(b) The cash account balance in the general ledger on July 31 was $13,343.

(c) Outstanding checks at July 31 were $2,695. Undeposited receipts on July 31 were $1,016.

(d) The bank statement on August 31 had a balance of $15,653, recognizing receipts of $21,072, and disbursements of $20,394. The disbursements included a service charge for August of $54 not yet reported to RTB Corporation.

(e) The cash account balance in the general ledger on August 31 was $16,087, recognizing receipts of $20,881 for August and checks written during August of $18,090. Receipts of $825 are in transit to the bank, and checks of $445 have not yet cleared the bank.

Instructions:

(1) Prepare a four-column bank reconciliation as of August 31. Use the form that reconciles the bank statement balance with the unadjusted balance per books.

(2) Give any entries at August 31 that may be required on the company's books.

5-5. The following information is related to Dolan, Inc.:

	1977	
	August	September
Bank statement balance — at month end	$ 4,830	$ 5,570
Cash account balance — at month end	3,910	4,549
Bank charges for N.S.F. check returned (normally written off in month following return)...	75	160
Outstanding checks — at month end..	1,200	1,930
Deposits in transit — at month end	600	940
Bank service charges (normally recorded in month following bank charge)...	5	9
Drafts collected by bank (not recorded by company until month following collection)..	400	300
Total credits to cash account...	29,705	35,961
Total deposits on bank statement..		36,160
Check #411 was erroneously recorded in the company checkbook and journal as $286; the correct amount is $186. (This check was not outstanding on September 30.)		

The outstanding checks on September 30 include a company check for $200 certified by the bank on September 18.

All disbursements were made by check.

> ***Instructions:*** Prepare a four-column bank reconciliation for the month of September, 1977. Use the form where both bank and book balances are brought to a corrected cash balance.

5-6. The following information concerning the cash accounts of Penetration Company is available:

(a) Balance per bank:

November 30, 1977..	$18,570
December 31, 1977...	19,362

(b) Balance per books:

November 30, 1977	$12,368
December 31, 1977	18,808

(c) Outstanding checks:

November 30, 1977	$6,352
December 31, 1977	7,504

(d) December deposits, per bank statement, $135,040.

(e) December cash receipts, per cash receipts journal, $170,510.

(f) N.S.F. checks returned by the bank are recorded as a reduction in the cash receipts journal. Those redeposited are recorded as regular cash receipts. Data regarding N.S.F. checks are as follows:

   (1) Returned by bank in November and recorded by company as a reduction in cash receipts in December, $150.

   (2) Returned by bank in December and recorded by company as a reduction in cash receipts in December, $1,350.

   (3) Returned by the bank in December and recorded by company as a reduction in cash receipts in January, $230.

   (4) Redeposited by company during December, $800.

(g) According to the repayment terms of a large loan with the bank, the bank credits the company's checking account with 80% of the amount presented for deposit. The remaining 20% is applied to reduce the unpaid balance of the loan. The following summary entries, recorded in the cash receipts and cash disbursements journals, for December indicate the company's treatment of the deposits and resulting loan reductions:

Cash in Bank	172,010	
Cash on Hand		172,010

Bank Loan	34,402	
Cash in Bank		34,402

(h) The above summary entries include one deposit in transit on December 31, in the amount of $3,210. There were no deposits in transit on November 30, 1977. There was no undeposited cash on hand on December 31, 1977.

(i) Interest on the bank loan for the month of December was charged by the bank against the checking account, $1,829.

(j) On December 31, 1977, a $2,323 check of Precision Company was charged to the company's account in error.

Instructions:

   (1) Prepare a four-column reconciliation of receipts, disbursements, and bank balance for December 31, 1977. Use the form where both bank and book balances are brought to a corrected cash balance.

   (2) Give the December 31, 1977 adjusting entries relating to the cash accounts of Penetration Company.

5-7. A bank statement for Elner, Inc., shows a balance as of December 31, 1977, of $2,943.14. The cash account for the company as of this date shows an overdraft of $135.56. In reconciling the statement with the books, the following items are discovered:

   (a) The cash balance includes $150 representing change cash on hand. When the cash on hand is counted, only $129.25 is found.

   (b) The cash balance includes $200 representing a petty cash fund. Inspection of the petty cash fund reveals cash of $160 on hand and a replenishing check drawn on December 31 for $40.

   (c) Proceeds from cash sales of $295 for December 27 were stolen. The company expects to recover this amount from the insurance company and has made no entry for the loss.

   (d) The bank statement shows the depositor charged with a customer's N.S.F. check for $23.50, bank service charges of $7.80, and a check for $65 drawn by Elmer, Inc., and incorrectly cleared through this account.

   (e) The bank statement does not show receipts of December 31 of $832.50, which were deposited on January 3.

(f) Checks outstanding were found to be $4,652.50. This includes the check transferred to the petty cash fund and also two checks for $57 each payable to J. Miner. Miner had notified the company she had lost the original check and had been sent a second one, the company stopping payment on the first check.

Instructions:
(1) Prepare a bank reconciliation statement, using the form in which both bank and book balances are brought to a corrected cash balance.
(2) Give the correcting entries for Elner, Inc. required by the foregoing.
(3) List the cash items as they should appear on the balance sheet on December 31.

5-8. Lexicon Corporation reports the following on their December 31, 1976, balance sheet:

Marketable securities (at cost).. $225,850
Less allowance for decline in value of marketable securities........   2,260 $223,590

Supporting records of Lexicon's temporary holdings show marketable securities as follows:

	Cost	Market
200 shares of Lampex Co. common..............	$ 25,450	$ 24,300
$80,000 U.S. Treasury 7% bonds...............	79,650	77,400
$120,000 U.S. Treasury 7½% bonds.............	120,750	121,890
	$225,850	$223,590

Interest dates on the treasury bonds are January 1 and July 1. Lexicon Corporation makes reversing entries and uses the revenue approach to recording the purchase of bonds with accrued interest.

During 1977 and 1978, Lexicon Corporation completed the following transactions related to their temporary investments:

1977

Jan. 1 Received semiannual interest on U.S. Treasury bonds. (The entry to reverse the interest accrual at the end of the last year has already been made.)

Apr. 1 Sold $60,000 of the 7½% U.S. Treasury bonds at 102 plus accrued interest. Brokerage fees were $200.

May 21 Received dividends of 25 cents per share on the Lampex Co. common stock. The dividend had not been recorded on the declaration date.

July 1 Received semiannual interest on U.S. Treasury bonds, then sold the 7% treasury bonds at 97½. Brokerage fees were $250.

Aug. 15 Purchased 100 shares of Norris Nets, Inc., common stock at 116 plus brokerage fees of $50.

Nov. 1 Purchased $50,000 of 8% U.S. Treasury bonds at 101 plus accrued interest. Brokerage fees were $125. Interest dates are January 1 and July 1.

Dec. 31 Market prices of securities were: Lampex Co. common, 110; 7½% U.S. Treasury bonds, 101¾; 8% U.S. Treasury bonds, 101; Norris Nets, Inc., common, 116¾. Lexicon Corporation reports all marketable securities at the lower of aggregate cost or market.

1978

Jan. 2 Recorded the receipt of semiannual interest on the U.S. Treasury bonds.

Feb. 1 Sold the 7½% U.S. Treasury bonds at 101 plus accrued interest. Brokerage fees were $300.

Instructions:
(1) Prepare journal entries for the foregoing transactions and accrue required interest on December 31. Give computations in support of your entries.
(2) Show how marketable securities would be presented on the December 31, 1977, balance sheet.

5-9. Jordan, Inc., purchased marketable securities during 1977 with the following costs and year-end market values:

	Cost	Market
600 shares of Briner Co. common..............	$22,400	$26,250
200 shares of Bilbo Bearings common..........	34,640	31,180
$20,000 Morepark Municipal 7% bonds..........	18,360	13,420
	$75,400	$70,850

Jordan, Inc., values marketable securities at the lower of cost or market on an aggregate basis. On August 10, 1978, Jordan, Inc., sold 150 shares of Bilbo Bearings common for $23,550. Market prices of the remaining securities on December 31, 1978, were: Briner Co. common, 42; Bilbo Bearings common, 157; and Morepark Municipal 7% bonds, 71¼.

> **Instructions:** Give all required entries for the valuation and sale of securities in 1977 and 1978. Ignore entries for interest revenue on the bonds.

5-10. Instex Sales Co. made the following investments in marketable securities in 1976:

Shield Hardware	400 shares @ 45¾	$18,300
Collins Instruments	500 shares @ 22⅝	11,312
Rider first-mortgage 8% bonds	30 $1,000 bonds at par	30,000
		$59,612

Collins Instruments were sold at the end of 1978 for $8,500. The market values of the securities at the end of 1976, 1977, and 1978 were as follows:

	1976	1977	1978
Shield Hardware	$19,500	$15,900	$17,250
Collins Instruments	10,200	8,600	
Rider first-mortgage 8% bonds	31,000	31,500	30,100

> **Instructions:** Give whatever entries are required in 1976, 1977, and 1978 for the valuation and for the sale of securities, and show how the securities would be reported on the balance sheet prepared at the end of 1976, 1977, and 1978 under each of the following assumptions:
> (1) Securities are valued at cost.
> (2) Securities are valued at the lower of cost or market (aggregate basis).
> (3) Securities are valued at market.

5-11. The balance sheet of Rector and Towle, Inc., shows the following balances for cash and temporary investments within its "Current assets" section as of December 31, 1977:

Current assets:		
Cash	$ 76,429	
Temporary investments	173,291	$249,720

In examining the books, the following information is revealed with respect to the current assets:

> Cash consists of: a demand deposit of $16,337 at the First Security Bank; a time deposit of $5,500 that cannot be withdrawn until after April 1, 1979; customers' checks not yet deposited, $500, and customers' returned N.S.F. checks, $200; a demand deposit of $9,184, which is unavailable, being in a bank in a foreign country at war; an overdraft of $192 in the Merchants Bank; a time deposit of $4,500 in a closed building and loan savings association; advances of $1,675 to officers; sinking fund cash of $16,525; a pension fund of $22,000 for employees; and a petty cash fund of $200, of which $65 is cash, $45 is in the form of employees' IOU's, and $90 is supported by the receipts for expenses paid out of the fund.

The following securities are included under the temporary investments heading:

	Cost	Market Value (Including Accrued Interest)
Rector and Towle, Inc., treasury stock	$ 6,920	$ 7,358
Eastern Corporation common stock (temporary holding)	3,490	3,250
Prairie Company, 8% bonds (interest payable March 1 and Sept. 1). Face value, $9,000. Acquired on Sept. 1, 1977 (temporary holding)	9,190	9,140
7% United States Treasury bonds (interest payable March 1 and September 1). Face value, $30,000. Purchased with pension sinking fund cash. Acquired Sept. 1, 1977	30,600	30,750
Goins Co. common stock (temporary holding)	7,235	5,500
Tonka Co. common stock (stock of subsidiary company)	112,000	106,300
ACC Corp. preferred stock (temporary holding)	4,900	6,300

Instructions: Show cash and temporary investments as these items should properly appear in the "Current assets" section of the balance sheet. Provide schedules to indicate how foregoing balances are determined and what disposition is to be made of items not appropriately shown under the cash and temporary investment headings. Assume that marketable securities are reported at cost or aggregate market, whichever is lower, by means of a valuation account.

5-12. You have completed your examination of the cash on hand and in banks in your audit of the Hoosier Company's financial statements for the year ended December 31, 1977, and note the following:

(a) The company maintains a general bank account at The National Bank and an imprest payroll bank account at The City Bank. All checks are signed by the company president, Carolyn Hoosier.

(b) Data and reconciliations prepared by Donald Hume, the company bookkeeper, at November 30, 1977, indicated that the payroll account had a $1,000 general ledger and bank balance with no in-transit or outstanding items, and the general bank account had a $12,405 general ledger balance with checks outstanding aggregating $918 (#1202 for $575 and #1205 for $343) and one deposit of $492 in transit.

(c) Your surprise cash count on Tuesday, January 2, 1978, revealed customers' checks totaling $540 and a National Bank deposit slip for that amount dated December 30, 1977, were in the company safe and that no cash was in transit to the bank at that time. Your examination of the general account check book had revealed check #1219 to be the first unused check.

(d) Company general ledger accounts are prepared on a posting machine and all transactions are posted in chronological sequence. The ledger card for the general bank account is reproduced below.

LEDGER

General Bank Account

The National Bank

DATE	FOLIO	DEBITS	CREDITS	BALANCE
11/30/77			BALANCE FORWARD →	12,405
12/01/77		496		12,901
12/05/77	1206		1,675	11,226
12/06/77	1207		645	10,581
12/06/77		832		11,413
12/08/77	1208		1,706	9,707
12/08/77		975		10,682
12/08/77	1209		2,062	8,620
12/08/77	1210		3,945	4,675
12/11/77	1211		6,237	(1,562)
12/12/77		8,045		6,483
12/15/77		9,549		16,032
12/15/77	1212		1,845	14,187
12/21/77	RT		241	13,946
12/21/77	1213		350	13,596
12/21/77	1214		2,072	11,524
12/22/77		1,513		13,037
12/23/77	1215		2,597	10,440
12/27/77	1216		1,739	8,701
12/29/77		540		9,241
12/29/77		942		10,183
12/29/77	1217		1,987	8,196
01/03/78	1218		1,120	7,076
		22,892	28,221	

(e) The December statements from both banks were delivered unopened to you. The City Bank statement contained deposits for $1,675; $1,706; $1,845; and $2,597; and 72 paid checks totaling $7,823. The National Bank statement is reproduced below.

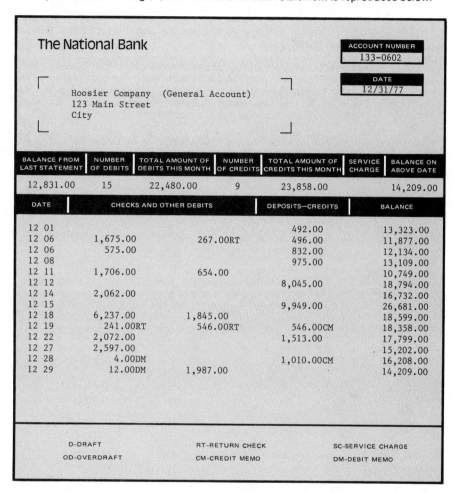

The National Bank

ACCOUNT NUMBER
133-0602

DATE
12/31/77

Hoosier Company (General Account)
123 Main Street
City

BALANCE FROM LAST STATEMENT	NUMBER OF DEBITS	TOTAL AMOUNT OF DEBITS THIS MONTH	NUMBER OF CREDITS	TOTAL AMOUNT OF CREDITS THIS MONTH	SERVICE CHARGE	BALANCE ON ABOVE DATE
12,831.00	15	22,480.00	9	23,858.00		14,209.00

DATE	CHECKS AND OTHER DEBITS		DEPOSITS—CREDITS	BALANCE
12 01			492.00	13,323.00
12 06	1,675.00	267.00RT	496.00	11,877.00
12 06	575.00		832.00	12,134.00
12 08			975.00	13,109.00
12 11	1,706.00	654.00		10,749.00
12 12			8,045.00	18,794.00
12 14	2,062.00			16,732.00
12 15			9,949.00	26,681.00
12 18	6,237.00	1,845.00		18,599.00
12 19	241.00RT	546.00RT	546.00CM	18,358.00
12 22	2,072.00		1,513.00	17,799.00
12 27	2,597.00			15,202.00
12 28	4.00DM		1,010.00CM	16,208.00
12 29	12.00DM	1,987.00		14,209.00

D-DRAFT	RT-RETURN CHECK	SC-SERVICE CHARGE
OD-OVERDRAFT	CM-CREDIT MEMO	DM-DEBIT MEMO

(f) A special bank statement was secured by you personally from both banks on January 8, 1978, and The National Bank statement is reproduced below.

BALANCE FROM LAST STATEMENT	NUMBER OF DEBITS	TOTAL AMOUNT OF DEBITS THIS MONTH	NUMBER OF CREDITS	TOTAL AMOUNT OF CREDITS THIS MONTH	SERVICE CHARGE	BALANCE ON ABOVE DATE
14,209.00	3	6,034.00	2	1,482.00		9,657.00

DATE	CHECKS AND OTHER DEBITS		DEPOSITS—CREDITS	BALANCE
1 03	1,739.00	3,945.00	540.00	9,065.00
1 05	350.00		942.00	9,657.00

(g) You determine the bank statements are correct except that The National Bank incorrectly charged a returned check on December 19 but credited the account the same day.

(h) On December 28 a 60-day, 10%, $1,000 note was collected by The National Bank for Hoosier for a $4 collection fee.

(i) The $12 debit memo from The National Bank was a charge for printed checks.

(j) Check #1213 was issued to replace check #1205 when the latter was reported not received by a vendor. Because of the delay in paying this account, Hoosier Company was no longer entitled to the 2% cash discount it had taken in preparing the original check.

Instructions: Prepare a proof of cash for December for Hoosier's general bank account in The National Bank. Your proof of cash should show the computation of the adjusted balances for both the bank statement and the general ledger account of The National Bank for cash in bank November 30, December receipts, December disbursements, and cash in bank December 31. The following column headings are recommended:

Description	Beginning Reconciliation November 30	December Receipts	December Disbursements	Ending Reconciliation December 31

(AICPA adapted)

6

Receivables

In its broadest sense, the term *receivables* is applicable to all claims against others, whether these are claims for money, for goods, or for services. For accounting purposes, however, the term is employed in a narrower sense to designate claims expected to be settled by the receipt of money.

Usually, the chief source of receivables is found in the normal activities of the operating cycle of a business. Business today is largely based on credit. Goods and services are sold on account; the collection of the accounts following some time after the sales. In the meantime, the seller has claims against the buyers. Other receivables arise as a result of such diverse activities as advances made by a company, the sale of properties and equipment items, and the sale of capital stock.

COMPOSITION OF RECEIVABLES

Receivables are composed of two classes: (1) those supported by formal promises to pay in the form of notes, referred to as *notes receivable*, and (2) those not so supported, referred to as *accounts receivable*. Accounts receivable may be divided into groupings as follows: (a) receivables from customers; (b) receivables from others; and (c) accrued receivables. Receivables are established in the accounts only when supportable claims exist and it can be assumed the claims will be realized.

Notes Receivable

A note is an unconditional written promise by one party to another to pay a certain sum of money at a specified time. The note may be negotiable or nonnegotiable. It is negotiable, i.e., legally transferable by endorsement and delivery, only if it provides for payment to the order of the second party or bearer. Such notes are commonly accepted by commercial banks for discount; hence, they are considered more liquid than are other classes of receivables.

The term *notes* is used to include not only promissory notes but also time drafts and trade acceptances. If time drafts and trade acceptances are material in amount, they may be summarized separately.

The notes receivable designation for reporting purposes should be limited to negotiable short-term instruments acquired from trade debtors and not yet due. When a written instrument fails to meet these requirements, it should be reported separately under an appropriately descriptive title. For example, notes arising from loans to customers, officers, employees, and affiliated companies should be reported separately.

Accounts Receivable

As previously indicated, accounts receivable broadly include all receivables other than those supported by some form of commercial paper. Although it would be appropriate to refer to open accounts with customers arising from the sale of goods and services as Trade Debtors or Trade Receivables to distinguish these from other receivables, it has become established practice to use the designation Accounts Receivable to represent these claims. Accounts receivable for reporting purposes should be limited to trade accounts expected to be converted into cash in the regular course of business. The account balances, for example, should not include receivables arising from charges for containers[1] if such charges will be canceled when containers are returned.

A receivable arising from the sale of goods is generally recognized when the title to goods passes to the buyer. Because the point at which title passes may vary with the terms of the sale, it is general practice to recognize the receivable when goods are shipped to the customer. Receivables should not be recognized for goods shipped on approval where the shipper retains title to the goods until there is a formal acceptance, or for goods shipped on consignment where the shipper retains title to the goods until they are sold by the consignee.

Receivables for services to customers are properly recognized when the services are performed. When work under a contract has not been completed at the end of the period, the amount due as of the balance sheet date will have to be calculated. Receivables should be recognized for the portion of work completed under construction contracts and for reimbursable costs and accrued fees on cost-plus-fixed-fee contracts.

Ordinarily, detailed records of customer transactions and customers' balances are carried in subsidiary records. Entries to subsidiary records may be made from original business documents evidencing the transactions. With machine methods, subsidiary records are frequently maintained simultaneously with the preparation of invoices and remittance records.

Nontrade receivables should be summarized in appropriately titled accounts and reported separately. The following are examples of the receivables that should be carried separately: claims arising from the sale of securities or property other than goods or services; advances to stockholders, directors, officers, employees, and affiliated companies; deposits with creditors, utilities, and other agencies; purchase prepayments; de-

---

[1]The use of the term *containers* refers to bottles, cartons, or other packaging devices for which a deposit is normally collected at the time of sale and then is refunded when the containers are returned.

posits to guarantee contract performance or expense payment; claims for losses or damages; claims for rebates and tax refunds; subscriptions for capital stock; and dividends receivable.

Certain revenues for services or goods accrue with the passage of time and are most conveniently recognized when collections are made. At the end of the period, it is necessary to calculate the amounts accrued since the last collections and to establish appropriate accrued receivables. Accrued interest is recognized on assets, such as bank deposits, notes, bonds, and annuities. Rentals may accrue on real estate holdings. Royalties and patent fees may accrue on certain rights and properties. For some business units, accrued receivables may be small in total; for others, they may involve large amounts.

It was indicated in an earlier chapter that the "Current assets" classification as broadly conceived comprehends all receivables identified with the normal operating cycle. Installment and other deferred collection contracts are current regardless of their terms. But receivables arising outside of the inventory-to-cash cycle qualify as current only if they are expected to be collected within one year. For classification purposes, each nontrade item requires separate analysis to determine whether it is reasonable to assume it will be collected within one year. Noncurrent receivables are reported under the "Long-term investments" or "Other long-term assets" caption, whichever may be considered appropriate.

Amounts due from officers, directors, and major stockholders arising out of sales and subject to the usual credit terms are normally considered current; however, when claims have arisen from transactions other than sales and current recovery is not assured, such items are properly classified as noncurrent. Sales to affiliated companies give rise to current claims, but advances are generally regarded as long-term in nature. Deposits on materials and merchandise ordered will soon represent inventories and are reported as current, but deposits on utility contracts are reported as long-term. Deposits for machinery and equipment ordered are noncurrent in view of the ultimate application of the deposit. Claims from the sale of assets other than merchandise and calling for periodic collections over a period exceeding one year require special analysis to determine the portion of the claim to be reported as current and the portion to be reported as noncurrent.

Subscriptions to capital stock are current only if they are currently collectible; when current collection is not probable or when payments may be deferred indefinitely, such balances are reported as noncurrent assets or in some instances more appropriately as subtractions from capital balances so that no more than the amount actually paid in by stockholders and subscribers is reported as paid-in capital.

When income tax refund claims or other claims have been granted and collection is expected within one year, they qualify for current presentation. When claims are still being processed and recovery is assured although the period required for such processing is uncertain, they are shown under a noncurrent heading. Certain claims may be in dispute.

When a claim does not involve a material amount and there is little likelihood of recovery, no reference needs to be made to it on the balance sheet. On the other hand, if a material amount is involved and there is prospect of a favorable settlement, the claim is properly viewed as a contingent receivable and should be disclosed by a special note or by an appropriate comment under a separate contingent asset heading as was discussed in Chapter 3.

Creditor and customer accounts with contra balances require special attention. These balances are found by an analysis of subsidiary ledger detail. For example, assume the accounts payable control account reports a balance of $10,000. Inspection of subsidiary account detail reveals accounts with credit balances of $10,500 and accounts with debit balances of $500. The nature of the debit balances should be investigated. If the debit balances have arisen as a result of overpayments or returns and allowances after payment, they are reportable as current assets in view of the claims they represent for cash or merchandise from vendors. Such balances are properly reported under a title, such as Creditors' Accounts with Debit Balances or Sundry Claims. If debit balances represent advance payments on the purchase of raw materials or merchandise, these too are current assets reportable under some descriptive title, such as Advances on Purchase Contracts. In either case, Accounts Payable is reported at $10,500. Although both an asset and a liability are reported, no adjustment to the control account or the subsidiary ledger detail is required. Debit balances in the subsidiary ledger are carried forward and are ultimately canceled by purchases or cash settlement.

Customer ledger detail needs similar analysis. Customers' accounts with credit balances may result from overpayments, from customer returns after full payment, or from advance payments by customers. Such credits should be recognized as current liabilities, and accounts receivable should be reported at the sum of the debit balances in the subsidiary ledger.

When contra balances in customer and creditor accounts are not material in amount, they are frequently disregarded and only the net receivable or payable balance is reported on the balance sheet.

VALUATION OF RECEIVABLES

Theoretically, receivables arising from the sale of property, goods, or services should be reported at their net realizable or cash value. This would suggest that receivables should be reduced by any interest implicit in their face amount, unearned finance or interest charges reported in their face amounts, and uncollectible items anticipated in the course of their collection.

Reporting Receivables at Present Values

When a sale is made at an amount that is collectible at some future date, the amount collectible may be regarded as consisting of both a sales price and a charge for interest for the period of the payment deferral. In the absence of an established exchange or sales price, the *present value* of the receivable should be determined by reducing the face amount of the receivable by an interest rate regarded as appropriate under the circumstances for the period that payment is deferred. The interest rate approximated for this period is generally referred to as the *imputed rate*; the process of arriving at the present value of the sum is generally referred to as *discounting* the sum. The difference between the face value of the receivable and its present value is recognized as a discount.[1] This discount is amortized as a credit to Interest Revenue over the life of the receivable; in preparing a balance sheet, any unamortized discount is reported as a direct subtraction from the face amount of the receivable.

To illustrate, assume on January 1, 1977, Alpha Corporation sells used equipment with a book value of $600 receiving a note for $1,000 due in two years with no stated interest. If the equipment had an established sales price, the difference between the sales price and the face amount of the notes would be considered the charge for interest to be recognized over the two years. However, in this case, the value of the equipment is unknown but the interest rate for this type of note is estimated to be 10%. The following entry is made to record the sale:

Notes Receivable	1,000.00	
Equipment		600.00
Gain on Sale of Equipment		226.40
Discount on Notes Receivable		173.60

Computation:

Discount on notes receivable:
$1,000 note discounted for two years at 10% ($1,000 × .8264 = $826.40); $1,000.00 − $826.40 = $173.60[2]

The amount of the discount amortized every year is found by applying the imputed interest rate to the net balance of the note, the face value less unamortized discount. Amortization for the two years is as shown in the schedule below:

Year	(1) Face Amount of Note	(2) Unamortized Discount	(3) Net Amount (1) − (2)	(4) Discount Amortization 10% × (3)
1	$1,000	$173.60	$826.40	$ 82.64
2	1,000	90.96	909.04	90.96*
				$173.60

*The 6¢ discrepancy is due to rounding.

The entry for the first year's amortization would be:

Discount on Notes Receivable	82.64	
Interest Revenue		82.64

---

[1] An interest rate provided by terms of the receivable that is higher or lower than a rate regarded as appropriate under the circumstances would call for similar analysis and the recognition of a premium or discount on the receivable.

[2] The present value of $1 due in two years at an interest rate of 10% is $0.8264. This is found in Table II of Appendix A on page 838.

Although the proper valuation of receivables calls for the procedure just described, exceptions to this procedure may be appropriate in special instances because of certain special limitations or practical considerations. The Accounting Principles Board in Opinion No. 21 provided guidelines for the recognition of interest on receivables and payables and the accounting subsequently to be employed. However, the Board indicated that this process is not to be regarded as applicable under all circumstances. Among the exceptions are the following:

> . . . receivables and payables arising from transactions with customers or suppliers in the normal course of business which are due in customary trade terms not exceeding approximately one year.[1]

Accordingly, short-term notes and accounts receivable arising from trade sales may be properly recorded at the amounts collectible in the customary sales terms.

Unearned Finance Charges Included in Receivables

In many instances, the amounts charged to customers on sales contracts include finance, interest, and other charges. These charges are actually earned with the passage of time and should be recognized as unearned at the time of the sale. The Accounting Principles Board in Opinion No. 6 makes the following observation:

> Unearned discounts (other than cash or quantity discounts and the like), finance charges and interest included in the face amount of receivables should be shown as a deduction from the related receivables.[2]

The entry at the time of sale should establish the unearned customer charges, and periodic adjustments should then be made to recognize the amounts earned. To illustrate, assume that installment sales contracts of $27,600 for a year include finance charges of 2% a month, or approximately $3,277. Payments are to be made in 12 equal monthly installments. Installment sales would be reported as follows:

Installment Accounts Receivable	27,600	
Sales		24,323
Unearned Customer Finance Charges		3,277
To record installment sales.		

Computation:
$PV_n = R(PVAF_{\overline{n}|i})$
$PV_n = (\$27,600 \div 12) (PVAF_{\overline{12}|2\%})$; $PV_n = \$2,300 (10.5753) = \$24,323$.
See Appendix A, Table IV on page 840.

As collections are made on installment accounts, the finance charges on the net receivable balance would be recognized as earned. Assuming the monthly finance charge of 2%, the entry for the first month is shown at the top of the next page.

---

[1]*Opinions of the Accounting Principles Board, No. 21*, "Interest on Receivables and Payables" (New York: American Institute of Certified Public Accountants, 1972), par. 3(a). It may be noted that the primary objective of the Opinion was not to suggest new principles but simply to clarify and refine the manner of applying existing principles.

[2]*Opinions of the Accounting Principles Board, No. 6*, "Status of Accounting Research Bulletins" (New York: American Institute of Certified Public Accountants, 1965), par. 14.

Cash..	2,300.00	
Unearned Customer Finance Charges	486.46	
Installment Accounts Receivable..		2,300.00
Revenue from Customer Finance Charges		486.46

Computation:

Finance charge:
2% × $24,323 ($27,600 − $3,277) = $486.46

In preparing a balance sheet, any unearned balance would be reported as a deduction from the related receivable account. The revenue from customer finance charges will be included in "Other operating revenues" in the income statement.

Estimated Uncollectible Accounts

Almost invariably some of the receivables arising from sales will prove uncollectible. Uncollectible amounts will have to be anticipated if the charge for them is to be related to the period of the sale and receivables are to be stated at their estimated realizable amounts.

The amount of receivables estimated uncollectible is recorded by a debit to expense and a credit to an allowance account. The terminology for these account titles has changed somewhat over time. The term Allowance for Doubtful Accounts has largely replaced the earlier term of Reserve for Bad Debts following the recommendation of the AICPA terminology bulletin regarding restrictive use of the term "reserve." Other possible secondary terms besides Doubtful Accounts which may be used are Losses, Uncollectible Accounts, or Bad Debts. The expense terminology usually is consistent with the secondary term, and thus becomes Doubtful Accounts Expense, Uncollectible Accounts Expense, or Bad Debts Expense. The charge for doubtful accounts may be reported as a deduction from sales on the theory that it is net sales — sales after uncollectibles — that must cover current charges and yield a profit. Instead of being treated as a contra-sales balance, however, the bad debts item is usually regarded as emerging from a failure of management, and, hence, is reported as a selling, general and administrative, or financial charge, depending upon the division held responsible for approving sales on account. The allowance account is then reported as a subtraction from accounts receivable. Use of the allowance account avoids premature adjustments to individual receivable accounts while making possible a continuing control of subsidiary ledger detail by the accounts receivable account in the general ledger.

When positive evidence is available concerning the partial or complete worthlessness of an account, the allowance account is debited and the receivable is credited. Positive evidence of worthlessness is found in the bankruptcy, death, or disappearance of a debtor, failure to enforce collection legally, or a barring of collection by the statute of limitations. Write-offs should be supported by evidence of the uncollectibility of the accounts from appropriate parties, such as courts, lawyers, or credit agencies, and should be authorized in writing by appropriate company officers.

Bases for Estimating Charge for Doubtful Accounts

The estimate for doubtful accounts may be based upon (1) the amount of sales or (2) the amount of receivables. When sales are used as the basis for calculation, the problem of estimating the charge for doubtful accounts is viewed as one involving primarily the proper measurement of income. When receivables are used as the basis for calculation, the problem is viewed as one involving primarily the proper valuation of receivables.

If the sales basis is used, the periodic charge for bad debts is strictly related to sales of the current period. Any previous balance in the allowance account resulting from past period charges is disregarded. For example, if 2% of sales are considered doubtful in terms of collection and sales for the period are $100,000, the charge for doubtful accounts expense would be 2% of the current period's sales, or $2,000, regardless of the carryover balance in the allowance account. On the other hand, if the amount of receivables is used as a basis for estimating the charge for doubtful accounts, a corrected allowance figure is established each period by adjusting the existing balance. For example, if it is determined that the allowance for doubtful accounts should be $1,500 and the current credit balance in the allowance account is $600, the debit to Doubtful Accounts Expense and corresponding credit to the allowance account would be $900. The methods employed under each of these bases are described in the paragraphs that follow.

Adjustment for Doubtful Accounts Based on Sales. The charges for doubtful accounts of recent periods are related to the sales of these periods in developing a percentage of the charge for doubtful accounts to sales. This percentage may be modified by expectations in the light of current experience. Since doubtful accounts occur only with credit sales, it would seem logical to develop a percentage of doubtful accounts to credit sales of past periods. This percentage would be applied to credit sales of the current period. However, since extra work may be required in maintaining records of cash and credit sales or in analyzing sales data, the percentage is frequently developed in terms of total sales. Unless there is considerable fluctuation in the proportion of cash and credit sales periodically, the total sales method will give satisfactory results.

The *sales percentage method* for anticipating doubtful accounts is widely used in practice because it is sound in theory and simple to apply. Although normally offering a satisfactory approach to income measurement by providing equitable charges to periodic revenue, the method may not offer a "cash realizable" valuation for receivables. This shortcoming can be overcome by analyzing receivables at different intervals and correcting the allowance for any significant excess or deficiency.

Adjustment for Doubtful Accounts Based on Receivables. There are two methods of establishing and maintaining an allowance for doubtful accounts when receivables are used as the basis for the adjustment:

1. The allowance is adjusted to a certain percentage of receivables.
2. The allowance is adjusted to an amount determined by aging the accounts.

Adjusting Allowance to a Certain Percentage of Receivables. The uncollectible accounts experiences of recent periods are related to accounts outstanding in these periods and the data are considered in terms of special current conditions. An estimate of the probable uncollectibles is developed and Doubtful Accounts Expense is debited and Allowance for Doubtful Accounts credited for an amount bringing the allowance to the desired balance. To illustrate, assume receivables of $60,000 and a credit balance of $200 in the allowance account at the end of the period. Doubtful accounts are estimated at 2% of accounts receivable, or $1,200. The following entry brings the allowance to the desired amount:

Doubtful Accounts Expense	1,000	
Allowance for Doubtful Accounts		1,000

Although this method provides a satisfactory approach to the valuation of receivables, it may fail to provide equitable period charges to revenue. This is particularly true in view of the irregular determinations of actual uncollectibles as well as the lag in their recognition. After the first year, periodic provisions are directly affected by the current reductions in the allowance resulting from a recognition of uncollectible accounts originating in prior periods.

Adjusting Allowance to an Amount Determined by Aging the Accounts. The most commonly used method for establishing an allowance in terms of receivables involves *aging* receivables. Individual accounts are analyzed to determine those not yet due and those past due. Past-due accounts are classified in terms of the length of the period past due. An analysis sheet used in aging accounts receivable is shown below:

Parker and Pope
Analysis of Receivables — December 31, 1977

Customer	Amount	Not Yet Due	Not More Than 30 Days Past Due	31–60 Days Past Due	61–90 Days Past Due	91–180 Days Past Due	181–365 Days Past Due	More Than One Year Past Due
A. B. Andrews	$ 450			$ 450				
B. T. Brooks	300				$ 100			
B. Bryant	200		$ 200			$ 200		
L. B. Devine	2,100	$ 2,100						
K. Martinez	200							$ 200
M. A. Young	1,400	1,000		100	300			
Total	$47,550	$40,000	$3,000	$1,200	$ 650	$ 500	$ 800	$1,400

It is desirable to review each overdue balance with an appropriate company official and to arrive at estimates concerning the degree of collectibility of each item listed. An alternative procedure is to develop a series of estimated loss percentages and apply these to the different receivable classifications. The calculation of the allowance on the latter basis is illustrated on page 160.

Doubtful Accounts Expense is debited and Allowance for Doubtful Accounts is credited for an amount bringing the allowance account to the

Parker and Pope
Estimated Amount of Uncollectible Accounts — December 31, 1977

Classification	Balances	Uncollectible Accounts Experience Percentage	Estimated Amount of Uncollectible Accounts
Not yet due	$40,000	2%	$ 800
Not more than 30 days past due	3,000	5%	150
31–60 days past due	1,200	10%	120
61–90 days past due	650	20%	130
91–180 days past due	500	30%	150
181–365 days past due	800	50%	400
More than one year past due	1,400	80%	1,120
	$47,550		$2,870

required balance. Assuming uncollectibles estimated at $2,870 as shown in the tabulation and a credit balance of $620 in the allowance before adjustment, the following entry would be made:

Doubtful Accounts Expense	2,250	
Allowance for Doubtful Accounts		2,250

The aging method provides the most satisfactory approach to the valuation of receivables at their cash realizable amounts. Furthermore, data developed through aging receivables may be quite useful to management for purposes of credit analysis and control. On the other hand, application of this method may require considerable time and may prove expensive. The method still involves estimates, and the added refinement achieved by the aging process may not warrant the additional cost. As in the preceding method, charges based upon the recognizable impairment of asset values rather than upon sales may fail to provide equitable periodic charges against revenue.

Corrections in Allowance for Doubtful Accounts

As previously indicated, the allowance for doubtful accounts balance is established and maintained by means of adjusting entries at the close of each accounting period. If the allowance provisions are too large, the allowance account balance will be unnecessarily inflated and earnings will be understated; if the allowance provisions are too small, the allowance account balance will be inadequate and earnings will be overstated.

Care must be taken to see that the allowance balance follows the credit experience of the particular business. The process of aging receivables at different intervals may be employed as a means of checking the allowance balance to be certain that it is being maintained satisfactorily. Such periodic reviews may indicate the need for a correction in the allowance as well as a change in the rate or in the method.

When the uncollectible accounts experience approximates the anticipation of the losses, the allowance procedure may be considered satisfactory and no adjustment is required. When it appears there has been a failure to estimate uncollectible accounts satisfactorily, resulting in an allowance balance clearly inadequate or excessive, an adjustment is in order. Since publication of APB Opinion No. 9, such an adjustment is to be reported as an ordinary item on the income statement, usually as an addition to or subtraction from Doubtful Accounts Expense.

The recognition of current period receivables as uncollectible by debits to the allowance and credits to the receivable accounts may result in a debit balance in the allowance account. A debit balance arising in this manner does not indicate the allowance is inadequate; debits to the allowance simply predate the current provision for uncollectible accounts, and the adjustment at the end of the period should cover uncollectibles already determined as well as those yet to be recognized.

Occasionally, accounts that have been charged off as uncollectible are unexpectedly collected. Entries are required to reverse the original entry and record the collection. Assuming an account of $1,500 was determined to be uncollectible but was subsequently collected, the entries would be as follows:

Allowance for Doubtful Accounts	1,500	
Accounts Receivable		1,500
To write off a customer's account as uncollectible.		
Accounts Receivable	1,500	
Allowance for Doubtful Accounts		1,500
To reverse the original entry made in writing off the account.		
Cash	1,500	
Accounts Receivable		1,500
To record collection of account.		

Many businesses may feel that the accounting refinement to be gained by anticipating uncollectibles hardly warrants the additional work required. Instead of anticipating uncollectible accounts, these businesses may prefer simply to recognize them in the periods in which accounts are determined to be uncollectible (direct write-off method). When the loss is not anticipated by the establishment of an allowance, uncollectible accounts are written off by a debit to Uncollectible Accounts Expense or Bad Debts and a credit to the customer's account. Because the loss is now certain, and the write-off is made directly to the customer's account rather than to an allowance, the term Doubtful Accounts Expense is not appropriate.

The recognition of uncollectibles in the period of their discovery is practiced because of its simplicity and convenience. However, accounting theory supports the anticipation of uncollectibles so that current revenue may carry its full burden of expenses.

Anticipation of Discounts and Other Charges in Valuation of Receivables

The foregoing discussion has been restricted to the provision for uncollectible items. Conditions of sales and collections may suggest the anticipation of other charges that will emerge in the realization of accounts receivable and hence should properly be matched against current revenue. These charges and the procedures for handling them are equally applicable to notes receivable and to trade accounts receivable.

For example, if customers generally take cash discounts in making remittances, it may be argued that reporting revenue and receivables in terms of customer billings involves some overstatement of these balances. Under these circumstances, it may be desirable to anticipate the discounts by a debit to Sales Discounts and a credit to Allowance for Sales Discounts. Allowance for Sales Discounts would be subtracted from Accounts Receivable so that receivables are reported at their estimated cash realizable value. Discounts on the collection of old accounts in the new period can be debited to the allowance account. However, it would be more convenient to debit all discounts taken to the sales discounts account. The allowance account can then be adjusted to its correct balance at the end of the new period.

To illustrate, assume customers generally take sales discounts averaging 1% of gross billings and the accounts receivable balance on December 31, 1976, is $50,000. The following adjusting entry may be made:

Sales Discounts	500	
Allowance for Sales Discounts		500

Computation:
1% × $50,000 = $500

During 1977, discounts taken on the collection of accounts receivable may be debited to Sales Discounts regardless of the period in which the account originated. Thus, the allowance for sales discounts account remains with a balance of $500. If at the end of 1977, Accounts Receivable has a balance of $40,000, the Allowance for Sales Discounts should have a balance of $400 ($400,000 × 1% = $400). Therefore, the following adjusting entry would be required:

Allowance for Sales Discounts	100	
Sales Discounts		100

Similar recognition may be suggested for probable allowances yet to be made to customers for shipment shortages and defects, for price adjustments, and also for probable losses on sales returns. Customer's claims for freight charges paid on the receipt or return of goods may call for consideration. Probable future expenses involved in the realization of accounts, such as billing and collection expenses and attorneys' fees may likewise warrant consideration. The anticipation of charges for the items just mentioned is seldom found in practice and is not allowed for income tax purposes. When these charges are not anticipated and the volume of activities and experiences with respect to these charges do not vary significantly from period to period, the recognition of such charges in the period in which they are finally determined will have little effect upon periodic net income, although the receivables balance may be slightly overstated.

USE OF RECEIVABLES IN CASH PLANNING

A business may require cash for current purposes exceeding the amount on hand and the amount to become available in the normal course of operations. The business may use accounts receivable or notes receivable as a basis for a cash advance from a bank or a finance company. These procedures are described in the following sections.

Customers' Accounts as a Source of Cash

In order to obtain immediate cash, accounts receivable owned by the business may be (1) pledged, (2) assigned, or (3) sold.

Pledge of Accounts Receivable. Advances are frequently obtained from banks or other lending institutions by pledging accounts receivable as security on a loan. Ordinarily, collections are made by the borrower who is required to use this cash in meeting the obligation to the lender. The lender may be given access to the borrower's records to determine whether remittances are being properly made on pledged accounts.

Assignment of Accounts Receivable. Finance companies may agree to advance cash over a period of time as accounts receivable are assigned to them. The assignments carry a guarantee on the part of the assignor to make up any deficiency if the accounts fail to realize required amounts. Assignments thus represent, in effect, sale of accounts on a *recourse* basis. The cash advanced by the finance company is normally less than the assigned accounts by a percentage considered adequate to cover uncollectible items, returns and allowances, offsets, and amounts subject to dispute. When amounts actually recovered on assigned accounts exceed the sum of the advance and the finance company's charges, such excess accrues to the assignor. Charges made by the finance company frequently consist of a commission on the amount advanced, plus interest on the unrecovered balance of the advance computed on a daily basis. Assignments are usually made on a *non-notification basis*, customers remaining uninformed concerning the assignment; customers, then, make their payments to the assignor who is then required to turn the collections over to the assignee. When assignments are made on a *notification basis*, customers are instructed to make their payments directly to the finance company.

Sale of Accounts Receivable. Certain dealers or finance companies purchase accounts receivable outright on a *without recourse* basis. This is known as accounts receivable *factoring*, and the buyer is referred to as a *factor.* Customers are notified that their bills are payable to the factor, and this party assumes the burden of billing and collecting accounts. In many instances, factoring may involve more than simply the purchase and collection of accounts receivable. Factoring frequently involves a continuing agreement whereby a financing institution assumes the credit function as well as the collection function. Under such an arrangement, the factor grants or denies credit, handles the accounts receivable bookkeeping, bills customers, and makes collections. The business unit is relieved of all these activities. The sale of goods provides immediate cash for business use. Because the factor absorbs the losses from bad accounts and frequently assumes credit and collection responsibilities, the charge made exceeds the interest charge involved in borrowing cash or the commission and interest charges involved in the assignment of receivables. In some instances, the factor may withhold a portion of the purchase price for possible future charges for customer returns and allowances or other special adjustments. Final settlement is made after receivables have been collected.

Accounting Procedures for Accounts Receivable Financing. No special accounting problems are encountered in the pledge or the sale of receivables. When receivables are pledged, the books simply report the loan and the subsequent settlement. Disclosure should be made on the balance sheet by parenthetical comment or note of the receivables pledged to secure the obligation to the lending agency. When receivables are sold outright, Cash is debited, receivables and related allowance balances are closed, and an expense account is debited for factoring charges. When part of the purchase price is withheld by the factor, a receivable is established pending final settlement.

The accounting treatment required for assignment of accounts receivable is illustrated by the following example. Assume the Bronson Co. on March 1 assigns accounts receivable of $25,000 to the Weber Finance Co. and receives $19,500 representing an advance of 80% of receivables less a commission on the advance of 2½%. Collections are to be made by the assignor who is to deposit such receipts intact to the credit of the assignee. The entries on the books of the assignor and assignee are given on the following page.

It will be observed that the assignor makes two entries at the time of assignment: one entry sets the assigned accounts receivable apart under separate control; a second entry establishes a credit representing the equity in the receivables of the assignee, accompanied by debits to Cash for the cash received, and to Assignment Expense for the charges made by the assignee. Thereafter, as cash is collected on assigned accounts, the assigned receivables balance is reduced and cash is remitted to reduce the assignee's equity. Entries are made to reduce the assigned receivables balance for such items as returns, allowances, and write-offs. Upon final settlement with the assignee, any balance in Accounts Receivable Assigned is returned to the unassigned accounts control. The equity of the assignor in the accounts is always the remaining balance in the assigned accounts less the equity of the assignee.

On the books of the assignee, the advance of cash is recorded by a debit to an asset account for the total receivables assigned, a credit to an account with the assignor for the latter's equity in this total, a credit to Commission Revenue for the charges made, and a credit to Cash for the cash paid. As cash is received, Cash is debited and the assigned accounts and Interest Revenue are credited. Reductions in assigned accounts involving charges to be absorbed by the assignor are recognized by reductions in the assignor's equity. Upon final settlement, any balance remaining in the assignor's equity in assigned accounts is offset against the assigned receivables balance.

If a balance sheet is prepared before the finance company has received full payment, the assignor recognizes the difference between the total accounts assigned and the portion required to cover the claim of the finance company as an asset. Disclosure is also made of the responsibilities to the finance company if assigned accounts do not realize enough to liquidate the loan. The assignee in preparing a balance sheet would report the interest in assigned accounts as an asset.

TRANSACTION	ENTRIES ON ASSIGNOR'S BOOKS (BRONSON COMPANY)			ENTRIES ON ASSIGNEE'S BOOKS (WEBER FINANCE CO.)		
March 1 Bronson Co. assigned accounts receivable of $25,000 to Weber Finance Co. receiving $19,500 representing an advance of 80% of receivables less a commission on the advance of 2½%.	Accounts Receivable Assigned	25,000		Bronson Co. Accounts	25,000	
	Accounts Receivable		25,000	Equity of Bronson Co. in Assigned Accounts		5,000
	Cash	19,500		Commission Revenue		500
	Assignment Expense	500		Cash		19,500
	Equity of Weber Finance Co. in Assigned Accounts		20,000			
March 31 Bronson Co. collected $15,000 on assigned accounts. This amount together with interest at 12% for one month on the amount advanced, or $200, was remitted to Weber Finance Co.	Cash	15,000		Cash	15,200	
	Accounts Receivable Assigned		15,000	Bronson Co. Accounts		15,000
	Equity of Weber Finance Co. in Assigned Accounts	15,000		Interest Revenue		200
	Interest Expense	200				
	Cash		15,200			
March 31 Sales returns and allowances granted by Bronson Co. on assigned accounts during March totaled $1,000.	Sales Returns and Allowance	1,000		Equity of Bronson Co. in Assigned Accounts	1,000	
	Accounts Receivable Assigned		1,000	Bronson Co. Accounts		1,000
May 31 Bronson Co. collected $8,500 on assigned accounts. Balance due, $5,000, together with interest at 12% for two months on this amount, or $100, was remitted to Weber Finance Co. in final settlement; $3,500 was retained. Remaining account balances relative to assignment were closed.	Cash	8,500		Cash	5,100	
	Accounts Receivable Assigned		8,500	Bronson Co. Accounts		5,000
	Equity of Weber Finance Co. in Assigned Accounts	5,000		Interest Revenue		100
	Interest Expense	100		Equity of Bronson Co. in Assigned Accounts	4,000	
	Cash		5,100	Bronson Co. Accounts		4,000
	Accounts Receivable	500				
	Accounts Receivable Assigned		500			

To illustrate, if in the preceding example balance sheets are prepared on March 31, information relating to assigned accounts may be reported as shown below.

Bronson Co. (Assignor)

Current assets:
Accounts receivable — unassigned		$50,000
Company's equity in assigned accounts receivable:		
Assigned accounts	$9,000	
Less equity of Weber Finance Co. in assigned accounts (company is contingently liable as guarantor of assigned accounts)	5,000	4,000
Total accounts receivable		$54,000

Weber Finance Co. (Assignee)

Current assets:
Bronson Co. accounts	$9,000	
Less equity of Bronson Co. in assigned accounts	4,000	$ 5,000

When collections are made by the finance company, procedures similar to those illustrated can still be employed. In these instances, however, entries are made by the assignor when information is received from the finance company concerning collections, interest charges, and the return of accounts in excess of claims.

Managements may employ accounts receivable financing as a temporary or emergency matter after exhausting the limited line of unsecured credit available from a lending institution. On the other hand, managements may engage in accounts receivable financing as a continuing policy. Recent years have witnessed an increasing number of factoring arrangements involving the full delegation of credit and collection responsibilities to specialists. Financial assistance to business through the factoring of open accounts today amounts to millions of dollars.

Notes Receivable as a Source of Cash

Cash may be obtained by selling notes receivable to a bank or to some other agency willing to accept such instruments. If a note is non-interest-bearing, cash is received for the face value of the note less a charge for interest, known as *discount*, for the period from the date the note is discounted to the date of its maturity. If the note is interest-bearing, the maturity value of the note is first determined. The amount received from the bank (*proceeds*) is the maturity value of the note less a discount calculated on this maturity value from the date the note is discounted to its maturity.

To illustrate entries for a non-interest-bearing note, assume a 90-day, $1,000 note dated December 1 is received; the note is discounted on December 16 at 10%. The following entries are made:

Dec. 1	Notes Receivable	1,000.00	
	Accounts Receivable		1,000.00
Dec. 16	Cash	979.17	
	Interest Expense	20.83	
	Notes Receivable		1,000.00

Computation:
Interest: $1,000 \times .10 \times 75/360 = $20.83

To illustrate the accounting for an interest-bearing note, assume the note received in the previous example provides for the payment of interest at 10% at its maturity and it is discounted at the bank at 10%. Under these circumstances, the following entries would be appropriate:

Dec. 1	Notes Receivable	1,000.00	
	Accounts Receivable		1,000.00
Dec. 16	Cash	1,003.65	
	Notes Receivable		1,000.00
	Interest Revenue		3.65

Computation:

Maturity value of note: Proceeds:

$1,000 + interest ($1,000 × .10 × 90/360) = $1,025 $1,025 − $21.35 = $1,003.65

Discount: Net interest revenue:

$1,025 × .10 × 75/360 = $21.35 $1,003.65 − $1,000 = $3.65

A note endorsed "without recourse" relieves the endorser of any liability for the inability of the maker of the note or any prior endorser to pay the note upon its maturity. When a note is endorsed without making any qualification, the endorser becomes liable to subsequent holders of the note if it is not paid at maturity. However, if the endorser is held liable on the note, that person has the right to recover amounts paid from the maker of the note or prior endorsers who failed to comply with its terms.

Normally, endorsement without qualification is required in discounting a note, and the endorser becomes contingently liable on the note. Under these circumstances Notes Receivable Discounted instead of Notes Receivable may be credited when the note is discounted. Pending final settlement on the note, the discounted portion of notes receivable would be regarded as a contingent asset. Notes Receivable Discounted, in turn, would be an accompanying contingent liability. When the person who holds the note at maturity receives payment from the maker, both payment and recovery contingencies are ended, and Notes Receivable Discounted can be applied against Notes Receivable.

The use of the notes receivable discounted account gives the same final result as that obtained when Notes Receivable is credited for notes discounted. Since data concerning the contingent liability are of concern only on the balance sheet date and these can be determined readily at the end of the period from an examination of the detailed record of notes discounted, the extra work involved in maintaining a notes receivable discounted account may not be warranted. When a notes receivable discounted balance is carried in the accounts, this balance is subtracted from Notes Receivable in reporting the notes receivable balance. When a notes receivable discounted account is not used, information concerning the contingent liability is provided on the balance sheet by means of a parenthetical remark or note or by special reference under a separate contingent liabilities heading.

If a note is not paid when it is due, the holder of the note must give the endorser prompt notice of such dishonor. The endorser is then required to make payment to the holder. Payment consists of the face value of the note plus interest and plus any fees and costs relating to collection. The full amount paid is recoverable from the maker of the note, and Accounts Receivable, Notes Receivable Dishonored, or Notes Receivable Past Due may be debited. If Notes Receivable Discounted were credited at the time the note was discounted, this balance, together with the original notes receivable balance, should be canceled. Subsequent recovery on the note is recorded by a debit to Cash and a credit to the account with the debtor; failure to recover any portion of the balance due would call for writing off the unpaid balance.

To illustrate, assume in the preceding example Notes Receivable Discounted instead of Notes Receivable was credited when the note was discounted. The following entry would be made when the note is paid at maturity.

Notes Receivable Discounted	1,000	
Notes Receivable		1,000

If the note was not paid at maturity and the bank charged the endorser with a $2.50 protest fee, an entry would be made as follows:

Accounts Receivable	1,027.50	
Notes Receivable Discounted	1,000.00	
Cash		1,027.50
Notes Receivable		1,000.00

Computation:
Maturity value of note, $1,025.00 + $2.50 protest fee = $1,027.50

Subsequent payment from the customer is recorded as follows:

Cash	1,027.50	
Accounts Receivable		1,027.50

PRESENTATION OF RECEIVABLES ON THE BALANCE SHEET

Normally, the receivables qualifying as current items are grouped for presentation in the following classes: (1) notes — trade debtors, (2) accounts — trade debtors, (3) other receivables, and (4) accrued receivables. Reporting should disclose nonnegotiable notes. The detail reported for other receivables depends upon the relative significance of the various items included. When trade accounts or installment contracts are properly reported as current but involve collections beyond one year, particulars of such deferred collections should be provided. Valuation accounts are deducted from the individual receivable balances or combined balances to which they relate. Notes receivable may be reported gross with notes receivable discounted shown as a deduction from this balance, or notes may be reported net with appropriate reference to the contingent liability arising from notes discounted. Accounts receivable assigned may be reported gross with the interest of the assignee in such balance shown as a subtraction item, or the company's interest in receivables may be reported net; here too, appropriate reference would be made to the contingent liability involved. When receivables are supported by pledges of collateral to assure their collectibility, the nature of the pledge and the fact that the receivables are wholly or partly secured should be disclosed. On the other hand, when receivables have been pledged or otherwise hypothecated on obligations of the company, these facts, too, should be disclosed and reference made to the obligation thus secured.

Current receivable items as they might appear on the balance sheet are shown below. An alternative to parenthetical disclosure would be to present the supplemental information in a note to the financial statements.

Receivables:

Trade notes and drafts receivable (notes of $20,000 have been pledged to secure bank borrowing)	$ 39,500	
Less discount on notes receivable	1,500	$ 38,000
Trade accounts receivable (including installment contracts of approximately $30,000 not due for 12–18 months)	$112,000	
Less allowance for doubtful accounts and repossession charges	2,500	109,500
Miscellaneous notes and accounts, including short-term loans to employees of $6,500		12,000
Accrued receivables		4,500
Total receivables		$164,000

QUESTIONS

1. The Philips Corporation shows on its balance sheet one receivable balance including the following items: (a) advances to officers, (b) deposits on machinery and equipment being produced by various companies for the Philips Corporation, (c) advances for traveling expenses, (d) damage claims against transportation companies approved by such companies, (e) estimated federal income tax refunds, (f) accrued interest on notes receivable, (g) overdue notes, (h) receivables from a foreign subsidiary company, (i) subscriptions receivable · on a new bond issue, and (j) creditor overpayments. Suggest the proper treatment of each item.

2. The Belnap Co. includes in its current receivable total an investment in a joint venture with the Conner Corporation. Officials of the Belnap Co. justify this practice on the grounds the assets of the joint venture are all in current form. Comment on this practice.

3. The Aldwin Manufacturing Co. ships merchandise on a consignment basis to customers, title to such goods passing only at the time the goods are sold by the consignees. The Aldwin Manufacturing Co. debits accounts receivable for the cost of the goods shipped until sales are reported, when it increases the receivable accounts with the con-

signee to the regular billing price. Goods on consignment appear on the balance sheet as receivables. (a) Would you approve such practice? (b) Suggest an alternative procedure.

4. Suggest several methods for reporting income tax refund claims approved or under review and the circumstances supporting the appropriate use of each method.

5. What kinds of receivables should be reported at their present values?

6. (a) Give three methods for the establishment and the maintenance of an allowance for doubtful accounts. (b) What are the advantages and disadvantages of each method?

7. How would the percentages used in estimating uncollectible accounts be determined under any of the methods of maintaining an allowance for doubtful accounts?

8. The bookkeeper for Warne, Inc., believes a more accurate valuation of notes and accounts receivable can be shown by aging the notes and accounts and establishing an allowance on this basis than by crediting the allowance account with a percentage of net sales on account. Do you agree? Give the advantages of each procedure.

9. (a) What entries are necessary when an account previously written off is collected? (b) Why would the collection of an account written off in a previous year not be a prior period adjustment?

10. An analysis of the accounts receivable balance of $8,702 on the records of Books, Inc., on December 31 reveals the following:

Accounts from sales of last three months (appear to be fully collectible)	$7,460
Accounts from sales prior to October 1 (of doubtful value)	1,312
Accounts known to be worthless	320
Dishonored notes charged back to customers' accounts	800
Credit balances in customers' accounts	1,190

(a) What adjustments are required?
(b) How should the various balances be shown on the balance sheet?

11. How do the accounting procedures for recognizing uncollectible accounts in the period of discovery (direct write-off) differ from those of anticipating uncollectible accounts?

12. List and explain at least four deductions that may be applied under certain circumstances in the valuation of accounts receivable.

13. The Ferrer Corporation sells home air-conditioning units. The cash price of these units is $800; the price on a deferred payment plan is $900. Those acquiring the units on the deferred payment plan sign a note providing for payments of $50 per month for eighteen months. How would you recommend the deferred payment sales and subsequent collections be reported in the accounts?

14. If unearned customer finance charges for installment receivables are carried as a separate valuation account balance, what difficulties do you foresee in calculating a proper allowance for doubtful accounts?

15. In what section of the income statement would you report (a) doubtful accounts expense, (b) sales discounts?

16. (a) Distinguish between the practices of (1) pledging, (2) assigning, and (3) selling accounts receivable. (b) Describe the accounting procedure to be followed in each instance.

17. The Barker Co. enters into a continuing agreement with Mercantile Finance, Inc., whereby the latter company buys without recourse all of the trade receivables as they arise and assumes all credit and collection functions. Describe the advantages that may accrue to the Barker Co. as a result of the factoring agreement.

18. The Beaner Company discounts at 8% the following three notes at the Security First Bank on July 1 of the current year. Compute the proceeds on each note using 360 days to a year.

(a) A 90-day, 9% note receivable for $10,000 dated June 1.
(b) A 6-month, 7% note receivable for $14,000 dated May 13.
(c) A 4-month note payable dated July 1 with face value of $5,000.

19. A. B. Crowell, who has been recording a contingent liability on notes receivable discounted, has noticed that he has been held liable on nearly as many customers' checks as he has on notes. He suggests setting up a "checks endorsed" account to show his contingent liability on checks. Is this advisable? Why?

20. Indicate several methods for presenting information on the balance sheet relating to (a) notes receivable discounted, and (b) accounts receivable assigned.

EXERCISES

1. The accounts receivable control account for the Arlo Co. shows a debit balance of $96,950; the Allowance for Doubtful Accounts shows a credit balance of $3,800. Subsidiary ledger detail reveals the following:

Trade accounts receivable — assigned (Finance Co. equity in assigned accounts is $8,000)	$10,000
Subscriptions receivable for common stock due in 60 days	50,000
Interest receivable on bonds	2,500
Installment receivables, due 1–18 months hence (including unearned finance charges of $500)	3,500
Trade receivables from officers, due currently	1,250

Customers' accounts reporting credit balances arising from sales returns	$ 250
Advance payments to creditors on purchase orders...	3,000
Advance payments to creditors on orders for machinery......................................	5,000
Customers' accounts reporting credit balances arising from advance payments	1,000
Accounts known to be worthless	450
Trade accounts on which post-dated checks are held (no entries were made on receipt of checks)...	500
Advances to affiliated companies	10,000
Other trade accounts receivable — unassigned...	12,000

Show how this information would be reported on the balance sheet.

2. Accounts Receivable of the Manta Motors Company on December 31, 1977, showed a balance of $50,000. The Allowance for Doubtful Accounts showed a $1,500 debit balance. Sales in 1977 were $375,000 less sales discounts taken of $3,000.

Give the adjusting entry for estimated doubtful accounts expense, assuming:

(a) One-half of 1% of 1977 net sales will never be collected.
(b) Two percent of outstanding accounts receivable are worthless.
(c) An aging schedule shows that $2,500 of the outstanding accounts receivable are worthless.

3. Prior to 1978, the James Company followed the percentage-of-sales method of estimating doubtful accounts. The following data are gathered by the accounting department.

	1974	1975	1976	1977
Total sales	$350,000	$600,000	$1,200,000	$2,100,000
Charge sales	200,000	320,000	650,000	1,200,000
Accounts receivable (end-of-year balance)	62,000	78,000	120,000	250,000
Allowance for doubtful accounts (end-of-year credit balance)..............	2,000	6,000	4,000	22,000
Accounts written off.............................	9,000	2,000	14,000	3,000

(a) What amount was debited to expense for 1975, 1976, and 1977?
(b) Compute the balance in the valuation account at the beginning of 1974 assuming there has been no change in the percentage of sales used over the four-year period.
(c) What explanation can be given for the fluctuating amount of write-off?
(d) Why do the actual write-offs fail to give the correct charge to expense?

4. The Hernandez Lumber Company follows the procedure of debiting doubtful accounts expense for 2% of all new sales. The following balances were found in using this method:

Year	Sales	Allowance for Doubtful Accounts (end-of-year credit balance)
1974	$3,530,000	$ 43,000
1975	3,800,000	71,000
1976	3,400,000	100,000
1977	3,985,000	132,000

(a) Compute the amount of accounts written off for the years 1975, 1976, and 1977.
(b) The external auditors are concerned with the growing amount in the allowance account. What action do you recommend the auditors take?
(c) What arguments might Hernandez use to justify the balance in the valuation account? Allowance for Doubtful Accounts is the only accounts receivable valuation account used by Hernandez.

5. Yamada Sales Co. assigns accounts of $60,000 to the Warren Finance Co., guaranteeing these accounts and receiving an 80% advance less a flat commission of 2% on the amount of the advance. Accounts of $45,000 are collected and remittance is made to the finance company. Uncollectible accounts of $2,000 are written off against an allowance for doubtful accounts; remaining accounts are collected and settlement is made with the finance company together with payment of $1,200 for interest. What entries are required on the books of Yamada Sales Co. and on the books of Warren Finance Co. to record the assignment and the subsequent transactions?

6. The Plow Co. decides to employ accounts receivable as a basis for financing. Its current position at this time is as follows:

Accounts receivable	$30,000	Cash overdraft	$ 550
Inventories	35,000	Accounts payable	28,000

Prepare a statement of its current position, assuming cash is obtained as indicated in each case below:

(a) Cash of $20,000 is borrowed on short-term notes and $15,000 is applied to the payment of creditors; accounts of $25,000 are pledged to secure the loan.

(b) Cash of $20,000 is advanced to the company by High Finance Co., the advance representing 80% of accounts assigned to it; assignment is made on a with recourse basis, and amounts collected in excess of the loan balance and charges accrue to the Plow Co.

(c) Cash of $20,000 is received on the sale of accounts receivable of $22,500 on a no recourse basis.

7. On December 21, the following notes are discounted by the bank at 9%. Give the cash proceeds from each note.

(a) 30-day, $2,000, non-interest-bearing note dated December 15.
(b) 60-day, $1,925, 7% note dated December 1.
(c) 60-day, $1,356, 9% note dated November 6.
(d) 90-day, $4,800, 12% note dated November 24.

8. Mike Owne received from Joe Last, a customer, a 90-day, 8% note for $3,000, dated November 6, 1976. On December 6, Owne had Last's note discounted at 7% and recorded the contingent liability. The bank protested nonpayment of the note and charged the endorser with protest fees of $2.75 in addition to the amount of the note. On February 28, 1977, the note was collected with interest at 10% from the maturity date on the face value of the note. What entries would appear on Owne's books as a result of the foregoing?

9. On June 1, 1977, L. Wagner received a $3,000 note from a customer on an overdue account. The note matures on August 30 and bears interest at 7%. On July 1, Wagner discounted the note at 8% and applied the proceeds to the payment of creditors. On August 30, the customer is unable to make payment to the bank and the bank charges Wagner's account for the maturity value of the note plus a $3 protest fee. On September 29, Wagner accepted the customer's offer to cancel the liability in exchange for marketable securities valued at $3,075. Give all entries on Wagner's books to record the foregoing.

PROBLEMS

6-1. Accounts receivable for the Tool Co. were reported on the balance sheet prepared at the end of 1977 as follows:

Accounts receivable		$62,400	
Less: Allowance for doubtful accounts	$2,630		
Allowance for sales discounts	870	3,500	$58,900

The company sells goods on terms of 3/10 e.o.m., n/30. At the end of the year accounts receivable are aged and the following percentages are applied in arriving at an estimate of the charge for doubtful accounts:

	Estimated Loss
Accounts not more than two months overdue	8%
Accounts more than two months but not more than six months overdue	25%
Accounts more than six months but not more than one year overdue	60%
Accounts more than one year overdue	100%

At the end of the year the company also anticipates sales discounts on all receivables not yet due for payment.

In 1978, the following transactions took place:

Sales on account	$426,582
Cash collected on account	408,970
Cash discounts allowed	5,862
Sales returns and allowances	2,320
Accounts written off	1,950
Accounts previously written off but recovered	430

At the end of the year overdue accounts are as follows:

Accounts not more than two months overdue	$6,500
Accounts more than two months but not more than six months overdue	3,100
Accounts more than six months but not more than one year overdue	1,200
Accounts more than one year overdue	1,380

> **Instructions:**
> (1) Give the entries required to record the transactions listed above and also to adjust the accounts.
> (2) Calculate the balances for accounts receivable and the related allowances as of December 31, 1978, and show these as they will appear on the balance sheet.

6-2. The balance sheet for the Valentine Co. on December 31, 1977, includes the following receivable balances:

Interest receivable		$ 300
Notes receivable	$32,500	
Less notes receivable discounted	15,500	17,000
Accounts receivable	$75,000	
Less allowance for doubtful accounts	3,750	71,250

Transactions during 1978 included the following:

(a) Sales on account were $642,200.

(b) Cash collected on accounts totaled $492,000, which included accounts of $104,000 on which cash discounts of 2% were allowed.

(c) Notes received in payment of accounts totaled $83,000.

(d) Notes receivable discounted as of December 31, 1977, were paid at maturity with the exception of one $8,000 note on which the company has to pay $8,090, which included interest and protest fees. It is expected that recovery will be made on this note in 1978.

(e) Customers' notes of $50,000 were discounted during the year, proceeds from their sale being $48,500. Of this total, $34,500 matured during the year without notice of protest.

(f) Customers' accounts of $9,610 were written off during the year as worthless.

(g) Recoveries of doubtful accounts written off in prior years were $740.

(h) Notes receivable collected during the year totaled $18,000 and interest collected was $1,200.

(i) On December 31, accrued interest on notes receivable was $580.

(j) Uncollectible accounts are estimated to be 5% of the December 31, 1978, Accounts Receivable balance.

(k) Cash of $20,000 was borrowed from the bank, accounts receivable of $25,000 being pledged on the loan. Collections of $13,000 had been made on these receivables (included in the total given in transaction [b]) and this amount was applied on December 31, 1978, to payment of accrued interest on the loan of $400, and the balance to partial payment of the loan.

> **Instructions:**
> (1) Prepare journal entries summarizing the transactions and information given above.
> (2) Prepare a summary of current receivables for balance sheet presentation.

6-3. The following transactions affecting the accounts receivable of Landfall Corporation took place during the year ended January 31, 1977:

Sales (cash and credit)	$236,420
Cash received from credit customers (customers who paid $119,560 took advantage of the discount feature of the corporation's credit terms, 2/10, n/30)	121,102

Cash received from cash customers	$ 82,070
Accounts receivable written off as worthless	1,982
Credit memoranda issued to credit customers for sales returns and allowances	22,510
Cash refunds given to cash customers for sales returns and allowances	6,789
Recoveries on accounts receivable written off as uncollectible in prior periods (not included in cash amount stated above)	4,246

The following two balances were taken from the January 31, 1976 balance sheet:

Accounts receivable	$38,337
Allowance for doubtful accounts	3,896

The corporation provides for its net uncollectible account losses by crediting Allowance for Doubtful Accounts for 1½% of net credit sales for the fiscal period.

Instructions:
(1) Prepare the journal entries to record the transactions for the year ended January 31, 1977.
(2) Prepare the adjusting journal entry for estimated uncollectible accounts on January 31, 1977.

6-4. The Mosher Company completed the following transactions during 1977 related to accounts receivable.

Apr. 1 Assigned accounts of $60,000 to Farns Finance Co. for a cash advance of 80% of receivables less a commission on the advance of 1½%.

Apr. 30 Collections during April on assigned accounts were $22,440. This amount plus 10% interest for one month on the amount advanced was remitted to Farns Finance Co.

Apr. 30 Wrote off against the allowance account, $3,500 of uncollectible accounts of which $2,000 were assigned accounts.

May 31 Collections during May on assigned accounts were $24,000. This amount plus 10% interest for one month on the unpaid balance was remitted to Farns Finance Co.

May 31 Granted sales returns of $5,000 on assigned accounts during May.

June 30 Collections during June on assigned accounts were $500. Balance due Farns Finance Co. plus 10% interest for one month on the unpaid balance was remitted. Remaining account balances relative to assignment were closed.

Instructions:
(1) Give the entries required to record the above transactions on the Mosher Company's books.
(2) Give the entries required to record the same transactions on the books of the Farns Finance Company.

6-5. The Hallock Fur Company has run into financial difficulties. It decides to improve its cash position by factoring one third of its accounts receivable and assigning one half of the remaining receivables to the local bank. Details of these arrangements were as follows:

Accounts receivable, Dec. 31, 1977 ....$240,000	(before financing)
Allowance for doubtful accounts, Dec. 31, 1977 1,500	(credit)
Estimated uncollectibles, Dec. 31, 1977	2% of accounts receivable balance
Factor discount rate	15% of gross receivables financed
Assignment withholding rate	10% of gross receivables financed
Assignment service charge rate	2% of amount advanced, payable in advance

Instructions:
(1) Prepare the journal entries to record the receipt of cash from (a) factoring, and (b) assigning the accounts receivable.
(2) Prepare the journal entry to record the necessary adjustment to Allowance for Doubtful Accounts.
(3) Prepare the accounts receivable section of the balance sheet as it would appear after these transactions.
(4) What entry would be made on the company books of the Hallock Fur Company when factored accounts have been collected?

6-6. The Galvez Corporation sold equipment on the installment basis. A balance sheet prepared December 31, 1976, indicated the following information under the heading "Notes and accounts receivable."

Installment notes assigned to PMA Corporation, including amounts due after one year..	$190,268	
Less amounts due PMA	82,967	$107,301
Installment notes, unassigned, including amounts due after one year		407,071
Accounts receivable..		59,155
		$573,527
Less:		
Unearned interest on installment notes	$ 92,305	
Allowance for doubtful accounts..	65,300	157,605
Net balance...		$415,922

During 1977, the following transactions occurred:

(a) New installment sales of $1,250,000 were made during the year. Included in these notes was $120,000 of unearned interest.

(b) $650,000 of these notes were assigned to PMA Corporation. Proceeds from PMA amounted to $530,000; an interest charge of $30,000 was made for the advance and added to the amount owed PMA.

(c) Interest earned on installment loans during 1977 amounted to $136,000.

(d) Collections on assigned notes were $580,000 of which $475,000 was paid to PMA.

(e) Assigned notes for $26,500 were written off as uncollectible; $1,500 unearned interest charge was included in the accounts written off.

(f) Estimated uncollectible notes as of December 31, 1977, were $72,300 exclusive of unearned interest charges.

Instructions: Prepare journal entries for 1977 to record the above summarized transactions.

6-7. J. P. Loax completed the following transactions, among others:

Oct. 5 Received a $6,000, 60-day, 8% note dated October 5 from B. R. Sonsen, a customer.

24 Received a $1,600, 90-day, non-interest-bearing note dated October 23 from E. L. Manwaring as settlement for unpaid balance of $1,564.

25 Had Sonsen's note discounted at the bank at 9%.

Nov. 7 Had Manwaring's note discounted at the bank at 8%.

25 Received from O. R. Malt, a customer, a $4,000, 90-day, 8% note dated November 5, payable to O. R. Malt and signed by the Beneficial Corporation. Upon endorsement, gave the customer credit for the maturity value of the note less discount at 7%.

29 Received a $3,000, 60-day, 7% note dated November 29 from M. R. Jones, a customer.

Dec. 5 Received notice from the bank that Sonsen's note was not paid at maturity. Protest fees of $2.50 were charged by the bank.

21 Received payment from Sonsen on the dishonored note, including interest at 9% on the face value of the note from maturity date.

Instructions:

(1) Give the journal entries to record the above transactions, showing contingent liabilities in the accounts. (Show data used in calculations with each entry.)

(2) Give the adjusting entries required on December 31.

6-8. The following transactions were completed by A. W. Fields over a three-month period:

June 10 Received from J. L. Norman, a customer, a $4,000, 60-day, 9% note dated June 9.

June 11 Received from G. R. Johnson on account, a $1,800, 60-day, 12% note dated June 10.

June 20 Discounted Johnson's note at the bank at 10%.

June 24 Discounted Norman's note at the bank at 10%.

July 3 Received a $2,950, 30-day, non-interest-bearing note dated July 1 from O. P. Fine, crediting Fine's account at face value.

July   7 Discounted Fine's note at the bank at 9%.

July 29 Received from J. D. Waddell, a $500, 90-day, 12% note dated July 14 and made by the Windel Company. Gave the customer credit for the maturity value of the note less discount at 10%.

July 29 Received a $3,500, 10-day, 7% note dated July 29 from L. Smathers, a customer.

Aug. 10 Received notice from the bank that Norman's note was not paid at maturity. A protest fee of $2.50 was charged by the bank.

Aug. 22 Received a $15,000, 120-day, 9% note dated August 22 from R. J. Roxy, a customer.

Aug. 28 Received payment on Smather's note, including interest at 10%, the legal rate, on the face value from the maturity date.

Instructions:

(1) Give the entries to record the above transactions showing the contingent liabilities in the accounts. (Show data used in calculations with each entry.)

(2) Give the necessary adjusting entries on August 31.

6-9. On December 31, 1977, the notes receivable account of the Imbler Company consisted of the following notes:

Trade notes receivable, considered good:	
Due in 12 months or less	$ 68,000
Due in more than 12 months	10,000
Trade notes receivable, considered 80% collectible:	
Due in 12 months or less	51,000
Trade notes receivable, considered worthless	3,500
Trade notes receivable, considered good, and discounted with the First National Bank (with offsetting credits to Notes Receivable Discounted). Of these notes, $21,000 have been paid.	65,000
Notes receivable accepted on sale of diesel equipment (fixed asset), $18,000. This amount was payable $500 monthly, and the purchaser was considered a good credit risk.	18,000
Note receivable of Ivan Imbler, president, payable on demand. This note was received in payment of his subscription to 1,000 shares of common stock of Imbler Company at par. Upon receipt of this note, the corporation issued a certificate of capital stock for 1,000 shares.	100,000
	$315,500

Instructions: Indicate how each of the company's notes receivable would be classified on the balance sheet of December 31, 1977.

6-10. Current assets for the Klein Company are listed as follows on the balance sheet prepared on December 31, 1977:

Current assets:	
Cash	$ 11,600
Marketable securities	32,575
Notes receivable	16,900
Accounts receivable	74,485
Merchandise inventory	82,300
	$217,860

An examination of the books revealed the following information concerning the current assets:

(a) Cash included:

Petty cash funds (of which $490 is cash, $130 is in the form of employees' IOU's, and $30 is in the form of postage stamps)	$ 650
Customers' checks not yet deposited	2,100
Demand deposit at the First National Bank	8,200
An overdraft at the Central City Bank	(300)
Customer's non-interest-bearing note (due January 2, 1978) deposited at the First National Bank for collection	950
	$11,600

(b) Marketable securities included:

Glendale Company Common (a subsidiary company), reported at cost	$16,155
Klein Company Preferred (treasury stock), reported at cost	12,100
9% Hamilton Company Bonds (interest payable January 1 and July 1), $4,000 face value, purchased September 1, 1977, as a temporary investment, reported at cost plus accrued interest to date of purchase.............	4,320
	$32,575

(c) Notes receivable included:

Customers' notes (due in 1978)..	$ 8,750
Glendale Company note (due March 1, 1978)...	6,000
Note receivable from sale of equipment (due July 1, 1979)	6,150
Notes receivable discounted (customers' notes)...	(4,000)
	$16,900

(d) Accounts receivable included:

Creditor's accounts with debit balances..	$ 1,000
Customers' accounts (regular)...	37,770
Dividends receivable on investments...	500
Deposit on equipment (ordered for delivery in December, 1979).................	1,000
Installment accounts receivable ($17,800 due in 1978; $9,200 due in 1979).	27,000
Interest receivable on bond investment..	120
Interest receivable on notes..	270
Receivables from consignees (representing the merchandise at cost transferred to consignees and still unsold on December 31, 1977)	2,100
Refundable income taxes of prior periods (believed to be collectible in 1978)..	1,250
Travel advances to employees..	975
Subscriptions receivable on capital stock (due in 1979)...............................	4,500
Allowance for doubtful accounts (on regular and installment accounts)	(2,000)
	$74,485

(e) Merchandise inventory (representing a physical count of goods on hand), at cost.. $82,300

Instructions: Revise the "Current assets" section of the balance sheet presenting individual items appropriately included therein in a proper manner. Prepare schedules stating what disposition was made of those items excluded in the revised presentation.

6-11. The Eastern Gas Company follows the practice of cycle billing in order to minimize peak work loads for its clerical employees. All customers are billed monthly on various dates, except in those cases when the meter readers are unable to enter the premises to obtain a reading.

The company presents the following information for the year ended September 30, 1977.

		Customers Billed		Customers
Cycle	Billing Period	Number	Amount	Not Billed
1	Aug. 7–Sept. 5 (inclusive)..............................	2760	$13,800.00	324
2	Aug. 12–Sept. 10 (inclusive)..............................	3426	13,704.00	411
3	Aug. 17–Sept. 15 (inclusive)..............................	3265	14,692.50	335
4	Aug. 22–Sept. 20 (inclusive)..............................	2630	12,492.50	370
5	Aug. 27–Sept. 25 (inclusive)..............................	3132	13,311.00	468

You are further advised that all customers have been billed for prior periods and that the company's experience shows that charges for those customers whose meters were not read average the same amount as the charges for the customers billed in their cycle. In addition, the company assumes that the customers' usage will be uniform from month to month.

Instructions: Compute the unbilled revenues of the company as of September 30, 1977, arising from cycles No. 1 and No. 3. (*Do not* compute revenues from cycles 2, 4 and 5.) (AICPA adapted)

6-12. The Comity Loan Company is engaged in the consumer finance business. Prior to 1977 the company followed the direct write-off method of recording uncollectible loans. The company also provided a reserve for uncollectible loans by an appropriation of retained earnings.

During 1977 the Comity Loan Company decided to change to the allowance method of recognizing losses due to uncollectible loans. Permission was received to use this method for income tax purposes. The books, however, were continued on the direct write-off method for the full year of 1977. An analysis of the company's loss experience showed that 4% of the loans receivable at the end of each year prove uncollectible and are written off in the following year.

The following are condensed trial balances:

The Comity Loan Company
Trial Balances
December 31, 1977 and 1976

	December 31, 1977		December 31, 1976 (Post-closing)	
Cash	49,300		86,500	
Loans receivable	712,500		687,500	
Other assets	27,000		25,000	
Liabilities other than income tax		520,700		543,500
Income tax payable		21,300		20,000
Capital stock		100,000		100,000
Retained earnings		108,000		108,000
Reserve for uncollectible loans		27,500		27,500
Dividends paid	10,000			
Interest revenue		165,000		
Operating expenses	49,500			
Uncollectible loans written off	13,400			
Interest expense	59,500			
Income tax	21,300			
	942,500	942,500	799,000	799,000

Instructions: (Assume that the current income tax rate is 45%).
   (1) Prepare the formal journal entries at December 31, 1977, to record the change in accounting method for 1977.
   (2) Prepare an income and retained earnings statement for the year ended December 31, 1977. (AICPA adapted)

6-13. Hoffman Factors, Inc., was incorporated December 31, 1976. The capital stock of the company consists of 100,000 shares of $10 par value each, all of which were paid in at par. The company was organized for the purpose of factoring the accounts receivable of various businesses requiring this service.

Hoffman Factors, Inc., charges a commission to its clients of 2% of all receivables factored and assumes all credit risks. Besides the commission, an additional 10% of gross receivables is withheld on all purchases and is credited to Client Retainer. This retainer is used for merchandise returns, etc., made by customers of the clients for which a credit memo would be due. Payments are made to the clients by Hoffman Factors, Inc., at the end of each month to adjust the retainer so that it equals 10% of the unpaid receivables at the month's end.

Based on the collection experience of other factoring companies in this area, officials of Hoffman Factors, Inc., have decided to make monthly provisions to Allowance for Doubtful Accounts based on ¼% of all receivables purchased during the month.

The company also decided to recognize commission revenue on only the factored receivables which have been collected; however, for bookkeeping simplicity all commissions are originally credited to Commission Revenue and an adjustment is made to Unearned Commissions at the end of each quarter based on 2% of receivables then outstanding.

Operations of the company during the first quarter of 1977 resulted in the following:
Accounts receivable factored:

January	$200,000
February	400,000
March	300,000

Collections on the above receivables totaled $700,000.

General and administrative expenses paid during the period:

Salaries	$5,000
Office rent	900
Advertising	500
Equipment rent	1,600
Miscellaneous	1,000

On February 1, 1977, a three-month 10% bank loan was obtained for $500,000 with interest payable at maturity.

For the first three months of the year, the company rented all of its office furniture and equipment; however, on March 31, 1977, it purchased various equipment at a cost of $5,000, the liability for which had not been recorded as of March 31.

Instructions:

(1) Give all entries necessary to record the above transactions and to close the books as of March 31, 1977. (Disregard all taxes.)

(2) Prepare a balance sheet and an income statement as of March 31, 1977. (AICPA adapted)

7

Inventories —
Cost Procedures

The term *inventories* is a designation for goods held for sale in the normal course of business, as well as for goods in production or to be placed in production. Practically all tangible items fall into this classification at one time or another. Gasoline, oil, and automotive supplies are included in the inventory of a service station; crops and livestock are included in the inventory of a farmer; machinery and equipment are included in the inventory of a manufacturer producing such items for sale. The sale of inventories normally provides a business with its chief source of revenue.

Inventories represent one of the most active elements in business operations, being continuously acquired, converted, and resold. A large part of a company's resources is frequently invested in goods purchased or manufactured. The cost of goods must be recorded, grouped, and summarized during the period. At the end of the period, costs must be allocated to current activities and to future activities. This allocation normally occupies a central role in the measurement of periodic operating results as well as in the determination of financial position. Failure to allocate costs properly can result in serious distortions of financial progress and position.

Accounting for inventory costs presents a number of theoretical and practical problems. Members of the accounting profession have directed much thought to these problems in recent years. This and the next two chapters consider these problems.

CLASSES OF INVENTORIES

The term *merchandise inventory* is generally applied to goods held by a merchandising concern, either wholesale or retail, when such goods have been acquired in a condition for resale. The terms *raw materials, goods in process,* and *finished goods* refer to the inventories of a manufacturing concern. The latter items require description.

Raw Materials

Raw materials are those tangible goods acquired for use in the productive process. Raw materials may be obtained directly from natural sources. Ordinarily, however, raw materials are acquired from other companies and represent the finished products of the companies from which they were purchased. For example, newsprint is the finished product of the paper mill but represents raw material to the printer who acquires it.

Although the term raw materials can be used broadly to cover all of the materials used in manufacturing, this designation is frequently restricted to materials that will be physically incorporated in the products being manufactured. The term *factory supplies*, or *manufacturing supplies*, is then used to refer to auxiliary materials, that is, materials that although necessary in the productive process are not directly incorporated in the products. Oils, fuels, cleaning supplies, etc., fall into this grouping since these items are not incorporated in a product but simply facilitate production as a whole; paint, nails, bolts, etc., although physically embodied in the final product, are normally of such minor significance as to warrant inclusion within the auxiliary grouping. Raw materials directly associated with the production of certain goods are frequently referred to as *direct materials*; factory supplies are referred to as *indirect materials*.

Although factory supplies may be summarized separately, they should be reported as a part of a company's inventories since they will ultimately be applied to the productive process. Factory supplies should be distinguished from other supplies that make contributions to the delivery, sales, and general administrative functions of the enterprise. Such other supplies should not be reported as part of the inventories but as prepaid expenses.

Goods in Process

Goods in process, alternately referred to as *work in process*, consists of materials partly processed and requiring further work before they can be sold. This inventory is considered to be made up of three cost elements: (1) *direct materials*, (2) *direct labor*, and (3) *manufacturing overhead* or *burden*. The cost of materials that can be directly identified with the goods in production is included under (1). The cost of labor that can be directly identified with goods in production is included under (2). The portion of manufacturing overhead assignable to goods still in production forms the third element of cost.

Manufacturing overhead consists of all manufacturing costs other than direct materials and direct labor. It includes factory supplies and labor not directly identified with the production of specific products. It also includes general manufacturing costs such as depreciation, maintenance, repairs, property taxes, insurance, and light, heat, and power, as well as a reasonable share of the managerial costs other than those relating solely to the selling and administrative functions of the business. Overhead may be designated as *fixed*, *variable*, or *semivariable*. Overhead charges that remain constant in amount regardless of the volume of production are referred to as fixed. Depreciation, insurance, rent, and property taxes normally fall into this category. Charges that fluctuate in proportion to the volume of production are called variable. Indirect materials, indirect labor, and repairs vary with production. Some charges vary, but the variations are not in direct proportion to the volume. These charges have both fixed and variable components and are designated as semivariable items. Factory supervision is an example of a semivariable item when it is fixed within a certain range of production but changes when production is not within this range.

Finished Goods   *Finished goods* are the manufactured products awaiting sale. The cost of the finished product consists of the direct materials, direct labor, and manufacturing overhead costs assigned to it. Finished parts purchased and used in the production of the finished product are normally classified as raw materials; finished parts held for purposes of sale may be reported as finished goods.

INVENTORIES IN THE MEASUREMENT OF INCOME

When goods purchased or manufactured are sold within a fiscal period, the determination of the gross profit on sales is a simple matter. The total cost of goods purchased or manufactured is also the cost of goods sold properly chargeable to revenue. Such a situation, however, is seldom found in practice. Normally a part of the goods acquired remains on hand at the end of the period. A value must be assigned to these goods. This value is subtracted from the total merchandise acquisition costs and is carried into the subsequent period to be charged against future revenue. Adequate records are required in providing cost data for statement purposes. These records are also required for the proper internal control of goods on hand.

Two classes of questions arise in the determination of the inventory to be reported on the statements: (1) What items are properly included in the inventory? and (2) What values are to be assigned to such items?

INVENTORY SYSTEMS

Quantities of inventories on hand are ascertained either through a *periodic system* requiring *physical inventories* at the end of each period, or a *perpetual system* requiring *perpetual* or *book inventories*.

The periodic system requires counting, measuring, or weighing goods at the end of the period to determine the quantities on hand. Values are then assigned to such quantities to determine the portion of the recorded costs to be carried forward.

The perpetual inventory system requires the maintenance of records that offer a continuous summary of inventory items on hand. Individual accounts are kept for each class of goods. Inventory increases and decreases are recorded in the individual accounts, the resulting balances representing the amounts on hand. In a manufacturing organization, a perpetual system applied to inventories requires recording the full movement of goods through individual accounts for raw materials, goods in process, and finished goods. Perpetual records may be kept in terms of quantities only or in terms of both quantities and costs.

When the perpetual system is employed, physical counts of the units on hand should be made at least once a year to confirm the balances found on the books. The frequency of physical inventories will vary depending upon the nature of the goods, their rate of turnover, and the degree of internal control. A plan for continuous counting of inventory items on a rotation basis is frequently employed. Variations between the book record and the amounts actually on hand resulting from errors in recording, shrinkage, breakage, theft, and other causes should be recognized, and the book inventories should be brought into agreement with the physical count with offsetting debits and credits to an inventory adjustment account. The explanation for the discrepancy will determine whether the inventory adjustment balance should be regarded as an adjustment to cost of goods sold or as an operating expense. Normal adjustments for shrinkage and breakage are recorded as adjustments to cost of goods sold. Abnormal shortages or thefts may be reported separately as operating expenses.

Practically all large trading and manufacturing enterprises, as well as many relatively small organizations, have adopted the perpetual inventory system as an integral part of their record keeping and internal control. This sytem offers a continuous check and control over inventories as well as immediate data concerning inventory position. Purchasing and production planning are facilitated, adequate supplies on hand are assured, and losses incurred through damage and theft are fully disclosed. The additional costs of maintaining such a system are usually well repaid by the benefits provided to management through its adoption.

ITEMS TO BE INCLUDED IN INVENTORY

As a general rule, goods should be included in the inventory of the party holding title. The passing of title is a legal term designating the point at which ownership changes. There are instances where the legal rule may be waived for practical reasons or because of certain limitations found in its application. When the circumstances are such that the rule of passing of title does not need to be observed, there should be appropriate disclosure on the statements of the special practice followed and the factors supporting such practice. Application of the legal test under a number of special circumstances is described in the following paragraphs.

Goods in Transit   When terms of sale are *FOB (free on board) shipping point*, title passes to the buyer with the loading of goods at the point of shipment. Application of the legal rule to a year-end shipment calls for recognition of a sale and an accompanying decrease in goods on hand on the books of the seller. On the other hand, the buyer should recognize such *goods in transit* as a purchase and an accompanying inventory increase even though there is no physical possession. A determination of the goods in transit at year-end is made by a review of the incoming orders during the early part of the new period. The purchase records may be kept open beyond the fiscal period to permit the recognition of goods in transit as of the end of the period, or goods in transit may be recorded by means of an adjusting entry. Although no objection to the application of the legal rule can be raised by a seller, the buyer, in the interests of expediency, may prefer to ignore such a rule and employ receipt as a basis for the recognition of a purchase and the related inventory increase. The latter approach is not objectionable when amounts in transit are not material and the inclusion of such items before their receipt and acceptance offers practical difficulties.

When terms of a sale are *FOB destination*, application of the legal test calls for no recognition of the transaction until goods are received by the buyer. In this case, it is the seller who may prefer to ignore the legal rule and employ shipment as a basis for booking a sale and the accompanying inventory decrease. In view of the difficulties involved in ascertaining whether goods have reached their destination at year-end, application of a shipment rule is not objectionable under normal circumstances.

Segregated Goods

When goods are prepared on special order and segregated for shipment, title may pass with such segregation. When goods are segregated at the end of the period and title has passed, the seller may properly recognize a sale and exclude *segregated goods* from the inventory, while the buyer may properly recognize both a purchase and an inventory increase. Frequently, one encounters practical problems in arriving at the portion of the inventory segregated as well as perplexing legal problems in defining their precise status. These difficulties normally result in the adoption of a policy whereby entries for both sale and purchase await formal shipment of goods by the seller.

Goods on Consignment

Goods are frequently transferred to dealers on a consignment basis, the consignor retaining title to the goods until their sale by the consignee. Until the goods are sold and cash or a receivable can be recognized, the goods should continue to be reported as a part of the inventory of the consignor. *Consigned goods* are properly reported at the sum of their cost and the handling and shipping costs involved in their transfer to the consignee. The goods may be separately designated on the balance sheet as merchandise on consignment. The consignee does not own the consigned goods; hence neither consigned goods nor obligations for such goods are reported on the consignee's financial statements. Other merchandise owned by a business but in the possession of others, such as goods in the hands of salespersons and agents, goods held by customers on approval, and goods held by others for storage, processing, or shipment, should also be shown as a part of the owner's ending inventory.

**Conditional
and
Installment
Sales**

Conditional sales and installment sales contracts may provide for a retention of title by the seller until the sales price is fully recovered. Under these circumstances, the seller, who retains title, may continue to show the goods, reduced by the buyer's equity in such goods as established by collections; the buyer, in turn, can report an equity in the goods accruing through payments made. However, in the usual case when the possibilities of returns and defaults are negligible, the test of passing of title should be relinquished and the transaction recorded in terms of the expected outcome: the seller, anticipating completion of the contract and the ultimate passing of title, recognizes the transaction as a regular sale involving deferred collections; the buyer, intending to comply with the contract and acquire title, recognizes the transaction as a regular purchase.

INVENTORY VALUATION

In viewing the inventory in its dual position as (1) a value reported on the income statement representing charges properly applicable to current revenue and (2) a value reported on the balance sheet representing the charges properly assignable to future revenues, the profession has accepted cost as the primary basis for inventory valuation. A marked change in the value of the inventory between the purchase date and the date of inventory raises the question as to whether some recognition should be given to current inventory replacement values. With a rise in prices, accountants generally answer this question in the negative, insisting that income must await sale of the goods; with a decline in prices, however, there is wide support for recognizing such decline by applying the "cost or market, whichever is lower" valuation procedure. In a few special instances full departure from cost and the use of a sales price or a modified sales price basis is considered acceptable.

Income measurement rather than balance sheet valuation is generally regarded as the major criterion in accounting for inventories. The American Institute of Certified Public Accountants has taken this position. The AICPA supports reporting inventories at cost, but recommends modifications in cost under certain circumstances.

> In accounting for the goods in the inventory at any point of time, the major objective is the matching of appropriate costs against revenues in order that there may be a proper determination of the realized income. Thus, the inventory at any given date is the balance of costs applicable to goods on hand remaining after the matching of absorbed costs with concurrent revenues. This balance is appropriately carried to future periods provided it does not exceed an amount properly chargeable against the revenues expected to be obtained from ultimate disposition of the goods carried forward.[1]

In contrast, the American Accounting Association's Special Committee on Inventories recognized market value for inventories as being very

---

[1]*Accounting Research and Terminology Bulletins — Final Edition*, "No. 43, Restatement and Revision of Accounting Research Bulletins" (New York: American Institute of Certified Public Accountants, 1961), Ch. 4, par. 4.

important, and recommended preparing multi-column statements reporting both cost and market valuations. This view was also supported in the AAA's *A Statement of Basic Accounting Theory*.[1]

INVENTORY COST METHODS

The principal inventory valuation methods and their special applicabilities will be considered in detail. Attention is directed in this chapter to the measurement of cost when cost is required for inventory valuation as well as when cost is to be used as the first step in the development of a lower of cost or market value.

Determination of Cost

The determination of the cost of inventory may not be a simple matter. First, it involves determining the expenditures for the cost of the goods that were acquired. Second, it involves applying a method for relating the different costs of the goods acquired to periodic revenue.

Inventory cost consists of all expenditures, both direct and indirect, relating to inventory acquisition, preparation, and placement for sale. In the case of raw materials or goods acquired for resale, cost includes, in addition to the purchase price, buying, freight, receiving, storage, and all other expenditures incurred to the time goods are ready for sale. Certain expenditures can be traced to specific acquisitions or can be allocated to inventory items in some equitable manner. Other expenditures may be relatively small and difficult to allocate. Such items are normally excluded in the calculation of inventory cost and are thus charged in full against current revenue as *period costs*.

The charges to be included in the cost of manufactured products have already been mentioned. Proper accounting for materials, labor, and manufacturing overhead items and their identification with goods in process and finished goods inventories may be best achieved through adoption of a cost accounting system designed to meet the needs of a particular business unit. Certain costs relating to the acquisition or the manufacture of goods may be considered abnormal and may be excluded in arriving at inventory cost. For example, costs arising from idle capacity, excessive spoilage, and reprocessing are normally considered abnormal items chargeable to current revenue. Only those portions of general and administrative costs that are clearly related to procurement or production should be included in inventory cost.

In practice, companies take different positions in classifying inventoriable costs. For example, costs of the purchasing department, costs of accounting for manufacturing activities, and costs of pensions for production personnel may be found either as part of the inventoriable costs or as direct deductions from revenue.

---

[1]*A Statement of Basic Accounting Theory* (Evanston, Illinois: American Accounting Association, 1966), p. 11.

Discounts as Reductions in Cost

Discounts treated as a reduction of cost in recording the acquisition of goods should similarly be treated as a reduction in the cost assigned to the inventory. *Trade discounts* are discounts converting a printed price list to the prices actually charged to a buyer. Frequently, trade discounts are stated in a series, e.g., 30/20/10 or 30%, then 20%, then 10%. Each discount is taken on the net invoice cost after taking the earlier discounts. [1]

Cost, then, is list price less the trade discount; purchases and inventory should be reported at such cost with no accounting recognition given to the discount. *Cash discounts* are reductions in prices allowed only upon payment of invoices within a limited period. Inventory treatment depends upon whether cash discounts are regarded as a reduction in cost or as a source of revenue. If cash discounts are treated as subtraction from purchases, the more common practice, the inventory balance should be correspondingly reduced; if cash discounts are reported as other revenue, inventories should be at invoice cost without reference to the discounts taken.

Treatment of purchase discounts as a subtraction from purchases recognizes the discounts as an adjustment in the purchase price. When settlement is not made within the discount period, a failure on the part of financial management is indicated either through carelessness in considering payment alternatives or through financial inability to avoid the extra charge. The inefficiency of management can be disclosed by recording purchases net and recognizing any amounts paid in excess of these amounts as Purchase Discounts Lost, a financial management expense item. When such a practice is to be followed, two methods may be employed: (1) accounts payable may be reported at the invoice price net or (2) accounts payable may be reported at the gross invoice price with a payable offset balance or liability valuation account reporting the purchase discounts available. The two methods are illustrated at the top of page 188.

Although recording purchases net and recognizing cash discounts lost as an expense has obvious merit, it has failed to gain wide adoption. Chief objection is made on practical grounds. Use of this method requires converting gross amounts into net amounts relating to individual acquisitions and using converted values throughout the accounting for inventories. This is normally less convenient than accounting in terms of gross invoice charges.

---

[1] An equivalent composite discount rate may be computed as follows:

(1) Discount Rate	(2) Percentage of Original Invoice Cost	(3) Composite Discount Rate (1) × (2)
30%	100%	30.0%
20%	70% (100% − 30%)	14.0
10%	56% (100% − 44%)	5.6
		49.6%

TRANSACTION	ACCOUNTS PAYABLE REPORTED NET		ACCOUNTS PAYABLE REPORTED GROSS	

Purchase of merchandise priced at $2,500 less trade discount of 30%/20% and a cash discount of 2%:
$2,500 less 30% = $1,750
$1,750 less 20% = $1,400
$1,400 less 2% = $1,372
	Purchases (or
	Inventory) 1,372
	    Accounts Payable ...
		1,372	Purchases (or
			Inventory) 1,372
			Allowance for
			Purchase Discounts ... 28
			    Accounts Payable ...
				1,400

(a) Assuming payment of the invoice within discount period.	Accounts Payable 1,372
	    Cash ....
		1,372	Accounts Payable 1,400
			    Allowance for
			    Purchase Discounts
			    Cash ....
				28
				1,372

(b) Assuming payment of the invoice after discount period.	Accounts Payable 1,372
	Purchase Discounts
	Lost 28
	    Cash ....
		1,400	Accounts Payable 1,400
			    Cash ....
			Purchase Discounts
			Lost 28
			    Allowance for
			    Purchase Discounts
				1,400
				28

(c) Required adjustment at the end of the period assuming that the invoice was not paid and the discount period has lapsed.	Purchase Discounts
	Lost 28
	    Accounts Payable ...
		28	Purchase Discounts
			Lost 28
			    Allowance for
			    Purchase Discounts
				28

Specific Identification of Costs with Inventory Items

Revenue may be charged for goods sold on the basis of identified costs of the specific items sold. Such practice calls for the identification of a cost with each item acquired. When perpetual inventories are maintained, the sale of goods requires the transfer of articles and their identified costs to the cost of goods sold. When a system of physical inventories is maintained, goods on hand require identification with specific invoices. In each instance, costs related to units sold are reported as cost of goods sold and costs identified with goods on hand remain to be reported as the ending inventory.

Although such identification procedure may be considered a highly satisfactory approach in matching costs with revenues because of its objectivity and adherence to empirical fact,[1] the practice may be difficult or impossible to apply or may be considered inadequate because of special existing conditions. When an inventory is composed of a great many items, some being similar items acquired at different times and at different prices, cost identification procedures may prove to be slow, burdensome, and costly. When identical items have been acquired at different times, their identities may be lost and cost identification thus denied. Furthermore, when units are identical and interchangeable, this method opens the doors to possible profit manipulation through the choice of particular units for delivery. Finally marked changes in costs

---

[1]This point is stressed in Accounting Research Study No. 13 as follows: "There appears to be little theoretical argument against the use of specific identification of cost with units of product if that method of determining inventory costs is practicable." Horace G. Barden, *The Accounting Basis of Inventories*, Accounting Research Study No. 13 (New York: American Institute of Certified Public Accountants, 1973), p. 82.

during a period may warrant charges to revenue on a basis other than past identifiable costs.

TRADITIONAL COST FLOW METHODS

When specific identification procedures are considered inappropriate, it is necessary to adopt some assumption with respect to the flow of costs associated with the movement of goods. Three methods, each with a different assumption as to an orderly flow of costs, have achieved widest application. These are: (1) *first-in, first-out*, (2) *weighted average*, and (3) *last-in, first-out*.

First-In, First-Out Method

The first-in, first-out method (*fifo* method) is based on the assumption that costs should be charged to revenue in the order in which incurred. Inventories are thus stated in terms of most recent costs. To illustrate the application of this method, assume the following data:

Jan.	1	Inventory	200 units at $10	$ 2,000
	12	Purchase	400 units at 12	4,800
	26	Purchase	300 units at 11	3,300
	30	Purchase	100 units at 12	1,200
		Total	1,000	$11,300

A physical inventory on January 31 shows 300 units on hand. The inventory would be considered to be composed of the most recent costs as follows:

Most recent purchase, Jan. 30	100 units at $12	$1,200
Next most recent purchase, Jan. 26	200 units at 11	2,200
Total	300	$3,400

If the ending inventory is recorded at $3,400, cost of goods sold is $7,900 ($11,300 − $3,400), and revenue is charged with the earliest costs.

When perpetual inventory accounts are maintained, a form similar to that illustrated at the top of page 190 is used to record the cost of units issued and the cost relating to the goods on hand. The columns show the quantities and values relating to goods acquired, goods issued, and balances on hand. It should be observed that identical values for physical and perpetual inventories are obtained when fifo is applied.

Fifo can be supported as a logical and realistic approach to the flow of costs when it is impractical or impossible to achieve specific cost identification. Fifo assumes a cost flow closely paralleling the actual physical flow of goods sold. Revenue is charged with costs considered applicable to those goods involved in the realization of revenue; ending inventories are reported in terms of most recent costs — costs fairly presenting the latest acquisitions and costs equitably assigned to revenues of the subsequent period. Fifo affords little opportunity for profit manipulation; assignment of costs against revenue is determined by the order in which costs are incurred.

COMMODITY: X (fifo)

DATE	RECEIVED			ISSUED			BALANCE		
	QUANTITY	UNIT COST	TOTAL COST	QUANTITY	UNIT COST	TOTAL COST	QUANTITY	UNIT COST	TOTAL COST
Jan. 1							200	$10	$2,000
12	400	$12	$4,800				200 400	10 12	2,000 4,800
16				200 300	$10 12	$2,000 3,600	100	12	1,200
26	300	11	3,300				100 300	12 11	1,200 3,300
29				100 100	12 11	1,200 1,100	200	11	2,200
30	100	12	1,200				200 100	11 12	2,200 1,200

Weighted Average Method   The weighted average method is based on the assumption that goods sold should be charged at an average cost, such average being influenced by the number of units acquired at each price. Inventories are stated at the same weighted average cost. Assuming the cost data in the preceding section, the weighted average cost of a physical inventory of 300 units on January 31 would be as follows:

Jan.	1	Inventory	200 units at $10	$ 2,000
	12	Purchase	400 units at 12	4,800
	26	Purchase	300 units at 11	3,300
	30	Purchase	100 units at 12	1,200
		Total	1,000	$11,300

Weighted average cost ....$11,300 ÷ 1,000 = $11.30.
Ending inventory...300 units at $11.30 = $3,390.

If the ending inventory is recorded at a cost of $3,390, cost of goods sold is $7,910 ($11,300 − $3,390), and revenue is charged with a weighted average cost. Calculations above were made for costs of one month. Similar calculations could be developed in terms of data for a quarter or for a year.

When perpetual inventories are maintained but the costs of units issued are not recorded until the end of a period, a weighted average cost for the period may be calculated at that time and the accounts may be credited for the cost of total units issued. Frequently, however, costs relating to issues are recorded currently, and it is necessary to calculate costs on the basis of the weighted average on the date of issue. This requires calculating a new weighted average cost immediately after the receipt of each additional lot of merchandise. This method, involving successive average recalculations, is referred to as a *moving average method*. The use of this method is illustrated at the top of the next page.

On January 12 the new unit cost of $11.33 was found by dividing $6,800, the total cost, by 600, the number of units on hand. Then on

COMMODITY: X (moving average)

DATE	RECEIVED			ISSUED			BALANCE		
	QUANTITY	UNIT COST	TOTAL COST	QUANTITY	UNIT COST	TOTAL COST	QUANTITY	UNIT COST	TOTAL COST
Jan. 1							200	$10.00	$2,000
12	400	$12	$4,800				600	11.33	6,800
16				500	$11.33	$5,665	100	11.35	1,135
26	300	11	3,300				400	11.09	4,435
29				200	11.09	2,218	200	11.09	2,217
30	100	12	1,200				300	11.39	3,417

January 16, the dollar balance, $1,135, represented the previous balance, $6,800, less $5,665, the cost assigned to the 500 units issued on this date. New unit costs were calculated on January 26 and 30 when additional units were acquired.

With successive recalculations of cost and the use of such different costs during the period, the cost identified with the ending inventory will differ from that determined when cost is assigned to the ending inventory in terms of average cost for all goods available during the period. A physical inventory and use of the weighted average method resulted in a value for the ending inventory of $3,390; a perpetual inventory and use of the moving average method resulted in a value for the ending inventory of $3,417.

The average cost approach can be supported as realistic and as paralleling the physical flow of goods, particularly where there is an intermingling of identical inventory units. Unlike the other inventory methods, the average approach provides the same cost for similar items of equal utility. The method does not permit profit manipulation. Limitations of the average method are inventory values that perpetually contain some degree of influence of earliest costs and inventory values that may lag significantly behind current prices in periods of rapidly rising or falling prices.

Last-In, First-Out Method   The last-in, first-out method (*lifo* method) is based on the assumption that the latest costs of a specific good be charged to cost of goods sold (*specific goods method*). Inventories are thus stated at earliest costs. Assuming the cost data in the preceding section, a physical inventory of 300 units on January 31 would have a cost as follows:

Earliest costs relating to goods, Jan. 1 ....200 units at $10 ....$2,000
Next earliest cost, Jan. 12 ....100 units at 12 1,200
           Total ....300 ....$3,200

If the ending inventory is recorded at a cost of $3,200, then cost of goods sold is $8,100 ($11,300 − $3,200), and revenue is charged with the latest costs.

When perpetual inventories are maintained but the cost of units issued is not recorded until the end of the period, the most recent costs relating to the total units issued for the period may be determined and the inventory account credited for this cost. Cost, then, is the same as reported on the preceding page. If costs relating to issues are recorded currently, it is necessary to calculate costs on a last-in, first-out basis using the cost data on the date of issue. This is illustrated below.

COMMODITY: X (lifo)

DATE	RECEIVED			ISSUED			BALANCE		
	QUANTITY	UNIT COST	TOTAL COST	QUANTITY	UNIT COST	TOTAL COST	QUANTITY	UNIT COST	TOTAL COST
Jan. 1							200	$10	$2,000
12	400	$12	$4,800				200 400	10 12	2,000 4,800
16				400 100	$12 10	$4,800 1,000	100	10	1,000
26	300	11	3,300				100 300	10 11	1,000 3,300
29				200	11	2,200	100 100	10 11	1,000 1,100
30	100	12	1,200				100 100 100	10 11 12	1,000 1,100 1,200

It should be noted that in applying lifo, physical and perpetual inventory values are not usually the same. In the example, a cost of $3,200 was obtained for the periodic inventory, whereas $3,300 was obtained when costs were calculated as goods were issued. This difference results because it was necessary to charge out 100 units of the beginning inventory at $10 in the issue of January 16. The ending inventory thus reflects only 100 units of the beginning inventory.

These temporary liquidations of inventory frequently do occur during the year, especially for companies with seasonal business. These liquidations cause monthly reports prepared on the lifo basis to be unrealistic and meaningless. Because of this, most companies using lifo maintain their internal records using other inventory methods, such as fifo or weighted average, and adjust the statements to lifo at the end of the year with a lifo allowance account.[1]

Specific-Goods Pools. With large and diversified inventories, application of the lifo procedures to specific goods has proved to be extremely burdensome. Because of the complexity and cost involved, companies frequently selected only a few very important inventory items, usually raw

---

[1]Companies frequently refer to this account as the *lifo reserve* account. Because the profession has recommended that the word reserve not be used for asset valuation accounts, the term allowance is used in this text.

materials, for application of the lifo method. As a means of simplifying the valuation process, and extending its applicability to more items, an adaptation of the specific goods method was developed permitting the establishment of inventory pools of substantially identical goods. Under this adaptation, the total quantity of items in the pool and the total costs of these units are determined. Average unit costs for goods within each pool are calculated, units being regarded as having been acquired at the same time. At the end of a period, units in each pool equal to the beginning number are assigned the beginning unit costs. As with all lifo applications, an increase in the number of units in an inventory pool during a period is regarded as an incremental layer, and such incremental layer is valued at current costs applied on the basis of (1) actual costs of earliest acquisitions within the period (lifo), (2) the average cost of acquisitions within the period, or (3) actual costs of the latest acquisitions within the period (fifo). Increments in subsequent periods form successive inventory layers. A decrease in the number of units in an inventory pool during a period is regarded as a reduction in the most recently added layer, then in successively lower layers, and finally in the original or base quantity. Once a specific layer is reduced or eliminated, it is not restored.

To illustrate the lifo valuation process, assume inventory pools and changes in pools as listed below. The inventory calculations that follow the listing are based on the assumption average costs are used in valuing annual incremental layers.

Inventory pool increments and liquidations:

	Class A Goods	Class B Goods	Class C Goods
Inv., Dec. 31, 1976	3,000 @ $6	3,000 @ $5	2,000 @ $10
Purchases — 1977	3,000 @ $7	2,000 @ $6	3,000 @ $11
	1,000 @ $9		
	7,000	5,000	5,000
Sales — 1977	3,000	1,000	3,500
Inv., Dec. 31, 1977	4,000	4,000	1,500
Purchases — 1978	1,000 @ $8	2,000 @ $6	3,000 @ $11
	3,000 @ $10		
	8,000	6,000	4,500
Sales — 1978	3,500	2,500	2,000
Inv., Dec. 31, 1978	4,500	3,500	2,500

Unit-lifo inventory valuations:

	Class A Goods		Class B Goods		Class C Goods	
Inv., Dec. 31, 1976	3,000 @ $6	$18,000	3,000 @ $5	$15,000	2,000 @ $10	$20,000
Inv., Dec. 31, 1977	3,000 @ $6	$18,000	3,000 @ $5	$15,000	1,500 @ $10	$15,000
	1,000 @ $7.50[1]	7,500	1,000 @ $6	6,000		
	4,000	$25,500	4,000	$21,000	1,500	$15,000
Inv., Dec. 31, 1978	3,000 @ $6	$18,000	3,000 @ $5	$15,000	1,500 @ $10	$15,000
	1,000 @ $7.50	7,500	500 @ $6	3,000	1,000 @ $11	11,000
	500 @ $9.50[2]	4,750				
	4,500	$30,250	3,500	$18,000	2,500	$26,000

---

[1]Cost of units acquired in 1977, $30,000, divided by number of units acquired, 4,000, or $7.50.
[2]Cost of units acquired in 1978, $38,000, divided by number of units acquired, 4,000, or $9.50.

The layer process for lifo inventories may be further illustrated in the following manner:

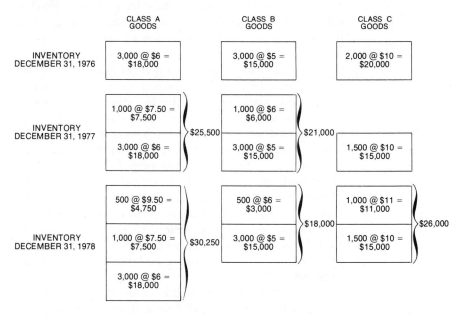

A new layer was added to the inventory of Class A goods each year. Previously established layers were reduced in 1978 for Class B goods and in 1977 for Class C goods.

Dollar-Value Pools. Even the grouping of substantially identical items into quantity pools does not produce all the benefits desired from the use of the lifo method. Technological changes sometimes introduce new products thus requiring the elimination of inventory in old pools, and requiring the establishment of new pools for the new product that no longer qualifies as being substantially identical. For example, the introduction of synthetic fabrics to replace cotton meant that "cotton" pools were eliminated and new "synthetic fabric" pools established. This change resulted in the loss of lower lifo bases by companies changing the type of fabrics they used. To overcome this type of problem and to further simplify the clerical work involved, the dollar-value method was developed. Under this method, the unit of measurement is the dollar rather than the quantity of goods. All similar items, such as all raw materials for a given line of business, are grouped into a pool and layers are determined based upon total dollar changes. The dollar value method is the most widely used adaptation of the lifo concept and is now acceptable for tax purposes. The procedures to apply this adaptation of lifo are discussed in Chapter 9.

Theoretical Arguments Concerning Lifo. The cost assignment resulting from the application of lifo cannot normally be considered in harmony with a movement of goods through the business. One would seldom encounter in practice priorities for the use or transfer of goods representing latest acquisitions. Sequences involved in the physical movement of goods are disregarded so that charges may be made to revenue in terms of most-current costs, that is, cost more nearly representative of the cost of replacing the inventory resulting from sales.[1]

However, it is argued that lifo offers a more accurate statement of earnings accruing to the ownership group than alternate methods. When fifo is used in a period of rising prices, for example, earnings reported are not fully available to owners but rather must be applied in part or in whole to higher-cost inventory replacement; in a period of falling prices, reported earnings fail to show the full resources accruing to owners from sales activities plus the amounts made available through lower cost inventory replacement. Lifo, on the other hand, by charging revenue with latest costs, avoids the recognition of "paper gain or loss" on an inventory that the company must continue to hold as long as it operates as a going concern. This aspect of the measurement process may be illustrated as follows:

	Inventory Cost	Sales Price	Latest Purchase Price	Fifo "Profit"	Lifo "Profit"	Dollars Available After Unit Replacement at Latest Purchase Price
With rising prices:	$10	$15	$12	$5	$3	$3
With falling prices:	$10	$12	$ 8	$2	$4	$4

Under lifo, that portion of sales proceeds that is required for the replacement of the inventory at higher costs receives recognition as net income only when it is freed through a subsequent replacement of inventories at lower costs.

Lifo is acceptable for income tax purposes; however, if it is used for tax purposes, the federal income tax provisions in the Internal Revenue Code require that it also be used for financial statement purposes. Its use for tax purposes in a period of rising prices serves to postpone taxes until earnings are reflected in a company's net monetary assets. It was for this reason that many companies changed the valuation method to lifo in the mid 1970's when prices rose sharply.[2] The savings in income tax were felt to be more important than reporting the larger profits resulting from using other inventory methods.

Although arguments for lifo as a means of achieving satisfactory income measurement are impressive, one must consider the deficiencies of this method as applied to the recognition of inventory position for balance sheet purposes. The lifo inventory consists of an assembly of congealed costs or cost layers dating back to original acquisitions — costs

---

[1] If the inventory turnover is slow, and if prices are rising or falling rapidly, current costs could differ significantly from lifo. Some accountants would go beyond lifo and charge revenue with the replacement cost of goods sold (next-in, first-out, or nifo) rather than with latest acquisition costs.

[2] In 1973, *Accounting Trends & Techniques* reported 150 of 600 companies used lifo. In 1974, the number increased to 303 of 600. *Accounting Trends & Techniques* (30th ed.; New York: American Institute of Certified Public Accountants, 1976), p. 89.

often differing materially from current prices. Such inventory costs enter into the determination of working capital and may seriously distort this measurement. Inventory position is also a determinant of total assets and capital. Adoption of lifo in a period of rising prices results in inventory understatement, a practice that is normally rationalized as acceptable on conservative grounds. Adoption of lifo in a period of falling prices results in inventory overstatement; here, it is fair to assume, there would be strong pressure for special action to write-down inventory balances to replacement cost.

In certain instances, the use of lifo may produce highly unrealistic operating results. Assume, for example, that special conditions make it necessary for a company to temporarily liquidate a significant part or an entire inventory carried at costs that are materially different from current costs. Under these circumstances, the lifo gross profit margin would not be the steady percentage offered by the recurring application of current costs to current revenues but instead a highly distorted figure resulting from the need to charge off original inventory costs. Two specific examples may clarify this weakness.

1. Many companies who rely upon steel as a basic raw material for their production processes use the lifo inventory method. Assume during an extended steel strike many manufacturing companies find their steel stock dwindling as their fiscal year-end approaches. Unless they can restock their inventories, they will be forced to use lower priced inventory costs to match against current revenue, thus creating a substantial current profit. Assume, for instance, that company sales for the year are $6,000,000 and that the cost of goods sold using current year prices is $5,000,000, but using a mixture of current year and earlier years lower priced lifo layers, the cost of goods sold is $4,000,000. The resulting increase in profit of $1,000,000 is effected only because of the inability of the company to replace its normal stocks.

2. The failure to protect lifo layers may be caused by a timing error in requesting shipments of purchases. Assume that a lumber company normally received its lumber by ship, but that at year-end orders were mishandled and a boat load was not received as planned. The company, in failing to record the boat load of lumber as a current year purchase, would have to apply older lifo costs against sales. The resulting profit could lead to conclusions that would not be justified by the facts.

To avoid the distortion caused by a temporary reduction of lifo layers at the end of a year, some accountants advocate establishing a replacement allowance that charges the current period for the extra replacement cost to be incurred in the subsequent period when the inventory is replenished. However, because the use of an allowance for temporary liquidation of lifo layers is in reality application of the base stock method, it is not permitted by the federal income tax regulations. The use of this type of allowance on the books could disqualify a company from filing its tax returns on the lifo basis, and therefore, it is seldom used in practice.

Lifo may also invite profit manipulation practices. For example, purchases, though required to maintain an inventory position, may be postponed at the end of the period so that costs of prior periods may be used in measuring net income. On the other hand, purchases may be made at the end of the period, though goods are not required, so that costs of the latest purchases may be used in arriving at net income.

Last-in, first-out has been widely adopted largely because of its ability to smooth the profit curve and its income tax advantages in a period of steadily rising prices. However, it is not the effects of a procedure but its merit as a means of sound measurement that should determine its acceptance for general accounting purposes. Depreciation and amortization charges, for example, could be recorded in accordance with the ability of revenue to absorb such charges in smoothing the profit curve. Such practices would not lead to measurements of what actually took place; instead, they would serve to obscure measurements and thus contradict the aim of accounting to report financial activities fairly.

It is interesting to note that the American Institute of Certified Public Accountants and the American Accounting Association differ in the criteria that each would consider in the choice of method for assigning costs. The AICPA views income measurement as the primary factor in making a choice. The Committee on Accounting Procedure has stated:

> Cost for inventory purposes may be determined under any one of several assumptions as to the flow of cost factors (such as first-in first-out, average, and last-in first-out), the major objective in selecting a method should be to choose the one which, under the circumstances, most clearly reflects periodic income.[1]

The American Accounting Association, however, has questioned the adoption of a cost flow assumption that is unrelated to the actual movement of goods.

> A flow assumption can be *realistic*, in that it reflects the dominant characteristics of the actual flow of goods; thus it may reflect the actual dominance of first-in, first-out (FIFO), average, or last-in, first-out (LIFO) movement. A flow assumption can be *artificial*, on the other hand, in that it premises a flow of costs that is clearly in contrast with actual physical movement.
>
> The LIFO flow assumption now has wide usage although in very few, if any, instances of its application can the assumption be justified on the ground that it corresponds even approximately with the actual flow of goods. *Artificial LIFO* has appeal to some during periods of markedly changing price levels as a means of approaching a matching of current cost (dollar costs adjusted to reflect changes in the general purchasing power of the monetary unit) with current revenues; however, grave doubt exists as to whether the accuracy of such artificial matching is sufficient to justify the resultant departure from realism. Present use of the method should be considered a transitory step which may ultimately be supplanted by better methods of accomplishing the intended result."[2]

---

[1] *Accounting Research and Terminology Bulletins — Final Edition*, "No. 43, Restatement and Revision of Accounting Research Bulletins" (New York: American Institute of Certified Public Accountants, 1961), Ch. 4, statement 4.

[2] *Accounting and Reporting Standards for Corporate Financial Statements and Preceding Statements and Supplements*, "Supplementary Statement No. 6, Inventory Pricing and Changes in Price Levels" (Madison, Wisconsin: American Accounting Association, 1957), pp. 36–37.

Effects of Traditional Cost Flow Procedures Compared

In using the first-in, first-out procedure, inventories are reported on the balance sheet at or near current costs. In using last-in, first-out, inventories not changing significantly in quantity are reported at more or less fixed amounts relating back to the earliest purchases. Use of the average method generally provides inventory values closely paralleling first-in, first-out values, since purchases during a period are normally several times the opening inventory balance and average costs are thus heavily influenced by current costs. When the prices paid for merchandise do not fluctuate significantly, alternative inventory methods may provide only minor differences on the financial statements. However, in periods of steadily rising or falling prices, the alternative methods may produce relatively material differences. Differences in inventory valuations on the balance sheet are accompanied by differences in earnings on the income statement for the period.

Use of first-in, first-out in a period of rising prices matches oldest low-cost inventory with rising sales prices, thus expanding the gross profit margin. In a period of declining prices, oldest high-cost inventory is matched with declining sales prices, thus narrowing the gross profit margin. On the other hand, use of last-in, first-out in a period of rising prices relates current high costs of acquiring goods with rising sales prices, and in a period of falling prices, low costs of acquiring goods with declining sales prices. Average methods that provide inventory costs closely comparable with first-in, first-out costs offer operating results approximating first-in, first-out results.

The application of the different methods in periods of rising and falling prices is illustrated in the following example. Assume that the Welch Sales Co. sells its goods at 50% in excess of prevailing costs from 1975 to 1978. The company sells its inventories and terminates activities at the end of 1978. Sales, costs, and gross profits using each of the three methods are shown in the tabulation below and at the top of the next page.

	FIFO			WEIGHTED AVERAGE[1]			LIFO		
1975:									
Sales, 500 units @ $9			$4,500			$4,500			$4,500
Inventory, 200 units	@ $5	$1,000		200 @ $5	$1,000		200 @ $5	$1,000	
Purchases, 500 units	@ $6	3,000		500 @ $6	3,000		500 @ $6	3,000	
		$4,000			$4,000			$4,000	
Ending Inv., 200 units	@ $6	1,200	2,800	200 @ $5.71 ($4,000 ÷ 700)	1,142	2,858	200 @ $5	1,000	3,000
Gross Profit on Sales			$1,700			$1,642			$1,500
1976:									
Sales, 450 units @ $12			$5,400			$5,400			$5,400
Inventory, 200 units	@ $6	$1,200		200 @ $5.71	$1,142		200 @ $5	$1,000	
Purchases, 500 units	@ $8	4,000		500 @ $8	4,000		500 @ $8	4,000	
		$5,200			$5,142			$5,000	
Ending Inv., 250 units	@ $8	2,000	3,200	250 @ $7.35 ($5,142 ÷ 700)	1,838	3,304	200 @ $5 ⎱ 50 @ $8 ⎰	1,400	3,600
Gross Profit on Sales			$2,200			$2,096			$1,800

[1]Totals in the illustration are calculated to the nearest dollar.

	FIFO		WEIGHTED AVERAGE		LIFO	
1977:						
Sales, 475 units @ $10.50		$4,988		$4,988		$4,988
Inventory, 250 units	@ $8 $2,000		250 @ $7.35 $1,838		200 @ $5 ⎱ $1,400	
					50 @ $8 ⎰	
Purchases, 450 units	@ $7 3,150		450 @ $7 3,150		450 @ $7 3,150	
	$5,150		$4,988		$4,550	
Ending Inv., 225 units	@ $7 1,575 3,575		225 @ $7.13 ($4,988 ÷ 700) 1,604 3,384		200 @ $5 ⎱ 1,200 3,350	
					25 @ $8 ⎰	
Gross Profit on Sales		$1,413		$1,604		$1,638
1978:						
Sales, 625 units @ $7.50		$4,688		$4,688		$4,688
Inventory, 225 units	@ $7 $1,575		225 @ $7.13 $1,604		200 @ $5 ⎱ $1,200	
					25 @ $8 ⎰	
Purchases, 400 units	@ $5 2,000 3,575		400 @ $5 2,000 3,604		400 @ $5 2,000 3,200	
Gross Profit on Sales		$1,113		$1,084		$1,488

Although the different methods give the same total gross profit on sales for the four-year period, use of first-in, first-out resulted in increased gross profit percentages in periods of rising prices and a contraction of gross profit percentages in a period of falling prices, while last-in, first-out resulted in relatively steady gross profit percentages in spite of fluctuating prices. The weighted average method offered results closely comparable to those obtained by first-in, first-out. Assuming operating expenses at 30% of sales, use of last-in, first-out would result in a net income for each of the four years; first-in, first-out would result in larger net incomes in 1975 and 1976, but net losses in 1977 and 1978. Inventory valuation on the last-in, first-out basis tends to smooth the peaks and fill the troughs of business fluctuations.

The foregoing transactions are summarized below:

Year	Sales	FIFO			WEIGHTED AVERAGE			LIFO		
		Cost of Goods Sold	Gross Profit on Sales	Gross Profit % to Sales	Cost of Goods Sold	Gross Profit on Sales	Gross Profit % to Sales	Cost of Goods Sold	Gross Profit on Sales	Gross Profit % to Sales
1975	$ 4,500	$ 2,800	$1,700	37.8%	$ 2,858	$1,642	36.5%	$ 3,000	$1,500	33.3%
1976	5,400	3,200	2,200	40.7	3,304	2,096	38.8	3,600	1,800	33.3
1977	4,988	3,575	1,413	28.3	3,384	1,604	32.2	3,350	1,638	32.8
1978	4,688	3,575	1,113	23.7	3,604	1,084	23.1	3,200	1,488	31.7
	$19,576	$13,150	$6,426	32.8%	$13,150	$6,426	32.8%	$13,150	$6,426	32.8%

OTHER COST PROCEDURES

The methods previously described for arriving at inventory cost are the ones most widely used. Several other procedures are sometimes encountered and deserve mention.

Cost of Latest Purchases

Sometimes goods are valued at cost of the latest purchase regardless of quantities on hand. When the inventory consists largely of recent purchases, this method may give results closely approximating those obtained through specific cost identification or first-in, first-out procedures with considerably less work. However, when the quantities of goods on hand are significantly in excess of the latest quantities purchased and major price changes have taken place, use of latest costs may result in significant cost misstatement.

Simple Average of Costs

Goods on hand are sometimes valued at a simple average of all of the costs for the period without regard to the number of units acquired on each purchase. With significant differences in quantities acquired, the disregard of the weight factor may result in unrepresentative costs.

Base Stock Method

This method assumes that a minimum stock is a normal and permanent requirement of the business; current purchases are means of satisfying current sales requirements, and hence their cost is properly applicable to revenues. The base stock inventory is regarded as fixed as to both quantity and price. The price is frequently the lowest cost experienced for the stock by the business unit. At the end of the period the amount of goods on hand is determined. The base stock quantity is valued at the lowest value experienced since the adoption of the method. An amount in excess of the base stock quantity is regarded as a temporary inventory increase and is valued at current costs, applied on a first-in, first-out, average, or other basis. A reduction in the base stock quantity is viewed as an amount temporarily "borrowed" to meet sales requirements, and this is charged to sales at current replacement value in view of the cost to be incurred in restoring the inventory deficiency.

To illustrate use of the base stock method, assume a base stock of 100,000 units at $1 per unit that has increased to a total of 120,000 units. If the current cost is $1.60 per unit, the inventory is valued as follows:

Base stock..................................	100,000 units @ $1.00..........................	$100,000
Add base stock quantity excess at current cost............	20,000 units @ $1.60...........................	32,000
Inventory value	120,000 units...	$132,000

Assume an inventory of only 90,000 units, and a current cost for units of $1.60. The inventory would be valued as follows:

Base stock..................................	100,000 units @ $1.00..........................	$100,000
Deduct base stock quantity deficiency at current cost......	10,000 units @ $1.60...........................	16,000
Inventory value	90,000 units...	$ 84,000

Instead of reporting $84,000, the inventory may be left at $100,000 by establishing an allowance for the deficiency with a credit balance of $16,000 offset by a debit to Cost of Goods Sold. Initial purchases in the next period of $16,000 would be applied against the allowance to cancel this balance.

As indicated previously, the base stock is regarded as a permanent asset; operations are charged with the costs of maintaining the normal stock. Results obtained through the base stock method are closely comparable with those obtained by the last-in, first-out method and the arguments for and against last-in, first-out can be applied here. Charges to revenue are costs currently experienced. The inventory, normally reported at the lowest value in the experience of the organization, may be seriously understated in terms of current prices. Use of the base stock method is not permitted for income tax purposes.

Standard Costs

Manufacturing inventories are frequently reported at *standard costs* — predetermined costs based upon representative or normal conditions of efficiency and volume of operations. Differences between actual costs and standard costs for materials, labor, and manufacturing overhead result in *standard cost variances* indicating favorable and unfavorable operational or cost experiences. Excessive materials usage, inefficient labor application, excessive spoilage, and idle time, for example, produce unfavorable variances, and these would be separately summarized in variance accounts.

Standard costs are developed from a variety of sources. Past manufacturing experiences may be carefully analyzed; time and motion studies, as well as job and process studies, may be undertaken; data from industry and economy-wide sources may be consulted. Standards should be reviewed at frequent intervals to determine whether they continue to offer reliable cost criteria. Changing conditions require adjustment in the standards, so that at the balance sheet date, standard costs will reasonably approximate costs computed under one of the recognized bases.

Direct Costing

A practice widely debated for many years is referred to as *direct costing, marginal costing,* or *variable costing.* Inventories under direct costing are assigned only the variable costs incurred in production — direct materials, direct labor, and the variable components of manufacturing overhead. Fixed costs are treated as periodic charges and assigned to current revenue. Only costs directly related to output are assigned to goods and charged to the period in which the goods are sold; costs that are a function of time and that are continuing regardless of the volume of output — for example, supervisory salaries, depreciation, and property tax — are charged against revenue of the period in which they are incurred.

These differences may be illustrated by the information given at the top of the next page.

With conventional *full costing* applied to inventories, a high gross profit may emerge in a period of high production even though sales are declining. With direct costing, cost of goods sold varies directly with sales and a high gross profit emerges in a period of high sales; changes in the volume of production have no effect upon gross profit. For example,

	Full Costing		Direct Costing	
Sales		$200,000		$200,000
Variable cost of goods sold	$110,000		$110,000	
Fixed cost of goods sold............	55,000		62,500	
Total cost of goods sold		165,000		172,500
Gross profit		$ 35,000		$ 27,500
Inventory value:				
Variable costs.........................		$ 15,000		$ 15,000
Fixed costs.............................		7,500		—
Total cost of inventory		$ 22,500		$ 15,000

assume in the illustration above that, although sales remained the same, production had been greater and as a result the ending inventory was double the amount shown. Variable costs identified with the inventory would amount to $30,000. Under full costing, a different allocation of fixed costs would be appropriate. Assuming that $12,500 in fixed costs is allocated to the inventory reducing the fixed costs assigned to operations by $5,000, the gross profit would increase to $40,000. Under direct costing, the gross profit would remain unchanged at $27,500.

Support for direct costing is made on the grounds that it provides more meaningful and useful data to management than full costing. Direct costing enables management to appraise the effects of sales fluctuations on net income. Sales, current and potential, can be evaluated in terms of out-of-pocket costs to achieve such sales. The direct costing approach becomes a valuable tool for planning and control and offers management highly useful approaches to cost, price, and volume relationships.

Although no objection can be raised to the use of direct costing when it is used for internal reporting and as a means for assisting management in decision-making, objection can be raised to the extension of direct costing procedures to the annual financial statements. In measuring financial position and the results of operations, inventories must carry their full costs including a satisfactory allocation of the fixed overhead costs. Fixed costs, no less than variable costs, are incurred in contemplation of future benefits and should be matched against the revenues ultimately produced through such efforts. When inventories are valued by direct costing procedures for internal reporting, they should be restated in terms of full costing whenever financial statements are to be prepared.

Cost Apportionment by Relative Sales Value Method

A special accounting problem arises when different commodities are purchased for a single sum. The apportionment of the cost to the units acquired must be made in some equitable manner. This cost apportionment should recognize the utility found in the different units. Ordinarily, the estimated sales value of the different units provides the best measure of respective utilities, and accordingly cost is allocated on the basis of such estimated sales value. This procedure is referred to as the *relative sales value method*. Costs derived through apportionment in terms of sales value are charged to revenue as units are sold.

To illustrate application of the relative sales value method, assume the purchase by a realty company of 60 acres of land for $220,000. The costs of grading, landscaping, streets, walks, water mains, lighting, and other improvements total $300,000. The property is divided into three groups of lots as follows: Class A, 100 lots to sell for $2,000 each; Class B, 200 lots to sell for $2,500 each; and Class C, 20 lots to sell for $5,000 each. The total cost of the inventory, $520,000, is apportioned to the lots on the basis of their relative sales values. The cost apportionment is made as follows:

Class A lots, 100 at $2,000	$200,000
Class B lots, 200 at $2,500	500,000
Class C lots, 20 at $5,000	100,000
Total sales value of Class A, B, and C lots	$800,000

	Total	No. of Lots	Cost Assigned to Each Lot
Cost apportioned to Class A lots:			
200,000/800,000 × $520,000	$130,000	100	$1,300
Cost apportioned to Class B lots:			
500,000/800,000 × $520,000	325,000	200	$1,625
Cost apportioned to Class C lots:			
100,000/800,000 × $520,000	65,000	20	$3,250
Total	$520,000		

The sale of a lot of any class results in a constant gross profit of 35% of sales.[1] Sale of a Class A lot would be recorded as follows:

Contracts Receivable	2,000	
Real Estate — Lot A-56		1,300
Gross Profit on Sale of Real Estate		700

Products that are manufactured simultaneously by a common process are referred to as *joint products*. When it is impractical or perhaps impossible to identify raw material and processing costs with the individual products produced, such costs may be assigned to the different products in a manner similar to that just illustrated. The sales value of each product is determined, and the total production cost is allocated according to the relative sales values of the respective products.

Products of relatively little value that are produced in the course of manufacturing the primary products are referred to as *by-products*. By-products are frequently valued at their sales prices or at sales prices less expenses of disposal, and costs identified with the primary products are reduced by the amounts assigned to the by-products. Total costs are thus identified with the entire output; earnings, however, emerge only upon the sale of the primary products.

---

[1]The same cost allocation can be developed by calculating the percentage of total cost to total estimated sales value, and applying such percentage to the sales price for the individual unit. In the example, cost is 65% of the total estimated sales value of the properties (520,000 ÷ 800,000). Each lot, then, is assigned a cost equal to 65% of its sales value: Class A lots have a cost of 65% of $2,000, or $1,300; Class B lots a cost of 65% of $2,500, or $1,625; Class C lots a cost of 65% of $5,000, or $3,250.

EFFECTS OF ERRORS IN RECORDING INVENTORY POSITION

Failures to report the inventory position accurately result in misstatements on both the balance sheet and the income statement. The effects of common inventory errors on the financial statements prepared at the end of the fiscal period are indicated in the summary that follows.

1. Overstatement of the ending inventory through errors in the count of goods on hand, pricing, or the inclusion in inventory of goods not owned or goods already sold:

   Current year:
   Income statement — overstatement of the ending inventory will cause the cost of goods sold to be understated and the net income to be overstated.
   Balance sheet — the inventory will be overstated and the owners' equity will be overstated.

   Succeeding year:
   Income statement — overstatement of the beginning inventory will cause the cost of goods sold to be overstated and the net income to be understated.
   Balance sheet — the error of the previous year will have been counterbalanced on the succeeding income statement and the balance sheet will be correctly stated.

2. Understatement of ending inventory through errors in the count of goods on hand, pricing, or the failure to include in inventory goods purchased or goods transferred but not yet sold:

   Misstatements indicated in (1) above are reversed.

3. Overstatement of ending inventory accompanied by failure to recognize sales and corresponding receivables at end of period:

   Current year:
   Income statement — sales are understated by the sales price of the goods and cost of goods sold is understated by the cost of the goods relating to the sales; gross profit and net income are thus understated by the gross profit on the sales.
   Balance sheet — receivables are understated by the sales price of the goods and the inventory is overstated by the cost of the goods that were sold; current assets and owners' equity are thus understated by the gross profit on the sales.

   Succeeding year:
   Income statement — sales of the preceding year are recognized in this year in sales and cost of sales; gross profit and net income, therefore, are overstated by the gross profit on such sales.
   Balance sheet — the error of the previous year is counterbalanced on the succeeding income statement and the balance sheet will be correctly stated.

4. Understatement of ending inventory accompanied by failure to recognize purchases and corresponding payables at end of period:

   Current year:
   Income statement — purchases are understated, but this is counterbalanced by the understatement of the ending inventory; gross profit and net income are correctly stated as a result of the counterbalancing effect of the error.
   Balance sheet — although owners' equity is reported correctly, both current assets and current liabilities are understated.

Succeeding year:
Income statement — the beginning inventory is understated, but this is counterbalanced by an overstatement of purchases, as purchases at the end of the prior year are recognized currently; gross profit and net income are correctly stated as a result of the counterbalancing effect of the error.
Balance sheet — the error of the previous year no longer affects balance sheet data.

Discoveries of inventory errors call for careful analyses of the effects of such errors and the preparation of entries to correct real and nominal accounts in order that both current and future activities may be accurately stated.

If the error is not discovered until a succeeding period, correct accounting standards require that inventory errors described in this section, if material, should be recorded as prior period adjustments. If trend statistics are included in the annual reports, prior years' balances should be adjusted to reflect the correction of the error. Because of present-day audit techniques, it is probable that material inventory counting and cut-off errors will occur only rarely.

QUESTIONS

1. (a) What are the three cost elements entering into goods in process and finished goods? (b) What items enter into manufacturing overhead? (c) Define fixed overhead, variable overhead, and semivariable overhead and give an example of each.

2. (a) What charges may be considered to compose the cost of raw material acquisitions? (b) Which of these charges are normally included as a part of raw material cost for inventory purposes? (c) Which of these are normally excluded? Why? What disposition would be made of such items?

3. What are the advantages of using the perpetual inventory system as compared with the periodic system?

4. Under what normal conditions is merchandise in transit reported as inventory?

5. Under what normal conditions would an accounting failure to recognize incoming merchandise in transit that was shipped FOB shipping point have no effect on the income statement?

6. The Miller Company has followed the practice of recording all consignment sales as current period sales and has not carried goods on consignment as inventory. Under what conditions would this practice have no effect upon income?

7. State how you would report each of the following items on the financial statements:

(a) Manufacturing supplies.
(b) Goods on hand received on a consignment basis.
(c) Materials of a customer held for processing.
(d) Goods received without an accompanying invoice.
(e) Goods in stock to be delivered to customers in subsequent periods.
(f) Goods in hands of agents and consignees.
(g) Deposits with vendors for merchandise to be delivered next period.
(h) Goods in hands of customers on approval.
(i) Defective goods requiring reprocessing.

8. (a) What are the theoretical arguments for recording purchases net of cash discounts? (b) What are the practical reasons for recording purchases gross rather than net?

9. What are the advantages of using the cost method of inventory valuation? Do you see any disadvantages?

10. Trade discounts are frequently used to avoid extra catalog printing costs. Describe in what way trade discounts could affect these savings.

11. What objections can be raised to inventory valuation by specific cost identification procedures?

12. What is the difference between a weighted average and a moving average cost method? Which may be preferred and why?

13. The Wallace Co. decides to adopt specific goods lifo as of the beginning of 1977, and determines the cost of the different lines of merchandise carried as of this date. (a) What three different methods may be employed at the end of each period in assigning costs to quantity increases in specific lines? (b) What procedure is employed at the end of each period for quantity decreases in specific lines?

14. Why did the AAA Committee on Inventories refer to lifo as an "artificial" pricing system?

15. The CPA for Reliance Steel Co. recommends that the company change its method of inventory from fifo to lifo because of an increase in the rate of inflation. Evaluate this recommendation including the advantages and disadvantages of such a change in inventory methods.

16. Compare the positions that are taken by the AICPA and the AAA relative to cost flow assumptions that may be considered valid in arriving at inventory cost.

17. (a) Describe the base stock method. (b) How does this method differ from inventory valuation by lifo?

18. (a) What type of company is likely to use standard costs? (b) What precautions are necessary in the use of standard costs?

19. What effect would each of the following situations have upon the current year's net income for a company manufacturing a single product if it used direct costing to value its ending inventory rather than full costing? Assume fixed costs are the same for each year.

(a) Quantity of items produced and sold are the same for the year.
(b) Quantity of items produced exceeds the quantity sold.
(c) Quantity of items sold exceeds the quantity produced.

20. Under what circumstances would you recommend use of cost apportionment by the relative sales method?

21. State the effect of each of the following errors made by Cole, Inc., upon the balance sheet and the income statement (1) of the current period and (2) of the succeeding period:

(a) The company fails to record a sale of merchandise on account; goods sold are excluded in recording the ending inventory.
(b) The company fails to record a sale of merchandise on account; the goods sold are included, however, in recording the ending inventory.
(c) The company fails to record a purchase of merchandise on account; goods purchased are included in recording the ending inventory.
(d) The company fails to record a purchase of merchandise on account; goods purchased are not recognized in recording the ending inventory.
(e) The ending inventory is understated as the result of a miscount of goods on hand.
(f) The ending inventory is overstated as the result of inclusion of goods held on a consignment basis and never recognized as a purchase.

22. The Carol Mfg. Co. reviewed its in-transit inventory and found the following items. Indicate which items should be included in the inventory balance at December 31, 1977. Give reasons for the treatment.

(a) Merchandise costing $2,350 was received on January 3, 1978, and the related purchase invoice recorded January 5. The invoice showed the shipment was made on December 29, 1977, FOB destination.
(b) Merchandise costing $625 was received on December 28, 1977, and the invoice was not recorded. You located it in the hands of the purchasing agent; it was marked on consignment.
(c) A packing case containing a product costing $816 was standing in the shipping room when the physical inventory was taken. It was not included in the inventory because it was marked "Hold for shipping instructions." Your investigation revealed that the customer's order was dated December 18, 1977, but that the case was shipped and the customer billed on January 10, 1978. The product was a stock item of your client.
(d) Merchandise received on January 6, 1978, costing $720 was entered in the purchase register on January 7, 1978. The invoice showed shipment was made FOB supplier's warehouse on December 31, 1977. Since it was not on hand at December 31, it was not included in inventory.
(e) A special machine, fabricated to order for a customer, was finished and in the shipping room on December 31, 1977. The customer was billed on that date and the machine excluded from inventory although it was shipped January 4, 1978. (AICPA adapted)

EXERCISES

1. Transactions of the McKinnon Co. relating to goods purchased during December are summarized below:

> Purchases were $15,000, terms 2/10, n/30.
> Accounts of $12,500 were paid, including accounts of $11,500 paid within the discount period.

Give the entries to record purchases and invoice payments in December, assuming that:

> (a) Accounts payable are recorded at invoice price and purchase discounts earned are summarized in the accounts.
> (b) Accounts payable are recorded net and purchase discounts lost are summarized in the accounts.
> (c) Accounts payable are recorded at invoice price and purchase discounts lost are summarized in the accounts.

2. Minson Body and Paint Shop purchases its supplies from Rankin Auto Wholesale. Rankin gives Minson a trade discount of 5/20/15 with a cash discount of 2/10, n/30. During March, Minson purchased supplies with a list price of $70,000. Eighty percent of the supplies bought were sold during March.

> (a) What is the cost of goods sold if purchases are recorded net?
> (b) What is the equivalent composite discount rate?

3. Changes in Commodity X during March are:

Mar. 1 Balance 700 units @ $6	Mar. 10 Sale 600 units @ $12
12 Purchase 150 units @ 8	30 Sale 150 units @ 14
28 Purchase 300 units @ 9	

> (a) Assuming that perpetual inventories are maintained and that accounts are kept up to date currently, what is the cost of the ending inventory for Commodity X using: (1) fifo; (2) lifo; (3) average? (Carry your calculations to four places and round to three.)
> (b) Assuming that perpetual inventories are not maintained and that a physical count at the end of the month shows 400 units to be on hand, what is the cost of the ending inventory using each of the three methods listed in part (a)?

4. The Parker Store shows the following information relating to Commodity A which it handles:

Inventory, January 1	100 units @ $7.50
Purchases, January 10	300 units @ $8.00
Purchases, January 20	400 units @ $9.00
Sales, January 8	50 units
Sales, January 18	200 units
Sales, January 25	400 units

What are the values of ending inventory under (1) perpetual and (2) periodic methods assuming the cost flows below? (Carry your calculations to four places and round to three.)

> (a) Fifo
> (b) Lifo
> (c) Average

5. The Alvarez Wholesale Company record for Material No. 101-2 follows:

Mar. 1 Balance 150 units at $10	$1,500
10 Received 200 units at 9	1,800
20 Received 100 units at 12	1,200
28 Received 100 units at 11	1,100

At the end of the month, 250 units are on hand. Give the cost of the ending inventory, assuming that it is calculated by each method listed at the top of the next page. (Carry your calculations to four places and round to three.)

(a) First-in, first-out.
(b) Weighted average.
(c) Last-in, first-out.
(d) Cost of latest purchase.
(e) Simple average of costs.

6. Genola Farm Supply's records show purchases of Commodity A as follows:

	No. of Units		Cost
March	1,500		$1,905
April	2,000		2,380
May	1,250		1,650

The inventory at the end of May of Commodity A using fifo is valued at $2,721. Assuming that none of Commodity A was sold during March and April, what value would be shown at the end of May if a lifo cost flow was assumed?

7. First-in, first-out has been used for inventory valuation by the Harper Co. since it was organized in 1974. Using the data that follow, redetermine the net incomes for each year on the assumption of inventory valuation on the last-in, first-out basis:

	1974	1975	1976	1977
Reported net income	$ 17,500	$ 30,000	$ 32,500	$ 45,000
Reported ending inventories — fifo basis	61,500	102,000	126,000	130,000
Inventories — lifo basis	59,000	75,100	95,000	105,000

8. Clement Corporation uses direct costing for internal reporting. It has been suggested that use of direct costing on the balance sheet would understate income because of the complete write-off of fixed costs. Information concerning the valuation of inventory for the year 1977 is as follows:

Inventory, January 1, 1977	20,000 units
Variable costs	$6.00 per unit
Fixed costs (if inventory valued at full costs)	$2.00 per unit
Units produced in 1977	140,000
Total fixed costs	$280,000
Inventory, December 31, 1977	25,000 units
Variable costs	$6.50 per unit

(a) Compute the effect on net income for 1977 of using direct costing to value the inventory as compared with full costing. Assume that there is no change in work in process between the beginning and the end of the year, and that the fifo cost flow method is used.
(b) What is the effect on net income if the ending inventory consisted of only 10,000 units?

9. The Hi-Land Realty Co. acquires land for $105,000 and incurs additional costs of $45,000 in improving the land. The land is divided into lots that are classified as follows:

Class	No. of Lots		Sales Price per Lot
100	20		$3,500
200	20		2,300
300	42		2,000

(a) What is the cost of each lot to the company?
(b) What entry should be made if five Class 200 lots are sold on contract?

10. Annual income for the Robinson Co. for the period 1973–1977 appears below. However, a review of the records for the company reveals inventory misstatements as listed. Calculate corrected net income for each year.

	1973	1974	1975	1976	1977
Reported net income (loss)	$19,500	$20,000	$1,500	$(7,500)	$15,000
Inventory overstatement, end of year	2,500		2,800		1,600
Inventory understatement, end of year				4,000	

PROBLEMS

7-1. The Geneva Corporation uses raw material A in a manufacturing process. Information as to balances on hand, purchases, and requisitions of material A are given in the following table:

| | Quantities | | | Unit Price |
Date	Received	Issued	Balance	of Purchase
Jan. 11	—	—	100	$1.50
Jan. 24	300	—	400	1.72
Feb. 8	—	80	320	—
Mar. 16	—	140	180	—
June 10	150	—	330	1.75
Aug. 18	—	130	200	—
Sept. 6	—	110	90	—
Oct. 14	200	—	290	2.00
Dec. 29	—	120	170	—

Instructions: What is the closing inventory under each of the following pricing methods? (Carry calculations to four places and round.)

(1) Perpetual fifo
(2) Perpetual lifo
(3) Moving average

(4) Periodic fifo
(5) Periodic lifo
(6) Weighted average

7-2. Records of the Stratton Sales Co. show the following data relative to Commodity Z:

Jan. 1 Inventory..............325 units at $25.50
3 Purchase.............300 units at 26.00
12 Purchase.............350 units at 27.00
24 Purchase............. 75 units at 27.50

Jan. 2 Sales ....300 units at $37.50
18 Sales ....200 units at 35.70
29 Sales ....150 units at 36.00

Instructions: Calculate the inventory balance and the gross profit on sales for the month on each of the following bases:

(1) First-in, first-out. Perpetual inventories are maintained and costs are charged out currently.
(2) First-in, first-out. No book inventory is maintained.
(3) Last-in, first-out. Perpetual inventories are maintained and costs are charged out currently.
(4) Last-in, first-out. No book inventory is maintained.
(5) Moving average. Perpetual inventories are maintained and costs are charged out currently. (Carry calculations to four places and round to three.)
(6) Weighted average. No book inventory is maintained.

7-3. The Brown Mfg. Co. was organized in 1975 to produce a single product. Its production and sales records for the period 1975–1978 are summarized below:

	Units Produced		Sales	
	No. of Units	Production Costs	No. of Units	Sales Revenue
1975	320,000	$ 86,400	200,000	$122,500
1976	310,000	130,200	290,000	175,000
1977	270,000	129,600	290,000	203,000
1978	220,000	99,000	200,000	150,000

Instructions: Calculate the gross profit for each of the four years assuming that inventory balances are calculated in terms of:

(1) First-in, first-out.
(2) Last-in, first-out.

7-4. Hoover's, Inc., sells a single commodity. Purchases, sales, and expenses for May, June, and July are summarized at the top of the next page.

	Purchases	
	Units	Cost per Unit
May 1–15...	2,000	$3.50
16–31...	3,000	3.75
June 1–15...	1,500	4.25
16–30...	2,000	4.75
July 1–15...	—	—
16–31...	2,000	4.25

	Sales	
	Units	Sales Price per Unit	Operating Expenses
May	2,000	$6.75	$2,700
June	3,200	7.50	4,100
July	3,100	7.75	3,700

Instructions: Prepare a comparative income statement summarizing operations for the months of May, June, and July for each case below:

(1) Assume that monthly inventories are calculated at cost on a first-in, first-out basis.
(2) Assume that monthly inventories are calculated at cost on a last-in, first-out basis.
(3) Assume that monthly inventories are calculated at cost on a weighted average basis. (Unit costs are calculated to the nearest cent.)

7-5. The Bramble Products Company reports its inventories at lifo. Inventories are composed of three classes of goods. Values are assigned to each class as follows: units equal to the number on hand when lifo was adopted are assigned average costs as of this date; annual incremental layers thereafter are assigned the average cost for the period. Lifo was adopted in 1975. The inventory on January 1, 1978, and purchases and sales for 1978 were as follows:

Inventory, January 1, 1978

	Model A			Model B			Model C		
	Quantity	Unit Cost	Total Cost	Quantity	Unit Cost	Total Cost	Quantity	Unit Cost	Total Cost
1975, Balance..................	40,000	$.10	$ 4,000	20,000	$ .60	$12,000	5,000	$3.00	$15,000
1976, Increment..............	20,000	.15	3,000	1,500	1.00	1,500			
1977, Increment..............	10,000	.17	1,700				2,000	3.25	6,500
Total	70,000		$ 8,700	21,500		$13,500	7,000		$21,500
1978, Purchase................	250,000		$50,000	60,000		$61,200	12,500		$42,500
1978, Sales.......................	265,000		79,500	64,500		96,750	12,000		48,000

Instructions: Prepare a statement reporting sales, cost of goods sold (including purchases and inventory detail), and gross profits for each class of goods handled and for combined activities as of December 31, 1978. Provide supporting schedules to show how the ending inventory balances are developed for each class of goods.

7-6. The Ames Construction Company purchased 50 acres of land in the suburbs of a large city with the intention of improving, subdividing, and selling it in one-acre lots. The purchase price for the tract of land was $210,000. The lots are given numbers and similar lots are grouped numerically. Lots 1–15 are choice lots and did not require extra improvements. They will sell for $8,000 each. Lots 16–30 required some extra improvements costing $34,000. They will sell for $7,000 each. Lots 31–50 required extensive drainage and clearing costing $40,000. They will sell for $6,500 each.

Instructions: Using the relative sales method, allocate the purchase and improvement costs to the various lots.

7-7. The Strasser Company's inventory record appears at the top of the next page.

	Purchases		Sales
	Quantity	Unit Cost	Quantity
1975...	8,000	$5.60	5,500
1976...	9,500	5.75	10,000
1977...	7,200	5.80	5,000

The company uses a lifo cost flow assumption. It reported ending inventories as follows:

1975...	$14,000
1976...	11,500
1977...	24,360

Instructions: Determine if the Strasser Company has reported their inventory correctly. Assuming that 1977 accounts are not yet closed, make any necessary correcting entries.

7-8. The Image Corporation has used the lifo inventory system for several years. The inventory contained ten different products, and historical lifo layers were maintained for each of them. The lifo layers for one of their products, Glamor Tool, was as follows at December 31, 1976:

1975 layer	2,000 @ $50
1970 layer	2,000 @ $30
1965 layer	1,000 @ $40
1960 layer	3,000 @ $35

Instructions:
(1) What was the value of the ending inventory of Glamor Tool at December 31, 1976?
(2) How did the December 31, 1976 quantity of tools compare with the December 31, 1975 quantity of tools?
(3) What was the value of the ending inventory of Glamor Tool at December 31, 1977, assuming there were 7,000 units of this tool on hand?
(4) How would income in part (3) be affected if, in addition to the quantity on hand, 1,500 units were in transit to us at December 31, 1977? The shipment was made on December 26, 1977, terms FOB shipping point. Total invoice cost was $90,000.

7-9. The errors listed below were made by the Scoll Sales Corporation in 1977.
(a) The company failed to record a sale on account of $210 at the end of 1977. The merchandise had been shipped and was not included in the ending inventory. The sale was recorded in 1978 when cash was collected from the customer.
(b) On January 2, 1978, the company received goods costing $780 which were shipped on December 30, 1977. The terms of the sale were FOB shipping point. The purchase was recorded and the merchandise was included in inventory when payment was made in 1978.
(c) The company included in its physical count of goods $560 for goods which had been custom built and are being held for the customer. The sale was recorded in 1978, sales value, $720.
(d) The company failed to make an entry for a purchase on account of $60 at the end of 1977, although it included this merchandise in the inventory count. The purchase was recorded when payment was made to the creditor in 1978.
(e) The company overlooked goods of $360 in the physical count of goods at the end of 1977.
(f) The company included goods of $270 in the physical count which were returned on January 2, 1978, by a consignee who was unable to sell them.

Instructions: Give the entry required in 1978 to correct each error. Assume that the company arrives at its inventory position by physical count and that the books for 1977 have been closed. Assume that all amounts are material.

7-10. The Brooksby Metal Products Co. adjusted and closed its books at the end of 1977, the summary of 1977 activities showing a net loss of $8,000. The following errors, made in 1977, all regarded as material, are discovered upon an audit of the books of the company made in March, 1978:

    (a) Merchandise, cost $3,000, was recorded as a purchase at the end of 1977 but was not included in the ending inventory since it was received on January 3, 1978.

    (b) Merchandise, cost $700, was received in 1977 and included in the ending inventory; however, the entry recording the purchase was made on January 4, 1978, when the invoice was received.

    (c) 800 units of Commodity Z, costing $5.36 per unit, were recorded at a per unit cost of $3.56 in summarizing the ending inventory.

    (d) Goods in the hands of a consignee costing $4,000 were included in the inventory; however, $2,400 of such goods had been sold as of December 31, and the sale was not recorded until January 31, 1978, when the consignee made a full remittance of $3,200 on this item.

    (e) Merchandise, cost $600, sold for $760 and shipped on December 31, 1977, was not included in the ending inventory; however, the sale was not recorded until January 12, 1978, when the customer made payment on the sale.

Instructions:
    (1) Compute the corrected net income or loss for 1977.
    (2) Give the entries that are required in 1978 to correct the accounts assuming the company uses the periodic inventory method.

7-11. You have been engaged for the audit of the Y Company for the year ended December 31, 1977. The Y Company is engaged in the wholesale chemical business and makes all sales at 25% over cost.

Portions of the client's sales and purchases accounts for the calendar year 1977 follow.

Sales

Date	Reference	Amount	Date	Reference	Amount
12/31	Closing entry	$699,860	Balance forward		$658,320
			12/27	SI#965	5,195
			12/28	SI#966	19,270
			12/28	SI#967	1,302
			12/31	SI#969	5,841
			12/31	SI#970	7,922
			12/31	SI#971	2,010
		$699,860			$699,860

Purchases

Date	Reference	Amount	Date	Reference	Amount
Balance forward		$360,300	12/31	Closing entry	$385,346
12/28	RR#1059	3,100			
12/30	RR#1061	8,965			
12/31	RR#1062	4,861			
12/31	RR#1063	8,120			
		$385,346			$385,346

    RR = Receiving report.
    SI = Sales invoice.

You observed the physical inventory of goods in the warehouse on December 31, 1977, and were satisfied that it was properly taken.

When performing a sales and purchases cutoff test, you found that at December 31, 1977, the last receiving report that had been used was No. 1063 and that no shipments had been made on any sales invoices with numbers larger than No. 968. You also obtained the following additional information:

    (a) Included in the warehouse physical inventory at December 31, 1977, were chemicals that had been purchased and received on receiving report No. 1060 but for which an invoice was not received until 1978. Cost was $2,183.

(b) In the warehouse at December 31, 1977, were goods that had been sold and paid for by the customer but that were not shipped out until 1978. They were all sold on sales invoice No. 965 and were not inventoried.

(c) On the evening of December 31, 1977, there were two cars on the Y Company siding:
1. Car #AR38162 was unloaded on January 2, 1978, and received on receiving report No. 1063. The freight was paid by the vendor.
2. Car #BAE74123 was loaded and sealed on December 31, 1977, and was switched off the company's siding on January 2, 1978. The sales price was $12,700 and the freight was paid by the customer. This order was sold on sales invoice No. 968.

(d) Temporarily stranded at December 31, 1977, on a railroad siding were two cars of chemicals enroute to the Z Pulp and Paper Co. They were sold on sales invoice No. 966 and the terms were FOB destination.

(e) Enroute to the Y Company on December 31, 1977, was a truckload of material that was received on receiving report No. 1064. The material was shipped FOB destination and freight of $75 was paid by the Y Company. However, the freight was deducted from the purchase price of $975.

(f) Included in the physical inventory were chemicals exposed to rain in transit and deemed unsalable. Their invoice cost was $1,250, and freight charges of $350 had been paid on the chemicals.

Instructions:
(1) Compute the adjustments that should be made to the client's physical inventory at December 31, 1977.
(2) Prepare the adjusting entries that are required as of December 31, 1977. (AICPA adapted)

7-12. You are engaged in an audit of The Wayne Mfg. Company for the year ended December 31, 1977. To reduce the work load at year end, the company took its annual physical inventory under your observation on November 30, 1977. The company's inventory account, which includes raw materials and work in process, is on a perpetual basis and the first-in, first-out method of pricing is used. There is no finished goods inventory. The company's physical inventory revealed that the book inventory of $60,570 was understated by $3,000. To avoid distorting the interim financial statements, the company decided not to adjust the book inventory until year end except for obsolete inventory items. Your audit revealed this information about the November 30th inventory:

(a) Pricing tests showed that the physical inventory was overpriced by $2,200.
(b) Footing and extension errors resulted in a $150 understatement of the physical inventory.
(c) Direct labor included in the physical inventory amounted to $10,000. Overhead was included at the rate of 200% of direct labor. You determined that the amount of direct labor was correct and the overhead rate was proper.
(d) The physical inventory included obsolete materials recorded at $250. During December these obsolete materials were removed from the inventory account by a charge to cost of sales.

Your audit also disclosed the following information about the December 31st inventory:

(e) Total debits to certain accounts during December are listed below:

	December
Purchases	$24,700
Direct labor	12,100
Manufacturing overhead expense	25,200
Cost of sales	68,600

(f) The cost of sales of $68,600 included direct labor of $13,800.
(g) Normal scrap loss on established product lines is negligible. However, a special order started and completed during December had excessive scrap loss of $800, which was charged to Manufacturing Overhead Expense.

Instructions:
(1) Compute the correct amount of the physical inventory at November 30, 1977.
(2) Without prejudice to your solution to part (1), assume that the correct amount of the inventory at November 30, 1977, was $57,700. Compute the amount of the inventory at December 31, 1977. (AICPA adapted)

Inventories — Special Valuation Procedures

Although inventories are typically valued at their cost, there are situations in which deviations from cost appear warranted. Some of these deviations are regarded as generally accepted; others are under careful study within the profession. These special valuation procedures will be described and discussed in this chapter.

INVENTORY VALUATION AT COST OR MARKET, WHICHEVER IS LOWER

One circumstance justifying a departure from cost occurs when replacement costs for goods on hand fall below original acquisition costs. Because wholesale and retail prices are generally related, declines in replacement costs usually indicate selling prices also have declined since the goods were purchased. However, the selling price of inventory may decline for other reasons. Perhaps an inventory item has been used as a demonstrator which reduces its marketability as a new product. Or perhaps an inventory item is damaged in storage or becomes shopworn through excessive handling. In each of these instances, a decline in utility is indicated, suggesting a departure from cost. The AICPA provides for this departure in the following statement:

> A departure from the cost basis of pricing the inventory is required when the utility of the goods is no longer as great as its cost. Where there is evidence that the utility of goods, in their disposal in the ordinary course of business, will be less than cost, whether due to physical deterioration, obsolescence, changes in price levels, or other causes, the difference should be recognized as a loss of the current period. This is generally accomplished by stating such goods at a lower level commonly designated as *market*.[1]

---

[1]*Accounting Research and Terminology Bulletins — Final Edition*, "No. 43, Restatement and Revision of Accounting Research Bulletins" (New York: American Institute of Certified Public Accountants, 1961), Ch. 4, statement 5.

Recognition of a decline in the value of inventory identifies the loss with the period in which the loss occurred. This practice is referred to as *valuation at cost or market, whichever is lower,* or simply valuation at the *lower of cost or market.*

Definition of Market

Market in "cost or market" is generally interpreted to be inventory replacement cost by purchase or manufacture. Replacement cost usually includes the purchase price of the product plus freight, duties, and other costs incidental to the acquisition of the goods. Replacement cost is sometimes referred to as *entry cost.* However, declines in entry cost are not always reflected immediately in the exit values, or selling prices. If there has been no decline in selling prices, no loss in utility has occurred and a write-down in inventory values is not justified. Thus, the entry cost definition of market must be modified to consider the utility of the inventory as measured by the selling prices. This modification is generally expressed in terms of the inventory's *net realizable value,* or estimated selling price less the cost of completion and disposal.

The American Institute of Certified Public Accountants has included this modification in their definition of market as follows:

> As used in the phrase *lower of cost or market*, the term *market* means current replacement cost (by purchase or by reproduction, as the case may be) except that:
> (1) Market should not exceed the net realizable value (i.e., estimated selling price in the ordinary course of business less reasonably predictable costs of completion and disposal); and
> (2) Market should not be less than net realizable value reduced by an allowance for an approximately normal profit margin.[1]

This definition establishes a ceiling for the market value at sales price less costs of completion and disposal and a floor for market at sales price less both the costs of completion and disposal and the normal profit margin. The ceiling limitation is applied so the inventory is not valued at more than its net realizable value. Failure to observe this limitation would result in charges to future revenue that exceed the utility carried forward and an ultimate loss on the sale of the inventory. The floor limitation is applied so the inventory is not valued at less than its net realizable value minus a normal profit. The concept of normal profit is a difficult one to measure objectively. Profits vary by item and over time. Records are seldom accurate enough to determine a normal profit by individual inventory item. Despite these difficulties, however, the use of a floor prevents a definition of market that would result in a write-down of inventory values in one period to create an abnormally high profit in future periods.

To illustrate, assume that a certain commodity sells for one dollar; selling expenses are twenty cents; the normal profit is 25% or twenty-five cents. The lower of cost or market as modified by the AICPA is developed in each case as shown in the illustration on the next page.

---

[1]*Ibid.,* statement 6.

| CASE | COST | MARKET | | | | LOWER OF COST OR MARKET |
		REPLACE-MENT COST	FLOOR (ESTIMATED SALES PRICE LESS SELLING EXPENSES AND NORMAL PROFIT)	CEILING (ESTIMATED SALES PRICE LESS SELLING EXPENSES)	MARKET (LIMITED BY FLOOR AND CEILING VALUES)	
A	$.65	$ .70	$.55	$.80	$.70	$.65
B	.65	.60	.55	.80	.60	.60
C	.65	.50	.55	.80	.55	.55
D	.50	.45	.55	.80	.55	.50
E	.75	.85	.55	.80	.80	.75
F	.90	1.00	.55	.80	.80	.80

A: Market is not limited by floor or ceiling; cost is less than market.
B: Market is not limited by floor or ceiling; market is less than cost.
C: Market is limited to floor; market is less than cost.
D: Market is limited to floor; cost is less than market.
E: Market is limited to ceiling; cost is less than market.
F: Market is limited to ceiling; market is less than cost.

The dollar line below graphically illustrates the floor and ceiling range. B and A replacement costs clearly are within bounds and therefore are defined as market. D and C are below the floor and thus the market is the floor; E and F are above the ceiling and market therefore is the ceiling.

Replacement cost is abandoned as a test of subsequent utility as long as cost is recoverable in the selling price. It should also be noted that the market value is always the middle value of three amounts; replacement cost, floor, and ceiling.

Methods of Applying Lower of Cost or Market Procedure

The lower of cost or market procedure may be applied to each inventory item, to the major classes or categories of inventory items, or to the inventory as a whole. Application of this procedure to the individual inventory items will result in the lowest inventory value. However, application to inventory groups or to the inventory as a whole may provide a sufficiently conservative valuation with considerably less effort. For example, assume that balanced stocks of raw materials are on hand, some of which have gone down and others have gone up. When raw materials are used as components of a single finished product, a loss in the value of certain materials may be considered to be counterbalanced by the gains that are found in other materials, and the lower of cost or market applied to this category as a whole may provide an adequate measure of the utility of the goods.

The illustration at the top of the next page shows the valuation procedure applied to (1) individual inventory items, (2) independent classes of the inventory, and (3) inventory as a whole.

In valuing manufacturing inventories, raw materials declines are applicable to the raw materials inventory and also to raw materials costs in goods in process and finished goods inventories. Declines in direct labor

	Quan-tities	Unit Cost	Market	Totals		Cost or Market, Whichever is Lower		
				Cost	Market	(1) If Applied to Individual Inventory Items	(2) If Applied to Inventory Classes	(3) If Applied to Inventory as a Whole
Material A............................	4,000	$1.20	$1.10	$ 4,800	$ 4,400	$ 4,400		
Material B	5,000	.50	.40	2,500	2,000	2,000		
Material C	2,000	1.00	1.10	2,000	2,200	2,000		
Total raw materials				$ 9,300	$ 8,600		$ 8,600	
Goods in Process D.........	10,000	1.60	1.40	$16,000	$14,000	14,000		
Goods in Process E	12,000	1.00	1.20	12,000	14,400	12,000		
Total goods in process....				$28,000	$28,400		28,000	
Finished Goods F.............	3,000	2.00	1.70	$ 6,000	$ 5,100	5,100		
Finished Goods G.............	2,000	1.50	1.60	3,000	3,200	3,000		
Total finished goods........				$ 9,000	$ 8,300		8,300	
				$46,300	$45,300			$45,300
Inventory valuation						$42,500	$44,900	$45,300

and manufacturing overhead costs also affect the values of goods in process and finished goods, but these are usually ignored when they are relatively minor.

The method that is chosen for reducing an inventory to a lower value should be applied consistently in successive valuations. When valuing inventories by individual items, a lower market value assigned to goods at the end of a period is considered to be its cost for purposes of inventory valuation in subsequent periods; cost reductions once made, then, are not restored in subsequent inventory determinations. This restriction does not apply to inventories valued by major classes or as a whole when a record of the individual price changes is not maintained. [1]

Application of Lower of Cost or Market in the Accounts

When an inventory value decline takes place, the decline may be reflected directly in the inventory account and thus cost is not reported separately on the balance sheet. When this is done, the decline is included in the cost of goods sold and there is no separate recognition on the income statement of the effect of the price change. Because price changes may or may not recur, the effect of these changes should be reflected separately in the financial statements as price or holding gains or losses. This will provide readers with increased information to forecast operations and cash flows, information considered essential by the Trueblood Committee in their report on the *Objectives of Financial Statements*. [2]

---

[1]Tax requirements limit the application of cost or market to individual items. Reg. 1.471-4(c).
[2]*Objectives of Financial Statements* (New York: American Institute of Certified Public Accountants, 1973), p. 46.

This separation can be accomplished by using an inventory valuation or allowance account reflecting the reduction of the inventory from cost to market and a separate cost account adjusting the cost of goods sold to reflect the market decline in the inventory value. The allowance account serves as a contra asset on the balance sheet, and the cost account adjusts the cost of goods sold in the income statement to reflect the inventory valuation change. The allowance account is adjusted at the end of each year to reflect the net change that has occurred between the ending inventory at cost and the ending inventory at market. If the difference at the end of the year is greater than the difference at the beginning of the year, the difference is added to the cost of goods sold. If the difference at the end of the year is less than the difference at the beginning, a reduction in the cost of goods sold must be reported.

To illustrate these two alternative approaches to recording the decline in inventory valuation, assume the inventory values given at the top of the next page for a company using the periodic inventory method.

	(1) FAILURE TO RECOGNIZE SEPARATELY EFFECTS OF FLUCTUATIONS IN INVENTORY VALUE		(2) SEPARATE RECOGNITION OF EFFECT OF FLUCTUATIONS IN INVENTORY VALUE	
December 31, 1977 To close beginning inventory.	Income Summary .... 50,000 Merchandise Inventory	 50,000	Income Summary .... 50,000 Merchandise Inventory	 50,000
December 31, 1977 To record ending inventory.	Merchandise Inventory .... 52,000 Income Summary .	 52,000	Merchandise Inventory .... 60,000 Income Summary .	 60,000
December 31, 1977 To establish allowance account.	No entry		Loss on Reduction of Inventory to Market .... 8,000 Allowance for Inventory Decline to Market	 8,000
Partial income statement for period ending Dec. 31, 1977	Sales .... Cost of goods sold: Merchandise inv., Jan. 1, 1977.... $ 50,000 Purchases .... 130,000 Mdse. available for sale.............. $180,000 Less mdse. inv., Dec. 31, 1977 (lower of cost or market)....... 52,000 Gross profit on sales	$240,000 128,000 $112,000	Sales................... Cost of goods sold: Merchandise inv., Jan. 1, 1977.... $ 50,000 Purchases .... 130,000 Mdse. available for sale.............. $180,000 Less mdse. inv., Dec. 31, 1977 (cost) .... 60,000 120,000 Gross profit on sales (cost) .... Loss on reduction of inv. to market...... Adjusted gross profit on sales	$240,000 $120,000 8,000 $112,000

	Cost	Market
January 1, 1977	$50,000	$50,000
December 31, 1977	60,000	52,000
December 31, 1978	75,000	70,000

The entries required for these two methods at the end of 1977 and 1978 and their effects upon the income statement would be as shown below and at the bottom of page 218.

In the first example, cost of goods sold each year reflects both goods sold and the effects of inventory declines. In the second example, cost of goods sold is reported in terms of original cost. Inventory price fluctuations are screened out of this section and the net effect of such price changes is reported separately as an adjustment to the cost of goods sold. This separation provides the user with more information to forecast future operating results. If the price changes are expected to continue at the same magnitude and in the same direction, the past can be extrapolated to the future. If conditions are expected to change, the effect of the change can be more easily determined.

	(1) FAILURE TO RECOGNIZE SEPARATELY EFFECTS OF FLUCTUATIONS IN INVENTORY VALUE	(2) SEPARATE RECOGNITION OF EFFECT OF FLUCTUATIONS IN INVENTORY VALUE

December 31, 1978 To close beginning inventory.	Income Summary 52,000
	  Merchandise
	  Inventory 52,000
		Income Summary.... 60,000
		  Merchandise
		  Inventory........ 60,000

December 31, 1978 To record ending inventory.	Merchandise
	Inventory 70,000
	  Income Summary . 70,000
		Merchandise
		Inventory 75,000
		  Income Summary . 75,000

December 31, 1978 To adjust allowance account.	No entry	Allowance for
		Inventory Decline
		to Market.......... 3,000
		  Gain from
		  Decrease in
		  Inventory
		  Allowance 3,000

Partial income statement for period ending Dec. 31, 1978	Sales $280,000
	Cost of goods sold:
	  Merchandise inv.,
	  Jan. 1, 1978
	  (lower of cost
	  or market)....... $ 52,000
	  Purchases 163,000
	  Mdse. available for
	  sale.............. $215,000
	  Less mdse. inv.,
	  Dec. 31, 1978
	  (lower of cost
	  or market)....... 70,000 145,000
	Gross profit on sales $135,000
		Sales $280,000
		Cost of goods sold:
		  Merchandise inv.,
		  Jan. 1, 1978
		  (cost) .... $ 60,000
		  Purchases 163,000
		  Mdse. available for
		  sale.............. $223,000
		  Less mdse. inv.,
		  Dec. 31, 1978
		  (cost) 75,000 148,000
		Gross profit on sales
		  (cost) $132,000
		Gain from decrease
		  in inv. allow....... 3,000
		Adjusted gross profit
		  on sales $135,000

**Evaluation of
Lower of Cost
or Market
Procedure**

The lower of cost or market rule is an evidence of the concept of accounting conservatism. Its strict application has been applied to avoid valuing inventory on the balance sheet at more than replacement cost. As discussed earlier, the AICPA replaced this strict entry valuation with a utility measure that relies partially upon the exit prices. If selling prices for the inventory have declined and the decline is expected to hold until the inventory is sold, the adjustment of income in the period of the decline seems justified. The value of the inventory has been impaired which requires current adjustment. However, care must be taken in using this method not to manipulate income by allowing excessive charges against income in one period to be offset by excessive income in the next period.

Some accountants have argued against the use of lower of cost or market because it violates the cost concept. Market valuations are often subjective and based upon expectations. To the extent these expectations are not realized, misleading financial statements will be produced. To illustrate, assume activities summarized in terms of cost provide the following results over a three year period:

	1976		1977		1978	
Sales..................................		$200,000		$225,000		$250,000
Cost of goods sold:						
Beginning inventory.....	$ 60,000		$ 80,000		$127,500	
Purchases	120,000		160,000		90,000	
	$180,000		$240,000		$217,500	
Less ending inventory..	80,000	100,000	127,500	112,500	92,500	125,000
Gross profit on sales........		$100,000		$112,500		$125,000
Operating expenses.........		80,000		90,000		100,000
Net income		$ 20,000		$ 22,500		$ 25,000
Rate of income to sales...		10%		10%		10%

Assume estimates as to the future utility of ending inventories indicated market values as follows:

1976	1977	1978
$75,000	$110,000	$92,500

If sales remained the same for the three years, inventory valuation at the lower of cost or market would provide the results shown at the top of the next page.

Reduction of an inventory below cost reduces the net income of the period in which the reduction is made and increases the net income of a subsequent period. In the example just given, total net income for the three-year period is the same under either set of calculations. But the reduction of inventories to lower market values reduced the net income for 1976 and for 1977 and increased the net income for 1978. The fact that inventory reductions were not followed by decreases in the sales prices resulted in net income determinations that varied considerably from

	1976		1977		1978	
Sales.................................		$200,000		$225,000		$250,000
Cost of goods sold:						
Beginning inventory.....	$ 60,000		$ 75,000		$110,000	
Purchases	120,000		160,000		90,000	
	$180,000		$235,000		$200,000	
Less ending inventory..	75,000	105,000	110,000	125,000	92,500	107,500
Gross profit on sales........		$ 95,000		$100,000		$142,500
Operating expenses.........		80,000		90,000		100,000
Net income		$ 15,000		$ 10,000		$ 42,500
Rate of income to sales...		7.5%		4.4%		17.0%

those that might reasonably have been expected from increasing sales and costs that normally vary with sales volume.

Objection to valuation at the lower of cost or market is also raised on the grounds it produces inconsistencies in the measurements of both the financial position and the operations of the enterprise. Market decreases are recognized but increases are not. Although this system does produce some inconsistent application to the upward and downward movement of market, the authors feel that the lower of cost or market concept is preferable to a strict cost measurement. A loss in the utility of any asset should be reflected in the period the impairment is first recognized and a reasonable estimate of its significance can be determined.

LOSSES ON PURCHASE COMMITMENTS

Commitments are frequently made for the future purchase of goods at fixed prices. When price declines take place subsequent to such commitments, it is considered appropriate to measure and recognize these losses on the books just as losses on goods on hand. A decline is recorded by a debit to a special loss account and a credit to an accrued liability account, such as Estimated Losses on Purchase Commitments. Acquisition of the goods in a subsequent period is recorded by a credit to Accounts Payable, a debit canceling the accrued liability, and a debit to Purchases for the difference.

For example, assume that Travis Manufacturing Company entered into a purchase contract for $120,000 of materials to be delivered in March of the following year. At the end of the current year, the market price for this order had fallen to $100,000. The entry to record this decline and subsequent delivery of the materials would be as follows:

Dec. 31	Loss on Purchase Commitments....................................	20,000	
	Estimated Loss on Purchase Commitments..............		20,000
Mar. 1	Estimated Loss on Purchase Commitments..................	20,000	
	Purchases...	100,000	
	Accounts Payable...		120,000

The loss is thus assigned to the period in which the decline took place, and a subsequent period is charged for no more than the economic utility of the goods it receives. Current loss recognition would not be appropriate when commitments can be canceled, when commitments provide for price adjustments, when hedging transactions prevent losses, or when declines do not suggest reductions in sales prices. Losses expected to arise from future sales commitments are not normally recognized as a charge against income. They may be recognized by footnote disclosure or by an appropriation of retained earnings.

VALUATION AT MARKET

There has been increasing support, particularly in recent years, for reporting inventories on the financial statements at their net realizable values or current replacement costs. Such valuation would recognize gains as well as losses when market or replacement costs differ from the costs of purchase or production. Earnings would emerge in two stages: (1) part of the earnings would be related to the periods in which goods are acquired, processed, and held; (2) the balance of the earnings would be related to the periods goods are sold. Supporters of valuation at market insist this is necessary if inventories and working capital are to be fairly stated on the balance sheet. They also maintain that valuation at market is necessary if net income is to be measured in a fair and consistent manner.

A strong appeal for inventory valuation at market was made by Robert T. Sprouse and Maurice Moonitz in Accounting Research Study No. 3, "A Tentative Set of Broad Accounting Principles for Business Enterprises." Two statements by committees of the American Accounting Association have also stressed the need for these values. The AAA Committee on Concepts and Standards for Inventory Measurement indicated that, although no single method for pricing inventory quantities had been found, the majority of Committee members felt replacement cost was the best of the several available measurements. They concluded that the best solution to current reporting was a "simultaneous presentation of statements based on historical (acquisition) cost and the best estimate of 'current value' in order to disclose adequately the status and progress of the enterprise."[1]

The special committee of the AAA authorized to produce a basic statement of accounting theory recommended the acceptance of multi-valued reports that included current replacement cost data. The committee also indicated means of obtaining current-cost data. The committee concluded by stating:

> . . . techniques presently used to determine current replacement cost produce information which is sufficiently verifiable, quantifiable, and free from bias to justify their use in stating inventories of merchandise, materials, and supplies at their current replacement cost.[2]

[1]"A Discussion of Various Approaches to Inventory Measurement, Supplementary Statement No. 2," *Accounting Review* (July, 1964), p. 700.
[2]*A Statement of Basic Accounting Theory* (Evanston, Illinois: American Accounting Association, 1966), p. 74.

The Securities and Exchange Commission now requires larger companies to include footnote disclosure of the current replacement cost of inventories at each fiscal year-end for which a balance sheet is provided.[1]

Despite such support, there has been little general acceptance to date by practitioners of inventory valuation at market. This procedure has been challenged chiefly on the grounds it represents a departure from the cost concept and violates the accounting standards of verifiability and objectivity. In special instances, however, there is support for valuation of inventory at sales prices less costs to be incurred in their sale even though such values may exceed cost. This valuation is accepted only when it is a regular trade practice and arises from either (1) assured market conditions that make possible the immediate sale of the goods at stated prices, or (2) standard products, a ready market, plus the inability to arrive at reasonable determination of costs. Inventories, such as certain precious metals, may be accorded this exceptional treatment in view of their immediate marketability at a relatively fixed sales price. Similar treatment may be accorded a farmer's inventory in view of the difficulty of arriving at satisfactory costs. When inventories are reported at more than cost, the special valuation procedure should be disclosed in the financial statements.

VALUATION OF TRADE-INS AND REPOSSESSIONS

When goods are acquired in secondhand condition as a result of repossessions and trade-ins, they should be recorded at their estimated cash purchase price. However, when this is difficult or impossible to define, the consistent application of *floor values* — amounts which, after increase by reconditioning charges, will permit the recognition of normal profits — would be appropriate. Sales efforts are required in the sale of repossessions and trade-ins just as in the sale of new items; recording the goods at floor values will permit the recognition of normal profits when goods are sold.

The accounting for trade-ins is illustrated by the following example: Daynes Department Store sells a new washing machine to a customer for $350 cash and a trade-in of an old washer. It is estimated that a realistic floor value for the trade-in is $50. Reconditioning costs of $30 are incurred after which the trade-in washer is sold for $120, an amount that provides a normal profit. Perpetual inventory records are maintained for trade-ins but not for the regular inventory. The entries shown below and at the top of the next page reflect these transactions:

Cash	350	
Trade-In Inventory	50	
Sales		400
Trade-In Inventory	30	
Cash		30

---

[1]Securities and Exchange Commission, *Accounting Series Release No. 190*, "Disclosure of Replacement Cost Data" (Washington: U.S. Government Printing Office, 1976).

```
Cash ....................................................................................................  120
    Sales — Trade-Ins..................................................................................        120
Cost of Trade-Ins Sold ................................................................................   80
    Trade-In Inventory ................................................................................          80
```

Assume Daynes Department Store sold another washing machine on account for $350 plus interest on the unpaid balance. The customer made principal payments of $200 on the machine and then defaulted on the contract. The machine was repossessed and overhauled at a cost of $40. It was then sold for $150, a price that provided a normal profit of 50% on cost.

The following entries reflect the repossession and subsequent resale.

```
Loss on Repossession...............................................................................   90
Repossessed Inventory..............................................................................   60
    Accounts Receivable...........................................................................         150
```

Computation:

Value of repossession established to permit 50% normal profit on cost. (33⅓% on selling price.)

Selling price...	$150
Less profit at 33⅓%	50
Cost of repossessed goods sold	$100
Less cost of overhaul..............................	40
Value of repossessed inventory..............	$ 60

```
Repossessed Inventory..............................................................................   40
    Cash.....................................................................................................        40
        Cost to overhaul repossessed washing machine.
Cash .......................................................................................................  150
    Sales — Repossessed Inventory .................................................................        150
        Sale of repossessed washing machine.
Cost of Repossessed Goods Sold................................................................  100
    Repossessed Inventory ........................................................................        100
        Cost of repossessed washing machine.
```

UNCOMPLETED CONTRACTS — INCOME BASED ON THE DEGREE OF COMPLETION

A special valuation problem is encountered in those instances where a contractor engages in certain construction work requiring months or perhaps years for completion. In these instances, projects are in various degrees of completion at the end of the contractor's fiscal period.

It is possible for a contractor engaged in a long-term project to carry such work in process at cost until it is completed, accepted by the customer, and the full income can be calculated. This practice, referred to as the *completed-contract method*, is in conformity with the concept that revenue is not realized until a sale is completed and there can be formal recognition of new assets; revenue emerges from sales, not production.

However, the application of a sales basis concept of revenue for long-term contracts may lead to serious distortions of periodic achievement. If income recognition is to await contract completion, the full income will be related to the year the project is completed even though only a small part of the earnings may be attributable to productive effort in that period. Previous periods receive no credit for their productive efforts; as a matter of fact, they may be penalized through the absorption of selling, general and administrative, and other overhead costs relating to construction in progress but not considered chargeable to the construction inventory. Authorities are in general agreement that circumstances such as those described may justify departure from the sales standard as a basis for the recognition of revenue. Accordingly, they would support a valuation procedure providing for an accrual of income over the life of the contract in some equitable and systematic manner.

The AICPA comments on the point at which income should be recognized as follows:

> It is recognized that income should be recorded and stated in accordance with certain accounting principles as to time and amount; that profit is deemed to be realized when a sale in the ordinary course of business is effected unless the circumstances are such that collection of the sales price is not reasonably assured; and that delivery of goods sold under contract is normally regarded as the test of realization of profit and loss. . . .
>
> It is, however, a generally accepted accounting procedure to accrue revenues under certain types of contracts and thereby recognize profits, on the basis of partial performance, where the circumstances are such that total profit can be estimated with reasonable accuracy and ultimate realization is reasonably assured.[1]

A satisfactory approach to periodic income recognition on long-term construction contracts may be achieved by use of the *percentage-of-completion method*. Use of the percentage-of-completion method calls for the selection of either of the following approaches to determine the degree of contract completion.

1. *Percentage-of-cost.* The degree of completion is developed by comparing costs already incurred with the most recent estimates as to total estimated costs to complete the project. The percentage that costs incurred bear to total estimated costs is applied to the estimated net income on the project in arriving at the earnings to date. Income is thus recognized in terms of a *percentage-of-cost completion.*
2. *Engineers' and Architects' Estimates.* Estimates of the progress of a project in terms of the work performed are obtained from qualified engineers and architects. Such estimates are applied to total contract price, and costs incurred to date are subtracted from estimated revenues in arriving at current earnings.

To illustrate the application of the percentage-of-completion method using the percentage-of-cost approach, assume that a dam is to be constructed over a two-year period commencing in September, 1976, at a contract price of $750,000. Summaries of construction progress and the estimated earnings for each year calculated on a degree of completion basis appear at the top of the next page.

---

[1]*Accounting Research and Terminology Bulletins — Final Edition*, "No. 43, Restatement and Revision of Accounting Research Bulletins," *op. cit.*, Ch. 11, sect. A, par. 11 and 13.

1976: Contract price..		$750,000
Less estimated cost:		
Cost to date..	$ 50,000	
Estimated cost to complete project....................................	550,000	600,000
Estimated total income		$150,000
Percentage completed ($50,000/$600,000)...........................		8⅓%
Estimated income — 1976:		
($150,000 × 8⅓%)..		$ 12,500[1]
1977: Contract price..		$750,000
Less estimated cost:		
Cost to date..	$450,000	
Estimated cost to complete project....................................	175,000	625,000
Estimated total income...		$125,000
Percentage completed ($450,000/$625,000).........................		72%
Estimated income to date:		
($125,000 × 72%)...		$ 90,000
Less income recognized in 1976		12,500
Estimated income — 1977..		$ 77,500
1978: Contract price..		$750,000
Less total cost:		
Cost of prior periods...	$450,000	
Current cost to complete...	167,500	617,500
Total income...		$132,500
Less income recognized to date ($12,500 + $77,500)		90,000
Income — 1978..		$ 42,500

The financing of long-term construction contracts usually requires progress billings by the contractor and advance payments by the customer on these billings. Generally, long-term construction contracts require inspection before final settlement is made. As a protection for the customer, the contract frequently provides for an amount to be held out from the progress payment. This retention is usually a percentage of the progress billings, 10% to 20%, and is paid upon final acceptance of the construction.

In the preceding example, recognition of income only upon project completion would have resulted in income of $132,500 in 1978. In the series of entries on page 227, recognition of income on the basis of degree of completion is compared with recognition of income only upon project completion based upon the facts in the example.

---

[1]The same estimated earnings are developed if the relationship of cost incurred to total estimated cost is applied to the total contract price in arriving at the contract price considered earned, and this balance is then reduced by cost incurred to date. Calculations in the example would be:

Contract price considered earned: $50,000/$600,000 × $750,000....................................	$62,500
Cost to date	50,000
Estimated income — 1976	$12,500

TRANSACTION	INCOME RECOGNITION BY PERCENTAGE-OF-COMPLETION METHOD		INCOME RECOGNITION BY COMPLETED-CONTRACT METHOD	
1976 Cost of construction.	Construction in Progress .... Materials, Cash, etc...................	50,000 50,000	Construction in Progress .... Materials, Cash, etc...................	50,000 50,000
Progress billings.	Progress Billings Receivable .... Progress Billings on Construction Contracts...........	60,000 60,000	Progress Billings Receivable .... Progress Billings on Construction Contracts...........	60,000 60,000
Payments from customer on contract. 10% retention.	Cash .... Progress Billings Receivable	54,000 54,000	Cash .... Progress Billings Receivable	54,000 54,000
Recognition of income for year.	Construction in Progress .... Income on Construction Contracts...........	12,500 12,500	No entry	
1977 Costs of construction.	Construction in Progress .... Materials, Cash, etc...................	400,000 400,000	Construction in Progress .... Materials, Cash, etc...................	400,000 400,000
Progress billings.	Progress Billings Receivable .... Progress Billings on Construction Contracts...........	425,000 425,000	Progress Billings Receivable .... Progress Billings on Construction Contracts...........	425,000 425,000
Payments from customer on contract. 10% retention.	Cash .... Progress Billings Receivable	382,500 382,500	Cash .... Progress Billings Receivable	382,500 382,500
Recognition of income for year.	Construction in Progress .... Income on Construction Contracts...........	77,500 77,500	No entry.	
1978 Cost of construction in completing contract.	Construction in Progress .... Materials, Cash, etc...................	167,500 167,500	Construction in Progress .... Materials, Cash, etc...................	167,500 167,500
Final billing.	Progress Billings Receivable .... Progress Billings on Construction Contracts...........	265,000 265,000	Progress Billings Receivable .... Progress Billings on Construction Contracts...........	265,000 265,000
Completion of contract: (a) Recognition of income for year.	Construction in Progress .... Income on Construction Contracts...........	42,500 42,500	Construction in Progress .... Income on Construction Contracts...........	132,500 132,500
(b) Final payment in settlement including retention.	Cash .... Progress Billings Receivable	313,500 313,500	Cash .... Progress Billings Receivable	313,500 313,500
(c) Approval of completed projects by customer.	Progress Billings on Construction Contracts............. Construction in Progress	750,000 750,000	Progress Billings on Construction Contracts............. Construction in Progress	750,000 750,000

The practice of recognizing earnings on a job still in progress is a departure from normal valuation procedures. It should be applied only when there is a firm sales contract for the job, and when the estimate of either the remaining costs to be incurred or the degree of physical completion can be objectively determined by qualified architects or engineers. When reliable estimates cannot be obtained or when possible future contingencies may operate to reduce or cancel what appear to be accruing profits, conservatism requires the recognition of income only upon project completion. In the event that estimates indicate an ultimate loss on the contract, the full amount of the loss should be immediately recognized in the accounts. This is true regardless of which method of income recognition is used. Thus, income estimates must be made throughout the contract, even if the completed contract method is used.

Financial statements should disclose the valuation method used for construction in progress as well as the full implications of using the method. When sales or transfers of partnership interests or of capital stock are involved, the status of contracts in progress and the degree of recognition of profits on the contracts in the asset and the capital sections assume vital significance.

In preparing the balance sheet, Progress Billings Receivable and the account Construction in Progress summarizing construction costs and recorded income on construction to date are properly recognized as current assets. The credit balance in the account Progress Billings on Construction Contracts is properly reported as a subtraction from the construction in progress balance. An excess of progress billings over the balance in the asset account Construction in Progress should be recognized as a current liability. Any advances from customers representing loans or deposits should be reported as liabilities. Using the previous example for both the percentage-of-completion method and the completed-contract method the balance sheet at the end of 1976 would include the following accounts:

Percentage-of-completion method:
Current assets:
    Progress billings receivable .... $ 6,000
    Construction in progress $62,500
        Less progress billings on construction contracts 60,000   2,500

Completed-contract method:
Current assets:
    Progress billings receivable .... $ 6,000
Current liabilities:
    Progress billings on construction contracts $60,000
        Less construction in progress 50,000 $10,000

When a building, installation, or construction contract covers more than one year, federal income tax regulations permit the taxpayer to recognize income on a percentage-of-completion basis over the life of the project or in the year when the project is completed and accepted. Salaries, taxes, and other expenses not directly attributable to the contract must be deducted in the year incurred.

Consistent application of the method of accounting chosen is required for tax purposes; a change from the percentage-of-completion method to the completed-contract method, or a change from the completed-contract method to the percentage-of-completion method, requires special permission. The use of different methods for financial statements and for income tax purposes will require the application of interperiod tax allocation procedures, which will be discussed in Chapter 16.

QUESTIONS

1. Define market for purposes of inventory valuation at cost or market whichever is lower.

2. Under what circumstances would a decline in replacement cost of an item not justify a departure from the cost basis of valuing inventory?

3. The use of cost or market, whichever is lower, is an archaic continuation of conservative accounting. Comment on this view.

4. Does normal profit in the AICPA definition of market refer to gross profit or some other profit? How is it determined?

5. Why is a ceiling and floor limitation on replacement cost considered necessary by the AICPA?

6. Why does the individual item inventory procedure result in a more conservative inventory valuation than either the inventory class or inventory as a whole procedure?

7. The inventory of the Prince Co. on December 31, 1977, had a cost of $85,000. However, prices had been declining and the replacement cost of the inventory on this date was $70,000. Prices continued to decline and in early March, 1978, when the statements were being drawn up, the replacement cost for the inventory was only $55,000. How would you recommend that the inventory be reported on the statements for 1977?

8. What arguments can be presented for separate reporting in the income statement of the effect of using the lower of cost or market procedure?

9. Under what circumstances would the account Allowance for Inventory Decline be debited? Could it ever have a debit balance at the end of an accounting period?

10. How does the accounting treatment for losses on purchase commitments differ between actual losses which have already occurred and losses which may occur in the future?

11. There has been increasing support for the use of market values in reporting inventories on the financial statements. What are the major arguments that are raised in supporting such use?

12. What is the justification for valuing trade-ins or repossessions so that a normal profit can be realized upon their sale?

13. How should repossessed goods be valued for inventory purposes? Give reasons for your answers.

14. The Berg Corporation began business on January 1, 1976. Information about inventories, as of December 31, under different valuation methods is shown below. Using this information you are to choose the phrase which best answers each of the following questions:

	Lifo Cost	Fifo Cost	Market	Lower of Cost or Market*
1976	$10,200	$10,000	$ 9,600	$ 8,900
1977	9,100	9,000	8,800	8,500
1978	10,300	11,000	12,000	10,900

*Fifo cost, item by item valuation.

(a) The inventory basis that would result in the highest net income for 1976 is: (1) Lifo cost, (2) Fifo cost, (3) Market, (4) Lower of cost or market.

(b) The inventory basis that would result in the highest net income for 1977 is: (1) Lifo cost, (2) Fifo cost, (3) Market, (4) Lower of cost or market.

(c) The inventory basis that would result in the lowest net income for the three years combined is: (1) Lifo cost, (2) Fifo cost, (3) Market, (4) Lower of cost or market.

(d) For the year 1977, how much higher or lower would net income be on the fifo cost basis than on the lower of cost or market basis? (1) $400 higher, (2) $400 lower, (3) $600 higher, (4) $600 lower, (5) $1,000 higher, (6) $1,000 lower, (7) $1,400 higher, (8) $1,400 lower.

15. Percentage-of-completion contracts are considered to be very difficult and risky to audit. Why?

16. J. M. Livasy, a building contractor, states, "I do not use the percentage-of-completion method. It is just too difficult to apply." What problems are associated with valuation of inventories by the percentage-of-completion method? How can they be overcome?

17. How would the following accounts be classified on the financial statements? (a) Progress Billings Receivable, (b) Construction in Progress, (c) Income on Construction Contracts, (d) Progress Billings on Construction Contracts.

EXERCISES

1. Sanchez, Inc., carries five products. Units on hand, costs, and market prices of these items on January 31, 1977, are as follows:

	Units	Unit Cost	Unit Market
Product 100	3,900	$2.50	$2.30
101	1,800	4.20	4.15
102	4,800	3.00	3.10
103	3,200	5.60	5.05
104	1,600	1.65	1.80

Prepare a statement to show the calculation of the inventory for statement purposes on the basis of cost or market, whichever is lower, as applied to individual products.

2. Determine the proper carrying value of the following inventory items if priced in accordance with the recommendations of the AICPA on inventory pricing.

Item	Cost	Replacement Cost	Sales Price	Cost of Completion	Normal Profit
A	$1.75	$1.80	$2.25	$.30	$.17
B	.68	.65	1.00	.30	.04
C	.29	.27	.50	.15	.05
D	.83	.83	1.05	.24	.05
E	.79	.74	.90	.11	.07
F	1.19	1.15	1.25	.13	.07

3. The Merrill Manufacturing Co. has the following items in its inventory on December 31, 1977:

	Units	Unit Cost	Unit Market
Raw Material A	2,000	$1.10	$1.00
Raw Material B	6,500	2.40	2.50
Raw Material C	6,000	3.00	3.20
Goods in Process #1	8,000	3.75	3.80
Goods in Process #2	4,000	5.20	5.10
Finished Goods X	3,000	7.00	7.20
Finished Goods Y	2,500	8.00	7.50

Calculate the value of the company's inventory using cost or market, whichever is lower, assuming that this valuation procedure is applied:

(a) To individual inventory items.
(b) To each class of inventory.
(c) To the inventory as a whole.

4. The Hartz Company summarizes inventory data at the end of 1977 and 1978 as follows:

	1977	1978
Invoice cost	$22,000	$25,000
Lower of cost or market	19,500	23,000

What entries are required (1) at the end of 1977 in recording the ending inventory and (2) at the end of 1978 in closing the beginning inventory and recording the ending inventory, assuming each of the following accounting procedures:

(a) The company calculates cost of goods sold in terms of inventories at the lower of cost or market without separate recognition of the effect of inventory market fluctuations.

(b) The company makes periodic recognition of the effects of market fluctuation identified with the inventory through valuation at the lower of cost or market.

5. The Hubbard Products Co. entered into a 6-month $800,000 purchase commitment for a supply of its major raw material on October 1, 1977. On December 31, 1977, the market value of this material has fallen so that current acquisition of the ordered quantity would cost $675,000. It is anticipated that a further decline will occur during the next three months and that market at date of delivery will be approximately $525,000. What entries would you make on December 31, 1977, to recognize these facts?

6. The Gordan Supply Company specializes in hardware used in plumbing. Severe price competition forced the company to reduce the prices on parts A and C by 15%, effective January 1, 1978. On the same date Gordan's suppliers reduced their prices on all parts by 12%. Gordan's inventory records indicated the following as of December 31, 1977.

Part	Units	Unit Cost	Unit Sales Price
A..	1,500	$2.00	$3.00
B..	2,000	3.80	4.00
C..	300	5.00	6.00

Gordan has selling costs of 10% of selling price and expects a normal profit after selling costs of 20% of sales price. Determine the value of Gordan's inventory at December 31, 1977, on the basis of cost or market, whichever is lower, as applied to individual products. Round all amounts to nearest cent.

7. Davis Construction Company is building a new home for L. Woodbury at a contracted price of $45,000. The estimated cost at the time the contract is signed (January 2, 1977) is $39,000. At December 31, 1977, the total cost incurred is $24,000 with estimated costs to complete of $16,000. Davis has billed $25,000 on the job and has received a $22,000 payment. This is the only contract in process. Prepare the sections of the balance sheet and the income statement of Davis Construction Company affected by these events assuming use of (a) the percentage-of-completion method and (b) the completed-contract method.

8. Gonzales Construction Co. has used the percentage-of-completion method of recognizing profits. Juan Gonzales recently died and his son, Manuel, has assumed leadership of the business. In reviewing the records, Manuel finds the following information regarding a recently completed building project for which the total contract was $500,000.

	1975	1976	1977
Income (loss)	$10,000	$35,000	$ (5,000)
Cost incurred to date	90,000	?	205,000

Manuel wants to know how effectively the company operated during the last three years on this project. Since the information is not complete, he has asked you to help him by answering the following questions:

(a) How much cost was incurred in 1976?
(b) What percentage of the project was completed by the end of 1976?
(c) What was the total estimated income on the project by the end of 1976?
(d) What was the estimated cost to complete the project at the end of 1976?

9. Wonder Builders, Inc., entered into a contract to construct an office building at a contract price of $10,000,000. Income is to be reported using the percentage-of-completion method as determined by estimates made by the architect. The data below summarizes the activities on the construction for the years 1976 through 1978. What entries are required to record this information?

Year	Cost Incurred	Estimated Cost to Complete	Percentage Complete — Architect's Estimate	Project Billings	Collections on Billings
1976	$3,200,000	$5,800,000	25%	$3,300,000	$3,100,000
1977	4,100,000	1,200,000	75%	4,200,000	4,000,000
1978	1,300,000	0	100%	2,500,000	2,900,000

PROBLEMS

8-1. The Western Supply Co. uses the first-in, first-out method in calculating cost of goods sold for the three products that it handles. Inventories and purchases of these products during January and the market price of these products on January 31 are as follows:

		Commodity A	Commodity B	Commodity C
Jan. 1	Inventory	2,000 units at $ 6.00	3,000 units at $10.00	4,500 units at $ .90
Jan. 1–15	Purchases	2,000 units at 6.50	4,500 units at 10.50	2,000 units at 1.20
Jan. 16–31	Purchases	1,000 units at 7.50		
Jan. 31	Inventory	2,000 units	2,500 units	4,000 units
Jan. 31	Sales price	$8.00 per unit	$11.00 per unit	$1.60 per unit

On January 31, Western's suppliers reduced their price from the last purchase price by these percentages: Commodity A, 10%; Commodity B, 6%; Commodity C, 15%. Accordingly, Western decided to reduce their sales prices on all items by 10% effective February 1. Western's selling cost is 5% of sales price and they have a normal profit after selling costs of 20% on sales prices.

> **Instructions:**
> (1) Calculate the cost of the inventory at January 31.
> (2) Calculate the cost of goods sold for January.
> (3) Calculate the balance to be provided by means of an allowance account to reduce the inventory as of January 31 to a basis of cost or market, whichever is lower, as applied to the individual items.

8-2. Robinson, Inc., carries five items in their inventory. The following data are relative to such goods at the end of 1977:

			Per Unit			
	Units	Cost	Replacement Cost	Estimated Sales Price	Selling Cost	Normal Profit
Commodity A	1,000	$ 2.90	$ 3.05	$ 5.00	$ 1.50	$ 1.25
Commodity B	1,200	3.50	3.50	6.00	.80	1.00
Commodity C	2,000	5.50	5.00	8.00	.90	2.00
Commodity D	2,500	7.00	7.50	9.00	1.20	1.75
Commodity E	250	12.30	12.00	12.00	1.00	2.50

> **Instructions:** Calculate the value of the inventory under each of the following methods:
> (1) Cost.
> (2) The lower of cost or market without regard to market floor and ceiling limitations, applied to the individual inventory items.
> (3) The lower of cost or market without regard to market floor and ceiling limitations applied to the inventory as a whole.
> (4) The lower of cost or net realizable value applied to the individual inventory items.
> (5) The lower of cost or market recognizing floor and ceiling limitations applied to the individual inventory items.

8-3. The Waggener Bros. Mfg. Co. manufactures parts for drilling wells. They use the fifo inventory method and follow the practice of valuing the inventory at the lower of cost or market. Severe competition has resulted in a sale price reduction at year end of 10% on all completed parts and a decrease of 20% in the replacement cost of raw materials. At the end of the current fiscal year, the following cost information pertained to the closing inventories:

Raw materials	$40,000
Goods in process:	
Raw materials	25,000
Labor	30,000
Overhead	15,000
Finished goods (replacement cost $51,000)	60,000

> **Instructions:** Make the adjustment necessary to record the ending inventory at the lower of cost or market applied to each *class* of inventory. (Assume normal markup of 30% of manufacturing costs for these parts. Selling costs are 10% of manufacturing costs.)

8-4. The Taylor Company accounts for fluctuations in the valuation of inventory by using the lower of cost or market method with an allowance account. The following data summarized inventory data for the years 1974 through 1977.

	Cost	Replacement Cost	Sales Price	Selling Cost	Normal Profit
1974	$65,000	$60,000	$70,000	$15,000	$15,000
1975	68,000	60,000	65,000	3,000	9,000
1976	58,000	59,000	75,000	15,000	10,000
1977	70,000	59,000	82,000	15,000	5,000

Instructions: Give the entries which would be required to recognize gains and losses due to changes in inventory value.

8-5. The Scott Sales Co. sells three products. Inventories and purchases during February and the market prices of these goods on February 28 are as follows:

		Product A	Product B	Product C
Feb. 1	Inventory	200 units at $ 65	200 units at $110	60 units at $145
1–28	Purchases	60 units at 50	120 units at 105	60 units at 200
	Total available for sale	260	320	120
Feb. 1–28	Sales	50 units at 95	40 units at 145	10 units at 220
		130 units at 100	110 units at 150	40 units at 210
Total sales		180	150	50
Feb. 28	Inventory	80	170	70
Feb. 28	Market values per unit	$ 55	$ 95	$140

Selling, general, and administrative expenses for February were $15,300.

Instructions:
(1) Prepare an income statement for February, assuming that the ending inventory is valued at cost on a first-in, first-out basis.
(2) Prepare an income statement for February, assuming that the inventory is reduced to cost or market, whichever is lower, applied to individual products, and the inventory loss is reported separately on the income statement. (First-in, first-out is used in arriving at cost.)

8-6. A condensed comparative income statement for the Forest Company appears below. Inventories have been reported periodically at cost. An analysis discloses that replacement costs for inventories on hand at the end of each year had been as follows:

Forest Company
Comparative Income Statement
For Years Ended December 31

	1978		1977		1976	
Sales		$88,500		$82,500		$67,500
Cost of goods sold:						
Merchandise inventory, Jan. 1	$18,000		$13,000		$10,000	
Purchases	50,000		46,000		40,000	
Merchandise available for sale	$68,000		$59,000		$50,000	
Less merchandise inventory, Dec. 31	22,000	46,000	18,000	41,000	13,000	37,000
Gross profit on sales		$42,500		$41,500		$30,500
Selling and general expenses		25,000		23,500		20,000
Net income		$17,500		$18,000		$10,500
Inventory at market		$23,000		$14,500		$12,500

Instructions: Prepare a set of comparative income statements on each assumption presented below and at the top of the next page.
(1) Inventories are recorded in the "Cost of goods sold" section on the basis of cost or market, whichever is lower.

(2) Inventories are recorded at cost in the "Cost of goods sold" section but at the lower of cost or market for balance sheet purposes. The effect of fluctuations in price on beginning and ending inventories is reflected as a special adjustment to gross profit on the income statement.

8-7. The Napa Appliance Company began business on January 1, 1976. The company decided from the beginning to grant allowances on merchandise traded in as part payment on new sales. During 1977 the company granted trade-in allowances of $42,690. The wholesale value of merchandise traded in was $27,250. Trade-ins recorded at $26,000 were sold for their wholesale value of $18,000 during the year.

The following summary entries were made to record annual sales and trade-in sales:

Accounts Receivable	293,260	
Trade-In Inventory	42,690	
Sales		335,950
Cash	18,000	
Loss on Trade-In Inventory	8,000	
Trade-In Inventory		26,000

When a customer defaults on the accounts receivable contract, the appliance is repossessed. During 1977 the following repossessions occurred:

	Original Sales Price	Unpaid Contract Balance
On 1976 contracts	$25,000	$13,500
On 1977 contracts	16,000	12,500

The wholesale value of these goods is estimated by the trade as follows:

(a) Goods repossessed during year of sale are valued at 50% of original sales price.
(b) Goods repossessed in later years are valued at 25% of original sales price.

Instructions:

(1) At what values should Napa Appliance report the trade-in and repossessed inventory at December 31, 1977?
(2) Give the entry that should have been made to record the repossessions of 1977.
(3) Give the entry that is required to correct the trade-in summary entries.

8-8. The Swenson Company values its perpetual inventory at the lower of fifo cost or market. The inventory accounts at December 31, 1976, had the following balances:

Raw Materials	$135,000
Allowance to Reduce Raw Material Inventory from Cost to Market	9,500
Work in Process	219,200
Finished Goods	342,000

The following are some of the transactions that affected the inventory of the Swenson Company during 1977:

Feb. 10 Purchased raw materials at an invoice price of $50,000; terms 3/15, n/30. Swenson Company uses the net method of valuing inventories.

Mar. 15 Swenson Company repossessed an inventory item from a customer who was overdue in making payment. The unpaid balance on the sale was $175. The repossessed merchandise is to be refinished and placed on sale. It is expected that the item can be sold for $250 after estimated refinishing cost of $50. The normal profit for this item is considered to be $40.

Apr. 1 Refinishing costs of $45 are incurred on the repossessed item.

Apr. 10 The repossessed item is resold for $230 on account; 20% down.

May 30 A sale on account is made of finished goods that have a list price of $740 and a cost of $480. A reduction from the list price of $100 is granted as a trade-in allowance. The trade-in item is to be priced to sell at $80 as is. The normal profit on this type of inventory is 25% of the sales price.

Nov. 30 Ordered materials to be delivered January 31, 1978, at a cost of $36,000. No discount terms were included.

Dec. 31 The following information was available to adjust the accounts for the annual statements:

(a) The market value of the items ordered on November 30 had declined to $30,000.
(b) The raw material inventory account had a cost balance of $184,000. Current market value was $169,000.
(c) The finished goods inventory account had a cost balance of $296,000. Current market value was $315,000.

Instructions: Record this information in journal entry form, including any required adjusting entries at December 31, 1977.

8-9. Joyce Rundo is a contractor for the construction of large office buildings. At the beginning of 1977 she had three buildings in progress. The following data describe the status of these buildings at the beginning of the year.

	Contract Price	Costs Incurred to 1/1/77	Estimated Costs to Complete 1/1/77
Building 1	$5,400,000	$2,064,000	$2,736,000
Building 2	9,000,000	6,318,000	1,782,000
Building 3	3,150,000	800,000	2,000,000

During 1977 the following costs were incurred:

Building 1 $2,436,000 (estimated cost to complete as of 12/31/77, $500,000)
Building 2 2,000,000 (job completed)
Building 3 1,000,000 (estimated cost to complete as of 12/31/77, $1,400,000)
Building 4   800,000 (contract price, $2,500,000; estimated cost to complete at 12/31/77, $1,200,000)

Instructions:
(1) Compute the gross profit in 1977 if Ms. Rundo uses the percentage-of-completion method. (Round to the nearest thousandths.)
(2) Compute the gross profit for 1977 if Ms. Rundo uses the completed-contract method.

8-10. Kimball Construction Company reports its income for tax purposes on a completed-contract basis and income for financial statement purposes on a percentage-of-completion basis. A record of construction activities for 1977 and 1978 follows:

		1977		1978	
	Contract Price	Cost Incurred 1977	Estimated Cost to Complete	Cost Incurred 1978	Estimated Cost to Complete
Project A	$1,450,000	$910,000	$390,000	$410,000	0
Project B	1,700,000	720,000	880,000	340,000	$650,000
Project C	850,000	160,000	640,000	431,500	253,500
Project D	1,000,000			280,000	520,000

General and administrative expenses for 1977 and 1978 were $50,000 for each year.

Instructions:
(1) Calculate the income for 1977 and 1978 that should be reported for financial statement purposes.
(2) Calculate the income for 1978 to be reported on a completed-contract basis.

8-11. Tall Construction Co. signed a long-term construction contract in 1975. The contract price was $600,000 and the company expected to earn $90,000 on the contract. The following schedule summarizes the contract to its completion.

Year	Actual Cost	Estimated Cost to Complete	Billings on Contract	Collections on Contract
1975	$ 50,000	$450,000	$ 55,000	$ 48,000
1976	184,000	286,000	190,000	170,000
1977	280,000	0	355,000	382,000
	$514,000		$600,000	$600,000

(continued)

Instructions:

    (1) Prepare a schedule showing the income earned each year under the percentage-of-completion method.

    (2) Prepare all journal entries required relative to the contract assuming the use of the percentage-of-completion method.

    (3) Assuming proper entries have been made for 1975 and 1976, prepare journal entries for 1977 assuming the use of the completed-contract method.

8-12. The Highcrest Bridge Company obtained a construction contract to build a highway and bridge over the Mississippi River. It estimated at the beginning of the contract that it would take three years to complete the project at an expected cost of $50,000,000. The contract price was $60,000,000. The project actually took four years, being accepted as completed late in 1977. The following information describes the status of the job as of the close of each production year.

	1974	1975	1976	1977	1978
Costs incurred	$12,000,000	$15,000,000	$18,000,000	$10,000,000	
Estimated cost to complete	38,000,000	27,000,000	11,250,000		
Collections on contract	12,000,000	13,000,000	15,000,000	15,000,000	$ 5,000,000
Billings on contract	13,000,000	15,500,000	17,000,000	14,500,000	

Instructions:

    (1) What is the income for each of the years 1974–1978 under (a) the percentage-of-completion method, (b) the completed-contract method?

    (2) Give combined journal entries for each year assuming that the percentage-of-completion method is used.

8-13. The Metro Construction Company commenced doing business in January, 1977. Construction activities for the year 1977 are summarized as follows:

Project	Total Contract Price	Contract Expenditures to Dec. 31, 1977	Estimated Additional Costs to Complete Contracts	Cash Collections to Dec. 31, 1977	Billings to Dec. 31, 1977
A	$ 310,000	$187,500	$ 12,500	$155,000	$155,000
B	415,000	195,000	255,000	210,000	249,000
C	350,000	320,000	—	300,000	350,000
D	300,000	16,500	183,500	—	4,000
	$1,375,000	$719,000	$451,000	$665,000	$758,000

The company is your client. The president has asked you to compute the amounts of revenue for the year ended December 31, 1977, that would be reported under the completed-contract method and the percentage-of-completion method of accounting for long-term contracts.

The following information is available:

    (a) All contracts are with different customers.

    (b) Any work remaining to be done on the contracts is expected to be completed in 1978.

    (c) The company's accounts have been maintained on the completed-contract method.

Instructions:

    (1) Prepare a schedule computing the amount of income (loss) by project for the year ended December 31, 1977, to be reported under (a) the completed-contract method, and (b) the percentage-of-completion method. (Round to the nearest thousandths.)

    (2) Prepare a schedule under the completed-contract method computing the amounts that would appear in the company's balance sheet at December 31, 1977, for (a) costs in excess of billings, and (b) billings in excess of costs.

    (3) Prepare a schedule under the percentage-of-completion method that would appear in the company's balance sheet at December 31, 1977, for (a) costs and estimated earnings in excess of billings, and (b) billings in excess of costs and estimated earnings. (AICPA adapted)

9

Inventories — Estimating Procedures in Valuation

Estimates are frequently employed in developing inventory quantities and inventory costs. Certain estimating procedures must be applied when inventories are lost by fire or other casualty. Estimating procedures are frequently employed in arriving at inventories of the mercantile enterprise when such procedures can offer satisfactory measurements without the counting and costing routines that would otherwise be necessary. Also, estimates of the impact of inflation on inventory values are employed using dollar-value lifo techniques. Widely used estimating procedures and the circumstances under which they are employed are described in the following pages.

GROSS PROFIT METHOD

Estimates of merchandise on hand may be developed by means of the *gross profit method*. In using the gross profit method, the company's gross profit percentage is applied to sales to determine cost of goods sold; cost of goods sold is subtracted from the cost of goods available for sale in arriving at an estimated inventory balance.

The gross profit method of arriving at an inventory is applicable:

1. When inventories are required for interim statements, or for the determination of the week-to-week or month-to-month inventory position, and the cost of taking physical inventories would be excessive for such purposes.
2. When an inventory has been destroyed by fire or other cause and the specific data required for its valuation are not available.
3. When it is desired to test or check on the validity of inventory figures determined by other means. Such application is referred to as the *gross profit test*.

The gross profit percentage used in reducing sales to a cost of goods sold balance must be a reliable measure of current sales experience. In developing a reliable rate, reference is usually made to past rates and these are adjusted for variations considered to exist currently. For example, past gross profit rates may require adjustment when they are affected by inventories valued at the lower of cost or market; rates affected by reductions applied to beginning or ending inventories may not be regarded as applicable under current experiences. Past gross profit rates may also require adjustment when inventories are valued at last-in, first-out, and significant fluctuations in inventory position and in prices have affected gross profits in a manner not representative of current experiences. Current changes in cost-price relationships or in the sales mix of specific products further create a need for modifying past rates.

The calculation of cost of goods sold depends upon whether the gross profit percentage is developed and stated in terms of sales or in terms of cost. The procedures to be followed in each case are illustrated below:

Example 1 — Gross profit as a percentage of sales. Assume sales are $100,000 and goods are sold at a gross profit of 40% of sales.

If gross profit is 40% of sales, then cost of goods sold must be 60% of sales:

Sales	100%		Sales	100%
Cost of goods sold	?	=	Cost of goods sold	60%
Gross profit	40%		Gross profit	40%

Cost of goods sold, then, is 60% of $100,000, or $60,000. Goods available for sale less the estimated cost of goods sold gives the estimated cost of the remaining inventory. Assuming the cost of goods available for sale is $85,000, this balance less the estimated cost of goods sold, $60,000, gives an estimated inventory of $25,000.

Example 2 — Gross profit as a percentage of cost. Assume sales are $100,000 and goods are sold at a gross profit that is 60% of their cost.

(a) If sales are made at a gross profit of 60% of cost, then sales must be equal to the sum of cost, considered 100%, and the gross profit on cost, 60%. Sales, then, are 160% of cost:

Sales	?		Sales	160%
Cost of goods sold	100%	=	Cost of goods sold	100%
Gross profit	60%		Gross profit	60%

To find cost, or 100%, sales may be divided by 160 and multiplied by 100, or sales may simply be divided by 1.60. Cost of goods sold, then, is $100,000 ÷ 1.60 = $62,500. This amount is subtracted from the cost of goods available for sale to determine the estimated inventory.

(b) The cost of goods sold can be developed through an alternate calculation. If sales are 60% above cost, then the cost relationship to sales must be 100/160, or 62.5%.

Sales	160%	But in terms		Sales.........................	100.0%	
Cost of goods sold ..	100%	of sales as	=	Cost of goods sold ..	62.5%	(100/160)
Gross profit	60%	100%		Gross profit	37.5%	(60/160)

Cost of goods sold, then, is 62.5% ×$100,000 = $62,500.

Example 3 — Sales as a percentage increase above cost. Assume sales are $100,000 and goods are sold at 20% above cost. This is the same as saying that the gross profit is 20% of cost, and the answer would be developed as in Example 2 above. Sales, then, would be divided by 1.20, as in (a) above, or multiplied by .83⅓ (100/120), as in (b) above, in arriving at the estimated cost of goods sold.

When various lines of merchandise are sold at different gross profit rates, it may be possible to develop a reliable inventory value only by making separate calculations for each line. Under such circumstances, it is necessary to develop summaries of sales, goods available, and gross profit data for the different sections of the inventory.

Use of Gross Profit Method for Monthly Inventory Calculations   The gross profit method may be employed in developing a series of inventory values. For example, assume the merchandise turnover is to be determined for a retail store whose gross profit calculation is as follows:

Sales		$500,000
Cost of goods sold:		
Merchandise inventory, January 1	$ 20,000	
Purchases	310,000	
Merchandise available for sale	$330,000	
Merchandise inventory, December 31	30,000	
Cost of goods sold		300,000
Gross profit on sales		$200,000

If only these data are available, the average inventory is $25,000, the sum of the beginning and ending balances divided by 2. The merchandise turnover, the number of times the average inventory has been replenished during the fiscal period, is 12 times, calculated as follows:

$$\frac{\text{Cost of goods sold}}{\text{Average inventory (using year-end balances)}} = \frac{\$300,000}{\$25,000} = 12$$

A more representative average inventory may be obtained by analyzing sales and purchases and computing monthly inventories by the gross profit method. These computations are given below.

	A Purchases	B Sales	C Cost as a Percentage of Sales	D Cost of Goods Sold (B × C)	E Inventory Increase or (Decrease) (A − D)	F Inventory (F + E)
			Cost of Goods Sold			
January 1						$ 20,000
January	$ 20,000	$ 30,000	60%	$ 18,000	$ 2,000	22,000
February	20,000	30,000	60	18,000	2,000	24,000
March	20,000	30,000	60	18,000	2,000	26,000
April	20,000	30,000	60	18,000	2,000	28,000
May	30,000	40,000	60	24,000	6,000	34,000
June	30,000	40,000	60	24,000	6,000	40,000
July	30,000	60,000	60	36,000	(6,000)	34,000
August	30,000	40,000	60	24,000	6,000	40,000
September	40,000	40,000	60	24,000	16,000	56,000
October	40,000	50,000	60	30,000	10,000	66,000
November	20,000	50,000	60	30,000	(10,000)	56,000
December	10,000	60,000	60	36,000	(26,000)	30,000
	$310,000	$500,000	60%	$300,000	$ 10,000	$476,000

The average inventory is calculated from the monthly inventory balances, and the merchandise turnover is determined as follows:

$$\frac{\text{Total of inventories}}{\text{Number of inventories}} = \frac{\$476,000}{13} = \$36,615$$

$$\frac{\text{Cost of goods sold}}{\text{Average inventory (using monthly balances)}} = \frac{\$300,000}{\$36,615} = 8.2$$

This figure is more accurate than the one developed on the basis of the year-end inventories which were unusually low and unrepresentative.

Use of Gross Profit Method for Computation of Fire Loss

A common application of the gross profit method occurs when a physical count of an inventory is impossible because of its physical destruction. For example, assume that on October 31, 1977, a wholesale distributing company had a fire in a warehouse which totally destroyed the contents, including many accounting records. Remaining records indicated that the last physical inventory was taken on December 31, 1976, and that the inventory at that date was $329,500. Microfilm bank records of canceled checks disclosed that during 1977 payments to suppliers for inventory items were $1,015,000. Unpaid invoices at the beginning of 1977 amounted to $260,000, and circularization of suppliers indicated a balance due at the time of the fire of $315,000. Bank deposits for the ten months amounted to $1,605,000. All deposits came from customers for merchandise except for a loan of $100,000 obtained from the bank during the year. Accounts receivable at the beginning of the year were $328,000, and an analysis of the available records indicated that accounts receivable on October 31 totaled $275,000. Gross profit percentages on sales were computed for the preceding four years as follows:

1973	28%	1975	23%
1974	25%	1976	24%

From these facts, the inventory in the warehouse at the time of the fire could be estimated as follows:

Estimate of sales January 1 to October 31, 1977:

Collection of accounts receivable ($1,605,000 − $100,000)	$1,505,000
Add accounts receivable at October 31, 1977	275,000
	$1,780,000
Deduct accounts receivable at January 1, 1977	328,000
Estimate of sales January 1 to October 31, 1977	$1,452,000
Average gross profit percentage on sales for past 4 years	25%
Average cost percentage on sales for past 4 years	75%
Estimate of cost of goods sold to October 31, 1977 ($1,452,000 × 75%)	$1,089,000

Estimate of inventory on October 31, 1977:

Merchandise inventory January 1, 1977		$ 329,500
Add: Payments to suppliers — 1977	$1,015,000	
Amounts payable to suppliers, October 31, 1977	315,000	
	$1,330,000	
Deduct accounts payable to suppliers, January 1, 1977	260,000	
Estimate of purchases January 1 to October 31, 1977		1,070,000
Merchandise available for sale		$1,399,500
Estimate of cost of goods sold for 1977 (from above)		1,089,000
Estimated merchandise inventory, October 31, 1977		$ 310,500

RETAIL INVENTORY METHOD

The *retail inventory method* is widely employed by retail concerns, particularly by department stores, as a means of arriving at reliable estimates of the business unit's inventory position whenever desired. When this method is employed, records of goods purchased are maintained in terms of costs and also at marked retail prices. The goods on hand at retail may be calculated at any time by subtracting sales for the period from the total goods available at retail. Cost and retail pricings of goods available are used in developing the percentage that cost bears to retail, and this percentage is applied to the goods on hand at retail in arriving at the estimated cost of such goods.

The determination of a company's inventory at the end of a month by using the retail inventory method follows:

	Cost	Retail
Merchandise inventory, January 1	$30,000	$45,000
Purchases in January	20,000	35,000
Merchandise available for sale	$50,000	$80,000
Cost percentage ($50,000/$80,000) = 62½%		
Deduct sales for January		25,000
Merchandise inventory, January 31, at retail		$55,000
Merchandise inventory, January 31, at estimated cost ($55,000 × 62½%)	$34,375	

It should be observed that the effect of the above procedure is to provide an inventory valuation in terms of average cost. No cost sequence is recognized; the percentage of cost to retail for the ending inventory is the same as the percentage of cost to retail for goods sold.

Use of the retail inventory method offers the following advantages:

1. Estimated interim inventories can be obtained without a physical count.
2. When a physical inventory is actually taken for periodic statement purposes, it can be taken at retail and then converted to cost without reference to individual costs and invoices, thus saving time and expense.
3. Checks are afforded on the movement of goods, since physical counts at retail should compare closely with inventories calculated at retail.

A physical count of the inventory to be reported on the annual statements is generally required at least once a year. Relatively significant discrepancies between a physical inventory and the inventory postion as derived from book calculations should be investigated. Such inquiry may lead to sources of inventory misappropriations. Retail inventory records should be adjusted for variations shown by the physical count so that records reflect the actual status of the inventory for purpose of future estimates and control.

Markups and Markdowns

The earlier inventory calculation assumed that after the goods were originally marked at retail prices, no further changes in such prices were made. Frequently, however, because of changes in the price level, changes in consumer demand, or other reasons, original retail prices are changed. The items listed below and at the top of the next page must ordinarily be considered in employing the retail method:

1. *Original retail* — the established sales price, including the original increase over cost variously referred to as the *markon* or *initial markup*.
2. *Additional markups* — increases that raise sales prices above original retail.
3. *Markup cancellations* — decreases in additional markups that do not reduce sales prices below original retail.

4. *Markdowns* — decreases that reduce sales prices below original retail.
5. *Markdown cancellations* — decreases in the markdowns that do not raise the sales prices above original retail.

The difference between cost and retail as adjusted for the described changes is referred to as the *maintained markup*.

To illustrate the use of the five terms, assume that goods originally placed for sale are marked at 50% above cost. Certain merchandise costing $4 a unit, then, is marked at $6, which is termed the original retail. This increase in cost is variously referred to as a "50% markon on cost" or a "33⅓% markon on sales price." In anticipation of a heavy demand for the article, the retail price of the goods is subsequently increased to $7.50. This represents an additional markup of $1.50. At a later date the price is reduced to $7. This is a markup cancellation of 50 cents and not a markdown since the retail price has not been reduced below the original sales price. But assume that goods originally marked to sell at $6 are subsequently marked down to $5. This represents a markdown of $1. At a later date the goods are marked to sell at $5.25. This is a markdown cancellation of 25 cents and not a markup since sales price does not exceed the original retail.

In determining the goods on hand without a physical inventory, a record of each of the foregoing adjustments is required. The beginning inventory and purchases at retail are increased by net markups to arrive at goods available for sale at retail. Subtractions from goods available at retail are then made for sales, net markdowns, inventory breakage, spoilage, and other losses. The ending inventory at retail may be reduced to cost by applying the percentage that cost bears to retail.

In obtaining the cost percentage, the cost of goods available for sale (including any freight in) is normally related to the original retail plus the net markups, without taking into account the net markdowns. Calculation of the inventory in this manner is illustrated below.

	Cost	Retail
Beginning inventory	$ 8,600	$ 14,000
Purchases	69,000	110,000
Freight in	3,100	
Additional markups		13,000
Markup cancellations		(2,500)
Goods available for sale	$80,700	$134,500
Cost percentage ($80,700 ÷ $134,500) = 60%		
Deduct: Sales		$108,000
Markdowns		4,800
Markdown cancellations		(800)
		$112,000
Ending inventory at retail		$ 22,500
Ending inventory at estimated cost ($22,500 × 60%)	$ 13,500	

Excluding markdowns in calculating the cost percentage results in a lower percentage and consequently a lower inventory figure than would otherwise be obtained. This lower inventory figure represents a lower of average cost or market valuation. It is sometimes referred to as the *conventional retail inventory* method, and is the more common type of retail inventory method used.

Markdowns may be made for special sales or clearance purposes, or they may be made as a result of market fluctuations and a decline in the replacement cost of goods. In either case their omission in calculating the cost percentage is necessary in order to value the inventory at the lower of cost or market. This is illustrated in the two examples below:

Example 1 — Markdowns for special sales purposes. Assume that merchandise costing $50,000 is marked to sell for $100,000. To dispose of part of the goods immediately, one fourth of the stock is marked down $5,000 and is sold. The cost of the ending inventory is calculated as follows:

	Cost	Retail
Purchases	$50,000	$100,000
Cost percentage ($50,000 ÷ $100,000) = 50%		
Deduct: Sales		$ 20,000
Markdowns		5,000
		$ 25,000
Ending inventory at retail		$ 75,000
Ending inventory at estimated cost ($75,000 × 50%)	$ 37,500	

If cost, $50,000, had been related to sales price after markdowns, $95,000, a cost percentage of 52.6% would have been obtained, and the inventory, which is three fourths of the merchandise originally acquired, would have been reported at 52.6% of $75,000, or $39,450. The inventory would thus be stated above the $37,500 cost of the remaining inventory and cost of goods sold would be understated by $1,950. A markdown relating to goods no longer on hand would have been recognized in the development of a cost percentage to be applied to the inventory. Reductions in the goods available at sales prices resulting from shortages or damaged goods should likewise be disregarded in calculating the cost percentage.

Example 2 — Markdowns as a result of market declines. Assume that merchandise costing $50,000 is marked to sell for $100,000. With a drop in replacement cost of the merchandise to $40,000, sales prices are marked down to $80,000. One half of the merchandise is sold. The cost of the ending inventory is calculated as follows:

	Cost	Retail
Purchases	$50,000	$100,000
Cost percentage ($50,000 ÷ $100,000) = 50%		
Deduct: Sales		$ 40,000
Markdowns		20,000
		$ 60,000
Ending inventory at retail		$ 40,000
Ending inventory at estimated cost ($40,000 × 50%)	$ 20,000	

If cost, $50,000, had been related to sales price after markdowns, $80,000, a cost percentage of 62.5% would have been obtained and the inventory would have been reported at 62.5% of $40,000, or $25,000. The use of the 50% cost percentage in the example reduces the inventory to $20,000, a balance providing the usual gross profit in subsequent periods if current prices and relationships between cost and retail prices prevail.

Discounts, Returns, and Allowances

Purchases should be shown net of cash discounts and purchase returns and allowances. A purchase return affects both the cost and the retail computations, while a purchase allowance affects only the cost total unless a change in retail price is made as a result of the allowance. Sales returns and allowances are proper adjustments to gross sales; however, sales discounts are not deducted to determine the ending retail inventory since retail prices for goods purchased are recorded at gross amounts.

Limitations of Retail Method

The calculation of a cost percentage for all goods carried is valid only when goods on hand can be regarded as a representative slice of the total goods handled. Varying markon percentages and sales of high- and low-margin items in proportions that differ from purchases will require separate records and the development of separate cost percentages for the different classes of goods. For example, assume that a store operates three departments and that for July the following information pertains to these departments:

	Department A		Department B		Department C		Total	
	Cost	Retail	Cost	Retail	Cost	Retail	Cost	Retail
Beginning inventory..............	$20,000	$ 28,000	$10,000	$15,000	$16,000	$ 40,000	$ 46,000	$ 83,000
Net purchases.......................	57,000	82,000	20,000	35,000	20,000	60,000	97,000	177,000
Goods available for sale	$77,000	$110,000	$30,000	$50,000	$36,000	$100,000	$143,000	$260,000
Cost percentage		70%		60%		36%		55%
Sales.....................................		80,000		30,000		40,000		150,000
Inventory at retail..................		$ 30,000		$20,000		$ 60,000		$110,000
Inventory at cost...................		$ 21,000		$12,000		$ 21,600		$ 60,500

($54,600)

Because of the range in cost percentages from 36% to 70% and the difference in mix of the purchases and ending inventory, the ending inventory balance, using an overall cost percentage, is $5,900 higher ($60,500 − $54,600), than when the departmental rates are used. When material variations exist in the cost percentages by departments, separate departmental rates should be computed and applied.

The retail method is acceptable for income tax purposes, provided the taxpayer maintains adequate and satisfactory records supporting inventory calculations and applies the method consistently on successive tax returns.

DOLLAR-VALUE LIFO PROCEDURES

The use of dollar-value lifo requires estimates of the price-level changes for specific inventories. For department stores, indexes furnished by the U.S. Bureau of Labor Statistics have been accepted for tax purposes by the Internal Revenue Service as the estimate of the price changes. For other types of companies, a specific set of indexes must be developed relating directly to a specific inventory. Because dollar-value lifo is acceptable for tax purposes only if fairly rigid requirements are met, the procedures used on the books generally correspond with the income tax regulations.

General Procedures— Dollar-Value Lifo

Dollar-value lifo views all goods in the inventory or in the separate pools to which it is to be applied as though they were similar items. Physical inventories are taken in terms of current replacement prices. Beginning and ending inventory values are then converted by means of appropriate price indexes to base-year prices, i.e., prices existing at the time the lifo method was adopted. The difference between beginning and ending dollar balances as converted is regarded as a measure of the inventory quantity change for the year. An inventory increase is recognized as an inventory layer to be added to the beginning inventory, and such increase is converted at the current price index and added to the dollars identified with the beginning balance. An inventory decrease is recognized as a shrinkage to be applied to the most recent or top layer and to successively lower layers of the beginning inventory, and this decrease is converted at the price indexes applying to such layers and subtracted from the dollars identified with the beginning inventory.

The example presented below and at the top of the next page illustrates dollar-value lifo calculations. The index numbers were as follows:

Year	Index
December 31, 1973	100
December 31, 1974	120
December 31, 1975	132
December 31, 1976	140
December 31, 1977	125

January 1, 1974 – Date of adoption of dollar-value lifo.
January 1, 1974 inventory at base prices (cost).. $38,000

December 31, 1974 – end of first year:
(a) December 31, 1974 inventory at year-end prices................................. $54,000
(b) December 31, 1974 inventory at base prices (a ÷ 1.20) 45,000
(c) January 1, 1974 inventory at base prices.. 38,000
(d) 1974 inventory increase at base prices, $45,000 − $38,000 (b − c) 7,000
(e) 1974 layer increase, $7,000 × 1.20... 8,400
(f) December 31, 1974 inventory at dollar-value lifo, $38,000 + $8,400
    (c + e) 46,400

Inventory composition:	Base Prices	Index	Cost
1974 layer	$ 7,000	120	$ 8,400
Base quantity	38,000	100	38,000
	$45,000		$46,400

December 31, 1975 – end of second year:
(a) December 31, 1975 inventory at year-end prices................................. $66,000
(b) December 31, 1975 inventory at base prices (a ÷ 1.32) 50,000
(c) January 1, 1975 inventory at base prices.. 45,000
(d) 1975 inventory increase at base prices, $50,000 − $45,000 (b − c) 5,000
(e) 1975 layer increase, $5,000 × 1.32... 6,600
(f) December 31, 1975 inventory at dollar-value lifo, $46,400 + $6,600
    (1974f + e) 53,000

	Base Prices	Index	Cost
Inventory composition: 1975 layer	$ 5,000	132	$ 6,600
1974 layer	7,000	120	8,400
Base quantity	38,000	100	38,000
	$50,000		$53,000

December 31, 1976 – end of third year:
(a) December 31, 1976 inventory at year-end prices................................. $56,000
(b) December 31, 1976 inventory at base prices (a ÷ 1.40)   40,000
(c) January 1, 1976 inventory at base prices....................................   50,000
(d) 1976 inventory decrease at base prices, $50,000 − $40,000 (c − b)...   10,000
(e) 1976 decrease: 1975 layer, $5,000 × 1.32 = $6,600
                         1974 layer,   5,000 × 1.20 =   6,000.........................   12,600
(f) December 31, 1976 inventory at dollar-value lifo, $53,000 − $12,600
     (1975f − e)   40,400

	Base Prices	Index	Cost
Inventory composition: 1974 layer	$ 2,000	120	$ 2,400
Base quantity	38,000	100	38,000
	$40,000		$40,400

December 31, 1977 – end of fourth year:
(a) December 31, 1977 inventory at year-end prices................................. $55,000
(b) December 31, 1977 inventory at base prices (a ÷ 1.25)   44,000
(c) January 1, 1977 inventory at base prices....................................   40,000
(d) 1977 inventory increase at base prices, $44,000 − $40,000 (b − c)   4,000
(e) 1977 layer increase, $4,000 × 1.25 (d × e).................................   5,000
(f) December 31, 1977 inventory at dollar-value lifo, $40,400 + $5,000
     (1976f + e)   45,400

	Base Prices	Index	Cost
Inventory composition: 1977 layer	$ 4,000	125	$ 5,000
1974 layer	2,000	120	2,400
Base quantity	38,000	100	38,000
	$44,000		$45,400

This example can be illustrated by highlighting the layers as follows:

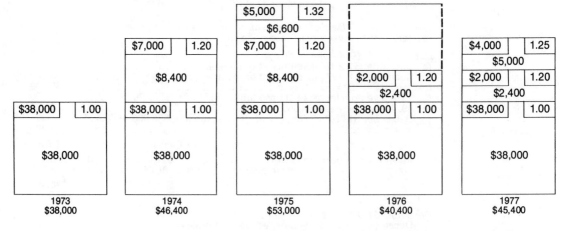

The amount of each layer is determined by multiplying together the
amounts in the corner boxes. The amount in the upper left hand box is
the base cost of the layer; the amount in the upper right hand box is
the price index for the layer year.

The following items should be observed in the example:

December 31, 1974 — With an ending inventory of $45,000 in terms of base prices, the inventory has increased in 1974 by $7,000; however, the $7,000 increase is stated in terms of the pricing when lifo was adopted and needs to be restated in terms of year-end prices which are 120% of the base level.

December 31, 1975 — With an ending inventory of $50,000 in terms of base prices, the inventory has increased in 1975 by another $5,000; however, the $5,000 increase is stated in terms of the pricing when lifo was adopted and needs to be restated in terms of year-end costs which are 132% of the base level.

December 31, 1976 — With an ending inventory of $40,000 in terms of base prices, the inventory has decreased in 1976 by $10,000; however, the $10,000 decrease is stated in terms of pricing when lifo was adopted and needs to be restated in terms of the pricing of the inventory layers that are eliminated or reduced. The decrease is applied first to elimination of the 1975 $5,000 layer and next to the reduction of the 1974 $7,000 layer; decreases are restated in terms of the percentages at which these layers were included in the inventory cost — for 1975, 132% of the base level, and for 1974, 120% of the base level.

December 31, 1977 — The ending inventory of $44,000 in terms of the base prices indicates an inventory increase for 1977 of $4,000; this increase requires restatement in terms of year-end prices which are 125% of the base level.

In the previous examples, it was assumed that the base year index was 100. If the base year index is not 100, a relative index can be computed from a fraction in which the numerator is the current year index and the denominator is the base year index. For example, assume that the current index is 140 and the base year index is 112. The relative index for the current year conversions would therefore be 140 ÷ 112 = 125.

Retail-Lifo Procedures

Dollar-value lifo procedures just described can be applied to the retail inventory method in developing inventory values reflecting a last-in, first-out valuation approach. *Retail lifo* requires that index numbers be applied to inventories stated at retail in arriving at the quantitative changes in inventories. When the quantitative changes have been developed, ending inventories are restated in terms of the retail base amounts, and the layers involved in their composition and related cost percentages are applied to such values.

The retail-lifo process calls for two modifications to the conventional retail procedures to determine a cost percentage.

1. Beginning inventory values are disregarded. The lifo inventory is composed of a base cost and subsequent cost layers that have not been assigned to revenues. With costs for prior periods to remain unchanged, only the cost of a current incremental layer requires calculation.

2. Markdowns, as well as markups, are recognized in calculating the cost percentage applicable to goods stated at retail. Markdowns were not recognized in arriving at the cost percentage when the objective was to arrive at a lower of cost or market valuation. However, with lifo measurements requiring inventory valuation in terms of cost, the recognition of both markups and markdowns becomes appropriate.

These modifications in calculating cost percentages are illustrated in the following example:

	Cost	Retail
Purchases..	$63,000	$ 98,000
Purchase returns..	(2,000)	(3,000)
Purchase discounts	(1,000)	
Freight in...	2,220	
Markups, net of cancellations..		8,000
Markdowns, net of cancellations......................................		(1,000)
Total current period purchases adjusted for markups and markdowns..	$62,220	$102,000

Cost percentage ($62,220 ÷ $102,000) = 61%

It is important to note that this cost percentage will be used only if an incremental layer is added to the inventory in the current period. If the inventory level has declined, previous inventory layers will be reduced.

Retail-lifo procedures are illustrated in the example that follows. To simplify the example, it is assumed that any net markups or net markdowns are already included in the net purchase figures. To determine the December 31, 1974, inventory at retail, two calculations are necessary. First add beginning inventory at retail to the net purchases for the period to determine goods available for sale at retail ($60,000 + $200,000 = $260,000). Then subtract the net sales for the period from the goods available for sale at retail ($260,000 − $190,700) and this is the ending inventory at retail. Similar computations are done for each year to determine the ending inventory at retail. Year-end price indexes expressed in terms of prices as of December 31, 1973, are: 1974, 105; 1975, 110; 1976, 112; 1977, 108.

	Retail	Index	Cost Percentage	Cost
January 1, 1974 – Date of adoption of retail lifo.				
January 1, 1974 inventory..	$ 60,000	100	60	$ 36,000
December 31, 1974 – end of first year:				
Net purchases..	200,000		62	124,000
Net sales..	(190,700)			
December 31, 1974 inventory at retail	69,300			
December 31, 1974 inventory at retail base prices, $69,300 ÷ 1.05..	66,000			
1974 inventory increase at retail base prices, $66,000 − $60,000..	6,000			
1974 layer increase — 1974 index, 105; 1974 cost percentage, 62%	6,000	105	62	3,906
Inventory composition: 1974 layer	$ 6,000	105	62	$ 3,906
Base quantity	60,000	100	60	36,000
	$ 66,000			$ 39,906

	Retail	Index	Cost Percentage	Cost
December 31, 1975 – end of second year:				
January 1, 1975 inventory at retail	$ 69,300			
Net purchases..	210,000		64	$134,400
Net sales..	(202,300)			
December 31, 1975 inventory at retail	77,000			
December 31, 1975 inventory at retail base prices, $77,000 ÷ 1.10..	70,000			
1975 inventory increase at retail base prices, $70,000 – $66,000..	4,000			
1975 layer increase — 1975 index, 110; 1975 cost percentage, 64%	4,000	110	64	2,816
Inventory composition: 1975 layer	$ 4,000	110	64	$ 2,816
1974 layer	6,000	105	62	3,906
Base quantity	60,000	100	60	36,000
	$ 70,000			$ 42,722
December 31, 1976 – end of third year:				
January 1, 1976 inventory at retail	$ 77,000			
Net purchases..	180,000		65	$117,000
Net sales..	(179,720)			
December 31, 1976 inventory at retail	77,280			
December 31, 1976 inventory at retail base prices, $77,280 ÷ 1.12..	69,000			
1976 inventory decrease at retail base prices, $70,000 – $69,000..	1,000			
1976 decrease — 1975 layer..	1,000	110	64	704
Inventory composition: 1975 layer	$ 3,000	110	64	$ 2,112
1974 layer	6,000	105	62	3,906
Base quantity	60,000	100	60	36,000
	$ 69,000			$ 42,018
December 31, 1977 – end of fourth year:				
January 1, 1977 inventory at retail	$ 77,280			
Net purchases..	220,000		60	$132,000
Net sales..	(218,980)			
December 31, 1977 inventory at retail	78,300			
December 31, 1977 inventory at retail base prices, $78,300 ÷ 1.08..	72,500			
1977 inventory increase at retail base prices, $72,500 – $69,000..	3,500			
1977 layer increase — 1977 index, 108; cost percentage, 60%	3,500	108	60	2,268
Inventory composition: 1977 layer	$ 3,500	108	60	$ 2,268
1975 layer	3,000	110	64	2,112
1974 layer	6,000	105	62	3,906
Base quantity	60,000	100	60	36,000
	$ 72,500			$ 44,286

With the cost percentage included in the lower left hand corner, the layers of this example can be illustrated as shown at the top of the following page.

The amount of each layer is determined by multiplying together the amounts in the three corner boxes.

The foregoing example assumed that retail-lifo was used from the beginning of the company's existence. However, if a company has been using the conventional retail method and decides to change to retail-lifo, the beginning inventory in the year of change must be adjusted from a

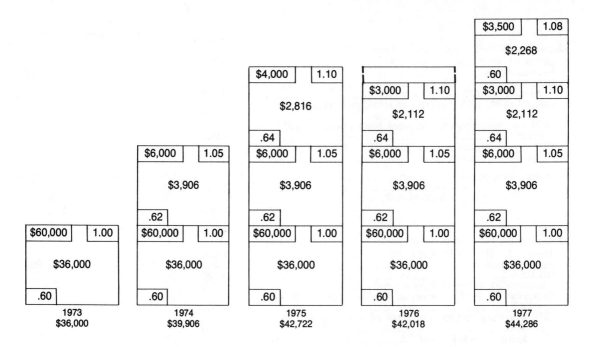

lower of cost or market valuation to a cost valuation. This can be done by including markdowns before computing the cost percentage. Any gain arising from the increase in the beginning inventory valuation should be reported in the current period income statement.

Determination of Price Indexes

There are two generally accepted methods for determining price indexes for a particular inventory: (1) using a published index relating to the inventory; or (2) developing a specific index from the company's inventory records.

Although many price-level indexes are published by governmental and private agencies, only the Bureau of Labor Statistics' department store indexes are automatically acceptable for income tax purposes. These indexes are computed twice a year, January and July, and are available about March 15 and September 15. The BLS department store indexes are divided into twenty groups, and each group becomes a separate dollar-value pool for department stores using these indexes. Indexes for other retail establishments and industries might be used if they can be shown to be appropriate for the special inventory pool to which they are applied. However, industry averages are generally not acceptable because they do not take into consideration the specific variables affecting a given company.

When published indexes are not acceptable, specific indexes must be developed from the company's inventory records. The most widely adopted method of developing indexes for dollar-value lifo is *double extension*. This index is computed by extending a representative portion of a specific inventory at both base-year prices and at current prices. Thus, if the total ending inventory was $126,500 valued at current prices and $105,400 when the individual items in the ending inventory were valued at base-year prices, the index relationship between these values would be 120 ($126,500 ÷ $105,400). The double extension method may use a sample of items, but the Internal Revenue Service has stated that a representative sample must include at least 50% of the items and represent 75% or more of the dollar value.

This method has two principal disadvantages: (1) it is time consuming and costly for companies having a large number of different inventory items; and (2) if the inventory items are changing, it may be difficult to determine base year prices for newly added items. This latter disadvantage is overcome with the *link chain* method. This modification of the double extension method requires extending a statistically representative portion of the ending inventory at both end-of-year prices and beginning-of-year prices. The index computed from this valuation is then multiplied by the cumulative index carried forward from previous years to determine the current index. The BLS department store indexes are established using this method.

The computations of the link chain method are illustrated as follows:

Valuation at year-end prices of representative portion of inventory	$215,040
Valuation at beginning-of-year prices of above portion of inventory	$204,800
Yearly index ($215,040 ÷ $204,800)	105
Cumulative index from previous years	140
Cumulative index as of end of current year (1.40 × 1.05 = 1.47)	147

This method has the advantage of simplicity because historical records of base year costs are not necessary. It permits changing inventory items without causing difficulty in computing base year prices for the new items.

Selection of Pools   The selection of inventory pools is very critical in dollar-value lifo. A company should have a minimum of pools to benefit most by the use of the lifo concept. The Internal Revenue Service, however, requires separate pools when inventory items are quite dissimilar. The organization of the company is a major factor in determining the pools to be used.

INVENTORIES ON THE BALANCE SHEET

It is customary for business units to report trading as well as manufacturing inventories as current assets even though in some instances it may take considerable time before portions of such inventories are realized in cash. Among the items that are generally reported separately under the inventories heading are merchandise inventory or finished goods, goods in process, raw materials, factory supplies, goods and materials in transit, goods on consignment, and goods in the hands of agents and salespersons. Inventories are normally listed in the order of their liquidity.

Purchase orders should not be treated as additions to inventories, nor should sales orders be treated as deductions as long as title to goods has not passed. When goods have been formally set aside and the title is transferred, purchases or sales may be recognized with proper recognition of the effect of such transactions on the inventory position. Any advance payments on purchase commitments should not be included in inventories but should be reported separately. Such advances are preferably listed after inventories in the current asset section since they still await entry into the inventory phase of the operating cycle.

The valuation procedures employed must be disclosed in a note to the financial statements outlining all significant accounting policies followed.[1] The basis of valuation (such as cost or lower of cost or market), together with the method of arriving at cost (lifo, fifo, average, or other method), should be indicated. The reader of a statement may assume that the valuation procedures indicated have been consistently applied and financial statements are comparable with those of past periods. If this is not the case, a special note should be provided stating the change in the method and the effects of the change upon the financial statements. Further discussion of reporting changes in accounting methods is found in Chapter 22.

When the inventory method provides values that are materially less than current replacement costs, disclosure of replacement costs should be offered. The use of lifo, for example, may result in a serious distortion of working capital measurements. Data concerning replacement costs should be given if the reader of the statement is to be adequately informed on financial position.

An inventory allowance to reduce an inventory to a lower of cost or market basis is reported as a subtraction from the inventory at cost. However, an appropriation of retained earnings to preserve earnings within the business for possible future market decline in the inventory value is reported as a part of the stockholders' equity. If the decline fails to materialize, the appropriation balance is no longer required and is returned to the retained earnings account. If the decline does materialize, the appropriation is still returned to the retained earnings account where it will absorb the inventory loss ultimately carried to the latter account through net income.

If significant inventory price declines take place between the balance sheet date and the date the statement is prepared, such declines should be disclosed by parenthetical remark or note. When relatively large orders for merchandise have been placed in a period of widely fluctuating prices, but the title to such goods has not yet passed, such commitments should be described by special note. Information should also be provided concerning possible losses on purchase commitments. Similar information may be appropriate for possible losses on sales commitments.

---

[1] *Opinions of the Accounting Principles Board, No. 22,* "Disclosure of Accounting Policies" (New York: American Institute of Certified Public Accountants, 1972), par. 12.

When inventories or sections of an inventory have been pledged as security on loans from banks, finance companies, or factors, the amounts pledged should be disclosed parenthetically in the inventory section of the balance sheet.

Inventory items may be reported as follows:

Inventories:			
Raw materials:			
On hand	$228,000		
Less allowance to reduce inventory from cost to market	18,000	$210,000	
In transit from supplier		30,000	$240,000
Goods in process			300,000
Finished goods:			
On hand (goods of $100,000 have been pledged as security on loans of $75,000 from First State Bank)		$300,000	
On consignment		15,000	315,000
Factory supplies			12,000
Total inventories			$867,000

QUESTIONS

1. Give certain instances in which estimates of inventory costs are necessary or appropriate and state what procedure would be followed in developing satisfactory estimates of such costs.

2. What is your understanding of the meaning of the "gross profit test"?

3. Distinguish between: (a) gross profit as a percentage of cost and gross profit as a percentage of sales; (b) markup cancellation and markdown; (c) the gross profit method of calculating estimated inventory cost and the retail inventory method of calculating estimated inventory cost.

4. What effect would the use of the lifo inventory method have upon the applicability of the gross profit method of valuing inventory?

5. How can a company verify that the use of the gross profit percentage approximates the cost of the inventory?

6. How can the retail inventory method be considered a perpetual inventory method?

7. Define (a) initial markup, (b) additional markup, (c) markup cancellation, (d) markdown, (e) markdown cancellation, and (f) maintained markup.

8. How should the cost percentage be calculated for the conventional retail inventory method?

9. How are sales discounts recognized in using the retail inventory method?

10. A merchant taking inventory by the retail method maintains no separate record of markup cancellations and markdown cancellations. Instead she includes the former in markdowns and the latter in markups, as "these represent price decreases and increases respectively." How will this procedure affect her inventory at (a) retail? (b) cost?

11. What are the major advantages of dollar-value lifo?

12. Describe the application of dollar-value lifo procedures.

13. What kind of an enterprise will benefit most from the adoption of dollar-value lifo?

14. What are the similarities between dollar-value lifo and retail-lifo?

15. Compute a relative index assuming the current year index is 150 and the base year index is 90.

16. (a) Describe retail-lifo. (b) What modifications in the conventional retail procedures are required in adopting and applying retail-lifo?

17. Why must the beginning inventory be adjusted when a company changes from conventional retail to retail-lifo?

18. How would a company determine appropriate indexes for either the dollar-value lifo or retail-lifo methods?

19. How would you recommend that the items listed at the top of the next page be reported on the balance sheet?

(a) Unsold goods in the hands of consignees.
(b) Purchase orders outstanding.
(c) Advance payments on purchase commitments.
(d) Raw materials pledged by means of warehouse receipts on notes payable to bank.
(e) Raw materials in transit from suppliers.
(f) An allowance to reduce the inventory cost to market.
(g) An appropriation of retained earnings for possible future inventory declines.

(h) Materials received from a customer for processing.
(i) Merchandise produced by special order and set aside to be picked up by customer.
(j) Raw materials set aside to be used in connection with plant rehabilitation activities.
(k) Finished parts to be used in the assembly of final products.
(l) Janitorial supplies.

EXERCISES

1. Sales for a period are $100,000. What is the cost of goods sold under each assumption below?

(a) Gross profit on sales is 20%.
(b) Gross profit on cost of sales is 60%.
(c) Goods are marked up ¼ above cost.
(d) Gross profit on cost of sales is 150%.
(e) Goods are marked up 200% above cost.
(f) Gross profit on sales is 18%.
(g) Gross profit on cost is 18%.

2. On March 29, 1977, a warehouse of Paige Company was destroyed by fire. The following information was taken from Paige's books.

Merchandise inventory, December 31, 1976.. $70,000

	Sales	Purchases
January, 1977	$55,000	$30,000
February, 1977...	40,000	50,000
March, 1977	38,000	45,000

Determine the cost of the merchandise destroyed by the fire assuming:

(a) Gross profit margin is 30% of selling price.
(b) Gross profit percentage is 40% of cost.

3. The sales and purchases data for the Minton Co. follow:

	Sales	Purchases
January	$50,000	$40,000
February..	60,000	45,000
March..	65,000	50,000

The merchandise inventory at cost on January 1 was $30,000. Goods are sold at a gross profit of 20% on sales. Compute the monthly inventory balances for interim statement purposes.

4. M. Wilde requires an estimate of the cost of goods lost by fire on March 7. Merchandise on hand on January 1 was $60,000. Purchases since January 1 were $45,000; freight in, $5,000; purchase returns and allowances, $3,000. Sales are made at 20% above cost and totaled $48,000 to March 7. Goods costing $12,250 were left undamaged by the fire; remaining goods were destroyed. (a) What was the cost of goods destroyed? (b) What would your answer be if sales are made at a gross profit of 20% of sales?

5. Records for the Fox Department Store disclose the following data:

	Cost	Retail
Merchandise inventory, January 1	$ 30,000	$ 60,000
Purchases, January 1 — December 31	180,000	
Sales, January 1 — December 31...		205,000
Sales returns, January 1 — December 31......................................		5,000
Freight in, January 1 — December 31..	12,500	
Purchase discounts taken, January 1 — December 31	2,500	

A physical inventory taken on December 31 shows merchandise on hand valued at retail at $120,000. Compute the estimated cost of ending inventory.

6. From the following information, compute the cost of inventory shortage for the Brandenburg Discount Stores for 1977. The company uses conventional retail inventory procedures.

	Cost	Retail
Inventory, January 1, 1977 (cost ratio — 80%)	$ 9,600	
Purchases	59,000	$80,000

Total sales for the year amounted to $70,000. Markups were $6,000; markup cancellations were $1,500; markdowns, $3,000; freight in, $2,845; sales discounts, $2,000; and purchase discounts, $1,000. The physical inventory on December 31, 1977, was $20,000 (prices as shown on sales tags on items).

7. If the retail-lifo inventory method had been used in Exercise 6, what cost percentage would be used for 1977?

8. Snow White, Inc., employs dollar-value lifo for periodic inventories. The inventory on January 1, 1977, was reported at $80,000; the inventory on December 31, 1977, was $94,500. The December 31 inventory at January 1 prices was $90,000. What cost would be assigned to the ending inventory using the double extension method?

9. You assemble the following information for the Pratt Department Store which computes its inventory at retail-lifo.

	Cost	Retail
Inventory, January 1, 1977	$117,000	$150,000
Net purchases	208,000	250,000
Markups		10,000
Markdowns		5,000
Increase in price level for year		5%

Calculate the cost of the inventory on December 31, 1977, assuming that the inventory at retail is (a) $147,000, (b) $168,000.

10. The Jenkins Wholesale Company took a statistical sample of their inventory at December 31, 1977. The inventory revealed the following information:

		Cost	
Commodity	Quantity	1976	1977
A	100	$ 7.00	$ 7.50
B	250	2.40	2.60
C	75	10.00	10.60

The price-index in 1976 was 141. Calculate the index for 1977 using the link-chain method.

PROBLEMS

9-1. Quarterly purchases and sales for Lane Electrical, Inc., are listed below. The corporation began business in 1977 with a merchandise inventory of $44,500. Goods have been sold at a uniform markup of 33⅓%.

	Purchases	Sales
January 1–March 31	$30,520	$38,600
April 1–June 30	30,900	51,620
July 1–September 30	50,200	58,300
October 1–December 31	27,000	72,000

Instructions:
(1) Compute the inventory for the end of each quarter.
(2) Compute the merchandise turnover rate for the year based upon quarterly data.

9-2. The following information was taken from the records of the Lucky Company.

	1/1/76–12/31/76	1/1/77–9/30/77
Sales (net of returns)	$1,250,000	$750,000
Beginning inventory	210,000	365,000
Purchases	1,076,000	530,500
Freight in	58,000	36,000
Purchase discounts	15,000	7,500
Purchase returns	20,000	6,500
Purchase allowances	4,000	2,500
Ending inventory	365,000	
Selling and general expenses	225,000	160,000

Instructions: Compute by the gross-profit method the value to be assigned to the inventory as of September 30, 1977, and prepare an interim statement summarizing operations for the nine-month period ending on this date.

9-3. In December, 1977, Target Merchandise, Inc., had a significant portion of their inventory stolen. The company determined the cost of their inventory not stolen to be $31,705. The following information was taken from the records of the company.

	January 1, 1977 to Date of Theft	1976
Purchases	$129,045	$134,433
Purchase returns and allowances	6,021	7,017
Sales	196,677	203,317
Sales returns and allowances	2,402	2,167
Wages	17,743	18,356
Salaries	8,000	9,000
Taxes other than income	3,732	3,648
Rent	5,400	5,400
Insurance	967	982
Light, heat, and water	1,134	1,271
Advertising	4,250	2,680
Interest expense	2,755	3,020
Depreciation expense	1,255	1,280
Furniture and fixtures	10,065	10,570
Miscellaneous expense	6,634	6,877
Beginning inventory	47,880	49,200

Instructions: Estimate the cost of the stolen inventory.

9-4. The records of the appliance department for Bargain Basement Discount Store show the following data for the month of March:

Sales	$201,500	Purchase returns (at cost price)	$ 2,500
Sales returns	2,000	Purchase returns (at sales price)	3,400
Additional markups	17,900	Markup cancellations	4,000
Markdowns	24,000		
Markdown cancellations	3,500	Beginning inventory (at cost price)	125,000
Freight on purchases	3,500		
Purchases (at cost price)	61,000	Beginning inventory (at sales price)	170,000
Purchases (at sales price)	94,500		

Instructions: Compute the inventory using the conventional retail inventory method.

9-5. The following information was taken from the records of Gardens, Inc., for the years 1976 and 1977.

	1977	1976
Sales	$173,250	$169,500
Sales discounts	2,300	1,500
Sales returns	2,250	2,000
Freight in	5,000	4,550
Purchases (at cost)	97,500	85,700
Purchases (at retail)	125,700	115,600
Purchase discounts	1,472	1,250
Beginning inventory (at cost)		82,000
Beginning inventory (at retail)		109,400

Instructions: Compute the value of the inventory at the end of 1976 and 1977 using the conventional retail inventory method.

9-6. Information concerning the inventory of Home Manufacturing Corp. is shown below. Business was started in 1972.

Date	Price Index	Inventory At Year-End Prices
December 31, 1972	100	$ 15,000
December 31, 1973	115	28,750
December 31, 1974	150	45,000
December 31, 1975	125	35,000
December 31, 1976	170	68,000
December 31, 1977	200	100,000

Instructions: Compute the December 31, 1977, inventory under the dollar-value lifo method.

9-7. Perez Industrial, Inc., decided in December, 1976, to adopt the dollar-value lifo method for calculating the ending inventory for 1977 and each year thereafter. Perez decided to compute the index of price changes by sampling from the stock of goods. The inventory at December 31, 1976, was $3,200. This value is considered the base cost for applying the dollar-value technique.

The following data have been taken from Perez's books and are to be used as the basis for inventory valuation:

Description	Inventory Quantities (sample items) 1977	1978	Inventory Prices (end of year) 1976	1977	1978
A	40	40	$10.00	$12.70	$12.00
B	80	100	12.00	13.78	13.92
C	30	50	8.00	10.00	7.74
D	100	100	10.00	10.80	13.41
Total inventory cost at end-of-year prices.............			$3,200	$4,140	$4,473

Instructions:
  (1) Compute the price index to be used by Perez for 1977 and 1978.
  (2) Compute the dollar-value lifo inventory for 1977 and 1978 using the double extension method.

9-8. Havican, Inc., has adopted the retail-lifo method for stating its inventories. The following data are available for a four-year period ending December 31, 1978.

		Cost	Retail
1975	Inventory, January 1...	$ 56,700	$ 90,000
	Purchases	155,000	250,000
	Sales..		230,000
	Price index (1/1/75 = 100)...		110
1976	Purchases	145,200	220,000
	Sales..		237,250
	Price index (1/1/75 = 100)...		106
1977	Purchases	156,000	260,000
	Sales..		250,150
	Price index (1/1/75 = 100)...		108
1978	Purchases	201,600	320,000
	Sales..		305,000
	Price index (1/1/75 = 100)...		112

Instructions: Calculate the inventories to be reported at the end of 1975, 1976, 1977, and 1978.

9-9. The Goldstein Department Store provides you with the following information for 1977:

	Cost	Retail
Beginning inventory...	$ 72,000	$ 90,000
Sales		183,000
Markups (net)...		15,000
Sales discounts..		1,000
Markdowns (net)..		8,000

(continued)

	Cost	Retail
Purchases...	$150,000	$193,000
Freight in	8,000	
Purchase allowances...	2,000	
Purchase discounts..	2,000	
Price level — beginning of year (base)	100	
Price level — 1977	107	

Instructions:
(1) Determine the conventional retail cost percentage for the inventory.
(2) Calculate the retail value of the physical inventory at the end of the period assuming there was no shrinkage.
(3) Using retail-lifo procedures, compute retail and cost values for the inventory at December 31, 1977. Give your computations.

9-10. The Cougar Sports Shop values its inventory on the retail-lifo basis. At December 31, 1976, the inventory was valued as follows:

Lifo Layer Year	Cost	Actual Retail	Price Index for Year	Retail at Base of 100
1970	$ 4,920	$ 8,200	100	$ 8,200
1972	3,160	4,515	105	4,300
1974	4,480	8,961	103	8,700
1975	1,500	2,000	110	1,818
	$14,060	$23,676		$23,018

The following data were also compiled.

December 31, 1976 inventory at 1976 retail prices	$ 25,780
Purchases — cost	145,200
Purchases — selling price..	224,615
Freight in	3,300
Sales returns	3,740
Sales discounts	650
Markups	1,580
Markup cancellations	360
Markdowns	835
Gross sales	234,000
Price index for 1977..	108

Instructions: Based upon the above information for 1977, compute (1) the 1977 cost ratio, and (2) the inventory amount that would be reported on the balance sheet at December 31, 1977.

9-11. The Borow Corporation is an importer and wholesaler. Its merchandise is purchased from a number of suppliers and is warehoused by Borow Corporation until sold to consumers.

In conducting the audit for the year ended June 30, 1978, the company's CPA determined that the system of internal control was good. Accordingly, the physical inventory was observed at an interim date, May 31, 1978, instead of at year end.

The following information was obtained from the general ledger:

Inventory, July 1, 1977	$ 87,500
Physical inventory, May 31, 1978..	95,000
Sales for 11 months ended May 31, 1978	840,000
Sales for year ended June 30, 1978...	960,000
Purchases for 11 months ended May 31, 1978 (before audit adjustments)	675,000
Purchases for year ended June 30, 1978 (before audit adjustments)	800,000

The CPA's audit disclosed the following information:

Shipments received in May and included in the physical inventory but recorded as June purchases	7,500
Shipments received in unsalable condition and excluded from physical inventory. Credit memos had not been received nor had chargebacks to vendors been recorded.	
Total at May 31, 1978..	1,000
Total at June 30, 1978 (including the May unrecorded chargebacks)	1,500

Deposit made with vendor and charged to purchases in April, 1978. Product was shipped in July, 1978... $2,000

Deposit made with vendor and charged to purchases in May 1978. Product was shipped, FOB destination, on May 29, 1978, and was included in May 31, 1978, physical inventory as goods in transit 5,500

Through the carelessness of the receiving department a June shipment was damaged by rain. This shipment was later sold in June at its cost of $10,000.

In audit engagements in which interim physical inventories are observed, a frequently used auditing procedure is to test the reasonableness of the year-end inventory by the application of gross profit ratios.

> **Instructions:** Prepare the following schedules:
> (1) Computation of the gross profit ratio for 11 months ended May 31, 1978.
> (2) Computation by the gross profit method of cost of goods sold during June 1978.
> (3) Computation by the gross profit method of the inventory at June 30, 1978. (AICPA adapted)

9-12. The operations of a department of a retail store that uses the conventional retail method of inventory determination are given in the figures presented below:

Opening inventory — cost...	$14,250
Opening inventory — sales price..	19,105
Purchases — cost	33,771
Purchases — sales price	46,312
Purchase allowances..	1,093
Freight in	845
Departmental transfers (debit) — cost..	100
Departmental transfers (debit) — sales price	140
Additional markups..	1,207
Markup cancellations	274
Inventory shortage — sales price	704
Sales (including sales of $4,460 of items that were marked down from $5,920).	37,246

> **Instructions:** Set up a computation showing the ending inventory at sales price and at cost as determined by the conventional retail method. (AICPA adapted)

9-13. Lopez Department Store converted from the conventional retail method to the retail-lifo method on January 1, 1977. Management requested during your examination of the financial statements for the year ended December 31, 1978, that you furnish a summary showing certain computations of inventory costs for the past three years.

Available information follows:
(a) The inventory at January 1, 1976, had a retail value of $45,000 and a cost of $27,500 based on the conventional retail method. (There were no markdowns in 1975.)
(b) Transactions during 1976 were as follows:

	Cost	Retail
Gross purchases	$282,000	$490,000
Purchase returns...	6,500	10,000
Purchase discounts	5,000	
Gross sales		492,000
Sales returns		5,000
Employee discounts		3,000
Freight in	26,500	
Net markups...		25,000
Net markdowns		10,000

(c) The retail value of the December 31, 1977 inventory was $56,100, the cost percentage for 1977 under the retail-lifo method was 62%, and the regional price index was 102% of the January 1, 1977 price level.
(d) The retail value of the December 31, 1978 inventory was $48,300, the cost percentage for 1978 under the retail-lifo method was 61%, and the regional price index was 105% of the January 1, 1977 price level.

(continued)

Instructions:

(1) Prepare a schedule showing the computation of the cost of inventory on hand at December 31, 1976, based on the conventional retail method.

(2) Prepare a schedule showing the computation of the cost of inventory on hand at the store on December 31, 1976, based on the retail-lifo method. Lopez Department Store does not consider beginning inventories in computing its retail-lifo cost ratio. Assume that the retail value of the inventory on December 31, 1976, was $50,000.

(3) Without prejudice to your solution to part (2), assume that you computed the inventory on December 31, 1976, (retail value $50,000) under the retail-lifo method at a cost of $28,000. Prepare a schedule showing the computations of the cost of the 1977 and 1978 year-end inventories under the retail-lifo method. (AICPA adapted)

9-14. The E.A.P. Company is engaged in manufacturing. Its products are made principally from one raw material, and in order to insure uninterrupted production, it normally maintains a substantial inventory of the raw material. Because of advancing prices, the company in 1965 adopted the last-in, first-out method of pricing out its material requisitions, and thereafter valued its inventory at the prices shown by its perpetual inventory records.

As of December 31, 1976, the inventory consisted of 380,000 pounds carried on its books at an average price of $.90 per pound. The market price on December 31, 1976, was $1.50 per pound. As of December 31, 1977, the inventory was 420,000 pounds with a market price of $1.60 per pound. This was carried at the prices shown on the stock records, 270,000 pounds of this being valued at $.90 per pound and the remainder at prices which averaged $1.54 per pound. The purchases during the year were also made at an average price of about $1.54 per pound.

The operating accounts for the year ended December 31, 1977, included the following:

Sales	$2,100,000
Goods in Process Inventory, 1/1/77	146,600
Finished Goods Inventory, 1/1/77	90,000
Direct Labor	344,000
Cost of Materials Used	1,217,000
Manufacturing Overhead	302,000
Goods in Process Inventory, 12/31/77	180,000
Finished Goods Inventory, 12/31/77	100,000

On March 30, 1978, the warehouse in which the raw material inventory was stored was badly damaged by fire. The stock records were destroyed, but from other records the following figures were obtained:

Sales to March 30	$820,000
Purchases of materials	551,425
Direct labor	132,405
Manufacturing overhead	117,604
Goods in process inventory, March 30	175,000
Finished goods inventory, March 30	105,000
Salvage value of damaged materials	25,000

The purchase price of raw material during the three months had averaged $1.61 per pound with the price on March 30, at $1.62 per pound. The sales price during the period had varied only with the current material, labor and overhead cost existing at date of acceptance of the order, as is normal in this business.

Instructions: Calculate the amount of a claim for fire loss, assuming full insurance coverage. Show all computations to support the claim. (AICPA adapted)

10

Current Liabilities

Liabilities are obligations arising from past actions, i.e., transactions to pay sums of money, to convey certain other assets, or to perform certain services. In an economic system based largely on credit, many indications of debt will be found on the balance sheet. Most goods and services are purchased on account. Funds are borrowed from commercial banks for working capital purposes. Large sums are provided by bond issues to finance new buildings and equipment. During the life of such obligations, interest accrues as an additional liability. Taxes accrued but not yet due appear as liabilities until paid. Employees of the enterprise are creditors until they are paid for their services.

Liabilities of a business unit must be fully recognized and properly measured on the balance sheet if both the amounts owed and the owners' equity in business assets are to be reported accurately. In presenting liabilities, appropriate distinction must be made between current and noncurrent items if the company's working capital position is to be accurately defined. Also, any *contingent liabilities*, those liabilities that may materialize in the event of certain acts or circumstances, must be recognized.

Valuation problems arise in the measurement of payables just as they do in the measurement of receivables. In reporting receivables, it was recognized that theoretical accuracy would require reporting at present values. It was further observed that valuation accounts should be established for amounts estimated to be uncollectible and that further reductions should be recognized when receivables included finance and interest charges in their face amounts. In reporting payables, similar considerations apply. When properties, goods, or services are acquired at an amount payable at some future date, this amount may be regarded as composed of a purchase price and a charge for interest for the period of payment deferral. If determinable, an established exchange or purchase price may be used to arrive at the present value of the payable. In the absence of such a price, the present value of the payable should be determined by discounting the amount payable at an appropriate interest rate for the period payment is deferred. The acquisition, then, is recorded by a debit to the account reporting the purchase at the amount computed, a debit to the discount on the payable, and a credit to the payable at its face amount. The discount is amortized over the life of the payable as a debit to interest expense; in preparing a balance sheet, any unamortized discount is reported as a direct subtraction from the payable.

As indicated in the earlier chapter on receivables, the Accounting Principles Board in Opinion No. 21 has concluded that the discounting procedure is not regarded as appropriate in all instances, and exempts from such practice payables arising from creditors in the normal course of business due in customary trade terms not exceeding one year. Deductions should also be recognized for such items as discounts that can be anticipated in the course of settlement, and also for any finance or interest charges included in the face amounts of the payables.

Not all obligations are definite in amount at the time financial statements are prepared. For example, obligations whose amounts cannot be exactly determined include payments under certain pension plan agreements and payments under product service warranties where experience shows that liabilities do exist. Such obligations are often referred to as *estimated liabilities.*[1] Even though the exact amounts to be paid are not determinable, proper matching of revenues and expenses, as well as the proper inclusion of all of the amounts owed by a business, requires that estimates of these obligations be made as accurately as possible.

It was indicated in Chapter 3 that *current liabilities* are broadly defined to include (1) all obligations arising from operations related to the operating cycle, and (2) all other obligations to be paid within a year. These liabilities make a claim against resources classified as current. Current liabilities are subtracted from current assets in arriving at *working capital.*

CURRENT LIABILITIES THAT ARE DEFINITE IN AMOUNT

Representative of current liabilities that are definite in amount and that are frequently found on the balance sheet are notes and accounts currently payable, current maturities of long-term obligations, cash dividends payable, deposits and agency obligations, sales and use taxes, payroll taxes and income tax withholdings, and liabilities under bonus agreements. Some of the problems arising in determining the balance to be reported for these items are described in the following sections.

Notes and Accounts Currently Payable

Both notes and accounts currently payable originate from the purchase of goods and services and from short-term borrowings. Notes currently payable may include notes issued to trade creditors for the purchase of goods and services, to banks for loans, to officers and stockholders for advances, and to others for the purchase of equipment.

---

[1]Estimated liabilities should be distinguished from contingent liabilities. The former category includes definite obligations whose exact amounts are not determinable and must be estimated on an accrual basis. The latter category includes items for which it is not certain there is a liability, even though an amount may be known, e.g., in a pending lawsuit.

Accounts currently payable may consist of a wide variety of items, including obligations to trade creditors for the purchase of goods and services, obligations for the purchase of property items and securities, credit balances in customers' accounts, customers' refundable deposits, advances from officers and stockholders, and guaranteed interest and dividends on securities of affiliated companies.

In presenting current payables on the balance sheet, it is normally desirable to classify notes and accounts in terms of their origin. Such presentation affords information concerning the sources of business indebtedness as well as the extent to which the business has relied upon each source in financing its activities.

In arriving at the total amount owed trade creditors, particular attention must be given to the purchase of goods and services at the end of the fiscal period. Both the goods and the services acquired, as well as the accompanying obligations, must be reported on the statements even though invoices evidencing the charges are not received until the following period.

Individual notes and accounts are frequently secured by the pledge of certain assets. Assets pledged may consist of marketable securities, notes receivable, accounts receivable, inventories, or land, buildings, and equipment items. The pledge of an asset limits the use or the disposition of the asset or its proceeds until the related obligation is liquidated. In the event of bankruptcy, the cash realized on a pledged asset must first be applied to the satisfaction of the related obligation. A liability is *partly secured* or *fully secured* depending upon whether the value of the pledged property is less than the amount of the obligation or whether such value is equal to or in excess of the obligation. It has already been stated that reference is made to a lien on an asset by a parenthetical remark in the "Assets" section of the balance sheet. It is also desirable to provide a parenthetical remark in connection with the liability item identifying the asset pledged and indicating its present market value.

There are many kinds of notes. However, two types frequently create difficulty in recording: (1) the note with no stated interest rate, and (2) the note that is discounted. An example of each of these types is included in the following paragraphs:

1. Assume equipment is purchased on terms calling for issue of a $10,000 non-interest-bearing note for one year. If the equipment and the related obligation are recorded at $10,000, this would fail to recognize the charge for interest implicit in the deferred payment arrangement and both asset and liability balances would be overstated. If money is worth 8% per year, the asset, as well as the liability, must be recognized at a cash-equivalent value of $9,259.26 ($10,000 ÷ 1.08). The following entry should be made:

Equipment	9,259.26	
Discount on Notes Payable	740.74	
Notes Payable		10,000.00

In reporting the note on the balance sheet prior to its payment, an adjustment should be made to recognize the accrual of interest at 8% on the amount of the debt of $9,259.26 to the date of the balance sheet. The accrual of interest is recorded by a debit to Interest Expense and a credit to Discount on Notes Payable. The balance of the discount on notes payable is subtracted from notes payable in reporting the liability on the balance sheet. A similar procedure would be required if a note provided for a nominal interest rate that was substantially lower than the current market rate.

2. Assume a company discounts a $10,000 one-year, non-interest-bearing note at the bank, receiving $10,000 less a discount of 8%, or $9,200. If the amount of the discount is recognized as prepaid interest and the note is recorded at $10,000, both asset and liability balances would be overstated: interest has not been paid in advance but is still to be paid; the obligation at the time of borrowing is no greater than the amount borrowed. The following entry should be made:

Cash...	9,200	
Discount on Notes Payable	800	
Notes Payable		10,000

In reporting the note on the balance sheet prior to its payment, an adjustment should be made to recognize the accrual of interest just as in the first example. However, a discount of 8% is, in effect, a charge for interest at the rate of 8.7% ($800 ÷ $9,200). The accrual of interest, then, is computed at 8.7% on the amount of the debt of $9,200 to the date of the balance sheet.

Current Maturities of Long-Term Obligations

Bonds, mortgage notes, and other long-term indebtedness are reported as current liabilities if they are to be paid within a twelve-month period. When only a part of a long-term obligation is to be paid currently, as in the case of bonds payable in a series of annual installments, the maturing portion of the debt is reported as current, the balance as noncurrent. But if the maturing obligation is payable out of a special retirement fund or if it is to be retired from the proceeds of a new bond issue or by conversion into capital stock, the obligation will not call for the use of current funds and therefore should continue to be listed as noncurrent.[1] Reference to the plan for liquidation should be made parenthetically or by special note.

Dividends Payable

A cash dividend declared by appropriate action of the board of directors is recorded by a debit to Retained Earnings and a credit to Dividends Payable. The latter balance is reported as a current liability. The

[1]As noted in Chapter 3, the Financial Accounting Standards Board has specified two conditions which help demonstrate a company's ability to consummate refinancing on a long-term basis: (1) the post-balance-sheet-date issuance of a long-term obligation or equity security, and (2) the existence of a specific financing agreement. *Statement of Financial Accounting Standard No. 6*, "Classification of Short-Term Obligations Expected to be Refinanced" (Stamford, Conn.: Financial Accounting Standards Board, 1975). However, where payment is made on a obligation after the balance sheet date and then long-term financing is arranged or equity securities are issued with the proceeds being used to replenish the current assets prior to issuance of the balance sheet, the obligation should not be excluded from the current liabilities. *FASB Interpretation No. 8*, "Classification of a Short-Term Obligation Repaid Prior to Being Replaced by a Long-Term Security" (Stamford, Conn.: Financial Accounting Standards Board, 1976).

declaration of a dividend payable in the form of additional shares of stock is recorded by a debit to Retained Earnings and a credit to Stock Dividends Distributable. The latter balance is not recognized as a liability but is reported in the "Stockholders' equity" section since it represents retained earnings in the process of transfer to paid-in capital.

A company with cumulative preferred stock outstanding may have sufficient retained earnings to legally declare a dividend but may fail to declare a dividend in order to preserve cash for other purposes. No liability is recognized because dividends are not payable until formal action is taken by the corporate board of directors authorizing the distribution of earnings. Nevertheless, the amount of unpaid cumulative dividends should be reported on the balance sheet. This amount may be shown parenthetically in the "Stockholders' equity" section following a description of the stock or it may be reported by a special note.

Deposits and Agency Obligations   Current resources of a company may include monies deposited with it and returnable to depositors, or monies collected or otherwise accumulated and payable to third parties. A company may have received deposits as guarantees of contract performance, and a current liability needs to be recognized until the deposits are returned. In other instances, companies will make payroll deductions for such items as employees' income tax, payroll taxes, insurance plans, or saving plans. These current liabilities payable to third parties need to be recognized until payments are made and the company fulfills its responsibilities as an agent.

Sales and Use Taxes   With the passage of sales and use tax laws by state and local governments, additional duties are required of a business unit. Laws generally provide that the business unit must act as an agent for the governmental authority in the collection from customers of sales tax on the transfers of tangible personal properties. Laws may also provide that the business unit is additionally liable for sales tax or use tax on goods it buys for its own use. The buyer is responsible for the payment of sales tax to the seller when both buyer and seller are in the same tax jurisdiction; however, the buyer is responsible for the payment of use tax directly to the tax authority when the seller is outside the jurisdiction of such authority. Provision must be made in the accounts for the liability to the government for the tax collected from customers and the additional tax that the business must absorb.

Sales Tax Collections Included in Sales Balance. The sales tax payable is generally a stated percentage of sales. When the sales tax collections as well as sales are recorded in total in the sales account, it becomes necessary to divide this amount into its component parts, sales and sales tax payable. For example, if the sales tax is 5% of sales, then the amount recorded in the sales account is equal to sales + .05 of sales, or 1.05 times the sales total. The amount of sales is obtained by dividing the sales account balance by 1.05, and 5% of the sales amount as thus derived is the tax liability. To illustrate, assume that the sales account balance is

$100,000, which includes sales tax of 5%. Sales, then, are $100,000 ÷ 1.05% = $95,238.10. The sales tax liability is then 5% of $95,238.10 = $4,761.90. The liability can also be determined by subtracting the sales figure, $95,238.10 from $100,000.00. To record the liability, Sales would be debited and Sales Tax Payable would be credited for $4,761.90.

Sales Tax Collections Recorded Separately. Frequently, the actual sales total and the sales tax collections are recorded separately at the time of sale. The sales tax payable account then accumulates the sales tax liability. If sales tax collections are not exactly equal to the sales tax liability for the period as computed under the law, the payable account will require adjustment to bring it to the balance due. In making this adjustment a gain or a loss on sales tax collections is recognized.

Sales Tax or Use Tax on Acquisitions. The recognition in the accounts of obligations for sales tax, use tax, or for tax on goods purchased by a business unit for its own use should be accompanied by debits to the asset or expense accounts in which the original purchases are recorded. For example, sales or use tax on the purchase of furniture and fixtures is recorded as a part of the cost of the asset; sales or use tax on the purchase of supplies representing a selling expense would be recorded as such.

Payroll Taxes and Income Tax Withheld

Social security and income tax legislation impose four taxes based upon payrolls:

1. Federal old-age, survivors, disability, and hospital insurance
2. Federal unemployment insurance
3. State unemployment insurance
4. Income tax withheld.

Federal Old-Age, Survivors, Disability, and Hospital Insurance. The Federal Insurance Contributions Act (FICA), generally referred to as the federal old-age retirement legislation, provides for equal taxes on employer and employee to provide funds for federal old-age, survivors, disability, and hospital insurance benefits for certain individuals and members of their families. At one time only employees were covered by this legislation; however, coverage now includes most individuals who are self-employed.

Provisions of the legislation provide for an equal matching of contributions by the employee and the employer. The contribution is based upon a tax rate applied to gross wages.[1] The tax has gradually increased since the inception of the social security legislation to provide for increasing benefits. The tax rate is applied to all wages up to a designated maximum. This wage limit has also been raised through the years as the total cost of the program has increased.

Employers of one or more persons, with certain exceptions, come under the law. The amount of the employee's tax is withheld from the

---

[1]The rate for 1977 is 5.85%; for 1978–1980 the rate is scheduled to be increased to 6.05%.

wage payment by the employer. The employer remits this amount together with a matched amount. The employer is required to maintain complete records and submit detailed support for the tax remittance. The employer also is responsible for the full amount of the tax even when the employee contributions are not withheld. Self-employed persons who carry on a trade or business are assessed tax rates somewhat higher than the employees rates but less than the sum of the employee and employer contributions.

Federal Unemployment Insurance. The Federal Social Security Act and the Federal Unemployment Tax Act provide for the establishment of unemployment insurance plans. Employers with covered workers employed in each of 20 weeks during a calendar year or who pay $1,500 or more in wages during any calendar quarter are affected.

Under present provisions of the law, the federal government taxes eligible employers on the first $4,200 paid to every employee during the calendar year at 3.2% but allows the employer a tax credit limited to 2.7% for taxes paid under state unemployment compensation laws. No tax is levied on the employee. When an employer is subject to a tax of 2.7% or more as a result of state unemployment legislation, the federal unemployment tax, then, is 0.5% of the wages. Payment to the federal government is required quarterly. Unemployment benefits are provided by the systems created by the individual states. Revenues of the federal government under the acts are used to meet the cost of administering state and federal unemployment plans as well as to provide supplemental unemployment benefits.

State Unemployment Insurance. State unemployment compensation laws are not the same in all states. In most states, laws provide for tax only on employers; but in a few states, taxes are applicable to both employers and employees. Each state law specifies the classes of exempt employees, the number of employees required, or the amount of wages paid before the tax is applicable, and the contributions that are to be made by employers and employees. The legislation applies to all employers of one or more employees. Exemptions are frequently similar to those under the federal act. Tax payment is generally required on or before the last day of the month following each calendar quarter.

Although the normal tax on employers may be 2.7%, states have merit rating or experience plans providing for lower rates based upon employers' individual employment experiences. Employers with stable employment records are taxed at a rate in keeping with the limited amount of benefits required for their employees; employers with less satisfactory employment records contribute at a rate more nearly approaching 2.7% in view of the greater amount of benefits paid to their employees. Savings under state merit systems are allowed as credits in the calculation of the federal contribution, so the federal tax does not exceed 0.5% even though payment of less than 2.7% is made by an employer entitled to a lower rate under the merit rating system.

Income Tax Withheld. Federal income tax on the wages of an individual are collected in the period in which the wages are paid. The "pay-as-you-go" plan requires employers to withhold income tax from wages paid to their employees. Withholding is required not only of employers engaged in a trade or business, but also of religious and charitable organizations, educational institutions, social organizations, and governments of the United States, the states, the territories, and their agencies, instrumentalities, and political subdivisions. Certain classes of wage payments are exempt from withholding although these are still subject to income tax.

An employer must meet withholding requirements under the law even if wages of no more than one employee are subject to such withholdings. The amounts to be withheld by the employer are developed from formulas provided by the law or from tax withholding tables made available by the government. Withholding is based upon the length of the payroll period, the amount earned, and the number of withholding exemptions claimed by the employee. Taxes required under the Federal Insurance Contributions Act (both employees' and employer's portions) and income tax that has been withheld by the employer are paid to the federal government at the same time. These combined taxes are deposited in an authorized bank quarterly, monthly, or quarter-monthly (four deposits a month) depending upon the amount of the liability. A quarterly statement must also be filed providing summary of all wages paid by the employer.

Accounting for Payroll Taxes and Income Tax Withheld. To illustrate the accounting procedures for payroll taxes and income tax withheld, assume that in January, 1977, salaries for a retail store with 15 employees are $10,000. The state unemployment compensation law provides for a tax on employers of 2.7%. Income tax withholdings for the month are $1,020. Assume FICA rates are 6% for employer and employee. Entries for the payroll and the employer's payroll taxes follow:

Salaries..	10,000	
FICA Tax Payable..		600
Employees Income Tax Payable...		1,020
Cash..		8,380
To record payment of payroll.		
Payroll Taxes Expense..	920	
FICA Tax Payable..		600
State Unemployment Tax Payable		270
Federal Unemployment Tax Payable		50
To record the payroll tax liability of the employer.		

Computation:

Tax under Federal Insurance Contributions Act: 6% × $10,000..	$600
Tax under state unemployment insurance legislation: 2.7% × $10,000..................................	270
Tax under Federal Unemployment Tax Act: 0.5% (3.2% − credit of 2.7%) × $10,000...........	50
Total payroll taxes expense	$920

When tax payments are made to the proper agencies, the tax liability accounts are debited and Cash is credited.

The employer's payroll taxes, as well as the taxes withheld from employees, are based upon amounts paid to employees during the period regardless of the basis employed for reporting income. When financial reports are prepared on the accrual basis, the employer will have to recognize both accrued payroll and the employer's payroll taxes relating thereto by adjustments at the end of the accounting period. In adjusting the accounts for accrued payroll, however, recognition of the amounts to be withheld for employees' taxes may be ignored. The entries recording the accrued payroll and the employer's payroll taxes may be reversed at the start of the new period. The next regular payment of wages can then be recorded in the usual manner, giving recognition to the employees' taxes based upon the entire payroll and the balances payable to employees; a second entry is made at this time recording the accrual of the employer's payroll taxes based upon the full amount of the payroll. The accrual of payroll and taxes at the end of the period as indicated provides more accurate statements while deferring the analysis of payroll as to amounts payable to the government and to employees until the wage payment date.

Agreements with employees may provide for payroll deductions and employer contributions for other items, such as group insurance plans, pension plans, savings bonds purchases, or union dues. Such agreements call for accounting procedures similar to those described for payroll taxes and income tax withholdings.

Liability Under Bonus Agreements

Bonuses accruing to officers, managers, or employees at the end of a period are recorded by a debit to an expense account and a credit to a liability account. Employee bonuses, even though they may be defined as a sharing of profits with the employees, are deductible expenses for purposes of income tax.

Special problems frequently arise in the computation of the amount of the bonus accruing to personnel. An agreement may provide for a bonus computed on the basis of gross revenue or sales or on the basis of earnings. When earnings are to be used, the computation will depend upon whether the bonus is based on: (1) income before deductions for bonus or income tax, (2) income after deduction for bonus but before deduction for income tax, (3) income after deduction for income tax but before deduction for bonus, or (4) net income after deductions for both bonus and income tax. To illustrate the computations required in each case, assume the following: Barker Sales, Inc., gives the sales managers of its individual stores a bonus of 10% of store earnings. Income for 1977 for store No. 1 before any charges for bonus or income tax was $100,000. The income tax was 40% of income before income tax.

$$\text{Let } B = \text{Bonus}$$
$$T = \text{Income Tax}$$

1. *Assuming the bonus is based on income before deductions for bonus or income tax:*

$$B = .10 \times \$100,000$$
$$B = \$10,000$$

2. *Assuming the bonus is based on income after deduction for bonus but before deduction for income tax:*

$$B = .10 \; (\$100,000 - B)$$
$$B = \$10,000 - .10B$$
$$B + \;.10B = \$10,000$$
$$1.10B = \$10,000$$
$$B = \$9,090.91$$

Calculation of the bonus may be proved as follows:

Income before bonus and income tax	$100,000.00
Deduct bonus	9,090.91
Income after bonus but before income tax	$ 90,909.09
Bonus rate	10%
Bonus	$ 9,090.91

3. *Assuming the bonus is based on income after deduction for income tax but before deduction for bonus:*

$$B = .10 \; (\$100,000 - T)$$
$$T = .40 \; (\$100,000 - B)$$

Substituting for T in the first equation and solving for B:

$$B = .10 \; [\$100,000 - .40 \; (\$100,000 - B)]$$
$$B = .10 \; (\$100,000 - \$40,000 + .40B)$$
$$B = \$10,000 - \$4,000 + .04B$$
$$B - .04B = \$6,000$$
$$.96B = \$6,000$$
$$B = \$6,250$$

Substituting for B in the second equation and solving for T:

$$T = .40 \; (\$100,000 - \$6,250)$$
$$T = .40 \times \$93,750$$
$$T = \$37,500$$

Calculation of the bonus may be proved as follows:

Income before bonus and income tax	$100,000
Deduct income tax	37,500
Income after income tax but before bonus	$ 62,500
Bonus rate	10%
Bonus	$ 6,250

4. *Assuming the bonus is based on net income after deductions for bonus and income tax:*

$$B = .10 \; (\$100,000 - B - T)$$
$$T = .40 \; (\$100,000 - B)$$

Substituting for T in the first equation and solving for B:

$$B = .10 \; [\$100,000 - B - .40 \; (\$100,000 - B)]$$
$$B = .10 \; (\$100,000 - B - \$40,000 + .40B)$$
$$B = \$10,000 - .1B - \$4,000 + .04B$$
$$B + .1B - \;.04B = \$10,000 - \$4,000$$
$$1.06B = \$6,000$$
$$B = \$5,660.38$$

Substituting for B in the second equation and solving for T:

$$T = .40 \; (\$100,000 - \$5,660.38)$$
$$T = .40 \times \$94,339.62$$
$$T = \$37,735.85$$

Calculation of the bonus is proved in the following summary:

Income before bonus and income tax		$100,000.00
Deduct: Bonus	$ 5,660.38	
Income tax	37,735.85	43,396.23
Net income after bonus and income tax		$ 56,603.77
Bonus rate		10%
Bonus		$ 5,660.38

The bonus should be reported on the income statement as an expense before arriving at net income regardless of the method employed in its computation.

Other Accrued Liabilities
The accrued liabilities most commonly found were described on the preceding pages. Other accruals that may be found include obligations for salaries, interest, and rent. Frequently, these miscellaneous accruals are combined and reported on the balance sheet classification as *other liabilities.*

ESTIMATED CURRENT LIABILITIES

The amount of an obligation is generally established by contract or accrues at a certain rate. There are instances, however, when an obligation clearly exists on a balance sheet date but the amount ultimately to be paid cannot be definitely determined. Because the amount to be paid is not definite does not mean the liability can be ignored or given a contingent status. The claim must be estimated from whatever data are available. The amount to be paid in the form of income tax, for example, must be estimated in preparing interim statements or statements at the end of the period if the tax return has not yet been prepared. Although the exact amount ultimately payable is not known, the obligation is unquestioned and requires recognition. Expenditures arising from current operations, for example, the cost of meeting warranties for service and repairs on goods sold, also call for estimates when prior experience indicates there is a definite liability. Here, uncertainty as to the amount to be expended is accompanied by an inability to identify the payees as well as to determine the time of payments; but the fact that there are charges yet to be absorbed is certain. Liabilities established to meet estimated charges arising from current activities are sometimes referred to as *operating reserves.* These liabilities generally call for current liquidation and hence are classified under the current heading.

Representative of short-term liabilities that are estimated in amount and are frequently found on financial statements are the following:

1. *Estimated tax liabilities*, reporting the estimated income, state franchise, property, and other tax obligations.
2. *Estimated liabilities on customer premium offers*, reporting the estimated value of premiums or prizes to be distributed as a result of past sales or sales promotion activities.
3. *Estimated liabilities under warranties for service and replacements*, reporting the estimated future claims by customers as a result of past guarantees of services or product or product part replacement.
4. *Estimated liabilities on tickets, tokens, and gift certificates outstanding*, reporting the estimated obligations in the form of services or merchandise arising from the receipt of cash in past periods.

Some of the problems arising in the development of the balances to be reported for these items are described in the sections that follow.

Estimated Tax Liabilities

Estimates are required for all taxes related to current operations but not finally known at the time financial statements are prepared. Estimates may thus be called for in the case of federal income tax, state income or franchise tax, real and personal property taxes, and various other licenses and fees. Tax rates may vary from year to year. Normally the best guide as to current tax rates is found in the rates applicable in the preceding period. When legislative bodies are considering revisions in tax rates and their application, the best available information should be used in developing estimates. Not only may estimates have to be made relative to rates but also to the bases on which such rates are applicable. In the case of real and personal property taxes, for example, the valuation to be assigned to properties owned may have to be estimated in arriving at an estimated tax liability. In the case of income tax, estimates of the income subject to tax are required unless tax data are fully compiled before the financial statements are prepared.

Estimated taxes are recorded by debits to expense and credits to liability accounts. Liabilities are closed when the taxes are paid. Any difference between the amount paid and the obligation originally recognized may be reported in the expense account in the period of payment.

Real and Personal Property Taxes. Real and personal property taxes are based upon the assessed valuation of properties as of a given date. This has given rise to the view held by courts and others that taxes accrue as of a given date. Generally the date of accrual has been held to be the date of property assessment. However, accounting treatment, in general, has been to charge taxes ratably over a tax year rather than to recognize these at the time the legal obligation arises.

Real and personal property taxes have been charged against the revenue of various periods, including (1) the year in which paid (cash basis), (2) the year ending (or beginning) on the assessment (or lien) date, and (3) the fiscal year of the governing body levying the tax.

The Committee on Accounting Procedure of the AICPA in considering the various alternatives for tax accounting has suggested, "generally, the most acceptable basis of providing for property taxes is monthly accrual on the taxpayer's books during the fiscal period of the taxing authority for which the taxes are levied."[1] This would relate the tax charge to the period in which taxes provide benefits through governmental services. However, the Committee indicates that special circumstances may suggest the use of alternative accrual periods, and it concludes, "consistency of application from year to year is the important consideration and selection of any of the periods mentioned is a matter for individual judgment."[2]

---

[1] *Accounting Research and Terminology Bulletins — Final Edition*, "No. 43, Restatement and Revision of Accounting Research Bulletins" (New York: American Institute of Certified Public Accountants, 1961), Ch. 10A, par. 14.

[2] *Ibid.*, par. 13.

Accounting for tax when accrual is made over the fiscal year of the taxing authority is illustrated in the example that follows. Assume the accounting period for the Reid Co. is the calendar year. The fiscal year for the city in which this company is located begins on July 1 and ends on the following June 30. Real and personal property taxes are assessed in March, but bills are sent out in November covering the year ending June 30 of the following year. Tax payments in equal installments are due on December 10 and the following April 10. The Reid Co. accrues taxes on its books monthly in terms of the fiscal period of the governmental unit.

On July 1, 1977, the Reid Co. estimated total property tax for the year July 1, 1977, to June 30, 1978, at $1,800. On November 4 the company received a tax bill for 1977–78 of $1,842. Entries to record the monthly tax charges and tax payments are shown below.

TRANSACTION	ENTRY
At the end of July, August, September, October: Estimated tax for 1977–78.................................. $1,800 Monthly accrual, 1/12 × $1,800 150	Property Tax Expense........................... 150.00 Property Tax Payable........................ 150.00

At the end of November:
Amount of tax for year $1,842.00
 	
Amount chargeable to date
  4 × $153.50 ($1,842 ÷ 12) .... $ 614.00
Accrual recognized to date
  4 × $150.. 600.00
Tax deficiency — prior periods.................... $ 14.00
Add accrual for November........................... 153.50
Total charge.. $ 167.50
	Property Tax Expense........................... 167.50
	   Property Tax Payable........................ 167.50

December 10:
Payment of first installment, 50% × $1,842 = $921,
  chargeable as follows:
July–November (accrued)................................ $767.50
December (current period)............................. 153.50
	Property Tax Payable........................... 767.50
	Property Tax Expense........................... 153.50
	   Cash.. 921.00

At the end of January, February, March: Monthly accrual.	Property Tax Expense........................... 153.50 Property Tax Payable........................ 153.50

April 10:
Payment of second installment, 50% × $1,842 = $921,
  chargeable as follows:
January–March (accrued)............................... $460.50
April (current period) 153.50
May and June (prepaid)................................. 307.00
	Property Tax Payable........................... 460.50
	Property Tax Expense........................... 153.50
	Prepaid Property Tax 307.00
	   Cash.. 921.00

At the end of May, June: Monthly amortization of prepaid property tax.	Property Tax Expense........................... 153.50 Prepaid Property Tax........................ 153.50

It should be noted that when the actual tax charge became known in November, an adjustment was made for charges of previous months.[1]

---

[1] An alternative treatment would apply the adjustment over the remaining months of the fiscal year of the taxing authority.

Estimated Liabilities on Customer Premium Offers

Many companies offer special premiums to those purchasing their products. These offers to stimulate the regular purchase of certain products may be open for a limited time or may be of a continuing nature. The premium is normally made available when the customer submits the required number of product labels, box tops, wrappers, or certificates. In certain instances the premium offer may provide for an optional cash payment.

If a premium offer expires at the end of the company's fiscal period, adjustments in the accounts are not required. Premium requirements are fully met and the premium expense account summarizes the full charge for the period. However, when a premium offer is continuing, an adjustment must be made at the end of the period to recognize the liability that is found in the continuing costs of the offer — Premium Expense is debited and an appropriate liability account is credited. The expense is thus charged to the period benefiting from the premium plan and current liabilities reflect the claim for premiums outstanding. If premium distributions are debited to an expense account, the liability balance may be reversed at the beginning of the new period.

To illustrate the accounting for a premium offer, assume the following: Smart Foods offers a set of breakfast bowls upon the receipt of 20 certificates, one certificate being included in each package of the cereal distributed by this company. The cost of each set of bowls to the company is $1. It is estimated that only 40% of the coupons will be redeemed. Transactions and entries are as follows:

TRANSACTION	ENTRY		
1977:			
Premium purchases:	Premiums — Bowl Sets	10,000	
10,000 sets × $1 = $10,000	Cash		10,000
Sales:	Cash	240,000	
400,000 packages × $.60 = $240,000	Sales		240,000
Premium claim redemptions:	Premium Expense	6,000	
120,000 certificates, or 6,000 sets × $1 = $6,000.	Premiums — Bowl Sets		6,000
December 31, 1977:			
Coupons estimated redeemable in future periods:	Premium Expense	2,000	
Total estimated redemptions —	Estimated Premium Claims Outstanding		2,000
40% of 400,000 160,000			
Redemptions in 1977 120,000			
Estimated future redemptions 40,000			
Estimated claim outstanding:			
40,000 certificates, or 2,000 sets @ $1 ..... $ 2,000			
January 1, 1978 (optional):	Estimated Premium		
Reversal of accrued liability balance.	Claims Outstanding	2,000	
	Premium Expense		2,000

The balance sheet at the end of 1977 will show premiums of $4,000 as a current asset and estimated premium claims outstanding of $2,000 as a current liability; the income statement for 1977 will show premium expense of $8,000 as a selling expense.

Experience indicating a redemption percentage that differs from the assumed rate will call for an appropriate adjustment in the subsequent period and the revision of future redemption estimates.

The estimated cost of the premiums may be shown as a direct reduction of sales by recording the premium claim at the time of the sale. This requires an estimate of the premium cost at the time of the sale. For example, in the previous illustration, the entry to be made at the time of the sale, employing the sales reduction approach, would be as follows:

```
Cash.......................................................................................  240,000
    Sales .................................................................................              232,000
    Estimated Premium Claims Outstanding...............................                8,000
```

The redemption of premium claims would call for debits to the liability account. Either the expense method or the sales reduction method is acceptable and both are found in practice.

Some organizations have adopted plans for the issuance to customers of trading stamps, cash register tapes, or other media redeemable in merchandise, premiums, or cash. The accounting procedure followed will depend upon the nature of the plan. A business may establish its own plan, prepare its own stamps or other trading media, and assume redemption responsibilities. Under these circumstances, the accounting procedure would parallel that just illustrated for specific premium offers. On the other hand, a business unit may enter into an agreement for a stamp plan with a trading-stamp company. The latter normally assumes full responsibility for the redemption of stamps and sells the trading stamps for a set unit price whether they are redeemed or not. The business would report stamps purchased as an asset and stamps issued as a selling expense; the trading-stamp company would recognize on its books the sale of stamps, purchase of premiums, distributions of premiums, and the estimated liability for the costs of merchandise and related services identified with stamps expected to be redeemed.

Estimated Liabilities Under Warranties

Some companies agree to provide free service on units failing to perform satisfactorily or to replace defective goods. When agreements involve only minor costs, such costs may be recognized in the periods incurred. When agreements involve significant future costs and when experience indicates a definite future obligation exists, estimates of such costs should be made. Such estimates are recorded by a debit to an expense account and a credit to a liability account. Subsequent costs of fulfilling warranties are debited to the liability account. Adjustments to the liability account will be required if experience differs from the estimates. The anticipation of costs results in appropriate charges during the period in which revenue is realized and in recognition of the obligation outstanding. To illustrate this procedure, consider the following example. Supersonic Sound, Inc., sells compact stereo systems with a two-year warranty. It estimated that 10% of all sets sold will need repairs in the first year, and 20% will need repairs in the second year. The average repair cost is $50 per system. The number of systems sold in 1977 and 1978 was 5,000 and 6,000, respectively. Associated repairs were $28,000 in 1977 and $60,000 in 1978.

TRANSACTION	ENTRY

1977
Warranty Expense:
Stereo systems sold 5,000
Repair rate (.10 + .20) .... .30
Systems ultimately to be repaired................ 1,500
Cost to repair each system .... × $50
Warranty expense... $75,000
Repairs actually made: $28,000
	Warranty Expense 75,000
	   Estimated Liability
	   Under Warranties.............................. 75,000
	
	Estimated Liability
	Under Warranties................................ 28,000
	   Cash 28,000

1978
Warranty Expense:
Stereo systems sold 6,000
Repair rate (.10 + .20) .... .30
Systems ultimately to be repaired................ 1,800
Cost to repair each system .... × $50
Warranty expense... $90,000
Repairs actually made: $60,000
	Warranty Expense 90,000
	   Estimated Liability
	   Under Warranties.............................. 90,000
	
	Estimated Liability
	Under Warranties................................ 60,000
	   Cash 60,000

In certain cases customers are charged special fees for a service or replacement warranty covering a specific period. In such cases, a customers' advances account is credited. Expenditures in meeting contract requirements are debited to expense, and the advances balance is recognized as revenue over the warranty period. Recognition of revenue in excess of expenses indicates a profit on such service contracts; revenue less than expenses indicates a loss on such contracts. The customers' advances balance should be reported as a current liability in view of the claim it makes upon current assets.

Estimated Liabilities on Tickets, Tokens, and Gift Certificates Outstanding

Many companies sell tickets, tokens, and gift certificates that entitle the owner to services or merchandise: for example, airlines issue tickets used for travel; local transit companies issue tokens good for fares; department stores sell gift certificates redeemable in merchandise.

When instruments redeemable in services or merchandise are outstanding at the end of the period, accounts should be adjusted to reflect the obligations under such arrangements. The nature of the adjustment will depend upon the entries originally made in recording the sale of the instruments.

Ordinarily, the sale of instruments redeemable in services or merchandise is recorded by a debit to Cash and a credit to a liability account. As instruments are redeemed, the liability balance is debited and Sales or an appropriate revenue account is credited. Certain claims may be rendered void by lapse of time or for some other reason as defined by the sales agreement. In addition, experience may indicate a certain percentage of outstanding claims will never be presented for redemption. These factors must be considered at the end of the period, when the liability balance is reduced to the balance of the claim estimated to be outstanding and a revenue account is credited for the gain indicated from forfeitures. If Sales or a special revenue account is originally credited on the sale of the redemption instrument, the adjustment at the end of the period calls for a debit to the revenue account and a credit to a liability account for the claim still outstanding.

CURRENT LIABILITIES ON THE BALANCE SHEET

The nature of the detail to be presented for current liabilities depends upon the use to be made of the financial statement. A balance sheet prepared for stockholders might report little detail; on the other hand, creditors may insist on full detail concerning current debts.

Current assets are normally recorded in the order of their liquidity, and consistency would suggest liabilities be reported in the order of their maturity. The latter practice may be followed only to the extent it is practical: observance of this procedure would require an analysis of the different classes of obligations and separate reporting for classes with varying maturity dates. A bank overdraft should be listed first in view of the immediate demand it makes on cash. In some cases a distinction is made between liabilities that have matured and are presently payable and others that have not matured though they are current.

Current liabilities should not be reduced by assets to be applied to their liquidation. Disclosure as to future debt liquidation, however, may be provided by an appropriate parenthetical remark or note. Disclosure of liabilities secured by specific assets should also be made by a parenthetical remark or note.

The current liabilities section of a balance sheet prepared on December 31, 1977, might appear as shown below:

Current liabilities:			
Notes payable:			
Trade creditors	$12,000		
Banks (secured by assignment of monies to become due under certain contracts totaling $36,000 included in asset section)	20,000		
Officers	10,000		
Miscellaneous	2,500	$44,500	
Accounts payable:			
Trade creditors	$30,500		
Credit balances in customers' accounts	1,250		
Miscellaneous	3,500	35,250	
Long-term liability installments due in 1978		10,000	
Cash dividends payable		4,500	
Income tax payable		6,000	
Other liabilities:			
Salaries and wages payable	$ 1,250		
Real and personal property taxes	1,550		
Miscellaneous liabilities	1,400		
Customer advances	7,500		
Estimated repair costs on goods sold with service warranties	2,500	14,200	$114,450

QUESTIONS

1. (a) Define liabilities. (b) Distinguish between contingent and estimated liabilities.

2. What problems arise in the proper valuation of liabilities?

3. (a) Distinguish between current and non-current liabilities. (b) Indicate the major classifications for current liabilities.

4. The Cable Co. issues a non-interest-bearing note due in one year in payment for equipment. Describe the accounting procedures that should be employed for the purchase.

5. Under what circumstances would an interest-bearing note be reported at an amount that is less than its maturity value?

6. When does (a) a cash dividend become a liability and (b) a stock dividend become a liability?

7. What is the nature of a firm's liability for sales and use taxes?

8. What are the purposes of the various payroll taxes?

9. The hourly wage of an employee is $3, but the total employee labor cost, including tax-related expenses, is greater than $3 an hour. Explain.

10. The sales manager for the Bonneville Sales Co. is entitled to a bonus of 12% of profits. What difficulties may arise in the interpretation of this profit-sharing agreement?

11. When the fiscal year of the taxpayer is different from that of the taxing authority, how should the taxpayer account for property taxes?

12. What information must a firm accumulate in order to adequately account for estimated liabilities on tickets, tokens, and gift certificates?

13. Where would each of the following items be reported on the balance sheet?

    (a) Bank overdraft.
    (b) Cash dividends declared.
    (c) Dividends in arrears on preferred stock.
    (d) Estimated income tax.
    (e) Stamps issued and redeemable by customers for certain premiums.
    (f) Deposits received in connection with meter installations by a public utility.
    (g) Current maturities of a serial bond issue.
    (h) Customer accounts with credit balances.
    (i) Purchase money obligation maturing in five annual installments.
    (j) Gift certificates sold to customers but not yet presented for redemption.
    (k) Service warranties on equipment sales.
    (l) Contract entered into with contractors for the construction of a new building.
    (m) Stock dividend payable.
    (n) Accrued vacation pay.
    (o) Strike settlement calling for retroactive wage payments.

EXERCISES

1. The following notes were issued by the Sunshine Co.:

    (a) Note issued to purchase machinery. Face amount $12,960; no stated interest rate; market rate of interest, 8%; term of note, one year; date of note, November 1, 1977.

    (b) Note issued to bank for a cash loan. Maturity value of note, $5,000; bank discount rate, 9%; term of note, one year; date of note, October 1, 1977.

(1) Give the entries required at the time the notes were issued. (2) Give the adjusting entries required on December 31, 1977, to recognize the accrual of the interest on each note.

2. Total sales plus sales tax for the Geronimo Electric Company in 1977 were $99,750; 60% of the sales are normally made on account. Prepare an entry summarizing these data for 1977 if the sales tax rate is 5%.

3. Molton, Inc., paid $1,600 in cash (net pay) to its ten employees, which represented one week's wages. Income tax withholdings were equal to 16% of the gross payroll and the only other deductions were 5% for FICA tax and $59 for union dues. Give the entries that should be made on the books of the store to record the payroll and the tax accruals to be recognized by the employer, assuming that the company is subject to unemployment taxes of 2.7% (state) and 0.5% (federal).

4. The Laredo Company provides a special bonus for its executive officers based upon income before bonus or income tax. Income before bonus and income tax for 1977 was $300,000. The income tax rate is 45% and the income tax liability for 1977 is $114,750. What was the bonus rate?

5. Western Sales, Inc., has an agreement with its sales manager whereby the latter is entitled to 6% of company earnings as a bonus. Company income for a calendar year before bonus and income tax is $150,000. Income tax is 45% of income after bonus. Compute the amount of the bonus under each of the conditions below.

 (a) The bonus is calculated on income before deductions for bonus and income tax.
 (b) The bonus is calculated on income after deduction for bonus but before deduction for income tax.
 (c) The bonus is calculated on income after deduction for income tax but before deduction for bonus.
 (d) The bonus is calculated on net income after deductions for both bonus and income tax.

6. On July 1, 1977, the Stephens Company estimated total property tax for the year July 1, 1977, through June 30, 1978, at $960. On November 7, the company received the tax bill of $1,080. One half of the tax bill is paid on December 8, 1977. Give all required entries for 1977 to record monthly tax charges and the tax payment in December.

7. The Melvin Co. includes one coupon in each box of cereal that it packs, 15 coupons being redeemable for a premium consisting of a toy. In 1977, the Melvin Co. purchased 6,000 premiums at 75¢, and sold 125,000 boxes of cereal at 79¢ each. 22,500 coupons are presented for redemption. It is estimated that 60% of the coupons issued will be presented for redemption. Make all journal entries required in 1977 to properly account for the above information.

8. The Klear Kolor Appliance Company sells color television sets with a three-year repair warranty. The sales price for each set is $550. The average expense of repairing a set is $20. Research has shown that 10% of all sets sold are repaired in the first year, 15% in the second year, and 40% in the third year. The number of sets sold were as follows: 3,000 in 1977; 5,000 in 1978; and 6,000 in 1979. Total payment for repairs associated with the warranties were $5,500 in 1977, $14,500 in 1978, and $30,000 in 1979. Sales were made on account evenly throughout the year. Sales tax is charged at 5%.

Give the entries to record sales, the liability for warranties, and the payment made in connection with warranties for 1977, 1978, and 1979.

9. Prepare the "Current liabilities" section of the balance sheet for the Worthmore Co. on December 31, 1977, from the information appearing below:

 (a) Notes payable: arising from purchases of goods, $32,600; arising from loans from banks, $10,000, on which marketable securities valued at $14,500 have been pledged as security; arising from advances by officers, $12,000.
 (b) Accounts payable: arising from purchase of goods, $31,000.
 (c) Cash balance with Farmers Bank, $5,500; cash overdraft with Merchants Bank, $3,320.
 (d) Dividends in arrears on preferred stock, $18,000.
 (e) Employees income tax payable, $880.
 (f) First-mortgage serial bonds, $125,000, payable in semiannual installments of $5,000 due on March 1 and September 1 of each year.
 (g) Advances received from customers on purchase orders, $2,300.
 (h) Customers' accounts with credit balances arising from purchase returns, $1,200.
 (i) Estimated expense of meeting warranty for service requirements on merchandise sold, $2,700.

PROBLEMS

10-1. The information below and at the top of page 280 is selected from the books of Jenkins Lumber Co. for the year 1978:

Sales on account (including sales tax of 5%).....................................	$183,750
Net income	14,500
Cash dividends (declared December 30, 1978)	10,000
Stock dividends (declared December 30, 1978)	7,000
Machinery purchased (a non-interest-bearing note was issued in payment)	20,000

Notes payable (a note for $5,000 was discounted at the bank at 9%)	$ 5,000
Marketable securities	8,000
Bonds payable	25,000
Common stock, $100 par	50,000

> **Instructions:** Prepare necessary journal entries to record the following transactions:
> (1) Discounting the note payable.
> (2) Purchase of machinery (money is worth 12% per year).
> (3) Declaration of cash dividend.
> (4) Declaration of stock dividend.
> (5) Sales tax.

10-2. Ultra-Modern Mobile Homes, Inc., pays bonuses to its sales manager and two sales agents. The company had income for 1977 of $900,000 before bonuses and income tax. Income taxes average 45%.

> **Instructions:** Compute the bonuses assuming:
> (1) Sales manager gets 6% and sales agents get 5% of income before tax and bonuses.
> (2) Each bonus is 9% of income after income tax but before bonuses.
> (3) Each bonus is 12% of net income after income tax and bonuses.
> (4) Sales manager gets 12% and sales agents get 10% of income after bonuses but before income tax.

10-3. The real and personal property taxes paid by the Crow Corp. for 1976–1977 were $5,210. The taxes cover the city's fiscal year which is July 1, 1976–June 30, 1977, and the company follows the policy of accruing taxes over the fiscal period of the taxing authority. The company has made property improvements and estimates the tax for 1977–1978 at $6,300. On October 31, 1977, the company receives its tax bill reporting a liability of $6,900. The assessment is protested. The company pays 50% of the tax bill on December 10, 1977. On March 20, 1978, the company is advised that its tax liability for 1977–1978 was reduced to $6,480. The balance of the amount due, $3,030, is paid on April 10, 1978.

> **Instructions:** Give the entries relating to the property taxes that will appear on the books of the Crow Corp. over the period July 1, 1977–June 30, 1978, including monthly adjustments required for the preparation of monthly financial statements.

10-4. The Super-Soap Corp. manufactures a special type of low-suds laundry soap. A package of three golf balls is offered as a premium to customers who send in two proof-of-purchase seals from these soap boxes and a remittance of $1. Data for the premium offer are summarized below:

	1978	1977
Soap sales ($1.20 per package)	$1,500,000	$1,200,000
Golf ball purchases ($2.50 per package)	$75,000	$62,000
Number of golf ball packages distributed as premiums	28,500	20,000
Estimated number of golf ball packages to be distributed in subsequent periods	1,000	3,500
Mailing costs are 26¢ per package.		

> **Instructions:**
> (1) Give the entries for 1977 and 1978 to record product sales, premium purchases and redemptions, and year-end adjustments.
> (2) Present "T" accounts with appropriate amounts as of the end of 1977 and 1978.

10-5. During the year 1977, the Mass Transit Authority sold the following tokens at 25¢ each.

Month	Tokens Sold
January	20,000
February	22,000
March	23,000
April	25,000
May	30,000
June	37,000
July	38,000
August	39,000
September	26,000
October	25,000
November	21,000
December	18,000

Past experience has shown that 60% of the tokens are used in the month of sale, 30% in the following month, 5% in the next month, and 5% are rendered void after six months.

> ***Instructions:*** Give entries for 1977 to account for the tokens:
> (1) Assuming a liability account is originally credited.
> (2) Assuming a revenue account is originally credited.

10-6. The following data are made available for purposes of stating the financial position of the Salt Water Corp. on December 31, 1977.

Cash in bank..	$20,000
Petty cash, which includes IOU's of employees totaling $350 that are to be repaid to the petty cash fund	2,000
Marketable securities, valued at $48,900; securities valued at $25,000 having been pledged on a note payable to the bank for $20,000, reported on the books at cost	45,000
Notes receivable, which have been reduced by notes discounted of $10,000 that are not yet due and on which the company is contingently liable...........	15,500
Accounts receivable, which include accounts with credit balances of $560 and past-due accounts of $2,650 on which a loss of 80% is anticipated	34,700
Merchandise inventory, which includes goods held on a consignment basis, $1,800, and goods received on December 31, $2,600, neither of these items having been recorded as a purchase	29,600
Prepaid insurance, which includes cash surrender value of life insurance policies, $4,200	9,100
Rents paid in advance	830

Furniture and fixtures, which include fixtures that were fully depreciated and that have just been scrapped, $4,500:		
Cost..	$25,000	
Accumulated depreciation...	11,750	13,250

Notes payable, which are trade notes with the exception of a 6-month, $20,000 note payable to Commerce First National Bank on June 15, 1978	30,500
Accounts payable, which include accounts with debit balances of $675...........	18,100
Miscellaneous accrued expenses..	3,650
Long-term notes, which are payable in annual installments of $2,500 on February 1 of each year...	10,000
Preferred 6% stock, $15 par, cumulative, on which dividends for 3 years are in arrears	45,000
No-par common stock, 40,000 shares authorized and outstanding...................	60,000
Retained earnings..	2,730

The following data are not included in the above account balances:

> (a) A special sales offer made in December will result in redemption of premiums estimated at a cost of $4,000 during the next year.
> (b) Product replacement warranties outstanding are estimated to result in costs to the company of $6,000.

> ***Instructions:*** Prepare a classified balance sheet, including whatever notes are appropriate in support of balance sheet data.

10-7. In January, 1978, you were examining the financial statements of Lang Manufacturing Company for the year ended December 31, 1977. Lang filed the necessary payroll tax returns for the first three quarters of 1977 and had prepared drafts of the returns scheduled to be filed by January 31, 1978.

The information below and on page 282 was available from the general ledger, copies and drafts of payroll tax returns and other sources:

General Ledger

Account	Balance December 31, 1977	Composition of Balance
Wages (various expense accounts)	$121,800	12 monthly entries from payroll summaries.
Payroll Tax Expense.....................................	7,488	FICA (5% of $103,000), $5,150; state unemployment tax (2.7% of $59,000), $1,593; federal unemployment tax (.5% of $59,000), $295; amounts withheld from employees for FICA tax in October and November and paid to depositary, $450.

General Ledger (continued)

Account	Balance December 31, 1977	Composition of Balance
Employees Payroll Taxes Payable...............	$ 2,285	December income tax, $1,530; October through December FICA, $755
Employer's Payroll Taxes Payable...............	561	December FICA, $305; October through December state unemployment tax, $216; 1977 federal unemployment tax, $40 for last quarter.

Copies of 1977 Tax Returns

	Totals for Year	First Three Quarters (Duplicate Copies of Returns)	Last Quarter (Pencil Draft)
Gross wages...	$121,800	$95,870	$25,930
Wages taxable for FICA..	103,000	87,900	15,100
FICA tax	10,300	8,790	1,510
Income tax withheld	15,740	11,490	4,250
Wages taxable for state and federal unemployment tax	59,000	51,000	8,000
Total state unemployment tax (employer only)..................	1,593	1,377	216
Total federal unemployment tax (employer only)	295	255	40

Information from other sources:

(a) In August, 1977, six laborers were hired to tear down an old warehouse building located on the site where a new warehouse would soon be constructed. The laborers' 1977 wages totaling $1,000 were debited to the land and buildings account. Payroll taxes were not withheld.

(b) Included in a 1977 wages expense account is one month's salary of $1,400 paid to the president on December 30, 1977, for a 1976 vacation allowance.

(c) In December, 1977, a contractor was paid $2,000 for making repairs to machinery usually made by company employees and the amount was debited to Wages Expense. No payroll taxes were withheld and none were required.

Instructions:

(1) Prepare a schedule presenting the computation of total taxable wages to be reported on the 1977 payroll tax returns for FICA and for state unemployment tax.

(2) Prepare a schedule presenting the computation of the amounts (to the nearest dollar) that should be paid with each of the year-end payroll tax returns to be filed in January, 1978, for (a) FICA tax and income tax withheld, (b) state unemployment tax and (c) federal unemployment tax.

(3) Prepare a schedule to reconcile the differences between the amounts which should be paid with payroll tax returns to be filed in January, 1978, as computed for (2), and the balances shown at December 31, 1977, in the related general ledger liability accounts. (AICPA adapted)

10-8. The Miracle Radio Corporation, a client, requests that you compute the appropriate balance for its estimated liability for product warranty account for a statement as of June 30, 1977.

The Miracle Radio Corporation manufactures television tubes and sells them with a six-month warranty under which defective tubes will be replaced without a charge. On December 31, 1976, the Estimated Liability for Product Warranty had a balance of $510,000. By June 30, 1977, this balance had been reduced to $80,250 by debits for estimated net cost of tubes returned which had been sold in 1976.

The company started out in 1977 expecting 8% of the dollar volume of sales to be returned. However, due to the introduction of new models during the year, this estimated percentage of returns was increased to 10% on May 1. It is assumed that no tubes sold during a given month are returned in that month. Each tube is stamped with a date at time of sale so that the warranty may be properly administered. The table of percentages at the top of page 283 indicates the likely pattern of sales returns during the six-month period of the warranty, starting with the month following the sale of tubes.

Month Following Sale	Percentage of Total Returns Expected
First..	20%
Second	30
Third	20
Fourth through sixth — 10% each month	30
Total..	100%

Gross sales of tubes were as follows for the first six months of 1977:

Month	Amount	Month	Amount
January	$3,600,000	April..	$2,850,000
February....................................	3,300,000	May...	2,000,000
March	4,100,000	June..	1,800,000

The company's warranty also covers the payment of freight cost on defective tubes returned and on new tubes sent out as replacements. This freight cost runs approximately 10% of the sales price of the tubes returned. The manufacturing cost of the tubes is roughly 80% of the sales price, and the salvage value of returned tubes averages 15% of their sales price. Returned tubes on hand at December 31, 1976, were thus valued in inventory at 15% of their original sales price.

> *Instructions:* Using the data given, draw up a suitable working-paper schedule for arriving at the balance of the estimated liability for product warranty account and give the proposed adjusting entry. Assume that proper recognition of costs for financial accounting will be allowed for income tax purposes. (AICPA adapted)

10-9. The Novelties Co., Inc., is engaged in manufacturing and wholesaling two principal products. As their accountant, you have been asked to advise management on its sales policy for the coming year.

Two different plans are being considered by management, either of which, they believe, will (1) increase the volume of sales, (2) reduce the ratio of selling expense to sales, and (3) decrease unit production costs. These proposals are presented below and on page 284.

> *Plan 1 — Premium Stamp Books*
>
> It is proposed that each package of Product A will contain 8 premium stamps, and each package of Product B will contain 4 premium stamps. Premium stamp books will be distributed to consumers, and when a book is filled with stamps (100 stamps), it will be redeemed by the award of a cash prize in an amount indicated under an unbroken seal attached to the book at the time of distribution. Every 10,000 books distributed will provide for prizes in accordance with the following schedule.
>
> | Number of Books | Prize for Each | Total Prizes |
> |---|---|---|
> | 1 .... | $150.00 | $ 150 |
> | 5 .... | 50.00 | 250 |
> | 14 .... | 20.00 | 280 |
> | 50 .... | 10.00 | 500 |
> | 160 .... | 5.00 | 800 |
> | 1,020 .... | 1.00 | 1,020 |
> | 8,750 .... | .40 | 3,500 |
> | 10,000 | | $6,500 |

This schedule is fixed and not subject to alteration or modification. The cost of this plan will be as follows:

Books, including distribution cost	$15 per 1,000 books
Stamps	$1 per 1,000 stamps
Prizes...	$650 per 1,000 books

The premium stamp book plan will take the place of all previous advertising, and previously established selling prices will be maintained.

Plan 2 — Reduced Selling Prices

It is proposed that the selling price of Product A will be reduced by 8⅓% and of Product B by 5% and to increase the advertising expenditures over those of the prior year. This plan is an alternative to Plan 1, and only one will be adopted.

Management has provided you with the following information as to the previous year's operations, and as to anticipated changes:

	Product A	Product B
Prior year's operations:		
Quantity sold	200,000 units	600,000 units
Production cost per unit	$.40	$.30
Selling price per unit	.60	.40
Selling expenses were 18% of sales, of which one third was for advertising. Administrative expenses were 5% of sales.		
Expected changes:		
Increase in unit sales volume:		
Plan 1	50%	50%
Plan 2	40%	25%
Decrease in unit production cost:		
Plan 1	5%	10%
Plan 2	7½%	6⅔%
Advertising:		
Plan 1	None	None
Plan 2	8% of sales	7% of sales
Other selling expenses:		
Plan 1	15% of sales	12% of sales
Plan 2	12% of sales	12% of sales
Premium book expenses:		
Plan 1	As indicated	
Plan 2	None	None
Administrative expenses:		
Plan 1	4% of sales	4% of sales
Plan 2	Same dollar amount as prior year.	

Instructions: Prepare a schedule for submission to management comparing operations of the previous year with those under both proposed plans. (AICPA adapted)

Land, Buildings, and Equipment — Acquisition, Use, and Retirement

Land, buildings, and equipment is a classification heading for those tangible properties of a relatively permanent character used in the normal conduct of a business. Many other terms have been and are being used to describe such properties. *Fixed assets* has been frequently used in the past; however, it must be modified by *tangible* or *intangible* to distinguish between these two classes of assets. *Plant and equipment* is ambiguous because of the several connotations to the word *plant*. Plant could mean only the buildings, or perhaps buildings and land. *Property, plant, and equipment* has been used by the Accounting Principles Board in its opinions. In this use, property means land, but in a more normal connotation, both plant and equipment are also property and this title is ambiguous. The heading "Land, buildings, and equipment" is used throughout this text. "Property" is used as a general term referring to all three classes of items.

As in the case of other noncurrent assets, land, buildings, and equipment items do not turn over as frequently as current assets. Land, buildings, and equipment are acquired, used, and retired. Although these properties as a class remain as long as the business continues, the individual items, with the exception of land, have limited service lives. The costs of buildings and equipment are assigned to operations by means of periodic depreciation charges. When an item is no longer of economic benefit to the business, its cost should have been fully absorbed through these periodic charges.

COMPOSITION OF LAND, BUILDINGS, AND EQUIPMENT

Land refers to earth surface and includes building sites, yards, and parking areas. When natural resources in the form of mineral deposits, oil and gas wells, and timber are found on land, they are frequently reported separately. Buildings refer to improvements permanently affixed to land and include not only structures in the form of factories, office buildings, storage quarters, and garages, but also structure facilities and appurtenances such as loading docks, heating and air conditioning systems, and walks and drives. Equipment consists of a wide variety of items including factory machines, hand and machine tools, patterns and dies, store and office equipment, and motor vehicles and other transport equipment. Items in the equipment group are frequently referred to as *personal property* or *personalty* as distinguished from the land and buildings group referred to as *real property* or *realty*.

CAPITAL AND REVENUE EXPENDITURES

The proper treatment of expenditures relative to the acquisition and use of property presents many accounting problems. Expenditures for property are made in anticipation of their favorable effects upon operations. In recording such expenditures, it must be determined whether favorable effects are limited to the current period or whether they extend into future periods. The underlying concept involved is the matching principle already described. An expenditure benefiting only the current period is called a *revenue expenditure* and is recorded as an expense. An expenditure benefiting operations beyond the current period is called a *capital expenditure* and is recorded as an asset. A property expenditure recorded as an asset is said to be *capitalized*.

Income cannot be fairly measured unless expenditures are properly identified and recorded as revenue or capital charges. For example, an incorrect debit to an equipment item instead of an expense results in the current overstatement of earnings on the income statement and the overstatement of assets and capital on the balance sheet. As the charge is assigned to operations in subsequent periods, earnings of such periods will be understated; assets and capital on the successive balance sheets will continue to be overstated, although by lesser amounts each year, until the asset is written off and the original error is fully counterbalanced. On the other hand, an incorrect debit to an expense instead of an equipment item results in the current understatement of earnings and the understatement of assets and capital. Earnings of subsequent periods will be overstated in the absence of debits for depreciation; assets and capital will continue to be understated, although by lesser amounts each year, until the original error is counterbalanced.

Although all property expenditures providing benefits beyond the current period should be capitalized, companies frequently adopt an arbitrary practice of debiting to expense all expenditures not exceeding a certain amount, perhaps $50 or $100. Such practice is adopted for the sake of expediency: the analysis of relatively small expenditures, as well as the application of depreciation procedures for them, is avoided. Adherence to such a practice is acceptable if it results in no material misstatement of property costs and periodic income.

VALUATION OF PROPERTY

Property items, just as all other facilities acquired by a business entity, are recognized initially at cost — the original bargained price. When payment for an asset is not made in the form of cash, the cash value of the consideration given in exchange must be established to arrive at cost. When it is not possible to arrive at a satisfactory cash value for the consideration transferred, the asset is reported at its present fair market value or, stated differently, the amount which would have been paid if it had been acquired in a cash transaction.[1] A similar procedure is followed for assets acquired through gift or discovery.

The cost of property includes not only the original purchase price or equivalent value, but also any other expenditures required in obtaining and preparing it for its intended use. Any taxes and duties, freight or cartage, and installation and other expenditures related to the acquisition should be added to the original outlay.

Property items are presented on the balance sheet at cost less the portion of cost assigned to past revenues. Land is normally considered to have an unlimited service life and, therefore, is reported at its original cost. In special cases where agricultural land may lose its fertility through use or erosion, or a building site may lose its utility through physical or environmental changes, reductions in cost to reflect the decline in asset usefulness may be appropriate. Natural resources are subject to exhaustion and are normally reported at cost less the portion of cost related to removed resources. This expired cost is referred to as *depletion*. All other property items are considered to have a limited service life and are normally reported at *cost less accumulated depreciation. Accumulated depreciation* is the portion of the asset cost written off by periodic depreciation charges since the acquisition of the asset. The difference between asset cost and accumulated depreciation is referred to as the asset *book value*. Historically, no reference to market values or replacement values has been made in presenting property on the balance sheet. However, there is increasing interest in reporting property items at their current values or at their costs adjusted for general price-level changes. These matters are discussed in later chapters.

ACQUISITION OF PROPERTY

There are a number of different ways in which property is acquired and each presents special problems relating to asset cost. The acquisition of properties is discussed under the following headings: (1) purchase for cash, (2) purchase on long-term contract, (3) exchange, (4) issuance of securities, (5) self-construction, and (6) donation or discovery.

Purchase for Cash   Property acquired for cash is recorded at the amount of the cash outlay, including all incidental outlays relating to its purchase or preparation for use.

As suggested in an earlier chapter, sound accounting theory requires discounts on purchases to be regarded as reductions in costs: earnings

---

[1]*Opinions of the Accounting Principles Board, No. 29*, "Accounting for Nonmonetary Transactions" (New York: American Institute of Certified Public Accountants, 1973), par. 18.

arise from sales, not from purchases. In applying this theory, any available discounts on property acquisitions should be treated as reductions to the asset cost. Failure to take such discounts should be reported as Discounts Lost or Interest Expense.

A number of property items may be acquired for one lump sum. Some of the assets may be depreciable, others nondepreciable. Depreciable assets may have different useful lives. If there is to be accountability for the assets on an individual basis, the total purchase price must be allocated among the individual assets. When part of a purchase price can be clearly identified with specific assets, such cost assignment should be made and the balance of the purchase price allocated among the remaining assets. When no part of the purchase price can be related to specific assets, the entire amount must be allocated among the different assets acquired. Appraisal values or similar evidence provided by a competent independent authority should be sought to support such allocation.

To illustrate the allocation of a joint asset cost, assume land, buildings, and equipment are acquired for $80,000. Assume further that assessed values for the individual assets as reported on the property tax bill are considered to provide an equitable basis for cost allocation. The allocation is made as shown below.

	Assessed Values	Cost Allocation According to Relative Assessed Values	Cost Assigned to Individual Assets
Real properties:			
Land	$14,000	14,000/50,000 × $80,000	$22,400
Improvements (building)	30,000	30,000/50,000 × $80,000	48,000
Personal property (equipment)	6,000	6,000/50,000 × $80,000	9,600
	$50,000		$80,000

An asset acquired in secondhand or used condition should be set up at its cost without reference to the balance found on the seller's books. Expenditures to repair, recondition, or improve the asset before it is placed in use should be added to cost. It must be assumed that the buyer knew additional expenditures would be required when the purchase was made.

Purchase on Long-Term Contract

Real estate or other property is frequently acquired under contracts whereby payments are to be made over a number of years. Interest charged on the unpaid balance of the contract should be recognized as an expense. To illustrate the accounting for a long-term purchase contract, assume land is acquired for $100,000; $25,000 is paid at the time of purchase and the balance is to be paid in semiannual installments of $5,000, including interest on the unpaid principal at 8% per year. Entries for the purchase and for the first and second payments on the contract are shown at the top of the next page.

In the preceding example, the contract specified both a purchase price and interest at a stated rate on the unpaid balance. Sometimes, however, a contract may simply provide for a series of payments without

TRANSACTION	ENTRY

January 2, 1977
Purchased land for $100,000 paying $25,000 down, the balance to be paid in semiannual payments of $5,000 including interest at 8%.
	Land 100,000
	   Cash... 25,000
	   Contract Payable......................... 75,000

June 30, 1977 Made first payment: Amount of payment .... $5,000 Amount representing interest, 4% of unpaid balance of $75,000 .... 3,000 Balance — reduction in principal.................. $2,000	Interest Expense .... 3,000 Contract Payable............................. 2,000 Cash... 5,000
December 31, 1977 Made second payment: Amount of payment .... $5,000 Amount representing interest, 4% of unpaid balance of $73,000 ($75,000 − $2,000) ...... 2,920 Balance — reduction in principal.................. $2,080	Interest Expense .... 2,920 Contract Payable............................. 2,080 Cash... 5,000

reference to interest or may provide for a stated interest rate that is unreasonable in relation to the market. The Accounting Principles Board identified this type of contract in Opinion No. 21, "Interest on Receivables and Payables," and stated that:

> . . . In these circumstances, the note, the sales price, and the cost of the property, goods, or service exchanged for the note should be recorded at the fair value of the property, goods or services or at an amount that reasonably approximates the market value of the note, whichever is the more clearly determinable. That amount may or may not be the same as its face amount, and any resulting discount or premium should be accounted for as an element of interest over the life of the note. In the absence of established exchange prices for the related property, goods, or service or evidence of the market value of the note, the present value of a note that stipulates either no interest or a rate of interest that is clearly unreasonable should be determined by discounting all future payments on the notes using an imputed rate of interest. . .[1]

To illustrate the accounting for this type of long-term contract, assume that certain equipment is acquired at a price of $40,000; the down payment is $10,000, and the balance is payable in four equal annual installments of $7,500. Assume further that, although there is no interest rate specified in the contract, it is fair to assume that the contract price involves implicit interest at 8%. The cost of the equipment, then, should be regarded as the discounted value at 8% of installments of $7,500 due in one, two, three, and four years. The present value of the contract, including the down payment, is $34,840.75.[2] The obligation is recorded by a credit to Contract Payable for $30,000 and a debit to a discount on the payable for $5,159.25, or a net contract price of $24,840.75. The 8%

---

[1]*Opinions of the Accounting Principles Board, No. 21*, "Interest on Receivables and Payables" (New York: American Institute of Certified Public Accountants, 1971), par. 12.

[2]$PV_n = R(PVAF_{\overline{n}|\,i})$

$PV_n = \$7,500(\text{Table IV}_{\overline{4}|\,8\%}) = \$7,500(3.3121) = \$24,840.75$. The total contract equals the down payment plus the present value of four installments: ($10,000 + $24,840.75 = $34,840.75).

rate is applied to the declining debt balance in subsequent periods in amortizing the debt discount. Entries for the acquisition of the property item, and the first periodic payment are as follows:

TRANSACTION	ENTRY

January 2, 1977
Purchased equipment at a price of $40,000 paying $10,000 down, the balance in four equal installments of $7,500. It is assumed that interest at 8% is implicit in the purchase price and the obligation is recorded at its present value of $24,840.75 ($30,000.00 − $5,159.25).
	Equipment.................................... 34,840.75
	Discount on Equipment Contract Payable 5,159.25
	   Cash 10,000.00
	   Equipment Contract Payable . 30,000.00

December 31, 1977
Made first payment of $7,500.
Amortization of debt discount:
8% × $24,840.75 = $1,987.26.
	Equipment Contract Payable..... 7,500.00
	   Cash 7,500.00
	Interest Expense......................... 1,987.26
	   Discount on Equipment Contract Payable........................... 1,987.26

When a cash price is quoted for a property item, this amount may be used in recording the property item and in recognizing the present value of the debt. In such instances, the debt discount may be amortized either by (1) calculating the effective or implicit interest rate and applying this to the declining debt balance as in the previous example, or (2) developing fractions expressing the dollar debt for the period to the dollar debt for the life of the contract and applying them to the debt discount.

To illustrate the second procedure, assume that in the preceding example the equipment is quoted at a cash price of $35,000. The equipment, then, would be reported at $35,000, cash would be credited for the down payment of $10,000, and a payable would be recognized for $30,000 less a discount of $5,000. Discount amortization may be calculated as follows:

Year	Liability Balance	Fraction of Discount to be Amortized	Annual Discount Amortization (Fraction × $5,000)
1977	$30,000	300/750	$2,000
1978	22,500	225/750	1,500
1979	15,000	150/750	1,000
1980	7,500	75/750	500
	$75,000	750/750	$5,000

Property may be acquired under a conditional sales contract whereby legal title to the asset is retained by the seller until payments are completed. The failure to acquire legal title may be disregarded by the buyer and the transaction recognized in terms of its substance — the acquisition of an asset and the assumption of a liability. The buyer has the possession and use of the asset and must absorb any decline in its value; title to the asset is retained by the seller simply as a means of assuring payment on the purchase contract. In reporting the asset on the balance sheet prior to full settlement, there should be disclosure by parenthetical remark or note indicating legal title to the asset still remains with the seller.

Acquisition by Exchange — General Case

When one nonmonetary asset[1] is traded for another, the new asset generally should be recorded at the fair market value of the asset given up, or the fair market value of the asset received if its fair market value is more clearly evident.[2] If a used asset is surrendered for a new asset, the fair market value of the new asset is often more clearly evident than the market value of the old asset, and thus would be used to value the exchange. Care must be taken to determine the true market value of the new asset. Frequently, the quoted list price is not a good indicator of market and is higher than the actual cash price for the new asset. The inflation of the list price permits the seller to inflate the trade-in allowance for the used asset. The price for which the asset could be acquired in a strictly cash transaction is the fair market value that should be used.

Any difference between the fair market value assigned to the asset received and the book value (carrying value) of the old asset should be recognized as a gain or loss on the exchange. If the exchange involves a monetary payment, or *boot*, the new asset should be recorded at the sum of the value of the monetary asset and the fair market value of the surrendered asset. Any trade-in allowance should be carefully examined to determine whether it measures fairly the value of the asset exchanged. The use of an inflated trade-in allowance as representative of the market value of the surrendered asset will result in the overstatement of the newly acquired asset and also in the subsequent overstatement of depreciation charges.

To illustrate an exchange involving nonsimilar, nonmonetary assets, assume equipment with an original cost of $5,000 and a book value of $3,000 is accepted at a trade-in value of $2,600 in part payment on a truck with a fair market value of $3,200. The difference of $600 is paid in cash. The following entry would be made to record the exchange:

Trucks	3,200	
Accumulated Depreciation — Equipment	2,000	
Loss on Exchange of Equipment	400	
Equipment		5,000
Cash		600

Computation:
Accumulated depreciation:
$5,000 cost — $3,000 book value = $2,000 accumulated depreciation.
Loss:
$3,000 book value — $2,600 trade-in allowance = $400 loss.

If, in the above example, the truck could have been acquired at a cash price of $2,800, this value should have been used in recording the asset rather than the inflated trade-in allowance. Although the trade-in allowance on the old equipment was stated at $2,600, this asset apparently had an actual worth of no more than $2,200 ($2,800 − $600); the loss on the exchange was $800, the difference between the actual trade-in value of the surrendered asset, $2,200 and its book value, $3,000.

---

[1]*Monetary assets* are those whose amounts are fixed in terms of units of currency by contract or otherwise. Examples include cash and short or long-term accounts receivable. *Nonmonetary assets* include all other assets, such as inventories, land, buildings, and equipment.
[2]*Opinions of the Accounting Principles Board*, No. 29, *op. cit.*, par. 18.

In the example, the asset was assumed to have been exchanged at the beginning of a fiscal period. When a depreciable asset is exchanged within a fiscal period, depreciation should be recognized to the time of the exchange, and the entry to record the exchange should recognize the book value of the asset at that date.

Acquisition by Exchange — Special Cases

The Accounting Principles Board recognized three exceptions to the general rule of using market values to determine the gain or loss on exchange of nonmonetary assets. They are:

1. If market values are not determinable within reasonable limits.
2. If the exchange indicates a gain, but does not culminate the earnings process:
   a. Exchange of inventory between dealers to facilitate sales to customers other than the parties involved in the exchange.
   b. Exchange of *similar productive assets* not held for sale.
3. If nonmonetary assets are transferred to owners in a spin-off, or other form of reorganization.[1]

In the first case, since there are no market values available, the new asset is recorded at the book value of the old asset and no gain or loss is recognized. In the second case, market values are available and indicated gains or losses can be computed. However, the Board concluded that both the exchanges identified above are interim transactions, and do not culminate the earnings process. Inventories are often swapped between dealers or other firms to obtain a different model, style, or color for a specific sale. The Board felt that no income should be recognized until a sale actually was made to an external customer. Likewise, they felt that income from an exchange of similar productive assets occurs from the sale of items produced by the productive assets, not from their exchange. Thus, any gain indicated by comparing market values with book values is deferred unless boot is involved, and the asset acquired is valued at the book value of the asset relinquished. However, if a loss is indicated from the market value involved in the transaction, the entire loss should be recognized. If boot is *received* in the exchange, a partial culmination of the earnings process has occurred and part of the gain represented by the boot should be recognized immediately. Because of the complexities of accounting for exchanges not culminating the earning process, the following examples will illustrate journal entries for exchange with and without monetary asset transfers.

Exchanges Not Culminating the Earnings Process — No Boot Involved. To illustrate the exchange of similar assets when no boot is involved, assume Company A exchanged equipment costing $9,000, with accumulated depreciation of $6,000 and a fair market value of $5,000, for similar equipment from Company B costing $12,000, with accumulated depreciation on Company B's books of $7,500, and a fair market value of $5,000. The entries on the books of Company A and Company B would be:

---

[1]*Ibid.*, par. 20–23. Further discussion of Exception 3 is beyond the scope of this textbook.

Company A

Equipment	3,000	
Accumulated Depreciation — Equipment...	6,000	
Equipment..		9,000

Computation:

$9,000 cost of old equipment − $6,000 accumulated depreciation = $3,000 carrying value of the old equipment.

Company B

Equipment	4,500	
Accumulated Depreciation — Equipment...	7,500	
Equipment..		12,000

Computation:

$12,000 cost of old equipment − $7,500 accumulated depreciation = $4,500 carrying value of the old equipment.

Since the fair market value ($5,000) exceeded the book value of each asset involved in the exchange, each company had an indicated gain ($2,000 for Company A and $500 for Company B), but it is deferred and not recognized.

If the fair market values of the assets exchanged had been $4,000 at the time of the exchange, Company A would still have an indicated gain ($1,000) and would record the exchange as above with the gain deferred. However, Company B would have an indicated loss of $500 on the exchange, $4,500 − $4,000, and would value the new equipment at $4,000 after recognizing the loss of $500. This latter treatment differs from the income tax treatment for exchanges with an indicated loss. Under income tax regulations, no gain *or* loss is recognized on exchange of productive, like-kind assets.[1]

Exchange Not Culminating the Earnings Process — Boot Involved. When a small amount of monetary consideration (boot) is *given* in an exchange, the same procedures apply as when no boot is involved.[2] No indicated gain is recognized and the new asset is recorded at the carrying value of the old asset plus the cash given. However, if boot is *received* in the exchange, and there is an indicated gain on the transaction, a portion of the gain is recognized to the extent the boot received exceeds a proportionate share of the carrying value of the surrendered assets. The formula for the amount of gain recognized is as follows:[3]

$$\text{Recognized Gain} = \text{Boot Received} - \left(\frac{\text{Boot}}{\text{Boot} + \text{Fair Market Value of Acquired Asset}} \times \text{Carrying Value of Surrendered Asset} \right)$$

To illustrate this situation, assume Company A exchanged equipment costing $15,000 with accumulated depreciation of $9,000 and a fair market value of $8,000 plus cash of $500 for similar equipment from

---

[1]Internal Revenue Code, Sec. 1031.

[2]Opinion No. 29 does not define a "small amount of monetary consideration." Presumably, if the monetary amount exceeds the concept of being small, the transaction no longer qualifies as a nonmonetary exchange and the exchange would be accounted for as a monetary exchange with any gain or loss recognized.

[3]*Opinions of the Accounting Principles Board, No. 29, op. cit.*, par. 22.

Company B costing $12,000 with accumulated depreciation on Company B's books of $5,000 and a fair market value of $8,500. Company A would have an indicated gain of $2,000 ($8,500 fair market value of the asset received less a carrying value of the asset exchanged of $6,000 plus boot paid of $500). Because the exchange is not viewed as culminating the earnings process, the gain is deferred. The entries on the books of Company A would be as follows:

Company A

Equipment	6,500	
Accumulated Depreciation — Equipment	9,000	
Cash		500
Equipment		15,000

Computation:

$15,000 cost of old equipment − $9,000 accumulated depreciation + $500 cash = $6,500 carrying value of the old equipment plus cash paid.

Company B would have an indicated gain of $1,500 ($8,500 − $7,000, the carrying value of the asset exchanged). However, since Company B received the boot, a portion of the gain will be recognized and the balance deferred. The gain is computed from the formula as follows:

$$\text{Recognized Gain} = \$500 - \left(\frac{\$500}{\$500 + \$8,000} \times \$7,000 \right)$$
$$= \$500 - \$412^* = \$88$$

*Rounded to the nearest dollar.

The entries on the books of Company B would be as follows:

Company B

Equipment	6,588	
Accumulated Depreciation — Equipment	5,000	
Cash	500	
Equipment		12,000
Gain on Exchange of Equipment		88

Computation:

$12,000 cost of old equipment − $5,000 accumulated depreciation − $500 cash = $6,500 carrying value of the old equipment minus cash paid. $6,500 + $88 gain = $6,588.

For income tax purposes, Company B would recognize any indicated gain to the extent boot is received. Thus, Company B would recognize for tax purposes the entire cash received as a gain.

Acquisition by Issuance of Securities

A company may acquire certain property by issuing its own bonds or stock. When a market value for the securities can be determined, such value is assigned to the asset; in the absence of a market value for the securities, the fair market value of the asset would be sought. If bonds or stock are selling at more or less than par value, the asset should be reported at the current cash value; Bonds Payable or Capital Stock should be credited at par and a premium or discount should be established for the difference. To illustrate, assume a company issues bonds of $100,000 in acquiring land; the bonds are currently selling on the market at 95. An entry should be made as follows:

Land..	95,000	
Discount on Bonds Payable	5,000	
Bonds Payable		100,000

Thus, the value of the securities is set as of the time of the issuance and at a price established by market transactions.

When securities do not have an established market value, appraisal of the assets by an independent authority may be required to arrive at an objective determination of their fair market value. If satisfactory market values cannot be obtained for either securities issued or the assets acquired, values as established by the board of directors may have to be accepted for accounting purposes. For example, assume a corporation issues stock in payment for certain mining property. A market value cannot be established for the stock, and there are no means of arriving at a fair market value for the property received. If the board of directors values the property at $100,000, the property value and the issuing price of the stock are thereby set at this amount. Disclosure should be provided on the balance sheet of the source of the valuation. The assignment of values by the board of directors is normally not subject to challenge unless it can be shown that the board has acted fraudulently. Nevertheless, evidence should be sought to validate the fairness of original valuations, and if within a short time after an acquisition, the sale of stock or other information indicates that original valuations were erroneous, appropriate action should be taken to restate asset and owners' equity accounts.

Property is frequently acquired in exchange for securities pursuant to a corporate merger or consolidation. When such combination represents the transfer of properties to a new owner, the combination is designated a *purchase* and acquired assets are reported at their cost to the new owner. But when such combination represents essentially no more than a continuation of the original ownership in the enlarged entity, the combination is designated a *pooling of interests* and accounting authorities have approved the practice of recording properties at the original book values as shown on the books of the acquired company. Specific guidelines for distinguishing between a purchase and a pooling of interests are included in APB Opinion No. 16.[1]

Acquisition by Self-Construction

Sometimes buildings or equipment items are constructed by a company for its own use. This may be done to save on construction costs, to utilize idle facilities, or to achieve a higher quality of construction. When construction takes place, a number of special problems arise in arriving at asset cost.

Overhead Chargeable to Self-Construction. All costs that can be related to construction should be charged to the assets under construction. There is no question about the inclusion of charges directly attributable to the new construction. However, there is a difference of opinion regarding

---

[1]The pooling of interests concept is discussed in greater detail in *Advanced Accounting*, Fourth Edition, by Simons and Karrenbrock.

the amount of overhead properly assignable to the construction activity. Some accountants take the position that assets under construction should be charged with no more than the incremental overhead — the increase in a company's total overhead resulting from the special construction activity. Others maintain that overhead should be assigned to construction just as it is assigned to normal operations. This would call for the inclusion of not only the increase in overhead resulting from construction activities but also a pro rata share of the company's fixed overhead.

Those supporting charges for overhead limited to incremental amounts maintain that the cost of construction is actually no more than the extra costs incurred. Normal operations should receive no special favors as a result of construction. Management is aware of the cost of normal operations and decides to undertake a project on the basis of the anticipated added costs. Those taking the position that construction should carry a fair share of the fixed overhead maintain this must be done if the full cost of the asset is to be reported. It is their view that construction is entitled to no special favors, and this practice should be followed even though general operations are relieved of a portion of the overhead that they would normally carry; overhead has served a double purpose during the construction period and this is properly reflected in reduced operating costs. The latter argument may be particularly persuasive if construction takes place during a period of subnormal operations and utilizes what would otherwise represent idle capacity cost, or if construction restricts production or other regular business activities.

The assignment to construction of normal overhead otherwise chargeable to current operations will increase net income during the construction period. The recognition of a portion of overhead is postponed and related to subsequent periods through charges in the form of depreciation.

Companies have not been successful in coming to an agreement on this issue. Authors of a research study for the AICPA have suggested the following criteria to help resolve the issue.

> . . . in the absence of compelling evidence to the contrary, overhead costs considered to have "discernible future benefits" for the purpose of determining the cost of inventory should be presumed to have "discernible future benefits" for the purpose of determining the cost of a self-constructed depreciable asset.[1]

This criterion would charge both normal and incremental overhead costs to self-constructed fixed assets and have the advantage of providing consistency within a company in the treatment of overhead costs.

Saving or Loss on Self-Construction. When the cost of self-construction of an asset is less than the cost to acquire it through purchase or construction by outsiders, the difference for accounting purposes is not a profit but a *saving*. The construction is properly reported at its actual cost. The

---

[1]Charles Lamden, Dale L. Gerboth, and Thomas McRae, "Accounting for Depreciable Assets," *Accounting Research Monograph No. 1* (New York: American Institute of Certified Public Accountants, 1975), pp. 57.

saving will emerge as income over the life of the asset as lower deprecia-tion is charged against periodic revenue. Assume, on the other hand, the cost of self-construction is greater than bids originally received for the construction. There is generally no assurance that the asset under alter-native arrangements might have been equal in quality to that which was self-constructed. In recording this transaction, just as in recording others, accounts should reflect those courses of action taken, not the al-ternatives that might have been selected. At the same time, if there is evidence indicating cost has been materially excessive because of certain construction inefficiencies or failures, the excess is properly recognized as a loss; subsequent periods should not be burdened with charges for depreciation arising from costs that could have been avoided.

Interest During Period of Construction. In public utility accounting, inter-est during a period of building construction is recognized as a part of asset cost. This practice applies both to interest actually paid and to an implicit interest charge if the public utility uses its own funds. Interest, then, emerges as a charge for depreciation in the periods in which the properties are income-producing. Service rates established by regulatory bodies are based upon current charges and may provide for a recovery of past interest in this manner.

The practice of capitalizing interest has sometimes been carried into accounting for industrial companies. Support for this practice is made on the grounds that interest is a cost of construction, and the proper match-ing of revenues and expenses suggests it be deferred and charged over the life of the constructed asset. It can also be argued that if buildings or equipment were acquired by purchase rather than by self-construction, a charge for interest during the construction period would be implicit in the purchase price.

Arguments advanced against this practice are:

1. It is difficult to follow cash once it is invested in a firm. Is the interest charge really related to the constructed asset, or is it a payment made to meet general financial needs? Even when a loan is made for specific pur-poses, it frees cash raised by other means to be used for other projects.
2. To be consistent, implicit interest on all funds used, not just borrowed funds, should be charged to the asset cost. This practice is followed in utility accounting and requires determining a cost of capital for internal funds used, a very difficult task.

Traditionally, nonutility companies have not capitalized interest. However, in the mid 1970's an increasing number of companies changed their accounting method to a policy of capitalizing interest, an action that tended to increase net income. In reaction to these changes, the Securi-ties and Exchange Commission, in 1974, declared a moratorium on com-panies changing their methods of accounting for interest costs pending study of the issue by the Financial Accounting Standards Board.[1]

---

[1]Securities and Exchange Commission, *Accounting Series Release No. 163*, "Capitalization of Interest by Companies Other than Public Utilities" (Washington: U.S. Government Printing Office, 1974).

Development Stage Expenditures

Some have maintained that all charges for interest, taxes, and general and administrative services during the development stage of a new company should be capitalized. Support for this procedure is based on the theory that future periods are benefited by necessary initial costs and it is unreasonable to assume losses have been incurred before sales activities begin. The Financial Accounting Standards Board reviewed this practice and concluded that accounting principles for companies in the organizational or developmental stage should be the same as for more mature companies. No special rules or principles should apply. Therefore, capitalization policies would not be different for these companies, and the above expenditures should be expensed in the period incurred.[1]

Acquisition by Donation or Discovery

When property is received through donation by a governmental unit or other source, there is no cost that can be used as a basis for its valuation. It is classified as a nonreciprocal transfer of a nonmonetary asset.[2] Even though certain expenditures may have to be made incident to the gift, these expenditures are generally considerably less than the value of the property. Here cost obviously fails to provide a satisfactory basis for asset accountability as well as for future income measurement.

Property acquired through donation should be appraised and recorded at its fair market value.[3] A donation increases owners' equity, therefore Donated Capital is credited. To illustrate, if the Beverly Hills Chamber of Commerce donates land and buildings appraised at $50,000 and $150,000 respectively, the entry on the books of the donee would be:

Land	50,000	
Buildings	150,000	
Donated Capital		200,000

Depreciation of an asset acquired by gift should be recorded in the usual manner; the value assigned to the asset providing the basis for the depreciation charge.

If a gift is contingent upon some act to be performed by the donee, the contingent nature of the asset and the capital item should be indicated in the account titles. Account balances should be reported "short" or a special note should be made on the balance sheet. When conditions of the gift have been met, both the increase in assets and in owners' equity should be recognized in the accounts and on the financial statements.

Occasionally, valuable resources are discovered on already owned land. The discovery greatly increases the value of the property. However, because the cost of the land is not affected by the discovery, it is common practice to ignore this increase in value. Similarly, the increase in value for assets that change over time, such as growing timber or aging wine, is ignored in common practice. Failure to recognize these discovery or accretion values ignores the economic reality of the situation and

---

[1]*Statement of Financial Accounting Standards No. 7*, "Accounting and Reporting by Development Stage Enterprises" (Stamford, Conn.: Financial Accounting Standards Board, 1975), par. 10.

[2]*Opinions of the Accounting Principles Board, No. 29, op. cit.*, par 3(d).

[3]*Ibid.*, par. 18.

tends to materially understate the assets of the entity. More meaningful decisions could probably be made if the user of the statements was aware of these changes in value.

Special Problems

Special accounting problems arise in recording the acquisition of certain property items. Attention is directed in the following sections to specific properties and their special problems.

Land. Rights to land arising from *purchase* should be distinguished from rights under *leaseholds* and under *easements*. With a purchase, the buyer acquires title and ownership *in fee simple*, and the property is properly recognized as an asset. A leasehold provides rights for the *possession and profits* of land for a certain period. An easement provides rights for the *use* of land as in the case of rights-of-way or other special privileges. Recognition of asset balances for leaseholds and easements is limited to prepayments of rents and fees to the owners of land for the acquired rights unless the leasehold or easement is in substance a purchase. In this case, the present value of future rental payments is capitalized.[1]

When land is purchased, its cost includes not only the negotiated purchase price but also all other costs related to the acquisition including brokers' commissions, legal fees, title, recording, and escrow fees, and surveying fees. Any existing unpaid tax, interest, or other liens on the property assumed by the buyer are added to cost.

Costs of clearing, grading, subdividing, landscaping, or otherwise permanently improving the land after its acquisition should also be treated as increases in the cost of land. When a site secured for a new plant is already occupied by a building that must be torn down, the cost of removing the old structure less any recovery from salvage is added to land cost. If salvage exceeds the cost of razing buildings, the excess may be considered a reduction of land cost. Special assessments by local governments for certain local benefits, such as streets and sidewalks, lighting, and sewers and drainage systems that will be maintained by the government, may be regarded as permanently improving land and thus chargeable to this asset. When expenditures are incurred for land improvements having a limited life and requiring ultimate replacement as, for example, paving, fencing, and water and sewage systems, such costs should be summarized separately in an account entitled Land Improvements and depreciated over the estimated useful life of the improvements. The useful life of some improvements may be limited to the life of the buildings on the land; other improvements may have an independent service life.

Land qualifies for presentation in the land, buildings, and equipment category only when it is being used in the normal activities of the business. For example, land held for future use or for speculation should be reported under the long-term investments heading; land held for current sale should be reported as a current asset. A descriptive account title

---

[1]See Chapter 17 for discussion of capitalization of leases.

should be used to distinguish land not used in normal operations from the land in use.

When land is acquired and held for future use or as a speculative venture, a question arises as to the proper treatment of the charges of carrying such property. Should expenditures for tax and interest on mortgages, for example, be charged to periodic revenue or be added to the cost of the land? There is strong support for adding these charges to land. The buyer knows that costs will be involved in holding the land before it can be applied to the specific purpose for which it is acquired and makes the purchase with the expectation that the investment will yield benefits exceeding both the original cost and carrying charges. When carrying charges are capitalized, the full cost of the investment can be assigned to the purpose for which it is ultimately applied.

To illustrate, assume in 1977 a company acquires land for expansion purposes although it does not expect to use the land until 1987. Cost of the land is $40,000; tax and other carrying charges are estimated at $20,000 for the ten-year period. Under these circumstances, the company has actually made a decision to invest $60,000 in land instead of delaying action until some later date when efforts toward expansion might find circumstances less favorable. Or assume in 1977 land is acquired as a speculative investment for $40,000 and it is ultimately sold in 1987 for $75,000, carrying charges during the ten-year period having totaled $20,000. Here, too, the investment in land may be regarded as $60,000 and the gain as $15,000. The land represented, in effect, goods in process during the holding period; $75,000 is ultimately realized on an investment totaling $60,000. If carrying charges had been assigned to the periodic revenues, net income during the ten-year holding period would have been reduced by $20,000 and a gain of $35,000 would be reported on the sale of the property. The latter treatment fails to offer a satisfactory accounting for period earnings and for the gain emerging from the investment.

It is difficult to support capitalizing expenditures for carrying assets when market values fail to confirm increasing property values; here conservatism requires the treatment of such expenditures as charges to periodic revenues. The capitalization procedure is likewise inappropriate when land is used for such purposes as rental or farming and produces current revenue; expenditures under these circumstances should be treated as charges against such revenue.

Carrying charges on investments in land are sometimes recorded as expenses rather than as part of the cost of land. In reporting land held as a long-term investment on the balance sheet, it is desirable to indicate in parenthetical or note form the cost procedure employed for the asset as well as its current fair market value when this can be supported by objective evidence.

Buildings. A purchase involving the acquisition of both land and buildings requires the cost to be allocated between the two assets. Allocable cost consists of the purchase price plus all charges incident to the purchase. The cost allocated to buildings is increased by expenditures for reconditioning and repairs in preparing the asset for use as well as by expenditures for improvements and additions.

When buildings are constructed, their cost consists of materials, labor, and overhead related to construction. Costs of excavation or grading and filling required for purposes of the specific project, rather than for making land usable, are charged to buildings. Charges for architects' fees, building permits and fees, workmen's compensation and accident insurance, fire insurance for the period of construction, and temporary buildings used for construction activities, form part of the total building cost. Tax on property improvements, as well as financing costs during a period of construction, are generally capitalized as a cost of buildings.

It was suggested earlier that when land and buildings are acquired and buildings are immediately demolished, the cost of demolishing buildings is added to land as a cost of preparing land for its intended use. However, the cost of demolishing buildings that have been previously occupied by the company requires different treatment. This is a cost that should be identified with the life of the original buildings. The recovery of salvage upon asset retirement serves to reduce the cost arising from the use of an asset and is frequently anticipated in calculating periodic charges for depreciation; a cost arising from asset retirement serves to increase the cost of asset use but is seldom anticipated in developing periodic charges.

In many instances, careful analysis is required in determining whether an expenditure should be recognized as buildings or whether it should be identified with the land or equipment categories. For example, expenditures for sidewalks and roads that are part of a building program are normally reported as buildings, but these would be properly reported as land improvements when they improve land regardless of its use; expenditures for items such as shelving, cabinets, or partitions in the course of building construction are normally reported as buildings, but these would be properly reported as equipment items when they are movable, can be used in different centers, and are considered to have independent lives. Particular care should be directed to charges against revenues under different classification and recording alternatives. Frequently alternative classifications can be supported and the ultimate choice will be a matter of judgment.

If depreciation on buildings is to be recognized satisfactorily, separate accounts should be maintained for each building with a different life as well as for those structural elements of a building requiring modification or replacement before the building is fully depreciated, such as loading and shipping quarters, storage facilities, and garages. Separate recording should also be extended to building equipment and appurtenances requiring replacement before the building is fully depreciated, such as boilers, heating and ventilating systems, plumbing and lighting systems, elevators, and wiring and piping installations. The latter items are frequently summarized in an account titled Building Equipment or Building Improvements, but detailed records will be required in support of this balance because of the different service lives of the individual items.

Equipment. Equipment covers a wide range of items that vary with the particular enterprise and its activities. The discussion in the following paragraphs is limited to machinery, tools, patterns and dies, furniture and fixtures, motor vehicles, and returnable containers.

Machinery of the manufacturing concern includes such items as lathes, stamping machines, ovens, and conveyor systems. The machinery account is debited for all expenditures identified with the acquisition and the preparation for use of factory machines. Machinery cost includes the purchase price, tax and duties on purchase, freight charges, insurance charges while in transit, installation charges, expenditures for testing and final preparation for use, and costs for reconditioning used equipment when purchased.

Two classes of tools are employed in productive activities: (1) machine tools, representing detachable parts of a machine, such as dies, drills, and punches; and (2) hand tools, such as hammers, wrenches, and saws. Both classes of tools are normally of small individual cost and are relatively short-lived as a result of wear, breakage, and loss. These factors frequently suggest that these items be accounted for as a single asset. Replacement of these small tools may then either be charged directly to expense or added to the single asset account and written off by reasonable annual amortization charges.

Patterns and dies are acquired for designing, stamping, cutting, or forging out a particular object. The cost of patterns and dies is either a purchase cost or a developmental cost composed of labor, materials, and overhead. When patterns and dies are used in normal productive activities, their cost is reported as an asset and the asset values are written off over the period of their usefulness. When the use of such items is limited to the manufacture of a single job, their cost is recognized as a part of the cost of that job.

Furniture and fixtures include such items as desks, chairs, carpets, showcases, and display fixtures. Acquisitions should be identified with production, selling, or general and administrative functions. Such classification makes it possible to assign depreciation accurately to the different business activities. Furniture and fixtures are recorded at cost, which includes purchase price, tax, freight, and installation charges.

Automobile and truck acquisitions should also be identified with production, selling, or general and administrative functions. Depreciation can then be accurately related to the different activities. Automotive equipment is recorded at its purchase price increased by any sales and excise tax and delivery charges paid. When payment for equipment includes charges for items, such as current license fees, personal property tax, and insurance, these should be recognized separately as expenses relating to both the current and the future use of the equipment.

Goods are frequently delivered in containers to be returned and reused. Returnable containers consist of such items as tanks, drums, and barrels. Containers are depreciable assets used in the business and are included in the equipment group. Adjustments must be made periodically to reduce the asset account and its related accumulated depreciation for containers not expected to be returned. The reduction is reported as a current loss.

The Investment Credit

In order to encourage investment in productive facilities, the Revenue Act of 1962 permitted taxpayers to reduce their federal income tax by an *investment credit* equal to a specified percentage of the cost of certain depreciable properties acquired after January 1, 1962. This act thus provided certain tax benefits as a stimulant to the economy. The investment credit has had a turbulent history both in politics and in accounting practice. The credit provisions were significantly amended in 1964; the credit was temporarily suspended in 1966 and suspended again in 1969 when the economy was in an inflationary period. The credit was reinstated in 1971, but the rate and coverage have changed through the years.

Accounting for the credit has also been the subject of much controversy and change. Essentially, there are two methods that can be used to record the tax reduction: (1) The credit can be used to reduce the income tax expense for the year in which it is received, commonly referred to as the *flow-through method*, or (2) the credit can be deferred and reflected as a reduction of tax expense over the period during which the asset is depreciated, commonly referred to as the *deferred method*.

To illustrate the two approaches, assume that a business acquired machinery in 1977 for $100,000 when the investment credit rate was 10% on new assets. The asset has an estimated useful life of 10 years with no salvage value and is to be depreciated on a straight-line basis. Assume further that federal income tax for 1977 is $40,000 reduced by an investment credit of $10,000 (10% of $100,000). Entries in 1977 would be:

TRANSACTION	ASSUMING THAT THE INVESTMENT CREDIT IS TREATED AS A REDUCTION IN TAX (FLOW-THROUGH METHOD)		ASSUMING THAT THE INVESTMENT CREDIT IS TREATED AS A DEFERRED CREDIT (DEFERRED METHOD)	
Purchase of machinery for $100,000.	Machinery .... 100,000 　Cash....................	100,000	Machinery .... 100,000 　Cash....................	100,000
Recognition of income tax, $40,000 less investment credit, $10,000.	Income Tax .... 30,000 　Income Tax 　Payable..............	30,000	Income Tax .... 40,000 　Deferred 　Investment Tax 　Credit .... 　Income Tax 　Payable..............	10,000 30,000
Amortization of deferred investment tax credit and depreciation for 1977.	Depreciation Expense .... 10,000 　Accumulated 　Depreciation — 　Machinery..........	10,000	Depreciation Expense .... 10,000 Deferred Investment Tax Credit..................... 1,000 　Income Tax........ 　Accumulated 　Depreciation — 　Machinery..........	1,000 10,000

The Accounting Principles Board favored the deferred method and approved it in Opinion No. 2. Lack of support for this view among many prominent accountants led to the issuance in 1964 of Opinion No. 4 in which the Board accepted both methods although still stating a preference for the deferred method. In 1968, a further attempt was made by the Accounting Principles Board to restore the deferred method as a single uniform method. Again, differences of opinion resulted in failure to adopt the original conclusions. In 1971, the Board once again made serious effort to restore the deferred method. However, they had to postpone such effort as a result of congressional action permitting the taxpayer to choose the method to be used in recognizing the benefit arising from the credit.

Good theoretical arguments can be presented for either of the methods. Those who advocate using the deferred method argue that the cost of the asset is effectively reduced by the investment credit, and the tax benefit should be spread over the acquired asset's useful life. This point of view is strengthened by the current tax requirement that a company must hold the asset for a specified period of time or return part of the allowed credit. Those who advocate using the flow-through method argue that the tax credit is in reality a tax reduction in the current period. They argue that tax regulations establish the tax liability each year, and that amount is the proper expense to match against current revenues. This latter treatment affects current income more and is favored by political leaders when the investment tax credit is being used to stimulate a sluggish economy.

It is unfortunate that this issue has become such a political item. It is an example of an area where there seems to be no justification for having two methods. It is difficult to see how different economic circumstances among companies would justify dual treatment. Uniformity in treatment of the investment tax credit is definitely preferable to the alternatives presently available under generally accepted accounting principles.

EXPENDITURES INCURRED DURING SERVICE LIFE OF PROPERTY ITEMS

During the lives of property items, regular as well as special expenditures are incurred. Certain expenditures are required to maintain and repair assets; others are incurred to increase their capacity or efficiency or to extend their useful lives. Each expenditure requires careful analysis to determine whether it should be assigned to revenue of the current period, hence charged to an expense account, or whether it should be assigned to revenue of more than one period, which calls for a debit to an asset account or to an accumulated depreciation account. In many cases the answer may not be clear, and the procedure chosen may be a matter of judgment.

The terms maintenance, repairs, betterments, improvements, additions, and rearrangements are used in describing expenditures made in the course of asset use. These are described in the following sections.

Maintenance   Expenditures to maintain assets in fit condition are referred to as *maintenance*. Among these are expenditures for painting, lubricating, and adjusting equipment. Maintenance items are ordinary and recurring and do not improve the asset or add to its life; therefore, they are recorded as expenses.

Repairs   Expenditures to restore assets to a fit condition upon their breakdown or to restore and replace broken parts are referred to as *repairs*. When these expenditures are ordinary and benefit only current operations, they are debited to expense. When they are extraordinary and extend the life of the asset, they may be debited to the accumulated depreciation account. The depreciation rate is then redetermined in view of changes in the asset book value and estimated life. Debits for repairs extending the useful life of the asset are made against the accumulated depreciation account to avoid a build-up of gross asset values. The book value of the asset will be the same whether the debit is made to the asset account directly or to the accumulated depreciation account.

Repairs involving the overhauling of certain assets are frequently referred to as *renewals*. Substitutions of parts or entire units are referred to as *replacements*. The cost of the replacement may be expensed or capitalized depending upon how the property unit is defined. For example, components of a major piece of equipment, such as the motor, the frame, and the attachments, may be considered separate property units, or the entire machine may be considered the property unit. If the component parts are the property units, replacement of a component requires entries cancelling the book value related to the old component and capitalizing the cost of the new equipment. If the property unit is the entire machine, the replacement of the component would be debited to an expense if it is considered to be a normal replacement, or debited to accumulated depreciation if it is considered to be an extraordinary replacement. General criteria as to what constitutes a property unit have not been developed by the profession. Companies have had to establish their own guidelines and consistently apply them. Research indicates that companies do not feel that this lack of guidelines has led to serious abuses in practice.[1]

Repairs arising from flood, fire, or other casualty require special analysis. An expenditure to restore an asset to its previous condition should be reported as a loss from casualties.

Betterments or Improvements   Changes in assets designed to provide increased or improved services are referred to as *betterments* or *improvements*. Installation of improved lighting systems, heating systems, or sanitary systems represent betterments. Minor expenditures for betterments may be recorded as ordinary repairs. Major expenditures call for entries to cancel the book value related to the old asset and to establish the new, or entries to reduce the accumulated depreciation related to the original asset. The latter method is sometimes required when the cost of the item replaced is not readily separable from the whole unit.

---

[1]Lamden, Gerboth, and McRae, *op. cit.*, pp. 48–49.

Additions
Enlargements and extensions of existing facilities are referred to as *additions*. A new plant wing, additional loading docks, or the expansion of a paved parking lot represent additions. These expenditures are capitalized, and the cost is written off over the service life of the addition.

Rearrangements
Movement of machinery and equipment items and reinstallations to secure economies or greater efficiencies are referred to as *rearrangements*. Costs related to rearrangements should be assigned to those periods benefiting from such changes. When more than one period is benefited, an asset account — appropriately designated to indicate the nature of the cost deferral — should be established and this balance allocated systematically to revenue. When rearrangements involve reinstallation costs, the portion of asset book value related to an original installation should be canceled; the cost of the new installation should be added to the asset and written off over its remaining life.

Establishment of Allowance for Repairs and Parts Replacements
When certain relatively large repair and parts replacement charges are expected at irregular intervals during the life of an asset, provision may be made to charge operations not only with a share of the original cost of the asset but also with a share of the total repair and replacement charges anticipated over the life of the asset. An expense account may be debited periodically and a repairs and replacements allowance account credited for the estimated repairs and replacements. If this is done, repairs and replacements, when incurred, are properly debited to the allowance. To illustrate, a new roof for a building does not increase the original estimated service life of the building, but it may represent a relatively heavy charge if made against the revenue of a single fiscal period. If an allowance for repairs and replacements has been set up by periodic charges to operations, the expenditure for the new roof can be debited to this allowance. Each period is thus charged with its share of the charges of this kind, and an unreasonably large charge against the revenue of a single period is avoided. In preparing the balance sheet, the building account would be reduced by both accumulated depreciation and the allowance for repairs and replacements. The allowance for repairs and replacements may be regarded as reflecting the above-normal depreciation of certain components of the property item.

If a business has many equipment items of different ages in service, total repairs and replacements charges may not vary significantly from period to period, and little may be gained by establishing an allowance. Charges for repairs and replacements are deductible for tax purposes only when the expenditures are made.

It should be observed that irregular charges for major repairs and parts replacements are largely avoided when individual accounts are established for each separate component of an asset item deemed to have an independent life. Instead of a single depreciation rate applied to a composite asset, individual rates are applied to the separate asset components. Major expenditures during the life of the property item are reported as newly acquired asset components, and balances related to original components are canceled. Although it may require considerable analysis and detailed records, this procedure has merit in achieving fairer assignments of expenses to revenue.

PROPERTY RETIREMENTS

Properties may be retired by sale, trade, scrapping and removal, or abandonment. When properties are disposed of, both property and accumulated depreciation accounts are canceled and a gain or loss is recognized for the difference between the amount recovered on the asset and its book value.

In recording a disposal, it is necessary to follow the practice adopted by the entity for recognizing depreciation for fractional periods. Various practices are employed including the following:

1. Depreciation is recognized on the asset from the time it is acquired to the time it is retired.
2. Depreciation is recognized at the annual rate on the beginning-of-year balance in the asset account plus or minus depreciation at one half the annual rate on the net additions or subtractions in the account for the year. The effect of this procedure is to recognize depreciation for one-half year on all acquisitions and all retirements.
3. Depreciation is recognized at the annual rate on the beginning-of-year balance in the asset account. Thus, no depreciation is recognized on acquisitions during the year but depreciation for a full year is recognized on retirements.
4. Depreciation is recognized at the annual rate on the end-of-year balance in the asset account. Thus, depreciation is recognized for a full year on acquisitions during the year but no depreciation is recognized on retirements.

Methods (2), (3), and (4) are attractive because of their simplicity. However, method (1) provides greatest accuracy and its use is assumed unless some alternate policy is specifically stated. In applying method (1), depreciation, rather than being recognized on as short a period as a day or a week, would normally be calculated to the nearest month: no charge would be made for an asset used for less than half of a month; a charge for a full month would be recognized for an asset used for more than half of a month. This practice is assumed in the examples and problems in the text.

To illustrate the entries for asset retirement, assume it is decided to sell certain machinery. The machinery was originally acquired on November 20, 1968, for $10,000 and had been depreciated at 10% per year. The asset is sold on April 10, 1977, for $1,250. The entries to record depreciation for 1977 and sale of the property item follow:

Depreciation Expense — Machinery	250.00	
Accumulated Depreciation — Machinery		250.00
To record depreciation for three months in 1977.		

Computation:
$10,000 × 10% × $^3/_{12}$ = $250.

Cash...	1,250.00	
Accumulated Depreciation — Machinery	8,333.33	
Loss on Sale of Machinery	416.67	
Machinery..		10,000.00
To record sale of machinery.		

Computation:

Cost	$10,000.00	
Depreciation to date of sale:		
November 20, 1968 — April 10, 1977 (10% per year for		
8⁴/₁₂ years)...	8,333.33	
Asset book value..	$ 1,666.67	
Proceeds from sale..	1,250.00	
Loss on sale...	$ 416.67	

The preceding entries can be combined in the form of a single compound entry as follows:

Cash..	1,250.00	
Depreciation Expense — Machinery	250.00	
Accumulated Depreciation — Machinery.................................	8,083.33	
Loss on Sale of Machinery	416.67	
Machinery..		10,000.00

If a property item is scrapped or abandoned without cash recovery, a loss would be recognized equal to the asset book value; if the full cost of the asset has been written off, the asset and its offset balances would simply be canceled. If a property item is retired from active or standby service but is not immediately disposed of, asset and accumulated depreciation balances should be closed and the salvage value of the asset established as a separate asset.

In the examples in this chapter a difference between the amount recovered and the book value of a depreciable asset exchanged, sold, or scrapped, was recognized as a gain or loss related to the current decision to dispose of the asset. The gain or loss would be reported as an ordinary income item in the year of asset disposition.

Property Damage or Destruction

Special accounting problems arise when property is damaged or destroyed as a result of fire, flood, storm, or other casualty. When a company owns many properties and these are widely distributed, the company itself may assume the risk of loss. However, companies ordinarily carry insurance for casualties that may involve large sums.

When uninsured properties are partly or wholly destroyed, asset book values should be reduced or canceled and a loss recorded for such reductions. Generally, these losses will be classified as ordinary; however, they may be classified as extraordinary, if they meet the criteria as established in APB Opinion 30 — materiality, unusual nature, and infrequency of occurrence.[1] When property items are insured and these are damaged or destroyed, entries on the books must be made to report asset losses and also the insurance claims arising from such losses.

---

[1]*Opinions of the Accounting Principles Board, No. 30,* "Reporting the Results of Operations" (New York: American Institute of Certified Public Accountants, 1973), par. 20.

The most common casualty loss incurred by a business is that from fire. Of all of the various types of protection offered by insurance, fire is the risk most widely covered. Because of the importance of fire insurance in business and because of the special accounting problems that arise in the event of fire, the remaining pages of this chapter are devoted to a detailed discussion of this matter.

Fire Insurance

Fire insurance policies are usually written in $100 or $1,000 units for a period of three years. Insurance premiums are normally paid annually in advance. The amount of the premium is determined by the conditions prevailing in each case.

The insurance contract may be canceled by either the insurer or the insured. When the insurance company cancels the policy, a refund is made on a pro rata basis. When the policyholder cancels the policy, a refund may be made on what is known as a short-rate basis that provides for a higher insurance rate for the shorter period of coverage.

A *coinsurance clause* is frequently written into a policy by the insurance companies to offset the tendency by the buyer to purchase only a minimum insurance coverage. A business with assets worth $100,000 at fair market value, for example, may estimate that any single loss could not destroy more than one half of these assets and might consider itself adequately protected by insurance of $50,000. With an 80% coinsurance clause, however, the business would have to carry insurance equal to 80% of the fair market value of the property, or $80,000, to recover the full amount on claims up to the face of the policy. When less than this percentage is carried, the insured shares in the risk with the insurer.

To illustrate the calculation of the amount recoverable on a policy failing to meet coinsurance requirements, assume the following: assets are insured for $70,000 under a policy containing an 80% coinsurance clause; on the date of a fire, assets have a fair market value of $100,000. Because insurance of only $70,000 is carried when coinsurance requirements are $80,000, any loss will be borne 7/8 by the insurance company and 1/8 by the policyholder; furthermore, whatever the loss, the maximum to be borne by the insurance company is $70,000, the face of the policy. The amount recoverable from the insurance company if a fire loss is $50,000, for example, is calculated as follows:

$$\frac{70,000 \text{ (policy)}}{80,000 \text{ (coinsurance requirement)}} \times \$50,000 \text{ (loss)} = \$43,750$$

The same calculations are made when the loss is greater than the face of the policy. Assume the same facts given above, but assume a fire loss of $75,000. The amount recoverable from insurance is calculated as follows:

$$\frac{70,000 \text{ (policy)}}{80,000 \text{ (coinsurance requirement)}} \times \$75,000 \text{ (loss)} = \$65,625$$

In the example above, application of the formula gives an amount still less than the face of the policy and hence fully recoverable. But if application of the formula results in an amount exceeding the face value of the policy, the claim is limited to the latter amount. If, for example, the loss is $90,000, the following calculation is made:

$$\frac{70{,}000 \text{ (policy)}}{80{,}000 \text{ (coinsurance requirement)}} \times \$90{,}000 \text{ (loss)} = \$78{,}750$$

Recovery from the insurance company, however, is limited to $70,000, the ceiling set by the policy.

When the insurance coverage is equal to or greater than the percentage required by the coinsurance clause, the formula need not be applied since any loss is paid in full up to the face value of the policy. It is important to note that coinsurance requirements are based not on the cost or book value of the insured property but upon the actual market value of the property on the date of a fire. If coinsurance requirements are to be met, a rise in the value of insured assets requires that insurance coverage be increased.

The following general rules may be formulated:

1. In the absence of a coinsurance clause the amount recoverable is the lower of the loss or the face of the policy.
2. When a policy includes a coinsurance clause, the amount recoverable is the lower of the loss as adjusted by the coinsurance formula or the face of the policy.

Insurance policies normally include a *contribution clause* that provides that if other policies are carried on the same property, recovery of a loss on a policy shall be limited to the ratio which the face of the policy bears to the total insurance carried. Such a limitation on the amount to be paid eliminates the possibility of recovery by the insured of amounts in excess of the actual loss. When coinsurance clauses are found on the different policies, the recoverable amount on each is limited to the ratio of the face of the policy to the higher of (a) the total insurance carried, or (b) the total insurance required to be carried by the policy. To illustrate the limitations set by contribution clauses, assume a fire loss of $30,000 on property with a value of $100,000 on which policies are carried as follows: Co. A, $50,000; Co. B, $15,000; Co. C, $10,000.

1. Assuming policies have no coinsurance clauses, amounts that may be recovered from each company are as follows:

Co. A: $\frac{50{,}000 \text{ (policy)}}{75{,}000 \text{ (total policies)}} \times \$30{,}000 \text{ (loss)}$ $20,000

Co. B: $\frac{15{,}000 \text{ (policy)}}{75{,}000 \text{ (total policies)}} \times \$30{,}000 \text{ (loss)}$ 6,000

Co. C: $\frac{10{,}000 \text{ (policy)}}{75{,}000 \text{ (total policies)}} \times \$30{,}000 \text{ (loss)}$ 4,000

Total amount recoverable $30,000

2. Assuming each policy includes an 80% coinsurance clause, coinsurance requirements on each policy would exceed the total insurance carried and amounts recoverable from each company are as follows:

Co. A: $\dfrac{50{,}000 \text{ (policy)}}{80{,}000 \text{ (coinsurance requirement)}} \times \$30{,}000 \text{ (loss)}$ $18,750

Co. B: $\dfrac{15{,}000 \text{ (policy)}}{80{,}000 \text{ (coinsurance requirement)}} \times \$30{,}000 \text{ (loss)}$ 5,625

Co. C: $\dfrac{10{,}000 \text{ (policy)}}{80{,}000 \text{ (coinsurance requirement)}} \times \$30{,}000 \text{ (loss)}$ 3,750

Total amount recoverable $28,125

3. Assuming each policy includes a 70% coinsurance clause, total insurance carried exceeds coinsurance requirements on each policy and amounts recoverable from each company are the same as in (1).

4. Assuming that coinsurance requirements are Co. A — none, Co. B — 70%, and Co. C — 80%, recovery on each policy is based on its relationship to the total insurance carried or the coinsurance requirement where this is higher, as follows:

Co. A: $\dfrac{50{,}000 \text{ (policy)}}{75{,}000 \text{ (total policies)}} \times \$30{,}000 \text{ (loss)}$ $20,000

Co. B: $\dfrac{15{,}000 \text{ (policy)}}{75{,}000 \text{ (total policies)}} \times \$30{,}000 \text{ (loss)}$ 6,000

Co. C: $\dfrac{10{,}000 \text{ (policy)}}{80{,}000 \text{ (coinsurance requirement)}} \times \$30{,}000 \text{ (loss)}$ 3,750

Total amount recoverable $29,750

Accounting for Fire Losses

When a fire occurs and books of account are destroyed, account balances to the date of the fire will have to be reconstructed from the best available evidence. As the first step in summarizing the fire loss, books as maintained or as reconstructed are adjusted as of the date of the fire. With accounts brought up to date, the loss may be summarized in a fire loss account. The fire loss account is debited for the book value of properties destroyed, and it is credited for amounts recoverable from insurance companies and amounts recoverable from salvage. The balance of the account is normally recognized as an ordinary loss and is closed into the income summary account.

A number of special problems are encountered in arriving at the charges to be made to the fire loss account. When depreciable assets are destroyed, the book values of the properties must be brought up to date and these balances in total or in part transferred to the fire loss account. When merchandise is destroyed, the estimated cost of the merchandise on hand at the time of the fire must be determined. If perpetual inventory records are available, the goods on hand may be obtained from this source. In the absence of such records, the inventory is generally calculated by the gross profit method. The inventory may be set up by a debit to the inventory account and a credit to the income summary account. The inventory total or portion destroyed may now be transferred to the fire loss account.

Insurance expired to the date of the fire is recorded as an expense. The balance in the unexpired insurance account is carried forward when policies continue in force and offer original protection on rehabilitated properties or newly acquired replacements. If a business does not plan to repair or replace the assets, it may cancel a part or all of a policy and recover cash on a short-rate basis. The difference between the unexpired insurance balance and the amount received on the short-rate basis is a loss from insurance cancellation brought about by the fire and is recorded as an addition to the fire loss balance.[1]

To illustrate the accounting for a fire loss, assume the following facts: J. J. Bailey, a retailer, suffers a fire loss after the close of business on March 31, 1977. Assets destroyed and amounts recoverable from insurance and salvage are summarized below:

ITEM	LOSS — BOOK VALUES	AMOUNT RECOVERABLE
Inventory	Entire inventory, estimated to have a cost of $18,000.	Policy carried..................................... $12,500 Value of property at date of fire as agreed by insured and insurer .... 18,000 Salvage goods valued at.................. 1,400 Amount recoverable from insurance company: Full amount of policy 12,500
Equipment	One third of equipment: Cost of equipment........................... $15,000 Accumulated depr., 1/1/77 $9,000 Add depr. at 10% for 3 months .... 375 9,375 Asset book value .... $ 5,625 Book value of portion lost: ⅓ × $5,625..................................... $ 1,875	Policy carried..................................... $ 6,000 Value of equipment at date of fire, as agreed by insured and insurer 7,800 Amount recoverable from insurance company: ⅓ × $7,800................................... 2,600
Buildings	One fourth of buildings: Cost of buildings............................. $32,000 Accumulated depr., 1/1/77. $4,000 Add depr. at 2½% for 3 months........................ 200 4,200 Asset book value .... $27,800 Book value of portion lost: ¼ × $27,800.................................... $ 6,950	Policy carried..................................... $35,000 Value of buildings at date of fire, as agreed by insured and insurer 32,000 Amount recoverable from insurance company: ¼ × $32,000.................................... 8,000

Entries for the fire loss are given on the following page. These are given in three groups: (1) entries that bring asset book values up to date so that the loss may be determined, (2) entries that record the assets lost, and (3) entries that record the amounts recoverable from salvage and due from the insurance companies. Explanations for the entries are not given; however, each entry requires an explanation accompanied by the data used in arriving at the reported amounts.

Entries to adjust the accounts and to record the fire loss may be transferred to the ledger, but nominal accounts may be left open and transactions for the remainder of the fiscal period recorded therein. At the end

---

[1]Under policies written in some states, payment by the insurer on a policy may serve to cancel that portion of the policy paid by the insurer. When this is the case, any unexpired insurance balance applicable to the portion of the policy paid should be written off as an addition to the fire loss account.

of the period, nominal accounts will reflect activities for the entire period and statements can be prepared summarizing activities in the usual manner. Any differences that are found during the period between amounts originally stated to be recoverable from insurance and amounts actually recovered should be debited or credited to the fire loss account, thus correcting this balance to the loss actually sustained.

Entries to Bring Asset Book Values up to Date

(a)	Income Summary..	12,250	
	Inventory[1]...		12,250
(b)	Inventory..	18,000	
	Income Summary		18,000
(c)	Depreciation Expense — Equipment...	375	
	Accumulated Depreciation — Equipment		375
(d)	Depreciation Expense — Buildings	200	
	Accumulated Depreciation — Buildings.................................		200

Entries to Record Assets Lost by Fire

(e)	Fire Loss..	18,000	
	Inventory		18,000
(f)	Fire Loss..	1,875	
	Accumulated Depreciation — Equipment	3,125	
	Equipment		5,000
(g)	Fire Loss..	6,950	
	Accumulated Depreciation — Buildings	1,050	
	Buildings..		8,000

Entries to Record Amounts Recoverable
from Salvage and Due from Insurance Companies

(h)	Salvage Goods...	1,400	
	Fire Loss		1,400
(i)	Recoverable from Insurance Companies	12,500	
	Fire Loss		12,500
(j)	Recoverable from Insurance Companies	2,600	
	Fire Loss		2,600
(k)	Recoverable from Insurance Companies	8,000	
	Fire Loss		8,000

The total amount recoverable from the insurance companies is $23,100 and this balance would be reported as a current asset if current settlement is anticipated. The fire loss account reports a debit balance of $2,325; this is the loss from the fire.

Because the insurance proceeds are based upon appraised values, insurance proceeds may exceed the book value of assets destroyed, resulting in a credit balance in the fire loss account. If the assets destroyed must be replaced at current market prices, the credit balance can hardly be viewed as indicating an economic gain. The credit balance may be designated for reporting purposes as "Excess of Insurance and Salvage over Book Value of Assets Lost by Fire."

---

[1]It is assumed the opening inventory balance is $12,250; this balance is closed to Income Summary. The inventory on the date of the fire is recorded in entry (b) by a debit to the asset and a credit to Income Summary; the credit represents a subtraction item from goods available for the period in arriving at the cost of goods sold. The inventory balance as of the date of the fire is transferred to the fire loss account in entry (e).

QUESTIONS

1. Distinguish among the terms *plant, property, tangible fixed assets,* and *intangible fixed assets.*

2. Which of the following items are properly shown under the heading "Land, buildings, and equipment"?

(a) Deposits on machinery not yet received.
(b) Idle equipment awaiting sale.
(c) Property held for investment purposes.
(d) Land held for possible future plant site.

3. (a) Distinguish between capital expenditures and revenue expenditures. (b) Give five examples of each.

4. Which of the following items would be recorded as a revenue expenditure and which would be recorded as a capital expenditure?

(a) Cost of installing machinery.
(b) Cost of moving and reinstalling machinery.
(c) Extensive repairs as a result of fire.
(d) Cost of grading land.
(e) Insurance on machinery in transit.
(f) Bond discount amortization during construction period.
(g) Cost of major overhaul on machinery.
(h) New safety guards on machinery.
(i) Commission on purchase of real estate.
(j) Special tax assessment for street improvements.
(k) Cost of repainting offices.

5. Indicate the effects of the following errors on the balance sheet and the income statement in the current year and in succeeding years:

(a) The cost of a depreciable asset is incorrectly recorded as a revenue expenditure.
(b) A revenue expenditure is incorrectly recorded as an addition to the cost of a depreciable asset.

6. What additional accounting problems are introduced when a company purchases equipment on a long-term contract rather than with cash?

7. Under what circumstances is a gain or loss recognized when a productive asset is exchanged for a similar productive asset?

8. What is the rationale behind requiring the recognition of part of the gain when boot is received in an exchange of similar productive assets, but not when boot is given?

9. What is meant by a business *pooling of interests*? How does this differ from a business *purchase*?

10. Christie, Inc., decides to construct a building for itself and plans to use whatever plant facilities it has to further such construction. (a) What costs will enter into the cost of construction? (b) What two positions can the company take with respect to general overhead allocation during the period of construction? Evaluate each position and indicate your preference.

11. The Waters Co. decides to construct a piece of specialized machinery using personnel from the maintenance department. Personnel were instructed to schedule their work so that all overtime hours were charged to the machinery. Evaluate the practice as it relates to the resulting cost of the machine.

12. When the Boatman Corporation finds that the lowest bid it can get on the construction of an addition to its building is $40,000, it proceeds to erect the building with its own workers and equipment. (a) Assuming that the cost of construction is $35,000, how would you treat the savings? (b) Assuming the cost of construction is $50,000, how would you treat the excess cost?

13. Evaluate the practice of including interest as a cost of construction for (a) public utilities, (b) commercial entities.

14. The Parkhurst Corporation acquires land and buildings valued at $250,000 as a gift from Industrial City. The president of the company maintains that since there was no cost for the acquisition, neither cost of the facilities nor depreciation needs to be recognized for financial statement purposes. Evaluate the president's position assuming (a) the donation is unconditional; (b) the donation is contingent upon the employment by the company of a certain number of employees for a ten-year period.

15. In the balance sheets of many companies, the largest classification of assets in amount is fixed assets. Name the items, in addition to the amount paid to the former owner or contractor, that may be properly included as part of the acquisition cost of the following property items: (a) land, (b) buildings, and (c) equipment.

16. Distinguish between (a) maintenance and repairs, (b) ordinary repairs and extraordinary repairs, (c) betterments and additions.

17. Machinery in the finishing department of the Gerhardt Co., although less than 50% depreciated, has been replaced by new machinery. The company expects to find a buyer for the old machinery, and on December 31 the machinery is in the yards and available for inspection. How should it be reported on the balance sheet?

18. (a) What is a coinsurance clause and why is it found in policies? (b) What is a contribution clause? How does it affect recovery of a loss?

EXERCISES

1. Hillcrest, Inc., acquires a machine priced at $72,000. Payment of this amount may be made within 60 days; a 5% discount is allowed if cash is paid at time of purchase. Give the entry to record the acquisition, assuming:

(a) Cash is paid at time of purchase.
(b) Payment is to be made at the end of 60 days.
(c) A long-term contract is signed whereby a down payment of $12,000 is made with 12 payments of $6,000 to be made at monthly intervals thereafter.

2. The Webber Natralist Co. acquired land, buildings, and equipment items at a lump-sum price of $125,000. An appraisal of the assets at the time of acquisition disclosed the following values:

Land	$80,000
Buildings	70,000
Equipment	50,000

What cost should be assigned to each asset?

3. Timpanogas, Inc., purchases equipment costing $80,000 with a down payment of $20,000 and sufficient semiannual installments of $7,000 (including interest on the unpaid principal at 10% per year) to pay the balance.

(a) Give the entries to record the purchase and the first two semiannual payments.
(b) Assume that there was no known cash price and ten semiannual installments were to be made. Give the entries to record the purchase and the first two semiannual payments.

4. Concepcion Co. purchased a new milling machine. The following data relate to the purchase:

Invoice price of new machine to Concepcion Co. — $55,000.
Cash price of new machine with no trade-in — $48,700.
The Concepcion Co. received a trade-in allowance of $15,000 on a dissimilar machine
  costing $25,000 new and having a present book value of $12,000.
The Express Delivery Service charged Concepcion Co. $1,200 to deliver the machine.

Give the entry to record the acquisition of the new machine.

5. Assume Nebo Corporation has a machine that cost $12,000, has a book value of $6,000, and has a market value of $10,000. For each of the following situations, indicate the value at which Nebo should record the new asset and why it should be recorded at that value.

(a) Nebo exchanged the machine for a truck with a list price of $11,000.
(b) Nebo exchanged the machine for another machine qualifying as a similar productive asset with a list price of $10,500.
(c) Nebo exchanged the machine for a newer model machine with a list price of $14,000. Nebo paid $1,000 in the transaction.
(d) Nebo exchanged the machine and $750 cash for a similar machine from Quin Co. The newly acquired machine is carried on Quin's books at $15,000 with accumulated depreciation of $5,000; its fair market value is $10,750. In addition to determining the value, give the journal entries for both companies to record the exchange.

6. The Eagle Co. enters into a contract with the Taulbee Construction Co. for construction of an office building at a cost of $720,000. Upon completion of construction, the Taulbee Construction Co. agrees to accept in full payment of the contract price Eagle Co. 6% bonds with a face value of $400,000 and common stock with a par value of $300,000. Eagle Co. bonds are selling on the market at this time at 95. How would you recommend the building acquisition be recorded?

7. The Ross Company acquired land and an old building in exchange for 5,000 shares of its common stock, par $10, and cash of $25,000. The auditor ascertains that the company's stock was selling on the market at $12 when the purchase was made. The following additional costs were incurred to complete the transaction.

Escrow cost to complete transaction	$1,000
Property tax for previous year	500
Cost of building demolition	8,000
Salvage value of demolished building	4,000

What entry should be made to record the acquisition of the property?

8. The Hansen Corporation summarizes manufacturing and construction activities for 1977 as follows:

	Product Manufacture	Building Wing Construction
Materials	$150,000	$32,000
Direct labor	220,000	45,000

Overhead for 1976 was 80% of the direct labor cost. Overhead in 1977 related to both product manufacture and construction activities totaled $199,810.

(a) Calculate the cost of the building addition, assuming manufacturing activities are to be charged with overhead at the rate experienced in 1976 and construction activities are to be charged with the excess.

(b) Calculate the cost of the addition if manufacturing and construction activities are to be charged with overhead at the same rate.

9. The following expenditures were incurred by the Watson Co. in 1977: purchase of land, $120,000; land survey, $1,500; fees for search of title on land, $350; building permit, $250; temporary quarters for construction crews, $2,750; payment to tenants of old building for vacating premises, $2,000; razing of old building, $2,000; excavation for basement, $10,000; special assessment tax for street project, $2,000; dividends, $5,000; damages awarded for injuries sustained in construction, $4,200 (no insurance was carried; the cost of insurance would have been $200); costs of construction, $225,000; cost of paving parking lot adjoining building, $12,500; cost of shrubs, trees, and other landscaping, $1,500. What is the cost of the land and the cost of the building?

10. Stornetta's Dairy bills its customers for milk bottles. During July the total amount billed for milk and bottles was $78,350. Of this amount, $4,780 was for the bottles. Bottles were returned by customers and customers were given credit for $3,620 on these returns. The cost of bottles not returned was determined to be $750 and the accumulated depreciation on these bottles was $300. The cost of bottles is carried in a property account entitled Containers.

Give the entries to record the transactions for July.

11. The Marx Company purchased a new machine on January 1, 1977, for $150,000. The machine had a 10-year life and was depreciated by the straight-line method. Assuming a 10% investment tax credit, give the entries to record the purchase of the machine and the recognition and payment of tax for the first two years under (a) the flow-through method and (b) the deferred method. (Income tax before the credit in 1977 and 1978 was $40,000 and $25,000 respectively.)

12. One of the most difficult problems facing an accountant is the determination of which expenditures should be deferred as assets and which should be immediately charged off as expenses. What position would you take in each of the following instances?

(a) Painting of partitions in a large room recently divided into four sections.
(b) Labor cost of tearing down a wall to permit extension of assembly line.
(c) Replacement of motor on a machine. Life used to depreciate the machine is 8 years. The machine is 4 years old. Replacement of the motor was anticipated when the machine was purchased.
(d) Cost of grading land prior to construction.
(e) Assessment for street paving.
(f) Cost of moving and reinstalling equipment.
(g) Cost of tearing down an old building in preparation for new construction; old building is fully depreciated.

13. The Stoddard Company purchased a building for $120,000 on August 1, 1969. Depreciation was recorded at 3% a year. On October 31, 1977, 50% of the building was destroyed. On this date the building had a fair market value of $100,000. A policy for $60,000 was carried on the building, the policy containing a 80% coinsurance clause. What entries would be made to record (a) the loss from destruction of the building, and (b) the amount due from the insurance company? (Assume the company's fiscal period is the calendar year.)

PROBLEMS

11-1. The following transactions were completed by the St. Helena Co. during 1977:

Mar. 1	Purchased real property for $178,925 which included a charge of $3,925 representing property tax for March 1–June 30 that had been prepaid by the vendor. Twenty percent of the purchase price is deemed applicable to land and the balance to buildings. A mortgage of $125,000 was assumed by the St. Helena Co. on the purchase.
Mar. 2–30	Previous owners had failed to take care of normal maintenance and repair requirements on the building, necessitating current reconditioning at a cost of $8,300.
Apr. 1–May 15	Garages in the rear of the buildings were demolished, $1,500 being recovered on the lumber salvage. The company itself proceeded to construct a warehouse. The cost of such construction was $12,500 which was almost exactly the same as bids made on the construction by independent contractors. Upon completion of construction, city inspectors ordered extensive modifications in the buildings as a result of failure on the part of the company to comply with the Building Safety Code. Such modifications, which could have been avoided, cost $2,800.
Nov. 5–20	The company contracted for parking lots and landscaping at a cost of $15,000 and $3,200 respectively. The work was completed and billed on November 20.
Dec. 29–31	The business was closed to permit taking the year-end inventory. During this period, required redecorating and repairs were completed at a cost of $1,500.

Instructions: Give journal entries to record each of the preceding transactions. (Disregard depreciation.)

11-2. On December 31, 1977, the Danville Co. shows the following account for machinery it had assembled for its own use during 1977:

ACCOUNT   Machinery (Job Order #62)

ITEM	DEBIT	CREDIT	BALANCE DEBIT	BALANCE CREDIT
Cost of dismantling old machine..............	3,120		3,120	
Cash proceeds from sale of old machine .		2,500	620	
Raw materials used in construction of new machine..........:	15,750		16,370	
Labor in construction of new machine.....	12,250		28,620	
Cost of installation..................................	2,800		31,420	
Materials spoiled in machine trial runs.....	600		32,020	
Profit on construction	6,900		38,920	
Purchase of machine tools	3,600		42,520	
Depreciation for 1977, 10% of $42,520......		4,252	38,268	

An analysis of the detail in the account discloses the following:

   (a) The old machine, which was removed in the installation of the new one, had been fully depreciated.

(continued)

(b) Cash discounts received on the payments for materials used in construction totaled $400 and these were reported in the purchase discounts account.
(c) The factory overhead account shows a balance of $73,000 for the year ended December 31, 1977; this balance exceeds normal overhead on regular plant activities by approximately $3,700 and is attributable to machine construction.
(d) A profit was recognized on construction for the difference between costs incurred and the price at which the machine could have been purchased.
(e) Machine tools have an estimated life of 3 years; machinery has an estimated life of 10 years. The machinery was used for production beginning on September 1, 1977. (Depreciation should be computed to nearest month.)

Instructions:
(1) Determine the machinery and machine tools balances as of December 31, 1977.
(2) Give individual journal entries necessary to correct the accounts as of December 31, 1977, assuming the nominal accounts are still open.

11-3. The Calistoga Wholesale Company incurred the following expenses in 1977 for their office building acquired on July 1, 1977, the beginning of the fiscal year:

Cost of land	$ 30,000
Cost of building	170,000
Remodeling and repairs prior to occupancy	27,000
Escrow fee	1,500
Landscaping	10,000
Unpaid property tax for period prior to acquisition	3,500
Real estate commission	6,000

The company signed a non-interest-bearing note for $200,000 on the acquisition. The implicit interest rate is 8%. Payments of $11,000 are to be made semiannually beginning January 1, 1978, for 10 years.

Instructions: Give the required journal entries to record (1) the acquisition of the land and building (assume cash is paid to equalize the cost of the assets and the present value of the note), and (2) the first two semiannual payments, including amortization of bond discount.

11-4. You are given the following information about equipment held by Woolley Manufacturing.

	Asset A	Asset B	Asset C
Cost	$25,000	$100,000	$78,000
Accumulated depreciation (12/31/76)	12,500	20,000	70,200
Fair market value	20,000	60,000	10,000
Depreciation (per year — straight-line)	10%	5%	10%

Asset A is exchanged on March 31, 1977, for a similar piece of equipment plus cash of $2,000. Assets B and C are sold for $80,000 on June 30, 1977.

Instructions: Give the required journal entries to record the above transactions.

11-5. The Thompson Company planned to open a new store. The company narrowed the possible sites to two lots and decided to take purchase options on both lots while they studied traffic densities in both areas. They paid $2,400 for the option on Lot A and $4,800 for the option on Lot B. After studying traffic densities, they decided to purchase Lot B. The company opened a single real estate account that shows the following:

Debits:	Option on Lot A	$ 2,400
	Option on Lot B	4,800
	Payment of balance on Lot B	40,000
	Title insurance	700
	Assessment for street improvements	1,700
	Recording fee for deed	100
	Cost of razing old building on Lot B	3,000
	Payment for erection of new building	100,000
Credit:	Sale of salvaged materials from old building	3,000

The salvage value of material obtained from the old building and used in the erection of the new building was $2,500. The depreciated value of the old building, as shown by the books of the company from which the purchase was made, was $18,000. The old building was razed immediately after the purchase.

Instructions:
(1) Determine the cost of the land, listing the items included in the total.
(2) Determine the cost of the new building, listing the items included in the total.

11-6. The Pageant Corporation was organized in June 1977. In auditing the books of the company, you find a land, buildings, and equipment account with the following detail:

ACCOUNT   Land, Buildings, and Equipment

DATE		ITEM	DEBIT	CREDIT	BALANCE DEBIT	BALANCE CREDIT
1977						
June	8	Organization fees paid to the state	2,500		2,500	
	16	Land site and old building	325,000		327,500	
	30	Corporate organization costs	2,500		330,000	
July	2	Title clearance fees...	2,100		332,100	
Aug.	28	Cost of razing old building	4,000		336,100	
Sept.	1	Salaries of Pageant Corporation executives.....	15,000		351,100	
Dec.	12	Stock bonus to corporate promoters, 2,000 shares of common stock, $10 par..................	20,000		371,100	
	15	County real estate tax......................................	3,600		374,700	
	15	Cost of new building completed and occupied on this date..	620,000		994,700	

An analysis of the foregoing account and of other accounts disclosed the following additional information:

(a) The building acquired on June 16, 1977, was valued at $35,000.
(b) The company paid $4,000 for the demolition of the old building, then sold the scrap for $200 and credited the proceeds to Miscellaneous Revenue.
(c) The company executives did not participate in the construction of the new building.
(d) The county real estate tax was for the six-month period ended December 31, 1977, and was assessed by the county on the land.

Instructions: Prepare journal entries to correct the books of the Pageant Corporation. Each entry should include an explanation.

11-7. The Lucci Company completed a program of expansion and improvement of its plant during 1977. You are provided with the following information concerning its buildings account:

(a) On October 31, 1977, a 30-foot extension to the present factory building was completed at a contract cost of $72,000.
(b) During the course of construction, the following costs were incurred for the removal of the end wall of the building where the extension was being constructed:
(1) Payroll costs during the month of April arising from employees' time spent in removal of the wall, $4,627.
(2) Payments to a salvage company for removing unusual debris, $520.
(c) The cost of the original structure allocable to the end wall was estimated to be $17,600, with accumulated depreciation thereon of $7,400; $4,721 was received by Lucci Company from the construction company for windows and other assorted materials salvaged from the old wall.
(d) The old flooring was covered with a new type long-lasting floor covering at a cost of $3,257.
(e) The interior of the plant was painted in new bright colors for a contract price of $3,250.
(f) New and improved shelving was installed at a cost of $572.
(g) Old electrical wiring was replaced at a cost of $6,812. Cost of the old wiring was determined to be $3,100 with accumulated depreciation to date of $1,370.
(h) New electrical fixtures using fluorescent bulbs were installed. The new fixtures were purchased on the installment plan; the schedule of monthly payments showed total payments of $6,200, which included interest and carrying charges of $480. The old fixtures were carried at a cost of $1,860, with accumulated depreciation to date of $796. The old fixtures had no scrap value.

Instructions: Prepare journal entries including explanations for the above information. Briefly justify the capitalization v. revenue decision for each item.

11-8. On March 1, 1975, the Torrez Co. took out a $500,000, 4-year fire insurance policy on a building that was completed at a cost of $880,000 at the end of June, 1959. The insurance policy contains an 80% coinsurance clause. Depreciation is calculated at 2½% annually. On July 5, 1977, the building was 50% destroyed by fire. The insurance company accepted a value for the property of $687,500 and agreed to make settlement on this basis. The fiscal period for the Torrez Co. is the calendar year.

> **Instructions:** Prepare the journal entries necessary as of July 5, 1977, to summarize the foregoing information in the fire loss account and to close the account to Income Summary.

11-9. In your examination of the financial statements of Gaar Corporation at December 31, 1977, you observe the contents of certain accounts and other pertinent information as follows:

ACCOUNT   Building

DATE		ITEM	POST. REF.	DEBIT	CREDIT	BALANCE DEBIT	CREDIT
1976 Dec.	31	Balance	X	100,000		100,000	
1977 July	1	New boiler...............................	CD	16,480	1,480	115,000	
Sept.	1	Insurance recovery.............................	CR		2,000	113,000	

ACCOUNT   Accumulated Depreciation — Building

DATE		ITEM	POST. REF.	DEBIT	CREDIT	BALANCE DEBIT	CREDIT
1976 Dec.	31	Balance — 15 years at 4% of $100,000.	X		60,000		60,000
1977 Dec.	31	Annual depreciation..............................	GJ		4,440		64,440

You learn that on June 15 the company's old high-pressure boiler exploded. Damage to the building was insignificant but the boiler was replaced by a more efficient oil-burning boiler. The company received $2,000 as an insurance adjustment under terms of its policy for damage to the boiler.

The disbursement voucher charged to the building account on July 1, 1977, follows:

> To: REX HEATING COMPANY
> List price — new oil-burning boiler
>   (including fuel oil tank and 5,000 gallons fuel oil) $16,000
> Sales tax — 3% of $16,000... 480
>   Total.. $16,480
> Less allowance for old coal-burning boiler in building — to be removed at the
>   expense of the Rex Heating Company... 1,480
>   Total price $15,000

In vouching the expenditure you determine that the terms included a 2% cash discount which was properly computed and taken. The sales tax, fuel oil, and trade-in allowance are not subject to discount.

Your audit discloses that a voucher for $1,000 was paid to Emment Co. on July 2, 1977, and debited to the repair expense account. The voucher is adequately supported and is marked "installation costs for new oil-burning boiler."

The company's fuel oil supplier advises that fuel oil had a market price of 16¢ per gallon July 1 and 18¢ per gallon December 31. The fuel oil inventory at December 31 was 2,000 gallons.

A review of subsidiary property records discloses that the replaced coal-burning boiler was installed when the building was constructed and was recorded at a cost of $10,000. According to its manufacturers the new boiler should be serviceable for 15 years.

In computing depreciation for retirements Gaar Corporation consistently treats a fraction of a month as a full month.

Instructions: Prepare the adjusting journal entries that you would suggest for the books of Gaar Corporation. The books have not been closed. Support your entries with computations in good form. (AICPA adapted)

11-10. Ellford Corporation received a $400,000 low bid from a reputable manufacturer for the construction of special production equipment needed by Ellford in an expansion program. Because the company's own plant was not operating at capacity, Ellford decided to construct the equipment there and recorded the following production costs related to the construction:

Services of consulting engineer	$ 10,000
Work subcontracted	20,000
Materials	200,000
Plant labor normally assigned to production	65,000
Plant labor normally assigned to maintenance	100,000
Total	$395,000

Management prefers to record the cost of the equipment under the incremental cost method. Approximately 40% of the corporation's production is devoted to government supply contracts which are all based in some way on cost. The contracts require that any self-constructed equipment be allocated its full share of all costs related to the construction.

The following information is also available:

    (a) The above production labor was for partial fabrication of the equipment in the plant. Skilled personnel were required and were assigned from other projects. The maintenance labor would have been idle time of nonproduction plant employees who would have been retained on the payroll whether or not their services were utilized.

    (b) Payroll taxes and employee fringe benefits are approximately 30% of labor cost and are included in manufacturing overhead cost. Total manufacturing overhead for the year was $5,630,000 including the $100,000 maintenance labor used to construct the equipment.

    (c) Manufacturing overhead is approximately 50% variable and is applied on the basis of production labor cost. Production labor cost for the year for the corporation's normal products totaled $6,810,000.

    (d) General and administrative expenses include $22,500 of executive salary cost and $10,500 of postage, telephone, supplies, and miscellaneous expenses identifiable with this equipment construction.

Instructions:

    (1) Prepare a schedule computing the amount that should be reported as the full cost of the constructed equipment to meet the requirements of the government contracts. Any supporting computations should be in good form.

    (2) Prepare a schedule computing the incremental cost of the constructed equipment.

    (3) What is the greatest amount that should be capitalized as the cost of the equipment? Why? (AICPA adapted)

11-11. The ABC Corporation is a small manufacturing company producing a highly flammable cleaning fluid. On May 31, 1977, the company had a fire which completely destroyed the processing building and the in-process inventory; some of the equipment was saved.

The cost of the fixed assets destroyed and their related accumulated depreciation accounts at May 31, 1977 were as follows:

	Cost	Accumulated Depreciation
Buildings	$40,000	$24,667
Equipment	15,000	4,375

At present prices, the cost to replace the destroyed property would be: building, $80,000; equipment, $37,500. At the time of the fire, it was determined that the destroyed building was 62½% depreciated, and the destroyed equipment was 33⅓% depreciated. The insurable value of the building and equipment was determined to be $75,000.

After the fire a physical inventory was taken. The raw materials were valued at $30,000, the finished goods at $60,000, and supplies at $5,000.

(continued)

The inventories on January 1, 1977 consisted of:

Raw materials	$ 15,000
Goods in process	50,000
Finished goods	70,000
Supplies	2,000
Total	$137,000

A review of the accounts showed that the sales and gross profit for the last five years were:

	Sales	Gross Profit
1972	$300,000	$ 86,200
1973	320,000	102,400
1974	330,000	108,900
1975	250,000	62,500
1976	280,000	84,000

The sales for the first five months of 1977 were $150,000. Raw materials purchases were $50,000. Freight on purchases was $5,000. Direct labor for the five months was $40,000; for the past five years manufacturing overhead was 50% of direct labor.

Insurance on the property and inventory was carried with three companies. Each policy included an 80% coinsurance clause. The amount of insurance carried with the various companies was:

	Buildings and Equipment	Inventories
Company A	$30,000	$38,000
Company B	20,000	35,000
Company C	15,000	35,000

The cost of cleaning up the debris was $7,000. The value of the scrap salvaged from the fire was $600.

Instructions:
(1) Compute the value of inventory lost.
(2) Compute the expected recovery from each insurance company. (AICPA adapted)

Land, Buildings, and Equipment — Depreciation and Depletion

In spite of expenditures for maintenance and repairs, the time ultimately comes when all building and equipment items can no longer make a favorable contribution to business activities and must be retired. The costs of these assets must be allocated to revenues over the limited duration of the assets' usefulness. *Depreciation* represents an estimate of the decline in service potential of the asset occurring during the period.

The Committee on Terminology of the American Institute of Certified Public Accountants has defined depreciation accounting as follows:

> *Depreciation accounting* is a system of accounting which aims to distribute the cost or other basic value of tangible capital assets, less salvage (if any), over the estimated useful life of the unit (which may be a group of assets) in a systematic and rational manner. It is a process of allocation, not of valuation. *Depreciation for the year* is the portion of the total charge under such a system that is allocated to the year. Although the allocation may properly take into account occurrences during the year, it is not intended to be a measurement of the effect of all such occurrences.[1]

It should be noted that the term depreciation is used in a specialized sense in accounting. It is the systematic allocation of cost in recognition of the exhaustion of asset life and is applicable only to those tangible assets used by the business. Depreciation is not used to designate a decline in market value as the term is popularly employed. Nor is the term used to designate the physical change in an asset, for an asset may show little physical decline in the early years and may have significant physical utility even at the time of its retirement. It is not used to designate the charge for using wasting assets, which is termed *depletion*, nor to designate the allocation of costs over a period of time for limited-life intangible assets, which is termed *amortization*. Depreciation does not refer to a decrease in value assigned to marketable securities as a result of market decline, or to a decrease in value assigned to inventories as a result of obsolescence, spoilage, or other deterioration.

---

[1]*Accounting Research and Terminology Bulletins — Final Edition*, "Accounting Terminology Bulletins, No. 1, Review and Résumé" (New York: American Institute of Certified Public Accountants, 1961), par. 56.

FACTORS DETERMINING THE PERIODIC DEPRECIATION CHARGE

Four factors must be recognized in arriving at the periodic charge for the use of a depreciable property item: (1) *asset cost*, (2) *residual or salvage value*, (3) *useful life*, and (4) *pattern of use*.

Asset Cost

The *cost* of a property item includes all of the expenditures relating to its acquisition and preparation for use as described in Chapter 11. Expenditures considered to be related to revenues of future periods are capitalized and form the base for depreciation charges.

Residual or Salvage Value

The *residual* or *salvage value* of a depreciable asset is the amount which can reasonably be expected to be realized upon retirement of an asset. This may depend upon the retirement policy of the company as well as market conditions and other factors. If, for example, the company normally uses equipment until it is physically exhausted and no longer serviceable, the residual value, represented by the scrap or junk that may be salvaged, may be only nominal. But if the company normally trades its equipment after a relatively short period of use, the residual value, represented by the value in trade, may be relatively high. In some cases the cost of dismantling and removing an asset may equal or exceed the residual value. From a theoretical point of view, any estimated residual value should be subtracted from cost in arriving at the depreciable cost of the asset; on the other hand, dismantling and removal costs expected to exceed the ultimate salvage value should be added to the cost in arriving at an asset's depreciable cost.

In practice, both salvage values and dismantling and removal costs are frequently ignored in developing periodic depreciation charges. Disregard of these items is not objectionable when they are relatively small and not subject to reasonable estimation and when it is doubtful whether greater accuracy will be gained through such refinement of the depreciation estimate.

Useful Life

Buildings and equipment items have a limited *useful life* as a result of certain *physical* and *functional* factors. The physical factors that move a property item towards its ultimate retirement are (1) *wear and tear*, (2) *deterioration and decay*, and (3) *damage or destruction*. Everyone is familiar with the processes of wear and tear that render an automobile, a typewriter, or furniture no longer usable. The deterioration and the decay of an asset through aging, whether the asset is used or not, is also well known. Finally, fire, flood, earthquake, or accident may reduce or terminate the useful life of an asset.

The functional factors limiting the life of a property item are (1) *inadequacy* and (2) *obsolescence*. An asset may lose its usefulness when, as a result of altered business requirements, it can no longer carry the productive load and requires replacement. Although the asset is still usable, its inadequacy for present purposes has cut short its service life. An asset may also lose its usefulness as a result of consumer demand for new and different products or services or as a result of technical progress and the availability of other assets that can be more economically employed. In such instances, obsolescence is the factor operating to limit service life.

Depreciation accounting calls for the recognition of both the physical and functional factors limiting the useful life of an asset. This recognition requires estimating what events will take place in the future and requires careful judgment on the part of the accountant.[1] Physical factors are more readily apparent than functional factors in predicting the asset life. But when certain functional factors are expected to hasten the retirement of an asset, these must also be recognized. Both physical and functional factors may operate gradually or may emerge in sudden fashion. Recognition of depreciation is usually limited to the conditions that operate gradually and are reasonably foreseeable. For example, a sudden change in demand for a certain product may make a property item worthless, or an accident may destroy a property item, but these are unforeseeable events requiring recognition when they occur.

Since the service life of an asset is affected by maintenance and repairs, the policy operating with respect to these matters must be considered in estimating useful life. Low standards of maintenance and repair keep these charges at a minimum but may hasten the physical deterioration of the asset, thus requiring higher-than-normal allocations for depreciation. On the other hand, high standards of maintenance and repairs will mean higher charges for these items; but with a policy prolonging the usefulness of assets, allocations for depreciation may be reduced.

The useful life of a property item may be expressed in terms of either an estimated *time* factor or an estimated *use* factor. The time factor may be a period of months or years; the use factor may be a number of hours of service or a number of units of output. The cost of the property item flows into production in accordance with the lapse of time or degrees of use. The rate of cost flow may be modified by other factors, but basically depreciation must be measured on a time or use basis.[2]

Pattern of Use

In arriving at the useful life of an asset, it is necessary to consider the *pattern of use* and focus upon how the asset's services are actually to be used over that life. Service cost is being matched against revenue. If the

---

[1]Although the concept of useful life is generally recognized to be difficult to apply, there has been relatively little written on it in accounting literature. For a thorough discussion of the topic, see Charles Lamden, Dale L. Gerboth, and Thomas McRae, "Accounting for Depreciable Assets," *Accounting Research Monograph No. 1* (New York: American Institute of Certified Public Accountants, 1975), Chap. 5.

[2]Prior to 1962 the Internal Revenue Service in *Bulletin "F"* offered a compilation of different assets and their probable useful lives on a time basis as found by normal experiences in various industries to assist taxpayers in establishing appropriate depreciation rates. This publication was superseded in July, 1962, by *Revenue Procedure 62-21*. While the original publication listed depreciation guidelines for thousands of individual items, the present guidelines are limited to 75 broad classes of property items. A further modification of the present guidelines was made in 1971 when the Asset Depreciation Range (ADR) system was installed by the Treasury Department. Under this system, the life of each class of asset has a range 20% above and 20% below the guideline life. This latter modification adds flexibility to the allowed depreciation.

asset produces a varying revenue pattern, then the depreciation charges should vary in a corresponding manner. When depreciation is measured in terms of a time factor, the pattern of use must be estimated. Several somewhat arbitrary methods have come into common use. Each method represents a different pattern and is designed to make the time basis approximate the use basis.[1] The time factor is employed in two general classes of methods, *straight-line depreciation* and *decreasing-charge depreciation*. When depreciation is measured in terms of a use factor, the units of use must be estimated. The depreciation charge varies periodically in accordance with the services provided by the asset. The use factor is employed in *service-hours depreciation* and in *productive-output depreciation*.

RECORDING DEPRECIATION

Periodic depreciation could be recorded by a debit to operations and a credit to the property item. However, it is customary to report the reduction in a depreciable asset in a separate valuation account. When cost allocation is reported in a separate account, original cost, as well as that part of the cost already allocated to revenues, can be provided on the balance sheet. This practice also serves to emphasize the estimates inherent in the allocation process.

A variety of titles are used to designate the valuation balance, such as Accumulated Depreciation, Allowance for Depreciation, and Depreciation Allocated to Past Operations. The term Reserve for Depreciation has also been widely used, but since this title may suggest the existence of a fund available for asset replacement, its use has been discouraged.

A separate valuation account is maintained for each asset or class of assets requiring the use of a separate depreciation rate. When a subsidiary ledger is maintained for land, buildings, and equipment, such record normally provides for the accumulation of depreciation allocations on the individual assets. Separate debits relating to individual property items in the subsidiary ledger support the land, buildings, and equipment balance in the general ledger; separate credits representing individual property item cost allocations in the subsidiary ledger support the accumulated depreciation balance in the general ledger.

When a property item consists of a number of units or structural elements with varying lives and these units are recorded separately, depreciation is recognized in terms of the respective lives of the different units. Retirement of an individual unit and its replacement by a new unit requires the cancellation of cost and accumulated depreciation balances related to the old unit and recognition of the new.

---

[1]The Cost Accounting Standards Board (CASB) has considered guidelines for accounting for depreciation on government contracts. Generally, the standard for depreciation requires that the method selected "shall reflect the expected consumption of services in each accounting period." ("Depreciation of Tangible Capital Assets," *Code of Federal Regulations*, Title 4, Chap. III, Part 409[3]).

METHODS OF COST ALLOCATION

As mentioned earlier, there are a number of different methods for allocating the costs of depreciable assets. The method used in any specific instance is a matter of judgment and should be selected to most closely approximate the actual pattern of use expected from the asset. The following methods are described in this chapter:

Time-Factor Methods
1. Straight-line depreciation
2. Decreasing-charge depreciation
   (a) Sum-of-the-years-digits method
   (b) Declining-balance method
   (c) Double-declining-balance method

Use-Factor Methods
1. Service-hours method
2. Productive-output method

Group-Rate and Composite-Rate Methods
1. Group depreciation
2. Composite depreciation

Two other time-factor methods each providing for increasing charges, the *annuity method* and the *sinking fund method*, require the use of compound interest calculations. These methods are rarely encountered in practice.

The examples that follow assume the acquisition of a machine at a cost of $10,000 with a salvage value at the end of its useful life of $500. The following symbols are employed in the formulas for the development of depreciation rates:

C = Asset cost
S = Estimated salvage value
n = Estimated life in years, hours of service, or units of output
r = Depreciation rate per period, per hour of service, or per unit of output
D = Annual depreciation charge

Straight-Line Depreciation

Straight-line depreciation relates cost allocation to the passage of time and recognizes equal periodic charges over the life of the asset. The depreciation charge assumes equal usefulness per time period, and in applying this assumption, the charge is not affected by asset productivity or efficiency variations. In developing the periodic charge, an estimate is made of the useful life of the asset in terms of months or years. The difference between the asset cost and residual value is divided by the useful life of the asset in arriving at the cost assigned to each time unit.

Using data for the machine referred to earlier and assuming a 10-year life, annual depreciation is determined as follows:

$$D = \frac{C - S}{n}, \text{ or } \frac{\$10,000 - \$500}{10} = \$950$$

The depreciation rate is commonly expressed as a percentage to be applied periodically to asset cost. The depreciation rate in the example is calculated as follows: $(100\% - 5\%) \div 10 = 9.5\%$. This percentage applied to cost provides a periodic charge of $950. The rate may also be expressed as a percentage to be applied to depreciable cost — cost less residual value. Expressed in this way the rate is simply the reciprocal value of the useful life expressed in periods, or r (per period) $= 1 \div n$. In the example, then, the annual rate would be $1 \div 10 = 10\%$, and this rate applied to depreciable cost, $9,500, gives an annual charge of $950. A table to summarize the process of cost allocation follows:

| | Asset Cost Allocation — Straight-Line Method | | |
End of Year	Debit to Depreciation and Credit to Accumulated Depreciation	Balance of Accumulated Depreciation	Asset Book Value
			$10,000
1	$ 950	$ 950	9,050
2	950	1,900	8,100
3	950	2,850	7,150
4	950	3,800	6,200
5	950	4,750	5,250
6	950	5,700	4,300
7	950	6,650	3,350
8	950	7,600	2,400
9	950	8,550	1,450
10	950	9,500	500
	$9,500		

It was indicated earlier that residual value is frequently ignored when this is only a relatively minor amount. If this were done in the example, a ten-year life would call for the use of a 10% rate; depreciation, then, would be recognized at $1,000 per year instead of $950.

In using the straight-line method, depreciation is a constant or fixed charge of each period. Net income measurements become particularly sensitive to changes in the volume of business activity: with above-normal activity, there is no increase in the depreciation charge; with below-normal activity, revenue is still charged with the costs of assets standing ready to serve. When the life of a property item is affected primarily by the lapse of time rather than by the degree of use, recognition of depreciation as a constant charge is particularly appropriate.

Straight-line depreciation is a widely used procedure. It is readily understood and frequently parallels observable asset deterioration. It has the advantage of simplicity and under normal property conditions offers a satisfactory means of cost allocation. Normal property conditions mean (1) properties that have been accumulated over a period of years so that the total of depreciation plus maintenance is comparatively even from period to period, and (2) properties whose service potentials are being steadily reduced by functional as well as physical factors. The absence of either of these conditions may suggest the use of some method other than the straight-line method.

Decreasing-Charge Depreciation

Decreasing-charge or *accelerated depreciation methods* also relate charges for depreciation to time. However, they provide for the highest depreciation charge in the first year of asset use and declining depreciation charges in ensuing years. Such plans are based largely on the assumption that there will be reductions in asset efficiency, output, or other benefits as the asset ages. Such reductions may be accompanied by increased charges for maintenance and repairs. Charges for depreciation decline, then, as the economic advantages afforded through ownership of the asset decline.

Sum-of-the-Years-Digits Method. The *sum-of-the-years-digits method* provides decreasing charges by applying a series of fractions, each of a smaller value, to depreciable asset cost. Fractions are developed in terms of the sum of the asset life periods. Weights for purposes of developing reducing fractions are the years-digits listed in reverse order. The denominator for the fraction is obtained by adding these weights; the numerator is the weight assigned to the specific year. The denominator for the fraction can be obtained by an alternate calculation: the sum of the digits for the first and last years can be divided by 2 and multiplied by the number of years of asset life. In the example, the denominator can be determined as follows: ([10 + 1] ÷ 2) × 10 = 55. Periodic charges for depreciation using the sum-of-the-years-digits method for the asset previously described are developed as follows:

	Reducing Weights	Reducing Fractions
First year	10	10/55
Second year	9	9/55
Third year	8	8/55
Fourth year	7	7/55
Fifth year	6	6/55
Sixth year	5	5/55
Seventh year	4	4/55
Eighth year	3	3/55
Ninth year	2	2/55
Tenth year	1	1/55
	55	55/55

Depreciation computed by the application of reducing fractions to depreciable cost is summarized in the table below:

Asset Cost Allocation — Sum-of-the-Years-Digits Method

End of Year	Debit to Depreciation and Credit to Accumulated Depreciation		Balance of Accumulated Depreciation	Asset Book Value
				$10,000.00
1	(10/55 × $9,500)	$1,727.27	$1,727.27	8,272.73
2	(9/55 × 9,500)	1,554.55	3,281.82	6,718.18
3	(8/55 × 9,500)	1,381.82	4,663.64	5,336.36
4	(7/55 × 9,500)	1,209.09	5,872.73	4,127.27
5	(6/55 × 9,500)	1,036.36	6,909.09	3,090.91
6	(5/55 × 9,500)	863.64	7,772.73	2,227.27
7	(4/55 × 9,500)	690.91	8,463.64	1,536.36
8	(3/55 × 9,500)	518.18	8,981.82	1,018.18
9	(2/55 × 9,500)	345.45	9,327.27	672.73
10	(1/55 × 9,500)	172.73	9,500.00	500.00
		$9,500.00		

Declining-Balance Method. The *declining-balance method* provides decreasing charges by applying a constant percentage rate to a declining asset book value. The rate to be applied to the declining book value in producing the estimated salvage value at the end of the useful life of the asset is calculated by the following formula:

$$r \text{ (rate per period applicable to declining book value)} = 1 - \sqrt[n]{S \div C}$$

Using the previous asset data and assuming a 10-year asset life, the depreciation rate is determined as follows:

$$1 - \sqrt[n]{500 \div 10,000} = 1 - \sqrt[n]{.05} = 1 - .74113 = .25887, \text{ or } 25.887\%$$

Dividing the estimated salvage value by cost in the formula above gives .05, the value that the salvage value at the end of 10 years should bear to cost. The tenth root of this value is .74113. Multiplying cost and the successive declining book values by .74113 ten times will reduce the asset to .05 of its cost. The difference between 1 and .74113, or .25887, then, is the rate of decrease to be applied successively in bringing the asset down to .05 of its original balance. Since it is impossible to bring a value down to zero by a constant multiplier, a residual value must be assigned to the asset in using the formula. In the absence of an expected residual value, a nominal value of $1 can be assumed for this purpose.

Depreciation calculated by application of the 25.887% rate to the declining book value is summarized in the following table:

Asset Cost Allocation — Declining-Balance Method

End of Year	Debit to Depreciation and Credit to Accumulated Depreciation		Balance of Accumulated Depreciation	Asset Book Value
				$10,000.00
1	(25.887% × $10,000.00)	$2,588.70	$2,588.70	7,411.30
2	(25.887% × 7,411.30)	1,918.56	4,507.26	5,492.74
3	(25.887% × 5,492.74)	1,421.91	5,929.17	4,070.83
4	(25.887% × 4,070.83)	1,053.82	6,982.99	3,017.01
5	(25.887% × 3,017.01)	781.01	7,764.00	2,236.00
6	(25.887% × 2,236.00)	578.83	8,342.83	1,657.17
7	(25.887% × 1,657.17)	428.99	8,771.82	1,228.18
8	(25.887% × 1,228.18)	317.94	9,089.76	910.24
9	(25.887% × 910.24)	235.63	9,325.39	674.61
10	(25.887% × 674.61)	174.61*	9,500.00	500.00
		$9,500.00		

*Discrepancy due to rounding.

Instead of developing an exact rate that will produce a salvage value of $500, it is usually more convenient to approximate a rate that will provide satisfactory cost allocation; since depreciation involves an estimate, there is little assurance that rate refinement will produce more accurate results. In the previous illustration, the use of a rate of 25% is more convenient than 25.887%; differences are not material.

Double-Declining-Balance Method. Federal income tax regulations provide that for certain assets, depreciation is allowed at a fixed percentage equal to double the straight-line rate. This is referred to as the *double-declining-balance method.* Although a residual value is not taken into account in employing this method as in other methods, depreciation charges should not be made after reaching the residual balance. The double-declining-balance method was initially introduced into the income tax laws in 1954. Since that time, this method has gained increased acceptability for both financial accounting as well as for tax reporting. The percentage is readily calculated as follows:

Estimated Life in Years	Straight-Line Rate	Double-Declining-Balance Rate
3	33⅓%	66⅔%
5	20	40
6	16⅔	33⅓
8	12½	25
10	10	20
20	5	10

Depreciation using the double-declining-balance method for the asset described earlier is summarized in the table that follows:

End of Year	Debit to Depreciation and Credit to Accumulated Depreciation		Balance of Accumulated Depreciation	Asset Book Value
	Asset Cost Allocation — Double-Declining-Balance Method			
				$10,000.00
1	(20% × $10,000.00)	$2,000.00	$2,000.00	8,000.00
2	(20% × 8,000.00)	1,600.00	3,600.00	6,400.00
3	(20% × 6,400.00)	1,280.00	4,880.00	5,120.00
4	(20% × 5,120.00)	1,024.00	5,904.00	4,096.00
5	(20% × 4,096.00)	819.20	6,723.20	3,276.80
6	(20% × 3,276.80)	655.36	7,378.56	2,621.44
7	(20% × 2,621.44)	524.29	7,902.85	2,097.15
8	(20% × 2,097.15)	419.43	8,322.28	1,677.72
9	(20% × 1,677.72)	335.54	8,657.82	1,342.18
10	(20% × 1,342.18)	268.44	8,926.26	1,073.74
		$8,926.26		

It should be noted that the rate of 20% is applied to the book value of the asset each year. In applying this rate, the book value after ten years exceeds the residual value by $573.74 ($1,073.74 − $500.00). This condition arises wherever residual values are relatively low in amount. One way to make the book value equal the residual value is to change from the double-declining-balance method to another acceptable method prior to the end of the asset's useful life. This change is permitted for tax purposes.

The optimal time to make the change is at the point when depreciation for the year using another acceptable method exceeds that computed using the double-declining-balance method. This comes earliest by changing to the sum-of-the-years-digits method. The exact time to change depends upon the estimated residual value of the asset. In the above example, the change should be made in the third year when the depreciation using the sum-of-the-years-digits method for the remaining life of the asset would be $1,311.11 rather than $1,280 under the double-declining-balance method. The determination of which year is the best time to change can be made each year by comparing the depreciation using the sum-of-the-years-digits method for the remaining life of the asset to the depreciation using the double-declining-balance method. This is illustrated at the top of the next page.

Year	Reducing Fraction Based Upon Remaining Life		Asset Book Value Less Salvage at Beginning of Year Using Double-Declining-Balance Depreciation	Depreciation Using Sum-of-the-Years-Digits Method for Remaining Life of the Asset	Depreciation Using Double-Declining-Balance Method (See Preceding Schedule)
1	10/55	×	$9,500	$1,727.27	$2,000
2	9/45	×	7,500	1,500.00	1,600
3	8/36	×	5,900	1,311.11	1,280

A new schedule combining both methods can be prepared. The reducing fraction for the sum-of-the-years-digits method will be 8/36, 7/36, 6/36, etc., since the asset has eight years of remaining life when the change takes place.

End of Year	Debit to Depreciation and Credit to Accumulated Depreciation			Balance of Accumulated Depreciation	Asset Book Value
					$10,000.00
1		(20% × $10,000)	$2,000.00	$2,000.00	8,000.00
2		(20% × 8,000)	1,600.00	3,600.00	6,400.00
3	8/36($9,500	−	3,600) 1,311.11	4,911.11	5,088.89
4	7/36(9,500	−	3,600) 1,147.22	6,058.33	3,941.67
5	6/36(9,500	−	3,600) 983.33	7,041.66	2,958.34
6	5/36(9,500	−	3,600) 819.44	7,861.10	2,138.90
7	4/36(9,500	−	3,600) 655.56	8,516.66	1,483.34
8	3/36(9,500	−	3,600) 491.67	9,008.33	991.67
9	2/36(9,500	−	3,600) 327.78	9,336.11	663.89
10	1/36(9,500	−	3,600) 163.89	9,500.00	500.00

Evaluation of Decreasing-Charge Methods. Decreasing-charge methods can be supported as reasonable approaches to asset cost allocation when the benefits provided by a property item decline as it grows older. These methods, too, are suggested when a property item calls for increasing maintenance and repairs over its useful life.[1] When straight-line depreciation is employed, the combined charges for depreciation, maintenance, and repairs will increase over the life of the asset; when the decreasing-charge methods are used, the combined charges will tend to be equalized.

Other factors suggesting the use of a decreasing-charge method include: (1) the anticipation of a significant contribution in early periods with the extent of the contribution to be equalized in later periods less definite; (2) the possibility that inadequacy or obsolescence may result in premature retirement of the asset. In the event of premature retirement, depreciation charges will have absorbed what would otherwise require recognition as a loss.

---

[1]The AICPA Committee on Accounting Procedure has stated, "The declining-balance method is one of those which meets the requirements of being 'systematic and rational.' In those cases where the expected productivity or revenue-earning power of the asset is relatively greater during the earlier years of its life, or where maintenance charges tend to increase during the later years, the declining-balance method may well provide the most satisfactory allocation of cost." The Committee would apply these conclusions to other decreasing-charge methods, including the sum-of-the-years-digits method, that produce substantially similar results. See *Accounting Research and Terminology Bulletins — Final Edition*, "No. 44 (Revised), Declining-Balance Depreciation" (New York: American Institute of Certified Public Accountants, 1961), par. 2.

Decreasing-charge or accelerated methods are frequently used for income tax purposes. Although total depreciation over the asset life is no greater than that provided by alternative methods, the recognition of higher depreciation in the early years of an asset's life serves to postpone the income tax otherwise payable and thus provides interest-free working capital to the business. Many taxpayers use accelerated depreciation methods on their tax returns but straight-line depreciation on their books. This requires income tax allocation adjustments to be made on the books in view of the timing differences in recognizing depreciation charge.[1]

Use-Factor Methods

Use-factor methods view asset exhaustion as related primarily to asset use or output and provide periodic charges varying with the degree of such service. Service life for certain assets can best be expressed in terms of hours of services; for others in terms of units of production.

Service-Hours Method. *Service-hours* depreciation is based on the theory that purchase of an asset represents the purchase of a number of hours of direct service. This method requires an estimate of the life of the asset in terms of service hours. Depreciable cost is divided by total service hours in arriving at the depreciation rate to be assigned for each hour of asset use. The use of the asset during the period is measured, and the number of service hours is multiplied by the depreciation rate in arriving at the depreciation charge. Depreciation charges fluctuate periodically according to the contribution the asset makes in service hours.

Using asset data previously given and an estimated service life of 20,000 hours, the rate to be applied for each service hour is determined as follows:

$$r \text{ (per hour)} = \frac{C - S}{n}, \text{ or } \frac{\$10,000 - \$500}{20,000} = \$.475$$

Allocation of asset cost in terms of service hours is summarized in the table below:

End of Year	Service Hours	Debit to Depreciation and Credit to Accumulated Depreciation		Balance of Accumulated Depreciation	Asset Book Value
		Asset Cost Allocation — Service-Hours Method			
					$10,000.00
1	1,500	(1,500 × $.475)	$ 712.50	$ 712.50	9,287.50
2	2,500	(2,500 × .475)	1,187.50	1,900.00	8,100.00
3	2,500	(2,500 × .475)	1,187.50	3,087.50	6,912.50
4	2,000	(2,000 × .475)	950.00	4,037.50	5,962.50
5	1,500	(1,500 × .475)	712.50	4,750.00	5,250.00
6	1,500	(1,500 × .475)	712.50	5,462.50	4,537.50
7	3,000	(3,000 × .475)	1,425.00	6,887.50	3,112.50
8	2,500	(2,500 × .475)	1,187.50	8,075.00	1,925.00
9	2,000	(2,000 × .475)	950.00	9,025.00	975.00
10	1,000	(1,000 × .475)	475.00	9,500.00	500.00
	20,000		$9,500.00		

[1]See discussion in Chapter 16.

It is assumed that the original estimate of service hours is confirmed and the asset is retired after 20,000 hours are reached in the tenth year. Such precise confirmation would seldom be found in practice.

It should be observed that straight-line depreciation resulted in an annual charge of $950 regardless of fluctuations in productive activity. When asset life is affected directly by the degree of use, and when there are significant fluctuations in such use in successive periods, the service-hours method, which recognizes hours used instead of hours available for use, normally provides the more equitable charges to operations.

Productive-Output Method. *Productive-output* depreciation is based on the theory that an asset is acquired for the service it can provide in the form of production output. This method requires an estimate of the total unit output of the property item. Depreciable cost divided by the total output gives the equal depreciation debit to be assigned for each unit of output. The measured production for a period multiplied by the depreciation charge per unit gives the charge to be made for depreciation. Depreciation charges fluctuate periodically according to the contribution the asset makes in unit output.

Using the previous asset data and an estimated productive life of 2,500,000 units, the rate to be applied for each thousand units produced is determined as follows:

$$r \text{ (per thousand units)} = \frac{C - S}{n}, \text{ or } \frac{\$10,000 - \$500}{2,500} = \$3.80$$

Asset cost allocation in terms of productive output is summarized in the tabulation below:

Asset Cost Allocation — Productive-Output Method

End of Year	Unit Output	Debit to Depreciation and Credit to Accumulated Depreciation		Balance of Accumulated Depreciation	Asset Book Value
					$10,000
1	80,000	(80 × $3.80)	$ 304	$ 304	9,696
2	250,000	(250 × 3.80)	950	1,254	8,746
3	400,000	(400 × 3.80)	1,520	2,774	7,226
4	320,000	(320 × 3.80)	1,216	3,990	6,010
5	440,000	(440 × 3.80)	1,672	5,662	4,338
6	360,000	(360 × 3.80)	1,368	7,030	2,970
7	280,000	(280 × 3.80)	1,064	8,094	1,906
8	210,000	(210 × 3.80)	798	8,892	1,108
9	120,000	(120 × 3.80)	456	9,348	652
10	40,000	(40 × 3.80)	152	9,500	500
	2,500,000		$9,500		

Evaluation of Use-Factor Methods. When quantitative uses of depreciable properties can be reasonably estimated and readily measured, the use-factor methods provide highly satisfactory approaches to asset cost allocation. Depreciation is a fluctuating charge tending to follow the revenue curve: high depreciation charges are assigned to periods of high activity; low depreciation charges are assigned to periods of low activity. When the useful life of an asset is affected primarily by the degree of its use, recognition of depreciation as a variable charge is particularly appropriate.

However, certain limitations in using the use-factor methods need to be pointed out. Asset performance in terms of service hours or productive output may be difficult to estimate. Measurement solely in terms of these factors could fail to recognize special conditions, such as increasing maintenance and repair costs as well as possible inadequacy and obsolescence. Furthermore, when service life expires even in the absence of use, a use-factor method may serve to conceal actual fluctuations in earnings; by relating periodic depreciation to the volume of operations, periodic operating results may be smoothed out, thus creating a false appearance of stability.

Group-Rate and Composite-Rate Methods   It was assumed in preceding discussions that depreciation is associated with individual property items and is applied to each separate unit. This practice is commonly referred to as *unit depreciation*. However, there may be certain advantages in associating depreciation with a group of properties and applying a single rate to the collective cost of the group. Group cost allocation procedures are referred to as *group depreciation* and *composite depreciation*.

Group Depreciation. When useful life is affected primarily by physical factors, a group of similar items purchased at one time should have the same expected life, but in fact some will probably remain useful longer than others. In recording depreciation on a unit basis, the sale or retirement of an asset before or after its anticipated lifetime requires recognition of a gain or loss. Such gains and losses, however, can usually be attributed to normal variations in useful life rather than to unforeseen disasters and windfalls.

The *group-depreciation* procedure treats a collection of similar assets as a single group. Depreciation is accumulated in a single valuation account, and the depreciation rate is based on the average life of assets in the group. Because the accumulated depreciation account under the group procedure applies to the entire group of assets, it is not related to any specific asset. Thus, there are no fully depreciated assets and the depreciation rate is applied to the cost of all assets remaining in service, regardless of age, in arriving at the periodic depreciation charge.

When an item in the group is retired, no gain or loss is recognized; the asset account is credited with the cost of the item and the valuation account is debited for the difference between cost and any salvage. With normal variations in asset lives, the losses not recognized on early retirements are offset by the continued depreciation charges on those assets still in service after the average life has elapsed.

To illustrate, assume 100 similar machines having an average expected useful life of 5 years are purchased at a total cost of $200,000. Of this group, 30 machines are retired at the end of four years, 40 at the end of five years, and the remaining 30 at the end of the sixth year. Based on the average expected useful life of 5 years, a depreciation charge of 20% is reported on those assets in service each year. The charges for depreciation and the changes in the group asset and accumulated depreciation accounts are summarized below.

Asset Cost Allocation — Group Depreciation

End of Year	Debit to Depreciation (20% of Cost)	Asset			Accumulated Depreciation			Asset Book Value
		Debit	Credit	Balance	Debit	Credit	Balance	
		$200,000		$200,000				$200,000
1	$ 40,000			200,000		$ 40,000	$ 40,000	160,000
2	40,000			200,000		40,000	80,000	120,000
3	40,000			200,000		40,000	120,000	80,000
4	40,000		$ 60,000	140,000	$ 60,000	40,000	100,000	40,000
5	28,000		80,000	60,000	80,000	28,000	48,000	12,000
6	12,000		60,000	—	60,000	12,000	—	—
	$200,000	$200,000	$200,000		$200,000	$200,000		

It should be noted that the depreciation charge is exactly $400 per machine-year. In each of the first four years, 100 machine-years of service are utilized, and the annual depreciation charge is $40,000. In the fifth year, when only 70 machines are in operation, the charge is $28,000. In the sixth year, when 30 units are still in service, a proportionate charge for such use of $12,000 is made. Under unit depreciation a loss of $12,000 would have been recognized at the end of the fourth year when 30 machines were scrapped prematurely. However, no charge for depreciation would have been recognized in the sixth year when the 30 machines remaining in service would have been fully depreciated.[1]

Application of the group depreciation procedure under circumstances such as the foregoing provides an annual charge that is more closely related to the quantity of productive facilities being used. Gains and losses due solely to normal variations in asset lives are not recognized, and operating results are more meaningfully stated. The convenience of applying a uniform depreciation rate to a number of similar items may also represent a substantial advantage.

Composite Depreciation. The basic procedures employed under the group method for allocating the cost of substantially identical assets may be extended to include dissimilar assets. This special application of the group procedure is known as *composite depreciation*. The composite method retains the convenience of the group method, but because assets with varying service-lives are aggregated to determine an average life, it is unlikely to provide all the reporting advantages of the group method.

A composite rate is established by analyzing the various assets or classes of assets in use and computing the depreciation as follows:

---

[1]It should be observed that in the example the original estimates of an average useful life of 5 years is confirmed in the use of the assets. Such precise confirmation would seldom be the case. In instances where assets in a group are continued in use after their cost has been assigned to operations, no further depreciation charges would be recognized. On the other hand, where all of the assets in a group are retired before their cost has been assigned to operations, a special charge related to such retirement would have to be recognized.

Asset	Cost	Residual Value	Depreciable Cost	Estimated Life in Years	Annual Depreciation
A	$ 2,000	$ 120	$ 1,880	4	$ 470
B	6,000	300	5,700	6	950
C	12,000	1,200	10,800	10	1,080
	$20,000	$1,620	$18,380		$2,500

Composite depreciation rate to be applied to cost: $2,500 ÷ $20,000 = 12.5%.
Composite or average life of assets: $18,380 ÷ $2,500 = 7.35 years.

It will be observed that a rate of 12.5% applied to the cost of the assets, $20,000, results in annual depreciation of $2,500. Annual depreciation of $2,500 will accumulate to a total of $18,380 in 7.35 years; hence 7.35 years may be considered the composite or average life of the assets. Composite depreciation would be reported in a single valuation account. Upon the retirement of an individual asset, the asset account is closed and the valuation account is debited with the difference between cost and residual value. As with the group procedure, no gains or losses are recognized at the time individual assets are retired.

After a composite rate has been set, it is ordinarily continued in the absence of significant changes in the lives of assets or asset additions and retirements having a material effect upon the rate. It is assumed in the preceding example that the assets are replaced with similar assets when retired. If they are not replaced, continuation of the 12.5% rate will misstate depreciation charges.

DEPRECIATION FOR PARTIAL PERIODS

The discussion thus far has assumed that assets were purchased or sold on the first day of a company's fiscal period. In reality, of course, asset transactions occur throughout the year. Company policy determines how partial periods will be handled for depreciation purposes. The following are some alternatives commonly followed:

1. Compute depreciation to the nearest whole month. Assets acquired on or before the 15th of the month are considered owned for the entire month; assets acquired after the 15th are not considered owned for any part of the month. Conversely, assets sold on or before the 15th of the month are not considered owned for any part of the month; assets sold after the 15th are considered owned for the entire month.
2. Compute depreciation to the nearest whole year. Assets acquired during the first six months are considered held for the entire year; assets acquired during the last six months are not considered in the depreciation computation. Conversely, no depreciation is recorded on assets sold during the first six months and a full year's depreciation is recorded on assets sold during the last six months.
3. One-half year's depreciation is taken on all assets purchased or sold during the year. A full year's depreciation is taken on all other assets.

If a company uses the sum-of-the-years-digits method of depreciation and recognizes partial year's depreciation on assets purchased or sold, each year's computation after the first year must be divided into two parts. The depreciation expense for each full year must be computed and then prorated over the partial periods. For example, assume the asset discussed on page 327 was acquired midway through a fiscal period. The computation of depreciation for the first two years recognizing partial period depreciation would be as follows:

First Year
Depreciation for first full year (see page 329)..............................$1,727.27
One-half year's depreciation .... $ 863.64

Second Year
Depreciation for balance of first year .... $ 863.63
Depreciation for second full year (see page 329)........................$1,554.55
One-half year's depreciation 777.28
  Total depreciation — second year $1,640.91

DEPRECIATION ACCOUNTING AND PROPERTY REPLACEMENT

There has been a tendency on the part of many readers of financial statements to interpret depreciation accounting as somehow related to the accumulation of a fund for asset replacement. The use of such terms as "provision for depreciation" and "reserve for depreciation" has contributed toward this misinterpretation.

The charge for depreciation originates from the recognition of the movement of a property item towards ultimate exhaustion. The nature of this charge is no different from those made to recognize the expiration of insurance premiums or patent rights. It is true that revenues equal to or in excess of expenses for a period result in a recovery of these expenses; salary expense is thus recovered by revenues, as is insurance expense, patent amortization, and charges for depreciation. But this does not mean that the cash equivalent to the recorded depreciation will necessarily be segregated to use for property replacement. Resources from revenues may be applied to many uses: to the increase in receivables, inventories, or other working capital items; to the acquisition of new property or other noncurrent items; to the retirement of debt or the redemption of stock; or to the payment of dividends. If a special fund is to be available for the replacement of property, special authorization by management would be required. Such a fund is seldom found, however, because good financial management would require fund earnings exceeding those accruing from alternative uses of the resources.

PROPERTY RECORDS

Data concerning individual property items are required in accounting for past activities, in planning future activities, and for insurance, tax, and other purposes. Data requirements can be met only by detailed records systematically and efficiently maintained. Such records are variously termed Unit Property Records, Property Ledger, and Fixed Asset Control Records. They usually involve the control account principle; property items being summarized in the general ledger, and detail being recorded in subsidiary ledgers.

Subsidiary records are commonly found in the form of a property register or a property file. When a property register is used, special sections are usually assigned to the assets of each department so depreciation charges may be accumulated departmentally. One line is provided for each asset, and significant information regarding the asset is reported in special columns. A register prepared in a form that summarizes periodic depreciation charges is generally referred to as a *lapsing schedule*. Individual assets are listed as they are acquired and periodic depreciation charges for the entire life of each depreciable asset are reported in a series of columns representing successive years. The charge for depreciation is readily determined by adding the debits appearing in the column for the particular year.

The use of a property file consisting of cards or separate sheets frequently provides a more flexible record than the register form since assets can be arranged in an order other than date of acquisition. One card or one sheet is provided for each asset on which all information with respect to the item is listed. For buildings and equipment, this information usually includes the name of the asset, location, name of the vendor, guarantee period, insurance carried, date acquired, original cost, transportation charges, installation cost, estimated life, estimated residual value, depreciation rate, depreciation to date, major expenditures for repairs and improvements, and proceeds from final disposal. Property files are frequently maintained on tabulating cards, magnetic tapes, or in the memory of an electronic computer. When the information is maintained and stored in this form, it may be easily sorted and used to make depreciation computations and accounting entries.

DISCLOSURE OF DEPRECIATION METHODS IN FINANCIAL STATEMENTS

Because of the alternative methods available to compute depreciation, the method used must be disclosed in the financial statements. Without disclosure, a user of the statements might be misled in trying to compare the financial results of one company with another.

The Accounting Principles Board detailed the following information as being pertinent to full disclosure.

> Because of the significant effects on financial position and results of operations of the depreciation method or methods used, the following disclosures should be made in the financial statements or in notes thereto:
>
> a. Depreciation expense for the period,
> b. Balances of major classes of depreciable assets, by nature or function, at the balance sheet date,
> c. Accumulated depreciation, either by major classes of depreciable assets or in total, at the balance sheet date, and
> d. A general description of the method or methods used in computing depreciation with respect to major classes of depreciable assets.[1]

---

[1]Opinions of the Accounting Principles Board, No. 12, "Omnibus Opinion — 1967" (New York: American Institute of Certified Public Accountants, 1967), par. 5.

DEPLETION

Natural resources, also called *wasting assets*, move toward exhaustion as the physical units representing these resources are removed and sold. The withdrawal of oil or gas, the cutting of timber, and the mining of coal, sulphur, iron, copper, or silver ore are examples of processes leading to the exhaustion of natural resources. The reduction in the cost or value of natural resources as a result of the withdrawal of resources is referred to as *depletion*.

Depletion may be distinguished from depreciation in these respects:

1. Depletion is recognition of the quantitative exhaustion taking place in a natural resource, while depreciation is recognition of the service exhaustion taking place in a building or equipment item.
2. Related to (1), depletion is recognized as the cost of the material that becomes directly embodied in the product of the company; through depreciation, the cost of an asset may be allocated to production but the asset itself does not become a part of the finished product.
3. Depletion involves a distinctive asset that cannot be directly replaced in kind upon its exhaustion; depreciation involves an asset that can generally be replaced upon its exhaustion.

The measurement of net income calls for the recognition of depletion. If the natural resource is sold directly upon its emergence or withdrawal, the recognition of depletion is, in effect, the recognition of cost of goods sold; if the natural resource is processed and stored before sale, depletion is initially recognized as a part of inventory cost.

When natural resources are acquired together with land for a lump sum, the total cost of the property must be allocated to the two property items. Separate accounts may be established for land and for the resources. The cost of the latter asset divided by the estimated quantity of resources that can profitably be removed gives the charge to be recognized for each unit removed, or the *unit depletion charge*. Depletion for the period is computed in the same way as productive-output depreciation; i.e., the measured number of units removed during the period are multiplied by the unit depletion charge.

To illustrate, assume the following facts: Land containing natural resources is purchased at a cost of $5,500,000. The land has an estimated value after removal of the resources of $250,000; the natural resource supply is estimated at 1,000,000 tons. The unit depletion charge and the total depletion charge for the first year, assuming the withdrawal of 80,000 tons, are calculated as follows:

Depletion charge per ton: ($5,500,000 − $250,000) ÷ 1,000,000 = $5.25
Depletion charge for the first year: 80,000 tons × $5.25 = $420,000

When developmental costs, such as costs of drilling, sinking mine shafts, and constructing roads, are related to the removal of the resource, these should be added to the original cost of the property in arriving at the total cost subject to depletion. These costs may be incurred before normal activities begin. On the other hand, they may be continuing and, therefore, may call for estimates in arriving at a depletion charge to be used uniformly for all recoverable units. It should be observed that the capitalization of developmental costs is an application of the matching process requiring that costs incurred in anticipation of subsequent revenue be deferred. In practice, however, in view of a variety of special situations encountered by companies with wasting assets, practices ranging from the full capitalization of periodic developmental expenditures to the full assignment to current revenue of such expenditures are encountered. Support for charging current revenue for developmental costs is made on the grounds this practice affords the conservatism required in view of the general uncertainty of the benefits the costs may provide. Because a number of companies report developmental costs as expenses, there is a need to review carefully the financial statements of companies with wasting assets if operating results are to be properly evaluated.[1] When costs will be required to restore land for use after the resources are exhausted, these should also be added to depletable cost.

The charge for resource exhaustion is recorded by a debit to Depletion Expense and a credit directly to the resource account or to Accumulated Depletion. If an accumulated depletion account is established, it should be subtracted from the resource account in reporting the asset.

The charge for depletion, increased by labor and overhead relating to removal and processing, is reported in the "Cost of goods sold" section of the income statement. If all of the units represented by the depletion charge are sold, depletion, labor, and overhead costs measure the cost of goods sold to be applied against revenue in arriving at gross profit on sales; if some of the units remain on hand, the total for depletion, labor, and overhead related to such units is recognized as inventory and subtracted from total costs in arriving at cost of goods sold. Depletion, therefore, is comparable to raw materials purchases.

When developmental costs differ significantly from original estimates and when estimates of the available unit supply change as a result of further discoveries or improved extraction processes, revisions in the unit depletion charge often become necessary. Revisions may also be required when changes in sales prices indicate changes in the number of units that can profitably be extracted.

In revising depletion charges, no adjustment would be made for past charges; the current annual charge would be established by dividing the resource cost balance as found at the end of the year by the estimated remaining recoverable units as of the beginning of the year (units recovered during the year plus the estimated recoverable units at the end of the year). To illustrate, assume in the preceding example that additional developmental costs of $525,000 are incurred in the second year and recoverable units are estimated at 950,000 tons after second-year withdrawals of 100,000 tons. The depletion charge for the second year is then determined as shown at the top of the next page.

---

[1] A discussion memorandum, "Financial Accounting and Reporting in the Extractive Industries," was issued by the FASB in December, 1976. The U.S. Congress has given the profession only until December, 1977, to develop more uniform standards for these industries. Title V, Sec. 503, Public Law 94–163, *Energy Policy and Conservation Act.*

Cost assignable to recoverable tons as of the beginning of the second year:

Original costs applicable to depletable resources............................	$5,250,000
Add additional costs incurred in the second year	525,000
	$5,775,000
Deduct depletion charge for the first year...	420,000
Balance of cost subject to depletion...	$5,355,000

Estimated recoverable tons as of the beginning of the second year:

Number of tons withdrawn in the second year.................................	100,000
Estimated recoverable tons as of the end of the second year	950,000
Total recoverable tons at the beginning of the second year............	1,050,000

Depletion charge per ton for the second year: $5,355,000 ÷ 1,050,000 = $5.10
Depletion charge for the second year: 100,000 × $5.10 = $510,000

When buildings and improvements are constructed in connection with the removal of natural resources and their usefulness is limited to the duration of the project, it is reasonable to recognize depreciation on such properties on an output basis consistent with the charges to be recognized for the natural resources themselves. For example, assume buildings are constructed at a cost of $250,000; the useful lives of the buildings are expected to terminate upon exhaustion of the natural resource consisting of 1,000,000 units. Under these circumstances, a depreciation charge of $.25 ($250,000 ÷ 1,000,000) should accompany the depletion charge recognized for each unit. When improvements provide benefits expected to terminate prior to the exhaustion of the natural resource, the cost of such improvements may be allocated on the basis of the units to be removed during the life of the improvements or on a time basis, whichever is considered more appropriate.

DIVIDENDS REPRESENTING PROCEEDS FROM WASTING ASSETS

When a company's stock in trade is its wasting assets, revenue represents a recovery of the cost of such wasting assets charged to operations, a recovery of other expenses, and earnings. When operations are to cease upon exhaustion of the resources, dividends need not be limited to net income but may be paid in amounts equal to such net income increased by the amount charged against revenue as depletion. To limit dividends to net income would be to retain the amount recovered from wasting assets, possibly in unproductive form, until the time the business is liquidated. In the absence of effective utilization of revenue proceeds for new properties or other productive purposes, these assets should be made available to stockholders. Amounts received by stockholders, then, would represent in part a distribution of earnings and in part a return of invested capital.

To illustrate the nature of the foregoing, assume the Midas Mines Co. in 1977 issues capital stock in exchange for certain mineral properties valued at $100,000. During the course of the fiscal period, natural resources costing $25,000 are sold for $50,000 and operating expenses of $10,000 are incurred. At the end of the period, the balance sheet reports the following:

Midas Mines Co.
Balance Sheet
December 31, 1977

Assets			Liabilities and Stockholders' Equity	
Cash		$ 35,000	Liabilities	$ 5,000
Receivables		10,000	Capital stock	100,000
Mineral properties	$100,000		Retained earnings	15,000
Less accumulated				
depletion	25,000	75,000		
			Total liabilities and	
Total assets		$120,000	stockholders' equity	$120,000

Management here does not need to limit dividends to the retained earnings balance of $15,000 but may consider the limitation to be $40,000 — net income, $15,000, increased by the recovery of the asset depletion, $25,000. However, since revenue has not been fully realized in cash, and since some cash is required for a continuation of operations, dividends of a lesser amount would be in order. If a dividend of $28,000 is paid, it is regarded as representing first a distribution of earnings of $15,000, and the balance is regarded as a return of invested capital to owners. The return of invested capital could be reported by a debit to a capital stock offset balance rather than by a debit to Capital Stock. The entry to record the $28,000 dividend distribution follows:

```
Retained Earnings ...................................................................... 15,000
Capital Distributions to Stockholders................................. 13,000
    Cash............................................................................................          28,000
```

The stockholders' equity would then be reported as follows:

```
Capital stock.................................................................................. $100,000
    Less capital distributions to stockholders............................    13,000
Total stockholders' equity.......................................................... $ 87,000
```

The distribution to stockholders of amounts equal to net income increased by the depletion charge is permitted by state laws. It is sanctioned on the theory that creditors are aware of the shrinking investment requirements peculiar to operations involving wasting assets not subject to replacement. When dividends are in part liquidating, stockholders should be informed of the portion of the dividend representing a distribution of corporate earnings and of the portion representing a return of invested capital.

QUESTIONS

1. There are several different methods that may be used to allocate the cost of property items against revenue. Wouldn't it be better to require all companies to use the same method? Discuss briefly.

2. What factors must be considered to determine the periodic depreciation charges that should be made for a company's assets?

3. What rationale can be given for ignoring salvage or residual values when computing depreciation?

4. Distinguish between functional depreciation and physical depreciation of assets.

5. After reading an article on the allocation of costs, the controller for a client corporation asks you to explain the excerpt on page 344.

Depreciation may be either a fixed cost or a variable cost, depending on the method used to compute it.

6. The president of the Vega Co. recommends that no depreciation be recorded for 1977 since the depreciation rate is 5% per year and indexes show that prices during the year have risen by more than this figure. Evaluate this argument.

7. The policy of the Lyons Co. is to recondition its building and equipment each year so they may be maintained in perfect repair. In view of the extensive periodic costs involved in keeping the property in such condition, officials of the company feel the need for recognizing depreciation is eliminated. Evaluate this argument.

8. The Egnew Manufacturing Company purchased a new machine especially built to perform one particular function on their assembly line. A difference of opinion has arisen as to the method of depreciation to be used in connection with this machine. Three methods are now being considered:

    (a) The straight-line method.
    (b) The productive-output method.
    (c) The sum-of-the-years-digits method.

List separately the arguments for and against each of the proposed methods from both the theoretical and the practical viewpoints. In your answer, you need not express your preference and you are to disregard income tax consequences.

9. In what ways, if any, do accelerated methods of depreciation increase the flow of cash funds into a company?

10. Why is it frequently necessary to change from the double-declining-balance method of depreciation to another of the accepted methods? What factors determine when the change should be made?

11. The president of the Canter Co. objects to the use of straight-line depreciation on the grounds that sale of the asset at the end of the first year of its life would result in a loss significantly greater than the depreciation charge. The vice-president objects to the use of the straight-line method on the grounds that an appraisal of the asset at the end of the first year would hardly show a physical decline equal to the depreciation charge. Evaluate each position.

12. The certified public accountant is frequently called upon by management for advice regarding methods of computing depreciation. Although the question arises less frequently, of comparable importance is whether the depreciation method should be based on the consideration of the property items as units, as groups, or as having a composite life.

    (a) Briefly describe the depreciation methods based on recognizing property items as (1) units, (2) groups, or (3) as having a composite life.
    (b) Present the arguments for and against the use of each of these methods.
    (c) Describe how retirements are recorded under each of these methods.

13. The recognition of depreciation has no essential relation to the problem of replacement. Do you agree?

14. The computer has greatly simplified accounting for buildings and equipment. In what ways has this simplification taken place?

15. (a) Define wasting assets. (b) Give five examples of wasting assets.

16. What are the similarities and the differences in recognizing depreciation on buildings and equipment and depletion on wasting assets?

17. What procedures must be followed when the estimate of recoverable wasting assets is changed due to subsequent developmental work?

18. Justify the practice, followed in the case of a company with wasting assets, of adding the charge for depletion to net income in arriving at the amount available for dividends.

EXERCISES

1. A machine is purchased at the beginning of 1977 for $25,500. Its estimated life is 6 years. Freight in on the machine is $400. Installation costs are $300. The machine is estimated to have a residual value of $1,000, and a useful life of 40,000 hours. It was used 5,000 hours in 1977.

    (a) What is the cost of the machine for accounting purposes?
    (b) Compare the depreciation charge for 1977 using (1) the straight-line method, and (2) the service-hours method.

2. Sun, Inc., purchased equipment costing $65,000 on June 30, 1977, having an estimated life of 5 years and a residual value of $5,000. The company uses the sum-of-the-years-digits method of depreciation, and takes one-half year's depreciation on assets in the year of purchase. The asset was sold on December 31, 1979, for $21,000. Give the entry to record the sale of the equipment.

3. Ham Manufacturing Co. acquired machinery at a cost of $200,000. The asset had a 10-year life and a scrap value of $14,000. Depreciation was to be recorded at a rate double the straight-line rate. However, realizing that a continuation of depreciation at the same rate would require the recognition of a significant loss in the last year of asset life, the company decided to change to the sum-of-the-years-digits method and write off the remaining asset book value over the remaining asset life beginning with the year in which the declining-balance method produced a smaller charge than the straight-line depreciation. Prepare a table indicating the optimum year to change methods and listing annual depreciation charges and the accumulated depreciation for the 10-year period. Round depreciation to the nearest dollar amount.

4. The Piper Manufacturing Co. acquired a machine at a cost of $9,540 on March 1, 1971. The machine is estimated to have a life of 10 years except for a special unit that will require replacement at the end of 6 years. The asset is recorded in two accounts, $7,200 being assigned to the main unit, and $2,340 to the special unit. Depreciation is recorded by the straight-line method to the nearest month, salvage values being disregarded. On March 1, 1977, the special unit is scrapped and is replaced with a similar unit; the cost of the replacement at this time is $5,600, and it is estimated that the unit will have a residual value of approximately 25% of cost at the end of the useful life of the main unit. What are the depreciation charges to be recognized for the years 1971, 1977, and 1978?

5. Equipment was purchased at the beginning of 1975 for $100,000 with an estimated product life of 600,000 units. The equipment has a salvage value of $10,000. During 1975, 1976, and 1977, the unit production of the equipment was 80,000 units, 120,000 units, and 40,000 units respectively. The machine was damaged at the beginning of 1978, and the equipment was scrapped with no salvage value. (1) Determine depreciation taken during 1975, 1976, and 1977. (2) Give the entry to write off the equipment.

6. The Quartz Co. records show the following assets:

	Acquired	Cost	Salvage	Estimated Useful Life
Machinery	7/1/76	$70,000	$5,000	10 years
Equipment	1/1/77	22,000	1,000	7 years
Fixtures	1/1/77	30,000	3,000	4 years

What is (a) the composite depreciation rate to be applied to cost and (b) the composite life of the asset?

7. The Salvador Co. obtains a lease for 20 years on a piece of land upon which it erects a building at a cost of $300,000 with an estimated life of 30 years. Buildings belong to the lessor at the end of the lease period. It also leases another piece of land for 30 years and erects a factory building at a cost of $262,500 with an estimated life of 25 years. What is the annual depreciation charge on each piece of property, assuming use of the straight-line method?

8. The Cervantes Mining Co. in 1974 paid $1,600,000 for property with a supply of natural resources estimated at 1,000,000 tons. The property was estimated to be worth $200,000 after removal of the natural resource. Developmental costs of $300,000 were incurred in 1975 before withdrawals of the resource could be made. In 1976, resources removed totaled 200,000 tons. In 1977 resources removed totaled 300,000 tons. During 1977 discoveries were made indicating that available resources subsequent to 1977 will total 1,500,000 tons. Additional developmental costs of $440,000 were incurred in 1977. What entries should be made to recognize depletion for 1976 and 1977?

9. On July 1, 1977, Miller Mining, a calendar-year corporation, purchased the rights to a copper mine. Of the total purchase price, $2,800,000 was appropriately allocable to the copper. Estimated reserves were 800,000 tons of copper. Miller expects to extract and sell 10,000 tons of copper per month. Production began immediately. The selling price is $25 per ton. *(continued)*

To aid production, Miller also purchased some new equipment on July 1, 1977. The equipment cost $76,000 and had an estimated useful life of 8 years. However, after all the copper is removed from this mine, the equipment will be of no use to Miller and will be sold for an estimated $4,000.

If sales and production conform to expectations, what is Miller's depletion expense on this mine and depreciation expense on the new equipment for financial accounting purposes for the calendar year 1977?

PROBLEMS

12-1. The Bacon Company purchased a machine for $60,000 on June 15, 1977. It is estimated that the machine will have a 10-year life and will have a salvage value of $6,000. Its working hours and production in units are estimated at 36,000 and 600,000 respectively. It is the company's policy to take a half-year's depreciation on all assets for which they use the straight-line or double-declining-balance depreciation method in the year of purchase. During 1977, the machine was operated 4,050 hours and produced 67,000 units.

> *Instructions:* Which of the following methods will give the greatest depreciation expense for 1977: (1) double-declining balance; (2) productive-output; or (3) service-hours. (Show computations for all three methods.)

12-2. A delivery truck was acquired by Big Bag, Inc., for $5,000 on January 1, 1976. The truck was estimated to have a 3-year life and a trade-in value at the end of that time of $500. The following depreciation methods are being considered.

> (a) Depreciation is to be calculated by the straight-line method.
> (b) Depreciation is to be calculated by the sum-of-the-years-digits method.
> (c) Depreciation is to be calculated by applying a fixed percentage to the declining book value of the asset that will reduce the asset book value to its residual value at the end of the third year. (The third root of .10 = .464.)
> (d) Repair charges are estimated at $70 for the first year and are estimated to increase by $50 in each succeeding year; depreciation charges are to be made on a diminishing scale so that the sum of depreciation and estimated repairs is the same for each year over the life of the asset.

> *Instructions:* Prepare tables reporting periodic depreciation and asset book value over the 3-year period for each assumption listed above.

12-3. A company buys a machine for $4,800. The maintenance costs for the years 1975–1978 are as follows:

1975 ....$	50	
1976	55	
1977	1,274	(Includes $1,248 for cost of a new motor installed in December, 1977.)
1978	70	

> *Instructions:*
> (1) Assume the machine is recorded in a single account at a cost of $4,800. No record is kept of the cost of the component parts. Straight-line depreciation is used and the asset is estimated to have a useful life of 8 years. It is assumed there will be no residual value at the end of the useful life. What is the sum of the depreciation and maintenance charges for each of the first four years?
> (2) Assume the cost of the frame of the machine was recorded in one account at a cost of $3,600 and the motor was recorded in a second account at a cost of $1,200. Straight-line depreciation is used with a useful life of 10 years for the frame and 4 years for the motor. Neither item is assumed to have any residual value at the end of its useful life. What is the sum of depreciation and maintenance charges for each of the first four years?
> (3) Evaluate the two methods.

12-4. The Boswell Company purchased machinery costing $220,000 in 1976. In 1977, $80,000 of machinery was purchased. All machinery has an estimated useful life of 20 years. The machinery purchased at $220,000 has an estimated salvage value of $40,000, and the machinery purchased for $80,000 has an estimated salvage value of $4,000. It is the company policy to take a full year's depreciation in the year of purchase. At the beginning of 1979, the company changed the method of depreciation on the 1976 purchase from double-declining balance to sum-of-the-years-digits in order to fully depreciate the machinery. On December 31, 1980, the company sold machinery for $30,000 that cost $55,000 in 1976.

> **Instructions:** Determine the gain or loss on the sale of the machinery. (Round depreciation computations to the nearest dollar.)

12-5. The Majestic Manufacturing Co. acquired 25 similar machines at the beginning of 1972 for $100,000. Machines have an average life of 5 years and no residual value. The group-depreciation method is employed in writing off the cost of the machines. Machines were retired as follows:

2 machines at the end of 1974	11 machines at the end of 1976
6 machines at the end of 1975	6 machines at the end of 1977

> **Instructions:** Give the entries to record the retirement of machines and the periodic depreciation for the years 1972–1977 inclusive.

12-6. Machines are acquired by McEwan, Inc., on March 1, 1977, as follows:

	Cost	Estimated Salvage Value	Estimated Life in Years
Machine 101	$27,000	$6,000	6
102	10,000	1,000	8
103	1,000	400	8
104	9,000	850	10
105	3,500	None	10

> **Instructions:**
> (1) Calculate the composite depreciation rate for this group.
> (2) Calculate the composite or average life in years for the group.
> (3) Give the entry to record the depreciation for the year ending December 31, 1977.

12-7. Head Steel Products Company uses a number of electric cranes, each consisting of a chassis, motor, and truck. The crane chassis has a normal service life of 10 years, the truck lasts 5 years and must be overhauled at the end of every 3 years, and the motor normally requires a major overhaul at the end of every 2 years and must be replaced every 4 years.

The operating history of crane No. 315 is as follows:

Jan. 1968	Purchased crane for $70,000. Estimated cost of components: chassis, $35,000; truck, $25,000; motor, $10,000.
Dec. 1969	Overhauled motor at cost of $1,000.
Dec. 1970	Overhauled truck at cost of $3,000.
Dec. 1971	Replaced motor at cost of $10,200.
Dec. 1972	Overhauled motor at cost of $700; replaced truck at cost of $28,000.
Dec. 1974	Overhauled truck at cost of $3,300; replaced motor at cost of $11,000.
Dec. 1975	Overhauled motor at cost of $1,100.
Dec. 1977	Scrapped crane; proceeds from scrap was equal to the cost of dismantling and removing the asset.

The company depreciates its cranes at an average straight-line rate of 15% per year. The cost of motor and truck overhauls is debited to expense, and the cost of replacing motors and trucks is debited to the accumulated depreciation account.

The assistant controller has suggested the company revise its accounting procedure as follows: separate property records would be maintained for motors, trucks, and chassis. Annual depreciation on each component would be computed by totaling the cost of the component and the estimated cost of the overhaul (in the case of motors and trucks) and dividing by the estimated service life. The cost of major overhauls would be debited to Accumulated Depreciation, and components would be retired from the property account with any gain or loss recorded at the time of replacement.

The controller feels this procedure would not make any significant difference in the pattern of operating charges and asks the assistant to prepare a comparative history, using crane No. 315 as an example, showing the results under the company's present policy and the results under the assistant's suggested procedure.

> **Instructions:**
> (1) Prepare a schedule summarizing the operating history of crane No. 315 if the company's present procedures are followed showing the total debit to expense for depreciation and repairs for each of the 10 years. Assume any difference between asset cost and accumulated depreciation is added to or deducted from the depreciation charged in the tenth year.
> (2) Prepare a similar schedule summarizing the operating history of crane No. 315 assuming the company had followed the assistant's suggested procedure. Assume the cost of the first overhaul is estimated as follows: motor, $1,000; truck, $3,000. Subsequent overhauls are estimated at the cost actually incurred in making the last previous overhaul. Include supporting schedules showing the computation of revised depreciation charges after the replacement of a component and the gain or loss at the time of retirement.
> (3) Evaluate the two procedures and explain why you would or would not recommend that the assistant's suggestion be adopted.

12-8. The Gold Mining Company paid $1,800,000 in 1976 for property with a supply of natural resources estimated at 2,000,000 tons. The estimated cost of restoring the land for use after the resources are exhausted is $150,000. After the land is restored, it will have an estimated value of $375,000. Development costs, such as drilling and road construction, were $550,000. Buildings, such as bunk houses and mess hall, were constructed on the site for $75,000. The useful lives of the buildings are expected to terminate upon exhaustion of the natural resources. Operations were not begun until January 1, 1977. In 1977, resources removed totaled 600,000 tons. During 1978, an additional discovery was made indicating that available resources subsequent to 1978 will total 1,800,000 tons. Because of a strike, only 400,000 tons of resources were removed during 1978.

> **Instructions:** Compute the debits to Depletion Expense for 1976, 1977, and 1978.

12-9. The Squires Corp. was organized on January 2, 1977. It was authorized to issue 80,000 shares of common stock, par $50. On the date of organization it sold 20,000 shares at par and gave the remaining shares in exchange for certain land bearing recoverable ore deposits estimated by geologists at 800,000 tons. The property is deemed to have a value of $3,000,000.

During 1977 mine improvements totaled $45,000. Miscellaneous buildings and sheds were constructed at a cost of $99,000. During the year 50,000 tons were mined; 4,000 tons of this amount were on hand unsold on December 31, the balance of the tonnage being sold for cash at $16 per ton. Expenses incurred and paid for during the year, exclusive of depletion and depreciation, were as follows:

Mining	$151,750
Delivery	15,000
General and administrative	12,800

Cash dividends of $2 per share were declared on December 31, payable January 15, 1978.

It is believed that buildings and sheds will be useful only over the life of the mine; hence depreciation is to be recognized in terms of the mine output.

> **Instructions:** Prepare an income statement and a balance sheet for 1977. Submit working papers showing the development of statement data.

12-10. A depreciation schedule for auto trucks of the Way Mfg. Company was requested by an income tax revenue agent soon after December 31, 1977, showing the additions, retirements, depreciation, and other data affecting the taxable income of the company in the four-year period 1974 to 1977, inclusive. The following data were ascertained:

Balance of auto trucks account January 1, 1974:	
Truck No. 1 purchased January 1, 1971, cost	$6,000
Truck No. 2 purchased July 1, 1971, cost	5,400
Truck No. 3 purchased January 1, 1973, cost	4,800
Truck No. 4 purchased July 1, 1973, cost	5,000
Balance January 1, 1974	$21,200

The auto trucks accumulated depreciation account, previously adjusted by a revenue agent to January 1, 1974, and duly entered in the ledger, had a balance on that date of $7,760, this amount being depreciation on the four trucks from the respective dates of purchase, based on a five-year life. No charges had been made against this account prior to January 1, 1974.

Transactions between January 1, 1974, and December 31, 1977, and their record in the ledger were as follows:

(a) July 1, 1974: Truck No. 1 was sold for $2,000 cash. The entry made was a debit to Cash and a credit to Auto Trucks, $2,000.

(b) January 1, 1975: Truck No. 3 was traded for a larger one (No. 5), the agreed purchase price of which was $5,000. The Way Mfg. Company paid the automobile dealer $1,780 cash on the transaction. The entry was a debit to Auto Trucks and a credit to Cash, $1,780.

(c) July 1, 1976: Truck No. 4 was damaged in a wreck to such an extent that it was sold as junk for $50 cash. Way Mfg. Company received $950 from the insurance company. The entry made by the bookkeeper was a debit to Cash, $1,000, and credits to Miscellaneous Revenue, $50, and Auto Trucks, $950.

(d) July 1, 1976: A new truck (No. 6) was acquired for $6,500 cash and debited at that amount to the auto trucks account.

Entries for depreciation had been made at the close of each year as follows: 1974, $3,600; 1975, $3,000; 1976, $3,200; 1977, $4,000.

Instructions:

(1) For each of the four years, calculate separately the increase or decrease in earnings arising from the company's errors in determining or entering depreciation or in recording transactions affecting trucks.

(2) Prove your work by one compound journal entry as of December 31, 1977; the adjustment of the auto trucks account is to reflect the correct balances assuming the books have not been closed for 1977. (AICPA adapted)

12-11. Thompson Corporation, a manufacturer of steel products, began operations on October 1, 1977. The accounting department of Thompson has started the fixed asset and depreciation schedule presented below. You have been asked to assist in completing this schedule. In addition to ascertaining that the data already on the schedule are correct, you have obtained from the company's records and personnel the information shown below the schedule and on page 350.

Thompson Corporation
Fixed Asset and Depreciation Schedule
For Years Ended September 30, 1978, and September 30, 1979

Assets	Acquisition Date	Cost	Salvage	Depreciation Method	Estimated Life in Years	Depreciation Expense Year Ended September 30,	
						1978	1979
Land A..................	October 1, 1977	$ (1)	N/A*	N/A	N/A	N/A	N/A
Building A	October 1, 1977	(2)	$47,500	Straight Line	(3)	$14,000	(4)
Land B..................	October 2, 1977	(5)	N/A	N/A	N/A	N/A	N/A
Building B	Under Construction	210,000 to date	—	Straight Line	30	—	(6)
Donated Equipment..........	October 2, 1977	(7)	2,000	150% Declining Balance	10	(8)	(9)
Machinery A...........	October 2, 1977	(10)	5,500	Sum-of-the-Years-Digits	10	(11)	(12)
Machinery B..........	October 1, 1978	(13)	—	Straight Line	15	—	(14)

*N/A — Not Applicable

(a) Depreciation is computed from the first of the month of acquisition to the first of the month of disposition.

(b) Land A and Building A were acquired from a predecessor corporation. Thompson paid $812,500 for the land and building together. At the time of acquisition, the land had an appraised value of $72,000 and the building had an appraised value of $828,000.

(c) Land B was acquired on October 2, 1977, in exchange for 3,000 newly issued shares of Thompson's common stock. At the date of acquisition, the stock had a par value of $5 per share and a fair value of $25 per share. During October, 1977, Thompson paid $10,400 to demolish an existing building on this land so it could construct a new building.

(d) Construction of Building B on the newly acquired land began on October 1, 1978. By September 30, 1979, Thompson had paid $210,000 of the estimated total construction costs of $300,000. Estimated completion and occupancy are July, 1980.

(e) Certain equipment was donated to the corporation by a local university. An independent appraisal of the equipment when donated placed the fair value at $16,000 and the salvage value at $2,000.

(f) Machinery A's total cost of $110,000 includes installation expense of $550 and normal repairs and maintenance of $11,000. Salvage value is estimated at $5,500. Machinery A was sold on February 1, 1979.

(g) On October 1, 1978, Machinery B was acquired with a down payment of $4,000 and the remaining payments to be made in ten annual installments of $4,000 each beginning October 1, 1979. The prevailing interest rate was 8%.

Instructions: For each numbered item on the preceding schedule determine the correct amount. Round each answer to the nearest dollar. (AICPA adapted)

12-12. You are engaged in the examination of the financial statements of The Smoky Mountain Mfg. Company and are auditing the machinery and equipment account and the related depreciation accounts for the year ended December 31, 1977.

Your permanent file contains the following schedules:

Machinery and Equipment

Year	Balance 12/31/75	1976 Retirements	1976 Additions	Balance 12/31/76
1963–66	$ 8,000	$2,100	—	$ 5,900
1967	400	—	—	400
1968	—	—	—	—
1969	—	—	—	—
1970	3,900	—	—	3,900
1971	—	—	—	—
1972	5,300	—	—	5,300
1973	—	—	—	—
1974	4,200	—	—	4,200
1975	—	—	—	—
1976	—	—	$5,700	5,700
	$21,800	$2,100	$5,700	$25,400

Accumulated Depreciation

Year	Balance 12/31/75	1976 Retirements	1976 Provision	Balance 12/31/76
1963–66	$ 7,840	$2,100	$ 160	$ 5,900
1967	340	—	40	380
1968	—	—	—	—
1969	—	—	—	—
1970	2,145	—	390	2,535
1971	—	—	—	—
1972	1,855	—	530	2,385
1973	—	—	—	—
1974	630	—	420	1,050
1975	—	—	—	—
1976	—	—	285	285
	$12,810	$2,100	$1,825	$12,535

A transcript of the machinery and equipment account for 1977 follows:

Machinery and Equipment

Date	Item	Debit	Credit
1977 Jan. 1 Mar. 1 May 1 June 1 June 1 Aug. 1 Nov. 1 Nov. 1 Dec. 1	Balance forward.. Burnham grinder... Air compressor.. Power lawnmower .... Lift truck battery... Rockwood saw... Electric spot welder...................................... Baking oven.. Baking oven..	$25,400 1,200 4,500 600 320 4,500 2,800 236	 $ 150
		$39,556	$ 150
Dec. 31	Balance...		39,406
		$39,556	$39,556

Your examination reveals the following information:

(a) The company uses a ten-year life for all machinery and equipment for depreciation purposes. Depreciation is computed by the straight-line method. Six months' depreciation is recorded in the year of acquisition or retirement. For 1977 the company recorded depreciation of $2,800 on machinery and equipment.

(b) The Burnham grinder was purchased for cash from a firm in financial distress. The chief engineer and a used machinery dealer agreed that the practically new machine was worth $2,100 in the open market.

(c) For production reasons the new air compressor was installed in a small building that was erected in 1977 to house the machine and will also be used for general storage. The cost of the building, which has a 25-year life, was $2,000 and is included in the $4,500 voucher for the air compressor.

(d) The power lawnmower was delivered to the home of the company president for personal use.

(e) On June 1 the battery in a battery-powered lift truck was accidentally damaged beyond repair. The damaged battery was included at a price of $600 in the $4,200 cost of the lift truck purchased on July 1, 1974. The company decided to rent a replacement battery rather than buy a new battery. The $320 expenditure is the annual rental for the battery paid in advance, net of a $40 allowance for the scrap value of the damaged battery that was returned to the battery company.

(f) The Rockwood saw sold on August 1 had been purchased on August 1, 1964, for $1,500. The saw was in use until it was sold.

(g) On September 1 the company determined that a production casting machine was no longer needed and advertised it for sale for $1,800 after determining from a used machinery dealer that this was its market value. The casting machine had been purchased for $5,000 on September 1, 1972.

(h) The company elected to exercise an option under a lease-purchase agreement to buy the electric spot welder. The welder had been installed on February 1, 1977, at a monthly rental of $100.

(i) On November 1 a baking oven was purchased for $10,000. A $2,800 down-payment was made and the balance will be paid in monthly installments over a three-year period. The December 1 payment includes interest charges of $36. Legal title to the oven will not pass to the company until the payments are completed.

Instructions: Prepare the auditor's adjusting journal entries required at December 31, 1977, for equipment and the related depreciation. (AICPA adapted)

12-13. You are engaged in the examination of the financial statements of the Ute Corp. for the year ended December 31, 1976. Schedules for the land, buildings, and equipment and related accumulated depreciation accounts have been prepared by the client and are shown on page 352. You have checked the opening balances to your prior year's audit working papers.

Assets

Description	Final 12/31/76	Additions	Retirements	Per Books 12/31/77
Land...	$ 22,500	$ 5,000		$ 27,500
Buildings.......................................	120,000	17,500		137,500
Machinery and equipment....................	385,000	40,400	$26,000	399,400
	$527,500	$62,900	$26,000	$564,400

Accumulated Depreciation

Description	Final 12/31/76	Additions*	Retirements	Per Books 12/31/77
Buildings...................................	$ 60,000	$ 5,150		$ 65,150
Machinery and equipment....................	173,250	39,220		212,470
	$233,250	$44,370		$277,620

*Depreciation expense for the year.

Your examination reveals the following information:

(a) All equipment is depreciated on the straight-line basis (no salvage value taken into consideration) based on the following estimated lives: buildings, 25 years; all other items, 10 years. The company's policy is to take one-half year's depreciation on all asset acquisitions and disposals during the year.

(b) On April 1, the company entered into a ten-year lease contract for a die casting machine with annual rentals of $5,000 payable in advance every April 1. The lease is cancelable by either party (sixty days written notice is required) and there is no option to renew the lease or buy the equipment at the end of the lease. The estimated useful life of the machine is ten years with no salvage value. The company recorded the die casting machine in the machinery and equipment account at $40,400, the present discounted value at the date of the lease, and $2,020 applicable to the machine has been included in depreciation expense for the year.

(c) The company completed the construction of a wing on the plant building on June 30. The useful life of the building was not extended by this addition. The lowest construction bid received was $17,500, the amount recorded in the buildings account. Company personnel were used to construct the addition at a cost of $16,000 (materials, $7,500; labor, $5,500; and overhead, $3,000).

(d) On August 18, $5,000 was paid for paving and fencing a portion of land owned by the company and used as a parking lot for employees. The expenditure was charged to the land account.

(e) The amount shown in the machinery and equipment asset retirement column represents cash received on September 5 upon disposal of a machine purchased in July, 1973, for $48,000. The bookkeeper recorded depreciation expense of $3,500 on this machine in 1977.

(f) Crux City donated land and building appraised at $10,000 and $40,000 respectively to the Ute Corporation for a plant. On September 1, the company began operating the plant. Since no costs were involved, the bookkeeper made no entry for the above transaction.

Instructions: Prepare the formal adjusting journal entries that you would suggest at December 31, 1977, to adjust the accounts for the above transactions. Disregard income tax implications. The books have not been closed. Computations should be rounded off to the nearest dollar. (AICPA adapted)

13

Intangible Assets

The term *intangible assets* is used in accounting to denote long-term property items not having physical characteristics. From a strictly legal point of view, such assets as shares of stock, bonds, and claims against customers may be regarded as intangibles. In accounting, however, the term is generally restricted in use to include such items as patents, copyrights, trademarks, franchises, leaseholds,[1] and goodwill.

Intangible assets derive their values by affording special rights or advantages expected to contribute to the earnings of a business. Special rights contributing to earnings may be found, for example, in the ownership of patents; special advantages contributing to earnings may arise from the skill of employees, the ability of management, the desirable location of a business, and good customer relationships — elements of a company's goodwill.

The intangible assets designation is perhaps unfortunate since it has contributed to a general misunderstanding of the nature of these assets and of their accounting treatment. Mere physical existence does not affect an item's economic significance. A factory building about to be razed may be reported on the balance sheet at little or no value despite its massive physical dimensions. On the other hand, a patent without physical qualities could be the most valuable property item owned by a company. Intangible assets, no less than tangible properties, require a full accounting.

VALUATION OF INTANGIBLE ASSETS AT TIME OF ACQUISITION

In general, valuation for intangible assets should follow the standards employed for tangible assets. Intangible assets should be recorded at cost. Cost should include all expenditures specifically related to the development or the purchase of the assets. When an intangible asset is

---

[1]The subject of leases is treated in Chapter 17.

acquired in exchange for an asset other than cash, the fair market value of the asset exchanged or that of the intangible asset, whichever is more clearly determinable, should be used to record the acquisition. When shares of stock or bonds are issued in exchange for an intangible asset, the fair market value of the securities issued or the intangible asset acquired should be used in recording the exchange. When several intangible assets or a combination of tangible and intangible assets are acquired for a lump sum, amounts must be allocated to the individual assets in some equitable manner, normally on the basis of the relative market values of the individual assets acquired.

Costs are reported for intangible assets only when expenditures can be specifically related to their acquisition. For example, no value should appear on the books for a franchise acquired without cost or for a company's goodwill developed internally over a period of years. But when an intangible asset without an accountable cost makes a significant contribution to the earnings of a business, reference on the balance sheet to this right or advantage by means of a special note is appropriate.

VALUATION OF INTANGIBLE ASSETS SUBSEQUENT TO THE TIME OF ACQUISITION

The subject of accounting for intangible assets subsequent to their acquisition has received wide attention. The costs of intangible assets have been charged off in many different ways. The process of assigning the costs of intangible assets to operations in a systematic manner is called *amortization*. Amortization is recorded by a debit to an expense account and a credit to the asset account or to an asset valuation account.

The terms of existence of certain intangible assets are limited by law, regulation, contract, or economic factors. The terms of existence of other intangible assets are not limited and the periods of their usefulness are indefinite or indeterminate. The cost of a limited-life intangible asset historically has been assigned to revenue according to an estimate of its useful economic life. The cost of an intangible asset having no limited term of existence and no indication of limited life at the time of acquisition has generally been carried forward until it appeared that any benefits would be of limited duration or that there was no longer any contribution to revenue. At that time, the cost of the asset either was assigned to revenue over the period of the remaining estimated life or was written off entirely.

In 1970 the Accounting Principles Board issued Opinion No. 17 on intangible assets, and made the following observation:

> Present accounting for goodwill and other unidentifiable intangible assets is often criticized because alternative methods of accounting for costs are acceptable. Some companies amortize the cost of acquired intangible assets over a short arbitrary period to reduce the amount of the asset as rapidly as practicable, while others retain the cost as an asset until evidence shows a loss of value and then record a material reduction in a single

period. Selecting an arbitrary period of amortization is criticized because it may understate net income during the amortization period and overstate later net income. Retaining the cost as an asset is criticized because it may overstate net income before the loss of value is recognized and understate net income in the period of write-off.[1]

In answer to criticisms of past practice, the Board established a maximum amortization period for all intangible assets. The Board reasoned that few, if any, intangible assets last forever; that those intangible assets with an indeterminate life, such as goodwill, should be amortized over a limited term because their usefulness will almost surely eventually disappear. Factors to be considered in estimating the useful lives of intangible assets include:

a. Legal, regulatory, or contractual provisions may limit the maximum useful life.
b. Provisions for renewal or extension may alter a specified limit on useful life.
c. Effects of obsolescence, demand, competition, and other economic factors may reduce a useful life.
d. A useful life may parallel the service life expectancies of individuals or groups of employees.
e. Expected actions of competitors and others may restrict present competitive advantages.
f. An apparently unlimited useful life may in fact be indefinite and benefits cannot be reasonably projected.
g. An intangible asset may be a composite of many individual factors with varying effective lives.[2]

Within these general guidelines for estimating a useful life for an intangible asset, the Board established a maximum amortization period of forty years. If analysis indicates that the life of an intangible asset is likely to exceed forty years, the cost of the asset should be amortized over the maximum forty-year period and not some arbitrary shorter period. The Board also concluded that the straight-line method of amortization should be applied unless it can be shown that another systematic method would be more appropriate.[3]

A company should evaluate periodically the estimated life selected for each intangible asset to determine whether current events or circumstances warrant a revision of the original estimated lives. When a change is indicated, the amortization plan may be modified as described earlier for tangible assets. Thus, a change in the period of usefulness of an intangible asset would be recognized by an increase or a decrease in the rate of amortization for the remainder of the asset life. When a revised life for an intangible asset is indicated, this should not exceed forty years from the original date of acquisition. Under some conditions, a significant reduction in the unamortized cost of an intangible asset may be warranted. If such reduction is material, it may be reported as a separate component of income from operations and disclosure made of the effects

---

[1]*Opinions of the Accounting Principles Board, No. 17,* "Intangible Assets" (New York: American Institute of Certified Public Accountants, 1970), par. 14.
[2]*Ibid.*, par. 27.
[3]*Ibid.*, par. 29 and 30.

of the transaction.[1] However, if periodic reviews are made of the estimated future benefits of recorded intangible assets, the need for recognizing these unusual write-offs would be minimized.

Intangible assets subject to amortization are reported on the balance sheet at unamortized cost or at original cost less accumulated amortization summarized in a valuation account. If an intangible asset is reported at a value other than cost, full information concerning the valuation should be provided. The periodic charge for amortization is reported as a manufacturing cost or as an operating expense depending upon the nature of the contribution made by the intangible asset.

Federal income tax regulations allow the taxpayer to write off the cost of an intangible asset by periodic charges when its term of existence is definitely limited in duration. Periodic deductions would be recognized for income tax purposes on patents, copyrights, licenses, franchises, and similar properties. Present income tax regulations do not allow a deduction for goodwill. However, upon the sale or termination of a business, a deduction would be allowed for the portion of goodwill not realized.[2]

Because of their relationship to certain intangible assets, research and development costs are discussed in the next section. Additional accounting problems related to specific intangibles are then discussed in the remaining sections of this chapter.

RESEARCH AND DEVELOPMENT COSTS

Enterprises often engage in research and development activities designed to discover new products or processes, or to improve existing ones. Historically, there has been considerable diversity in accounting for research and development (R & D) costs. Expenditures for general research have frequently been recorded as a part of regular manufacturing overhead, being regarded as a continuous cost of keeping abreast of current technological advances. On other occasions, especially when research was directed toward particular product improvements, research costs have been capitalized.

A major factor in the decision to capitalize or expense R & D costs is the extent to which current research costs can be identified with specific future benefits. If a current research expenditure has a definite causal relationship with identifiable future benefits, accounting theory would suggest capitalization. On the other hand, where no measurable cause and effect relationship can be determined, the current expensing of research costs is more appropriate.

---

[1] *Opinions of the Accounting Principles Board, No. 30*, "Reporting the Results of Operations — Reporting the Effects of Disposal of a Segment of a Business, and Extraordinary, Unusual and Infrequently Occuring Events and Transactions" (New York: American Institute of Certified Public Accountants, 1973), par. 26.

[2] The APB does not view the difference between accounting for goodwill for accounting purposes and for income tax purposes as a timing difference and hence observed that the allocation of income taxes under these circumstances is inappropriate. *Opinions of the Accounting Principles Board, No. 17, op. cit.*, par. 30.

In 1974, the Financial Accounting Standards Board issued a statement dealing specifically with the accounting treatment for research and development costs. The FASB recognized the need for more uniform treatment of costs relating to research and development activities. It also recognized the uncertainty of future benefits of research costs and the difficulty in measuring the cause and effect relationships of those costs. As a result, the FASB concluded that all costs associated with research and development activities should be debited to expense when incurred.[1]

As defined by the FASB in Statement No. 2, research and development costs include those costs of materials, personnel, purchased intangibles, contract services, and a reasonable allocation of indirect costs which are specifically related to research and development activities and which have no alternative future uses.[2] Such activities include:

1. Laboratory research aimed at discovery of new knowledge.
2. Searching for applications of new research findings or other knowledge.
3. Conceptual formulation and design of possible product or process alternatives.
4. Testing in search for or evaluation of product or process alternatives.
5. Modification of the formulation or design of a product or process.
6. Design, construction, and testing of pre-production prototypes and models.
7. Design of tools, jigs, molds, and dies involving new technology.
8. Design, construction, and operation of a pilot plant that is not of a scale economically feasible to the enterprise for commercial production.
9. Engineering activity required to advance the design of a product to the point that it meets specific functional and economic requirements and is ready for manufacture.[3]

The recognition of research and development costs as current period expenses modifies the accounting treatment given certain intangibles, e.g., patents, as explained in later sections.

IDENTIFIABLE INTANGIBLE ASSETS

Intangible assets may be divided between those assets identified with a specific right or type of activity, and those assets not specifically identified but which are regarded as related to the enterprise as a whole. The latter are generally lumped together and designated as *goodwill*. Managements involved in the purchase of a company carefully value all tangible assets as well as all identifiable intangible assets. An amount paid on the purchase of a company exceeding the sum of identifiable net assets is normally recorded as goodwill.

Patents   A *patent* is an exclusive right granted by the government to an inventor enabling the inventor to control the manufacture, sale, or other use of

---

[1]*Statement of Financial Accounting Standards No. 2*, "Accounting for Research and Development Costs" (Stamford, Conn.: Financial Accounting Standards Board, 1974), par. 12.
[2]*Ibid.*, par. 11.
[3]*Ibid.*, par. 9.

the invention for a specified period of time. The United States Patent Office issues patents which are valid for seventeen years from the date of issuance. Patents are not renewable although effective control of an invention is frequently maintained beyond the expiration of the original patent through new patents covering improvements or changes. The owner of a patent may grant its use to others under royalty agreements or the patent may be sold.

The issuance of a patent does not necessarily indicate the existence of a valuable right. The value of a patent stems from whatever advantage it might afford its owner in excluding competitors from utilizing a process resulting in lower costs or superior products. Many patents cover inventions that cannot be exploited commercially and may actually be worthless.

Patents are recorded at their acquisition costs. When a patent is purchased, it is recorded at the new owner's purchase price. When a patent is developed through company-sponsored research, the accounting treatment falls under FASB Statement No. 2 described previously. Only patent licensing and related legal fees are included as its costs. All related experimental and developmental expenditures, along with the cost of models and drawings not required by the patent application, are considered research and development costs and are to be debited to expense when incurred.[1]

The validity of a patent may be challenged in the courts. The cost of successfully prosecuting or defending infringement suits is regarded as a cost of establishing the legal rights of the holder and may be added to the other costs of the patent. In the event of unsuccessful litigation, the litigation cost, as well as other patent costs, should be written off as a loss.

Patent costs should be amortized over the useful life of the patent. The legal life of a patent is used for amortization only when the patent is expected to provide benefits during its full legal life. The economic or useful life of a patent is usually much shorter than its legal life because of obsolescence. New and more efficient inventions or changes in demand for certain products may result in loss of patent value; processes developed by competitors sufficiently different to qualify as new inventions, yet so similar to a company's own process as to destroy the economic advantages enjoyed through patent protection, may also result in the loss of patent value. In some instances, the useful life of a patent is expressed in terms of productive output rather than in years, and cost is assigned to operations on the basis of units produced.

The classification of the charge for patent amortization depends upon the nature and the use of the patent. A charge for a patent used in the manufacturing process would be recognized as a manufacturing cost. A charge for a patent used in shipping department activities would be recognized as a selling expense.

---

[1]*Ibid*., par. 10(i).

Copyrights   *Copyrights* are exclusive rights granted by the federal government permitting an author or an artist to publish, sell, or otherwise control literary, musical, or artistic works. The right to exclusive control is issued for a period of twenty-eight years with the privilege of renewal for another twenty-eight years. Copyrights, like patents, may be licensed to others or sold.

The cost assigned to a copyright consists of those charges required to establish the right. When a copyright is purchased, the copyright is recorded at its purchase price.

The useful life of a copyright is generally considerably less than its legal life. The cost of a copyright may be amortized over the number of years in which sales or royalties can be expected, or cost may be assigned in terms of the estimated sales units relating to such rights.

Franchises   A *franchise* is a contract, often between a governmental unit and a private company, giving the latter exclusive rights to perform certain functions or to sell certain products or services. The rights may be granted for a specified number of years or in perpetuity; in certain instances, the rights may be revoked by the grantor.

The cost of a franchise includes any sum paid specifically for a franchise as well as legal fees and other costs incurred in obtaining it. Although the value of a franchise at the time of its acquisition may be substantially in excess of its cost, the amount recorded should be limited to actual outlays. When a franchise is purchased from another company, the amount paid is recorded as the franchise cost.

When a franchise has a limited life, its cost should be amortized over that limited life. When the life of a franchise can be terminated at the option of the granting authority, the cost is best amortized over a relatively short period. The cost of a perpetual franchise appearing to be of continuing economic value should be amortized over a period of forty years.

A franchise may require that periodic payments be made to the grantor. Payments may be fixed amounts or they may be variable amounts depending upon revenue, utilization, or other factors. These payments should be recognized as charges to periodic revenue. When certain property improvements are required under terms of the franchise, the costs of the improvements should be capitalized and charged to revenue over the life of the franchise.

Trademarks and Trade Names   *Trademarks* and *trade names*, together with distinctive symbols, labels, and designs, are important to all companies that depend upon a public demand for their products. It is by means of these distinctive markings that particular products are differentiated from competing brands. In building up the reputation of a product, relatively large costs may be involved. The federal government offers legal protection for trademarks through their registry with the United States Patent Office.

Prior and continuous use is the important factor in determining the ownership of a particular trademark. The right to a trademark is retained as long as continuous use is made of it. Protection of trade names and brands that cannot be registered must be sought in the common law. Distinctive trademarks, trade names, and brands can be assigned or sold.

The cost assigned to a trademark consists of those expenditures required to establish it, including filing and registry fees, and expenditures for successful litigation in defense of the trademark. When a trademark is purchased, it is recorded at its purchase price.

Even though the legal life of a trademark is not limited, the trademark cost is frequently amortized over a relatively short period on the theory that changes in consumer demand may limit its usefulness.

Organization Costs

In forming a corporation, certain expenditures are incurred including legal fees, promotional costs, stock certificate costs, underwriting costs, and incorporation fees. The benefits to be derived from these expenditures normally extend beyond the first fiscal period. Further, the recognition of these expenditures as expenses at the time of organization would commit the corporation to a deficit before it actually begins operations. These factors support the practice of recognizing the initial costs of organization as an intangible asset.

Expenditures relating to organization may be considered to benefit the corporation during its entire life. Thus, when the life of a company is not limited, there is theoretical support for carrying organization costs as an intangible asset for the maximum period of forty years. On the other hand, it may be argued that the organizational and start-up costs of a business are of primary benefit during the first few years of operation. Beyond that point, these costs generally become insignificant in terms of impact on the success or failure of the enterprise. In addition, newly organized corporations are permitted to amortize their organization costs for tax purposes fairly quickly. The amortization period allowed can be as short as five years. These reasons have led to the widespread practice of writing off organization costs within a relatively short period, generally five years, from the date of corporate organization.

It is sometimes suggested that operating losses of the first few years should be capitalized as organization costs or as goodwill. It is argued that the losses cannot be avoided in the early years when the business is being developed, and hence it is reasonable that these losses should be absorbed in later years. Although losses may be inevitable, they do not necessarily carry any future service potential. To report these losses as intangible assets would result in the overstatement of assets and owners' equity. This practice cannot be condoned.

A related question deals with so-called development stage companies which are trying to establish a new business. In order to clarify the accounting and reporting practices for developmental stage enterprises, the FASB issued *Statement of Financial Accounting Standards No. 7*. The FASB concluded that the accounting practices and reporting standards for developmental stage companies should be no different than for other companies. The same set of generally accepted accounting principles should govern the recognition of revenues and the determination of costs as expenses or assets for both developmental stage enterprises and established operating enterprises.[1]

GOODWILL

Goodwill is generally regarded as the summation of all the special advantages, not otherwise identifiable, related to a going concern. It includes such items as a good name, capable staff and personnel, high credit standing, reputation for superior products and services, and favorable location. Unlike most other assets, tangible or intangible, goodwill cannot be transferred without transferring the entire business.

From an accounting point of view, goodwill is recognized as the ability of a business to earn above-normal earnings with the identifiable assets employed in the business. Above-normal earnings mean a rate of return greater than that normally required to attract investors into a particular type of business.

Valuation of Goodwill
Goodwill is recorded on the books only when it is acquired by purchase or otherwise established through a business transaction. The latter condition includes its recognition in connection with a merger or a reorganization of a corporation, a purchase or a partial purchase of a business, or a change of partners in a partnership. Recognition only under these circumstances assures an objective approach to the valuation of goodwill. To permit the recognition of goodwill on the basis of judgment and estimates by owners and other interested parties would encourage abuse and misrepresentation. Goodwill reported on the balance sheet arises from a purchase or a contractual arrangement calling for its recognition.

In the purchase of a going business, the actual price to be paid for goodwill usually results from bargaining and compromises between the parties concerned. A basis for negotiation in arriving at a price for goodwill normally involves the following steps:

1. Projection of the level of future earnings.
2. Determination of an appropriate rate of return.
3. Current valuation of the net business assets other than goodwill.
4. Use of projected future earnings and rate of return in developing a value for goodwill.

Projection of the Level of Future Earnings. Past earnings ordinarily offer the best basis upon which to develop a specific value for goodwill. However, it is not these past earnings but projected future earnings that are being purchased. In considering past earnings as a basis for projection

---

[1]*Statement of Financial Accounting Standards No. 7,* "Accounting and Reporting by Development Stage Enterprises" (Stamford, Conn.: Financial Accounting Standards Board, 1975), par. 10.

into the future, reference should be made to earnings most recently experienced. A sufficient number of periods should be included in the analysis so a representative measurement of business performance is available.

In certain instances, it may be considered necessary to restate revenue and expense balances to give effect to alternative depreciation or amortization methods, inventory methods, or other measurement processes considered desirable in summarizing past operations. Unusual or infrequently occuring and extraordinary gains and losses which cannot be considered a part of normal activities would be excluded from past operating results. Depending on the circumstances, these items may include gains and losses from the sale of investments and land, buildings, and equipment, gains and losses from the retirement of debt, and losses from casualties.

The normal earnings from operations should be analyzed to determine their trend and stability. If earnings over a period of years show a tendency to decline, careful analysis is necessary to determine whether this decline may be expected to continue. There may be greater confidence in possible future earnings when past earnings have been relatively stable rather than when widely fluctuating.

Any changes in the operations of the business which may be anticipated after the transfer of ownership should also be considered. The elimination of a division, the disposal of substantial property items, or the retirement of long-term debt, for example, could materially affect future earnings.

The normal earnings of the past are used as a basis for estimating earnings of the future. Business conditions, the business cycle, sources of supply, demand for the company's products or services, price structure, competition, and other significant factors must be studied in developing data making it possible to convert past earnings into estimated future earnings.

Determination of an Appropriate Rate of Return. The existence of above-normal earnings, if any, can be determined only by reference to a normal rate of return. The *normal earnings rate* is that which would ordinarily be required to attract investors in the particular type of business being acquired. In judging this rate, consideration must be given to such factors as money rates, business conditions at the time of the purchase, competitive factors, risks involved, entrepreneurial abilities required, and alternative investment opportunities.

In general, the greater the risk entailed in an investment, the higher the rate of return required. Because most business enterprises are subject to a considerable amount of risk, investors generally expect a relatively high rate of return to justify their investment. A long history of stable earnings or the existence of certain tangible assets that can be easily sold reduce the degree of risk in acquiring a business and thus reduce the rate of return required by a potential investor.

If goodwill is to be purchased, it should be looked upon as an investment and must offer the prospect of sufficient return to justify the commitment. Special risks are associated with goodwill. The value of goodwill is uncertain and fluctuating. It cannot be separated from the business as a whole and sold, as can most other business properties. Furthermore, it is subject to rapid deterioration and may be totally lost in the event of business sale or liquidation. As a result, a higher rate of return would normally be required on the purchase of goodwill than on the purchase of other business properties.

Current Valuation of Net Business Assets Other than Goodwill. Because goodwill is associated with the earnings that cannot be attributed to a normal return on identifiable assets, the ultimate evaluation of goodwill depends upon the valuation of those identified business properties. In appraising properties for this purpose, current market values should be sought rather than the values reported in the accounts. Receivables should be stated at amounts estimated to be realized. Inventories and securities should be restated in terms of current market values. Land, buildings, and equipment items may require special appraisals in arriving at their present replacement or reproduction values. Intangible assets, such as patents and franchises, should be included at their current values even though, originally, expenditures were reported as expenses or were reported as assets and amortized against revenue. Care should be taken to determine that liabilities are fully recognized. Assets at their current fair market values less the liabilities to be assumed provide the net assets total that, together with estimated future earnings, is used in arriving at a purchase price.

Use of Projected Future Earnings and Rate of Return in Developing a Value for Goodwill. A number of methods may be employed in arriving at a goodwill figure. Several of these will be described. Assume the following information for Company A:

Net earnings after adjustment and elimination of unusual and extraordinary items:

1973	$140,000
1974	90,000
1975	110,000
1976	85,000
1977	115,000
Total	$540,000

Average net earnings 1973–1977: $540,000 ÷ 5 = $108,000.
Estimated future net earnings, $100,000.
Net assets as appraised on January 2, 1978, before recognizing goodwill, $1,000,000. (Land, buildings, equipment, inventories, and receivables, $1,200,000; liabilities to be assumed by purchaser, $200,000.)

The average net earnings figure of $108,000 for the five-year period 1973–1977 was used in arriving at an estimate of the probable future net earnings. It is assumed the prospective buyer after analyzing the assembled data concludes future earnings may reasonably be estimated at $100,000 a year.

Capitalization of Average Net Earnings. The amount to be paid for a business may be determined by capitalizing expected future earnings at a rate representing the required return on the investment. Capitalization of earnings, as used in this sense, means calculation of the principal value that will yield the stated earnings at the specified rate. This is accomplished by dividing the earnings by the specified rate.[1] The difference between the amount to be paid for the business as thus obtained and the appraised values of the individual property items may be considered the price paid for goodwill.

If, in the example, a return of 8% were required on the investment and earnings were estimated at $100,000 per year, the business would be valued at $1,250,000 ($100,000 ÷ .08). Since net assets, with the exception of goodwill, were appraised at $1,000,000, goodwill would be valued at $250,000. If a 10% return were required on the investment, the business would be worth only $1,000,000. In acquiring the business for $1,000,000, there would be no payment for goodwill.

Capitalization of Average Excess Net Earnings. In the above method, a single rate of return was applied to the earnings in arriving at the value of the business. No consideration was given to the extent the earnings were attributable to net identifiable assets and the extent the earnings were attributable to goodwill. It would seem reasonable, however, to expect a higher return on an investment in goodwill than on the other assets acquired. To illustrate, assume the following facts:

	Company A	Company B
Net assets as appraised	$1,000,000	$500,000
Estimated future net earnings	100,000	100,000

If the estimated earnings are capitalized at a uniform rate of 8%, the value of each company is found to be $1,250,000. The goodwill for Company A is then $250,000, and for Company B, $750,000 as shown:

	Company A	Company B
Total net asset valuation (earnings capitalized at 8%)	$1,250,000	$1,250,000
Deduct net assets as appraised	1,000,000	500,000
Goodwill	$ 250,000	$ 750,000

These calculations ignore the fact that the appraised value of the net assets identified with Company A exceed those of Company B. Company A, whose earnings of $100,000 are accompanied by net assets valued at $1,000,000, would certainly command a higher price than Company B, whose earnings of $100,000 are accompanied by net assets valued at only $500,000.

Satisfactory recognition of both earnings and asset contributions is generally effected by (1) requiring a fair return on identifiable net assets,

---

[1]This may be shown as follows: P = principal amount or the capitalized earnings to be computed; r = the specified rate of return; E = expected annual earnings. Then, E = P × r, and P = E ÷ r.

and (2) viewing any excess earnings as attributable to goodwill and capitalizing the excess at a higher rate in recognition of the degree of risk that characterizes goodwill. To illustrate, assume in the previous cases that 8% is considered a normal return on identifiable net assets and that excess earnings are capitalized at 20% in determining the amount to be paid for goodwill. Amounts to be paid for Companies A and B would be calculated as follows:

	Company A	Company B
Estimated net earnings..	$ 100,000	$ 100,000
Normal return on net assets:		
Company A — 8% of $1,000,000...........................	80,000	
Company B — 8% of $ 500,000		40,000
Excess net earnings...	$ 20,000	$ 60,000
Excess net earnings capitalized at 20%....................	÷ .20	÷ .20
Value of goodwill	$ 100,000	$ 300,000

	Company A	Company B
Value of net assets offering normal return of 8%.....	$1,000,000	$ 500,000
Value of goodwill, excess net earnings capitalized		
at 20%...	100,000	300,000
Total net asset valuation..	$1,100,000	$ 800,000

Number of Years' Purchase. Behind each of the capitalization methods just described, there is an implicit assumption that the superior earning power attributed to the existence of goodwill will continue indefinitely. The very nature of goodwill, however, makes it subject to rapid decline. A business with unusually high earnings may expect the competition from other companies to reduce earnings over a period of years. Furthermore, the high levels of earnings may frequently be maintained only by special efforts on the part of the new owners, and they cannot be expected to pay for something they themselves must achieve.

As the goodwill being purchased cannot be expected to last beyond a specific number of years, one frequently finds payment for excess earnings stated in terms of *years' purchase* rather than capitalization in perpetuity.[1] For example, if excess annual earnings of $20,000 are expected and payment is to be made for excess earnings for a five-year period, the purchase price for goodwill would be $100,000. If the excess annual earnings are expected to be $60,000 and the payment is to be made for four years' excess earnings, the price for goodwill would be $240,000.

The years' purchase method has the advantage of conceptual simplicity. It is related to the common business practice of evaluating investment opportunities in terms of their *payback period* — the number of years expected for recovery of the initial investment.

---

[1]Calculation of goodwill in terms of number of years' purchase will yield results identical to the capitalization method when the number of years used is equal to the reciprocal of the capitalization rate. Payment for five years' earnings, for example, is equivalent to capitalizing earnings at a 20% rate $(1 \div .20 = 5)$. Payment of four years' earnings is equivalent to capitalization at a 25% rate $(1 \div .25 = 4)$.

Present Value Method. The concept of number of years' purchase can be combined with the concept of a rate of return on investment. Excess earnings can be expected to continue for only a limited number of years, but an investment in these earnings should provide an adequate return, considering the risks involved. The amount to be paid for goodwill, then, is the discounted or present value of the excess earnings amounts expected to become available in future periods.

To illustrate the calculation of goodwill by the present value method, assume the earnings of Company A exceed a normal return on the net identifiable assets used in the business by $20,000 per year. These excess earnings are expected to continue for a period of five years, and a return of 8% is considered necessary to attract investors in this industry. The amount to be paid for goodwill, then, may be regarded as the discounted value at 8% of five installments of $20,000 to be received at annual intervals. Present value tables may be used in determining the present value of the series of payments. The present value of 5 annual payments of $1 each, to provide a return of 8%, is found to be 3.9927.[1] The present value of five payments of $20,000 each would then be calculated as $20,000 × 3.9927 = $79,854.

It may be noted that the calculation of goodwill by the present value method, using a five-year period and an 8% return, produced approximately the same result as would have been obtained by purchasing four years' excess earnings, or by capitalizing these earnings at 25%. The principal advantage of the present value method is the explicit recognition of the anticipated duration of excess earnings together with the use of a realistic rate of return. Thus it focuses on the factors most relevant to the goodwill evaluation.

Implied Goodwill   When a lump sum amount is paid for an established business and no explicit evaluation is made of goodwill as illustrated in the preceding section, goodwill may still be recognized. In this case the identifiable net assets require appraisal, and the difference between the full purchase price and the value of identifiable net assets can be attributed to the purchase of goodwill.

Failure to recognize the payment for goodwill separately may result in attaching this cost to identifiable assets and thus result in their overvaluation. If this cost is attributed to depreciable assets, the periodic depreciation charges and net income, as well as financial position, may then be misstated.

When capital stock is issued in exchange for a business, the value of the stock determines the consideration paid for the assets. Care must be exercised so that what in effect represents a discount on the stock is not reported as goodwill. For example, assume a company exchanges 100,000 shares of common stock, par $10, selling on the market at 7½, for a business with assets appraised at $800,000 and liabilities of $200,000. The acquisition should be recorded as follows:

---

[1]See Appendix A Table IV on page 840.

Assets..	800,000	
Goodwill..	150,000	
Discount on Common Stock..	250,000	
Liabilities..		200,000
Common Stock, $10 par..		1,000,000

If the discount is not recognized and goodwill is established at $400,000, both assets and paid-in capital will be misstated.

The entry given above recognizes the exchange as a *purchase*. Not all exchanges are recognized in this manner. As indicated in an earlier chapter, under certain conditions the issuance of stock in exchange for the owners' equity in the net assets of a company is recognized as a *pooling of interests*. In applying this concept, the company issuing the stock reports the net asset balances at the same amounts previously reported. No changes to reflect current market values for property items are made and no additional intangible assets are recognized. The increase in net assets is accompanied by an increase in the stockholders' equity, and in certain instances this increase is recorded in the invested capital and retained earnings accounts at the same amounts previously reported. The Accounting Principles Board has been concerned that the pooling of interests method might not be fair and realistic in its application to certain combinations, and in Opinion No. 16, "Business Combinations," it established definite guidelines to govern the use of this method. [1]

Adjustment of Goodwill after Acquisition

The amortization of goodwill, as well as of all other intangible assets, is now governed by APB Opinion No. 17. As indicated earlier in this chapter, a maximum period of forty years is used in the amortization of all intangible assets, including goodwill. In some cases goodwill may be considered to have a measurable life less than forty years and the amortization period selected can be based upon this life.

Some accountants have suggested that goodwill should be written off immediately after acquisition. Justification for this action is given as follows:

1. Goodwill is not a resource or property right that is consumed or utilized in the production of earnings. It is the result of expectations of future earnings by investors and thus is not subject to normal amortization procedures.
2. Goodwill is subject to sudden and wide fluctuations. That value has no reliable or continuing relation to costs incurred in its creation.
3. Under existing practices of accounting, neither the cost nor the value of nonpurchased goodwill is reported in the balance sheet. Purchased goodwill has no continuing, separately measurable existence after the combination and is merged with the total goodwill value of the continuing business entity. As such, its write-off cannot be measured with any validity.
4. Goodwill as an asset account is not relevant to an investor. Most analysts ignore any reported goodwill when analyzing a company's status and operations. [2]

---

[1] The subject of business combinations, including accounting by the pooling of interests method, is discussed fully in *Advanced Accounting* by Simons and Karrenbrock.

[2] George R. Catlett and Norman O. Olson, *Accounting for Goodwill*, Accounting Research Study No. 10 (New York: American Institute of Certified Public Accountants, 1968). The authors of this research study recommended the write-off of goodwill immediately upon acquisition.

This position has consistently been rejected by the committees of the AICPA, and the lump-sum write-off of goodwill and other intangible assets is strongly discouraged. In opposing the arbitrary write-off of goodwill or any other intangible asset, it can be maintained that asset and owners' equity balances are misstated and the ratio of earnings to owners' equity is distorted. Earnings thus appear to be more favorable than is actually the case as a result of this conservative practice.

INTANGIBLE ASSETS ON THE BALANCE SHEET

When a single long-term asset classification is given on the balance sheet, tangible and intangible asset subheadings should be provided and summaries developed for each group. When separate classifications are given for tangible and intangible assets, the intangible asset classification usually follows the tangible asset classifications. Each intangible asset should be listed separately. If an intangible asset has been acquired for consideration other than cash, disclosure should be made of the properties or securities exchanged and the data used in arriving at the original cost assigned to the asset. Disclosure should also be made of the valuation procedures employed for intangible assets subsequent to their acquisition.

Intangible assets as they might appear on the balance sheet follow:

Intangible assets:		
Goodwill, at cost less amortization on 25-year basis	$220,000	
Licenses, at costs less amortization based on estimated useful lives..	18,000	
Patents, acquired through issue of 12,000 shares of common stock with a market value of $12.50 per share and reported at such value, less amortization based on an estimated useful life of 10 years	107,500	$345,500

QUESTIONS

1. What are the characteristics that distinguish intangible assets from tangible assets?

2. How would a trademark worth $5,000,000 be reported on the balance sheet if (a) the trademark were purchased for $5,000,000 or (b) the trademark gradually became identified over the years as a company symbol?

3. What factors should be considered in estimating the useful lives of intangible assets?

4. What types of activities are considered research and development activities?

5. How are identifiable intangible assets more similar to tangible assets than to the intangible asset, goodwill?

6. (a) What items enter into the cost of a patent developed by a business? (b) What factors should be considered in establishing a schedule for amortization of patent cost?

7. What costs are capitalized as (a) copyrights, (b) franchises, (c) trademarks?

8. How should the following assets be amortized: (a) copyrights; (b) franchises; (c) trademarks; (d) organization costs?

9. (a) What items are normally considered to compose the organization costs of a company? (b) Would you approve the inclusion of the following items: (1) common stock discount; (2) first-year advertising costs; (3) first-year loss from operations?

10. How should development stage enterprises report (a) their organization costs and (b) any net operating losses?

11. (a) Under what conditions may goodwill be reported as an asset? (b) The Radcliff Company engages in a widespread advertising campaign on behalf of new products, charging above-normal expenditures to goodwill. Do you approve of this practice? Why or why not?

12. What factors should be considered in estimating the future earnings of a business in order to develop a fair valuation of goodwill?

13. Give four methods for arriving at a goodwill valuation, using estimated future earnings as a basis for these calculations. Which method do you think would give the most relevant valuation of goodwill?

14. The transactions that result in recording goodwill are primarily related to the acquisition and merger of companies. Describe an accounting method for recording such mergers that has eliminated the need for recognizing goodwill.

15. Wells, Inc., has valuable patent rights that are being amortized over their legal lives. The president of the company believes these pat-

ents are contributing substantially to company goodwill and recommends patent amortization be capitalized as company goodwill. What is your opinion of this proposal?

16. What are the major arguments for writing off goodwill immediately after acquisition? What effect would an immediate write-off of goodwill have on a company's ratio of earnings to owners' equity?

17. The Reno Corporation purchased the Stardust Club for $500,000 which included $100,000 for goodwill. Reno Corporation incurs large promotional and advertising expenses to maintain Stardust Club's popularity. The Reno Corporation controller feels that amortization of the purchased goodwill in the same periods that heavy expenses are incurred to maintain the goodwill in effect creates a double charge against income of the period. Do you agree?

EXERCISES

1. The Beacon Corporation purchased land, a building, and a franchise for the lump sum of $150,000. A real estate appraiser estimated the building to have a resale value of $90,000 (75% of the total worth of the land and building). The franchise had no established resale value.

The estimated useful life of the franchise on the acquisition date was 20 years. After 15 years, Beacon Corporation management decided that the franchise would be of economic value for an additional 30 years.

    (a) Give the journal entry to record the acquisition of the assets.
    (b) Give the journal entry to record the amortization of the franchise in the sixteenth year, assuming straight-line amortization.

2. The Qualis Co. applied for and received numerous patents at a total cost of $14,450 at the beginning of 1972. It is assumed the patents will be useful during their full legal life. At the beginning of 1974, the company paid $3,750 in successfully prosecuting an attempted infringement of these patent rights. At the beginning of 1977, $12,000 was paid to acquire patents that could make its own patents worthless: the patents acquired have a remaining life of 15 years but will not be used.

    (a) Give the entries to record the expenditures relative to patents.
    (b) Give the entries to record patent amortization for the years 1972, 1974, and 1977.

3. Flex Corporation acquired the following assets at the beginning of 1977. (1) Give the entries to record the acquisition of the assets. (2) Give the entries for the amortization for 1977, if any. (3) In each case justify the useful life estimated.

    (a) Paperback copyright to a best-seller novel in exchange for 240 shares of Flex Corporation stock; $50 par, common stock selling for $224 per share. The copyright has a 28-year legal life. Paperback sales of the novel are estimated to be 500,000 copies in 1977, 300,000 in 1978, 100,000 in 1979, 20,000 in 1980, and no sales thereafter.
    (b) A fast foods franchise in exchange for one acre of prime real estate. Franchises of this type are selling for $100,000 cash. The land was purchased 10 years ago for $5,000. The franchise has an unlimited life as long as Flex Corporation maintains the quality standards of the grantor.
    (c) Enoc Enterprises for $425,000 cash. Net identifiable assets of Enoc Enterprises are fairly valued at $375,000. The purchased goodwill is expected to grow every year as Flex Corporation plans to expend substantial resources for advertising and other promotional activities.

4. (1) Which of the following activities of the All-World Aerodynamics Corporation would be considered research and development activities?

(a) Testing of electronic instrument components during their production.
(b) Development of a new, more efficient wing design.
(c) Construction of a prototype for a new jet model.
(d) Start-up activities for the production of a newly developed jet.
(e) Study of the possible uses of a newly developed fuel.

(2) Which of the following costs are considered research and development costs of the *current period*?

(a) The portion of the president's salary allocable to research and development activities.
(b) The cost of a market research study.
(c) Costs of a pension plan for employees engaged in research and development activities.
(d) Current period depreciation taken on the company's laboratory research facilities.

5. The Bronco Mfg. Co. was incorporated on January 1, 1977. In reviewing the accounts in 1978, you find the organization costs account appears as follows:

ACCOUNT Organization Costs

ITEM	DEBIT	CREDIT	BALANCE DEBIT	BALANCE CREDIT
Discount on common stock issued	62,400		62,400	
Incorporation fees............................	2,500		64,900	
Legal fees relative to organization .	14,100		79,000	
Stock certificate cost......................	4,000		83,000	
Cost of rehabilitating building acquired at beginning of 1977 and estimated to have a remaining life of 10 years...............................	48,000		131,000	
Advertising expenditures to promote company products.............	12,000		143,000	
Amortization of organization costs for 1977, 20% of balance of organization cost (per board of director's resolution)....................		28,600	114,400	
Net loss for 1977.............................	36,000		150,400	

Give the entry or entries required to correct the account.

6. In analyzing the accounts of Oliver's, Inc., in an attempt to measure goodwill, you find pretax earnings of $200,000 for 1977 after debits and credits for the items listed below. Land, buildings, and equipment are appraised at 50% above cost for purposes of the sale.

Depreciation of land, buildings, and equipment (at cost)......................................	$30,000
Special year-end bonus to president of company	10,000
Gain on sale of securities...	18,000
Gain on revaluation of securities	6,000
Write-off of goodwill...	60,000
Amortization of patents and leaseholds	25,000
Income tax refund for 1975..	8,000

What is the normal pretax earnings balance for purposes of your calculations?

7. The appraised value of net assets of the Cassidy Co. on December 31, 1977, was $100,000. Average net earnings for the past 5 years after elimination of unusual or extraordinary gains and losses were $16,500. Calculate the amount to be paid for goodwill under each assumption given below and at the top of the next page:

(a) Earnings are capitalized at 15% in arriving at the business worth.
(b) A return of 9% is considered normal on net assets at their appraised value; excess earnings are to be capitalized at 15% in arriving at the value of goodwill.
(c) A return of 12% is considered normal on net assets at their appraised value; goodwill is to be valued at 5 years' excess earnings.

(d) A return of 10% is considered normal on net identifiable assets at their appraised value. Excess earnings are expected to continue for 6 years. Goodwill is to be valued by the present value method using a rate of 12%. (Use present value table in Appendix A.)

8. Because of superior earning power, Hanks & Co. is considering paying $301,915 for the Gage Proprietorship with the following assets and liabilities:

	Cost	Fair Market Value
Accounts receivable..	$120,000	$110,000
Inventory	70,000	75,000
Prepaid insurance	5,000	5,000
Buildings & equipment (net)...........................	85,000	150,000
Accounts payable..	(80,000)	(80,000)
Net assets..	$200,000	$260,000

Estimated future earnings are expected to exceed normal earnings by $13,800 for four years. Hanks & Co. uses the present value method of valuing goodwill. Hanks is willing to purchase Gage if the normal rate of return for Gage exceeds 10%. Should Hanks & Co. purchase Gage Proprietorship? (Use present value table in Appendix A.)

PROBLEMS

13-1. On January 10, 1969, the Banks Company spent $12,000 to apply for and obtain a patent on a newly developed product. The patent had an estimated useful life of 10 years. At the beginning of 1973, the company spent $9,000 in successfully prosecuting an attempted infringement of the patent. At the beginning of 1974, the company purchased for $25,000 a patent that was expected to prolong the life of its original patent by 5 years. On July 1, 1977, a competitor obtained rights to a patent which made the company's patent obsolete.

> **Instructions:** Give all of the entries that would be made relative to the patent for the period 1969–1977, including entries to record the purchase of the patent, annual patent amortization, and ultimate patent obsolescence. (Assume the company's accounting period is the calendar year.)

13-2. In your audit of the books of Flagg Corporation for the year ending September 30, 1977, you found the following items in connection with the company's patents account:

> (a) The company had spent $102,000 during its fiscal year ended September 30, 1976, for research and development costs and debited this amount to its patents account. Your review of the company's cost records indicated the company had spent a total of $123,500 for the research and development of its patents, of which only $21,500 spent in its fiscal year ended September 30, 1975, had been debited to Research and Development Expense.
> (b) The patents were issued on April 1, 1976. Legal expenses in connection with the issuance of the patents of $14,280 were debited to Legal and Professional Fees.
> (c) The company paid a retainer of $7,500 on October 5, 1976, for legal services in connection with an infringement suit brought against it. This amount was debited to Deferred Costs.
> (d) A letter dated October 15, 1977, from the company's attorneys in reply to your inquiry as to liabilities of the company existing at September 30, 1977, indicated that a settlement of the infringement suit had been arranged. The other party had agreed to drop the suit and to release the company from all future liabilities for $16,000. Additional fees due to the attorneys amounted to $590.
> (e) The balance of the patents account on September 30, 1977, was $96,000. No amortization had been recognized on the patents for the fiscal year ended September 30, 1977.

(continued)

Instructions:
(1) From the information given, prepare correcting journal entries as of September 30, 1977. (Assume an estimated life for the patents of 17 years from date of issuance.)
(2) Give the entry to record amortization on patents for the year ended September 30, 1977.

13-3. Transactions during 1977 of the newly organized Brook Corporation included the following:

Jan. 2 Paid legal fees of $5,000 and stock certificate costs of $1,600 to complete organization of the corporation. Organization costs will be amortized over the maximum period allowable.

     15 Hired a clown to stand in front of the corporate office for two weeks and hand out pamphlets and candy to create goodwill for the new enterprise. Clown cost $800; candy and pamphlets, $500.

Apr. 1 Patented a newly developed process with the following costs:

Legal fees to obtain patent	$11,200
Patent application and licensing fees	400
Total	$11,600

It is estimated that in five years other companies will have developed improved processes making the Brook Corporation process obsolete.

May 1 Acquired both a license to use a special type of container and a distinctive trademark to be printed on the container in exchange for 600 shares of Brook Corporation common stock selling for $80 per share. The license is worth twice as much as the trademark, both of which may be used for 6 years.

July 1 Constructed a shed for $50,000 to house prototypes of experimental models to be developed in future research projects. The shed has a 10-year life and will be depreciated on a straight-line basis.

Dec. 31 Salaries for an engineer and a chemist involved in product development totaled $75,000 in 1977.

     31 Amortized all intangible assets. Brook Corporation takes a full year's amortization in the year of acquisition of intangible assets.

Instructions:
(1) Give journal entries to record the foregoing transactions. (Give explanations in support of your entries.)
(2) Present in good form the "Intangible assets" section of the Brook Corporation balance sheet at December 31, 1977.

13-4. The Aurora Corp. in considering acquisition of the Cherryhill Company assembles the following information relative to the company.

Cherryhill Company
Balance Sheet
December 31, 1977

Assets	Per Company's Books	As Adjusted by Appraisal and Audit
Current assets	$120,000	$115,000
Investments	40,000	35,000
Land, buildings, and equipment (net)	349,000	325,000
Goodwill	80,000	80,000
	$589,000	$555,000
Liabilities and Stockholders' Equity		
Current liabilities	$ 18,750	$ 18,750
Long-term liabilities	200,000	200,000
Capital stock	200,000	200,000
Retained earnings	170,250	136,250
	$589,000	$555,000

An analysis of retained earnings discloses the following information:

	Per Company's Books	As Adjusted by Appraisal and Audit
Retained earnings, January 1, 1975	$144,450	$118,250
Add net income, 1975–1977*	61,800	54,000
Deduct dividends, 1975–1977	(36,000)	(36,000)
Retained earnings, December 31, 1977	$170,250	$136,250
*After loss on sale of assets in 1977	$ 61,200	$ 66,000

Instructions:

(1) Calculate the amount to be paid for goodwill, assuming that earnings of the future are expected to be the same as average normal earnings of the past 3 years, 8% is accepted as a reasonable return on net assets other than goodwill as of December 31, 1977, and average earnings in excess of 8% are capitalized at 15% in determining goodwill.

(2) Give the entry on the books of the Aurora Corp., assuming purchase of the assets of the Cherryhill Company and assumption of its liabilities on the basis as indicated in (1). Cash is paid for net assets acquired.

13-5. East Coast Industries, Inc., assembles the following data relative to the Cape Cod Corp. in determining the amount to be paid for the net assets and goodwill of the latter company:

Assets at appraised values (before goodwill)	$850,000
Liabilities	320,000
Stockholders' equity	$530,000

Net earnings (after elimination of extraordinary items):

1973	$ 90,000
1974	72,000
1975	97,000
1976	95,000
1977	101,000

Instructions: Calculate the amount to be paid for goodwill under each of the following assumptions:

(1) Average earnings are capitalized at 16% in arriving at the business worth.

(2) A return of 12% is considered normal on net assets at appraised values; goodwill is valued at 5 years' excess earnings.

(3) A return of 14% is considered normal on net assets at appraised values; excess earnings are to be capitalized at 20%.

(4) Goodwill is valued at the sum of the earnings of the last 3 years in excess of a 10% annual yield on net assets at appraised values. (Assume that net assets are the same for the 3-year period.)

(5) A return of 10% is considered normal on net identifiable assets at their appraised values. Excess earnings are expected to continue for 10 years. Goodwill is to be valued by the present value method using a 20% rate. (Use Appendix A present value table.)

13-6. The Rocca Corporation is considering the acquisition of the assets and business of the Holiday Corporation as of June 30, 1977. The Rocca Corporation is willing to pay the appraised value of the net identifiable assets of Holiday plus a reasonable amount for goodwill. The net assets other than goodwill are appraised at $2,600,000 on June 30, 1977.

All-inclusive income statements prepared by the Holiday Corporation show the following pretax income for the four years preceding the proposed acquisition:

Year Ending June 30	Pretax Income
1974	$345,000
1975	382,000
1976	375,000
1977	385,000

(continued)

Similar operating results are expected in the future except for the following items:

(a) A review of Holiday Corporation accounting records reveals that equipment acquired in July, 1972, at a cost of $300,000 has been depreciated on a straight-line basis with a 20-year useful life and no estimated salvage value. This equipment was included in the appraisal of net tangible assets at a current value of $452,000. Company engineers estimate that the equipment will probably be retired with an estimated salvage value of $40,000 in approximately 16 years.

(b) Holiday had been paying $15,000 per year in interest charges on bonds that were redeemed at a gain of $16,000 on June 30, 1977. Funds for bond retirement were provided by sale in June, 1977, of the company's Consumer Products division for $500,000. This division had constant losses of approximately $30,000 annually.

(c) Normal maintenance on the equipment of Holiday Corporation has been inadequate by approximately $19,000 annually.

Both parties agree that a return of 14% before tax is normal on assets employed in the type of business engaged in by Holiday Corporation. Earnings in excess of this amount are expected to continue for another 5 years but since there is less certainty about excess earnings, a return of 20% is considered reasonable for an investment in above-normal pretax earnings.

Instructions: Prepare a summary showing how the amount to be paid for goodwill of the Holiday Corporation is determined using the present value method of calculating goodwill. (Use Appendix A present value table.)

13-7. Sorenson Manufacturing Corporation was incorporated on January 3, 1976. The corporation's financial statements for its first year's operations were not examined by a CPA. You have been engaged to examine the financial statements for the year ended December 31, 1977, and your examination is substantially completed. The trial balance at December 31, 1977, appears below:

Sorenson Manufacturing Corporation
Trial Balance
December 31, 1977

Cash	37,000	
Accounts Receivable	42,500	
Allowance for Doubtful Accounts		500
Inventories	38,500	
Machinery	75,000	
Equipment	29,000	
Accumulated Depreciation		10,000
Patents	85,000	
Prepaid Expenses	10,500	
Organization Costs	29,000	
Goodwill	24,000	
Licensing Agreement No. 1	50,000	
Licensing Agreement No. 2	49,000	
Accounts Payable		147,500
Deferred Credits		12,500
Capital Stock		300,000
Retained Earnings, January 1, 1977	27,000	
Sales		668,500
Cost of Goods Sold	454,000	
Selling and General Expenses	173,000	
Interest Expense	3,500	
Extraordinary Losses	12,000	
	1,139,000	1,139,000

The following information relates to accounts that may yet require adjustment:

(a) Patents for Sorenson's manufacturing process were purchased January 2, 1977, at a cost of $68,000. An additional $17,000 was spent in December, 1977, to improve machinery covered by the patents and debited to the patents account. Depreciation on fixed assets has been properly recorded for 1977 in accordance with Sorenson's practice which provides a full year's depreciation for property on hand June 30 and no depreciation otherwise. Sorenson uses the straight-line method for all depreciation and amortization.

(b) On January 3, 1976, Sorenson purchased two licensing agreements that were then believed to have unlimited useful lives. The balance in the licensing agreement No. 1 account includes its purchase price of $48,000 and expenses of $2,000 related to the acquisition. The balance in the licensing agreement No. 2 account includes its $48,000 purchase price and $2,000 in acquisition expenses, but it has been reduced by a credit of $1,000 for the advance collection of 1978 revenue from the agreement. In December, 1976, an explosion caused a permanent 60% reduction in the expected revenue-producing value of licensing agreement No. 1 and in January, 1978, a flood caused additional damage that rendered the agreement worthless.

A study of licensing agreement No. 2 made by Sorenson in January, 1977, revealed that its estimated remaining life expectancy was only 10 years as of January 1, 1977.

(c) The balance in the goodwill account includes (1) legal expenses of $16,000 incurred for Sorenson's incorporation on January 3, 1976, and (2) $8,000 paid January 15, 1977, for an advertising program that is expected to increase Sorenson's sales over a period of 3 to 5 years following the disbursement.

(d) The balance in the organization costs account properly includes costs incurred during the organizational period. The corporation has exercised its option to amortize organization costs over a 60-month period beginning January, 1976, for federal income tax purposes and wishes to amortize these costs for accounting purposes in the same manner. No amortization has yet been taken.

Instructions: Prepare the journal entries in 1977 required by the information given. (*Note:* Licensing Agreement No. 1 is amortized after explosion damage loss is determined.) (AICPA adapted)

14

Long-Term Investments: Stocks, Funds, and Miscellaneous

A company must invest funds in inventories, receivables, land, buildings and equipment, and other assets in order to engage in the sale of goods and services. But a portion of its available funds may be applied to assets not directly identified with primary activities. Assets that occupy an auxiliary relationship to central revenue-producing activities are referred to as *investments*. Investments are expected to contribute to the success of the business either by exercising certain favorable effects upon sales and operations generally, or by making an independent contribution to business earnings over the long term.

CLASSIFICATION OF INVESTMENTS

From the standpoint of the owner, investments are either temporary or long-term. As suggested earlier, investments are classified as current only where they are readily marketable and it is management's intent to use them in meeting current cash requirements. Investments not meeting these tests are considered *long-term* or *permanent investments* and are usually reported on the balance sheet under a separate noncurrent heading. The purpose to be served by the investment as well as its marketability govern its classification.

Long-term or permanent investments include a variety of items. For discussion purposes, long-term investments will be classified in four groups: (1) investments in stocks, both preferred and common; (2) investments in bonds, mortgages, and similar debt instruments; (3) funds for bond retirement, stock redemption, and other special purposes; and (4) miscellaneous investments including real estate held for appreciation or for future use, advances to affiliates, interests in life insurance contracts, ownership equities in partnerships and joint ventures, and interests in trusts and estates. The accounting problems relating to all long-term investments except bonds are considered in this chapter; those relating to bonds are considered in the next chapter.

LONG-TERM INVESTMENT IN STOCKS

Companies frequently invest in common or preferred stocks of other companies. Often these investments are made to permit the purchaser to exercise a significant influence over the operating and financial policies of the company whose stock was acquired. Ownership of stock may permit the purchaser to be guaranteed a supplier of a major raw material or a critical assembled part, or it may provide a sales outlet for the finished products. The intent is generally to hold the stock for control purposes, and the investment is therefore classified as a noncurrent asset.

The ability to exercise significant influence by stock ownership may be indicated in several ways, such as representation on the board of directors, participation in policy-making processes, material intercompany transactions, interchange of managerial personnel, or technological dependency. Another important consideration is the extent of ownership by an investor in relation to the concentration of other shareholdings. If the investment represents more than 50% of the voting stock, a controlling interest obviously exists. Under these conditions, the company holding the stock is usually referred to as a *parent* company; the company controlled is referred to as a *subsidiary* company. However, control may effectively be achieved with an investment significantly lower than 50%. The Accounting Principles Board addressed this problem in Opinion No. 18. They recognized that control factors will not always be clear and that judgment will be required in assessing the status of each investment. To achieve a reasonable degree of uniformity in the application of its position, the Board set 20% as an ownership standard: the ownership of 20% or more of the voting stock of the company carries the presumption, in the absence of evidence to the contrary, that an investor has the ability to exercise significant influence over that company. Conversely, ownership of less than 20% leads to the presumption that the investor does not have the ability to exercise significant influence unless such ability can be demonstrated.[1]

The valuation of long-term investment in stocks differs depending upon whether the stockholder's investment is considered to be a controlling interest. If the investment represents less than 20% of the outstanding voting stock, it is generally presumed that no control exists and the investment is carried at the lower of cost or market. If the investment represents 20% or more of the outstanding voting stock, significant influence is assumed and the investment is carried at its original cost as adjusted by a portion of the acquired company's periodic net income or loss, and any distributions in the form of dividends to the stockholder. This procedure is referred to as the *equity method.*

---

[1]*Opinions of the Accounting Principles Board, No. 18,* "The Equity Method of Accounting for Investments in Common Stock" (New York: American Institute of Certified Public Accountants, 1971).

The following discussion of investment in stocks relates to both the cost and equity methods unless otherwise indicated.

Stock Purchases

Shares of stock may be acquired on the New York Stock Exchange, the American Stock Exchange, and other exchanges in the different regions of the country. Stock not listed on the exchanges is acquired over the counter through stockbrokers. Stock may also be acquired directly from an issuing company or from a private investor.

When stock is purchased for cash, it is recorded at the amount paid, including brokers' commissions, taxes, and other fees incidental to the purchase. When stock is acquired *on margin*,[1] the stock should be recorded at its full cost and a liability should be recognized for the unpaid balance: to report only the amount invested would be, in effect, to offset the obligation to the broker against the investment account. An agreement or *subscription* entered into with a corporation for the purchase of stock is recognized by a debit to an asset account for the security to be received and a credit to a liability account for the amount to be paid. A charge for interest on an obligation arising from a stock purchase should be reported as expense. When stock is acquired in exchange for properties or services, the fair market value of such considerations or the value at which the stock is currently selling, whichever may be more clearly determinable, should be used as a basis for recording the investment. In the absence of clearly defined values for assets or services exchanged or a market price for the security acquired, appraisals and estimates are required in arriving at cost.

When two or more securities are acquired for a lump-sum price, this cost should be allocated in some equitable manner to the different acquisitions. When market prices are available for each security, cost may be apportioned on the basis of the relative market prices. When there is a market price for one security but not for the other, it may be reasonable to assign the market price to the one and the cost excess to the other. When market prices are not available, it may be necessary to postpone cost apportionment until support for an equitable division becomes available. In certain instances it may be desirable to carry the two securities in a single account and to treat the proceeds from the sale of one as a subtraction from total cost, the residual cost then to be identified with the other. To illustrate these procedures, assume the purchase of 100 units of preferred and common stock at $75 per unit; each unit consists of one share of preferred and two shares of common. Market prices at the time the stock is acquired are $60 per share for preferred and $10 per share for common. The investment cost is recorded in terms of the relative market values of the securities, as follows:

Investment in Preferred Stock	5,625	
Investment in Common Stock	1,875	
Cash		7,500

---

[1] A deposit or advance by an investor with or to a broker representing a part payment on the purchase price of a security or commodity is defined as a purchase on margin.

Computation:
Value of preferred: 100 × $60 = $6,000
Value of common: 200 × $10 = 2,000
                           $8,000

Cost assigned to preferred: 6,000/8,000 × $7,500 = $5,625.
Cost assigned to common: 2,000/8,000 × $7,500 = $1,875.

If there is no market value for common stock, the investment may be recorded as follows:

Investment in Preferred Stock	6,000	
Investment in Common Stock	1,500	
Cash		7,500

Computation:

Cost of preferred and common stock	$7,500
Cost identified with preferred stock (market)	6,000
Remaining cost identified with common stock	$1,500

If the division of cost must be deferred, the following entry is made:

Investment in Preferred and Common Stock	7,500	
Cash		7,500

The joint investment balance may be eliminated when a basis for apportionment is established and costs can be assigned to individual classes.

When stock is subject to special calls or assessments and such payments are made to the corporation, these are recorded as additions to the costs of the holdings. Pro rata contributions by the stockholders to the corporation to eliminate a deficit, to retire bonds, or to effect a reorganization, are also treated as additions to investment cost.

Revenue from Long-Term Investment in Stocks

The revenue recognized from investment in stocks depends upon whether the investment is considered to be of a magnitude to warrant use of the equity method as opposed to the cost method. As indicated earlier, ownership of 20% or more of the voting stock is generally considered to be the cut-off between long-term stock investments held for control and other long-term stock investments.

Equity Method. The equity method of recognizing revenue reflects the economic substance of the relationship between the controlling stockholder and its related company rather than the legal distinction of the separate entities. Although the earnings of the owned company (investee) are not legally available to stockholders until their distribution as dividends has been authorized by the board of directors, the timing of the distribution can be influenced significantly by the controlling stockholder. Failure to recognize income as earned would permit the controlling stockholder to affect its income by the distribution policy followed.

Under the equity method of accounting for controlled investments, a proportionate share of the earnings or losses of the investee is recognized by the investor in the year earned or incurred. The earnings are generally reflected in a single account unless the investee has extraordinary gains or losses. In this case, separate revenue accounts should be used for both ordinary and extraordinary earnings or losses. The investment account is increased by the proportionate share of the earnings and decreased by the proportionate share of losses and the proportionate distribution of dividends.

For example, assume Probert Manufacturing Co. held a 40% interest in the common stock of Stewart, Inc. In 1977, Stewart, Inc., reported net income of $150,000, including an extraordinary gain of $30,000. Dividends of $70,000 were distributed to stockholders. The following entries would be made on the books of Probert Manufacturing Co. to record its share of the 1977 earnings of Stewart, Inc.

```
Investment in Stewart, Inc., Common Stock .................................  60,000
    Share of Ordinary Income — Stewart, Inc., Common Stock .....            48,000
    Share of Extraordinary Income — Stewart, Inc., Common
    Stock ........................................................................................            12,000
        To recognize 40% of the income earned by Stewart, Inc.,
        common stock.


Cash .....................................................................................................  28,000
    Investment in Stewart, Inc., Common Stock .............................            28,000
        To record receipt of cash dividend.
```

Special adjustments are necessary in recognizing the proportionate share of the investee's income, if the amount paid for the stock exceeds the proportionate share of the investee's underlying assets at the date of purchase. The excess must either be attributed to an excess of market value over carrying value of identifiable tangible and intangible assets, or to the intangible asset goodwill. If the assets involved have limited lives, an adjustment to the proportionate share of the income to be recognized must be made to reflect the depreciation of the market value excess for depreciable assets or the amortization of goodwill.

For example, assume the total stockholders' equity of Stewart, Inc., was $500,000 at the time Probert Manufacturing Co. purchased 40% of its shares for $250,000. The implied value of the total stockholders' equity of Stewart, Inc., would be $625,000 ($250,000 ÷ .40), or $125,000 in excess of the recorded stockholders' equity. Assume that review of the asset values discloses that the market value of depreciable properties with an average remaining life of ten years exceeds the carrying value of these assets by $50,000. The remaining $75,000 difference ($125,000 − $50,000) is attributed to goodwill. The adjustment to Stewart, Inc.'s revenue to be recognized by Probert Manufacturing Co. would be a deduction of $2,000 for the proportionate depreciation of the excess market value on depreciable property, ($50,000 × .40) ÷ 10, and a deduction of $750 for the proportionate amortization of goodwill over a forty year period, ($75,000 × .40) ÷ 40. The entry for this adjustment would be as follows:

```
Share of Ordinary Income — Stewart, Inc., Common Stock ..............  2,750
    Investment in Stewart, Inc., Common Stock ....................................            2,750
        To adjust share of ordinary income on Stewart, Inc., common
        stock for proportionate depreciation on excess market value
        of depreciable property, $2,000, and for amortization of im-
        plied goodwill from acquisition, $750.
```

In some cases, the cost may be less than the underlying book value at the time of acquisition. In this situation, it is assumed that specific assets of the investee are overvalued and an adjustment is necessary to reduce the depreciation or amortization taken by the investee. The journal entry to reflect this adjustment is the reverse of that just illustrated.

If the investor and the investee are engaged in intercompany revenue producing activities, adjustments must also be made to eliminate intercompany profits. These adjustments are similar to those made when consolidated statements are prepared for parents and 50% or more owned subsidiaries. A more complete description of these intercompany problems is found in *Advanced Accounting* of this series.

Cost Method. When the investment in another company's stock does not involve a controlling interest, the revenue recognized is limited to the distribution of the dividends declared by the investee. The receipt of cash dividends by a stockholder is recorded by a debit to Cash and a credit to Dividend Revenue. Three dates are generally included in the formal dividend announcement: (1) date of declaration, (2) record date, and (3) date of payment. The formal dividend announcement may read somewhat as follows: "The Board of Directors at their meeting on November 5, 1976, declared a regular quarterly dividend on outstanding common stock of 50 cents per share payable on January 15, 1977, to stockholders of record at the close of business, December 29, 1976." The stockholder becomes aware of the dividend action upon its announcement. But if the holdings are sold and a new owner is recognized by the corporation prior to the record date, the dividend is paid to the new owner. If the stockholder retains the holdings until the record date, he or she will be entitled to the dividends when paid. After the record date, stock no longer carries a right to dividends and sells *ex-dividend*.[1] Accordingly, a stockholder is justified in recognizing the corporate dividend action on the record date. At this time a receivable account may be debited and Dividend Revenue credited. Upon receipt of the dividend, Cash is debited and the receivable credited.

There are some who would accrue dividends in the same manner as interest when the declaration of a regular dividend at a certain date is virtually assured by the nature of the security, the position and earnings of the company, and the policies of the board of directors. The recognition of accrued dividends under such circumstances is not objectionable if disclosure is made on the statements that such special practice is followed.

Federal income tax regulations provide that dividends are taxable only when unqualifiedly made subject to the demand of the stockholder. Hence, even though preparing the tax return on an accrual basis, the

---

[1]Stock on the New York Stock Exchange is normally quoted ex-dividend or ex-rights four full trading days prior to the record date because of the time required to deliver the stock and to record the stock transfer.

taxpayer recognizes dividends as revenue only when these become available. Ordinarily, the taxpayer maintains the books in accordance with the tax rule and recognizes revenue when the dividends are received.

Liquidating Dividends

Dividends are sometimes identified as liquidating dividends. A *liquidating dividend* involves a return of the invested capital of a company to its stockholders. Although liquidating dividends can occur in any company, they are most common in a company consuming natural resources in its operations. When natural resources are limited and irreplaceable, the company may choose to distribute full proceeds becoming available from operations. Dividends paid, then, represent in part a distribution of earnings and in part a distribution of invested capital. Distributions involving both earnings and invested capital may also be found when a company makes full distribution of the proceeds from the sale of certain properties, such as land or securities, or when a distribution represents the proceeds from business liquidation.

A stockholder, receiving a dividend consisting of both a distribution of earnings and return of invested capital, credits revenue for the amount representing earnings and the investment account for the amount representing invested capital. To illustrate, assume that Lucky Mines, Inc., pays a dividend of $500,000, 60% representing a distribution of earnings and 40% representing a distribution of the cost recovery of certain wasting assets. A stockholder receiving a dividend of $1,200 makes the following entry:

Cash	1,200	
Dividend Revenue..		720
Investment in Lucky Mines, Inc., Common Stock............................		480
To record receipt of cash dividend; 40% liquidating dividend.		

Information regarding the portion of dividends representing earnings and the portion representing invested capital should be reported to the stockholder by the corporation making the distribution. This report may not accompany each dividend check but instead may be provided annually and may cover the total dividends paid during the year. If dividends have been recorded as revenue during the year, the revenue account is debited and the investment account is credited when notification is received of the amount to be recognized as a distribution of invested capital.

When liquidating dividends exceed investment cost, excess distributions are reported as a gain from the investment. If liquidation is completed and the investment cost is not fully recovered, the balance of the investment account should be written off as a loss.

Property Dividends

Dividends that are distributed in the form of assets other than cash are referred to as *property dividends*. In distributing earnings by means of a property dividend, the corporation credits the asset account for the cost of the asset distributed, debits Retained Earnings for the market value of the asset distributed, if determinable, and accounts for the difference as a gain or a loss. APB Opinion No. 29 defines this type of transaction as a nonreciprocal transfer to an owner.[1] The stockholder debits an asset account and credits Dividend Revenue. The stockholder also recognizes the dividend in terms of the market value of the property item at the date of its distribution. To illustrate these situations, assume that the Wells Corporation with 1,000,000 shares of common stock outstanding distributes as a dividend its holdings of 50,000 shares of Barnes Co. stock acquired at a cost of $11 per share. The distribution of one share of Barnes Co. stock for every 20 shares of Wells Corporation held is made when Barnes Co. shares are selling at $16. Wells Corporation would record the dividend as follows:

```
Retained Earnings ..................................................................... 800,000
   Investment in Barnes Co. Common Stock ................................        550,000
   Gain from Distribution of Barnes Co. Common Stock .............        250,000
      To record distribution of 50,000 shares of Barnes Co. stock
      as a property dividend.
```

A stockholder owning 100 shares of Wells Corporation stock would make the following entry in recording the receipt of the dividend:

```
Investment in Barnes Co. Common Stock ....................................    80
   Dividend Revenue .................................................................        80
      Received 5 shares of Barnes Co. common stock, market
      price $16 per share, as a dividend on 100 shares of Wells
      Corporation.
```

Stock Dividends

A company may distribute a dividend in the form of additional shares that are the same as those held by its stockholders. Such a dividend does not affect company assets but simply results in the transfer of retained earnings to invested capital. The increase in total shares outstanding is distributed pro rata to individual stockholders. The receipt of additional shares by stockholders leaves their respective equities exactly as they were. Although the number of shares held by individual stockholders has gone up, there are now a greater number of shares outstanding and proportionate interests remain unchanged. The division of equities into a greater number of parts cannot be regarded as giving rise to revenue. To illustrate, assume that Eagle Corporation has 10,000 shares of common stock outstanding. The total of the stockholders' equity is $330,000; the book value per share is $33. If a 10% stock dividend is declared, an additional 1,000 shares of stock will be issued and the book value per share will decline to $30. A stockholder who held 10 shares with a book value of $330 (10 × $33) will hold 11 shares after the stock dividend, with the book value remaining at $330 (11 × $30).

The market value of the stock may or may not react in a similar manner. Theoretically the same relative decrease should occur in the market value as occurred in the book value; however, there are many variables

---

[1]*Opinions of the Accounting Principles Board, No. 29*, "Accounting for Nonmonetary Transactions" (New York: American Institute of Certified Public Accountants, 1973), par. 3.

influencing the market price of securities. If the percentage of the stock dividend issued is comparatively low, under 20–25%, there is generally less than a pro rata immediate effect on the stock market price. This means that while a stockholder after receiving a stock dividend will have no greater interest in the company, the investment may have a greater market value.

Because there is no effect on the underlying book value of the investment, only a memorandum entry needs to be made by the stockholder in recognizing the receipt of additional shares. Original investment cost applies to a greater number of shares, and this cost is divided by the total shares now held in arriving at the cost per share to be used upon subsequent disposition of holdings. The new per-share cost basis is indicated in the memorandum entry.

When stock has been acquired at different dates and at different costs, the stock dividend will have to be related to each different acquisition. Adjusted costs for shares comprising each lot held can then be developed. To illustrate, assume that H. C. De Soto owns stock of the Banner Corporation acquired as follows:

	Shares	Cost per Share	Total Cost
Lot 1	50	$120	$6,000
Lot 2	30	90	2,700

A stock dividend of 1 share for every 2 held is distributed by the Banner Corporation. A memorandum entry on De Soto's books to report the number of shares now held and the cost per share within each lot would be made as follows:

> Received 40 shares of Banner Corporation stock, representing a 50% stock dividend on 80 shares held. Number of shares held and costs assigned to shares are now as follows:

	Shares	Total Cost	Revised Cost per Share
Lot 1	75 (50 + 25)	$6,000	$80 ($6,000 ÷ 75)
Lot 2	45 (30 + 15)	2,700	60 ($2,700 ÷ 45)

The number of shares to be issued as a stock dividend may include fractional shares. Usually a cash payment is made to the stockholder by the issuing company in lieu of issuing fractional shares.

When stock of a class different from that held is received as a stock dividend, such a dividend, too, should not be regarded as revenue. As in the case of a like dividend, a portion of the retained earnings relating to the original holdings is formally labeled invested capital. All owners of the stock on which the dividend is declared participate pro rata in the distribution and now own two classes of stock instead of a single class. A book value is now identified with the new stock, but this is accompanied by a corresponding decrease in the book value identified with the original holdings. A similar position can be taken when an investor receives dividends in the form of bonds or other contractual obligations of the corporation.

One difference between the receipt of stock of the same class and securities of a different class needs to be noted. When common stock is received on common, all shares are alike and original cost may be equitably assigned in terms of the total number of units held after the dividend. When different securities are received whose value is not the same as that of the shares originally held, it would not be proper to assign an equal amount of original cost to both old and new units. Instead, equitable apportionment of cost would require use of the relative market values of the two classes of securities. To illustrate, assume the ownership of 100 shares of Bell Co. common stock acquired at $100 per share. A stock dividend of 50 shares of $25 par preferred stock is received on the common stock held. On the date of distribution the common stock is selling for $65 and the preferred stock for $20. The receipt of the dividend and the apportionment of cost is recorded as follows:

Investment in Bell Co. Preferred Stock...................................... 1,333.33
   Investment in Bell Co. Common Stock..................................   1,333.33
      To record receipt of 50 shares of preferred stock as a
      dividend on 100 shares of common.

Computation:

Cost of common apportioned to common and preferred shares on the basis of relative market values of the two securities on the date of distribution:

Value of preferred: 50 × $20 = $1,000
Value of common: 100 × $65 = 6,500
                          $7,500

Cost assigned to preferred: 1,000/7,500 × $10,000 = $1,333.33.
(Cost per share: $1,333.33 ÷ 50 = $26.67.)
Cost assigned to common: 6,500/7,500 × $10,000 = $8,666.67.
(Cost per share: $8,666.67 ÷ 100 = $86.67.)

Stock dividends may be reported as revenue if they are regarded as having been made in lieu of cash. The distribution is regarded as having been made in lieu of cash if (1) it is made in discharge of preference dividends for the current year or for the preceding taxable year, or (2) the stockholder is given the option of receiving cash or other property instead of stock.

Stock Splits   A corporation may effect a *stock split* by reducing the par or the stated value of capital stock and increasing the number of shares outstanding accordingly. For example, a corporation with 1,000,000 shares outstanding may decide to split its stock on a 3-for-1 basis. After the split the corporation will have 3,000,000 shares outstanding: each stockholder will have three shares for every share originally held. However, each share will now represent only one third of the interest previously represented; furthermore, each share of stock can be expected to sell for approximately one third of its previous value.

The stockholders ledger is revised to show the increased number of shares identified with each stockholder and the reduced par value, if any. Accounting for a stock split on the books of the investor is the same as that for a stock dividend. With an increase in the number of shares, each share now carries only a portion of the original cost. When shares have been acquired at different dates and at different prices, the shares received in a split will have to be associated with the original acquisitions and per-share costs for each lot revised. A memorandum entry is made to report the increase in the number of shares and the allocation of cost to the shares held after the split.

Stock Rights

A corporation that wishes to raise cash by the sale of additional stock may be required to offer existing stockholders the right to subscribe to the new stock. This privilege attaching to stock is called the *preemptive right* and is designed to enable stockholders to retain their respective interest in the corporation. For example, assume that a stockholder owns 50% of a company's outstanding stock. If the stock is doubled and the additional shares are offered and sold to other parties, that stockholder's interest in the company would drop to 25%. With the right to subscribe to the pro rata share of any new offering, the stockholder can maintain the same proportionate interest in the corporation. Although the preemptive right is a general requirement in most state corporation laws, the right may be nullified in the articles of incorporation of a company. There is an increasing movement by corporations to eliminate the preemptive right.

In order to make subscription privileges attractive and to insure sale of the stock, it is customary for corporations to offer the additional issues to its stockholders at less than the market price of the stock. Certificates known as *rights* or *warrants* are issued to stockholders enabling them to subscribe for stock in proportion to the holdings on which they are issued. One right is offered for each share held. But more than one right is generally required in subscribing for each new share. Rights may be sold by stockholders who do not care to exercise them.

As in the case of cash and other dividends, the directors of the corporation in declaring rights to subscribe for additional shares designate a record date that follows the declaration date. All stockholders on the record date are entitled to the rights. Up to the record date, stock sells *rights-on*, since parties acquiring the stock will receive the rights when they are issued; after the record date, the stock sells *ex-rights*, and the rights may be sold separately by those owning the rights as of the record date. A date on which the rights expire is also designated when the rights are declared. Rights not exercised are worthless beyond the expiration date. Generally, rights have a limited life of only a few weeks.

Accounting for Stock Rights. The receipt of stock rights is comparable to the receipt of a stock dividend. The corporation has made no asset distribution; stockholders' equities remain unchanged. However, the stockholders' investment is evidenced by shares originally acquired and rights that have a value of their own since they permit the purchase of shares at less than market price. These circumstances call for an allocation of cost between the original shares and the rights. Since the shares and the rights have different values, an apportionment should be made in terms of the relative market values as of the date the right distribution is declared. A separate accounting for each class of security is subsequently followed. The accounting for stock rights is illustrated in the following example.

Assume that in 1973 Eva Montano acquired 100 shares of Superior Products no-par common at $180 per share. In 1977 the corporation issues rights to purchase 1 share of common at $100 for every 5 shares owned. Montano thus receives 100 rights — one right for each share owned. However, since 5 rights are required for the acquisition of a single share, the 100 rights enable her to subscribe for only 20 new shares. Montano's original investment of $18,000 now applies to two assets, the shares and the rights. This cost is apportioned on the basis of the relative market values of each security as of the date that the rights are distributed to the stockholders. The cost allocation may be expressed as follows:

$$\text{Cost assigned to rights:} \frac{\text{Market Value of Rights}}{\substack{\text{Market Value of Stock Ex-rights} \\ + \text{ Market Value of Rights}}} \times \substack{\text{Original} \\ \text{Cost of} \\ \text{Stock}}$$

$$\text{Cost assigned to stock:} \frac{\text{Market Value of Stock Ex-rights}}{\substack{\text{Market Value of Stock Ex-rights} \\ + \text{ Market Value of Rights}}} \times \substack{\text{Original} \\ \text{Cost of} \\ \text{Stock}}$$

Assume that Superior Products common is selling ex-rights at $121 per share and rights are selling at $4 each. The cost allocation would be made as follows:

To rights: $\dfrac{4}{121 + 4} \times \$18,000 = \$576$ ($576 ÷ 100 = $5.76, cost per right)

To stock (balance): $18,000 − $576 = $17,424 ($17,424 ÷ 100 = $174.24, cost per share)

The following entry may be made at this time:

Investment in Superior Products Stock Rights...	576	
Investment in Superior Products Common Stock		576
Received 100 rights permitting the purchase of 20 shares at $100. Cost of stock was apportioned on the basis of the relative market values of stock and rights on the date rights were distributed.		

The cost apportioned to the rights is used in determining the gain or the loss arising from the sale of rights. Assume that the rights in the preceding example are sold at 4½. The following entry would be made:

Cash..	450	
Loss on Sale of Superior Products Stock Rights	126	
Investment in Superior Products Stock Rights		576
Sold 100 rights at 4½.		

If the rights are exercised, the cost of the new shares acquired consists of the cost assigned to the rights plus the cash that is paid in the exercise of the rights. Assume that, instead of selling the rights, Montano exercises her privilege to purchase 20 additional shares at $100. The entry at the top of the next page is made.

Investment in Superior Products Common Stock..............................	2,576	
Investment in Superior Products Stock Rights...............................		576
Cash..		2,000
Exercised rights acquiring 20 shares at $100.		

Upon exercising the rights, Montano's records show an investment balance of $20,000 consisting of two lots of stock as follows:

Lot 1 (1973 acquisition) 100 shares:	
($17,424 ÷ 100 = $174.24, cost per share as adjusted)	$17,424
Lot 2 (1977 acquisition) 20 shares:	
($2,576 ÷ 20 = $128.80, cost per share acquired through rights)	2,576
Total	$20,000

These costs provide the basis for calculating gains or losses upon subsequent sales of the stock.

Frequently the receipt of rights includes one or more rights that cannot be used in the purchase of a whole share. For example, assume that the owner of 100 shares receives 100 rights; 6 rights are required for the purchase of 1 share. Here the holder uses 96 rights in purchasing 16 shares. Several options are available to the holder: allow the remaining 4 rights to lapse; sell the rights and report a gain or a loss on such sale; or supplement the rights held by the purchase of 2 more rights making possible the purchase of an additional share of stock.

If the owner of valuable rights allows them to lapse, it would appear that the cost assigned to such rights should be written off as a loss. This can be supported on the theory that the issuance of stock by the corporation at less than current market price results in some dilution in the equities identified with original holdings. However, when changes in the market price of the stock make the exercise of rights unattractive and none of the rights can be sold, no dilution has occurred and any cost of rights reported separately should be returned to the investment account.

Disposition of Stock

Long-term investments in stock may be disposed of by sale, redemption, or exchange for another type of security. It is necessary to maintain sufficient records so the carrying value of the stock can be determined.

Sale of Stock. If there is a difference between the sales proceeds and the carrying value of the investment, the sale of stock results in a recognition of a gain or loss. Because stock certificates are identified by number, the carrying value can usually be specifically determined. In some cases, however, companies use the first-in, first-out method for stock sold from lots acquired at different dates and prices. The gain or loss on the sale of long-term investments is generally recognized as ordinary income. Either specific identification or first-in, first-out are acceptable methods for income tax purposes.

Redemption of Stock. Stock, particularly preferred issues, may be called in for redemption and cancellation by the corporation under conditions set by the issue. The call price is ordinarily set at a figure higher than the price at which the stock was originally issued, but this call price may be more or less than the cost to the holder who acquired the stock from another person after its original issue. When stock is surrendered to the corporation, an entry is made debiting Cash and crediting the investment account. Any difference between the cash proceeds and the investment cost is recorded as a gain or a loss. For example, assume that an investor acquires 100 shares of Y Co. 6% , $100 par preferred stock at 97. These shares are subsequently called in at 105. The redemption is recorded on the stockholder's books by the following entry.

```
Cash ....................................................................................... 10,500
    Investment in Y Co. 6% Preferred Stock .........................................         9,700
    Gain on Redemption of Y Co. Preferred Stock...............................            800
        Received $10,500 on call of Y Co. preferred stock, cost $9,700.
```

Exchange of Stock. When shares of stock are exchanged for other securities, the investor opens an account for the newly acquired security and closes the account of the security originally held. The new securities should be recorded at their fair market value or at the fair market value of the shares given up, whichever may be more clearly determinable, and a gain or loss is recognized on the exchange for the difference between the value assigned to the securities acquired and the carrying value of the shares given up. In the absence of a market value for either old or new securities, the carrying value of the shares given up will have to be recognized as the cost of the new securities. To illustrate, assume that the Z Co. offers its preferred stockholders two shares of no-par common stock in exchange for each share of $100 par preferred. An investor exchanges 100 shares of preferred stock carried at a cost of $10,000 for 200 shares of common stock. Common shares are quoted on the market at the time of exchange at $65. The exchange is recorded on the books of the stockholder by the following entry:

```
Investment in Z Co. Common Stock...................................................... 13,000
    Investment in Z Co. Preferred Stock..............................................       10,000
    Gain on Conversion of Z Co. Preferred Stock ...............................        3,000
        Acquired 200 shares of common stock valued at $65 in ex-
        change for 100 shares of preferred stock costing $100.
```

Recognition of a gain or a loss on a security exchange can be supported on the grounds that the exchange closes the transaction cycle relating to the original asset and opens a new cycle, the newly acquired asset requiring valuation in terms of current market. This view received authoritative support in APB Opinion No. 29.[1]

Stock Valuation at Lower of Cost or Market   Reference was made in Chapter 5 to the valuation of equity securities held as a temporary investment and included with current assets. In general, current marketable equity securities are valued at the lower of aggregate cost or market, and an allowance account is used to reduce the

---

[1]*Opinions of the Accounting Principles Board, No. 29, op. cit.*, par. 23.

cost to market. Any change in the allowance account is recognized in the income statement in the period of change.

When equity securities are classified as long-term investments because management's intent is not to use the securities as a current source of cash, the advantages of market valuations are less certain. Stock market prices can fluctuate greatly while the stock is being held, and if the investment is to be retained for long-range purposes, the impact of gains or losses on the net income could be misleading. The Financial Accounting Standards Board in its Statement No. 12 considered this classification difference to be significant, and recommended a different treatment for valuation of noncurrent equity investments than for current equity investments.[1] Unless the investment is accounted for under the equity method,[2] the lower of aggregated cost or market is to be used for valuation of the asset exactly as is recommended for equity securities classified as current assets. However, the offset entry does not affect current net income. Instead, a negative stockholders' equity account is created. This account, which (in FASB Statement No. 12) is entitled Net Unrealized Loss on Noncurrent Marketable Equity Securities, is to be deducted from the total stockholders' equity balance in the balance sheet. Both the allowance account that reduces the cost to market and the negative stockholders' equity account should have the same balance at all times. As the market price of the noncurrent equity security portfolio varies, these accounts will be adjusted to bring the valuation to the lower of aggregate cost or market. When equity securities are sold, the transaction is recorded on the historical cost basis and a gain or loss recognized. These transactions are illustrated in the following example.

A company carries a long-term investment equity portfolio that has a cost of $125,000. At December 31, 1977, the market value of the securities held has fallen to $110,000. There is no indication that the decline is permanent. The following entries would be required to reduce the securities valuation from cost to market.

Net Unrealized Loss in Noncurrent Marketable Equity Securities..... 15,000
    Allowance for Decline in Value of Noncurrent Marketable Equity
    Securities 15,000

At the end of 1978, the portfolio has increased to an original cost of $155,000. The market value of the portfolio is $148,000. The amount in the allowance account and in the negative equity account can now be reduced to $7,000 as follows:

Allowance for Decline in Value of Noncurrent Marketable Equity
    Securities 8,000
    Net Unrealized Loss in Noncurrent Marketable Equity Securities.   8,000

If the decline in market value is judged to be other than temporary, the cost basis of the property should be written down (no allowance),

---

[1] *Statement of Financial Accounting Standards No. 12*, "Accounting for Certain Marketable Securities" (Stamford, Conn.: Financial Accounting Standards Board, 1975), par. 9.
[2] Statement No. 12 does not apply to investments accounted for by the equity method.

and the write-down should be accounted for as a realized loss.[1] The new cost basis is not to be changed for subsequent increases in market value.

If the reduction in value at December 31, 1977, in the preceding example is judged to be permanent, the entry would be altered as follows:

Realized Loss from Permanent Decline in Market Value of Noncurrent Marketable Equity Securities	15,000	
Long-Term Investment in Marketable Securities		15,000

Assume the portfolio cost at the end of 1978, after adjusting for the permanent decline in securities at the end of 1977, was $140,000, and the market was still $148,000. In this situation, no entry would be necessary in 1978. The investment would continue to be carried at the new cost of $140,000.

If there is a change in the classification of a marketable equity security between current and noncurrent assets, the transfer should be made at the lower of cost or market at the date of the transfer, and the lower figure is defined as the new cost base with a loss being recorded in the current period.

The above action of the Financial Accounting Standards Board places a high premium on the classification of these types of investments. Because the classification is determined on the basis of subjective criteria, such as the intent of management to hold or sell, there is much concern that the classification might be used to manipulate the net income. The adoption of a consistent valuation for all investments, regardless of their classification, seems preferable to the differentiated treatment outlined in Statement No. 12.

LONG-TERM INVESTMENT IN FUNDS

Cash and other assets set apart for certain common purposes are called *funds, sinking funds,* or *redemption funds.* Some funds are to be used for specified current purposes, such as the payment of expenses or the discharge of current obligations, and are appropriately reported as current assets. Examples of these are petty cash funds, payroll funds, interest funds, dividend funds, and withholding, social security, and other tax funds. Other funds are accumulated over a long term for such purposes as the acquisition or the replacement of properties, the retirement of long-term indebtedness, the redemption of capital stock, the operation of a pension plan, or possible future contingencies. These funds are properly considered noncurrent and are reported under the long-term investment heading.

Establishment of Funds   A fund may be established through the voluntary action of management or it may be established as a result of contractual requirements. It may arise from a single deposit or from a series of deposits, or it may be composed of the sum of the deposits plus the earnings identified with such deposits. The fund may be used for a single purpose, such as the

---

[1]*Statement of Financial Accounting Standards No. 12, op. cit.,* par. 21.

redemption of preferred stock, or it may be used for several related purposes, such as the periodic payment of interest on bonds, the retirement of bonds at various intervals, and the ultimate retirement of the remaining bonded indebtedness.

When a fund is voluntarily created by management, control of the fund and its disposition is an arbitrary matter depending upon the wishes of management. When a fund is created through some legal requirement, it must be administered and applied in accordance therewith. Such a fund may be administered by one or more independent trustees under an agreement known as a *trust indenture*. If the trustee assumes responsibility for the fulfillment of the requirement, such as may be true for a bond retirement or a pension program, the fund is not carried as an asset on the company's books. However, if the indenture does not free the company from further obligation, the fund must be accounted for as if there were no trustee.

Fund Accumulation

When a corporation is required by agreement to establish a fund for a certain purpose, such as the retirement of bonds or the redemption of stock, the agreement generally provides that fund deposits (1) shall be fixed amounts, (2) shall vary according to gross revenue, net income, or units of product sold, or (3) shall be equal periodic sums which, together with earnings, will produce a certain amount at some future date. The latter arrangement is based on compound-interest factors, and compound-interest or annuity tables are used to determine the equal periodic deposits. In order to accumulate a fund of $100,000 by a series of 5 equal annual deposits at 8% compounded annually, a periodic deposit of $17,045.65 is required.[1] A schedule can be developed to show the planned fund accumulation through deposits and earnings. Such a schedule is illustrated below:

Fund Accumulation Schedule

Year	Earnings on Fund Balance for Year	Amount Deposited in Fund	Total Increase in Fund for Year	Accumulated Fund Total
1		$17,045.65	$17,045.65	$ 17,045.65
2	$1,363.65	17,045.65	18,409.30	35,454.95
3	2,836.40	17,045.65	19,882.05	55,337.00
4	4,426.96	17,045.65	21,472.61	76,809.61
5	6,144.74	17,045.65	23,190.39	100,000.00

Assuming deposits at the end of each year, the table shows a fund balance at the end of the first year of $17,045.65 resulting from the first deposit. At the end of the second year the fund is increased by (1) earnings at 8% on the investment in the fund during the year, $1,363.65, and (2) the second deposit to the fund, $17,045.65. The total in the fund at

---

[1]This amount can be determined from Table III, Appendix A, on page 839. The rent or annual payment for an annuity whose amount is $100,000 at 8% for 5 periods is computed as follows:

$$R = \frac{FV_n}{FVAF_{\overline{n}|\,i}} = \frac{FV_n}{\text{Table III }_{\overline{5}|\,8\%}} = \frac{100,000}{5.8666} = \$17,045.65$$

this time is $35,454.95. Fund earnings in the following year are based on a total investment of $35,454.95 as of the beginning of the year.

The schedule is developed on the assumption of annual earnings of 8%. However, various factors, such as fluctuations in the earnings rate and gains and losses on investments, may provide earnings that differ from the assumed amounts. If the fund is to be maintained in accordance with the accumulation schedule, deposits may be adjusted for earnings that differ from estimated amounts. Smaller deposits, then, can be made in periods when earnings exceed the assumed rate; larger deposits are necessary when earnings fail to meet the assumed rate.

Accounting for Funds

A fund is usually composed of cash and securities. The accounting for stock held in a fund is the same as that described earlier in this chapter except the securities are reported as part of the fund balance. The accounting for investments in bonds will be discussed in the next chapter.

To illustrate the accounting for a fund held by a company, assume a preferred stock redemption fund is established with annual payments to the fund of $20,000. The fund administrator invests 90% of its assets in stock and places the remainder in bank certificates of deposit paying 6% interest. Journal entries for the first year's transactions are as follows:

Stock Redemption Fund Cash	20,000	
Cash		20,000
Annual fund contribution.		
Stock Redemption Fund Securities	18,000	
Stock Redemption Fund Cash		18,000
Investment of fund cash in securities.		
Stock Redemption Fund Certificates of Deposit	2,000	
Stock Redemption Fund Cash		2,000
Investment of fund cash in certificates of deposit.		
Stock Redemption Fund Cash	1,400	
Stock Redemption Fund Revenue		1,400
Dividends on fund securities.		
Stock Redemption Fund Cash	120	
Stock Redemption Fund Revenue		120
Interest on certificates of deposit.		
Stock Redemption Fund Expenses	200	
Stock Redemption Fund Cash		200
Expenses to operate fund.		

At the end of the year, the stock redemption fund assets are as follows:

Stock redemption fund cash	$ 1,320
Stock redemption fund certificate of deposit	2,000
Stock redemption fund securities	18,000
Total	$21,320

This total amount would be reported under the "Long-term investments" heading on the balance sheet.

Stock redemption fund revenue for the year is $1,520 and stock redemption fund expense is $200, resulting in a net income from the fund operation of $1,320. This amount is reported on the income statement as other revenue. When stock is redeemed, the payment is made from the Stock Redemption Fund Cash after the securities are converted to cash.

CASH SURRENDER VALUE OF LIFE INSURANCE

Many business enterprises carry life insurance policies on the lives of their executives because the business has a definite stake in the continuing services of its officers. In some cases the insurance plan affords a financial cushion in the event of loss of such personnel. In other instances the insurance offers a means of purchasing a deceased owner's interest in the business, thus avoiding a transfer of such interest to some outside party or the need to liquidate the business in effecting settlement with the estate of the deceased.

Insurance premiums normally consist of an amount for insurance protection and the balance for a form of investment. The investment portion is manifest in a growing *cash surrender value* available to the insured in the event of policy surrender and cancellation. If this cash surrender value belongs to the business, it should be reported as a long-term investment. Insurance expense for a fiscal period is the difference between the insurance premium paid and the increase in the cash surrender value of the policy. The increase in the cash surrender value is relatively uniform after the first year of the policy. At the end of the first year there may be no cash surrender value, or, if there is such a value, it may be quite low because the insurance company must recover certain costs connected with selling and initiating the policy. The cost of life insurance to the business, then, may be considered higher during the first year of the policy than in later years because of the starting costs involved.

An insurance policy with a cash surrender value also has a *loan value*; this is the amount that the insurance company will permit the insured to borrow on the policy. When the insured uses the policy as a basis for a loan, the amount borrowed should be recorded as a liability and not as a reduction in the cash value. Such a loan may be liquidated by payments of principal and interest, or the loan may be continuing, to be applied against the insurance proceeds upon policy cancellation or ultimate settlement.

The loan an insurance company will make on a policy is normally limited to the policy cash surrender value at the end of the policy year less discount from the loan date to the cash surrender value date. For example, assume a cash surrender value of $3,000 at the end of a fifth policy year. The maximum loan value on the policy at the beginning of the fifth policy year, assuming the insurance premium for the fifth year is paid, is $3,000 discounted for one year. If the discount rate applied by the insurance company is 5%, the policy loan value is calculated as follows: $3,000 ÷ 1.05 = $2,857.14.

Although it is possible for the insured to recognize policy loan values instead of cash surrender values, the latter values are generally used.

The insured may authorize the insurance company to apply any dividends declared upon insurance policies to the reduction of the annual premium payment or to the increase in insurance cash surrender value, or the dividends may be collected in cash. Dividends should be viewed as a reduction in the cost of carrying insurance rather than as a source of supplementary revenue. Hence, if dividends are applied to the reduction of the annual premium, Insurance Expense is simply debited for the net amount paid. If the dividend is applied to the increase in the policy cash surrender value or if it is collected in cash, it should still be treated as an offset to the periodic expense of carrying the policy; the policy cash surrender value or Cash, then, is debited and Insurance Expense is credited. After a number of years, the periodic dividends plus increases in the cash surrender value may exceed the premium payments, thus resulting in revenue rather than expense on policy holdings.

Collection of a policy upon death of the insured requires cancellation of any cash surrender balance. The difference between the insurance proceeds and the balances relating to the insurance policy is recognized as a gain in the period of the death. The nature of the insurance policies carried and their coverage should be disclosed by appropriate comment on the balance sheet.

For income tax purposes no deduction may be taken by an employer for the payment of life insurance premiums on officers or employees when the employer is directly or indirectly the policy beneficiary. The amount recovered on the surrender of an insurance contract represents taxable income to the extent this exceeds total policy payments; the policy here is viewed as an investment that has realized an amount exceeding its cost. However, amounts collected on a policy by reason of the death of the insured are not subject to income tax.

The entries to be made for an insurance contract are illustrated in the following example. The Andrews Manufacturing Company insured the life of its president, W. E. Andrews, on October 1, 1975. The amount of the policy was $50,000; the annual premiums were $2,100.

Year	Gross Premium	Dividend	Net Premium	Increase in Cash Value	Insurance Expense for Year
1	$2,100	——	$2,100	——	$2,100
2	2,100	——	2,100	$1,150	950
3	2,100	$272	1,828	1,300	528

The fiscal period for the company is the calendar year. Mr. Andrews died on July 1, 1978. The entries made in recording transactions relating to the insurance contract are shown on the next page.

Cash surrender value increases are recognized on the books whenever a premium is paid. The periodic insurance premium includes a charge for the increase in the policy cash surrender value but the increase actually becomes effective as of the end of the policy year. Hence, anticipation of the cash surrender value on the date of the premium payment needs to be accompanied by a notation as to its effective date. Anticipation of the cash surrender value should also be disclosed in

TRANSACTION	ENTRY
October 1, 1975 Paid first annual premium, $2,100.	Prepaid Insurance............................ 2,100.00 Cash.. 2,100.00
December 31, 1975 To record insurance expense for Oct. 1–Dec. 31: ¼ × $2,100 = $525.	Life Insurance Expense.................. 525.00 Prepaid Insurance 525.00

October 1, 1976
Paid second annual premium, $2,100.
  Premium.. $2,100
  Less cash surrender value.............................. 1,150
  Net insurance charge..................................... $ 950
	Cash Surrender Value of Life Insurance (as of 9/30/77).................... 1,150.00
	Prepaid Insurance............................ 950.00
	   Cash.. 2,100.00

December 31, 1976
To record insurance expense for the year:
  ¾ × $2,100 (Jan. 1–Sept. 30)..................... $1,575.00
  ¼ × $950   (Oct. 1–Dec. 31)...................... 237.50
                             $1,812.50
	Life Insurance Expense.................. 1,812.50
	   Prepaid Insurance 1,812.50

October 1, 1977
Paid third annual premium, $2,100.
  Premium $2,100
  Less: Cash surrender value credit.... $1,300
         Dividend credit......................... 272   1,572
  Net insurance charge..................................... $ 528
	Cash Surrender Value of Life Insurance (as of 9/30/78).................... 1,300.00
	Prepaid Insurance............................ 528.00
	   Cash.. 1,828.00

December 31, 1977
To record insurance expense for the year:
  ¾ × $950 (Jan. 1–Sept. 30) $712.50
  ¼ × $528 (Oct. 1–Dec. 31).............................. 132.00
                             $844.50
	Life Insurance Expense 844.50
	   Prepaid Insurance 844.50

July 1, 1978 To record insurance expense for Jan. 1–July 1: ½ × $528 = $264.	Life Insurance Expense .... 264.00 Prepaid Insurance...................... 264.00

July 1, 1978
To record cancellation of policy upon death of insured:
Amount recoverable on policy:
  Face of policy... $50,000
  Premium rebate for period July 1–Oct. 1
  and current year dividend 735
                             $50,735
 	
Cancellation of asset values:
  Cash surrender value............................... $ 2,450
  Prepaid insurance................................... 132
                             $ 2,582
Gain on policy settlement........................... $48,153
	Receivable from Insurance Company... 50,735.00
	   Cash Surrender Value of Life
	   Insurance.................................... 2,450.00
	   Prepaid Insurance...................... 132.00
	   Gain on Settlement of Life Insurance..................................... 48,153.00

presenting this asset on the balance sheet. If loan values instead of cash surrender values were recognized, no notation would be required since the loan values become effective immediately upon meeting premium requirements for the policy year. Dividends in the example reduce the insurance charge of the period in which they are applied against a premium. Actually the dividend applied against the premium for the third year accrues at the end of the second year and could be considered as a correction in the expense of the second year. Dividends received in the period of policy termination are recognized as a part of policy proceeds in final settlement rather than as a correction of insurance expense. The procedures illustrated involve certain concessions in theoretical accuracy but are normally preferred because of their practicality.

INTERESTS IN REAL ESTATE

Improved property purchased for supplementary income and possible price appreciation or for future use is shown under the long-term investment heading. The expenses relating to such holdings should be deducted from any revenue produced by the property. Unimproved property is frequently acquired for possible future use or for sale. Land while unused makes no contribution to periodic revenue. Costs incident to holding the land should be added to the investment balance. When the land is used for construction purposes or is sold, its cost will include all expenditures incident to its acquisition and holding. Market or appraised values, when available, may be reported parenthetically.

MISCELLANEOUS LONG-TERM INVESTMENTS

Many assets could be named that are of an auxiliary character in terms of central business activities and are properly reportable under the "Long-term investments" heading. Long-term investments include such items as: advances to subsidiaries that are of a permanent nature; deposits made to guarantee contract performance; and equity interests in partnerships, trusts, and estates. Most of these assets produce either current revenue or have a favorable business effect in some other way. Although cost is the underlying basis for these miscellaneous investments, the accounting procedure varies according to the type of investment involved.

LONG-TERM INVESTMENTS ON THE BALANCE SHEET

Long-term investments are generally reported on the balance sheet following the current assets classification. The long-term investment section should not include temporary investments held as a ready source of cash. Headings should be provided for the different long-term investment categories and individual long-term investments reported within such groupings. Detailed information relative to individual long-term investments may be provided in separate supporting schedules. Long-term investment costs should be supplemented by market quotations in parenthetical or note form if market exceeds cost. Information concerning the pledge of long-term investments as collateral on loans should be provided. When long-term investments are carried at amounts other than cost, the valuation that is employed should be described.

In reporting funds to be applied to specific purposes or paid to specific parties, disclosure should be made by special note of the conditions relative to their establishment and ultimate application. A fund arrearage or other failure to meet contractual requirements should be pointed out;

the demand to be made upon current assets by deposit requirements in the succeeding fiscal period should also be disclosed when material. Offset of a fund balance against a liability item is proper only when an asset transfer to a trustee is irrevocable and actually serves to discharge the obligation.

The "Long-term investments" section of a balance sheet might appear as follows:

```
Long-term investments:
  Affiliated companies:
    Investment in Wilson Co. common
      stock, reported by the equity method
      (Investment consists of 90,000 shares
      representing a 40% interest acquired
      on July 1, 1973, for $1,500,000. Re-
      tained earnings of the subsidiary
      since date of acquisition have in-
      creased by $120,000; 40% of this
      amount, or $48,000, is identified with
      the parent company equity and has
      been recognized in the accounts.)......  $1,548,000
    Advances to Wilson Co. ..........................     115,000   $1,663,000

  Miscellaneous stock investments, at cost
    (stock has an aggregate quoted market
    value of $112,000; stock has been de-
    posited as security on bank loan —
    refer to notes payable, contra)...............                    100,000
  Stock redemption fund, composed of:
    Cash ......................................................  $    15,000
    Stocks and bonds, at cost (aggregate
      quoted market value, $420,000)..........      410,500
    Dividends and interest receivable...........        4,500        430,000
  Investment in land and unused facilities...                       125,000
  Cash surrender value of life insurance
    carried on officers' lives..........................              12,500
  Total long-term investments.......................                            $2,330,500
```

QUESTIONS

1. Why would a manufacturing company invest funds in stocks, bonds and other securities?

2. How should each of the following be classified on the balance sheet?

(a) Stock held for purposes of controlling the activities of a subsidiary.
(b) Listed stock rights to be sold.
(c) Stock intended to be transferred to a supplier in cancellation of an amount owed.

3. Under what conditions may an investor owning less than a majority interest in the stock of an investee exercise significant control over the investee's operating and financial policies?

4. (a) Define: (1) parent company, (2) subsidiary company. (b) How much stock ownership is required to exercise control?

5. How would you record the purchase of stock and bond units acquired for a lump sum when (a) only one of the securities is quoted on the market? (b) both securities are quoted? (c) neither security is quoted?

6. R. S. Doug purchases 1,000 shares of Abbott Motors at $90 a share in November, paying his broker $65,000. The market value of the stock on December 31 is $125 a share; Doug has made no further payment to his broker. On this date he shows on his balance sheet Abbott Motors Stock, $100,000, the difference between market value and the unpaid balance to the broker. Do you approve of this report? Explain.

7. What conflict, if any, exists between the equity method of reporting subsidiary company earnings on parent company statements and the entity theory?

8. When using the equity method, what special adjustments are necessary in recognizing the proportionate share of the investee's income?

9. What dates are significant in the declaration of a dividend?

10. Distinguish between the following types of dividends: (a) cash, (b) liquidating, (c) stock, (d) property.

11. What reasons may be offered for the infrequent use of property dividends by a corporation?

12. B. A. Lopez receives $400 representing a dividend of $4 per share on Atlas Securities Co. common stock, accompanied by a statement that $1.56 represents a distribution of income and $2.44 represents a dividend in partial liquidation. (a) What is the meaning of this statement? (b) What entry should Lopez make in recording the dividend?

13. Some accounting writers have suggested that certain stock dividends should constitute revenue to the recipients. What is the basis for this view?

14. Distinguish between a stock dividend and a stock split.

15. If stock rights lapse and are not used, what disposition should be made of the investment cost allocated to the rights?

16. The Parker Co. accepts 2,000 shares of Murdock common stock in full payment of a claim of $12,000 against the latter company. State how this transaction would be recorded on the books of the Parker Co., assuming that (a) Murdock stock is closely held and no market value is available; (b) Murdock stock is

quoted on the market at $5; (c) Murdock stock is quoted on the market at $6.50 bid, $7.50 asked.

17. Distinguish between the valuation method recommended for current marketable equity securities and that recommended for noncurrent marketable equity securities.

18. Name and describe five funds that would be listed as current assets and five that would be listed as long-term investments.

19. The Duane Co. has made certain major modifications in property that was leased for a ten-year period. The leasehold contract provides that in addition to the payment of monthly rents Duane Co. was to make monthly deposits to a sinking fund that will be used to restore the properties to their original condition upon termination of the leasehold. How would you record the payments required by the terms of the contract?

20. (a) Distinguish between life insurance cash surrender value and loan value. (b) How is the loan value on a life insurance policy calculated?

21. The Meadows Company collects in cash the dividends on the life insurance policies that it carries. The Nielson Company uses dividend credits to reduce the life insurance premium it pays. The Ogg Corporation authorizes the insurance companies to apply dividend credits to the increase of policy surrender value. What entries will each company make in recognizing dividends?

22. Name ten items properly reported under the "Long-term investments" heading on the balance sheet.

EXERCISES

1. The Leisure Life Co. acquired on margin 2,000 shares of Alloy, Inc., preferred stock and 20,000 shares of Alloy, Inc., common stock for $450,000 plus broker's commission of 1%. Market prices at the time the stock was acquired were $50 per share for preferred and $20 per share for common. Terms of the margin agreement provided for payment at acquisition date of 25% of the stock purchase price plus the broker's commission. The balance due the broker, plus 8% interest, must be paid within six months.

      (a) What entry should have been made to record the purchase?

      (b) What entry would be made to pay the balance due the broker three months after purchase?

2. The Crawford Co. holds stock of Russell Co. acquired as follows:

	Shares	Total Cost
1975	100	$5,600
1976	150	7,350
1977	50	2,410

(continued)

Give the entries that would be made upon the sale of 150 shares in 1978 at $53 per share assuming that cost is determined by (a) the first-in, first-out method, (b) the weighted average cost method, (c) identification of lot sold as the 1976 purchase.

3. In 1976, Fred Alpaka acquired 15,000 shares of Tropi-Cal & Co. for a cost of $375,000. He was also appointed chairman of the board of directors, a position that gave him significant control over the affairs of the company. Tropi-Cal & Co. has 100,000 shares of stock outstanding. What entries would be made by Alpaka in 1977 for the following events?

 (a) Tropi-Cal announces net income of $45,000 for the first six months and pays a dividend of 6¢ per share.
 (b) Alpaka acquires an additional 5,000 shares of Tropi-Cal & Co. at 15.
 (c) Tropi-Cal & Co. announces ordinary income of $60,000 for the second six months and an extraordinary loss of $100,000.

4. On January 1, 1977, M. Wilde and Company purchased 20,000 shares of Storms Corporation common stock for $100,000. At that date there were 50,000 shares of Storms common stock authorized and outstanding. The net assets of Storms at January 1 were valued at $200,000. You determine that fixed assets with a remaining life of 15 years have a fair market value of $30,000 above their net book value, and that the remainder of the excess is attributed to goodwill and amortized over 40 years.

What entries are required to report adjusted net income or loss for (a) 1978, reported proportionate share of income, $10,000; and (b) 1997, reported proportionate share of loss, $2,000?

5. Joseph Moi owns stock of Blackburn & Co. acquired in two lots as follows:

	Shares	Cost per Share	Total Cost
February 10, 1975	100	$45	$4,500
April 23, 1976	100	50	5,000

In 1977, a stock dividend of 50 shares was received. Because Joseph Moi needed cash, he sold the 50 shares at $32 per share and credited the proceeds to a revenue account, Gain on Sale of Blackburn Co. Stock. If the first-in, first-out method is used to record stock sales, what correction in the accounts is necessary assuming (a) the books are still open for 1977; (b) the error is not detected until 1978 after the 1977 financial reports were prepared?

6. Jill Hagen owns 400 shares of Automat Co. common acquired at $50 per share. Give the cost basis per share for her investment holdings if:

 (a) She receives a common stock dividend of 1 for 4.
 (b) Common stock is exchanged in a 5-for-1 split.
 (c) She receives a preferred stock dividend of 1 share for every 4 shares of common held; common is selling ex-dividend at $75; preferred is selling at $200.
 (d) She receives a property dividend of 1 share of Jasper Co. common, market price $7, for every 5 shares held.

7. On March 1, R. Wallace purchased 1,000 shares of Georgia Corp. common stock, par $5, at $32. On May 3, Wallace received a stock dividend of 1 share for every 4 owned. On September 13, he received a cash dividend of 40¢ on the stock and was granted the right to purchase 1 share at $10 for every 4 shares held. On this date stock had a market value ex-rights of $15, and each right had a value of $1; stock cost was allocated on this basis. On November 15, Wallace sold 450 rights at $1.50 each and exercised the remaining rights. What entries will appear on Wallace's books as a result of the foregoing?

8. The Flavor Co. holds stock of Santos, Inc., acquired as follows:

	Shares	Total Cost
Lot A, 1975	100	$8,400
Lot B, 1976	50	4,300

In 1977, Flavor Co. receives 150 rights to purchase Santos, Inc., stock at $75 per share. Four rights are required to purchase one share. At issue date, rights had a market value of $5 each and stock was selling ex-rights at $95. Flavor Co. used rights to purchase 20 additional shares of Santos, Inc., and allowed the unexercised rights to lapse. Assume use of the first-in, first-out method of identifying stock rights used. What entries are required to record the above events?

9. On March 1, 1977, Gilkes Corporation invested $75,000 stock redemption fund cash in 8% preferred stock of Wilkens, Inc., par value of $80,000. Wilkens normally declares and pays dividends on the preferred stock semiannually: May 1 and November 1. On April 1, 1978, Gilkes exchanged the stock with another investor for 2,000 shares of Simmons Corporation common stock. The market value of the common at the date of exchange was 42½.

Give all the entries necessary to record the above transactions assuming semiannual dividends were paid.

10. Sinking fund tables show that 5 annual deposits of $18,097.48 accruing interest at 5% compounded annually will result in a total accumulation of $100,000 immediately after the fifth payment. (a) Prepare a fund accumulation schedule showing the theoretical growth of the fund over the 5-year period. (b) Give all of the entries that would appear on the books for the increases in the property acquisition fund balance for the first three years.

11. The Dobb Company insured the life of its president for $100,000. Annual premiums of $4,200 are paid beginning July 1, 1977. A dividend of $600 is to be paid annually beginning July 1, 1978. Cash surrender value after the second year is $2,200; after the third year, $4,460. The president died January 1, 1980, and a premium refund of $1,500 is made in addition to the face value of the policy. If Dobb Company closes its books on December 31, give the required entries on its books for the years 1977–1980.

12. In 1967, the Cragen Appliance Corporation purchased for $78,000 ten acres adjoining its manufacturing plant to provide for possible future expansion. From 1967–1977 the company paid $20,000 in taxes and $30,000 in special assessments. In 1977 it sold one half of the land for $87,000 and erected a building at a cost of $300,000 on the other half. The company books on December 31, 1977, show a "plant" account balance of $341,000. Give the journal entries to correct the accounts.

PROBLEMS

14-1. The Roger Corp. and the Martin Corp. each have 150,000 shares of no-par stock outstanding. Water's, Inc., acquired 25,000 shares of Roger stock and 60,000 shares of Martin stock in 1972. Changes in retained earnings for Roger and Martin for 1976 and 1977 are as follows:

		Roger Corp.		Martin Corp.
Retained earnings (deficit), January 1, 1976		$140,000		$ (20,000)
Cash dividends, 1976		(30,000)		0
		$110,000		$ (20,000)
Income before extraordinary items	$20,000		$ 80,000	
Extraordinary gain	30,000		20,000	
Net income, 1976		50,000		100,000
Retained earnings, December 31, 1976		$160,000		$ 80,000
Cash dividends, 1977			$ (20,000)	
Market value of stock dividends issued — 7,500 shares (transferred to paid-in capital section)			(30,000)	(50,000)
				$ 30,000
Net income (loss), 1977		(60,000)		(10,000)
Retained earnings, December 31, 1977		$100,000		$ 20,000

> *Instructions:* Give the entries required on the books of Water's, Inc., for 1976 and 1977 to account for its investments.

14-2. J. Takashi owns 800 shares of Gino, Inc., acquired on May 1, 1973, for $30,000.

During 1976 and 1977, the following transactions took place with respect to this investment:

1976
Mar. 1 Received cash dividend of 50¢ per share and stock dividend of 25%.
Oct. 15 Received stock rights offering the purchase of 1 share at $70 for every 5 shares held. At this time stock was quoted ex-rights at $95 and rights were quoted at $5; stock cost was apportioned on this basis. Rights were exercised.

(continued)

1977
Mar. 1 Received a cash dividend of 50¢ per share and a stock dividend of 20%.
Dec. 5 Received stock rights offering the purchase of 1 share at $68 for every 5 shares held. At this time stock was quoted ex-rights at $78 and rights were quoted at $2; stock cost was apportioned on this basis. Rights were sold at $3, less brokerage charges of $75.

Instructions:
(1) Give journal entries to record the foregoing transactions.
(2) Give the investment account balance as of December 31, 1977, including shares and costs in support of this balance.

14-3. On January 1, 1977, Shaw, Inc., purchased 100,000 shares of Squires Corporation common stock for $600,000. At the time, Squires had 400,000 shares authorized and issued. You are given the following information:

(a) Squires Corporation asset values at January 1, 1977, are as follows:

	Book Value	Market Value
Net current assets	$1,250,000	$1,250,000
Land	350,000	350,000
Buildings (10-year remaining life)	900,000	700,000
	$2,500,000	$2,300,000

(b) Squires Corporation reported income for 1977 of $400,000.
(c) On February 1, 1978, Squires paid a dividend of $1 per share.
(d) Squires Corporation reported income for 1978 of $350,000.

Instructions: Give the necessary journal entries to record the above information. (Assume income is earned evenly throughout the year.)

14-4. The following balances appeared in the ledger of the Fleming Company on December 31, 1974:

Investment in Ace Co. Common Stock, par $100, 250 shares	$24,000
Investment in Ace Co. 6% Preferred Stock, par $100, 50 shares	$ 3,950

The Fleming Company uses the first-in, first-out method in accounting for stock transactions. In 1975, 1976, and 1977 the following transactions took place relative to the above investments:

1975
Jan. 20 Holders of Ace Co. 6% preferred were given the right to exchange their holdings for an equal number of Ace Co. common, and the Fleming Co. made such exchange. Common shares on the date of exchange were quoted on the market at $120 per share.
Dec. 29 Received cash dividends of $3 per share on Ace Co. common.
1976
July 30 Received additional shares of Ace Co. common in a 4-for-1 stock split. (Par value of common was reduced to $25.)
Dec. 28 Exercised option to receive one share of Ace Co. common for each 40 shares held in lieu of a cash dividend of $1 per share held. The market value of Ace Co. common on the date of distribution was $50 per share. Dividend revenue was recognized at the value of the shares received.
1977
July 1 Received a stock dividend of 10% on Ace Co. common.
Oct. 15 Received warrants representing right to purchase at par 1 share of Ace Co. common for every 4 shares held. On date of warrants issue, the market value of shares ex-rights was $37, and the market value of rights was $3; cost of the stock was allocated on this basis.
Oct. 31 Exercised 440 rights identified with the first lot of stock acquired and sold remaining rights at $2.50 per right less brokerage charges of $30.
Dec. 31 Sold 660 shares of Ace Co. common at $43 per share less brokerage charges of $330.

Instructions:

(1) Prepare journal entries to record the transactions in Ace Co. holdings.
(2) Prepare a schedule showing the balance of Ace Co. Common Stock held by Fleming Company on December 31, 1977.

14-5. The Tong Co. has the following securities on hand on January 1, 1977.

Investment in North Co. 6% Preferred Stock, par $60, 75 shares .... $ 2,700
Investment in Ontario Iron Common Stock, 500 shares $30,250

During 1977, the following transactions were completed relative to investments.

Jan. 24 Purchased 150 shares of Wyler Co. common for $8,400.
Feb. 1 Received a cash dividend of 50¢ and stock dividend of 10% on Ontario Iron common.
Apr. 12 Purchased 200 shares of Wyler Co. common for $14,000.
May 20 Received the semiannual dividend on North Co. 6% preferred.
July 1 Wyler Co. common was split on a 2-for-1 basis.
Aug. 11 Received a dividend of $2 on Wyler Co. common.
11 Received a cash dividend of 50¢ and a stock dividend of 10% on Ontario Iron common.
Oct. 10 Sold 200 shares of Wyler Co. common for $9,100 and also sold the 75 shares of North Co. 6% preferred for $5,000.
28 Received rights on Wyler Co. common to subscribe for additional shares as follows: 1 share could be acquired at $40 for every 4 shares held. On this date stock was selling for 48 and rights were selling at 2; stock cost was apportioned on this basis.
Nov. 15 Sold all of the Wyler rights for $815.
Dec. 20 Received a special year-end dividend on Ontario Iron common of $3.

Instructions:

(1) Assuming the use of first-in, first-out in assigning costs to sales, give journal entries to record the foregoing transactions. (Give calculations in support of your entries.)
(2) Give the investment account balance as of December 31, 1977, including the number of shares and costs comprising such balances.

14-6. Transactions of Merrill Machines, Inc., during 1977 included the following:

Jan. 15 Purchased 600 units of Joel Co. preferred and common stock at $60 per unit: each unit consists of one share of preferred and two shares of common. No market costs are available. Brokerage charges were $540.
Feb. 10 Received a 20% stock dividend on the common stock.
Feb. 15 Sold all the preferred stock for $16 per share less brokerage charges of $420.
Mar. 10 Received stock rights permitting the purchase of one share at $14 of common for every 5 shares held. On this day, rights were being traded at $1 each and stock was being traded ex-rights at $19 per share.
Mar. 21 Exercised 1,000 rights pertaining to the stock acquired on January 15, and sold remaining rights at $1 less brokerage charges of $6.
June 30 Received a stock dividend of 82 shares of $25 par preferred stock on the common stock held. On the date of distribution common stock was selling for $20 and the preferred stock for $30. Because Merrill Machines, Inc., keeps its stock records on the fifo method, it is necessary to allocate cost according to the different lots held.
Aug. 15 Sold the shares acquired on March 21 plus 300 shares from the holdings acquired on January 15 at $22 less brokerage charges of $225.
Dec. 15 Redeemed the preferred stock at a call price of $35.

Instructions:

(1) Give journal entries to record the foregoing transactions. (Give computations in support of your entries.)
(2) Give the investment account balance on December 31, 1977, and the shares and costs making up this balance.

14-7. During your December 31, 1977 audit of Rich, Inc., you find the following items in the account summarizing the investment in Musket Motors & Co. common stock:

ACCOUNT   **Investment in Musket Motors & Co. Common Stock**

DATE	ITEM	DEBIT	CREDIT	BALANCE DEBIT	BALANCE CREDIT
1977 Jan. 1	Purchased 5,000 shares at $30	150,000		150,000	
Mar. 31	Cash dividend..................................		3,000	147,000	
June 30	Share of net income for first half of 1977	20,000		167,000	
Nov. 10	Received stock rights		16,700	150,300	
30	Cash dividend..............................		5,000	145,300	
Dec. 30	Exercised stock rights to purchase 1,000 shares at $34	40,680		185,980	
31	Share of net income for second half of 1977................................	18,000		203,980	

After inquiry, the following additional data were obtained.

    (a) Musket Motors & Co. net income for the first and second halves of 1977 was $400,000 and $450,000 respectively.

    (b) Broker's fees of $2,500 on the original purchase were recorded as an expense.

    (c) The dividend of March 31 represented a distribution of earnings from the second half of 1976.

    (d) The dividend of November 30 was $1 per share; 70¢ per share represents earnings and the balance represents a liquidating dividend.

    (e) Musket Motors & Co. offered its stockholders the opportunity to subscribe to new stock at $34 per share up to 50% of their holdings. At distribution date, stock rights were selling for $5. Rich, Inc., was informed that 10% of stock cost was applicable to rights.

Instructions:

    (1) Give the individual entries for each correction required in the Musket Motors & Co. investment account on December 31, 1977, to bring this account in conformity with generally accepted accounting principles.

    (2) Give the corrected balance for the investment account on December 31, 1977, and the shares and costs making up this balance.

14-8. Transactions of Coleman Service Co. in securities during 1977 were as follows:

    Feb. 10 Purchased 1,000 shares of Harper, Inc., common stock for $37,000.

    Mar. 15 Purchased 9,000 shares of Fisher Co. preferred stock for $72,000.

    Oct.   24 Sold 500 shares of Harper, Inc., common stock for $15,000.

The fair market value of Fisher Co. preferred and Harper, Inc., common stock on December 31, 1977, the date of the annual audit, was $7 and $25 per share respectively. The president of the company recommends that the cost balance in the investments account be retained because the investments are in reality long-term and the declines in market values seem to be temporary. The auditor counters that since one half of the Harper, Inc., common stock has been sold during the year and since the investment in Fisher Co. is in preferred stock, the investments appear to be current assets rather than long-term investments.

Instructions:

    (1) Give journal entries to record any valuation adjustments that would be made if the auditor's recommendations are followed.

    (2) Give journal entries to record any valuation adjustments that would be made if the president's recommendations are followed.

    (3) Give journal entries to record any valuation adjustments that would be made if the Harper, Inc., common is identified as long-term, but the decline is felt to be permanent. The Fisher Co. stock is still classified as a current asset.

14-9. On December 31, 1977, a four-payment fund is set up to redeem $30,000 of preferred stock. The fund is guaranteed to earn 6% compounded annually, and must generate enough income to enable the company to retire the stock after the fourth payment. The annual installments paid to the fund trustee are $6,857.75. The first deposit is made immediately.

Instructions:
(1) Give the journal entries in connection with the fund for the years 1977 and 1978. (Assume the company keeps its books on the calendar year basis.)
(2) Suppose that on December 31, 1981, the fund balance of $30,000 consisted of $8,000 cash and $22,000 in securities. The securities are sold for $24,000. Give all of the journal entries that would be made to sell the securities, retire the $30,000 of preferred stock, and liquidate any balance in the fund account.

14-10. During the course of the audit of the Harlen Lee Company, which closes its accounts on December 31, you examine the life insurance policies, premium receipts, and confirmations returned by the insurance companies in response to your request for information. You find that in 1977 the company had paid premiums on the life of the president, Harlen Lee, as shown below:

Sole Owner and Beneficiary	Face of Policy	Annual Billed Premium 1977	Cash Dividend Used to Reduce Premium	Annual Premium Date	Cash Surrender Value December 31 1977	1976
1. Harlen Lee Company	$100,000	$2,500	$700	June 30	$32,000	$30,000
2. Dorothy Lee, wife of Harlen Lee	50,000	1,600	300	Sept. 30	15,000	14,000
3. Harlen Lee Company	100,000	3,600	800	April 1	22,000	21,000

Instructions:
(1) Prepare all of the journal entries required for the year 1977.
(2) What balances relating to these insurance policies would appear on the balance sheet prepared on December 31, 1977?

14-11. The analysis below and on page 406 relates to the Craig Corporation investment account:

Craig Corporation
Analysis of Investments
For Year Ended December 31, 1977

Date		Debit	Credit
	(1)		
1977	**Ace Tool Company Common Stock**		
Mar. 15	Purchased 1,000 shares at $25 per share........................	$ 25,000	
June 28	Received 50 shares of Bymore Sales Company common stock as a dividend on Ace Tool Company common stock (memorandum entry in general ledger).		
Sept. 30	Sold 50 shares of Bymore Sales Company common stock at $14 per share		$ 700
Oct. 31	Awarded 500 shares of Ace Tool Company common stock to selected members of Craig's management as an incentive award and accounted for as employee compensation		12,500
	(2)		
	Mascot, Inc., Common and Preferred Stock		
Mar. 15	Purchased 600 units of common and preferred stock at $36 per unit. Each unit consists of one share of preferred and two shares of common stock..............	21,600	
Apr. 30	Sold 300 shares of common stock at $13 per share......		3,900
June 28	Received 900 common stock rights. Each right entitles the holder to purchase one share of common stock for $12 (memorandum entry in general ledger).		
Sept. 30	Exercised 450 common stock rights to acquire 450 shares of common stock at $12 per share..................	5,400	
Sept. 30	Sold remaining 450 common stock rights at $4 per right...		1,800

Date			Debit	Credit
		(3) Standard Service, Inc., Common Stock		
Mar.	15	Purchased 10,000 shares at $17 per share.....................	170,000	
Oct.	31	Received dividend of 75¢ per share...............................		7,500
		(4) Kevin Instruments, Inc., Common Stock		
Mar.	15	Purchased 4,000 shares at $28 per share......................	112,000	
Apr.	30	Purchased 2,000 shares at $30 per share......................	60,000	
June	28	Received dividend of 40¢ per share..............................		2,400
		(5) Other Investment		
Oct.	31	Reacquired 1,600 shares of its own (Craig) outstanding common stock at $14 per share with the intention of retiring them..		22,400

Additional information follows:

(a) The fair market value for each security as of the 1977 date of each transaction follows:

Security	March 15	April 30	June 28	Sept. 30	Oct. 31
Ace Tool Company common stock.....	$25				$42
Bymore Sales Company common stock...			$ 8	$14	
Mascot, Inc., preferred stock	20				
Mascot, Inc., common stock	10	$13	15*	16	
Mascot, Inc., common stock rights			3	4	
Standard Service, Inc., common stock...	17				
Kevin Instruments, Inc., common stock...	28	30			
Craig Corporation common stock					14

*Ex-rights

(b) Standard Service, Inc., has only one class of stock authorized and there were 30,000 shares of its common stock outstanding throughout 1977. Craig's cost of its investment in Standard was not materially different from its equity in the recorded values of Standard's net assets; recorded values were not materially different from fair values (individually or collectively). Standard's net income from the date of acquisition of Craig's investment to December 31, 1977, was $336,000. There were no intercompany transactions requiring elimination.

(c) Kevin Instruments, Inc., has only one class of stock authorized and there were 40,000 shares of its common stock outstanding throughout 1977. Craig's cost of its investment in Kevin was not materially different from its equity in the recorded values of Kevin's net assets; recorded values were not materially different from fair values (individually or collectively). Kevin's net income from the date of acquisition of Craig's investment to December 31, 1977, was $120,000. There were no intercompany transactions requiring elimination.

(d) All other investments of Craig are widely held, and Craig's percentage of ownership in each is nominal (5% or less).

(e) At December 31, 1977, Craig Corporation had 98,400 shares of its $10 par value common stock outstanding. The balance in the premium on common stock account was $100,000.

Instructions: Prepare necessary adjusting journal entries classified by each of the securities analyzed in (a) through (e) to properly adjust the investment account. Identify each security by type (preferred stock, common stock, rights, etc.) as well as by company. Schedules supporting calculations should be in good form and either included as part of the journal entry explanation or properly cross-referenced to the appropriate journal entry. (Ignore brokers' fees, transfer and income taxes.) (AICPA adapted)

14-12. During your audit of the 1977 financial statements of Longwood, Inc., you find a new account titled Miscellaneous Assets. Your examination reveals that in 1977 Longwood, Inc., began investing cash in securities and the corporation's bookkeeper entered all transactions believed related to investments in this account. Information summarized from the miscellaneous assets account appears below:

Longwood, Inc.
Information Summarized from
the Miscellaneous Assets Account
For Year Ended December 31, 1977

Date			Folio	Debit	Credit
		Compudata Common Stock			
1977					
Mar.	31	Purchased 500 shares at 48.........................	CD	$24,000	
July	31	Received cash dividend of $2 per share......	CR		$ 1,000
July	31	Sold 100 shares at 60..................................	CR		6,000
Nov.	15	Pledged 100 shares as security for $4,000 bank loan payable February 15, 1978......	CR		4,000
Nov.	30	Received 150 shares by donation from stockholder whose cost in 1970 was $10 per share...	JE	1,500	
		Standard Atomic Common Stock			
Mar.	31	Purchased 900 shares at 26..........................	CD	23,400	
June	30	Received dividend (25¢ per share in cash and 1 share Standard Atomic preferred for each 5 shares common owned)..........	CR		225
		Standard Atomic Preferred Stock			
June	30	Received 180 shares as stock dividend on Standard Atomic common	MEMO		
July	31	Sold 80 shares at 17.....................................	CR		1,360
		Other			
Dec.	29	Paid 1978 rental charge on safe deposit box used for investments..........................	CD	35	
		Total..		$48,935	$12,585

All security purchases include brokers' fees, and sales are net of brokers' fees and transfer taxes when applicable. The fair market values (net of brokers' fees and transfer taxes) for each security as of the 1977 date of each transaction were:

Security	3/31	6/30	7/31	11/15	11/30
Compudata common.................................	48		60	61¼	62
Standard Atomic common	26	30			
Standard Atomic preferred		16⅔	17		

Instructions: Prepare a work sheet to distribute or correct each of the transactions entered in the miscellaneous assets account. Ignore income tax in your solution. Formal adjusting entries are not required. Make separate entries for each transaction; do not combine adjustments. In addition to columns for entries in the miscellaneous assets account, the following column headings are recommended for your work sheet:

Adjustments to Distribute and Correct Items Entered
in the Miscellaneous Assets Account

Miscellaneous Assets	Investments	(Gain) Loss from Sale of Investments	(Revenue) from Dividends and Interest	Other Accounts	
Debit (Credit)	Debit (Credit)			Name of Account	Debit (Credit)

(AICPA adapted)

Accounting for Bonds

Long-term financing of a corporation is accomplished either through the issuance of long-term debt instruments, usually bonds, or through the sale of additional ownership equity, usually stock. The issuance of bonds instead of stock may be preferred by stockholders for the following reasons: (1) the charge against earnings for bond interest is normally less than the share of earnings that would otherwise be payable as dividends on a new issue of preferred stock or on the sale of additional common stock; (2) present owners continue in control of the corporation; and (3) interest is a deductible expense in arriving at taxable income while dividends are not.

But there are certain limitations and disadvantages of financing through bonds. Bond financing is possible only when a company is in a satisfactory financial condition and can offer adequate security to a new creditor group. Furthermore, interest must be paid regardless of the company's earnings and financial position. With operating losses and the inability of a company to raise sufficient cash to meet the periodic interest payments, bondholders may take legal action to assume control of company properties.

Bonds are purchased for both short-term and long-term purposes by corporations, principally insurance companies, banks, trust companies, and educational and charitable institutions. Because of the similarity in accounting for bonds as a liability and as a long-term investment, both sides of a bond transaction will be discussed in this chapter.

NATURE OF BONDS

The power of a corporation to create bonded indebtedness is found in the corporation laws of the state and may be specifically granted by charter. In some cases formal authorization by a majority of stockholders is required before a board of directors can approve a bond issue.

Borrowing by means of bonds involves the issuance of a number of certificates of indebtedness. Bond certificates may represent equal parts of the bond issue or they may be of varying denominations. Bonds of a business unit are commonly issued in $1,000 denominations, referred to as the *bond face, par*, or *maturity value*.

The group contract between the corporation and the bondholders is known as the *bond* or *trust indenture*. The indenture details the rights and obligations of the contracting parties, indicates the property pledged as well as the protection offered on the loan, and names the bank or trust company that is to represent the bondholders.

Bonds may be sold by the company directly to investors, or they may be underwritten by investment bankers or a syndicate. The underwriters may agree to purchase the entire bond issue or that part of the issue which is not sold by the company, or they may agree simply to manage the sale of the security on a commission basis.

Types of Bonds

Bonds may be classified in many different ways. When all of the bonds mature on a single date, they are called *term bonds*; when bonds mature in installments, they are known as *serial bonds*. Bonds issued by private corporations may be *secured* or *unsecured*. Secured bonds provide protection to the investor in the form of a mortgage covering the company's real estate and perhaps other property, or a pledge in the form of certain collateral. A *first-mortgage bond* represents a first claim against the property of a corporation in the event of the company's inability to meet bond interest and principal payments. A *second-mortgage bond* is a secondary claim ranking only after the claim of the first-mortgage bonds or senior issue has been completely satisfied. A *collateral trust bond* is usually secured by stocks and bonds of other corporations owned by the issuing company. Such securities are generally transferred to a trustee who holds them as collateral on behalf of the bondholders and, if necessary, will sell them to satisfy the bondholders' claim.

Unsecured bonds are not protected by the pledge of certain property and are frequently termed *debenture bonds*. Holders of debenture bonds simply rank as general creditors with other unsecured parties. The risk involved in these securities varies with the financial strength of the debtor. Debentures issued by a strong company may involve little risk; debentures issued by a weak company whose properties are already heavily mortgaged may involve considerable risk.

When another party promises to make payment on bonds if the issuing company fails to do so, the bonds are referred to as *guaranteed bonds*. A parent company, for example, may guarantee payment of the bonds issued by its subsidiaries.

Obligations known as *income bonds* have been issued when business failure has resulted in corporate reorganization. These bonds require the payment of interest only to the extent of a company's current earnings. Income bonds may be cumulative or noncumulative. If cumulative, interest that cannot be paid in one year is carried over as a lien against future earnings; if noncumulative, no future lien arises from inability to meet interest payments.

The investor acquiring governmental obligations looks to the taxing authority of the issuing unit for the measure of its ability to raise money to meet debt service requirements. Certain government obligations are identified with government-owned enterprises, and principal and interest payments are made from the revenues accruing from such operations. These are known as *revenue bonds*.

Bonds may provide for their conversion into some other security at the option of the bondholder. Such bonds are known as *convertible bonds*. The conversion feature generally permits the owner of bonds to exchange holdings into common stock. The bondholder is thus able to exchange the claim into an ownership interest if corporate operations prove successful and conversion becomes attractive; in the meantime the special rights of a creditor are maintained.

Other bond features may serve the issuer's interests. For example, bond indentures frequently give the issuing company the right to call and retire the bonds prior to their maturity. Such bonds are termed *callable bonds*. When a corporation wishes to reduce its outstanding indebtedness, bondholders are notified of the portion of the issue to be surrendered, and they are paid in accordance with call provisions. Interest does not accrue after the call date.

Bonds may be classified as (1) *registered bonds* and (2) *bearer* or *coupon bonds*. Registered bonds call for the registry of the owner's name on the corporation books. Transfer of bond ownership is similar to that for stock. When a bond is sold, the corporate transfer agent cancels the bond certificate surrendered by the seller and issues a new certificate to the buyer. Interest checks are mailed periodically to the bondholders of record. Bearer or coupon bonds are not recorded in the name of the owner, title to such bonds passing with delivery. Each bond is accompanied by coupons for individual interest payments covering the life of the issue. Coupons are clipped by the owner of the bond and presented to a bank for deposit or collection. The issue of bearer bonds eliminates the need for recording bond ownership changes and preparing and mailing periodic interest checks. But coupon bonds fail to offer the bondholder the protection found in registered bonds in the event bonds are lost or stolen. In some cases, bonds provide interest coupons but require registry as to principal. Here, ownership safeguards are afforded while the time-consuming routines involved in making interest payments are avoided. Most bonds of recent issue are registered.

Bond Market Price

The market price of bonds varies with the safety of the investment. When the financial condition and earnings of a corporation are such that payment of interest and principal on bonded indebtedness is assured, the interest rate a company must offer to dispose of a bond issue is relatively low. As the risk factor increases, a higher interest return is necessary to attract investors. The interest rate on the bonds is known as the *stated* or *contract rate*. Although bonds provide for the payment of interest at a certain rate, this rate may not be the same as the prevailing or *market rate* for bonds of similar quality at the time the issue is sold. Furthermore, the market rate constantly fluctuates. These factors often result in a difference between bond face values and the prices at which the bonds sell on the market.

The purchase of bonds at face value implies agreement between the bond rate of interest and the prevailing market rate of interest. If the bond rate exceeds the market rate, the bonds will sell at a premium; if the bond rate is less than the market rate, the bonds will sell at a discount. The premium or the discount is the discounted value of the difference between the contract rate and the market rate of the series of interest payments. A declining market rate of interest subsequent to issuance of the bonds results in an increase in the market value of the bonds; a rising market rate of interest results in a decrease in their market value. The contract rate corrected for the premium or the discount on the purchase gives the actual return on the bonds, known as the *effective rate*. Bonds are quoted on the market as a percentage of face value. Thus, a bond quotation of 96 means the market price is 96% of face value, or at a discount; a bond quotation of 104 means the market price is 104% of face value, or at a premium.

The market price of a bond at any date can be determined by discounting the maturity value of the bond and each remaining interest payment at the effective rate of interest for similar debt on that date. Present value tables that can be used for discounting are included in Appendix A.

To illustrate the computation of a bond market price from the tables, assume 10-year, 8% bonds of $100,000 are to be sold on the bond issue date. The effective interest rate for these bonds is 10%, compounded semiannually. The computation may be divided into two parts:

1. *Present Value of Maturity Value:*
   Maturity value of bonds after ten years or twenty semiannual periods = $100,000
   Effective interest rate — 10% per year, or 5% per semiannual period:
   $PV_n = A(PVF_{\overline{n}|\,i}) = \$100,000(\text{Table II}_{\overline{20}|\,5\%}) = \$100,000(.3769) = \$37,690.$
2. *Present Value of Twenty Interest Payments:*
   Semiannual payment, 4% of $100,000 = $4,000
   Effective interest rate — 10% per year, or 5% per semiannual period:
   $PV_n = R(PVAF_{\overline{n}|\,i}) = \$4,000(\text{Table IV}_{\overline{20}|\,5\%}) = \$4,000(12.4622) = \$49,849$

The market price for the bonds would thus be $87,539, the sum of the two parts. Because the effective interest rate is higher than the stated interest rate, the bonds would sell at a $12,461 discount at the issuance date.

Special adaptation of present value tables are available to determine the price to be paid for the bonds if they are to provide a certain return. A portion of such a bond table is illustrated at the top of the next page.

Note that the present value from the table of 8% bonds to return 10% in 10 years is $87,539, the same amount computed above. If the bond return were 7.5%, the present value would be $103,476.

Values to the Nearest Dollar of 8% Bond for $100,000
Interest Payable Semiannually

Yield	8 years	8½ years	9 years	9½ Years	10 Years
7.00	$106,046	$106,325	$106,595	$106,855	$107,107
7.25	104,495	104,699	104,896	105,090	105,272
7.50	102,971	103,100	103,232	103,360	103,476
7.75	101,472	101,537	101,595	101,658	101,718
8.00	100,000	100,000	100,000	100,000	100,000
8.25	98,552	98,494	98,437	98,372	98,325
8.50	97,141	97,012	96,893	96,787	96,678
8.75	95,746	95,568	95,398	95,232	95,070
9.00	94,383	94,147	93,920	93,703	93,496
9.25	93,042	92,757	92,480	92,214	91,953
9.50	91,723	91,380	91,055	90,751	90,452
9.75	90,350	89,960	89,588	89,238	88,902
10.00	89,162	88,726	88,310	87,914	87,539

This table can also be used to determine the effective rate on a bond acquired at a certain price. To illustrate, assume that a $1,000, 8% bond due in 10 years is selling at $951. Reference to the column "10 years" for $95,070 shows a return of 8.75% is provided on an investment of $950.70.

BOND ISSUANCE

Bonds may be issued directly by the issuer or they may be sold on the open market through securities exchanges or through investment bankers.

The issuer normally records bonds at their face value — the amount that the company must pay at maturity. Hence, when bonds are issued at an amount other than face value, a bond discount or premium balance is established for the difference between the cash received and the bond face value. This amount is added to or subtracted from the bond face value in the liability section of the balance sheet.

The investor normally records an investment in bonds at cost, which includes brokerage fees and any other costs incident to the purchase. No separate premium or discount account is therefore required. Bonds acquired in exchange for assets or services are recorded at the fair market value of such consideration. When bonds and other securities are acquired for a lump sum, an apportionment of such cost among the securities is required. Purchase of bonds on a deferred payment basis calls for recognition of both the asset and the liability balances.

The purchase, as well as the issuance of bonds, when made between interest payment dates requires calculation of the accrued interest which is added to the bond price. The amount paid for accrued interest on a purchase is subtracted from subsequent interest collections in measuring interest revenue; the amount received for accrued interest on an issuance is subtracted from subsequent interest payments in measuring interest expense.

To illustrate the accounting for bond issuance, assume a 10-year, $200,000, 8% bond issue is sold at 103, on May 1. Interest payment dates are February 1 and August 1. The entries on the books of the issuer and the investor would be as follows:

Issuer's Books

May 1	Cash	210,000	
	Bonds Payable		200,000
	Premium on Bonds		6,000
	Interest Expense[1]		4,000
	To record issuance of bonds.		

Computation:

$200,000 × 103 = $206,000 purchase price.
Interest: $200,000 × .08 × 3/12 = $4,000

Investor's Books

May 1	Investment in Bonds	206,000	
	Interest Revenue[1]	4,000	
	Cash		210,000
	To record investment in bonds.		

A 360-day year was assumed in the illustration for convenience. A 365-day year is frequently used for governmental obligations and is increasingly used by many banks.

When bonds are issued in exchange for property, the transaction should be recorded at the cash price at which the bonds could be issued. When difficulties are encountered in arriving at a cash price, the market or appraised value of the property acquired would be used. A difference between the face value of the bonds and the cash value of the bonds or the value of the property acquired is recognized as bond discount or bond premium.

The issuance of bonds normally involves costs for legal services, printing and engraving, taxes, and underwriting. These costs should be summarized separately as issuing costs, classified as deferred charges, and charged to revenue over the life of the bond issue.[2]

Issuance of Convertible Bonds

The issuance of *convertible debt securities*, most frequently bonds, has become very popular. These securities are convertible into the common stock of the issuing company or an affiliate at a specified price and at the option of the holder. These securities usually have the following characteristics:[3]

1. An interest rate lower than the issuer could establish for nonconvertible debt.
2. An initial conversion price higher than the market value of the common stock at time of issuance.
3. A callable option retained by the issuer.

---

[1]As indicated in Chapter 2, the real accounts Interest Payable and Interest Receivable could have been used rather than Interest Expense and Interest Revenue. These real accounts could then be reduced when the interest payments are made or received, or they could be adjusted to their proper balances at the end of the reporting period.

[2]*Opinions of the Accounting Principles Board, No. 21,* "Interest on Receivables and Payables" (New York: American Institute of Certified Public Accountants, 1971), par. 16.

[3]*Opinions of the Accounting Principles Board, No. 14,* "Accounting for Convertible Debt and Debt Issued with Stock Purchase Warrants" (New York: American Institute of Certified Public Accountants, 1969), par. 3.

The popularity of these securities may be attributed to the advantages to both the issuer and the holder. The issuer is able to obtain financing at a lower interest rate because of the value of the conversion feature to the holder. Because of the call provision, the issuer is in a position to exert influence upon the holders to exchange the debt into equity capital if stock values increase; he or she has had the use of relatively low interest rate financing if stock values do not increase. On the other hand, the holder has the advantage of the security of a debt instrument that, barring default, assures the return of investment plus a fixed return, and at the same time offers an option to transfer his or her interest to equity capital should such transfer become attractive.

Differences of opinion exist as to whether convertible debt securities should be treated by the issuer solely as debt, or whether part of the proceeds received from the issuance of debt should be recognized as equity capital. One view holds that the debt and the conversion privilege are inseparably connected, and therefore the debt and equity portions of the security should not be separately valued. The holder cannot sell part of the instrument and retain the other. An alternate view holds that there are two distinct elements in these securities and that each should be recognized in the accounts: that portion of the issuance price attributable to the conversion privilege should be recorded as a credit to Paid-In Capital; the balance of the issuance price should be assigned to the debt. This would decrease the premium otherwise recognized on the debt or perhaps result in a discount.

These views are compared in the illustration that follows. Assume 500 ten-year bonds, face value $1,000, are sold at 105. The bonds contain a conversion privilege that provides for exchange of a $1,000 bond for 20 shares of stock, par value $40. The interest rate on the bonds is 8%. It is established that without the conversion privilege, the bonds would sell at 96. The journal entries to record the issuance on the issuer's books under the two approaches follow.

Debt and Equity Not Separated

Cash	525,000	
Bonds Payable		500,000
Premium on Bonds Payable		25,000

Debt and Equity Separated

Cash	525,000	
Discount on Bonds Payable	20,000	
Bonds Payable		500,000
Paid-In Capital Arising from Bond Conversion Privilege		45,000

The periodic charge for interest will differ depending upon which method is employed. Under the first approach, the annual interest charge would be $37,500 ($40,000 paid less $2,500 straight-line premium amortization). Under the second approach, the annual interest charge would be $42,000 ($40,000 paid plus $2,000 straight-line discount amortization).

In 1969, the Accounting Principles Board in APB Opinion No. 14 stated that when convertible debt is sold at a price or with a value at issuance not significantly in excess of the face amount, "... no portion of the proceeds from the issuance ... should be accounted for as attributable to the conversion feature."[1]

The Opinion stated that greater weight for this decision was placed upon the inseparability of the debt and the conversion option than upon the practical problems of valuing the separate parts. However, the practical problems are considerable. Separate valuation requires asking the question: How much would the security sell for without the conversion feature? In many instances this question would appear to be unanswerable. Investment banks responsible for selling these issues are frequently unable to separate the two features for valuation purposes. The cash required simply could not be raised, they contend, without the conversion privilege.

There would seem to be strong theoretical support for separating the debt and equity portions of the proceeds from the issuance of convertible debt on the issuer's books. The conversion privilege does have a value, and this situation is only an example of the complex transactions requiring special analysis for proper recording. Present practical considerations may make it difficult to always separate the debt and conversion privileges. This means that valuation techniques require additional study. In applying present guidelines, even when separate values are determinable, they are not recorded.

Issuance of Bonds with Stock Purchase Warrants Attached

In addition to an increasing volume of convertible debt issues, bonds with detachable stock purchase warrants have been issued. Because the debt instrument and the warrant are separate, they can and do trade on the market separately Unlike convertible debt, of which repayment is uncertain, the presumption in debt with detachable warrants is that the debt will be repaid upon maturity. The decision to exercise the warrants depends upon the movement of the stock market.

Because the warrants are separable from the debt instrument, a value can be assigned to the warrants based on the relative fair value of the debt security without the warrants and the value of the warrants themselves at the time of issuance. Assume the same example used in the discussion of convertible bonds except that stock warrants are substituted for the conversion feature: 500 ten-year bonds, face value $1,000, are sold at 105. Each bond is accompanied by one warrant that permits the holder to purchase 20 shares of stock, par value $40. Each bond without the warrant has a market value of $960, and each warrant has a market value of $90. The proceeds of $525,000 would be allocated $480,000 to the debt and $45,000 to the owners' equity on the issuer's books as follows:

Cash	525,000	
Discount on Bonds Payable	20,000	
Bonds Payable		500,000
Common Stock Purchase Warrants		45,000

---

[1]*Ibid.*, par. 12.

In the preceding example, the sum of the market value for bonds and stock warrants equaled the issue price of the joint offering. Market imperfections rarely provide such perfect relationships. When such relationship is not found, sales proceeds should be allocated between the two securities on the basis of their relative market values at the time of their issuance. When the purchase warrants are used to acquire stock, the amount allocated to equity is transferred to the account Premium on Common Stock.

BOND INTEREST — TERM BONDS

When coupon bonds are issued, cash is paid by the company in exchange for interest coupons on the interest dates. Payments on coupons may be made by the company directly to bondholders, or payments may be cleared through a bank or other disbursing agent. Subsidiary records with bondholders are not maintained since coupons are redeemable by bearers. In the case of registered bonds, interest checks are mailed either by the company or its agent. When bonds are registered, the bonds account requires subsidiary ledger support. The subsidiary ledger shows holdings by individuals and changes in such holdings. Checks are sent to bondholders of record as of the interest payment dates.

When an agent is to make interest payments, the company normally transfers cash to the agent in advance of the interest payment date. Since the company is not freed from its obligation to bondholders until payment has been made by its agent, it records the cash transfer by a debit to Cash Deposited with Agent for Bond Interest and a credit to Cash. On the date the interest is due, the company debits Interest Expense and credits Interest Payable. Upon receipt from the agent of paid interest coupons, a certificate of coupon receipt and appropriate disposal, or other evidence that the interest was paid, the company debits Interest Payable and credits Cash Deposited with Agent for Bond Interest.

Amortization of Premium or Discount

When bonds are issued at a premium or discount, the market acts to adjust the stated interest rate to a market or effective interest rate. Because of the initial premium or discount, the periodic interest payments made over the bond life by the issuer to the investors do not represent the complete revenue and expense for the periods involved. An adjustment to the cash transfer for the periodic write-off of the premium or discount is necessary to reflect the effective interest rate being incurred or earned on the bonds. The periodic adjustment of bonds to their face value is referred to as *bond premium* or *discount amortization*.

A premium on bonds issued recognizes that the stated interest rate is higher than the market interest rate. Amortization of the premium reduces the interest revenue or expense below the amount of cash transferred. As the bond approaches the maturity date, reduction of the premium balance through amortization results in a bond investment or liability account that approaches the maturity value.

A discount on bonds issued recognizes that the stated interest rate is lower than the market interest rate. Amortization of the discount increases the amount of interest revenue or expense above the amount of cash transferred. As with the premium amortization, reduction of the discount through amortization results in a bond investment or liability balance that approaches the maturity value.

Two principal methods are used to amortize the premium or discount on the books of both the issuer and the investor. These are (1) the straight-line method and (2) the interest method.

Straight-Line Method. The straight-line method provides for the recognition of an equal amount of premium or discount amortization each period. The amount of monthly amortization is determined by dividing the premium or discount at purchase or issuance by the number of months remaining to the bond maturity date. For example, if a 10-year, 8% bond issue with a maturity value of $200,000 were sold on the issuance date at 103, the $6,000 premium would be amortized evenly over the 120 months until maturity, or at a rate of $50 per month, ($6,000 ÷ 120). If the bonds were sold three months after the issuance date, the $6,000 premium would be amortized evenly over 117 months, or a rate of $51.28 per month, ($6,000 ÷ 117). The premium amortization would reduce both interest expense on the issuer's books and interest revenue on the investor's books. A discount amortization would have the opposite results: both accounts would be increased.

It is necessary to set some arbitrary minimum time unit in the straight-line amortization of bond premium or bond discount. The month is used in this text as the minimum unit. Transactions occurring during the first half of the month are treated as though they were made at the beginning of the month; transactions occurring during the second half are treated as though made at the start of the following month. Use of a longer term, such as the quarter or half year, is possible, although this offers less accuracy than the use of a shorter time unit.

Interest Method. The interest method of amortization uses a uniform interest rate based upon a changing investment balance and provides for an increasing premium or discount amortization each period. In order to use this method, the effective interest rate for the bonds must first be determined. This is the rate of interest at bond issuance that discounts the maturity value of the bonds and the periodic interest payments to the market price of the bonds. This rate is used to determine the effective revenue or expense to be recorded on the books.

For example, as shown on page 411, $100,000, 10-year, 8% bonds sold to return 10% would sell for $87,539, or at a discount of $12,461. If the bonds were sold on the issuance date, the discount amortization for the first six months would be computed as illustrated at the top of the following page.

Investment balance at beginning of first period	$87,539
Effective rate per semiannual period...	5%
Stated rate per semiannual period	4%
Interest amount based on effective rate ($87,539 × .05)	$ 4,377
Interest payment based on stated rate ($100,000 × .04).............................	4,000
Difference between interest amount based on effective rate and stated rate..	$ 377

This difference is the discount amortization for the first period using the interest method. For the second semiannual period, the bond carrying value increases by the discount amortization. The amortization for the second semiannual period would be computed as follows:

Investment balance at beginning of second period ($87,539 + $377).........	$87,916
Interest amount based on effective rate ($87,916 × .05)	$ 4,396
Interest payment based on stated rate ($100,000 × .04).............................	4,000
Difference between interest amount based on effective rate and stated rate..	$ 396

The amount of interest for each period is computed at a uniform rate on an increasing balance. This results in an increasing discount amortization over the life of the bonds that is graphically demonstrated below:

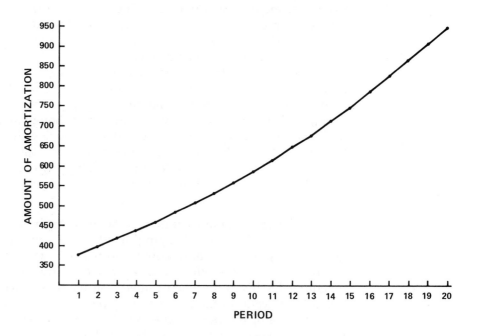

Premium amortization would be computed in a similar way except that the interest amount based on the stated interest rate would be higher than the amount based on the effective rate. For example, $100,000, 10-year, 8% bonds sold to return 6% would sell for $114,880, or at a premium of $14,880. If the bonds were sold on the issuance date, the premium amortization for the first and second six-month periods would be computed as follows:

Investment balance at beginning of first period...	$114,880
Effective rate per semiannual period	3%
Stated rate per semiannual period	4%
Interest payment based on stated rate ($100,000 × .04)........................	$ 4,000
Interest amount based on effective rate ($114,880 × .03)........................	3,446
Difference between interest amount based on stated rate and effective rate, or premium amortization..	$ 554
Investment balance at beginning of second period ($114,880 − $554)	$114,326
Interest payment based on stated rate ($100,000 × .04)...........................	$ 4,000
Interest amount based on effective rate ($114,326 × .03)........................	3,430
Difference between interest amount based on stated rate and effective rate..	$ 570

As illustrated, as the investment or liability balance is reduced by the premium amortization, the interest based upon the effective rate also decreases. The difference between the interest payment and the interest based upon the effective rate increases in a manner similar to discount amortization. Special bond amortization tables, such as the partial one illustrated below, may be prepared to determine the periodic adjustments to the bond carrying value.

Amortization of Premium — Interest Method
$100,000, 10-Year Bonds, Interest at 8% Payable Semiannually,
Sold at $114,880 to Yield 6%

Inter-est Pay-ment	A Interest Paid (4% of Face Value)	B Interest Expense (3% of Bond Carrying Value)	C Premium Amortization (A − B)	D Unamortized Premium (D − C)	E Bond Carrying Value ($100,000 + D)
				$14,880	$114,880
1	$4,000	$3,446 (3% of $114,880)	$554	14,326	114,326
2	4,000	3,430 (3% of 114,326)	570	13,756	113,756
3	4,000	3,413 (3% of 113,756)	587	13,169	113,169
4	4,000	3,395 (3% of 113,169)	605	12,564	112,564
5	4,000	3,377 (3% of 112,564)	623	11,941	111,941
6	4,000	3,358 (3% of 111,941)	642	11,299	111,299
7	4,000	3,339 (3% of 111,299)	661	10,638	110,638
8	4,000	3,319 (3% of 110,638)	681	9,957	109,957
9	4,000	3,299 (3% of 109,957)	701	9,256	109,256
10	4,000	3,278 (3% of 109,256)	722	8,534	108,534
⋮	⋮	⋮	⋮	⋮	⋮

Because the interest method adjusts the stated interest rate to an effective interest rate, it is theoretically more accurate as an amortization method than is the straight-line method. Since the issuance of APB Opinion No. 21, it is the recommended amortization method. The more popular straight-line method may be used by a company if the results of using it do not differ materially from the amortization using the interest method.[1]

---

[1]*Opinions of the Accounting Principles Board, No. 21*, "Interest on Receivables and Payables" (New York: American Institute of Certified Public Accountants, 1972), par. 15.

Accounting for Bond Interest   Entries for premium or discount amortization may be made as adjusting entries at the end of a company's fiscal year or interim period, or as each interest payment is made. The accounting entries for bond interest and first year discount amortization on both the issuer's and investor's books would be as follows. Assume the bonds are issued at a discount as described on page 417, and the discount is amortized by the interest method when each payment is made or received.

Issuer's Books

First payment:	Interest Expense	4,377	
	Cash		4,000
	Discount on Bonds Payable		377
Second payment:	Interest Expense	4,396	
	Cash		4,000
	Discount on Bonds Payable		396

Investor's Books

First payment:	Cash	4,000	
	Investment in Bonds	377	
	Interest Revenue		4,377
Second payment:	Cash	4,000	
	Investment in Bonds	396	
	Interest Revenue		4,396

If the bonds were sold at a premium, the investment or liability balance would be reduced over the life of the bonds to maturity value. Assume a 10-year, $200,000, 8% bond issue is sold at 103 on May 1 and is recorded as shown on page 413. Interest payment dates are February 1 and August 1, and the straight-line method of amortization is used. The following entries on both the issuer's and investor's books for the first year would be required. (Adjusting entries at end of fiscal year are not included.)

Issuer's Books

Aug. 1	Interest Expense	7,846	
	Premium on Bonds Payable	154	
	Cash		8,000

Computation:
Premium amortization for 3 months:
$6,000/117 = $51.28 per month
$51.28 × 3 = $153.84, or $154

Feb. 1	Interest Expense	7,692	
	Premium on Bonds Payable	308	
	Cash		8,000

Computation:
Premium amortization for 6 months:
$51.28 × 6 = $307.68, or $308

Investor's Books

Aug. 1	Cash	8,000	
	Investment in Bonds		154
	Interest Revenue		7,846
Feb. 1	Cash	8,000	
	Investment in Bonds		308
	Interest Revenue		7,692

When bonds are acquired as a temporary investment, investment cost is maintained in the accounts without adjustment for premium or discount amortization. Any difference between the purchase and sales price is recognized as a gain or loss at the time of the sale.

BOND INTEREST — SERIAL BONDS

When serial bonds are issued, the amortization schedule for bond premium or discount requires recognition of a declining debt principal. Successive bond years cannot be charged with equal amounts of premium or discount because of a shrinking debt and successively smaller interest payments.

Premium or discount on serial bonds may be amortized by the straight-line method or by the interest method. The straight-line procedure is referred to as the *bonds-outstanding method* and calls for decreases in the amortization schedule proportionate to the decrease in the loan balance. The interest method is as described for term bonds but is applied to a declining total debt.

Bonds-Outstanding Method

Amortization by the bonds-outstanding method is illustrated in the example that follows. Assume that bonds of $100,000, dated January 1, 1977, are issued on this date for $101,260. Bonds of $20,000 mature at the beginning of each year. The bonds pay interest of 8% annually. The company's accounting period ends on December 31; the accounting period and the bond year thus coincide. A table showing the premium to be amortized each year is developed as shown on the schedule below.

Amortization Schedule — Bonds-Outstanding Method

Year	Bonds Outstanding	Fraction of Premium to be Amortized	Annual Premium Amortization (Fraction × $1,260)
1977	$100,000	100,000/300,000 (or 10/30)	$ 420
1978	80,000	80,000/300,000 (or 8/30)	336
1979	60,000	60,000/300,000 (or 6/30)	252
1980	40,000	40,000/300,000 (or 4/30)	168
1981	20,000	20,000/300,000 (or 2/30)	84
	$300,000	300,000/300,000 (or 30/30)	$1,260

The annual premium amortization is found by multiplying the premium by a fraction whose numerator is the number of bond dollars outstanding in that year and whose denominator is the total number of bond dollars outstanding for the life of the bond issue. As bonds are retired, the amounts of premium amortization decline accordingly.

Periodic amortization may be incorporated in a table summarizing the interest charges and changes in bond carrying values as shown below.

Amortization of Premium — Serial Bonds
Bonds-Outstanding Method

Date	A Interest Payment (8% of Face Value)	B Premium Amortization	C Interest Expense (A−B)	D Principal Payment	E Bond Carrying Value Decrease (B+D)	F Bond Carrying Value (F−E)
Jan. 1, 1977						$101,260
Dec. 31, 1977	$8,000	$420	$7,580	$20,000	$20,420	80,840
Dec. 31, 1978	6,400	336	6,064	20,000	20,336	60,504
Dec. 31, 1979	4,800	252	4,548	20,000	20,252	40,252
Dec. 31, 1980	3,200	168	3,032	20,000	20,168	20,084
Dec. 31, 1981	1,600	84	1,516	20,000	20,084	——

Interest Method   Tables show that the bonds discussed on the preceding page were sold to return approximately 7½%. Use of this rate results in the following interest charges and premium amortization:

Amortization of Premium — Serial Bonds
Interest Method

Date	A Interest Payment (8% of Face Value)	B Interest Expense (7½% of Bond Carrying Value)	C Premium Amortiza-tion (A−B)	D Principal Payment	E Bond Carry-ing Value Decrease (C+D)	F Bond Carrying Value (F−E)
Jan. 1, 1977						$101,260
Dec. 31, 1977	$8,000	$7,595	$405	$20,000	$20,405	80,855
Dec. 31, 1978	6,400	6,064	336	20,000	20,336	60,519
Dec. 31, 1979	4,800	4,539	261	20,000	20,261	40,258
Dec. 31, 1980	3,200	3,019	181	20,000	20,181	20,077
Dec. 31, 1981	1,600	1,523[1]	77[1]	20,000	20,077	——

The bonds-outstanding method of amortization provides for the recognition of uniform amounts of amortization in terms of the par value of bonds outstanding. The interest method provides for the recognition of interest at a uniform rate on the declining debt balance.

Amortization Procedures when Bond Year and Fiscal Year Do Not Coincide   When serial bond retirement dates do not agree with the company's fiscal year, the amortization schedule must provide for amortization other than for full annual periods. To illustrate, assume that $500,000, 5% serial bonds, dated March 1, 1977, are sold on April 1, 1977, at a discount of $35,000. Bonds of $100,000 mature on March 1 of each year. The discount should be amortized over 59 months. Assuming that the fiscal period for the issuer is the calendar year, an amortization schedule that uses *bond month-dollars* may be prepared as follows:

Amortization Schedule When Bond Year and Fiscal Year
Do Not Coincide — Bonds-Outstanding Method

Year	Bonds Outstanding	Months Outstanding	Bond Month-Dollars (Months Times Bonds Outstanding)	Total Bond Month-Dollars	Fraction of Discount to be Amortized	Annual Discount Amortization (Fraction × $35,000)
1977	$500,000	9	$4,500,000	$ 4,500,000	45/175	$ 9,000
1978	500,000	2	1,000,000⎱	5,000,000	50/175	10,000
	400,000	10	4,000,000⎰			
1979	400,000	2	800,000⎱	3,800,000	38/175	7,600
	300,000	10	3,000,000⎰			
1980	300,000	2	600,000⎱	2,600,000	26/175	5,200
	200,000	10	2,000,000⎰			
1981	200,000	2	400,000⎱	1,400,000	14/175	2,800
	100,000	10	1,000,000⎰			
1982	100,000	2	200,000	200,000	2/175	400
		59		$17,500,000	175/175	$35,000

---

[1]The last payment is adjusted because the effective rate was not exactly 7½%. On the final payment the premium balance is closed and interest expense is reduced by this amount.

CONVERSION OF BONDS

Convertible bonds grant to the investor the right to convert debt equity to stock equity under certain conditions. The conversion privilege is granted when the bonds are sold, but as discussed earlier, the value of the conversion privilege is normally combined with the cost of the debt instrument. When conversion takes place, a special valuation question must be answered. Should the market value of the securities be used to compute a gain or loss on the transaction? If the security is viewed as debt, then the conversion to equity would seem to be a significant economic transaction and a gain or loss would be recognized. If, however, the security is viewed as equity, the conversion is really an exchange of one type of equity capital for another, and the historical cost principle would seem to indicate that no gain or loss would be recognized. In practice, the latter approach seems to be most commonly followed by both the issuer and investor of the bonds. No gain or loss is recognized either for book or tax purposes. The book value of the bonds is transferred to become the book value of the stock issued. However, this treatment seems inconsistent with APB Opinion No. 14 as discussed earlier in this chapter.[1] In that opinion, convertible debt was considered to be debt rather than equity.

If the investor viewed the security as debt, conversion of the debt could be viewed as an exchange of one asset for another. The general rule for the exchange of nonmonetary assets is that the market value of the asset exchanged should be used to measure any gain or loss on the transaction.[2] If there is no market value of the asset surrendered or if its value is undeterminable, the market value of the asset received should be used. The market value of convertible bonds should reflect the market value of the stock to be issued on the conversion, and thus the market value of the two securities should be similar. Before an exchange is recorded, the investment account should be brought up to date for premium or discount amortization.

To illustrate bond conversion for the investor recognizing a gain or loss on conversion, assume Carl Co. offers bondholders 40 shares of Carl Co. common stock, $25 par, in exchange for each $1,000, 8% bond held. An investor exchanges bonds of $10,000 (book value as brought up to date, $9,850) for 400 shares of common stock having a market price at the time of the exchange of $26 per share. The exchange is completed three months after an interest payment date. The exchange is recorded as follows:

Cash	200	
Investment in Carl Co. Common Stock	10,400	
Investment in Carl Co. 8's		9,850
Gain on Conversion of Carl Co. Bonds		550
Interest Revenue		200

---

[1]See page 415.

[2]*Opinions of Accounting Principles Board, No. 29*, "Accounting for Nonmonetary Transactions" (New York: American Institute of Certified Public Accountants, 1973), par. 18.

If the investor chose not to recognize a gain or loss, the journal entry would be as follows:

Cash	200	
Investment in Carl Co. Common Stock	9,850	
Investment in Carl Co. 8's		9,850
Interest Revenue		200

Similar differences would occur on the issuer's books depending upon the viewpoint assumed. If the issuer desired to recognize the conversion of the convertible debt as a significant transaction, the market value of the securities would be used to record the conversion. To illustrate the journal entries for the issuer using this reasoning, assume 100 bonds, face value $1,000, are exchanged for 2,000 shares of common stock, $40 par value, $55 market value. At the time of the conversion, there is an unamortized premium on the bond issue of $3,000. The conversion would be recorded as follows:

Bonds Payable	100,000	
Premium on Bonds Payable	3,000	
Loss on Conversion of Bonds	7,000	
Common Stock		80,000
Premium on Common Stock		30,000

Computation:

Market value of stock issued (2,000 shares at $55)..		$110,000
Face value of bonds payable	$100,000	
Plus unamortized premium	3,000	103,000
Loss to company on conversion of bonds		$ 7,000

If the issuer did not consider the conversion as a culminating transaction, no gain or loss would be recognized. The bond carrying value would be transferred to the capital stock account on the theory that the company upon issuing the bonds is aware of the fact that bond proceeds may ultimately represent the consideration identified with stock. Thus, when bondholders exercise their conversion privileges, the value identified with the obligation is transferred to the security that replaces it. Under this assumption, the conversion would be recorded as follows:

Bonds Payable	100,000	
Premium on Bonds Payable	3,000	
Common Stock, $40 par		80,000
Premium on Common Stock		23,000

The profession has not resolved the accounting issues surrounding convertible debt. Although the practice of not recognizing gain or loss on either the issuer's or the investor's books is widespread, it seems inconsistent with the treatment of other items that are transferred by an entity. The economic reality of the transaction would seem to require a recognition of the change in value at least at the time conversion takes place. The movement toward the use of current values in the accounts, as discussed in Chapter 25, would require recognition of gains or losses on these securities at even earlier dates if the market reflected a change in value. Perhaps the resolution of this issue must await more specific definitions that will distinguish between debt and equity.

TERMINATION OF BONDS

Bonds always include a specified termination or maturity date. At that time, the issuer must pay the current investor the maturity or face value of the bond. Bonds may be terminated earlier than the maturity date in one of two ways: (1) the issuer may *reacquire* individual bonds on the market and retire them, or (2) the issuer may utilize the call provision frequently included in bond indentures and *redeem* all or part of the issue prior to maturity. Issuing companies frequently finance the termination of bonds by issuing new debt securities. When the two transactions are merged into one, such financing is referred to as *bond refunding*. The following sections discuss the special accounting problems for both the issuer and the investor dealing with termination of bonds.

Bond Retirement at Maturity	Most bond issues are payable at the end of a specified period. When bond discount or premium and issue cost balances have been satisfactorily amortized over the life of the bonds, bond retirement simply calls for elimination of the liability or the investment by a cash transaction. Any bonds not presented for payment at their maturity date should be removed from the bonds payable balance on the issuer's books and reported separately as Matured Bonds Payable; these are reported as a current liability except when they are to be paid out of a sinking fund. Interest does not accrue on matured bonds not presented for payment.

If a bond fund is used to pay off a bond issue, any cash remaining in the fund may be returned to the cash account. Appropriations of retained earnings established during the life of the issue may be returned to retained earnings. |

Bond Reacquisition Prior to Maturity	Corporations frequently reacquire their own bonds on the market when prices or other factors make such action desirable. Reacquisition of bonds prior to their maturity calls for the recognition of a gain or a loss for the difference between the bond carrying value and the amount paid. This gain or loss is classified as an *early extinguishment of debt*, and is reported as an extraordinary item on the income statement.[1] Payment of accrued interest on bond reacquisition is separately reported as a debit to Interest Expense.

When bonds are reacquired, amortization of bond premium, discount, and issue costs should be brought up to date. Reacquisition calls for the cancellation of the bond face value together with any related premium, discount, or issue costs as of the reacquisition date.

When bonds are reacquired and canceled, Bonds Payable is debited. When bonds are reacquired but are held for possible future reissue, |

---

[1]*Opinions of the Accounting Principles Board, No. 26*, "Early Extinguishment of Debt" (New York: American Institute of Certified Public Accountants, 1972), par. 20; *Statement of Financial Accounting Standards No. 4*, "Reporting Gains and Losses from Extinguishment of Debt" (Stamford, Conn.: Financial Accounting Standards Board, 1975).

Treasury Bonds instead of Bonds Payable may be debited. Treasury bonds are evidence of a liquidated liability. Although treasury bonds may represent a ready source of cash, their sale creates new creditors, a situation that is no different from the debt created by any other type of borrowing. Treasury bonds, then, should be recorded at their face value and subtracted from the bonds payable balance in reporting bonds issued and outstanding. If treasury bonds are sold at a price other than face value, Cash is debited, Treasury Bonds is credited, thus reinstating the bond liability, and a premium or a discount on the sale is recorded, the latter balance to be amortized over the remaining life of this specific bond group. While held, treasury bonds occupy the same legal status as unissued bonds. At the maturity of the bond issue, any balance in a treasury bonds account is applied against Bonds Payable.

To illustrate bond reacquisition, assume $100,000, 8% bonds of Atlas, Inc., are not held until maturity, but are sold back to the issuer on February 1, 1979, at 97 plus accrued interest. The book value of the bonds on both the issuer's and investor's books is $97,700 as of January 1. Discount amortization has been recorded at $50 a month using the straight-line method. Interest payment dates on the bonds are November 1 and May 1; accrued interest adjustments are reversed. Entries on both the issuer's and investor's books at the time of bond redemption would be as follows:

Issuer's Books

Feb. 1	Interest Expense	50	
	Discount on Bonds Payable		50
	To record discount amortization for January, 1979.		
Feb. 1	Bonds Payable (*or* Treasury Bonds)	100,000	
	Interest Expense	2,000	
	Discount on Bonds Payable		2,250
	Cash		99,000
	Gain on Bond Reacquisition		750
	To record reacquisition of bonds and payment of three months' interest.		

Computation:

Book value of bonds, January 1, 1979	$97,700
Discount amortization for January	50
Book value of bonds, February 1, 1979	$97,750
Sales proceeds	97,000
Gain on sale	$ 750

Interest expense for 3 months:
$100,000 × .08 × ¼ = $2,000

Investor's Books

Feb. 1	Investment in Atlas, Inc., 8's	50	
	Interest Revenue		50
	To record discount amortization for January, 1979.		
Feb. 1	Cash	99,000	
	Loss on Sale of Bonds	750	
	Investment in Atlas, Inc., 8's		97,750
	Interest Revenue		2,000
	To record reacquisition of bonds and receipt of three month's interest.		

Bond Redemption Prior to Maturity— Term Bonds
Provisions of the bond indenture frequently give the issuer the option of calling bonds for payment prior to maturity. Ordinarily the call must be made on an interest payment date and no further interest accrues on the bonds not presented at this time. When only a part of the issue is to be retired, the bonds called may be determined by lot.

The inclusion of call provisions in the bond agreement is a feature favoring the issuer. The company is in a position to terminate the bond agreement and eliminate future interest charges whenever its financial position makes such action feasible. Furthermore, the company is protected in the event of a fall in the market interest rate by being able to retire the old issue from proceeds of a new issue paying a lower rate of interest. The bond contract normally requires payment of a premium if bonds are called. The bondholder is thus offered special compensation if the investment is terminated.

When bonds are called, the difference between the amount paid and the bond carrying value is reported as a gain or a loss on both the issuer's and investor's books. Any interest paid at the time of the call is recorded as a debit to Interest Expense or a credit to Interest Revenue. The entries to be made are the same as illustrated previously for the sale and reacquisition of bonds.

When an investor acquires callable bonds at a premium, conservatism calls for an amortization policy that prevents the bonds from being reported at more than their redemption values at the various call dates. To illustrate, assume bonds of $10,000 are acquired for $10,800 on January 1, 1978. The bonds were originally issued on January 1, 1976, and have a maturity date of January 1, 1996. The following table of redemption values is included in the indenture.

Redeemable January 1, 1981, to December 31, 1985, at 105
Redeemable January 1, 1986, to December 31, 1990, at 102½
Redeemable January 1, 1991, to December 31, 1995, at 101

Regular premium amortization and accelerated amortization based upon bond redemption values of $10,500, $10,250 and $10,100, are compared below:

Regular Amortization	Accelerated Amortization
$800 ÷ 18 years = $44.44 per year (1978–1996)	($10,800 − $10,500) ÷ 3 years (1978–1980) = $100 per year ($10,500 − $10,250) ÷ 5 years (1981–1985) = $ 50 per year ($10,250 − $10,100) ÷ 5 years (1986–1990) = $ 30 per year ($10,100 − $10,000) ÷ 5 years (1991–1995) = $ 20 per year

If regular amortization procedures are followed on the books of the investor, bond redemption prior to maturity will result in a recovery of cash that is less than bond carrying value and will require recognition of a loss that nullifies in part the earnings recognized in the past. Accelerated amortization reduces the investment to its redemption value; bond redemption values are used for income measurement purposes and the need for recognition of a loss upon redemption is avoided. Obviously, bonds reported at a discount, or bonds reported at a premium reduced by normal amortization to an amount that is not greater than redemption value, require no special treatment.

Bond Redemption Prior to Maturity — Serial Bonds

When serial bonds are reacquired prior to their maturities, it is necessary to cancel the unamortized premium or discount relating to that part of the bond issue that is liquidated. For example, assume the issuance of serial bonds previously described on page 421 and amortization of the premium by the bonds-outstanding method as given on page 421. On April 1, 1978, $10,000 of bonds due January 1, 1980, and $10,000 of bonds due January 1, 1981, are reacquired at 100½ plus accrued interest. The premium for the period January 1 — April 1, 1978, relating to retired bonds affects bond interest for the current period and will be written off as an adjustment to expense. The balance of the premium from the retirement date to the respective maturity date of the series retired must be canceled. The premium balance relating to retired bonds is calculated as follows:

Premium Identified with 1978: 20,000/80,000 × $336 × 9/12 = $ 63
Premium Identified with 1979: 20,000/60,000 ×   252   =   84
Premium Identified with 1980: 10,000/40,000 ×   168   =   42
Premium Identified with Retired Bonds $189

Instead of the above procedure, the premium amortization per year on each $1,000 bond may first be calculated and this rate applied to bonds of each period that are canceled. The annual amortization rate per $1,000 bond is calculated as follows:

$$\frac{\$1,260 \text{ (Total Premium: Life of Bonds)}}{300 \text{ (Total \$1,000 Bonds Outstanding: Life of Bonds)}} = \$4.20$$

The premium to be canceled may now be determined as follows:

Year	Number of $1,000 Bonds	×	Annual Premium Amortization per $1,000 Bond	×	Fractional Part of Year	=	Total Premium Cancellation
1978	20		$4.20		9/12		$ 63
1979	20		4.20				84
1980	10		4.20				42
Premium Identified with Retired Bonds							$189

Bonds, carrying value $20,189, are retired at a cost of $20,100 resulting in a gain of $89. Payment is also made for interest on bonds of $20,000 for three months at 8%, or $400. The entry to record the retirement of bonds and the payment of interest on the series retired follows:

Bonds Payable..	20,000	
Premium on Bonds Payable..	189	
Interest Expense..	400	
Cash..		20,500
Gain on Bond Retirement.....................................		89

A revised schedule for the amortization of bond premium follows:

Amortization Schedule — Bonds-Outstanding Method
Revised for Bond Retirement

Year	Annual Premium Amortization per Original Schedule	Premium Cancellation on Bond Retirement	Annual Premium Amortization Adjusted for Bond Retirement
1977	$ 420		$ 420
1978	336	$ 63	273
1979	252	84	168
1980	168	42	126
1981	84		84
	$1,260	$189	$1,071

**Bond
Refunding**   Cash for the retirement of a bond issue is frequently raised through the sale of a new issue and is referred to as bond refunding; the original issue is said to be *refunded*. Bond refunding may take place when an issue matures. Bonds may also be refunded prior to their maturity when the interest rate has dropped and the interest savings on a new issue will more than offset the costs of retiring the old issue. To illustrate, assume a corporation has outstanding 8% bonds of $1,000,000 callable at 102 and with a remaining 10-year term, and similar 10-year bonds can be marketed currently at an interest rate of only 6½%. Under these circumstances it would be advantageous to retire the old issue with the proceeds from a new 6½% issue since the future savings in interest will exceed by a considerable amount the premium to be paid on the call of the old issue.

The desirability of refunding may not be so obvious as in the preceding instance. In determining whether refunding is warranted in marginal cases, careful consideration must be given to such factors as the different maturity dates of the two issues, possible future changes in interest rates, changed loan requirements, different indenture provisions, income tax effects of refunding, and legal fees, printing costs, and marketing costs involved in refunding.

When refunding takes place before the maturity date of the old issue, the problem arises as to how to dispose of the call premium and unamortized discount and issue costs of the original bonds. Three positions have been taken with respect to disposition of these items:

1. Such charges are considered a loss on bond retirement.
2. Such charges are considered deferrable and to be amortized systematically over the remaining life of the original issue.
3. Such charges are considered deferrable and to be amortized systematically over the life of the new issue.

Although arguments can be presented supporting each of these alternatives, the Accounting Principles Board concluded that "all extinguishments of debt before scheduled maturities are fundamentally alike. The accounting for such transactions should be the same regardless of the means used to achieve the extinguishment."[1] The first position, immediate recognition of the gain or loss, was selected by the Board for all early

---

[1] *Opinions of the Accounting Principles Board, No. 26, op. cit.*, par. 19.

extinguishment of debt. The Financial Accounting Standards Board considered the nature of this gain or loss and defined it as being an extraordinary item requiring separate income statement disclosure.[1]

BOND FUNDS

Bond indentures for term bonds frequently require the issuing company to establish a *sinking fund* to be used to retire the bonds at maturity. The annual amount to be paid into the fund is computed using compound interest tables as illustrated in Chapter 14. Bond funds may be administered directly by a company or by an independent trustee.

The example on pages 432–433 illustrates the accounting that may be employed when (1) information is recorded currently on the company's books, and (2) information is recorded at the end of the period on the company's books from summaries provided by separate books maintained by a trustee. The example assumes the establishment of a fund for the retirement of bonds and gives the entries for the fund accumulation in the first year and for debt retirement in the last year.

It should be observed that when separate books are maintained by a trustee, assets are balanced by a *company* account summarizing the trustee's accountability to the company. This account is credited for assets received from the company as well as for net asset increases resulting from earnings; it is debited for assets applied to the purpose for which the fund was established as well as for assets transferred to the company. The *fund* account on the company's books, in turn, reports the company's equity in the fund. This account is debited for assets transferred to the trustee and for net asset increases resulting from fund earnings; it is credited for assets applied to the purpose for which the fund was established and for the assets transferred to the company. The company account on the trustee's books and the fund account on the company's books are *reciprocal accounts* since the credit balance in the company account is equal to the debit balance in the fund account when both sets of books are up to date. When a company administers a fund but wishes to remove fund detail from the general ledger, a separate ledger can be provided in a form similar to that employed by the trustee.

In the example, the bond fund assets as shown on the company's books or as reported to the company by the trustee at the end of 1977 are as follows:

Bond fund cash	$44,950
Bond fund securities	35,500
Accrued interest on bond fund securities	225
Total	$80,675

Bond fund revenue for 1977 is $875 and bond fund expense is $200; the difference, $675, represents the fund earnings. This amount is reported on the income statement as "Other revenue." A gain or a loss on the

---

[1]*Statement of Financial Accounting Standards No. 4, op. cit.*

sale of fund securities would be recognized as an other revenue or expense item. The individual assets in the fund would be reported under the long-term investments heading on the balance sheet.

The foregoing illustration assumed purchase of securities other than bonds originally issued by the company. Bond fund cash is commonly used to purchase a company's own bonds. Such fund use frequently operates to support a firm market price for the issue since the company can enter the market whenever the market price makes retirement of the company's bonds attractive.

When a company retires its own bonds through bond fund cash, the liability is canceled, the bond fund cash account is credited, and a loss or gain on the retirement is recorded. For example, assume that the books of a company show bonds of $100,000 outstanding with an unamortized bond discount balance relating to this issue of $3,500. The company acquires and formally retires bonds with a face value of $20,000 at a cost of $19,500. The entry to record the bond retirement follows:

Bonds Payable	20,000	
Loss on Bond Retirement	200	
Bond Fund Cash		19,500
Unamortized Bond Discount		700
To record bond retirement.		

Computation:

Amount paid on retirement	$19,500
Book value of bonds retired: face value of bonds, $20,000, less unamortized discount applicable to bonds, $700	19,300
Loss on retirement	$ 200

When bonds are acquired by a trustee and kept *alive*, such bonds are sometimes carried on the books the same as any other investment. The trustee records the bonds at cost, collects interest on the bonds and records collections as revenue, applies accumulation and amortization procedures in calculating effective earnings, and reports a gain or a loss on the resale of bonds to outsiders. The treatment of reacquired bonds as an investment results in periodic cash transfers to the trustee representing bond interest and permits fund accumulation in accordance with scheduled requirements. Interest paid by the corporation on its own bonds is counterbalanced by interest received by the trustee. Any difference between the book value of the liability and the amount paid for the bonds is recognized over the remaining life of the bonds by the entries for discount accumulation and premium amortization by the corporation and by the trustee.

The treatment of bond reacquisition as an investment is not supportable in theory. Reacquired bonds, even though in the hands of a corporate agent, cannot be considered an asset by the corporation. Such bonds are, in effect, evidence of debt retirement. Reacquired bonds may be sold and thus provide additional cash, but this is also true of unissued bonds; both reacquired and unissued bonds are no more than instruments that may be used in future borrowing.

TRANSACTION	FUND TRANSACTIONS RECORDED CURRENTLY ON COMPANY'S BOOKS
	ENTRY
1977: **June 30, 1977** The Powell Corporation made the first of a series of 20 equal semiannual deposits of $40,000 to bond fund.	Bond Fund Cash......................... 40,000 Cash 40,000
July 6, 1977 Purchased bond fund securities for $35,750, which included accrued interest of $150.	Bond Fund Securities................. 35,600 Bond Fund Revenue.................... 150 Bond Fund Cash 35,750
December 1, 1977 Received interest on bond fund securities, $900.	Bond Fund Cash......................... 900 Bond Fund Revenue 900
December 31, 1977 Paid bond fund custodian fees, $200.	Bond Fund Expenses .... 200 Bond Fund Cash 200
Made second deposit of $40,000 to bond fund.	Bond Fund Cash......................... 40,000 Cash 40,000
To record accrued interest on bond fund securities and cash deposits, $225.	Interest on Bond Fund Securities Receivable........................... 225 Bond Fund Revenue 225
To record amortization of premium on bond fund securities, $100.	Bond Fund Revenue................... 100 Bond Fund Securities............. 100

(a) To recognize bond fund revenue and expense.
(b) To close bond fund revenue and expense balances.
	(b) Bond Fund Revenue 875
	        Bond Fund Expenses 200
	        Income Summary.............. 675

1986
December 31, 1986
Sold bond fund securities, book value after entries for amortization, $1,060,000, for $1,100,000, which included accrued interest, $8,000; total proceeds were added to bond fund cash on hand on this date of $15,000.
	Bond Fund Cash......................... 1,100,000
	    Bond Fund Securities............. 1,060,000
	    Bond Fund Revenue 8,000
	    Gain on Sale of Bond Fund Securities 32,000

Paid bonded indebtedness from bond fund cash, $1,000,000.	Bonds Payable............................ 1,000,000 Bond Fund Cash 1,000,000
Transferred bond fund cash on hand after payment of bonds to cash account.	Cash... 115,000 Bond Fund Cash 115,000

(a) To recognize bond fund income or loss.
(b) To close nominal accounts relating to bond fund activities.
	(b) Bond Fund Revenue 8,000
	    Gain on Sale of Bond Fund Securities 32,000
	        Income Summary.............. 40,000

FUND TRANSACTIONS RECORDED CURRENTLY ON TRUSTEE'S BOOKS

ENTRY ON CORPORATION'S BOOKS			ENTRY ON TRUSTEE'S BOOKS		
Bond Fund — A. G. Shaw, Trustee	40,000		Cash	40,000	
Cash		40,000	The Powell Corporation		40,000
			Investment in Securities	35,600	
			Interest Revenue	150	
			Cash		35,750
			Cash	900	
			Interest Revenue		900
			Expenses	200	
			Cash		200
Bond Fund — A. G. Shaw, Trustee	40,000		Cash	40,000	
Cash		40,000	The Powell Corporation		40,000
			Interest on Securities Receivable	225	
			Interest Revenue		225
			Interest Revenue	100	
			Investment in Securities		100
(a) Bond Fund — A. G. Shaw, Trustee	675		Interest Revenue	875	
Bond Fund Expenses	200		Expenses		200
Interest Revenue		875	The Powell Corporation		675
(b) Interest Revenue	875				
Bond Fund Expense		200			
Income Summary		675			
			Cash	1,100,000	
			Investments in Securities		1,060,000
			Interest Revenue		8,000
			Gain on Sale of Securities		32,000
Bonds Payable	1,000,000		The Powell Corporation	1,000,000	
Bond Fund — A. G. Shaw, Trustee		1,000,000	Cash		1,000,000
Cash	115,000		The Powell Corporation	115,000	
Bond Fund — A. G. Shaw, Trustee		115,000	Cash		115,000
(a) Bond Fund — A. G. Shaw, Trustee	40,000		Interest Revenue	8,000	
Interest Revenue		8,000	Gain on Sale of Securities	32,000	
Gain on Sale of Bond Fund Securities		32,000	The Powell Corporation		40,000
(b) Interest Revenue	8,000				
Gain on Sale of Bond Fund Securities	32,000				
Income Summary		40,000			

The treatment of bond reacquisition as a retirement by an entry similar to that on page 431 may call for an increase in the deposit schedule to compensate for the loss of interest in the fund accumulation. The larger transfers to the fund, however, are accompanied by reduced interest payments in the absence of interest accruals on bonds reacquired by the trustee. If bonds are resold, the sale is treated just as an original issue, any premium or discount on the reissue being identified with the remaining life of the bond lot resold. The treatment of bond reacquisitions as bond retirement should be followed even though this calls for adjustments in a plan for systematic fund accumulation.

In some instances, the trustee may assume the liability for payment of the bonds. In these circumstances, the bond liability is reduced as payments are made to the trustee and no fund investment is reported on the issuer's balance sheet.

The issuance of serial bonds eliminates the need for a bond sinking fund. When a sinking fund cannot produce earnings at a rate equivalent to that paid on the bond issue, serial bonds are advantageous to the issuing company. In this case, cash otherwise deposited in the fund is applied directly to the retirement of debt, and the payment of interest relating to that portion of the debt is terminated.

BOND RESTRUCTURING

Economic conditions sometimes arise making it difficult for the issuer of bonds to make the cash payments required by the bond indenture. These payments include interest payments, principal payments to retire serial bonds, periodic payments into bond sinking funds, or even payments at the maturity of the debt.[1] To avoid bankruptcy proceedings or foreclosure on the bonds, investors in such situations may agree to revise the original terms of the bond issue to permit the issuer to recover from financial problems. The restructuring may take many different forms. For example, there may be a suspension of interest payments for a period of time, a reduction in the interest rate, an extension of the maturity date of the debt, or even an exchange of equity securities for the debt. The principal accounting question in these cases, on both the books of the issuer and the investor, is whether a gain or loss should be recognized upon the restructuring of the debt.

If the restructuring agreement is not viewed as a significant economic transaction, no special entry is required unless the debt is actually exchanged at carrying value for a different type of security. No gain or loss is recognized on the restructuring, and future interest and principal payments are recorded as they are made under the new agreement. If, however, the restructuring agreement is viewed as a transaction to be accounted for on the books, a gain or loss should be determined based

---

[1]For a detailed discussion of the problems involved in restructuring of debt, see *FASB Discussion Memorandum*, "Accounting by Debtors and Creditors When Debt is Restructured" (Stamford, Conn.: Financial Accounting Standards Board, 1976).

upon newly computed present values of the debt. This would be necessary on both the books of the issuer and the investor.

To illustrate the accounting problems arising upon debt restructuring, assume the issuing company has outstanding $1,000,000, 8% bonds issued at an effective interest rate of 10% with a present carrying value of $922,768 on the books. The bonds are scheduled to mature in five years. Because of financial difficulties, the company is behind in its interest payments and in payments to the bond sinking fund. In order to avoid foreclosure on the bonds, the holders of the bonds, principally large financial institutions, agree to a reduction in the interest rate to 5% per year. The current rate of interest for similar debt is 12% per year.

The present value of the restructured debt may be computed using one of at least two possible interest rates; the interest rate implied in the original debt before restructuring or the current interest rate for similar debt. If the restructuring is viewed as a new lending situation, the current rate of interest would be used. If it is viewed as a modification of an existing lending situation, the effective interest rate in the original debt instrument would be used.[1] The difference in the computed present value between these methods is illustrated as follows:

Assume the current rate of interest is used to find the present value of the restructured debt.

1. *Present Value of Maturity Value:*
   Maturity value of bonds after five years or ten semiannual periods = $1,000,000
   Effective interest rate — 12% per year, or 6% per semiannual period:
   $PV_n = A(PVF_{\overline{n}\,i}) = \$1,000,000(\text{Table II}_{\overline{10}\,6\%}) = \$1,000,000(.5584) = \$558,400.$

2. *Present Value of Ten Semiannual Interest Payments at Current Rate:*
   Semiannual payment, 2½% of $1,000,000 = $25,000
   Interest rate — 12% per year, or 6% per semiannual period:
   $PV_n = R(PVAF_{\overline{n}\,i}) = \$25,000(\text{Table IV}_{\overline{10}\,6\%}) = \$25,000(7.3601) = \$184,002.$

The present value of the restructured debt using the current market interest rate is $742,402 ($558,400 + $184,002).

Assume the effective rate of interest of the original debt is used to find the present value of the restructured debt.

1. *Present Value of Maturity Value:*
   Maturity value of bonds after five years or ten semiannual periods = $1,000,000
   Effective interest rate — 10% per year, or 5% per semiannual period:
   $PV_n = A(PVF_{\overline{n}\,i}) = \$1,000,000(\text{Table II}_{\overline{10}\,5\%}) = \$1,000,000(.6139) = \$613,900.$

2. *Present Value of Ten Semiannual Interest Payments at Effective Interest Rate of Original Bonds:*
   Semiannual payments, 2½% of $1,000,000 = $25,000
   Effective interest rate — 10% per year, or 5% per semiannual period:
   $PV_n = R(PVAF_{\overline{n}\,i}) = \$25,000(\text{Table IV}_{\overline{10}\,5\%}) = \$25,000(7.7217) = \$193,042$

The present value of the restructured debt using the effective rate of interest of the original debt is $806,942 ($613,900 + $193,042).

---

[1]*Ibid.*, p. 7.

The gain on the issuer's books and the loss on the investor's books on the restructuring would be $180,366 ($922,768 − $742,402) if the current interest rate is used, or $115,826 ($922,768 − $806,942) if the effective interest rate on the original debt is used.

To illustrate the entries required to record the restructuring of the debt, assume the effective rate of interest on the original debt is used to compute the present value of the restructured debt. The entries would be as follows:

Issuer's Books

Discount on Bonds Payable..	115,826	
Gain on Restructuring of Bonds Payable		115,826

Investor's Books

Loss on Restructuring of Bonds Held as Investment....................	115,826	
Investment in Bonds		115,826

These entries would reduce the carrying value of the liability and the investment to $806,942. The larger discount would be amortized over the remaining ten years of the bond life, preferably by the interest method of amortization. Thus, in the first semiannual period, the new interest payment would be $25,000 (2½% of $1,000,000) but the amount of expense or revenue, assuming the original interest rate is used and the interest method of amortization is applied, would be $40,347 ($806,942 × .05). While this amount is lower than the $46,138 ($922,768 × .05) expense and revenue before restructuring, there is less impact on income than would be reflected if no gain or loss were recognized on the restructuring and the expense and revenue were reduced by the entire difference in cash interest payments of $15,000 ($40,000 − $25,000).

Similar adjustments of present value could be made for an extension of the bond maturity date or other modification of bond terms.

The profession has not yet agreed on whether the restructuring should be viewed as a new lending situation or a modification of an existing lending situation. Practice seems to favor the latter view, which, with rising interest rates, tends to produce a lower amount of gain or loss than would be true using the former view. Many companies are in opposition to any recognition of a gain or loss on the grounds that no recordable transaction has occurred and future interest expense should reflect the new bond terms, not those existing before the restructuring. They argue that it seems unrealistic and misleading for the income statement of companies in financial difficulty to report significant gains from restructuring. The restructuring of debt illustrates another example of the complexities introduced to accounting as economic conditions change. To be most useful to users of financial statements, it seems reasonable that economic change should be recognized in the accounts, and that a gain or loss should be reported upon the restructuring of debt.

REPORTING OF BONDS ON THE BALANCE SHEET

Bond accounts are frequently very significant items on the balance sheet of both the investor and the issuer. Generally, bonds are reported in the noncurrent section; however, under some circumstances they may be reported as current items. The valuation and reporting problems for the investor and the issuer will be considered separately.

Reporting Bond Investments

The market value of bonds varies with changes in the financial strength of the issuing company, changes in the level of interest rates, and shrinkage in the remaining life of the issue. In the absence of material price declines, bonds held as long-term investments are reported on the balance sheet at book value. This book value approaches par as the bonds move closer to maturity. To this extent, then, the accounting can be considered to follow a similar change that is taking place on the market as the bond life is reduced and a correspondingly lower valuation is attached to the difference between the actual rate and the market rate of remaining interest payments. Although investments are properly reported at book value, parenthetical disclosure of the aggregate market value of the securities makes the financial statements more informative.

A material decline in bond value, however, as a result of unfavorable developments relating to the issuer cannot be ignored. Assume, for example, that the issuing company has found it impossible to meet redemption fund requirements, which suggests it may have difficulties in paying off the obligation at its maturity. Even more serious, assume that there has been default on bond interest payments. These conditions may lead to a restructuring of debt as discussed earlier. However, even before restructuring occurs, if significant investment loss is indicated, there is a strong argument for recording a loss. Such loss may be established by referring to current market quotations, by an investigation of prices at which similar bonds are sold, or by special appraisal of the assets that are pledged as security on the bonded indebtedness. Since the threatened default of New York City bonds, some investors question whether a loss needs to be reported on bonds of large municipalities if it is unlikely they would ever be allowed to default on their principal. However, even in these cases, recovery usually requires substantial restructuring of the debt resulting in an economic loss to the investor over the life of the investment. When it becomes evident this type of loss will occur, it seems reasonable the loss should be reflected in the accounts of the investor.

When bonds are purchased *flat*, that is, when interest on bonds is in arrears and one price is paid for the bonds together with all accrued and unpaid interest, this price is recorded as the bond investment cost. Any amounts subsequently received on the bonds, whether designated as payments of principal or defaulted interest, should be treated as a recovery of investment cost as long as there is uncertainty of ultimate recovery of more than the amount invested. No interest should be accrued on the bonds until solvency of the debtor is restored and the regular receipt of interest is assured. Such bonds are reported at their unrecovered cost with full information as to the nature of the investment.

Bond funds are also normally classified as long-term investments. Even when the maturity date of term bonds will occur during the next fiscal period, the fund and the liability continue to be reported as non-current items.

Data relative to bond investments might be reported as follows:

Long-term investments:		
Investment in Wilkins Co. 8's, $100,000 face value, due July 1, 1982 (reported at cost as adjusted for amortized discount)		$ 98,250
Bond retirement fund in hands of trustee, composed of:		
Cash	$ 15,000	
Stocks and bonds (reported at cost; aggregate quoted market value, $240,000)	210,500	
Dividends and interest receivable	4,500	230,000

Reporting Bond Liabilities

In reporting bond liabilities on the balance sheet, the nature of the liabilities, maturity dates, interest rates, methods of liquidation, conversion privileges, and other significant matters should be indicated. When assets have been pledged to secure a liability, full particulars of the pledge should be indicated in the description of the obligation. This may be accompanied by identification on the asset side of the balance sheet of the specific assets pledged. When an agreement with a creditor limits the ability of a company to pay dividends, such limitation should be disclosed.

The portion of serial bonds payable within one year and other long-term debt maturing within one year should be reported as a current liability only if retirement will claim current assets. If the debt is to be paid from a bond retirement fund or is to be retired through some form of refinancing, it would continue to be reported as noncurrent with an explanation of the method to be used in its liquidation.[1]

Bond liabilities may be reported on a balance sheet as of December 31, 1977, as follows:

Current liabilities:		
Serial 7% debentures, installment due May 1, 1978		$ 10,000
Long-term liabilities:		
20-year, 6% First-mortgage bonds outstanding, due January 1, 1989	$210,000	
Less unamortized bond discount	4,500	205,500
Serial 7% debentures, due May 1, 1979 to May 1, 1988, inclusive		100,000

[1]*Statement of Financial Accounting Standards No. 6*, "Balance Sheet Classification of Short-Term Obligations Expected to be Refinanced" (Stamford, Conn.: Financial Accounting Standards Board, 1975).

QUESTIONS

1. What factors should be considered in determining whether cash should be raised by the issue of bonds or by the sale of additional stock?

2. Distinguish between (a) secured and unsecured bonds, (b) collateral trust and debenture bonds, (c) guaranteed bonds and income bonds, (d) convertible bonds and callable bonds, and (e) coupon bonds and registered bonds.

3. What is meant by bond market rate, stated or contract rate, and effective rate? Which of these rates changes during the lifetime of the bond issue?

4. An investor purchases bonds of $100,000. Payment for the bonds includes charges for (a) a premium, (b) accrued interest, and (c) brokerage fees. How would each of these charges be recorded and what disposition would ultimately be made of each of these charges?

5. (a) Why do companies find the issuance of convertible bonds a desirable method of financing? (b) What are the normal characteristics of convertible bonds?

6. Convertible bonds provide something extra over a regular bond. That "extra" is really part of the owners' equity of the company, and part of the bond proceeds should be allocated to the stockholders' equity. What are the chief arguments against this proposal?

7. (a) What is the difference in the accounting treatment between convertible bonds and bonds issued with detachable stock warrants? (b) Do you think this difference is justified? Give your reasons.

8. Distinguish between straight-line and interest methods of bond premium amortization. What arguments can be offered in support of each method?

9. The interest method of bond premium or discount amortization is not desirable for the issuer because it results in higher net income than would be found with straight-line amortization. Under what conditions would this be true?

10. (a) Describe the bonds-outstanding method for premium or discount amortization. (b) How does this method differ from the interest method of amortization?

11. The conversion of convertible bonds to common stock by an investor may be viewed as an exchange involving no gain or loss, or as a transaction for which market values should be recognized and a gain or loss reported. What arguments support each of these views for the investor and for the issuer?

12. What is the difference between bond reacquisition and bond redemption?

13. What purpose is served by using callable bonds? What effect does a call feature have upon the amortization of a bond premium?

14. What is meant by refunding a bond issue? Why may refunding be advisable?

15. Because of favorable market prices, the trustee of Wilson Company's bond sinking fund invested the current year's contributions to the fund in the company's own bonds. The bonds are kept alive in the fund and are not canceled. The fund also includes cash and securities of other companies. What are the arguments for and against carrying these bonds as an investment on Wilson Company's balance sheet?

16. (a) What is meant by purchase of bonds *flat*? (b) What special accounting procedure should be followed for such an investment?

17. Restructuring of bond debt may be accomplished in several ways. Why is restructuring sometimes necessary, and what are some of the more common ways it can take place?

18. The Madesen Company has $40,000,000 of 8% bonds outstanding. Because of cash flow problems, the company is behind in interest payments and in contributions to its sinking fund. The market value of the bonds has declined until it is currently only 50% of the face value of the bonds. After lengthy negotiations, the principal bondholders have agreed to exchange their bonds for preferred stock that also has a current market value of $20,000,000. What are the arguments for and against recognizing a gain on the issuer's books for this restructuring?

EXERCISES

1. What is the market value of each of the following bond issues? Round to nearest dollar.

(a) 5% bond of $50,000 sold on the bond issue date; 10-year life, interest payable semiannually, effective rate 8%.

(b) 6% bond of $200,000 sold on bond issue date; 20-year life, interest payable semiannually, effective rate 4%.

(c) 8% bond of $100,000 sold 30 months after bond issue date; 15-year life, interest payable semiannually, effective rate 6%.

2. The Riggs Co. has issued 10,000 shares of $100 par common stock. The company requires additional working capital and finds it can sell 5,000 additional shares of common at $60, or it can issue $300,000 of 10% bonds at par. Earnings of the company before income tax have been $80,000 annually, and it is expected that these will increase 30% (before additional interest charges) as a result of the additional funds. Assuming that the income tax rate is estimated at 45%, which method of financing would you recommend as a common stockholder? Why? (Show calculations.)

3. Herde Insurance decides to finance expansion of its physical facilities by issuing convertible debenture bonds. The terms of the bonds are: maturity date 20 years after May 1, 1976, the date of issuance; conversion at option of holder after 2 years, 40 shares of $30 par value stock for each $1,000 bond held; interest rate of 6% and call provision on the bonds of 104. The bonds were sold at 102. (a) Give the entry on Herde's books to record the sale of 1,000 bonds on July 1, 1977; interest payment dates are May 1 and November 1. (b) Assume the same condition as in (a) above, except that the sale of the bonds is to be recorded in a manner that will recognize a value related to the conversion privilege. The estimated sales price of the bonds without the conversion privilege is 98.

4. Assume $100,000 Valley School District 5% bonds are purchased on the bond issue date for $96,193. Interest is payable semiannually and the bonds mature in 10 years. The purchase price provides a return of 5.5% on the investment.

> (a) What entries would be made on the investor's books for the receipt of the first two interest payments, assuming discount amortization on each interest date by (1) the straight-line method and (2) the interest method? Round to nearest dollar.
> (b) What entries would be made on Valley School District's books to record the first two interest payments, assuming discount amortization on each interest date by (1) the straight-line method and (2) the interest method? Round to nearest dollar.

5. On January 1, 1977, Tony Bell purchased $20,000 of Derek Company 6% bonds at 108. Bonds are due on January 1, 1992, but can be redeemed by the company at earlier dates at premium values as follows:

> January 1, 1985, to December 31, 1988, at 103
> January 1, 1989, to December 31, 1991, at 101

> (a) What alternatives does Bell have as to the method of recognizing the amortization of premium? Which is preferable? Why?
> (b) What amortization amounts should Bell recognize over the life of the bond issue?

6. The NAPA Corporation issued $100,000 of 5% debenture bonds on a basis to return 7%, receiving $91,684. Interest is payable semiannually and the bonds mature in 5 years.

> (a) What entries would be made for the first two interest payments, assuming discount amortization on interest dates by (1) the straight-line method and (2) the interest method? Round to nearest dollar.
> (b) If the sale is made on a 4% return, $104,491 being received, what entries would be made for the first two interest payments, assuming premium amortization on interest dates by (1) the straight-line method and (2) the interest method? Round to nearest dollar.
> (c) What entries would be made on the books of the investor assuming one party obtained all the bonds and the straight-line method of amortization was used? Round to nearest dollar.

7. Craven Corporation purchased 8% serial bonds on April 1, 1977, for $2,000,000. The bonds mature in $400,000 lots on April 1 of each of the following years. Interest is payable semiannually; the issue has a discount of $50,000. Assuming that Craven operates on a calendar year, prepare a table summarizing interest charges and bond carrying values by the bonds-outstanding method.

8. On June 30, 1977, the original issue date, Toni Taylor purchased $500,000 of 20-year, 7% convertible bonds of Moore Corporation at 104. Moore bonds are convertible to 25 shares of $20 par common stock for each $1,000 bond. The bond interest is payable semiannually, June 30 and December 31. On March 31, 1982, Taylor converts $200,000 of the bonds. Both Taylor and Moore Corporation use the calendar year as their fiscal year and amortize the bond premium on the straight-line basis.

> (a) Give entries on both Taylor's and Moore Corporation's books to record the conversion in the absence of a market value for the stock.
> (b) Give entries on both Taylor's and Moore Corporation's books if the market value of the stock was $50 at the conversion date and a gain or loss is to be recognized on the conversion.

9. On December 1, 1975, the Haymond Company issues 10-year bonds of $100,000 at 104. Interest is payable on December 1 and June 1 at 8%. On April 1, 1977, the Haymond Company reacquires and retires 20 of its own $1,000 bonds at 98 plus accrued interest. The fiscal period for the Haymond Company is the calendar year. What entries are made to record (a) the issuance of the bonds, (b) the interest payments and adjustments relating to the debt in 1976, (c) the reacquisition and retirement of bonds in 1977, and (d) the interest payments and adjustments relating to the debt in 1977? Round to nearest dollar.

10. B. Jenkins acquired $40,000 of Texacana Corp. 9% bonds on July 1, 1975. The bonds were acquired at 92; interest is paid semiannually on March 1 and September 1. The bonds mature September 1, 1982. Jenkins' books are kept on a calendar year basis. On February 1, 1978, Jenkins sold the bonds for 97 plus accrued interest. Assuming a straight-line discount amortization, give the entry to record the sale of the bonds on February 1. Round to nearest dollar.

11. Give the entries that would be made for each of the following bond retirement fund transactions, assuming that (1) transactions are recorded only on the books of the corporation, and (2) the transactions are recorded in a double-entry set of books maintained by the trustee and are summarized on the books of the corporation.

     (a) Cash is transferred to the bond retirement fund trustee, $78,000.
     (b) Securities are purchased out of bond retirement fund cash, $73,000.
     (c) Income is collected on bond retirement fund securities, $8,100.
     (d) Expenses are paid out of bond retirement fund cash, $550.
     (e) All of the bond retirement fund securities are sold for $89,000.
     (f) Bonds are redeemed at maturity date out of bond retirement fund cash, $100,000.
     (g) Remaining cash in bond retirement fund is deposited in general cash account.
     (h) Nominal accounts are closed.

PROBLEMS

15-1. Sellers Products decided to issue $1,000,000 in 10-year bonds. The interest rate on the bonds is stated at 7%, payable semiannually. At the time the bonds were sold, the market rate had increased to 8%.

Instructions:
     (1) Determine the maximum amount an investor should pay for these bonds. Round to nearest dollar.
     (2) Assuming that the amount in (1) is paid, compute the amount at which the bonds would be reported after being held for one year. Use two recognized methods of handling amortization of the difference in cost and maturity value of the bonds, and give support for the method you prefer. Round to nearest dollar.

15-2. Brooksby and Brooksby, Inc., was authorized to issue 8-year, 9% bonds of $1,000,000. The bonds are dated January 1, 1976, and interest is payable semiannually on January 1 and July 1. Checks for interest are mailed on June 30 and December 31. Bond sales were as follows:

     April 1, 1976..$500,000 at 96 plus accrued interest.
     July 1, 1977..$300,000 at 102.

On September 1, 1977, remaining unissued bonds were pledged as collateral on the issue of $166,000 of short-term notes.

Instructions:
     (1) Give the journal entries relating to bonds that would appear on the corporation's books in 1976 and 1977. (Straight-line amortization is used. Adjustments are made annually.) Round to nearest dollar.
     (2) Show how information relative to the bond issue will appear on the balance sheet prepared on December 31, 1977. (Give balance sheet section headings and accounts and account balances appearing within such sections.)

15-3. The Roman Co. acquired $20,000 of Mapleton Sales Co. 7% bonds, interest payable semiannually, bonds maturing in 5 years. The bonds were acquired at $20,850, a price to return approximately 6%.

Instructions:

(1) Prepare tables to show the periodic adjustments to the investment account and the annual bond earnings, assuming adjustment by each of the following methods: (a) the straight-line method, and (b) the interest method. Round to nearest dollar.

(2) Assuming use of the interest method, give entries for the first year on the books of both companies.

15-4. The Hiller Manufacturing Company issued $2,000,000 of 8% serial bonds on January 1, 1970, at 98. The bonds mature in units of $250,000 beginning January 1, 1975, with interest payable semiannually on January 1 and July 1. On June 1, 1978, Hiller reacquired at 101 plus accrued interest, $200,000 of bonds due January 1, 1980, and $100,000 due January 1, 1981.

Instructions:

(1) Assuming discount amortization by the bonds-outstanding method and bond retirements as scheduled, prepare a table summarizing interest charges and bond carrying values for the bond life, supported by a schedule showing the calculation of amortization amounts. Round to nearest dollar.

(2) Prepare a similar table summarizing interest charges and bond carrying values for the bond life taking into consideration bond redemptions in advance of maturity dates as indicated (round to nearest dollar).

(3) Record in general journal form the retirement of bonds on June 1, 1978.

15-5. Upon inspecting the records of the Ile Corporation you find that $200,000 of 6½% first-mortgage serial bonds were authorized and dated July 1, 1974, with interest payable semiannually. The issue was sold on October 1, 1974, at $196,950 which included accrued interest. Bonds of $20,000 mature at annual intervals; the first maturity date is July 1, 1975. Bonds are callable on any interest payment date. On January 1, 1977, the company called in the 1979 maturities at 103. The company maintained a single account for the bond issue, and on December 31, 1977, the close of an annual fiscal period, this account showed a balance of $116,350, and appeared as follows:

ACCOUNT 6½% First-Mortgage Serial Bonds

DATE		ITEM	DEBIT	CREDIT	BALANCE DEBIT	BALANCE CREDIT
1974 Oct.	1	Proceeds from sale of bonds............		196,950		196,950
1975 July	1	Retirement of 1975 maturities	20,000			176,950
1976 July	1	Retirement of 1976 maturities	20,000			156,950
1977 Jan.	1	Retirement of 1979 maturities	20,600			136,350
July	1	Retirement of 1977 maturities	20,000			116,350

Instructions:

(1) Give the correcting journal entries on the issuer's books as well as any adjusting entries required as of December 31, 1977. (Assume the books for 1977 have not been closed. Give any schedules that may be required in developing the entries.)

(2) What account balances and amounts relating to the bond issue would appear on the balance sheet as of December 31, 1977, and on the income statement for the year ending December 31, 1977?

15-6. The Fir Company issued $10 million of 7% convertible bonds with interest payment dates of April 1 and October 1. The bonds were issued on July 1, 1967, and mature on April 1, 1987. The bond discount totaled $533,250. The bond contract entitles the bondholders to receive 25 shares of $15 par value common stock in exchange for each $1,000 bond. On April 1, 1977, the holders of bonds, face value $1,000,000, exercised their conversion privilege. On July 1, 1977, the Fir Company reacquired bonds, paying the face value of $500,000 on the open market. The balances in the capital accounts as of December 31, 1976 were:

Common Stock, $15 par, authorized 3 million shares, issued and outstanding, 250,000 shares $3,750,000
Premium on Common Stock 2,500,000

Market value of the common stock and bonds were as follows:

Date	Bonds (per $1,000)	Common Stock (per share)
April 1, 1977	$1,220	$47
July 1, 1977	1,250	51

Instructions: Prepare journal entries on the issuer's books for each of the following transactions. (Use straight-line amortization for the bond discount.)
(1) Issuance of the bonds on July 1, 1967.
(2) Interest payment on October 1, 1967.
(3) Interest accrual on December 31, 1967, including bond discount amortization.
(4) Conversion of bonds on April 1, 1977. (Assume that interest and discount amortization are correctly shown as of April 1, 1977. No gain or loss on conversion is recognized.)
(5) Reacquisition and retirement of bonds on July 1, 1977. (Interest and discount amortization are correctly reported as of July 1, 1977.)

15-7. Jackson Company issued $1,000,000 of 8%, 10-year debentures on January 1, 1972. Interest is payable on January 1 and July 1. The entire issue was sold on April 1, 1972, at 102. On April 1, 1977, $500,000 of the bond issue was reacquired and retired at 99 plus accrued interest. On June 30, 1977, the remaining bonds were reacquired at 96 and refunded with a $400,000, 6% bond issue sold at 100.

Instructions: Give the journal entries for 1972 and 1977 (through June 30) on the Jackson Company books. The company's books are kept on a calendar year basis. Round to nearest dollar.

15-8. On May 1, 1974, the Nebo Co. acquired $20,000 of ABC Corp. 9% bonds at 97 plus accrued interest. Interest on bonds is payable semiannually on March 1 and September 1, and bonds mature on September 1, 1977.

On May 1, 1975, the Nebo Co. sold bonds of $6,000 for 103 plus accrued interest.

On July 1, 1976, bonds of $8,000 were exchanged for 2,250 shares of ABC Corp. no-par common, quoted on the market on this date at 4. Interest was received on bonds to date of exchange.

On September 1, 1977, remaining bonds were redeemed.

Instructions:
(1) Give journal entries for 1974–1977 to record the foregoing transactions on the books of the Nebo Co. including any adjustments that are required at the end of each fiscal year ending on December 31. (Show all calculations.)
(2) Give the journal entries on the books of ABC Corp. for 1976.

15-9. In auditing the books for the Hunsaker Corporation as of December 31, 1977, before the accounts are closed, you find the following long-term investment account balance:

ACCOUNT Investment in Corey Steel 6's (Maturity Date, April 1, 1981)

DATE		ITEM	DEBIT	CREDIT	BALANCE DEBIT	BALANCE CREDIT
1977 Jan.	22	Bonds, $100,000 par, acquired at 102 plus accrued interest............	102,850		102,850	
Mar.	10	Proceeds from sale of bonds, $50,000 par and accrued interest		53,000	49,850	
June	1	Interest received		1,500	48,350	
Nov.	1	Amount received on call of bonds, $20,000 par, at 101 and accrued interest...		20,700	27,650	
Dec.	1	Interest received		900	26,750	

(continued)

Instructions:

(1) Give the entries that should have been made relative to the investment in bonds, including any adjusting entries that would be made on December 31, the end of the fiscal year. (Assume bond premium amortization by the straight-line method.)

(2) Give the journal entries required at the end of 1977 to correct and bring the accounts up to date in view of the entries actually made.

15-10. D. A. Davis Company established a bond retirement fund to retire their recently issued bonds. The fund is held by a trustee who maintains a separate record of transactions.

You obtain the following information:

1977

Mar. 31   Davis transferred $125,000 to the bond retirement fund.

Apr. 1   The trustee bought $50,000 of Jensen 6% bonds at 110, including interest. The bonds pay interest on March 1 and September 1; they mature in five years.

May 1   The trustee purchased $30,000 of Blacker Corp. 6% bonds for $28,000, including interest. Interest is paid on January 1 and July 1; the bonds mature in ten years.

Dec. 1   Sold Jensen bonds for $52,000, including accrued interest.

Dec. 1   Exchanged Blacker bonds for 2,000 shares of Peterman Corporation common stock with a market price of 15½.

Instructions: Give the necessary entries to record the transactions in 1977 on the books of both the trustee and the company. Round to nearest dollar.

15-11. The Catalina Co. issued $1,000,000 of convertible 10-year debentures on July 1, 1976. The debentures provide for 9% interest payable semiannually on January 1 and July 1. The discount in connection with the issue was $19,500 which is being amortized monthly on a straight-line basis.

The debentures are convertible after one year into 7 shares of the Catalina Co.'s $100 par value common stock for each $1,000 of debentures.

On August 1, 1977, $100,000 of debentures were turned in for conversion into common. Interest has been accrued monthly and paid as due. Accrued interest on debentures is paid in cash upon conversion.

Instructions: Prepare the journal entries to record the conversion, amortization and interest in connection with the debentures as of: August 1, 1977; August 31, 1977; and December 31, 1977 — including closing entries for end of year. No gain or loss is to be recognized on the conversion. Round to nearest cent. (AICPA adapted)

15-12. The Arden Company issued $3,000,000 of 8% first-mortgage bonds on October 1, 1969, at $2,873,640 plus accrued interest. The bonds were dated July 1, 1969; interest payable semiannually on January 1 and July 1; redeemable after June 30, 1974, and to June 30, 1976, at 104, and thereafter until maturity at 102; and convertible into $100 par value common stock as follows:

Until June 30, 1974, at the rate of 6 shares for each $1,000 of bonds.
From July 1, 1974, to June 30, 1977, at the rate of 5 shares of each $1,000 of bonds.
After June 30, 1977, at the rate of 4 shares for each $1,000 of bonds.

The bonds mature in 10 years from their date. The company adjusts its books monthly and closes its books as of December 31 each year. It follows the practice of writing off all unamortized bond discount in the period of bond retirement.

The following transactions occur in connection with the bonds:

1975

July 1 $500,000 of bonds were converted into stock.

1976

Dec. 31 $500,000 face amount of bonds were reacquired at 99¼ and accrued interest. These were immediately retired.

1977

July 1   The remaining bonds were called for redemption. For purpose of obtaining funds for redemption and business expansion, a $4,000,000 issue of 6% bonds was sold at 98¾. These bonds were dated July 1, 1977, and were due in 20 years.

Instructions: Prepare in journal form the entries necessary for the company in connection with the preceding transactions, including monthly adjustments where appropriate, as of the following dates. Round to nearest dollar.

(1) October 1, 1969
(2) December 31, 1969
(3) July 1, 1975

(4) December 31, 1976
(5) July 1, 1977
(AICPA adapted)

15-13. Zakin Co. recently issued $1,000,000 face value, 8%, 30-year subordinated debentures at 97. The debentures are redeemable at 103 upon demand by the issuer at any date upon 30 days notice ten years after issue. The debentures are convertible into $10 par value common stock of the company at the conversion price of $12.50 per share for each $500 or multiple thereof of the principal amount of the debentures.

Assume that no value is assigned to the conversion feature upon issue of the debentures. Assume further that five years after issue, debentures with a face value of $100,000 and book value of $97,500 are tendered for conversion on an interest payment date when the market price of the debentures is 104 and the common stock is selling at $14 per share and that the company records the conversion as follows:

Bonds Payable	100,000	
Discount on Bonds Payable		2,500
Common Stock		80,000
Premium on Common Stock		17,500

Instructions: Do you agree with this entry? If not, prepare a correct one. (AICPA adapted)

16

Accounting for Income Tax

Accounting for federal and state income taxes has become an increasingly complex topic for the accounting profession. A direct tax based upon income has become a chief source of revenue for both federal and state governments. Although the first income tax was levied by the federal government during the Civil War, it was not until the Constitution was amended in 1913 by the 16th Amendment that the legality of such a tax was established. The tax rates were sufficiently low in the first years after the 16th Amendment that not too much attention was paid to this new tax outlay for individuals and businesses. However, as the services provided by governments have expanded, the rates have increased and the significance of the income tax on personal and business decision making has greatly expanded.

NATURE OF INCOME TAX

Theoretically, income tax could be viewed as either an expense of operating a business or as a distribution of profits between the governmental unit and the owners of the business. The private enterprise philosophy of the United States has led to an acceptance of the former view; income tax is a levy placed by a government on all businesses and thus it is a necessary expense of doing business within our society. Because the amount of tax expense is directly related to the income earned, control of the expense is limited to tax planning that will take advantage of income tax regulations to minimize the present value of tax outlays over the life of the business. Usually, this means taking advantage of provisions to minimize the tax payment for each year. This strategy often makes the income reported for tax purposes different from that reported on the published financial statements, and this difference creates the need for an income tax adjustment on the books referred to as *interperiod income tax allocation*. This adjustment and ramifications from it have created the greatest problems in accounting for income tax.

Although the federal income tax is the most significant income tax in most cases, state and local income taxes are also generally an important expense outlay. Many states and local governments pattern their income tax regulations after the federal government. This simplifies the preparation of income tax returns for businesses and permits more efficient tax planning. Although the emphasis in this chapter will be on the federal tax, accounting for state and local income taxes would be handled in a similar manner with variations depending upon the particular state laws involved.

Because income tax affects almost every business entity, accounting for income tax has widespread interest. The federal tax laws and regulations are complex, and specialists on income tax are usually employed to do the tax planning and tax return preparation. The purpose of this chapter is not to discuss the income tax laws specifically, except as they might have an impact upon the timing of tax payments. Most problems in accounting for income tax may be divided into three categories.

1. Accounting for intraperiod income tax allocation
2. Accounting for interperiod income tax allocation
3. Accounting for operating loss carrybacks and carryforwards

Each of these areas will be discussed in the remainder of this chapter.

INTRAPERIOD INCOME TAX ALLOCATION

Because income tax is related specifically to income items, the reporting of the income tax should be directly related to the income involved. If all income items were classified in one place on the financial statements, the income tax expense could be reported directly as a deduction against that income. However, as discussed in Chapter 4, the income statement is separated into several major divisions: operating income, income from continuing operations, income from discontinued operations, extraordinary items, and cumulative effect of accounting changes. Each of these items usually has income tax consequences. For example, an extraordinary gain on retirement of a long-term debt would be reported for income tax purposes and a tax would be paid. A loss from disposing of a business segment would be deductible from other taxable income and thus the loss would reduce the income tax otherwise payable.[1] The intraperiod income tax allocation principle requires that income tax expense or tax reduction be related to the specific classification of the financial statement involved. In the past, prior period adjustments reported as a direct adjustment to retained earnings but reported currently on income tax returns also required intraperiod tax allocation. However, if prior period adjustments are limited to correction of accounting errors, the

---

[1]A cumulative change in accounting principles will also have tax effects arising from the change of principles; however, the exact nature of the effect depends upon whether the change was also made for tax purposes and if it was applied retroactively in the current year's tax return. If the current year's tax return is not affected by the retroactive change, the tax effects arise as a result of interperiod tax allocation which is discussed later in the chapter rather than as a result of intraperiod tax allocation.

income tax effect of the error can be calculated directly and an amended return filed for the year of the error. No allocation of current income tax to prior periods is necessary.

Intraperiod Income Tax Allocation Assuming a Level Tax Rate

Income tax rates usually are either graduated and increase as income increases, or have a limited number of rates for different levels of income. The federal corporate tax rate is currently a three-level tax: 20% on the first $25,000 of income, 22% on the second $25,000, and 48% on all income over $50,000. To simplify the discussion, it will be assumed in this section that the income tax rate is 45% and is constant over all income. Assume examination of Springer Corporation's income tax return for 1977 revealed the following information before computation of the income tax.

Income classified as ordinary income from continuing operations	$ 225,000
Income from discontinued operations	62,000
Loss on sale of segment of business	(100,000)
Extraordinary loss from earthquake	(50,000)
Taxable income on income tax return	$ 137,000

Using a 45% tax rate, the income tax of $61,650 ($137,000 × .45) would be allocated as follows:

Income tax on ordinary income from continuing operations ($225,000 × .45)	$101,250
Income tax on income from discontinued operations ($62,000 × .45)	27,900
Income tax reduction from loss arising from disposal of a business segment ($100,000 × .45)	(45,000)
Income tax reduction from extraordinary loss ($50,000 × .45)	(22,500)
Income tax payable for current year	$ 61,650

The journal entry required to record the computations on the books would be as follows:

Income Tax on Income from Continuing Operations	101,250	
Income Tax on Income from Discontinued Operations	27,900	
Income Tax Reduction from Loss on Disposal of a Business Segment		45,000
Income Tax Reduction from Extraordinary Loss		22,500
Income Tax Payable		61,650

The abbreviated income statement at the top of the next page shows how the information would be reported. Alternatively, the detail for the "Provision for income tax" section could be presented in notes to the financial statement.

The illustration demonstrates how the amount of income tax applicable to each section might be disclosed. In addition, notes are usually included with the financial statements to provide more detail of these transactions. Sometimes the amount of income tax expense or tax reduction is included in the note rather than in the body of the financial statements, and the item is reported "net of income tax effect." Either method of disclosure is acceptable.[1]

---

[1] *Opinions of the Accounting Principles Board, No. 30*, "Reporting the Results of Operations" (New York: American Institute of Certified Public Accountants, 1973), par. 11.

Springer Corporation
Income Statement (Partial)
For Year Ended December 31, 1977

Income from continuing operations before income tax.....................		$225,000
Provision for income tax:		
Income tax currently payable................................	$ 61,650	
Income tax reduction from extraordinary loss.............................	22,500	
Income tax reduction from loss arising from disposal of a business segment	45,000	
Income tax on income from discontinued operations	(27,900)	101,250
Income from continuing operations..		$123,750
Discontinued operations:		
Income from operations of discontinued business segment (less applicable income tax of $27,900).....................	$ 34,100	
Loss on disposal of business segment (less applicable income tax of $45,000)	(55,000)	(20,900)
Extraordinary loss from earthquake damage (less applicable income tax of $22,500)		(27,500)
Net income..		$ 75,350

Intraperiod Income Tax Allocation Assuming Differential Tax Rates

As indicated earlier, the corporate income tax rate structure in the United States involves three steps. If income before and after the special items considered separately or in the aggregate always exceeds the last rate break of $50,000, the tax applicable to the special item would simply be 48%, the highest rate. The lower tax rates of 20% and 22% are thus applied to the first $50,000 of ordinary income from continuing operations. If excluding the special items considered separately causes income to cross over either the $25,000 or the $50,000 break, an allocation must be made by computing the impact of each special item considered separately, and then allocating the aggregate tax effect among the special items in proportion to the individual tax effects. This, in effect, uses a weighted average rate for the special items.

To illustrate, assume the Martinez Company had income from operations of $60,000, an extraordinary loss of $40,000, and a loss from disposal of a business segment of $5,000. The aggregate income tax effect of these two special items would be computed as follows:

Income tax on taxable income after special items ($15,000* × .20)...		$ 3,000
Less income tax on $60,000 income from operations:		
First $25,000 × .20	$5,000	
Next $25,000 × .22	5,500	
Next $10,000 × .48	4,800	15,300
Aggregate tax effect of special items............................		$(12,300)

*($60,000 − $40,000 − $5,000)

The income tax impact of each special item considered separately as an adjustment to taxable income would be computed as follows:

Loss on disposal of a business segment, $5,000:		
Income tax on $15,000 taxable income (as above)		$ 3,000
Less income tax on $20,000 taxable income after adding back $5,000 loss on disposal of a business segment ($20,000 × .20)..		4,000
Income tax impact of loss on disposal of a business segment considered separately..		$ (1,000)

Extraordinary loss, $40,000:
  Income tax on $15,000 taxable income (as on page 449).......... $ 3,000
  Less income tax on $55,000 taxable income after adding
    back $40,000 extraordinary loss:
      First $25,000 × .20... $5,000
      Next $25,000 × .22... 5,500
      Next $5,000 × .48... 2,400   12,900
Tax impact of extraordinary loss considered separately.......... $ (9,900)

The total impact of the two items considered separately is $10,900 ($9,900 + $1,000), or $1,400 less than the aggregate income tax effect ($12,300 − $10,900). Therefore, the income tax allocation for reporting purposes must be made in the proportion of each impact to the total impact as follows:

Income tax allocation for loss from disposal of a business seg-
  ment ($1,000 ÷ $10,900) × $12,300... $ (1,128)
Income tax allocation for extraordinary loss ($9,900 ÷ $10,900)
  × $12,300..   (11,172)
                                                                                                         $(12,300)

The required journal entry to record the income tax for the year would be as follows:

Income Tax... 15,300
  Income Tax Reduction from Loss on Disposal of a Business
    Segment...   1,128
  Income Tax Reduction from Extraordinary Loss   11,172
  Income Tax Payable..   3,000

Sometimes the income tax rate for the different items may not be the same because of the income tax regulations. For example, items qualifying as capital gain items may be taxed at rates differing from the rate for income from normal operations. The capital gain rate should be used in making intraperiod income tax allocations for these items.

INTERPERIOD INCOME TAX ALLOCATION

Perhaps the most complex area involving accounting for income tax is the adjustment necessary to apply the accrual concept to income tax expense. Income tax regulations do not always follow generally accepted principles of accounting. This is not necessarily a weakness in the regulations. The objective of income tax is to raise revenue for federal, state, and local governments. Tax considerations, such as taxing according to the ability of taxpayers to pay the tax, taxing according to the benefits the taxpayers receive, and taxing to depress or stimulate various portions of the economy, are not the same objectives accountants have in determining a fair amount of income. Consequently, income for tax purposes can and usually does differ from income for external reporting purposes.

These differences between taxable and accounting income may be divided into two categories: timing differences and permanent differences. Timing differences are temporary in nature. An expense may be deducted for income tax purposes in the current year, but on the external financial statements in a subsequent year. A revenue item may have to be reported on the income tax return in the current year, but won't be reported on the external financial statements until it is earned in subsequent years. In order to match the tax expense with its appropriate revenue, interperiod income tax allocation is necessary for timing differences. Essentially, it means that the income tax expense reported on the financial statements is the tax that would have been paid if the income on the financial statements had been used for income tax purposes. The difference between the amount reported as income tax expense and the amount currently payable is reported as a deferred charge or a deferred credit depending upon the nature of its balance. When the item *reverses* in subsequent periods, the deferred balance is eliminated.

On the other hand, permanent differences between the income reported for external purposes and on the income tax return are not subject to interperiod income tax allocation. Permanent differences are directly related to the tax regulations and vary in their impact over time. Permanent differences include nontaxable revenue, such as interest revenue from municipal securities and proceeds from life insurance policies received by a company upon the death of a company officer. They also include expenses not deductible for tax purposes, such as fines for violation of government regulations, goodwill amortization, and amounts deductible in excess of actual expenditures such as the excess of percentage depletion on wasting assets over cost depletion.

Historical Development	The principle of interperiod income tax allocation was recognized by the Committee on Accounting Procedure in Bulletin No. 43, but the Committee recognized an exception to such allocation when it could be presumed that ". . . particular differences between the tax return and the income statement will recur regularly over a comparatively long period of time."[1] This led to varied interpretations and alternative procedures by different companies. For example, if a company uses an accelerated depreciation method for equipment on the income tax return but straight-line depreciation on the books, the amount of depreciation expense for tax purposes will exceed that for reporting purposes every year as long as the company is growing and adding new equipment faster than it is retiring the old equipment. This type of timing difference is defined as a *recurring timing difference* because, in total, the tax deferral will never reverse due to recurring purchase of new equipment. Some companies interpreted Bulletin No. 43 as applying to this type of item, and did not provide for interperiod income tax allocation for depreciation differences. This procedure is referred to as *partial allocation*. Other companies included these depreciation differences in their computation of interperiod income tax allocation balances. The Accounting Principles

[1]*Accounting Research and Terminology Bulletins — Final Edition*, "No. 43, Restatement and Revision of Accounting Research Bulletins" (New York: American Institute of Certified Public Accountants, 1961), Ch. 10, sect. B, par. 1.

Board in Opinion No. 11 sought to extend the principle of income tax allocation, as well as to achieve uniformity in practice, by modifying the original position and concluding that ". . . comprehensive interperiod tax allocation is an integral part of the determination of income tax expense."[1] Comprehensive income tax allocation requires allocation for all timing differences whether they are expected to recur in the future or not. The Board reasoned that although the total difference between accelerated depreciation and straight-line depreciation may increase each year, under the revolving account theory, depreciation on a specific asset does reverse itself in time so that in the latter part of an asset's life more depreciation is charged on the books than on the income tax return.

Although comprehensive income tax allocation is widely accepted, there is still concern as to the true nature of the deferred amount reported on the balance sheet. If the amount is a credit, it is usually reported as a long-term deferred credit with long-term liabilities unless it is clearly going to reverse in the next period or unless it arises from transactions such as installment sales whose asset balance is reported in current assets. If the amount is a debit, it is usually reported as a long-term deferred charge after land, buildings, and equipment. Because the deferred tax is payable only when the items reverse, and then only if there is sufficient income in that year to be taxed, analysts often delete the amount from the liability section of the balance sheet when they are computing ratios for comparative purposes. Interperiod income tax allocation places principal emphasis on the income statement and proper matching of expenses with revenues. If the Financial Accounting Standards Board continues to place increased emphasis on the balance sheet, the attractiveness of interperiod income tax allocation may diminish and the profession may return to some form of partial allocation.

Accounting for Different Types of Timing Differences

Timing differences may be classified into the following categories. Examples of items fitting into each category are also included.

1. Reported book income before tax is less than taxable income.
    (a) Revenue is deferred for reporting purposes but is currently recognized for tax purposes.
        (1) Rent revenue received in advance of period earned and deferred for reporting purposes, but taxable in period of receipt.
        (2) Subscription revenue received in advance of period earned and deferred for reporting purposes but taxable in period of receipt.
    (b) Expense is currently recognized for reporting purposes but is deferred for tax purposes.
        (1) Warranty expense accrued in advance for reporting purposes but allowed for tax purposes only when costs are incurred under the warranty.
        (2) Reduction in market value of current marketable securities deducted for reporting purposes in the current period, but allowed for tax purposes only when securities are sold.

---

[1] *Opinions of the Accounting Principles Board, No. 11*, "Accounting for Income Taxes" (New York: American Institute of Certified Public Accountants, 1967), par. 34.

2. Reported book income before tax is more than taxable income.
   (a) Revenue is currently recognized for reporting purposes, but is deferred for tax purposes.
      (1) Installment sales method used for tax purposes but accrual method of sales used for reporting purposes.
      (2) Construction revenue recognized using the percentage-of-completion method for reporting purposes, but using the completed-contract method for tax purposes.
   (b) Expense is deferred for reporting purposes, but is currently recognized for tax purposes.
      (1) Straight-line depreciation used for reporting purposes, but accelerated depreciation used for tax purposes.
      (2) Intangible drilling costs for extractive industry capitalized and deferred for reporting purposes, but written off as incurred for tax purposes.

Accounting for Interperiod Income Tax Allocation — No Change in Rates

To illustrate the accounting for interperiod income tax allocation when income tax rates are constant at 45%, assume the following:

Year	Reported Book Income Before Tax	Excess of Accelerated Depreciation Over Straight-Line	Excess of Rent Revenue Received in Advance Over Rent Revenue Earned	Taxable Income
1977	$100,000	$15,000	$10,000	$ 95,000
1978	130,000	25,000	(6,000)	99,000
1979	175,000	(5,000)	15,000	195,000

The excess of rent revenue received in advance over rent earned causes reported income to be lower than taxable income. The excess of accelerated depreciation over straight-line depreciation causes the opposite effect: reported income exceeds taxable income. If the item is reversed in a particular year, reported and taxable income are affected in the opposite direction. Different kinds of timing differences should be maintained separately for computation purposes, although they may be combined for reporting purposes.

The income tax expense for the period is computed on the reported income adjusted for any permanent difference effects. The current income tax liability for the period is computed on the taxable income for the period. The difference between the computed income tax expense and the computed income tax liability is recorded as a deferred charge or a deferred credit. To illustrate, the entries given below and on page 454 would be recorded for the years 1977–79 for the preceding example:

```
1977: Income Tax ..................................................................... 45,000
      Deferred Income Tax — Rent Revenue¹ ................................  4,500
        Deferred Income Tax — Depreciation¹ ...............................          6,750
        Income Tax Payable .................................................................          42,750
```

Computation:
Income tax: 45% × $100,000 = $45,000
Deferred income tax — rent revenue: 45% × $10,000 = $4,500
Deferred income tax — depreciation: 45% × $15,000 = $6,750
Income tax payable: 45% × $95,000 = $42,750

---

[1]These accounts may be combined and only the net effect reported as long as they are both current or both noncurrent items.

1978: Income Tax 58,500
          Deferred Income Tax — Rent Revenue................................   2,700
          Deferred Income Tax — Depreciation................................   11,250
          Income Tax Payable   44,550

Computation:

Income tax: 45% × $130,000 = $58,500
Deferred income tax — rent revenue: 45% × $6,000 = $2,700
Deferred income tax — depreciation: 45% × $25,000 = $11,250
Income tax payable: 45% × $99,000 = $44,550

1979: Income Tax 78,750
          Deferred Income Tax — Rent Revenue...................................   6,750
          Deferred Income Tax — Depreciation   2,250
          Income Tax Payable   87,750

Computation:

Income tax: 45% × $175,000 = $78,750
Deferred income tax — rent revenue: 45% × $15,000 = $6,750
Deferred income tax — depreciation: 45% × $5,000 = $2,250
Income tax payable: 45% × $195,000 = $87,750

A comparison of reported results with and without interperiod income tax allocation is given below:

Year	Reported Results Without Interperiod Income Tax Allocation			Reported Results With Interperiod Income Tax Allocation		
	Reported Book Income Before Income Tax	Income Tax	Net Income	Reported Book Income Before Income Tax	Income Tax	Net Income
1977	$100,000	$42,750	$57,250	$100,000	$45,000	$55,000
1978	130,000	44,550	85,450	130,000	58,500	71,500
1979	175,000	87,750	87,250	175,000	78,750	96,250

Examination of the table shows that without interperiod income tax allocation, the income tax expense in 1978 is almost the same as for 1977 even though reported income was $28,200 higher in 1978 than in 1977. The results using interperiod income tax allocation more accurately portray the accrual concept of matching expense against revenue.

The balance sheet classification of deferred income tax depends upon whether it has a debit or a credit balance. If it has a credit balance, it is classified as a liability; if it has a debit balance, it is classified as an asset. If it arose from a nonrecurring timing difference, and the difference is expected to reverse in the subsequent period, the asset or liability is classified as current. If the deferred income tax arises from recurring timing differences, and is related to another asset or liability balance, the classification of deferred income tax will depend upon the classification of the related account. For example, if the deferral arises from installment sales, it will be classified as current because unpaid installment receivables are always classified as a current asset. In the above example, Rent Revenue Received in Advance is normally classified as a noncurrent item on the grounds that there is an insignificant demand on current assets necessary to realize the revenue. Rent revenue is related more closely to Land, Buildings, and Equipment, noncurrent accounts. Therefore, the deferred income tax related to rent revenue would be classified as noncurrent. A similar classification would apply to deferred income tax arising from depreciation differences. Because both of the deferred income tax accounts are noncurrent, they would generally be netted for purpose of balance sheet disclosure. Thus, the balance in the noncurrent deferred income tax account for each year in the example would be as follows:

| | Deferred Income Tax Balance Arising From | | |
	(1) Rent Revenue Received in Advance Debit (Credit)	(2) Accelerated Depreciation Debit (Credit)	(3) Net Balance (2) − (1)
1977	$4,500	$(6,750)	$(2,250)
1978	1,800	(18,000)	(16,200)
1979	8,550	(15,750)	(7,200)

Computation:
(1) 1977: 45% × $10,000 = $ 4,500
    1978: 45% × $ 6,000 = $ 2,700 $ 4,500 − $ 2,700 = $ 1,800
    1979: 45% × $15,000 = $ 6,750 $ 1,800 + $ 6,750 = $ 8,550
(2) 1977: 45% × $15,000 = $ 6,750
    1978: 45% × $25,000 = $11,250 $ 6,750 + $11,250 = $18,000
    $18,000 − $ 2,250 = $15,750

The income statement would disclose the income tax effect of all timing differences. For example, the income tax effect for 1977 in the above example might be disclosed as follows:

Income before income tax		$100,000
Less provision for income tax:		
Income tax currently payable	$42,750	
Deferred income tax from timing differences	2,250	45,000
Net income		$ 55,000

If in 1977, $20,000 of the $100,000 book income was from tax exempt municipal securities, the taxable income would be $75,000 rather than $95,000, and the tax computation on reported income would be based on $80,000 rather than the $100,000 reported income because of this permanent difference. The revised entry would then be as follows:

1977: Income Tax	36,000	
Deferred Income Tax — Rent Revenue	4,500	
Deferred Income Tax — Depreciation		6,750
Income Tax Payable		33,750

Computation:
Income tax: 45% × $80,000 = $36,000
Deferred income tax — rent revenue: 45% × $10,000 = $4,500
Deferred income tax — depreciation: 45% × $15,000 = $6,750
Income tax payable: 45% × $75,000 = $33,750

Interperiod Income Tax Allocation — With Change in Rates

If income tax rates change over time, the change in rates must be accounted for in some manner, either currently or in the future. Two methods of accounting for income tax rate changes have been proposed, the deferred method and the liability method. Under the *deferred method*, the current income tax rate is used to accrue the difference between reported and taxable income. No adjustment is made when tax rates change unless the item reverses itself as discussed later. Under the *liability method*, the income tax rate used is the rate estimated to be in effect when the item reverses. Since this future rate is very uncertain, the current rate is often used as an estimate of the future rate, and it is adjusted as the actual rate changes. Thus, if the rate decreased, and a deferred income tax credit was on the books, a gain from the change in rates would be reported. Prior to the issuance of Accounting Principles Board Opinion No. 11, both methods were being used in practice. However, the Accounting Principles Board expressed its preference for the deferred method, and it is now the generally accepted method.

For each kind of timing difference under the deferred tax method, a company may choose to compute income tax expense on either an individual basis or for groups of transactions. Under the individual basis, any change in rates would be reflected as a gain or loss when the item is reversed. More commonly, similar timing differences are grouped. If similar timing differences are grouped, and if the income tax rate changes over time, income tax allocation under the group method may be accounted for either by the gross change or net change method. Under the *gross change method*, new timing differences arising in the current period are accrued at the current income tax rates and reversals of prior period timing differences are removed from the deferred accounts at the income tax rate reflected in the accounts at the beginning of the current period. This may be done using either a weighted average rate, or a specified rate based upon a fifo flow. The gain or loss on the rate change is reflected in the current period. Under the *net change method*, the current income tax rate is applied to the net change in timing differences for the current period, and no gain or loss on rate change is reported currently. No more deferred tax can be amortized than was provided for a particular type of timing difference. Thus, until an item almost completely reverses, an adjustment for the change in rates may not be required. Once one of these methods is adopted, it should be consistently applied. If a change is made, it is subject to the principles of reporting accounting changes discussed more fully in Chapter 22.

Illustration of Gross and Net Change Methods. The following example illustrates the difference between the gross change and net change methods. Assume in the example on page 453 that the income tax rate in 1978 changed from 45% to 48%. Also assume the $25,000 depreciation was a net figure composed of equipment whose depreciation using the accelerated depreciation method exceeded the depreciation using the straight-line method by $60,000, and equipment whose depreciation had reversed and whose straight-line depreciation exceeded depreciation on the accelerated depreciation method by $35,000. The net excess of rent revenue earned over rent revenue received was composed of $30,000 rent revenue received in advance and $36,000 rent revenue earned during the period.

Under the net change method, all of the computations would be made using the 48% rate. No adjustment would be made for the change in rates, and none would be made unless the deferred income tax account was reduced to zero. The entry for 1978 would be as follows:

Income Tax	62,400	
Deferred Income Tax — Rent Revenue		2,880
Deferred Income Tax — Depreciation		12,000
Income Tax Payable		47,520

Computation:
Income tax: 48% × $130,000 = $62,400
Deferred income tax — rent revenue: 48% × $6,000 = $2,880
Deferred income tax — depreciation: 48% × $25,000 = $12,000
Income tax payable: 48% × $99,000 = $47,520

Under the gross change method, new or originating balances would be added at the 48% rate; reversals would be deducted at the 1977 rate since only one prior year was involved. Weighted average or fifo may be used when multiple years exist. Thus, the computation for 1978 under the gross change method would be as follows:

Rent revenue timing differences:	
Originating in 1978 ($30,000 × .48)	$14,400
Reversing in 1978 ($36,000 × .45)..	16,200
Net change in 1978...	$ (1,800)
Depreciation timing differences:	
Originating in 1978 ($60,000 × .48)	$28,800
Reversing in 1978 ($35,000 × .45)..	15,750
Net change in 1978...	$13,050

The entry for 1978 would be as follows:

Income Tax	62,370	
Deferred Income Tax — Rent Revenue		1,800
Deferred Income Tax — Depreciation		13,050
Income Tax Payable		47,520

Computation:
Income tax payable: $99,000 × .48 = $47,520

The debit to income tax, $62,370, is the net effect of the tax on current taxable income as adjusted by the effect of the change in rates. It can be compared with the $62,400 debited to income tax under the net method. The effect of the tax rate change, $30 in this example, could be reported separately; however, it is generally netted against income tax expense because of the immateriality of the rate change adjustment.

Because of its simplicity, the net change method is most commonly followed in practice, although both methods are currently acceptable.

Problem Areas in Interperiod Income Tax Allocation

Several difficult questions have arisen concerning interperiod income tax allocation as it relates to specific industries and situations. For example, the equity method of accounting for investment revenue results in accounting income in excess of taxable income. Income from investments is taxable only when distributed. If the distribution never occurs, the difference is really a permanent difference rather than a timing difference. The Accounting Principles Board considered this situation, and concluded that it should be presumed all undistributed earnings from an investment included in income should be accounted for as timing differences and a deferred tax credit recognized as if the earnings remittance had occurred in the current period.[1]

Similar reasoning was used to justify calling undistributed earnings of a subsidiary to its parent as timing differences unless "sufficient evidence shows that the subsidiary has invested or will invest the undistributed earnings indefinitely or that earnings will be remitted in a tax-free liquidation."[2]

The provisions of the Internal Revenue Code permit companies such as savings and loan associations and life insurance companies to exclude from taxable income amounts determined by formulae for bad debt reserves and policyholders' surplus. In both cases, the Board concluded that the entity involved controls the decision as to whether the item would or would not reverse. Therefore, no interperiod income tax allocation is required for these items.[3]

Another question that has been extensively discussed is whether the deferred tax credit should be discounted to report the amount at the present value of the expected future payments. In Accounting Principles Board Opinion No. 10, the Board concluded that because of the uncertainty of the reversal date, deferred income tax should not be accounted for on a discount basis.[4]

ACCOUNTING FOR OPERATING LOSSES

Since income tax is based upon the amount of income earned, no tax is payable if a company experiences an operating loss. As an incentive to those businesses that experience alternate periods of income and losses, the income tax regulations provide a way to ease the risk of loss years. This is done through a carryback and carryforward provision that permits a company to apply an operating loss occurring in one year against income of other years. The number of years the loss can be carried backward and forward has varied over time. The current tax code (1976) provides for a three-year carryback and a seven-year carryforward. As of 1976, a company has a choice for any given year's operating loss as to whether or not it desires to use the carryback provision. It may choose only to go forward. If it chooses to go backward, a company experiencing an operating loss for the current year first applies the loss to the income of the third previous year and an income tax refund claim is filed. If the income in the third previous year is not sufficient to use all of the operating loss, the remainder is carried back two years; then one year. Operating loss carrybacks result in an entry establishing a receivable for the

[1]*Opinions of the Accounting Principles Board, No. 24*, "Accounting for Income Taxes" (New York: American Institute of Certified Public Accountants, 1972), par. 7–9. Current tax regulations permit corporations to deduct a 85% dividends-received credit against dividend revenue.

[2]*Ibid.*, par. 12.

[3]*Ibid.*, par. 23–28.

[4]*Opinions of the Accounting Principles Board, No. 10*, "Omnibus Opinion No. 10" (New York: American Institute of Certified Public Accountants, 1966), par. 6.

refund claim and reducing the operating loss for the current year reflecting the tax savings arising from recovery of the prior years' income taxes.

To illustrate, assume Superior Company had the following pattern of income and losses for the years 1974–1977. For simplicity, complicating assumptions of capital gains, investment credit, etc., are not included as part of this example.

Year	Income (Loss)	Income Tax at 45%
1974	$ 15,000	$6,750
1975	10,000	4,500
1976	14,000	6,300
1977	(29,000)	0

The $29,000 operating loss would be carried back to 1974 first, then to 1975, and finally, $4,000 to 1976. The income tax rate for these former years was 45%. Therefore, an income tax refund claim of $13,050 would be filed for the three years ($29,000 × .45). The entry to record the income tax receivable would be as follows:

Income Tax Refund Receivable..	13,050	
Refund of Income Tax from Operating Loss Carryback...............		13,050
Refund from applying operating loss carryback.		

The refund will be reflected on the income statement as a reduction of the operating loss as follows:

Operating loss before refundable income tax..	$29,000
Refund of prior years' income tax arising from carryback of operating loss	13,050
Net loss	$15,950

If an operating loss also occurred in 1978, only $10,000 of income from carryback years would be available against which to apply the loss. Any additional loss could be carried forward against future income, if earned. Current federal income tax provisions provide for a seven-year carryforward period. Because the ability to earn income in the future is generally not assured, the Accounting Principles Board recommended that carryforward of operating losses be reflected in the accounts only when its earning is assured beyond reasonable doubt. This will exist only if both of the following conditions exist, "(a) the loss results from an identifiable, isolated and nonrecurring cause and the company either has been continuously profitable over a long period or has suffered occasional losses which were more than offset by taxable income in subsequent years, and (b) taxable income is virtually certain to be large enough to offset the loss carryforward and will occur soon enough to provide realization during the carryforward period."[1] The Securities and Exchange Commission has given further guidelines to the virtual certainty test in its Staff Accounting Bulletin No. 8. Virtual certainty requires meeting the conditions given at the top of the next page.

---

[1]*Opinions of the Accounting Principles Board, No. 11, op. cit.,* par. 47.

1. The company has a strong earnings history.
2. The loss was not caused by a general economic or industry decline.
3. The company has reasonable alternative tax strategies available.
4. A forecast based on reasonable assumptions indicates more than enough future income to offset the carryforward.[1]

When these requirements are met, the carryforward may be recognized in the loss period in a similar manner as was done for loss carrybacks.

When this assurance of future earnings does not exist, no entry is made in the loss period. When the carryforward benefit can be applied against subsequent income, the income tax benefit should be reported as an extraordinary gain in the year of realization.[2]

Assume a company had used up its carryback years, but had a $40,000 carryforward in the current year. In the subsequent year, net income is $15,000, and income tax without the carryforward would have been $6,750, or 45% of $15,000. The carryforward benefit would eliminate the income tax liability. The following entries would be required to record the tax provision:

```
Income Tax.................................................................................. 6,750
      Income Tax Payable........................................................           6,750
            Income tax liability assuming no carryforward.

Income Tax Payable ................................................................ 6,750
      Extraordinary Gain from Use of Operating Loss Carryforward ..........           6,750
            Application of carryforward provision against current year's in-
            come tax.
```

The income statement would reflect the carryover application as follows:

Income before income tax and extraordinary item...........................		$15,000
Less provision for income tax:		
Income tax currently payable	$ 0	
Income tax reduction from carryforward of operating loss.........	6,750	6,750
Income before extraordinary item		$ 8,250
Extraordinary item from reduction of income tax arising from		
carryforward of prior year's operating loss..................................		6,750
Net income..		$15,000

Operating Losses and Deferred Tax Credits

The payment of deferred income tax is contingent upon an earnings for the year of the reversal. If an operating loss occurs in the year of a reversal, an adjustment must be made to reduce the deferred credit and increase income for the adjustment. In addition, if there is an operating loss carryforward, an adjustment may be necessary for the expected reversal in the subsequent periods when the carryforward may be applied.

The issues involving income tax are still evolving. Although interperiod income tax allocation is being applied extensively, there are still many who doubt its usefulness, especially as the liability continues to increase in amount on the balance sheet. Continual attention needs to be given to the accounting for this significant cost of doing business in today's economy.

---

[1]Securities and Exchange Commission, *Staff Accounting Bulletin No. 8*, "Corrections or Changes to Bulletin No. 1 — New Interpretations" (Washington, D.C.: U.S. Government Printing Office, 1976).

[2]*Opinions of the Accounting Principles Board, No. 11, op. cit.*

QUESTIONS

1. Accounting methods used by a company to determine income for reporting purposes frequently differ from those used to determine taxable income. What is the justification for these differences?

2. What is meant by intraperiod income tax allocation?

3. Describe the entries that would be made in recognizing the income tax for the period in each case below:

(a) There are earnings from ordinary operations and an extraordinary loss that is less than such earnings.

(b) There are earnings from ordinary operations and a credit for a correction of an error recorded directly to Retained Earnings. An amended income tax return has been filed.

(c) There is a loss from ordinary operations, an extraordinary gain that is greater than the loss, and a debit for a correction of an error recorded directly to Retained Earnings. A claim for an income tax refund has been filed.

4. How is income tax allocated among the various classifications in the financial statements when differential tax rates exist?

5. What theoretical support exists for interperiod income tax allocation?

6. Distinguish between a timing difference and a permanent difference when accounting for interperiod income tax allocation.

7. Distinguish between partial interperiod income tax allocation and comprehensive interperiod income tax allocation. Which method is generally accepted and why?

8. How would the balance sheet account for deferred income tax differ if a company used the liability concept of interperiod income tax allocation as opposed to the deferred concept?

9. When a company grows, all liabilities grow in amount. The growth in the credit balance of deferred income tax is no different than the growth in accounts payable. Do you agree?

10. In adopting income tax allocation procedures for timing differences between reported book and taxable income, what adjustments are made when (a) reported book income before tax is less than taxable income, and (b) reported book income before tax is more than

taxable income? What timing differences are most commonly found?

11. (a) Under what circumstances would Deferred Income Tax be classified as a current liability on the balance sheet?

(b) Under what circumstances would Deferred Income Tax be classified as a current asset on the balance sheet?

12. Under what circumstances will a Deferred Income Tax credit balance be reduced to zero? Why do most companies report an increasing balance in this account?

13. The net change method of accounting for interperiod income tax allocation under the deferred concept is more generally followed than the gross change method. Since both were recognized as acceptable methods by the Accounting Principles Board, why has this preference developed?

14. For each of the following situations, indicate whether or not interperiod income tax allocation would be required. Justify your answers.

(a) Undistributed earnings from investment accounted for under the equity method.

(b) Income tax refund from previous year.

(c) Bad debt reserve for a savings and loan association.

(d) Fine because of a violation of equal opportunity law.

(e) Depreciation using the sum-of-the-years-digits method for tax purposes and straight-line on the books.

(f) Undistributed earnings from subsidiary to parent.

(g) Interest on municipal bonds.

(h) Policyholders' surplus for life insurance companies.

15. How do the operating loss carryback and carryforward provisions of the Internal Revenue Code reduce the risk to a corporation?

16. In applying the operating loss carryback and carryforward provisions, what order of application must be followed?

17. Under what conditions should an anticipated operating loss carryforward be recorded on the books?

18. (a) How would an operating loss carryback be reflected in the financial statements?

(b) How would a realized operating loss carryforward be reflected in the financial statements?

EXERCISES

1. In 1977, the Broer Co. reported taxable operating income of $120,000 and a fully taxable extraordinary gain of $30,000. Assume income tax rates for 1977 of 45% on all items. (a) Give the entry to record the income tax payment for 1977. (b) Assuming there was a fully deductible extraordinary loss of $30,000 rather than an extraordinary gain, give the entry to record the income tax payment for 1977.

2. The Atlanta Corporation reported the following income items before tax for the year 1977.

Income from continuing operations before income tax	$230,000
Loss from operations of a discontinued business segment	10,000
Loss from disposal of a business segment	30,000
Extraordinary gain on retirement of debt	70,000

The income tax rate is 45% on all items. Prepare the portion of the income statement beginning with "Income from continuing operations before income tax" for the year ended December 31, 1977, after applying proper intraperiod income tax allocation procedures.

3. The Hawkins Corporation reported taxable income in 1977 of $65,000. Included in taxable income were the following special items:

Extraordinary gain	$20,000
Gain on disposal of a business segment	15,000

The income tax rate for all items has three levels: 20% on the first $25,000 of income, 22% on the next $25,000 of income, and 48% on all income over $50,000. Based upon these data, compute the income tax that would be allocated to income from continuing operations, extraordinary gain, and gain from disposal of a business segment for the year 1977.

4. For each of the following items, indicate whether it is a timing difference or a permanent difference. For each timing difference, indicate whether it is a deferred credit or a deferred debit.

(a) Tax depreciation in excess of book depreciation, $240,000.
(b) Excess of income on installment sales over income reportable for tax purposes, $170,000.
(c) Proceeds from life insurance policy on recently deceased president, $950,000.
(d) Earnings of foreign subsidiary currently recognized as income, but not yet remitted (remitted in subsequent year), $430,000.
(e) Fine paid for violation of Occupational Safety and Health Act, $250,000.
(f) Royalties collected in advance of period earned, $100,000.
(g) Provision for warranty repairs in excess of actual expenditure for current year, $70,000.
(h) Interest revenue received on municipal bonds, $15,000.

5. Using the information given in Exercise 4, and assuming a pretax reported book income of $2,450,000 and an income tax rate of 45%, calculate taxable income and give the entry to record income tax for the year. Your entry may "net" the various deferred income tax accounts into one account.

6. The Barbara Elaine Foods Corporation reports income of $155,000 on its income tax return for the year ended December 31, 1977. Timing differences between pretax operating income and taxable income for the year are:

Book depreciation in excess of tax depreciation	$35,000
Estimated premium expense in excess of actual premiums redeemed	5,000
Earnings of a foreign subsidiary not yet remitted	10,000

The premium expense arose as a result of a product promotion by the Barbara Elaine Foods Corporation that was initiated on April 1, 1977. According to the rules, a customer could redeem 10 coupons, available in company products, for a cooking utensil set. The company estimated that $12,000 worth of premiums relating to 1977 sales would be redeemed. By year-end, only $7,000 worth of premiums had been redeemed.

The earnings of the foreign subsidiary, Alimientos de Barbara Elaine, S.A., had not been remitted by December 31, 1977, but were expected early in the following year.

Assuming an income tax rate of 45%, compute the income tax per books, deferred income tax, and income tax payable. Give the necessary journal entry to record these amounts. Use one deferred income tax account.

7. The Waltrip Co. shows reported book income before income tax and taxable income for 1976 and 1977 as follows:

	Reported Book Income before Income Tax	Taxable Income
1976	$ 95,400	$149,400
1977	115,800	103,800

The discrepancies arose because the company, organized in the middle of 1976, wrote off against revenue of that year organization costs totaling $60,000. For federal income tax purposes, however, the organization costs can be written off ratably over a period of not less than 60 months. For income tax purposes, then, the company deducted 6/60 of the costs in 1976 and 12/60 of the costs in 1977. Income tax is to be calculated at 45% of taxable income.

Give the entries that would be made on the books of the company at the end of 1976 and 1977 to recognize the income tax liability and to provide for a proper allocation of income tax in view of the differences in book and income tax reporting.

8. The following historical information of the Evensen Corporation shows timing differences for the past three years along with their effects on the deferred income tax liability.

Year	Timing Difference	Tax Rate	Deferred Tax
1974	$ 3,000	48%	$1,440
1975	5,000	49%	2,450
1976	7,000	50%	3,500
	$15,000		$7,390

Pretax book income for 1977 was $75,000. The only timing difference for 1977 was broken down as follows:

Originating timing differences — tax depreciation in excess of book depreciation — $10,000

Reversing timing differences — book depreciation in excess of tax depreciation — $4,000

The tax rate for 1977 is 45%.

(a) Using the gross change method, determine how much would be added to the deferred income tax liability and how much would be removed from it in 1977. Show the computation using both the fifo and the average rate methods.

(b) Using the net change method, determine the net change in the deferred income tax account for the 1977 transactions.

9. The following historical financial data are available for the Mendoza Manufacturing Company.

Year	Income	Tax Rate	Tax Paid
1974	$ 5,000	48%	$2,400
1975	15,000	48%	7,200
1976	20,000	45%	9,000

In 1977, the Mendoza Company suffered a $50,000 net operating loss due to an economic recession. The company elects to use the carryback provision in the tax law.

(a) Using the information given, calculate the refund due arising from the loss carryback and the amount of the loss available to carryforward to future periods. Assume a 1977 tax rate of 45%. Also, assume that no adjustments need to be made to prior years' net income for purposes of the loss carryback and that there is no guarantee that future periods will be profitable.

(b) Give the entry necessary to record the refund due and the loss reduction.

(c) Using the answer from (a), prepare the bottom portion of the income statement reflecting the effect of the loss carryback on the 1977 income statement.

PROBLEMS

16-1. The Hansen Manufacturing Co. reported taxable income for the fiscal year ended October 31, 1977, of $620,000. Ordinary income tax rates were 45%. Included in the $620,000 was a gain of $75,000 properly classified as extraordinary. The gain was taxed at 30%. Also included in taxable income was a loss from the disposal of a business segment of $80,000. The loss was deductible from ordinary income. The annual audit disclosed a $60,000 overstatement in income of the previous year. An amended income tax return will be filed. The income tax rate on the refund will be 45%.

Instructions:
(1) Prepare journal entries to record the income tax liability and income tax refund claim, including proper intraperiod income tax allocation.
(2) Prepare the income statement for the fiscal year ending October 31, 1977, beginning with "Income before income tax, extraordinary items, and loss from disposal of a business segment."

16-2. Zollinger Electronics, Inc., reported the following items of income for the period ended December 31, 1977.

Income before income tax, extraordinary items, and loss from discontinued operations	$ 80,000
Extraordinary loss	(40,000)
Loss from discontinued operations	(15,000)

The following income tax rates are in effect:

First $25,000	20%
Next $25,000	22%
Over $50,000	48%

Instructions:
(1) Allocate the income tax to the various components of income.
(2) Give the entry necessary to allocate income tax to the various categories of income and to record the income tax liability.
(3) Prepare the income statement beginning with the line "Income from continuing operations before income tax, extraordinary items, and loss from discontinued operations."

16-3. The Krahl Corporation accrued certain revenue on its books in 1975 and 1976 of $6,500 and $5,000 respectively, but such revenue was not subject to income tax until 1977. Reported book income before tax and taxable income for the three-year period are as follows:

	Reported Book Income Before Income Tax	Taxable Income
1975	$18,000	$11,500
1976	17,000	12,000
1977	12,000	23,500

Assume the income tax rate applicable to taxable income is 45% in each year.

Instructions: Give the entries that would be made at the end of each year to recognize the income tax liability and to provide for a proper allocation of income tax in view of the differences between reported book income before income tax and taxable income.

16-4. Income data of the Edwards Company for the first five years of its operations are summarized below:

	1973	1974	1975	1976	1977
Sales	$1,250,000	$1,300,000	$1,400,000	$1,400,000	$1,500,000
Cost of goods sold	750,000	780,000	820,000	840,000	900,000
Gross profit on sales	$ 500,000	$ 520,000	$ 580,000	$ 560,000	$ 600,000
Operating expenses	200,000	210,000	230,000	220,000	240,000
Income before income tax	$ 300,000	$ 310,000	$ 350,000	$ 340,000	$ 360,000

Cost of goods sold includes depreciation on buildings and equipment items calculated by the straight-line method. However, for income tax purposes, the company employed the accelerated depreciation methods providing for higher charges in the early years of asset life and correspondingly lower charges in the later years. Depreciation charges on the books as compared with charges recognized for income tax purposes during the five-year period were as follows:

	1973	1974	1975	1976	1977
Depreciation per books	$165,000	$170,000	$170,000	$175,000	$175,000
Accelerated depreciation per tax return	270,000	226,000	180,000	155,000	125,000

All of the revenue of the company is taxable; all of the expenses are deductible for income tax purposes. Income tax rates in each year were 45% of taxable income.

Instructions:
    (1) Give the entries that would be made by the company for the years 1973 through 1977 to record the accrual of income tax if income is debited with income tax allocable to such income.
    (2) Prepare comparative income statements for the Edwards Company for the five-year period assuming the use of interperiod income tax allocation procedures.
    (3) Prepare comparative income statements for the Edwards Company for the five-year period assuming the interperiod income tax allocation procedures were not used and charges for income tax was recognized at the amounts actually becoming payable each year.

16-5. The Trueberg Corporation has taxable income of $2,544,000 for the year ended December 31, 1977. The controller is unfamiliar with the treatment of timing and permanent differences in reconciling from taxable income to reported book income, and has requested your assistance. You are given the following list of differences.

Book depreciation in excess of tax depreciation..	$375,000
Proceeds from life insurance policy upon death of officer................................	240,000
Unremitted earnings of foreign subsidiary, reported as income on the books. Remittance highly unlikely	175,000

Instructions: Using the above information:
    (1) Compute reported book income before income tax.
    (2) Assuming an income tax rate of 45%, give the journal entry to record the income tax for the year.
    (3) Prepare a partial income statement beginning with "Income before income tax."

16-6. You have been asked by the Aust Development Co. to review their books and to indicate what effect income tax allocation procedures will have on their statements. The following reconciliations of book and taxable income are made available to you for the three years.

	1975	1976	1977
Reported book income before tax....................................	$150,000	$225,000	$300,000
Add: Nondeductible expense for tax purposes		75,000	
Excess of book depreciation over tax depreciation..			25,000
Deferred revenue taxable in period of collection...	40,000	35,000	20,000
	$190,000	$335,000	$345,000
Less: Excess of reported book income on installment sales over taxable income	30,000	45,000	40,000
Excess of tax depreciation over book depreciation..	30,000	10,000	
Taxable income	$130,000	$280,000	$305,000

Instructions:
    (1) Assume tax rates are 45% on taxable income for all years. For each of the three years prepare journal entries to record the income tax liability. Assume the net change method is used.
    (2) Assume the rate changed in 1977 to 48%. Prepare the journal entry to record the income tax liability for that year if the net change method is used.

16-7. The Bartholomew Manufacturing Company prepared the following reconciliation between taxable and reported book income for 1977:

Income per tax return	$2,750,000
Add excess depreciation taken on the tax return as compared with books	200,000
	$2,950,000
Less: Extraordinary gain on early extinguishment of debt.............................	150,000
Estimated expenses of future warranties not allowable for tax purposes until expenses are actually incurred..	100,000
Advance rent revenue taxable in period of receipt	50,000
Reported book income before income tax and extraordinary items.................	$2,650,000

A prior period adjustment for the correction of an error was debited directly against Retained Earnings. An income tax refund claim has been filed for this adjustment. Ordinary income tax rates apply.

Instructions:

(1) Assuming an ordinary income tax rate of 45%, prepare required journal entries to record the income tax liability at December 31, 1977.

(2) Prepare the income statement for 1977 beginning with "Income before income tax."

16-8. The books of Rupcich Company for the year ended December 31, 1977, showed a pretax book income of $150,000. In computing the year's taxable income for federal income tax purposes, the following timing differences were taken into account:

(a) Originating timing differences:

(1) Tax depreciation in excess of book depreciation, $12,000.

(2) Installment sales income recognized in excess of income reported for tax purposes, $5,000.

(b) Reversing timing differences:

(1) Book depreciation in excess of tax depreciation, $8,000.

(2) Installment sales income reportable for tax purposes in excess of income recognized on the books, $7,000.

The income tax rate was reduced on January 1, 1977, from 48% to 45%. Prior to that date it was 48%, which was the rate in effect when the Rupcich Company was organized.

Instructions:

(1) Using the net change method, calculate: (a) income tax payable, (b) the change in the deferred income tax account, and (c) income tax debit to operating income.

(2) Calculate each of the above items using the gross change method.

16-9. The following data were taken from the financial statements of the Whipple Company:

Year	Taxable and Book Income	Tax Rate	Income Tax Paid
1973	$ 10,000	45%	$4,500
1974	15,000	45%	6,750
1975	17,000	48%	8,160
1976	13,000	52%	6,760
1977	(50,000)	48%	0

The company elects to use the carryback provision in the tax law.

Instructions:

(1) Calculate the income tax refund due as a result of the 1977 operating loss.

(2) What is the amount, if any, of the operating loss carryforward?

(3) (a) Assume the loss for 1977 was $35,000. Calculate the refund due and prepare the journal entry to record the claim for income tax refund.

(b) Assume in addition to (a) there was another loss in 1978 of $20,000. How much could be carried back and how much would be carried forward?

16-10. The following financial history shows the income and losses for McBride Corporation for the ten-year period 1968–1977.

Year	Income (Loss)	Tax Rate	Tax Paid
1968	$ 5,000	52%	$2,600
1969	6,000	52%	3,120
1970	7,000	48%	3,360
1971	(15,000)	48%	0
1972	4,000	48%	1,920
1973	(12,000)	50%	0
1974	10,000	50%	?
1975	20,000	45%	9,000
1976	(35,000)	45%	0
1977	40,000	45%	?

Assume that no adjustments to taxable income are necessary for purposes of the net operating loss carryback and the company elects to use the carryback provisions of the tax code.

Instructions:

(1) For each of the loss years, calculate the income tax refund due from the loss carryback and the amount of the carryforward (if any).
(2) For 1974 and 1977, calculate the amount of income tax paid, showing the benefit of the loss carryforward.
(3) For 1977, give the entry to record the income tax liability.
(4) For 1977, prepare the income statement beginning with "Income before income tax and extraordinary items."

16-11. Your firm has been appointed to examine the financial statements of Clark Engineering, Inc., (CEI), for the two years ended December 31, 1977, in conjunction with an application for a bank loan. CEI was formed on January 2, 1966, by the nontaxable incorporation of the Clark family partnership.

Early in the engagement you learned that the controller was unfamiliar with income tax accounting and that no income tax allocations have been recorded.

During the examination considerable information was gathered from the accounting records and client employees regarding interperiod income tax allocation. This information has been audited and is as follows (with dollar amounts rounded to the nearest $100):

(a) CEI uses a bad debt write-off method for income tax purposes and a full accrual method for book purposes. The balance of Allowance for Doubtful Accounts at December 31, 1975, was $62,000. Following is a schedule of accounts written off and the corresponding year(s) in which the related sales were made.

Year(s) in Which Sales Were Made	Year in Which Accounts Written Off	
	1977	1976
1975 and prior	$19,800	$29,000
1976	7,200	
1977		
	$27,000	$29,000

The following is a schedule of changes in Allowance for Doubtful Accounts for the two years ended December 31, 1977.

	Year Ended December 31	
	1977	1976
Balance at beginning of year	$ 66,000	$ 62,000
Accounts written off during the year	(27,000)	(29,000)
Doubtful accounts expense for the year	38,000	33,000
Balance at end of year	$ 77,000	$ 66,000

(b) At the top of the next page is a reconciliation between net income per books and taxable income.

	Year Ended December 31	
	1977	1976
(1) Income per books	$333,100	$262,800
(2) Federal income tax payable during year	182,300	236,800
(3) Taxable income not recorded on the books this year: Deferred sales commissions	10,000	
(4) Expenses recorded on the books this year not deducted on the income tax return:		
a. Allowance for doubtful accounts	11,000	4,000
b. Amortization of goodwill	8,000	8,000
(5) Total of lines (1) through (4)	$544,400	$511,600
(6) Income recorded on the books this year not included on the income tax return: Tax exempt interest — Watertown 5% municipal bonds	$ 5,000	
(7) Deductions on the income tax return and charged against book income this year: Depreciation	83,700	$ 38,000
(8) Total of lines (6) and (7)	$ 88,700	$ 38,000
(9) Taxable income [line (5) less line (8)]	$455,700	$473,600

(c) Assume that the effective rates are as follows: 1975 and prior years, 60%; 1976, 50%; 1977, 40%.

(d) In December 1977, CEI entered into a contract to serve as distributor for Brown Manufacturer, Inc.'s engineering products. The contract became effective December 31, 1977, and $10,000 of advance commissions on the contract were received and deposited on December 31, 1977. Since the commissions had not been earned, they were accounted for as a deferred credit to income on the balance sheet at December 31, 1977.

(e) Goodwill represents the excess of cost over fair value of the net tangible assets of a retiring competitor that were acquired for cash on January 2, 1972. The original balance was $80,000.

(f) Depreciation on plant assets transferred at incorporation and acquisitions through December 31, 1975, have been accounted for on a straight-line basis for both financial and tax reporting. Beginning in 1976 all additions of machinery and equipment have been depreciated using the declining-balance method for tax reporting but the straight-line method for financial reporting. Company policy is to take a full year's depreciation in the year of acquisition and none in the year of retirement. There have been no sales, trade-ins, or retirements since incorporation. Following is a schedule disclosing significant data about depreciable property and related depreciation:

Asset	Cost	Life	Annual Straight-Line Amount*	Declining-Balance Depreciation		Depreciation Taken Through December 31, 1975
				1977	1976	
Buildings	$1,190,000	20 & 50 yrs.	$31,000			$380,000
Machinery and equipment:						
Transferred at incorporation or acquired through December 31, 1975	834,000	Various	45,900			495,800
Acquisitions since December 31, 1975:						
1976	267,000	6 yrs.	38,000	$ 63,700	$ 76,000	
1977	395,000	6 yrs.	58,000	116,000		
Total asset cost	$2,686,000					

	Total Depreciation Expense		
	1977	1976	Through December 31, 1975
For book purposes	$172,900	$114,900	$875,800
For tax purposes	$256,600	$152,900	$875,800

*After giving appropriate consideration to salvage value.

Instructions:

(1) Which of the reconciling items between reported book and taxable income are permanent differences?

(2) For each timing difference, calculate the originating and reversing differences for both 1976 and 1977. Round to nearest $100.

(3) Compute the amount to be reported as income tax expense for both 1976 and 1977.

(4) Independent of your solution in (3) and assuming data shown below, prepare the section of the income statement beginning with "Income before income tax" to disclose properly income tax expense for the years ended December 31, 1977 and 1976.

	1977	1976
Income before income tax	$480,400	$465,600
Taxes payable currently	182,300	236,800
Year's net timing differences — Dr. (Cr.)	28,100	(24,500)
Balance of deferred tax at end of year — Dr. (Cr.)	(44,200)	(16,100)

(AICPA adapted)

17

Accounting for Leases and Pension Costs

One of the more interesting and challenging aspects of accounting is the need to continually adjust methods and techniques to account for changes in the type of business transactions occurring in the economy. Few types of transactions in recent years have created more discussion and controversy in accounting than have those involving leases and pension plans. Because of the attention devoted to these two topics by the accounting profession, they have been segregated from the other chapter material, and the latest developments are presented in this separate chapter.

LEASES

The use of leases as a means of transferring property to others has experienced a great growth in the decades since World War II. Indeed, much of the growth that has occurred in American businesses can be attributed to the added flexibility lease financing offers both to the one transferring the property (lessor) as well as the one receiving and using the property (lessee). The Financial Accounting Standards Board has recognized this growth, and has commented upon it as follows:

> Leasing as a means of acquiring the right to use property has proliferated markedly throughout the post-war period. But it was the decade of the 1960s that saw the greatest expansion, not only in the volume of leasing transactions, but also in the variety of application and degree of sophistication of the techniques employed. During that period, according to some estimates, leasing grew at an average annual rate of between 15 percent and 20 percent. It was estimated that over $11 billion in new equipment was leased in 1974 and that by the end of 1975 equipment on lease would total $100 billion.[1]

Simple lease rental contracts have, of course, existed for many decades. Lessees frequently rented equipment for short periods of time

---

[1]*Financial Accounting Standards Board Exposure Draft (Revised): Proposed Statement of Financial Accounting Standards*, "Accounting for Leases" (Stamford, Conn.: Financial Accounting Standards Board, 1976), par. 51.

with no intent of using it throughout the equipment's economic life. Lease payments were debited to an expense account as they were made. But as the lease arrangements became more sophisticated, it became more difficult to distinguish between a rental contract and a sale and purchase of an asset. Leases were frequently noncancelable or cancelable only with severe penalty. They contained terms that extended over the life of the asset, required the lessee to pay the costs of ownership, including taxes and maintenance, and even included options to purchase or renew the lease at bargain amounts. Since there was no recording of the implied liability arising from the lease agreement, there was increasing concern among accountants that accounting for these types of leases as simple rentals no longer described the true nature of the transaction. The legal form of the transaction was different from a purchase/sale transaction, but the substance of the transaction was frequently the same.

Historical Development of Lease Accounting

Perhaps the earliest accounting recognition of the importance of leasing as a financial investment occurred in 1949 when the Committee on Accounting Procedures issued Accounting Research Bulletin No. 38, "Disclosure of Long-Term Leases in Financial Statements of Lessees." When the Accounting Principles Board and Accounting Research Division were formed in 1959, the topic of leases was one of the initial ones to be considered by the Accounting Research Division. This resulted in the publication of Accounting Research Study No. 4, "Reporting of Leases in Financial Statements."[1] The Accounting Principles Board responded to this research and continued need with four opinions on the subject spread over its brief fourteen-year history. Two of the opinions, Number 5 and Number 31, dealt with accounting for leases by lessees. The other two, Number 7 and Number 27, dealt with accounting for leases by lessors. But the profession was not satisfied with the results of these opinions. Inconsistencies developed between accounting for lessees and lessors, and much of the opinions dealt with footnote disclosure rather than the accounting procedures themselves. Rules for requiring capitalization of leases on the balance sheet were vague, and few companies actually reported leases as assets with the accompanying liabilities.

The Financial Accounting Standards Board put the topic of leases on its original topical agenda. In 1974, a comprehensive discussion memorandum on lease accounting was published by the Board. Public hearings were held and in August, 1975, an exposure draft of a proposed Statement of Financial Accounting Standards was issued. Reaction to the exposure draft was generally negative, especially as it dealt with the criteria to distinguish between operating and financing leases and with the period of transition. As a result, the Board issued a revised exposure draft a year later, July, 1976, that made many modifications to the earlier

---

[1]John Myers, *Accounting Research Study No. 4*, "Reporting of Leases in Financial Statements" (New York: American Institute of Certified Public Accountants, 1962).

draft. After exposure, a final FASB statement was adopted in November, 1976. The material in this chapter is based upon that statement.[1]

Leases vary widely in their contractual terms. Variables include length of the lease term, renewal and purchase options, noncancelable provisions, guarantees by lessees of residual values, amount of lease payments, interest rates implicit in the lease agreement, and the degree of risk assumed by lessee, including payment of certain executory costs, such as maintenance, insurance, and taxes. All types of assets are subject to lease: manufacturing equipment, automotive equipment, buildings, land, and tools have all been transferred by some form of lease contract. Although the lease terms apply both to lessees and lessors, there are different accounting problems associated with each side of the lease transaction. Because of these differences, accounting for leases by lessees will be presented first, followed by a discussion of accounting for leases by lessors.

Accounting for Leases — Lessee

A lessee has access to designated leased property during the term of the lease, perhaps with some specific renewal or purchase privileges. Title to the property remains with the lessor; however, many of the normal ownership responsibilities may be transferred to the lessee by contract. These could include payment of such executory costs as maintenance, insurance, and taxes. Basically, all leases as viewed by the lessee may be divided into two types: *operating* and *capital* leases. Accounting for these two types differs materially. Accounting for operating leases essentially requires all rental payments to be debited to an expense when incurred. If rent is prepaid, it is debited to an expense as the period for which the rent applies is reached. No asset for the leased asset or liability for the long-term commitment is recognized on the balance sheet, and information concerning the lease is limited to disclosure by notes to the statements. Accounting for a capital lease essentially requires the lessee to report on the balance sheet the present value of the future lease payments, both as an asset and a liability. The asset is amortized as though the asset had been purchased and was owned by the lessee. The liability is accounted for in the same manner as would be a mortgage on the property. The difference in the impact of these two methods on the financial statements is frequently significant.

Accounting for Operating Leases — Lessee. Operating leases are considered to be the same as simple rental agreements with debits being made annually to an expense account as the payments are made. For example, assume the lease terms for manufacturing equipment were $40,000 a year on a year-to-year basis. The entry to record the payment for a year's rent would be as follows:

Rent Expense	40,000	
Cash		40,000

---

[1]*Statement of Financial Accounting Standards No. 13*, "Accounting for Leases" (Stamford, Conn.: Financial Accounting Standards Board, 1976).

Rent payments are frequently made in advance. In this event, if the lease period does not coincide with the lessee's fiscal year, or if the lessee prepares interim reports, a prepaid rent account would be required to record the unexpired portion of rent at the end of the accounting period involved. Amortization of the prepayment should be made on a straight-line basis. In some cases, the terms of an operating lease provide for a large initial payment, and smaller annual charges in the future. Other patterns that vary from straight-line may also be encountered, including patterns with small payments in the early years and larger payments in the later years. In these instances, recording of rent expense should approximate a straight-line pattern, and differences between the actual payments and the debit to expense would be reported either as Prepaid Rent or Rent Payable. For example, assume the terms of the lease were $70,000 rent each year for the first two years of a five-year lease, with annual payments for the last three years reduced to $20,000 a year. The total lease payments for the five years would be $200,000, or $40,000 a year on a straight-line basis. The required entries in the first two years would be as follows:

```
Prepaid Rent.....................................................................................   30,000
Rent Expense ...................................................................................   40,000
    Cash..........................................................................................            70,000
```

The entries for each of the last three years would be as follows:

```
Rent Expense ...................................................................................   40,000
    Prepaid Rent.............................................................................            20,000
    Cash..........................................................................................            20,000
```

Even though a lease is accounted for by the lessee as an operating lease, users of financial statements need to be informed as to the nature of the agreement if the amounts involved are significant. Illustrative of the disclosure suggested for operating leases are the following recommendations of the Financial Accounting Standards Board.

1. For operating leases having initial or remaining noncancelable lease terms in excess of one year:
   (a) Future minimum rental payments required as of the date of the latest balance sheet presented, in the aggregate and for each of the five succeeding fiscal years.
   (b) The total minimum rentals to be received in the future under noncancelable subleases as of the date of the latest balance sheet presented.
2. For all operating leases:
   (a) Rental expense for each period for which an income statement is presented, with separate amounts for minimum rentals, contingent rentals, and sublease rentals. Rental payments under leases with terms of a month or less that were not renewed need not be included.[1]

In addition, disclosure of restrictions on such items as dividends, additional debt, and further leasing should be included for all leases.

---

[1]*Ibid*., par. 16b.

Accounting for Capital Leases — Lessee. Capital leases are considered to be more like a purchase of property than a rental. Consequently, the accounting for capital leases requires entries similar to those required for the purchase of an asset with long-term credit terms. The amount to be recorded as an asset and a liability should represent the present value of future minimum rental payments, including the present value of any *bargain purchase*[1] or other guarantee of the residual value[2] made by the lessee. The minimum rental payment would not include payments representing executory costs such as insurance, maintenance, or taxes paid by the lessee plus any profit thereon. These latter costs are considered period costs, and would be recorded as a lease expense when paid or accrued. The lease term to be used to establish the minimum rental payments is the fixed noncancelable term of the lease plus all periods covered by *bargain renewal* options,[3] or renewal periods for which failure to renew the lease imposes penalty provisions so severe that renewal appears reasonably assured. The lease term does not, however, extend beyond the date a bargain purchase option becomes exercisable. The recommended discount rate to be used by the lessee is the lessee's *incremental borrowing rate*, the rate that, at the inception of the lease, the lessee would have incurred to borrow over a similar term the funds necessary to purchase the leased asset.[4]

For example, assume Buehner Corporation leases equipment from Universal Leasing Company with the following terms:

Lease Period: Five years, beginning January 1, 1977. Noncancelable.
Rental Amount: $40,000 a year plus $3,000 a year executory costs. Payable in advance.
Incremental Borrowing Rate of Lessee: 8%
Expected Residual Value of Equipment at End of Lease Period: None

Because the rental payments are payable in advance, the formula to find the present value of the lease is the annuity-due formula described in Appendix A, page 832. The present value for the Buehner lease would be $172,484[5] computed as follows:

$$PV_n = R(PVAF_{\overline{n-1}|i} + 1)$$
$$PV_n = \$40,000(\text{Table IV}_{\overline{4}|8\%} + 1)$$
$$PV_n = \$40,000(3.3121 + 1)$$
$$PV_n = \$172,484$$

---

[1]A provision allowing the lessee, at his or her option, to purchase the leased property for a price which is sufficiently lower than the expected fair value of the property at the date the option becomes exercisable when that exercise of the option appears, at the inception of the lease, to be reasonably assured. *Ibid.*, par. 5d.

[2]The use of the term residual value will be discussed on page 483.

[3]A provision allowing the lessee, at his or her option, to renew the lease for a rental sufficiently lower than the fair rental of the property at the date the option becomes exercisable when that exercise of the option appears, at the inception of the lease, to be reasonably assured. *Ibid.*, par. 5e.

[4]*Ibid.*, par. 5l. An exception was made to using this rate if the lessee knows the lessor's computation of the implicit rate of interest (see page 481) of the lease, and if that rate is lower than the lessee's incremental borrowing rate. *Ibid.*, par. 10.

[5]All computations of present value in this chapter will be rounded to the nearest dollar. This will require some adjustment at times to the final figures in tables to balance the amounts.

The journal entry to record the lease at its inception would be as follows:

```
1977
Jan.  1  Leased Equipment Under Capital Leases...................  172,484
            Obligations Under Capital Leases........................           172,484¹
      1  Lease Expense.................................................    3,000
            Obligations Under Capital Leases.............................   40,000
            Cash ........................................................           43,000
```

Although the asset and liability balances are the same at the inception of the lease, they seldom remain the same during the lease period. The asset value should be amortized in accordance with the lessee's normal depreciation policy over the asset's life.[2] The liability should be reduced each period so as to produce a constant rate of interest expense on the remaining balance of the obligation. The lessee's incremental borrowing rate is the constant interest rate for the lessee under the provisions of FASB Statement No. 13. Table 1 below shows how the $40,000 payments (excluding executory costs) would be separated between payment on the obligation and interest expense to produce this constant rate of return. If the normal company depreciation policy for this type of equipment were straight-line, the required entry at December 31, 1977, for amortization of the asset would be as follows:

```
1977
Dec.  31  Amortization Expense on Leased Equipment....................  34,497
              Accumulated  Amortization  of  Leased  Equipment
              Under Capital Leases........................................           34,497
```
Computation:
$172,484 ÷ 5 = $34,497

TABLE 1
Schedule of Lease Payments and Interest Accruals
[Five-Year Lease, $40,000 Annual Payments (Exclusive of Executory Costs) 8% Interest]

Date	Description	Interest Expense*	Lease Payment Amount	Lease Payment Interest	Lease Payment Principal	Lease Obligation	Interest Payable
1- 1-77	Initial balance					$172,484	
1- 1-77	Payment		$40,000		$40,000	132,484	
12-31-77	Interest accrual	$10,599				132,484	$10,599
1- 1-78	Payment		40,000	$10,599	29,401	103,083	0
12-31-78	Interest accrual	8,247				103,083	8,247
1- 1-79	Payment		40,000	8,247	31,753	71,330	0
12-31-79	Interest accrual	5,706				71,330	5,706
1- 1-80	Payment		40,000	5,706	34,294	37,036	0
12-31-80	Interest accrual	2,964				37,036	2,964
1- 1-81	Payment		40,000	2,964	37,036	0	0

*Preceding lease obligation × 8%.

[1]It is also possible to record the liability at the gross amount of the payments ($200,000) and offset it with a discount account. The net method is more common in accounting for leases by the lessee and will be used in this chapter.

[2]FASB Statement No. 13 identifies four criteria to be used to determine whether a lease is an operating lease or a capital lease. (See page 485.) If the lease qualifies under the first two criteria as a capital lease, the asset life should be used for amortizing the capitalized value of the leased asset. If the lease qualifies under the second two criteria, the lease term (period) should be used for amortization purposes. *Statement of Financial Accounting Standards No. 13, op. cit.*, par. 11.

Similar entries would be made for each of the remaining four years. Although the credit could be made directly against the asset account, the use of a contra asset account provides the necessary disclosure information about the original lease value and accumulated amortization to date.

Another entry is required at December 31 to record the accrual of the interest expense for the year. As indicated in Table 1, the interest accrual for 1977 would be computed by applying the incremental borrowing rate of 8% against the initial present value of the obligation less the immediate $40,000 first payment, or $10,599[($172,484 − $40,000) × .08].

```
1977
Dec.  31 Interest Expense ................................................................. 10,599
           Interest Payable on Obligations Under Capital Leases...           10,599
```

The December 31, 1977, balance sheet of Buehner Corporation would include information concerning the lease as illustrated below:

Buehner Corporation
Balance Sheet
December 31, 1977

Assets		Liabilities	
Land, buildings, and equipment:		Current liabilities:	
Leased equipment under capital leases	$172,484	Obligations under capital leases, current portion	$ 29,401
Less accumulated amortization of leased equipment under capital leases	34,497	Interest payable on obligations under capital leases...	10,599
Net value	$137,987		$ 40,000
		Long-term liabilities:	
		Obligations under capital leases, exclusive of $29,401 included in current liabilities	$103,083

The income statement would include the amortization on leased property of $34,497, interest expense of $10,599, and executory costs of $3,000 as expenses for the period. The total expense of $48,096 exceeds the $43,000 rental payment made in the first year. As the amount of interest expense declines each period, the total expense will be reduced and, for the last two years, will be less than the $43,000 payments (Table 2). The total amount debited to expense over the life of the lease will, of course, be the same regardless of whether the lease is accounted for as an operating lease or as a capital lease. If a declining balance of amortization is used,

TABLE 2
Schedule of Amounts Charged to Operations —
Capital and Operating Leases Compared

	Charge to Operations — Capital Lease				Charge to Operations — Operating Lease	Difference
Year	Interest	Executory Costs	Amortization	Total		
1	$10,599	$ 3,000	$ 34,497	$ 48,096	$ 43,000	$ 5,096
2	8,247	3,000	34,497	45,744	43,000	2,744
3	5,706	3,000	34,497	43,203	43,000	203
4	2,964	3,000	34,497	40,461	43,000	(2,539)
5	—	3,000	34,496	37,496	43,000	(5,504)
	$27,516	$15,000	$172,484	$215,000	$215,000	$ 0

the difference in the early years between the expense and the payment would be even larger. In addition to this statement disclosure, a note to the financial statements would be necessary to explain the terms of the lease and future rental payments in more detail.

The second lease payment on January 1, 1978, would be recorded as follows:

```
1978
Jan. 1  Lease Expense................................................................  3,000
        Interest Payable on Obligations Under Capital Leases .........  10,599
        Obligations Under Capital Leases .........................................  29,401
           Cash .................................................................................            43,000
```

Similar entries would be made for each year of the lease. At the end of the five years, both the asset and liability balances would be reduced to zero.

In many leases, the lessee is given the option of purchasing the property at some future date at a bargain price. When this option exists, the present value of the purchase option should be included in the capitalized value of the lease. Assume in the above example that there was a bargain purchase option of $60,000 exercisable after five years, and the economic life of the equipment was expected to be ten years. The other lease terms remain the same. The present value of the revised lease would be increased by the present value of the bargain purchase amount of $60,000, or $40,836 computed as follows:

$$PV = A(PVF_{\overline{n}|i})$$
$$PV = \$60,000(\text{Table II}_{\overline{5}|8\%})$$
$$PV = \$60,000(.6806)$$
$$PV = \$40,836$$

The total present value of the lease is $213,320 ($172,484 + $40,836). This amount will be used to record the initial asset and liability. The asset balance of $213,320 will be amortized over the asset life of ten years because of the existence of the bargain purchase option which makes the transaction in reality a sale. The liability balance will be reduced as shown in Table 3. At the date of exercising the option, the net balance in

TABLE 3
Schedule of Lease Payments and Interest Accruals
[Five-Year Lease with Bargain Purchase Option of $60,000 after Five Years,
$40,000 Annual Payments (Exclusive of Executory Costs) 8% Interest]

Date	Description	Interest Expense	Lease Payment			Lease Obligation	Interest Payable
			Amount	Interest	Principal		
1– 1–77	Initial balance					$213,320	
1– 1–77	Payment		$40,000			173,320	
12–31–77	Interest accrual	$13,866				173,320	$13,866
1– 1–78	Payment		40,000	$13,866	$26,134	147,186	0
12–31–78	Interest accrual	11,775				147,186	11,775
1– 1–79	Payment		40,000	11,775	28,225	118,961	0
12–31–79	Interest accrual	9,517				118,961	9,517
1– 1–80	Payment		40,000	9,517	30,483	88,478	0
12–31–80	Interest accrual	7,078				88,478	7,078
1– 1–81	Payment		40,000	7,078	32,922	55,556	0
12–31–81	Interest accrual	4,444				55,556	4,444
1– 1–82	Purchase		60,000	4,444	55,556	0	0

the asset account, Leased Equipment Under Capital Leases, and its related accumulated amortization account would be transferred to the regular equipment account. If the equipment is not purchased and the lease is permitted to lapse, a loss in the amount of the net remaining balance in the asset account, less any remaining liabilities, would have to be recognized by the following entry:

Loss from Failure to Exercise Bargain Purchase Option on Capital Lease..	46,660	
Obligations Under Capital Leases...	55,556	
Interest Payable on Obligations Under Capital Leases.................	4,444	
Accumulated Amortization of Leased Equipment Under Capital Leases...	106,660	
Leased Equipment Under Capital Leases...................................		213,320

Computation:

Accumulated Amortization:
One half amortized after five years of a ten-year life: $213,320 \div 2 = \$106,660$
Obligation Under Capital Lease: See Table 3

If, under the conditions given, a renewal of the lease is negotiated, the lease would be considered a new one and adjustments would be made to the accounts to bring them into proper balance for the new lease terms.

Accounting for Leases— Lessor

The lessor in a lease transaction gives up the physical possession of the property to the lessee. If the transaction is considered temporary in nature, the lessor will continue to carry the leased asset as an owned asset on the balance sheet, and the revenue from the lease will be reported as it is received and earned. Depreciation of the leased asset will be debited against the revenue. This type of lease is described as an operating lease and is similar to the operating lease described for the lessee. However, the lease may have terms that in effect make the transaction similar in substance to a sale or a permanent transfer of the asset to the lessee. Under these conditions, the lessor should no longer report the asset as though it were owned, but should reflect the transfer and the future minimum rental payments as a receivable with revenue recognized according to the substance of the transaction. These types of leases may be classified into two major types: (1) *Sales-type leases* and (2) *direct financing leases*. Sales-type lease transactions are in effect similar to a sale of property carried by the lessor at a cost lower (or in some cases higher) than the current fair market value of the property. The difference between the fair market value and the cost of the asset is referred to as the manufacturer's or dealer's profit, or loss if cost exceeds the fair market value. A second revenue exists for these leases. The difference between the gross amount of future rentals and the current fair market value of the asset is considered to be interest revenue, and is recognized over the life of the lease. Direct-financing lease transactions involve no manufacturer's or dealer's profit. They are essentially financial arrangements between a financial institution and the lessee, and the revenue is recognized only over the life of the lease.

Thus, from the lessor's point of view, leases may be divided into three categories: operating leases, sales-type leases, and direct-financing leases. As is true for the lessee, the accounting for these types of leases is usually materially different.

Accounting for Operating Leases — Lessor. Accounting for operating leases for the lessor is very similar to that described for the lessee. The lessor recognizes the payments as they are received as revenue. If there are significant variations in the payment terms, entries will be necessary to reflect a straight-line pattern of revenue recognition. To illustrate accounting for an operating lease on the lessor's books, assume the equipment leased by Buehner Corporation for $40,000 a year plus executory costs of $3,000 per year had a cost of $300,000 to the lessor. It is expected that the equipment has a ten-year life, with no salvage value at the end of the ten years. If the lease contract is on a year-to-year basis, it would usually qualify as an operating lease. The entry to record the first-year's receipt of rent would be as follows:

```
1977
Jan.   1 Cash .................................................................. 43,000
            Rent Revenue .................................................          43,000
```

Assuming the lessor depreciates the equipment on a straight-line basis, the depreciation entry at the end of the first year would be:

```
1977
Dec. 31 Depreciation Expense on Leased Equipment ................... 30,000
            Accumulated Depreciation on Leased Equipment .........          30,000
```

If the rental period and the lessor's fiscal year do not coincide or if the lessor prepares interim reports, a rent received in advance account would be required to record the unearned rent revenue at the end of the accounting period.

There are no special disclosure problems on the financial statements for this type of lease; however, a note disclosure of the lease terms similar to those included by the lessee (page 473) is recommended. The leased property with its accumulated depreciation should be disclosed separately in the category "Land, buildings, and equipment" on the balance sheet. If there are any initial direct costs associated with the lease, they should be deferred and allocated over the lease period.

Accounting for Sales-Type Leases — Lessor. If the lessor uses leases as an alternative means of financing its sales, there is usually manufacturer's or dealer's profit identifiable from the lease terms. Normally, leases used to market products by manufacturers or dealers will have three identifiable values:[1] (1) the maximum value, or gross amount of rental payments excluding periodic payments of executory costs but including any bargain purchase amount; (2) the fair market value of the asset; and (3) the cost or

---

[1]This discussion assumes there is no residual value accruing to the lessor. See pages 483–484 for discussion of modification when unguaranteed residual values exist.

carrying value of the asset to the lessor including any initial costs to acquire the lease. The manufacturer's or dealer's profit is the difference between the fair market value of the asset [(2) above] and the cost or carrying value of the asset to the lessor [(3) above]. If cost exceeds the fair market value, a loss will be reported. The difference between the gross rentals [(1) above] and the fair market value of the asset [(2) above] is interest revenue and arises because of the time delay in paying for the asset as described by the lease terms. The relationship between these three values can be demonstrated as follows:

1. Gross rentals, including bargain purchase...................... ⎤
                                                 Financial Revenue
                                                 (Interest)
2. Fair market value of leased asset....................................... ⎦
                                                 Manufacturer's or
                                                 Dealer's Profit
3. Cost or carrying value of leased asset to lessor .... ⎦

To illustrate this type of lease, assume the equipment described on page 474 had a fair market value equal to its present value at 8% interest or $172,484 and a cost of $125,000. The three values and their related revenue amounts would be as follows:

Gross rentals: ($43,000 − $3,000) × 5.......... $200,000 ⎤
                                                    $27,516 (Interest Revenue)
Fair market value of equipment.................... $172,484 ⎦
                                                    $47,484 (Manufacturer's Profit)
Cost of leased equipment to lessor.............. $125,000 ⎦

The interest revenue is recognized as revenue over the life of the lease so as to produce a constant periodic rate of return on the net investment of the lease in a similar manner to the recognition of interest expense on the lessee's books (see Table 1). The manufacturer's profit is recognized as revenue in the current period by including the fair market value of the asset as a sale and debiting the cost of the equipment carried in the finished goods inventory to Cost of Sales. The reimbursement of executory costs to the lessor is either credited to Miscellaneous Revenue or to the executory expense accounts involved. The entries to record this information on the lessor's books at the inception of the lease would be as follows:

```
1977
Jan. 1 Lease Payments Receivable .........................................  200,000¹
        Cost of Leased Equipment Recorded as a Sale..........  125,000
           Finished Goods Inventory ......................................            125,000
           Unearned Interest Revenue.....................................             27,516
           Sales.......................................................................            172,484
     1 Cash...............................................................................   43,000
           Miscellaneous Revenue (or Executory Expenses) ..             3,000
           Lease Payments Receivable.....................................             40,000
              First year lease receipts.
```

¹It is also possible to record the receivable at the net difference between the gross receivable and the unearned interest revenue. The gross method is more common in accounting for the lessor and is used in this chapter.

At the end of the first year, interest revenue would be recognized in the same amount as indicated in Table 4 and recorded as follows:

```
1977
Dec. 31  Unearned Interest Revenue................................................  10,599
              Interest Revenue...........................................................          10,599
              Earned interest.
```

TABLE 4
Schedule of Lease Receipts and Interest Revenue
[Five-Year Lease, $40,000 Annual Payments
(Exclusive of Executory Costs) 8% Interest]

Date	Description	Interest Revenue*	Lease Receipt	Lease Payments Receivable	Unearned Interest Revenue
1- 1-77	Initial balance			$200,000	$27,516
1- 1-77	Receipt		$40,000	160,000	27,516
12-31-77	Interest revenue	$10,599		160,000	16,917
1- 1-78	Receipt		40,000	120,000	16,917
12-31-78	Interest revenue	8,247		120,000	8,670
1- 1-79	Receipt		40,000	80,000	8,670
12-31-79	Interest revenue	5,706		80,000	2,964
1- 1-80	Receipt		40,000	40,000	2,964
12-31-80	Interest revenue	2,964		40,000	0
1- 1-81	Receipt		40,000	0	0

*Preceding lease payment receivable less unearned interest revenue × 8%.

The balance sheet of the lessor at December 31, 1977, will report the lease receivable less the unearned interest revenue as follows:

Universal Leasing Company
Balance Sheet
December 31, 1977

Assets

Current assets:		
Lease payment receivable		$ 40,000
Long-term assets:		
Lease payments receivable (exclusive of $40,000 included in current assets)..	$120,000	
Less unearned interest revenue	16,917	103,083

The income statement would include the sales and cost of sales amounts yielding the manufacturer's profit of $47,484, and interest revenue of $10,599. A note to the statements would describe in more detail the nature of the lease and its terms.

This example paralleled the illustration of accounting for a capital lease by the lessee because it was assumed the fair market value was equal to the present value discounted at the lessee's incremental borrowing rate. This condition would not be normal, but was used to highlight the accounting entries required on the lessor's books. In the more normal situation, the fair market value of the equipment is known, and the interest rate must be computed from the terms of the lease. The interest rate that will discount future lease rentals, including residual value to the lessor, to the fair market value of the leased asset is referred to as the *implicit interest rate* of the lease. The method of determining this rate from the present value annuity tables is illustrated in Appendix A, page 833. Thus, if the fair market value of the above lease had been $166,796 rather than $172,484, the computation of the implicit interest rate would have been made as follows:

$$PV_n = R(PVAF_{\overline{n-1}|i} + 1)$$

$$PVAF_{\overline{n-1}|i} + 1 = \frac{PV_n}{R}$$

$$PVAF_{\overline{4}|i} = \frac{\$166,796}{\$40,000} - 1$$

$$\text{Table IV}_{\overline{4}|i} = 3.1699$$

By moving horizontally across Table IV for n = 4, the implicit rate is seen to be 10%. If the table does not have the exact value, interpolation is required as illustrated in Appendix A, pages 829–830.

For complex lease situations involving something besides equal annual lease payments, computation of the implicit rate of interest must be done from the present value formulas themselves. This computation is facilitated by use of a computer.

The Financial Accounting Standards Board has recommended that the lessor use the fair market value of the leased asset to record the net receivable, and the implicit rate of interest to recognize the earned interest revenue. As indicated in the discussion of accounting for the lessee, the Board recommended that the lessee use its incremental borrowing rate to determine the present value of the lease agreement unless it is practicable for the lessee to learn the lessor's computed implicit interest rate, and that rate is lower than the lessee's incremental borrowing rate. Thus, the amount capitalized as an asset by the lessee and the amount recorded as a net receivable by the lessor may often be different.

Accounting for Direct Financing Leases — Lessor. If the cost of the leased property and its fair market value are the same, no manufacturer's or dealer's profit exists, and the entire difference between the gross amount of the lease payments plus unguaranteed residual value and the cost is considered to be interest revenue to be recognized over the life of the lease. Usually, the lessors of direct financing leases are primarily engaged in financing operations rather than in manufacturing or dealerships. Renewals of sales-type leases are frequently considered to be direct financing leases inasmuch as no manufacturer's or dealer's profits could exist at the time of the renewal.

To illustrate the accounting for a direct financing lease, assume the cost of the leased equipment in the above example was $172,484, the same amount as the fair market value, and the purchase had been entered into the account Equipment Purchased for Lease. The entry to record the initial lease would be as follows:

Lease Payments Receivable	200,000	
Equipment Purchased for Lease		172,484
Unearned Interest Revenue		27,516

No sales or cost of sales figures would be reported. The entries for recognition of interest revenue would be the same as in the example for a sales-type lease.

Accounting
for Residual
Values

One of the most difficult questions in accounting for leases has involved the treatment of expected salvage or residual value of the property at the end of the lease term. Frequently, the economic life of a leased asset exceeds the initial lease term, and thus a significant economic value may still exist at the end of the initial lease term. In some leases, the lessee guarantees payment of the residual value at the expiration of the lease term which may or may not constitute a purchase of the property. For example, the lessee may agree to make up a deficiency below a stated amount in the lessor's realization, and the stated amount thus becomes a guaranteed residual value. In leases involving the guaranty of the residual value, the minimum lease payment includes the amount of the guaranty, and both the lessee and the lessor include the present value of the guaranteed residual value in the valuation of the lease. In many leases, however, no bargain purchase or guarantee of the residual value exists, and the lessor receives the benefit of the residual value at the expiration of the lease. The original lease exposure draft proposed that the unguaranteed residual value be classified separately on the lessor's balance sheet at its undiscounted value, and in effect recognized as an immediate increase in manufacturer's or dealer's profit for sales-type leases in the amount of the undiscounted residual value. Because of considerable opposition to this approach, the final statement requires that lessors of both sales-type leases and direct financing leases add the expected unguaranteed residual value of leased property to the minimum lease rentals to determine the gross investment in the lease. No consideration for possible changes in the purchasing power of the monetary unit is to be included in this estimate of residual value. The present value of the residual value computed using the new implicit interest rate is deducted from the cost, thus increasing the manufacturer's or dealer's profit by the present value of the residual value rather than by the gross amount. The difference between the gross amount of residual value plus the gross amount of minimum lease payments and their present values is recognized over the life of the lease as interest revenue. Sales for the transaction is computed either by applying the implicit interest rate to the minimum lease rentals or by deducting the present value of the residual value from the fair market value of the leased asset.

To illustrate this approach to accounting for residual values, assume in the example of the Universal Leasing Company lease on page 474 that there was an expected unguaranteed residual value of $60,000 at the end of the five-year period with no bargain purchase option. The residual value would be added to the gross lease receivable to determine the gross investment by the lessor in the leased asset ($200,000 + $60,000 = $260,000). Because the asset now includes both the residual value and the lease receivable, a change in the account title of the asset from Lease Payments Receivable to Gross Investment in Leases is recommended. Assume the fair market value of the property with residual value was $213,320. Because the terms of the lease now include both an annuity and a future lump-sum value, the computation of the implicit interest rate is more complex and would require use of the formulas rather than the normally established tables. In this example, the implicit rate is 8%. The present value of the residual value using this rate is $40,836 ($60,000 × .6806), and the entry to record the lease initially on the lessor's books would be as follows:

```
1977
Jan.  1  Gross Investment in Leased Assets ................................   260,000
         Cost of Leased Equipment Recorded as a Sale ..............    84,164
             Finished Goods Inventory ..........................................              125,000
             Unearned Interest Revenue .......................................               46,680
             Sales ..........................................................................              172,484
```

Computations:

Cost of leased equipment recorded as a sale:	
Cost from finished goods	$125,000
Less present value of residual value	40,836
	$ 84,164

Unearned interest revenue:	
Gross investment in lease	$260,000
Less fair market value of lease	213,320
	$ 46,680

Sales:
     Same as computation on page 474. Also equals fair market value of property less present value of residual value ($213,320 − $40,836 = $172,484).

The manufacturer's profit in this case would be $88,320 ($172,484 − $84,164), or $40,836 (present value of unguaranteed residual value) more than the example on page 480. The annual recognition of interest revenue would also differ from the earlier example because of the higher interest rate applied to a higher net investment base that includes the present value of the residual amount. For example, the interest revenue for the first year would be $13,866 (Table 3) rather than $10,599 (Table 1) computed without the residual value (see page 481).

Because of the significance of the residual value in lease accounting, the estimate of its amount should be reviewed at least annually. If it is felt to be excessive and the decline is other than temporary, the accounting should be revised to reflect the changed estimate. The resulting reduction in the net investment is recognized as a loss in the period when the estimate is changed. If the residual value is felt to be too low, adjustment would result in a gain. The Financial Accounting Standards Board has recommended that no upward adjustment be made in the estimate, again demonstrating the conservative bias of accounting principle seeking bodies.[1]

Criteria for Distinguishing Between Types of Leases

The previous sections have described the accounting entries and reporting necessary for different classifications of leases on both the lessee's and lessor's books. The remaining problem is how to determine which classification fits a particular lease. This is another area that has generated considerable discussion and controversy. In the Discussion Memorandum issued by the Financial Accounting Standards Board in

[1]*Statement of Financial Accounting Standards No. 13, op. cit.*, par. 17d.

1974, the Board identified fourteen criteria that might be considered to have some support for lessee classification purposes. Five additional criteria were listed for possible use in classifying leases by lessors. Subsequent public hearings and correspondence disclosed that several of the criteria were overlapping and/or were embodied in other criteria. The Board considered the recommendations carefully; and in Statement No. 13, the criteria have been distilled to four criteria covering both lessees and lessors, plus two additional criteria for lessors.[1] The Board has proposed that if a lease meets any one of the four criteria, it is considered to be a capital lease to the lessee; otherwise, it is an operating lease.[2] If it meets any one of the four criteria *and* meets both of the additional criteria for lessors, it is considered to be a sales-type or direct financing lease to the lessor depending upon the existence of manufacturer's or dealer's profit; otherwise, it is an operating lease.

Criteria Applying to Both Lessee and Lessor. A lease must meet at least one of the following criteria to qualify as a capital, sales-type, or direct financing lease.[3]

1. The lease transfers ownership of the property to the lessee by the end of the lease term.
2. The lease contains a bargain purchase option.
3. The lease term is equal to 75% or more of the estimated economic life of the leased property.[4]
4. The present value of the minimum lease payments excluding that portion representing executory costs, such as insurance, maintenance, and taxes to be paid by the lessor, but including any profit thereon, equals or exceeds 90% of the fair market value of the leased property.[5] The lessor shall compute the present value of the minimum lease payments using the interest rate implicit in the lease.[6] The lessee shall compute the present value of the minimum lease payments using the incremental borrowing rate unless it is practicable to learn the implicit rate computed by the lessor, and it is less than the lessee's incremental borrowing rate. In this case, the lower implicit rate should be used.

Criteria Applying Only to Lessor. In addition to meeting at least one of the above criteria, the lease must meet both of the criteria given at the top of the next page to qualify as a sales-type or direct financing lease.

---

[1]For a full discussion of the FASB's reaction to all criteria included in the Discussion Memorandum, see Appendix B of Statement No. 13.

[2]If land is involved in the lease, and if its fair market value exceeds 25% of the total fair market value of all leased property at the inception of the lease, different combinations of criteria are recommended. *Statement of Financial Accounting Standards No. 13, op. cit.*, par. 26. In this chapter it is assumed that the leases do not involve land.

[3]*Ibid.*, par. 7 and 8.

[4]If the beginning of the lease term falls within the last 25% of the total estimated economic life of the leased property, neither criterion 3 nor 4 applies.

[5]After adjustment for related investment tax credit (see page 486).

[6]The computation of the implicit rate includes as part of the gross receivable any unguaranteed residual value as discussed on page 483. If there is no unguaranteed residual value of the leased property, the implicit rate will always reduce the minimum lease payments to a present value equal to 100% of the fair value of the leased property, and the lease would meet the fourth criterion for the lessor. If there is an unguaranteed residual value, the implicit interest rate will be computed using the unguaranteed residual value, but will be applied to the minimum lease payments without residual values for applying the 90% test; e.g., in the given example, the lease would not meet the 90% test: $172,484 ÷ $213,320 = 80.9%.

1. Collectibility of the payments required from the lessee is reasonably predictable.
2. No important uncertainties surround the amount of unreimbursable costs yet to be incurred by the lessor under the lease.

The objective of these criteria is to identify leases that are in substance more like purchases and sales of property than like simple rentals. The complexity of the criteria is dictated by the complex nature of lease terms now in existence in our economy.

Complications in Lease Accounting

The discussion of leases included in this chapter and the examples used to illustrate leases have not dealt with many of the complexities that may be encountered in accounting for the various types of leases that are currently being used. For example, a special type of lease, known as a *leveraged lease*, involves three parties — the lessee, a long-term creditor, and the lessor. Several accounting problems arise with this type of lease; they are considered in paragraphs 40–47 of Statement No. 13. These complex leases are considered beyond the scope of this discussion of lease accounting.

One of the complications that may arise in recording leases is the existence of an investment tax credit on the leased property. Income tax laws permit lessors in some circumstances to retain the benefit of the investment tax credit. When an investment tax credit exists, the fair market value of the leased property should be reduced by the amount of the investment tax credit in computing the implicit interest rate and in applying the fourth criterion for lessees and lessors.

Another type of lease that sometimes occurs is identified as a *sale-leaseback* transaction. Typical of this lease is an arrangement whereby one party sells the property to a second party, and then the first party leases the property back. Thus, the seller becomes a seller-lessee and the purchaser a purchaser-lessor. The accounting problem raised by this transaction is whether the seller-lessee should recognize the profit from the original sale immediately, or defer it over the lease term. The Financial Accounting Standards Board has recommended that if the initial sale produces a profit, it should be deferred and amortized in proportion to the amortization of the leased asset if it is a capital lease or in proportion to the rental payments if it is an operating lease. If the transaction produces a loss because the fair market value of the asset is less than the undepreciated cost, an immediate loss should be recognized.[1]

Summary of Accounting for Leases

Accounting for leases has occupied much of the agenda for both the Accounting Principles Board and more recently the Financial Accounting Standards Board. Industries and companies have been especially concerned as to the final conclusion because of the extent to which they are engaged in leases. The increase in liabilities on the lessee's books when leases are capitalized may create debt to equity ratios that will cause a company to be in violation of long-term bond covenants. The computa-

---

[1]*Statement of Financial Accounting Standards No. 13, op. cit.*, par. 32–33.

tions necessary to implement retroactively full-scale lease accounting will be difficult because of a lack of necessary information. These implementation difficulties have led to the conclusion by the Board that there be an interim transition period when accounting for leases is modified. FASB Statement No. 13 requires that the provisions be effected for all lease transactions and agreements entered into after January 1, 1977. After a four-year transition period (December 31, 1980), the statement provisions are to be retroactively applied. This interim period will give companies the chance to make whatever adjustments are necessary to loan indentures and give companies time to develop the information necessary to make retroactive adjustments to the accounts.

PENSION COSTS

Accounting for pension costs is another area that has demanded considerable attention by accounting principle-making bodies. After much discussion during the 1960's, the Accounting Principles Board issued Opinion No. 8, "Accounting for the Cost of Pension Plans," that resulted in more consistent accounting treatment for these items.[1] Recent developments in the mid-1970's have again brought the accounting problem of pension plans before the Financial Accounting Standards Board. This portion of the chapter will highlight the development of pension plans and the principal accounting problems surrounding pension plan accounting. The currently accepted methods of accounting for pension costs are presented, and areas where changes may occur are identified.

Growth of Pension Plans

The number of pension plans and the size of their investment portfolios have grown sharply in the period since World War II. As inflation has made it more difficult for Social Security benefits to provide employees with an adequate retirement, labor negotiations between unions and managements have generally included provisions for company-sponsored pension programs. Generally, these plans have been given special income tax considerations permitting the corporations to deduct contributions to the plan as expenses, but allowing the employees to defer recognition of income until retirement benefits are received. Because individuals working as employees for corporations or other identified institutions had definite tax advantages in the pension plan area, additional tax provisions were enacted giving similar tax incentives to self-employed individuals or to those whose employers did not have a definite pension plan. This has led to an entire industry of individual retirement plans and has extended significantly the number of those persons affected by pensions.

Pension plans historically have varied widely, with many different types of plans, methods of funding, and concepts of benefits. The Internal Revenue Service has instituted many provisions to control the tax

---

[1]*Opinions of the Accounting Principles Board, No. 8,* "Accounting for the Cost of Pension Plans" (New York: American Institute of Certified Public Accountants, 1966).

consequences of pension plans and their effect on employee's income. However, little control has been exercised to protect employees from under-funded plans, termination before the benefits are available to the employees, i.e., *vested*,[1] and protection in the event the plan was terminated due to employer bankruptcy. Trustees of pension plans assumed responsibility for determining the contribution necessary and for investing the portfolios to meet established goals. Institutions, such as insurance companies, banks, unions, and other associations, assumed the trustee role. Yet, very few plans were subject to independent financial audit. As a result of pension plan irregularities and abuses, Congress enacted a massive piece of legislation in 1974 officially known as the Employment Retirement Income Security Act of 1974 (ERISA), commonly called the Pension Reform Act of 1974. The act effected a wide spectrum of reforms and many regulations covering all pensions, and will probably require several years to fully interpret and implement. Included in the act were provisions requiring minimum funding of plans, minimum vesting rights to employees, minimum disclosure and audit requirements, and minimum requirements for trustees of pension plans. Although the act is having a great impact upon pension plans themselves and their reporting requirements, it is not clear how extensively the act will affect accounting for pension costs by the employer. The Financial Accounting Standards Board issued an interpretation shortly after the Pension Reform Act was passed in which they stated that nothing in the act was immediately recognizable as requiring modification of currently accepted pension cost accounting.[2] They then directed most of their attention to the accounting principles and procedures involved in accounting for the pension plans. In October 1975, a discussion memorandum, "Accounting and Reporting for Employee Benefit Plans," was issued. Public hearings were held and consideration is being given for a standard in this area.

In addition, the Financial Accounting Standards Board has a project under way involving accounting for pension costs; however, nothing has been published on this project as yet. While the task force working with the discussion memorandum for employee benefit plans did not address itself to accounting for the employer, they did recognize that implications for employer accounting for pension costs could be found in their study.[3]

Principal Pension Cost Accounting Problems of Employers

The issues involved in accounting for pension costs are well defined. They may be summarized as follows: (1) How much should be debited to pension expense each period for current employee service performed? (2) How much should be recorded as a liability for unfunded pension costs on the employer's balance sheet? (3) How should actuarial gains and

---

[1]Vested benefits are those benefits that are not contingent upon any future services by employees. These benefits are thus available to the employee should he or she leave the employer.

[2]*FASB Interpretation of APB Opinion No. 8, Interpretation No. 3*, "Accounting for the Employee Retirement Income Security Act of 1974" (Stamford, Conn.: Financial Accounting Standards Board, 1975).

[3]*FASB Discussion Memorandum*, "Accounting and Reporting for Employee Benefit Plans" (Stamford, Conn.: Financial Accounting Standards Board, 1975), p. 4.

losses on pension plans be recognized on the employer's income statement? Other accounting issues connected with pension costs are either subsets of these three areas or are of relatively minor effect. Each of these three issues will be discussed separately.

Amount of Periodic Pension Cost. Most pension plans are administered by an outside trustee, one not directly connected with the employer. The plan itself identifies the benefits that will be paid to employees upon retirement based upon variables such as length of service, amount earned, and position in the company. Contributions are made to the trustee based upon accepted actuarial assumptions and Federal requirements. Traditionally an employer has tended to debit to expense the actual amount contributed to the trustee. If the contributions made follow a well-defined pattern, the resulting debit to expense may be reasonable. However, if the contributions to the trustee are made somewhat arbitrarily, erratic expense patterns may arise and net income may be manipulated.

Contributions to the trustee usually consist of two principal items: (1) normal costs and (2) past service costs. *Normal costs* are the current annual costs assigned under the actuarial cost method in use to years subsequent to the inception of a pension plan. They are the present value of the future increase in benefits arising from the current year's service to the company by covered employees. *Past service costs* are the costs related to the past service of the employees before the adoption of a pension plan. They are the present value of the future benefits arising from services performed by the employees before the pension plan was initiated. At any date subsequent to the adoption of a pension plan, a company may need to determine the total of all past normal costs plus past service costs under the pension plan. The date of such determination is identified as a *valuation date*, and the sum of these costs is defined as *prior service costs*. These costs may be illustrated by the following time line for an individual employee:

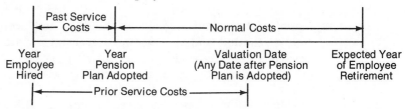

The pattern of funding these items depends upon the actuarial cost method required by the provisions of the pension plan.

Actuarial Cost Methods. There are several well-defined methods of funding being used; however, they can all be divided into two major classifications: (1) *accrued benefit cost method* and (2) *projected benefit cost methods*. The accrued benefit cost method, also referred to as the *unit credit method*, identifies a distinct unit of retirement benefit with each year of credited service, and the present value of the unit can be computed at any date. The computation of past service costs under this method is easily made. The projected benefit cost methods relate the cost to the prospective benefits of a closed group of employees. Costs are computed so as to remain constant over the life of the employee. Projected benefit methods include the following popular methods:

1. Entry age normal
2. Attained age normal
3. Aggregate
4. Individual level premium

The pattern of funding under these methods is illustrated in Figure 1 on page 491. The latter two methods spread past service costs over the entire pension period rather than over just a predetermined number of years (twenty in this illustration), and thus do not provide for a separate computation of past service costs. Consistent use of any plan provides for an orderly accrual of funds for the plan.

Accrual Requirement for Pension Costs. After considerable discussion, the Accounting Principles Board issued Opinion No. 8 recommending that the employer charge pension costs to income in a consistent manner; and because past service costs are incurred in contemplation of future services to be rendered, that they be charged against current and future revenues and not against prior periods. This recommendation became known as the accrual requirement. Because funding requirements were often very loose and did not always follow one of the established methods, the practice of debiting expense for the actual contribution made was not considered acceptable unless the contribution also met certain restrictions. APB Opinion No. 8 required all employers to select one of the actuarial cost methods identified above, and to use it consistently over the years. It did not have to be the method used for funding purposes; however, it could be the same method. Thus, in practice, the contribution and the accrual are frequently identical because the same actuarial cost method is used for funding and accrual purposes. If the amount funded and the amount expensed are not the same, the difference is to be recorded as a Liability Under Pension Plan or a Deferred Pension Expense depending upon the nature of its balance.

Minimum-Maximum Provision. In order to add some measure of control over the amount of pension cost debited to current income, the opinion specified a *minimum* and a *maximum* amount of pension cost that could be debited to a given period. This range was designed to set limits to the cost method used. In practice, these limits have seldom been restrictive, and most contribution methods fit well into the rather wide range.

The computation of the minimum and maximum limits are complex and are usually made by the trustee's actuaries. While accountants will

FIGURE 1
Annual Cost Patterns for a Typical Pension Plan Under Five Actuarial Cost
Methods Currently Acceptable for Accounting Purposes[1]

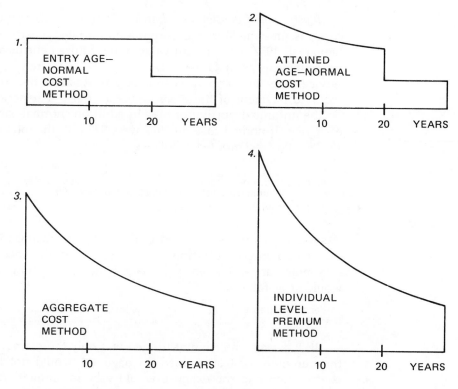

ACCRUED BENEFIT COST METHOD

ACCRUED BENEFIT
(UNIT CREDIT)
METHOD

10   20   YEARS

PROJECTED BENEFIT COST METHODS

1.
ENTRY AGE—
NORMAL
COST
METHOD

10   20   YEARS

2.
ATTAINED
AGE—NORMAL
COST
METHOD

10   20   YEARS

3.
AGGREGATE
COST
METHOD

10   20   YEARS

4.
INDIVIDUAL
LEVEL
PREMIUM
METHOD

10   20   YEARS

seldom have to compute them, it is important that they be able to identify the variables used in their computation.

   1. Minimum. The annual provision for pension cost should not be less than the total of:
   (a) The normal cost.
   (b) An amount equivalent to interest on any unfunded prior service cost.
   (c) If indicated, a provision for vested benefits.

---

[1]William A. Dreher, "Alternatives Available Under APB Opinion No. 8: An Actuary's View," *Journal of Accountancy* (September, 1967), p. 41.

2. Maximum. The annual provision for pension cost should not be more than the total of:
   (a) The normal cost.
   (b) Ten percent of the past service cost (until fully amortized).
   (c) Ten percent of the amounts of any increases or decreases in prior service cost arising on amendments of the plan (until fully amortized).
   (d) Interest equivalents on the difference between provisions and the amount funded.

If past service costs are being amortized over a period between ten and forty years, the debit to pension expense will usually meet these limits.

Because the Pension Reform Act requires funding of past service costs within a thirty-year period, the forty-year limitation included in the analysis for vested benefit provision will probably be revised by the FASB.

Illustration of Pension Cost Entries. To illustrate accounting for pension costs, assume the Marlowe Corporation initiated a pension plan effective January 1, 1977. The present value of the future benefits assumed earned by employees as of January 1, 1977, were separately identified as past service costs and amounted to $150,000. Assume the contribution plan required payment of these costs over a fifteen-year period plus interest on the unfunded portion of 8%. In addition, normal costs were funded each year. If normal costs in 1977 were $22,000, the total contribution for 1977 would be computed as follows:

Normal costs	$22,000
Amortization of past service costs	10,000
Interest on unfunded past service costs (8% of $150,000)	12,000
Total contribution	$44,000

Assume the employer decided to debit expense using the same method as used for the contribution and it falls within the specified minimum-maximum range. The entry to record the contribution and the accrual would be as follows:

Pension Expense	44,000	
Cash		44,000

If, however, the amount funded was only the normal cost of $22,000, the minimum cost as defined on page 491 would not be met and the contribution and the expense would vary in amount. Assume the employer made the decision to accrue the pension cost according to the pattern described above even though the contribution was for the normal cost only. The entry to record this situation would be as follows:

Pension Expense	44,000	
Cash		22,000
Liability Under Pension Plan		22,000

The liability would be classified on the balance sheet according to the expected contribution date. It should be emphasized that the minimum-maximum rule does not usually determine the amount of expense to be debited against revenue. The formula for the minimum or the maximum is not recognized as an accepted actuarial method.

There can be cases where the amount funded could exceed the amount accrued, in which case a deferred pension expense account would be debited. For example, assume in the previous example that the contribution for the first year was $55,000. The journal entry would be as follows:

Pension Expense	44,000	
Deferred Pension Expense	11,000	
Cash		55,000

In the above examples, the pension expense for the first year was the same regardless of how the plan was funded. Subsequent year's expense would vary according to the amount of interest on unfunded past service costs. In many cases, pension plans are written to fund past service costs by equal contributions over a specified number of years. The interest on unfunded past service costs is included in the payment and the annual contribution is computed from annuity tables. If a company expenses the same amount as funded, no asset or liability for pension costs is created on the balance sheet. However, if the company desires to expense past service costs equally, but over a number of years that differs from the number of years used for funding purposes, asset or liability balances will be created.

To illustrate these conditions, assume the past service costs for the Andrus Co. at the adoption of a pension plan is $310,500. The interest rate used in the plan is 10%. If contributions are made at the end of each year for twelve years, the amount of each contribution (rent) would be computed as follows:

$$PV_n = R(PVAF_{\overline{n}|i})$$
$$R = \frac{PV_n}{PVAF_{\overline{n}|i}}$$
$$R = \frac{\$310,500}{\text{Table IV}_{\overline{12}|10\%}}$$
$$R = \frac{\$310,500}{6.8137}$$
$$R = \$45,570$$

Thus, payments of $45,570 for twelve years would liquidate the past service cost liability. If the company decides to amortize the past service costs equally over a ten-year period to pension expense, computations similar to the above would be made to determine that the annual amortization would be $50,532 ($310,500 ÷ 6.1446). Similarly, if a fifteen-year amortization is used, the annual charge would be $40,822 ($310,500 ÷ 7.6061). If the amortization period differs from the contribution period, an interest adjustment to pension expense will be necessary. If the contribution period covers fewer years than the amortization period, the trustee has funds in advance of the accrual period and a reduction in pension expense for the lower interest is necessary. If the contribution period covers more years than the amortization period, the trustee has deferred receiving funds and an addition to pension expense for the additional interest paid must be made.

The effects of these different patterns of contribution and amortization on balance sheet accounts are illustrated in the following two tables:

TABLE 5
Andrus Company
Past Service Cost Accounting
Accrual of Pension Liability
Amortization — 10 Years

Year	(A) Funding Contribution 12 Years	(B) Annuity Amortization	(C) Add Interest (10%) on Previous Liability Balance	(D) Pension Expense (B + C)	(E) Liability Increase (Decrease) (D − A)	(F) Liability Balance
1	$45,570	$50,532	$ 0	$50,532	$ 4,962	$ 4,962
2	45,570	50,532	496	51,028	5,458	10,420
3	45,570	50,532	1,042	51,574	6,004	16,424
4	45,570	50,532	1,642	52,174	6,604	23,028
5	45,570	50,532	2,303	52,835	7,265	30,293
6	45,570	50,532	3,029	53,561	7,991	38,284
7	45,570	50,532	3,828	54,360	8,790	47,074
8	45,570	50,532	4,707	55,239	9,669	56,743
9	45,570	50,532	5,674	56,206	10,636	67,379
10	45,570	50,532	6,738	57,270	11,700	79,079
11	45,570	0	7,908	7,908	(37,662)	41,417
12	45,570	0	4,153*	4,153	(41,417)	0

*Adjusted for rounding differences.

TABLE 6
Andrus Company
Past Service Cost Accounting
Accrual of Deferred Pension Expense
Amortization — 15 Years

Year	(A) Funding Contribution 12 Years	(B) Annuity Amortization	(C) Less Interest (10%) on Previous Deferred Charge Balance	(D) Pension Expense (B − C)	(E) Deferred Charge Increase (Decrease) (A − D)	(F) Deferred Pension Expense Balance
1	$45,570	$40,822	$ 0	$40,822	$ 4,748	$ 4,748
2	45,570	40,822	475	40,347	5,223	9,971
3	45,570	40,822	997	39,825	5,745	15,716
4	45,570	40,822	1,572	39,250	6,320	22,036
5	45,570	40,822	2,204	38,618	6,952	28,988
6	45,570	40,822	2,899	37,923	7,647	36,635
7	45,570	40,822	3,664	37,158	8,412	45,047
8	45,570	40,822	4,505	36,317	9,253	54,300
9	45,570	40,822	5,430	35,392	10,178	64,478
10	45,570	40,822	6,448	34,374	11,196	75,674
11	45,570	40,822	7,568	33,255	12,315	87,989
12	45,570	40,822	8,799	32,023	13,547	101,536
13	0	40,822	10,154	30,668	(30,668)	70,868
14	0	40,822	7,087	33,735	(33,735)	37,133
15	0	40,822	3,689*	37,133	(37,133)	0

*Adjusted for rounding differences.

Journal entries to record the past service pension cost amortization and contribution to the pension fund may be made directly from the tables for any year included. Thus, the entry for Year 8 assuming a ten-year amortization period for past service costs would be as follows:

Pension Expense	55,239	
Cash		45,570
Liability Under Pension Plan		9,669

The entry for Year 8 assuming a fifteen-year amortization period would be as follows:

Pension Expense	36,317	
Deferred Pension Expense	9,253	
Cash		45,570

Of course, normal pension costs would be added to the amortization of past service costs to arrive at the total pension expense for the year.

As a result of the Pension Reform Act, contributions to pension plans may have to be accelerated. If the accrual method is not changed, deferred pension costs will begin to appear in the asset section of employer balance sheets. If an employer changes the accrual method to agree with the accelerated contribution, a note disclosing the change would seem essential.

Liability for Unfunded Prior Service Costs. Unfunded prior service costs are those prior pension costs, both past service costs and past normal costs, not yet funded to the trustee. APB Opinion No. 8 does not require reporting of this amount as a liability "unless the company clearly has a legal obligation for pension cost in excess of amounts paid or accrued."[1] Prior to the Pension Reform Act, an employer often had only limited liability for unfunded prior service costs. In the event bankruptcy occurred, claims against the plan by the employee were usually limited to the amount of funds in the plan. Many accountants have felt that this failure to record as a liability unfunded prior service costs is a serious deficiency in APB Opinion No. 8. They advocate reporting these unfunded prior service costs offset by a deferred charge for the portion of prior-service costs not yet charged against revenue. With the tightening of funding requirements in the new Pension Reform Act and the requirement for accelerated vesting privileges, it seems likely that the definition of legal liability will be restated by the FASB.

Actuarial Gains and Losses. The amount of required contributions to a pension plan is based upon many actuarial assumptions including mortality tables for employees, expected employee turnover rates, anticipated investment revenue from dividends, interest and sales of securities, amount of future compensation to be paid to employees, and vesting benefits. When these variables differ from the estimates, more or less funds are provided than planned. These differences are referred to as *actuarial gains* and *losses*. Alternative ways of accounting for these gains and losses are *immediate recognition*, *spreading* in a consistent manner over a reasonable number of years, defined as between ten and twenty years, or determining on an *average* basis, the average being determined from past experience.

---

[1]*Opinions of the Accounting Principles Board, No. 8, op. cit.*, par. 18.

The Accounting Principles Board rejected the immediate recognition method because of its fluctuating impact upon the amount of pension expense. Accordingly, it recommended that actuarial gains and losses should be spread over the current and future years by either the spreading or averaging technique. Some of the actuarial cost methods used to determine periodic pension costs automatically provide for spreading. If the method used does not accomplish this, special amortization adjustments to normal costs may be required, as illustrated in the following tables adapted from the interpretations of APB Opinion No. 8.[1] The

TABLE 7
Actuarial Gains and Losses
Spreading Technique
10-Year Straight-Line

Year	(A) Actual Gain (Loss)	(B) Cumulative Actual (B + A)	(C) Applied to Reduce Pension Expense (B ÷ 10)	(D) Increase (Decrease) in Deferred Amount (A − C)	(E) Deferred to Future Years (E + D)
1	$ 5,000	$ 5,000	$ 500	$ 4,500	$ 4,500
2	2,000	7,000	700	1,300	5,800
3	6,000	13,000	1,300	4,700	10,500
4	(1,000)	12,000	1,200	(2,200)	8,300
5	7,000	19,000	1,900	5,100	13,400
6	3,000	22,000	2,200	800	14,200
7	(8,000)	14,000	1,400	(9,400)	4,800
8	1,000	15,000	1,500	(500)	4,300
9	10,000	25,000	2,500	7,500	11,800
10	1,000	26,000	2,600	(1,600)	10,200

TABLE 8
Actuarial Gains and Losses
Averaging Technique
5-Year Moving-Average

Year	(A) Actual Gain (Loss)	(B) 5-Year Total	(C) Applied to Reduce Pension Expense (B ÷ 5)	(D) Increases in Deferred Amount (A − C)	(E) Deferred to Future Years (E + D)
−4	$ 1,000*				
−3	4,000*				
−2	(2,000)*				
−1	3,000*				
1	5,000	$11,000	$2,200	$ 2,800	$ 2,800
2	2,000	12,000**	2,400	(400)	2,400
3	6,000	14,000	2,800	3,200	5,600
4	(1,000)	15,000	3,000	(4,000)	1,600
5	7,000	19,000	3,800	3,200	4,800
6	3,000	17,000	3,400	(400)	4,400
7	(8,000)	7,000	1,400	(9,400)	(5,000)
8	1,000	2,000	400	600	(4,400)
9	10,000	13,000	2,600	7,400	3,000
10	1,000	7,000	1,400	(400)	2,600

*Before Year 1, the gains and losses were recognized in the year of determination; they are used here, however, to develop a starting point in the averaging computation.
**$4,000 − $2,000 + $3,000 + $5,000 + $2,000 = $12,000. Each year the previous earliest year is dropped from the average and the new year is added.

[1]*Accounting Interpretations of APB Opinion No. 8,* "Accounting for the Cost of Pension Plans" (New York: American Institute of Certified Public Accountants, 1966), par. 15, Exhibit D.

methods used in this illustration are only examples of those that are acceptable. More complex methods of spreading and averaging are permitted. The major objective of these methods is to avoid significant year-to-year fluctuations due to actuarial gains and losses. The journal entries required to record actuarial gains and losses when they are considered a separate component of pension expense are illustrated for Year 3 from the spreading table as follows. Assume normal costs without actuarial gain are $20,000.

Pension Expense	20,000	
Liability Under Pension Plan		20,000
Normal costs for year.		
Liability Under Pension Plan	6,000	
Pension Expense		1,300
Deferred Actuarial Gain		4,700
Actuarial gains and losses using spreading technique.		

Assume normal costs are again $20,000 and the spreading technique is used, the entries for Year 4 would be as follows:

Pension Expense	20,000	
Liability Under Pension Plan		20,000
Normal costs for year.		
Deferred Actuarial Gain	2,200	
Pension Expense		1,200
Liability Under Pension Plan		1,000
Actuarial gains and losses using spreading technique.		

Disclosure Requirements

Pension plans are of great importance to the proper understanding of both financial position and the results of operations. There is a need for the adequate disclosure of such plans. The Accounting Principles Board suggested that disclosure be made in financial statements or by notes as follows:

1. A statement that such plans exist, identifying or describing the employee groups covered.
2. A statement of the company's accounting and funding policies.
3. The provision for pension cost for the period.
4. The excess, if any, of the actuarially computed value of vested benefits over the total of the pension fund and any balance sheet pension accruals, less any pension prepayments or deferred charges.
5. Nature and effect of significant matters affecting comparability for all periods presented, such as changes in accounting methods (actuarial cost method, amortization of past and prior service cost, treatment of actuarial gains and losses, etc.), changes in circumstances (actuarial assumptions, etc.), or adoption or amendment of a plan. [1]

Future Outlook

Accounting for pension costs and pension plans is still in a transition period. While much greater consistency exists in pension cost accounting today than was true before APB Opinion No. 8, the provisions of the Pension Reform Act may still provide additional stimulus to better control over this important cost area.

---

[1]*Ibid*., par. 4b.

QUESTIONS

1. Why has leasing as a means of financing and investing enjoyed such a remarkable growth rate since the end of World War II?

2. What is the basic difference between an operating lease and a capital lease from the viewpoint of the lessee?

3. If a lease defined as an operating lease requires the payment of uneven rental amounts over its life, how should the lessee recognize rental expense?

4. What disclosure would be required on the lessee's financial statements for operating leases with six-month terms?

5. What amount should be recorded as an asset and a liability for capital leases on the books of the lessee?

6. Why do asset and liability balances for capital leases usually differ after the first year?

7. The use of the capital lease method for a given lease will always result in a lower net income than the operating lease method. Do you agree? Explain fully.

8. If a lease contains a bargain purchase option, what entries are required on the books of the lessee under each of the following conditions?

   (a) The bargain purchase option is exercised.
   (b) The bargain purchase option is not exercised and no renewal of the lease is made.
   (c) The bargain purchase option is not exercised, but a renewal of the lease is obtained.

9. How does classification of leases by the lessor differ from the classification by the lessee?

10. Contrast a sales-type lease from a direct financing lease.

11. Under what circumstances would a lessor recognize as interest revenue over the lease term an amount greater than the difference between the gross amount of lease receivables and the cost of the asset to the lessor?

12. How would a lessor report future lease payments receivable on the balance sheet?

13. What is meant by an implicit rate of interest on a lease contract? How is it computed?

14. Unguaranteed residual values may accrue to the lessor at the expiration of the lease. How should the lessor reflect these values on the financial statements during the lease term?

15. What criteria must be met before a lease can be properly accounted for as a capital lease on the books of the lessee?

16. In determining the classification of a lease, a lessor uses the criteria of the lessee plus two other criteria. What are these other criteria and why are they included in the determination of the classification of lessors' leases?

17. What are the principal accounting problems relating to pension costs?

18. Define (a) normal costs, (b) past service costs, (c) prior service costs, (d) vested benefits.

19. What portion of past service costs must be reported as a liability under current accounting principles?

20. What are the variables in computing (a) minimum limits on pension expense, and (b) maximum limits on pension expense?

21. Why are past service costs considered a charge against future earnings rather than an adjustment of past earnings?

22. (a) Define actuarial gains and losses. (b) What are the three alternative ways of accounting for these gains and losses? Which do you recommend?

23. What pension information should be disclosed in annual reports?

EXERCISES

1. The Clark Construction Company leases a bulldozer from Universal Leasing Company for $2,500 a month plus a surcharge of $5 an hour for all hours used in excess of 200 hours per month. The lease is from month to month. The bulldozer was used 198 hours in April, 205 hours in May, and 215 hours in June. Give the entries necessary to record the rent expense for each of the three months.

2. Wagstaff, Inc., leases equipment on a five-year lease. The lease payments are to be made in advance as shown at the top of page 499.

The equipment is to be used evenly over the five-year period. For each of the five years, give the entry that should be made at the time the lease payment is made to allocate the proper share of rent expense to each period. The lease is classified as an operating lease by Wagstaff, Inc.

January 1, 1977	$ 75,000
January 1, 1978	65,000
January 1, 1979	60,000
January 1, 1980	50,000
January 1, 1981	40,000
Total..	$290,000

3. Smetena Smelting Company entered into a lease beginning January 1, 1977, for equipment to use in its smelting operations. The term of the lease is essentially the expected economic life of the equipment. Smetena uses straight-line depreciation on all its owned assets. The operating terms of the lease call for annual payments of $75,000 in advance plus $4,000 per year as payment for executory costs, such as taxes and insurance, for the fifteen-year period of the lease. At the end of the fifteen years, the equipment is expected to be junked. The incremental borrowing rate of Smetena is 10%. The lessor's computed implicit interest rate is unknown to Smetena.

Record the lease on the books of Smetena and give all the entries necessary to record the lease for its first year plus the entry to record the second lease payment on January 2, 1978. Round to nearest dollar.

4. On January 2, 1977, the Midland Company entered into a noncancelable lease for a new warehouse. The warehouse was built to the Midland Company's specifications and is in an area where rental to another lessee would be difficult. Rental payments are $125,000 a year for ten years, payable in advance. The warehouse has an estimated economic life of twenty years. The taxes and maintenance are to be paid by the Midland Company, and they have an option to purchase the property at the conclusion of the lease for a nominal amount. Assume the cost of borrowing funds for this type of an asset by Midland Company is 8%. (a) Give the entry that should be made at the inception of the lease. (b) Give the entries that should be made for 1977 and 1978 relative to the amortization of the warehouse value assuming amortization by the straight-line method.

5. Union Rent-All leases equipment to Lindsay Manufacturing Company. The lease is for five years and is classified as an operating lease. The lease requires advance payments of $5,000 per year. Union has a calendar year accounting period. The lease began April 1, 1977, at which time the first payment was made. The equipment has a cost of $50,000 and an economic life of twenty years. Union uses the double-declining balance method of depreciation on all equipment owned. What entries should be made by Union Rent-All for the first year of the lease?

6. A-1 Leasing leases equipment to A-1 Manufacturing (an unrelated company). The fair market value of the equipment is $221,487. Lease payments, excluding executory costs, are $35,000 per year, payable in advance, for ten years. What is the implicit rate of interest A-1 Leasing should use to record this capital lease on its books?

7. The Northwestern Finance Company purchased a printing press to lease to the Apex Printing Company. The lease was structured so that at the end of the lease period of fifteen years Apex would own the printing press. Lease payments required in this lease were $50,000 per year, the annual payment being payable in advance. The cost of the press to Northwest was $418,335, which is also considered to be its fair market value at the time of the lease. (a) Is this lease a sales-type or a direct financing lease? Why? (b) Give the entry to record the lease transaction on the books of Northwestern Finance Company. (c) Give the entry at the end of the first year on Northwestern Finance Company's books to recognize interest revenue.

8. The Lind Leasing and Manufacturing Company uses leases as a means of financing sale of its equipment. Lind leased a machine to Ace Awning for $10,000 per year, payable in advance, for a ten-year period. The cost of the machine to Lind was $65,000. The fair market value at the date of the lease was $75,000. Assume a residual value of zero at the end of the lease. (a) Give the entry required to record the lease on Lind's books. (b) How much profit will Lind recognize initially on the lease, excluding any interest revenue? (c) How much interest revenue would be recognized in the first year?

9. The Bellows Corporation leases a machine to the Furness Company. The lease payments are $10,000 per year payable in advance for ten years. The machine cost Bellows $55,000. The fair market value of the machine at the lease date is $72,942. The machine is expected to have an unguaranteed residual value of $30,000 at the end of the lease. Bellows' computed implicit interest rate on the lease is 12%. Furness Company's incremental borrowing rate is 10%. The economic life of the machine is 12 years. Give the entries necessary to record the lease on the books of both the lessee and the lessor at the inception of the lease.

10. All-Rite Cleaners leases its dry cleaning equipment from Rite-Way Leasing Company. In each of the following cases, assuming none of the other criteria for capitalizing leases is met, determine whether the lease would be a capital lease or an operating lease under FASB Statement No. 13 on leases. Your decision is to be based only on the terms presented, considering each case independent of the others.

(a) At the end of the lease, the market value of the equipment is expected to be $5,000. All-Rite has the option of purchasing it for $2,500.

(b) The fair market value of the equipment is $25,000. The present value of the lease payments is $22,250 (excluding any executory costs).

(c) All-Rite obtains the property at the end of the lease.

(d) The economic life of the equipment is 15 years. The lease term is for 12 years.

(e) The lease requires payments of $5,500 per year in advance, plus executory costs of $500 per year. The lease period is for three years, and All-Rite's incremental borrowing rate is 8%. The fair market value of the equipment is $17,000.

(f) The lease requires payments of $5,500 per year in advance which includes executory costs of $500 per year. The lease period is for three years, and All-Rite's incremental borrowing rate is 8%. The fair market value of the equipment is $17,000.

11. The Torres Company accrued pension costs of $25,000 for 1977. Give the entry to record pension costs for 1977 if the company funds (a) $25,000, (b) $19,000, and (c) $28,000.

12. The Morris Company funds its pension plan as follows: 1977, $276,000; 1978, $255,000.

(a) Give the entry to record pension costs in 1977 if the maximum limit is computed to be $270,000.

(b) Give the entry to record pension expense in 1978 if the minimum limit is computed to be $260,000.

13. The Suzuki Corporation funds its past service pension costs over fifteen years and amortizes them over ten years. Past service pension costs at the adoption of the pension plan are $360,000 and the interest rate is 10%. The corporation accountant has prepared the following four-year table accounting for past service pension costs.

Suzuki Corporation
Past-Service Pension Costs
Accrual of Pension Liability
Amortization — 10 Years

Year	Funding Contribution 15 Years	Annuity Amortization	Add Interest (10%) on Previous Liability Balance	Pension Expense	Increase (Decrease)	Liability Balance
1975	$47,330	$58,000	0	$58,000	$10,670	$10,670
1976	47,330	58,000	$1,067	59,067	11,737	22,407
1977	47,330	58,000	2,041	60,241	10,911	33,318
1978	47,330	58,000	3,332	60,000	14,000	47,318

(a) Prepare a corrected table for 1975–1978.

(b) Give the entry to record past service pension cost for 1977 assuming the entry has not been made.

14. Actuarial gains and losses for 1971–1977 are shown below:

1971	$(1,000)
1972	5,000
1973	2,000
1974	(500)
1975	1,000
1976	4,000
1977	(2,000)

(a) Using the five-year averaging technique, compute the amount applied to reduce pension expense in 1976 and 1977 if the actuarial gains and losses are computed separately each year.

(b) Prepare the journal entries in 1977 if normal costs are $15,000.

PROBLEMS

17-1. Mendoza Mining and Manufacturing Company leases from Wasatch Leasing Company three machines under the following terms:

> Machine #1   Lease Period — ten years, beginning April 1, 1971.
>   Lease Payment — $9,000 per year, payable in advance.
> Machine #2   Lease Period — ten years, beginning July 1, 1975.
>   Lease Payment — $15,000 per year, payable in advance.
> Machine #3   Lease Period — fifteen years, beginning January 1, 1976.
>   Lease Payment — $12,500 per year, payable in advance.

All of the above leases are classified as operating leases.

> **Instructions:** Prepare the note to the 1977 financial statements that would be required to disclose the lease commitments of Mendoza Mining and Manufacturing Company. Mendoza uses the calendar year as its accounting period.

17-2. The 3-N Company leased a machine on July 1, 1977, under a ten-year lease. The economic life of the machine is estimated to be 15 years. Title to the machine passes to 3-N Company at the expiration of the lease and thus the lease is a capital lease. The lease payments are $27,000 per year, including executory costs of $2,000 per year, all payable in advance annually. The incremental borrowing rate of the company is 10%. The 3-N Company uses the straight-line method of depreciation.

> **Instructions:**
>   (1) Record the entry on the books of the lessee, and give all entries necessary to record the operation of the lease for the first year.
>   (2) Assume the lessor retains title to the machine at the expiration of the lease, there is no bargain renewal or purchase option, and that the fair market value of the equipment was $180,000 as of the lease date. Using the criteria for distinguishing between operating and capital leases according to FASB Statement No. 13, what would be the amortization or depreciation expense for 1977?

17-3. Randall Electric Company has a policy of acquiring its equipment by leasing. On January 2, 1977, the company signed a lease for a coiling machine. The lease stipulates that payments of $45,000 will be made annually for five years. The payments are to be made in advance. At the end of the five-year period, the company may purchase the machine for $20,000. Its estimated fair market value at that date is $75,000. The company's incremental borrowing rate is 8%. The estimated economic life of the equipment is eight years. Randall Electric Company uses the calendar year for reporting purposes.

> **Instructions:**
>   (1) Compute the amount to be capitalized as an asset for the lease of the coiling machine.
>   (2) Prepare a table similar to Table 3, page 477, that shows the computation of the interest expense for each period.
>   (3) Give the journal entries that would be made on Randall Electric Company's books for the first two years of the lease.
>   (4) Assume on January 2, 1982, the purchase option is exercised. Give the journal entry to record the exercise of the option on Randall Electric Company's books.

17-4. The Royal Shipbuilding Company uses leases as a method of selling its products. In 1976, the company constructed a ferry to ply the waters of the Puget Sound between Seattle and Bremerton. The ferry was leased to Sea Brem Ferry Line on April 1, 1977, for a total lease payment of $150,000 per year for twenty years, paid annually in advance. The fair market value of the ferry on the lease date was $1,404,735. The cost of the ferry was $1,294,855. At the end of the lease period, the title to the property passes to Sea Brem.

> **Instructions:**
>   (1) From the information given above, compute the amount of financial revenue that will be earned over the lease term and the manufacturer's profit that will be earned immediately by Royal.

(continued)

(2) Give the entries to record the lease on Royal's books. What is the implicit rate of interest on the lease?

(3) Give all the entries necessary to record the operating of the lease for the first three years, exclusive of the initial entry. Royal's accounting period is the calendar year.

(4) What would be the balance in each of the following accounts at December 31, 1979: Unearned Interest Revenue; and Lease Payments Receivable?

17-5. The Granada Manufacturing Company both leases and sells its equipment to its customers. The most popular line of equipment includes a machine that costs $120,000 to manufacture and sells normally for $175,136. The lease terms provide for five annual payments of $42,000 each, with the first payment due when the lease is signed. The implicit rate of interest in the contract is 10% per year. Boise Powder Co. leases one of these pieces of equipment on January 2, 1977. Their incremental borrowing rate is determined to be 8% per year. The equipment is very specialized, and it is assumed it will have no salvage value after five years. Assume the lease qualifies as a capital lease and a sales-type lease for the lessee and lessor respectively. Also assume that both the lessee and the lessor are on a calendar year basis.

Instructions:

(1) Give all entries required on the books of Boise Powder Co. to record the lease of equipment from Granada Manufacturing Company for the year 1977. The depreciation on owned equipment is computed once a year on the straight-line basis.

(2) Give entries required on the books of Granada Manufacturing Company to record the lease of equipment to Boise Powder Co. for the year 1977.

(3) Prepare the Balance Sheet section involving lease balances for both the lessee's and lessor's financial statements at December 31, 1977.

(4) Determine the amount of expense Boise Powder Co. will report relative to the lease for 1977 and the amount of revenue Granada Manufacturing Company will report for the same period.

17-6. The Colton Leasing Company buys equipment for leasing to various manufacturing companies. On October 1, 1976, Colton leases a strap press to the Hermes Shoe Company. The cost of the machine to Colton, which approximated its fair market value on the lease date, was $163,590. The lease payments stipulated in the lease are $27,500 per year in advance for the ten-year period of the lease. The payments include executory costs of $2,500 per year. The expected economic life of the equipment is also ten years. The title to the equipment remains in the hands of Colton Leasing Company at the end of the lease term, although only nominal scrap value is expected at that time. Hermes incremental borrowing rate is 8% and it uses the straight-line method of depreciation on all owned equipment. Both Hermes and Colton have a fiscal year-end of September 30.

Instructions:

(1) Prepare the entries to record the lease on the books of the lessor and lessee assuming the lease meets the criteria of a direct-financing lease for the lessor and a capital lease for the lessee.

(2) Compute the implicit rate of interest of the lessor.

(3) Give all entries required to account for the lease on both the lessee's and lessor's books for the fiscal years 1977, 1978, and 1979 [exclusive of the initial entry required in (1)].

17-7. Clyde Manufacturing Company manufactures and leases a variety of items. On January 2, 1977, Clyde leased a hydraulic left-handed skyhook to Astro Industries Co. The lease is for six years with an annual amount of $38,000 payable annually in advance. The skyhook has an estimated useful life of eight years, and was manufactured by Clyde at a cost of $130,000. The lease payment includes executory costs of $1,500 per year. It is estimated that the skyhook will have a residual value of $50,000 at the end of the six-year lease term. There is no guarantee by the lessee of this amount, nor is there any provision for purchase or renewal of the skyhook by Astro at the end of the lease term. The skyhook has a fair market value at the lease inception of $203,089. The implicit rate of interest in the contract is 10%, the same rate at which Astro Industries Co. can borrow money at their bank. Astro depreciates assets on a straight-line basis.

Instructions:
     (1) Give the entries required on the books of lessor and lessee to record the incurrance of the lease and its operation for the first year, assuming the lease meets the qualifications for a capital lease for the lessee and a sales-type lease for the lessor.
     (2) Show how the lease would appear on the balance sheets of Clyde Manufacturing Company and Astro Industries Co. (if applicable) as of December 31, 1977.
     (3) Assume Clyde Manufacturing Co. sold the skyhook at the end of the six-year lease for $60,000. Give the entry to record the sale assuming all lease entries have been properly made.

17-8. The Snarr Corporation institutes a pension plan on January 2, 1977. Normal costs for 1977 are $20,000. Other information is as follows:

     (a) Past-service costs are $175,000.
     (b) The Snarr Corporation accrues past-service costs over a 25-year period.
     (c) Minimum pension cost for 1977 is computed to be $30,000.
     (d) Interest on unfunded prior service costs is 8% and is added to the annual accrual of pension costs.
     (e) Maximum pension cost for 1977 is computed to be $60,000.

Instructions: Compute pension expense for 1977 and give the entries to record pension expense if the Snarr Corporation funds equal (1) $41,000, (2) $46,000, and (3) $35,000.

17-9. The Hawkins Company adopts a pension plan on January 2, 1977. Past-service costs at that date are $250,000, and the plan calls for payment of these costs plus interest at 8% over a 20-year period. The company decides to write off past service pension costs over a 25-year period, plus interest of 8% on the unfunded portion. Normal costs for 1977 and 1978 are $40,000 and $42,000 respectively and are funded each year.

Instructions: Give the entries required in 1977 and 1978 to record pension expense and pension contributions to the fund. Show all computations.

17-10. The Connors Corporation adopted a pension plan on January 6, 1976. Past service costs are estimated by the firm's actuary to be $427,975. The plan will be funded over fifteen years and earn an average earnings rate of 8%. Past service costs will be amortized over twelve years.

Instructions:
     (1) Construct the first four years of a table showing the computation of annual past service pension expense and accrued pension liability.
     (2) Prepare journal entries to record pension related transactions for 1978.

17-11. The Andrus Company experienced actuarial gains and losses in relation to its pension plan as follows:

Year	
1	$ 7,000
2	2,000
3	(3,000)
4	(1,500)
5	4,000

Actuarial gains and losses are spread over ten years using a straight-line basis.

Instructions:
     (1) Construct a table showing the spreading of Andrus Company's actuarial gains and losses for the five years.
     (2) Assuming past service costs are being amortized according to Table 5 on page 494, record pension expense for Year 4. Normal costs are $125,000.

18

Paid-In Capital — Capital Upon Formation

The corporation is an artificial entity created by law that has an existence separate from its owners and may engage in business within prescribed limits just as a natural person. The modern corporation makes it possible for large amounts of property to be assembled under one management. This property is transferred to the corporation by the individual owners because they believe they can earn a greater rate of return through the corporation's efficient use of the property than would be possible from alternative investments. In exchange for this property, the corporation issues ownership interests in the form of shares of stock. Managements elected by stockholders supervise the use, operation, and disposition of the property. Unless the life of the corporation is limited by law, it has perpetual existence.

Corporations are the dominant form of organization in today's economy. Not only are they the major source of our national output, but they also provide the majority of the employment opportunities. Accounting for corporations has become very important because of the division between ownership and management and the widespread holding of ownership securities.

FORMING THE CORPORATION

Business corporations may be created under the corporation laws of any one of the fifty states or of the federal government. Since the states do not follow a uniform incorporating act, the conditions under which corporations may be created and under which they may operate are somewhat varied.

In most states at least three individuals must join in applying for a corporate charter. Application is made by submitting *articles of incorporation* to the secretary of state or other appropriate official. The articles must set forth the name of the corporation, its purpose and nature, the stock to be issued, those persons who are to act as first directors, and other data required by law. If the articles conform to the state's laws governing corporate formation, they are approved and are recognized as the *charter* for the new corporate entity.[1] Subscriptions to capital stock then become effective. A stockholders' meeting is called at which a code of rules or *bylaws* governing meetings, voting procedures, and other internal operations are adopted, a *board of directors* is elected, and the board appoints company administrative officers. Corporate activities may now proceed in conformance with laws of the state of incorporation and charter authorization. A complete record of the proceedings of both the stockholders' and the directors' meetings must be maintained in a *minutes book*.

Corporations are classified as *public* when they represent governmental subdivisions or government-owned units and as *private* when they are privately owned. The private group includes *nonstock* companies where operations are of a nonprofit nature and stock is not issued, as in the case of hospitals, charities, and religious organizations, and *stock* companies where operations are for profit and stock is issued as evidence of an ownership interest. Corporations are also classified as *domestic* and *foreign*. In state corporation laws, a corporation is termed domestic in the state of its incorporation and foreign in all other states. In the federal income tax law, a United States corporation is termed domestic and corporations formed under the laws of another country are foreign. A corporation whose stock is widely held and is available for purchase is known as an *open corporation*; a corporation whose stock is held by relatively few individuals and is not available for purchase is called a *close corporation*.

NATURE OF CAPITAL STOCK

An ownership interest in a corporate entity is evidenced by shares of stock in the form of certificates. When a value is assigned to each share and is reported on the stock certificate, the stock is said to have a *par value*; stock without such an assigned value is called *no-par* stock.

Most companies generally issue a single class of stock. However, in assembling property for a corporation there are advantages in issuing more than one kind of stock with varying rights and priorities. When a single class of stock is issued, shares are all alike and are known as *common stock*. When more than one class is issued, stock given certain preferences over the common issue is called *preferred stock*.

Because of the increased need for financial expansion, many other types of securities have been used. Some types have both debt and equity qualities and can be converted into straight equity securities at the option of the holders. The use of these securities changes as economic conditions change, and they increase in variety as the acquisition of new investment funds becomes more difficult.

---

[1]When stock of a corporation is to be distributed outside the state in which it is incorporated, registration with the Securities and Exchange Commission may be required. The objective of such registration is to assure that all of the facts relative to the business and its securities will be adequately and honestly disclosed.

Unless restricted or withheld by terms of the stock contract, certain basic rights are held by each stockholder. These rights are as follows:

1. To share in distributions of corporate earnings.
2. To vote in the election of directors and in the determination of certain corporate policies.
3. To maintain one's proportional interest in the corporation through purchase of additional capital stock if issued, known as the *preemptive right*.
4. To share in distributions of cash or other properties upon liquidation of the corporation.

If preferred and common stocks are issued, the special features of each class of stock are stated in the articles of incorporation or in the corporation bylaws and become a part of the stock contract between the corporation and its stockholders. One must be familiar with the overall capital structure to understand fully the nature of the equity found in any single class of stock. Frequently, the stock certificate describes the rights and restrictions relative to the ownership interest it represents together with those pertaining to other securities issued. Shares of stock represent personal property and may be freely transferred by their owners.

Legal or Stated Value of Stock

When stock is issued by a corporation, a portion or all of the capital arising from the issue is designated *legal* or *stated capital*. State incorporation laws provide that dividends cannot reduce corporate capital below legal capital. Modern corporation laws normally go beyond these limitations and add that legal capital cannot be impaired by the reacquisition of capital stock. Creditors of a corporation cannot hold individual stockholders liable for claims against the company. But with a portion of the corporate capital restricted as to distribution, creditors can rely on the absorption by the ownership group of losses equal to the legal capital before losses are applied to the creditors' equity.

When shares have a par value, the legal or stated capital is normally the aggregate par value of all shares issued and subscribed. When shares are no-par, laws of certain states require that the total consideration received for the shares, even when they are sold at different prices, be recognized as legal capital. Laws of a number of states, however, permit the corporate directors to establish legal capital by assigning an arbitrary value to each share regardless of issue price, although in some instances the value cannot be less than a certain minimum amount. The value fixed by the board of directors or the minimum value required by law is known as the share's *stated value*. No-par shares whose full proceeds must be regarded as legal capital are referred to as *true* or *pure no-par stock* to distinguish these from no-par issues with a stated value.

The full amount invested by stockholders is recognized as *paid-in capital* or *invested capital*. The portion of the paid-in capital representing legal capital is reported as *capital stock*; any amount in excess of the legal capital portion is reported as *paid-in capital* or *premium*.

Legal or stated capital arises from the issuance of capital stock. It may be increased by a stock dividend or by other appropriate action of the board of directors transferring additional paid-in capital or retained earnings to capital stock. It is decreased by the formal retirement of capital stock. It may also be decreased by action of the board of directors reducing the par or stated value of shares as permitted by law.

Par and No-Par Stock

When a corporation is authorized to issue capital stock with a par value, the incorporation laws of some states permit such issue only for an amount equal to or in excess of par. Par value may be any amount, for example, $100, $5, or 25 cents. An amount received on the sale of capital stock for an amount in excess of its par value is recorded as a premium; the premium is added to capital stock at par in reporting total paid-in capital.

In certain states corporations may be permitted to sell stock at a discount. Capital stock is still reported at par, but the discount is reported as a subtraction item in presenting paid-in capital. Persons subscribing for stock at a discount fulfill their obligation to the corporation upon payment of the agreed price. However, the laws of the state may provide that if the assets of a corporation are insufficient to meet its obligations, creditors may hold stockholders personally liable for deficiencies up to the amounts of the discount. Creditors are thus protected by the full legal capital as reported in the capital stock account.

Prior to 1912, corporations were permitted to issue only stock with a par value. In 1912, however, New York state changed its corporation laws to permit the issuance of stock without a par value, and since that time all other states have followed with similar statutory provisions. Today many of the common stocks, as well as some of the preferred stocks, listed on the large securities exchanges are no-par. Usually, no-par stock must have a stated value for reporting purposes. This makes it very similar to par stock and defines a separation of the stock proceeds between stated value and additional paid-in capital.

Use of no-par issues was originally encouraged on the grounds that: (1) such stock could be sold as *fully paid* without making the subscriber contingently liable to creditors as in the case of par stock issued at a discount; (2) investors would not be misled by a less-than-par *bargain* price, but in the absence of a value appearing on stock certificates would investigate the value of a stock; and (3) assets acquired in exchange for stock would be recorded at their actual worth rather than at inflated amounts set by the par value of the stock as a means of enabling stockholders to avoid the contingent liability for the discount.

It is questionable whether investors have subjected no-par stock to closer investigation than stock with a par value. It is also questionable whether more satisfactory valuations have been applied to properties received in exchange for no-par stock as compared with stock with a par value. Moreover, certain undesirable practices have arisen in the treatment of the paid-in capital arising from the sale of no-par stock at more than its stated value: (1) this portion of paid-in capital has been reported on financial statements in a manner suggesting accumulated earnings rather than invested capital; (2) such paid-in capital has been used to absorb operating losses, the balance sheet thus failing to disclose operating deficits; and (3) such paid-in capital has been used as a basis for dividends without disclosure to stockholders that dividends under such circumstances represent no more than a return of original investment. A disadvantage in the issue of no-par stock has been that transfer fees, stock taxes, and other fees and taxes on no-par stock are frequently based on an arbitrary share value that may be grossly in excess of the issuing price or market price of the stock.

PREFERRED STOCK

When a corporation issues both preferred and common stock, the preference attaching to preferred stock normally consists of a prior claim to dividends. A dividend preference does not assure stockholders of dividends on the preferred issue but simply means that dividend requirements must be met on preferred stock before anything may be paid on common stock. Dividends do not legally accrue; a dividend on preferred stock, as on common stock, requires the legal ability on the part of the company to make such a distribution as well as appropriate action by the board of directors.[1] When the board of directors fails to declare a dividend at the time such action would be called for, the dividend is said to be *passed*. Although preferred stockholders have a prior claim on dividends, such preference is usually accompanied by limitations on the amount of dividends they may receive.

Preferred stock is generally issued with a par value. When preferred stock has a par value, the dividend preference is stated in terms of percentage of par value. When preferred stock is no-par, the dividend must be stated in terms of dollars and cents. Thus, holders of 5% preferred stock with a $50 par value are entitled to an annual dividend of $2.50 per share before any distribution is made to common stockholders; holders of $5 no-par preferred stock are entitled to an annual dividend of $5 per share before dividends are paid to common stockholders.

A corporation may issue more than one class of preferred stock. For example, preferred issues may be designated first preferred or second preferred with the first preferred issue having a first claim on earnings and the second preferred having a second claim on earnings. Some companies refer to second preferred as *preference stock*. In other instances the claim to earnings on the part of several preferred issues may have equal priority, but dividend rates or other preferences may vary. Holders of the common stock may receive dividends only after the satisfaction of all preferred dividend requirements.

Other characteristics and conditions are frequently added to preferred stock in the extension of certain advantages or in the limitation of

---

[1]Although a company can make no guarantee of dividends on its own stock, it can guarantee dividends on stock of another company. Hence, one may find a company guaranteeing dividends of another in consideration for certain services or properties.

certain rights. Such factors may be expressed in adjectives modifying preferred stock, as *cumulative* preferred stock, *convertible* preferred stock, and *callable* preferred stock. More than one of these characteristics may be applicable to a specific issue of preferred stock.

Cumulative and Non-cumulative Preferred Stock

Cumulative preferred stock provides that whenever the corporation fails to declare dividends on this class, such dividends accumulate and require payment in the future before any dividends may be paid to common stockholders. For example, assume a corporation has outstanding 100,000 shares of 9% cumulative preferred stock, $10 par. Dividends were last paid through December 31, 1974, and the company wishes to resume payments at the end of 1977. The company will have to declare dividends on preferred for three years, or $270,000, before it may declare any dividends on common stock. Preferred dividends on cumulative preferred stock that are passed are referred to as *dividends in arrears*. Although these dividends are not a liability until declared by the board of directors, this information is of importance to stockholders and other users of the financial statements. Disclosure of the amount of the dividends in arrears is made by special note on the balance sheet.

If preferred stock is *noncumulative*, it is not necessary to provide for passed dividends. A dividend omission on preferred stock in any one year means it is irretrievably lost. Dividends may be declared on common stock as long as the preferred stock receives the preferred rate for the current period. Preferred stock contracts normally provide for cumulative dividends. Courts have generally held that dividend rights on preferred stock are cumulative in the absence of specific conditions to the contrary.

Convertible Preferred Stock

Preferred stock is *convertible* when terms of the issue provide that it can be exchanged by its owner for some other security of the issuing corporation. Conversion rights generally provide for the exchange of preferred stock into common stock. Since preferred stock normally has a prior but limited right on earnings, large earnings resulting from successful operations accrue to the common stockholders. The conversion privilege gives the preferred stockholder the opportunity to exchange his or her holdings for stock in which the rights to earnings are not limited. In some instances, preferred stock may also be convertible into bonds. Here the investor has the option of changing his or her position from stockholder to that of a creditor. Convertible preferred issues have become increasingly popular in recent years.

The decision by a stockholder of when to convert preferred holdings into common stock is a difficult one and involves many factors including the time limitation, if any, on the conversion privilege, the relative dividend returns on common stock as compared with preferred stock, as well as other provisions related to the two classes of securities.

Callable Preferred Stock

Preferred stock is *callable* when it can be called or redeemed at the option of the corporation. Many preferred issues are callable. The *call price* is usually specified in the original agreement and provides for payment of dividends in arrears as part of the repurchase price. When convertible stock has a call provision, the holder of the stock frequently is given the option of converting his or her holdings into common stock. The decision made by the investor will be based on the market price of the common stock.

Asset and Dividend Preferences upon Corporate Liquidation

Preferred stock is generally preferred as to assets upon corporate liquidation. Such a preference, however, cannot be assumed but must be specifically stated in the preferred stock contract. The asset preference for stock with a par value is an amount equal to par, or par plus a premium; in the absence of a par value it is a stated amount. Terms of the preferred contract may also provide for the full payment of any dividends in arrears upon liquidation, regardless of the retained earnings balance reported by the company. When this is the case and there are insufficient retained earnings, i.e., a deficit, such dividend priorities must be met from paid-in capital of the common issue; common stockholders receive whatever assets remain after settlement with the preferred group.

COMMON STOCK

Strictly speaking, there should be but one kind of common stock. Common stock represents the residual ownership equity and carries the greatest risk. In return for this risk, common stock ordinarily shares in earnings to the greatest extent if the corporation is successful. There is no inherent distinction in voting rights between preferred and common stocks; however, voting rights are frequently given exclusively to common stockholders as long as dividends are paid regularly on preferred stock. Upon failure to meet preferred dividend requirements, special voting rights may be granted to preferred stockholders, thus affording this group a more prominent role in the management. In some states, voting rights cannot be withheld on any class of stock.

Because of certain legal restrictions on preferred stock, some corporations have issued two types of common stock, known as Class A stock and Class B stock. One of the two types will have special preferences or rights that the other type does not have, such as dividend preferences or voting rights. The distinction between Class A and Class B stock, then, may be similar to that normally found between a company's preferred and common issues. The use of such classified common stocks has been so abused that some stock exchanges have refused to list such issues, and this form of corporate financing has been largely discontinued.

RECORDING ISSUANCE OF CAPITAL STOCK

The capital stock of a corporation may be authorized but unissued; it may be subscribed for and held for issuance pending receipt of cash on stock subscriptions; it may be outstanding in the hands of stockholders; it may be reacquired and held by the corporation for subsequent resale or bonus distribution; it may be canceled by appropriate corporate action. An accurate record of the position of the corporation as a result of the exchanges of property between stockholders and the corporation must be maintained in the accounts. Each class of stock requires separate accounting.

Recording the Stock Subscription

The agreement to purchase stock, known as a *subscription*, states the number of shares subscribed for, the subscription price, terms of payment, and other conditions of the transaction. This is a legally binding contract on the subscriber and the corporation. By express provisions, however, the contract may be binding only if the corporation receives subscriptions for a stated number of shares. A subscription, while giving the corporation a legal claim for the contract price, also gives the subscriber the legal status of a stockholder unless certain rights as a stockholder are specifically withheld by law or by terms of the contract. Ordinarily stock certificates evidencing share ownership are not issued until the full subscription price has been received by the corporation.

Upon receiving subscriptions, Capital Stock Subscriptions Receivable is debited for the subscription price, Capital Stock Subscribed is credited for the amount to be recognized as capital stock when subscriptions have been collected, and a paid-in capital account is credited for the amount of the subscription price in excess of par or stated value.[1] When stock has a par value, such excess may simply be designated Premium on Capital Stock; when a stock is no-par with a stated value, the excess is designated Paid-In Capital from Sale of Capital Stock at More Than Stated Value. When no-par stock is without a stated value, Capital Stock Subscribed is credited for the full amount of the subscription. If the laws of the state of incorporation permit stock with a par value to be sold at a discount and subscriptions are received on this basis, Capital Stock Subscriptions Receivable is debited for the subscription price, Discount on Capital Stock is debited for the discount, and Capital Stock Subscribed is credited for the stock par value. A special *subscribers journal* may be used in recording capital stock subscriptions.

Capital Stock Subscriptions Receivable is a control account, individual subscriptions being reported in the subsidiary *subscribers ledger*. Subscriptions Receivable is regarded as a current asset only when the corporation expects to collect the balance currently, which is the usual situation. Balances currently receivable are recognized as current assets; remaining balances are regarded as noncurrent. When subscription balances are to be collected only if cash is required by the company, these balances may be appropriately considered a subtraction item in reporting paid-in capital.

---

[1]The term *Capital Stock* is used in account titles in the text when the class of stock is not specifically designated. When preferred and common designations are given, these are used in the account titles.

Recording Collection of Subscriptions

Subscriptions may be collected in cash or in other properties accepted by the corporation. When collections are made, the appropriate asset account is debited and the receivable account is credited. Credits are also made to subscribers' accounts in the subsidiary ledger.

Recording the Issuance of Stock

The issuance of stock is recorded by a debit to Capital Stock Subscribed and a credit to Capital Stock. A *stockholders ledger*, in which accounts are maintained for each stockholder, is controlled by the capital stock account. The issuance of stock by the corporation calls for a credit to a stockholder's account for the shares issued. A transfer of stock ownership is recorded by a debit to the account of the person making the transfer and a credit to the account of the person acquiring the stock; since the capital stock outstanding remains the same after transfer of individual holdings, general ledger accounts are not affected.

A *stock certificate book* also reports shares outstanding. Certificates in the book are usually serially numbered. As certificates are issued, the number of shares issued is reported on the certificate stubs. When ownership transfers, the original certificates submitted by the sellers are canceled and attached to the original stubs and new certificates are issued to the buyers. Frequently, a corporation will appoint banks or trust companies to serve as *registrars* and *transfer agents*. These parties are assigned

TRANSACTION	ASSUMING STOCK IS $10 PAR VALUE	
November 1 Received cash of $10,000 and equipment valued at $20,000 in exchange for 3,000 shares.	Cash.. 10,000 Equipment... 20,000 Capital Stock....................................	 30,000

November 1–30
Received subscriptions for 5,000 shares at 12½ with 50% down payment, balance payable in 60 days.
	Capital Stock Subscriptions Receivable.. 62,500
	    Capital Stock Subscribed..................
	    Premium on Capital Stock ....
		
		50,000
		12,500

	Cash.. 31,250 Capital Stock Subscriptions Receivable..	 31,250
December 1–31 Received balance due on one half of subscriptions and issued stock to the fully paid subscribers, 2,500 shares.	Cash.. 15,625 Capital Stock Subscriptions Receivable..	 15,625
	Capital Stock Subscribed .... 25,000 Capital Stock....................................	 25,000

Stockholders' equity after the above transactions:	Stockholders' Equity
	Paid-in capital:
	    Capital stock, $10 par, 10,000 shares authorized, 5,500 shares issued and outstanding.. $55,000
	    Capital stock subscribed, 2,500 shares 25,000
	    Premium on capital stock 12,500
	
	    Total stockholders' equity $92,500	

various responsibilities, such as transferring stock certificates, maintaining the stockholders ledger, preparing lists of stockholders for meetings, and making dividend distributions.

Issuance of Capital Stock Illustrated The examples presented at the bottom of page 512 and below illustrate the entries for the sale of stock when: (1) stock has a par value; (2) stock is no-par but has a stated value; and (3) stock is no-par and without a stated value. It is assumed that the Welch Corporation is granted permission to issue 10,000 shares of capital stock.

SUBSCRIPTION DEFAULTS

If a subscriber defaults on a subscription by failing to make a payment when it is due, the corporation may (1) return to the subscriber the amount paid, (2) return to the subscriber the amount paid less any reduction in price or expense incurred upon the resale of the stock, (3) declare the full amount paid as forfeited, or (4) issue to the subscriber shares equal to the number paid for in full. The practice followed will depend upon the policy adopted by the corporation within the legal limitations set by the state in which it is incorporated. To illustrate the entries under these different circumstances, assume the subscription of $10

ASSUMING STOCK IS NO-PAR BUT HAS A STATED VALUE OF $10			ASSUMING STOCK IS NO-PAR AND HAS NO STATED VALUE		
Cash	10,000		Cash	10,000	
Equipment	20,000		Equipment	20,000	
Capital Stock		30,000	Capital Stock		30,000
Capital Stock Subscriptions Receivable	62,500		Capital Stock Subscriptions Receivable	62,500	
Capital Stock Subscribed		50,000	Capital Stock Subscribed		62,500
Paid-In Capital from Sale of Capital Stock at More Than Stated Value		12,500	Cash	31,250	
Cash	31,250		Capital Stock Subscriptions Receivable		31,250
Capital Stock Subscriptions Receivable		31,250			
Cash	15,625		Cash	15,625	
Capital Stock Subscriptions Receivable		15,625	Capital Stock Subscriptions Receivable		15,625
Capital Stock Subscribed	25,000		Capital Stock Subscribed	31,250	
Capital Stock		25,000	Capital Stock		31,250

Stockholders' Equity			Stockholders' Equity		
Paid-in capital:			Paid-in capital:		
Capital stock, $10 stated value, 10,000 shares authorized, 5,500 shares issued and outstanding		$55,000	Capital stock, no-par, 10,000 shares authorized, 5,500 shares issued and outstanding		$61,250
Capital stock subscribed, 2,500 shares		25,000	Capital stock subscribed, 2,500 shares		31,250
Paid-in capital from sale of capital stock at more than stated value		12,500			
Total stockholders' equity		$92,500	Total stockholders' equity		$92,500

par capital stock at 12½. One subscriber for 100 shares defaults after making a 50% down payment. Defaulted shares are subsequently resold at 11. The entries to record the default by the subscriber and the subsequent resale of the defaulted shares would be as follows:

1. *Assuming the amount paid in is returned:*

Capital Stock Subscribed	1,000	
Premium on Capital Stock	250	
Capital Stock Subscriptions Receivable		625
Cash		625
Cash	1,100	
Capital Stock		1,000
Premium on Capital Stock		100

2. *Assuming the amount paid in less the price reduction on the resale is returned:*

Capital Stock Subscribed	1,000	
Premium on Capital Stock	250	
Capital Stock Subscriptions Receivable		625
Payable to Defaulting Subscriber (*payment withheld pending stock resale*)		625
Cash	1,100	
Payable to Defaulting Subscriber	150	
Capital Stock		1,000
Premium on Capital Stock		250
Payable to Defaulting Subscriber	475	
Cash		475

3. *Assuming the full amount paid in is declared to be forfeited:*

Capital Stock Subscribed	1,000	
Premium on Capital Stock	250	
Capital Stock Subscriptions Receivable		625
Paid-In Capital from Forfeited Stock Subscriptions		625
Cash	1,100	
Capital Stock		1,000
Premium on Capital Stock		100

4. *Assuming shares equal to the number paid for in full are issued:*

Capital Stock Subscribed	1,000	
Premium on Capital Stock	125	
Capital Stock		500
Capital Stock Subscriptions Receivable		625
Cash	550	
Capital Stock		500
Premium on Capital Stock		50

SALE OF SECURITY UNITS FOR A SINGLE SUM

Corporations sometimes sell for a single sum *security units* consisting of two or more classes of securities. In recording sales of this kind, the sales proceeds must be allocated among the different issues. When a sale consists of two different securities and both have a known market value, the single sum may be allocated to the securities according to their relative fair market values. If only one of the securities has a known market value, the sales price of the other may be determined by subtracting the known value from the sales price of the unit. To illustrate, assume one share of common stock, par $50, is offered with each $1,000, 6% bond at $1,050. If the common stock is selling for $80 per share, this value is assigned to common and the sales price applicable to the bonds is calculated as follows:

Unit price of $1,000 bond together with 1 share of common	$1,050
Price identified with common share (market price)	80
Price identified with bond	$ 970

A discount should thus be identified with the bonds and a premium with the common shares. The entry to record the sale of 100 units would be:

Cash	105,000	
Discount on Bonds Payable	3,000	
Common Stock, $50 par		5,000
Premium on Common Stock		3,000
Bonds Payable		100,000

If market prices are known for each security, an allocation is necessary. For example, assume two shares of common, par $25, are offered with five shares of preferred, par $100, at $580 per unit. If the preferred and common stocks have a per share market price of $102 and $45 respectively, the sales price applicable to common stock is calculated as follows:

Market price — preferred stock ($102 × 5)	$510
Market price — common stock ($45 × 2)	90
	$600

Cost allocated to preferred: $510/$600 × $580	$493
Cost allocated to common: $90/$600 × $580	87
	$580

The entry to record the sale of 100 units, consisting of 500 shares of preferred and 200 shares of common, at $580 per unit would be:

Cash	58,000	
Discount on Preferred Stock	700	
Preferred Stock, $100 par		50,000
Common Stock, $25 par		5,000
Premium on Common Stock		3,700

If neither preferred nor common stock has a market price, it may be necessary to record the acquisition in a combined account until one of the securities develops a market price that can be used to separate the securities.

CAPITAL STOCK ISSUED FOR CONSIDERATION OTHER THAN CASH

When capital stock is issued for consideration in the form of property other than cash or for services, particular care is required in recording the transaction. When, at the time of the exchange, stock is sold by the company for cash or is quoted on the open market at a certain price, this price can be used in recording the consideration received and the capital increase. When means for arriving at the cash value of the securities are not available, it will be necessary to arrive at a value for the acquired consideration.

It may be possible to arrive at a satisfactory valuation of property received in exchange for stock through an appraisal by a competent outside authority. But this solution may not be available in arriving at a valuation for consideration in the form of certain services as, for example, promotional services in organizing the corporation.

Normally the board of directors is given the right by law to establish valuations for consideration other than cash received for stock. Such values will stand for all legal purposes in the absence of proof that fraud was involved in the action. The assignment of values by the board of directors should be subject to particularly careful scrutiny. There have been instances where directors have assigned excessive values to the consideration for stock to avoid the recognition of a discount on the issue of stock or to improve the company's reported financial position. When the value of the consideration cannot be clearly established and the directors' valuations are used in reporting assets and invested capital, the source of the valuations should be disclosed on the balance sheet. When there is evidence that improper values have been assigned to the consideration received for stock, such values should be restated.

Stock is said to be *watered* when assets are overstated and capital items are correspondingly overstated. On the other hand, the balance sheet is said to contain *secret reserves* when there is an understatement of assets or an overstatement of liabilities accompanied by a corresponding understatement of capital. These misstatements may be intentional or unintentional. The accountant cannot condone either overstatement or understatement of net assets and capital. It should be observed once more that any failures in accounting for assets are not limited to the balance sheet: the overstatement of assets will result in understatements of net income as asset cost is assigned to revenue; the understatement of assets will result in overstatements of net income as asset cost is assigned to revenue.

TREATMENT OF PREMIUM AND DISCOUNT ON SALE OF CAPITAL STOCK

Amounts received on the sale of capital stock give rise to paid-in capital. When the amount received on the sale of stock is greater than the par or stated value assigned to the stock, the excess is recorded separately as a premium or special paid-in capital balance and is carried on the books as long as the stock to which it relates is outstanding. When stock is retired, the capital stock balance, as well as any related paid-in capital balance, is canceled.

When capital stock is sold at less than par or stated value, a discount is recorded. As stated previously, a discount indicates a claim may be made by creditors upon stockholders in the event the company becomes insolvent; from a going-concern point of view, however, the discount should be recognized as a subtraction item in presenting the company's paid-in capital. There have been cases in practice where discounts on stock have been applied directly against paid-in capital balances arising from stock premiums or other sources. In other instances, discounts have been recognized as intangible assets or deferred costs and have been written off against periodic revenue. Such practices are objectionable. The absorption of a discount by positive paid-in capital balances serves only to obscure the original stockholders' investment as well as the claim that may be made upon stockholders by creditors. An account balance reporting a discount on stock does not indicate the ownership of an asset. Write-off of the discount against revenue is even more objectionable, for this not only obscures significant information relative to the stockholders' equity but also distorts periodic income. The discount should be carried on the books as long as the capital stock to which it relates is outstanding.

ISSUANCE OF CAPITAL STOCK IN EXCHANGE FOR A BUSINESS

A corporation, upon its formation or at some later date, may take over a going business, issuing capital stock in exchange for the properties acquired. In determining the amount of the stock to be issued for business assets, the fair market value of the stock, as well as the values of the properties acquired, must be considered. Frequently the value of the stock transferred by the corporation will exceed the value of the identifiable assets acquired because of the favorable earnings record of the business acquired. If the exchange is recognized as a *purchase*, the value of the stock in excess of the values assigned to identifiable assets is recognized as goodwill. On the other hand, if the exchange is recognized as a *pooling of interests*, neither the revaluation of assets nor the recognition of goodwill is recorded. Assets are stated at the amounts previously reported; stockholders' equity is increased by the amount of the net increase in assets.

INCORPORATION OF A SOLE PROPRIETORSHIP OR PARTNERSHIP

When a sole proprietorship or partnership is incorporated to secure the advantages of the corporate form of organization, the books of the old organization may be used after the changes that have taken place as a result of the incorporation are recorded, or a new set of records may be opened. The accounting procedure to be followed in each instance will be illustrated. Assume Rodriguez and Jones, partners who share earnings and losses in a ratio of 3:2 respectively, desire to retire from active participation in their business, and they form a corporation to take over partnership assets. The partnership balance sheet just before incorporation on March 15, 1977, appears at the top of the next page.

The corporation is organized as the Raleigh Corporation and is authorized to issue 25,000 shares of no-par stock. Fifteen thousand shares

Rodriguez and Jones
Balance Sheet
March 15, 1977

Assets			Liabilities and Owners' Equity		
Cash		$ 8,600	Accounts payable		$12,000
Accounts receivable	$15,000		Rodriguez, capital		50,000
Less allowance for doubtful accounts	400	14,600	Jones, capital		16,200
Inventories		20,000			
Equipment	$50,000				
Less accumulated depreciation — equipment	15,000	35,000			
			Total liabilities and owners'		
Total assets		$78,200	equity		$78,200

are sold at $10. The corporation takes over partnership assets other than cash and assumes partnership liabilities in exchange for the remaining 10,000 shares. In taking over net assets, the corporation makes the following adjustments:

1. The allowance for doubtful accounts is increased to $1,000.
2. Inventories are recorded at their present market value of $23,500.
3. Equipment is recorded at its appraised value of $52,500.
4. Accrued liabilities of $400 are recorded.

The 10,000 shares received by the partners are divided as follows: Rodriguez, 7,500 shares; Jones, 2,500 shares. The cash of $8,600 is then withdrawn by the partners according to the balances remaining in their capital accounts.

If Original Books Are Retained   If the partnership books are retained, entries are first made to indicate any revaluation in assets and adjustments to partners' interests at the time of incorporation. A revaluation account may be debited with losses and credited with gains resulting from revaluations, and the balance in this account may subsequently be closed into the capital accounts in the earnings distribution ratio. However, with relatively few changes in asset balances, gains and losses may be reported directly in the capital accounts. In recording the issuance of stock in exchange for the partners' equities, the partners' capital accounts are debited and Capital Stock is credited. Subsequent corporate transactions are recorded in the old books that have become the records for the newly-formed corporation. The entries to record the incorporation follow:

TRANSACTION	ENTRY		
(a) To record revaluation of assets upon transfer to Raleigh Corporation, the net gain from revaluation and adjustments of $20,000 being credited to Rodriguez and Jones in the earnings distribution ratio of 3:2 respectively.	Inventories	3,500	
	Equipment	2,500	
	Accumulated Depreciation — Equipment	15,000	
	Allowance for Doubtful Accounts		600
	Accrued Liabilities		400
	Rodriguez, Capital		12,000
	Jones, Capital		8,000

TRANSACTION	ENTRY		
(b) To record goodwill as indicated by excess of value of stock issued to partners over the appraised value of net assets transferred:	Goodwill...	22,400	
	Rodriguez, Capital........................		13,440
	Jones, Capital		8,960
Value of stock issued (10,000 shares at $10, price at which stock is currently being sold)... $100,000			
Value of net assets transferred:			
Assets........................... $90,000			
Less liabilities.......................... 12,400 77,600			
Goodwill credited to partners in earnings distribution ratio.. $ 22,400			
(c) To record distribution of capital stock according to agreement:	Rodriguez, Capital	75,000	
	Jones, Capital....................................	25,000	
Rodriguez — 7,500 shares valued at $10..... $ 75,000	Capital Stock....................................		100,000
Jones — 2,500 shares valued at $10............ $ 25,000			
(d) To record distribution of cash in final settlement of partners' claims according to balances in capital accounts:	Rodriguez, Capital	440	
	Jones, Capital....................................	8,160	
	Cash...		8,600
	Rodriguez	Jones	
Capital after adjustment............. $75,440	$33,160		
Less payment in stock................ 75,000	25,000		
Balance paid in cash .... $ 440	$ 8,160		
(e) To record sale of 15,000 shares at $10.	Cash	150,000	
	Capital Stock....................................		150,000

A balance sheet for the corporation after the foregoing transactions is shown below:

Raleigh Corporation
Balance Sheet
March 15, 1977

Assets		Liabilities	
Cash	$150,000	Accounts payable........................	$ 12,000
Accounts receivable...... $15,000		Accrued liabilities	400
Less allowance for			$ 12,400
doubtful accounts.. 1,000	14,000		
Inventories	23,500	**Stockholders' Equity**	
Equipment	52,500	Capital stock, no-par, 25,000	
Goodwill..........................	22,400	shares authorized and issued .	250,000
		Total liabilities and stockhold-	
Total assets....................	$262,400	ers' equity..................................	$262,400

If New Books Are Opened for the Corporation   If new books are opened for the corporation, all of the accounts on the partnership books are closed and partnership assets and liabilities are recorded on the new records. In closing the partnership books, entries are made to record the transfer of assets and liabilities to the corporation, the receipt of capital stock, and the distribution of stock and cash in payment of partners' respective interests. If desired, it would be possible to record the revaluation of assets and the recognition of goodwill before recording the transfer of assets and liabilities. Entries to close the partnership books for Rodriguez and Jones may be made as shown on the following page.

TRANSACTION	ENTRY		
To record the transfer of assets and liabilities to Raleigh Corporation, the difference between claim against vendee, $100,000 (10,000 shares of stock valued at $10), and book value of net assets transferred, $57,600, representing gain on sale of business of $42,400. The gain is distributed to partners in the ratio of 3:2 as follows: To Rodriguez: 3/5 of $42,400 .... $25,440 To Jones: 2/5 of $42,400 .... 16,960 $42,400	Receivable from Raleigh Corporation .... Accounts Payable .... Allowance for Doubtful Accounts... Accumulated Depreciation — Equipment .... Accounts Receivable................... Inventories................................. Equipment................................. Rodriguez, Capital....................... Jones, Capital	100,000 12,000 400 15,000	 15,000 20,000 50,000 25,440 16,960
To record the receipt of capital stock in payment of net assets transferred.	Stock of Raleigh Corporation .... Receivable from Raleigh Corporation	100,000	 100,000
To record distribution of capital stock according to agreement.	Rodriguez, Capital .... Jones, Capital................................. Stock of Raleigh Corporation......	75,000 25,000	 100,000
To record distribution of cash in final settlement of partners' claims according to balances in capital accounts.	Rodriguez, Capital .... Jones, Capital................................. Cash...	440 8,160	 8,600

The entries on the separate corporation books would be as follows:

TRANSACTION	ENTRY		
To record acquisition of assets and liabilities from Rodriguez and Jones.	Accounts Receivable .... Inventories .... Equipment .... Goodwill.. Allowance for Doubtful Accounts.................................... Accounts Payable........................ Accrued Liabilities....................... Payable to Rodriguez and Jones	15,000 23,500 52,500 22,400	 1,000 12,000 400 100,000
To record issuance of 10,000 shares of stock in payment of net assets acquired.	Payable to Rodriguez and Jones .... Capital Stock...............................	100,000	 100,000
To record sale of 15,000 shares of stock for cash.	Cash .... Capital Stock...............................	150,000	 150,000

QUESTIONS

1. Mark Good has been operating a small machine shop for several months. His business has grown, and he has given some thought to incorporating his business. What advantages and disadvantages would there be to such a change?

2. Distinguish between the following: (a) a domestic corporation and a foreign corporation, (b) a stock corporation and a nonstock corporation, (c) an open corporation and a close corporation.

3. What are the four basic rights of stockholders?

4. (a) Define legal capital. (b) What limitations are placed upon the corporation by law to safeguard legal capital?

5. Name the advantages and the disadvantages applying to no-par stock as compared with par-value stock.

6. (a) What preferences are usually granted preferred stockholders? (b) What is callable preferred stock? (c) What is convertible preferred stock? (d) Distinguish between cumulative and noncumulative preferred stock. (e) What limitations on stockholders' rights are generally found in preferred stock?

7. A new company decides to issue both preferred and common stock. The par value for both types is $100. An investor decides to purchase the preferred stock. Under what conditions would this be a wise decision?

8. Describe each of the following records: (a) minutes book, (b) subscribers ledger, (c) stockholders ledger, (d) stock certificate book.

9. Although subscriptions receivable are generally presented as an asset, the propriety of such presentation has been questioned and it has been suggested that they be treated as a subtraction item in reporting the stockholders' equity. What questions can you raise as to the general treatment and what support can you provide for the alternate presentation?

10. The Holmes Co. treats proceeds from capital stock subscription defaults as miscellaneous revenue. Would you approve of this practice?

11. (a) What alternatives may a company have when a subscriber defaults on a subscription? (b) What limits the choice between these alternatives?

12. (a) How should cash proceeds be assigned to individual securities when two different securities are sold for a single sum? (b) Would your answer differ if one of the securities is designated a bonus? Give reasons for your answer.

13. (a) What are "secret reserves"? (b) The treasurer of your client is in favor of secret reserves as a means of achieving "balance sheet conservatism." What is your comment?

14. The Paxton Co. issues 5,000 shares of common stock to persons organizing and promoting the company and another 20,000 shares in exchange for properties believed to have valuable mineral rights. The par value of the stock, $10 per share, is used in recording the consideration for the shares. Shortly after organization the company decides to sell the properties and use the proceeds for another venture. The property is sold for cash of $65,000. How would you record the sale of the properties?

15. The Warner Corporation issues 100,000 shares of common stock, $10 par value, in exchange for certain patents and secret processes. The board of directors authorizes that the assets acquired be reported at $1,000,000. Would you accept this valuation in auditing the financial statements for this company? Explain your position fully.

16. The Bailey Co. records the discount on common stock issued as organization cost and writes this balance off against periodic revenue. What objections do you have to this treatment?

17. The Welch Company acquires the assets of the Goodman Company in exchange for 10,000 shares of its common stock, par value $10. (a) Assuming the appraised value of the property acquired exceeds the par value of the stock issued, how would you record the acquisition? (b) Assuming the par value of the stock issued exceeds the appraised value of the property acquired, suggest different methods for recording the acquisition. What factors will determine the method to be used?

18. What entries are made upon incorporation of a partnership when the original partnership books are retained?

EXERCISES

1. The Holt Company pays out dividends at the end of each year as follows: 1975, $75,000; 1976, $120,000; 1977, $280,000. Give the amount that will be paid per share on common and preferred stock for each year, assuming capital structures as follows:

  (a) 250,000 shares of no-par common; 10,000 shares of $100 par, 7%, noncumulative preferred.
  (b) 250,000 shares of no-par common; 10,000 shares of $100 par, 7%, cumulative preferred, dividends three years in arrears at the beginning of 1975.
  (c) 250,000 shares of $10 par common; 15,000 shares of $100 par, 7%, cumulative preferred, no dividends in arrears at the beginning of 1975.

2. Ferris Corporation has 400,000 shares of $10 par common and 200,000 shares of $100 par, 7% preferred outstanding. The preferred is cumulative. Give the amounts paid on each share of common and preferred stock each year, assuming dividend distributions as follows: 1975, $700,000; 1976, $2,600,000; 1977, $4,000,000. There were no dividends in arrears at the beginning of 1975.

3. The stockholders' equity for the Folsom Corporation on July 1, 1977, is as given on page 522.

Paid-in capital:
    Preferred stock, cumulative, $1 stated value, 10,000 shares outstanding, en-
       titled upon involuntary liquidation to $20 per share plus dividends in ar-
       rears amounting to $8 per share on July 1, 1977 .... $185,000
    Common stock, $1 stated value, 90,000 shares outstanding 90,000
    Paid-in capital from sale of common stock at more than stated value 100,000
    Retained earnings.. 28,000
    Total stockholders' equity... $403,000

Give the amounts that would be paid to each class of stockholders if the company is liquidated on this date, assuming cash available for stockholders after meeting all of the creditors'
claims is: (a) $150,000; (b) $250,000; (c) $320,000.

4. The Hunter Corporation is organized with authorized capital as follows: 30,000 shares of no-
par common and 4,000 shares of 8% preferred, par $100. Give the entries required for each of the
following transactions:

        (a) Assets formerly owned by E. Hansen are accepted as payment for 10,000 shares of
            common stock. Assets are recorded at values as follows: land, $30,000; buildings,
            $35,000; inventories, $95,000.
        (b) Remaining common stock is sold at $18.50.
        (c) Subscriptions are received for 2,500 shares of preferred stock at $103. A 30% down
            payment is made on preferred.
        (d) One subscriber for 250 shares of preferred defaults and her down payment is re-
            tained pending sale of this lot. Remaining subscribers pay the balances due and the
            stock is issued.
        (e) Lot of 250 shares of preferred is sold at $101. Loss on resale is charged against the
            account of the defaulting subscriber, and the down payment less the loss is returned
            to her.

5. On January 1, 1977, Nance Corporation received authorization to issue 100,000 shares of no-
par common stock with a stated value of $10 per share. The stock was offered to subscribers at a
subscription price of $50 per share. Subscriptions were recorded by a debit to Subscriptions Re-
ceivable and credits to Common Stock Subscribed and to a paid-in capital account. Subsequently
a subscriber who had contracted to purchase 500 shares defaulted after paying 50% of the subscription price. Give four methods of accounting for the default, and give the journal entry to
record the default under each method.

6. D. Ekman subscribed to 100 shares of Knapp Industries no-par stock on July 30 at $40. A
down payment of 20% was required, and she paid 50% of the remaining balance due on August 30.
In September, a business loss made it necessary for Ekman to default on her subscription. The
shares were then sold by the company at $30. (a) What rule for the default was applied if the
amount of the refund was (1) $2,400, (2) $1,400, (3) None. (b) Give the journal entries on the books
of the corporation for the subscription, for the subsequent payment on the subscription, and for
the refund of $1,400 under the second assumption above.

7. The Bancroft Corporation has 200,000 authorized shares of common stock, par value $10 per
share. Its trial balance at the end of 1977 includes the following account balances: Capital Stock,
$1,630,000; Premium on Capital Stock, $80,000; Capital Stock Subscribed, $300,000; Deficit,
$20,000.

        (a) Summarize the stockholders' equity as it would be reported on the balance sheet.
        (b) Assuming the trial balance also reports receivables from subscribers at this date of
            $60,000, how much has been paid into the company by stockholders to date?

8. The Athey Co. issues 20,000 shares of preferred stock and 90,000 shares of common stock,
each with a par value of $10, in exchange for properties appraised at $1,200,000. Give the entry to
record the exchange on the books of the corporation assuming:

        (a) No price can be assigned at date of issuance to the preferred stock or common stock
            issues.
        (b) Common stock is selling on the market at $11 per share; there was no preferred
            stock issued prior to this issue.
        (c) Common stock is selling on the market at $10 per share; preferred stock is selling on
            the market at $15 per share.

9. $2,000,000 in Dodd Company bonds are sold at 105. The price includes a bonus of 3 shares of Dodd Company common stock, $20 par, with each $1,000 bond. At the time the bonds were sold, the stock was selling on the market at $23.50 per share. What entry would be made to record the sale of the bonds?

10. Clock, Inc., sells 4,000 shares of its 5% cumulative preferred stock, par $100, to an investment group for $460,000, giving 1 share of common stock, par $50, as a bonus with every 4 shares of preferred. The market value of the preferred stock immediately following the sale is $103 per share. What is the entry for the sale?

11. A balance sheet for Aston and Barker, prepared on June 30, appears below. Partners share earnings and losses in the ratio of 3:1 respectively.

Aston and Barker
Balance Sheet
June 30, 1977

Assets			Liabilities and Owners' Equity	
Cash		$ 2,000	Accounts payable	$ 5,100
Accounts receivable......	$ 6,200		Aston, capital	19,700
Less allowance for doubtful accounts..	600	5,600	Barker, capital	20,100
Inventories		10,300		
Equipment	$30,000			
Less accumulated depreciation	8,000	22,000		
Goodwill		5,000		
Total assets		$44,900	Total liabilities and owners' equity	$44,900

An appraisal of the assets discloses the following current values:

Inventories	$14,800
Equipment...	26,000

Aston and Barker decide to incorporate as Bushnell Co.; 7,000 shares of $2 par common stock are issued to the partners in exchange for partnership assets other than cash. The corporation also agrees to assume partnership obligations. On this date the corporation stock has a market value of $7 per share. In dissolving the partnership, Aston agrees to take 4,000 shares and Barker, 3,000 shares. The partnership cash is then appropriately divided between the partners. Give the entries to record the foregoing on the books of the partnership and on the new books of the corporation.

PROBLEMS

18-1. The Yoko Co. was organized on May 25, 1977, and was authorized to issue 250,000 shares of no-par common stock, stated value $15, and 10,000 shares of 8% preferred stock, par value $50. The following were the company's capital stock transactions through September 15, 1977.

June 1 Issued 50,000 shares of common stock to an investment group at $20.

June 15 Assets were obtained from Tom Co. in exchange for 75,000 shares of common stock. The assets were appraised as follows:

Merchandise inventory	$300,000
Furniture and fixtures	75,000
Machinery and equipment	475,000
Land	375,000

July 1 Subscriptions were received for 100,000 shares of common stock at $25 and for 5,000 shares of preferred 8% stock at $55; each class of stock is to be paid for in two installments, 25% on the date of subscription and 75% within 90 days.

Sept. 15 The second installments on the common stock and preferred stock were paid in full and the stock was issued.

(continued)

    (1) Give the journal entries to record the preceding transactions.
    (2) Prepare a balance sheet based on results of the preceding transactions.

18-2. The Chambers Co., organized on April 10, 1977, was authorized to issue stock as follows:

    100,000 shares of $10 par common stock
    5,000 shares of 8% preferred stock with a par value of $100

Capital stock transactions through September 15, 1977, were as follows:

May 15 Subscriptions were received for 50,000 shares of common stock at $15 on the following terms: 10% was paid in cash at the time of subscription, the balance being payable in three equal installments due on the fifteenth day of each succeeding month.

June   1 All of the preferred stock was sold to an investment company for cash at $96 and stock was issued.

June 15 The first installment on subscriptions to 48,800 shares was collected. Terms of the subscription contract provided that defaulting subscribers have 30 days in which to make payment and obtain reinstatement; failure to make payment within the specified period will result in the forfeiture of amounts already paid in.

July 15 The second installment on common subscriptions was collected. Collections included receipt of the first and second installment on 200 shares from subscribers who defaulted on their first installment; however, subscribers to 250 shares defaulted in addition to subscribers already in default.

Aug. 15 The third installment on common subscriptions was collected. Collections included receipt of the second and third installment from subscribers to 200 shares who defaulted on their second installment. Stock certificates were issued to fully paid subscribers.

Sept.   1 Stock in default was sold to an investment company at 13.

    (1) Give the journal entries to record these transactions.
    (2) Prepare the "Stockholders' equity" section of the balance sheet on September 15, 1977.

18-3. The Williams Corporation was organized on September 1, 1977, with authorized capital stock of 100,000 shares of 8% cumulative preferred with a $30 par value and 500,000 shares of no-par common with a $25 stated value. During the balance of the year, the following transactions relating to capital stock were completed:

Oct.   1 Subscriptions were received for 150,000 shares of common stock at $40, payable $15 down and the balance in two equal installments due November 1 and December 1. On the same date 15,000 shares of common stock were issued to Jim Williams in exchange for his business. Assets transferred to the corporation were valued as follows: land, $180,000; buildings, $210,000; equipment, $60,000; merchandise, $104,500. Liabilities of the business assumed by the corporation were: mortgage payable, $37,000; accounts payable, $10,500; accrued interest on mortgage, $450. No goodwill is recognized in recording the issuance of the stock for net assets.

Oct.   3 Subscriptions were received for 60,000 shares of preferred stock at $32, payable $12 down and the balance in two equal installments due November 1 and December 1.

Nov.   1 Amounts due on this date were collected from all common and preferred stock subscribers.

Nov. 12 Subscriptions were received for 240,000 shares of common stock at $38, payable $15 down and the balance in two equal installments due December 1 and January 1.

Dec.   1 Amounts due on this date were collected from all common stock subscribers and stock fully paid for was issued. The final installment on preferred stock subscriptions was received from all subscribers except one whose installment due on this date was $6,000. State corporation laws provide that the company is liable for the return to the subscriber of the amount received less the loss on the subsequent resale of the stock. Preferred stock fully paid for was issued.

Dec. 6 Preferred stock defaulted on December 1 was sold for cash at $27. Stock was issued, and settlement was made with the defaulting subscriber.

Instructions:
(1) Prepare journal entries to record the foregoing transactions.
(2) Prepare the "Stockholders' equity" section for the corporation as of December 31.

18-4. The Addison Company had the following account balances in its balance sheet at December 31, 1977, the end of its first year of operations. All stock was sold on a subscription basis, and the state laws permit the company to retain all partial subscriptions paid by defaulting subscribers.

Common Stock Subscriptions Receivable	$50,000
Common Stock, $25 par	25,000
Common Stock Subscribed	75,000
Premium on Common Stock	20,000
Preferred 8% Stock, $100 par	50,000
Premium on Preferred Stock	25,000
Paid-In Capital from Default on Preferred Stock (100 shares)	5,000
Preference 10% Stock, $50 par	10,000
Retained Earnings	10,000

The reported net income for 1977 was $20,000.

Instructions: From the above data, reconstruct in summary form the journal entries to record all transactions involving the company's stockholders. Indicate the amount of dividends distributed to each class of stockholders.

18-5. The Toko Machine Co. was incorporated on January 31, 1977, with authorized common stock of $1,000,000 and 7% cumulative preferred stock of $225,000, each class with a par value of $50.

Subscriptions were received for 4,000 shares of common stock at $60 a share, to be paid in four equal installments on March 1, April 1, May 1, and June 1. The first installment was paid in full. Subscribers for 300 shares defaulted on the second installment, and the amounts already received from these subscribers were returned. The second, third, and fourth installments were paid in full on their due dates by the remaining subscribers, and the stock was issued.

During March, preferred stock was offered for sale at $65, 1 share of common stock being offered with each subscription for 10 shares of preferred. During March, the market price for the common stock was $60 per share. On this basis subscriptions were received for all of the preferred stock. Subscriptions were payable in two equal installments: the first was payable by the end of March and the second was payable at any time prior to June 15. The first installment was paid in full. By June 1, $117,000 had been received on the second installment, and stock was issued to the fully paid subscribers.

Instructions:
(1) Journalize the above transactions.
(2) Prepare the "Stockholders' equity" section of the balance sheet as of June 1 reflecting the foregoing.

18-6. San Miguel and Thorsen, partners, who share earnings and losses in a ratio of 3:2 respectively, wish to retire from active participation in their manufacturing business and decide to form a corporation to take over the partnership assets. The partnership balance sheet prepared on March 1, 1977, appears at the top of the next page.

The partners, together with Baldwin and Casper who wish to join the new enterprise, agree to the following:

(a) The corporation shall be known as the Super Scope Company, and its authorized stock shall consist of 100,000 shares of common stock, $10 par, and 7,500 shares of preferred 7% stock, $50 par.

(b) Partnership assets other than cash are to be transferred to the corporation and the liabilities are to be assumed by the corporation. The corporation is to issue 4,000 shares of preferred stock in payment for net assets acquired. (It is assumed the stock is worth par value.) The stock is to be divided equally between San Miguel and Thorsen, and the partnership cash is then to be withdrawn by the partners in settlement

San Miguel and Thorsen
Balance Sheet
March 1, 1977

Assets			Liabilities and Owners' Equity	
Cash		$ 26,000	Notes payable	$ 42,000
Notes receivable		49,000	Accounts payable	80,000
Accounts receivable		60,000	San Miguel, capital	75,000
Inventories		70,500	Thorsen, capital	87,500
Land		30,000		
Buildings	$50,000			
Less accumulated depreciation — buildings	32,000	18,000		
Machinery	$80,000			
Less accumulated depreciation — machinery	49,000	31,000	Total liabilities and owners'	
Total assets		$284,500	equity	$284,500

of their interests. Partnership properties other than land, buildings, and machinery are to be recorded on the corporation records at book value. Land, buildings, and machinery items are to be recorded at current fair market values as follows:

Land	$42,000
Buildings	22,000
Machinery	32,000

(c) Baldwin will take charge of the organization of the corporation and will be allowed 2,000 shares of common stock in full payment for his services.

(d) Casper, who owns valuable patent rights, will be given 8,000 shares of common stock upon transfer of these rights to the corporation.

The Super Scope Company is incorporated on March 1 and the foregoing transactions are completed.

Instructions:

(1) Prepare the entries to record the transfer of assets and liabilities to the corporation, and the distribution of stock and cash on the partnership books.

(2) Prepare the entries for the separate corporation books.

(3) Prepare a balance sheet for the corporation on March 1, 1977, after the foregoing transactions have been recorded.

18-7. Hanks, Ison, and Jackson, partners sharing earnings and losses 3:3:2 respectively, draw up the following partnership balance sheet on November 1, 1977:

Hanks, Ison, and Jackson
Balance Sheet
November 1, 1977

Assets			Liabilities and Owners' Equity	
Cash		$ 31,450	Notes payable	$ 15,000
Accounts receivable		35,000	Accounts payable	21,400
Merchandise inventory		62,000	Hanks, capital	40,250
Furniture and fixtures	$21,450		Ison, capital	35,000
Less accumulated depreciation — furniture and fixtures	7,250	14,200	Jackson, capital	31,000
Total assets		$142,650	Total liabilities and owners' equity	$142,650

The partners incorporate on this date as HIJ, Inc., with authorized capital stock as follows:

Preferred stock, 5,000 shares, $25 par
Common stock, 20,000 shares, $10 par

The partners agree to the following:

    (a) Adjustments are to be made in asset values as follows:
        (1) An allowance for doubtful accounts is to be established at 5% of accounts receivable.
        (2) Furniture and fixtures are to be restated at present replacement cost of $30,000 less accumulated depreciation of 30% on replacement cost.
        (3) Expenses of $550 have been prepaid and are to be recognized as an asset.
    (b) Partners are to be paid for their partnership interest as follows, it being assumed that stock has a value equal to its par:
        (1) 1,200 shares of preferred are to be allowed to each partner.
        (2) Remaining capital interests are to be paid for with common stock, in even multiples of 100 shares, each partner to be paid cash for his or her capital balance in excess of the highest 100-share multiple that can be issued.

The above adjustments and transactions are completed and shares not required for the settlement of the partners' interests are immediately sold at par.

Instructions:
    (1) Give journal entries to record the incorporation, assuming that it is to be reflected on the partnership books, no new books being opened by the corporation.
    (2) Prepare a balance sheet for the corporation. (Assume transactions are completed on November 1.)

18-8. Howard & Sanders Electrical Contracting Co., a partnership, and Grover Wholesale Electricians' Hardware Co., a proprietorship, have agreed to transfer the assets and liabilities of their companies on November 1, 1977, to a newly chartered corporation, Major Electrical, Inc., in exchange for Major Electrical, Inc.'s stock. The agreement provides:

    (a) Preferred stock shall be issued at par value of $100 per share to each of the parties in exchange for his or her share of the net assets (assets minus liabilities) transferred to Major Electrical, Inc. Jill Grover shall receive at least 900 shares of preferred stock and Bill Howard and Joe Sanders shall receive together a total of not more than 480 shares of preferred stock. Cash shall be contributed to the companies by the respective parties or distributed by the companies to the parties to accomplish the proper net asset transfers.
    (b) Common stock shall be issued in a total amount equal to the earnings expected to be contributed by the companies to Major Electrical, Inc., for the next five years to the extent that the earnings of each company respectively, based on the past three calendar years, exceed the average earnings of its industry. The common stock shall be issued at par value of $10 per share to the owners of the companies in the ratio of the amount that each company's average earnings are expected to exceed the average industry earnings of the company with the lesser earnings.

Additional information includes the following:

    (c) Trial balances at October 31, 1977, for both companies are given at the top of the following page.
    (d) Howard and Sanders maintain the partnership books on the cash basis of accounting and Grover maintains her proprietorship books on the accrual basis. Major Electrical, Inc.'s books are to be maintained on the accrual basis. Items not recorded on Howard and Sanders' books at October 31, 1977, follow:

Accounts receivable	$20,300
Allowance for doubtful accounts	400
Unbilled contract in progress	8,000
Prepaid expenses	1,200
Accounts payable	6,200
Accrued liabilities	2,400

All accounts receivable are for jobs completed and billed. The unbilled contract in progress is for a $10,000 contract which was 80% complete and upon which a $2,500 deposit was paid to Howard & Sanders when the contract was signed. Cash payments for work on the contract to October 31, 1977, total $3,500 and were recorded on the partnership books as inventory. Accounts payable include $2,800 owed to Grover Wholesale Electricians' Hardware Co. *(continued)*

Grover Hardware Co. and
Howard & Sanders Co.
Trial Balances
October 31, 1977

	Grover Hardware		Howard & Sanders	
Cash	17,000		20,700	
Accounts Receivable	43,000			
Allowance for Doubtful Accounts............................		3,000		
Inventory...	63,000		3,500	
Prepaid Expenses	2,000		1,300	
Land, Buildings, and Equipment	44,000		26,000	
Accumulated Depr. — Buildings and Equip.		27,000		12,000
Accounts Payable...		54,000		
Miscellaneous Expenses Payable...........................		4,000		
Deposit on Contract...				2,500
Grover, Capital		75,000		
Grover, Drawing...	5,000			
Howard, Capital..				11,300
Sanders, Capital..				7,700
Revenues		200,000		70,000
Cost of Producing Revenues	160,000		31,000	
Howard, Salary			4,000	
Sanders, Salary			3,000	
Operating Expenses..	29,000		14,000	
	363,000	363,000	103,500	103,500

(e) The partnership agreement specified Bill Howard would receive a salary of $12,000 per year and share 60% of any earnings or loss and Joe Sanders would receive a salary of $9,000 per year and share 40% of any earnings or loss. Each partner will receive the same annual salary from the corporation.

(f) Jill Grover withdraws an amount each month from her proprietorship equal to a normal salary. Grover's annual salary from the corporation will be $15,000.

(g) Based on the past three years, Jill Grover could expect her proprietorship to earn an average of $39,000 per year for the next five years before any salary allowance with average expected sales of $600,000 per year. The industry average net income (after deducting all salaries and income tax) for electrical hardware wholesalers for the next five years is expected to be 1.35% of sales.

(h) Based on the past three years, Bill Howard and Joe Sanders could expect their partnership to earn an average of $55,500 per year for the next five years before deducting partners' salaries with average expected revenues of $240,000 per year. The industry average net income (after deducting all salaries and income tax) for electrical contractors for the next five years is expected to be 7.5% of sales.

(i) The parties expect the corporation to pay income tax at an average of 40% during the next five years.

Instructions: Complete a work sheet with the columnar headings indicated below to determine the opening account balances of Major Electrical, Inc., giving effect to the agreement to transfer the assets and liabilities and issue stock.

Your work sheet would include space to list the names of accounts followed by a pair of columns for each of the following headings:

> Grover Hardware Trial Balance
> Howard & Sanders Trial Balance
> Grover Hardware Adjusting and Closing Entries
> Howard & Sanders Adjusting and Closing Entries
> Major Electrical, Inc., Opening Account Balances

Prepare supporting schedules computing (1) any cash contributions or distributions necessary and preferred stock to be issued to each party and (2) the number of shares of common stock to be issued to each party. Formal adjusting and closing entries and formal financial statements are not required. (AICPA adapted)

19

Paid-In Capital — Changes Subsequent to Corporate Formation

Corporate capital originates from different sources. These different sources need to be identified in providing information concerning the character of the stockholders' equity. These must also be known to determine the amounts legally distributable as dividends. Corporate capital originates from two primary sources: (1) investments by those acquiring stock; and (2) retention of net assets arising from earnings.

1. *Investments by those acquiring stock.* Net assets received by a corporation in exchange for its stock are the source of a company's invested capital. Invested capital is divided into (a) an amount forming the corporate legal or stated capital, and (b) the balance not classified as legal capital. The amount of the investment representing the legal or stated capital is reported as *capital stock*. The balance is recognized as *additional paid-in capital*. Contributions of properties by outsiders may also be included in the additional paid-in capital grouping, although it would be possible to recognize these in a separate *donated capital* category.
2. *Retention of net assets arising from earnings.* Changes in net assets arising from the sale of goods and services give rise to earnings and losses that are summarized as *retained earnings*. When a portion of retained earnings is unavailable for dividends, it is referred to as *appropriated* or *reserved*; any balance is then regarded as *unappropriated* or *free*. A debit balance in retained earnings resulting from losses is termed a *deficit* and is subtracted from paid-in capital in arriving at the total corporate capital.

Individual accounts should be maintained in the ledger for each separate source of capital within each of the classifications listed. For example, separate accounts should be provided for preferred stock and for common stock, for a premium on preferred stock and for a premium on common stock, for a retained earnings appropriation related to a bond redemption fund and for a retained earnings appropriation related to the acquisition of treasury stock. In reporting the stockholders' equity on the balance sheet, however, individual paid-in capital and retained earnings balances are frequently combined and presented under class headings. Whether reported separately or in combined form, the capital accounts simply designate the source of the stockholders' equity and are not related to specific assets.

Remaining pages of this chapter consider the transactions affecting paid-in capital balances after formation of the corporation. The next chapter considers those transactions affecting retained earnings.

CAPITAL STOCK REACQUISITION AND RETIREMENT

A corporation may have the right to call certain classes of stock for redemption and may choose to exercise this right. In other cases, it may purchase stock on the open market and formally retire shares. Whether obtained through call for redemption or through purchase on the market, retirement of stock at a cost differing from the original issuance price presents special accounting problems.

The reacquisition and retirement of stock cannot be considered to give rise to income or loss. A company in issuing stock raises capital which it hopes to employ profitably; in reacquiring and retiring shares it reduces the capital to be employed in subsequent operations. Income or loss arises from the utilization of resources placed in the hands of the corporation, not from capital transactions between the company and its stockholders. Although there is general agreement on this matter, there are still certain problems in recording stock retirement.

If a class of stock is retired at the same amount originally recognized as capital stock, the capital stock account is debited and Cash is credited. All reference to the investment by the stockholders, then, is cancelled. However, when the purchase price of the stock retired exceeds the par or stated value of the stock, the excess must be assigned in some satisfactory manner to paid-in capital and retained earnings.

The Accounting Principles Board in Opinion No. 6 commented upon the procedure to be followed when stock of a corporation is retired:

> i. *an excess of purchase price over par or stated value* may be allocated between capital surplus [paid-in capital] and retained earnings. The portion of the excess allocated to capital surplus should be limited to the sum of (a) all capital surplus arising from previous retirements and net "gains" on sales of treasury stock of the same issue and (b) the pro rata portion of capital surplus paid in, voluntary transfers of retained earnings, capitalization of stock dividends, etc., on the same issue. For this purpose, any remaining capital surplus applicable to issues fully retired (formal or constructive) is deemed to be applicable pro rata to shares of common stock. Alternatively, the excess may be charged entirely to retained earnings in recognition of the fact that a corporation can always capitalize or allocate retained earnings for such purposes.
> ii. *an excess of par or stated value over purchase price* should be credited to capital surplus.[1]

The effects of these provisions are illustrated in the following examples. Assume a corporation reports the following balances related to an issue of preferred stock:

---

[1] *Opinions of the Accounting Principles Board, No. 6,* "Status of Accounting Research Bulletins" (New York: American Institute of Certified Public Accountants, 1965), par. 12a.

Preferred stock outstanding, par $10, 10,000 shares $100,000
Premium on preferred stock.. 10,000

1. Assume the corporation redeems and retires 2,000 shares, or 20%, of the preferred stock at $12.50 per share. Reductions are made in the preferred stock account for 2,000 shares, par $10, or $20,000, and in the premium on preferred stock for a pro rata share of the premium, 20% of $10,000, or $2,000, and the difference between the sum of these amounts and the amount paid is debited to Retained Earnings. The entry, then, is as follows:

Preferred Stock 20,000
Premium on Preferred Stock 2,000
Retained Earnings.. 3,000
    Cash 25,000

If the alternate method indicated by the Accounting Principles Board is followed, the entire amount paid over par or stated value of the retired shares would be debited to Retained Earnings. In the example, then, the entry would be:

Preferred Stock 20,000
Retained Earnings.. 5,000
    Cash 25,000

2. Assume the corporation redeems and retires the 2,000 shares of preferred stock at only $9 per share. The preferred stock account is reduced by the par value of the shares, $20,000, and the difference between the debit to Preferred Stock and the amount paid is credited to a paid-in capital account. The following entry is made:

Preferred Stock 20,000
    Cash 18,000
    Paid-In Capital from Preferred Stock Reacquisition......... 2,000

It would also be possible to reduce Premium on Preferred Stock for a pro rata share of the premium, $2,000, and report the Paid-In Capital from Preferred Stock Reacquisition at the difference between the amount at which the preferred shares were originally issued and the amount paid on their retirement. The following entry can be made:

Preferred Stock 20,000
Premium on Preferred Stock 2,000
    Cash 18,000
    Paid-In Capital from Preferred Stock Reacquisition......... 4,000

If additional shares of preferred stock are subsequently retired at amounts in excess of par, the differences between the amounts paid and the par value of the preferred stock retired can be debited to the paid-in capital from the earlier preferred stock acquisition.

When stock is formally retired, there is a reduction in the corporate legal or stated capital. State laws normally do not bar the reduction of legal or stated capital when stock is issued subject to redemption and redemption is made at the price provided by terms of the stock issue.

TREASURY STOCK

When a company's own stock, paid for and issued, is reacquired and held in the name of the company rather than formally retired, it is known as *treasury stock*. A company may acquire its own stock by purchase, by acceptance in satisfaction of a claim, or by donation from stockholders. Treasury shares may subsequently be sold or formally retired.

There are many reasons a company finds it desirable to repurchase its own stock. A survey by the Conference Board cited seven major reasons for repurchasing shares.

1. To obtain shares for executive stock options and other compensation programs.
2. To obtain stock to be used in acquisitions.
3. To improve per-share earnings by reducing the number of shares outstanding.
4. To obtain shares for conversion from other securities.
5. To invest surplus cash temporarily.
6. To support the market price of the stock.
7. To increase the rate of debt to equity.[1]

State laws vary widely in their regulations concerning treasury stock. In some states, accounting for treasury stock is governed largely by statute. In other states, only general restrictions are applied. The accounting for treasury stock requires careful review of the state laws. State laws normally provide that the reacquisition of stock must serve some legitimate corporate purpose and must be made without injury or prejudice to the creditors or to the remaining stockholders. In almost every state, it is provided that the legal or stated capital of the corporation may not be reduced by reacquisition.[2] Accordingly, purchases are limited to a company's retained earnings, or in some instances to the sum of its retained earnings and paid-in capital balances; they also reduce the amount otherwise available for distribution as dividends. To illustrate the effects of such legislation, assume the capital of a corporation is as follows:

Capital stock, $10 par, 100,000 shares outstanding.................................. $1,000,000
Retained earnings   500,000

The company can declare dividends of $500,000 and creditors will continue to be safeguarded by the stockholders' investment of $1,000,000 as reported in the capital stock account. But assume the reacquisition by the company of a part of its outstanding stock for $400,000. If dividends of $500,000 were still permitted and were paid, protection to creditors would shrink to $600,000. With the company's ability to pay dividends reduced to $100,000 upon the purchase of treasury stock for $400,000, the original protection to the creditor group is assured; the sum of payments for treasury stock and dividends will not reduce net assets below the legal capital reported in capital stock, $1,000,000.

Despite the fact that the legal capital remains the same after a company has reacquired shares of its own stock, the treasury stock cannot

---

[1]Francis J. Walsh, Jr., *Repurchasing Common Stock* (New York: The Conference Board, Inc., 1975), p. 5.

[2]Corporation laws of a few jurisdictions specifically provide that the purchase of treasury stock reduces the retained earnings balance. The purchase of shares thus has the same effect as a dividend. In California, for example, the purchase of shares is restricted to the amount of retained earnings and reduces this balance; the legal or stated capital remains the same even though there has been a decrease in the number of shares outstanding. If reacquired shares are retired, there are no changes in stated capital and retained earnings balances; if the shares are resold, the entire proceeds must be recognized as additional paid-in capital.

normally be viewed as an asset but should be regarded as a reduction in corporate capital. A company cannot have an ownership interest in itself; treasury stock confers upon the corporation no dividend, voting, or subscription rights.

The AICPA has discouraged the recognition of treasury stock as an asset in the following statement:

> While it is perhaps in some circumstances permissible to show stock of a corporation held in its own treasury as an asset, if adequately disclosed, the dividends on stock so held should not be treated as a credit to the income account of the company.[1]

Although treasury stock has a number of similarities to unissued stock, there are some significant differences. Among these differences are the following: (1) stockholders' preemptive rights do not apply to treasury stock; (2) treasury stock may be reissued without authorization by stockholders; (3) having already been issued in accordance with legal requirements governing legal or stated capital, treasury stock may be reissued without the conditions imposed upon its original issue, for example, the discount liability on the original issue; and (4) treasury stock remains a part of legal capital in most states.

The sale of treasury stock increases the number of shares outstanding. However, the legal capital, remaining unchanged upon its purchase, is not increased through its sale. If treasury stock is to be retired, such retirement is formalized by the preparation of a certificate or notice of reduction filed with appropriate state officials. Upon the formal retirement of shares, these revert to the status of unissued shares and there is a reduction in the corporate legal or stated capital. For federal income tax purposes, treasury stock transactions provide no taxable gain or loss; stock reacquisition, as well as stock reissue or retirement, is regarded as a transaction related to a company's invested capital.

Purchase of Treasury Stock

A number of different methods for recording the purchase of treasury stock have been suggested. These methods are the products of two general approaches to the problem of treasury stock purchases:

1. The purchase of treasury stock may be viewed as the retirement of outstanding stock.
2. The purchase of treasury stock may be viewed as giving rise to a capital element whose ultimate disposition still remains to be resolved.

The two approaches are described in the following sections. Descriptions are accompanied by examples illustrating the different approaches.

---

[1] *Accounting Research and Terminology Bulletins — Final Edition*, "No. 43, Restatement and Revision of Accounting Research Bulletins" (New York: American Institute of Certified Public Accountants, 1961), Ch. 1, sec. A, par. 4. In 1975, 8 of the 600 companies listed in *Accounting Trends & Techniques* reported treasury stock as an asset. A bonus agreement specifying that a liability to employees for a bonus that can be satisfied by issuing to the employees shares of company stock is an example where support is given for reporting treasury stock as an asset. *Accounting Trends & Techniques* (30th ed.; New York: American Institute of Certified Public Accountants, 1976), p. 189.

First Approach: Treasury Stock Purchase Viewed as Capital Retirement (Par or Stated Value Method). The purchase of treasury stock may be regarded as the withdrawal of a group of stockholders calling for the cancellation of capital balances identified with this group. It follows that the sale of treasury stock represents the admission of a new group of stockholders calling for entries to give effect to the investment by this group. Thus, there are two separate transactions that must be recorded, the purchase and the sale.

When the purchase of stock is viewed as stock retirement, alternate methods may be employed in reporting the reduction in the capital stock balance: (1) the capital stock account may be debited directly; or (2) a treasury stock account may be debited and the balance treated as an offset account to capital stock; this procedure preserves capital at the legal or stated amount as reported by the capital stock account. The alternate methods are illustrated on pages 536 and 537. The transactions for each case are described below.

Treasury Stock Reported as a Reduction in Capital Stock

Transaction 1:
Treasury stock is acquired at a price exceeding the original issue price. Debits are made to capital stock and to additional paid-in capital and retained earnings balances applying the alternatives stated on page 530. If treasury stock is acquired at a price less than the original issue price, a separate paid-in capital account should be credited for the difference in values.

Transaction 2:
When the stock is sold at more than its par or stated value, Capital Stock is credited at par or stated value and Paid-In Capital from Sale of Treasury Stock at More Than Par or Stated Value is credited for the excess. When the stock is sold at less than par or stated value, Capital Stock is credited at par or stated value and a debit for the difference is made to any paid-in capital from earlier sales or retirements of treasury stock of the same class, or to Retained Earnings.

Treasury Stock Account Used to Report Reduction in Capital Stock

Transaction 1:
When treasury stock is acquired at a price exceeding its par or stated value, a treasury stock account instead of capital stock may be debited for the amount of the reduction in the capital stock. The treasury stock account subtracted from the capital stock account reporting the amount issued then gives the capital stock outstanding. Debits to other paid-in capital and retained earnings balances would be made as described in the preceding section.

Transaction 2:
When the treasury stock is sold, the treasury stock account is credited for the amount at which treasury stock is carried, and any difference between the sales price and the carrying amount is treated as described in the preceding section.

Second Approach: Treasury Stock Purchase Viewed as Giving Rise to Capital Element Awaiting Ultimate Disposition (Cost Method). The purchase of treasury stock may be viewed as an application of cash to a capital purpose that has not been finally defined or consummated. Upon the purchase of treasury stock, a treasury stock account is debited for the cost of the purchase regardless of whether this cost is more or less than the original stock issue price. This balance is recognized as a negative stockholders' equity element that does not call for specific identification with paid-in capital or retained earnings at this time. If treasury stock is subsequently retired, the debit balance in the treasury stock account can be allocated to the appropriate equity balances as in the first approach. If the treasury stock is sold, the difference between the acquisition cost and the selling price is reported as an increase or decrease in stockholders' equity. It is the retirement or the sale of treasury stock that makes possible a determination of the effect of treasury stock transactions upon the elements of corporate capital.

The application of this approach is illustrated on pages 536 and 537. The transactions in the example are described below.

Transaction 1:
When treasury stock is purchased, it is recorded at its cost regardless of whether this cost is more or less than the original stock issue price. In a presentation of corporate capital at this time, treasury stock, consisting of a cost unallocated as to the different capital elements, would normally be reported as a subtraction from the sum of paid-in capital and retained earnings.[1]

Transaction 2:
When treasury stock is sold at more than its cost, Treasury Stock is credited at cost and Paid-In Capital from Sale of Treasury Stock at More Than Cost is credited. When the stock is sold at less than cost, Treasury Stock is credited at cost and a debit is made to any paid-in capital from earlier sales or retirements of treasury stock of the same class, or to Retained Earnings.

When retained earnings are restricted for dividend purposes while treasury stock is held, there are several ways these restrictions may be shown on the balance sheet. The most common are (1) as an appropriation of retained earnings, (2) as a parenthetical remark in the body of the statement, and (3) as a note to the financial statements. The restriction would be reported regardless of the method used to record the purchase of the stock.

Evaluation of the Two Approaches to Entries for Treasury Stock. Neither the AICPA, through the Accounting Principles Board, nor the Financial Accounting Standards Board has expressed a preference between the two approaches of reporting treasury stock purchases.

The American Accounting Association's Committee on Concepts and Standards Underlying Corporate Financial Statements would recognize the acquisition of treasury stock as equivalent to the retirement of stock. The Committee's comment appears on page 536.

---

[1]"When a corporation's stock is acquired for purposes other than retirement (formal or constructive), or when ultimate disposition has not yet been decided, the cost of acquired stock may be shown separately as a deduction from the total of capital stock, capital surplus [paid-in capital], and retained earnings or may be accorded the accounting treatment appropriate for retired stock ...."
Opinions of the Accounting Principles Board, No. 6, op. cit., par. 12b.

TRANSACTION	FIRST APPROACH: TREASURY STOCK PURCHASE VIEWED AS CAPITAL RETIREMENT
	TREASURY STOCK PURCHASE REPORTED AS REDUCTION IN CAPITAL STOCK

1976
Issue of stock, 10,000 shares, $10 par, at 15.
	Cash 150,000
	    Capital Stock............................... 100,000
	    Premium on Capital Stock.......... 50,000

Net income for year, $30,000.	Income Summary .... 30,000 Retained Earnings........................ 30,000
1977 (1) Reacquisition of 1,000 shares at 16.	Capital Stock .... 10,000 Premium on Capital Stock* .... 5,000 Retained Earnings............................ 1,000 Cash... 16,000

(2) Sale of treasury stock at 20.	Cash 20,000
	    Capital Stock............................... 10,000
	    Paid-In Capital from Sale of
	    Treasury Stock at More Than
	    Par.. 10,000

"Stockholders' equity" section after sale of treasury stock:	Stockholders' Equity
	
	Paid-in capital:
	  Capital Stock.. $100,000
	  Premium on capital stock 45,000
	  Paid-in capital from sale of treasury
	    stock at more than par.......................... 10,000
	Retained earnings 29,000
	Total stockholders' equity $184,000

      The acquisition of its own shares by a corporation represents a contraction of its capital structure. However, statutory requirements are particularly restrictive in this area of corporate activity and, to an important degree, are controlling in the reporting of such transactions. Preferably, the outlay by a corporation for its own shares is reflected as a reduction of the aggregate of contributed capital, and any excess of outlay over the pro rata portion of contributed capital as a distribution of retained earnings. The issuance of reacquired shares should be accounted for in the same way as the issuance of previously unissued shares, that is, the entire proceeds should be credited to contributed capital.[1]

    Although there is theoretical support for each of the approaches presented, laws of the states may take different views relative to the effects of treasury stock transactions upon corporate capital. As already indicated, state laws generally provide that legal or stated capital is not reduced by the purchase by a company of its own shares. This provision is accompanied by restrictions on the availability of retained earnings and perhaps of paid-in capital for dividends. Upon the sale or retirement of treasury stock, some states cancel these restrictions, thus reinstating the reductions applied to specific capital balances. Other states do not cancel

[1]*Accounting and Reporting Standards for Corporate Financial Statements and Preceding Statements and Supplements* (Madison, Wisconsin: American Accounting Association, 1957), p. 7.

FIRST APPROACH: TREASURY STOCK PURCHASE VIEWED AS CAPITAL RETIREMENT		SECOND APPROACH: TREASURY STOCK PURCHASE VIEWED AS GIVING RISE TO CAPITAL ELEMENT AWAITING ULTIMATE DISPOSITION	
TREASURY STOCK ACCOUNT USED TO REPORT REDUCTION IN CAPITAL STOCK			
Cash 150,000		Cash 150,000	
Capital Stock..............................	100,000	Capital Stock..............................	100,000
Premium on Capital Stock...........	50,000	Premium on Capital Stock..........	50,000
Income Summary 30,000		Income Summary 30,000	
Retained Earnings........................	30,000	Retained Earnings........................	30,000
Treasury Stock 10,000		Treasury Stock 16,000	
Premium on Capital Stock* 5,000		Cash...	16,000
Retained Earnings............................ 1,000			
Cash..	16,000		
Cash 20,000		Cash 20,000	
Treasury Stock.............................	10,000	Treasury Stock.............................	16,000
Paid-In Capital from Sale of Treasury Stock at More Than Par..	10,000	Paid-In Capital from Sale of Treasury Stock at More Than Par..	4,000
Stockholders' Equity		Stockholders' Equity	
Paid-in capital:		Paid-in capital:	
Capital stock..	$100,000	Capital stock..	$100,000
Premium on capital stock	45,000	Premium on capital stock	50,000
Paid-in capital from sale of treasury stock at more than par..........................	10,000	Paid-in capital from sale of treasury stock at more than cost........................	4,000
Retained earnings	29,000	Retained earnings	30,000
Total stockholders' equity	$184,000	Total stockholders' equity	$184,000

*As indicated earlier, the entire difference between the debit to Capital Stock and the amount paid may be debited to Retained Earnings.

such restrictions but require that if treasury stock is sold, the proceeds from the sale be recognized as an increase in paid-in capital, and if treasury stock is retired, a transfer be made from the legal capital to additional paid-in capital.

The procedures illustrated in this chapter may be modified to meet existing legal requirements relative to the status of treasury stock and to the effects upon capital balances when treasury stock is sold or retired.[1]

Acquisition of No-Par Treasury Stock

Previous illustrations assumed the purchase and sale of treasury stock with a par value. The purchase of stock with a stated value provides no new problems; the stated value instead of the par value is used in reducing capital stock or in reporting treasury stock. When there is no stated or par value and the capital stock account has been credited with the proceeds from stock issued at different prices, a special problem arises. Under these circumstances, the capital stock offset is usually considered to be either (1) the original issuing price of the particular lot

---

[1]In practice, the cost method appears to be the preferred method for recording treasury stock. In 1975, 357 of the companies reported in *Accounting Trends & Techniques* used this approach for common stock and 70 used the par or stated value approach. *Accounting Trends & Techniques* (30th ed.; New York: American Institute of Certified Public Accountants, 1976), p. 189.

reacquired, or (2) the weighted average price at which the stock of the company was originally sold. For example, assume no-par stock has been issued as follows:

2,000 shares @ $18	$36,000
2,000 shares @ $20	40,000
1,000 shares @ $22	22,000
5,000 shares	$98,000

Assume 1,000 shares are reacquired at $16.50. The acquisition is identified as the second lot sold, and treasury stock is to be recorded at the original issuing price. The following entry is made:

Treasury Stock	20,000	
Cash		16,500
Paid-In Capital from Capital Stock Reacquisition		3,500

Assume treasury stock is to be recorded at the average issuing price. The average price per share is calculated as follows:

$98,000 (proceeds from sales) ÷ 5,000 (number of shares issued) = $19.60

The entry to record the acquisition would be:

Treasury Stock	19,600	
Cash		16,500
Paid-In Capital from Capital Stock Reacquisition		3,100

Conclusions Relative to Treasury Stock Transactions

From the discussion of treasury stock and the presentation of the different methods that may be followed when treasury stock is purchased, the current approaches may be summarized as follows:

1. Treasury stock is rarely includible as an asset on corporation books and does not qualify for dividends.
2. Neither gain nor loss can be recognized on the income statement relative to transactions in a company's own stock.
3. Retained earnings can be decreased as a result of capital transactions; however, retained earnings cannot be increased through such transactions.
4. In most states, retained earnings equal to the cost of treasury stock is legally unavailable for dividends. This restriction on retained earnings is reported on the balance sheet by an appropriation of retained earnings, by parenthetical remark, or by a note to the financial statements.
5. The total stockholders' equity is not affected by the method used; however, the amounts reported for paid-in capital and retained earnings can be affected by the recording procedure followed.

DONATED STOCK

Treasury stock may be acquired by donation from the stockholders. Shares may be donated to raise company working capital through their sale. In other instances, shares may be donated to eliminate a deficit. Ordinarily, all of the stockholders participate in the donation, each party donating a certain percentage of holdings so that relative interests in the corporation remain unchanged.

Donations of stock are sometimes found where large blocks of stock were originally issued in exchange for properties of uncertain values, for example, mining properties, patents, and leaseholds. Such stock, which is considered fully paid, may be resold at any price without involving the purchaser in a possible liability to creditors for the difference between par and a lower purchase price. Such a donation may represent a sacrifice on the part of the donors of the stock; frequently, however, it represents no more than return of a stock overissue. The issuance of an excessive number of shares of stock for properties and the subsequent donation of stock that may be sold without a discount liability has been referred to as *treasury stock subterfuge*.

In the absence of any cost, the acquisition of treasury stock by donation may be reported on the corporation books by a memorandum entry. Assuming the assets of the company have been fairly valued, the sale of donated stock is then recorded by a debit to Cash and a credit to Donated Capital. If assets of the company have been overvalued, however, it would be improper to recognize an increase in capital arising from the sale of donated shares. Under these circumstances, the sale price for the stock should be employed as a basis for restating the company assets and paid-in capital.

To illustrate the latter instance, assume the Bonanza Mining Co. is formed to take over the mining properties of partners Clark and Davis, and the corporation issues 10,000 shares of no-par stock to the partners in exchange for the properties. A value of $250,000 is assigned to the properties and an entry is made for the acquisition as follows:

Mining Properties...	250,000	
Capital Stock..		250,000

Shortly after corporate formation, Clark and Davis donate 4,000 shares to the corporation, and the corporation sells these for $15 per share. If $15 can be regarded as a measure of the fair value of the stock exchanged for the properties, properties should be restated at $90,000, or $15 × 6,000, the number of shares actually exchanged for the properties. Upon the sale of the donated shares, then, entries should be made (1) to correct the property account and capital stock for both the stock overissue and the property overvaluation, and (2) to record the sale of the donated shares. These entries are:

Capital Stock..	160,000	
Mining Properties..		160,000
Cash...	60,000	
Capital Stock..		60,000

The balance sheet for the corporation would now show the following balances:

Cash......................................	$60,000	Capital stock, no-par, 10,000	
Mining properties..................	90,000	shares outstanding............	$150,000

The membership of the AICPA has adopted the rule on page 540 relative to the donation of shares to an issuing company.

> ... If capital stock is issued nominally for the acquisition of property and it appears that at about the same time, and pursuant to a previous agreement or understanding, some portion of the stock so issued is donated to the corporation, it is not permissible to treat the par value of the stock nominally issued for the property as the cost of that property. If stock so donated is subsequently sold, it is not permissible to treat the proceeds as a credit to surplus [paid-in capital] of the corporation.[1]

When stock is donated so that a company may cancel a deficit, the company should take formal action to retire donated shares. Upon retirement, Capital Stock is debited for the decrease in legal capital and additional paid-in capital is credited. The deficit can then be applied against the additional paid-in capital balance.

STOCK RIGHTS AND OPTIONS

As discussed in Chapter 14, a company may grant rights and options to buy its stock. These grants generally arise under the following circumstances:

1. A company requiring additional capital may offer stockholders subscription rights to make the purchase of additional shares attractive to them.
2. A company may provide subscription rights with the issue of various classes of securities to promote the sale of these securities.
3. A company may offer promoters, officers, or employees special subscription rights or options as compensation for services or other contributions.

Rights to purchase stock are evidenced by certificates called *stock purchase warrants*. The rights enable their owners to purchase shares at a specified price or a variable price dependent upon future events. The period for exercise is usually limited. Because the rights are represented by separate purchase warrants, they also have a market value and are traded on the exchange. The rights have a value because of the difference between the exercise price of the right as compared with a higher market value for the security, either present or potential.

The accounting problems faced by the issuing company under each of the circumstances listed above are described in the following paragraphs.

Rights Issued to Existing Stockholders

When rights are issued to stockholders, only a memorandum entry is made on the issuing company's books stating the number of shares that may be claimed under the outstanding rights. This information is required so the corporation may retain sufficient unissued or reacquired stock to meet the exercise of the rights. Upon surrender of the rights and payments as specified by the rights, the stock is issued. At this time a memorandum entry is made to record the decrease in the number of rights outstanding accompanied by an entry to record the stock sale. The entry for the sale depends upon the amount paid for the shares:

---

[1]*Accounting Research and Terminology Bulletins — Final Edition*, "No. 43, Restatement and Revision of Accounting Research Bulletins," *op. cit.*, par. 4.

1. When the cash received in the exercise of rights is less than par or stated value, the difference must be debited to Retained Earnings; retained earnings are permanently capitalized under these conditions.
2. When the cash received is equal to the par or stated value of the stock, Cash is debited and Capital Stock is credited.
3. When the cash received is more than the par or the stated value of the stock, the excess is recorded as a credit to Premium on Capital Stock or Paid-In Capital from Sale of Capital Stock at More Than Stated Value.

Usually the time period to exercise this type of right is very limited. As indicated in Chapter 14, some state laws require corporations to give existing stockholders first right to purchase new issues of stock to protect their percentage ownership in the business. This is known as the stock-holders' *preemptive right*. Because this process is often cumbersome and time consuming, corporate articles of incorporation are frequently written to limit this right.

Information concerning outstanding rights should be reported on the balance sheet so the effects of the exercise of future rights may be ascertained.

Rights Issued with Various Classes of Securities

When rights are issued with various classes of securities, such as debt or preferred stock, separate stock purchase warrants are issued to accompany the basic security. As described in Chapter 15, the Accounting Principles Board in Opinion No. 14 recommended assigning part of the issuance price of debt to any detachable stock purchase warrants and classifying it as part of the owners' equity.[1] The value assigned to the warrants is the relative fair market value of the warrants to the fair market value of the security without the warrants plus the fair market value of the warrants. Although Opinion No. 14 is directed only to warrants attached to debt, it appears logical to extend the conclusions of that Opinion to warrants attached to preferred stock. Thus, if a market value does exist for the purchase warrants at the issuance date, a separate equity account is credited with that portion of the issuance price assigned to the warrants. If the rights are exercised, the value assigned to the common stock is the value assigned to the warrants plus the cash proceeds from the issuance of the common stock. If the rights are allowed to lapse because of a change in stock market conditions, the value assigned to the warrants may be transferred to a permanent paid-in capital account.

Accounting for rights attached to a preferred stock issue is illustrated as follows: assume the Matson Co. sells 1,000 shares of $50 par preferred stock for $60 per share. As an incentive for the sale, Matson Co. gives the purchaser separate warrants enabling holders to subscribe to 1,000 shares of $20 par common stock for $25 per share. The rights expire after one year. Immediately following the issuance of the stock, the stock purchase warrants are selling at $5 per warrant. Assume the fair market value of

---

[1]*Opinions of the Accounting Principles Board, No. 14*, "Accounting for Convertible Debt and Debt Issued with Stock Purchase Warrants" (New York: American Institute of Certified Public Accountants, 1969), par. 14.

the preferred stock without the warrant attached is $55. The proceeds of $60,000 should be allocated as follows:

Value Assigned to the Purchase Warrants .... $\frac{\$5}{\$55 + \$5} \times \$60,000 = \$5,000$

The entry to record the sale of the preferred stock with detachable warrants is as follows:

Cash	60,000	
Preferred Stock, $50 par		50,000
Premium on Preferred Stock		5,000
Common Stock Purchase Warrants		5,000

If the rights are exercised, the entry to record the issuance of common stock would be as follows:

Common Stock Purchase Warrants	5,000	
Cash	25,000	
Common Stock		20,000
Premium on Common Stock		10,000

This entry would be the same regardless of the market price of the common stock at the issuance date.

If the rights in the above example were allowed to lapse, the following entry is recommended.

Common Stock Purchase Warrants	5,000	
Paid-In Capital from Lapsed Warrants		5,000

Rights or Options Issued to Employees

Many corporations have adopted various plans, contracts, and other agreements giving employees the opportunity to purchase stock in the employer corporation. These plans may be part of a corporate program to secure equity capital and to spread the ownership to the employee group. They may also be intended as a form of compensation to employees for services rendered to the corporation. Depending upon the principal objectives of the corporation in initiating the plan, plans may be classified as *noncompensatory* or *compensatory*. No special accounting problems arise if the plan is classified as noncompensatory; no compensation is recognized by the employer corporation when the stock is issued — the cash price is the issue price. If the plan is compensatory, compensation may or may not be recorded depending upon the provisions of the issue.

Noncompensatory Plans. Because of the difference in accounting between compensatory and noncompensatory plans, the Accounting Principles Board in Opinion No. 25 identified four characteristics essential in a noncompensatory program.

1. Substantially all full-time employees who meet limited employment qualifications may participate.
2. Stock is offered to eligible employees equally or based on a uniform percentage of salary or wages.

3. The time period for exercise of an option or purchase right is limited to a reasonable period.
4. The discount from the market price of the stock is no greater than would be reasonable in an offer of stock to stockholders or others.[1]

Compensatory Plans. Stock purchase plans not meeting the four characteristics of noncompensatory plans are classified as compensatory plans. The major accounting questions associated with compensatory plans are: (1) what amount, if any, should be recognized as compensation, and (2) what periods should be charged with the cost? Opinion No. 25 specifies that "compensation for services that a corporation receives as consideration for stock issued through employee stock option plans should be measured by the quoted market price of the stock at the measurement date, less the amount, if any, that the employee is required to pay."[2]

If a quoted market price is not available, the best estimate of the market value should be used. Most of the accounting controversy with compensatory plans has been determining the measurement date. The AICPA Committee on Accounting Procedures has pointed out that six dates may be considered for this purpose: (1) the date of the adoption of an option plan; (2) the date on which an option is granted to a specific individual; (3) the date on which the grantee has performed any conditions precedent to exercise of the option; (4) the date on which the grantee may first exercise the option; (5) the date on which the option is exercised by the grantee; and (6) the date on which the grantee disposes of the stock acquired.[3]

Additional date options are available if the purchase plan includes variable factors depending on future events; for example, a plan that awards a variable number of shares of stock as an option with a variable option price.

The Accounting Principles Board has considered these options and has defined the measurement date as the first date on which are known both (1) the number of shares that an individual employee is entitled to receive, and (2) the option or purchase price, if any.[4] For many plans, that date is the date of the option agreement. However, plans with variable terms would use a later measurement date. It is felt that this is the date on which the company acknowledges the claim and takes action precluding any alternative use of the shares covered by the option. Dates prior to this time are not pertinent: plans calling for services are no more than proposed courses of action until services are formally recognized and the liability becomes effective. Dates after this time are not pertinent: changes in the values of the compensation award after its accrual are beyond the scope of the plan and represent matters of concern only to

---

[1]*Opinions of the Accounting Principles Board, No. 25*, "Accounting for Stock Issued to Employees" (New York: American Institute of Certified Public Accountants, 1972), par. 7.

[2]*Ibid.*, par. 10.

[3]*Accounting Research and Terminology Bulletins — Final Edition*, "No. 43, Restatement and Revision of Accounting Research Bulletins," *op. cit.*, Ch. 13, sec. B, par. 6.

[4]*Opinions of the Accounting Principles Board, No. 25, op. cit.*, par. 10b.

the grantee. Thus, a corporation will recognize compensation expense for compensatory plans unless the employee pays an amount at least equal to the quoted market price at the measurement date.

The other date for valuing an option that has received strong support from some members of the accounting profession is the exercisable date, the date on which the grantee may first exercise the option. The argument supporting this view is that prior to the exercisable date, the employee has no right to exercise the option and thus is unable to appraise its value. The rights are given with the anticipation of a rise in market and if such condition does occur, the intended compensation is realized. A difficult measurement problem exists with the exercisable date, however, since the market price at the exercisable date is unknown until it is reached. Thus, the total amount of compensation is uncertain and it would be difficult to determine compensation for the periods between the measurement date and the exercisable date. This difficulty has resulted in the rejection of this alternative.

If compensation expense is to be recognized, the remaining accounting problem is the determination of what period should be charged for the cost. Generally, the compensation should be charged to the current and future periods in which the employee performs the services for which the stock is issued. Past periods should not be adjusted. The grant may specify the period or periods during which the service is to be performed, or it may be inferred from the past pattern of grants or awards. When several periods of employment are involved before the stock is issued, the employer corporation should accrue compensation expense in each period involved. If the measurement date is later than the award date, the compensation expense each period must be estimated based upon the quoted market price of the stock at the end of each period.[1] If stock is issued before some or all of the services are performed, part of the consideration received should be recorded in an unearned compensation account. Because it is related to issued stock, this account should be classified as a separate reduction of stockholders' equity rather than as a deferred charge in the asset section.

Options are sometimes issued as a payment for services that should be capitalized. For example, the employee receiving the option may be involved in producing specialized equipment for the company's own use, or in producing specialized inventory. In these cases, the appropriate asset account should be debited for the implicit value of the services included in the option. Upon exercise of the options, the sum of the cash received and the value previously assigned to options represents the consideration related to the issue of the stock.

Illustrative Entries for Recording Compensatory Stock Options. Accounting for compensatory plans can be illustrated by the following examples: Assume on December 31, 1974, the board of directors of the Laredo Co. authorizes the grant of nontransferable stock options to supplement the

---

[1] *Ibid.*, par. 13.

salaries of certain executives. Options permit the purchase of 10,000 shares of $10 par common stock at a price of $47.50. Stock is currently selling at $50. Options can be exercised beginning January 1, 1977, but only if executives are still in the employ of the company; options expire at the end of 1978. All of the options are exercised on December 31, 1977, when the $10 par stock is quoted on the market at $60.

The value of the stock options at the date of the grant (compensation expense) is determined as follows:

Market value of common stock on December 31, 1974, 10,000 shares at $50	$500,000
Option price, 10,000 shares at $47.50	475,000
Value of stock options (compensation expense)	$ 25,000

The terms of the grant indicate that the services are being performed for the period from the grant date to the exercisable date, or for 1975 and 1976.

The following entries are made by the corporation to record the grant of the options, the annual accrual of option rights, and the exercise of the options.

TRANSACTION	ENTRY
December 31, 1974 Grant of nontransferable stock options.	(Memorandum entry) Granted nontransferable options to executives for the purchase of 10,000 shares of common stock at $47.50. Options are exercisable beginning January 1, 1977, providing officers are in the employ of the company on that date. Options expire on December 31, 1978. Value of options on December 31, 1974, is $25,000 (market value of stock, $500,000; option price, $475,000).
December 31, 1975 To record compensation and option credit accrual for 1975: value of stock options, $25,000; period of service covered by plan, 1975 and 1976; cost assigned to 1975: ½ × $25,000 = $12,500.	Executive Compensation Expense. 12,500 Credit Under Stock Option Plan.. 12,500
December 31, 1976 To record compensation and option credit accrual for 1976: ½ × $25,000 = $12,500.	Executive Compensation Expense. 12,500 Credit Under Stock Option Plan.. 12,500

December 31, 1977
To record exercise of stock options: cash received for stock, 10,000 shares at $47.50, or $475,000; par value of stock issued, 10,000 shares at $10, or $100,000.
	Cash 475,000
	Credit Under Stock Option Plan 25,000
	   Common Stock............................ 100,000
	   Premium on Common Stock 400,000

The accrued compensation reported in Credit Under Stock Option Plan is properly reported as a part of paid-in capital because it will be liquidated by the issuance of stock. If options expire through a failure of employees to meet the conditions of the option or through changes in the price of the stock making exercise of options unattractive, the balance of the account should be eliminated by decreasing compensation expense in the period of forfeiture.[1]

---

[1]*Ibid.*, par. 15.

If the grant provisions offered by Laredo Co. were variable and the measurement date occurred after the option date, different entries would be required. Assume on December 31, 1974, the executives of Laredo Co. are given the right to purchase 10,000 shares of $10 par stock at 80% of the market price on December 31, 1976, two years after the grant date. In order to be eligible for the stock, the executives must remain with the company until the exercisable date, December 31, 1977. The market price for the stock is as follows: December 31, 1974, date of grant, $50; December 31, 1975, end of first year of service period, $60; December 31, 1976, end of second year of service period, $65; and December 31, 1977, exercisable date, $80.

The following entries would be made to record the annual accruals of option rights and the exercise of the options:

TRANSACTION	ENTRY		
December 31, 1975 To record estimate of compensation expense accrual for 1975: market price of stock, December 31, 1975, $60; option price, 80% of $60, or $48; estimated value of option per share, $12 ($60 − $48); total, $120,000 ($12 × 10,000). Period of services rendered, three years or $40,000 each year.	Executive Compensation Expense. Credit Under Stock Option Plan..	40,000	40,000
December 31, 1976 To record estimate of compensation expense accrual for 1976: market price of stock, December 31, 1976, $65; estimated option price, 80% of $65, or $52. Value of option per share, $13 ($65 − $52); total, $130,000 ($13 × 10,000). Compensation recognized 1975, $40,000. Compensation to be recognized 1976 and 1977, $90,000, or $45,000 per year.	Executive Compensation Expense. Credit Under Stock Option Plan..	45,000	45,000
December 31, 1977 To record compensation expense for 1977 and issuance of stock.	Executive Compensation Expense. Credit Under Stock Option Plan..	45,000	45,000
	Cash .... Credit Under Stock Option Plan ..... Common Stock............................. Premium on Common Stock	520,000 130,000	100,000 550,000

Income Tax Treatment of Compensatory Stock Plans. The detailed nature of stock option plans offered by employers are greatly affected by the provisions of the Internal Revenue Code in effect at the time the options are granted. Compensatory plans have frequently been awarded to key executives whose cash salaries place them in higher tax rate brackets. Before 1976, if the plan met certain conditions, it was classified by the Code as a *qualified plan* and some or all of the benefits received by the executives were deferred beyond the period of exercising the option. Subsequent sale of stock purchased through options in a qualified plan were taxed at lower capital gain rates.

For many years, qualified plans were the most common type of stock option plan offered to key executives by corporate employers. However, as the tax benefits of such plans were reduced, especially for executives in the higher income brackets, many plans for key executives were non-qualified and thus involved a recognition of compensation expense for the difference between the option price and the market price at the measurement date. The erosion of the attractiveness of qualified stock options was made complete by the Tax Reform Act of 1976 that repealed qualified stock option benefits for all options granted after May 20, 1976.

Disclosure of Stock Options   When stock option plans are in existence, disclosure should be made as to the status of the option or plan at the end of the period of report, including the number of shares under option, the option price, and the number of shares which were exercisable. Information on options exercised should also be provided, including the number of shares exercised and the option price.

STOCK CONVERSIONS

Stockholders may be permitted by the terms of their stock agreement or by special action by the corporation to exchange their holdings for stock of other classes. No gain or loss is recognized on these conversions because it is the exchange of one equity for another. In certain instances, the exchanges may affect only corporate paid-in capital accounts; in other instances, the exchanges may affect both paid-in capital and retained earnings accounts.

To illustrate the different conditions, assume that the capital of the Washington Corporation on December 31, 1977, is as follows:

Preferred stock, $100 par, 10,000 shares	$1,000,000
Premium on preferred stock	100,000
Common stock, $25 stated value, 100,000 shares	2,500,000
Paid-in capital from sale of common stock at more than stated value	500,000
Retained earnings	1,000,000

Preferred shares are convertible into common shares at any time at the option of the shareholder.

Case 1 — Assume conditions of conversion permit the exchange of each share of preferred for 4 shares of common. On December 31, 1977, 1,000 shares of preferred stock are exchanged on the above basis. The amount originally paid for the preferred, $110,000, is now the consideration identified with 4,000 shares of common stock with a total stated value of $100,000. The conversion is recorded as follows:

Preferred Stock, $100 par	100,000	
Premium on Preferred Stock	10,000	
Common Stock, $25 stated value		100,000
Paid-In Capital from Conversion of Preferred Stock into Common Stock		10,000

Case 2 — Assume conditions of conversion permit the exchange of each share of preferred for 5 shares of common. In converting 1,000 shares of preferred for common, an increase in common stock of $125,000 must be recognized although it is accompanied by a decrease in the preferred equity of only $110,000;

the increase in the legal capital related to the new issue can be accomplished only by a debit to Retained Earnings. The conversion, then, is recorded as follows:

Preferred Stock, $100 par	100,000	
Premium on Preferred Stock	10,000	
Retained Earnings	15,000	
Common Stock, $25 stated value		125,000

The problems relating to the conversion of bonds for capital stock were described in Chapter 15. When either stocks or bonds have conversion rights, the company must be in a position to issue securities of the required class. Unissued or reacquired securities may be maintained by the company for this purpose. Detailed information should be given on the balance sheet relative to security conversion features as well as the means for meeting conversion requirements.

RECAPITALIZATIONS

Corporate recapitalization occurs when an entire issue of stock is changed by appropriate action of the corporation. In some states, recapitalizations, including changes in the legal capital, are possible by action of the board of directors and stockholders; in other states, recapitalizations also require the approval of state authorities.

A common type of recapitalization is a change from par to no-par stock. If the capital stock balance is to remain the same after the change, the original capital stock account is closed and an account for the new issue is opened. Any premium relating to the original stock issue should be transferred to some other paid-in capital account appropriately labeled. If the capital stock balance is to exceed the consideration received on the original sale of the stock, a new capital stock account is credited for the value assigned to the new issue, original paid-in capital balances are closed, and the retained earnings account is debited for the difference. If the capital stock balance is to be reduced, the original account, as well as any premium account, is closed, a new capital stock account is credited for the value assigned to the new stock, and an appropriately titled paid-in capital account is credited for the difference.

To illustrate, assume capital for the Signal Corporation as follows:

Capital stock, $10 par, 100,000 shares	$1,000,000
Premium on capital stock	100,000
Retained earnings	250,000

Entries for each of the three possibilities follow:

Case 1 — Assume the original stock is exchanged for no-par stock with a stated value of $10:

Capital Stock, $10 par	1,000,000	
Premium on Capital Stock	100,000	
Capital Stock, $10 stated value		1,000,000
Paid-In Capital from Exchange of Par for No-Par Stock		100,000

Case 2 — Assume the original stock is exchanged for no-par stock with a stated value of $12.50:

Capital Stock, $10 par...	1,000,000	
Premium on Capital Stock...	100,000	
Retained Earnings..	150,000	
Capital Stock, $12.50 stated value....................................		1,250,000

Case 3 — Assume the original stock is exchanged for no-par stock with a stated value of $5:

Capital Stock, $10 par...	1,000,000	
Premium on Capital Stock...	100,000	
Capital Stock, $5 stated value...		500,000
Paid-In Capital from Reduction in Value Assigned to		
Capital Stock...		600,000

Recapitalizations involving changes in the stated values of no-par stock or changes from no-par stock to stock with a par value call for similar procedures.

QUASI-REORGANIZATION

A situation may arise in which a company's properties were acquired at costs that do not permit earnings under current conditions. There may also be a deficit from previous operations or a retained earnings balance insufficient to absorb a reduction in the carrying value of the property items. Yet such a reduction may be warranted by current conditions and indeed may be necessary if the company is to be able to report profitable operations in future periods. The company erred in acquiring property which could not be employed profitably in the business, but it should be recognized that a mistake was made and that the future operations of the company should not be burdened with past mistakes.

Under such circumstances a company may elect to write down property items and to accompany such action with a restatement of the capital structure, eliminating the deficit found after the write-off. The elimination of a deficit through a restatement of invested capital balances providing, in effect, a fresh start accounting-wise on the part of the corporation, is called a *quasi-reorganization* or *corporate readjustment*. The quasi-reorganization procedure does not require recourse to the courts as in formal reorganization procedures; there is no change in the legal corporate entity or interruption in business activity.

To illustrate the nature of a quasi-reorganization, assume the Baldwin Corporation has suffered losses from operations for some time and both current and future revenues appear to be insufficient to cover the depreciation on properties acquired when prices were considerably higher than at present. The company decides upon a restatement of assets and also the restatement of paid-in capital to remove the deficit and make possible the declaration of dividends upon a return to profitable operations. A balance sheet for the company just prior to this action is given at the top of page 550.

The quasi-reorganization is to be accomplished as follows:

1. Land, buildings, and equipment are to be reduced to their present fair market value of $600,000 by reductions in the asset and accumulated depreciation balances of 33⅓%.

Baldwin Corporation
Balance Sheet
June 30, 1977

Assets			Liabilities and Stockholders' Equity		
Current assets..........		$ 250,000	Liabilities		$ 300,000
Land, buildings, and			Capital stock, $10		
equipment............	$1,500,000		par, 100,000		
Less accumulated			shares...................	$1,000,000	
depreciation......	600,000	900,000	Less deficit..............	150,000	850,000
			Total liabilities and		
			stockholders' eq-		
Total assets		$1,150,000	uity........................		$1,150,000

2. Capital stock is to be reduced to a par of $5, $500,000 in capital stock thus being converted into "additional paid-in capital."
3. The deficit of $450,000 ($150,000 as reported on the balance sheet increased by $300,000 arising from the write-down of land, buildings, and equipment) is to be applied against the capital from the reduction of the par value of stock.

Entries to record the changes follow:

TRANSACTION	ENTRY		
(1) To write down land, buildings, and equipment and accumulated depreciation balances by 33⅓%.	Retained Earnings (Deficit).......... Accumulated Depreciation........... Land, Buildings, and Equipment..	300,000 200,000	500,000
(2) To reduce the capital stock balance from $10 par to $5 par and to establish paid-in capital from reduction in stock par value.	Capital Stock, $10 par.................. Capital Stock, $5 par................. Paid-In Capital from Reduction in Stock Par Value....................	1,000,000	500,000 500,000
(3) To apply the deficit after asset devaluation against paid-in capital from reduction in stock par value.	Paid-In Capital from Reduction in Stock Par Value........................ Retained Earnings (Deficit)	450,000	450,000

The balance sheet after the quasi-reorganization is shown below:

Baldwin Corporation
Balance Sheet
June 30, 1977

Assets			Liabilities and Stockholders' Equity	
Current assets..........		$250,000	Liabilities	$300,000
Land, buildings, and			Capital stock, $5 par, 100,000	
equipment............	$1,000,000		shares.....................................	500,000
Less accumulated			Paid-in capital from reduction	
depreciation......	400,000	600,000	in stock par value	50,000
			Total liabilities and stockhold-	
Total assets		$850,000	ers' equity	$850,000

Following the quasi-reorganization, the accounting for the company's operations is similar to that for a new company. Earnings subsequent to the quasi-reorganization, however, should be accumulated in a *dated retained earnings* account. On future balance sheets, retained earnings dated as of the time of account readjustment will inform readers of the date of such action and of the fresh start in earnings accumulation.

The AICPA Committee on Accounting Procedure has recommended that a company electing to bring about a legitimate restatement of its assets, capital stock, and retained earnings through a quasi-reorganization, relieving future income or retained earnings of charges that would otherwise be made against these, should meet the following conditions:

1. It should make a clear report to stockholders of the proposed changes and should obtain their formal consent.
2. It should present a fair balance sheet with a reasonably complete restatement of values so that there will be no continuation of the circumstances that justify charges to invested capital.
3. Assets should be carried forward as of the date of the quasi-reorganization at fair and not unduly conservative amounts, determined with due regard for the accounting to be employed thereafter. Excessive writedowns that will result in the overstatement of earnings or retained earnings on the ultimate realization of assets should be avoided.[1]

The Committee recognized that in some cases the fair value of an asset or the amount of potential losses or charges cannot be measured satisfactorily as of the date of a quasi-reorganization and estimates of asset and liability values will be required. In such cases, material differences between book values and ultimate realization or liquidation amounts that cannot be attributed to events or circumstances originating after the date of the readjustment should not be recognized as losses but should be reported as corrections identified with the readjustment.

STOCK SPLITS AND REVERSE STOCK SPLITS

When the market price of shares is high and it is felt that a lower price will result in a better market and a wider distribution of ownership, a corporation may authorize the shares outstanding to be replaced by a larger number of shares. For example, 100,000 shares of stock, par value $100, are called in and exchanged for 500,000 shares of stock, par value $20. Each stockholder receives 5 new shares for each share owned. The increase in shares outstanding in this manner is known as a *stock split* or *stock split-up*. The reverse procedure, replacement of shares outstanding by a smaller number of shares, may be desirable when the price of shares is low and it is felt there may be certain advantages in having a higher price for shares. The reduction of shares outstanding by combining shares is referred to as a *reverse stock split* or a *stock split-down*.

After a stock split or reverse stock split, the capital stock balance remains the same; however, the change in the number of shares of stock outstanding is accompanied by a change in the par or stated value of the stock. The change in the number of shares outstanding, as well as the change in the par or stated value, may be recorded by means of a memorandum entry. However, it would normally be desirable to establish a new account reporting the nature and the amount of the new issue. In

---

[1]*Accounting Research and Terminology Bulletins — Final Edition*, "No. 43, Restatement and Revision of Accounting Research Bulletins" (New York: American Institute of Certified Public Accountants, 1961), Ch. 7, sec. A.

any event, notations will be required in the subsidiary stockholders ledger to report the exchange of stock and the change in the number of shares held by each stockholder.

Stock splits are sometimes effected by issuing a large stock dividend. In this case, the par value of the stock is not changed and an amount equal to the par value of the newly issued shares is transferred to the capital account from either additional paid-in capital or from retained earnings. A further discussion of this type of stock split is included in Chapter 20.

PAID-IN CAPITAL NOT DESIGNATED AS LEGAL CAPITAL

Although it is common practice to report on the balance sheet a single value for additional paid-in capital, separate accounts should be provided in the ledger to identify the individual sources of such capital. Sources of additional paid-in capital and the accounts summarizing these are listed below.

SOURCE	ADDITIONAL PAID-IN CAPITAL ACCOUNT
Sale of stock at more than par value	Premium on Capital Stock (or Paid-In Capital from Sale of Stock at More Than Par)
Sale of stock at more than stated value	Paid-In Capital from Sale of Capital Stock at More Than Stated Value
Stock subscription defaults resulting in forfeiture of amounts paid in	Paid-In Capital from Forfeited Stock Subscriptions
Assessments levied on stockholders	Paid-In Capital from Capital Stock Assessments (except where stock was originally sold at a discount and stock assessments are considered to be proper credits to such discount)
Reacquisition of stock at less than original sales price	Paid-In Capital from Capital Stock Reacquisition (or Paid-In Capital from Capital Stock Redemption)
Conversion of outstanding stock into a new issue with a smaller total par or stated value	Paid-In Capital from Conversion of Capital Stock
Reduction in corporate stated capital as a result of recapitalization	Paid-In Capital from Reduction in Value Assigned to Capital Stock
Sale of treasury stock at more than cost	Paid-In Capital from Sale of Treasury Stock at More Than Cost
Donation of stock or properties or forgiveness of corporate indebtedness by stockholders	Donated (or Paid-In) Capital from Contributions by Stockholders
Donation of properties or forgiveness of corporate indebtedness by governmental authorities or other outsiders	Donated (or Paid-In) Capital from Contributions by Governmental Authority (or others)

Debits should be made to paid-in capital balances only when (1) transactions may be regarded as reducing such balances, or (2) there is an express authorization by the board of directors for such reduction. To illustrate (1) above, the redemption and retirement of a preferred stock issue may properly be recorded by cancellation of the preferred stock balance as well as any other paid-in capital balance relating to the original issue; all reference to paid-in capital relating to the preferred stock is thus canceled with the redemption of this class of stock. To illustrate (2) on page 552, authorization by the board of directors for the capitalization of a portion of a particular paid-in capital balance would call for a reduction in the additional paid-in capital account and an increase in the capital stock account.

Paid-in capital balances should not be charged with losses whether from normal operations or from extraordinary sources, nor should such paid-in capital be used for the cancellation of a deficit in the absence of formal steps taken to effect a quasi-reorganization. The membership of the AICPA adopted the following rule on this matter:

> ... Capital surplus, however created, should not be used to relieve the income account of the current or future years of charges which would otherwise fall to be made thereagainst. This rule might be subject to the exception that where, upon reorganization, a reorganized company would be relieved of charges which would require to be made against income if the existing corporation were continued, it might be regarded as permissible to accomplish the same result without reorganization provided the facts were as fully revealed to and the action as formally approved by the shareholders as in reorganization.[1]

The availability as a basis for dividends of paid-in capital not designated as legal capital depends upon the laws of the state of incorporation. In the absence of legal restrictions, paid-in capital can be used as a basis for dividends. Laws may provide restrictions upon the use of all of the paid-in capital or upon the use of only certain kinds of paid-in capital. Separate accounts in the ledger summarizing paid-in capital by source make possible the ready determination of distributable capital. When capital other than retained earnings is used as a basis for dividends, stockholders should be informed by the corporation concerning the source of such distribution, since stockholders have the right to assume that dividends represent distributions of earnings unless they are notified to the contrary.

---

[1]*Ibid.*, Ch. 1, sec. A, par. 2.

QUESTIONS

1. The controller for the Scott Co. contends that the redemption of preferred stock at less than its issuance price should be reported as an increase in retained earnings since redemption at more than issuance price calls for a decrease in retained earnings. How would you answer this argument?

2. Why might a company purchase its own stock?

3. What is the purpose of legislation limiting the purchase by a company of its own stock to its retained earnings balance?

4. The Waters Co. reports treasury stock as a current asset, explaining that it intends to sell the stock soon to acquire working capital. Do you approve of this reporting?

5. The Accounting Principles Board suggests alternate methods for the reacquisition and retirement by a company of its own shares at more than par or stated value. What are the alternate methods and what support can you give for each?

6. (a) Describe two approaches that may be taken in recording the reacquisition of treasury stock. (b) What are the entries in each case assuming: (1) the stock is purchased at more than its par or stated value; (2) the stock is purchased at less than its par or stated value?

7. There is frequently a difference between the purchase price and the sales price of treasury stock. Why isn't this difference properly shown as an income statement item, especially in view of the APB opinions which restrict entries to Retained Earnings?

8. Describe, in order of preference, alternative methods of accounting for the receipt and immediate disposition of donated treasury stock which was originally issued at its fair market value and had no aspects of a treasury stock subterfuge.

9. The Walsh Co. issues 10,000,000 shares of no-par common stock in exchange for certain mineral lands. Property is established on the books at $5,000,000. Shortly thereafter, stockholders donate to the corporation 20% of their shares. The stock is resold by the company at 10¢ per share. What accounting problems arise as a result of the stock donation and resale?

10. (a) What entries should be made on the books when stock rights are issued to stockholders? (b) What entries should be made when stock is issued on rights? (c) What information, if any, should appear on the balance sheet relative to outstanding rights?

11. What characteristics are essential for a stock-option plan to be classified as noncompensatory?

12. Under what conditions would a compensatory stock option program for key executives not result in a charge to compensation expense upon exercise of the option?

13. Some users of accounting reports believe that net income is overstated on certain income statements because of the currently accepted procedure for recording employee stock options. (a) Describe how the net income may be overstated. (b) What alternative procedures would more satisfactorily match revenue and expense?

14. What determines the measurement date for purposes of a stock option valuation?

15. What accounting periods should be charged for compensation expense recognized upon the exercise of stock options?

16. What tax benefits are available to employees if a stock option plan initiated before May 20, 1976, meets the Internal Revenue Service requirements for a qualified stock option plan?

17. Preferred stockholders of the Beacon Corporation exchange their holdings for no-par common stock in accordance with terms of the preferred issue. How should this conversion be reported on the corporation books?

18. The president of Meyer Corporation, your client, has asked you for an explanation of a quasi-reorganization. He is unfamiliar with the procedure and is concerned that a competitor might have an advantage since undergoing a quasi-reorganization. Prepare a report for the president explaining the quasi-reorganization. Your report should include the following parts:

  (a) Definition and accounting features of the procedure.
  (b) The purposes of the procedure and the conditions under which it should be considered.
  (c) The authorization necessary.
  (d) The disclosure required in the financial statements.
  (e) Does the competitor have an advantage? Discuss briefly.

19. Define a stock split and identify the major objectives of this corporate action.

20. The Mellon Corporation was formed in July, 1977. At date of incorporation it issued $1,000,000 of $100 par value common stock at par for cash. Operations during the remainder of 1977 resulted in net income of $75,000. At a directors' meeting in January, 1978, it was decided that $700,000 of contributed capital would be adequate to meet foreseeable operating needs and provide for reasonable expansion. The following individual suggestions were made to provide for the excess capitalization:

  (a) Reduce shares from $100 to $70 par value.
  (b) Invest $300,000 of excess cash in the company's own shares.
  (c) Distribute a cash dividend of $30 per share.
  (d) Resort to a quasi-reorganization and write down various assets by $300,000.

In your opinion, how sound is each of these suggestions in accomplishing the desired purpose?

EXERCISES

1. The Willich Co. reported the following balances related to an issuance of common stock:

Common Stock, $10 par, 25,000 shares issued and outstanding $250,000
Premium on Common Stock 50,000

On June 1, 1977, and December 31, 1977, the company purchased and retired 5,000 shares at $14 and 10,000 shares at $9 respectively. Give the entries to record the acquisition and retirement of the common stock.

2. The capital accounts for the Williams Co. were as follows on June 1, 1977:

Common Stock, $15 par, 80,000 shares $1,200,000
Premium on Common Stock 160,000
Retained Earnings 300,000

On this date the company purchased 5,000 shares of stock at $16; and in December of the same year it sold this stock at $19. (a) What entries should be made for the stock purchase and the sale if the purchase is viewed as a capital stock retirement and treasury stock is reported at par? (If alternate treatments are possible, justify your selection.) (b) What entries should be made for the stock purchase and the sale if the purchase is viewed as giving rise to a capital element awaiting ultimate disposition and treasury stock is reported at cost? (c) After the sale of the treasury stock, how does the stockholders' equity differ under the two methods?

3. The Yoshi Company issued 20,000 shares of no-par stock at $32 and 40,000 shares at $50. The state in which Yoshi is incorporated does not require any stated capital. During 1977, 4,000 shares were reacquired at $42. Assume the treasury stock is to be carried at the weighted average price per share. Prepare the journal entry to record the reacquisition.

4. The assets of the Meed Company are properly valued at $5,000,000. The outstanding common stock of the company is no-par with a stated value of $15. The principal shareholders donated 20,000 shares of stock on June 30, 1977, when the market value was $23. The shares were then resold on September 15, 1977, at $25. Give the entries to record the donation and resale of the treasury stock.

5. In your first audit of a mining company, you note the following facts with respect to its capital stock transactions:

Authorized capital consists of 5,000,000 shares of $1 par value common stock.
All of the shares were issued initially in exchange for certain mineral properties. The properties were recorded on the company books at $10,000,000.
Two million shares were received by the company as a donation shortly after incorporation and were sold immediately for cash of $3,000,000. This amount was recorded as a credit to Donated Capital.

(a) What values should be assigned to the mineral properties and the stockholders' equity? Discuss. (b) Prepare any required correcting entry.

6. The Gividen Company needs to raise additional equity capital. After analysis of the available options, the company decides to issue 1,000 shares of $100 par preferred stock with detachable warrants attached. The package of the stock and warrants sells for 108. The warrants enable the holder to purchase 1,000 shares of $25 par common stock at $30 per share. Immediately following the issuance of the stock, the stock purchase warrants are selling at $8 per share. The market value of the preferred stock without the warrants is 102. What journal entries would be required to record the sale of the stock and subsequent use of the warrants to purchase the common stock? Round answers to the nearest dollar.

7. The stockholders of the Johnson Co. on December 24, 1971, approved a plan granting certain officers of the company nontransferable options to buy 50,000 shares of no-par common at $8 per share. Stock was selling at this time at $10 per share. The option plan provides that the officers must be employed by the company for the next five years, that options can be exercised after January 1, 1977, and that options will expire at the end of 1978. One of the officers who had been granted options for 10,000 shares left the company at the beginning of 1975; remaining officers exercised their rights under the option plan at the end of 1978. Give the entries that should be made on the books of the corporation at the end of each year for 1971–1978 inclusive. The market price of the stock at January 1, 1977, was $15 per share.

8. Capital accounts for the Kelly Co. on December 31 are as follows:

Preferred Stock, $25 par, 25,000 shares issued and outstanding......................	$ 625,000
Premium on Preferred Stock...	31,250
Common Stock, $5 par, 200,000 shares issued and outstanding......................	1,000,000
Premium on Common Stock..	110,000
Retained Earnings..	1,450,000

Preferred stock is convertible into common stock. Give the entry made on the corporation books assuming 1,600 shares of preferred are converted under each assumption listed:

   (a) Preferred shares are convertible into common on a share-for-share basis.
   (b) Each preferred share is convertible into 8 shares of common.
   (c) Each preferred share is convertible into 4 shares of common.

9. The Bullock Company has 10,000 shares of convertible preferred stock, $25 par, and 25,000 shares of common stock, $10 par, outstanding. Proceeds from the sale of the preferred stock and common stock were $280,000 and $250,000 respectively. Give the entries to record the following transactions (consider each transaction as being independent of the others). Assume retained earnings balance is $500,000.

   (a) Each preferred share is converted into 5 shares of common stock.
   (b) Each common stock shareholder receives 2 shares of new no-par common stock with a stated value of $2 in exchange for each share of common stock owned.
   (c) Each common stock shareholder receives 5 shares of new stock, $2 par, in exchange for each share of common stock owned.
   (d) Each common stock shareholder receives 1 share of new $8 par value common stock in exchange for each share of common stock owned.

10. The Luedke Co. reports its stockholders' equity as follows:

Common stock, $10 par, 750,000 shares..	$7,500,000
Additional paid-in capital...	530,000
Deficit..	(880,000)
Total stockholders' equity..	$7,150,000

The company wishes to cancel the deficit and is considering each of the possibilities listed below. Give the entries required and prepare the "Stockholders' equity" section for each assumption.

   (a) Stockholders are to donate 30% of their shares to the company and these are to be formally retired.
   (b) The par value of shares is to be reduced to $7.50.
   (c) One new share of no-par stock is to be exchanged for each share of common stock outstanding and the legal capital for the company is to be restated at $7,150,000.
   (d) One new share of no-par stock with a stated value of $25 is to be exchanged for every three shares of common.

11. From the following information, reconstruct the journal entries that were made by the Gouro Corporation during 1977:

	Dec. 31, 1977		Dec. 31, 1976	
	Amount	Shares	Amount	Shares
Common stock...................................	$175,000	8,750	$150,000	7,500
Premium on common stock............................	62,500		52,500	
Paid-in capital from sale of treasury stock at more than cost..	1,000	200	—	—
Retained earnings...	66,500*	—	39,000	—
Treasury stock..	12,000	300	—	—

*Includes net income for 1977 of $30,000. There were no dividends.

Twenty-five hundred shares of common stock issued when the company was formed were purchased and retired during 1977. The cost method is used to record treasury stock transactions.

12. The Pearson Company has a deficit in retained earnings of $120,000. Business appears to be turning around so the president wants the company to go through a quasi-reorganization. The balance sheet of the company prior to the reorganization contains the following information: current assets, $200,000; land, $100,000; buildings, $300,000; accumulated depreciation, $150,000; liabilities, $220,000; capital stock, $10 par value, $350,000. As part of the reorganization, the building is to be written down to its fair value of $120,000 and the common stock is to be canceled and reissued at $5 par. Give the entries to record the quasi-reorganization.

PROBLEMS

19-1. The capital accounts of the Harris Company were as follows on June 1, 1977:

Preferred 8% Stock, $50 par, 10,000 shares issued and outstanding...............	$ 500,000
Premium on Preferred Stock...	10,000
Common Stock, $15 par, 80,000 shares issued and outstanding.....................	1,200,000
Premium on Common Stock..	240,000
Retained Earnings..	160,000

During the remainder of 1977, the Harris Company called the preferred stock at $55 per share and then retired the stock. Also, the company reacquired 30,000 shares of common stock at $14, and 20,000 of the reacquired common shares were reissued (resold) at $20 per share.

> *Instructions:*
> (1) Give the entries to record the reacquisition and retirement of the preferred stock and the acquisition and reissue of the common stock assuming the common stock is viewed as a capital retirement and the treasury stock account is to be debited.
> (2) Give the entry to record the acquisition and resale of the common stock assuming the common stock purchase is viewed as a capital element awaiting ultimate disposition.

19-2. The Hansen Company has two classes of capital stock outstanding: 8%, $10 par preferred and $50 par common. During the fiscal year ending November 30, 1977, the company was active in transactions affecting the stockholders' equity. The following summarizes these transactions:

Type of Transaction	Number of Shares	Price per Share
(a) Issue of preferred stock...	10,000	$14
(b) Issue of common stock	35,000	50
(c) Retirement of preferred stock.......................................	2,000	16
(d) Purchase of treasury stock — common (reported at cost)	5,000	70
(e) Stock split — common (par value reduced to $25)....................	2 for 1	
(f) Reissue of treasury stock — common	5,000	45

Balances of the accounts in the "Stockholders' equity" section on November 30, 1976, were:

Preferred Stock, 50,000 shares	$ 500,000
Common Stock, 100,000 shares...	5,000,000
Premium on Preferred Stock..	200,000
Premium on Common Stock	1,000,000
Retained Earnings..	520,000

Dividends were paid at the end of the fiscal year on the common stock at $1 per share, and on the preferred stock at the preferred rate. Net income for the year was $500,000.

> *Instructions:* Based upon the above data, prepare the "Stockholders' equity" section of the balance sheet as of November 30, 1977. (Note: A work sheet beginning with November 30, 1976 balances and providing for transactions for the current year will facilitate the preparation of this section of the balance sheet.)

19-3. Transactions of the Shrub Company during 1977, the first year of operations, that affected its stockholders' equity are given at the top of the next page.

(a) Sold 20,000 shares of 9% preferred stock, $10 par, at $14.
(b) Sold 50,000 shares of $25 par common stock at $27.
(c) Purchased and retired 4,000 shares of preferred stock at $15.
(d) Purchased 6,000 shares of its own common stock at $29.
(e) Sold 1,000 shares of treasury stock at $31.
(f) Stockholders donated to the company 4,000 shares of common when shares had a market price of $30. One half of these shares were sold for $35.

No dividends were declared in 1977 and net income for 1977 was $150,000.

Instructions:
(1) Record each of the above transactions. Assume treasury stock acquisitions are recorded at cost.
(2) Give the entries for (d) and (e) assuming treasury stock acquisitions are reported as capital stock retirement.
(3) Prepare the "Stockholders' equity" section of the balance sheet assuming treasury stock is recorded at cost and assuming retained earnings restrictions are shown by parenthetical remarks.
(4) Prepare the "Stockholders' equity" section of the balance sheet assuming treasury stock is recorded at par value and assuming retained earnings restrictions are shown as appropriations.

19-4. The board of directors of the Queen Production Co. adopted a stock option plan to supplement the salaries of certain executives of the company. Options to buy common stock were granted as follows:

	No. of Shares	Option Price	Price of Shares at Date of Grant
Jan. 10, 1974..............John Hancock.....................	75,000	16	17
June 30, 1974..............Donald Norton	50,000	21	22
Maynard Erickson...............	20,000		

Options are nontransferable and can be exercised three years after date of grant providing the executive is still in the employ of the company. Options expire two years after the date they can first be exercised.

Maynard Erickson left the employ of the company at the beginning of 1976.

Stock options were exercised as follows:

	No. of Shares	Price of Shares at Date of Exercise
Jan. 15, 1977.......................John Hancock	60,000	41
Dec. 20, 1977.......................John Hancock	15,000	32
Dec. 22, 1977.......................Donald Norton........................	50,000	28

Stock of the company has a $10 par value. The accounting period for the company is the calendar year.

Instructions: Give all of the entries that would be made on the books of the corporation relative to the stock option agreement for the period 1974 to 1977 inclusive.

19-5. The "Stockholders' equity" section of the Stars, Inc., showed the following data on December 31, 1976: common stock, $25 par, 200,000 shares authorized, 100,000 shares issued and outstanding, $2,500,000; premium on common stock, $300,000; credit under stock option plan, $100,000; retained earnings, $320,000. The stock options were granted to key executives and provided them the right to acquire 20,000 shares of common stock at $30 per share. The stock was selling at $35 at the time the options were granted.

The following transactions occurred during 1977:

Mar. 31 3,000 options outstanding at December 31, 1976, were exercised. The market price per share was $42 at this time.
Apr. 1 The company issued bonds of $1,500,000 at par, giving with each $1,000 bond a warrant enabling the holder to purchase two shares of stock at $35 for a one-year period. The stock was selling for $42 per share at that date.
June 30 The company issued rights to stockholders (one right on each share) permitting holders to acquire for a thirty-day period one share at $40 with every eight

rights submitted. Shares were selling for $45 at this time. All but 7,000 rights were exercised on July 31, and the additional stock was issued.

Sept. 30 All shares were issued in connection with rights issued on the sale of bonds.

Nov. 30 The market price per share dropped to $25 and options came due. Since the market price was below the option price, no remaining options were exercised.

Instructions:

(1) Give entries to record the foregoing transactions.

(2) Prepare the "Stockholders' equity" section of the balance sheet as of December 31, 1977, (assume net income of $175,000 for 1977).

19-6. The Hanford Co., organized on June 1, 1976, was authorized to issue stock as follows:

50,000 shares of preferred 8% stock, convertible, $100 par
200,000 shares of common stock, $10 par

During the remainder of Hanford Co.'s fiscal year, the following transactions were completed in the order given.

(a) 25,000 shares of preferred stock were subscribed for at $105, and 75,000 shares of the common stock were subscribed for at $15. Both subscriptions were payable 50% upon subscription, the balance in one payment.

(b) The second subscription payment was made, except one subscriber for 5,000 shares of common stock defaulted on his payment. The full amount paid by him was returned and all of the fully paid stock was issued.

(c) 10,000 shares of common stock were reacquired by purchase at $8. (Treasury stock is recorded at cost.)

(d) Each share of preferred stock is converted into five shares of common stock.

(e) The treasury stock was exchanged for machinery with a fair market of $100,000.

(f) There is a 2:1 stock split and the par value of the new common stock is $5.

(g) A major stockholder donated 90,000 shares of common stock to the company.

(h) All of the common stock outstanding is exchanged for no-par common with a stated value of $2 per share.

(i) Net income was $80,000.

Instructions:

(1) Give the journal entries to record the transactions described above. (For net income, give the entry to close the income summary account to Retained Earnings.)

(2) Prepare the "Stockholders' equity" section as of May 31, 1977.

19-7. Capital accounts for the Lopez Company on January 1 are as follows:

Preferred Stock, $50 par, 50,000 shares issued and outstanding.....................	$2,500,000
Premium on Preferred Stock..	37,500
Common Stock, $10 par, 450,000 shares authorized, 200,000 shares issued and outstanding..	2,000,000
Premium on Common Stock	200,000
Retained Earnings..	1,000,000

Each share of preferred stock is convertible into 4 shares of common stock. The following transactions affected the "Stockholders' equity" section during 1977.

(a) 800 shares of common stock were reacquired by purchase at $8. (Capital retirement method; the treasury stock account is used to report reduction in common stock.)

(b) Each preferred stockholder exercised the convertible feature of the preferred stock.

(c) 150 shares of common stock were used to settle an account payable of $2,000. The market price of the stock at the time of settlement was $20 per share.

(d) Annual cash dividends of $1 on common stock were declared and paid.

(e) 400 shares of treasury stock were sold for $11. The remaining treasury stock was used to acquire machinery with a list price of $5,000.

(f) All of the common stock was exchanged for no-par common with a stated value of $5 per share.

(g) Net income was $175,000.

Instructions:

(1) Record each of the above transactions.

(2) Prepare the "Stockholders' equity" section of the balance sheet as of year end.

19-8. You have been assigned to the audit of Wright, Inc., a manufacturing company. You have been asked to summarize the transactions for the year ended December 31, 1978, affecting stockholders' equity and other related accounts. The "Stockholders' equity" section of Wright's December 31, 1977, balance sheet follows:

Stockholders' Equity

Paid-in capital:

Common stock, $10 par value, 500,000 shares authorized, 90,000 shares issued	$900,000	
Paid-in capital from treasury stock transactions	11,250	
Premium on common stock	100,000	$1,011,250
Retained earnings	$324,689	
Less cost of 1,210 shares of common stock in treasury	36,300	288,389
Total stockholders' equity		$1,299,639

You have extracted the following information from the accounting records and audit working papers.

1978

Jan. 15 Six hundred fifty shares of treasury stock were sold for $20 per share. The 1,210 shares of treasury stock on hand at December 31, 1977, were purchased in one block in 1973. Wright used the cost method for recording the treasury shares purchased.

Jan. 26 A 5% stock dividend was declared and issued in early February to stockholders of record on January 31. Market price of the stock was $21 on January 26 and $23 on January 31.

Feb. 2 Ninety, $1,000, 5½% bonds due February 1, 1981, were sold at 104 with one detachable stock purchase warrant attached to each bond. Interest is payable annually on February 1. The fair value of the bonds without the stock warrants is 98 4/5. The detached warrants have a fair value of $52 each and expire on February 1, 1979. Each warrant entitles the holder to purchase ten shares of common stock at $30 per share.

Mar. 6 Subscriptions for 1,400 shares of common stock were issued at $22 per share, payable 50% down and the balance by March 20.

Mar. 20 The balance due on 1,200 shares was received and those shares were issued. The subscriber who defaulted on the 200 remaining shares forfeited the down payment in accordance with the subscription agreement.

Nov. 1 Fifty-five stock warrants detached from the bonds were exercised.

Instructions: Give journal entries required to summarize the above transactions. (AICPA adapted)

19-9. The McAllister Company has experienced several poor earnings years and has several assets on its books that are overvalued. It desires to revalue its assets downward and eliminate the deficit. At December 31, 1977, the company owns the following land, buildings, and equipment:

	Cost	Accumulated Depreciation	Book Value	Current Value
Land	$250,000	——	$250,000	$150,000
Buildings	375,000	$175,000	200,000	100,000
Machinery and equipment	175,000	75,000	100,000	75,000
	$800,000	$250,000	$550,000	$325,000

The balance sheet on December 31, 1977, reported the following balances in the "Stockholders' equity" section:

Common stock, $10 par, 100,000 shares	$1,000,000
Additional paid-in capital	100,000
Retained earnings (deficit)	(150,000)
Total	$ 950,000

As part of the reorganization, the common stock is to be canceled and reissued at $5 par.

Instructions:

(1) Prepare the journal entries to record the quasi-reorganization.
(2) Give the property section and "Stockholders' equity" section of the company's balance sheet as they would appear after the entries are posted.

19-10. The Shaky Company at December 31, 1977, is insolvent and must declare bankruptcy unless a large loan can be obtained immediately. A lender who is willing to advance $450,000 to the company has been located, but will only make the loan subject to the following conditions:

(a) A $600,000, 6% mortgage payable on the company's land and buildings held by a major stockholder will be canceled along with four months' accrued interest. The mortgage will be replaced by 5,000 shares of $100 par value, 6%, cumulative if earned, nonparticipating, preferred stock.
(b) A $450,000, 8% mortgage payable over 15 years on the land and buildings will be given as security on the new loan.
(c) On May 1, 1976, the company's trade creditors accepted $360,000 in notes payable on demand at 6% interest in settlement of all past-due accounts. No payment has been made to date. The company will offer to settle these liabilities at $.75 per $1.00 owed or to replace the notes payable on demand with new notes payable for full indebtedness over five years at 6% interest. It is estimated that $200,000 of the demand notes will be exchanged for the longer-term notes and that the remainder will accept the offer of a reduced cash settlement.
(d) A new issue of 500 shares of $100 par value, 5%, noncumulative, nonparticipating, preferred stock will replace 500 outstanding shares of $100 par value, 7%, cumulative, participating preferred stock. Preferred stockholders will repudiate all claims to $21,000 of dividends in arrears. The dividends have never been formally declared.
(e) A new issue of 600 shares of $50 par value, class A common stock will replace 600 outstanding shares of $100 par value, class A common stock.
(f) A new issue of 650 shares of $40 par value, class B common stock will replace 650 outstanding shares of $100 par value, class B common stock.

The following condensed account balances are on the books at December 31, 1976:

Bank overdraft	$ 15,000
Other current assets	410,000
Land, buildings, and equipment	840,000
Trade accounts payable	235,000
Other current liabilities	85,000
Paid-in capital at more than par value	125,000
Retained earnings deficit	345,000

Instructions:

(1) Prepare pro forma journal entries you would suggest to give effect to the foregoing transactions as of January 1, 1978. Entries should be keyed to lettered information in order.
(2) Prepare a pro forma balance sheet for the Shaky Company at January 1, 1978, as if the recapitalization had been consummated. (AICPA adapted)

19-11. The Columbia Corporation had $105,000 of dividends in arrears on its preferred stock as of March 31, 1977. While retained earnings were adequate to meet the accumulated dividends, the company's management did not wish to weaken its working capital position. The management also realized that a portion of the fixed assets were no longer used or useful in their operation. Therefore, the following reorganization was proposed, which was approved by stockholders to be effective as of April 1, 1977:

(a) The preferred stock was to be exchanged for $300,000 of 5% debenture bonds. Dividends in arrears were to be settled by the issuance of $120,000 of $10 par value, 5%, noncumulative preferred stock.
(b) Common stock was to be assigned a value of $50 per share.
(c) Goodwill was to be written off.
(d) Land, buildings, and equipment were to be written down, based on appraisal and estimates of useful value, by a total of $103,200, consisting of an $85,400 increase in accumulated depreciation and a $17,800 decrease in certain assets.
(e) Current assets were to be written down by $10,460 to reduce certain items to expected realizable values.

(continued)

The condensed balance sheet as of March 31, 1977, was as follows:

Columbia Corporation
Balance Sheet
March 31, 1977

Assets

Cash		$ 34,690
Other current assets		252,890
Land, buildings, and equipment	$1,458,731	
Less accumulated depreciation	512,481	946,250
Goodwill		50,000
Total assets		$1,283,830

Liabilities and Stockholders' Equity

Current liabilities		$ 136,860
Preferred 7% stock, cumulative, $100 par*		300,000
Common stock, no-par, 9,000 shares		648,430
Premium on preferred stock		22,470
Retained earnings		176,070
Total liabilities and stockholders' equity		$1,283,830

*$105,000 dividends in arrears.

Instructions:

(1) Prepare journal entries to give effect to the reorganization as of April 1, 1977. Give complete explanations with each entry and comment on any possible options in recording the reorganization.

(2) Prepare a balance sheet as of April 30, 1977, assuming that net income for April was $10,320 after provision for tax. The operations resulted in a $5,290 increase in cash, a $10,660 increase in other current assets, a $2,010 increase in current liabilities, and a $3,620 increase in accumulated depreciation.

(3) In making an audit of the Columbia Corporation as of December 31, 1977, you find that the following items had been debited or credited directly to Retained Earnings during the nine months since April 1, 1977:

  (a) A debit of $14,496 arising from correction of an error applicable to prior years.

  (b) A debit of $7,492 resulting from a loss on fixed assets destroyed in a fire on November 2, 1977.

  (c) A debit of $13,500 representing dividends declared on common and' preferred stock.

  For each of these items, state whether you believe it to be correctly debited or credited to Retained Earnings. Give the reasons for your conclusion. If the item is not handled properly, prepare the necessary correcting entry. (AICPA adapted)

20

Retained Earnings — Earnings and Earnings Distributions

The difference between assets and liabilities is proprietorship or capital: the owners' equity in assets. In a sole proprietorship, a single capital account reports the owner's entire equity in assets resulting from investments, withdrawals, and earnings. In a partnership, capital balances for the individual partners normally report partners' full equities resulting from investments, withdrawals, and earnings. Because of the nature of the corporate form, it is necessary to distinguish between the capital originating from the stockholders' investment, designated as *paid-in* or *invested capital*, and the capital originating from earnings, designated as *retained earnings*.

Retained earnings is essentially the meeting place of the balance sheet accounts and the income statement accounts. In successive periods retained earnings are increased by income and decreased by losses and dividends. As a result, the retained earnings balance represents the net accumulated earnings of the corporation. If the retained earnings account were affected only by income or losses and dividends, there would be little confusion in its interpretation. But a number of factors tend to complicate the nature of retained earnings. Among these factors are: transactions between the corporation and its stockholders affecting retained earnings; stock dividends resulting in transfers from retained earnings to paid-in capital; recapitalizations resulting in transfers between retained earnings and capital stock; quasi-reorganizations and "fresh-start" retained earnings; legal restrictions upon retained earnings in protecting the stockholder and creditor groups; and contractual limitations upon the use of retained earnings for dividends. The nature of retained earnings is frequently misunderstood and this misunderstanding may lead to seriously misleading inferences in reading the balance sheet.

SOURCE OF RETAINED EARNINGS

Retained earnings is the terminus of all accounting for earnings. The retained earnings account is increased by net income from the activities of a business unit and is reduced by net losses from these activities. The retained earnings account is also affected by items defined as prior period adjustments. It should never be increased as a result of a company dealing in its own stock; however, as indicated in Chapter 19, it may be decreased.

Corporate earnings transferred to retained earnings originate from transactions with individuals or businesses outside of the company. No earnings are recognized in the construction of machinery or other plant items for a company's own use, even though the cost of such construction is below the market price for similar assets: self-construction at less than the asset purchase price is regarded simply as a savings in cost. No increases in retained earnings are recognized on transactions with stockholders involving treasury stock; however, decreases may be recognized. The receipt of properties through donation is not recognized as earnings, but as paid-in capital.

The earnings of a corporation may be distributed to the stockholders or retained to provide for expanding operations. When earnings are retained, they may be appropriated so as to be reported as unavailable for dividend declaration. Appropriations are canceled after the purpose of the appropriation has been fulfilled. When operating losses or other debits to the retained earnings account produce a debit balance in this account, the debit balance is referred to as a *deficit*.

DIVIDENDS

Dividends are distributions to stockholders of a corporation in proportion to the number of shares held by the respective owners. Distributions may take the form of (1) cash, (2) other assets, (3) evidences of corporate indebtedness, in effect, deferred cash dividends, and (4) shares of a company's own stock. All dividends involve reductions in retained earnings except dividends in corporate liquidation, which represent a return to stockholders of a portion or all of the corporate legal capital and call for reductions in invested capital.

Use of the term *dividend* without qualification normally implies the distribution of cash. Dividends in a form other than cash should be designated by their special form, and dividends declared from a capital source other than retained earnings should carry a description of their special origin. The terms *property dividend, scrip dividend,* and *stock dividend* suggest distributions of a special form; designations such as *liquidating dividend* and *dividend distribution of paid-in capital* identify the special origin of the distribution.

"Dividends paid out of retained earnings" is an expression frequently encountered. Accuracy, however, would require the statement that dividends are paid out of cash, which serves to reduce retained earnings. Earnings of the corporation increase net assets and also the stockholders' equity. Dividend distributions represent no more than asset withdrawals that reduce net assets and the stockholders' equity.

Among the powers delegated by the stockholders to the board of directors is controlling the dividend policy. Whether dividends shall or shall not be paid, as well as the nature and the amount of dividends, are matters the board determines. In declaring dividends, the board of directors must observe the legal requirements governing the maintenance of legal or stated capital. These requirements vary with the individual states. In addition, the board of directors must consider the financial aspects of dividend distributions — the company asset position, the present asset requirements, and the future asset requirements. The board of directors must answer two questions: Do we have the legal right to declare a dividend? Is such a distribution financially advisable?[1]

When a dividend is legally declared and announced, its revocation is not possible. In the event of corporate insolvency prior to payment of the dividend, stockholders have claims as a creditor group to the dividend, and as an ownership group to any assets remaining after all corporate liabilities have been paid. A dividend that was illegally declared is revocable; in the event of insolvency, such action is nullified and stockholders participate in asset distributions only after creditors have been paid in full.

The Formal Dividend Announcement

Three dates are essential in the formal dividend statement: (1) date of declaration, (2) date of stockholders of record, (3) date of payment. Dividends are made payable to stockholders of record as of a date following the date of declaration and preceding the date of payment. The liability for dividends payable is recorded on the declaration date and is canceled on the payment date. No entry is required on the record date, but a list of the stockholders is made as of the close of business on this date. These are the persons who receive dividends on the payment date. The stock is said to sell ex-dividend on the day following the date of record. A full record of the dividend action must be provided in the minutes book.

Cash Dividends

The most common type of dividend is a *cash dividend*. For the corporation, these dividends involve a reduction in retained earnings and in cash. A current liability for dividends payable is recognized on the declaration date; this is canceled when dividend checks are sent to stockholders. Entries to record the declaration and the payment of a cash dividend follow:

Retained Earnings	100,000	
Dividends Payable		100,000
Dividends Payable	100,000	
Cash		100,000

[1]Laws of the different states range from those making any part of capital other than legal capital available for dividends to those permitting dividends only from retained earnings and under specified conditions. In most states dividends cannot be declared in the event of a deficit; in a few states, however, dividends equal to current earnings may be distributed despite a previously accumulated deficit. The availability of capital as a basis for dividends is a determination to be made by the attorney and not by the accountant. The accountant must report accurately the sources of each capital increase; the attorney investigates the availability of such sources as bases for dividend distributions.

In declaring a dividend, the board of directors must consider the limitations set by the current position and the cash balance. For example, a corporation may have retained earnings of $500,000. If it has cash of only $150,000, however, cash dividends must be limited to this amount unless it converts certain assets into cash or borrows cash. If the cash required for regular operations is $100,000, the cash available for dividends is only $50,000. Although legally able to declare dividends of $500,000, the company would be able to distribute no more than one tenth of such amount at this time.

Scrip Dividends

If a corporation has retained earnings that may be used as a basis for dividend declaration but does not have sufficient funds at the time for a cash dividend, it may declare a *scrip dividend* which consists of a written promise to pay certain amounts at some future date. The corporation can thus take regular dividend action although it is temporarily short of cash. Stockholders, in turn, are provided currently with instruments they may sell for cash if they wish. Such dividends are rare.

Assume the declaration of a scrip dividend of $150,000, payable in six months together with interest at the rate of 6% for the period of payment deferment. The declaration is recorded as follows:

Retained Earnings	150,000	
Scrip Dividends Payable		150,000

When the scrip matures and scrip and interest payments are made, the entry is:

Scrip Dividends Payable	150,000	
Interest Expense	4,500	
Cash		154,500

Property Dividends

A distribution to stockholders that is payable in some asset other than cash is generally referred to as a *property dividend*. Frequently the assets to be distributed are securities of other companies owned by the corporation. The corporation thus transfers to its stockholders its ownership interest in such securities.

This transfer is sometimes referred to as a *nonreciprocal transfer to owners* inasmuch as nothing is received by the company in return for their distribution to the stockholders. This type of transfer should be recorded using the fair market value (as of the day of declaration) of the assets distributed, and a gain or loss recognized for the difference between the carrying value on the books of the issuing company and the fair market value of the assets.[1]

To illustrate the entries for a property dividend, assume the State Oil Corporation owns 100,000 shares in the Valley Oil Co., cost $2,000,000, fair market value $3,000,000, which it wishes to distribute to its stockholders. There are 1,000,000 shares of State Oil Corporation stock out-

---

[1]*Opinions of the Accounting Principles Board, No. 29,* "Accounting for Nonmonetary Transactions" (New York: American Institute of Certified Public Accountants, 1973), par. 18.

standing. Accordingly, a dividend of 1/10 of a share of Valley Oil Co. stock is declared on each share of State Oil Corporation stock outstanding. The entries for the dividend declaration and payment are:

Retained Earnings	3,000,000	
Property Dividends Payable		3,000,000
Property Dividends Payable	3,000,000	
Investment in Valley Oil Co. Stock		2,000,000
Gain on Distribution of Property Dividends		1,000,000

Stock Dividends   A corporation may distribute to stockholders additional shares of the company's own stock as a *stock dividend*. A stock dividend permits the corporation to retain within the business net assets produced by earnings while at the same time offering stockholders tangible evidence of the growth of their equity.

A stock dividend usually involves (1) the capitalization of retained earnings, and (2) a distribution of common stock to common stockholders. These distributions are sometimes referred to as *ordinary stock dividends*. In some states, stock dividends may be effected by the capitalization of certain paid-in capital balances. In some instances, common stock is issued to holders of preferred stock or preferred stock is issued to holders of common stock. These distributions are sometimes referred to as *special stock dividends*.

A stock dividend makes a portion of retained earnings no longer available for distribution while raising the legal capital of the corporation. In recording the dividend, a debit is made to Retained Earnings and credits are made to appropriate paid-in capital balances. The stock dividend may be viewed as consisting, in effect, of two transactions: (1) the payment by the corporation of a cash dividend; and (2) the return of the cash to the corporation in exchange for capital stock.

In distributing stock as a dividend, the issuing corporation must meet legal requirements relative to the amounts to be capitalized. If stock has a par or a stated value, an amount equal to the par or stated value of the shares issued will have to be transferred to capital stock; if stock is no-par and without a stated value, the laws of the state of incorporation may provide specific requirements as to amounts to be transferred, or they may leave such determinations to the corporate directors.

Although the minimum amounts to be transferred to legal or stated capital balances upon the issuance of additional stock are set by law, the board of directors is not prevented from going beyond legal requirements and authorizing increases in both capital stock and paid-in capital balances. For example, assume that $100 par stock was originally issued at $120. Legal requirements may call for the capitalization of no more than the par value of the additional shares issued. The board of directors, however, in order to preserve the paid-in capital relationship, may authorize a transfer from retained earnings of $120 per share; for every share issued, capital stock would be increased $100 and a paid-in capital balance $20; or the board of directors may decide that the retained earnings transfer shall be made in terms of the fair value of shares which exceeds the legal value. Here, too, the credit to capital stock is accompanied by a credit to a paid-in capital account.

The Committee on Accounting Procedure of the AICPA, in commenting on the issuance by a corporation of its own common stock to its common stockholders, has indicated that proper corporate policy in certain situations would call for the capitalization of an amount equal to the fair value of shares issued. The Committee pointed out:

> . . . a stock dividend does not, in fact, give rise to any change whatsoever in either the corporation's assets or its respective shareholders' proportionate interests therein. However, it cannot fail to be recognized that, merely as a consequence of the expressed purpose of the transaction and its characterization as a *dividend* in related notices to shareholders and the public at large, many recipients of stock dividends look upon them as distributions of corporate earnings and usually in an amount equivalent to the fair value of the additional shares received. Furthermore, it is to be presumed that such views of recipients are materially strengthened in those instances, which are by far the most numerous, where the issuances are so small in comparison with the shares previously outstanding that they do not have any apparent effect upon the share market price and, consequently, the market value of the shares previously held remains substantially unchanged. The committee therefore believes that where these circumstances exist the corporation should in the public interest account for the transaction by transferring from earned surplus to the category of permanent capitalization (represented by the capital stock and capital surplus accounts) an amount equal to the fair value of the additional shares issued. Unless this is done, the amount of earnings which the shareholder may believe to have been distributed to him will be left, except to the extent otherwise dictated by legal requirements, in earned surplus subject to possible further similar stock issuances or cash distributions.[1]

However, the Committee indicated that certain circumstances would suggest that retained earnings be debited for no more than the stock's par, stated, or other value as required by law. The Committee stated:

> . . . Where the number of additional shares issued as a stock dividend is so great that it has, or may reasonably be expected to have, the effect of materially reducing the share market value, the committee believes that the implications and possible constructions discussed . . . are not likely to exist and that the transaction clearly partakes of the nature of a stock split-up. . . . Consequently, the committee considers that under such circumstances there is no need to capitalize earned surplus, other than to the extent occasioned by legal requirements. It recommends, however, that in such instances every effort be made to avoid the use of the word *dividend* in related corporate resolutions, notices, and announcements and that, in those cases where because of legal requirements this cannot be done, the transaction be described, for example, as a *split-up effected in the form of a dividend*.[2]

The Committee indicated that the majority of stock dividends would probably fall within the first category stated above, suggesting debits to retained earnings of amounts exceeding legal requirements. Although reluctant to name a dividend percentage that would require adherence to this practice, the Committee did suggest that in stock distributions in-

---

[1] *Accounting Research and Terminology Bulletins —Final Edition*, "No. 43, Restatement and Revision of Accounting Research Bulletins" (New York: American Institute of Certified Public Accountants, 1961), Ch. 7, sec. B, par 10.
[2] *Ibid.*, par. 11.

volving the issuance of less than 20% to 25% of the number of shares previously outstanding, there would be but few instances where debits to retained earnings at the fair value of additional shares issued would not be appropriate.

The following examples illustrate the entries for the declaration and the issue of a stock dividend. Assume the capital for the Bradford Co. on July 1 is as follows:

Capital stock, $10 par, 100,000 shares outstanding	$1,000,000
Premium on capital stock	1,100,000
Retained earnings	750,000

The company declares a 10% stock dividend, or a dividend of 1 share for every 10 held. Shares are selling on the market on this date at $16 per share. The stock dividend is to be recorded at the market value of the shares issued, or $160,000 (10,000 shares at $16). The entries to record the declaration of the dividend and the issue of stock follow:

Retained Earnings	160,000	
Stock Dividends Distributable		100,000
Paid-In Capital from Stock Dividends		60,000
Stock Dividends Distributable	100,000	
Capital Stock, $10 par		100,000

Assume, however, that the company declares a 50% stock dividend, or a dividend of 1 share for every 2 held. Legal requirements call for the transfer to capital stock of an amount equal to the par value of the shares issued. This transfer may be made from retained earnings or paid-in capital. When the transfer is made from paid-in capital, it is preferable to refer to the transaction as a stock split effected in the form of a dividend rather than as a stock dividend. Entries for the declaration of the dividend and the issue of stock follow:

Retained Earnings (*or* Premium on Capital Stock)	500,000	
Stock Dividends Distributable		500,000
Stock Dividends Distributable	500,000	
Capital Stock, $10 par		500,000

Fractional Share Warrants. When stock dividends are issued by a company, it may be necessary to issue *fractional share warrants* to certain stockholders. For example, when a 10% stock dividend is issued, a stockholder owning 25 shares can be given no more than 2 full shares; however, the holdings in excess of an even multiple of 10 shares are recognized by the issue of a fractional share warrant for ½ share. The warrant for ½ share may be sold, or a warrant for an additional ½ share may be purchased so a full share may be claimed from the company. In some instances, the corporation may arrange for the payment of cash in lieu of fractional warrants or it may issue a full share of stock in exchange for warrants accompanied by cash for the fractional share deficiency.

Assume that the Miller Company in distributing a stock dividend issues fractional share warrants totaling 500 shares, par $50. The entry for the fractional share warrants issued would be as given on page 570.

| Stock Dividends Distributable | 25,000 | |
| Fractional Share Warrants Issued | | 25,000 |

Assuming 80% of the warrants are ultimately turned in for shares and the remaining warrants expire, the following entry would be made:

Fractional Share Warrants Issued	25,000	
Capital Stock, $50 par		20,000
Paid-In Capital from Forfeitures of Fractional Share Warrants		5,000

Stock Dividends on the Balance Sheet. If a balance sheet is prepared after the declaration of a stock dividend but before issue of the shares, Stock Dividends Distributable is reported in the "Stockholders' equity" section as an addition to Capital Stock Outstanding. By the declaration of the dividend, the corporation has reduced its retained earnings balance and is committed to the increase of capital stock. The stock the corporation may still sell is limited to the difference between capital stock authorized and the sum of (1) capital stock issued, (2) capital stock subscribed, (3) stock reserved for the exercise of stock rights and stock options, and (4) stock dividends distributable.

Although a stock dividend can be compared to a stock split from the investors' point of view, its effects upon corporate capital differ from those of the stock split. A stock dividend results in an increase in the number of shares outstanding and in an increase in the capital stock balance, no change being made in the value assigned to each share of stock on the company records; the increase in capital stock outstanding is effected by a transfer from the retained earnings balance, retained earnings available for dividends being permanently reduced by this transfer. A stock split merely divides the existing capital stock balance into more parts with a reduction in the stated or legal value related to each share; there is no change in the retained earnings available for dividends, both the capital stock and the retained earnings balances remaining unchanged.

A stock split effected in the form of a large stock dividend is sometimes referred to simply as a stock split. This can be misleading because additional shares of stock are issued in this situation and the par value of the stock is not changed. A careful distinction should be made between a pure stock split as described in Chapter 19 and the large stock dividends discussed in this chapter.

There have been suggestions that special disclosure be provided on the balance sheet when retained earnings has been reclassified as paid-in capital as a result of stock dividends, recapitalizations, or other actions. Information concerning the amount of retained earnings transferred to paid-in capital will contribute to an understanding of the extent to which business growth has been financed through corporate earnings. For example, assume the information for the Bradford Co. on page 569 and the transfer to paid-in capital of $500,000 as a result of the 50% stock dividend. The stockholders' equity may be presented as illustrated at the top of the next page.

Paid-in capital:		
Capital stock, $10 par, 150,000 shares	$1,500,000	
Premium on capital stock..	1,100,000	$2,600,000
Retained earnings..	$ 750,000	
Less amount transferred to paid-in capital by stock div-		
idend	500,000	250,000
Total stockholders' equity...		$2,850,000

Liquidating Dividends   A corporation will declare a *liquidating dividend* when the dividend is to be considered a return to stockholders of a portion of their original investments. These distributions by the corporation represent reductions of invested capital balances. Instead of actually debiting capital stock and paid-in capital balances, however, it is possible to debit a separate account for the reduction in invested capital. This balance is subtracted from the invested capital balances in presenting the stockholders' equity on the balance sheet.

Corporations owning wasting assets may regularly declare dividends that are in part a distribution of earnings and in part a distribution of the corporation's invested capital. Entries on the corporation books for such dividend declarations should reflect the decrease in the two capital elements. This information should be reported to stockholders so they may recognize dividends as representing in part income and in part a return of investment.

Dividends on Preferred Stock   When dividends on preferred stock are cumulative, the payment of a stipulated amount on these shares is necessary before any dividends may be paid on common. When the board of directors fails to declare dividends on cumulative preferred stock, information concerning the amount of dividends in arrears should be reported parenthetically or in note form on the balance sheet; or retained earnings may be divided on the balance sheet to show the amount required to meet dividends in arrears and the free balance for other purposes. In this case retained earnings may be reported on the balance sheet in the following manner:

Retained earnings:		
Required to meet dividends in arrears on preferred stock ..	$40,000	
Balance..	60,000	
Total retained earnings..		$100,000

The board of directors may pay a portion of a cumulative preferred dividend or a portion of the total in arrears. For example, 2% may be paid annually on 7% cumulative preferred stock, allowing 5% to accumulate for future payment. Or a payment of $15 may be made on cumulative dividends in arrears of $50, leaving $35 still in arrears.

Dividends on No-Par Stock   Cash dividends on no-par stock must be expressed as a certain amount per share since there is no par value upon which a percentage may be applied. Dividends on capital stock with a par value are often expressed in the same manner.

When no-par stock is outstanding and the corporation desires to transfer an amount from Retained Earnings to Capital Stock, there is no need to declare a stock dividend. The board of directors can simply take action to raise the stated value of the no-par stock. An entry such as the following is made:

Retained Earnings..	500,000	
Capital Stock..		500,000
To raise $5 stated value on 100,000 shares of no-par stock to $10 in accordance with resolution by board of directors.		

Extraordinary Dividend Distributions

In the case of common stock, a corporation may establish a policy of *regular dividends* and may provide for greater payments when warranted through *extraordinary dividends* or *extra dividends*. For example, a corporation may have a regular rate of 50 cents a quarter or $2 a year per share on common stock. In a particular quarter it may wish to declare a dividend of 80 cents a share. Such a dividend may be expressed as a 50-cent regular dividend plus a 30-cent extra dividend.

APPRAISAL CAPITAL

Companies sometimes have chosen to report the impact of inflation on their assets by increasing the cost of some of their assets to current appraisal values. This increase is usually offset by creating a special stockholders' equity account, Appraisal Capital. At the present time, the use of appraisal accounting is not generally accepted. However, as discussed in Chapter 25, there is increasing pressure on accountants to reflect the impact of inflation on a company in the financial statements.

Appraisal capital should never be used to absorb operating losses or the write-down of properties other than those values representing the source of the appraisal increase. Appraisal capital, representing unrealized earnings, is not properly used as a basis for cash dividends; however, its use as a basis for stock dividends is permitted in some states.

Disposal of an asset that has been increased by appraisal results in cancellation of the asset balance at appraised value, cancellation of the related appraisal capital, and recognition of a gain or loss based upon cost.

USE OF TERM "RESERVE"

The term *reserve* has been employed in a variety of different senses in accounting practice. It has been used in the following ways:

1. *As a Valuation Account.* The reserve designation has been employed to report a valuation account related to a balance sheet item. For example, deductions may be required from the face amount of assets in arriving at the realizable amounts, as in the case of marketable securities, receivables, or inventories. Deductions may also be required from the face amount of assets in the recognition of cost expirations, as in the case of

assets subject to depreciation, depletion, or amortization. When such reductions are related to current revenues, expense accounts are debited and asset valuation accounts are credited. Valuation accounts are ultimately applied against the items to which they relate. The accounts receivable valuation account is used to absorb accounts that prove to be uncollectible; the property valuation account is applied against the property item when the latter is disposed of or scrapped. As suggested earlier, a term such as *allowance* should be substituted for the term reserve in designating valuation accounts.

2. *As an Estimate of a Liability of Uncertain Amount.* The reserve title has been employed to designate a liability of uncertain amount requiring an estimate. Estimates may be required for such items as unsettled claims for damages and injuries, premium claims outstanding, claims under guarantees for services and replacements, tax obligations, and obligations under pension plans. When these claims are related to current revenue, expense accounts are debited and liability accounts are credited. The liabilities are ultimately canceled through payment. Designation of the accounts in this class as *estimated liabilities* rather than as reserves would clarify the nature of the items presented.

3. *As an Appropriation of Retained Earnings.* The reserve title is used to indicate that retained earnings have been appropriated in accordance with legal or contractual requirements or as a result of authorization by the board of directors. The appropriation of retained earnings has no effect upon individual assets and liabilities nor does it change total capital; amounts are merely transferred from retained earnings to special retained earnings accounts and assets otherwise available for dividend distribution are kept within the business. The appropriation balance is no guarantee that cash or any other specific asset will be available to carry out the purpose of the appropriation. Resources represented by retained earnings may have been applied to the enlargement of plant, to the increase of working capital, or to the retirement of corporate indebtedness. If assets are to be made available for a particular purpose, special action relative to asset use would be required. When the purpose of the appropriation has been served, the appropriation balance is returned to Retained Earnings.

It was indicated in an earlier chapter that the American Institute Committee on Terminology has held that the use of the term reserve to indicate the retention of assets comes closest to its popular meaning. Accordingly, the Committee has recommended that the term reserve be limited to appropriations of retained earnings and any alternative use of the term on the financial statements be discontinued.[1] The American Accounting Association Committee on Concepts and Standards Underlying Corporate Financial Statements, however, would abandon the use of the term in financial statements. The Committee has maintained that although accounting terminology would be improved if the term were limited to balances includible in capital, the conflict between the general and the accounting connotations of the word would still be unresolved.[2]

---

[1]*Accounting Research and Terminology Bulletins — Final Edition*, "Accounting Terminology Bulletins, No. 1, Review and Résumé" (New York: American Institute of Certified Public Accountants, 1961), par. 57–64.

[2]*Accounting and Reporting Standards for Corporate Financial Statements and Preceding Statements and Supplements*, Supplementary Statement No. 1 (Madison, Wisconsin: American Accounting Association, 1957), p. 20.

There can be little question that greater clarity in financial statement presentation would be promoted through abandonment of the term *reserve* and the adoption of more descriptive terminology.

RETAINED EARNINGS APPROPRIATIONS

Appropriations of retained earnings may be classified as follows:

1. *Appropriations to Report Legal Restrictions on Retained Earnings.* Laws of the state of incorporation may require a company, upon reacquiring its own stock, to retain its earnings as a means of maintaining its legal capital. The restriction may be recognized in the accounts by the appropriation of retained earnings.
2. *Appropriations to Report Contractual Restrictions on Retained Earnings.* Agreements with creditors or stockholders may provide for the retention of earnings within the company to protect the interests of these parties and assure redemption of the securities they hold. The restriction may be indicated in the accounts by the appropriation of retained earnings.
3. *Appropriations to Report Discretionary Action by the Board of Directors in the Presentation of Retained Earnings.* The board of directors may authorize that a portion or all of the retained earnings be presented in a manner disclosing the actual use in the present or the planned use in the future of the resources represented by this part of the stockholders' equity. Discretionary action on the part of the board of directors may then be the basis for appropriations.

A number of appropriated retained earnings accounts and the purposes for which such balances are established are listed below:

ACCOUNT	PURPOSE
(1) Appropriations to report legal restrictions on retained earnings: Retained Earnings Appropriated for Purchase of Treasury Stock	To retain earnings upon the reacquisition of stock so that resources of the business and the stockholders' equity may be maintained at original legal or stated balances.
(2) Appropriations to report contractual restrictions on retained earnings: Retained Earnings Appropriated for Redemption of Bonds Retained Earnings Appropriated for Bond Redemption Fund	To retain earnings so that resources may be available for the redemption of bonds or for transfer to a fund for bond redemption.
Retained Earnings Appropriated for Redemption of Preferred Stock Retained Earnings Appropriated for Preferred Stock Redemption Fund	To retain earnings so that resources may be available for the redemption of preferred stock or for transfer to a fund for stock redemption.
(3) Appropriations to report discretionary action by the board of directors in the presentation of retained earnings: Retained Earnings Appropriated for General Contingencies Retained Earnings Appropriated for Possible Inventory Decline Retained Earnings Appropriated for Self-Insurance	To retain earnings in the business so that resources may be available for use in meeting possible future losses.
Retained Earnings Appropriated for Increased Working Capital Retained Earnings Appropriated for Plant Expansion	To report that resources from earnings are to be applied or have been applied to some particular business purpose and thus are unavailable for dividends.

Appropriations Relating to Stock Reacquisitions   A legal restriction upon retained earnings arising upon the reacquisition of the company's own stock is recorded by a debit to Retained Earnings and a credit to an appropriately titled appropriations account. Retained earnings thus replace the capital impairment arising from treasury stock acquisition. The appropriated balance may be returned to Retained Earnings when the legal restriction is removed. To illustrate, assume a corporation reacquires its own stock and subsequently resells this stock. Retained Earnings of $100,000 are restricted by law from use for dividends during the period the treasury stock is held. The entries for the appropriation and its subsequent cancellation follow:

Retained Earnings..	100,000	
Retained Earnings Appropriated for Purchase of Treasury Stock...		100,000
Retained Earnings Appropriated for Purchase of Treasury Stock	100,000	
Retained Earnings...		100,000

Appropriations Relating to Bond Redemption   A restriction upon retained earnings arising from a contract with creditors or stockholders is recorded by a debit to Retained Earnings and a credit to an appropriations account. When the restriction is removed, the appropriation is returned to Retained Earnings. To illustrate, assume that the corporation agrees to restrict retained earnings of $5,000,000 from dividend distribution during the full term of a bond issue. Entries when the loan is made and when it is liquidated follow:

Retained Earnings..	5,000,000	
Retained Earnings Appropriated for Redemption of Bonds		5,000,000
Retained Earnings Appropriated for Redemption of Bonds ...	5,000,000	
Retained Earnings...		5,000,000

When the agreement with creditors provides for the periodic appropriation of earnings during the life of the obligation, entries similar to the first entry above would be made each period.

The appropriation of retained earnings may be accompanied by the segregation of assets in a special fund for retirement of the obligation at maturity. The establishment of the fund may be voluntary or it may be required by the bond indenture. A retained earnings appropriation that is accompanied by the segregation of assets in a special fund is said to be *funded*. This practice results not only in the limitation of dividends but also in the accumulation of resources to meet the obligation. Liquidation of the obligation by means of the redemption fund and the termination of the contract with creditors releases previously existing restrictions, and the appropriated retained earnings may be returned to a free status. It may be observed, however, that when proceeds from a bond issue are used for expansion purposes and when resources from profitable operations have been used to retire the bonds, the expansion has in effect been financed by earnings. Under these circumstances, the board of directors may choose to report retained earnings equivalent to the amount applied to expansion under the designation "Retained Earnings

Appropriated for Plant Expansion," or it may choose to effect a permanent capitalization of such retained earnings by means of a stock dividend.

Appropriations Relating to Stock Redemption   Retained earnings may be appropriated at regular intervals as part of a plan to retire preferred stock from resources arising from earnings. The appropriation of earnings may be required by the contract with stockholders or it may be voluntary and established at the discretion of the board of directors. Stock may be reacquired out of cash or out of a redemption fund previously established by transfers from cash. In either case, upon the retirement of outstanding stock, the board of directors may authorize the return of the appropriation balance to retained earnings. However, it should be observed that retained earnings now take the place of the capital stock equity previously reported. In recognition of this factor, the board of directors may choose to designate these earnings as applied to the retirement of a previously existing stockholders' equity; on the other hand, it may choose to effect a permanent capitalization of such retained earnings by means of a stock dividend.

Appropriations for Possible Future Losses   Appropriations of retained earnings may be authorized by the board of directors in anticipation of possible future losses. A clear distinction must be made between those possible future losses which are certain enough that they can be accrued and shown as liabilities, and those so uncertain that only disclosure of their existence is required. The Financial Accounting Standards Board has established two conditions that "loss contingencies" must have if they are to be accrued as liabilities:

1. Information available prior to issuance of the financial statements indicates that it is probable that an asset has been impaired or a liability has been incurred at the date of the financial statement.
2. The amount of the loss can be reasonably estimated.[1]

If both of these conditions are not met, but there is at least a reasonable possibility that a loss may occur, disclosure of the contingency loss must be made. One form of disclosure may be through the appropriation of retained earnings.[2] Three examples of such appropriations are described in the following paragraphs: (1) the appropriation for possible inventory decline; (2) the appropriation for self-insurance; and (3) the general purpose contingency appropriation.

Appropriation for Possible Inventory Decline. When inventories are acquired in a high-price period, management may authorize that provision be made in the accounts for possible future inventory decline. Valuation accounts reducing inventory costs to a lower market are established by charges to current revenue; valuation accounts providing for inventory

---

[1]*Statement of Financial Accounting Standards No. 5*, "Accounting for Contingencies" (Stamford, Conn.: Financial Accounting Standards Board, 1975), par. 8.
[2]*Ibid.*, par. 15.

obsolescence, deterioration, and similar losses already incurred are also established by charges to current revenue. A provision for possible future inventory decline, however, cannot be viewed as an inventory valuation account but must be considered a part of retained earnings. Accordingly, an appropriation procedure is required. An appropriation for possible inventory decline is established by a debit to Retained Earnings, and the appropriated balance is ultimately returned to Retained Earnings; no costs or losses should be debited to the appropriation, nor should any part of the appropriation be transferred to income. A loss on inventories requires separate recognition in the period in which it actually emerges.

To illustrate the use of appropriation for possible inventory decline, assume the ending inventory of Crainer Corporation has a cost valuation of $325,000 and a lower of cost or market valuation of $310,000. Officers of the corporation anticipate that inventory prices will continue to decline in the subsequent year, and that before the inventory is sold, a further decline of $30,000 in the replacement cost of the inventory can be anticipated. Selling prices of the inventory by Crainer are expected to decline in a corresponding fashion.

The following entries would be required to reflect (1) the actual decline occurring prior to the balance sheet date, and (2) the anticipated future decline by appropriating retained earnings.

Loss on Reduction of Inventory to Market	15,000	
Allowance for Inventory Decline to Market		15,000
To record actual decline in market value from cost of $325,000.		
Retained Earnings	30,000	
Retained Earnings Appropriated for Possible Future Inventory Decline		30,000
To appropriate retained earnings for anticipated future inventory declines.		

The loss account in the first entry is closed through Income Summary to Retained Earnings. The allowance account is a contra inventory account in the balance sheet. The Retained Earnings Appropriated for Possible Future Inventory Decline is only a disclosure account. If prices do decline in the subsequent period, sales will be lower and income will thus be reduced. If the appropriation is no longer required at the end of the subsequent year, an entry reversing the establishment of the appropriation should be made as follows:

Retained Earnings Appropriated for Possible Future Inventory Decline	30,000	
Retained Earnings		30,000
To return reserve for possible future inventory decline to unappropriated retained earnings.		

As indicated earlier, under no conditions should the actual loss be debited to the appropriation.

Appropriation for Self-Insurance. A company may face certain risks but may not obtain insurance on the theory that the assumption of these risks will prove less expensive in the long run than the cost of outside protection. The FASB has concluded that self-insurance is in reality no insurance. The first guideline for recording contingency losses in the accounts as an expense is not met in the case of self-insurance because no asset has been impaired nor has a liability been incurred. Thus, in FASB Statement No. 5, the Board states:

> ... Fires, explosions, and other similar events that may cause loss or damage of an enterprise's property are random in their occurrence. With respect to events of that type, the condition for accrual in paragraph 8(a) is not satisfied prior to the occurrence of the event because until that time there is no diminution in the value of the property. There is no relationship of those events to the activities of the enterprise prior to their occurrence. Further, unlike an insurance company, which has a contractual obligation under policies in force to reimburse insureds for losses, an enterprise can have no such obligation to itself and, hence, no liability.[1]

Similar reasoning is used for self-insurance related to the risk of loss from injury to others, damages to the property of others, or losses from interruption of business operations.[2]

Because there is a possibility of future loss, disclosure of the contingency is required and appropriation of retained earnings is one acceptable method of such disclosure. Actual losses incurred are charged against revenue in the period the loss occurs. The balance in the appropriation account should be evaluated each year to determine its reasonableness relative to the risk assumed. In addition, the appropriation may be funded so that cash will be available for property replacement.

The following entries illustrate a self-insurance plan with funding for property replacement.

TRANSACTION	ENTRY		
Retained earnings appropriated under fire-loss, self-insurance plans.	Retained Earnings..................................	20,000	
	Retained Earnings Appropriated for Self-Insurance Fire Loss....................		20,000
Establishment of fund to meet self-insurance plans.	Property Replacement Fund.................	20,000	
	Cash		20,000
Fire loss: building book value, $15,000 (cost, $21,500; accumulated depreciation, $6,500); building replacement cost, $23,500, paid $20,000 from fund and $3,500 from regular cash balance.	Fire Loss...	15,000	
	Accumulated Depreciation — Buildings	6,500	
	Buildings...		21,500
Since the building has been replaced, there will still be a need for an appropriation for another possible fire loss; therefore, management may decide to retain the appropriation and rebuild the cash fund.	Buildings	23,500	
	Property Replacement Fund.............		20,000
	Cash		3,500

It should be observed that since self-insurance is simply a policy of no insurance, management, in considering such a policy, should evaluate carefully such factors as the size of the organization and how this affects risk, the protective measures available in minimizing risk, and the probable savings accruing through this action. Self-insurance should

[1]*Ibid.*, par. 28.
[2]*Ibid.*, par. 29 and 30.

be undertaken only when a company is financially prepared to assume the full responsibilities related to the risk-bearing role.

Appropriation for General Contingencies. Company management may authorize provision in the accounts for general undetermined contingencies. Such authorization may require appropriation of retained earnings to assure the availability of resources to absorb the losses if they materialize. The establishment of an asset valuation balance or a liability balance is not appropriate under these circumstances; the provision for contingencies is related to losses of the future that may or may not take place, not to losses of the past or of the present. In the event the contingencies fail to materialize, the board of directors may authorize cancellation of the provision for contingencies, and the appropriated balance would then be returned to retained earnings. If the contingencies do materialize, the appropriated balance is still returned to retained earnings and the losses are assigned to the period in which they materialized.

To illustrate the foregoing, assume that management, in reviewing business conditions at the end of 1975, concludes there may be a general business decline in the next year or two and authorizes an appropriation of $500,000 for general contingencies. In 1977, the company sells some investment land at a loss of $150,000. At the end of 1977, with prospects for business good, management decides to cancel the provision for general contingencies. The following entries record the appropriation for general contingencies, the recognition of the loss on the sale of the land, and the return of the appropriation to retained earnings.

1975:	Retained Earnings	500,000	
	Retained Earnings Appropriated for General Contingencies		500,000
1977:	Cash	250,000	
	Loss on Sale of Land	150,000	
	Land		400,000
	Retained Earnings Appropriated for General Contingencies	500,000	
	Retained Earnings		500,000

Appropriations to Describe Business Purposes Served by Retained Earnings

Corporate officials may authorize appropriations to show the use of retained earnings within the business. For example, assume earnings are to be retained by a company to finance the expansion of plant facilities. Or assume resources from earnings have already been applied to plant expansion. In either instance, instead of continuing to report undistributed profits in retained earnings, which may be interpreted by stockholders as amounts available for dividends, the company may authorize transfers from retained earnings to a special account describing the utilization of earnings. A permanent increase in a company's working capital position may likewise suggest an appropriation of earnings. Such appropriations may be carried forward indefinitely. On the other hand, in view of the permanent commitment of assets, the company may choose to effect a permanent capitalization of retained earnings by means of a stock dividend.

Objections to Appropriation Procedures

The Committee on Concepts and Standards Underlying Corporate Financial Statements of the American Accounting Association has taken issue with the general practice of earmarking retained earnings through the appropriation procedure, pointing out that such practice may serve to confuse and mislead those using the financial statements. When earnings are retained, the objectives of the retention are best explained, in the opinion of the Committee, by narrative materials accompanying the statements. Managerial policy arises from a number of complex factors; the "Stockholders' equity" section of the balance sheet is hardly the most practical vehicle for the description of this policy. In considering the problems presented by reserves and retained earnings, the Committee has recommended:

1. The term "reserve" should not be employed in published financial statements of business corporations.
2. The "reserve section" in corporate balance sheets should be eliminated and its elements exhibited as deduction-from-asset, or liability, or retained income amounts.
3. Appropriations of retained income should not be made or displayed in such a manner as to create misleading inferences.
(a) Appropriations of retained income which purport to reflect managerial policies relative to earnings retention are ineffective, and frequently misleading, unless all retained income which has in fact been committed to operating capital is earmarked. Partial appropriation fosters the implication that retained earnings not earmarked are available for distribution as dividends.
(b) Appropriations of retained income required by law or contract preferably should be disclosed by footnote. If required to be displayed as balance sheet amounts, such appropriations should be included in the proprietary section.
(c) Appropriations of retained income reflecting anticipated future losses, or conjectural past or present losses (when it is not established by reasonably objective evidence that any loss has been incurred) preferably should be disclosed by footnote. If displayed as balance sheet amounts, such appropriations should be included in the proprietary section.
(d) In any event, whenever appropriations are exhibited in a balance sheet, the retained income (excluding amounts formally capitalized) should be summarized in one total.
4. The determination of periodic earnings is not affected by the appropriation of retained income or the restoration of such appropriated amounts to unappropriated retained income.[1]

There can be little objection to the position taken by the Committee, and the use of appropriations is declining.

DEDUCTIONS FROM TOTAL STOCKHOLDERS' EQUITY

As previously discussed, there are now two situations in which a deduction may be taken from the total stockholders' equity: the cost of treasury stock,[2] and the accumulated changes in the valuation allowance for the marketable equity securities portfolio included in noncurrent assets.[3] These may be referred to as contra equity accounts.

---

[1] *Accounting and Reporting Standards for Corporate Financial Statements and Preceding Statements and Supplements, op. cit.,* p. 19.
[2] Chapter 19, page 535.
[3] Chapter 14, page 390.

These deductions from total stockholders' equity are dissimilar in origin, but both have the result of reducing the stockholders' equity position of the company. Some loan agreements may require a company to maintain a certain amount of stockholders' equity in relation to its debt. The reduction of stockholders' equity due to the decline in value of long-term investments could cause a violation of these requirements. For example, assume a company was required to maintain a debt-to-equity ratio of .66 or less, and that a market decline of $75,000 was incurred on long-term investments held by the company. Before the entry recognizing the market decline in long-term securities, the company had debt of $1,000,000 and stockholders' equity of $1,550,000, or a debt-to-equity ratio of .645 ($1,000,000 ÷ $1,550,000). This ratio thus meets the requirements. After the entry for the market decline, stockholders' equity would be reduced to $1,475,000 and the debt-to-equity ratio increased to .678, a figure that would be in violation of the loan agreement.

FINANCIAL STATEMENTS PREPARED FOR THE CORPORATION

Transactions affecting the stockholders' equity have been described in this and the preceding two chapters. The persons who refer to the financial statements of a corporation must be provided with a full explanation of the changes during the period in the individual balances comprising the stockholders' equity. In the remaining pages of this chapter, the financial statements for the General Manufacturing Company are illustrated with special attention directed to the stockholders' equity section of the balance sheet. The statements are prepared as of December 31, 1977, and summarize the position of the company as of this date and operations for the year ending on this date.

The Balance Sheet The balance sheet for the General Manufacturing Company as of December 31, 1977, is given on pages 582 and 583. Classifications and the presentation of financial data follow the standards developed in the preceding chapters. The following matters deserve special attention:

1. The stockholders' equity is reported in terms of its source: (a) the amount paid in by stockholders; and (b) the amount representing earnings retained in the business.
2. The classes of capital stock are reported separately and are described in detail. Information is offered concerning the nature of the stock, the number of shares authorized, the number of shares issued, and the number of shares reacquired and held as treasury stock.
3. The capital items representing paid-in capital and retained earnings are reported in detail; when paid-in capital and appropriated retained earnings are composed of a great many items, related balances are frequently combined and reported in total on the balance sheet.
4. In complying with legal requirements, the company has reported retained earnings equivalent to the cost of the treasury stock held as an appropriation of retained earnings.

Reference is made at the bottom of the balance sheet to the notes accompanying the financial statements. (These notes appear on page

General
Balance
December

Assets

Current assets:		
Cash on hand and on deposit..		$ 55,000
U.S. Government securities (reported at cost; market value, $87,500).......		86,000
Trade notes and accounts receivable..	$182,600	
Less allowance for doubtful accounts	2,600	180,000
Inventories (Note 1a):		
Finished goods..	$190,000	
Goods in process	200,000	
Raw materials and supplies..	185,000	575,000
Loans, advances, and accrued income items		20,000
Prepayments including taxes, insurance, and sundry current items		14,500
Total current assets...		$ 930,500
Long-term investments:		
Marketable equity securities (cost $124,000, less allowance to reduce valuation to market, $24,000)		$ 100,000
Fund consisting of U.S. Government securities to be used for property additions		150,000
Land held for future expansion		110,000
Total long-term investments...		360,000
Land, buildings, and equipment (Note 1b):		
Land, buildings, and equipment, at cost	$1,235,000	
Less accumulated depreciation	580,000	
Total land, buildings, and equipment...		655,000
Intangible assets (Note 1c):		
Patents, formulas, and goodwill — less amortization		120,000
Other assets:		
Advance payments on equipment purchase contracts		102,500
Total assets		$2,168,000

See accompanying notes to financial statements.

585.) This reference would also appear on the other financial statements prepared by the company.

The Income Statement   The income statement for the General Manufacturing Company is prepared in condensed single-step form. The income statement for the year ended December 31, 1977, is illustrated on page 584.

With single amounts reported for sales and for cost of goods sold, special supporting schedules may be provided to offer an analysis of these balances in terms of the major divisions of the business or of the different product lines. With single amounts reported for selling, general and administrative, and other expenses, supporting schedules may be provided to indicate the individual items composing such totals.

Manufacturing Company
Sheet
31, 1977

Liabilities			
Current liabilities:			
Notes and accounts payable..		$ 52,500	
Income tax payable...		12,000	
Payroll, interest, and taxes payable..		23,500	
Serial debenture bonds due May 1, 1978..		20,000	
Customers' deposits and sundry items...		24,000	
Total current liabilities..			$ 132,000
Long-term liabilities:			
Twenty-year 7% first-mortgage bonds..	$260,000		
Less unamortized discount on first-mortgage bonds............................	10,000	$ 250,000	
Serial 7½% debenture bonds due May 1, 1979, to May 1, 1987, inclusive..		180,000	
Deferred leasehold revenue (Note 1d)		200,000	
Liability under pension plan (Note 2)...		20,000	
Contingent liabilities (Note 3)			
Total long-term liabilities..			650,000
Total liabilities...			$ 782,000
Stockholders' Equity			
Paid-in capital:			
Preferred 6% stock, $100 par, cumulative, callable, 5,000 shares authorized and issued (Note 4)..	$500,000		
No-par common stock, $5 stated value, 100,000 shares authorized, 60,000 shares issued; treasury stock, 5,000 shares — deducted below..	300,000	$ 800,000	
Paid-in capital:			
From sale of common stock at more than stated value............................	$260,000		
From sale of treasury stock at more than cost	16,000	276,000	
Total paid-in capital..		$1,076,000	
Retained earnings:			
Appropriated:			
For purchase of treasury stock..	$40,000		
For contingencies...	85,000	$125,000	
Unappropriated..		225,000	
Total retained earnings..		350,000	
Total paid-in capital and retained earnings...		$1,426,000	
Deduct: Common treasury stock, at cost (2,000 shares acquired at $8).......	$ 16,000		
Net unrealized loss on noncurrent marketable equity securities (Note 4)..	24,000	40,000	
Total stockholders' equity			1,386,000
Total liabilities and stockholders' equity...			$2,168,000

Statements
Accounting
for the
Changes in
the
Stockholders'
Equity

Those who wish to be fully informed on the financial position and results of operations of the corporation require full information explaining the change in the stockholders' equity. When changes in paid-in capital have taken place, a *paid-in capital statement* may be prepared. This statement reports the paid-in capital balances at the beginning of the period and the changes in these balances during the period as a result of such transactions as the sale of capital stock, stock dividends, the retirement of stock, and the purchase and sale of treasury stock. The paid-in capital statement for the General Manufacturing Company for the year ended December 31, 1977, is shown on page 584.

The changes in retained earnings are summarized in the retained earnings statement. In some instances, it is necessary to recognize addi-

General Manufacturing Company
Income Statement
For Year Ended December 31, 1977

Revenues:		
Sales..	$1,550,000	
Other revenue...	100,000	$1,650,000
Expenses:		
Cost of goods sold..	$ 940,000	
Selling expense...	300,000	
General and administrative expense....................................	125,000	
Other expense...	80,000	
Income tax...	92,500	1,537,500
Income before extraordinary items...		$ 112,500
Extraordinary gain on early extinguishment of debt, net of tax .		7,500
Net income...		$ 120,000
Earnings per common share:[1]		
Income before extraordinary items		$1.50
Extraordinary income		.14
Net income...		$1.64

Condensed Single-Step Income Statement

General Manufacturing Company
Paid-In Capital Statement
For Year Ended December 31, 1977

	Preferred Stock	Common Stock	Paid-In Capital	Total
Paid-in capital, January 1, 1977	$300,000	$300,000	$260,000*	$ 860,000
Add: Increase from sale of 1,000 shares of preferred stock at the beginning of 1977 at par value..........	200,000			200,000
Increase from sale of 25,000 shares of treasury stock, common, at the beginning of 1977, cost $20,000, for $36,000			16,000	16,000
Paid-in capital, December 31, 1977	$500,000	$300,000	$276,000	$1,076,000

*From sale of common stock at more than stated value.

Paid-In Capital Statement

tional changes, such as those resulting from prior period adjustments, the acquisition of treasury stock, and transfers to paid-in capital. Frequently the retained earnings statement is expanded to show changes in both unappropriated and appropriated balances. The statement then summarizes transfers from the unappropriated retained earnings account to accounts reporting appropriations, and also transfers from accounts reporting appropriations to the unappropriated retained earnings account.

The form of statements reconciling paid-in capital and retained earnings vary greatly in practice. However, the following rules should be observed in their preparation:

---

[1]Preferred dividend requirements are subtracted from earnings to arrive at earnings related to common shares. This computation, as well as computations for more complex capital structures, are described in the following chapter.

1. Paid-in capital and retained earnings changes should be summarized separately.
2. The beginning balances should be those reported on the balance sheet at the end of the preceding period; the changes should provide the balances reported in the balance sheet at the end of the current period.
3. Changes in balances that have taken place during the period should be classified and listed in some consistent manner.

The General Manufacturing Company's retained earnings statement for the year ended December 31, 1977, is illustrated below.

General Manufacturing Company
Retained Earnings Statement
For Year Ended December 31, 1977

	Retained Earnings		
	Appropriated for Purchase of Treasury Stock	Appropriated for Contingencies	Unappropriated
Balances, January 1, 1977	$60,000	$50,000	$202,500
Prior period adjustment — correction of 1975 error, net of tax..			(25,000)
Balances, January 1, 1977, as adjusted...........................	$60,000	$50,000	$177,500
Return to retained earnings of earnings previously restricted through ownership of treasury stock..............	(20,000)		20,000
Retained earnings appropriated for contingencies		35,000	(35,000)
Cash dividends:			
Preferred stock, $6 on 5,000 shares, $30,000...............			
Common stock, 50¢ on 55,000 shares, $27,500			(57,500)
Net income for 1977......................................			120,000
Balances, December 31, 1977	$40,000	$85,000	$225,000

Retained Earnings Statement

**GENERAL MANUFACTURING COMPANY
NOTES TO FINANCIAL STATEMENTS — YEAR ENDED DECEMBER 31, 1977**

1. The following is a summary of significant accounting policies followed by General Manufacturing Company.

    (a) Inventories are valued at cost or market, whichever is lower. Cost is calculated by the first-in, first-out method.

    (b) Depreciation is computed for both the books and the tax return by the double-declining balance method.

    (c) Intangible assets are being amortized over the period of their estimated useful lives: patents, 10 years; formulas, 8 years; and goodwill, 20 years.

    (d) The company leased Sinclair Street properties for a 15-year period ending January 1, 1989. Leasehold payment received in advance is being recognized as revenue over the life of the lease.

2. The company has accrued $20,000 more under the pension plan than it has paid. At December 31, 1977, the balance in the pension fund exceeds the vested benefits as of that date. No further accrual of past service cost is therefore considered necessary.

3. The company is contingently liable on guaranteed notes and accounts totaling $40,000. Also, various suits are pending on which the ultimate payment cannot be determined. In the opinion of counsel and management, such liability, if any, will not be material. Retained earnings has been appropriated in anticipation of possible losses.

4. Preferred stock may be redeemed at the option of the board of directors at 105 plus accrued dividends on or before December 31, 1979, and at gradually reduced amounts but at not less than 102½ plus accrued dividends after January 1, 1985.

Statement Accounting for the Changes in Financial Position

Reference was made in earlier chapters to the statement of changes in financial position required to offer a full reporting of a company's operations. This statement is prepared from comparative balance sheets as of the beginning and end of the period and summarizes the financing and investing activities that resulted in the change in financial position. The preparation of this statement is described and illustrated in Chapter 24.

QUESTIONS

1. Accumulated earnings are in general supported by a cross section of all of the assets. Directors are criticized by stockholders for failure to declare dividends when accumulated earnings are present. Are these two statements related? Explain.

2. Which of the following transactions are a source of stockholders' equity? Indicate the class of stockholders' equity in each case.

   (a) Operating profits.
   (b) Cancellation of a part of a liability upon prompt payment of the balance.
   (c) Reduction of par value of stock outstanding.
   (d) Discovery of an understatement of income in a previous period.
   (e) Release of Retained Earnings Appropriated for Purchase of Treasury Stock upon the sale of treasury stock.
   (f) Issue of bonds at a premium.
   (g) Purchase of the corporation's own capital stock at a discount.
   (h) Increase in the company's earning capacity, taken to be evidence of considerable goodwill.
   (i) Construction of equipment for the company's own use at a cost less than the prevailing market price of identical equipment.
   (j) Donation to the corporation of its own stock.
   (k) Sale of land, buildings, and equipment at a gain.
   (l) Gain on bond retirement.
   (m) Revaluation of land, buildings, and equipment resulting in an increase in asset book value as a result of increase in asset replacement value.
   (n) Collection of stock assessments from stockholders.
   (o) Discovery of valuable resources on company property.
   (p) Conversion of bonds into common stock.
   (q) Conversion of preferred stock into common stock.

3. The following announcement appeared on the financial page of a newspaper:

"The Board of Directors of the Maxwell Co., at their meeting on June 15, 1977, declared the regular quarterly dividend on outstanding common stock of 50 cents per share and an extra dividend of $1 per share, both payable on July 10, 1977, to the stockholders of record at the close of business June 30, 1977."

   (a) What is the purpose of each of the three dates given in the declaration? (b) When would the stock become "ex-dividend"? (c) Why is the $1 designated as an "extra" dividend?

4. Dividends are sometimes said to have been paid "out of retained earnings." What is wrong with this statement?

5. The directors of Lenox Corporation are considering the issuance of a stock dividend. They have asked you to discuss the proposed action by answering the questions below:

   (a) What is a stock dividend? How is a stock dividend distinguished from a stock split: (1) from a legal standpoint? (2) from an accounting standpoint?
   (b) For what reasons does a corporation usually declare (1) a stock dividend? (2) a stock split? (3) a stock split in the form of a stock dividend?

6. The Blattner Co. has 1,000,000 shares of no-par common outstanding. Dividends have been limited to approximately 20% of annual earnings, remaining earnings being used to finance expansion. With pressure from stockholders for an increase in dividends, the board of directors takes action to issue to stockholders an additional 1,000,000 shares of stock, and the president of the company informs stockholders that the company will pay a 100% stock dividend in view of the conservative dividend policy in the past. What is your comment on this statement?

7. It has been recommended that the balance sheet maintain a permanent distinction between paid-in capital and retained earnings. How can such a distinction be maintained when action is taken to convert retained earnings into capital stock?

8. (a) What is a liquidating dividend? (b) Under what circumstances are such distributions made? (c) How would you recommend that liquidating dividends be recorded in the accounts of the corporation?

9. At the regular meeting of the board of directors of the May Corporation, a dividend payable in the stock of the June Corporation is to be declared. The stock of the June Corporation is recorded on the books of May Corporation at $87,000; the market value of the stock is $100,000.

The question is raised whether the amount to be recorded for the dividend payable should be the book value or the market value. What is the proper accounting treatment?

10. The Byron Corporation, acting within the law of the state of incorporation, paid a cash dividend to stockholders for which it debited Paid-In Capital from Sale of Stock at a Premium. A stockholder protested, saying that such a dividend was a partial liquidation of her holdings. Is this true?

11. What methods can be followed in reporting dividends in arrears on preferred stock on the balance sheet?

12. Why should Retained Earnings not be credited for gains arising from a company dealing in its own stock if losses for similar transactions are debited to the account?

13. (a) What criticisms have been made of the term *reserve*? (b) What position has been taken by the American Institute of Certified Public Accountants and by the American Accounting Association with respect to the use of the term? (c) What position would you take with respect to use of the term? What substitute terms would you employ?

14. Some of the following account titles use the term *reserve* improperly. For each account indicate (a) the proper account title, and (b) the heading under which it would appear in the balance sheet.

    (1) Reserve for Contingencies
    (2) Reserve for Doubtful Accounts
    (3) Reserve for Possible Inventory Decline
    (4) Reserve for Self-Insurance — Fire Loss
    (5) Reserve for Bond Retirement
    (6) Reserve for Income Tax
    (7) Reserve for Undeclared Dividends
    (8) Reserve for Increased Investment in Land, Buildings, and Equipment
    (9) Reserve for Depletion
   (10) Reserve for Redeemable Coupons Outstanding
   (11) Reserve for Repairs and Replacements
   (12) Reserve for Purchase of Treasury Stock
   (13) Reserve for Personal Injury Claims Pending
   (14) Reserve for Unrealized Building Appreciation
   (15) Reserve for Leasehold Amortization
   (16) Reserve for Restoration of Properties upon Termination of Lease
   (17) Reserve for Sales Discounts
   (18) Reserve for Reduction of Inventory to Market
   (19) Reserve for Vacation Pay for Employees

15. The use of appropriation accounts to disclose contingencies has declined. What method of disclosure has replaced appropriation accounts? Evaluate the disclosure methods as to their communication value for statement readers.

16. A stockholder of Barker, Inc., does not understand the purpose of the Appropriation for Bond Redemption Fund that has been set up by periodic debits to Retained Earnings. He is told that this balance will not be used to redeem the bonds at their maturity. (a) What account will be reduced by the payment of the bonds? (b) What purpose is accomplished by the Appropriation for Bond Redemption Fund? (c) What dispositions may be made of the appropriation?

17. Management Research, Inc., has appropriated retained earnings of $5,000,000 over a five-year period for plant expansion. In the sixth year the company completes an expansion program at a cost of $6,500,000; such expansion is financed through company funds of $4,500,000, and borrowed funds of $2,000,000. What disposition of the appropriation for plant expansion would you recommend?

18. Management of the Gilbert Co., considering the possibility of a strike by employees, authorized the establishment of an appropriation for contingencies at the end of 1976 by a charge to revenue. The strike was called in 1977, and company losses incurred to the date of the strike settlement were charged against the appropriation. The company management points out that it exercised good judgment in anticipating strike losses and providing a cushion for such losses. What criticism, if any, can you offer of the accounting procedures followed by the company?

19. Mr. Collins, President of Bolinder Corp., is concerned by the FASB Statement that prevents his company from accruing estimated losses from self-insurance for fire loss. Assets are scattered over a wide geographical area and Mr. Collins feels the company can economically carry its own insurance risks. But he feels that revenue of each period should bear part of the fire loss, not just the periods in which the losses occur. Explain to Mr. Collins the rationale supporting the FASB position.

20. What items are defined as contra equity accounts and deducted from the total stockholders' equity?

21. The Clark Co. reports appropriations as a subtraction from net income at the bottom of the income statement. When an appropriation is canceled, it is reported as an addition to net income on the income statement. What objections would you raise to such a practice?

22. Which of the following transactions change total stockholders' equity? What is the nature of the change?

(a) Declaration of a cash dividend.
(b) Payment of a cash dividend.
(c) Retirement of bonds payable for which both a redemption fund and an appropriation had been established.
(d) Declaration of a stock dividend.
(e) Payment of a stock dividend.
(f) Conversion of bonds payable into preferred stock.
(g) The passing of a dividend on cumulative preferred stock.
(h) Donation by the officers of shares of stock.
(i) Operating loss for the period.

23. How would you report the following items on the balance sheet: (a) dividends in arrears on cumulative preferred stock, (b) unclaimed bond interest and unclaimed dividends, (c) stock purchase rights issued but not exercised as of the balance sheet date, (d) stock that is callable at a premium at the option of the corporation?

EXERCISES

1. The retained earnings account for the Hobert Company shows the following debits and credits. Give whatever entries may be required to correct the account.

ACCOUNT   Retained Earnings

DATE		ITEM	DEBIT	CREDIT	BALANCE DEBIT	BALANCE CREDIT
Jan.	1	Balance..................................				75,200
(a)		Loss from fire..............................	750			74,450
(b)		Write-off of goodwill..................	7,500			66,950
(c)		Stock dividend	20,000			46,950
(d)		Loss on sale of equipment.........	6,900			40,050
(e)		Officers compensation related to income of prior periods — accrual overlooked	46,500		6,450	
(f)		Loss on retirement of preferred shares at more than issuance price	10,000		16,450	
(g)		Premium on common stock.......		18,500		2,050
(h)		Stock subscription defaults.......		1,210		3,260
(i)		Gain on retirement of preferred stock at less than issuance price		3,700		6,960
(j)		Gain on early retirement of bonds at less than book value......................................		2,150		9,110
(k)		Gain on life insurance policy settlement..............................		1,500		10,610
(l)		Correction of prior period error		7,150		17,760

2. The balance sheet of the Packard Corporation shows the following on July 1:

Cash	$200,000
Capital stock, $10 par, 100,000 shares authorized, 50,000 shares issued and outstanding..	500,000
Paid-in capital	100,000
Retained earnings..	230,000

On July 1, Packard Corporation declared a cash dividend of $1 per share payable on October 1. Then on October 1, the corporation issued a scrip dividend of $2 per share payable on December 31, with interest at a rate of 7%. Finally, on November 1, the corporation declared a 15% stock dividend with the shares to be issued on December 31. Market value on November 1 was $15 per share. Give the necessary entries to record the declaration and payment or issuance of the dividends.

3. The balance sheet of the Fast Corporation shows the following:

Capital stock, $5 stated value, 40,000 shares issued and outstanding	$200,000
Paid-in capital	400,000
Retained earnings	175,000

A 25% stock dividend is declared, the board of directors authorizing a transfer from Retained Earnings to Capital Stock at the stock stated value.

    (a) Give entries to record the declaration and payment of the dividend.
    (b) What was the effect of the issue of the stock dividend on the ownership equity of each stockholder in the corporation?
    (c) Give entries to record the declaration and payment of the dividend if the board of directors had elected to transfer amounts from Retained Earnings to Capital Stock equal to the market value of the stock ($10 per share).

4. The capital accounts for the Dean Co. on June 30, 1977, follow:

Capital Stock, $20 par, 100,000 shares	$2,000,000
Premium on Capital Stock	725,000
Retained Earnings	3,600,000

Shares of the company's stock are selling at this time at 36. What entries would you make in each case below?

    (a) A stock dividend of 10% is declared and issued.
    (b) A stock dividend of 100% is declared and issued.
    (c) A 2-for-1 stock split is declared and issued.

5. The dividend declarations and distributions by the Federal Company over a three-year period are listed below. Give the entry required in each case.

1975
July   1 Declared a 25% stock dividend on 1,000,000 shares of stock, par value $15. The stock was originally sold at $17, and Retained Earnings is to be debited for the stock dividend for an amount equal to the original stock issuance price.
July 15 Distributed the stock dividend declared on July 1, which included fractional warrants for 1,600 shares.
Sept. 1 1,000 shares were issued for fractional warrants; remaining fractional warrants expired.
1976
July   1 Declared a scrip dividend of $2 per share, payable on January 1, 1977, with interest at the rate of 8%.
1977
Jan.   1 Paid scrip dividend.
July   1 Declared a dividend of 1 share of Eastern Co. common stock on every share of Federal Company stock owned. Eastern Co. common stock is carried on the books of the Federal Company at a cost of $1.50 per share, and the market price is $2 per share.
July 15 Distributed Eastern Co. common stock to shareholders.

6. On January 1, 1975, the Fast Foods Corporation floated a $10,000,000 bond issue. The bond issue agreement with the underwriters required Fast Foods to appropriate earnings of $625,000 at the end of each year until the bonds are retired. During their 1977 board meeting, the directors decided to change the company's financing policy to just short-term debt and equity, and to drop their present insurance policy in favor of a self-insurance plan. On July 1, 1977, the company retired the bond issue and set up their first annual appropriation for self-insurance by debiting Self-Insurance Expense for $10,000 and crediting Retained Earnings Appropriated for Self-Insurance. *(continued)*

    (a) Give the entries to record the periodic appropriations under the bond issue agreement for 1975 and 1976 and their cancellation in 1977.

    (b) Did the company use generally accepted accounting principles in setting up their appropriation for self-insurance? Explain.

    (c) If the answer to (b) is no, what entry should have been made?

7. A physical inventory taken by the Fisher Co. on December 31, 1977, discloses goods on hand with a cost of $860,000; the inventory is recorded at this figure less an allowance of $36,000 to reduce it to the lower of cost or market. At the same time, the company authorizes that an appropriation for possible future inventory decline of $300,000 be established.

    (a) Give the entries to be made at the end of 1977 in recording the inventory and establishing the accounts as indicated.

    (b) Give the entries in 1978 to close the beginning inventory and balances established at the end of 1977, assuming that the estimated inventory decline does not materialize and that the inventory at the end of 1978 is properly reported at cost, which is lower than market.

    (c) Give the entries in 1978 to close the inventory and other account balances established at the end of 1977 if a decline in the value of the December 31, 1977 inventory of $160,000 is to be recognized; the inventory at the end of 1978 is properly reported at cost, which is lower than its market value at this date.

8. The Script Co. reports appropriated retained earnings on its balance sheet at the end of 1977 at $335,000. Analysis of the account balances in support of this total discloses the following:

Reserve for contingencies — to meet estimated claims arising from damage suits in 1977 for which the company has been held to be liable	$ 45,000
Reserve for self-insurance for fire loss — to meet possible fire losses as a result of self-insurance on this contingency..	40,000
Reserve for pensions — to meet estimated pension costs arising from contracts with employees	195,000
Reserve for possible declines on marketable securities — to meet possible future losses on marketable securities...	25,000
Reserve for property rehabilitation costs — to meet costs of rehabilitating plant at termination of lease in accordance with contractual requirements ...	30,000

    (a) Which of the above items, if any, would you exclude from the appropriated retained earnings classification?

    (b) State how you would classify such items, and what account title you would use.

9. For each of the following items, give the title of the account that would be credited and where it would be reported on financial statements.

    (a) 15% stock dividend declared on common stock.
    (b) Transfer to reserve for bond redemption fund.
    (c) Profit-sharing bonus to employees.
    (d) Gain on sale of treasury stock.
    (e) Donation of land by government agency.
    (f) Gain on sale of investment in securities.
    (g) Premium on sale of bonds.
    (h) Gain on sale of property originally acquired by exchange for capital stock.

10. The directors of Roof Corporation, whose $80 par value common stock is currently selling at $100 per share, have decided to issue a stock dividend. Roof has an authorization for 400,000 shares of common, has issued 220,000 shares of which 20,000 shares are now held as treasury stock, and desires to capitalize $1,600,000 of the retained earnings account balance. What percent stock dividend should be issued to accomplish this desire?

PROBLEMS

20-1. The Hansen Company was organized on June 30, 1975. After two and one-half years of profitable operations, the equity section of Hansen's balance sheet was as follows:

Paid-in capital:
Common stock, $20 par, 500,000 shares authorized, 100,000 shares issued
  and outstanding... $2,000,000
Premium on common stock..   500,000
Retained earnings   1,800,000
Total stockholders' equity $4,300,000

During 1978, the following transactions affected the stockholders' equity:

Jan. 31 10,000 shares of common stock were reacquired at $22.50; treasury stock is reported at cost.
Apr. 1 The company declared a 30% stock dividend.
Apr. 30 The company declared a 50-cent cash dividend.
June 1 The stock dividend was issued and the cash dividend was paid.
Aug. 31 The treasury stock was sold at $25.
Sept. 30 Since the company needs its cash to meet a debt obligation due on October 10, the board of directors declared a scrip dividend of 75 cents per share with interest at a rate of 8%.
Dec. 31 The scrip dividend was paid.

Instructions: Give journal entries to record the above stock transactions.

20-2. The stockholders' equity of the High Co. on June 30, 1977, was as follows:

Paid-in capital:
Preferred 8% stock, $50 par, cumulative, 20,000 shares issued, dividends
  5 years in arrears.. $1,000,000
Common stock, $20 par, 160,000 shares issued   3,200,000
                                                                                          $4,200,000
Less deficit from operations...   600,000
Total stockholders' equity $3,600,000

On this date the following action was taken:

(a) Common stockholders turned in their stock and received in exchange new common stock, 1 share of the new stock being exchanged for every 4 shares of the old. New stock was given a stated value of $40 per share.
(b) One-half share of the new common stock was issued on each share of preferred stock outstanding in liquidation of dividends in arrears on preferred stock.
(c) The deficit from operations was applied against the paid-in capital arising from the common stock restatement.

Transactions for the remainder of 1977 affecting the stockholders' equity were as follows:

Oct. 1 10,000 shares of preferred stock were called in at $55 plus dividends for 3 months at 8%. Stock was formally retired.
Nov. 10 60,000 shares of new common stock were sold at 42.
Dec. 31 Net income for the six months ended on this date was $170,000. (Debit Income Summary.) The semiannual dividend was declared on preferred shares and a 50-cent dividend on common shares, dividends being payable January 20, 1978.

Instructions:
(1) Record in journal form the transactions given above.
(2) Prepare the "Stockholders' equity" section of the balance sheet as of December 31, 1977.

20-3. The Max Co. was organized on January 2, 1976, with authorized stock consisting of 40,000 shares of 8%, nonparticipating, $100 par preferred, and 250,000 shares of no-par common. During the first two years of the company's existence, the following transactions took place:

1976
Jan. 2 Sold 10,600 shares of common stock at 8.
      2 Sold 2,600 shares of preferred stock at 108.
Mar. 2 Sold common stock as follows: 10,200 shares at 11; 2,400 shares at 12.

(continued)

1976

July   10   A nearby piece of land, appraised at $202,000 was acquired for 600 shares of preferred stock and 28,000 shares of common. (Preferred stock was recorded at 108, the balance being assigned to common.)

Dec.   16   The regular preferred and a 75 cent common dividend were declared.

        28   Dividends declared on December 16 were paid.

        31   The income summary account showed a credit balance of $204,000, which was transferred to retained earnings.

1977

Feb.   27   The corporation reacquired 12,000 shares of common stock at 9. The treasury stock is carried at cost. (State law requires that an appropriation of retained earnings be made for the purchase price of treasury stock. Appropriations are to be returned to retained earnings upon resale of the stock.)

June 17   Resold 10,000 shares of treasury stock at 10.

July 31   Resold all of the remaining treasury stock at 9½.

Sept. 30   The corporation sold 12,000 additional shares of common stock at 10½.

Dec. 16   The regular preferred dividend and a 40 cents common dividend were declared.

        28   Dividends declared on December 16 were paid.

        31   The income summary account showed a credit balance of $178,000, which was transferred to retained earnings.

Instructions:

(1)   Give the journal entries to record the foregoing transactions.

(2)   Prepare the "Stockholders' equity" section of the balance sheet as of December 31, 1977.

20-4. A condensed balance sheet for Ferris, Inc., as of December 31, 1974, appears below:

Ferris, Inc.
Balance Sheet
December 31, 1974

Assets		Liabilities and Stockholders' Equity	
Assets...................................	$350,000	Liabilities	$ 80,000
		Preferred 8% stock, $100 par.....	50,000
		Common stock, $50 par	100,000
		Premium on common stock.......	20,000
		Retained earnings......................	100,000
		Total liabilities and stock-	
Total assets	$350,000	holders' equity........................	$350,000

Capital stock authorized consists of: 500 shares of 8%, cumulative, nonparticipating preferred stock with a prior claim on assets, and 10,000 shares of common stock.

Information relating to operations of the succeeding three years follows:

	1975	1976	1977
Dividends declared on Dec. 20, payable on Jan. 10 of following year:			
Preferred stock	8% cash	8% cash	8% cash
Common stock.....................................	{ $1.00 cash 50% stock*	$1.25 cash	$1.00 cash
Net income for year................................	$45,000	$26,000	$34,000

*Retained earnings is reduced by the par value of the stock dividend.

1976

Feb.   12   Accumulated depreciation was reduced by $48,000 following an income tax investigation. (Assume that this was an error and qualifies as a prior period adjustment.) Additional income tax of $15,000 for prior years was paid.

Mar.   3   200 shares of common stock were purchased by the corporation at $54 per share; treasury stock is recorded at cost and retained earnings are appropriated equal to such cost.

1977

Aug. 10 All of the treasury stock was resold at $59 per share and the retained earnings appropriation was canceled.

Sept. 12 By vote of the stockholders, each share of the common stock was exchanged by the corporation for 4 shares of no-par common stock with a stated value of $15.

Instructions:

(1) Give the journal entries to record the foregoing transactions for the three-year period ended December 31, 1977.

(2) Prepare the "Stockholders' equity" section of the balance sheet as it would appear at the end of 1975, 1976, and 1977.

20-5. On March 31, 1977, the retained earnings account of Jamison, Inc., showed a balance of $3,500,000. The board of directors of Jamison, Inc., made the following decisions during the remainder of 1977 that possibly affect the retained earnings account.

Apr. 1 Jamison, Inc., decided to assume the risk for workmen's compensation. The estimated liability for the first quarter of 1977 is $30,000. Also, a fund was set up to cover the estimated liability.

Apr. 30 Jamison, Inc., has not experienced even a small fire since 1942; therefore, the board of directors decided to start a self-insurance plan. They decided to start with a $100,000 appropriation.

May 15 A fire did considerable damage to the outside warehouse. It cost $90,000 to repair the warehouse.

Aug. 20 The board of directors received a report from the plant engineer which indicated that the company is possibly in violation of pollution control standards. The fine for such a violation is $200,000. As a result of the engineer's report, the board decided to set up a general contingency reserve for $200,000.

Sept. 15 The company reacquired 20,000 shares of their own stock at $29; treasury stock is recorded at cost. Due to legal restrictions, Jamison has to set up an appropriation to cover the cost of the treasury stock.

Dec. 31 The company had to pay a $200,000 fine for pollution control violations and the treasury stock was sold at $31. No workmen's compensation was paid during the year.

Instructions: Prepare all of the necessary entries to record the above transactions.

20-6. Accounts of the Sierra Co. on December 31, 1977, show the balances listed below:

Accumulated Depreciation — Buildings		$ 340,000
Allowance for Purchase Discounts	$ 3,000	
Bonds Payable		400,000
Bond Retirement Fund	160,000	
Buildings	1,500,000	
Capital Stock (100,000 shares authorized)		790,000
Capital Stock Subscribed (5,000 shares)		50,000
Current Assets	960,000	
Current Liabilities — Other		325,000
Customers' Deposits		25,000
Dividends Payable — Cash		20,000
Income Tax Payable		50,000
Paid-In Capital from Sale of Treasury Stock at More Than Cost		40,000
Premium on Capital Stock		30,000
Retained Earnings Appropriated for Contingencies		125,000
Retained Earnings Appropriated for Bond Retirement Fund		160,000
Retained Earnings Appropriated for Purchase of Treasury Stock		70,000
Stock Dividends Distributable		82,000
Treasury Stock, 6,000 shares at cost	70,000	
Unappropriated Retained Earnings		186,000
	$2,693,000	$2,693,000

Instructions: From this data prepare the "Stockholders' equity" section as it would appear on the balance sheet.

20-7. The following accounts are taken from the ledger of Harris Co.

ACCOUNT   Retained Earnings Appropriated for Plant Expansion

DATE		ITEM	DEBIT	CREDIT	BALANCE DEBIT	BALANCE CREDIT
1977 Jan.	1	Balance....................................				150,000
Dec.	31			25,000		175,000

ACCOUNT   Retained Earnings Appropriated for Purchase of Treasury Stock

DATE		ITEM	DEBIT	CREDIT	BALANCE DEBIT	BALANCE CREDIT
1977 Jan.	1	Balance....................................				92,000
Apr.	1			31,000		123,000
July	1		42,000			81,000

ACCOUNT   Unappropriated Retained Earnings

DATE		ITEM	DEBIT	CREDIT	BALANCE DEBIT	BALANCE CREDIT
1977 Jan.	1	Balance....................................				750,000
Apr.	1	Appropriated for purchase of treasury stock........................	31,000			719,000
July	1	Appropriated for treasury stock acquisitions..................		42,000		761,000
Oct.	31	Preferred dividends.................	50,000			711,000
	31	Stock dividend on common stock....................................	200,000			511,000
Dec.	31	Appropriated for plant expansion..	25,000			486,000
	31	Net income for 1977		210,000		696,000

> *Instructions:* Prepare a retained earnings statement for 1977 in support of the retained earnings balance to be reported on the company's balance sheet at the end of the year.

20-8. The Board of Directors of the XYZ Corporation on December 1, 1977, declared a 2% stock dividend on the common stock of the corporation, payable on December 28, 1977, to the holders of record at the close of business December 15, 1977. They stipulated that cash dividends were to be paid in lieu of issuing any fractional shares. They also directed that the amount to be debited to Retained Earnings should be an amount equal to the market value of the stock on the record date multiplied by the total of (a) the number of shares issued as a stock dividend and (b) the number of shares upon which cash is paid in lieu of the issuance of fractional shares.

The following facts are given:

    (a)   At the dividend record date —
        (1) Shares of XYZ common issued 2,771,600
        (2) Shares of XYZ common held in treasury.. 1,000
        (3) Shares of XYZ common included in (1) held by persons who will receive cash in lieu of fractional shares 202,500
        (4) Shares of predecessor company stock which are exchangeable for XYZ common at the rate of 1¼ shares of XYZ common for each share of predecessor company stock (necessary number of shares of XYZ common have been reserved but not issued pending presentation of stock for exchange).. 600
             Provision was made for a cash dividend in lieu of fractional shares to holders of 240 of these 600 shares.
    (b)   Values of XYZ common were:
         Par value... $ 5
         Market value at December 1st and 15th (Bid)... 21
                               (Asked) 23

Book value at December 1st and 15th...	$16
Capital value at December 1st and 15th..	10

Instructions: Give journal entries and explanations to record the payment of the dividend. Assume no entry was made at the declaration date. (AICPA adapted)

20-9. The following trial balance was taken from the books of the Welcome Manufacturing Company as of April 30, 1977:

Welcome Manufacturing Company
Trial Balance
April 30, 1977

Cash..	$ 310,000	
Accounts Receivable...	800,000	
Finished Goods on Hand	500,000	
Finished Goods Out on Consignment	100,000	
Raw Materials on Hand	750,000	
Land, Buildings, and Equipment.................................	1,460,000	
Prepaid Expenses..	5,400	
Sales Returns and Allowances	25,000	
Administrative Salaries...	65,000	
Cost of Goods Sold	2,350,000	
Travel Expenses..	30,030	
Interest Expense	10,570	
Accounts Payable		$ 175,000
Notes Payable..		100,000
Payroll Payable		6,000
Interest Payable on 6% Bonds....................................		10,000
Capital Stock — 6% Preferred		1,000,000
Capital Stock — Common...		1,416,000
6% Bonds, due June 30, 1985....................................		500,000
Sales		2,500,000
Retained Earnings, December 31, 1976.......................		520
Paid-In Capital...		698,480
	$6,406,000	$6,406,000

The following transactions had been completed by the company:

(a) The company has purchased various lots of its $100 par value common stock, aggregating 840 shares, at an average price of $65.50 per share, for $55,020. In recording these transactions the company has canceled the stock certificates and debited the common stock account with the par value of $84,000 and credited the paid-in capital account with the difference of $28,980 between par and the cash paid.

(b) Paid-in capital was previously credited with (1) a premium at $20 per share on 15,000 shares of common stock issued, and (2) adjustments arising from the appraisal of land, buildings, and equipment bought at a receivers' sale, $398,000.

(c) 6% bonds of the face amount of $250,000 falling due on December 31, 1983, were issued on January 1, 1959, at a 10% discount. To June 30, 1975, $16,500 of this discount had been charged against revenues and as of this date the entire issue of these bonds was retired at par and the unamortized discount debited to Additional Paid-In Capital.

(d) A new issue of $500,000, 6% ten-year bonds was effected as of July 1, 1975, at par. Expenses incurred with respect to this issue in the amount of $20,000 were debited to Paid-In Capital.

Instructions: Prepare a balance sheet as of April 30, 1977, in which effect has been given to such changes as may be necessary in view of the treatment accorded by the company to the transactions described above. (AICPA adapted)

20-10. You are a senior accountant responsible for the annual audit of Desco, Inc., for the year ended December 31, 1977. The information available to you is presented on the following pages. You may assume that any pertinent information not presented has already been checked and found satisfactory.

(a) Excerpts from the December 31, 1977 trial balance are given at the top of the following page.

	Debit	Credit
Retained Earnings..		$40,000
Allowance for Inventory Decline to Market		7,500
Capital Stock, 600 shares		60,000

(b) The books have not been closed but all adjusting entries which the company expects to make have been posted. Their work sheet shows a $15,000 net income for the year.

(c) Selected ledger accounts follow:

ACCOUNT   Retained Earnings

DATE		ITEM	POST. REF.	DEBIT	CREDIT	BALANCE	
						DEBIT	CREDIT
1976 Dec.	31	Balance					52,960
1977 Apr.	29		CR8		200		53,160
Aug.	6		CD62	160			53,000
Oct.	10		J34	10,000			43,000
Dec.	31		J40	3,000			40,000

(*Note:* The balance at December 31, 1976, agrees with last year's working papers and represents the net difference over the years between credits from the income summary account and debits for dividends.)

ACCOUNT   Allowance for Inventory Decline to Market

DATE		ITEM	POST. REF.	DEBIT	CREDIT	BALANCE	
						DEBIT	CREDIT
1977 June	30		J19		5,000		5,000
Sept.	26		CD78	500			4,500
Dec.	31		J40		3,000		7,500

(d) Analysis of selected cash receipts.

Page	Date		Account Credited	Amount	Explanation
8	1977				
	Apr.	29	⎰ Capital Stock.......................	$10,000	Sold $100 par stock
			⎱ Retained Earnings.............	200	at $102
20	Oct.	10	Building...............................	20,000	See J34

(e) Analysis of selected cash disbursements.

Page	Date		Account Debited	Amount	Explanation
62	1977				
	Aug.	6	Retained Earnings..............	$ 160	Freak accident to company truck not covered by insurance; repair by Doe & Co.
78	Sept.	26	⎰ Allowance for Inventory Decline to Market............	500	Purchase of materials (X Co.) to be used on orders taken prior to June 30, 1977; $500 is price increase since June 30, 1977.
			⎱ Purchases...........................	6,300	

(f) Selected entries in the general journal.

Page	Date	Entry and Explanation	Debit	Credit
19	1977			
	June 30	Inventory Loss (Income Summary)....................	5,000	
		Allowance for Inventory Decline to Market ...		5,000
		Provision voted by board of directors for estimated future price increases in materials needed to complete orders on hand. (*Note:* Orders do not represent contractual obligations.)		

Page	Date	Entry and Explanation	Debit	Credit
34	1977			
	Oct. 10	Accumulated Depreciation..................................	50,000	
		Retained Earnings	10,000	
		Building..		60,000
		Sale of main office building, moved to rental quarters downtown. (See CR20)		
40	Dec. 31	Retained Earnings	3,000	
		Allowance for Inventory Decline to Market...		3,000
		Provision to value materials inventory at lower of cost or market in accordance with company pricing policy.		
		Cost... $30,000		
		Market... 27,000		
		$ 3,000		

Instructions: Prepare in good form:
    (1) Schedule of recommended correcting entries to be placed on the books to state the stockholders' equity accounts in accordance with generally accepted accounting principles.
    (2) Statement of retained earnings for 1977.
    (3) "Stockholders' equity" section of balance sheet. (AICPA adapted)

21

Book Value and Earnings Per Share

The financial statements of a corporation are illustrated in Chapter 20 and in Appendix B. The persons who refer to these statements are interested in certain special measurements that can be developed from the data concerning the stockholders' equity and the operations for the period. Two special measurements of particular interest are described in this chapter: (1) the *book value per share* as determined by an analysis of the stockholders' equity as reported on the balance sheet, and (2) the *earnings per share* as determined by an analysis of the capital structure of the company and the net income as reported on the income statement.

BOOK VALUE PER SHARE

The *book value per share* measurement is the dollar equity in corporate capital of each share of stock. It is the amount that would be paid on each share assuming the company is liquidated and the amount available to stockholders is exactly the amount reported as the stockholders' equity.[1] The book value measurement is used as a factor in evaluating stock worth. Both single values and comparative values may be required, the latter to afford data relative to trends and growth in the stockholders' equity.

One Class of Outstanding Stock
When only one class of stock is outstanding, the calculation of book value is relatively simple; the total stockholders' equity is divided by the number of shares of stock outstanding at the close of the reporting period. When stock has been reacquired and treasury stock is reported, its cost should be recognized as a subtraction item in arriving at the stockholders' equity, and the shares represented by the treasury stock should be subtracted from the shares issued in arriving at the shares outstanding. When shares of stock have been subscribed for but are unissued, capital stock subscribed should be included in the total for the

---

[1]Financial analysts frequently follow the practice of subtracting any amounts reported for intangible assets from the total reported for the stockholders' equity in calculating share book value.

stockholders' equity and the shares subscribed should be added to the shares outstanding. To illustrate, assume a stockholders' equity for the Moore Corporation as shown below:

Paid-in capital:		
Capital stock, $10 par, 100,000 shares issued, 5,000 shares reacquired and held as treasury stock (see below)		$1,000,000
Capital stock subscribed, 20,000 shares....................................		200,000
Additional paid-in capital...		350,000
Retained earnings:		
Appropriated	$200,000	
Unappropriated	450,000	650,000
		$2,200,000
Less stock reacquired and held as treasury stock, at cost (5,000 shares)..		75,000
Total stockholders' equity...		$2,125,000

The book value per share of stock is calculated as follows:

$2,125,000 (total capital) ÷ 115,000 (shares issued, 100,000, plus shares subscribed, 20,000, minus treasury shares, 5,000) = $18.48.

More than One Class of Outstanding Stock

When more than one class of stock has been issued, it is necessary to consider the rights of the different classes of stockholders. With preferred and common issues, for example, the prior rights of preferred stockholders must first be determined and the portion of the stockholders' equity related to preferred stockholders calculated. The preferred stockholders' equity when subtracted from the total stockholders' equity gives the equity related to the common stockholders, or the *residual equity*. The preferred equity divided by the number of preferred shares gives the book value of a preferred share; the common equity divided by the number of common shares gives the book value of a common share.

The portion of the stockholders' equity related to preferred would be that amount distributable to preferred stockholders in the event of corporate liquidation and calls for consideration of the liquidation value and also the special dividend rights of the preferred issue.

Liquidation Value. Preferred shares may have a liquidation value equal to par, to par plus a premium, or to a stated dollar amount. Capital equal to this value for the number of preferred shares outstanding should be assigned to preferred stock. A preferred call price differing from the amount to be paid to preferred stockholders upon liquidation would not be applicable for book value computations; the call of preferred stock is not obligatory, hence call prices are not relevant in the apportionment of values between preferred and common stockholders.

Dividend Rights. (1) Preferred stock may have certain rights in retained earnings as a result of special dividend privileges. For example, preferred shares may be entitled to dividends not yet declared for a portion of the current year, assuming liquidation; here a portion of retained earnings equal to the dividend requirements would be related to preferred shares. (2) Preferred stock may be cumulative with dividends in arrears. When terms of the preferred issue provide that dividends in arrears must be paid upon liquidation regardless of any retained earnings or deficit balance reported on the books, capital equivalent to the dividends in arrears must be assigned to preferred shares even though this impairs or eliminates the equity relating to common stockholders. When preferred stockholders are entitled to dividends in arrears only in the event of accumulated earnings, as much retained earnings as are available, but not in excess of such dividend requirements, are related to preferred stock.

The computation of book values for preferred and common shares is illustrated in the following series of examples. The examples are based upon the stockholders' equity reported by the Maxwell Corporation on December 31, 1977, which follows:

Preferred 6% stock, $50 par, 10,000 shares	$ 500,000
Common stock, $10 par, 100,000 shares	1,000,000
Retained earnings	250,000
Total stockholders' equity	$1,750,000

Example 1 — Assume preferred dividends have been paid to July 1, 1977. Preferred stock has a liquidation value of $52 and is entitled to current unpaid dividends. Book values on December 31, 1977, are developed as follows:

Total stockholders' equity		$1,750,000
Equity identified with preferred:		
Liquidation value, 10,000 shares @ $52	$520,000	
Current dividends, 3% of $500,000	15,000	535,000
Balance — equity identified with common		$1,215,000

Book values per share:		
Preferred: $ 535,000 ÷ 10,000		$53.50
Common: $1,215,000 ÷ 100,000		$12.15

Example 2 — Assume preferred stock has a liquidation value of $52. Preferred stock is cumulative with dividends 5 years in arrears that must be paid in the event of liquidation. Book values for common and preferred shares would be developed as follows:

Total stockholders' equity		$1,750,000
Equity identified with preferred:		
Liquidation value, 10,000 shares @ $52	$520,000	
Dividends in arrears, 30% of $500,000	150,000	670,000
Balance — equity identified with common		$1,080,000

Book values per share:		
Preferred: $ 670,000 ÷ 10,000		$67.00
Common: $1,080,000 ÷ 100,000		$10.80

Example 3 — Assume preferred stock has a liquidation value equal to its par value. Preferred is cumulative with dividends 10 years in arrears payable in the event of liquidation even though impairing the invested capital of the common shareholders. Book values for common and preferred shares are developed as follows:

Total stockholders' equity		$1,750,000
Equity identified with preferred:		
Liquidation value, 10,000 shares @ $50	$500,000	
Dividends in arrears, 60% of $500,000	300,000	800,000
Balance — equity identified with common		$ 950,000

Book values per share:
Preferred: $800,000 ÷ 10,000... $80.00
Common: $950,000 ÷ 100,000... $ 9.50

The nature and the limitations of the share book value measurements must be appreciated in using these data. Share book values are developed from the net asset values as reported on the books. Furthermore, calculations require the assumption of liquidation in the allocation of amounts to the several classes of stock. Book values of assets may vary materially from present fair values or immediate realizable values. Moreover, book values of property items are stated in terms of the "going concern"; the full implications of a "quitting concern" approach would call for many significant changes in the values as reported on the books.

EARNINGS PER SHARE PRESENTATION ON THE INCOME STATEMENT

The term *earnings per share* generally refers to the amount earned during a given period on each share of common stock outstanding. It is a more useful figure than net income for comparison purposes among accounting periods because it normalizes net income across periods that may have varying capital structures. As a successful company grows, net income will naturally increase. But the investor is interested in determining if it is growing relative to the size of the company's capital structure. Investors use earnings per share figures to evaluate the results of operations of a business in order to make investment decisions. For example, by dividing the earnings per share figure into the market price per share, a *price-earnings ratio* may be computed that will permit a comparison among different companies. Thus, if Company A earns $3 per share with a $21 per share market price, and Company B earns $6 per share on stock with a $54 per share market value, an investor can state that Company A stock is selling at seven times earnings and Company B stock is selling at nine times earnings. If other things were equal between these two companies, Company A's stock would be the better buy since its market price is lower in relation to earnings than is Company B's price.

Investors, however, may be more interested in dividends than in earnings. This information may be communicated to them by using earnings per share data to compute a *dividend payout percentage* or *payout rate*. This rate is computed by dividing earnings per share into dividends per share. Thus, if Company A in the previous example pays a dividend of $2 per share, and Company B pays $3 per share, the payout percentage would be 66⅔% for Company A and 50% for Company B.

Earnings per share data receive wide recognition in the annual reports issued by companies, in the press, and in financial reporting publications. This measurement is frequently regarded as an important determinant of the market price of the common stock. The American Institute of Certified Public Accountants has recognized the widespread use and importance attached to earnings per share data and has devoted considerable study to determine how this information might be presented on a consistent basis and in the most meaningful manner.

In 1969, the Accounting Principles Board reached the following conclusion:

> The Board believes that the significance attached by investors and others to earnings per share data, together with the importance of evaluating the data in conjunction with the financial statements, requires that such data be presented prominently in the financial statements. The Board has therefore concluded that earnings per share or net loss per share data should be shown on the face of the income statement. The extent of the data to be presented and the captions used will vary with the complexity of the company's capital structure. . . .

The Board further stated:

> The reporting of earnings per share data should be consistent with the income statement presentation called for by . . . Opinion No. 9. Earnings per share amounts should therefore be presented for (a) income before extraordinary items and (b) net income. It may also be desirable to present earnings per share amounts for extraordinary items, if any.[1]

The Accounting Principles Board in Opinion No. 15 has made recommendations for the calculation and presentation of earnings per share data under a variety of circumstances. Only the basic recommendations can be presented here. When the Opinion fails to state the specific procedures to be followed under special circumstances, the accountant will have to exercise judgment in developing supportable presentations within the recommended framework.

The many problems in developing earnings per share presentations arise because of the different securities making up the capital structure of a company. Many new and unique securities have been issued over the past several years. Some of these securities have elements similar to common stock, and their market price often reacts to the market price of the common stock. A principal use of earnings per share figures is to enable an investor to evaluate the company's future earnings potential per share of stock. The possible future conversion of securities and exercise of stock options, warrants, and other rights may materially alter the earnings per share figures. Because of this, modifications to the computations of earnings per share are necessary for many companies.

Simple and Complex Capital Structures

The capital structure of a company may be classified as *simple* or *complex*. If a company has only common stock outstanding and there are no convertible securities, stock options, warrants, or other rights outstanding, it is classified as a company with a simple capital structure. A single earnings per share figure is computed by dividing the net income for the period by the weighted average number of shares of common stock outstanding for the period.

---

[1]*Opinions of the Accounting Principles Board, No. 15*, "Earnings per Share" (New York: American Institute of Certified Public Accountants, 1969), par. 12 and 13.

Even if convertible securities, stock options, warrants or other rights do exist, the company structure may be classified as simple if there is no potential material dilution to earnings per share from the conversion or exercise of these items. Potential earnings per share dilution exists if the earnings per share would decrease or the loss per share would increase as a result of the conversion of securities or exercise of stock options, warrants, or other rights based upon the conditions existing at the financial statement date. The Accounting Principles Board defined *material dilution* as being a decrease of 3% or more in the aggregate earnings per share figure. If the conversion of securities or exercise of stock options, warrants, or rights would increase earnings per share or decrease loss per share, these securities would be classified as *anti-dilutive*. Thus, if earnings per share based upon actual common stock outstanding was $2.45, and assumed conversion of convertible preferred stock would increase the earnings per share to $2.50, the convertible preferred stock would be classified as an anti-dilutive security. Generally, no adjustment to earnings per share figures is required for anti-dilutive securities.

If a company's capital structure does not qualify as being simple, it is classified as complex and two earnings per share figures are required. The first, or *primary earnings per share* figure, is based upon common stock outstanding plus securities identified as common stock equivalents that are dilutive in effect. The second, or *fully diluted earnings per share* figure, is based upon common stock outstanding plus common stock equivalents and all other material, potentially dilutive convertible securities, stock options, warrants, or rights. Fully diluted earnings per share provides for the maximum possible dilution of earnings which might occur.

The Simple Capital Structure — Computational Guidelines

The simple capital structure calls for a single presentation on the face of the income statement designated *earnings per share*. The earnings per share computation presents no problem when only common stock has been issued and the number of shares outstanding has remained the same for the entire period. Earnings divided by the number of shares outstanding gives the amount of earnings per share. Frequently, however, consideration will have to be given to the following matters:

(1) When common shares have been issued or have been reacquired by a company during a period, the resources available to the company have changed and this change should affect earnings. Under these circumstances, a weighted average for shares outstanding should be computed.

The weighted average number of shares may be computed by determining month-shares of outstanding stock and dividing by 12 to obtain the weighted average for the year. For example, if a company has 10,000 shares outstanding at the beginning of the year, issues 5,000 more shares on May 1, and retires 2,000 shares on November 1, the weighted average number of shares would be computed as illustrated on page 604.

		Month-Shares
Jan. 1 to May 1...........................10,000 × 4 months......................		40,000
May 1 to Nov. 1..........................15,000 × 6 months......................		90,000
Nov. 1 to Dec. 1..........................13,000 × 2 months......................		26,000
Total month-shares..		156,000
Weighted average number of shares: 156,000 ÷ 12..		13,000

The same answer could be obtained by applying a weight to each period equivalent to the portion of the year since the last change in number of shares occurred, as follows:

Jan. 1 to May 1.................................10,000 × 4/12 year.............................	3,333
May 1 to Nov. 1...............................15,000 × 6/12 year.............................	7,500
Nov. 1 to Dec. 31............................13,000 × 2/12 year.............................	2,167
Weighted average number of shares..	13,000

(2) When the number of common shares outstanding has changed during a period as a result of a stock dividend, a stock split, or a reverse split, recognition of this change must be made in arriving at the amount of earnings per share. In developing comparative data, recognition of equivalent changes in the common stock of all prior periods included in the statements is necessary. To illustrate these changes, assume in the above example a two-for-one stock split occurred on November 1 before the retirement of the 2,000 shares of stock. The computation of the weighted average number of shares would be changed as follows:

Jan. 1 to May 1.................................10,000 × 200% (two-for-one stock split) × 4/12 year.............................	6,667
May 1 to Nov. 1...............................15,000 × 200% (two-for-one stock split) × 6/12 year.............................	15,000
Nov. 1 to Dec. 31............................28,000* × 2/12 year.............................	4,667
Weighted average number of shares..	26,334

*30,000 outstanding − 2,000 retired = 28,000 shares

Only with the retroactive recognition of changes in the number of shares can earnings per share presentations for prior periods be stated on a basis comparable with the earnings per share presentation for the current period. Similar retroactive adjustments must be made even if the stock dividend or stock split occurs after the end of the period but before the financial statements are prepared; disclosure of this situation should be made in a note to the financial statements.

(3) When a capital structure includes nonconvertible preferred stock, the claim of preferred stock should be deducted from net income and also from income before extraordinary or other special items when such items appear on the income statement, in arriving at the earnings related to common shares. If preferred dividends are not cumulative, only the dividends declared on preferred stock during the period are deducted. If preferred dividends are cumulative, the full amount of dividends on preferred stock for the period, whether declared or not, should be deducted from income before extraordinary or other special items in arriving at the earnings or loss balance related to the common stock. If there is a loss for

the period, the amount of dividends on cumulative preferred stock for the period is added to the loss in arriving at the full loss related to the common stock.

To illustrate the computation of earnings per share for a simple capital structure for a comparative two-year period, assume the following data:

Summary of changes in capital balances:

	6% Cumulative Preferred Stock $100 Par		Common Stock No Par		Retained Earnings
	Shares	Amount	Shares	Amount	
Dec. 31, 1975 Balances....	10,000	$1,000,000	200,000	$1,000,000	$4,000,000
June 30, 1976 Issuance of 100,000 shares of common stock.............			100,000	600,000	
June 30, 1976 Dividend on preferred stock, 6%					(60,000)
June 30, 1976 Dividend on common stock, 30¢					(90,000)
Dec. 31, 1976 Net income for year, including extraordinary gain of $75,000..........................					360,000
Dec. 31, 1976 Balances....	10,000	$1,000,000	300,000	$1,600,000	$4,210,000
May 1, 1977 50% Stock dividend on common stock.........................			150,000	800,000	(800,000)
June 30, 1977 Dividend on preferred stock, 6%					(60,000)
Dec. 31, 1977 Net loss for year...............................					(75,000)
	10,000	$1,000,000	450,000	$2,400,000	$3,275,000

Number of common shares expressed as weighted average of current equivalent shares:

1976:   Jan. 1–June 30 200,000 × 150% (50% stock dividend in 1977) × 6/12 year..   150,000

        July 1–Dec. 31 200,000 + 100,000 (sale of stock in 1976) × 150% (50% stock dividend in 1977) × 6/12 year...   225,000   375,000

1977:   Jan. 1–Dec. 31 300,000 × 150% (50% stock dividend in 1977) × 12/12 year..   450,000

Computation of earnings per share:

1976: Income before extraordinary gain	$285,000
Deduct preferred dividend	60,000
Income after preferred dividend	$225,000
Add extraordinary gain	75,000
Net income identified with common stock	$300,000
Earnings per common share before extraordinary gain, $225,000 ÷ 375,000	$ .60
Extraordinary gain, $75,000 ÷ 375,000	.20
Total earnings per share	$ .80
1977: Net loss for year	$ 75,000
Add cumulative preferred dividends	60,000
Loss identified with common stock	$135,000
Loss per share, $135,000 ÷ 450,000	$ .30

It would be inappropriate to report earnings per share on preferred stock in view of the limited dividend rights of such stock. In the case of preferred, however, it may be informative to indicate the number of times or the extent to which the dividend per share requirements were met. Such information should be designated as *earnings coverage on preferred stock* and in the foregoing example would be computed as follows:

1976: Earnings coverage on preferred stock, $360,000 ÷ $60,000 (cumulative preferred requirements) = 6.00 times*

1977: Earnings coverage on preferred stock. Because there was a loss in 1977, no earnings coverage on preferred stock can be computed.

*Earnings coverage on preferred stock before extraordinary gain, $285,000 ÷ $60,000, or 4.75 times.

The Complex Capital Structure — Computational Guidelines

As discussed above, complex capital structures call for a dual presentation of earnings per share data on the face of the income statement: (1) primary earnings per share — a presentation based upon the number of common shares outstanding plus the shares represented by common stock equivalents, securities that are in substance common shares and that have a dilutive effect on earnings per share; (2) fully diluted earnings per share — a second presentation based on the assumption that all of the contingent issuances of shares of common stock that would individually reduce earnings per share had taken place.

It should be recognized that the primary earnings per share for a complex structure with common stock equivalents is not the same as the basic earnings per share for a simple structure. APB Opinion No. 15 does not provide for an earnings per share figure for complex capital structures with common stock equivalents based solely upon common shares actually issued and outstanding.[1]

The difference between primary and fully diluted presentations indicates the maximum extent of dilution of earnings possible through the full conversion of securities not recognized as common stock equivalents. When a capital structure does not include common stock equivalents, the first presentation may be designated *earnings per share — assuming no dilution*, and the second *earnings per share — assuming full dilution*.

A schedule or note should be provided for a dual presentation explaining the bases upon which both primary and fully diluted earnings are calculated. Those issues included as common stock equivalents in arriving at primary earnings per share, as well as those issues included in the computation of fully diluted earnings per share, should be identified. All of the assumptions made and the resulting adjustments required in developing the earnings per share data should be indicated. Additional disclosures should be made of the number of shares of com-

---

[1]Many accountants feel this omission may result in the misinterpretation of the term "primary earnings per share." It may be noted that the Canadian Institute of Chartered Accountants issued a statement on earnings per share rejecting a "primary earnings per share" presentation calling for the computation of common stock equivalents and recommended a "basic earnings per share" presentation computed in terms of the number of common shares actually outstanding. *CICA Handbook, Section 3500*, "Earnings per Share" (Toronto: The Canadian Institute of Chartered Accountants, February, 1970).

mon stock issued upon conversion, exercise, or satisfaction of required conditions for at least the most recent annual fiscal period. [1]

Computation of dual earnings per share requires application of the procedures for the simple structure previously described as well as special analyses and additional computations described in the following sections. The first section describes the computation of primary earnings per share; the second section describes the computation of fully diluted earnings per share.

Primary Earnings Per Share

The computation of primary earnings per share requires an identification of those securities qualifying as common stock equivalents. A *common stock equivalent* is a security not in the form of common stock but one whose terms enable its holder to acquire common shares and whose terms indicate that acquisition is likely. Holders of these securities can expect to participate in the appreciation of the value of common stock resulting primarily from present and potential earnings of the issuing company. A security identified as a common stock equivalent enters into the computation of primary earnings per share only if its effects on earnings are dilutive. Once a security is recognized as a common stock equivalent, the Accounting Principles Board has indicated that it retains this status. However, depending upon its dilutive effect, it could enter into the computation of primary earnings per share in one period and not in another. Common stock equivalents are composed of the securities described in the following paragraphs.

Convertible Securities. A convertible security, whether bonds or preferred stock, which at the time of its issuance has terms indicating the purchaser is placing a premium on the conversion feature is recognized as a common stock equivalent. The Accounting Principles Board has indicated that if the cash yield of the convertible security at the time of its issuance is significantly less than a comparable security without the conversion option it is a common stock equivalent. Cash yield as used in Opinion No. 15 is the cash to be received annually expressed as a percentage of the market value of the security at the specified date. For example, a $1,000 bond paying interest at 4½% and selling for 90 would have a cash yield of 5% ($45/$900 = 5%). To make the determination both simple and objective, the Board, after considering a number of alternatives, concluded that a convertible security should be recognized as a common stock equivalent if it has a cash yield based upon its market price of less than 66⅔% of the bank prime interest rate for short-term loans at the

---

[1] APB Opinion No. 15 also recognizes the need for special disclosure on the financial statements of the capital structure in view of the variety and complexity of securities that have been issued. The Board states that "... financial statements should include a description, in summary form, sufficient to explain the pertinent rights and privileges of the various securities outstanding. Examples of information which should be disclosed are dividend and liquidation preferences, participation rights, call prices and dates, conversion or exercise prices or rates, and pertinent dates, sinking fund requirements, unusual voting rights, etc." *Opinions of the Accounting Principles Board, No. 15, op. cit.*, par. 19.

time of its issuance. The identification of a convertible security as a common stock equivalent is made at the time of its issuance, and it retains this identity as long as it remains outstanding.

For example, assume at December 31, 1977, the prime interest rate is 8½%. A $1,000, twenty-year, convertible, debenture bond with a stated interest rate of 6% is sold at 109 providing a cash yield of 5½% ($60/$1,090). Since the yield is less than ⅔ of the bank prime rate of 8½%, or 5⅔%, the bond is recognized as a common stock equivalent. The bond will retain this classification even though the future bank prime rate may fall and the cash yield exceed the ⅔ ratio.

In order to compute primary earnings per share when convertible securities exist, adjustments must be made to both net income and to the number of shares of common stock outstanding. These adjustments must reflect what these amounts would have been if the conversion had taken place at the beginning of the current year or at the date of issuance of the convertible securities, whichever comes later. If the securities are bonds, net income is adjusted by adding back the interest expense, net of tax, to net income; the number of shares of common stock outstanding is increased by the number of shares that would have been issued upon conversion.[1] If the convertible securities are shares of preferred stock, no reduction is made from net income for preferred dividends, as is done with the computation of earnings per share in a simple capital structure; the number of shares of common stock outstanding is increased by the number of shares that would have been issued upon conversion. If the convertible securities were issued during the year, adjustments would be made for only the portion of the year since the issuance date. In order to test for material dilution, it is necessary to compute earnings per share without common stock equivalents as well as primary earnings per share including common stock equivalents. As indicated earlier on page 603, if primary earnings per share exceed earnings per share without common stock equivalents, the common stock equivalents are anti-dilutive. If the primary earnings per share is less than earnings per share without common stock equivalents, the common stock equivalents are dilutive. The 3% test determines if they are materially dilutive.

The following examples illustrate the computation of primary earnings per share when convertible securities qualifying as common stock equivalents exist.

Summary of relevant information:

Maturity value of 6% convertible bonds	$500,000
Net income for the year	$ 83,000
Common shares outstanding (no change during year)	100,000
Conversion terms of convertible bonds	80 shares for each $1,000 bond
Assumed tax rate	45%

---

[1]In addition to adjustments for interest, adjustments to net income for nondiscretionary or indirect items would have to be made in many situations. These items would include profit-sharing bonuses and other payments whose amount is determined by the net income reported. For simplicity, no indirect effects are illustrated in this chapter. See Chapter 22 for impact of such effects on accounting changes.

Earnings per share without common stock equivalents:

Actual net income	$83,000
Actual number of shares outstanding	100,000
Earnings per share	$.83

Primary earnings per share including common stock equivalents:

Actual net income		$83,000
Add interest on convertible bonds, net of tax:		
Interest, $500,000 at 6%	$30,000	
Less income tax at 45%	13,500	16,500
Adjusted net income		$99,500
Actual number of shares outstanding		100,000
Additional shares issued upon assumed conversion of bonds, 500 × 80		40,000
Adjusted number of shares		140,000
Primary earnings per share, $99,500 ÷ 140,000		$.71

In this example, material dilution has occurred because primary earnings per share (71¢) is less than 80.51¢ [83¢ − .03(83¢)], the earnings per share without common stock equivalents reduced by 3%. Therefore, primary earnings per share would be reported.

If the convertible bonds had been issued on March 31 of the current year, the adjustments would be made to reflect only the period subsequent to the issuance date, or ¾ of a year.

Primary earnings per share including common stock equivalents (¾ year):

Actual net income		$83,000
Add interest on convertible bonds, net of tax:		
Interest, $500,000 at 6% for ¾ year	$22,500	
Less income tax at 45%	10,125	12,375
Adjusted net income		$95,375
Actual number of shares outstanding		100,000
Additional shares issued upon assumed conversion of bonds, 500 × 80 × ¾		30,000
Adjusted number of shares		130,000
Primary earnings per share, $95,375 ÷ 130,000		$.73

If the 6% convertible bonds had been 6% convertible preferred stock, and if the stock qualified as a common stock equivalent and was issued in a prior year, the computations would be as illustrated below and on page 610.

Earnings per share without common stock equivalents:

Net income, assuming no interest on bonds (as computed above)	$99,500
Less preferred dividends	30,000
Net income identified with common stock	$69,500
Actual number of shares outstanding	100,000
Earnings per share	$.70

Primary earnings per share including common stock equivalents:

Net income assuming no interest on bonds..	$99,500
Actual number of shares outstanding...	100,000
Additional shares issued upon assumed conversion of preferred stock, 500 × 80...	40,000
Adjusted number of shares..	140,000
Primary earnings per share, $99,500 ÷ 140,000..	$.71

In this latter case, the assumed conversion of preferred stock is anti-dilutive (70¢ as compared to 71¢). Thus the preferred stock conversion would not be assumed in computing earnings per share of common stock.

It is possible to determine if a convertible security is anti-dilutive without actually computing primary or fully diluted earnings per share assuming conversion. The anti-dilutive test is performed by computing what the convertible security is costing the existing common stockholders per assumed converted share, and comparing that rate with the earnings per common share assuming no conversion. If the cost rate on the convertible security exceeds the earnings per share assuming no conversion, the convertible security is anti-dilutive. If the cost rate is lower, it is dilutive. To illustrate, the after-tax interest on bonds in the previous example was $16,500. Conversion would have given the bondholders 40,000 shares. The cost rate to the existing common stockholders is 41¢ ($16,500 ÷ 40,000), which is lower than 83¢ earnings per common share, and thus the convertible bonds are dilutive. However, in the example dealing with preferred stock, the cost to the existing common stockholders for the preferred dividends is $30,000, with no tax deduction, and the cost rate to the existing common stockholders is 75¢ ($30,000 ÷ 40,000). This rate is higher than 70¢ earnings per common share, and the preferred stock conversion is thus anti-dilutive.

Stock Options and Warrants and Their Equivalents and Stock Purchase Contracts. Stock options, warrants, and similar arrangements may provide no cash yield, but have value because they offer rights for the acquisition of common shares at specified prices for an extended period. By definition of the APB, these items are always regarded as common stock equivalents. However, they are included in the computation of earnings per share only if they are dilutive. If the price for which stock can be acquired is lower than the current market price, the options, warrants and rights would probably be exercised and their effect would be dilutive. If the exercise price is higher than the current market price, no exercise would take place, and the arrangement would be considered anti-dilutive. The Board recommends that no assumption of exercise is necessary unless the market price has been in excess of the exercise price for substantially all of three consecutive months ending with the last month to which earnings per share data relate.[1]

---

[1]*Opinions of the Accounting Principles Board, No. 15, op. cit.*, par. 36. "Substantially all" has been defined as 11 of the 13 weeks.

If it is assumed that exercise of options, warrants, or other rights takes place as of the beginning of the year or at issuance date, whichever comes later, additional cash resources would have been available for the company's use. In order to compute primary earnings per share when these types of arrangements exist, either net income must be increased to take into consideration the additional revenue such additional resources would produce, or the cash must be assumed to be used for some non-revenue producing purpose. The latter approach was selected by the APB, and they have recommended it be assumed that the cash proceeds from the exercise of the options be used to purchase common stock on the market (treasury stock) at the average market price for the period involved. It is further assumed that the shares of treasury stock are issued to those exercising their rights, and the remaining shares required to be issued will be additional shares to be added to the actual number of shares outstanding to compute primary earnings per share. This method is known as the *treasury stock method*. To illustrate, assume employees have outstanding stock options to acquire 5,000 shares of common stock at $40. The current market price is $50, so exercise may be assumed and it will be dilutive. The proceeds from the issuance of the stock to the employees would be $200,000 (5,000 × $40). Assuming the average market price for the period was also $50, then, these proceeds would purchase 4,000 shares of treasury stock ($200,000 ÷ $50). If it is assumed that these 4,000 shares are issued to the employees, an additional 1,000 shares would have to be issued and the number of shares of stock for computation of primary earnings per share would be increased by 1,000 shares. The interpretations of Opinion No. 15 refer to these shares as *incremental shares*.[1]

To illustrate the use of the treasury stock method for computing common stock equivalent shares, assume the data below and on page 612.

Summary of relevant information:

Net income for the year (primary earnings)	$92,800
Common shares outstanding (no change during year)	100,000
Options outstanding to purchase equivalent shares	20,000
Exercise price per share on options	$ 6
Average market price for common shares	$10
Income tax rate	45%

Earnings per share without common stock equivalents:

Actual net income for the year	$92,800
Actual number of shares outstanding	100,000
Earnings per share	$.93

Application of proceeds from assumed exercise of options outstanding to purchase treasury stock:

Proceeds from assumed exercise of options outstanding, 20,000 × $6	$120,000
Number of outstanding shares assumed to be repurchased with proceeds from options, $120,000 ÷ $10	12,000

---

[1]*Accounting Interpretations of APB Opinion No. 15, Interpretation 51*, "Computing Earnings Per Share" (New York: American Institute of Certified Public Accountants, 1970).

Number of shares to be used in computing primary earnings per share:

Actual number of shares outstanding		100,000
Additional shares issued:		
On assumed exercise of options	20,000	
Less assumed repurchase of shares from proceeds of options	12,000	8,000
Total		108,000
Primary earnings per share, $92,800 ÷ 108,000		$.86

The dilution exceeds 3% (93¢ as compared to 86¢), so the common stock equivalent would be used in computing primary earnings per share.

If the number of common shares of stock involved in exercising options, warrants and other rights is large, the market price of the shares may not be a reliable figure because any attempt to purchase a large block of stock would drive the stock price upward. The Accounting Principles Board recognized this possibility, and declared the treasury stock method inappropriate for proceeds in excess of those required to purchase 20% of the outstanding shares. Proceeds beyond that required to purchase 20% of the common stock are assumed to be applied first to reduce any short-term or long-term borrowings and any remaining proceeds are assumed to be invested in U.S. Government securities or commercial paper with appropriate recognition of any income tax effect.

To illustrate the computation of primary earnings per share under these circumstances, assume the data that follow:

Summary of relevant information:

Net income for the year	$4,000,000
Common shares outstanding (no change during year)	3,000,000
6% First-mortgage bonds outstanding	$5,000,000
Options outstanding to purchase equivalent shares	1,000,000
Limitation on assumed repurchase of shares, 3,000,000 × 20%	600,000
Exercise price per share on options	$15
Market value per common share (average)	$20
Income tax rate	45%

Earnings per share without common stock equivalents:

Actual net income for the year	$4,000,000
Actual number of shares outstanding	3,000,000
Earnings per share	$1.33

Application of proceeds from assumed exercise of options outstanding:

Proceeds from assumed exercise of options outstanding, 1,000,000 × $15 .	$15,000,000
Maximum applied toward repurchase of outstanding shares, 600,000 × $20	12,000,000
Balance of proceeds applied to retirement of 6% first-mortgage bonds	$ 3,000,000

Net income to be used in computing primary earnings per share:

Actual net income		$4,000,000
Add interest on 6% first-mortgage bonds assumed retired, net of income tax:		
Interest, $3,000,000 × 6%	$180,000	
Less income tax ($180,000 × 45%)	81,000	99,000
Total		$4,099,000

Number of shares to be used in computing primary earnings per share:

Actual number of shares outstanding..		3,000,000
Additional shares issued:		
On assumed exercise of options...	1,000,000	
Less assumed repurchase of outstanding shares from proceeds of options	600,000	400,000
Total		3,400,000
Primary earnings per share, $4,099,000 ÷ 3,400,000..................		$1.21

The dilution again exceeds 3% ($1.33 as compared to $1.21), and the common stock equivalent options would be included.

Contingent Shares. Shares whose issuance depends merely upon the passage of time or shares held in escrow pending the satisfaction of conditions unrelated to earnings or market values, are recognized as common stock equivalents. If additional shares are issuable for little or no consideration after the satisfaction of certain conditions, they should be considered as outstanding when the conditions are met.

Fully Diluted Earnings Per Share

In calculating fully diluted earnings in the dual presentation of earnings per share, it is necessary to consider not only all common stock equivalents, but all other contingent issuances of a dilutive effect even though they do not qualify as common stock equivalents. For example, fully diluted earnings per share would include convertible securities whose cash yield exceeded $66\frac{2}{3}$% of the prime interest rate at the issuance date and that were dilutive. As with common stock equivalents, all such issuances are assumed to have taken place at the beginning of the period or at the time the convertible security was issued, if later. The maximum potential dilution of current earnings per share on a prospective basis is thus determined.

When primary earnings are diluted as a result of the inclusion of outstanding options and warrants, a modification in the application of the treasury stock method may be necessary for purposes of calculating the fully diluted earnings per share. To reflect maximum potential dilution, the market price of the common stock at the close of the period is used in computing the number of shares assumed to be reacquired if the ending market price is higher than the average price that had been used in computing primary earnings per share.

As indicated earlier, computations of fully diluted earnings should exclude those securities whose subsequent conversion, exercise, or other contingent issuance would increase the earnings per share amount or decrease the loss per share amount.

To continue with the example on page 612 and illustrate the computation of fully diluted earnings, assume that the following convertible security that did not qualify as a common stock equivalent had been outstanding during the year, and that the year-end market price was $23.

7½% Convertible bonds outstanding, issued at face value	$5,000,000

Each $1,000 bond is convertible into 60 shares of common stock.

Application of proceeds from assumed exercise of options outstanding:

Proceeds from assumed exercise of options outstanding, 1,000,000 × $15 .	$15,000,000
Maximum applied toward repurchase of outstanding shares, 600,000 × $23 (year-end market price)...	13,800,000
Balance of proceeds applied to retirement of 6% first-mortgage bonds	$ 1,200,000

Net income to be used in computing fully diluted earnings per share:

Actual net income...		$4,000,000
Add: Interest on 6% first-mortgage bonds assumed retired, net of income tax:		
Interest, $1,200,000 × 6%..	$ 72,000	
Less income tax ($72,000 × 45%).......................................	32,400	39,600
Interest on 7½% convertible bonds assumed converted, net of income tax:		
Interest, $5,000,000 × 7½%..	$375,000	
Less income tax ($375,000 × 45%).....................................	168,750	206,250
Total..		$4,245,850

Number of shares to be used in computing fully diluted earnings per share:

Number of shares used in computing primary earnings per share (as computed earlier)..	3,400,000
Additional shares assumed issued on conversion of convertible bonds, 5,000 × 60..	300,000
Total..	3,700,000
Fully diluted earnings per share, $4,245,850 ÷ 3,700,000................................	$1.15

Primary and fully diluted earnings in the example would be reported on the income statement as shown below. This presentation would be accompanied by notes explaining the nature of the calculations.

Primary earnings per share	$1.21
Fully diluted earnings per share...	1.15

Even if conversion or exercise actually takes place during the period, adjustment is made to reflect what the impact on earnings per share would have been if the conversion or exercise would have taken place at the beginning of the period or issuance date whichever comes later. For primary earnings per share, this adjustment is made only if the results are dilutive. For fully diluted earnings per share, the adjustment is made even if the results are anti-dilutive. When options or warrants are exercised, the adjustment for the period before exercise for primary earnings per share uses the average market price of the pre-exercise period; the adjustment for fully diluted earnings per share uses the market price at exercise date.

To illustrate, assume the options in the previous example were actually exercised on October 1 of the current year at a time when the market price was $20, and all proceeds were used to retire common shares. The average market price from January 1 to October 1 was $18.[1] The computation of the weighted average number of shares to be used in computing both primary and fully diluted earnings per share would be as follows:

---

[1] Since the average market price ($18) exceeded the exercise price ($15), the adjustment is dilutive.

Weighted average number of shares for primary earnings per share:

Actual number of shares outstanding for full year..........................		3,000,000
Additional shares issued on October 1:		
On exercise of options..	1,000,000	
Less repurchase of shares with proceeds, $15,000,000 ÷ $20......	750,000	
Incremental shares issued...	250,000	
Weighted average of incremental shares issued, 250,000 × ¼......		62,500
Additional shares if options had been exercised on January 1:		
On exercise of options..	1,000,000	
Less repurchase of shares with proceeds, $15,000,000 ÷ $18.......	833,333	
Incremental shares issued...	166,667	
Weighted average of incremental shares assumed to be issued, 166,667 × ¾...		125,000
Weighted average number of shares for primary earnings per share..		3,187,500

Weighted average number of shares for fully diluted earnings per share:

Actual number of shares outstanding for full year..........................		3,000,000
Additional shares issued on October 1:		
On exercise of options..	1,000,000	
Less repurchase of shares with proceeds, $15,000,000 ÷ $20	750,000	
Incremental shares issued	250,000	
Weighted average of incremental shares issued, 250,000 × ¼......		62,500
Additional shares issued on January 1:		
On exercise of options..	1,000,000	
Less repurchase of shares with proceeds, $15,000,000 ÷ $20.......	750,000	
Incremental shares issued...	250,000	
Weighted average of incremental shares assumed to be issued, 250,000 × ¾...		187,500
Weighted average number of shares for fully diluted earnings per share..		3,250,000

Multiple Potentially Dilutive Securities

When several potentially dilutive securities exist, the combination of securities and options, warrants and other rights that produce the lowest primary and fully diluted earnings per share should be determined and reported. This lowest figure is found by computing earnings per share for all possible combinations of potentially dilutive securities that are not anti-dilutive, and identifying the lowest figure. More efficient methods of testing for the lowest earnings per share have been developed for use, but they are beyond the scope of this text.[1]

Earnings Per Share Presentation

When earnings of a period include extraordinary items, income or loss from discontinued operations, or a cumulative effect of a change in accounting method, earnings per share amounts should be presented for amounts before these special items and for each of these special items and for net income, both on a primary share basis and on a fully diluted basis.

As will be discussed in Chapter 22, the Accounting Principles Board in Opinion No. 20, "Accounting Changes," recommended that the cumulative effect of a change in accounting principle be reported under a separate income statement heading between "extraordinary items" and

---

[1]For example, see Sidney Davidson and Romen L. Weil, "A Shortcut in Computing Earnings per Share," *Journal of Accountancy* (December, 1975), pp. 45–47.

"net income." The Board referred to earnings per share calculations and stated:

> The per share information shown on the face of the income statement should include the per share amount of the cumulative effect of the accounting change.[1]

A common stock equivalent or other dilutive security may dilute one of the several per share amounts required to be disclosed on the face of the income statement, while increasing another amount. In such a case, the common stock equivalent or other dilutive securities should be recognized for all computations even though they have an anti-dilutive effect on one or more of the per share amounts.[2]

Earnings per share data should be presented for all periods covered by the income statement. If potential dilution exists in any of the periods presented, the dual presentation of primary and fully diluted earnings per share should be made for all periods presented.[3] Whenever net income of prior periods has been restated as a result of a prior period adjustment, the earnings per share for these prior periods should be restated and the effect of the restatements disclosed in the year of restatement.[4]

It is important that great care be exercised in interpreting earnings per share data regardless of the degree of refinement applied in the development of the data. These values are the products of the principles and practices employed in the accounting process and are subject to the same limitations as found in the net income measurement reported on the income statement.

---

[1]*Opinions of the Accounting Principles Board, No. 20*, "Accounting Changes" (New York: American Institute of Certified Public Accountants, 1971), par. 20.
[2]*Opinions of the Accounting Principles Board, No. 15*, op. cit., par. 30.
[3]*Ibid.*, par. 17.
[4]*Ibid.*, par. 18.

QUESTIONS

1. Why is book value per share often a poor indicator of stock worth?

2. What adjustments are applied to the total stockholders' equity in computing book value per common share when there is more than one class of stock outstanding?

3. The liquidation value of preferred stock is 100 and the call price is 105. Which value should be used in computing book value for preferred stock? Why?

4. Earnings per share computations have been receiving increased prominence on the income statement. How would an investor use such information in making investment decisions?

5. What computation is reported for preferred stock instead of earnings per share? Why is such a computation more appropriate?

6. What distinguishes a simple from a complex capital structure?

7. What constitutes a common stock equivalent for calculating primary earnings per share?

8. What is meant by "dilution of earnings per share"?

9. What is an anti-dilutive security? Why are such securities generally excluded from the computation of earnings per share?

10. A dual presentation of earnings per share is required only if the introduction of dilutive securities is material. How does the profession define materiality in this case?

11. (a) Under what conditions is a convertible security recognized as a common stock equivalent? (b) Under what conditions are stock options and warrants recognized as common stock equivalents?

12. Why are earnings per share figures adjusted retroactively for stock dividends, stock splits, and reverse stock splits?

13. How are convertible securities converted during the period accounted for in computing fully diluted earnings per share?

14. What is the treasury stock method of accounting for outstanding stock options and warrants in computing primary earnings?

15. What modification to the treasury stock method is required if the number of shares obtainable from the exercise of outstanding options and warrants exceeds 20% of the number of shares outstanding?

16. Compare the concept of primary earnings per share with the concept of fully diluted earnings per share.

17. How is the treasury stock method for stock options and warrants modified in computing fully diluted earnings per share as compared with computing primary earnings per share?

18. In case convertible debentures are not considered as common stock equivalents, explain how they are handled for purposes of earnings per share computations.

19. What limitations should be recognized in using earnings per share data?

EXERCISES

1. As of December 31, the equity section of the McAllister, Inc., balance sheet contained the following information: capital stock, 60,000 shares issued, $600,000; capital stock subscribed, 10,000 shares, $100,000; additional paid-in capital, $200,000; retained earnings, $900,000; treasury stock at cost, 10,000 shares, $60,000. Compute the book value per share of common stock.

2. The stockholders' equity of Glidden, Inc., on December 31, 1977, follows:

Common stock, $10 par, 75,000 shares	$ 750,000
Preferred 6% stock, $25 par, 5,000 shares	125,000
Additional paid-in capital	75,000
Retained earnings	50,000
	$1,000,000

Compute the book values per share of preferred stock and common stock under each of the following assumptions:

(a) Preferred stock is noncumulative, callable at $30, and preferred as to assets at $27.50 upon corporate liquidation.

(b) Preferred stock is cumulative, with dividends in arrears for 6 years (including the current year). Upon corporate liquidation, shares are preferred as to assets up to par, and any dividends in arrears must be paid before distribution may be made to common shares.

3. Compute the weighted average number of shares outstanding for Meyers Construction Company assuming transactions in common stock occurred during the year as follows:

Date	Transactions in Common Stock	Number of Shares $10 Par Value
Jan. 1, 1977	Outstanding	16,000
Mar. 1, 1977	Issued for cash	3,200
April 1, 1977	Repurchased shares outstanding	(3,000)
June 1, 1977	Resold part of shares acquired April 1	1,400
Sept. 1, 1977	Issued in exchange for property	6,400
Dec. 1, 1977	50% stock dividend	50% of outstanding shares

4. The Updike Corporation had 500,000 shares of common stock outstanding at the end of 1975. During 1976 and 1977, the transactions on page 618 took place.

1976
Apr.   1 $5,000,000 of convertible bonds were converted with 25 shares issued for each $1,000 bond.
July   1   A 5% stock dividend was declared.
Oct.   1   Options to purchase 6,000 shares for $40 a share were exercised.
1977
Mar.   1   A 2-for-1 stock split was declared.
Aug.   1   150,000 shares were sold for $40 a share.

From the information given, compute the comparative number of weighted average shares outstanding for 1976 and 1977.

5. The income statement for the Braden Co. for the year ended December 31, 1977, shows the following:

Income before income tax	$660,000
Income tax	297,000
Income before extraordinary item	$363,000
Add extraordinary gain (net of income tax)	180,000
Net income	$543,000

Compute earnings per share amounts for 1977 under each of the following assumptions:

(a) The company has only one class of stock, the number of shares outstanding totaling 300,000.
(b) The company has shares outstanding as follows:
Preferred 6% stock, $50 par, cumulative, 20,000 shares; common, $25 par, 300,000 shares. Only the current year's dividends are unpaid.

6. Which of the following securities would qualify as common stock equivalents? If a common stock equivalent, would it be used in computing primary earnings per share? Give reasons supporting each answer.

(a) Employee stock options to purchase 1,000 shares of common stock at $40 are outstanding. The market price of the common stock has been in excess of $45 for the past three months.
(b) Warrants to purchase 2,000 shares at $30 are issued. The current market price is $25.
(c) 8% convertible bonds are sold: sales price, 120. The prime interest rate is 8½%.
(d) Preferred stock, 5%, convertible, is sold at par. The prime interest rate is 7%.
(e) An agreement was made with management to issue 2,000 shares of common stock in two years at a price equal to 75% of the market price at that date.

7. The Stewart Corporation has earnings per common share of $1.51 for the period ended December 31, 1977. For each of the following examples, decide whether the convertible security would be dilutive or anti-dilutive in computing primary earnings per share. Consider each example individually. All are common-stock equivalents. The tax rate is 45%.

(a) 8½% debentures, $1,000,000 face value, are convertible into common stock at the rate of 40 shares for each $1,000 bond.
(b) $4 preferred stock is convertible into common stock at the rate of 2 shares of common for 1 share of preferred. There are 50,000 shares of preferred stock outstanding.
(c) Options to purchase 200,000 shares of common stock are outstanding. The exercise price is $25 per share. Current market price is $20 per share.
(d) $500,000 of 8% debentures are convertible at the rate of 20 shares of common stock per each $1,000 bond.
(e) Preferred 6% stock, $100 par, 5,000 shares outstanding, convertible into 5 shares of common stock for each 1 share of preferred.

8. On January 2, 1977, Lang Co. issued at par $10,000 of 4% bonds convertible in total into 1,000 shares of Lang's common stock. These bonds are common stock equivalents for purposes of computing earnings per share. No bonds were converted during 1977.

Throughout 1977, Lang had 1,000 shares of common stock outstanding. Lang's 1977 net income was $1,000. Lang's tax rate is 45%.

No other potentially dilutive securities other than the convertible bonds were outstanding during 1977. For 1977, compute Lang's primary earnings per share.

9. The Ewing Manufacturing Company reports long-term liabilities and stockholders' equity balances at December 31, 1977, as follows:

Convertible 6% bonds (sold at par)	$ 500,000
Common stock, $25 par, 100,000 shares issued and outstanding....................	2,500,000

Additional information is determined as follows:

Conversion terms of bonds	40 shares for each $1,000 bond
Income before extraordinary gain — 1977	$180,000
Extraordinary gain	30,000
Net income — 1977	$210,000

What are the primary earnings per share for the company for 1977 assuming that the income tax rate is 45% and the prime interest rate at the date the bonds were sold was 9½%? No changes occurred in the above debt and equity balances during 1977.

10. On January 1, 1977, Hage Corporation granted options to purchase 9,000 shares of its common shares at $7 each. The market price of common was $10.50 per share on March 31, 1977, and averaged $9 per share during the quarter then ended. There was no change in the 50,000 shares of outstanding common stock during the quarter ended March 31, 1977. Net income for the quarter was $8,268. Compute the number of shares to be used in computing primary earnings per share and fully diluted earnings per share for the first quarter of 1977.

11. Options to purchase 4,000 common shares at $5 per share are outstanding. All of these options were outstanding during the entire year and are presently exercisable or will become exercisable within four years. The average market price of the company's common stock during the year was $20 and the price of the stock at the end of the year was $25. Compute the common stock equivalent incremental shares that would be used in arriving at (a) primary earnings per share, and (b) fully diluted earnings per share. (Assume less than 20% of outstanding stock is reacquired.)

PROBLEMS

21-1. The stockholders' equity for the Rice Realty and Development Company on December 31, 1977, follows:

Preferred 6% stock, $100 par, 20,000 shares..	$2,000,000
Common stock, $25 par, 200,000 shares..	5,000,000
Additional paid-in capital...	500,000
Retained earnings	750,000
Total stockholders' equity	$8,250,000

    Instructions: Calculate the book values of preferred shares and common shares as of December 31, 1977, under each of the following assumptions:
        (1) Preferred dividends have been paid to October 1, 1977; preferred shares have a call value of $110, a liquidation value of $105, and are entitled to current unpaid quarterly dividends.
        (2) Preferred shares have a liquidation value of $110; shares are cumulative, with dividends 4 years in arrears and fully payable in the event of liquidation.
        (3) Preferred shares have a liquidation value of par; shares are noncumulative, and no dividends have been paid for the past 5 years; however, the current year's dividend has been declared but not yet recorded on the books.

21-2. Transactions involving the common stock account of the French Company during the two-year period, 1976 and 1977, were as shown below and on page 620.

1976		
Jan.	1	Balance 50,000 shares of $20 par stock.
Mar.	31	Sold 10,000 shares at $27.
Apr.	26	Paid cash dividend of 50¢ per share.
July	31	Paid cash dividend of 25¢ per share, and 5% stock dividend.
Oct.	26	Paid cash dividend of 50¢ per share.

1977
Jan. 26   Paid cash dividend of 50¢ per share.
Feb. 28   Purchased 5,000 shares of treasury stock.
Apr. 30   Issued 3-for-1 stock split.
July 26   Paid cash dividend of 50¢ per share.
Oct. 26   Paid cash dividend of 50¢ per share.
Nov. 1   Sold 6,000 shares of treasury stock.

The French Company has a simple capital structure.

> **Instructions:** Compute the weighted average number of shares for 1976 and 1977 to be used for earnings per share computations at the end of 1977.

21-3. The following 1977 condensed financial statements for the Brooke Corporation were prepared by the accounting department:

Brooke Corporation
Income Statement
For Year Ended December 31, 1977

Sales		$10,000,000
Cost of goods sold		8,000,000
Gross profit on sales		$ 2,000,000
Expenses:		
Selling expense	$452,000	
Administrative expense	500,000	
Interest expense	48,000	1,000,000
Income from operations		$ 1,000,000
Income tax		450,000
Income before extraordinary items		$ 550,000
Extraordinary gain, net of tax		45,000
Net income		$ 595,000

Brooke Corporation
Balance Sheet
December 31, 1977

Assets	$3,500,000
Current liabilities	$1,000,000
8% Bonds, due December 31, 1984	600,000
Stockholders' equity:	
Common stock, $5 par, 250,000 shares authorized, issued and outstanding	1,250,000
Additional paid-in capital	400,000
Retained earnings	250,000
	$3,500,000

> **Instructions:** Compute the earnings per share under each of the following separate assumptions (the company has a simple capital structure):
> (1) No change in the capital structure occurred in 1977.
> (2) On December 31, 1976, there were 150,000 shares outstanding. On April 1, 1977, 80,000 shares were sold at par and on October 1, 1977, 20,000 shares were sold at par.
> (3) On December 31, 1976, there were 187,500 shares outstanding. On July 1, 1977, the company issued a 33⅓% stock dividend.

21-4. Fong Fast Foods, Inc., reported the comparative balances given at the top of the next page in the "Stockholders' equity" section of its balance sheet at the end of 1977.

The following transactions involving the stockholders' equity balances occurred during 1976 and 1977.

1976
Mar. 1   Sold 50,000 shares of $15 par value common stock for $18 per share.
July 31   Sold 3,000 shares of $50 par value preferred stock for $60 per share.

	December 31, 1977	December 31, 1976	December 31, 1975
Preferred stock..	$ 650,000	$ 550,000	$ 400,000
Premium on preferred stock	100,000	70,000	40,000
Common stock..	4,650,000	4,500,000	3,000,000
Premium on common stock	810,000	750,000	400,000
Paid-in capital from sale of treasury stock at more than cost	40,000	10,000	10,000
Retained earnings unappropriated........	3,146,400	2,142,000	2,250,000
Retained earnings appropriated for contingencies	800,000	950,000	950,000
Total stockholders' equity...............	$10,196,400	$8,972,000	$7,050,000

Sept. 1	Issued a 20% stock dividend on common stock. The market price for common stock at that time was $19.
Dec. 31	Paid cash dividends of 6% on preferred shares; $2 on common shares.
Dec. 31	Net income for the year was $1,475,000, including an extraordinary gain net of tax of $75,000.
1977	
Feb. 1	Sold 10,000 shares of common stock for $21.
May 31	Sold 2,000 shares of preferred stock for $65.
July 1	Split common stock 3-for-1.
Sept. 30	Purchased 6,000 shares of common stock for $13 to be held as treasury stock.
Dec. 1	Sold 6,000 shares of treasury stock for $18.
Dec. 31	Paid cash dividends: 6% on preferred shares; $1 on common shares.
Dec. 31	Net income for 1977 included an extraordinary loss net of tax savings of $40,000.

Fong Fast Foods, Inc., has a simple capital structure. The call price and liquidation price of the preferred stock are both $55 per share.

> *Instructions:* Compute the comparative book value per share and earnings per share amounts for 1976 and 1977.

21-5. The capital structure of the Santos Dumont Company as of December 31, 1976, follows:

$3 Preferred stock, $50 par, 5,000 shares issued and outstanding	$ 250,000
Premium on preferred stock	25,000
Common stock, $10 par, 100,000 shares issued and outstanding....................	1,000,000
Premium on common stock	250,000
Retained earnings	725,000

On April 1, 1977, the company issued 15,000 stock options to select executives, creditors, and others, allowing for the purchase of common stock for $20 a share. The market price for the stock at this date was $15. The price of the common stock rose steadily during the year and closed at $30. The average market price for the year was $24. The dividend on preferred stock was paid in 1977.

There were no other capital transactions during the year. Net income for 1977 was $200,000.

> *Instructions:* Using the information given above, compute primary and fully diluted earnings per share.

21-6. The following is an extract from the balance sheet of the Walker Corporation, for the year ended December 31, 1976:

7% convertible debentures	$10,000,000
Common stock, $10 par, 1,000,000 shares issued and outstanding	$10,000,000
Retained earnings	6,750,000
Total stockholders' equity	$16,750,000

The terms of conversion state that for each $1,000 bond tendered, the corporation will transfer to the creditor 40 shares of common stock.

On June 30, 1977, the complete issue of convertible debentures was converted into common stock. *(continued)*

Net income for 1977 was $2,350,000. The income tax rate was 45%.

No common stock was issued or repurchased during the year, other than that issued in the conversion.

> **Instructions:** Compute the primary earnings per share for the Walker Corporation for the year ended December 31, 1977.

21-7. The Middleton Manufacturing Co. provides the following data at December 31, 1977:

Operating revenue	$950,000
Operating expenses	$450,000
Income tax rate	45%
Common stock outstanding during the entire year	25,000 shares

On January 1, 1977, there were options outstanding to purchase 10,000 shares of common stock at $20 per share. During 1977, the average price per share was $25 but at December 31, 1977, the market price had risen to $30 per share. The balance sheet reports $200,000 of 8% nonconvertible bonds at December 31, 1977. (Interest expense is included in operating expenses.)

> **Instructions:** Compute for 1977:
> (1) Primary earnings per share.
> (2) Fully diluted earnings per share.

21-8. Data for the Mary Jan Cosmetics Company at the end of 1977 are listed below. All bonds are convertible as indicated and were issued at their face amounts.

Description of Bonds	Amount	Date Issued	Prime Interest Rate on Date Issued	Conversion Terms
10-year, 6% Convertible bonds	$ 500,000	1/1/75	9½%	60 shares of common for each $1,000 bond
20-year, 7% Convertible bonds	1,000,000	1/1/76	8½%	40 shares of common for each $1,000 bond
25-year, 6½% Convertible bonds	800,000	6/30/77	9¾%	100 shares of common for each $1,000 bond

Common shares outstanding at December 31, 1976	800,000
Net income for 1977	$850,000
Income tax rate	45%

> **Instructions:**
> (1) Compute primary earnings per share for 1977, assuming that no additional shares of common stock were issued during the year.
> (2) Compute fully diluted earnings per share for 1977, assuming that no additional shares of common stock were issued during the year.
> (3) Compute both primary and fully diluted earnings per share assuming that the 20-year bonds were converted on July 1, 1977, and that net income for the year was $869,250.

21-9. The "Stockholders' equity" section of Lowe Company's balance sheet as of December 31, 1977, contains the following:

$1 Cumulative preferred stock, $25 par, convertible, 1,600,000 shares authorized, 1,400,000 shares issued, 750,000 converted to common, 650,000 shares outstanding; involuntary liquidation value, $30 a share, aggregating $19,500,000	$16,250,000
Common stock, $.25 par, 15,000,000 shares authorized, 8,800,000 shares issued and outstanding	2,200,000
Additional paid-in capital	32,750,000
Retained earnings	40,595,000
Total stockholders' equity	$91,795,000

On April 1, 1977, Lowe Company acquired the business and assets and assumed the liabilities of Diane Corporation in a transaction accounted for as a pooling of interests. For each of Diane

Corporation's 2,400,000 shares of 25¢ par value common stock outstanding, the owner received one share of common stock of the Lowe Company.

Included in the liabilities of Lowe Company are 5½% convertible subordinated debentures issued at their face value of $20,000,000 in 1976. The debentures are due in 1996 and until then are convertible into the common stock of Lowe Company at the rate of five shares of common stock for each $100 debenture. To date none of these have been converted.

On April 2, 1977, Lowe Company issued 1,400,000 shares of convertible preferred stock at $40 per share. Quarterly dividends to December 31, 1977, have been paid on these shares. The preferred stock is convertible into common stock at the rate of two shares of common for each share of preferred. On October 1, 1977, 150,000 shares and on November 1, 1977, 600,000 shares of the preferred stock were converted into common stock.

During July 1976, Lowe Company granted options to its officers and key employees to purchase 500,000 shares of the company's common stock at a price of $20 a share. The options do not become exercisable until 1978.

During 1977 dividend payments and average market prices of the Lowe common stock have been as follows:

	Dividend per Share	Average Market Price per Share
First quarter	$.10	$20
Second quarter	.15	25
Third quarter	.10	30
Fourth quarter	.15	25
Average for the year		25

The December 31, 1977, closing price of the common stock was $25 a share.

Assume that the bank prime interest rate was 7% throughout 1976 and 1977. Lowe Company's consolidated net income for the year ended December 31, 1977, was $9,200,000. The provision for income tax was computed at a rate of 48%.

Instructions:
    (1) Prepare a schedule which shows the evaluation of the common stock equivalency status of the (a) convertible debentures, (b) convertible preferred stock, and (c) employee stock options.
    (2) Prepare a schedule which shows for 1977 the computation of:
        (a) The weighted average number of shares for computing primary earnings per share.
        (b) The weighted average number of shares for computing fully diluted earnings per share.
    (3) Prepare a schedule which shows for 1977 the computation to the nearest cent of:
        (a) Primary earnings per share.
        (b) Fully diluted earnings per share. (AICPA adapted)

21-10. On February 1, 1978, when your audit and report is nearly complete, the president of the Scooter Corporation asks you to prepare statistical schedules of comparative financial data for the past five years for inclusion in the company's annual report. Your working papers reveal the information given below and on page 624.

    (a) Income statements show net income amounts as follows:

1973 — $20,000*
1974 — (17,000) (loss)
1975 — 25,000
1976 — 38,000
1977 — 47,000

      *Includes extraordinary gain of $8,000.

    (b) On January 1, 1973, there were outstanding 1,000 shares of common stock, par value $100, and 500 shares of cumulative preferred 6% stock, par value $50.
    (c) A 5% dividend was paid in common stock to common stockholders on December 31, 1974. The fair market value of the stock was $150 per share at the time.
    (d) Four hundred shares of common stock were issued on March 31, 1975, to purchase another company.

(e) A dividend of cumulative preferred stock was distributed to common stockholders on July 1, 1975. One share of preferred stock was distributed for every five shares of common stock held. The fair market value of the preferred stock was $55 per share before the distribution and $53 per share immediately after the distribution.

(f) The common stock was split 2-for-1 on December 31, 1976, and December 31, 1977.

(g) Cash dividends are paid on the preferred stock on June 30 and December 31. Preferred stock dividends were paid in each year except 1974; the 1974 and 1975 dividends were paid in 1975.

(h) Cash dividends on common stock are paid semiannually. Dividends paid per share of stock outstanding at the respective dates were:

	June 30	December 31
1973	$ .50	$ .50
1974	None	None
1975	.75	.75
1976	1.00	.50*
1977	.75	.75**

*After 2-for-1 split.
**Before 2-for-1 split.

Instructions:

(1) In connection with your preparation of the statistical schedule of comparative financial data for the past five years:

    (a) Prepare a schedule computing the number of shares of common stock and preferred stock outstanding as of the respective year-end dates.

    (b) Prepare a schedule computing the current equivalent number of shares of common stock outstanding as of the respective year-end dates. The current equivalent shares means the number of shares outstanding in the respective prior periods in terms of the present stock position.

    (c) Compute the total cash dividends paid to holders of preferred stock and to holders of common stock for each of the five years.

(2) Prepare a five-year summary of financial statistics to be included in the annual report. The summary should show by years "Net Income (or Loss)," "Earnings per Share of Common Stock," and "Dividends per Share of Common Stock." Include any explanatory footnotes considered necessary. (AICPA adapted)

21-11. The controller of Lafayette Corporation has requested assistance in determining income, primary earnings per share and fully diluted earnings per share for presentation in the company's income statement for the year ended September 30, 1977. As currently calculated, the company's net income is $400,000 for fiscal year 1976–1977. The controller has indicated that the income figure might be adjusted for the following transactions which were recorded by charges or credits directly to retained earnings (the amounts are net of applicable income tax):

(a) The sum of $375,000, applicable to a breached 1973 contract, was received as a result of a lawsuit. Prior to the award, legal counsel was uncertain about the outcome of the suit.

(b) A gain of $300,000 was realized on the sale of a subsidiary.

(c) A gain of $80,000 was realized on the sale of treasury stock.

(d) A special inventory write-off of $150,000 was made, of which $125,000 applied to goods manufactured prior to October 1, 1976.

Your working papers disclose the following opening balances and transactions in the company's capital stock accounts during the year:

(e) Common stock (at October 1, 1976, stated value $10, authorized 300,000 shares; effective December 1, 1976, stated value $5, authorized 600,000 shares):
Balance, October 1, 1976 — issued and outstanding 60,000 shares.
December 1, 1976 — 60,000 shares issued in a 2-for-1 stock split.
December 1, 1976 — 280,000 shares (stated value $5) issued at $39 per share.

(f) Treasury stock common:
March 1, 1977 — purchased 40,000 shares at $38 per share.
April 1, 1977 — sold 40,000 shares at $40 per share.

(g) Stock purchase warrants, Series A (initially, each warrant was exchangeable with $60 for one common share; effective December 1, 1976, each warrant became exchangeable for two common shares at $30 per share):

October 1, 1976 — 25,000 warrants issued at $6 each.
(h) Stock purchase warrants, Series B (each warrant is exchangeable with $40 for one common share):
April 1, 1977 — 20,000 warrants authorized and issued at $10 each.
(i) First-mortgage bonds, 5½%, due 1985 (nonconvertible; priced to yield 5% when issued):
Balance, October 1, 1976 — authorized, issued and outstanding — the face value of $1,400,000.
(j) Convertible debentures, 7%, due 1989 (initially each $1,000 bond was convertible at any time until maturity into 12½ common shares; effective December 1, 1976, the conversion rate became 25 shares for each bond):
October 1, 1976 — authorized and issued at their face value (no premium or discount) of $2,400,000.

The following table shows market prices for the company's securities and the assumed bank prime interest rate during 1976–1977.

	Price (or Rate) at			Average for Year Ended
	October 1, 1976	April 1, 1977	September 30, 1977	September 30, 1977
Common stock	66	40	36¼	37½*
First-mortgage bonds	88½	87	86	87
Convertible debentures	100	120	119	115
Series A Warrants	6	22	19½	15
Series B Warrants	—	10	9	9½
Bank prime interest rate	8%	7¾%	7½%	7¾%

*Adjusted for stock split.

Instructions:

(1) Prepare a schedule computing net income as it should be presented in the company's income statement for the year ended September 30, 1977.
(2) Assuming net income for the year was $540,000 and that there were no extraordinary items, prepare a schedule computing (a) the primary earnings per share, and (b) the fully diluted earnings per share which should be presented in the company's income statement for the year ended September 30, 1977. A supporting schedule computing the number of shares to be used in these computations should also be prepared. (Because of the relative stability of the market price for its common shares, the annual average market price may be used where appropriate in your calculations. Assume an income tax rate of 48% with no surcharge.) (AICPA adapted)

21-12. The schedule at the top of the following page sets forth the current liabilities, long-term liabilities, and stockholders' equity of Darren Company as of December 31, 1977. The president of Darren has requested that you assist the controller in preparing figures for earnings per share computations.

Explanation of current liabilities, long-term liabilities, and stockholders' equity including transactions during the year ended December 31, 1977 follow:

(a) The "Other long-term liabilities" and the related amounts due within one year are amounts due on unsecured promissory notes which require payments each year to maturity. The interest rate on these borrowings range from 6% to 7%. At the time that these monies were borrowed, the bank prime interest rate was 7%.
(b) The 4% convertible debentures were issued at their face value of $30,000,000 in 1956 when the bank prime interest rate was 5%. The debentures are due in 1986 and until then are convertible into the common stock of Darren at the rate of 25 shares for each $1,000 debenture.
(c) The $4 cumulative, convertible preferred stock was issued in 1973. The stock had a market value of $75 at the time of issuance when the bank prime interest rate was 9%. On July 1, 1977, and on October 1, 1977, holders of the preferred stock converted 80,000 and 20,000 preferred shares, respectively, into common stock. Each share of preferred stock is convertible into 1.2 shares of common stock.
(d) On April 1, 1977, Darren acquired the assets and business of Brett Industries by the issuance of 800,000 shares of Darren common stock in a transaction appropriately accounted for as a purchase.

Current liabilities:

Notes payable — banks	$ 4,000,000
Current portion of long-term liabilities	10,000,000
Total current liabilities	$ 14,000,000

Long-term liabilities:

4% convertible debentures due April 15, 1986	$ 30,000,000
Other long-term liabilities less current portions	20,000,000
Total long-term liabilities	$ 50,000,000

Stockholders' equity:

$4 cumulative, convertible preferred stock, $20 par; 2,000,000 shares authorized; 1,200,000 issued and outstanding; liquidation preference $30 per share aggregating $36,000,000	$ 24,000,000
Common stock, $1 par; 20,000,000 shares authorized; 7,500,000 shares issued including 600,000 shares held in treasury	7,500,000
Additional paid-in capital	4,200,000
Retained earnings	76,500,000
Total paid-in capital and retained earnings	$112,200,000
Less cost of 600,000 shares of common stock held in treasury (acquired prior to 1977)	900,000
Total stockholders' equity	$111,300,000
Total long-term liabilities and stockholders' equity	$161,300,000

Additional information:

(e) Dividends on the preferred stock have been paid quarterly through December 31, 1977. Dividends paid on the common stock were 50¢ per share for each quarter.

(f) The net income of Darren Company for the year ended December 31, 1977, was $8,600,000. There were no extraordinary items. The provision for income tax was computed at a rate of 48%.

Instructions:

(1) Prepare a schedule which shows the adjusted number of shares for 1977 to compute:
    (a) Primary earnings per share.
    (b) Fully diluted earnings per share.

(2) Prepare a schedule which shows the adjusted net income for 1977 to compute:
    (a) Primary earnings per share.
    (b) Fully diluted earnings per share. Do not compute earnings per share. (AICPA adapted)

22

Accounting Changes and Correction of Errors

A major objective of published financial statements is to provide users with information to help them predict, compare, and evaluate future earning power and cash flows to the reporting entity.[1] When a reporting entity changes its accounting principles from one method to another, adjusts its past estimates of revenues earned or costs incurred, changes its nature as a reporting entity, or corrects past errors, it becomes more difficult for a user to predict the future from past historical statements. Is it better to record these changes and error corrections as adjustments of the prior periods' statements and thus increase their comparability with the current and future statements, or should the changes and error corrections affect only the current and future years? Would user confidence in the accuracy of statements be shaken if past figures were changed each year as these types of changes occurred, or should the full impact of the change be reflected only in the current and future periods?

At least four alternative procedures have been suggested as solutions for reporting accounting changes and correction of errors.

1. Adjust all prior periods' statements for the effect of the change or correction and adjust the beginning Retained Earnings balance for the cumulative amount of the change or correction.
2. Make no adjustment to prior periods' statements, but reflect all effects of the change only in current and future periods. Report the catch-up adjustment as it affects prior years in the current year
   a. as a special item in the income statement.
   b. as a direct entry to Retained Earnings in the current period.
3. Make an adjustment in the current period as in (2a), but also report limited pro forma statements for all prior years included in the financial statements reporting "what might have been" if the change or correction had been made in the prior years.
4. Make the change effective only for current and future periods. Allow no catch-up adjustment to be made. Correct errors only if they still affect the statements.

[1]*Objectives of Financial Statements* (New York: American Institute of Certified Public Accountants, 1973), pp. 20 and 24.

Each of these alternative methods for reporting an accounting change or correcting an error have been used by companies in the past, and strong arguments can be made for each alternative. Because of the diversity of practice and the resulting difficulty in user understandability of the financial statements, the Accounting Principles Board issued Opinion No. 20 to bring increased uniformity to reporting practice.[1] Only two-thirds of the Board approved the opinion, the minimum required. This indicates the degree of divergence in views concerning this matter. Evidence of compromise exists in the final opinion, as the Board attempted to reflect both its desire to increase comparability of financial statements and to improve user confidence in published financial statements.

The Accounting Principles Board defined three types of accounting changes:

1. Change in an accounting principle.
2. Change in an accounting estimate.
3. Change in the reporting entity.

The Board also made recommendations for reporting a correction of a past error, although they did not classify error correction as an accounting change. Each of these four items will be discussed and illustrated separately.

CHANGE IN AN ACCOUNTING PRINCIPLE[2]

As has been indicated in previous chapters, companies may select among several alternative accounting principles to account for a business transaction. For example, a company may depreciate its buildings and equipment using the straight-line depreciation method, the double-declining-balance method, the sum-of-the-years-digits method, or any other consistent and rational allocation procedure. Long-term construction contracts may be accounted for by the percentage-of-completion or the completed contract method. The investment tax credit may be accounted for by the flow-through method or the deferred method. These alternative methods are often equally available to a given company but in most instances criteria for selection among the methods is inadequate. As a result, companies have found it rather easy to justify changing from one method to another. The impact of the change on financial statements is frequently very significant.

The Securities and Exchange Commission is concerned by the practice of changing accounting principles and is putting increased pressure on the independent auditor to insist that justification for a change be provided by a company and that the auditor agree with the change. They have even begun to question auditors who permit a client to use one

---

[1] *Opinions of the Accounting Principles Board, No. 20*, "Accounting Changes" (New York: American Institute of Certified Public Accountants, 1971).

[2] The classification "change in accounting principle" includes changes in methods used to account for transactions. No attempt was made by the Accounting Principles Board to distinguish between a principle and a method in Opinion No. 20. *Ibid*.

accounting principle and then permit another client in similar circumstances to change to an alternative accounting principle.[1]

General Reporting Rule

The APB concluded that, in general, companies should not change their accounting principles from one period to the next. "Consistent use of accounting principles from one period to another enhances the utility of financial statements to users by facilitating analysis and understandability of comparative accounting data."[2] However, a company may change its accounting principles if it can justify a change because of a new accounting pronouncement by the authoritative accounting principle-making body, or because of a change in its economic circumstances.[3] The Board could not agree between the first two alternative methods outlined on page 627 for reporting the effects of the change: to adjust prior period statements or to reflect the change only in current and future periods. Thus, they chose the compromise third alternative for most accounting principle changes. The fourth alternative was rejected because it would create future financial statements that would be inconsistent with prior statements.

In general, the effect of a change from one accepted accounting principle to another is reflected by reporting the retroactive, cumulative effect of the change in the income statement in the period of the change. This cumulative adjustment is shown as a separate item on the income statement after extraordinary items and before net income. The financial statements for all prior periods reported for comparative purposes with the current year financial statements are to be presented as previously reported. However, to enhance trend analysis, pro forma income information is also required wherever possible to reflect the income before extraordinary items and net income that would have been reported if the new accounting principle had been in effect for the respective prior years. The pro forma information should include not only the direct effects of the change in method with its tax effect, but also any indirect or nondiscretionary adjustment that would have been necessary if the income had been different for the prior periods. The indirect adjustments include items such as bonuses, profit sharing, or royalty agreements based upon reported net income. Pro forma earnings per share figures should also be reported.

The cumulative effect of a change in accounting principle must usually be adjusted for the effect of interperiod tax allocation. The change is often from a method that was used for both tax and reporting purposes to a different method for reporting purposes. Retroactive changes in methods for tax purposes are generally not permitted. Thus, the current

---

[1] Securities and Exchange Commission, *Accounting Series Release No. 177*, "Interim Reporting in Form 10-Q and Annual Reports" (Washington: U.S. Government Printing Office, 1975).

[2] *Opinions of the Accounting Principles Board, No. 20, op. cit.*, par. 15.

[3] Just what constitutes an acceptable change in economic circumstances is not too clear. However, it presumably could include such things as a change in the competitive structure of an industry, a change in the rate of inflation in the economy, a change resulting from government restrictions due to economic or political crisis, etc.

income tax payable is usually not affected by the change; however, an adjustment is usually necessary to the deferred income tax account. For example, if a company has been using the double-declining-balance method of depreciation for both reporting and tax purposes but changes to the straight-line method for reporting purposes, the tax effect should be reflected as a reduction in the cumulative change account and as a credit to Deferred Income Tax. If the change for reporting purposes is to a method used for tax purposes, the books and the tax return would be in agreement after the change; and previously recorded amounts in Deferred Income Tax would be reversed. An exception to the above situations arises when the change is made from lifo inventory to another method. This is because the income tax regulations do require consistency between the books and the tax return whenever lifo inventory is involved. Thus, a change on the books must also be made on the tax return. Any additional tax arising from the change must be paid, although the income tax regulations do provide for some spreading of the liability over several future years.

To illustrate the general treatment of a change in accounting principle, assume Excelsior Company elected in 1977 to change from the double-declining-balance method of depreciation used for both reporting and tax purposes to the straight-line method to bring its reporting practice in agreement with the majority of its competitors. The income tax rate is 45%, and the company pays a 20% management bonus on operating income before tax. The following information was gathered reflecting the impact of the change upon net income.

| | Excess of Double-Declining-Balance Depreciation Over Straight-Line | Effect of Change | |
Year	Depreciation	Direct Effect Less Tax (45% Tax Rate)	Direct and Indirect Effect After 20% Management Bonus. Pro Forma Data
Prior to 1972	$ 80,000	$ 44,000 [.55($80,000)]*	$35,200 {.55[$80,000 − .20($80,000)]}
1972	25,000	13,750 [.55($25,000)]	11,000 {.55[$25,000 − .20($25,000)]}
1973	30,000	16,500 [.55($30,000)]	13,200 {.55[$30,000 − .20($30,000)]}
1974	28,000	15,400 [.55($28,000)]	12,320 {.55[$28,000 − .20($28,000)]}
1975	22,000	12,100 [.55($22,000)]	9,680 {.55[$22,000 − .20($22,000)]}
1976	25,000	13,750 [.55($25,000)]	11,000 {.55[$25,000 − .20($25,000)]}
	$210,000	$115,500	$92,400

*The direct effect could be computed as $80,000 − .45($80,000), or simply as the complement of the tax rate .55 ($80,000). The complement computation is used in this illustration.

The net income for prior years as originally reported was as listed below:

1972	$350,000	1975	$450,000
1973	400,000	1976	500,000
1974	410,000		

The income statement for 1977, the year of the change, would report the $115,500 after-tax, direct, retroactive adjustment as a separate item after any extraordinary items as follows:

Income before extraordinary items and cumulative effect of a change in accounting principle	$560,000
Extraordinary gain on refunding of long-term debt (less applicable income tax of $72,000)	88,000
Cumulative effect on prior years of changing from the double-declining-balance method of depreciation to the straight-line method (less applicable income tax of $94,500)	115,500
Net income..	$763,500

Earnings per share amounts would be shown for each of the above elements.

In addition to the above disclosure, pro forma income information would be disclosed by adding both direct and indirect effects to the net income as originally reported. These pro forma income amounts would be included on the face of the income statements reported.

	Pro Forma Income Data				
	1976	1975	1974	1973	1972
Net income as previously reported	$500,000	$450,000	$410,000	$400,000	$350,000
Effect of change in principle — direct and indirect	11,000	9,680	12,320	13,200	11,000
Pro forma net income	$511,000	$459,680	$422,320	$413,200	$361,000

Revised earnings per share figures would also be computed and disclosed reflecting the revised net income amounts. It is recognized that in rare instances, past records are inadequate to prepare the pro forma statements for individual years. This fact should be disclosed. For example, a change to the lifo method of inventory valuation is usually made effective with the beginning inventory in the year of change rather than with some prior year because of the difficulty in identifying prior year layers or dollar value pools. Thus, the beginning inventory in the year of change is the same as the previous inventory valued at cost, and this becomes the base lifo layer. No cumulative effect adjustment is required.

Exceptions to the General Reporting Rule

Although the general rule for recording changes in accounting principles provides for catch-up adjustments, three specific changes in accounting principles and one general condition change were identified by the Accounting Principles Board as being of such a nature that the "advantages of retroactive treatment in prior period reports outweigh the disadvantages."[1] The changes identified as exceptions to the general rule are given below and on page 632.

1. Change from lifo method of inventory pricing to another method.
2. Change in the method of accounting for long-term construction contracts.

---

[1]*Opinions of the Accounting Principles Board, No. 20, op. cit.*, par. 27.

3. Change to or from the "full cost" method of accounting used in the extractive industries.
4. Changes made at the time of an initial distribution of company stock.[1]

In these cases, the cumulative effect of the change is recorded directly as an adjustment to the beginning Retained Earnings balance and all prior income statement data reported for comparative purposes are adjusted to reflect the new principle. No justification is given by the Board for selecting these items for special treatment; however, these items usually would be material and data would generally be available to adjust the prior years' statements.

To illustrate the exceptions, assume Swiss Company compiles the following information concerning its change in 1977 from the completed-contract method of valuing long-term construction contracts to the percentage-of-completion method.

Year	Net Income — Completed-Contract Method	Net Income — Percentage-of-Completion Method
1972	$ 20,000	$ 40,000
1973	60,000	70,000
1974	80,000	75,000
1975	75,000	110,000
1976	90,000	85,000
Total at beginning of 1977	$325,000	$380,000

The retained earnings statement for 1977 would reflect the effect of the change on prior years as follows:

Swiss Company
Retained Earnings Statement
For Year Ended December 31, 1977

Retained earnings, January 1, 1977, as previously reported	$ 900,000
Add adjustment for the cumulative effect on prior years of applying retroactively the percentage-of-completion method of accounting for long-term construction contracts as opposed to the completed-contract method (less applicable income tax of $45,000)	55,000
January 1, 1977, balance, as adjusted	$ 955,000
Add net income per income statement	660,000
	$1,615,000
Deduct dividends declared	400,000
Retained earnings, December 31, 1977	$1,215,000

All prior period income statements would be adjusted to the amounts that would have been reported using the new principle. If the prior statements cannot be adjusted because of inadequate data, this fact should be disclosed and the cumulative impact would be reported only on the retained earnings statement. No pro forma information is required for these exceptions because the prior periods statements are changed directly; however, full disclosure of the effect of the change should be made for all periods presented. The earnings per share data would be recomputed taking into consideration any impact the new income

[1]This exception is available only once for a company, and may be used whenever a company first issues financial statements for (a) obtaining additional equity capital from investors, (b) effecting business combinations, or (c) registering securities. *ibid.*, par. 29.

amount would have upon the computation of primary or fully diluted shares outstanding.

If comparative retained earnings statements are prepared for 1976 and 1977, the cumulative adjustment to beginning retained earnings for each reported year would reflect only those years prior to that particular year. Thus, in the example, the 1976 beginning retained earnings balance would be adjusted by $60,000, the difference in net income under the two methods for the years 1972–1975 ($295,000 − $235,000).

If a change in accounting principle is caused by a new pronouncement of an accepted authoritative accounting body, the cumulative effect may be adjusted retroactively as a prior period adjustment or currently, depending upon the instructions contained in the pronouncement. In most cases, the Financial Accounting Standards Board has chosen to require retroactive adjustment for newly pronounced principles. For example, such adjustment was required by the FASB in Statement No. 2 concerning the mandatory writing off of all deferred research and development costs.[1] Originally, the FASB recommended the general or nonretroactive rule for changes resulting from Statement No. 5 "Accounting for Contingencies;"[2] however, they reversed themselves in Statement No. 11[3] and recommended retroactive adjustment where practicable.

CHANGE IN AN ACCOUNTING ESTIMATE

Accountants must always exercise judgment in preparing journal entries to adjust accounts prior to preparing meaningful financial statements. Items, such as the number of years to use for depreciating buildings and equipment balances, the amount to provide for uncollectible accounts, or the amount of warranty liability to record on the books, are based upon estimates using the best available information at the statement date. Conditions may change in subsequent periods, and the estimate may need to be revised. The APB stated in Opinion No. 20 that all such adjustments in estimates should be made either in the current period or in the current and future periods. No retroactive adjustment or pro forma statements are to be prepared for a change in estimate.[4] These adjustments are felt to be part of the normal accounting process and not a change of past periods.

For example, assume assets costing $30,000 are estimated initially to have a ten-year life. Depreciation of $3,000 is recorded for each of the first four years; however, in the fifth year the estimated life of the assets is changed from ten years to eight years. At the time of the new estimate, $12,000 has been accumulated in the accumulated depreciation account, and the assets have a remaining book value of $18,000. The new annual

---

[1]*Statement of Financial Accounting Standards No. 2*, "Accounting for Research and Development Costs" (Stamford, Conn.: Financial Accounting Standards Board, 1974), par. 15.

[2]*Statement of Financial Accounting Standards No. 5*, "Accounting for Contingencies" (Stamford, Conn.: Financial Accounting Standards Board, 1975), par. 20.

[3]*Statement of Financial Accounting Standards No. 11*, "Accounting for Contingencies — Transition Method" (Stamford, Conn.: Financial Accounting Standards Board, 1975), par. 10.

[4]*Opinions of the Accounting Principles Board, No. 20, op. cit.*, par 31.

depreciation amount will now be $4,500, or $18,000 ÷ 4 years. No separate disclosure is required for this type of change unless the amount is material. If it is material, separate disclosure of the change should be included in a note to the financial statements.

In some instances, an accounting principle and an estimate are both changed on the same asset simultaneously, and the effect of the change in principle and change in estimate cannot be separated. In this situation, the APB suggested the change be treated as a change in estimate rather than a change in principle.[1]

CHANGE IN REPORTING ENTITY

Companies sometimes change their nature or report their operations in such a way that the financial statements are in effect those of a different reporting entity. These changes include: (a) presenting consolidated or combined statements in place of statements of individual companies; (b) changing specific subsidiaries comprising the group of companies for which consolidated statements are presented; (c) changing the companies included in combined financial statements; and (d) a business combination accounted for as a pooling of interest.[2]

Because of the basic objective of preparing statements that assist in predicting future flows, the APB recommended that financial statements be adjusted retroactively to disclose what the statements would have looked like if the current entity had been in existence in the prior years. Of course, this requirement assumes that the companies acting as a unit would have made the same decisions as they did while acting alone. While this assumption is probably invalid, the retroactive adjustment will probably come closer to providing useful information for trend analysis than would statements clearly noncomparable because of the different components of the entity.

In the period of the change, the financial statements should describe the nature and reason for the change. They should also clearly show the effect of the change on income before extraordinary items, net income, and the related earnings per share amounts for all periods presented. Subsequent years' statements do not need to repeat the disclosure.[3]

CORRECTION OF AN ERROR

Accounting errors can result from mathematical mistakes, the failure to apply appropriate accounting principles and procedures, or the misuse or omission of certain information. A change from an accounting principle not generally accepted to one that is generally accepted is considered to be a correction of an error.[4] When errors are discovered, the accountant must be able to analyze these in determining what action is appropriate under the circumstances. This calls for an understanding of

---

[1]*Ibid.*, par. 32.
[2]*Ibid.*, par. 12.
[3]*Ibid.*, par. 35.
[4]*Ibid.*, par. 13.

the standards for a full and fair accounting as well as good judgment and skill in handling situations indicating a failure to meet such standards.

A number of special practices are usually adopted by a business unit to insure accuracy in recording and summarizing business transactions. A prime requisite in achieving accuracy, of course, is the establishment of an accounting system providing safeguards against both carelessness and dishonesty. Such a system should include orderly and integrated procedures and controls. Personnel should have well-defined responsibilities. An internal auditing staff may be established as a part of the accounting system to continuously reconcile and prove recorded data and also to evaluate information systems. Independent public accountants verify recorded data as a further means of insuring accounting accuracy.

Despite the accounting system established and the verification procedures employed, some misstatements will enter into the financial statements. Misstatements may be minor ones having little effect on the financial presentations; others may be of a major character, resulting in material misrepresentations of financial position and the results of operations. Misstatements may arise from intentional falsifications by employees or officers as well as from unintentional errors and omissions by employees.

Intentional Misstatements

When misstatements result from intentional falsification of entries or records, the motive or motives may be: (1) to evade taxes; (2) to influence the market price of the company's securities; (3) to obtain favorable decisions by regulatory bodies; (4) to conceal the theft of cash, securities, merchandise, or other assets; (5) to conceal facts that may embarrass certain parties; or (6) to improve the company's ability to borrow. When intentional misstatements arise, management personnel are often directly involved in the misstatement. Because accounting systems are usually built upon the assumptions of honest management, it is difficult to design a system to prevent this type of misstatement. Both internal and external audits can be a deterrent to this type of activity.

Unintentional Misstatements

It would be impossible to offer a complete list of the misstatements that might arise unintentionally. Unintentional misstatements arise from clerical errors and omissions or from failures in the application of accounting principles. The most common misstatements include entries in the wrong customer or creditor accounts, entries in the wrong revenue and expense accounts, errors in counting and valuing inventories, errors in calculating depreciation and amortization, failures to distinguish properly between capital and revenue expenditures, and the omission of adjustments for prepaid and accrued items. These and other unintentional errors can be kept to a minimum through effective systems of internal control and satisfactory procedures for the audit and review of accounting data.

Errors are generally discovered at times when the periodic adjusting entries are being made, when an audit is being undertaken, when a business is to be sold, when a change of ownership is to be made in a partnership, when questions of taxation are to be decided, when heirs of an estate are to be satisfied, when a business is to be incorporated and shares are to be sold to outsiders, or when two or more business units are to be combined in a merger or consolidation.

Kinds of Errors

There are a number of different kinds of errors. Some errors are discovered in the period in which they are made, and these are easily corrected. Others may not be discovered currently and are reflected on the financial statements until discovered. Some errors are never discovered; however, the effects of these errors are counterbalanced in subsequent periods and after this takes place, account balances are again accurately stated. Errors may be classified as follows.

Errors Discovered Currently in the Course of the Normal Accounting Procedures. Certain errors are of a clerical nature and are discovered in the course of the normal accounting processes. For example, an entry may be made that is not in balance and the entry is posted, an item may be posted to the wrong side of the account, an arithmetic mistake may be made in computing an account balance, an amount may be misstated or omitted in posting to a subsidiary ledger, or an account balance may be misstated or omitted in listing accounts on a trial balance or on a work sheet. Such errors, when not discovered during the period, will become evident at the end of the period in the regular course of summarizing operations. Errors are indicated when subsidiary account detail is not equal to the balance in the control account, when debit and credit totals on a trial balance are not equal, or when totals on a work sheet are not in balance. Normally the summarizing process points to the source of the error, and the error is readily corrected.

Errors Limited to Balance Sheet Accounts. Certain errors affect only the balance sheet accounts. For example, Marketable Securities may be debited instead of Notes Receivable, Interest Payable may be credited instead of Salaries Payable, or Prepaid Tax may be debited instead of Tax Payable. In other instances, the acquisition of a property item on a deferred payment plan may be misstated, or the exchange of convertible bonds for stock may be omitted. Such errors are frequently discovered in the period in which they are made in the course of recording subsequent transactions in the misstated accounts, or in the course of reviewing preliminary summaries and statements. When the errors are discovered currently, entries are made to correct account balances. When the errors are not discovered until a subsequent period, corrections are made at that time. However, memorandum entries should be made on the books to indicate which accounts were misstated so the balance sheet data may be restated when the statement is to be presented in subsequent periods for analysis purposes or for comparative reporting.

Errors Limited to Income Statement Accounts. Certain errors affect only the income statement accounts. For example, Office Salaries may be debited instead of Sales Salaries, Purchases may be debited instead of Sales Returns, or Interest Revenue may be credited instead of Dividend Revenue. The discovery of the errors in the period in which they are made calls for the correction of the revenue and expense balances. However, if the errors are not discovered in the period in which they are made, net income will still be stated correctly; in closing the accounts at the end of the period, the balance sheet accounts remaining open are accurately stated and carried into the next period. If the errors are discovered in a subsequent period, no corrections are necessary. However, memorandum entries should be made on the books to indicate the misstated accounts so the income statement data may be restated when the statement is to be presented in future periods for analysis purposes or for comparative reporting.

Errors Affecting Both Income Statement Accounts and Balance Sheet Accounts. Certain errors, when not discovered currently, result in the misstatement of net income and thus affect both the income statement accounts and the balance sheet accounts. The balance sheet accounts are carried into the succeeding period; hence, an error made currently and not detected will affect earnings of the future. Such errors may be classified into two groups:

1. *Errors in net income which, when not detected, are automatically counterbalanced in the following fiscal period.* Net income on the income statements for two successive periods are inaccurately stated; certain account balances on the balance sheet at the end of the first period are inaccurately stated, but the account balances in the balance sheet at the end of the succeeding period are accurately stated. In this class are errors, such as the misstatement of inventories and the omission of adjustments for prepaid and accrued items at the end of a period.
2. *Errors in net income which, when not detected, are not automatically counterbalanced in the following fiscal period.* Account balances on successive balance sheets are inaccurately stated until the time entries are made compensating for or correcting the errors. In this class are errors, such as the recognition of capital expenditures as revenue expenditures and the omission of charges for depreciation and amortization.

When these types of errors are discovered, careful analysis is required to determine the required action to correct the account balances.

When it is discovered that an error in stating net income of the past has been counterbalanced in subsequent periods, a memorandum entry is made to indicate the corrections required in the balance sheet and income statement in providing such presentations in the future. However, when errors of the past have not yet been counterbalanced, the APB has specified that if the error is material, it should be considered as a prior period adjustment and the adjustment should be made directly to Retained Earnings.[1] For example, assume the merchandise inventory at

---

[1]*Ibid.*, par. 36.

the end of the preceding period was materially overstated on the books of a corporation as the result of an error in the count; the error is corrected by a debit to Retained Earnings and a credit to the inventory balance. Assume a material cut-off error was made in recording sales on account at the end of the previous period; the error is corrected by a debit to Sales of the current period and a credit to Retained Earnings.

Disclosure of the nature of the error and the effect of its correction on prior period income before extraordinary items, net income, and the related earnings per share amounts should be made in the period in which the error was discovered and corrected. Future financial statements need not repeat the disclosure.[1] As indicated in earlier chapters, corporate annual reports generally provide comparative financial statements reporting the financial position and the results of operations for the current period and for one or more preceding periods. In preparing comparative statements, these should be restated to report the retroactive application of error corrections.

The remaining sections in this chapter are designed to describe and illustrate the procedures applied when error corrections qualify as prior period adjustments. Accordingly, it is assumed each of the errors named is material and calls for correction directly to the retained earnings account summarizing past earnings. When errors are discovered, they usually affect the income tax liability for a prior period. Adjusted tax returns are usually prepared to either claim a refund or to pay any additional tax assessment. For simplicity, the extended example on the following pages and the exercises and problems at the end of the chapter ignore the income tax effect of errors.

Illustrative Example of Error Correction

The following example illustrates the analysis required upon the discovery of errors of prior periods and the entries to correct these errors.

Assume the Monarch Wholesale Co. began operations at the beginning of 1976. An auditing firm is engaged for the first time in 1978. Before the accounts are adjusted and closed for 1978, the auditor reviews the books and accounts, and discovers the errors summarized on pages 640 and 641. Effects on the financial statements are listed before any correcting entries. A plus sign (+) indicates an overstatement in the statement section; a minus sign (−) indicates an understatement in the statement section. Each error correction is discussed in more detail in the following paragraphs.

(1) *Understatement of merchandise inventory.* It is discovered that the merchandise inventory as of December 31, 1976, was understated by $1,000. The effects of the misstatement were as shown at the top of page 639.

Since this type of error counterbalances after two years, no correcting entry is required in 1978.

If the error had been discovered in 1977 instead of 1978, an entry could have been made to correct the account balances so that operations

---
[1]*Ibid*., par. 37.

Income Statement	Balance Sheet
For 1976: Cost of goods sold overstated (ending inventory too low)	Assets understated (inventory too low)
Net income understated	Retained earnings understated
For 1977: Cost of goods sold understated (beginning inventory too low)	Balance sheet items not affected, retained earnings understatement for 1976 being corrected by net income overstatement for 1977.
Net income overstated	

for 1977 might be reported accurately. The beginning inventory would have to be increased by $1,000, the asset understatement, and Retained Earnings would have to be credited for this amount representing the income understatement in 1976. The correcting entry in 1977 would have been:

Merchandise Inventory	1,000	
Retained Earnings		1,000

(2) *Failure to record merchandise purchases.* It is discovered that purchase invoices as of December 28, 1976, for $850 were not recorded until 1977. The goods were included in the inventory at the end of 1976. The effects of the failure to record the purchases were as follows:

Income Statement	Balance Sheet
For 1976: Cost of goods sold understated (purchases too low)	Liabilities understated (accounts payable too low)
Net income overstated	Retained earnings overstated
For 1977: Cost of goods sold overstated (purchases too high)	Balance sheet items not affected, retained earnings overstatement for 1976 being corrected by net income understatement for 1977.
Net income understated	

Since this is a counterbalancing error, no correcting entry is required in 1978.

If the error had been discovered in 1977 instead of 1978, a correcting entry would have been necessary. In 1977, Purchases was debited and Accounts Payable credited for $850 for merchandise acquired in 1976 and included in the ending inventory of 1976. Retained Earnings would have to be debited for $850, representing the net income overstatement for 1976, and Purchases would have to be credited for a similar amount to reduce the Purchases balance in 1977. The correcting entry in 1977 would have been:

Retained Earnings	850	
Purchases		850

(3) *Failure to record merchandise sales.* It is discovered that sales on account for the last week of December, 1977, for $1,800 were not recorded until 1978. The goods sold were not included in the inventory at the end of 1977. The effects of the failure to report the revenue in 1977 were:

Income Statement	Balance Sheet
For 1977: Revenue understated (sales too low)	Assets understated (accounts receivable too low)
Net income understated	Retained earnings understated

ANALYSIS SHEET TO SHOW EFFECTS

| | AT END OF 1976 | | | |
| | INCOME STATEMENT | | BALANCE SHEET | |
	SECTION	NET INCOME	SECTION	RETAINED EARNINGS
(1) Understatement of merchandise inventory of $1,000 on December 31, 1976.	Cost of Goods Sold +	−	Current Assets −	−
(2) Failure to record merchandise purchases on account of $850 in 1976; purchases were recorded in 1977.	Cost of Goods Sold −	+	Current Liabilities −	+
(3) Failure to record merchandise sales on account of $1,800 in 1977. (It is assumed that the sales for 1977 were recognized as revenue in 1978.)				
(4) Failure to record accrued sales salaries; expense was recognized when payment was made. On December 31, 1976, $450.	Selling Expense −	+	Current Liabilities −	+
On December 31, 1977, $300.				
(5) Failure to record prepaid taxes of $275 on December 31, 1976; amount was included as miscellaneous general expense.	General Expense +	−	Current Assets −	−
(6) Failure to record reduction in prepaid insurance balance of $350 on December 31, 1976; insurance for 1976 was charged to 1977.	General Expense −	+	Current Assets +	+
(7) Failure to record accrued interest on notes receivable of $150 on December 31, 1976; revenue was recognized on collection in 1977.	Other Revenue −	−	Current Assets −	−
(8) Failure to record unearned service fees; amounts received were included in Miscellaneous Revenue. On December 31, 1976, $175.	Other Revenue +	+	Current Liabilities −	+
On December 31, 1977, $225.				
(9) Failure to record reduction in unearned rent revenue balance on December 31, 1977, $125. (It is assumed that the rent revenue for 1977 was recognized as revenue in 1978.)				
(10) Failure to record depreciation of delivery equipment. On December 31, 1976, $1,200.	Selling Expense −	+	Non-current Assets +	+
On December 31, 1977, $1,200.				

OF ERRORS ON FINANCIAL STATEMENTS

| AT END OF 1977 | | | | AT END OF 1978 | | | |
| INCOME STATEMENT | | BALANCE SHEET | | INCOME STATEMENT | | BALANCE SHEET | |
SECTION	NET INCOME	SECTION	RETAINED EARNINGS	SECTION	NET INCOME	SECTION	RETAINED EARNINGS
Cost of Goods Sold −	+						
Cost of Goods Sold +	−						
Sales −	−	Accounts Receivable −	−	Sales +	+		
Selling Expense +	−						
Selling Expense −	+	Current Liabilities −	+	Selling Expense +	−		
General Expense −	+						
General Expense +	−						
Other Revenue +	+						
Other Revenue −	−						
Other Revenue +	+	Current Liabilities −	+	Other Revenue −	−		
Other Revenue −	−	Deferred Revenues +	−	Other Revenue +	+		
		Non-current Assets +	+			Non-current Assets +	+
Selling Expense −	+	Non-current Assets +	+			Non-current Assets +	+

When the error is discovered in 1978, Sales is debited for $1,800 and Retained Earnings is credited for this amount representing the net income understatement for 1977. The following entry is made:

Sales...	1,800	
Retained Earnings..		1,800

(4) *Failure to record accrued expense.* Accrued sales salaries of $450 as of December 31, 1976, and $300 as of December 31, 1977, were overlooked in adjusting the accounts on each of these dates. Sales Salaries is debited for salary payments. The effects of the failure to record the accrued expense of $450 as of December 31, 1976, were as follows:

Income Statement	Balance Sheet
For 1976: Expenses understated (sales salaries too low) Net income overstated	Liabilities understated (accrued sales salaries not reported) Retained earnings overstated
For 1977: Expenses overstated (sales salaries too high) Net income understated	Balance sheet items not affected, retained earnings overstatement for 1976 being corrected by net income understatement for 1977.

The effects of the failure to recognize the accrued expense of $300 on December 31, 1976, were as follows:

Income Statement	Balance Sheet
For 1977: Expenses understated (sales salaries too low) Net income overstated	Liabilities understated (accrued sales salaries not reported) Retained earnings overstated

No entry is required in 1978 to correct the accounts for the failure to record the accrued expense at the end of 1976, the misstatement in 1976 having been counterbalanced by the misstatement in 1977. An entry is required, however, to correct the accounts for the failure to record the accrued expense at the end of 1977 if the net income for 1978 is not to be misstated. If accrued expenses were properly recorded at the end of 1978, Retained Earnings would be debited for $300, representing the net income overstatement for 1977, and Sales Salaries would be credited for a similar amount, representing the amount to be subtracted from salary payments in 1978. The correcting entry is:

Retained Earnings...	300	
Sales Salaries..		300

If the failure to adjust the accounts for the accrued expense of 1976 had been recognized in 1977, an entry similar to the one above would have been required in 1977 to correct the account balances. The entry in 1977 would have been:

Retained Earnings...	450	
Sales Salaries..		450

The accrued salaries of $300 as of the end of 1977 would be recorded at the end of that year by an appropriate adjustment.

(5) *Failure to record prepaid expense.* It is discovered that Miscellaneous General Expense for 1976 included taxes of $275 that should have been deferred in adjusting the accounts on December 31, 1976. The effects of the failure to record the prepaid expense were as follows:

Income Statement	Balance Sheet
For 1976: Expenses overstated (miscellaneous general expense too high) Net income understated	Assets understated (prepaid taxes not reported) Retained earnings understated
For 1977: Expenses understated (miscellaneous general expense too low) Net income overstated	Balance sheet items not affected, retained earnings understatement for 1976 being corrected by net income overstatement for 1977.

Since this is a counterbalancing error, no entry to correct the accounts is required in 1978.

If the error had been discovered in 1977 instead of 1978, a correcting entry would have been necessary. If prepaid taxes were properly recorded at the end of 1977, Miscellaneous General Expense would have to be debited for $275, the expense relating to operations of 1977, and Retained Earnings would have to be credited for a similar amount representing the net income understatement for 1976. The correcting entry in 1977 would have been:

Miscellaneous General Expense...	275	
Retained Earnings..		275

(6) *Overstatement of prepaid expense.* On January 2, 1976, $1,050 representing insurance for a three-year period was paid. The charge was made to the asset account, Prepaid Insurance. No adjustment was made at the end of 1976. At the end of 1977, the prepaid insurance account was reduced to the prepaid balance on that date, $350, insurance for two years, or $700, being charged to operations of 1977. The effects of the misstatements were as follows:

Income Statement	Balance Sheet
For 1976: Expenses understated (insurance expense not reported) Net income overstated	Assets overstated (prepaid insurance too high) Retained earnings overstated
For 1977: Expenses overstated (insurance expense too high) Net income understated	Balance sheet items not affected, retained earnings overstatement for 1976 being corrected by net income understatement for 1977.

Since the balance sheet items at the end of 1977 were correctly stated, no entry to correct the accounts is required in 1978.

If the error had been discovered in 1977 instead of 1978, an entry would have been necessary to correct the account balances. Prepaid Insurance would have been decreased for the expired insurance of $350 and Retained Earnings would be debited for this amount representing the net income overstatement for 1976. The correcting entry in 1977 would have been:

Retained Earnings..	350	
Prepaid Insurance		350

The expired insurance of $350 for 1977 would be recorded at the end of that year by an appropriate adjustment.

(7) *Failure to record accrued revenue.* Accrued interest on notes receivable of $150 was overlooked in adjusting the accounts on December 31, 1976. The revenue was recognized when the interest was collected in 1977. The effects of the failure to record the accrued revenue were:

	Income Statement	Balance Sheet
For 1976:	Revenue understated (interest revenue too low)	Assets understated (interest receivable not reported)
	Net income understated	Retained earnings understated
For 1977:	Revenue overstated (interest revenue too high) Net income overstated	Balance sheet items not affected, retained earnings understatement for 1976 being corrected by net income overstatement for 1977.

Since the balance sheet items at the end of 1977 were correctly stated, no entry to correct the accounts is required in 1978.

If the error had been discovered in 1977 instead of 1978, an entry would have been necessary to correct the account balances. If accrued interest on notes receivable had been properly recorded at the end of 1977, Interest Revenue would have to be debited for $150, the amount to be subtracted from receipts of 1977, and Retained Earnings would have to be credited for a similar amount representing the net income understatement for 1976. The correcting entry in 1977 would have been:

Interest Revenue	150	
Retained Earnings		150

(8) *Failure to record unearned revenue.* Fees received in advance for miscellaneous services of $175 as of December 31, 1976, and $225 as of December 31, 1977, were overlooked in adjusting the accounts on each of these dates. Miscellaneous Revenue had been credited when fees were received. The effects of the failure to recognize the unearned revenue of $175 at the end of 1976 were as follows:

	Income Statement	Balance Sheet
For 1976:	Revenue overstated (miscellaneous revenue too high)	Liabilities understated (unearned service fees not reported)
	Net income overstated	Retained earnings overstated
For 1977:	Revenue understated (miscellaneous revenue too low)	Balance sheet items not affected, retained earnings overstatement for 1976 being corrected by net income understatement for 1977.
	Net income understated	

The effects of the failure to recognize the unearned revenue of $225 at the end of 1977 were as follows:

	Income Statement	Balance Sheet
For 1977:	Revenue overstated (miscellaneous revenue too high)	Liabilities understated (unearned service fees not reported)
	Net income overstated	Retained earnings overstated

No entry is required in 1978 to correct the accounts for the failure to record the unearned revenue at the end of 1976, the misstatement in 1976 having been counterbalanced by the misstatement in 1977. An entry is required, however, to correct the accounts for the failure to record the unearned revenue at the end of 1977 if the net income for 1978 is not to be misstated. If the unearned revenue were properly recorded at the end of 1978, Retained Earnings would be debited for $225, representing the net income overstatement for 1977, and Miscellaneous Revenue would be credited for the same amount, representing the revenue that is to be identified with 1978. The correcting entry is:

Retained Earnings	225	
Miscellaneous Revenue		225

If the failure to adjust the accounts for the unearned revenue of 1976 had been recognized in 1977 instead of 1978, an entry similar to the one above would have been required in 1977 to correct the account balances. The entry at that time would have been:

Retained Earnings	175	
Miscellaneous Revenue		175

The unearned service fees of $225 as of the end of 1977 would be recorded at the end of that year by an appropriate adjustment.

(9) *Overstatement of unearned revenue.* Unearned Rent Revenue was credited for $375 representing revenue for December, 1977, and for January and February, 1978. No adjustment was made on December 31, 1977. The effects of the failure to adjust the accounts to show revenue of $125 for 1977 were as follows:

	Income Statement	Balance Sheet
For 1977:	Revenue understated (rent revenue too low)	Liabilities overstated (unearned rent revenue too high)
	Net income understated	Retained earnings understated

When the error is discovered in 1978, Unearned Rent Revenue is debited for $125 and Retained Earnings is credited for this amount representing the net income understatement in 1977. The following entry is made:

Unearned Rent Revenue	125	
Retained Earnings		125

(10) *Failure to record depreciation.* Delivery equipment was acquired at the beginning of 1976 at a cost of $6,000. The equipment has an estimated five-year life, and depreciation of $1,200 was overlooked at the end of 1976 and 1977. The effects of the failure to record depreciation for 1976 were as follows:

	Income Statement	Balance Sheet
For 1976:	Expenses understated (depreciation of delivery equipment too low)	Assets overstated (accumulated depreciation of delivery equipment too low)
	Net income overstated	Retained earnings overstated
For 1977:	Expenses not affected	Assets overstated (accumulated depreciation of delivery equipment too low)
	Net income not affected	Retained earnings overstated

It should be observed that the misstatements arising from the failure to record depreciation are not counterbalanced in the succeeding year.

Failure to record depreciation for 1977 affected the statements as shown below:

Income Statement	Balance Sheet
For 1977: Expenses understated (depreciation of delivery equipment too low) Net income overstated	Assets overstated (accumulated depreciation of delivery equipment understated) Retained earnings overstated

When the omission is recognized, Retained Earnings must be decreased by the net income overstatements of prior years and accumulated depreciation must be increased by the depreciation that should have been recorded. The correcting entry in 1978 for depreciation that should have been recognized for 1976 and 1977 is as follows:

Retained Earnings...	2,400	
Accumulated Depreciation — Delivery Equipment		2,400

Working Papers to Summarize Corrections

It is assumed in the following sections that the errors previously discussed are discovered in 1978 before the accounts for the year are adjusted and closed. Accounts are corrected so that revenue and expense accounts report the balances identified with the current period and asset, liability, and retained earnings accounts are accurately stated. Instead of preparing a separate entry for each correction, a single compound entry may be made for all of the errors discovered. The entry to correct earnings of prior years as well as to correct current earnings may be developed by the preparation of working papers. Assume the following retained earnings account for the Monarch Wholesale Co.:

ACCOUNT Retained Earnings

DATE	ITEM	DEBIT	CREDIT	BALANCE DEBIT	BALANCE CREDIT
1976 Dec. 31	Balance...				12,000
1977 Dec. 20	Dividends declared..............................	5,000			7,000
31	Net income..		15,000		22,000

The working papers to determine the corrected retained earnings balance on December 31, 1976, and the corrected net income for 1977 are shown on page 647. As indicated earlier, no adjustment is made for income tax effects in this example.

The working papers indicate that Retained Earnings is to be decreased by $1,000 as of January 1, 1978. The reduction arises from:

Retained earnings overstatement as of December 31, 1976:		
Retained earnings as originally reported.................................	$12,000	
Retained earnings as corrected..	10,400	$1,600
Retained earnings understatement in 1977:		
Net income as corrected..	$15,600	
Net income as originally reported..	15,000	600
Retained earnings overstatement as of January 1, 1978............		$1,000

Monarch Wholesale Co.
Working Papers for Correction of Account Balances
December 31, 1978

EXPLANATION	RETAINED EARNINGS DEC. 31, 1976 DEBIT	CREDIT	NET INCOME YEAR ENDED DEC. 31, 1977 DEBIT	CREDIT	ACCOUNTS REQUIRING CORRECTION IN 1978 DEBIT	CREDIT	ACCOUNT
Reported retained earnings balance, Dec. 31, 1976		12,000					
Reported net income for year ended Dec. 31, 1977				15,000			
Corrections:¹							
(1) Understatement of inventory on Dec. 31, 1976, $1,000		1,000	1,000				
(2) Failure to record merchandise purchases in 1976, $850	850			850			
(3) Failure to record merchandise sales in 1977, $1,800				1,800	1,800		Sales
(4) Failure to record accrued sales salaries:							
(a) On Dec. 31, 1976, $450	450			450			
(b) On Dec. 31, 1977, $300			300			300	Sales Salaries
(5) Failure to record prepaid taxes on Dec. 31, 1976, $275		275	275				
(6) Failure to record insurance expense on Dec. 31, 1976, $350, insurance of $700 for 1976 and 1977 being charged to 1977	350			350			
(7) Failure to record accrued interest on notes receivable on Dec. 31, 1976, $150		150	150				
(8) Failure to record unearned service fees:							
(a) On Dec. 31, 1976, $175	175			175			
(b) On Dec. 31, 1977, $225			225			225	Miscellaneous Revenue
(9) Failure to record rent revenue on Dec. 31, 1977, $125				125	125		Unearned Rent Revenue
(10) Failure to record depreciation of delivery equipment:							
(a) On Dec. 31, 1976, $1,200	1,200					1,200 ⎰	Accumulated Depr. — Delivery Equipment
(b) On Dec. 31, 1977, $1,200			1,200			1,200 ⎱	
Corrected retained earnings balance, Dec. 31, 1976	10,400						
	13,425	13,425					
Corrected net income for 1977			15,600				
			18,750	18,750			
Net correction to retained earnings as of Jan. 1, 1978					1,000		Retained Earnings
					2,925	2,925	

¹For a more detailed description of the individual errors and their correction, refer to pages 638–646.

The following entry is prepared from the working papers to correct the account balances in 1978:

Retained Earnings	1,000	
Sales	1,800	
Unearned Rent Revenue	125	
Sales Salaries		300
Miscellaneous Revenue		225
Accumulated Depreciation — Delivery Equipment		2,400

The retained earnings account after correction will appear with a balance of $21,000, as follows:

ACCOUNT   Retained Earnings

DATE		ITEM	DEBIT	CREDIT	BALANCE DEBIT	BALANCE CREDIT
1978 Jan.	1	Balance				22,000
Dec.	31	Corrections in net incomes of prior periods discovered during the course of the audit	1,000			21,000

The balance in Retained Earnings can be proved by reconstructing the account from the detail shown on the working papers. If the net incomes for 1976 and 1977 had been reported properly, Retained Earnings would have appeared as follows:

ACCOUNT   Retained Earnings

DATE		ITEM	DEBIT	CREDIT	BALANCE DEBIT	BALANCE CREDIT
1976 Dec.	31	Corrected balance per working papers				10,400
1977 Dec.	20	Dividends declared	5,000			5,400
	31	Corrected net income for 1977		15,600		21,000

In the foregoing example, a corrected net income figure for only 1977 was required; hence any corrections in earnings for years prior to this date were shown as affecting the retained earnings balance as of December 31, 1976. Working papers on page 647 were constructed to summarize this information by providing a pair of columns for retained earnings as of December 31, 1976, and a pair of columns for earnings data for 1977. It may be desirable to determine corrected earnings for a number of years. When this is to be done, a pair of columns must be provided for retained earnings as of the beginning of the period under review and a separate pair of columns for each year for which corrected earnings are to be determined. For example, assume that corrected earnings for the years 1975, 1976, and 1977 are to be determined. Working papers for the correction of account balances would be constructed with headings as shown at the top of the next page. Corrections for the omission of accrued sales salaries for a four-year period would appear as follows:

EXPLANATION	RETAINED EARNINGS DEC. 31, 1974		NET INCOME YEAR ENDED DEC. 31, 1975		NET INCOME YEAR ENDED DEC. 31, 1976		NET INCOME YEAR ENDED DEC. 31, 1977		ACCOUNTS REQUIRING CORRECTION IN 1978		
	DEBIT	CREDIT	DEBIT	CREDIT	DEBIT	CREDIT	DEBIT	CREDIT	DEBIT	CREDIT	ACCOUNT
Failure to record accrued sales salaries at end of:											
1974, $750..............................	750			750							
1975, $800..............................			800			800					
1976, $900..............................					900			900			
1977, $625..............................							625			625	Sales Salaries

QUESTIONS

1. Explain briefly the difference in treatments of (a) a change in an accounting principle, and (b) a change in an accounting estimate.

2. Why does the adoption of new and different accounting principles require justification, whereas the continuation of a principle already applied requires no such justification?

3. When should the effects of a change in accounting principle be shown as a restatement of prior periods? (Give examples.)

4. When should the effects of a change in accounting principles be shown as a cumulative effect on net income? (Give examples.)

5. Why isn't a change from the fifo to the lifo method of inventory evaluation always shown as a pro forma restatement of prior years?

6. Describe the effect on current net income, beginning retained earnings, deferred income tax payable, individual assets accounts and asset contra accounts when:

(a) Depreciation is converted from the straight-line method to the double-declining-balance method.

(b) Depreciation is converted from the sum-of-the-years-digits method to the straight-line method.

(c) Income on construction contracts which had been reported on a completed-projects basis is now reported on the percentage-of-completion basis.

(d) The valuation of inventories is changed from a fifo to a lifo basis. Records do not permit retroactive change in methods.

(e) It is determined that the warranty expenses for sales in prior years should have been 5% instead of 4%.

(f) The valuation of inventories is changed from a lifo to a fifo basis.

(g) Your accounts receivable clerk reads that a major customer has declared bankruptcy.

(h) Your patent lawyer informs you that your rival has perfected and patented a new invention making your product obsolete.

7. Name three errors that are counterbalanced in the following period and do not require corrections if discovered after such time.

8. Name three errors that will not be counterbalanced in the following period and require corrections upon their discovery.

9. Name three errors that result in misstatements on the income statement but do not affect the balance sheet at the end of the current period.

10. Name three errors that result in misstatements on the balance sheet but do not affect the income statement at the end of the current period.

11. The controller for the Lopez Co. states: "The understatement of an expense in one year calls for an overstatement of the same expense in the following year even when the error is discovered; if this is not done, expense will bypass the income statement." Comment on this opinion.

12. State the effect upon net income in 1976 and 1977 of each of the following errors that are made at the end of 1976:

(a) Salaries payable are understated.

(b) Interest receivable is understated.

(c) Discount on notes payable is overstated.

(d) Unearned rent revenue is understated.

(e) Depreciation on an equipment item is overlooked.

(f) Discount on notes receivable is overstated.

(g) Interest payable is overstated.

(h) Amortization on patents acquired in 1975 is computed on the 17-year legal life instead of the 5-year useful life.

(i) A full year's depreciation is taken on items sold in June, 1976.

(j) Machinery purchased in June, 1976, was debited to the furniture and fixtures account.

13. State the effect of each of the following errors made in 1976 upon the balance sheets and the income statements prepared in 1976 and 1977:

(a) The ending inventory is understated as a result of an error in the count of goods on hand.

(b) The ending inventory is overstated as a result of the inclusion of goods acquired and held on a consignment basis. No purchase was recorded on the books.

(c) A purchase of merchandise at the end of 1976 is not recorded until payment is made for the goods in 1977; the goods purchased were included in the inventory at the end of 1976.

(d) A sale of merchandise at the end of 1976 is not recorded until cash is received for the goods in 1977; the goods sold were excluded from the inventory at the end of 1976.

(e) Goods shipped to consignees in 1976 were reported as sales; goods in the hands of consignees at the end of 1976 were not recognized for inventory purposes; sale of such goods in 1977 and collections on such sales were recorded as credits to the receivables established with consignees in 1976.

(f) One week's sales total during 1976 was credited to Gain on Sales — Machinery.

(g) No depreciation is taken in 1976 for machinery sold in April, 1976. The company is on a calendar year and computes depreciation to the nearest month.

(h) No depreciation is taken in 1976 for machinery purchased in October, 1976. The company is on a calendar year and computes depreciation to the nearest month.

(i) Customers' notes receivable are debited to Accounts Receivable.

EXERCISES

1. The Layton Construction Company has used the completed-contract method of accounting since it began operations in 1974. In 1977, management decided, for justifiable reasons, to adopt the percentage-of-completion method.

The company had prepared the following statement reporting income for the years 1974–1976.

	1974	1975	1976
Total sales price of completed contracts..........................	0	$1,000,000	$800,000
Less cost of completed contracts plus anticipated loss on contract in process...	0	825,000	560,000
Income from operations	0	$ 175,000	$240,000
Extraordinary loss			35,000
Net income...	0	$ 175,000	$205,000

Analysis of the accounting records disclosed the following income by projects was earned for the years 1974–1976 using the percentage-of-completion method of inventory valuation:

	1974	1975	1976
Project A	$125,000	$ 50,000	0
Project B	90,000	180,000	$20,000
Project C	0	20,000	80,000
Project D	0	0	(50,000)

Give the journal entry required in 1977 to reflect the change in inventory methods. Use a 45% income tax rate.

2. The Sterling Sales Company decides to change from the double-declining-balance method of depreciation it has used for both reporting and tax purposes to the straight-line method for reporting purposes. From the information which follows, prepare the income statement for 1977. Assume a 45% tax rate.

Year	Net Income As Reported	Excess of Double-Declining Balance Depreciation Over Straight-Line Depreciation	Direct Effect Less Tax (45%)
Prior to 1974		$25,000	$13,750
1974	$125,000	12,500	6,875
1975	109,000	15,000	8,250
1976	156,000	22,500	12,375
		$75,000	$41,250

In 1977, net sales were $380,000; cost of goods sold, $185,000; selling expenses, $95,000; and general and administrative expenses, $28,000. In addition, Sterling had a tax deductible extraordinary loss of $45,000. Assume the fiscal year ends on December 31.

3. Assume the change in net income as shown in Exercise 2 is the result of a change from the lifo method of inventory pricing to another method. During 1977, dividends of $35,000 were announced and distributed. Based upon this information, prepare the retained earnings statement for 1977. The December 31, 1976, retained earnings balance as reported was $520,000.

4. On December 31, 1977, the Pullins Company determined that heavy machinery previously thought to have a 20-year life will actually last only 12 years. The machinery was purchased nine years ago for $60,000 with an expected salvage value of $10,000. The straight-line depreciation method is used. Give the adjusting journal entry required at December 31, 1977, to account for this change in the estimated life of the machinery, if no entry has yet been made for depreciation in 1977.

5. The Hews Corporation purchased a patent on January 2, 1972, for $135,000. The original life of the patent was estimated to be 15 years. However, in December of 1977, the controller of Hews received information proving conclusively that the product protected by the Hews Corporation patent would be obsolete within two years. Accordingly, the company decided to write off the unamortized portion of the patent cost over three years beginning in 1977. How would the change in estimate be reflected in the accounts for 1977 and subsequent years?

6. The Nielson Co. reports net incomes for a three-year period as follows: 1975, $18,000; 1976, $10,500; 1977, $12,500.

In reviewing the accounts in 1978, after the books for the prior year have been closed, you find that the following errors have been made in summarizing activities:

	1975	1976	1977
Overstatement of ending inventories as a result of errors in count...	$1,600	$2,800	$1,800
Understatement of advertising expense payable	300	600	450
Overstatement of interest receivable..	250	——	200
Omission of depreciation on property items still in use	900	800	750

   (a) Prepare working papers summarizing corrections and reporting corrected net incomes for 1975, 1976, and 1977.
   (b) Give the entry to bring the books of the company up to date in 1978.

7. The Huntsman Manufacturing Company has been in business since 1975 and produces a single product sold with a one-year warranty covering parts and labor. An audit is made of the company's records for the first time at the end of 1977 before the accounts for 1977 are closed, and it is found that charges for warranties have not been anticipated but have been recognized when incurred. The audit discloses the following data:

Year	Sales	Warranty Expense for Sales Made in		
		1975	1976	1977
1975......................	$ 900,000	$23,000	$20,000	
1976......................	800,000		18,000	$24,000
1977......................	1,100,000			29,000

The auditor decides the company should have recognized the full expense for warranties in the year in which the sales were made. She recommends the charges for warranties should be recognized as a percentage of sales and that experiences of past years should be used in arriving at such a percentage. Net incomes before correction have been as follows: 1975, $87,000; 1976, $85,000; 1977, $140,000.

   (a) What earnings would have been reported if warranty costs had been anticipated and the percentage as calculated had been applied?
   (b) What correcting entry should be made as of December 31, 1977?

PROBLEMS

22-1. In 1977, Bacastow Builders changed their method of depreciating equipment from the sum-of-the-years-digits method, used for both reporting and tax purposes, to the straight-line method. The following information shows the effect of this change on the amount of depreciation to be shown on the income statement.

Year	Net Income as Reported	Excess of Sum-of-the-Years-Digits Depreciation Over Straight-Line Depreciation
Prior to 1973		$ 80,000
1973	$400,000	30,000
1974	365,000	26,000
1975	380,000	28,000
1976	420,000	34,000
		$198,000

Assume the company has a tax rate of 45%. Employees have been given a 15% cash bonus on operating income during these years.

Instructions:
(1) Compute the effect of the change in accounting principle on income as follows: (a) the direct effect less the tax effect; (b) the direct and indirect effects.
(2) Prepare (a) a partial income statement for 1977 if income before extraordinary items in the year was $450,000 and an extraordinary loss of $72,000 before tax was incurred; and (b) pro forma income tax data for the years 1973–1976.

22-2. In 1977, the Fleming Company decided to change from the straight-line method of amortizing capitalized leases to the declining-balance method, which had been used on the tax return. The following information shows the effect of this change on the amount of amortization to be shown on the income statement.

Year	Net Income As Reported	Excess of Accelerated Amortization Over Straight-Line Amortization
Prior to 1972		$18,000
1972	$258,000	6,000
1973	295,000	8,000
1974	325,000	9,200
1975	310,000	10,800
1976	400,000	12,000
		$64,000

Assume the company has a tax rate of 45%. Management personnel have been given a bonus of 10% of operating income to purchase stock during these years.

Instructions:
(1) Compute the effect of the change in accounting principle on income as follows: (a) The direct effect less the tax effect; (b) The direct and indirect effects.
(2) Prepare (a) a partial income statement for 1977 if income after tax before extraordinary items in that year was $425,000 and an extraordinary gain of $100,000 before tax was received; and (b) pro forma income data for the years 1972–1976.

22-3. On January 1, 1977, Russell Retailers, Inc., decided to change from the lifo method of inventory pricing to the fifo method. The reported income for the four years Russell Retailers had been in business was as follows:

1973	$125,000	1975	$155,000
1974	130,000	1976	165,000

Analysis of the inventory records disclosed the following inventories were on hand at the end of each year as valued under both the lifo and fifo methods.

Date	Lifo Method	Fifo Method
January 1, 1973	0	0
December 31, 1973	$114,000	$128,000
December 31, 1974	120,000	119,000
December 31, 1975	135,000	151,000
December 31, 1976	144,000	176,000

The income tax rate is 45%.

> **Instructions:**
> (1) Compute the restated net income for the years 1973–1976.
> (2) Prepare the retained earnings statement for Russell Retailers, Inc., for 1977 if the 1976 ending balance had been previously reported at $300,000, 1977 net income using the fifo method is $180,000, and dividends of $100,000 were paid during 1977.

22-4. The first audit of the books for the Risenmay Corporation was made for the year ended December 31, 1977. In reviewing the books, the auditor discovered that certain adjustments had been overlooked at the end of 1976 and 1977, and also that other items had been improperly recorded. Omissions and other failures for each year are summarized below:

	December 31	
	1976	1977
Sales salaries payable	$1,300	$1,100
Interest receivable	325	215
Prepaid insurance...	450	300
Advances from customers	1,750	2,500
(Collections from customers had been included in sales but should have been recognized as advances from customers since goods were not shipped until the following year.)		
Equipment...	1,400	1,200
(Expenditures had been recognized as repairs but should have been recognized as cost of equipment; the depreciation rate on such equipment is 10% per year, but depreciation in the year of the expenditure is to be recognized at 5%).		

> **Instructions:** Prepare journal entries to correct revenue and expense accounts for 1977 and record assets and liabilities that require recognition on the balance sheet as of December 31, 1977. Assume the nominal accounts for 1977 have not yet been closed into the income summary account.

22-5. The Lawler Sales Co. has failed to recognize certain prepaid and accrued items in the years 1974–1977. The retained earnings account is as follows at the end of 1977.

ACCOUNT　　Retained Earnings

DATE		ITEM	DEBIT	CREDIT	BALANCE DEBIT	BALANCE CREDIT
1974 Dec.	31	Balance..				55,000
1975		Dividends...	18,300			36,700
		Net income..		25,500		62,200
1976		Dividends...	14,800			47,400
		Net income..		24,000		71,400
1977		Dividends...	20,500			50,900
		Net income..		33,000		83,900

	End of 1974	End of 1975	End of 1976	End of 1977
Prepaid expenses	$3,200	$2,500	$3,800	$5,400
Prepaid revenues..		1,500	800	
Expenses payable..	6,000	7,500		4,200
Revenues receivable	300			400

(continued)

Instructions:

(1) Prepare working papers as illustrated on pages 647 and 649 to correct the retained earnings balance as of December 31, 1974, and to correct earnings for 1975, 1976, and 1977. Assume that an income tax rate of 45% applies to all years.

(2) Prepare a statement of retained earnings for the three-year period ending December 31, 1977, reporting corrected earnings.

(3) Give the entry that is required at the beginning of 1978 to correct the accounts assuming that the books are closed for 1977.

22-6. The auditors for the Hansen Co. in inspecting accounts on December 31, 1977, the end of the fiscal year, find that certain prepaid and accrued items had been overlooked in prior years and in the current year as follows:

	End of			
	1974	1975	1976	1977
Prepaid expenses	$700	$600	$750	$1,900
Expenses payable	500	800	950	1,000
Prepaid revenues	140			420
Revenues receivable		150	125	200

Retained earnings on December 31, 1974, had been reported at $25,600; and net income for 1975 and for 1976 were reported at $9,500 and $12,250 respectively. Revenue and expense balances for 1977 were transferred to the income summary account and the latter shows a credit balance of $12,500 prior to correction by the auditors. No dividends had been declared in the three-year period.

Instructions:

(1) Prepare working papers as illustrated on pages 647 and 649 to develop a corrected retained earnings balance as of December 31, 1974, and corrected earnings for 1975, 1976, and 1977. Disregard effects of corrections on income tax.

(2) Prepare a corrected statement of retained earnings for the three-year period ending December 31, 1977.

(3) Give the entry or entries required as of December 31, 1977, to correct the income summary account and retained earnings account and to establish the appropriate balance sheet accounts as of this date.

22-7. An auditor is engaged by the Morrison Corp. in March, 1978, to examine the books and records and to make whatever corrections are necessary. The retained earnings account on the date of the audit is as follows:

ACCOUNT   Retained Earnings

DATE		ITEM	DEBIT	CREDIT	BALANCE	
					DEBIT	CREDIT
1975 Jan.	1	Balance				40,500
Dec.	31	Net income for year		9,000		49,500
1976 Jan.	10	Dividends paid	7,500			42,000
Mar.	6	Premium on capital stock		16,000		58,000
Dec.	31	Net loss for year	5,600			52,400
1977 Jan.	10	Dividends paid	7,500			44,900
Dec.	31	Net loss for year	6,200			38,700

An examination of the accounts discloses the following:

(a) Dividends had been declared on December 15 in 1975 and 1976 but had not been entered in the books until paid.

(b) Improvements in buildings and equipment of $4,800 had been debited to expense at the end of April, 1974. Improvements are estimated to have an eight-year life. The company uses the straight-line method in recording depreciation.

(c) The physical inventory of merchandise had been understated by $1,500 at the end of 1975 and by $2,150 at the end of 1977.

(d) The merchandise inventories at the end of 1976 and 1977 did not include merchandise that was then in transit and to which the company had title. These shipments of $1,900 and $2,750 were recorded as purchases in January of 1977 and 1978 respectively.

(e) The company had failed to record sales commissions payable of $1,050 and $850 at the end of 1976 and 1977 respectively.

(f) The company had failed to recognize supplies on hand of $600 and $1,250 at the end of 1976 and 1977 respectively.

Instructions:

(1) Prepare working papers for the correction of account balances similar to those illustrated on pages 647 and 649, using the following columns (disregard effects of corrections on income tax):

EXPLANATION	RETAINED EARNINGS JAN. 1, 1975		NET INCOME YEAR ENDED DEC. 31, 1975		NET INCOME YEAR ENDED DEC. 31, 1976		NET INCOME YEAR ENDED DEC. 31, 1977		ACCOUNTS REQUIRING CORRECTION IN 1978		
	DEBIT	CREDIT	DEBIT	CREDIT	DEBIT	CREDIT	DEBIT	CREDIT	DEBIT	CREDIT	ACCOUNT

(2) Journalize corrections required in March, 1978, in compound form.

(3) Prepare a statement of retained earnings covering the three-year period beginning January 1, 1975. The statement should report the corrected retained earnings balance on January 1, 1975, the annual changes in the account, and the corrected retained earnings balances as of December 31, 1975, 1976, and 1977.

(4) Set up an account for retained earnings before correction, and post correcting data to this account from part (2) above. Balance the account, showing the corrected retained earnings as of December 31, 1977.

22-8. The statements that follow were prepared for Garfield, Inc., at the end of 1977:

Income Statement
For Year Ended December 31, 1977

Sales	$257,000	
Less sales discount	7,000	$250,000
Cost of goods sold:		
Merchandise inventory, January 1, 1977	$ 73,000	
Purchases	170,000	
Merchandise available for sale	$243,000	
Less merchandise inventory, December 31, 1977	70,000	173,000
Gross profit on sales		$ 77,000
Operating expenses:		
Selling expense	$ 30,000	
General expense	32,000	62,000
Operating income		$ 15,000
Other revenue:		
Interest revenue		2,300
Net income		$ 17,300

Balance Sheet
December 31, 1977

Assets		
Cash	$ 40,000	
Petty cash	200	
Accounts receivable	97,000	
Merchandise inventory	70,000	
Investment in bonds	10,000	
Total assets		$217,200
Liabilities		
Accounts payable	$ 35,000	
Bonds payable	98,000	
Total liabilities		$133,000
Stockholders' Equity		
Capital stock, $5 par	$ 55,000	
Retained earnings	29,200	
Total stockholders' equity		84,200
Total liabilities and stockholders' equity		$217,200

During January, 1978, the following facts were discovered:

(a) A 25% dividend in stock, payable on February 1, 1978, was declared on December 15, 1977. No entry had been made.

(b) Accrued expenses of $105 for utilities had not been included in the adjustments at the end of 1977.

(c) On January 2, 1977, a 5-year fire insurance policy was purchased for $1,500 and debited to General Expense. No adjustment was made at the end of 1977 for the unexpired insurance.

(continued)

(d) Ten-year, 6% bonds of $100,000 par were issued at 98 on June 30, 1977. The bonds payable account was credited for the amount of cash received. The interest is payable annually on June 30. No adjustments were made at the end of 1977.

(e) 7% bonds, face value $10,000, had been purchased at face value on January 2, 1977. Interest is collected semiannually on January 1 and July 1. No adjustment for accrued interest was made at the end of 1977.

(f) The board of directors had authorized an appropriation of retained earnings of $10,000 for possible losses on damage suits at the end of 1977. No entry had been made.

(g) The petty cash fund, kept under the imprest system, had not been replenished at the end of the fiscal period. Payments had been made out of the fund as follows: $75 for General Expense and $65 for Selling Expense.

Instructions: Prepare adjusting journal entries at December 31, 1977. Disregard effects of corrections on income tax.

22-9. You have been asked by a client to review the records of the Reardon Manufacturing Company, a small manufacturer of precision tools and machines. Your client is interested in buying the business and arrangements have been made for you to review the accounting records. Your examination reveals the following:

(a) The Reardon Manufacturing Company commenced business on April 1, 1974, and has been reporting on a fiscal year ending March 31. The company has never been audited, but the annual statements prepared by the bookkeeper reflect the following income before closing and before deducting income tax:

Year Ended March 31	Income Before Tax
1975	$37,800
1976	56,200
1977	53,790

(b) A relatively small number of machines has been shipped on consignment. These transactions have been recorded as an ordinary sale and billed as such. On March 31 of each year, machines billed and in the hands of consignees amounted to:

Year	Amount
1975	$6,110
1976	none
1977	5,343

Sales price was determined by adding 30% to cost.

(c) On March 30, 1976, two machines were shipped to a customer on a C.O.D. basis. The sale was not entered until April 5, 1976, when cash was received in the amount of $5,800. The machines were not included in the inventory at March 31, 1976.

(d) All machines are sold subject to a five-year warranty. It is estimated that the expense ultimately to be incurred in connection with the warranty will amount to ½% of sales. The company has charged an expense account for warranty costs incurred. Sales per books and warranty costs were:

Year Ended March 31	Sales	Warranty Expense for Sales Made in 1975	1976	1977	Total
1975	$ 844,710	$680			$ 680
1976	905,000	320	$1,170		1,490
1977	1,604,110	290	1,450	$1,710	3,450

(e) A review of the corporate minutes reveals the manager is entitled to a bonus of ½% of the income before deducting income tax and his bonus. The bonuses have never been recorded or paid.

(f) The bank deducts 6% on all contracts financed. Of this amount ½% is placed in a reserve to the credit of the Reardon Manufacturing Company which is refunded to Reardon as finance contracts are paid in full. The reserve established by the bank has not been reflected in the books of Reardon. The excess of credits over debits (net increase) to the reserve account with Reardon on the books of the bank for each fiscal year were as follows:

1975	$ 2,800
1976	3,750
1977	4,960
	$11,510

(g) Commissions on sales have been entered when paid. Commissions payable on March 31 of each year were:

1975	$1,200
1976	700
1977	960

(h) On May 17, 1976, the building was sold to an insurance company for $890,000. Its book value at the date of sale was $880,000.

Instructions:

(1) Present a schedule showing the revised income before income tax for each of the years ended March 31, 1975, 1976, and 1977. Make computations to the nearest whole dollar.

(2) Prepare the journal entry or entries you would present the bookkeeper to correct the books. Assume the books have not yet been closed for the fiscal year ended March 31, 1977. Disregard correction of income tax.

(3) Compute the purchase price. Your client will pay the amount of the corrected book value of the net assets at March 31, 1977, plus goodwill equal to two times the average profits before tax in excess of a 6% return on the net assets. According to the books the net assets were $548,250 at March 31, 1977. Extraneous gains and losses are not to be considered in the calculation of average annual profits. (AICPA adapted)

Statements From Incomplete Records

The procedures leading to the preparation of financial statements that have been applied in the preceding chapters are those required in a *double-entry system*. This is the characteristic system employed in practice and requires the analysis of each transaction in terms of debits and credits. Any set of procedures that does not provide for the analysis of each transaction in terms of double entry is referred to as a *single-entry system*.

SINGLE-ENTRY SYSTEMS

Single-entry systems differ widely depending upon the needs of the organization and the originality of the person maintaining the system. Records found in a single-entry system may vary from a narrative of transactions recorded in a single journal, called a *daybook*, to a relatively complete set of journals and a ledger providing accounts for all significant items.

Single-entry procedures are frequently found in organizations whose activities do not warrant the employment of a bookkeeper. Such organizations might include unincorporated retail businesses, professional and service units, and nonprofit organizations. Persons acting in a fiduciary capacity, such as estate executors and trust custodians, may also limit their record keeping to single-entry procedures. When double-entry records are not maintained, a professional accountant is normally engaged at different intervals to prepare financial statements, tax returns, and any other required reports on an accrual basis.

RECORDS IN SINGLE-ENTRY SYSTEMS

All of the variations of a single-entry system encountered in practice cannot be described here. A characteristic single-entry system consists of the following records: (1) a daybook or general journal, (2) a cashbook, and (3) ledger accounts showing debtor and creditor balances.

Single-entry procedures commonly take the following form. A cashbook is maintained showing all of the transactions affecting cash. Instead of naming accounts to be debited or credited as a result of cash receipts and disbursements, a description of the transaction is offered and a column for the amount of cash is provided. Transactions not shown in the cashbook are recorded in a daybook in descriptive form. Whenever the account of a debtor, a creditor, or the owner is affected, attention is directed to the need for posting by indicating "dr" or "cr" before the amount. Offsetting debits or credits are not shown since accounts in the ledger are maintained only for customers, creditors, and the owner. At the end of the period, reports may be limited to summaries of customer and creditor balances. Of course, because it is single entry, there is no direct way to know if the balances are correct.

PREPARATION OF FINANCIAL STATEMENTS FROM SINGLE-ENTRY RECORDS[1]

When records do not offer a complete summary of transactions, the preparation of accurate financial statements raises a number of special problems. These are discussed in the following sections.

Preparation of the Balance Sheet

When the ledger consists of account balances for only customers and creditors, the preparation of the balance sheet calls for reference to a number of different sources. Cash is reported at the balance shown in the cashbook after this figure has been reconciled with the totals of cash on hand and on deposit with the bank. Receivables and payables are summarized from the accounts maintained with debtors and creditors. Merchandise and supplies balances are found by taking inventories. Past statements, cash records, and other documents are reviewed in determining the book values of depreciable assets. Other assets and liabilities, including accrued and prepaid items, are determined by a review of the records, including invoices, documents, and other available sources offering evidence or information concerning transactions of the past, present, and future. The owner's capital balance in a double-entry system represents an amount arrived at by combining beginning capital, additional investments and withdrawals, and revenue and expense account balances; in single-entry, capital is simply the difference between the total reported for assets less the total reported for liabilities.

Determination of the Net Income or Loss from Comparative Balance Sheet Data and Cash Summary

In the absence of revenue and expense accounts, net income may be calculated by the single-entry method. The owner's capital at the beginning of the period is subtracted from owner's capital at the end of the period. The difference is then increased for any withdrawals and decreased for any investments made by the owner during the period. Beginning and ending owner's capital balances are taken from the balance sheets prepared at the end of the previous period and at the end of current period. Investments and withdrawals are ascertained from owner's capital and drawing accounts maintained in the ledger, or in the absence of these, from the cashbook and other memorandum records.

---

[1]In addition to the statements discussed in this chapter, a statement of changes in financial position could also be prepared. A further discussion of this statement is contained in Chapter 24.

To illustrate the determination of the net income or loss, assume the owner's capital is reported on comparative balance sheets as follows: January 1, $20,000; December 31, $30,000. In the absence of investments or withdrawals by the owner, it must be concluded that the net income for the year was $10,000. However, assume the owner has invested $2,500 and has withdrawn $9,000 during the year. Net income is then computed as follows:

Owner's capital, December 31		$30,000
Owner's capital, January 1		20,000
Net increase in owner's capital		$10,000
Add excess of owner's withdrawals over investments:		
Withdrawals	$9,000	
Investments	2,500	6,500
Net income for the year		$16,500

Preparation of the Income Statement

A summary of the net income or loss calculated from comparative capital balances is generally inadequate. The owner needs a detailed statement of operation disclosing sales, cost of goods sold, operating expenses, and miscellaneous revenue and expense items to evaluate past success or failure and to plan future activities. Creditors may insist upon such statements. In addition, revenue and expense data must be itemized for income tax purposes.

An itemized income statement can be prepared by (1) rewriting transactions in double-entry form or (2) computing the individual revenue and expense balances by reference to cash receipts and disbursements and the changes in asset and liability balances. Obviously, little or nothing is saved by the adoption of a single-entry system if transactions are rewritten in double-entry form and posted to accounts. When the second procedure is followed, an analysis of all cash receipts and disbursements is required, unless this is already provided by special analysis columns in the cash journals. Cash receipts must be classified as: (1) receipts for goods sold for cash, (2) receipts of other revenue items, (3) collections on customers' accounts, (4) proceeds from the sale of assets other than merchandise, (5) amounts borrowed, and (6) investments by the owner. Cash payments must be classified as (1) payments for merchandise purchased for cash, (2) payments of other expense items, (3) payments on trade creditors' accounts, (4) payments for the purchase of assets other than merchandise, (5) loans paid off, and (6) withdrawals by the owner. These data, together with the data provided by the balance sheet, are used in the preparation of the income statement on an accrual basis. Obviously, the accuracy of the income statement will depend upon the accuracy of the information used in computing revenue and expense items. The procedures followed in computing revenue and expense balances on the accrual basis are illustrated in the following sections.

Sales. The amount to be reported for sales consists of the total of cash sales and sales on account. Sales are computed from the cash receipts analysis and comparative balance sheet data as follows:

Cash sales		$ 7,500
Sales on account:		
Notes and accounts receivable at the end of the period...........	$1,500	
Collections on notes and accounts receivable during the period	3,000	
	$4,500	
Deduct notes and accounts receivable at the beginning of the period..	2,000	2,500
Sales for the period		$10,000

Notes and accounts receivable in the foregoing tabulation are limited to those arising from sales of merchandise.

The computation of gross sales is complicated if sales discounts and returns and allowances exist, or if accounts thought to be collectible are written off. For example, assume sales data as follows:

Data from cash records:	
Cash sales..	$10,000
Collections on accounts receivable arising from sales	42,000
Data from balance sheets:	
Accounts receivable at the beginning of the period	$14,300
Accounts receivable at the end of the period..	12,500
Supplementary data from special analysis of records:	
Accounts written off during the period	$ 600
Sales discounts allowed customers during the period.............................	850
Sales returns and allowances during the period.......................................	300

The supplementary data indicate that uncollectible accounts of $600, sales discounts of $850, and sales returns and allowances of $300 are to be recognized. All of these amounts must be added to cash collections in arriving at gross sales, for there must have been sales equivalent to the reductions in accounts receivable from these sources. Gross sales for the period are computed as follows:

Cash sales		$10,000
Sales on account:		
Accounts receivable at the end of the period............................	$12,500	
Collections on accounts receivable	42,000	
Accounts receivable written off..	600	
Accounts receivable reduced by discounts...............................	850	
Accounts receivable reduced by sales returns and allowances	300	
	$56,250	
Deduct accounts receivable at the beginning of the period	14,300	41,950
Gross sales for the period...		$51,950

Failure to recognize uncollectible accounts, sales discounts, and sales returns and allowances will be counterbalanced by an understatement in gross sales. Although the omissions will have no effect on the net income balance, revenue and expense balances will not be stated accurately.

Cost of Goods Sold. The inventory balance shown on the balance sheet prepared at the end of the preceding fiscal period is reported on the income statement as the beginning inventory.

The amount to be reported for purchases consists of the total of cash purchases and purchases on account. Purchases are computed from the cash payments analysis and comparative balance sheet data as follows:

Cash purchases		$1,500
Purchases on account:		
Notes and accounts payable at the end of the period	$2,500	
Payments on notes and accounts payable during the period	5,000	
	$7,500	
Deduct notes and accounts payable at the beginning of the period	3,500	4,000
Purchases for the period		$5,500

Notes and accounts payable in the foregoing tabulation are limited to those arising from purchases of merchandise.

The inventory balance shown on the balance sheet at the end of the current period is reported on the income statement as the ending inventory. In the first year complete statements are prepared; an estimate of the beginning inventory must be made, using perhaps the gross profit method of inventory valuation described in Chapter 9.

When purchase discounts and purchase returns and allowances reduce accounts payable, the computation of purchases follows the same procedure as for gross sales. The purchases balance is increased by the total purchase discounts and purchase returns and allowances since there must have been purchases equivalent to the reductions in the accounts payable from these sources.

Expense Items. An expense balance is computed from the analysis of cash payments and comparative balance sheet data. The computation of an expense item is made as follows:

Cash payments representing expense		$1,000
Add amounts not included in cash payments but to be charged to current period:		
Amount prepaid at the beginning of the period	$250	
Amount accrued at the end of the period	150	400
		$1,400
Deduct amounts included in payments but not to be charged to current period:		
Amount prepaid at the end of the period	$200	
Amount accrued at the beginning of the period	100	300
Expense for the period		$1,100

The charge for depreciation or amortization to be recognized on the income statement may be made by special analysis of balance sheet as well as cash data, if the balance sheet reflects depreciation in the asset balances. For example, assume no acquisition or disposal of property during the period and beginning and ending store furniture balances of $30,000 and $28,500 respectively. Depreciation is reported at $1,500, the net decrease in the asset account. Assume, however, the following information is assembled at the end of a fiscal period:

Data from cash records:	
Payments for store furniture, including payments on notes arising from acquisition of store furniture	$ 2,500

Data from balance sheets:
Store furniture at the beginning of the period... $16,500
Store furniture at the end of the period 20,675
Installment notes payable arising from acquisition of store furniture...... 4,000

The charge for depreciation for the period is computed as follows:

Balance of store furniture at the beginning of the period $16,500
Add acquisitions of store furniture:
Cash paid on acquisition of store furniture............................... $2,500
Amount owed at the end of the period on acquisition of store
  furniture.. 4,000 6,500
Balance of store furniture before depreciation......................... $23,000
Deduct balance of store furniture at the end of the period 20,675
Depreciation of store furniture for period .... $ 2,325

The charge for depreciation developed from the cash records and balance sheet data should be confirmed by computations based upon the individual property items held. The inability to confirm depreciation may indicate that property balances are not reported accurately on the balance sheet. The following analysis is made to support the charge calculated above.

Property	Date Acquired	Cost	Accumulated Depreciation— Prior Years	Remaining Cost	Estimated Life	Remaining Life from Beginning of Year	Depreciation Current Year
Store furniture..	4/1/73	$24,000	$7,500	$16,500	12 yrs.	8¼ yrs.	$2,000
Store furniture..	7/1/77	6,500	. . . . .	6,500	10 yrs.	. . . . .	325 (½ yr.)
		$30,500	$7,500	$23,000			$2,325

Other Revenue Items. Other revenue balances are computed from the analysis of cash receipts and comparative balance sheet data as follows:

Cash receipts representing revenue.. $ 800
Add amounts not included in cash receipts but to be credited to
current period:
Amount prepaid at the beginning of the period........................... $300
Amount accrued at the end of the period................................... 50 350
  $1,150
Deduct amounts included in receipts but not to be credited to current period:
Amount prepaid at the end of the period.................................... $225
Amount accrued at the beginning of the period.......................... 175 400
Other revenue for the period.. $ 750

PREPARATION OF FINANCIAL STATEMENTS FROM SINGLE-ENTRY RECORDS ILLUSTRATED

The following example illustrates the preparation from single-entry records of (1) a balance sheet, (2) a summary of net income by analysis of capital changes, and (3) an income statement reporting revenue and expense detail. John Bolton does not maintain double-entry records. Balance sheet data, analyses of cash receipts and disbursements, and supplementary data required in the development of financial statements from the single-entry data are assembled at the end of 1977 as shown below.

Comparative Balance Sheet Data

	Dec. 31, 1977	Jan. 1, 1977
Assets		
Cash	$ 5,200	$ 3,200
Notes receivable	3,000	2,500
Accounts receivable	4,500	6,000
Interest receivable	50	150
Merchandise inventory	24,600	20,000
Supplies on hand	600	400
Prepaid miscellaneous expense	——	100
Long-term investments	2,200	9,700
Furniture and fixtures (cost less accumulated depreciation)	8,325	5,800
Total assets	$48,475	$47,850
Liabilities		
Accounts payable	$ 9,000	$ 7,500
Salaries payable	250	200
Miscellaneous expense payable	150	——
Unearned rent revenue	125	150
Total liabilities	$ 9,525	$ 7,850

Analyses of Cash Receipts and Disbursements

Cash balance, January 1, 1977		$ 3,200
Receipts:		
Cash sales	$ 9,200	
Accounts receivable arising from sales	42,000	
Notes receivable arising from sales	6,000	
From rental of store space	1,750	
From interest and dividends	400	
From sale of investments, cost $7,500	6,250	65,600
		$68,800
Disbursements:		
Accounts payable arising from purchases	$40,000	
For salaries	4,200	
For rent	4,400	
For supplies	1,000	
Acquisition of furniture and fixtures	3,500	
For miscellaneous expense	1,500	
Owner's withdrawals	9,000	63,600
Cash balance, December 31, 1977		$ 5,200

Supplementary data developed from an analysis of business documents include the following:

1. Purchase discounts of $600 were received on the payment of creditor invoices during the year. Sales returns and allowances amounted to $1,480.
2. Furniture and fixtures were acquired during the year for cash, $3,500. Depreciation is recognized at 10% per year; one half of the normal rate is used for current acquisitions.

A balance sheet as of December 31, 1977, prepared from the foregoing data, is illustrated at the top of the next page.

The net income or loss can be calculated from the comparative balance sheet data and a summary of the investments and withdrawals by the owner as provided by the cash records, as shown on page 665.

John Bolton
Balance Sheet
December 31, 1977

Assets			Liabilities and Owner's Equity		
Current assets:			Current liabilities:.		
Cash	$ 5,200		Accounts payable	$9,000	
Notes receivable	3,000		Salaries payable	250	
Accounts receivable	4,500		Miscellaneous expense payable	150	
Interest receivable	50		Unearned rent revenue	125	$ 9,525
Merchandise inventory	24,600				
Supplies on hand	600	$37,950	Owner's equity:		
Long-term investments		2,200	John Bolton, capital		38,950
Furniture and fixtures (cost, less					
accumulated depreciation)		8,325			
Total assets		$48,475	Total liabilities and owner's equity		$48,475

John Bolton
Summary of Changes in Owner's Equity
For Year Ended December 31, 1977

John Bolton, capital, December 31, 1977	$38,950
John Bolton, capital, January 1, 1977 (assets, $47,850, less liabilities, $7,850)	40,000
Net decrease in owner's equity	$ (1,050)
Withdrawals by owner during year	9,000
Net income for year	$ 7,950

An income statement with revenue and expense detail is shown below. Schedules in support of the balances reported on the income statement are included on the following pages.

John Bolton
Income Statement
For Year Ended December 31, 1977

Revenue from sales:				
Sales	(A)	$57,680		
Less sales returns and allowances	(A-1)	1,480	$56,200	
Cost of goods sold:				
Merchandise inventory, January 1, 1977			$20,000	
Purchases	(B)	$42,100		
Less purchase discounts	(B-1)	600	41,500	
Merchandise available for sale			$61,500	
Less merchandise inventory, December 31, 1977			24,600	36,900
Gross profit on sales				$19,300
Operating expenses:				
Salaries	(C)	$ 4,250		
Rent expense	(D)	4,400		
Supplies expense	(E)	800		
Depreciation expense — furniture and fixtures	(F)	975		
Miscellaneous expense	(G)	1,750	12,175	
Operating income				$ 7,125
Other revenue and expense items:				
Interest and dividend revenue	(H)	$ 300		
Rent revenue	(I)	1,775		
Loss on sale of investments	(J)	1,250	825	
Net income				$ 7,950

(A)   Computation of sales:
      Cash sales .... $ 9,200
      Sales on account:
          Notes and accounts receivable, December 31......... $ 7,500
          Collections on notes and accounts receivable.........   48,000
          (A-1) Notes and accounts receivable reduced by
              sales returns and allowances...........................   1,480
                                                                      $56,980
          Deduct notes and accounts receivable, January 1.....   8,500   48,480
      Gross sales for the year... $57,680

(B)   Computation of purchases:
      Purchases on account:
          Accounts payable, December 31...................................... $ 9,000
          Payments on accounts payable.......................................   40,000
          (B-1) Discounts allowed on accounts payable......................   600
                                                                          $49,600
          Deduct accounts payable, January 1................................   7,500
      Purchases for the year $42,100

Computation of operating expenses:
(C)   Salaries:
      Payments for salaries.. $ 4,200
      Add salaries payable, December 31......................................   250
                                                                          $ 4,450
      Deduct salaries payable, January 1......................................   200
      Salaries for the year... $ 4,250

(D)   Rent expense:
      Payments for rent .... $ 4,400

(E)   Supplies expense:
      Payments for supplies .... $ 1,000
      Add supplies on hand, January 1   400
                                                                          $ 1,400
      Deduct supplies on hand, December 31..............................   600
      Supplies used during the year .... $ 800

(F)   Depreciation expense — furniture and fixtures:
      Balance of furniture and fixtures, January 1.......................... $ 5,800
      Add cash paid on acquisition of furniture and fixtures...........   3,500
      Balance of furniture and fixtures before depreciation .... $ 9,300
      Deduct balance of furniture and fixtures, Dec. 31   8,325
      Depreciation of furniture and fixtures for the year................. $ 975

Depreciation charge is substantiated as follows:

Property	Date Acquired	Cost	Accumulated Depreciation—Prior Years	Remaining Cost	Estimated Life	Remaining Life from Beginning of Year	Depreciation Current Year
Furniture and fixtures.	1973	$ 6,000	$2,100	$3,900	10 years	6½ years	$600
Furniture and fixtures.	1976	2,000	100	1,900	10 years	9½ years	200
Furniture and fixtures.	1977	3,500	.....	3,500	10 years	.....	175 (½ yr.)
		$11,500	$2,200	$9,300			$975

(G) Miscellaneous expense:

Miscellaneous expense payments		$ 1,500
Add: Prepaid miscellaneous expense, January 1		100
Miscellaneous expense payable, December 31		150
Miscellaneous expense for the year		$ 1,750

(H) Computation of interest and dividend revenue:

Interest and dividend receipts		$ 400
Add interest receivable, December 31		50
		$ 450
Deduct interest receivable, January 1		150
Total interest and dividend revenue for the year		$ 300

(I) Computation of rent revenue:

Rent receipts		$ 1,750
Add unearned rent revenue, January 1		150
		$ 1,900
Deduct unearned rent revenue, December 31		125
Total rent revenue for the year		$ 1,775

(J) Computation of loss on sale of investments:

Cost of investments sold		$ 7,500
Proceeds from sale		6,250
Loss on sale of investments		$ 1,250

WORK SHEET FOR PREPARATION OF FINANCIAL STATEMENTS

In the preceding example, a balance sheet was prepared first. The income statement was then drawn up from special schedules that developed revenue and expense balances. These procedures are convenient under simple circumstances. However, when the preparation of the financial statements involves a number of special analyses and computations and when certain difficulties are anticipated, working papers may be employed in assembling the financial data.

The use of a work sheet for the preparation of a balance sheet and income statement in the previous example is illustrated on pages 668 and 669. Opening balances are listed in the first pair of columns. Summaries of the transactions for the year appear in the second pair of columns. Cash receipts and disbursements are summarized first, followed by entries to adjust the balance sheet accounts to the proper ending balances. This approach produces the same results as the separate schedules developed on pages 666 and 667. Data on the work sheet should be traced to the statements presented on page 665.

CHANGE FROM SINGLE ENTRY TO DOUBLE ENTRY

A business may find that single-entry procedures fail to meet its needs and may decide to change to double entry. Single-entry records may be converted to double entry by first drawing up a balance sheet as

John
Work
For Year Ended

#	ACCOUNT TITLE	BALANCE SHEET JANUARY 1, 1977 DEBIT	CREDIT	TRANSACTIONS 1977 DEBIT	CREDIT	#
1	Cash..	3,200		(a) 65,600	(b) 63,600	1
2	Notes Receivable................................	2,500		(d) 6,500	(a) 6,000	2
3	Accounts Receivable...........................	6,000		(d) 41,980	(a) 42,000	3
4					(c) 1,480	4
5	Interest Receivable.............................	150			(e) 100	5
6	Merchandise Inventory.........................	20,000				6
7	Supplies on Hand	400		(f) 200		7
8	Prepaid Miscellaneous Expense	100			(g) 100	8
9	Long-Term Investments	9,700			(a) 7,500	9
10	Furniture and Fixtures (cost less					10
11	accumulated depreciation)...............	5,800		(b) 3,500	(h) 975	11
12	Accounts Payable................................		7,500	(b) 40,000	(j) 42,100	12
13				(i) 600		13
14	Salaries Payable..................................		200		(k) 50	14
15	Unearned Rent Revenue		150	(l) 25		15
16	John Bolton, Capital............................		40,000			16
17		47,850	47,850			17
18						18
19						19
20	Sales				(a) 9,200	20
21					(d) 48,480	21
22	Sales Returns and Allowances.............			(c) 1,480		22
23	Purchases..			(j) 42,100		23
24	Purchase Discounts.............................				(i) 600	24
25	Salaries...			(b) 4,200		25
26				(k) 50		26
27	Rent Expense......................................			(b) 4,400		27
28	Supplies Expense................................			(b) 1,000	(f) 200	28
29	Depreciation Expense — Furniture					29
30	and Fixtures...................................			(h) 975		30
31	Miscellaneous Expense Payable				(m) 150	31
32	Miscellaneous Expense........................			(g) 100		32
33				(b) 1,500		33
34				(m) 150		34
35	Interest and Dividend Revenue.............			(e) 100	(a) 400	35
36	Rent Revenue......................................				(a) 1,750	36
37					(l) 25	37
38	Loss on Sale of Investments.................			(a) 1,250		38
39	John Bolton, Drawing...........................			(b) 9,000		39
40				224,710	224,710	40
41						41
42						42
43	Net Income..					43
44						44
45						45
46						46
47	Capital, December 31, 1977					47
48						48
49						49
50						50

Explanation of transactions and adjustments:
(a) To record cash receipts.
(b) To record cash disbursements.
(c) To record sales returns and allowances.
(d) To establish notes and accounts receivable balances at end of year.
(e) To establish interest receivable balance at end of year.
(f) To establish supplies on hand balance at end of year.

Bolton
Sheet
December 31, 1977

	INCOME STATEMENT 1977		CAPITAL DECEMBER 31, 1977		BALANCE SHEET DECEMBER 31, 1977		
	DEBIT	**CREDIT**	**DEBIT**	**CREDIT**	**DEBIT**	**CREDIT**	
1					5,200		1
2					3,000		2
3							3
4					4,500		4
5					50		5
6	20,000	24,600			24,600		6
7					600		7
8							8
9					2,200		9
10							10
11					8,325		11
12							12
13						9,000	13
14						250	14
15						125	15
16				40,000			16
17							17
18							18
19							19
20							20
21		57,680					21
22	1,480						22
23	42,100						23
24		600					24
25							25
26	4,250						26
27	4,400						27
28	800						28
29							29
30	975						30
31						150	31
32							32
33							33
34	1,750						34
35		300					35
36							36
37		1,775					37
38	1,250						38
39			9,000				39
40							40
41							41
42							42
43	77,005	84,955					43
44	7,950			7,950			44
45	84,955	84,955					45
46							46
47			9,000	47,950			47
48			38,950			38,950	48
49							49
50			47,950	47,950	48,475	48,475	50

(g) To eliminate prepaid miscellaneous expense.
(h) To record depreciation.
(i) To record purchase discounts.
(j) To establish accounts payable balance at end of year.
(k) To establish salaries payable balance at end of year.
(l) To establish unearned rent revenue balance at end of year.
(m) To establish miscellaneous expense payable balance at end of year.

of the date of change. This statement is used as the basis for a journal entry establishing all of the asset, asset valuation, liability, and capital accounts. If additional accounts are to be added to a ledger already in use, accounts are opened and balances recorded for those items not included. If new books are to be used, accounts are opened and balances are recorded for all of the items reported in the opening journal entry.

USE OF SINGLE-ENTRY SYSTEMS

Single entry is described here because it represents a system the accountant may encounter when called upon to prepare financial statements, audit books and records, and prepare government informational reports and income tax returns.

Among the advantages of single-entry systems are the following:

1. Record keeping is simplified and the cost of maintaining records is minimal.
2. Individuals sometimes use formal financial statements only for tax returns and occasional borrowing. When needed for these purposes, financial statements can be prepared from the single-entry records as demonstrated in this chapter.

Among the disadvantages of single-entry procedures are the following factors:

1. A trial balance offering a check on the mathematical accuracy of posting is not available.
2. Preparation of the balance sheet from miscellaneous sources and memoranda may result in omissions and misstatements.
3. Detailed analysis of transactions is necessary in arriving at a summary of operations. Misstatements of assets and liabilities, particularly failures to report assets at properly depreciated or amortized balances, affect revenue and expense balances and may result in material misstatement of net income or loss.
4. There is failure to provide a centralized and coordinated accounting system subject to internal control and available for satisfactory and convenient audit by public accountants and Internal Revenue agents.

QUESTIONS

1. Distinguish between single-entry and double-entry procedures.

2. Describe the records and the nature of recording under typical single-entry bookkeeping.

3. What are the sources of information for balance sheet items when the single-entry plan is followed?

4. Distinguish between the manner in which the owner's capital balance is computed in a double-entry system as compared with a single-entry system.

5. Mary Miles has her assets appraised at the end of each year and draws up a balance sheet using such appraisal values. She then calculates the change in capital for the year and adjusts this for investments and withdrawals in arriving at the net income or loss for the year. In your opinion, does this procedure provide a satisfactory measurement of earnings?

6. State how each of the following items is computed in preparing an income statement when single-entry procedures are followed and the accrual basis is used in reporting net income:

(a) Merchandise sales
(b) Merchandise purchases
(c) Depreciation on equipment

(d) Sales salaries
(e) Insurance expense
(f) Interest revenue
(g) Rent revenue
(h) Taxes

7. Single-entry systems are obsolete and have no place in modern business. Do you agree? Explain.

8. In developing the sales balance, the owner of a business recognizes cash collections from customers and the change in the receivables balance but ignores the write-off of uncollectible accounts. Indicate the effects, if any, that such omissions will have on net income.

9. Greater accuracy is achieved in financial statements prepared from double-entry data as compared with single-entry data. Do you agree?

10. What are the principle disadvantages of single-entry systems?

11. Describe the procedure to be followed in changing from a single-entry system to double entry.

EXERCISES

1. Service fee collections in 1977 are $14,500; service fee revenue reported on the income statement is $13,600. The balance sheet prepared at the beginning of the year reported service fees receivable, $600, and unearned service fees, $450; the balance sheet at the end of the year reported service fees receivable, $760. What is the amount of unearned service fees at the end of the year?

2. Salary payments in 1977 were $15,000; salary expense reported on the income statement was $14,750. The balance sheet prepared at the beginning of the year reported salary advances, $200, salaries payable, $600; the balance sheet at the end of the year reported salary advances, $450. What is the amount of salaries payable at the end of the year?

3. Sales salaries are reported on the income statement for 1977 at $10,700. Balance sheet data relating to sales salaries are as follows:

	January 1, 1977	December 31, 1977
Prepaid salaries (advances to sales agents)........	$250	$100
Salaries payable...	700	750

How much cash was paid during 1977 for sales salaries expense?

4. Rent revenue is reported on the income statement for 1977 at $25,000. Balance sheet data relating to rent revenue are as follows:

	January 1, 1977	December 31, 1977
Unearned rent revenue...	$4,500	$3,700
Rents receivable (delinquent rent)......................	400	1,650

How much cash was collected during 1977 for rent revenue?

5. Total accounts receivable for the Arc Canning Company were as follows: on January 1, $6,000; on January 31, $6,300. In January, $9,500 was collected on accounts, $600 was received for cash sales, accounts receivable of $700 were written off as uncollectible, and allowances on sales of $100 were made. What amount should be reported for gross sales on the income statement for January?

6. On November 1, the capital of G. T. Fisher was $3,400 and on November 30 the capital was $4,875. During the month, Fisher withdrew merchandise costing $200 and on November 25 she paid a $1,600 note payable of the business with interest at 10% for three months with a check drawn on her personal checking account. What was Fisher's net income or loss for the month of November?

7. An analysis of the records of J. L. Wilson disclosed changes in account balances for 1977 and the supplementary data listed below and on page 672. From these data, calculate the net income or loss for 1977.

Cash	$ 2,400 decrease
Accounts receivable	1,500 increase

Merchandise inventory	$15,500 increase
Accounts payable	2,100 increase

During the year, Wilson borrowed $20,000 in notes from the bank and paid off notes of $15,000 and interest of $750. Interest of $250 is accrued as of December 31, 1977. There was no interest payable at the end of 1976.

In 1977, Wilson also transferred certain marketable securities to the business and these were sold for $5,300 to finance the purchase of merchandise.

Wilson made weekly withdrawals in 1977 of $250.

8. On December 31, 1977, Porter Company showed stockholders' equity on its balance sheet of $327,600. During 1977, the stockholders' equity was affected by: (1) an adjustment to retained earnings for an understatement of net income in 1976 of $11,200; (2) declared dividends of $40,000 of which $20,000 were paid during the year; (3) Porter Company common stock split 2 for 1; and (4) net income for 1977 of $55,650. The capital stock balance of $200,000 remained unchanged during the year. What was the retained earnings balance on January 1, 1977?

PROBLEMS

23-1. The following information is obtained from the single-entry records of Wilford Clyde.

	March 31	January 1
Notes receivable	$1,200	$1,500
Accounts receivable	8,800	4,500
Interest receivable	80	100
Merchandise inventories	1,000	3,800
Prepaid operating expenses	220	250
Store equipment (net)	3,000	3,250
Notes payable	1,200	1,000
Accounts payable	2,500	3,500
Interest payable	50	30
Operating expenses payable	500	270

The cashbook shows the following:

Balance, January 1			$1,500
Receipts:	Accounts receivable	$3,600	
	Notes receivable	1,500	
	Interest revenue	200	
	Investment by Clyde	600	5,900
			$7,400
Payments:	Accounts payable	$5,200	
	Notes payable	800	
	Interest expense	150	
	Operating expenses	1,700	7,850
Balance, March 31 — bank overdraft			$ (450)

Instructions:
 (1) Compute the net income or loss for the three-month period by considering the changes in the owner's capital.
 (2) Prepare an income statement for the three-month period accompanied by schedules in support of revenue and expense balances.

23-2. The following data are obtained from a single-entry set of books kept by Mary Golden, proprietor of a retail store:

	June 30	January 1
Notes receivable	$ 3,000	$ 1,000
Accounts receivable	6,000	4,000
Interest receivable	150	100
Merchandise inventories	4,400	4,000
Store equipment (net)	3,800	3,000
Notes payable	1,250	1,800
Accounts payable	4,650	3,000
Interest payable	100	200

The cashbook shows the following information:

Balance, January 1			$ 3,000
Receipts:	Accounts receivable	$10,500	
	Notes receivable	2,400	
	Interest on notes	100	13,000
			$16,000
Payments:	Accounts payable	$ 3,800	
	Notes payable	3,200	
	Interest on notes	200	
	Operating expenses	2,100	
	Withdrawals by Golden	3,000	
	Store equipment	1,000	13,300
Balance, June 30			$ 2,700

The following supplementary information is available:

(a) Accounts receivable of $250 were written off as uncollectible.
(b) Allowances of $140 were received on merchandise purchases.
(c) All notes receivable arise from sales.
(d) All notes payable arise from purchases of merchandise inventory.

Instructions:

(1) Compute the net income or loss for the six-month period by considering the changes in owner's capital.
(2) Prepare an income statement for the six-month period accompanied by schedules in support of revenue and expense balances.

23-3. Balance sheets for the Bastian Company prepared in 1977 report the following balances:

Assets	June 30	January 1
Cash	$ 84,500	$ 33,000
Notes receivable	21,000	20,000
Accounts receivable	95,000	74,000
Merchandise inventories	150,000	160,000
Prepaid expenses	10,000	12,000
Long-term investments (at cost)	10,000	40,000
Buildings and equipment (net)	120,000	100,000
	$490,500	$439,000

Liabilities and Stockholders' Equity		
Notes payable	$ 58,000	$ 75,000
Accounts payable	75,000	60,000
Interest payable	900	———
Expenses payable	3,000	2,000
Bonds payable	———	50,000
Common stock, $100 par	130,000	100,000
Premium on common stock	150,000	100,000
Retained earnings	73,600	52,000
	$490,500	$439,000

An analysis of cash receipts and disbursements discloses the following:

Receipts		Disbursements	
Capital stock	$ 80,000	Trade creditors — notes and accounts	$210,000
Trade debtors — notes and accounts	230,000	Expenses	70,000
Cash sales	65,000	Dividends	40,000
Notes receivable discounted:		Equipment	28,000
face value, $20,000, proceeds	19,500	Bonds	50,000
12% note issued to bank, dated March 31,			
1977	30,000		
Sale of investments	25,000		

Instructions:

(1) Prepare an income statement supported by schedules showing computations of revenue and expense balances for the six-month period ended June 30, 1977.
(2) Prove the net income or loss determined in part (1) by preparing a retained earnings statement.

23-4. A comparative balance sheet prepared from the single-entry records of Wheat, Inc., follows:

Wheat, Inc.
Comparative Balance Sheet
December 31

	1977		1976	
Assets				
Current assets:				
Cash...	$ 4,200		$ 4,300	
Accounts receivable........................	20,000		16,000	
Notes receivable	7,000		8,000	
Merchandise inventory......................	28,000		21,600	
Prepaid expenses	1,850		1,800	
Total current assets		$61,050		$51,700
Furniture and fixtures (net)		24,700		22,200
Total assets...............................		$85,750		$73,900
Liabilities and Stockholders' Equity				
Current liabilities:				
Accounts payable..........................	$16,400		$15,200	
Notes payable — bank and trade creditors........	12,000		8,500	
Expenses payable..........................	1,350		1,200	
Total liabilities...........................		$29,750		$24,900
Stockholders' equity:				
Capital stock..............................	$50,000		$50,000	
Retained earnings (deficit)	6,000	56,000	(1,000)	49,000
Total liabilities and stockholders' equity		$85,750		$73,900

Cash receipts and disbursements for 1977 are classified as follows:

Receipts:
Cash sales	$ 7,000
Accounts receivable..	102,000
Notes payable (amount borrowed from bank)	7,500
	$116,500

Disbursements:
Accounts payable	$ 73,000
Notes payable	6,200
Expenses..	23,900
Furniture and fixtures	4,500
Dividends	9,000
	$116,600

Instructions:

(1) Compute the net income or loss for the year by considering the changes in retained earnings.

(2) Prepare an income statement for the year and schedules in support of revenue and expense balances.

23-5. Stevens and Emett operate a retail store, sharing profits equally. A balance sheet for the partnership on January 1, 1977, appears at the top of the next page.

On December 31, 1977, asset and liability balances are:

Assets		Liabilities	
Notes receivable...........................	$ 1,500	Cash overdraft..............................	$ 200
Accounts receivable	7,650	Notes payable...............................	2,500
Interest receivable........................	50	Accounts payable..........................	12,100
Merchandise inventory	10,000	Expenses payable	200
Prepaid expense	300		$15,000
Furniture and fixtures...................	5,000		
	$24,500		

Stevens and Emett
Balance Sheet
January 1, 1977

Assets		Liabilities and Owners' Equity	
Cash	$ 260	Accounts payable	$ 4,900
Notes receivable	1,500	Expenses payable	260
Accounts receivable	6,500	Stevens, capital	8,900
Interest receivable	40	Emett, capital	4,700
Merchandise inventory	7,000		
Prepaid expenses	260		
Furniture and fixtures	3,200		
Total assets	$18,760	Total liabilities and owners' equity	$18,760

Cash receipts and disbursements for the year were:

Receipts			Disbursements		
Investment by Stevens		$ 800	Withdrawals by Stevens ($225 monthly)		$ 2,700
Cash sales		4,450	Withdrawals by Emett ($225 monthly)		2,700
Receipts on accounts and notes	$30,000		On accounts payable	$22,300	
Less discounts	400	29,600	Less discounts	1,500	20,800
Interest on notes		80	Purchase of store fixtures on July 1, 1977		2,200
Amount borrowed from bank on September			Operating expenses		9,490
1; issued $2,500, 6% note due in one year		2,500			
		$37,430			$37,890

Interest of $50 on the note payable is included in the expenses payable total of $200 as of December 31.

Doubtful accounts written off during the year totaled $300.

Sales returns and allowances during the year were $600.

Instructions:

(1) Prepare a work sheet for the preparation of a balance sheet and income statement.

(2) Prepare for the year ended December 31, 1977, (a) a balance sheet, and (b) an income statement accompanied by a statement of changes in the partners' capitals.

23-6. Adams and Benson, partners, do not maintain double-entry records. In preparing statements for the year ended December 31, 1977, you assemble the data that follow.

A balance sheet as of December 31, 1976, showed the following balances.

Adams and Benson
Balance Sheet
December 31, 1976

Assets		Liabilities and Owners' Equity	
Cash	$ 6,025	Accounts payable	$ 4,800
Marketable securities (cost)	3,600	Taxes payable	250
Accounts receivable	10,515	Miscellaneous expenses payable	150
Allowance for doubtful accounts	(650)	Notes payable	5,000
Merchandise inventory	24,005	Adams, capital	14,450
Prepaid miscellaneous expenses	115	Benson, capital	21,450
Supplies	250		
Fixtures	4,650		
Accumulated depreciation	(2,410)		
Total assets	$46,100	Total liabilities and owners' equity	$46,100

Cash records for 1977 show the data given below and on page 676.

Deposits:

Collections from customers	$103,600
Investment by Adams	7,000
Dividend revenue	140
Sale of marketable securities, cost $3,600	4,000
	$114,740

Checks written:

Purchase of merchandise	$ 77,200
Salaries	6,880
Utilities	800
Rent	4,800
Supplies	1,000
Fixtures	5,000
Taxes	1,240
Notes payable (includes interest of $180)	4,180
Miscellaneous expense	6,300
Partners' salaries — Adams, $110 per week	5,720
— Benson, $125 per week	6,500
	$119,620

The following additional data are available:

    (a) Bank service charges during the year were $60. (Debit to Interest Expense.)

    (b) Accounts receivable at the end of the year total $11,550. Accounts of $1,200 had been written off as worthless during the year; it is estimated that another $700 in accounts on hand at the end of the year will prove uncollectible.

    (c) Accounts payable on December 31, 1977, total $5,580. Purchase discounts of $1,440 had been taken during the year and merchandise of $1,580 had been returned to suppliers.

    (d) The merchandise inventory at the end of the year is $30,600; the supplies inventory is $215; and prepaid miscellaneous expenses are $210. Taxes payable at the end of the year are $705, salaries payable are $160, miscellaneous expenses payable are $80, and interest payable is $60.

    (e) Depreciation is recognized on the fixtures at the rate of 10% per year, but only one half of this rate is applied on fixtures that are acquired during the year.

    (f) The partnership agreement provides that Adams and Benson are entitled to $110 and $125 per week respectively as salaries, and that any profits after salaries are to be divided equally.

Instructions:

    (1) Prepare a work sheet for the preparation of a balance sheet and income statement.

    (2) Prepare for the year ended December 31, 1977, (a) a balance sheet, and (b) an income statement accompanied by a statement of changes in the partners' capital.

23-7. From the following data relative to the operation of the Garden Homes, Inc., during 1977, you are requested to prepare a schedule showing cash collections related to rent for the year.

Gross potential rents	$211,688
Vacancies	42,609
Space occupied by corporation for own use	4,925
Prepaid rent:	
Beginning of period	302
End of period	984
Delinquent rent:	
Beginning of period	377
End of period	79
Deposits (tenants) forfeited	100
Refunds to tenants	20
Uncollectible rents	80

(AICPA adapted)

23-8. The Hardin Furniture Store (a sole proprietorship) did not have complete records on a double-entry basis. However, from an investigation of its records you have established the information shown below and on page 677.

    (a) The assets and the liabilities as of December 31, 1976, were:

Cash	$ 5,175	
Accounts receivable	10,556	
Allowance for doubtful accounts		$ 740
Fixtures	3,130	
Accumulated depreciation — fixtures		1,110
Prepaid insurance	158	
Prepaid supplies	79	

Accounts payable		$ 4,244
Miscellaneous expenses payable		206
Taxes payable..		202
Merchandise inventory..	$19,243	
Note payable		5,000
Hardin, capital..		26,839

(b) A summary of the transactions for 1977 as recorded in the checkbook shows the following:

Deposits for the year (including the redeposit of $304 of checks charged back by the bank)	$83,187
Checks drawn during the year	84,070
Customers' checks charged back by the bank	304
Bank service charges	22

(c) The following information is available as to accounts payable:

Purchases on account during year	$57,789
Returns of merchandise allowed as credits against accounts by vendors......	1,418
Payments of accounts by check	55,461

(d) Information as to accounts receivable shows the following:

Accounts written off	$ 812
Accounts collected	43,083
Balance of accounts December 31, 1977 (of this balance $700 is estimated to be uncollectible)	11,921

(e) Checks drawn during the year include checks for the following items:

Salaries	$10,988
Rent	3,600
Heat, light, and telephone	394
Supplies	280
Insurance	341
Taxes and licenses..	1,017
Drawings of proprietor	6,140
Miscellaneous expense	769
Merchandise purchases	2,080
Note payable..	3,000
	$28,609

(f) Merchandise inventory December 31, 1977, was $17,807. Prepaid insurance amounted to $122 and supplies on hand amounted to $105 as of December 31, 1977. Taxes payable were $216 and miscellaneous expenses payable were $73 at the year end.

(g) Cash sales for the year are assumed to account for all cash received other than that collected on accounts. Fixtures are to be depreciated at the rate of 10% per annum.

Instructions: Prepare an income statement for the year ended December 31, 1977, and a balance sheet as of December 31, 1977. (AICPA adapted)

23-9. The Braxton Printing Company is a proprietorship owned by Robert Braxton, who does not have the time to keep detailed accounting records. Mr. Braxton purchased the business on January 1, 1977. He asks you to prepare interim financial statements for the six months ended June 30, 1978, and he provides the following schedule:

	June 30, 1978	December 31, 1977
Cash...	$ 2,039	$ 1,650
Note receivable	600	—
Accounts receivable...	1,700	1,300
Supplies inventory...	3,140	2,370
Prepaid insurance..	264	315
Equipment (original cost)	10,200	8,600*
Total assets...	$17,943	$14,235
Accounts payable	$ 1,100	$ 890
Expenses payable..	100	55
Total liabilities..	$ 1,200	$ 945

*As at January 1, 1977.

You are able to accumulate the information given below and on page 678.

(a) The schedule for December 31, 1977, was taken from the financial statements you prepared for Mr. Braxton as of that date.

(b) The cash balance of $2,039 was taken from the bank statement. The client's checkbook reveals the following:

Deposits:

Collections from customers	$25,025
Sale of equipment	400
Loan from bank ($2,000, 4-month note due September 30, 1978)	1,960
	$27,385

Withdrawals:

Payments to suppliers	$20,221
Insurance premiums	264
Employee's salary	775
Payment on Mr. Braxton's income tax	300
Purchase of equipment	1,600
Withdrawn by Mr. Braxton as salary	2,400
Miscellaneous expenses, including rent	1,436
	$26,996

(c) A check for $450 was received from a customer on June 30, 1978, and mailed to the bank on that day. The payment was deducted from the accounts receivable as of June 30 but not recorded in the checkbook or by the bank until July 2.

(d) Mr. Braxton excluded from accounts receivable $150 that he says is uncollectible. He estimates that the cost of this sale was $120.

(e) The note receivable is non-interest bearing and is due on September 1, 1978. It was accepted on May 1, 1978, from a delinquent account receivable.

(f) Printing equipment that was included in the original purchase price at $1,000 was sold for $400 on March 31. New equipment costing $1,600 was installed on April 1. All equipment has an estimated life of 10 years. Disregard salvage value of assets.

(g) Mr. Braxton hired an assistant on April 1, 1978, at a salary of $3,200 per year. (Disregard any payroll taxes.)

(h) An examination of insurance policies reveals the following:

Policy	Acquired	Term	Premium	Unexpired December 31, 1977
#2479	Jan. 1, 1977	3 years	$360	$240
C2160	June 1, 1977	1 year	180	75
831	April 1, 1978	1 year	72	
C2380	June 1, 1978	1 year	192	
			$804	$315

(i) The expenses payable are miscellaneous public utility charges which you compute to be $70 at June 30. The $100 item at June 30 is an extra month's rent that Mr. Braxton paid in error. He listed the item when the landlord advised him of the overpayment.

Instructions: Prepare a work sheet showing the account balances on December 31, 1977, the adjustments required in reporting revenue and expenses on an accrual basis for the six months ended June 30, 1978, the results of operations for the six months ended June 30, 1978, and the financial position at June 30, 1978. Formal journal entries and financial statements are not required. (AICPA adapted)

23-10. On January 3, 1977, Nolan-Paszkowski, Inc., was organized with two stockholders, Richard Nolan and Lynn Paszkowski. Richard Nolan purchased 500 shares of $100 par value common stock for $50,000 cash; Lynn Paszkowski received 500 shares of common stock in exchange for the assets and liabilities of a men's clothing shop that she had operated as a sole proprietorship. The balance sheet immediately after incorporation appears on the work sheet shown on the opposite page.

No formal books have been kept during 1977. The following data have been gathered from the checkbooks, deposit slips, and other sources:

(a) Most balance sheet account balances at December 31, 1977, have been determined and recorded on the work sheet.

(b) Cash receipts for the year are summarized as follows:

Advances from customers..	$ 700
Cash sales and collections on accounts receivable (after sales discounts of $1,520 and sales returns and allowances of $1,940)............................	126,540
Sale of equipment costing $5,000 on which $1,000 of depreciation had accumulated	4,500
	$131,740

(c) Cash disbursements for the year are summarized as follows:

Insurance premiums	$ 825
Purchase of equipment	18,000
Addition to building	4,600
Cash purchases and payments on accounts payable (after purchase discounts of $1,150 and purchase returns and allowances of $1,800)	82,050
Remittance of payroll taxes (income tax of $3,200 and FICA tax of $1,250 — divided equally between employee withholdings and employer)...	4,450
Net salaries paid to employees	38,620
Utilities	1,850
Dividends paid..	1,500
Total cash disbursements	$151,895

(d) Dividends of 75¢ per share were declared on June 30, September 30, and December 31.

(e) For tax purposes the depreciation expense for 1977 was: building $800, equipment $3,350. For financial accounting purposes the depreciation expense was: building $400, equipment $1,750.

(f) Doubtful accounts are estimated to be 1.2% of total sales for the year. The ending accounts receivable balance of $18,700 has been reduced by $650 for specific accounts which were written off as uncollectible.

(g) Annual income tax rates are 50% of taxable income. Assume advances from customers are not included in taxable income.

Instructions: Complete a work sheet for the preparation of accrual basis financial statements with the columns and data as given below. Formal financial statements and journal entries are not required. (AICPA adapted)

Nolan — Paszkowski, Inc.
Work Sheet for Preparation of Accrual Basis Financial Statements
For Year Ended December 31, 1977

ITEM	BALANCE SHEET JAN. 3, 1977		SUMMARY AND ADJUSTING ENTRIES		INCOME STATEMENT 1977		BALANCE SHEET DEC. 31, 1977	
	DEBIT	CREDIT	DEBIT	CREDIT	DEBIT	CREDIT	DEBIT	CREDIT
Cash....................................	50,000							
Accounts rec........................	12,400						18,700	
Merchandise inv.	23,000						24,500	
Prepaid insurance...............	350						200	
Land....................................	15,000						15,000	
Buildings.............................	20,000							
Accum. depr. — buildings..		7,000						
Equipment...........................	8,000							
Accum. depr. — equip.		2,400						
Accounts payable................		17,300						8,679
Adv. from customers...........		900						550
Salaries payable		600						1,595
Employees inc. tax pay.		450						775
FICA tax payable.................		100						190
Capital stock.......................		100,000						100,000
	128,750	128,750						

24

The Statement of Changes in Financial Position

The primary financial statements for a business unit consist of statements reporting financial position, results of operations, and changes in financial position. The position of a business at a given time is reported on the balance sheet. The operations for a given period are reported on the income statement and on the statement of changes in financial position — the funds statement. The income statement summarizes the revenues and expenses for the period and accounts for the change in retained earnings in successive periods. When there are further transactions that must be recognized in explaining the change in owners' equity, these would be reported in a separate statement accompanying the income statement. The funds statement, on the other hand, offers a summary not only of the operations of the business but also of the financing and investing activities of the business for the period. Thus, it accounts for all of the changes in financial position as reported on successive balance sheets.

The funds statement has variously been referred to as *the statement of application of funds, the statement of sources and uses of funds, the source and application of funds statement, and the statement of resources provided and applied*. In reporting funds flow, it is possible to adopt a funds concept that provides for a limited recognition of financial changes or a funds concept broadened to cover all financial changes. The Accounting Principles Board recommended that the broadened concept be adopted, and in applying this concept, that the funds statement be called the *statement of changes in financial position*.

To simplify reference to the statement, the term *funds statement* is used in this chapter.

FUNDS DEFINED

One significant variation found in funds-flow reporting is the definition applied to the term funds. The term has been defined in different ways and the definition determines the character and the form of the statement. Funds has most frequently been used to mean working capital, and in these instances the funds statement reports financing and investing activities in terms of working capital. Defined in those terms, the funds statement provides a summary of the individual sources and uses of working capital for the period. In its narrowest sense, funds has been used simply to denote cash, and a funds statement applying this concept simply provides a presentation of the individual sources and uses of cash for the period and the resulting change in the cash balance. Intermediate views would define funds as net current monetary assets — current assets excluding inventory and prepaid items less current liabilities — all current monetary assets, or simply cash and temporary investments combined. In applying the alternative definitions, the funds statement would report the sources and applications of such "funds" and reconcile their change in successive balance sheets. In practice, funds reporting generally employs the working capital or cash concept, and subsequent discussions will describe the preparation of funds statements when these concepts are adopted.

THE BROADENED INTERPRETATION OF FUNDS

If the funds definitions were to be applied literally, a number of transactions involving highly significant information relative to financing and investing activities would be omitted from the funds statement and thus might not be recognized by the user. For example, debt and equity securities may be issued in exchange for land and buildings; long-term investments may be exchanged for machinery and equipment; shares of stock may be issued in payment of long-term debt; properties may be received as gifts. These transactions carry significant implications in analyzing the change in financial position even though they are not factors in reconciling the change in funds defined either as working capital or cash. This suggests that in order to make the funds statement more useful, the funds interpretation should be broadened to recognize transactions such as those mentioned. The broadened view, for example, would recognize the issuance of capital stock for a property item as funds provided by the issuance of stock offset by funds applied to the acquisition of the asset.[1] Because sources and applications from such transactions are equal in amount, the remaining items reported on the funds statement will serve to reconcile the change in funds for the period. As indicated earlier, the broadened interpretation of funds, often referred to as the *all financial resources* concept, was recommended by the Accounting Principles Board, and this interpretation is assumed throughout this chapter. It is important to recognize that the all financial resources concept can be applied on either the working capital or cash basis as illustrated in latter sections of this chapter.

---

[1]It may be observed that this treatment requires adoption of the hypothesis that the transfer of an item in exchange or a gift effectively provides the company with working capital or cash immediately applied to the acquisition of property, the liquidation of debt, or the retirement of capital stock.

NATURE OF THE FUNDS STATEMENT

The funds statement provides a summary of the sources from which funds became available during a period and the purposes to which funds were applied. An important part of the summary is the presentation of data concerning the extent to which funds were generated by income-oriented operations of the business. In addition to reporting funds provided by operations, funds inflow is also related to such sources as the sale of property items, the issuance of long-term obligations, and the issuance of capital stock. Funds outflow is related to such uses as the acquisition of property items, the retirement of long-term obligations, the reacquisition of outstanding stock, and the payment of dividends.

These primary inflows and outflows are illustrated diagrammatically below:

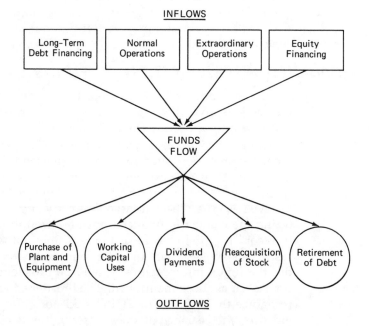

The funds statement helps answer directly questions such as: What use was made of profits? How was expansion financed? Why aren't dividend payments larger in view of rising earnings? Why did cash or working capital go down even though there was a substantial profit? How was bonded indebtedness paid off even though there was a substantial loss? These questions require answers if the various users of financial statements are to be provided the means of fully evaluating the operations of the business unit and the management of its resources.

USE OF THE FUNDS STATEMENT

The funds statement, although related to the balance sheet and the income statement, cannot be considered in any sense as a duplication or substitution for the other financial statements. The Accounting Principles Board, in Opinion No. 19, points out:

> The funds statement is related to both the income statement and the balance sheet and provides information that can be obtained only partially, or at most in piecemeal form, by interpreting them. An income statement together with a statement of retained earnings reports results of operations but does not show other changes in financial position. Comparative balance sheets can significantly augment that information, but the objectives of the funds statement require that all such information be selected, classified, and summarized in meaningful form. The funds statement cannot supplant either the income statement or the balance sheet but is intended to provide information that the other statements either do not provide or provide only indirectly about the flow of funds and changes in financial position during the period.[1]

To illustrate the special contribution made by the funds statement, consider the needs of a prospective creditor and the means for meeting these needs. An individual or group asked to make a long-term loan to a company is concerned with the company's proposed use of the loan, the ability of the company to meet the periodic interest payments on the loan, and the ability of the company ultimately to pay off the loan. Balance sheet analysis will provide answers to questions relative to the cash and near-cash items on hand, the working capital of the business — its amount and composition — present long-term indebtedness, and the implications on financial position if the loan is granted. Income statement analysis will provide answers to questions relative to the earnings of the company, the ability of earnings to cover current interest charges, and the implications as to earnings and interest charges if the loan is granted. Funds statement analysis will indicate the resources available to the company in the past and the uses made of those resources as well as the financing and investing implications if the loan is granted. Finally, funds data can be used in estimating the resources that will be generated in the future and the ability of the company to meet the added indebtedness.

It is obvious that in meeting the requirements of the users of financial statements, funds information will be most useful if offered in comparative form for two or more years. An additional statement reporting forecasted or budgeted funds-flow data may prove of equal or even greater value. Although suggestions have been made that the latter information be made available to the external users of financial information, this practice has not yet been adopted.

FUNDS STATEMENT APPLYING DIFFERENT FUNDS CONCEPTS

Regardless of how funds are defined, the funds statement is prepared from comparative balance sheets supplemented by explanations for the individual account balance changes. The preparation of the statement calls for the steps given at the top of the next page.

---

[1] *Opinions of the Accounting Principles Board, No. 19*, "Reporting Changes in Financial Position" (New York: American Institute of Certified Public Accountants, 1971), par. 5.

1. The definition to be used for "funds" is selected.
2. The funds accounts on the comparative balance sheets are listed and totaled; the net change in funds items found here should be the same as that computed in step (3).
3. The changes in each non-fund account on the comparative balance sheets are analyzed in order to classify the changes as sources or applications of funds, and the net increase or decrease arising from such changes is computed and compared with the amount determined in step (2).

To illustrate the process of analysis and the development of the funds statement applying the working capital and cash concepts, a relatively simple example will first be considered. Assume balance sheet information for the Goodspeed Company as shown below.

Assets	December 31, 1977	December 31, 1976
Cash	$ 75,000	$100,000
Accounts receivable	170,000	110,000
Inventories	195,000	160,000
Prepaid expenses	10,000	20,000
Land	160,000	160,000
Buildings and equipment	130,000	——
	$740,000	$550,000

Liabilities and Stockholders' Equity		
Accounts payable	$160,000	$100,000
Accrued expenses	20,000	30,000
Long-term liabilities	80,000	100,000
Preferred stock	100,000	100,000
Common stock	320,000	200,000
Retained earnings	60,000	20,000
	$740,000	$550,000

Funds Defined as Working Capital

When funds are defined as working capital, balance sheet changes must be analyzed in terms of their effects upon the working capital pool. Investigation of the balance sheet changes for the Goodspeed Company for 1977 reveals the following:

The increase in buildings and equipment reflects funds applied to the purchase of buildings and equipment, $130,000.

The decrease in long-term liabilities reflects funds applied to the retirement of long-term liabilities, $20,000.

The increase in common stock reflects funds provided from the sale of shares, $120,000.

Retained earnings went up as a result of net income for the period. The increase in retained earnings, then, reflects funds provided, $40,000 — working capital provided through sales exceeding the working capital consumed through cost of goods sold and expenses.

The foregoing analysis indicates that funds of $160,000 were provided from operations and from the sale of common stock, and funds of $150,000 were applied to the acquisition of buildings and equipment, to the retirement of long-term liabilities, and to a net increase in funds (working capital) of $10,000.

A statement for the Goodspeed Company summarizing working capital changes for the year is given on the following page.

Goodspeed Company
Statement of Changes in Financial Position — Working Capital Basis
For Year Ended December 31, 1977

Working capital was provided by:		
Operations...	$ 40,000	
Sale of common stock	120,000	$160,000
Working capital was applied to:		
Acquisition of buildings and equipment	$130,000	
Retirement of long-term liabilities	20,000	150,000
Increase in working capital		$ 10,000

The increase in working capital is accounted for as follows:

Working Capital Items	Dec. 31, 1977	Dec. 31, 1976	Increase (Decrease)
Current assets:			
Cash..	$ 75,000	$100,000	$ (25,000)
Accounts receivable....................................	170,000	110,000	60,000
Inventories	195,000	160,000	35,000
Prepaid expenses..	10,000	20,000	(10,000)
Current liabilities:			
Accounts payable..	160,000	100,000	(60,000)
Accrued expenses.......................................	20,000	30,000	10,000
Change in working capital..............................			$ 10,000

The funds statement shown is composed of two sections. The first section reports working capital inflow and outflow and the change in working capital for the period. The second section reports the individual changes within the working capital pool, summarizing and reconciling the individual changes with the total net change in working capital reported in the first section. Although working capital has increased by $10,000, which may be regarded as favorable, significant changes have taken place within the working capital pool which may not be similarly regarded, and the ratio of current assets to current liabilities has now changed from 3.0:1 to 2.5:1.

Instead of being prepared in two-section form, the statement may be limited to the presentation of the data in the first section and may refer to a separate supporting tabulation offering a summary of the changes in the individual working capital items.

Funds Defined as Cash   When the funds concept is used to denote cash, balance sheet account changes require analysis in terms of their effects upon the movement of cash. Cash is used in the same sense as that employed for cash recognized as a current asset — cash on hand and demand deposits in banks. The funds statement, then, describes the cash sources and cash uses and offers a reconciliation of the beginning and ending cash balances. This statement might be developed by simply classifying and summarizing cash receipts and disbursements as reported in the cash account. However, the statement is prepared to point out the broad sources and uses of cash, and such items as cash collected from customers, cash paid for merchandise, and cash paid for expenses are generally submerged in a cash-from-operations category. This information can be developed from comparative balance sheets supplemented by operating detail.

A statement for the Goodspeed Company giving effect to the cash concept follows.

Goodspeed Company
Statement of Changes in Financial Position — Cash Basis
For Year Ended December 31, 1977

Cash was provided by:			
Operations:			
Net income...		$ 40,000	
Items to be added to net income:			
Decrease in prepaid expenses...................................	$10,000		
Increase in accounts payable...................................	60,000	70,000	
		$110,000	
Items to be deducted from net income:			
Increase in accounts receivable..............................	$60,000		
Increase in inventories..	35,000		
Decrease in accrued expenses...............................	10,000	105,000	
Cash provided by operations...		$ 5,000	
Sale of common stock..		120,000	$125,000
Cash was applied to:			
Acquisition of buildings and equipment.........................		$130,000	
Retirement of long-term liabilities..................................		20,000	150,000
Decrease in cash..			$ 25,000

The decrease in cash of $25,000 is the same as that reported on the comparative balance sheets.

When funds are defined as cash, the analysis of the balance sheet changes is similar to that employed in the working capital example, but it must now be extended to include all of the working capital items except cash. A change in marketable securities is recognized as a source or an application of cash. Changes in other current assets and current liabilities related to operations are recognized by adjustments to net income. In the example, the following adjustments are required:

1. *Accounts receivable increase.* Net income is decreased since the cash receipts for goods and services sold were less than the revenue recognized in arriving at net income.
2. *Inventory increase.* Net income is decreased since purchases were greater than the charge made against revenue for cost of sales in arriving at net income.
3. *Prepaid expense decrease.* Net income is increased since the cash disbursements for expenses were less than the charges made against revenue for certain expenses in arriving at net income.
4. *Accounts payable increase.* Net income is increased since the cash disbursements for goods and services purchased were less than the charges made for these items in arriving at net income.
5. *Accrued expense decrease.* Net income is decreased since the cash disbursements for expenses were greater than the charges made against revenue for certain expenses in arriving at net income.

The cash-flow approach to the analysis of financial operations has received increasing attention in recent years.[1] The statement is readily

---

[1]See, for example, the emphasis placed on cash flows in the *Report of the Study Group on the Objectives of Financial Statements* (New York: American Institute of Certified Public Accountants, 1973).

interpreted by the reader, and it can be a highly useful tool for the fore-casting and planning of cash flow. However, a working capital analysis may still be required if questions are to be answered with respect to the effect of financial activities upon the working capital pool.

ANALYSIS OF ACCOUNT CHANGES IN PREPARATION OF FUNDS STATEMENT

As indicated earlier, the preparation of the funds statement requires comparative balance sheet information supplemented by explanations for account changes. Examples in the preceding sections were relatively simple and changes in account balances defined fund sources and applications. Ordinarily, however, more complex circumstances are encountered and it is not possible to rely on the net change in an account balance for a full explanation of the effect of that item on a company's funds flow. To illustrate, assume that comparative balance sheets report a $50,000 increase in bonds payable. Without further investigation, this might be interpreted as a source of funds of $50,000. However, reference to the liability account may disclose that bonds of $100,000 were retired during the period while new bonds of $150,000 were issued. A further analysis of the transactions affecting the liability account may reveal that a call premium of $2,000 was paid on bonds retired and a discount of $7,500 was identified with the new issue. The funds statement, then, should report that funds were provided by the new issue of $142,500 and that funds were applied to retirement of the old issue of $102,000.

Decreases in noncurrent assets and increases in noncurrent liabilities and in owners' equity require analysis in calculating funds provided; increases in noncurrent assets and decreases in noncurrent liabilities and in owners' equity require analysis in calculating funds applied.

Remaining pages of this chapter describe the nature of the analysis required as well as the procedures employed in developing a more complex funds statement.

Fund Sources The following examples indicate fund sources and suggest the nature of the analysis required in determining the actual amounts provided.

1. *Decreases in noncurrent asset accounts.* Balances in land, equipment, long-term investments, and other noncurrent asset accounts may decrease as a result of assets sold, thus representing fund sources. However, an analysis of the transactions accounting for each change is necessary; sale of investments at a gain, for example, provides funds exceeding the decrease in the asset account.
2. *Increases in noncurrent liabilities.* Balances in long-term notes, bonds, and other noncurrent liability accounts may increase as a result of amounts borrowed, thus representing fund sources. An analysis of the transactions accounting for each change is necessary; issuance of bonds at a discount, for example, provides less funds than the increase in the bond account.
3. *Increases in owners' equity.* Capital stock balances may increase as a result of the sale of stock, thus representing fund sources. However, the amounts received for shares must be determined, for these may differ

from the increases in the capital stock balances. When an increase in retained earnings cannot be explained solely by the net income for the period, an analysis of the retained earnings account is necessary. An increase in retained earnings resulting from profitable operations is recognized as a source of funds; a decrease in retained earnings resulting from cash dividends is separately recognized as an application of funds.

Fund Applications

The following examples indicate fund applications and suggest the nature of the analysis required in determining the actual amounts applied.

1. *Increases in noncurrent assets.* Balances in land, buildings, patents, and other noncurrent asset accounts may increase as a result of the acquisitions of such items, thus representing fund uses. An analysis of transactions accounting for the change is necessary; the amount paid for patents, for example, is greater than the increase in the patents account balance when the account is reduced during the period for patents cost amortization.

2. *Decreases in noncurrent liabilities.* The balances in mortgage, bond, and other noncurrent liability accounts may show decreases resulting from retirement of obligations, thus representing fund applications. An analysis of transactions accounting for each change is necessary; the amount paid bondholders, for example, exceeds the decrease in the bonds account when a call premium is paid upon bond retirement.

3. *Decreases in owners' equity.* Capital stock balances may show decreases as a result of the acquisition of shares previously issued, thus representing fund applications. However, the amounts paid for reacquired shares must be determined, for these may differ from the decreases in the capital stock balances. When a decrease in retained earnings cannot be explained solely by a net loss for the period, an analysis of the retained earnings account is necessary. A decrease in retained earnings resulting from operations at a loss is recognized as an application of funds; a further decrease resulting from cash dividends is separately recognized as an application of funds.

Changes in noncurrent asset and liability balances and in the owners' equity account balances must be analyzed and recognized as described regardless of the definition that is employed for funds. When the concept of funds is narrowed to cash, changes in certain current asset and current liability balances are also recognized in arriving at the amount of funds provided and applied.

Adjustments in Developing Amounts Provided and Applied

The preceding discussion has indicated that the changes in account balances require further analysis when they fail to report the amounts of funds actually provided or applied. When there are many adjustments to be made or when adjustments are complex, use of working papers may facilitate the preparation of the funds statement. In employing working papers, a special adjustments column is used to explain the changes in account balances in terms of the actual amounts of funds provided and applied by such changes.

The adjustments that are required in developing funds data may be classified under three headings:

1. *Adjustments to explain account changes not representing fund sources or applications.* Certain account changes may carry no funds-flow implications. For example, fully depreciated assets may have been applied against accumulated depreciation balances. Errors of prior periods may have been discovered requiring changes in property and owners' equity balances. Stock dividends may have been issued and retained earnings transferred to paid-in capital accounts. The foregoing items result in changes in account balances but these changes should be disregarded in reporting the flow of funds. When working papers are prepared, the adjustments made to explain such account changes do not affect the amount of funds provided or applied.
2. *Adjustments to report the individual fund sources and applications when several transactions are summarized in a single account.* The change in the balance of an account may result from funds provided by several different sources or applied to several different purposes, or from a combination of funds provided and applied. For example, the change in the land, buildings, and equipment balance may reflect funds applied to the construction of buildings and also to the purchase of equipment. The change in the bonds payable balance may reflect both funds applied to the retirement of an old bond issue and funds provided by a new issue. The change in the capital stock balance may reflect both funds provided by the issue of shares and funds applied to the reacquisition and retirement of shares. When working papers are prepared, adjustments are made to report separately the different fund sources and applications.
3. *Adjustments to report individual fund sources and applications when such information is reported in two or more accounts.* The amount of funds provided or applied as a result of a single transaction may be reflected in two or more accounts. For example, certain investments may have been sold for more than cost; the gain reported in net income and the decrease in the investment account must be combined in arriving at the actual amount provided by the sale. Bonds may have been issued at a discount; the increase in the discount account balance must be applied against the increase in the bond account in arriving at the actual amount provided by the issue. Stock may have been retired at a premium; the decreases in the paid-in capital and retained earnings account balances must be combined in arriving at the actual amount applied to the retirement. When working papers are prepared, adjustments are made to combine related changes.

Retained Earnings is an example of an account that may be affected by all three types of adjustments. To illustrate, assume that a retained earnings account shows an increase for a year of $10,000. Inspection of the account discloses the following:

ACCOUNT   Retained Earnings

DATE		ITEM	DEBIT	CREDIT	BALANCE	
					DEBIT	CREDIT
Jan.	1	Balance..				200,000
Mar.	1	Appropriation for bond sinking fund	20,000			180,000
July	10	Cash dividends......................................	30,000			150,000
Dec.	31	Net income for the year...........................		60,000		210,000

Retained earnings was reduced by the appropriation for bond sinking fund. Although both retained earnings and the appropriated retained earnings balance show changes of $20,000, the changes are without funds significance. If working papers are prepared, the decrease in retained earnings is explained by the increase in the appropriation for bond sinking fund; the account changes are thus explained and receive no recognition in developing the funds statement. Cash dividends of $30,000 are reported separately as funds applied. This leaves $60,000 in the retained earnings account to be reported as funds provided by operations.

If certain debits or credits recognized in arriving at net income carry no funds implications, the net income figure does not report the amount of funds actually made available by operations. For example, assume depreciation of $20,000 is recorded in computing net income. The entry for depreciation, although representing a proper charge in arriving at net income, is without funds significance; its effects, therefore, should be canceled. Funds from profitable operations, then, consist of $60,000, as reported, plus $20,000. If working papers are prepared, the increase in accumulated depreciation is explained by increasing funds provided by operations. To fully illustrate the nature of this adjustment, assume the following facts:

At the end of 1976, an attorney, in establishing a new office, invests cash of $15,000 and immediately acquires furniture and fixtures for $10,000. Furniture and fixtures are estimated to have a five-year life. Condensed comparative balance sheet and income statement data for 1976–1977 appear below.

	December 31, 1977		December 31, 1976
Working capital		$14,500	$ 5,000
Furniture and fixtures	$10,000		10,000
Less accumulated depreciation	2,000	8,000	
Capital		$22,500	$15,000
Fees received in cash or recognized as receivables		$20,000	
Expenses:			
Paid in cash or recognized as payables	$10,500		
Depreciation, recognized as reduction in furniture and fixtures balance	2,000	12,500	
Net income		$ 7,500	

Although there were no operating activities in 1976, funds of $10,000 were applied to the acquisition of furniture and fixtures and working capital changed from $15,000 to $5,000. In 1977, the income statement reported net income of $7,500 after a charge against revenue for depreciation of $2,000. However, operations provided working capital of $9,500 — fees providing working capital of $20,000 and expenses consuming working capital of $10,500. To arrive at the net increase in working capital, revenue representing working capital inflow is reduced only by those expenses involving working capital outflow or, alternately, net income is raised by the charge for depreciation involving no working capital outflow. Break-even operations would have recouped working capital equivalent to the reduction in the furniture and fixtures balance; profitable operations served to increase the working capital by an amount equal to both the charge for depreciation and the reported net income.

In calculating the funds provided by operations, net income must be increased by all charges that were recognized in arriving at net income from operations but involving no working capital outflow. Net income is increased for such charges as depletion, depreciation of buildings and equipment items, and amortization of patents, leaseholds, bond payable discounts, and bond investment premiums. Net income must be decreased by all credits recognized in arriving at net income but involving no working capital inflow. Net income is decreased for such items as the amortization of bond payable premiums and bond investment discounts. Any gains and losses included in net income but not related to normal operations must be identified with their particular sources; funds provided by operations are thus limited to amounts produced by normal and recurring activities.

PREPARATION OF THE FUNDS STATEMENT — FUNDS DEFINED ON A WORKING CAPITAL BASIS

In the examples given earlier, funds statements were prepared directly from comparative account balances. In the following example, comparative account balances require a number of adjustments and working papers are employed in developing the funds statement. In this section it is assumed the funds are defined as all financial resources on a working capital basis. The modifications in working papers and in statements when funds are defined as all financial resources on a cash basis are illustrated in a later section.

Assume for Atwood, Inc., the comparative balance sheet shown on page 692 and the supplementary data given below and on pages 692 and 693.

Supplementary data:

Changes in retained earnings during the year were as follows:

Balance, December 31, 1976		$125,500
Increases:		
Net income	$ 44,000	
Appropriation for building expansion returned to retained earnings	100,000	144,000
		$269,500
Decreases:		
Cash dividends	$ 12,000	
50% stock dividend on common stock	80,000	
Prior period adjustment resulting from omission of charges for depreciation on certain office equipment items	3,500	
Acquisition of treasury stock for $15,000; par value of stock, $12,000, originally issued at premium of $2,000	1,000	96,500
Balance, December 31, 1977		$173,000

The income statement for 1977 summarizes operations as follows:

Income before extraordinary items	$36,000
Add gain on involuntary conversion of buildings	8,000
Net income	$44,000

Buildings costing $40,000 with a book value of $2,000 were completely destroyed in an extraordinary disaster. The insurance company paid $10,000 cash; new buildings were then constructed at a cost of $105,000.

Building expansion fund investments, cost $96,000, were sold for $102,500.

Delivery equipment was acquired at a cost of $6,000; $2,000 was allowed on the trade-in of nonsimilar old equipment with an original cost of $4,800 and a book value of $2,800; and $4,000 was paid in cash. The entire loss is recognized.

Land was acquired for $108,500, the seller accepting in payment preferred stock, par $40,000, and cash of $68,500.

Atwood, Inc.
Comparative Balance Sheet
December 31

	1977		1976	
Assets				
Current assets:				
Cash in banks and on hand	$ 59,350		$ 65,000	
Accounts receivable (net)	60,000		70,500	
Interest receivable	250		2,400	
Inventories	75,000		76,500	
Prepaid operating expenses	16,500	$211,100	12,000	$226,400
Building expansion fund investments (at cost)		10,000		106,000
Land, buildings, and equipment:				
Land		$183,500		$ 75,000
Buildings	$290,000		$225,000	
Less accumulated depreciation	122,600	167,400	155,000	70,000
Machinery and equipment	$132,000		$120,000	
Less accumulated depreciation	32,800	99,200	43,500	76,500
Delivery equipment	$ 40,000		$ 38,800	
Less accumulated depreciation	26,000	14,000	20,000	18,800
Office equipment	$ 34,000		$ 26,000	
Less accumulated depreciation	12,500	21,500　485,600	6,000	20,000　260,300
Patents		35,000		40,000
Total assets		$741,700		$632,700
Liabilities				
Current liabilities:				
Income tax payable	$ 10,000		$ 9,500	
Accounts payable	65,000		81,200	
Salaries payable	5,000		1,500	
Dividends payable	4,400	$ 84,400		$ 92,200
Bonds payable	$ 60,000			
Less unamortized bond discount	2,700	57,300		
Deferred income tax payable		21,000		15,000
Total liabilities		$162,700		$107,200
Stockholders' Equity				
Preferred stock		$140,000		$100,000
Common stock	$240,000			160,000
Less treasury stock, common, at par	12,000	228,000		
Additional paid-in capital		38,000		40,000
Retained earnings appropriated for building expansion				100,000
Retained earnings		173,000　579,000		125,500　525,500
Total liabilities and stockholders' equity		$741,700		$632,700

New machinery was purchased for $12,000 cash. Additional machinery and equipment was overhauled which extended the useful life at a cost of $26,000, the cost being debited to the accumulated depreciation account.

The amortization of patents cost and depreciation expense on buildings and equipment were recorded as follows:

Buildings	$ 5,600
Machinery and equipment	15,300
Delivery equipment	8,000
Office equipment	3,000
Patents	5,000
Total	$36,900

Office equipment was acquired for $8,000 cash.

Ten-year bonds of $60,000 were issued at a discount of $3,000 at the beginning of the year; discount amortization for the year was $300.

The company recognizes depreciation on machines for tax purposes by the double-declining-balance method, and for accounting purposes by the straight-line method. This depreciation timing difference caused the income tax payable on 1977 taxable income to be $6,000 less than the income tax expense based on income per books.

In preparing a funds statement for Atwood, Inc., the first step is to decide to utilize the all financial resources concept of funds on a working capital basis. The second step is to determine the change in fund balances, in this case the working capital account balances. A schedule of changes in working capital for Atwood, Inc., is given below:

	December 31 1977	December 31 1976	Increase (Decrease)
Current assets:			
Cash in banks and on hand	$ 59,350	$ 65,000	$ (5,650)
Accounts receivable (net)	60,000	70,500	(10,500)
Interest receivable	250	2,400	(2,150)
Inventories	75,000	76,500	(1,500)
Prepaid operating expenses	16,500	12,000	4,500
Total	$211,100	$226,400	$ (15,300)
Current liabilities:			
Income tax payable	$ 10,000	$ 9,500	$ (500)
Accounts payable	65,000	81,200	16,200
Salaries payable	5,000	1,500	(3,500)
Dividends payable	4,400	0	(4,400)
Total	$ 84,400	$ 92,200	$ 7,800
Working capital	$126,700	$134,200	$ (7,500)

All nonfund accounts may then be analyzed using the working papers illustrated on pages 694 and 695. The funds statement is taken directly from the working papers and is illustrated on page 699.

It should be noted that the working papers contain a summary working capital fund account and the other nonfund accounts, in this instance nonworking capital accounts. These are the accounts which must be analyzed to determine the sources, uses, and net change in the fund balance already determined and shown above in the schedule of changes in working capital. The format of the working papers is straightforward. The first column contains the beginning balances, then there are two columns for analysis of transactions to arrive at the ending balances in the fourth column. The side headings added after the account titles are those to be used in preparing the formal funds statement.

In preparing working papers, accumulated depreciation balances, instead of being reported as credit balances in the debit section, may be more conveniently listed with liability and owners' equity balances in the credit section. Similarly, negative long-term liabilities and negative owners' equity balances are separately recognized and more conveniently listed with assets in the debit section.

Atwood, Inc.
Working Papers for Statement of Changes in Financial Position — Working Capital Basis
For Year Ended December 31, 1977

	ITEMS	BEGINNING BALANCE DEC. 31 1976	ANALYSIS OF TRANSACTIONS DEBIT		ANALYSIS OF TRANSACTIONS CREDIT		ENDING BALANCE DEC. 31 1977	
1	Debits							1
2	Working capital	134,200			(t)	7,500	126,700	2
3	Building expansion fund invest-							3
4	ments...................................	106,000			(i)	96,000	10,000	4
5	Land	75,000	(k)	108,500			183,500	5
6	Buildings...................................	225,000	(h)	105,000	(g)	40,000	290,000	6
7	Machinery and equipment......................	120,000	(m)	12,000			132,000	7
8	Delivery equipment.............................	38,800	(j)	6,000	(j)	4,800	40,000	8
9	Office equipment...............................	26,000	(p)	8,000			34,000	9
10	Patents	40,000			(o)	5,000	35,000	10
11	Unamortized bond discount..................		(q)	3,000	(r)	300	2,700	11
12	Treasury stock, common, at par...........		(f)	12,000			12,000	12
13	Totals.......................................	765,000					865,900	13
14								14
15	Credits							15
16	Accumulated depreciation—buildings...	155,000	(g)	38,000	(o)	5,600	122,600	16
17	Accumulated depreciation—machinery							17
18	and equipment.............................	43,500	(n)	26,000	(o)	15,300	32,800	18
19	Accumulated depreciation—delivery							19
20	equipment	20,000	(j)	2,000	(o)	8,000	26,000	20
21	Accumulated depreciation—office							21
22	equipment	6,000			(e)	3,500 }		22
23					(o)	3,000 /	12,500	23
24	Bonds payable..................................				(q)	60,000	60,000	24
25	Deferred income tax payable.................	15,000			(s)	6,000	21,000	25
26	Preferred stock.................................	100,000			(l)	40,000	140,000	26
27	Common stock	160,000			(d)	80,000	240,000	27
28	Additional paid-in capital	40,000	(f)	2,000			38,000	28
29	Retained earnings appropriated for							29
30	building expansion............................	100,000	(b)	100,000				30
31	Retained earnings...............................	125,500	(c)	12,000 }	(a)	44,000 }		31
32			(d)	80,000 {	(b)	100,000 {		32
33			(e)	3,500 {		{		33
34			(f)	1,000 }		}	173,000	34
35	Totals...	765,000		519,000		519,000	865,900	35
36								36

(Continued on next page.)

In developing working papers, it will normally prove most convenient to make the required analysis in the following order: (1) the change in retained earnings should be analyzed, and in the process the income from ordinary operations and the extraordinary items should be separately reported; (2) any extraordinary items should be related to appropriate asset or liability accounts; (3) the income statement and other supplementary data given, as well as any remaining accounts, should be reviewed to determine what additional adjustments are appropriate.

Explanations for individual adjustments recorded on the working papers for Atwood, Inc., are given on pages 696–699. The letter preceding each explanation corresponds with that used on the working papers.

	ITEMS	BEGINNING BALANCE DEC. 31 1976	ANALYSIS OF TRANSACTIONS DEBIT		ANALYSIS OF TRANSACTIONS CREDIT	ENDING BALANCE DEC. 31 1977	
37	Working capital was provided by:						37
38	Operations:						38
39	Income before extraordinary items .		(a)	36,000			39
40	Add items not requiring working						40
41	capital:						41
42	Loss on trade of delivery						42
43	equipment		(j)	800			43
44	Amortization of patents		(o)	5,000			44
45	Depreciation expense		(o)	31,900			45
46	Amortization of bond discount		(r)	300			46
47	Increase in deferred income						47
48	tax payable		(s)	6,000			48
49	Deduct item not providing						49
50	working capital:						50
51	Gain on sale of investments				(i) 6,500		51
52	Involuntary conversion of						52
53	buildings		(a)	8,000 ⎰			53
54			(g)	2,000 ⎱			54
55	Sale of building expansion						55
56	fund investments		(i)	102,500			56
57	Issuance of preferred stock						57
58	in part payment of land		(l)	40,000			58
59	Issuance of bonds at						59
60	discount		(q)	57,000			60
61	Working capital was applied to:						61
62	Dividends				(c) 12,000		62
63	Purchase treasury stock, common				(f) 15,000		63
64	Purchase land ($40,000 paid by						64
65	issuance of preferred stock)				(k) 108,500		65
66	Construct buildings				(h) 105,000		66
67	Purchase machinery and equipment ..				(m) 12,000		67
68	Overhaul machinery and equipment...				(n) 26,000		68
69	Purchase delivery equipment				(j) 4,000		69
70	Purchase office equipment				(p) 8,000		70
71	Decrease in working capital		(t)	7,500			71
72	Totals			297,000	297,000		72
73							73

(a) Net income included in the ending retained earnings balance is composed of income before extraordinary items and extraordinary items. The income before extraordinary items balance will require adjustment in arriving at the total funds provided by operations; the extraordinary items will require separate recognition as funds provided or applied and will later be combined with other asset or liability balances in arriving at the full amounts provided by or applied to the specific asset or liability items. Net income, then, is analyzed and is reported by an adjustment in compound form as follows:

Funds Provided by Income before Extraordinary Items	36,000	
Funds Provided by Involuntary Conversion of Buildings	8,000	
Retained Earnings		44,000

"Funds provided by income before extraordinary items" is reported on a separate line as a primary element of working capital provided from operations. Since a number of adjustments may be required in arriving at the actual amount of funds provided by operations, adequate space should be allowed after this line for these adjustments. The extraordinary items are listed below the space allowed for the income adjustments. Adequate space should also be allowed after each extraordinary item for adjustments necessary to show the actual amount of funds provided by or applied to the extraordinary transaction. Additional items requiring recognition are listed after the extraordinary items.

(b) The transfer of retained earnings appropriated for building expansion to retained earnings has no funds significance and the changes in the account balances are reconciled by the following entry:

Retained Earnings Appropriated for Building Expansion	100,000	
Retained Earnings		100,000

(c) The cash dividends reported in retained earnings are reported separately as an application of funds by the following entry:

Retained Earnings	12,000	
Funds Applied to Dividends		12,000

(d) The transfer of retained earnings to capital stock as a result of a common stock dividend has no funds significance and the changes in the account balances are reconciled by the following adjustment:

Retained Earnings	80,000	
Common Stock		80,000

(e) The recognition that depreciation had been omitted on certain office equipment items in prior periods is recorded by a debit to retained earnings and a credit to accumulated depreciation of office equipment. The correction of earnings of prior periods has no funds significance and the changes in the account balances may be reconciled as follows:

Retained Earnings	3,500	
Accumulated Depreciation — Office Equipment		3,500

(f) The acquisition of treasury stock, common, for $15,000 was recorded by a debit to Treasury Stock, Common at par, $12,000; a debit to Additional Paid-In Capital, $2,000; and a debit to Retained Earnings, $1,000. Funds applied to the acquisition of treasury stock are summarized by the following entry:

Treasury Stock, Common (at par)	12,000	
Additional Paid-In Capital	2,000	
Retained Earnings	1,000	
Funds Applied to Purchase Treasury Stock, Common		15,000

Debits to Retained Earnings of $96,500 and credits of $144,000 provide an ending balance of $173,000; fund sources and applications that were reflected in the retained earnings balance have been fully identified and given appropriate recognition.

(g) The destruction of the buildings and the subsequent insurance reimbursement produced an extraordinary gain of $8,000. This extraordinary gain was recorded as "Funds Provided by Involuntary Conversion of Buildings," in entry (a), as the result of the earlier recognition of the individual items comprising net income. Since the effect of the destruction was to provide funds of $10,000, the proceeds from the insurance company, the funds of $8,000 recognized in entry (a) may now be adjusted to show the true amount of funds provided by relating the required adjustment to the appropriate asset accounts:

Accumulated Depreciation — Buildings..	38,000	
Funds Provided by Involuntary Conversion of Buildings..............	2,000	
Buildings..		40,000

(h) The buildings account was increased by the cost of constructing new buildings, $105,000. The cost of new buildings is reported separately as an application of funds by the following entry:

Buildings	105,000	
Funds Applied to Construction of Buildings.............................		105,000

(i) The sale of building expansion fund investments was recorded by a credit to the asset account at cost, $96,000, and a credit to a gain on sale of investment. At the end of the period, the gain account was closed into retained earnings as part of income before extraordinary items. Since the effect of the sale was to provide funds of $102,500, this is reported on a separate line. The investments account balance is reduced and funds provided by operations are decreased by the amount of the gain. The following entry is made:

Funds Provided by Sale of Building Expansion Fund Investments...	102,500	
Building Expansion Fund Investments		96,000
Income before Extraordinary Items — Gain on Sale of Investments..		6,500

(j) Delivery equipment was purchased for $6,000; $2,000 was allowed on the trade-in of nonsimilar old delivery equipment, cost $4,800, with a book value of $2,800; and $4,000 was paid in cash. The loss of $800 on the equipment traded was closed into retained earnings as part of income before extraordinary items. Since the effect of the trade was to apply funds of $4,000, this is reported on a separate line. The changes in the delivery equipment balance and in the balance for accumulated depreciation on delivery equipment are explained, while the funds provided by operations are increased by the loss that did not involve current funds outflow. The following entry is made:

Delivery Equipment	6,000	
Accumulated Depreciation — Delivery Equipment......................	2,000	
Income before Extraordinary Items — Loss on Trade of Delivery Equipment..	800	
Delivery Equipment..		4,800
Funds Applied to Purchase Delivery Equipment.......................		4,000

(k) and (l) Land was acquired at a price of $108,500; payment was made in preferred stock valued at par, $40,000, and cash, $68,500. The analysis on the working papers is as follows: (k) the increase in the land balance, $108,500, is reported separately as an application of funds; (l) the increase in the preferred stock balance, $40,000, is reported separately as a source of funds applied to the purchase of land. The entries are:

Land...	108,500	
Funds Applied to Purchase Land		108,500
Funds Provided by Issuance of Preferred Stock in Part Payment of Land...	40,000	
Preferred Stock		40,000

(m) and (n) Machinery of $12,000 was acquired during the year. Payment was made in cash and is represented by funds applied to purchase machinery; the cost of overhauling other machinery and equipment also represents the application of funds and is reported separately. The cost was debited to the accumulated depreciation account. The entries are:

Machinery and Equipment..	12,000	
Funds Applied to Purchase Machinery and Equipment		12,000
Accumulated Depreciation — Machinery and Equipment............	26,000	
Funds Applied to Overhaul Machinery and Equipment.............		26,000

(o) The changes in the patents account and in the accumulated depreciation accounts result from the recognition of amortization of the patents and depreciation on the fixed assets. Funds provided by operations are increased by the charges against earnings not involving current funds outflow by the following adjustment:

Income before Extraordinary Items — Amortization of Patents...	5,000	
Income before Extraordinary Items — Depreciation Expense......	31,900	
Patents		5,000
Accumulated Depreciation — Buildings....................................		5,600
Accumulated Depreciation — Machinery and Equipment		15,300
Accumulated Depreciation — Delivery Equipment....................		8,000
Accumulated Depreciation — Office Equipment		3,000

(p) Office equipment of $8,000 was purchased during the year. The entry is as follows:

Office Equipment...	8,000	
Funds Applied to Purchase Office Equipment		8,000

(q) and (r) During the year, bonds were issued at a discount. The result of this transaction was to credit Bonds Payable for $60,000 and debit Unamortized Bond Discount for $3,000. The funds provided by the bond issuance of $57,000 are recognized by entry (q). Subsequently, the bond discount was amortized by reducing the unamortized bond discount account — entry (r). This decrease in the bond discount account is explained by increasing funds provided by operations by the amount of the charge against earnings not involving current fund outflow. The entries are as follows:

Unamortized Bond Discount	3,000	
Funds Provided by Issuance of Bonds	57,000	
Bonds Payable..		60,000
Income before Extraordinary Items — Amortization of Bond Discount	300	
Unamortized Bond Discount...		300

(s) The depreciation timing difference was recognized by a debit to Income Tax Expense and credits to Income Tax Payable and Deferred Income Tax Payable. The timing difference for 1977 is $6,000 and is shown on the work sheet by an increase in Deferred Income Tax Payable and an increase in funds provided by operations. The extra $6,000 debit to Income Tax Expense is thus added back to funds provided by operations because the extra charge against earnings did not involve current funds outflow. The following entry is made:

Income before Extraordinary Items — Increase in Deferred Income Tax Payable..	6,000	
Deferred Income Tax Payable...		6,000

(t) The change in working capital is explained by the following entry:

Decrease in Working Capital	7,500	
Working Capital...		7,500

This entry explains the net change occurring in all working capital accounts, and brings the working papers into balance.

A funds statement for Atwood, Inc., may be prepared from the working papers as follows:

Atwood, Inc.
Statement of Changes in Financial Position — Working Capital Basis
For Year Ended December 31, 1977

Working capital was provided by:			
Operations:			
Income before extraordinary items...............................		$ 36,000	
Add items not requiring working capital:			
Loss on trade of delivery equipment.........................	$ 800		
Amortization of patents..	5,000		
Depreciation expense...	31,900		
Amortization of bond discount	300		
Increase in deferred income tax payable.................	6,000		
	$44,000		
Deduct item not providing working capital:			
Gain on sale of investments......................................	6,500	37,500	
Working capital provided by operations		$ 73,500	
Involuntary conversion of buildings...............................		10,000	
Sale of building expansion fund investments.................		102,500	
Issuance of preferred stock in part payment of land			
(total cost of land, $108,500)......................................		40,000	
Issuance of bonds at a discount		57,000	$283,000
Working capital was applied to:			
Dividends		$ 12,000	
Purchase treasury stock, common		15,000	
Purchase land (cash paid, $68,500; preferred stock issued, $40,000)...		108,500	
Construct buildings...		105,000	
Purchase machinery and equipment...............................		12,000	
Overhaul machinery and equipment		26,000	
Purchase delivery equipment..		4,000	
Purchase office equipment		8,000	290,500
Decrease in working capital..			$ 7,500

The funds statement should begin with a summary of the funds related to normal operations. Income or loss before extraordinary items is listed. Those items reflected in this balance not requiring funds are added back while those items not providing funds are subtracted. The adjusted balance, representing funds provided by or applied to operations, is followed by any extraordinary items not related to normal financial transactions, but representing direct sources or applications of funds. Remaining sources and applications of funds are then listed in their respective sections in arriving at the net fund changes for the period.

Some persons object to the presentation of funds provided by operations in the form just illustrated. This form, they maintain, implies that the depreciation of assets generates funds. Actually, it is revenues that provide funds but the income from operations balance fails to report the full amount provided because of items such as depreciation. This objection is overcome by separately listing the individual revenues and expenses but excluding items and amounts not involving current fund inflows or outflows.

Special Problems

The analysis required in developing the funds statement may be simple or complex. In each instance where a noncurrent asset, a noncurrent liability, or an owners' equity account balance has changed, the question should be asked: Does this indicate a change in working capital? Frequently the answer to this question is obvious, but in some cases careful analysis is required. The following items suggest special analysis that may be required.

1. In the previous example, charges for depreciation on the tax return exceeded those on the books. This resulted in an increase in the deferred income tax payable account. When charges for depreciation on the books later exceed those on the tax return, or when an asset with a related deferred tax liability is retired early, the deferred tax credit will be decreased by a debit to Deferred Income Tax Payable and a credit to Income Tax Expense. This decrease in Income Tax Expense does not increase the amount of funds provided by operations nor does the decrease in Deferred Income Tax Payable indicate that funds have been applied; therefore, the decrease in Deferred Income Tax Payable must be recorded and funds provided by operations must be decreased by the reduction in income tax expense that did not involve current funds inflow.

2. Assume that retained earnings are reduced upon the declaration of a cash dividend payable in the following period. Declaration of the dividend has increased current liabilities and, thus, reduced working capital. Subsequent payment of the dividend will have no effect upon the amount of working capital, simply reducing both cash and the current liability. Declaration of a dividend, then, should be reported as funds applied. The reduction in working capital is confirmed in the summary of net change in working capital.

3. Assume that a long-term obligation becomes payable within a year, and requires change to the current classification. This change calls for a recognition of funds applied. The change in classification has resulted in a shrinkage of working capital; subsequent payment will have no effect upon the amount of working capital. The reduction in the long-term liability can be reported as "Funds applied to long-term obligations maturing currently." The change in working capital balances will confirm the reduction in working capital.

4. In previous examples, prepaid expenses were classified as current assets and therefore treated as working capital items in the analysis of the change in working capital. Prepaid expenses are sometimes listed under a separate heading or reported with noncurrent assets. This treatment calls for the special analysis of the prepaid expenses just as for other items classified as noncurrent, since their exclusion from the current group makes them part of the explanation for the change that took place in the current classification.

Alternative Methods for Developing a Funds Statement	It may be possible in some instances to analyze changes in comparative balance sheets and prepare the funds statement without the use of working papers, as was done in the first part of the chapter. In other instances, it may be desirable to arrive at fund changes by establishing several "T" accounts that will serve to control such an analysis; or it may be convenient to establish "T" accounts for all account balances reported at the beginning of the period and by the process of posting the changes in these accounts for the year, to list concurrently the funds provided and applied on a funds statement.

PREPARATION OF THE FUNDS STATEMENT — FUNDS DEFINED ON A CASH BASIS

In Chapter 23, the emphasis was on incomplete records and in going from a cash basis to financial statements on an accrual basis. When preparing a funds statement on a cash basis, the reverse analysis is required. That is, one must work from financial information on an accrual basis to the cash inflows and outflows provided and applied during the period. To illustrate, if sales for the period were $80,000 as reported on the income statement and the beginning and ending accounts receivable balances were $25,000 and $20,000 respectively, the cash provided from sales would be $85,000. The beginning accounts receivable balance would have been recorded as sales during the previous period, but collected in the current period; thus, the beginning balance should be added to the $80,000 sales figure. The ending balance is included in the $80,000 amount, but will not be collected until future periods; it should be subtracted. Therefore, the net decrease in accounts receivable should be added to the reported sales figure of $80,000 to arrive at the total cash provided from sales activity during the period.

If Atwood, Inc., wishes to prepare a funds statement using the all financial resources concept on a cash basis, working papers would be prepared as illustrated on pages 702 and 703. Adjustments are the same as those described on pages 696–699 but are supplemented by adjustments to show operations and also dividends in terms of cash. Income from operations as previously adjusted is further adjusted for the differences found in working capital items other than cash. The entry for cash dividends (c) is adjusted for the change in the dividends payable balance in arriving at the cash applied to dividends during the period. In the illustration, the entry (c) would be a debit to Retained Earnings, $12,000; a credit to Dividends Payable, $4,400; and a credit to Cash, $7,600. Entry (aa) serves the same purpose as entry (t) on page 695. The net change in cash is explained and the working papers are brought into balance by this entry. A statement of changes in financial position employing the cash concept for funds appears on page 704.

The working papers and the statement report the net amount of cash provided by operations, $70,950. When a full explanation of the cash provided by operations is desired, this can be provided by applying adjustments to the individual revenue and expense items rather than to the net

Atwood, Inc.
Working Papers for Statement of Changes in Financial Position — Cash Basis
For Year Ended December 31, 1977

	ITEMS	BEGINNING BALANCE DEC. 31 1976	ANALYSIS OF TRANSACTIONS DEBIT		ANALYSIS OF TRANSACTIONS CREDIT		ENDING BALANCE DEC. 31 1977	
1	Debits							1
2	Cash in banks and on hand....................	65,000			(aa)	5,650	59,350	2
3	Accounts receivable (net)........................	70,500			(t)	10,500	60,000	3
4	Interest receivable.................................	2,400			(u)	2,150	250	4
5	Inventories	76,500			(v)	1,500	75,000	5
6	Prepaid operating expenses	12,000	(w)	4,500			16,500	6
7	Building expansion fund invest-							7
8	ments..	106,000			(i)	96,000	10,000	8
9	Land	75,000	(k)	108,500			183,500	9
10	Buildings..	225,000	(h)	105,000	(g)	40,000	290,000	10
11	Machinery and equipment......................	120,000	(m)	12,000			132,000	11
12	Delivery equipment	38,800	(j)	6,000	(j)	4,800	40,000	12
13	Office equipment...................................	26,000	(p)	8,000			34,000	13
14	Patents	40,000			(o)	5,000	35,000	14
15	Unamortized bond discount...................		(q)	3,000	(r)	300	2,700	15
16	Treasury stock, common, at par		(f)	12,000			12,000	16
17	Totals	857,200					950,300	17
18								18
19	Credits							19
20	Accumulated depreciation —							20
21	buildings..	155,000	(g)	38,000	(o)	5,600	122,600	21
22	Accumulated depreciation —							22
23	machinery and equipment..................	43,500	(n)	26,000	(o)	15,300	32,800	23
24	Accumulated depreciation —							24
25	delivery equipment.............................	20,000	(j)	2,000	(o)	8,000	26,000	25
26	Accumulated depreciation —							26
27	office equipment................................	6,000			(e)	3,500 ⎱		27
28					(o)	3,000 ⎰	12,500	28
29	Income tax payable...............................	9,500			(x)	500	10,000	29
30	Accounts payable..................................	81,200	(y)	16,200			65,000	30
31	Salaries payable	1,500			(z)	3,500	5,000	31
32	Dividends payable.................................				(c)	4,400	4,400	32
33	Bonds payable.......................................				(q)	60,000	60,000	33
34	Deferred income tax payable.................	15,000			(s)	6,000	21,000	34
35	Preferred stock.....................................	100,000			(l)	40,000	140,000	35
36	Common stock	160,000			(d)	80,000	240,000	36
37	Additional paid-in capital	40,000	(f)	2,000			38,000	37
38	Retained earnings appropriated							38
39	for building expansion........................	100,000	(b)	100,000				39
40	Retained earnings.................................	125,500	(c)	12,000 ⎱	(a)	44,000 ⎱		40
41			(d)	80,000 ⎱	(b)	100,000 ⎰		41
42			(e)	3,500 ⎱				42
43			(f)	1,000 ⎰			173,000	43
44	Totals	857,200		539,700		539,700	950,300	44
45								45

(Continued on next page.)

	ITEMS	BEGINNING BALANCE DEC. 31 1976	ANALYSIS OF TRANSACTIONS				ENDING BALANCE DEC. 31 1977	
			DEBIT		CREDIT			
46	Cash was provided by:							46
47	Operations:							47
48	Income before extraordinary							48
49	items...............................		(a)	36,000				49
50	Items to be added to operating							50
51	income:							51
52	Loss on trade of delivery							52
53	equipment		(j)	800				53
54	Amortization of patents		(o)	5,000				54
55	Depreciation expense		(o)	31,900				55
56	Amortization of bond							56
57	discount....................................		(r)	300				57
58	Increase in deferred income							58
59	tax payable		(s)	6,000				59
60	Decrease in accounts							60
61	receivable (net)		(t)	10,500				61
62	Decrease in interest							62
63	receivable.................................		(u)	2,150				63
64	Decrease in inventories		(v)	1,500				64
65	Increase in income tax							65
66	payable		(x)	500				66
67	Increase in salaries							67
68	payable		(z)	3,500				68
69	Items to be deducted from							69
70	operating income:							70
71	Gain on sale of investment..........				(i)	6,500		71
72	Increase in prepaid operating							72
73	expenses..................................				(w)	4,500		73
74	Decrease in accounts							74
75	payable				(y)	16,200		75
76	Involuntary conversion of							76
77	buildings..		(a)	8,000				77
78			(g)	2,000				78
79	Sale of building expansion							79
80	fund investments.............................		(i)	102,500				80
81	Issuance of preferred stock							81
82	in part payment of land		(l)	40,000				82
83	Issuance of bonds at discount		(q)	57,000				83
84	Cash was applied to:							84
85	Pay dividends..................................				(c)	7,600		85
86	Purchase treasury stock,							86
87	common.....................................				(f)	15,000		87
88	Purchase land (cash paid,							88
89	$68,500; preferred stock							89
90	issued, $40,000).............................				(k)	108,500		90
91	Construct buildings............................				(h)	105,000		91
92	Purchase machinery and							92
93	equipment..................................				(m)	12,000		93
94	Overhaul machinery and							94
95	equipment..................................				(n)	26,000		95
96	Purchase delivery equipment.............				(j)	4,000		96
97	Purchase office equipment.................				(p)	8,000		97
98	Decrease in cash		(aa)	5,650				98
99	Totals			313,300		313,300		99

Atwood, Inc.
Statement of Changes in Financial Position — Cash Basis
For Year Ended December 31, 1977

Cash was provided by:			
Operations:			
Income before extraordinary items...............................		$ 36,000	
Items to be added to operating income:			
Loss on trade of delivery equipment.........................	$ 800		
Amortization of patents..	5,000		
Depreciation expense...	31,900		
Amortization of bond discount...................................	300		
Increase in deferred income tax payable.................	6,000		
Decrease in accounts receivable (net)......................	10,500		
Decrease in interest receivable.................................	2,150		
Decrease in inventories..	1,500		
Increase in income tax payable	500		
Increase in salaries payable	3,500	62,150	
		$ 98,150	
Items to be deducted from operating income:			
Gain on sale of investments......................................	$ 6,500		
Increase in prepaid operating expenses..................	4,500		
Decrease in accounts payable	16,200	27,200	
Cash provided by operations		$ 70,950	
Involuntary conversion of buildings		10,000	
Sale of building expansion fund investments................		102,500	
Issuance of preferred stock in part payment of land			
(total cost of land, $108,500).....................................		40,000	
Issuance of bonds at a discount		57,000	$280,450
Cash was applied to:			
Pay dividends...		$ 7,600	
Purchase treasury stock, common		15,000	
Purchase land (cash paid, $68,500; preferred stock issued, $40,000)...		108,500	
Construct buildings..		105,000	
Purchase machinery and equipment.............................		12,000	
Overhaul machinery and equipment		26,000	
Purchase delivery equipment..		4,000	
Purchase office equipment		8,000	286,100
Decrease in cash...			$ 5,650

income balance. The operations section of the working papers will require expansion in developing this detail. The operations section of the working papers just illustrated can be expanded as shown at the top of the next page. Adjustment (a), instead of reporting the results of operations as summarized on the income statement, lists the individual revenue and expense items. The adjustments required in developing the cash flow from operations are then applied to the individual revenue and expense balances.

Cash provided by operations as summarized on page 705 may be presented on the statement as follows:

Cash was provided by:			
Operations:			
Receipts — Sales		$760,500	
Interest revenue		6,750	$767,250
Payments — Cost of goods sold......................................		$538,800	
Selling and general expenses......................		136,400	
Interest expense..		3,600	
Income tax..		17,500	696,300
Cash provided by operations			$ 70,950

	Analysis of Transactions	
Item	Debit	Credit
Cash was provided by:		
Operations:		
Sales	(a) 750,000	
Add decrease in accounts receivable	(t) 10,500	
Cost of goods sold		(a) 550,000
Add decrease in accounts payable		(y) 16,200
Deduct:		
Depreciation of building, machinery, and equipment, amortization of patents	(o) 25,900	
Decrease in inventories	(v) 1,500	
Selling and general expenses		(a) 146,400
Add increase in prepaid operating expense		(w) 4,500
Deduct:		
Depreciation of office and delivery equipment	(o) 11,000	
Increase in salaries payable	(z) 3,500	
Other revenue — interest revenue	(a) 4,600	
Add decrease in interest receivable	(u) 2,150	
Other expense — interest expense		(a) 3,900
Deduct bond discount amortization	(r) 300	
Income tax expense		(a) 24,000
Deduct:		
Increase in income tax payable	(x) 500	
Increase in deferred income tax payable	(s) 6,000	
Loss on trade of delivery equipment		(a) 800
To cancel loss	(j) 800	
Gain on sale of building expansion fund investments	(a) 6,500	
To cancel gain		(i) 6,500

SPECIAL OBSERVATIONS

Alternate methods may be used for the presentation of exchanges interpreted as both financing and investing activities. For example, the acquisition of land for $30,000 cash and $50,000 of capital stock may be presented as follows:

Purchase of land	$80,000	
Less capital stock issued in part payment	50,000	$30,000

The difference represents the net amount of funds and would be shown in the application section. The financing and investing aspects of the transaction are related and the net effect on funds is reported. On the other hand, it may be maintained that the issuance of stock should be reported as funds provided and the acquisition of land at the full acquisition price as funds applied. This raises the totals for funds provided and applied but does not affect the increase or decrease in funds reported for the period. This is the approach used in the chapter illustrations and is consistent with APB Opinion No. 19.

The Accounting Principles Board in Opinion No. 19 recognized that the form, terminology, and content of the funds statement will not be the same for every company in meeting its objectives under different circumstances. Although recognizing the need for flexibility, the APB indicated that there is still a need for certain guides in the preparation of the statement and in its interpretation. At a minimum, disclosures should include the items listed at the top of the next page.

1. The amount of working capital or cash provided from operations;
2. The net changes in each element of working capital, either in the statement or a related tabulation;
3. Outlays for purchase of long-term assets;
4. Proceeds from sale of long-term assets not normally sold in the normal course of business;
5. Issuance, assumption, or redemption of long-term debt;
6. Issuance, redemption, or purchase of capital stock;
7. Conversion of long-term debt or preferred stock;
8. Dividends in cash or in kind, but not stock dividends or stock split-ups.[1]

The final recommendation of the board was that isolated statistics of working capital or cash provided from operations, especially per-share computations, should not be presented in annual reports to shareholders. The attempt has been made in this chapter to apply the above guidelines in funds-flow presentations.

The funds statement is now recognized as a primary statement, one which must be audited and which is considered essential for fully reporting the activities of a business unit. Even though not officially required for external reporting until APB Opinion No. 19 was issued in 1971, the funds statement has a long history of use. Many companies prepared the statement for management purposes long before actually presenting this information to external users. It is fortunate that this important statement is now readily available for all users of financial information.[2]

---

[1] *Opinions of the Accounting Principles Board, No. 19,* "Reporting Changes in Financial Position," *op. cit.,* pars. 12–14.
[2] See Appendix B for an illustrated funds statement for General Mills, Inc.

QUESTIONS

1. Describe the statement of changes in financial position. What information does it offer that is not provided by the income statement? What information does it offer that is not provided by comparative balance sheets?

2. What different concepts for funds may be applied in preparing the statement of changes in financial position? Describe the statement under each of the different fund concepts. Which approach do you support?

3. What is the "all financial resources" concept of funds? Why was this concept supported by the Accounting Principles Board?

4. What are the major categories of funds flows for a business entity?

5. Why must all "non-funds" account balances be analyzed in preparing a funds statement?

6. Name a source of funds originating from a transaction involving (a) noncurrent assets,

(b) noncurrent liabilities, (c) capital stock, (d) retained earnings. Name an application of funds identified with each group.

7. What three classes of adjustments are usually necessary in preparing the statement of changes in financial position?

8. (a) What adjustments are applied to the operating income figure when the funds statement summarizes working capital flow? (b) What adjustments are applied to operating income when the funds statement summarizes cash flow?

9. The American Co. had its worst year in 1977, operations resulting in a substantial loss. Nevertheless, without the sale of property items, borrowing, or the issue of additional stock, the company's working capital increased significantly. What possible explanation can you suggest for this increase?

10. Indicate how each of the following would be reported on a funds statement assuming that funds are regarded as working capital.

(a) Land and buildings are acquired for cash equal to 40% of the purchase price and a long-term mortgage note for the balance.
(b) Fully depreciated machinery is written off.
(c) Long-term notes are due within the year and their classification is changed to current.
(d) Capital stock is issued in exchange for land.

11. What alternatives exist to using working papers in developing funds statements?

12. What uses might each of the following find for a cash-flow statement?

(a) Manager of a small laundry.
(b) Stockholder interested in regular dividends.
(c) Bank granting short-term loans.
(d) Officer of a labor union.

13. Should a funds statement be audited by public accountants? Give your conclusion and reasons for your conclusion.

EXERCISES

1. State how each of the following items will be reflected on the statement of changes in financial position if funds are defined as all financial resources on (1) a working capital basis, and (2) a cash basis.

(a) Marketable securities were purchased for $20,000.
(b) At the beginning of the year, equipment, book value $7,000, was traded for non-similar equipment costing $15,000; a trade-in value of $3,000 is allowed on the old equipment, the balance of the purchase price to be paid in 12 monthly installments.
(c) Buildings were acquired for $75,000, the company paying $40,000 cash and signing a 6% mortgage note payable in 5 years for the balance.
(d) Uncollectible accounts of $900 were written off against the allowance for doubtful accounts.
(e) Cash of $250,000 was paid on the purchase of business assets consisting of: merchandise, $90,000; furniture and fixtures, $30,000; land and buildings, $95,000; and goodwill, $35,000.
(f) A cash dividend of $5,000 was declared in the current period, payable at the beginning of the next period.
(g) An adjustment was made increasing Deferred Income Tax Payable by $20,000.
(h) Accounts payable shows a decrease for the period of $15,000.

2. Give the adjustments needed for working papers in journal entry form for a statement of changes in financial position upon analyzing the following account:

ACCOUNT   Retained Earnings

DATE		ITEM	DEBIT	CREDIT	BALANCE	
					DEBIT	CREDIT
1977						
Jan.	1	Balance.................................				760,000
Mar.	20	Correction for error in inventory at end of 1976....................		15,000		775,000
June	1	Stock dividend...........................	200,000			575,000
Aug.	5	Discount on sale of treasury stock, par $150,000, for $125,000................................	25,000			550,000
Dec.	5	Cash dividends.........................	50,000			500,000
	31	Appropriated for loss contingencies................................	100,000			400,000
	31	Net income................................		75,000		475,000

3. The McCord Company prepared for 1977 and 1976 the balance sheet data shown at the top of the next page.

The cash needed to purchase the new equipment and to improve the company's working capital position was raised by selling marketable securities costing $117,000 for $120,000 and by issuing the mortgage. Equipment costing $25,000 with a book value of $5,000 was sold for $6,000;

	December 31	
	1977	**1976**
Cash	$ 116,500	$ 85,000
Marketable securities	23,000	140,000
Accounts receivable (net)	120,000	115,000
Merchandise inventory	250,000	218,000
Prepaid insurance	1,500	2,000
Buildings and equipment	1,838,500	1,450,000
Accumulated depreciation — buildings and equipment	(745,000)	(665,000)
Total	$1,604,500	$1,345,000
Accounts payable	$ 204,500	$ 315,000
Salaries payable	25,000	35,000
Notes payable — bank (current)	50,000	200,000
Mortgage payable	500,000	0
Capital stock, $5 par	800,000	800,000
Retained earnings (deficit)	25,000	(5,000)
Total	$1,604,500	$1,345,000

the gain on sale was included in net income. The McCord Company paid cash dividends of $30,000 during the year and reported earnings of $60,000 for 1977. There were no entries in the retained earnings account other than to record the dividend and the net income for the year. Marketable securities are carried at cost which is lower than market.

Prepare funds statements without the use of working papers:

(a) On a working capital basis.
(b) On a cash basis.

4. From the following information, give the necessary adjustments in journal entry form to explain the changes in accounts listed in preparing working papers for a statement of changes in financial position for 1977.

	Dec. 31, 1977	Dec. 31, 1976
Land	$ 25,000	$ 40,000
Buildings	100,000	100,000
Accumulated depreciation — buildings	68,500	62,500
Machinery	39,000	45,000
Accumulated depreciation — machinery	15,500	16,000
Delivery equipment	15,000	25,000
Accumulated depreciation — delivery equipment	6,500	12,500
Tools	14,000	12,000
Patents	3,500	4,500
Goodwill	0	40,000
Discount on bonds payable	0	6,000
Bonds payable	0	500,000
Capital stock	350,000	250,000
Treasury stock	22,000	0
Retained earnings appropriated for bond retirement fund	0	100,000
Retained earnings	179,500	180,000

ACCOUNT   Retained Earnings

DATE		ITEM	DEBIT	CREDIT	BALANCE	
					DEBIT	**CREDIT**
1977 Jan.	1	Balance				180,000
		Stock dividend	100,000			80,000
		Retained earnings appropriated for bond retirement fund		100,000		180,000
		Premium on purchase of treasury stock, par $22,000	8,000			172,000
		Cash dividends	10,000			162,000
Dec.	31	Net income		17,500		179,500

The income statement reports depreciation of buildings, $6,000; depreciation of machinery, $4,000; depreciation of delivery equipment, $2,000; tools amortization, $4,000; patents amortization, $1,000; and bond discount amortization, $1,000. The income statement also reports the following:

Operating income		$ 40,000
Other revenue and expense items:		
Gain on sale of land, cost $15,000, sold for $100,000	$85,000	
Gain on sale of delivery equipment, cost $10,000, book value $2,000, sold for $7,000	5,000	90,000
		$130,000
Loss on scrapping machinery, cost $6,000, on which accumulated depreciation of $4,500 had been recognized	$ 1,500	
Goodwill written off	40,000	41,500
Income before income tax		$ 88,500
Income tax		36,000
Income before extraordinary items		$ 52,500
Extraordinary loss on bond retirement (unamortized discount, $5,000 and call premium, $30,000)		35,000
Net income		$ 17,500

5. A summary of revenue and expense for the Convoy Corporation for 1977 follows:

Sales	$1,500,000
Cost of goods manufactured and sold	700,000
Gross profit	$ 800,000
Selling, general, and administrative expenses	500,000
Income before income tax	$ 300,000
Income tax	130,000
Net income	$170,000

Net changes in working capital items for 1977 were as follows:

	Dr.	Cr.
Cash	$ 26,000	
Trade accounts receivable (net)	100,000	
Inventories		$15,000
Prepaid expenses (selling and general)	2,500	
Accrued expenses (75% of increase related to manufacturing activities and 25% to general operating activities)		8,000
Income tax payable		12,000
Trade accounts payable		35,000

Depreciation on plant and equipment for the year totaled $150,000; 70% was related to manufacturing activities and 30% to general and administrative activities.

Prepare a summary of cash provided by operations for the year showing revenues and expenses in detail.

PROBLEMS

24-1. Comparative balance sheet data for the firm of Collins and Jones are given below and on page 710.

	December 31	
	1977	1976
Cash	$ 5,400	$ 3,900
Accounts receivable	8,800	10,200
Inventory	45,000	30,000
Prepaid expenses	1,200	1,700
Furniture and fixtures	25,800	16,000
Accumulated depreciation	(13,550)	(10,050)
Total	$72,650	$51,750

| | December 31 ||
	1977	1976
Accrued expenses	$ 2,600	$ 1,900
Accounts payable	7,650	9,950
Long-term note	7,000	0
Fenley Jones, capital	20,550	19,550
Peter Collins, capital	34,850	20,350
Total	$72,650	$51,750

Income from operations for the year was $15,000 and this was transferred in equal amounts to the partners' capital accounts. Further changes in the capital accounts arose from additional investments and withdrawals by the partners. The change in the furniture and fixtures account arose from a purchase of additional furniture; part of the purchase price was paid in cash and a long-term note was issued for the balance.

> *Instructions:* Prepare the following (working papers are not required):
> (1) A statement of changes in financial position applying the working capital concept of funds.
> (2) A statement of changes in financial position applying the cash concept of funds.

24-2. Comparative balance sheet data for Camera, Inc., follow:

| | December 31 ||
	1977	1976
Cash	$ 22,500	$ 40,000
Accounts receivable	60,000	50,000
Inventory	75,000	62,500
Prepaid expenses	12,500	10,000
Land, buildings, and equipment	160,000	95,000
Accumulated depreciation	(45,000)	(35,000)
	$285,000	$222,500
Accrued expenses	$ 7,500	$ 5,000
Accounts payable	52,500	42,500
Bonds payable	20,000	50,000
Capital stock, at par	125,000	100,000
Additional paid-in capital	25,000	10,000
Retained earnings	55,000	15,000
	$285,000	$222,500

Land and buildings were acquired in exchange for capital stock; the assets were recorded at $40,000, their appraised value. Equipment was acquired for $25,000 cash. Net income for the year transferred to retained earnings was $55,000; cash dividends accounted for the remaining change in retained earnings.

> *Instructions:* Prepare the following (working papers are not required):
> (1) A statement of changes in financial position applying the working capital concept of funds.
> (2) A statement of changes in financial position applying the cash concept of funds.

24-3. Ortiz's Optical reported net income of $12,320 for 1977 but has been showing an overdraft in its bank account in recent months. The manager has contacted you as the auditor for an explanation. The information at the top of page 711 was given to you for examination.

You also determine the following:

> (a) Equipment was sold for $3,000; its cost was $5,000 and its book value was $1,000. The gain was reported as Other Revenue.
> (b) Cash dividends of $9,000 were paid.

> *Instructions:* Prepare the following (working papers are not required):
> (1) A statement of changes in financial position applying the working capital concept of funds.
> (2) A statement of changes in financial position applying the cash concept of funds.

Ortiz's Optical
Comparative Balance Sheet
December 31

	1977		1976	
Assets				
Current assets:				
Cash	$ (1,920)		$ 9,560	
Accounts receivable	8,000		2,000	
Inventory	4,700		1,500	
Prepaid insurance	140		390	
Total current assets		$10,920		$13,450
Land, buildings, and equipment:				
Land	$25,000		$25,000	
Buildings	$50,000		$50,000	
Less accumulated depreciation	30,000	20,000	28,000	22,000
Equipment	$74,500		$61,700	
Less accumulated depreciation	45,000	29,500	36,800	24,900
Total land, buildings, and equipment		74,500		71,900
Total assets		$85,420		$85,350
Liabilities and Stockholders' Equity				
Current liabilities:				
Accounts payable	$ 8,500		$ 7,000	
Taxes payable	2,800		4,700	
Wages payable	1,500		3,350	
Notes payable — current portion	3,000		7,000	
Total current liabilities		$15,800		$22,050
Long-term liabilities:				
Notes payable		21,000		23,000
Capital stock	$35,000		$30,000	
Retained earnings	13,620		10,300	
Total stockholders' equity		48,620		40,300
Total liabilities and stockholders' equity		$85,420		$85,350

24-4. The Hubbard Company presented the following comparative information:

	1977	1976
Cash	$174,000	$150,000
Accounts receivable	95,000	80,000
Inventory (lower of cost or market)	180,000	175,000
Land, buildings, and equipment (net)	315,000	350,000
Current liabilities	(210,000)	(215,000)
Bonds payable	0	(200,000)
Bond premium	0	(6,000)
Common stock, $50 par	(450,000)	(250,000)
Additional paid-in capital	(35,000)	(15,000)
Retained earnings	(69,000)	(69,000)

ACCOUNT   Retained Earnings

DATE		ITEM	DEBIT	CREDIT	BALANCE	
					DEBIT	CREDIT
1976 Jan.	1	Balance				69,000
		Cash dividends paid during the year	10,000			59,000
		Correction of prior period inventory understatement		20,000		79,000
		Net loss (including $15,000 loss on bond conversion)	10,000			69,000

Buildings, with a book value of $80,000, were sold for $130,000 cash. Land was acquired from the proceeds of the sale for $60,000. Depreciation recorded for the year was $15,000. The bonds payable were converted to common stock on December 31, 1977, after the annual bond premium amortization of $1,000 had been recorded. The conversion privilege provided for exchange of a $1,000 bond for 20 shares of stock. Market value of the stock on December 31, 1977, was $55 per share.

> **Instructions:** Prepare a funds statement applying the working capital concept of funds (Working papers are not required.)

24-5. The following data were taken from the records of the Newbold Company.

Balance Sheet
December 31

	1977		1976	
Current assets..		$185,200		$148,300
Land, buildings, and equipment	$100,500		$96,000	
Less accumulated depreciation..................................	34,000	66,500	30,000	66,000
Investments in stocks and bonds................................		32,000		35,000
Goodwill		0		25,000
Total assets		$283,700		$274,300
Current liabilities		$ 58,800		$ 43,300
Bonds payable..		0		50,000
Unamortized bond discount....................................		0		(1,250)
Preferred stock, $100 par...		0		50,000
Common stock, $10 par..		165,000		105,000
Additional paid-in capital...		40,000		0
Retained earnings		19,900		27,250
Total liabilities and stockholders' equity......................		$283,700		$274,300

ACCOUNT   Retained Earnings

DATE		ITEM	DEBIT	CREDIT	BALANCE	
					DEBIT	CREDIT
1977 Jan.	1	Balance..				27,250
		Premium on retirement of preferred stock..............................	1,000			26,250
		Cash dividends............................	17,500			8,750
		Net income		11,150		19,900

Income statement data for the year ended December 31, 1977, summarized operations as follows:

Income before extraordinary items..	$14,650
Extraordinary loss on retirement of bonds..	3,500
Net income	$11,150

Fully depreciated equipment, original cost $10,500, was traded in on similar new equipment costing $16,500; $1,500 was allowed by the vendor on the trade-in. One hundred shares of Byler Co. preferred stock, cost $20,000, held as a long-term investment, were sold at a loss of $2,500 at the beginning of the year. Additional changes in the investments account resulted from the purchase of Carbon Co. bonds. The company issued common stock in April, and part of the proceeds was used to retire preferred stock at 102 shortly thereafter. On July 1, the company called in its bonds outstanding, paying a premium of 5% on the call. Discount amortization on the bonds to the date of call was $250. Depreciation for the year on buildings and equipment was $14,500. Goodwill was judged worthless and was written off.

> **Instructions:** Prepare working papers and a statement of changes in financial position applying the working capital concept of funds.

24-6. The information on page 713 is assembled for the Window Garden Corporation.

Balance Sheet
December 31

	1977		1976	
Cash (overdraft in 1976)...		$ 38,625		$ (5,625)
Accounts receivable..		82,000		95,500
Inventories..		73,250		50,000
Long-term investments		12,000		27,000
Land, buildings, and equipment	$130,000		$95,000	
Less accumulated depreciation................................	21,500	108,500	20,000	75,000
Patents...		0		35,000
Total assets		$314,375		$276,875
Accounts payable		$ 55,875		$ 49,375
Bonds payable..		50,000		20,000
Premium on bonds payable..		2,375		0
Preferred stock, $100 par..		0		50,000
Common stock, $10 par..		160,000		100,000
Premium on common stock		24,000		0
Retained earnings		22,125		57,500
Total liabilities and stockholders' equity.......................		$314,375		$276,875

ACCOUNT   Retained Earnings

DATE		ITEM	DEBIT	CREDIT	BALANCE	
					DEBIT	CREDIT
1977						
Jan.	1	Balance...				57,500
Oct.	15	Cash dividends..............................	25,000			32,500
Dec.	12	Premium on retirement of pre-				
		ferred stock.............................	5,000			27,500
Dec.	31	Net loss..	5,375			22,125

Income statement data for the year ended December 31, 1977, summarized operations as follows:

Loss before extraordinary items	$4,375
Extraordinary loss on retirement of bonds	1,000
Net loss...	$5,375

Equipment, cost $15,000, book value $3,000, was scrapped, salvage of $900 being recovered on the disposal. Additional equipment, cost $50,000, was acquired during the year. Long-term investments, cost $15,000, were sold for $18,250; 7% bonds, face value $20,000, were called in at 105, and new 10-year, 5% bonds of $50,000 were issued at 105 on July 1. Preferred stock was retired at a cost of 110 while 6,000 shares of common stock were issued at $14. Depreciation on buildings and equipment for the year was $13,500. Patents, costing $35,000, were written off.

Instructions:
(1) Prepare working papers and a statement of changes in financial position applying the working capital concept of funds.
(2) Prepare a statement of changes in financial position applying the cash concept of funds.

24-7. The Andersen Company prepared the comparative balance sheet shown on page 714 and the combined statement of income and retained earnings shown on page 715.

An analysis of the accounts reveals the following:
(a) The tax refund from correction of the inventory overstatement was received in cash during 1977.
(b) The usual annual cash dividend of $50,000 was declared on December 15, 1977, and paid on January 31, 1978.
(c) The 10% stock dividend was declared when Andersen Company stock was selling for $15 per share.

Andersen Company
Comparative Balance Sheet
December 31

	1977		1976	
Assets				
Current assets:				
Cash...		$ 320,000		$ 154,000
Marketable securities (cost)......................................	$ 90,000		$160,000	
Less allowance for decline in value of marketable securities...	8,000		10,000	
Marketable securities (market).................................		82,000		150,000
Accounts receivable (net)..		640,000		520,000
Inventories (lower of cost or market)........................		540,000		670,000
Prepaid expenses..		6,000		8,000
Total current assets...		$1,588,000		$1,502,000
Land, buildings, and equipment:				
Land		$ 50,000		$ 50,000
Buildings...	$825,000		$800,000	
Less accumulated depreciation — buildings..........	215,000	610,000	225,000	575,000
Machinery and equipment	$425,000		$380,000	
Less accumulated depreciation — machinery and equipment	75,000	350,000	120,000	260,000
Total land, buildings, and equipment		$1,010,000		$ 885,000
Investment in Tow Company (equity)		$ 970,000		$ 800,000
Goodwill		55,000		60,000
		$1,025,000		$ 860,000
Total assets		$3,623,000		$3,247,000
Liabilities				
Current liabilities:				
Accounts payable...		$ 464,000		$ 407,000
Mortgage payable in 6 months		20,000		0
Income tax payable..		115,000		150,000
Accrued payables..		80,000		75,000
Dividends payable..		50,000		50,000
Estimated liability under service contracts (current).		65,000		60,000
Long-term liabilities:				
Mortgage payable..		180,000		0
Debenture bonds payable..	$500,000		$500,000	
Plus unamortized premium	5,500	505,500	6,000	506,000
Long-term liability under service contracts...............		287,500		242,000
Other long-term liabilities:				
Deferred income tax payable		124,000		134,000
Total liabilities..		$1,891,000		$1,624,000
Stockholders' Equity				
Common stock, $10 par...	$880,000		$800,000	
Additional paid-in capital...	240,000		200,000	
Retained earnings	612,000	1,732,000	623,000	1,623,000
Total liabilities and stockholders' equity........................		$3,623,000		$3,247,000

(d) Equipment costing $300,000 with a book value of $220,000 was destroyed in an extraordinary disaster. The deferred income tax related to the difference between tax and book depreciation taken on the equipment was $35,000. This reduced the book income tax credit on the loss from $80,000 to an actual tax credit of $45,000. New equipment was purchased with cash raised by selling marketable securities, cost $150,000, for $145,000 and by taking out the mortgage for the balance due. The mortgage is due in 10 annual installments of $20,000.

(e) The allowance account for the decline in value of marketable securities was adjusted at year-end by a credit to the income account, Unrealized Gain on Marketable Securities.

(f) The ending inventory was written down by $50,000 to properly value the inventory at the lower of cost or market.

Andersen Company
Income and Retained Earnings Statement
For Year Ended December 31, 1977

Income before extraordinary items		$319,000
Extraordinary loss on equipment (net of income tax credit of $80,000)		140,000
Net income..		$179,000
Unadjusted retained earnings, January 1, 1977	$623,000	
Deduct: Prior period adjustment — correction of inventory overstatement, net of income tax refund of $18,000	20,000	603,000
Adjusted retained earnings, January 1, 1977......................................		$782,000
Deduct: Dividends declared	$ 50,000	
10% stock dividend	120,000	170,000
Retained earnings, December 31, 1977..		$612,000

(g) Tow Company, in which Andersen Company holds a 35% interest, paid dividends of $600,000 and reported earnings of $800,000 during 1977. Andersen Company made an additional investment in Tow Company on December 31, 1977.

(h) A warehouse costing $200,000, with a book value of $150,000 was destroyed by fire. The insurance proceeds were $210,000 cash. There was no tax on the gain of the old warehouse as a new warehouse costing $225,000 was built during the same year.

(i) Depreciation and amortization for 1977 were as follows:

Buildings...	$40,000
Machinery and equipment...	35,000
Goodwill...	5,000
Premium on bonds payable	500

Instructions: Prepare working papers and a statement of changes in financial position applying the cash concept of funds.

24-8. Financial data for the Logan Manufacturing Co. are presented below and on page 716.

Logan Manufacturing Co.
Comparative Balance Sheet
December 31

	1977		1976	
Assets				
Cash..		$ 33,550		$ 65,000
Accounts receivable...	$ 53,000		$ 27,625	
Less allowance for doubtful accounts.........................	2,500	50,500	2,125	25,500
Inventories...		75,000		32,000
Office supplies...		5,000		1,500
Miscellaneous prepaid expenses (selling and general)		3,500		3,000
Long-term investments......................................		115,000		20,000
Land..		75,000		25,000
Buildings..	$124,500		$ 90,000	
Less accumulated depreciation................................	40,000	84,500	36,000	54,000
Machinery...	$ 95,000		$ 75,000	
Less accumulated depreciation................................	44,000	51,000	40,000	35,000
Goodwill...		0		50,000
Total assets		$493,050		$311,000
Liabilities and Stockholders' Equity				
Accounts payable..		$ 23,000		$ 25,000
Miscellaneous accrued expenses (selling and general)..		6,500		4,000
Income tax payable		20,000		10,000
Bonds payable...	$225,000		$100,000	
Less bond discount	10,875	214,125	4,250	95,750
Capital stock, $10 par..		150,000		100,000
Additional paid-in capital..................................		55,000		30,000
Retained earnings...		24,425		46,250
Total liabilities and stockholders' equity.......................		$493,050		$311,000

Logan Manufacturing Co.
Condensed Income Statement
For Year Ended December 31, 1977

Sales		$218,900
Less expenses:		
Cost of goods sold (includes depreciation of machinery, $9,000, and depreciation of buildings, $6,000)	$118,000	
Selling, general, and administrative expenses	40,225	158,225
Operating income		$ 60,675
Other revenue and expense items:		
Gain on sale of investments		2,500
		$ 63,175
Loss on sale of machinery	$ 1,000	
Goodwill written off	50,000	51,000
Income before income tax		$ 12,175
Income tax		18,000
Net loss		$ 5,825

(a) Ten-year bonds of $100,000 had been issued on July 1, 1975, at 95. Additional 10-year bonds of $125,000 had been issued on July 1, 1977, at 94.

(b) Machinery no longer needed was sold for $7,000 in 1977; the machinery had an original cost of $13,000 and accumulated depreciation on the date of the sale totaled $5,000.

(c) Fully depreciated storage quarters were dismantled during the year; thus buildings, cost $2,000, were written off against the accumulated depreciation of buildings account. Long-term investments in outside companies that cost $16,000 were sold at the beginning of the year for $18,500, and additional long-term investments were subsequently made during the year. Additional capital stock was issued by the company during the year at 15 in order to raise working capital.

Instructions:

(1) Prepare working papers and a statement of changes in financial position applying the working capital concept of funds.

(2) Prepare working papers and a statement of changes in financial position applying the cash concept of funds and reporting revenue and expense detail.

24-9. Bencivenga Company has prepared its financial statements for the year ended December 31, 1976, and for the three months ended March 31, 1977. You have been asked to prepare a statement of changes in financial position on a working capital basis for the three months ended March 31, 1977. The company's balance sheet data at December 31, 1976, and March 31, 1977, and its income statement data for the three months ended March 31, 1977, follow. You have previously satisfied yourself as to the correctness of the amounts presented.

The balance sheet data are as follows:

	March 31, 1977	December 31, 1976
Cash	$ 87,400	$ 25,300
Marketable securities	7,300	16,500
Accounts receivable (net)	49,320	24,320
Inventory	48,590	31,090
Total current assets	$192,610	$ 97,210
Land	18,700	40,000
Buildings	250,000	250,000
Equipment	81,500	0
Accumulated depreciation	(16,250)	(15,000)
Investment in 30% owned company	67,100	61,220
Other assets	15,100	15,100
Total	$608,760	$448,530
Accounts payable	$ 17,330	$ 21,220
Dividends payable	8,000	0
Income tax payable	34,616	0
Total current liabilities	$ 59,946	$ 21,220

	March 31, 1977	December 31, 1976
Other liabilities	$186,000	$186,000
Bonds payable	115,000	50,000
Discount on bonds payable	(2,150)	(2,300)
Deferred income tax	846	510
Preferred stock	0	30,000
Common stock	110,000	80,000
Dividends declared	(8,000)	0
Retained earnings	147,118	83,100
Total	$608,760	$448,530

Income statement data for the three months ended March 31, 1977, are as follows:

Sales	$242,807
Gain on sale of marketable securities	2,400
Equity in earnings of 30% — owned company	5,880
Gain on condemnation of land (capital gains)	10,700
	$261,787
Cost of goods sold	$138,407
General and administrative expenses	22,010
Depreciation	1,250
Interest expense	1,150
Income tax	34,952
	$197,769
Net income	$ 64,018

Your discussion with the company's controller and a review of the financial records revealed the following information:

(a) On January 8, 1977, the company sold marketable securities for cash.

(b) The company's preferred stock is convertible into common stock at a rate of one share of preferred for two shares of common. The preferred stock and common stock have par values of $2 and $1 respectively.

(c) On January 17, 1977, three acres of land were extraordinarily condemned. An award of $32,000 in cash was received on March 22, 1977. Purchase of additional land as a replacement is not contemplated by the company.

(d) On March 25, 1977, the company purchased equipment for cash.

(e) On March 29, 1977, bonds payable were issued by the company at par for cash.

(f) The company's tax rate is 40% for regular income and 20% for capital gains.

Instructions: Prepare in good form a statement of changes in financial position on a working capital basis for Bencivenga Company for the three months ended March 31, 1977. (AICPA adapted)

24-10. The following schedule showing net changes in balance sheet accounts at December 31, 1977, compared to December 31, 1976, was prepared from the records of the Sodium Company. The statement of changes in financial position for the year ended December 31, 1977, has not yet been prepared.

Assets	Increase (Decrease)
Cash	$ 50,000
Accounts receivable (net)	76,000
Inventories	37,000
Prepaid expenses	1,000
Property, plant, and equipment (net)	64,000
Total assets	$228,000

(continued)

	Increase (Decrease)
Liabilities	
Accounts payable	$ (55,500)
Notes payable — current	(15,000)
Accrued expenses	33,000
Bonds payable	(28,000)
Less unamortized bond discount	1,200
Total liabilities	$ (64,300)
Stockholders' Equity	
Common stock, $10 par	$ 500,000
Paid-in capital in excess of par value	200,000
Retained earnings	(437,700)
Appropriation of retained earnings for possible future inventory price decline	30,000
Total stockholders' equity	$292,300
Total liabilities and stockholders' equity	$228,000

Additional information includes:

    (a) The net income for the year ended December 31, 1977, was $172,300. There were no extraordinary items.

    (b) During the year ended December 31, 1977, uncollectible accounts receivable of $26,400 were written off by a debit to Allowance for Doubtful Accounts.

    (c) A comparison of Property, Plant, and Equipment as of the end of each year follows:

	December 31		Increase
	1977	1976	(Decrease)
Property, plant, and equipment	$570,500	$510,000	$60,500
Less accumulated depreciation	224,500	228,000	(3,500)
Property, plant, and equipment (net)	$346,000	$282,000	$64,000

During 1977, machinery was purchased at a cost of $45,000. In addition, machinery that was acquired in 1970 at a cost of $48,000 was sold for $3,600. At the date of sale, the machinery had an undepreciated cost of $4,200. The remaining increase in Property, Plant, and Equipment resulted from the acquisition of a tract of land for a new plant site.

    (d) The bonds payable mature at the rate of $28,000 every year.

    (e) In January 1977, the company issued an additional 10,000 shares of its common stock at $14 per share upon the exercise of outstanding stock options held by key employees. In May 1977, the company declared and issued a 5% stock dividend on its outstanding stock. During the year, a cash dividend was paid on the common stock. On December 31, 1977, there were 840,000 shares of common stock outstanding.

    (f) The appropriation of retained earnings for possible future inventory price declines was provided by a debit to Retained Earnings, in anticipation of an expected future drop in the market related to goods in inventory.

Instructions:

    (1) Prepare a statement of changes in financial position for the year ended December 31, 1977, based upon the information presented. The statement should be prepared using a working capital format.

    (2) Prepare a schedule of changes in working capital for the year 1977. (AICPA adapted)

24-11. The schedule on page 719 shows the account balances of the Relgne Corporation at the beginning and end of the fiscal year ended October 31, 1977.

The following information was also available:

    (a) All purchases and sales were on account.

    (b) The sinking fund will be used to retire the long-term bonds.

    (c) Equipment with an original cost of $15,000 was sold for $7,000.

Debits	October 31, 1977	November 1, 1976	Increase (Decrease)
Cash	$ 226,000	$ 50,000	$176,000
Accounts Receivable	148,000	100,000	48,000
Inventories	291,000	300,000	(9,000)
Prepaid Insurance	2,500	2,000	500
Long-Term Investments (at cost)	10,000	40,000	(30,000)
Sinking Fund	90,000	80,000	10,000
Land and Building	195,000	195,000	
Equipment	215,000	90,000	125,000
Discount on Bonds Payable	8,500	9,000	(500)
Treasury Stock (at cost)	5,000	10,000	(5,000)
Cost of Goods Sold	539,000		
Selling and General Expenses	287,000		
Income Tax	35,000		
Loss on Sale of Equipment	1,000		
Total debits	$2,053,000	$876,000	

Credits			
Allowance for Doubtful Accounts	$ 8,000	$ 5,000	3,000
Accumulated Depreciation — Building	26,250	22,500	3,750
Accumulated Depreciation — Equipment	39,750	27,500	12,250
Accounts Payable	55,000	60,000	(5,000)
Notes Payable — current	70,000	20,000	50,000
Miscellaneous Expenses Payable	18,000	15,000	3,000
Taxes Payable	35,000	10,000	25,000
Unearned Revenue	1,000	9,000	(8,000)
Note Payable — Long-Term	40,000	60,000	(20,000)
Bonds Payable — Long-Term	250,000	250,000	
Common Stock	300,000	200,000	100,000
Retained Earnings Appropriated for Sinking Fund	90,000	80,000	10,000
Unappropriated Retained Earnings	94,000	112,000	(18,000)
Paid-In Capital in Excess of Par Value	116,000	5,000	111,000
Sales	898,000		
Gain on Sale of Investments	12,000		
Total credits	$2,053,000	$876,000	

(d) Selling and general expenses include the following expenses:

Building depreciation	$ 3,750
Equipment depreciation	19,250
Doubtful accounts expense	4,000
Interest expense	18,000

(e) A six-months note payable for $50,000 was issued toward the purchase of new equipment.

(f) The long-term note payable requires the payment of $20,000 per year plus interest until paid.

(g) Treasury stock was sold for $1,000 more than its cost.

(h) All dividends were paid by cash.

Instructions:

(1) Prepare schedules computing: (a) collections of accounts receivable; (b) payments of accounts payable.

(2) Prepare a statement of changes in financial position applying the cash concept of funds. Supporting computations should be in good form. (AICPA adapted)

24-12. You have been contacted by the president of Boulder Company, Inc. This company has never retained the services of a public accountant, all financial statements and tax returns having been prepared by the comptroller.

The president is disturbed that the net working capital and cash balances at December 31, 1977, are substantially lower than those of the previous year despite the fact that the income for 1977 before tax of $176,500 was $350,000.

You have been given the financial statements shown on page 720 and have satisfied yourself as to the correctness of the figures shown.

Boulder Company, Inc.
Comparative Balance Sheet
December 31

	1977	1976	Increase (Decrease)
Assets			
Cash in bank..	$ 42,000	$129,000	$ (87,000)
Accounts receivable (net of allowance for doubtful accounts)..	133,000	85,500	47,500
Inventories..	192,000	152,500	39,500
Land, buildings, and equipment (net of accumulated depreciation)..	500,000	260,000	240,000
Deposits — utilities	4,000	3,200	800
Prepaid expenses..	21,000	14,000	7,000
Total assets...	$892,000	$644,200	$247,800
Liabilities and Stockholders' Equity			
Accounts payable and miscellaneous payables.......	$263,000	$220,850	$ 42,150
Income tax payable..	176,500	61,850	114,650
Mortgage payable	—	125,000	(125,000)
Capital stock..	150,000	100,000	50,000
Retained earnings..	302,500	136,500	166,000
Total liabilities and stockholders' equity	$892,000	$644,200	$247,800

Boulder Company, Inc.
Retained Earnings Statement
For Year Ended December 31, 1977

Balance, January 1, 1977...	$136,500
Add net income for the year..	173,500
	$310,000
Deduct dividends paid	7,500
Balance, December 31, 1977..	$302,500

You also have obtained the following information:

      (a) At December 31, the accumulated depreciation on fixed assets was $180,000 in 1977 and $160,000 in 1976. Machinery costing $20,000, which was one-half depreciated, was abandoned and written off in 1977. Manufacturing costs absorbed depreciation of $27,000 and selling and administrative expense absorbed $3,000.

      (b) In 1977, sales were $3,300,000; cost of goods sold was $2,650,000 and selling and administrative expense (excluding taxes) was $290,000.

      (c) On January 2, 1977, two insurance policies on material stored in a public warehouse were canceled. The unexpired premiums on these policies amounted to $2,000, and refund of this amount was received from the insurance company. Insurance charged to manufacturing expense was $4,000 and to selling and administrative expense $500 for the year. Other prepaid expense write-offs were $12,000 to manufacturing expense.

      (d) The balance in the allowance for doubtful accounts at each year-end was 5% of the gross amount of receivables. Write-off of receivables amounted to $2,300 in 1977.

Instructions:

      (1) Prepare a statement reporting the changes in financial position accounting for the decrease in working capital.

      (2) Prepare a statement reporting the changes in financial position accounting for the decrease in cash. Support this statement with details in good form showing how you arrived at cash required for sales, cost of goods sold, and expenses. (AICPA adapted)

24-13. The comparative balance sheet for the Plainview Corporation is shown on page 721. Your workpapers and other sources disclose additional information on 1977 activities:

      (a) The retained earnings account was analyzed as shown below and on page 721.

Retained earnings, December 31, 1976	$758,200
Add net income...	236,580
	$994,780

Plainview Corporation
Comparative Balance Sheet
December 31

	1977	1976	Increase (Decrease)
Assets			
Cash	$ 142,100	$ 165,300	$ (23,200)
Marketable securities (at cost)	122,800	129,200	(6,400)
Accounts receivable (net)	312,000	371,200	(59,200)
Inventories	255,200	124,100	131,100
Prepaid expenses	23,400	22,000	1,400
Bond sinking fund		63,000	(63,000)
Investment in subsidiary (at equity)	134,080	152,000	(17,920)
Land, buildings, and equipment (net)	1,443,700	1,534,600	(90,900)
Total assets	$2,433,280	$2,561,400	$ (128,120)
Liabilities and Stockholders' Equity			
Accounts payable	$ 238,100	$ 213,300	$ 24,800
Notes payable — current		145,000	(145,000)
Miscellaneous payables	16,500	18,000	(1,500)
Income tax payable	97,500	31,000	66,500
Deferred income tax payable	53,900	43,400	10,500
6% Mortgage bonds (due 1989)		300,000	(300,000)
Premium on mortgage bonds		10,000	(10,000)
8% Debentures (due 1997)	125,000		125,000
Liability for estimated casualty losses	74,000	85,000	(11,000)
Common stock, $10 par value	1,033,500	950,000	83,500
Premium on common stock	67,700	51,000	16,700
Retained earnings	761,580	758,200	3,380
Treasury stock — at cost of $3 per share	(34,500)	(43,500)	9,000
Total liabilities and stockholders' equity	$2,433,280	$2,561,400	$ (128,120)

Deduct:		
Cash dividends	$130,000	
Loss on reissue of treasury stock	3,000	
10% stock dividend	100,200	$233,200
Retained earnings, December 31, 1977		$761,580

You noted that the client's determination of net income complied with Opinion No. 9 and Opinion No. 30 of the Accounting Principles Board and Statement No. 4 of the Financial Accounting Standards Board.

(b) On January 2, 1977, marketable securities costing $110,000 were sol. for $127,000. The proceeds from this sale, the funds in the bond sinking fund, and the amount received from the issuance of the 8% debentures were used to retire the 6% mortgage bonds.

(c) The treasury stock was reissued on February 28, 1977.

(d) The stock dividend was declared on October 31, 1977, when the market price of Plainview Corporation's stock was $12 per share.

(e) On April 30, 1977, a fire destroyed a warehouse costing $100,000 and upon which depreciation of $65,000 had accumulated. The deferred income tax payable relating to the difference between tax and book depreciation on the warehouse was $12,700. The loss was debited to Liability for Estimated Casualty Losses.

(f) Building and equipment transactions consisted of the sale of a building at its book value of $4,000 and the purchase of equipment for $28,000.

(g) In 1977, a $30,000 debit was made to accumulated depreciation for excessive depreciation taken in prior years but disallowed by the Internal Revenue Service. A tax deficiency of $16,000 was paid and debited to Deferred Income Tax.

(h) Accounts receivable written off as uncollectible were $16,300 in 1976 and $18,500 in 1977. Expired insurance recorded in 1976 was $4,100 and $3,900 in 1977.

(i) The subsidiary, which is 80% owned, reported a loss of $22,400 for 1977.

Instructions: Prepare a formal statement of changes in financial position (working capital) for the year ended December 31, 1977. Include supporting schedules in good form. (AICPA adapted)

Financial Statements Reporting Price Changes

Traditionally, financial statements have reflected transactions recorded in terms of the number of dollars exchanged. These statements are often referred to as *historical-cost* or *historical-dollar* statements. The primary reason for reporting original dollar amounts is their objectivity. Historical costs generally are based on arms-length transactions and measure appropriate exchange values at the transaction date.

With the steady increase in prices over the past several years, there has been a growing awareness of the limitations of historical-dollar statements. Fluctuations in the general purchasing power of the dollar and significantly increased replacement costs of certain assets make it difficult to interpret the dollar amounts reported in conventional statements. Thus, the validity of the analytical data provided by historical-dollar statements has been challenged and has caused accountants to consider providing financial data reflecting price changes.

GENERAL PRICE-LEVEL CHANGES VS. SPECIFIC PRICE CHANGES

There are two kinds of price changes that must be accounted for. The first deals with changes in the general price level for all commodities. In periods of rising prices this concept is generally referred to as *inflation*. The second kind of price change relates to changes in the specific prices of particular items. Prices for individual items may fluctuate up or down and by differing magnitudes; the average of all specific price changes determines the change in the general price level. With respect to terminology, accounting for the first kind of price change is referred to as general price-level adjusted accounting or simply *price-level accounting*. Accounting for the second kind of price change is referred to as *current or fair value accounting*. This distinction is important for understanding the reporting alternatives identified in the next section.

REPORTING ALTERNATIVES

Several alternatives to reporting financial statements on an historical-cost basis have been proposed. The major proposals, including the currently used historical-cost basis, may be classified as follows:

	Historical Cost Basis	Current Value Basis
Dollar Measurement	1	3
Purchasing Power Measurement	2	4

It is important to distinguish among the alternatives identified. Cell 1 represents the present basis of financial reporting. Historical costs, representing the exchange prices of transactions, are measured in terms of dollars. This is contrasted with Cell 2 which maintains the historical-cost valuation basis but changes the unit of measurement from dollars to *purchasing power units,* i.e., the amount of goods or services which can be purchased given a general price level. This concept is explained in greater detail later in this chapter. Cell 3 is a significant departure from current practice. While the dollar is still the measurement unit, a new basis of valuation is used. The current value basis may utilize replacement costs, sales values, net realizable values, or economic values (i.e., discounted cash flows). The issues relating to current values are also discussed in a later section of this chapter. The fourth cell is a combination of the concepts incorporated in Cells 2 and 3. Current values are used but adjustments are also made for purchasing power changes.

This chapter discusses these alternatives, with emphasis being placed on reporting general price-level changes (Cell 2) because this alternative has received considerable support for a number of years and because the concepts and techniques required for general price-level restatement are useful for understanding the other alternatives.

GENERAL PRICE-LEVEL ADJUSTMENTS

As mentioned, in the accounting process, transactions traditionally are recorded in terms of the number of dollars exchanged. Contrary to the assumption that the dollar is a stable monetary unit, dollar measurements represent diverse amounts of purchasing power. The dollar is an abstraction which has significance only in reference to a particular level of prices. Unless adjustments are made, a reader of financial statements is likely to regard a dollar in terms of its current general purchasing power rather than its general purchasing power at the time it was exchanged. Thus, the objective of general price-level adjustments is to convert all dollar measurements into equivalent purchasing power units so that a company's position and progress may be viewed in proper perspective.

To illustrate, it would not seem proper to add 100 U.S. dollars to 100 British pounds to obtain 200 of something. It would seem necessary to first convert one of the figures to its exchange equivalent before proceeding with arithmetic operations. Similarly, it would seem appropriate to convert the number of dollars expended years ago for land or buildings into equivalent purchasing power units of dollars expended currently for merchandise in arriving at a meaningful asset total. This conversion of historical-dollar amounts to equivalent purchasing power units is the essence of general price-level restatement. Note that historical costs, the original exchange values, are maintained as the valuation basis, but are adjusted for changes in the general price level. The basis of measurement changes from dollar amounts to equivalent purchasing power units. The conversion is accomplished by using price indexes.

Price-Level Indexes

The value or purchasing power of a monetary unit is inversely related to the price of goods or services for which it can be exchanged. Over a period of time, the prices of specific goods or services will move up or down depending upon their relative scarcity and desirability. It would be possible to adjust for specific items, but those prices may change more or less than, or in the opposite direction from, a change in the general price level. The movements of the price structure for goods and services as a whole are referred to as inflation or deflation.

The general level of prices cannot be measured in absolute terms, but the relative changes from period to period and the direction of change can be determined. To measure the changes in general price level, a sample of commodities is selected and the current prices of these items are compared with their prices during a base period. The prices during the base period are assigned a value of 100, and the prices of all other periods are expressed as percentages of this amount. The resulting series of numbers is called a *price-level index*.

Price-level indexes can be valuable aids in judging the extent of inflation or deflation. However, there are limitations in these measurements. In the first place, all price indexes are based upon a sampling process. Since all prices do not fluctuate in the same degree or direction, the selection of commodities to be included and their relative weights have important bearings on the computed values. In addition, improvements in the products included in the sample affect the general level of prices, but qualitative changes are difficult to measure.

Although no perfect means of measuring the changing value of the dollar has yet been devised, indexes have been developed providing reasonable estimates of the overall change in the dollar's general purchasing power. Among these are the Consumer Price Index and the Wholesale Price Index, both provided by the Bureau of Labor Statistics, and the GNP (Gross National Product) Implicit Price Deflator provided by the Department of Commerce.

Each of these indexes exhibits a similar pattern of price-level change, but the indexes report different values. This is because each index is based upon the prices of a different group of items. Users of financial statements represent a broader interest than just consumers or those concerned about a particular industry. Therefore, for general purpose statements adjusted for changes in the general price level, it makes sense to use a broadly based index. Because the GNP Implicit Price Deflator represents the most comprehensive indicator of the general price level in the United States, accounting authorities have recommended its use in restating financial statements for general price-level changes. The GNP Deflator provides price indexes in terms of annual averages beginning with 1929 and also quarterly averages beginning with 1947. In the absence of end-of-year price-level measurements, the deflator for the last quarter of the year is normally used to approximate the price index at the end of the year. A summary of annual averages for the GNP index follows:

GNP Index

Year	GNP Implicit Price Deflator
	(1972 = 100)
1945	40.9
1950	54.9
1955	62.2
1960	70.7
1965	75.9
1966	78.0
1967	80.3
1968	83.7
1969	88.0
1970	93.0
1971	96.8
1972	100.0
1973	105.9
1974	116.2
1975	126.4

Source: United States Department of Commerce, Bureau of Economic Analysis, Bureau of Labor Statistics.

Effects of General Price-Level Changes on Monetary and Nonmonetary Items

In recognizing the effects of general price-level changes, it is necessary to distinguish between monetary items and nonmonetary items. *Monetary items* are those assets and liabilities whose dollar balances are fixed in terms of numbers of dollars regardless of changes in the general price level. All other items not representing a right to receive or an obligation to pay a fixed sum are *nonmonetary*.

Monetary assets include cash as well as such items as accounts receivable, notes receivable, loans to employees, cash surrender value of life insurance, and certain marketable securities, such as bonds that are expected to be held to maturity and redeemed at a fixed number of dollars. Regardless of the changes taking place in the general price level, these balances are fixed and provide for the recovery of neither more nor less than the stated amounts. Monetary liabilities include such items as accounts payable, notes payable, cash dividends payable, and the fixed payment amounts for accruals under pension plans. Regardless of the changes taking place in the price level, these balances are fixed and call for the payment of neither more nor less than the stated amounts. By holding monetary assets or liabilities, one realizes purchasing-power gains or losses — price-level gains or losses not disclosed in conventional reporting.

For example, assume a person placed $1,000 in cash under the mattress for "safekeeping" when the price level was 100%. If the price level were to rise to 110% a year later, the individual would have suffered a purchasing-power loss because it would require $1,100 to purchase the same amount of goods that $1,000 would have bought a year ago. On the other hand, a debt of $1,000 payable a year later, again assuming an increase in the price level to 110% from 100%, would result in a purchasing-power gain. The equivalent purchasing power should be $1,100 yet the debt can be settled for the fixed amount of $1,000.

Nonmonetary assets include such items as inventories and supplies; prepaid expenses; land, buildings, and equipment; intangible assets; and deferred income tax debits. These items derive their nonmonetary classification because with changes in the general price level, the dollar amounts at which they are reported on the conventional financial statements will differ from the dollar resources they actually represent. On the other hand, nonmonetary liabilities include such items as deferred revenues, advances on sales contracts, deferred income tax credits, and warranties on goods sold. These items derive their nonmonetary classification because with changes in the general price level, the dollar demands they will actually make will differ from the dollar amounts reported on the conventional financial statements.[1]

The distinction between monetary and nonmonetary items is not related to the current and noncurrent classifications used for assets and liabilities. For example, monetary assets include current assets, such as accounts receivable, and also noncurrent assets, such as long-term investments in bonds; nonmonetary assets include current items, such as inventories and supplies, and noncurrent items, such as land, buildings, and equipment. Monetary liabilities include current items, such as accounts and notes payable, and noncurrent items, such as bonds payable; nonmonetary liabilities include current items, such as advances on sales contracts, and noncurrent items, such as long-term sales warranties.

The difference between a company's monetary assets and its monetary liabilities is referred to as its *net monetary position*. With the number of dollars relating to monetary items remaining fixed, and reflecting current dollars regardless of the change in the price level, general price-level gains and losses arise as prices change. In any given period, the gain or loss from holding monetary assets is offset by the loss or gain from maintaining monetary liabilities. The net gain or loss for a period, then, depends upon whether a company's position in net monetary items is positive — monetary assets exceeding monetary liabilities — or negative — monetary liabilities exceeding monetary assets. Gains and losses are associated with a company's monetary assets, monetary liabilities, and net monetary position as follows:

	Rising Prices	Declining Prices
Positive Net Monetary Position	Loss	Gain
Negative Net Monetary Position	Gain	Loss

[1]Ordinarily the stockholders' equity would be regarded as a nonmonetary item. However, an exception may be made with respect to the equity represented by nonconvertible, callable, preferred stock. When preferred stock can be retired at a fixed-dollar amount, it is regarded as a monetary item. A comprehensive list of balance sheet items and their classification as monetary and nonmonetary items, together with an explanation of the reason for classification, is given in Accounting Principles Board Statement No. 3, Appendix B.

Restating Financial Statements for General Price-Level Changes

The process of restating financial statements for general price-level changes involves restating the dollar balances in conventional statements to their equivalent purchasing power units, generally in terms of the current period.[1] The formula for restatement in terms of current year purchasing power units is:

$$\text{Historical-Cost Dollar Amounts of Nonmonetary Assets and Liabilities} \times \frac{\text{Index at End of Current Period}}{\text{Index at Date Nonmonetary Asset Was Acquired or Nonmonetary Liability Was Incurred}}$$

Nonmonetary assets are generally reported on the financial statements at the number of dollars originally paid upon acquisition; nonmonetary liabilities are reported at the number of dollars originally received; and nonmonetary capital balances are stated at the number of dollars originally received from stockholders and accumulated through earnings. Restating these balances requires recognition of the change in the price level since the time each transaction within these groups took place. The monetary assets and liabilities state amounts recognized as representing current dollars. These items, therefore, do not require restatement.

A number of simple examples will be given to illustrate the restatement of financial data in terms of dollars of uniform purchasing power and to suggest the nature of the analysis afforded by these data. These examples will be followed by an extended illustration in which financial statements summarizing operations of successive periods are restated. In each of the examples in the following section, the activities of a company for the first year of its life are given. It is assumed in the examples that the general price level moves up evenly throughout the year and produces a 5% rise for the year.

Example 1 — Nonmonetary assets are held during the year. Assume a company issues capital stock of $50,000 in exchange for land valued at $50,000. The company holds the land during the year without engaging in any other activities. A balance sheet prepared in conventional form at the end of the year will show both land and invested capital at their original amounts. In preparing a balance sheet expressing financial position in terms of the price level at the end of the year, however, land and capital stock will be reported as follows:

1. Land, a nonmonetary asset, needs to be restated for the change in price level since its acquisition. Land, with an acquisition cost of $50,000, is expressed in current dollars at $50,000 × 105/100, or $52,500.[2]
2. Capital stock, a nonmonetary item, also requires restatement so that it expresses the stockholders' investment in terms of the current price level. The capital stock balance is expressed in current dollars at $50,000 × 105/100, or $52,500.

---

[1]Obviously, it is possible to convert original costs to purchasing power units at a date other than the current period by using the index of whatever year is desired as the base year. However, it is usually more meaningful to convert to the current year.

[2]It is possible to use conversion rates which express the relationship of one index to another. Thus, in the example cited, 105/100 may be stated as a conversion rate of 1.05. When the restatement process is a lengthy one but requires the use of relatively few conversion factors, it is generally convenient to prepare a table of values stated in quotients and apply these values to the individual items requiring restatement.

A balance sheet restated to report resources and the stockholders' equity in terms of the price level prevailing at the end of the year follows:

Balance Sheet at End of Year Reporting General Price-Level Changes

	Historical Amount	Conversion Factor	Restated Amount
Land	$50,000	105/100	$52,500
Capital stock	$50,000	105/100	$52,500

A comparative balance sheet for the company prepared in conventional form will show the asset and stockholders' equity balances at the end of the year to be the same as the balances at the beginning of the year. A comparative balance sheet expressed in terms of the purchasing power of the dollar at the end of the year will also show account balances to have remained unchanged. In preparing adjusted comparative data, beginning balances must be updated or "rolled forward" so that they are stated in a manner permitting comparisons with the statements prepared currently. Updating the balance sheet does not indicate earlier balances were misstated; it is simply a means of changing the form of the information in terms of a later unit of measure. A balance sheet comparing beginning and ending balances in dollars of uniform purchasing power follows:

Comparative Balance Sheet Reporting General Price-Level Changes

	Beginning of Year			End of Year	Increase (Decrease)
	Historical Amount	Conversion Factor	Restated Amount		
Land	$50,000	105/100	$52,500	$52,500	——
Capital stock	$50,000	105/100	$52,500	$52,500	——

The comparative balance sheet shows that company resources and the stockholders' equity have not changed during the year. In the absence of monetary items, there has been neither price-level gain nor loss arising from the decline in the purchasing power of the dollar in a period of price-level advance.

Example 2 — Monetary and nonmonetary assets are held and monetary liabilities are maintained during the year. Assume a company issues capital stock of $75,000 in exchange for cash of $25,000 and land valued at $100,000 subject to a mortgage note of $50,000. This represents a negative net monetary position because monetary liabilities exceed monetary assets. As indicated in the diagram on page 726, in an inflationary trend, this will result in a gain. The assets are held and the liability is maintained throughout the year without any accrual of revenue or expense. A balance sheet prepared in conventional form at the end of the year shows asset, liability, and stockholders' equity balances at their original amounts. However, in preparing a balance sheet in terms of the price level at the end of the year, balances would be as follows:

1. Cash is a monetary asset, a resource of fixed-dollar amount, that has not changed with the change in the purchasing power of the dollar. The cash balance, then, is reported at $25,000.
2. Land is restated in terms of the current price level at $100,000 × 105/100, or $105,000.
3. The mortgage note is a monetary item, a legal obligation of fixed-dollar amount, that has not changed with the change in purchasing power of the dollar. The mortgage note, then, is reported at $50,000.
4. The capital stock balance is restated in terms of the current price level at $75,000 × 105/100, or $78,750.
5. The stockholders' equity must be reported at an amount equal to the net assets as restated, or $80,000. With the original investment by stockholders expressed in terms of the current price level at $78,750, there has been an increase in the stockholders' equity of $1,250. Since there were no transactions during the year, the increase in the stockholders' equity indicates a price-level gain from the increase in the purchasing power of the company's net monetary position during the year.

A balance sheet restated to report balances in terms of the price level prevailing at the end of the year and a schedule reporting the change in the stockholders' equity resulting from the change in price level during the year follow:

Balance Sheet at End of Year Reporting General Price-Level Changes

	Historical Amount	Conversion Factor	Restated Amount
Cash	$ 25,000		$ 25,000
Land	100,000	105/100	105,000
	$125,000		$130,000
Mortgage note payable	$ 50,000		$ 50,000
Capital stock	75,000	105/100	78,750
Retained earnings	—	(see schedule)	1,250
	$125,000		$130,000

Schedule Reporting General Price-Level Gain or Loss for Year

	Historical Amount	Conversion Factor	Restated Amount
Excess of monetary liabilities over monetary assets at beginning of year	$ 25,000	105/100	$ 26,250
Excess of monetary liabilities over monetary assets at end of year			25,000
General price-level gain			$ 1,250

A comparative balance sheet prepared in conventional form will show asset, liability, and stockholders' equity balances as unchanged for the year. However, a comparative balance sheet expressed in terms of the purchasing power of the dollar at the end of the year shows that changes did take place. A comparative balance sheet reporting beginning and ending balances in dollars of uniform purchasing power appears at the top of the next page.

Although no transactions took place during the year, the comparative balance sheet shows there was an increase in the stockholders' equity.

Comparative Balance Sheet Reporting General Price-Level Changes

	Beginning of Year			End of Year	Increase (Decrease)
	Historical Amount	Conversion Factor	Restated Amount		
Cash	$ 25,000	105/100	$ 26,250	$ 25,000	$(1,250)
Land	100,000	105/100	105,000	105,000	
	$125,000		$131,250	$130,000	$(1,250)
Mortgage note payable....	$ 50,000	105/100	$ 52,500	$ 50,000	$(2,500)
Capital stock...................	75,000	105/100	78,750	78,750	
Retained earnings............	——		——	1,250	1,250
	$125,000		$131,250	$130,000	$(1,250)

This increase resulted from a price-level gain identified with a financial position in which monetary liabilities exceeded monetary assets during a period of price-level advance.

Example 3 — Monetary assets are increased by proceeds from sale of property at year end and as a result of operations during the year. Assume a company issues capital stock of $75,000 in exchange for cash of $25,000 and land valued at $50,000. The land is sold at the end of the year for cash of $60,000. Services are performed during the year resulting in operating income of $20,000; earnings accrue evenly, and at the end of the year cash is $102,500 and accounts receivable are $2,500. A balance sheet prepared in conventional form will show increases in assets of $30,000 accompanied by a corresponding increase in retained earnings. However, in preparing a balance sheet in terms of the price level at the end of the year, balances are reported as follows:

1. Cash is reported at $102,500.
2. Accounts receivable is a monetary asset, a resource of fixed-dollar amount, and is reported at $2,500.
3. The capital stock balance is restated in terms of the current price level at $75,000 × 105/100, or $78,750.
4. The stockholders' equity must be reported at an amount equal to total net assets, or $105,000. Since the original investment by stockholders in terms of the current price level is $78,750, there has been an increase in the stockholders' equity for the year of $26,250. Three factors explain this change: (a) the sale of land, (b) operations for the year, and (c) the change in the price level. The gain on the sale of land expressed in terms of the price level at the end of the period is $7,500 — the cost of the land in terms of the year-end price level, $52,500 ($50,000 × 105/100), as compared with a sales price at the time of $60,000. The earnings from operations, $20,000, are assumed to have accrued evenly during the year and may be regarded as reflecting earnings in terms of the average price level for the year. The reported figure is adjusted to end-of-year dollars by the following computation:

$$\$20,000 \times 105/102.5 = \$20,488^{[1]}$$

The price-level loss for the year consists of that sustained on the monetary assets held throughout the year as well as on the monetary assets that became available during the year. The computations are shown in the Schedule Reporting General Price-Level Gain or Loss for Year on page 731.

---

[1]It may be observed that if the prices rose evenly during the year, the price rise for the first half-year would be 102.5/100 and the price rise for the second half-year would be 105/102.5: the rate of increase, then, in the second half of the year is not equal to that which took place in the first half of the year.

In reporting the stockholders' equity on the balance sheet, then, capital stock as restated is accompanied by retained earnings summarizing three factors responsible for the change in the stockholders' equity — the gain on the sale of land, operating income, and the price-level loss. A statement of income and retained earnings supported by a schedule to show the computation of the price-level loss, and a balance sheet follow:

Income and Retained Earnings Statement for Year
Reporting General Price-Level Changes

	Historical Amount	Conversion Factor	Restated Amount
Sale of land (at end of year)	$60,000	105/105	$60,000
Cost of land	50,000	105/100	52,500
Gain on sale of land	$10,000		$ 7,500
Operating income (realized evenly throughout year)	20,000	105/102.5	20,488
Total	$30,000		$27,988
Deduct general price-level loss (see schedule)	——		1,738
Retained earnings at end of year	$30,000		$26,250

Schedule Reporting General Price-Level Gain or Loss for Year

	Historical Amount	Conversion Factor	Restated Amount
Monetary position at beginning of year	$ 25,000	105/100	$ 26,250
Increase in monetary assets:			
From sale of land at end of year	60,000	105/105	60,000
From operations	20,000	105/102.5	20,488
			$106,738
Monetary position at end of year	$105,000		105,000
General price-level loss			$ 1,738

Balance Sheet at End of Year Reporting General Price-Level Changes

	Historical Amount	Conversion Factor	Restated Amount
Cash	$102,500		$102,500
Accounts receivable	2,500		2,500
	$105,000		$105,000
Capital stock	$ 75,000	105/100	$ 78,750
Retained earnings	30,000		26,250
	$105,000		$105,000

Assuming the facts given, a comparative balance sheet prepared in conventional form will show an increase in the stockholders' equity of $30,000. However, a comparative balance sheet expressed in terms of the purchasing power of the dollar at the end of the year will show an increase in the stockholders' equity of only $26,250. A balance sheet comparing beginning and ending balances in dollars of uniform purchasing power is shown at the top of the next page.

The comparative balance sheet shows the change in the financial position was not as favorable as that shown on a similar statement prepared in conventional form. The gain on the sale of property, when cost and

Comparative Balance Sheet Reporting General Price-Level Changes

| | Beginning of Year | | | | |
	Historical Amount	Conversion Factor	Restated Amount	End of Year	Increase (Decrease)
Cash	$25,000	105/100	$26,250	$102,500	$ 76,250
Accounts receivable	—			2,500	2,500
Land	50,000	105/100	52,500	—	(52,500)
	$75,000		$78,750	$105,000	$ 26,250
Capital stock	$75,000	105/100	$78,750	$ 78,750	—
Retained earnings	—		—	26,250	$ 26,250
	$75,000		$78,750	$105,000	$ 26,250

sales prices are expressed in terms of the purchasing power of the dollar at the end of the year, was only $7,500. The operating income, when restated in terms of the year-end level, was $20,488, providing a gross increase of $27,988. However, the net increase in the stockholders' equity after recognizing the price-level loss from holding monetary assets in a period of price-level advance was limited to $26,250.

PREPARATION OF FINANCIAL STATEMENTS RESTATED FOR GENERAL PRICE-LEVEL CHANGES ILLUSTRATED

The following illustration indicates the basic procedures followed in restating financial statements in successive periods to reflect general price-level changes. The illustration covers operations of a company for the first two years of its life. Financial statements for the first and second years are provided in their conventional forms. Financial statements are restated at the end of the first year and at the end of the second year in terms of the price levels prevailing at each of these times.[1]

The illustration assumes the following:

1. Price-level index numbers were:

At the time the business was formed	100
At the end of the first year	104
At the end of the second year	108

   The price level rose evenly throughout each year. The average index for the first year, then, was 102; the average index for the second year was 106.
2. Sales and purchases were made evenly and expenses were incurred evenly throughout each year.
3. Inventories were valued at cost calculated by the first-in, first-out method.
4. Dividends were declared and paid at the end of each year.
5. Buildings had a useful life of 10 years and depreciation was recognized at $5,000 per year.

A comparative income and retained earnings statement reporting operations of the company for the first and second years and a comparative

---

[1]The illustration is limited to the restatement of financial data presented on the income and retained earnings statement and on the balance sheet. In providing a full set of financial statements, a statement of changes in financial position would be required.

balance sheet reporting the financial position of the company upon its organization and at the end of the first and second years appear below.

Comparative Income and Retained Earnings Statement

	First Year	Second Year
Sales	$300,000	$400,000
Cost of goods sold:		
Beginning inventory	$ 55,000	$ 65,000
Purchases	200,000	280,000
Merchandise available for sale	$255,000	$345,000
Ending inventory	65,000	80,000
Cost of goods sold	$190,000	$265,000
Gross profit on sales	$110,000	$135,000
Expenses:		
Depreciation	$ 5,000	$ 5,000
Other expenses	90,000	100,000
Total expenses	$ 95,000	$105,000
Net income	$ 15,000	$ 30,000
Retained earnings at beginning of year	——	10,000
	$ 15,000	$ 40,000
Dividends paid	5,000	10,000
Retained earnings at end of year	$ 10,000	$ 30,000

Comparative Balance Sheet

	Beginning of Business	End of First Year	End of Second Year
Assets			
Cash	$ 60,000	$ 30,000	$ 40,000
Accounts receivable	——	40,000	50,000
Inventory	55,000	65,000	80,000
Land	35,000	35,000	35,000
Buildings (net)	50,000	45,000	40,000
Total assets	$200,000	$215,000	$245,000
Liabilities			
Accounts payable	$ 20,000	$ 25,000	$ 35,000
Mortgage payable	30,000	30,000	30,000
Total liabilities	$ 50,000	$ 55,000	$ 65,000
Stockholders' Equity			
Capital stock	$150,000	$150,000	$150,000
Retained earnings	——	10,000	30,000
Total stockholders' equity	$150,000	$160,000	$180,000
Total liabilities and stockholders' equity	$200,000	$215,000	$245,000

Restated Income and Retained Earnings Statement at the End of the First Year

An income and retained earnings statement for the first year as restated at the end of the first year and a schedule reporting the price-level loss are given on page 734. The following items should be noted.

Sales. Since sales were made evenly throughout the year, the sales balance reflects the average index for the year. To restate the sales balance to end-of-years dollars, it is multiplied by the ratio of the end-of-year index to the average index for the year.

Cost of Goods Sold. The inventory is reported on the first-in, first-out basis. Restatement of cost of goods sold to end-of-year dollars involves the following adjustments:

1. The beginning inventory balance reports costs incurred when the business was organized and therefore reflects the index at the beginning of the year, 100. To restate the beginning inventory to end-of-year dollars, it is multiplied by the ratio of the end-of-year index to the index at the beginning of the year.

Income and Retained Earnings Statement Restated for General Price-Level Changes
For First Year

	Historical Amount	Conversion Factor	Restated Amount
Sales	$300,000	104/102	$305,882
Cost of goods sold:			
Beginning inventory	$ 55,000	104/100	$ 57,200
Purchases	200,000	104/102	203,922
Merchandise available for sale	$255,000		$261,122
Ending inventory	65,000	104/102	66,275
Cost of goods sold	$190,000		$194,847
Gross profit on sales	$110,000		$111,035
Expenses:			
Depreciation	$ 5,000	104/100	$ 5,200
Other expenses	90,000	104/102	91,765
Total expenses	$ 95,000		$ 96,965
Income before adjustment for general price-level gain or loss	$ 15,000		$ 14,070
General price-level loss (see schedule)	—		595
Net income after adjustment for general price-level loss	$ 15,000		$ 13,475
Retained earnings at beginning of year	—		—
	$ 15,000		$ 13,475
Dividends paid	5,000	104/104	5,000
Retained earnings at end of year	$ 10,000		$ 8,475

Schedule Reporting General Price-Level Gain or Loss
For First Year

	Historical Amount		Conversion Factor	Restated Amount
Net monetary position at beginning of year:				
Assets (cash)	$60,000			
Liabilities (accounts payable and mortgage payable)	50,000	$ 10,000	104/100	$ 10,400
Increase in net monetary position during year:				
Sales		300,000	104/102	305,882
		$310,000		$316,282
Decrease in net monetary position during year:				
Purchases		$200,000	104/102	$203,922
Other expenses		90,000	104/102	91,765
Dividends		5,000	104/104	5,000
		$295,000		$300,687
				$ 15,595
Net monetary position at end of year:				
Assets (cash and accounts receivable)	$70,000			
Liabilities (accounts payable and mortgage payable)	55,000	$ 15,000		15,000
General price-level loss				$ 595

2. Purchases were made evenly throughout the year. To restate the purchases balance to end-of-year dollars, it is multiplied by the ratio of the end-of-year index to the average index.
3. In applying first-in, first-out, latest costs were assigned to the ending inventory. The ending inventory, then, may be regarded as composed of purchases of the current period. To restate the ending inventory to end-of-year dollars, it is multiplied by the ratio of the end-of-year index to the average index.[1]

Depreciation. Since the charge for depreciation represents the allocation of the cost of a property item to operations, the adjustment of the depreciation charge must be consistent with the adjustment applicable to the property item. To restate the buildings cost to end-of-year dollars, it is multiplied by the ratio of the end-of-year index to the index at the time the buildings were acquired, in this case the index at the beginning of the year, or 100; to restate the depreciation charge, it is similarly multiplied by the ratio expressing the price-level change since the date buildings were acquired. The charge for depreciation as restated can also be computed by applying the depreciation rate to the cost of the asset stated in terms of end-of-year dollars.

Other Expenses. The other expenses were incurred evenly throughout the year. To restate the other expenses total to end-of-year dollars, it is multiplied by the ratio of the end-of-year index to the average index.

Income before Adjustment for General Price-Level Gain or Loss. Revenue and expense items are summarized to arrive at the income for the year before adjustment for the general price-level gain or loss.

General Price-Level Gain or Loss. The income and retained earnings statement is supported by a schedule reporting the general price-level gain or loss from holding monetary assets and maintaining monetary liabilities in a period of changing prices. The schedule is developed as follows:

1. The difference between the monetary assets and liabilities, net monetary position, at the beginning of the period is restated to an end-of-year dollars balance.
2. Any monetary items becoming available during the year are expressed in terms of end-of-year dollars and are added to or subtracted from the beginning net monetary position balance.
3. The actual monetary assets and the liabilities as of the end of the year are determined. The balance of net monetary position at the end of the year is compared with the sum of (1) and (2) above. In the example, net monetary position at the end of the year would have been $15,595 if the company had maintained its net monetary position during the period of rising prices; since the net monetary position is only $15,000, a loss in purchasing power for the year of $595 was sustained.

---

[1]When there is evidence that the ending inventory is composed of goods acquired within the last half of the year or the last quarter, the average index for such shorter period is properly applied in restating the inventory.

The general price-level gain or loss is reported on the income and retained earnings statement, and the net income after adjustment for the gain or loss is determined.

Dividends. Dividends were declared and paid at the end of the year. The dividends balance, then, reflects end-of-year dollars and is reported without change.

Retained Earnings at the End of the Year. The dividends balance is subtracted from net income after adjustment for the general price-level loss in determining the retained earnings balance at the end of the first year in terms of year-end dollars.

Restated Balance Sheet at the End of the First Year

A balance sheet as restated at the end of the first year is given below.

Balance Sheet Restated for General Price-Level Changes
End of First Year

	Historical Amount	Conversion Factor	Restated Amount
Assets			
Cash	$ 30,000		$ 30,000
Accounts receivable	40,000		40,000
Inventory	65,000	104/102	66,275
Land	35,000	104/100	36,400
Buildings (net)	45,000	104/100	46,800
Total assets	$215,000		$219,475
Liabilities			
Accounts payable	$ 25,000		$ 25,000
Mortgage payable	30,000		30,000
Total liabilities	$ 55,000		$ 55,000
Stockholders' Equity			
Capital stock	$150,000	104/100	$156,000
Retained earnings	10,000*		8,475
Total stockholders' equity	$160,000		$164,475
Total liabilities and stockholders' equity	$215,000		$219,475

*See the income and retained earnings statement on page 734.

Monetary Assets. Monetary assets are reported without change.

Inventory. The ending inventory balance reflects the average index for the year. To restate this balance to end-of-year dollars, it is multiplied by the ratio of the end-of-year index to the average index. The dollar value for the inventory on the balance sheet must be the same as that reported in arriving at cost of goods sold on the income and retained earnings statement.

Land and Buildings. Land and buildings accounts report dollar costs at the time the assets were acquired. To restate land and buildings balances to end-of-year dollars, these are multiplied by the ratio expressing the price-level change since the time they were acquired.

Liabilities. Liabilities, because they are monetary, are reported without change.

Stockholders' Equity. Capital stock expressed in terms of original dollar investment is restated to end-of-year dollars. The retained earnings balance as summarized in terms of end-of-year dollars on the income and retained earnings statement is added to the capital stock balances in arriving at the stockholders' equity. If comparable assumptions and procedures have been employed in developing balances on the income and retained earnings statement and the balance sheet, the statements will be complementary and recognition of the stockholders' equity will bring the balance sheet into balance. If the stockholders' equity is not equal to the difference between the assets and the liabilities, errors or inconsistencies are indicated, and these must be found and corrected.

Restated Comparative Balance Sheet at the End of the First Year

A comparative balance sheet prepared in terms of the current price level is given below.

Comparative Balance Sheet Restated for General Price-Level Changes
End of First Year

	Beginning of Business			End of First Year	Increase (Decrease)
	Historical Amount	Conversion Factor	Restated Amount		
Assets					
Cash	$ 60,000	104/100	$ 62,400	$ 30,000	$ (32,400)
Accounts receivable				40,000	40,000
Inventory	55,000	104/100	57,200	66,275	9,075
Land	35,000	104/100	36,400	36,400	
Buildings (net)	50,000	104/100	52,000	46,800	(5,200)
Total assets	$200,000		$208,000	$219,475	$ 11,475
Liabilities					
Accounts payable	$ 20,000	104/100	$ 20,800	$ 25,000	$ 4,200
Mortgage payable	30,000	104/100	31,200	30,000	(1,200)
Total liabilities	$ 50,000		$ 52,000	$ 55,000	$ 3,000
Stockholders' Equity					
Capital stock	$150,000	104/100	$156,000	$156,000	
Retained earnings				8,475	$ 8,475
Total stockholders' equity	$150,000		$156,000	$164,475	$ 8,475
Total liabilities and stockholders' equity	$200,000		$208,000	$219,475	$ 11,475

Restated Income and Retained Earnings Statement at the End of the Second Year

A statement of income and retained earnings as restated at the end of the second year and a schedule reporting the price-level loss are given on page 738. The following items should be noted:

Income before Adjustment for General Price-Level Gain or Loss. In developing the income and retained earnings statement for the second year, sales, purchases, and other expense balances reflecting the average index for the year are multiplied by the ratio of the price-level index at the end of the second year to the average index for the second year. In developing cost of goods sold, the beginning inventory balance, stated at $65,000, reflecting acquisitions when the index was 102, must be adjusted to a dollar balance in terms of the price level at the end of the second year, 108, and hence is multiplied by 108/102; the ending inventory balance reflecting purchases during the second year is multiplied by the ratio of the index at the end of the second year to the average index for the second year, or 108/106. The charge for depreciation, reported in terms of asset cost, is multiplied by the ratio of the index at the end of

Income and Retained Earnings Statement Restated for General Price-Level Changes
For Second Year

	Historical Amount	Conversion Factor	Restated Amount
Sales	$400,000	108/106	$407,547
Cost of goods sold:			
Beginning inventory	$ 65,000	108/102	$ 68,824
Purchases	280,000	108/106	285,283
Merchandise available for sale	$345,000		$354,107
Ending inventory	80,000	108/106	81,509
Cost of goods sold	$265,000		$272,598
Gross profit on sales	$135,000		$134,949
Expenses:			
Depreciation	$ 5,000	108/100	$ 5,400
Other expenses	100,000	108/106	101,887
Total expenses	$105,000		$107,287
Income before adjustment for general price-level gain or loss	$ 30,000		$ 27,662
General price-level loss (see schedule)	—		954
Net income after adjustment for general price-level loss	$ 30,000		$ 26,708
Retained earnings at beginning of year	10,000	($8,475 × 108/104)	8,801
	$ 40,000		$ 35,509
Dividends paid	10,000	108/108	10,000
Retained earnings at end of year	$ 30,000		$ 25,509

Schedule Reporting General Price-Level Gain or Loss
For Second Year

	Historical Amount		Conversion Factor	Restated Amount
Net monetary position at beginning of year:				
Assets (cash and accounts receivable)	$70,000			
Liabilities (accounts payable and mortgage payable)	55,000	$ 15,000	108/104	$ 15,577
Increase in net monetary position during year:				
Sales		400,000	108/106	407,547
		$415,000		$423,124
Decrease in net monetary position during year:				
Purchases		$280,000	108/106	$285,283
Other expenses		100,000	108/106	101,887
Dividends		10,000	108/108	10,000
		$390,000		$397,170
				$ 25,954
Net monetary position at end of year:				
Assets (cash and accounts receivable)	$90,000			
Liabilities (accounts payable and mortgage payable)	65,000	$ 25,000		25,000
General price-level loss				$ 954

the second year to the index at the date of asset acquisition, or 108/100. Revenue and expense balances are summarized to arrive at the income for the year before adjustment for the general price-level gain or loss.

General Price-Level Gain or Loss. The computation of the price-level gain or loss for the second year is made just as it was for the first year. Beginning net monetary position adjusted for net monetary items becoming available to the company during the second year, expressed in terms of end-of-year balances, are compared with the actual ending net monetary position. This comparison indicates a further loss of purchasing power.

Retained Earnings at the Beginning of the Year. All stockholders' equity balances expressed in terms of end-of-dollars for the first year must be restated to end-of-year dollars for the second year. Retained earnings, then, as reported at the amount shown on the balance sheet at the end of the first year is updated to indicate its equivalent in dollars at the end of the second year.

Dividends. Dividends were declared and paid at the end of the year. The dividends balance, then, reflects end-of-year dollars and is reported without change.

Retained Earnings at the End of the Year. Having determined net income after adjustment for the general price-level change, this is increased by the beginning retained earnings balance as restated in end-of-year dollars and reduced by dividends to arrive at the ending retained earnings balance.

Restated Balance Sheet at the End of the Second Year

A balance sheet at the end of the second year is given below. Monetary assets and liabilities are reported without change. The inventory ac-

Balance Sheet Restated for General Price-Level Changes
End of Second Year

	Historical Amount	Conversion Factor	Restated Amount
Assets			
Cash	$ 40,000		$ 40,000
Accounts receivable	50,000		50,000
Inventory	80,000	108/106	81,509
Land	35,000	108/100	37,800
Building (net)	40,000	108/100	43,200
Total assets	$245,000		$252,509
Liabilities			
Accounts payable	$ 35,000		$ 35,000
Mortgage payable	30,000		30,000
Total liabilities	$ 65,000		$ 65,000
Stockholders' Equity			
Capital stock	$150,000	($156,000 × 108/104)	$162,000
Retained earnings	30,000		25,509
Total stockholders' equity	$180,000		$187,509
Total liabilities and stockholders' equity	$245,000		$252,509

quired during the second year is raised to an end-of-year-dollars balance. Land and buildings reported at dollar amounts at the time the business was organized are adjusted for the change in the price level for the two-year period. Capital stock reported on the balance sheet at the end of the preceding period is updated to report current end-of-year dollars. The retained earnings balance as summarized in terms of end-of-year dollars on the statement of income and retained earnings is added to the capital stock balances in arriving at the stockholders' equity. A schedule reconciling the end-of-year retained earnings figure as shown on the restated balance sheet may be presented as follows:

Schedule Reconciling Retained Earnings Restated for General Price-Level Changes
End of Second Year

	Historical Amount	Conversion Factor	Restated Amount
Retained earnings balance at beginning of second year	$ 8,475*	108/104	$ 8,801
Add item increasing retained earnings:			
Net income for year after adjustment for general price-level loss (from restated income statement)	30,000		26,708
Subtract item decreasing retained earnings:			
Dividends	(10,000)	108/108	(10,000)
Retained earnings balance at end of second year			$ 25,509

*Note that this is not the historical amount of $10,000, but is the restated retained earnings balance as of the end of the first year which needs to be "rolled forward" to report current dollars at the end of the second year.

Restated Comparative Statements at the End of the Second Year

A comparative statement of income and retained earnings and a comparative balance sheet prepared at the end of the second year are given below and on page 741.

Comparative Income and Retained Earnings Statement Restated for General Price-Level Changes
First and Second Years

	First Year Restated to End of First Year	Conversion Factor	Restated to End of Second Year	Second Year	Increase (Decrease)
Sales	$305,882	108/104	$317,647	$407,547	$ 89,900
Cost of goods sold:					
Beginning inventory	$ 57,200	108/104	$ 59,400	$ 68,824	$ 9,424
Purchases	203,922	108/104	211,765	285,283	73,518
Merchandise available for sale	$261,122		$271,165	$354,107	$ 82,942
Ending inventory	66,275	108/104	68,824	81,509	12,685
Cost of goods sold	$194,847		$202,341	$272,598	$ 70,257
Gross profit on sales	$111,035		$115,306	$134,949	$ 19,643
Expenses:					
Depreciation	$ 5,200	108/104	$ 5,400	$ 5,400	——
Other expenses	91,765	108/104	95,295	101,887	$ 6,592
Total expenses	$ 96,965	108/104	$100,695	$107,287	$ 6,592
Income before adjustment for general price-level gain or loss	$ 14,070		$ 14,611	$ 27,662	$ 13,051
General price-level loss	595	108/104	618	954	336
Net income after adjustment for general price-level loss	$ 13,475	108/104	$ 13,993	$ 26,708	$ 12,715
Retained earnings at beginning of year	——		——	8,801	8,801
	$ 13,475		$ 13,993	$ 35,509	$ 21,516
Dividends paid	5,000	108/104	5,192	10,000	4,808
Retained earnings at end of year	$ 8,475		$ 8,801	$ 25,509	$ 16,708

Comparative Balance Sheet Restated for General Price-Level Changes
End of Second Year

	Beginning of Business			End of First Year				Increase (Decrease)	
	Restated to End of First Year	Conversion Factor	Restated to End of Second Year	Restated to End of First Year	Conversion Factor	Restated to End of Second Year	End of Second Year	Beginning of Business to End of First Year	End of First Year to End of Second Year
Assets									
Cash	$ 62,400	108/104	$ 64,800	$ 30,000	108/104	$ 31,154	$ 40,000	$ (33,646)	$ 8,846
Accounts receivable				40,000	108/104	41,538	50,000	41,538	8,462
Inventory	57,200	108/104	59,400	66,275	108/104	68,824	81,509	9,424	12,685
Land	36,400	108/104	37,800	36,400	108/104	37,800	37,800		
Buildings (net)	52,000	108/104	54,000	46,800	108/104	48,600	43,200	(5,400)	(5,400)
Total assets	$208,000		$216,000	$219,475		$227,916	$252,509	$ 11,916	$ 24,593
Liabilities									
Accounts payable	$ 20,800	108/104	$ 21,600	$ 25,000	108/104	$ 25,961	$ 35,000	$ 4,361	$ 9,039
Mortgage payable	31,200	108/104	32,400	30,000	108/104	31,154	30,000	(1,246)	(1,154)
Total liabilities	$ 52,000		$ 54,000	$ 55,000		$ 57,115	$ 65,000	$ 3,115	$ 7,885
Stockholders' Equity									
Capital stock	$156,000	108/104	$162,000	$156,000	108/104	$162,000	$162,000		
Retained earnings				8,475	108/104	8,801	25,509	$ 8,801	$ 16,708
Total stockholders' equity	$156,000		$162,000	$164,475		$170,801	$187,509	$ 8,801	$ 16,708
Total liabilities and stockholders' equity	$208,000		$216,000	$219,475		$227,916	$252,509	$ 11,916	$ 24,593

GENERAL PRICE-LEVEL RESTATEMENTS APPLIED TO INVENTORIES REPORTED UNDER ALTERNATIVE COST-FLOW ASSUMPTIONS

In the preceding illustration, inventories were refelected on a first-in, first-out cost-flow assumption and the implications of this procedure were recognized in restating inventory and cost of goods sold balances. When other cost-flow assumptions are employed, restatements must be modified to recognize the costs reflected in the inventory balances as a result of the alternative assumptions. For example, using the first-in, first-out assumption, the inventory balance reports costs of the inventory in terms of most recent purchases, and accordingly the inventory is re-stated to the prevailing price level by applying an index expressing the price-level change from the time the goods were acquired. If the last-in, first-out procedure is employed, the inventory balance may report a number of cost layers, and different indexes must be applied to express the individual cost layers in terms of the prevailing price level.

To illustrate, assume price-level changes for a two-year period as given in the preceding illustration and a company's inventories and costs during the first two years of its operations as follows:

	First Year	Second Year
Beginning inventory	$100,000	$120,000
Purchases	300,000	400,000
Goods available for sale	$400,000	$520,000
Ending inventory (lifo)	120,000	105,000
Cost of goods sold	$280,000	$415,000

Inventory balances and the cost of goods sold balances would be re-stated as follows:

	Historical Amount		Conversion Factor	Restated Amount
First Year:				
Beginning inventory		$100,000	104/100	$104,000
Purchases		300,000	104/102	305,882
Goods available for sale		$400,000		$409,882
Ending inventory:				
Original balance	$100,000		104/100	$104,000
First-year layer increase	20,000		104/102	20,392
		120,000		124,392
Cost of goods sold		$280,000		$285,490
Second Year:				
Beginning inventory:				
Original balance	$100,000		108/100	$108,000
First-year layer increase	20,000		108/102	21,176
		$120,000		$129,176
Purchases		400,000	108/106	407,547
Goods available for sale		$520,000		$536,723
Ending inventory:				
Original balance	$100,000		108/100	$108,000
First-year layer increase	5,000		108/102	5,294
		105,000		113,294
Cost of goods sold		$415,000		$423,429

The inventory balance at the end of the first year was recognized as composed of two separate layers — a cost assigned to the original inventory balance and an incremental cost layer for the inventory increase for the year. The beginning cost is restated to report the change in the price level since the beginning of the year; the current cost layer is restated to report the difference between the end-of-year index and the average index for the year. The inventory at the end of the second year was recognized as composed of two layers — the cost assigned to the original inventory balance and a portion of the incremental cost related to the first year. The original cost is restated to report the change in the price level since the beginning of the first year; the incremental layer is restated to report the difference between the end-of-second-year index and the average index for the first year.

GENERAL PRICE-LEVEL RESTATEMENTS APPLIED TO DEPRECIABLE PROPERTIES ACQUIRED AT DIFFERENT TIMES

In the illustrations on pages 732–741, there was a single acquisition of depreciable property — the acquisition of buildings when the business was formed. When depreciable properties are acquired at different times, the restatement of depreciable properties becomes more involved. The acquisition dates for the individual property items must be determined and both property balances and depreciation charges must be restated to reflect price-level changes since the various acquisition dates.

To illustrate, assume the general price-level changes for a two-year period are the same as in the preceding illustration, and company purchases of depreciable properties as follows:

Date of Acquisition	Asset	Cost	Useful Life
Beginning of first year	Building	$100,000	25 years
Middle of first year	Equipment	$ 61,200	6 years
Middle of second year	Furniture	$ 42,400	8 years

Assume depreciation charges are calculated on the straight-line basis; salvage values are negligible and are not recognized. The cost of the property items would then be adjusted at the end of the first year as follows:

Asset	Historical Amount	Conversion Factor	Restated Amount
Building	$100,000	104/100	$104,000
Equipment	61,200	104/102	62,400
Total	$161,200		$166,400

The charges for depreciation may be obtained by applying depreciation rates to the restated costs. On the other hand, it is possible to compute depreciation charges by applying the individual conversion factors used in restating the property items to the depreciation charges based on cost. The latter procedure is illustrated at the top of the next page.

Asset	Historical Depreciation Charge	Conversion Factor	Restated Depreciation Charge
Building..	$4,000 (1 yr.)	104/100	$4,160
Equipment	5,100 (½ yr.)	104/102	5,200
Total...	$9,100		$9,360

In determining the balances for the property items to be reported on the balance sheet at the end of the first year, the individual conversion factors are applied to the separate acquisitions and to the related balances for accumulated depreciation. These balances at the end of the first year are derived as follows:

Asset	Historical Amount		Conversion Factor	Restated Amount	
Building cost...............................	$100,000		104/100	$104,000	
Accumulated depreciation.........	4,000		104/100	4,160	
Net..		$ 96,000			$ 99,840
Equipment cost...........................	$ 61,200		104/102	$ 62,400	
Accumulated depreciation.........	5,100		104/102	5,200	
Net..		56,100			57,200
Total....................................		$152,100			$157,040

At the end of the second year, depreciable assets would be restated as follows:

Asset	Historical Amount	Conversion Factor	Restated Amount
Building..	$100,000	108/100	$108,000
Equipment	61,200	108/102	64,800
Furniture	42,400	108/106	43,200
Total...	$203,600		$216,000

Depreciation for the second year would be computed as follows:

Asset	Historical Depreciation Charge	Conversion Factor	Restated Depreciation Charge
Building..	$ 4,000 (1 yr.)	108/100	$ 4,320
Equipment	10,200 (1 yr.)	108/102	10,800
Furniture	2,650 (½ yr.)	108/106	2,700
Total...	$16,850		$17,820

At the end of the second year, cost and accumulated depreciation balances would be restated as follows:

Asset	Historical Amount		Conversion Factor	Restated Amount	
Building cost...............................	$100,000		108/100	$108,000	
Accumulated depreciation.........	8,000		108/100	8,640	
Net..		$ 92,000			$ 99,360
Equipment cost...........................	$ 61,200		108/102	$ 64,800	
Accumulated depreciation.........	15,300		108/102	16,200	
Net..		45,900			48,600
Furniture cost.............................	$ 42,400		108/106	$ 43,200	
Accumulated depreciation.........	2,650		108/106	2,700	
Net..		39,750			40,500
Total....................................		$177,650			$188,460

CURRENT VALUE ACCOUNTING

Current value accounting, represented by Cell 3 in the diagram on page 723, is a term used to designate an alternative reporting model to traditional accounting which utilizes historical costs. A distinction may be made in defining current values as: (1) input prices, i.e., replacement costs; (2) exit prices, i.e., sales values; (3) net realizable values, i.e., expected sales prices less costs to complete and sell; and (4) economic values, i.e., present values of future cash flows. These distinctions are technical refinements in implementing the general approach of reflecting current values in financial statements. In this chapter, current values will refer to the amounts required to replace specific items, i.e., replacement costs. Discussion of possible refinements is beyond the scope of this book.[1]

Proponents of current value accounting argue that financial statements presented on an historical cost basis, even if adjusted for general price-level changes, do not adequately reflect the economic circumstances of a business. The balance sheet is deficient because only historical costs are presented which do not reflect the current financial picture of an enterprise. The income statement is deficient because charges against revenues are based on historical costs which may differ from current costs. Also, increases in net asset values are not recognized at the time of a change in asset value but must await realization at time of sale. Under current value accounting, assets would be reported at their current market prices, thus more closely reflecting the actual financial position of a business. The impact on the income statement is not certain. Some accountants would recognize revenues when there is evidence of an increase in net asset values; others would not recognize revenues until realized as evidenced by a sale. However, most would agree that expenses should be based on the expiration of current values of the assets utilized, thus providing a more meaningful income measure.

Concept of Well-Offness

From an income measurement perspective, current value accounting is based on a concept of *well-offness*. As indicated in Chapter 4, this concept is attributed to J. R. Hicks and maintains that operating gain, often called economic income, is the amount a firm can spend during a period and still be equally well-off at the end of the period as at the beginning. Operationalized, economic income (loss) is the difference between the sales price of an item and the cost to replace that item. Alternatively, it may be viewed as the change in net assets during a period measured on a current value basis. For example, if an entity's net assets, valued in terms of current values, equaled $250,000 at the beginning of a

---

[1]See for example, Robert R. Sterling, *Theory of the Measurement of Enterprise Income* (Lawrence, Kansas: University Press of Kansas, 1970); Edgar O. Edwards and Philip W. Bell, *The Theory and Measurement of Business Income* (Berkeley: University of California Press, 1961); Raymond T. Chambers, *Accounting Evaluation and Economic Behavior* (Englewood Cliffs, N.J.: Prentice-Hall, 1966).

period and $300,000 at the end of the period, given no additional investments or withdrawals and holding the general purchasing power constant, economic income would be $50,000.

Holding Gains or Losses   Current value accounting not only emphasizes economic income but it also makes it possible to isolate any gains or losses resulting from holding assets. To illustrate, assume Current Value Company had sales of $100,000, cost of goods sold of $65,000, and a cost of $80,000 to replace the inventory sold. There is an operating gain of $20,000, which is the difference between the sales price and the replacement cost of the inventory. A *realized holding gain* ($15,000) represents the difference between the historical cost and replacement cost of the inventory sold. The total gross profit traditionally recognized is $35,000. However, that amount includes some *inventory profits* which will have to be reinvested if the firm is to be in an equally well-off position at the end of the period. Thus, the gross profit in an economic sense is the $20,000 operating gain.

Sales..	$100,000	➤Operating gain
Replacement cost of inventory...............	80,000	➤Realized holding gain
Cost of goods sold	65,000	
Gross profit...	$ 35,000	

If, in the above example, Current Value Company has additional inventory which is not sold but which has had a change in value, it would have an *unrealized holding gain or loss*. Assume inventory that was not sold cost $50,000 and had a replacement cost of $70,000. There would be a $20,000 unrealized holding gain that some accountants would recognize, if not in income, in a separate report on changes in values.

Approaches to Implementing Current Value Accounting   There are at least two methods for incorporating current values into the financial statements: (1) Disclose current value information parenthetically or in the notes to financial statements; and (2) Record current values on the balance sheet.

Disclose Current Value Information Parenthetically or in the Notes to Financial Statements. This proposal would not really change the historical cost basis of accounting. Historical-dollar financial statements would still be presented, but additional data reporting the replacement costs of all or selected items would also be disclosed. The potential impact on income, for example, from depreciation charges and cost of goods sold on a replacement cost basis, might also be given.

In effect, this is the method required for all large companies filing with the SEC. Accounting Series Release No. 190 sets forth the final rules, effective for fiscal years ending on or after December 25, 1976, requiring disclosure of certain replacement cost information. The disclosures may be provided in a special section or in the notes to the financial statements but should include at least the following:

1. The current replacement cost of the ending inventory for each year for which a balance sheet is presented.
2. The estimated current replacement cost of the productive capacity (plant and equipment), including the depreciated cost of such productive capacity, for each year for which a balance sheet is presented.
3. The approximate cost of sales for the two most recent years computed as though on a replacement cost basis.
4. The approximate amount of depreciation expense for the two most recent years based on the average current replacement cost of productive capacity.[1]

The SEC also requires a description of the methods used to determine the information disclosed, and any additional information needed to prevent the information supplied from being misleading. Although the replacement cost disclosures may be labeled *unaudited*, Accounting Series Release No. 190 indicates an independent accountant should be "associated" with the information disclosed.

Record Current Values on the Balance Sheet. This approach would change the historical-cost basis of accounting and would report current values on the balance sheet. The emphasis is on the balance sheet, but operating income might reflect revenue transactions and related expenses measured on a current-cost basis. As indicated earlier, it is not exactly clear what the impact on income will be. Several alternatives have been proposed.

Some have suggested that holding gains or losses not be reported as income, but be disclosed in a special report showing changes in values. Another suggestion is to recognize only those holding gains or losses that have been validated by the realization test, generally a sale. Under this approach, net income would consist of operating income and realized holding gains or losses, each disclosed separately. Additional changes in net asset values might be shown in a separate report or as a special account in the "Owners' equity" section of the balance sheet.

Still a third alternative is to recognize all changes in the net asset values in income currently, whether realized or not. Under this approach, net income would consist of operating income plus realized and unrealized holding gains or losses. The total amount of net income would then be reflected in retained earnings and would offset the change in net asset values shown on the balance sheet.

Arguments Against Current Value Accounting

Opponents to current value accounting argue that determining current values is too subjective. For example, the replacement cost for a particular item may not be readily available, at least at a reasonable cost, and may have to be estimated by some method, such as an appraisal. It

---

[1]Securities and Exchange Commission, *Accounting Series Release No. 190*, "Notice of Adoption of Amendments to Regulation S-X Requiring Disclosure of Certain Replacement Cost Data" (Washington: U.S. Government Printing Office, 1976). In Item (2), there is a distinction between replacing productive capacity and replacing specific assets. Productive capacity deals with assets which may not be identical but which produce comparable results in terms of a company's ability to produce and distribute goods or services. The concept of replacing specific assets deals with identical assets. The *productive capacity* approach taken by the SEC may be contrasted to the *replacement of specific asset* approach advocated by the United Kingdom's Sandilands report.

may be difficult, if not impossible, to even find an identical item to consider its replacement cost. If an identical asset is not used, then a subjective adjustment for differences in the quality of a similar but not identical item would have to be made.

Another disadvantage is the increased subjectivity of the income measurement if changes in current values are recognized as income prior to the consumation of a transaction which offers confirmation of arms-length exchange values.

Additional arguments against current value accounting include the lack of understanding of the resulting financial statements, particularly the income statement; the question of whether the benefits are worth the extra costs involved; and the uncertainty of whether in the final analysis users of financial statements will be better served by current value accounting.

CURRENT VALUE ADJUSTED FOR GENERAL PRICE-LEVEL CHANGES

The fourth cell identified in the matrix diagram on page 723 represents a combination of shifting to a current value reporting basis but with common purchasing power units of measurement. This approach recognizes that adjusting for both specific and general price changes are not mutually exclusive and are not necessarily competing alternatives. Some accountants argue that this combination is conceptually the best reporting alternative. They feel adjustments must be made for both specific and general price changes.

In terms of the effect on the balance sheet, this approach is not significantly different from Cell 3. There would have to be some roll-forward changes for comparative balance sheets, but the primary effect of adding general price-level changes to current value accounting is on the income statement. The result is a further distinction among the income components. For example, in the illustration referred to earlier, the following elements of income were identified:

Sales	$100,000	Operating gain
Replacement cost of inventory	80,000	Realized holding gain
Cost of goods sold	65,000	
Gross profit	$ 35,000	

If general price-level adjustments were added, assuming 10% inflation for the year, the result would be:

Sales	$100,000	Operating gain
Replacement cost of inventory	80,000	Realized holding gain
Cost of goods sold adjusted for inflation.	71,500*	Inflationary holding gain
Cost of goods sold at historical costs	65,000	
Gross profit	$ 35,000	

*($65,000 × 1.10 = $71,500)

Note that the realized holding gain has been broken into two parts: the realized holding gain (the difference between the price-level adjusted historical cost and the replacement cost), and the inflationary holding gain (the difference between the historical costs and the price-level adjusted historical costs). In addition to the other shortcomings ascribed to the current value approach and price-level adjustments considered separately, a major disadvantage of this method is its complexity, caused by combining alternatives.

CHALLENGE TO ACCOUNTING PROFESSION

Most would agree that the traditional accounting model has served society well. The challenge to the accounting profession is to continually modify its practices to meet the changing demands of users of financial information. Inflation and other business environmental factors have already caused several countries to adopt accounting practices which reflect price changes; proposals for additional modification of accounting rules are also being considered.[1] This is a topic which is under study by the Financial Accounting Standards Board in the United States and by other authoritative accounting bodies throughout the world. The alternatives discussed in this chapter are deserving of careful consideration, and further research is needed to determine their practicality and usefulness for the future.

---

[1]See, for example, the "Sandilands Committee Report" (United Kingdom: Committee of Enquiry, 1975).

QUESTIONS

1. What has caused the increased interest in reporting financial statements adjusted for price changes?

2. Why do accountants prefer to report historical costs rather than market values in conventional statements?

3. (a) Identify three possible methods of overcoming objections to historical-cost financial statements. (b) Compare the concept of reporting market values in financial statements with the concept of restating original dollar costs for price-level changes.

4. How are general price-level indexes, e.g., the GNP Implicit Price Deflator, derived?

5. (a) Distinguish between monetary assets and nonmonetary assets. (b) Which of the following are monetary assets?

    (1) Cash
    (2) Investment in common stock
    (3) Investment in bonds
    (4) Merchandise on hand
    (5) Prepaid expenses
    (6) Buildings
    (7) Patents
    (8) Sinking fund — uninvested cash

    (9) Sinking fund — investments in real estate
    (10) Deferred developmental costs

6. Assume a company holds property or maintains the obligations listed below during a year in which there is an increase in the price level. State in each case whether the position of the company at the end of the year is better, worse, or unchanged.

    (a) Cash
    (b) Cash surrender value of life insurance
    (c) Land
    (d) Unearned subscription revenue
    (e) Accounts receivable
    (f) Notes payable
    (g) Merchandise on hand
    (h) Long-term warranties on sales

7. Indicate whether a company gains or loses under each condition described below and on page 750.

    (a) A company maintains an excess of monetary assets over monetary liabilities during a period of general price-level increase.
    (b) A company maintains an excess of monetary liabilities over monetary assets during a period of general price-level increase.

(c) A company maintains an excess of monetary assets over monetary liabilities during a period of general price-level decrease.

(d) A company maintains an excess of monetary liabilities over monetary assets during a period of general price-level decrease.

8. It has been suggested that although the stockholders' equity is nonmonetary in character, an exception should be made in the case of the equity of preferred stockholders and this equity should be treated as a monetary item. Would you agree? Give your reasons.

9. What is the general formula for restating financial statements to reflect general price-level changes?

10. Some have suggested that the restatement of accounting data in terms of current purchasing power be limited to land, buildings, and equipment and to related depreciation charges. Would you defend or reject such a proposal? Give your reasons.

11. Describe the restatement of inventories for general price-level changes when inventories are reported (a) on a first-in, first-out basis; (b) on a last-in, first-out basis.

12. The most time-consuming step in the restatement of accounts to report general price-level changes is the aging of the depreciable property and the corresponding restatement of the periodic depreciation. What is meant by aging as used here? Do you agree with this statement?

13. What special procedures are required when price-level statements are prepared for the first time for a company that has been operating for many years?

14. What are the advantages of current-value financial statements as compared to historical-cost financial statements?

15. What are two methods for incorporating current values into the financial statements?

EXERCISES

1. Compute in each case below the general price-level gain or loss assuming that assets are held and liabilities are maintained during a period in which the general price level rises by 8%.

(a)	Cash	$ 50,000
	Accounts receivable	20,000
(b)	Cash	100,000
	Accounts payable	25,000
	Long-term payables	55,000
(c)	Cash	25,000
	Land	50,000
	Accounts payable	25,000
(d)	Cash	25,000
	Land and buildings	100,000
	Mortgage note payable	40,000

2. Assuming prices rise evenly by 9% during a year, compute the amount of the expense stated in terms of year-end dollars in each of the following independent cases:

(a) Expenses of $500,000 were paid at the beginning of the year for services received during the first half of the year.

(b) Expenses of $125,000 were paid at the end of each quarter for services received during the quarter.

(c) Expenses of $125,000 were paid at the beginning of each quarter for services received during the quarter.

(d) Expenses of $500,000 were paid at the end of the year for services received during the year.

(e) Expenses of $500,000 were paid evenly throughout the year for services received during the year.

In terms of year-end dollars, when is the best time to pay for services received in periods of rising prices?

3. The Wilson Washerettes Co. will prepare for the first time price-level adjusted statements as of June 30, 1977. In connection with the restatement, an analysis of the equipment and related accumulated depreciation account was made before the 1977 adjustments for depreciation:

Year Acquired	Cost	Accumulated Depreciation Dec. 31, 1976	Estimated Useful Life
1971	$100,000	$ 73,786	10 years
1973	250,000	147,600	10 years
1975	300,000	74,667	15 years
1976	50,000	33,333	3 years
1977	130,000	——	5 years

The double-declining balance method of depreciation is used with a full year's depreciation taken in the year of acquisition and none taken in the year of retirement. Adjust for general price-level changes the equipment and related accumulated depreciation account as of June 30, 1977. Round to the nearest dollar. Assume the general price index rose as follows:

Year	Index
1971	100
1972	105
1973	110
1974	120
1975	130
1976	135
1977	145

4. A comparative income statement for the Panlow Company for the first two years of operations appears below.

	First Year		Second Year	
	Results of Operations			
Sales		$750,000		$900,000
Cost of goods sold:				
Beginning inventory	——		$300,000	
Purchases	$750,000		500,000	
Goods available for sales	$750,000		$800,000	
Ending inventory	300,000	450,000	400,000	400,000
Gross profit on sales		$300,000		$500,000
Operating expenses:				
Depreciation	$ 30,000		$ 30,000	
Other	240,000	270,000	350,000	380,000
Net income		$ 30,000		$120,000
Dividends		15,000		30,000
Increase in retained earnings		$ 15,000		$ 90,000

Prepare a comparative income and retained earnings statement expressing items in dollars of purchasing power at the end of the second year, considering the following data:

(a) Prices rose evenly and index numbers expressing the general price-level changes were:

Beginning of first year 100
End of first year 110
End of second year 140

(b) Sales and purchases were made and expenses were incurred evenly each year.

(c) Inventories were reported at cost using first-in, first-out pricing; average indexes for the year are applicable in restating inventories.

(d) Depreciation relates to equipment acquired at the beginning of the first year.

(e) Dividends were paid at the middle of each year.

(f) Assume no general price-level gain or loss in either year.

5. Comparative balance sheet data for Hiatt Industries, Inc., since its formation, appear below. The general price level during the two-year period went up steadily; index numbers expressing the general price-level changes are listed following the balance sheet. Restate the comparative balance sheet data in terms of the purchasing power at the end of the second year.

	End of First Year	End of Second Year
Cash	$ 75,000	$ 62,500
Receivables	50,000	70,000
Land, buildings, and equipment (net)*	130,000	115,000
	$255,000	$247,500
Payables	$ 67,500	$ 45,000
Capital stock	160,000	160,000
Retained earnings	27,500	42,500
	$255,000	$247,500

*Acquired at the beginning of the first year.

Price Level Index Numbers

At the beginning of the business	112
At the end of the first year	125
At the end of the second year	140

6. The income statement for Bingham Oil Company is given below. Using the income statement, together with the additional data provided, prepare an income statement restated in terms of end-of-year dollars accompanied by a schedule summarizing the general price-level gain or loss for the year.

Bingham Oil Company
Income Statement
For Year Ended December 31, 19—

Sales		$990,000
Cost of goods sold:		
Beginning inventory	$ 150,000	
Purchases	900,000	
Goods available for sale	$1,050,000	
Ending inventory	450,000	600,000
Gross profit on sales		$390,000
Operating expenses		270,000
Income before income tax		$120,000
Income tax		60,000
Net income		$ 60,000

The general price level rose evenly from 140 to 160 in the preceding year and from 160 to 200 in the current year. Sales and purchases were made evenly and expenses were incurred evenly during the year. The average index is regarded as applicable in stating inventories. All of the company's assets and liabilities, both at the beginning and at the end of the period, were classified as current and, except for inventories, monetary. Current assets were $600,000 and current liabilities were $200,000 at the beginning of the year.

7. On September 1, 1977, Carmen's Toy Store purchased 800 dolls at $2.50 per doll. As of December 31, 1977, Carmen's had sold three-fourths of the dolls at $6 per doll, and the doll manufacturer was selling to retailers at $3 per doll. With respect to the doll venture, how much should Carmen's Toy Store recognize as (a) operating gain, (b) realized holding gain, and (c) unrealized holding gain under the current value method of accounting?

PROBLEMS

25-1. Classify the following accounts as either monetary or nonmonetary.

Assets	Liabilities and Stockholders' Equity
Current assets:	Current liabilities:
Cash	Accounts and notes payable
Marketable securities (stocks)	Dividends payable
Receivables (net of allowance)	Refundable deposits on returnable containers
Inventories	Advances on sales contracts
Prepaid rent	Long-term liabilities:
Discount on notes payable	Bonds payable
Deferred income tax expense	Premium on bonds payable
Long-term investments:	Stockholders' equity:
Affiliated companies, at cost	Preferred stock (at fixed liquidation price)
Cash surrender value of life insurance	Common stock
Bond sinking fund	Retained earnings
Investment in bonds	
Land, buildings, and equipment:	
Land	
Buildings	
Equipment	
Intangible assets:	
Patents	
Goodwill	
Advances paid on purchase contracts	

25-2. The following information was taken from the books of the Sessions Hardware Store during its first two years of operations:

	Useful Life	1977	1978
Beginning inventory		$150,000	$200,000
Purchases		550,000	500,000
Ending inventory		200,000	160,000
Building (acquired 1/1/77)	25 years	400,000	——
Office equipment (acquired 7/1/77)	12 years	30,000	——
Machinery (acquired 10/1/77)	8 years	16,000	——
Price index (1/1)		190	202
Price index (12/31)		202	214

> **Instructions:**
> (1) Calculate the cost of goods sold for 1977 and 1978 in terms of respective year-end dollars assuming a lifo inventory cost flow with average costs used for any increments. Assume the 1977 beginning inventory was purchased on January 1, 1977. Round to the nearest dollar amount.
> (2) Restate depreciable assets and accumulated depreciation (straight-line, ignore salvage values) reporting the depreciation for 1977 and 1978 in terms of 1977 and 1978 year-end dollars respectively.

25-3. The Crow Co. began operations in 1950. At the end of 1974 it was decided to furnish stockholders with a balance sheet restated in terms of uniform 1974 dollars as a supplement to the conventional financial statements. This is the first time such a statement was prepared. The balance sheet prepared in conventional form at the end of 1974 was as follows:

Crow Co.
Balance Sheet
December 31, 1974

Cash	$ 187,600	Accounts payable	$ 379,900
Accounts receivable	342,400	Mortgage note payable	450,000
Inventory	742,300	Bonds payable	1,250,000
Land	1,720,000	Capital stock	1,000,000
Building	2,115,000	Premium on capital stock	200,000
Less accumulated depr.	(705,000)	Retained earnings	1,122,400
		Total liabilities and	
Total assets	$4,402,300	stockholders' equity	$4,402,300

(continued)

All of the stock was issued in 1950. Land was purchased subject to a mortgage note of $1,000,000 at the time the company was formed. The present building is being depreciated on a straight-line basis with a 30-year life and no salvage value. The bonds were issued in 1960. The company uses the first-in, first-out method in pricing inventories.

> **Instructions:** Prepare a balance sheet for the Crow Co. restated in terms of 1974 dollars. Use the GNP Deflator on page 725 in making adjustments; assume the index for each year is regarded as representative of the price level for the entire year.

25-4. The income statement prepared at the end of the year for the Wagner Corporation follows:

Wagner Corporation
Income Statement
For Year Ended December 31, 19––

Sales..		$350,000
Less sales discount...		15,000
Net sales..		$335,000
Cost of goods sold:		
Inventory, January 1	$125,000	
Purchases..	180,000	
Goods available for sale..	$305,000	
Inventory, December 31	120,000	
Cost of goods sold..		185,000
Gross profit on sales...		$150,000
Operating expenses:		
Depreciation...	$ 21,250	
Other operating expenses	50,000	
Total operating expenses...		71,250
Income before income tax..		$ 78,750
Income tax		31,300
Net income..		$ 47,450

The following additional data are available:

    (a) The price index rose evenly throughout the year from 120 on January 1 to 130 on December 31.

    (b) Sales were made evenly throughout the year; expenses were incurred evenly throughout the year.

    (c) The inventory was valued at cost using first-in, first-out pricing; average indexes for the year are used in restating inventories. The beginning inventory was acquired in the preceding period when the average index was 122.

    (d) The depreciation charge related to the following items:

	Asset Cost	Index Number at Date of Acquisition	Depreciation Rate
Building	$75,000	95	3 %
Equipment...	80,000	95	12½%
Equipment...	20,000	98	12½%
Equipment*..	39,000	120	16⅔%

    *Acquired at the beginning of the current year.

    (e) Semiannual dividends of $7,500 were declared and paid at the end of June and at the end of December.

    (f) The balance sheet position for the company changed during the year as follows:

	January 1	December 31
Current assets	$180,000	$174,700
Building and equipment (net)........................	120,000	137,750
	$300,000	$312,450
Current liabilities...	$ 55,000	$ 35,000
Capital stock..	200,000	200,000
Retained earnings...	45,000	77,450
	$300,000	$312,450

> *Instructions:* Prepare an income statement in which items are stated in end-of-year dollars accompanied by a schedule summarizing the general price-level gain or loss for the year.

25-5. Financial statements are prepared for the Ervin Co. at the end of each year in conventional form and also in price-level adjusted form. Balance sheet data summarized in conventional and in general price-level form at the end of 1976 are given below.

	Conventional Form		General Price-Level Form (Reporting Purchasing Power at End of Year)	
Assets:				
Cash.....................................		$ 23,000		$ 23,000
Accounts receivable		70,000		70,000
Inventory..		105,000		106,500
Buildings and equipment................	$120,000		$153,600	
Less accumulated depreciation....	48,000	72,000	61,440	92,160
Land		50,000		64,000
Total assets		$320,000		$355,660
Liabilities:				
Accounts payable..............................		$ 48,000		$ 48,000
Long-term liabilities..........................		40,000		40,000
Total liabilities..................................		$ 88,000		$ 88,000
Stockholders' equity:				
Capital stock......................................		$150,000		$192,000
Retained earnings.............................		82,000		75,660
Total stockholders' equity................		$232,000		$267,660
Total liabilities and stockholders' equity..		$320,000		$355,660

Data from statements prepared in conventional form at the end of 1977 are given below:

Balance Sheet

Assets	
Cash	$ 83,840
Accounts receivable	72,500
Inventory...	125,000
Buildings and equipment..........................	120,000
Accumulated depreciation........................	(56,000)
Land	50,000
	$395,340

Liabilities and Stockholders' Equity	
Accounts payable......................................	$ 37,000
Long-term liabilities..................................	40,000
Capital stock...	150,000
Retained earnings.....................................	168,340
	$395,340

Income Statement

Sales..		$1,100,000
Cost of goods sold.......................................		600,000
Gross profit on sales...................................		$ 500,000
Operating expenses.....................................		308,000
Income before income tax		$ 192,000
Income tax..		85,660
Net income		$ 106,340
Dividends..		20,000
Increase in retained earnings		$ 86,340

The following additional data are available at the end of 1977:

(a) Price-level index numbers were as follows for the year:

January 1	150
December 31	153

The price level rose steadily during the year.

(b) Sales and purchases were made evenly and expenses were incurred evenly throughout the year.

(c) The first-in, first-out method was used to compute inventory cost; average indexes for the year are used in restating inventories.

(d) All of the land, buildings, and equipment were acquired when the company was formed.

(e) Dividends were declared and paid at the end of the year.

(continued)

Instructions: Prepare in terms of end-of-year dollars: (1) an income and retained earnings statement accompanied by a schedule summarizing the general price-level gain or loss for 1977; (2) a balance sheet as of December 31, 1977.

25-6. Operations of the Alton Corporation for the two-year period after its organization are summarized on the comparative statements given below:

Comparative Income Statement

	First Year		Second Year	
Sales		$1,200,000		$1,400,000
Cost of goods sold:				
Beginning inventory	$200,000		$ 50,000	
Purchases	700,000		1,135,000	
Merchandise available for sale	$900,000		$1,185,000	
Ending inventory	50,000	850,000	210,000	975,000
Gross profit on sales		$ 350,000		$ 425,000
Expenses (including depreciation)		290,000		335,000
Net income		$ 60,000		$ 90,000
Dividends		50,000		50,000
Increase in retained earnings		$ 10,000		$ 40,000

Comparative Balance Sheet

	Beginning of Business	End of First Year	End of Second Year
Assets			
Cash	$140,000	$312,500	$ 60,000
Accounts receivable	—	150,000	175,000
Inventory	200,000	50,000	210,000
Land	60,000	60,000	60,000
Buildings (net)	250,000	237,500	225,000
Total assets	$650,000	$810,000	$730,000
Liabilities			
Accounts payable	—	$150,000	$180,000
Mortgage note payable	$150,000	150,000	—
Total liabilities	$150,000	$300,000	$180,000
Stockholders' Equity			
Capital stock	$500,000	$500,000	$500,000
Retained earnings	—	10,000	50,000
Total stockholders' equity	$500,000	$510,000	$550,000
Total liabilities and stockholders' equity	$650,000	$810,000	$730,000

Certain stockholders of the company request additional data that will enable them to judge the economic progress of the company during this period, and it is decided to prepare price-level statements for each year expressing the purchasing power of the dollar at the end of each year. The data and assumptions to be applied in the preparation of such statements follow:

(a) Price-level index numbers were:

Beginning of first year (at company formation) 115
End of first year 125
End of second year 135

The price level rose evenly throughout each year.
(b) Sales, purchases, and expenses were made or incurred evenly throughout each year.
(c) The first-in, first-out method was used in calculating inventory cost; average indexes for the year are used in restating inventories.
(d) Dividends were declared and paid in the middle of each year.
(e) The mortgage note was paid off at the end of the second year.
(f) Buildings were depreciated at the rate of 5%.

Price-level multipliers in ratio form are given below:

125/115	1.087	135/120	1.125
135/115	1.174	135/125	1.080
125/120	1.042	135/130	1.038

Instructions:

(1) Prepare in terms of end-of-year dollars an income and retained earnings statement accompanied by a schedule summarizing the general price-level gain or loss, and a balance sheet for the first year.

(2) Prepare similar statements for the second year.

25-7. To obtain a more realistic appraisal of his investment, Walter Abbott, your client, has asked you to adjust certain financial data of the Global Company for price-level changes. On January 1, 1975, Abbott invested $50,000 in the Global Company in return for 10,000 shares of common stock. Immediately after his investment, the trial balance data appeared as follows:

	Debit	Credit
Cash and Receivables	$ 65,200	
Merchandise Inventory	4,000	
Building	50,000	
Accumulated Depreciation — Building		$ 8,000
Equipment	36,000	
Accumulated Depreciation — Equipment		7,200
Land	10,000	
Current Liabilities		50,000
Capital Stock, $5 par		100,000
	$165,200	$165,200

Balances in certain selected accounts as of December 31 of each of the next three years were as follows:

	1975	1976	1977
Sales	$39,650	$39,000	$42,350
Inventory	4,500	5,600	5,347
Purchases	14,475	16,350	18,150
Operating expenses (excluding depreciation)	10,050	9,050	9,075

Assume the 1975 price level as the base year and all changes in the price level take place at the beginning of each year. Further assume the 1976 price level is 10% above the 1975 price level and the 1977 price level is 10% above the 1976 level.

The building was constructed in 1971 at a cost of $50,000 with an estimated life of 25 years. The price level at that time was 80% of the 1975 price level.

The equipment was purchased in 1973 at a cost of $36,000 with an estimated life of ten years. The price level at that time was 90% of the 1975 price level.

The lifo method of inventory valuation is used. The original inventory was acquired in the same year the building was constructed and was maintained at a constant $4,000 until 1975. In 1975 a gradual buildup of the inventory was begun in anticipation of an increase in the volume of business.

Abbott considers the return on his investment as the dividend he actually receives. In 1975 and also in 1977 the Global Company paid cash dividends in the amount of $4,000.

On July 1, 1976, there was a reverse stock split-up of the company's stock in the ratio of one-for-ten.

Instructions:

(1) Compute the 1977 earnings per share of common stock in terms of 1975 dollars.

(2) Compute the percentage return on the investment for 1975 and 1977 in terms of 1975 dollars. (AICPA adapted)

25-8. You have been engaged by the Charlton Corporation since the fall of 1976 to translate the corporation's financial statements from historical costs to current or replacement costs for internal use. You assisted in the determination at December 31, 1976 and 1977 of the amounts listed in the Replacement Costs columns on the balance sheet given on page 758.

Charlton Corporation
Comparative Balance Sheet
December 31

	Historical Costs		Replacement Costs	
	1976	1977	1976	1977
Assets				
Current assets:				
Cash	$ 238,500	$ 494,500	$ 238,500	$ 494,500
Receivables (net)	581,500	760,850	581,500	760,850
Marketable securities	27,500		28,600	
Inventories	407,000	434,500	440,000	462,000
Prepaid expenses	5,500	11,000	5,500	11,000
Total current assets	$1,260,000	$1,700,850	$1,294,100	$1,728,350
Investment in affiliated company	$ 440,000	$ 440,000	$ 660,000	$ 726,000
Long-term assets:				
Land	$ 110,000	$ 105,000	$ 231,000	$ 231,000
Buildings and equipment	3,850,000	3,850,000	5,390,000	5,713,400
Accumulated depreciation	(1,925,000)	(2,117,500)	(2,695,000)	(3,142,370)
Long-term lease	540,000	480,000	567,000	529,200
Total long-term assets	$2,575,000	$2,317,500	$3,493,000	$3,331,230
Patents (net)	$ 395,000	$ 345,000	$ 495,000	$ 440,000
Total assets	$4,670,000	$4,803,350	$5,942,100	$6,225,580
Liabilities				
Current liabilities:				
Accounts payable	$ 805,000	$ 709,400	$ 805,000	$ 709,400
Current portion of lease obligation	44,400	47,050	44,400	47,050
Total current liabilities	$ 849,400	$ 756,450	$ 849,400	$ 756,450
Long-term liabilities:				
5% Bonds payable, due 1986	$1,100,000	$1,100,000	$1,019,039	$1,025,181
Lease obligation	465,600	418,550	465,600	418,550
Deferred income tax payable	55,000	60,000	55,000	60,000
Estimated tax on increases to replacement costs			591,005	645,524
Total long-term liabilities	$1,620,600	$1,578,550	$2,130,644	$2,149,255
Total liabilities	$2,470,000	$2,335,000	$2,980,044	$2,905,705
Stockholders' Equity				
Common stock — $100 par value	$1,650,000	$1,650,000		
Premium on common stock	330,000	330,000		
Retained earnings	220,000	488,350		
Total stockholders' equity	$2,200,000	$2,468,350	$2,962,056	$3,319,875
Total liabilities and stockholders' equity	$4,670,000	$4,803,350	$5,942,100	$6,225,580

One of the factors considered in determining replacement costs was an increase in the price level, which at December 31, 1977, was 104% of the price-level index at December 31, 1976. Management has now engaged you to translate Charlton Corporation's 1977 income statement from historical costs as it appears on the opposite page to current costs.

The following information relative to current cost computations is also available:

(a) The general price level increased early in January 1977, to 104% of the 1976 index.
(b) The marketable securities were sold August 17, 1977, for $29,000.
(c) Prepaid expenses are for prepaid variable manufacturing costs.
(d) Land purchased in 1970 for $5,000 was sold November 20, 1977, for $12,000. The land had a replacement cost of $10,500 at December 31, 1976.
(e) Replacement costs of the land and the building and equipment increased by amounts greater than the increase in the general price level. Depreciation on building and equipment is computed by the straight-line method at 5% of the 1977 replacement cost. The accumulated depreciation was increased by depreciation for 1977 plus an adjustment for prior years based on 1977 replacement cost of the building and equipment.

Charlton Corporation
Income Statement
For Year Ended December 31, 1977

	Historical Costs	
Sales		$7,999,750
Cost of goods sold:		
Inventories, January 1, 1977	$ 407,000	
Variable manufacturing costs	2,175,250	
Fixed manufacturing costs	825,000	
Depreciation	154,000	
Amortization of lease	60,000	
Amortization of patents	50,000	
Total	$3,671,250	
Less inventories, December 31, 1977	434,500	3,236,750
Gross profit on sales		$4,763,000
Operating expenses:		
Variable selling expenses	$1,375,000	
Fixed selling expenses	825,000	
Variable administrative expenses	275,000	
Fixed administrative expenses	1,650,000	4,125,000
Operating income		$ 638,000
Other revenue and expense items:		
Dividends received	$ 8,350	
Bond interest expense	(55,000)	
Lease interest expense	(27,950)	
Gain (loss) from sale of securities	1,500	
Gain from sale of land	7,000	(66,100)
Income before income tax		$ 571,900
Income tax		279,150
Net income		$ 292,750

(f) Depreciation is allocated 80% to manufacturing operations and 10% each to fixed selling expenses and fixed administrative expenses and is included in the fixed selling and administrative expenses on the income statement.

(g) The long-term lease is for the use of manufacturing facilities during the period 1976 through 1985. The lease required the payment of $90,000 on January 1, 1976, and $75,000 on each January 1 through 1985. Charlton capitalized the lease at $600,000 and is amortizing it on a straight-line basis. The replacement cost for a comparable unexpired lease increased 5% each year for 1976 and 1977.

(h) The replacement cost of patents increased a total of $15,000 in 1977 and amortization amounted to $70,000 on a replacement cost basis.

(i) The 5% bonds were originally issued at par and are due December 31, 1986. At December 31, 1976, and December 31, 1977, these bonds were selling in the market to yield 6% interest. Interest is payable annually on December 31.

(j) The deferred income tax payable results from differences in treatment of items for income tax and financial reporting purposes. Management would like to have income tax in the current costs section of the income statement based on historical costs expressed in current dollars.

Instructions: Prepare an income statement that expresses all amounts in current costs and determines net income. Supporting schedules should be in good form. (In addition to income from transactions Charlton Corporation would also recognize gains from current cost valuations and from purchasing power gains on net debt on its current cost income statement, but these computations are not required.) (AICPA adapted)

25-9. The Melgar Company purchased a tract of land as an investment in 1974 for $100,000; late in that year the company decided to construct a shopping center on the site. Construction began in 1975 and was completed in 1977; one third of the construction was completed each year. Melgar originally estimated the costs of the project would be $1,200,000 for materials, $750,000 for labor, $150,000 for variable overhead, and $600,000 for depreciation.

Actual costs (excluding depreciation) incurred for construction were as listed at the top of the next page.

	1975	1976	1977
Materials	$418,950	$434,560	$462,000
Labor	236,250	274,400	282,000
Variable overhead	47,250	54,208	61,200

Shortly after construction began, Melgar sold the shopping center for $3,000,000 with payment to be made in full on completion in December 1977. One hundred fifty thousand dollars of the sales price was allocated for the land.

The transaction was completed as scheduled and now a controversy has developed between the two major stockholders of the company. One feels the company should have invested in land because a high rate of return was earned on the land. The other feels the original decision was sound and that changes in the price level which were not anticipated affected the original cost estimates.

You were engaged to furnish guidance to these stockholders in resolving their controversy. As an aid, you obtained the following information:

(a) Using 1974 as the base year, price-level indexes for relevant years are: 1971 = 90; 1972 = 93; 1973 = 96; 1974 = 100; 1975 = 105; 1976 = 112; and 1977 = 120.
(b) The company allocated $200,000 per year for depreciation of fixed assets allocated to this construction project; of that amount $25,000 was for a building purchased in 1971 and $175,000 was for equipment purchased in 1973.

Instructions:

(1) Prepare a schedule to restate in base year (1974) costs the actual costs, including depreciation, incurred each year. Disregard income tax and assume each price-level index was valid for the entire year.
(2) Prepare a schedule comparing the originally estimated costs of the project with the total actual costs for each element of cost (materials, labor, variable overhead, and depreciation) adjusted to the 1974 price-level.
(3) Prepare a schedule to restate the amount received on the sale in terms of base year (1974) purchasing power. The gain or loss should be determined separately for the land and the building in terms of base year purchasing power and should exclude depreciation. (AICPA adapted)

25-10. Skadden, Inc., a retailer, was organized during 1971. Skadden's management has decided to supplement its December 31, 1974 historical-dollar financial statements with general price-level financial statements. The following general ledger trial balance (historical dollar) and additional information have been furnished:

Skadden, Inc.
Trial Balance
December 31, 1974

Cash and Receivables (net)	540,000	
Marketable Securities (common stock)	400,000	
Inventory	440,000	
Equipment	650,000	
Accumulated Depreciation — Equipment		164,000
Accounts Payable		300,000
9% First-Mortgage Bonds, due 1992		500,000
Common Stock, $10 par		1,000,000
Retained Earnings, December 31, 1973	46,000	
Sales		1,900,000
Cost of Goods Sold	1,508,000	
Depreciation	65,000	
Other Operating Expenses and Interest	215,000	
	3,864,000	3,864,000

(a) Monetary assets (cash and receivables) exceeded monetary liabilities (accounts payable and bonds payable) by $445,000 at December 31, 1973. The amounts of monetary items are fixed in terms of numbers of dollars regardless of changes in specific prices or in the general price level.
(b) Purchases ($1,840,000 in 1974) and sales are made uniformly throughout the year.
(c) Depreciation is computed on a straight-line basis, with a full year's depreciation being taken in the year of acquisition and none in the year of retirement. The depre-

ciation rate is 10 percent and no salvage value is anticipated. Acquisitions and re-tirements have been made fairly evenly over each year and the retirements in 1974 consisted of assets purchased during 1972 which were scrapped. An analysis of the equipment account reveals the following:

Year	Beginning Balance	Additions	Retirements	Ending Balance
1972	——	$550,000	——	$550,000
1973	$550,000	10,000	——	560,000
1974	560,000	150,000	$60,000	650,000

(d) The bonds were issued in 1972 and the marketable securities were purchased fairly evenly over 1974. Other operating expenses and interest are assumed to be incurred evenly throughout the year.

(e) Assume that Gross National Product Implicit Price Deflators were as follows:

Annual Averages	Index	Conversion Factors (1974 4th Qtr. = 1.000)
1971	141.4	1.259
1972	146.1	1.218
1973	154.3	1.153
1974	170.2	1.046
Quarterly Averages		
1973 4th	158.9	1.120
1974 1st	163.6	1.088
2d	167.3	1.064
3d	172.1	1.034
4th	178.0	1.000

Instructions:

(1) Prepare a schedule to convert the equipment account balance at December 31, 1974, from historical cost to general price-level adjusted dollars.

(2) Prepare a schedule to analyze in historical dollars the accumulated depreciation account for equipment for the year 1974.

(3) Prepare a schedule to analyze in general price-level dollars the accumulated depreciation account for equipment for the year 1974.

(4) Prepare a schedule to compute Skadden, Inc.'s general price-level gain or loss on its net holdings of monetary assets for 1974 (ignore income tax implications). The schedule should give consideration to appropriate items on or related to the balance sheet and the income statement. (AICPA adapted)

Financial Statement Analysis — Use of Comparative Data

The analysis of financial data is directed toward the requirements of the users of such information; and the nature of the analysis will depend upon the questions raised. The information to be analyzed is normally provided by general purpose financial statements and whatever additional financial data are made available in a company's annual report. For example, questions are raised concerning matters such as a company's sales and earnings and the trends for these items, the amount of working capital and the changes that took place in working capital, the relationship of earnings to sales, and the relationship of earnings to investments. These questions require analysis of the data reported on the income statement, the balance sheet, and the statement of changes in financial position. Internal management is also highly concerned with questions whose answers are provided by analyzing the general purpose financial statements. However, management also requires special information in setting policies and arriving at decisions for which they are responsible. Questions may arise on such matters as the performance of various company divisions, the return from sales of the individual products or product lines, and whether to make or to buy product parts or equipment. These questions can be answered only by establishing internal information systems that provide the data required for the special analyses.

The analyses of financial data described in this and the following chapter are directed primarily to the questions raised by external users, such as investors and creditors, who must generally rely on the financial reports issued by a company.

GENERAL OBJECTIVES OF FINANCIAL ANALYSIS

The financial statements give vital information concerning the position of a business and the results of its operations. The many groups interested in the financial data found in these statements include:

1. The owners — sole proprietor, partners, or stockholders.
2. The management.

3. The creditors.
4. Government — local, state, and federal (including regulatory, taxing, and statistical units).
5. Prospective owners and prospective creditors.
6. Stock exchanges, investment bankers, and stock brokers.
7. Trade associations.
8. Employees of the business and their labor unions.
9. The general public (including students and researchers).

Questions raised by these groups can generally be answered by means of analyses that develop comparisons and measure relationships of the data provided by the financial statements. The analyses will form the basis for the interpretations made and the conclusions reached by the user.

Analysis is generally directed toward reaching answers to three broad questions concerning a business: (1) its liquidity, (2) its stability, and (3) its profitability.

To be liquid, a business must be able to meet its liabilities as they mature. The financial statements are analyzed to determine whether the business is currently liquid and whether it can retain its liquidity if it should experience a period of adversity. Such analysis includes studies of the relationship of current assets to current liabilities, the size and nature of the various creditor and ownership interests, the protection afforded the creditors and owners through the soundness of asset values, and the amounts and trends of periodic earnings.

Stability is measured by the ability of a business to meet interest and principal payment requirements on outstanding debt and also its ability to pay dividends to its stockholders regularly. In judging stability, data concerning operations and financial position require study. There must be a regular demand for the goods or services sold, and the margin on sales must be sufficient to cover operating expenses, interest, and dividends. There should be a satisfactory turnover of current assets and property items. All of the business resources should be productively employed.

Profitability is measured by the success of a business in maintaining a satisfactory dividend policy while at the same time being able to show a steadily increasing ownership equity. The nature and the amount of earnings, as well as their regularity and trend, are all significant factors in arriving at conclusions concerning profitability.

Although attention is normally directed to an evaluation of each of the foregoing matters, analysis must also serve the various groups having individual questions of special interest. For example, owners are interested in the ability of a company to obtain additional capital for current needs and for possible expansion. Creditors are interested not only in the position of a business as a going concern but also in its position if it should be forced to liquidate.

The various groups interested in the facts of business have looked to accountants, not only for general purpose statements concerning financial position and the results of operations, but also for the special analyses of financial data that may be required. They have regarded accountants as best qualified to develop analytical data in view of their knowledge of the conventions and processes applied in developing the statements that form the basis for analysis. It is not uncommon for accountants to submit, along with the regular financial statements, comprehensive analyses of significant financial information that will assist individuals in interpreting financial data and in reaching intelligent conclusions with respect to a particular business.

PRELIMINARY STUDY OF FINANCIAL STATEMENTS

If analytical data are to be reliable, they must be developed from financial statements that properly exhibit business position and operations. As a first step, statements to be used as a basis for analysis should be carefully reviewed to determine whether they display any shortcomings or discrepancies. In the course of the examination, the following questions should be asked: Is there full disclosure of all relevant financial data? Have proper accounting principles and procedures been employed? Have appropriate and consistent bases for valuation been used? Are the data properly classified? When necessary, statements should be corrected so they report the full financial story in conformance with accepted accounting principles.

ANALYTICAL PROCEDURES

Analytical procedures fall into two main categories: (1) comparisons and measurements based upon financial data for two or more periods, and (2) comparisons and measurements based upon the financial data of only the current fiscal period. The first category includes the preparation of comparative statements, the determination of ratios and trends for data on successive statements, and special analyses of changes in the balance sheet, income statement, and statement of changes in financial position. The second category includes the determination of current balance sheet and income statement relationships and special analyses of earnings and earning power. An adequate review of financial data usually requires both types of analysis.

The analytical procedures commonly employed are illustrated in this and the following chapter of the text. Although individual analyses will be presented in statement and tabular forms, data are frequently reported in graphic form for more effective presentation of significant relationships. It should be emphasized that the analyses illustrated herein are simply guides to the evaluation of financial data. Sound conclusions can be reached only through the intelligent use and interpretation of such data.

COMPARATIVE STATEMENTS

Financial data become more meaningful when they are compared with similar data for the preceding period or for a number of prior periods. Statements prepared in a form reflecting financial data for two or more periods are known as *comparative statements*. Annual data can be compared with similar data for prior years. Monthly or quarterly data can be compared with similar data for the previous months or quarters or with similar data for the same months or quarters of previous years. However, as discussed in a later section of the chapter, there are some difficulties in reporting on intervals of less than a full year.

Accounting authorities have strongly encouraged the preparation of statements in comparative form. The Committee on Accounting Procedure of the AICPA has commented:

> The presentation of comparative financial statements in annual and other reports enhances the usefulness of such reports and brings out more clearly the nature and trends of current changes affecting the enterprise. Such presentation emphasizes the fact that statements for a series of periods are far more significant than those for a single period and that the accounts for one period are but an installment of what is essentially a continuous history.[1]

The Accounting Principles Board in Statement No. 4 provides an extended discussion of comparative reporting and indicates that comparisons, whether made for the single enterprise or between two or more enterprises, are more informative and useful if the following conditions exist:

1. The presentations are in good form; that is, the arrangement within the statements is identical.
2. The content of the statements is identical; that is, the same items from the underlying accounting records are classified under the same captions.
3. Accounting principles are not changed or, if they are changed, the financial effects of the changes are disclosed.
4. Changes in circumstances or in the nature of the underlying transactions are disclosed.[2]

To the extent that the above criteria are not met, comparisons may be misleading. When comparisons are made for a single enterprise, the Accounting Principles Board would add the factors of consistency in practices and procedures and reporting periods of equal and regular lengths.

Horizontal Analysis   Operations and the financial position of a company may be viewed over a number of periods by preparing the financial statements in comparative form. The comparative statements may go beyond a simple listing of comparative values by offering analytical information in the form of dollar changes and percentage changes for the data presented. The absolute changes, together with the relative changes, are thus shown. The development of data measuring changes taking place over a number

---

[1]*Accounting Research and Terminology Bulletins — Final Edition*, "No. 43, Restatement and Revision of Accounting Research Bulletins" (New York: American Institute of Certified Public Accountants, 1961), Ch. 2, Sec. A, par. 1-2.

[2]*Statements of the Accounting Principles Board, No. 4*, "Basic Concepts and Accounting Principles Underlying Financial Statements of Business Enterprises" (New York: American Institute of Certified Public Accountants, 1970), par. 95–99.

of periods is known as *horizontal analysis*. Horizontal analysis is illustrated in the comparative income statement below. This statement reports income data for a three-year period together with the dollar changes and percentage changes for each item listed.

Chaparral Company
Condensed Comparative Income Statement
For Years Ended December 31

| | 1977 | 1976 | 1975 | Increase (Decrease) | | | |
| | | | | 1976–1977 | | 1975–1976 | |
				Amount	Percent	Amount	Percent
Gross sales	$1,500,000	$1,750,000	$1,000,000	$(250,000)	(14%)	$750,000	75%
Sales returns	75,000	100,000	50,000	(25,000)	(25%)	50,000	100%
Net sales	$1,425,000	$1,650,000	$ 950,000	$(225,000)	(14%)	$700,000	74%
Cost of goods sold	1,000,000	1,200,000	630,000	(200,000)	(17%)	570,000	90%
Gross profit on sales	$ 425,000	$ 450,000	$ 320,000	$ (25,000)	(6%)	$130,000	41%
Selling expense	$ 280,000	$ 300,000	$ 240,000	$ (20,000)	(7%)	$ 60,000	25%
General expense	100,000	110,000	100,000	(10,000)	(9%)	10,000	10%
Total operating expenses	$ 380,000	$ 410,000	$ 340,000	$ (30,000)	(7%)	$ 70,000	21%
Operating income (loss)	$ 45,000	$ 40,000	$ (20,000)	$ 5,000	13%	$ 60,000	——
Other revenue items	85,000	75,000	50,000	10,000	13%	25,000	50%
	$ 130,000	$ 115,000	$ 30,000	$ 15,000	13%	$ 85,000	283%
Other expense items	30,000	30,000	10,000	——	——	20,000	200%
Income before income tax	$ 100,000	$ 85,000	$ 20,000	$ 15,000	18%	$ 65,000	325%
Income tax	30,000	25,000	5,000	5,000	20%	20,000	400%
Net income	$ 70,000	$ 60,000	$ 15,000	$ 10,000	17%	$ 45,000	300%

The detail concerning cost of goods sold, operating expenses, and other revenue and expense items may be provided by expanding the statement or by preparing separate supporting schedules. A schedule reporting comparative cost of goods sold detail is illustrated below.

Chaparral Company
Comparative Schedule of Cost of Goods Sold
For Years Ended December 31

| | 1977 | 1976 | 1975 | Increase (Decrease) | | | |
| | | | | 1976–1977 | | 1975–1976 | |
				Amount	Percent	Amount	Percent
Merchandise inventory, January 1	$ 330,000	$ 125,000	$105,000	$ 205,000	164%	$ 20,000	19%
Purchases	895,000	1,405,000	650,000	(510,000)	(36%)	755,000	116%
Merchandise available for sale	$1,225,000	$1,530,000	$755,000	$(305,000)	(20%)	$775,000	103%
Less merchandise inventory, December 31	225,000	330,000	125,000	(105,000)	(32%)	205,000	164%
Cost of goods sold	$1,000,000	$1,200,000	$630,000	$(200,000)	(17%)	$570,000	90%

The effects of operations on financial position and the trends in financial position can be presented by means of a comparative balance sheet. Here, too, both dollar changes and percentage changes may be provided to show the absolute as well as the relative changes that have taken place. A comparative balance sheet for the Chaparral Company for the three-year period, 1975–1977 inclusive, is illustrated below.

Chaparral Company
Condensed Comparative Balance Sheet
December 31

| | 1977 | 1976 | 1975 | Increase (Decrease) | | | |
| | | | | 1976–1977 | | 1975–1976 | |
				Amount	Percent	Amount	Percent
Assets							
Current assets	$ 855,000	$ 955,500	$ 673,500	$(100,500)	(11%)	$282,000	42%
Long-term investments........	500,000	400,000	250,000	100,000	25%	150,000	60%
Land, buildings, and equipment (net)..........................	775,000	875,000	675,000	(100,000)	(11%)	200,000	30%
Intangible assets	100,000	100,000	100,000	——	——	——	——
Other assets..........................	48,000	60,500	61,500	(12,500)	(21%)	(1,000)	(2%)
Total assets...........................	$2,278,000	$2,391,000	$1,760,000	$(113,000)	(5%)	$631,000	36%
Liabilities							
Current liabilities.................	$ 410,000	$ 546,000	$ 130,000	$(136,000)	(25%)	$416,000	320%
Long-term liabilities — 8% bonds................................	400,000	400,000	300,000	——	——	100,000	33%
Total liabilities......................	$ 810,000	$ 946,000	$ 430,000	$(136,000)	(14%)	$516,000	120%
Stockholders' Equity							
Preferred 6% stock	$ 350,000	$ 350,000	$ 250,000	——	——	$100,000	40%
Common stock......................	750,000	750,000	750,000	——	——	——	——
Additional paid-in capital	100,000	100,000	100,000	——	——	——	——
Retained earnings.................	268,000	245,000	230,000	$ 23,000	9%	15,000	7%
Total stockholders' equity...	$1,468,000	$1,445,000	$1,330,000	$ 23,000	2%	$115,000	9%
Total liabilities and stockholders' equity.................	$2,278,000	$2,391,000	$1,760,000	$(113,000)	(5%)	$631,000	36%

Detail for the various asset, liability, and stockholders' equity categories may be provided by expanding the statement or by preparing separate supporting schedules as in the case of the income statement. A schedule reporting comparative current asset detail is given below:

Chaparral Company
Comparative Schedule of Current Assets
December 31

| | 1977 | 1976 | 1975 | Increase (Decrease) | | | |
| | | | | 1976–1977 | | 1975–1976 | |
				Amount	Percent	Amount	Percent
Cash.....................................	$ 60,000	$100,500	$115,000	$ (40,500)	(40%)	$ (14,500)	(13%)
Marketable securities	150,000	150,000	100,000	——	——	50,000	50%
Notes receivable...................	$ 50,000	$ 40,000	$ 10,000	$ 10,000	25%	$ 30,000	300%
Accounts receivable	380,000	350,000	328,500	30,000	9%	21,500	7%
Total receivables..................	$430,000	$390,000	$338,500	$ 40,000	10%	$ 51,500	15%
Less allowance for doubtful accounts............................	10,000	15,000	5,000	(5,000)	(33%)	10,000	200%
Net receivables.....................	$420,000	$375,000	$333,500	$ 45,000	12%	$ 41,500	12%
Merchandise inventory........	225,000	330,000	125,000	(105,000)	(32%)	205,000	164%
Total current assets	$855,000	$955,500	$673,500	$(100,500)	(11%)	$282,000	42%

Changes in retained earnings over a number of periods may be viewed by means of a comparative retained earnings statement. A comparative retained earnings statement for the Chaparral Company is illustrated below:

Chaparral Company
Comparative Retained Earnings Statement
For Years Ended December 31

| | 1977 | 1976 | 1975 | Increase (Decrease) | | | |
| | | | | 1976–1977 | | 1975–1976 | |
				Amount	Percent	Amount	Percent
Retained earnings, Jan. 1....	$245,000	$230,000	$240,000	$15,000	7%	$ (10,000)	(4%)
Net income per income statement	70,000	60,000	15,000	10,000	17%	45,000	300%
Total	$315,000	$290,000	$255,000	$25,000	9%	$ 35,000	14%
Dividends:							
Preferred stock	$ 21,000	$ 21,000	$ 15,000	——	——	$ 6,000	40%
Common stock	26,000	24,000	10,000	2,000	8%	14,000	140%
Total	$ 47,000	$ 45,000	$ 25,000	$ 2,000	4%	$ 20,000	80%
Retained earnings, December 31	$268,000	$245,000	$230,000	$23,000	9%	$ 15,000	7%

In viewing the operations of a company, there is a need for interpreting operations in terms of their profitability and also in terms of their effect upon financial resources. A comparative statement of changes in financial position providing absolute changes as well as percentage changes for the Chaparral Company is illustrated on page 769.

The absolute changes reported on the comparative statements may suggest further investigation in arriving at fully informed judgments with respect to the changes. For example, the comparative statement of changes in financial position shows that funds of $550,000 were made available during the three-year period through the issuance of bonds and preferred and common stock. During this same period, $450,000 was applied to investments. Investigation may indicate that the investments do not provide an adequate return on the capital provided by bondholder and stockholder groups. The statement also indicates that operations have provided significantly increasing amounts of working capital; it may be questioned whether such increases have been employed to the best advantage in view of the fact that net income for 1977 shows only a moderate increase over 1976.

The relative changes on the comparative statements may also suggest a need for further investigation in evaluating the changes. For example, the comparative schedule of current assets shows an increase in notes receivable for 1976 of $30,000. The indication that this is a 300% increase serves to emphasize the significance of the change. Investigation may disclose that collections on account are slow and that customers are postponing payments by the issuance of notes. The comparative income statement reports an increase in sales returns for 1976 of $50,000. This information becomes more meaningful when gross sales are shown to

Chaparral Company
Condensed Comparative Statement of Changes in Financial Position — Working Capital Basis
For Years Ended December 31

| | 1977 | 1976 | 1975 | Increase (Decrease) | | | |
| | | | | 1976–1977 | | 1975–1976 | |
				Amount	Percent	Amount	Percent
Working capital was provided by:							
Operations:							
Net income....................	$ 70,000	$ 60,000	$ 15,000	$ 10,000	17%	$ 45,000	300%
Add item not requiring working capital:							
Depreciation..............	125,000	100,000	75,000	25,000	25%	25,000	33%
Working capital provided by operations...............	$195,000	$ 160,000	$ 90,000	$ 35,000	22%	$ 70,000	78%
Other assets......................	12,500	1,000	10,000	11,500	1,150%	(9,000)	(90%)
Issuance of bonds...........	—	100,000	100,000	(100,000)	(100%)	—	—
Issuance of preferred stock............................	—	—	100,000	—	—	(100,000)	(100%)
Issuance of common stock............................	—	—	250,000	—	—	(250,000)	(100%)
Total..............................	$207,500	$ 261,000	$550,000	$ (53,500)	(20%)	$(289,000)	(53%)
Working capital was applied to:							
Dividends.........................	$ 47,000	$ 45,000	$ 25,000	$ (2,000)	4%	$ 20,000	80%
Investments......................	100,000	150,000	200,000	(50,000)	(33%)	(50,000)	(25%)
Land, buildings, and equipment.....................	25,000	300,000	100,000	(275,000)	(92%)	200,000	200%
Total..............................	$172,000	$ 495,000	$325,000	$(323,000)	(65%)	$ 170,000	52%
Increase (decrease) in working capital................	$ 35,500	$(234,000)	$225,000	$ 269,500	—	$(459,000)	(204%)

have increased by 75% for the year while sales returns have increased by 100%. Investigation of the causes for the disproportionate increase appears warranted. The income statement also shows that in 1976 net sales went up 74% while cost of goods sold went up 90%; in 1977 net sales went down 14% while cost of goods sold went down 17%. These data suggest that wholesale price changes are not promptly reflected in the company's sales prices, and further study of the cost-price relationship appears warranted. When absolute amounts or relative amounts appear out of line, conclusions, favorable or unfavorable, are not justified until investigation has disclosed all of the reasons for the changes.

Use of Base Year Percentages. Percentage changes in the previous examples were given in terms of the data for the year immediately preceding. With data covering more than two years, this procedure results in a changing base that makes the comparison of relative changes over a number of years difficult. When comparative data for more than two years are to be provided, it is generally desirable to develop all comparisons in terms of a base year. This may be the earliest year given, or some other year considered particularly appropriate. Each amount on the statement representing the base year is considered to be 100%. Each amount on all other statements is expressed as a percentage of the base-year amount. The set of percentages for several years may thus be interpreted as trend values or as a series of index numbers relating to the particular item. Assuming the Chaparral Company recognizes 1975 as the base year, comparative income statement data may be presented as illustrated below:

Chaparral Company
Condensed Comparative Income Statement
For Years Ended December 31

| | 1977 | 1976 | 1975 | Increase (Decrease) | | | |
| | | | | 1975–1977 | | 1975–1976 | |
				Amount	Percent	Amount	Percent
Gross sales	$1,500,000	$1,750,000	$1,000,000	$500,000	50%	$750,000	75%
Sales returns	75,000	100,000	50,000	25,000	50%	50,000	100%
Net sales	$1,425,000	$1,650,000	$ 950,000	$475,000	50%	$700,000	74%
Cost of goods sold	1,000,000	1,200,000	630,000	370,000	59%	570,000	90%
Gross profit on sales	$ 425,000	$ 450,000	$ 320,000	$105,000	33%	$130,000	41%
Selling expense	$ 280,000	$ 300,000	$ 240,000	$ 40,000	17%	$ 60,000	25%
General expense	100,000	110,000	100,000	——	——	10,000	10%
Total operating expenses	$ 380,000	$ 410,000	$ 340,000	$ 40,000	12%	$ 70,000	21%
Operating income (loss)	$ 45,000	$ 40,000	$ (20,000)	$ 65,000	——	$ 60,000	——
Other revenue items	85,000	75,000	50,000	35,000	70%	25,000	50%
	$ 130,000	$ 115,000	$ 30,000	$100,000	333%	$ 85,000	283%
Other expense items	30,000	30,000	10,000	20,000	200%	20,000	200%
Income before income tax	$ 100,000	$ 85,000	$ 20,000	$ 80,000	400%	$ 65,000	325%
Income tax	30,000	25,000	5,000	25,000	500%	20,000	400%
Net income	$ 70,000	$ 60,000	$ 15,000	$ 55,000	367%	$ 45,000	300%

When relationships for a certain base period can be regarded as "normal," a statement such as the one above serves as a clearer medium for interpretation than those previously illustrated. For example, the comparative income statement on page 766 shows that gross sales increased 75%, then decreased 14%; sales returns increased 100%, then decreased 25%. Analyses were based upon the data for the year immediately preceding. The illustration above shows that gross sales increased 75% and 50% in terms of 1975 amounts. It also shows that sales returns increased 100% and 50% as compared with 1975 amounts. It is thus shown that, while sales returns increased disproportionately as compared with sales in 1976, the increase was proportionate in 1977, both sales and sales returns increasing 50% in terms of 1975 data.

Analysis in terms of a base year is desirable, not only for the comparison of entire statements, but also for the comparison of various related single items, ratios, and other pertinent data. Data expressed in terms of a base year are also well adapted for graphic presentation.

Data expressed in terms of a base year are frequently useful for comparisons with similar data provided by business or industry sources or by governmental agencies. When the information to be used for making comparisons does not employ the same base period, it will have to be restated. Restatement calls for the expression of each value as a percentage of the value for the period that is recognized as the base year.

To illustrate, assume the net sales data for the Chaparral Company for 1975–1977 are to be compared with a sales index for its particular industry. The industry sales indexes are as follows:

	1977	1976	1975
(1968 – 1970 = 100)...	146	157	124

Recognizing 1975 as the base year, industry sales are restated as follows:

1975	100
1976 (157 ÷ 124)..	127
1977 (146 ÷ 124)..	118

Industry sales and net sales for the Chaparral Company can now be expressed in comparative form as follows:

	1977	1976	1975
Industry sales index...	118	127	100
Chaparral Company sales index*	150	174	100

*From comparative income statement on page 770.

Use of Ratios. Changes in the preceding examples were expressed in the form of percentages. Changes can be expressed in the form of ratios instead of percentages. A 50% increase in an item results in the designation of a ratio to the base figure of 1.50; a 25% decrease in an item results in a ratio to the base figure of .75. Plus and minus designations are thus avoided. Use of ratios instead of percentages is illustrated in the following statement:

Chaparral Company
Condensed Comparative Income Statement
For Years Ended December 31

	1977	1976	1975	Increase (Decrease) 1975–1977 Amount	Increase (Decrease) 1975–1977 Ratio	Increase (Decrease) 1975–1976 Amount	Increase (Decrease) 1975–1976 Ratio
Gross sales	$1,500,000	$1,750,000	$1,000,000	$500,000	1.50	$750,000	1.75
Sales returns	75,000	100,000	50,000	25,000	1.50	50,000	2.00
Net sales	$1,425,000	$1,650,000	$ 950,000	$475,000	1.50	$700,000	1.74
Cost of goods sold...............	1,000,000	1,200,000	630,000	370,000	1.59	570,000	1.90
Gross profit on sales............	$ 425,000	$ 450,000	$ 320,000	$105,000	1.33	$130,000	1.41
Selling expense.....................	$ 280,000	$ 300,000	$ 240,000	$ 40,000	1.17	$ 60,000	1.25
General expense...................	100,000	110,000	100,000	—	1.00	10,000	1.10
Total operating expenses....	$ 380,000	$ 410,000	$ 340,000	$ 40,000	1.12	$ 70,000	1.21
Operating income (loss)......	$ 45,000	$ 40,000	$ (20,000)	$ 65,000	—	$ 60,000	—
Other revenue items	85,000	75,000	50,000	35,000	1.70	25,000	1.50
	$ 130,000	$ 115,000	$ 30,000	$100,000	4.33	$ 85,000	3.83
Other expense items............	30,000	30,000	10,000	20,000	3.00	20,000	3.00
Income before income tax ..	$ 100,000	$ 85,000	$ 20,000	$ 80,000	5.00	$ 65,000	4.25
Income tax............................	30,000	25,000	5,000	25,000	6.00	20,000	5.00
Net income	$ 70,000	$ 60,000	$ 15,000	$ 55,000	4.67	$ 45,000	4.00

When a base figure is zero or is a minus value, it is possible to report a dollar change but the change cannot be expressed as a percentage. When a base figure is a positive value, however, a dollar change and also a percentage change can be stated. When ratio analysis is employed, ratios can be provided only when two positive values are given. The foregoing practices are illustrated in the examples below:

Net Income (Loss) for Year Ended December 31		Increase (Decrease)		
1977	1976	Amount	Percent	Ratio
$20,000	$ 0	$20,000	——	——
(2,000)	0	(2,000)	——	——
2,000	(5,000)	7,000	——	——
(10,000)	(5,000)	(5,000)	——	——
0	10,000	(10,000)	(100%)	——
(2,000)	10,000	(12,000)	(120%)	——
35,000	10,000	25,000	250%	3.50
8,000	10,000	(2,000)	(20%)	.80
10,000	10,000	——	——	1.00

Other Considerations. Although comparisons in previous examples have been limited to annual data, it is frequently desirable to develop comparisons for shorter periods. It would be possible, for example, to prepare comparative statements for monthly or quarterly periods. Furthermore, in the case of earnings data, it may be desirable to compare a current month with the same month of preceding years, or cumulative data for the current year to date with cumulative data for the corresponding period of preceding years.

A number of companies have adopted the *thirteen-month year*, dividing the calendar year into thirteen equal periods of four weeks. Variations for the total number of days and number of Saturdays and Sundays found in the calendar months are thus eliminated in the development of comparative "monthly" statements. More reliable conclusions can be drawn from analyses developed from data for periods of comparable length.

Vertical Analysis   Comparative data may include analyses in terms of percentages or ratios based upon the related data of each individual period. For example, in presenting comparative operating data, it may be desirable to show the relationship in each period of cost of goods sold, operating expenses, other revenue and expense items, and income tax to sales. The development of data expressing relationships within a single period is known as *vertical analysis*. Vertical analysis as applied to the comparative data on the income statement for the Chaparral Company is illustrated at the top of the next page. The net sales figure for each year is used as the base figure for that year and is expressed as 100%. The analysis can be expressed in the form of ratios rather than percentages. Net sales, then, would be expressed as 1.00 and revenue and expense items would be reported in terms of this base.

Chaparral Company
Condensed Comparative Income Statement
For Years Ended December 31

	1977		1976		1975	
	Amount	Percent	Amount	Percent	Amount	Percent
Gross sales	$1,500,000	105.3%	$1,750,000	106.1%	$1,000,000	105.3%
Sales returns.................................	75,000	5.3	100,000	6.1	50,000	5.3
Net sales...	$1,425,000	100.0%	$1,650,000	100.0%	$ 950,000	100.0%
Cost of goods sold	1,000,000	70.2	1,200,000	72.7	630,000	66.3
Gross profit on sales......................	$ 425,000	29.8%	$ 450,000	27.3%	$ 320,000	33.7%
Selling expense..............................	$ 280,000	19.7%	$ 300,000	18.2%	$ 240,000	25.3%
General expense	100,000	7.0	110,000	6.7	100,000	10.5
Total operating expenses...............	$ 380,000	26.7%	$ 410,000	24.9%	$ 340,000	35.8%
Operating income (loss)	$ 45,000	3.1%	$ 40,000	2.4%	$ (20,000)	(2.1%)
Other revenue items........................	85,000	6.0	75,000	4.5	50,000	5.3
	$ 130,000	9.1%	$ 115,000	6.9%	$ 30,000	3.2%
Other expense items........................	30,000	2.1	30,000	1.8	10,000	1.1
Income before income tax..............	$ 100,000	7.0%	$ 85,000	5.1%	$ 20,000	2.1%
Income tax	30,000	2.1	25,000	1.5	5,000	.5
Net income......................................	$ 70,000	4.9%	$ 60,000	3.6%	$ 15,000	1.6%

Although it may not be possible to specify a normal gross profit rate for the Chaparral Company, it can be determined from the comparative income statement that a significant decline in the gross profit rate took place in 1976 with a partial recovery in 1977. This would suggest that an analysis be made of the causes for the increase in the cost of goods sold percentage. Notwithstanding the reduction in the gross profit rate, the net income percentage on each dollar of sales increased in 1976 and again in 1977. These increases resulted from reductions in the expense percentage per dollar of sales that more than compensated for the increases in the cost of goods sold percentage. The comparative statement points to certain relationships and trends requiring further investigation in arriving at an explanation and an evaluation of the changes.

When supporting schedules are prepared for the detail relating to totals on the condensed income statement, individual items may be expressed in terms of net sales or in terms of the totals reported on the individual schedules. Sales salaries for the Chaparral Company for 1977, for example, may be reported as a certain percentage of net sales of $1,425,000, with the selling expense schedule listing expenses adding up to 19.7%; or the salaries may be reported as a percentage of total selling expenses of $280,000, with the individual items on the schedule adding to 100%.

Vertical analysis may also be employed in presenting a comparative balance sheet, a comparative statement of retained earnings, and a comparative statement of changes in financial position. On the balance sheet, individual items are expressed in terms of the total assets and the total liabilities and stockholders' equity; on the statement of retained earnings, individual items can be expressed in terms of the retained earnings balance at the beginning or at the end of the period; on the statement of changes in financial position, individual items are expressed in terms of total funds provided or total funds applied. The balance sheet for the Chaparral Company is provided as an illustration.

Chaparral Company
Condensed Comparative Balance Sheet
December 31

	1977		1976		1975	
	Amount	Percent	Amount	Percent	Amount	Percent
Assets						
Current assets	$ 855,000	38%	$ 955,500	40%	$ 673,500	38%
Long-term investments	500,000	22	400,000	17	250,000	14
Land, buildings, and equipment (net)	775,000	34	875,000	37	675,000	38
Intangible assets	100,000	4	100,000	4	100,000	6
Other assets	48,000	2	60,500	2	61,500	4
Total assets	$2,278,000	100%	$2,391,000	100%	$1,760,000	100%
Liabilities						
Current liabilities	$ 410,000	18%	$ 546,000	23%	$ 130,000	7%
Long-term liabilities — 8% bonds	400,000	18	400,000	17	300,000	17
Total liabilities	$ 810,000	36%	$ 946,000	40%	$ 430,000	24%
Stockholders' Equity						
Preferred 6% stock	$ 350,000	15%	$ 350,000	15%	$ 250,000	14%
Common stock	750,000	33	750,000	31	750,000	43
Additional paid-in capital	100,000	4	100,000	4	100,000	6
Retained earnings	268,000	12	245,000	10	230,000	13
Total stockholders' equity	$1,468,000	64%	$1,445,000	60%	$1,330,000	76%
Total liabilities and stockholders' equity	$2,278,000	100%	$2,391,000	100%	$1,760,000	100%

When a supporting schedule is prepared to show the detail for a group total, individual items may be expressed as a percentage of the base figure or as a percentage of the group total.

Both horizontal and vertical analyses are required if business trends and financial and operating relationships are to be fully understood. Measurements used in horizontal analyses are frequently referred to as *trend ratios*; measurements used in vertical analyses are frequently referred to as *structural ratios*. When vertical relationships are expressed for a number of periods, analyses of both a horizontal and vertical character are provided.

Interim Financial Statements

Statements showing financial position and operating results for intervals of less than a year are referred to as *interim financial statements*. As indicated earlier, there are inherent problems in preparing such statements, yet interim reports are considered essential in providing investors and others with more timely information as to the position and progress of an enterprise. This information is most useful in comparative form because of the relationship it shows to data for similar reporting intervals and to data in the annual report.

Some of the difficulties found in reporting interim results are caused by seasonal factors of certain businesses. For example, in some companies, revenues fluctuate widely among interim periods; in other businesses, significant fixed costs are incurred during a single period but are to benefit several periods. Not only must costs be allocated to appropriate periods of benefit, but they must be matched against the realized revenues for the interim period to determine a reasonable profit measurement.

In preparing interim reports, adjustments for accrued items, generally required only at year end, have to be considered at the end of each interim period. Because of the additional time and extra costs involved to develop complete information, many estimates of expenses will have to be made for interim reports. The increased number of estimates adds an element of subjectivity to the reports.

Another problem is that extraordinary items or the disposal of a business segment will have a greater impact on an interim period's earnings than on the results of operations for an entire year. In analyzing interim financial statements, special attention should be given to these and similar considerations.

Partially because of some of the above problems and partially because of differing views as to the objective of interim reports, there has been a variety of practice in presenting interim financial information. Two prominent viewpoints exist. One viewpoint is that each reporting interval is to be recognized as a separate accounting period. Thus, the results of operations for each interim period are determined in essentially the same manner as for the annual accounting period. Under this approach, the same judgments, estimations, accruals, and deferrals are recognized at the end of each interim period as for the annual period.

The other viewpoint, and the one accepted by the APB in Opinion No. 28, is that the interim period is an integral part of the annual period.[1] Essentially, the revenues and expenses for the total period are allocated among interim periods on some reasonable basis, e.g., time, sales volume, or productive activity.

Under the integral part of annual period concept, the same general accounting principles and reporting practices employed for annual reports are to be utilized for interim statements, except modifications may be required so the interim results will better relate to the total results of operations for the annual period. As an example of the type of modification that may be required, assume a company uses the lifo method of inventory valuation and encounters a situation where liquidation of the base period inventory occurs at an interim date but the inventory is expected to be replaced by the end of the annual period. Under these circumstances, the inventory reported at the interim date should not reflect the lifo liquidation, and the cost of goods sold for the interim period should include the expected cost of replacing the liquidated lifo base.[2]

---

[1]*Opinions of the Accounting Principles Board, No. 28*, "Interim Financial Reporting" (New York: American Institute of Certified Public Accountants, 1973), par. 9.
[2]*Ibid.*, par. 14.

Another example of a required modification deals with a change in accounting principle during an interim period. In general, these changes should follow the provisions of APB Opinion No. 20.[1] However, the FASB has concluded in Statement No. 3 that for any cumulative effect-type change, other than a change to lifo, if the change is made "in other than the first interim period of an enterprise's fiscal year, the cumulative effect of the change on retained earnings at the beginning of that year shall be included in the determination of net income of the first interim period of the year of change."[2]

Applying generally accepted accounting practices to interim financial statements can become complex. This is an area which is developing to meet the perceived needs of users. For example, the SEC has adopted rules requiring significantly increased disclosure of interim financial information. Accounting Series Release No. 177 requires additional quarterly report data in Form 10-Q as well as summarized quarterly operating data in an "unaudited" note to the annual financial statements included in SEC filings.[3] Interpretations of old standards and the development of new standards will assist in presenting interim financial data that should help investors and others in analyzing and interpreting the financial picture and operating results of a company.

Line of Business Reporting

Financial analysts and others argue that it is necessary to have disaggregated information about the major lines of business or segments of a company in order to effectively analyze a company's profitability. This is especially true for highly diversified companies which operate in several widely differing industries. For example, if a company were involved in each of the foods, clothing, and chemical industries, it would be difficult to compare total company data with any meaningful single industry standard. Each of these lines of business may have a different profit potential, rate of growth, or degree of risk. To effectively analyze the total company's profitability would require having information about each major segment of the company's business.

Reporting by lines of business presents several problems. For example, how does one determine which business segments should be reported upon? Certainly not all companies are organized in the same manner, even if they are engaged in similar business activities. Reporting on a particular division or profit-center in one company may not be comparable to another company. Another problem relates to transfer pricing. Not all companies use the same method of pricing goods or services that are "sold" among the different divisions or units of a company. This could lead to distorted segment profit data. Another related problem is the allo-

---

[1] *Opinions of the Accounting Principles Board, No. 20,* "Accounting Changes" (New York: American Institute of Certified Public Accountants, 1971).

[2] *Statement of Financial Accounting Standards No. 3,* "Reporting Accounting Changes in Interim Financial Statements" (Stamford, Conn.: Financial Accounting Standards Board, 1974), par. 4.

[3] Securities and Exchange Commission, *Accounting Series Release No. 177,* "Notice of Adoption of Amendments to Form 10-Q and Regulation S-X Regarding Interim Financial Reporting" (Washington, D.C.: U.S. Government Printing Office, 1975).

cation of common costs among segments of a company. Certain costs, such as general and administrative expenses, are very difficult to assign to particular segments of a company on anything other than an arbitrary basis. This, again, could lead to misleading information.

Notwithstanding the foregoing problems and recognizing the potential benefit to be obtained from disclosure of segment data, the FASB has issued Statement No. 14 which requires companies presenting financial statements to include information about operations in different industries, foreign operations and export sales, and major customers.[1] Information to be reported includes revenues, operating profit, and identifiable assets for each significant industry segment of a company. Essentially, a segment is considered significant if its sales, profit, or assets are 10 percent or more of the respective total company amounts. A practical limit of 10 segments is suggested, and at least 75 percent of total company sales must be accounted for. The segment profit data may be reported in the audited financial statements, notes to the financial statements, or in a separate schedule considered an integral part of the statements. Other provisions of Statement No. 14 require disclosure of revenues from major customers and provide guidelines for determining a company's foreign operations and export sales. Normally, the above requirements do not apply to interim financial reports.

COMMON-SIZE STATEMENTS

Comparative statements providing relationships of the individual items to the whole without giving dollar values are known as *common-size statements*. These relationships may be stated in terms of percentages or in terms of ratios. Common-size statements may be prepared for the same business as of different dates or periods or for two or more business units as of the same date or for the same period.

A common-size income statement for the Chaparral Company is given at the top of the next page. The statement is prepared simply by reporting the percentage figures that were shown on the comparative income statement on page 773. A common-size statement comparing balance sheet data for the Chaparral Company with that of the Baxter Company is also given on the next page. This statement provides a comparison of the relationships of balance sheet items for the two companies. It is readily seen, for example, that the relationship of the stockholders' equity to total assets is approximately the same for each company. Although the percentage of current liabilities to total assets for the Baxter Company is somewhat higher than that for the Chaparral Company, the ratio of current assets to current liabilities for the Baxter Company exceeds significantly that of the Chaparral Company. It would thus appear that the Baxter Company has the stronger working capital position. Further inquiry, however, is necessary. Reference to the items com-

---

[1]*Statement of Financial Accounting Standards No. 14*, "Financial Reporting for Segments of a Business Enterprise" (Stamford, Conn.: Financial Accounting Standards Board, 1976).

Chaparral Company
Condensed Common-Size Income Statement
For Years Ended December 31

	1977	1976	1975
Gross sales	105.3%	106.1%	105.3%
Sales returns	5.3	6.1	5.3
Net sales	100.0%	100.0%	100.0%
Cost of goods sold	70.2	72.7	66.3
Gross profit on sales	29.8%	27.3%	33.7%
Selling expense	19.7%	18.2%	25.3%
General expense	7.0	6.7	10.5
Total operating expenses	26.7%	24.9%	35.8%
Operating income (loss)	3.1%	2.4%	(2.1%)
Other revenue items	6.0	4.5	5.3
	9.1%	6.9%	3.2%
Other expense items	2.1	1.8	1.1
Income before income tax	7.0%	5.1%	2.1%
Income tax	2.1	1.5	0.5
Net income	4.9%	3.6%	1.6%

Chaparral Company and Baxter Company
Condensed Common-Size Balance Sheet
December 31, 1977

	Chaparral Company	Baxter Company
Assets		
Current assets	38%	64%
Long-term investments	22	—
Land, buildings, and equipment (net)	34	35
Intangible assets	4	—
Other assets	2	1
Total assets	100%	100%
Liabilities		
Current liabilities	18%	20%
Long-term liabilities	18	12
Deferred revenues	—	2
Total liabilities	36%	34%
Stockholders' Equity		
Preferred stock	15%	—
Common stock	33	46%
Additional paid-in capital	4	5
Retained earnings	12	15
Total stockholders' equity	64%	66%
Total liabilities and stockholders' equity	100%	100%

posing working capital may show that Baxter Company current assets consist primarily of slow-moving inventories, whereas Chaparral Company current assets consist primarily of cash and marketable securities, and inventories are only a small part of the total. It may be further disclosed that although the inventories of both companies are reported on the last-in, first-out basis, this method was adopted by the Chaparral Company some time prior to its adoption by the Baxter Company, and, as a result, inventories of the Chaparral Company reflect costs that are significantly lower than those of the Baxter Company.

In preparing common-size statements for two companies, it is important that the financial data for each company reflect comparable price levels. Furthermore, it should be determined that financial data were developed in terms of comparable accounting methods, classification procedures, and valuation bases. Comparisons should be limited to companies engaged in similar activities. When financial policies of the two companies are different, these differences should be recognized in evaluating comparative reports. For example, one company may lease its properties while the other may purchase such items; one company may resort to financing by means of long-term borrowing while the other may rely primarily on funds supplied by stockholders and by earnings. Operating results for the two companies under these circumstances cannot be wholly comparable.

The above suggests that comparisons between different companies should be approached with care, and when comparisons are made, these should be viewed with a full understanding of the limitations inherent in them. Reference was made earlier to the criteria that the Accounting Principles Board has set if comparisons are to be most meaningful under any circumstances. The Board is aware that comparability between and among enterprises is more difficult to obtain than comparability within a single enterprise. Ideally, differences in companies' financial reports should arise from basic differences in the companies themselves or from the nature of their transactions and not from differences in accounting practices and procedures. The Board remarks, "One of the most important unsolved problems at present is the general acceptance of alternative accounting practices under circumstances which themselves do not appear to be sufficiently different to justify different practices."[1]

STATEMENT ACCOUNTING FOR VARIATION IN NET INCOME

As previously illustrated, the comparative income statement shows comparative balances, changes in individual revenue and expense items, and also changes in the net income. Comparative income statement data may be used in the preparation of a statement accounting for the variation in net income. Here, comparative data are assembled and presented in a manner that calls attention to the various constituent factors responsible for the change in net income. A statement accounting for the increase in the net income for the Chaparral Company for 1977 over 1976 may be prepared from comparative income statement data as shown at the top of the next page.

The statement shows that although reductions in net income resulted from a decrease in the gross profit on sales and an increase in income tax, these were more than offset by a decrease in cost of goods sold, a decrease in operating expenses, and an increase in other revenue. It would appear, then, that increased operating efficiency was a significant factor in increasing net income.

---

[1]*Statements of the Accounting Principles Board, No. 4, op. cit.*, par. 101.

Chaparral Company
Statement Accounting for Variation in Net Income
1977 as Compared with 1976

Net income for year ended December 31, 1976.....................................					$60,000
Net income was increased as a result of:					
Decrease in selling expenses					
1976..	$300,000				
1977..	280,000	$20,000			
Decrease in general expenses					
1976..	$110,000				
1977..	100,000	10,000			
Increase in other revenue items					
1977..	$ 85,000				
1976..	75,000	10,000	$40,000		
Net income was decreased as a result of:					
Decrease in gross profit on sales:					
Decrease in net sales					
1976..	$1,650,000				
1977..	1,425,000	$225,000			
Less decrease in cost of goods sold					
1976..	$1,200,000				
1977..	1,000,000	200,000	$25,000		
Increase in income tax					
1977..	$ 30,000				
1976..	25,000	5,000	30,000	10,000	
Net income for year ended December 31, 1977.....................................					$70,000

STATEMENT ACCOUNTING FOR VARIATION IN GROSS PROFIT

Since gross profit is so significant in determining earnings, special analyses may be directed to the factors responsible for the periodic changes in gross profit. If these analyses are to go beyond simply reporting the effects of changes in sales and in cost of goods sold on gross profit, information will be required concerning the changes in the number of units sold. With this information it is possible to determine the volume and the price factors responsible for the changes in sales and the changes in cost of goods sold. The following summary indicates the volume and price variations that can be provided and the computations that they require.

Variations identified with the change in sales:
1. *Variations arising from the change in sales volume.* To calculate the change in sales arising from the change in the sales volume, the change in volume is multiplied by the sales price for the preceding period.
2. *Variations arising from the change in sales price.* To calculate the change in sales arising from the change in sales price, the volume of goods sold in the preceding period is multiplied by the change in sales price.
3. *Variations arising from the change in the joint sales price-volume factor.* Since the computation in (1) used the sales price of the preceding period as a base and the computation in (2) used the volume of goods sold in the preceding period as a base, a third price-volume factor must now be recognized to complete the explanation for the change in sales. The price-volume factor is computed by multiplying the change in sales volume by the change in sales price. An increase in both volume and price indicates an increase in sales; a decrease in volume or in price indicates a decrease in sales arising from the joint price-volume factor.

Variations identified with the change in the cost of goods sold:

1. *Variations arising from the change in sales volume.* To calculate the change in cost of goods sold arising from the change in the volume of goods sold, the change in volume is multiplied by the cost price for the preceding period.
2. *Variations arising from the change in cost price.* To calculate the change in cost of goods sold arising from the change in the cost price, the change in price is multiplied by the volume of goods sold in the preceding period.
3. *Variations arising from the change in the joint cost price-volume factor.* Since the computation in (1) used the cost price of the preceding period as a base and the computation in (2) used the volume of goods sold in the preceding period as a base, a third price-volume factor is computed by multiplying the change in the volume of goods sold by the change in cost price. An increase in both volume and cost indicates an addition to cost of goods sold; a decrease in volume or in cost indicates a reduction of cost of goods sold arising from the joint cost price-volume factor.

To illustrate the nature of the calculations, assume the following gross profit data:

	1977		1976		Change
Sales	120,000 @ $10.00	$1,200,000	100,000 @ $9.50	$950,000	$250,000
Cost of goods sold.	120,000 @ $ 7.00	840,000	100,000 @ $7.25	725,000	115,000
Gross profit		$ 360,000		$225,000	$135,000

The variation in gross profit can now be analyzed as follows:

Increase in sales:		
Variation arising from increase in sales volume (20,000 × $9.50)	$190,000	
Variation arising from increase in sales price (100,000 × $.50)	50,000	
Variation arising from joint increase in sales volume and increase in sales price (20,000 × $.50)	10,000	$250,000
Less increase in cost of goods sold:		
Variation arising from increase in cost volume (20,000 × $7.25)	$145,000	
Variation arising from decrease in cost price (100,000 × $.25)	(25,000)	
Variation arising from joint increase in volume and decrease in cost price (20,000 × $.25)	(5,000)	115,000
Increase in gross profit		$135,000

The analysis will now be applied to the Chaparral Company and the statement of the variation of gross profit will be illustrated in formal form. Assume that information concerning sales and costs for the Chaparral Company are as follows:

	1977		1976		Change
Sales...................	20,000 @ $71.25	$1,425,000	25,000 @ $66.00	$1,650,000	$(225,000)
Cost of goods sold.	20,000 @ $50.00	1,000,000	25,000 @ $48.00	1,200,000	(200,000)
Gross profit		$ 425,000		$ 450,000	$ (25,000)

Analysis of these data is summarized in the statement that appears at the top of the next page.

Chaparral Company
Statement Accounting for Variation in Gross Profit
1977 as Compared with 1976

Decrease in gross profit resulted from:			
Decrease in net sales:			
Decrease arising from decrease in number of units sold (5,000 × $66), in absence of change in sales price		$(330,000)	
Increase arising from increase in sales price (25,000 × $5.25), in absence of change in volume		131,250	
Decrease arising from joint decrease in number of units sold and increase in sales price (5,000 × $5.25)		(26,250)	$225,000
Less decrease in cost of goods sold:			
Decrease arising from decrease in number of units sold (5,000 × $48), in absence of change in cost price		$(240,000)	
Increase arising from increase in cost price (25,000 × $2), in absence of change in volume		50,000	
Decrease arising from joint decrease in number of units sold and increase in cost price (5,000 × $2)		(10,000)	200,000
Decrease in gross profit			$ 25,000

The above analysis indicates that although sales went down $225,000, the decline would have been even greater were it not for the increases in sales prices. The decreases in selling and general and administrative expenses for the year reported on the statement accounting for the variation in net income given on page 780 had been interpreted as evidence of increased operating efficiency. It would appear that this conclusion needs to be questioned in view of the analysis showing a significant reduction in the number of units sold. The gross profit analysis also shows that increases in sales prices exceeded the increased cost of goods sold, thus helping to maintain the gross profit at close to the total of the preceding year despite the reduction in sales. It thus appears that the increased net income for 1977 for the Chaparral Company was the result of rising sales prices rather than greater managerial efficiency.

It was assumed that the Chaparral Company sold a single commodity. If several commodities are sold, data would have to be assembled and separate schedules developed with respect to sales, sales prices, and costs for each. Analyses of the gross profit variations relating to each class of sales could then be prepared. When many commodities are sold and price changes are numerous, these refined analyses may become extremely complicated.

Although the analysis of gross profit variation may be of value to certain external groups, the analysis requires information concerning the change in the volume of sales not ordinarily found on the published financial statements. In some cases, these data may be provided in the annual reports. In other cases, information in the annual reports may have to be supplemented by reference to other sources, by special research and inquiry, or by estimates.

QUESTIONS

1. What groups may be interested in a company's financial statements?

2. What types of questions requiring financial statement analysis might be raised by external users, such as investors and creditors, as contrasted to internal management?

3. Explain how an understanding of accounting assists in the analysis and interpretation of financial statements.

4. What are the factors that one would look for in judging a company's (a) liquidity, (b) stability, (c) profitability?

5. Why are comparative financial statements considered more meaningful than statements prepared for a single period? What conditions increase the usefulness of comparative statements?

6. Distinguish between horizontal and vertical analytical procedures. What special purpose does each serve?

7. What type of information is provided by analysis of comparative changes in financial position that is not available from analysis of comparative balance sheets and income statements?

8. When data for more than two years are available, what are the advantages of developing comparisons in terms of the earliest year given? What are the advantages of developing comparisons in terms of the preceding year?

9. What are the relative advantages of changes reported as percentages as compared with changes reported as ratios?

10. What is meant by a *thirteen-month year*? What advantages and disadvantages can you suggest in the use of such a year for accounting purposes?

11. Distinguish between the two primary view-points concerning the preparation of interim financial statements.

12. What is meant by a *common-size* statement? What are its advantages?

13. Mention some factors that may limit the comparability of financial statements of two companies in the same industry.

14. What factors may be responsible for a change in a company's net income from one year to the next?

15. What factors may be responsible for a change in a company's gross profit from one year to the next?

16. (a) The Price Co. reports an increase in gross profit in 1977 over 1976 of $60,000. What other information would be useful in the evaluation of this increase? (b) Give possible unfavorable factors that might accompany an increase in gross profit.

17. The World Co. develops the following measurements for 1977 as compared with the year 1976. What additional information would you require before arriving at favorable or unfavorable conclusions for each item?

- (a) Net income has increased $70,000.
- (b) Sales returns and allowances have increased by $25,000.
- (c) The gross profit rate has increased by 5%.
- (d) Purchase discounts have increased by $5,000.
- (e) Working capital has increased by $85,000.
- (f) Accounts receivable have increased by $150,000.
- (g) Inventories have decreased by $100,000.
- (h) Retained earnings have decreased by $300,000.

18. What is meant by the joint sales price-volume factor? Why do total sales decline as a result of this factor if *either* sales price or sales volume declines?

EXERCISES

1. Indicate the dollar change, the percentage change, and also the ratio that would be reported for each case below, assuming horizontal analysis:

Gain (loss) on sale of investments:

	1977	1976			1977	1976
(a)	$45,000	$20,000		(f)	$(30,000)	0
(b)	20,000	40,000		(g)	5,000	$ (5,000)
(c)	30,000	0		(h)	(20,000)	5,000
(d)	0	40,000		(i)	(10,000)	(10,000)
(e)	(30,000)	10,000		(j)	20,000	20,000

2. Sales for the Carson Company for a five-year period and an industry sales index for this period are listed below. Convert both series into indexes employing 1973 as the base year.

	1977	1976	1975	1974	1973
Sales of Carson Company (in thousands of dollars)	$4,200	$4,515	$4,355	$4,425	$4,265
Industry sales index (1963–1965 = 100)	190	212	210	170	158

3. Cost of goods sold data for Bell, Inc., are presented below:

	1977	1976
Merchandise inventory, January 1	$ 40,000	$ 25,000
Purchases	100,000	90,000
Merchandise available for sale	$140,000	$115,000
Less merchandise inventory, December 31	35,000	40,000
Cost of goods sold	$105,000	$ 75,000

Prepare a comparative schedule of cost of goods sold showing dollar and percentage changes.

4. The financial position of the Dew Co., at the end of 1977 and 1976 is presented below:

	1977	1976
Assets		
Current assets	$ 40,000	$ 42,000
Long-term investments	15,000	14,000
Land, buildings, and equipment (net)	50,000	55,000
Intangible assets	10,000	10,000
Other assets	5,000	6,000
Total assets	$120,000	$127,000
Liabilities		
Current liabilities	$ 15,000	$ 20,000
Long-term liabilities	38,000	42,000
Total liabilities	$ 53,000	$ 62,000
Stockholders' Equity		
Preferred 6% stock	$ 10,000	$ 9,000
Common stock	39,000	39,000
Additional paid-in capital	5,000	5,000
Retained earnings	13,000	12,000
Total stockholders' equity	$ 67,000	$ 65,000
Total liabilities and stockholders' equity	$120,000	$127,000

Prepare a comparative balance sheet offering a percentage analysis of component items in terms of total assets and total liabilities and stockholders' equity for each year.

5. From the following data for Patrick Exports, explain the causes for the increase in net income supported by a detailed analysis of the causes for the change in gross profit.

	1977		1976	
Sales	100,000 units @ $6	$600,000	125,000 units @ $6.20	$775,000
Cost of goods sold		250,000		450,000
Gross profit on sales		$350,000		$325,000
Operating expenses		100,000		125,000
Net income		$250,000		$200,000

6. Comparative data for the Harris Company appear below:

	1977	1976
Sales	$6,000,000	$4,000,000
Cost of goods sold	3,500,000	2,000,000
Gross profit on sales	$2,500,000	$2,000,000

(a) Assume sales prices in 1977 average 20% above those for 1976. What part of the change in gross profit is due to changes in the sales volume, in the sales price, and in the gross profit rate?

(b) Assume, instead, a single commodity is sold, and the sales price of this commodity was $2 in 1976 and $2.40 in 1977. Prepare a statement analyzing the change in gross profit in terms of volume and price changes for both sales and costs.

PROBLEMS

26-1. Operations of the Teegarden Company for 1977 and 1976 are summarized below:

	1977	1976
Sales	$500,000	$450,000
Sales returns	20,000	10,000
Net sales	$480,000	$440,000
Cost of goods sold	350,000	240,000
Gross profit on sales	$130,000	$200,000
Selling and general expenses	100,000	120,000
Operating income	$ 30,000	$ 80,000
Other expenses	35,000	30,000
Income (loss) before income tax	$ (5,000)	$ 50,000
Income tax		22,500
Net income (loss)	$ (5,000)	$ 27,500

Instructions:

(1) Prepare a comparative income statement showing dollar changes and percentage changes for 1977 as compared with 1976.

(2) Prepare a comparative income statement offering a percentage analysis of component revenue and expense items in terms of net sales for each year.

(3) Prepare a statement accounting for the variation in net income for 1977 as compared with 1976.

26-2. The financial position of Teodoro, Inc., at the end of 1977 and at the end of 1976 is summarized below and on the next page.

	1977	1976
Assets		
Current assets:		
Cash	$ 70,000	$ 90,000
Marketable securities	90,000	100,000
Notes and accounts receivable, less allowance	400,000	300,000
Raw materials	350,000	300,000
Goods in process	200,000	160,000
Finished goods	400,000	350,000
Miscellaneous prepaid items	40,000	60,000
Total current assets	$1,550,000	$1,360,000
Long-term investments:		
Bond redemption fund	$ 400,000	$ 300,000
Investment in properties not in current use	250,000	250,000
Total long-term investments	$ 650,000	$ 550,000
Land, buildings, and equipment at cost, less accumulated depreciation	$ 920,000	$1,000,000
Intangible assets	$ 60,000	$ 70,000
Other assets:		
Unamortized bond issue costs	$ 34,000	$ 40,000
Machinery rearrangement costs	16,000	20,000
Total other assets	$ 50,000	$ 60,000
Total assets	$3,230,000	$3,040,000

	1977	1976
Liabilities		
Current liabilities:		
Notes and accounts payable	$ 250,000	$ 240,000
Income tax payable	80,000	50,000
Payrolls, interest, and tax payable	50,000	40,000
Dividends payable	10,000	15,000
Miscellaneous payables	10,000	15,000
Total current liabilities	$ 400,000	$ 360,000
Long-term liabilities — 8%, 10-year first-mortgage bonds	300,000	350,000
Estimated employee pensions payable	110,000	150,000
Deferred revenues	20,000	30,000
Total liabilities	$ 830,000	$ 890,000
Stockholders' Equity		
Paid-in capital:		
Preferred 6% stock, $25 par	$ 400,000	$ 400,000
No-par common stock, $10 stated value	600,000	600,000
Additional paid-in capital	700,000	700,000
Total paid-in capital	$1,700,000	$1,700,000
Retained earnings:		
Appropriated	$ 350,000	$ 300,000
Unappropriated	350,000	150,000
Total retained earnings	$ 700,000	$ 450,000
Total stockholders' equity	$2,400,000	$2,150,000
Total liabilities and stockholders' equity	$3,230,000	$3,040,000

Instructions:

(1) Prepare a comparative balance sheet showing dollar changes and changes in terms of ratios for 1977 as compared with 1976.

(2) Prepare a common-size balance sheet comparing financial structure ratios for 1977 with those for 1976.

26-3. Financial statements for the Baltzer Mfg. Co. are given below and on pages 787 and 788.

Baltzer Mfg. Co.
Balance Sheet
December 31

	1977	1976	1975
Assets			
Current assets	$1,130,000	$1,000,000	$ 600,000
Investments	300,000	230,000	350,000
Land, buildings, and equipment (net)	1,320,000	1,000,000	1,050,000
Intangible assets	140,000	130,000	130,000
Total assets	$2,890,000	$2,360,000	$2,130,000
Liabilities			
Current liabilities	$ 320,000	$ 412,000	$ 300,000
Long-term liabilities — 8% bonds	300,000	250,000	200,000
Deferred revenues	10,000	60,000	10,000
Total liabilities	$ 630,000	$ 722,000	$ 510,000
Stockholders' Equity			
Cumulative preferred 6% stock, $50 par and liquidating value	$ 500,000	$ 500,000	$ 500,000
Common stock, $50 par	1,500,000	1,000,000	1,000,000
Additional paid-in capital	152,000	125,000	125,000
Retained earnings (deficit)	108,000	13,000	(5,000)
Total stockholders' equity	$2,260,000	$1,638,000	$1,620,000
Total liabilities and stockholders' equity	$2,890,000	$2,360,000	$2,130,000

Baltzer Mfg. Co.
Income Statement
For Years Ended December 31

	1977	1976	1975
Gross sales	$3,000,000	$2,400,000	$1,700,000
Sales returns	100,000	80,000	50,000
Net sales	$2,900,000	$2,320,000	$1,650,000
Finished goods inventory, Jan. 1	$ 320,000	$ 300,000	$ 440,000
Cost of goods manufactured	1,770,000	1,560,000	950,000
Goods available for sale	$2,090,000	$1,860,000	$1,390,000
Finished goods inventory, Dec. 31	360,000	320,000	300,000
Cost of goods sold	$1,730,000	$1,540,000	$1,090,000
Gross profit on sales	$1,170,000	$ 780,000	$ 560,000
Selling expense	$ 600,000	$ 480,000	$ 420,000
General and administrative expense	280,000	160,000	150,000
Total operating expenses	$ 880,000	$ 640,000	$ 570,000
Operating income (loss)	$ 290,000	$ 140,000	$ (10,000)
Other revenue items	60,000	40,000	15,000
	$ 350,000	$ 180,000	$ 5,000
Other expense items	50,000	20,000	20,000
Income (loss) before income tax	$ 300,000	$ 160,000	$ (15,000)
Income tax	135,000	72,000	
Net income (loss)	$ 165,000	$ 88,000	$ (15,000)

Baltzer Mfg. Co.
Schedule of Cost of Goods Manufactured
For Years Ended December 31

	1977	1976	1975
Raw materials inventory, Jan. 1	$ 210,000	$ 300,000	$ 200,000
Raw materials purchases	1,080,000	920,000	700,000
	$1,290,000	$1,220,000	$ 900,000
Raw materials inventory, Dec. 31	300,000	210,000	300,000
Cost of raw materials used	$ 990,000	$1,010,000	$ 600,000
Direct labor	400,000	340,000	300,000
Manufacturing overhead	290,000	260,000	200,000
	$1,680,000	$1,610,000	$1,100,000
Goods in process inventory, Jan. 1	350,000	300,000	150,000
	$2,030,000	$1,910,000	$1,250,000
Goods in process inventory, Dec. 31	260,000	350,000	300,000
Cost of goods manufactured	$1,770,000	$1,560,000	$ 950,000

Baltzer Mfg. Co.
Retained Earnings Statement
For Years Ended December 31

	1977	1976	1975
Retained earnings (deficit), Jan. 1	$ 13,000	$ (5,000)	$ 10,000
Net income (loss) per income statement	165,000	88,000	(15,000)
	$178,000	$ 83,000	$ (5,000)
Dividends:			
Preferred stock	$ 30,000	$ 60,000	
Common stock	40,000	10,000	
Total	$ 70,000	$ 70,000	
Retained earnings (deficit), Dec. 31	$108,000	$ 13,000	$ (5,000)

Baltzer Mfg. Co.
Statement of Changes in Financial Position — Working Capital Basis
For Years Ended December 31

	1977	1976	1975
Working capital was provided by:			
Operations:			
Net income	$165,000	$ 88,000	$ (15,000)
Add items not requiring working capital:			
Depreciation	70,000	65,000	60,000
Increase in deferred revenues		50,000	
Total	$235,000	$203,000	$ 45,000
Deduct item not providing working capital:			
Deferred revenues	50,000		
Working capital provided by operations	$185,000	$203,000	$ 45,000
Issuance of bonds	50,000	50,000	
Issuance of common stock	527,000		
Sale of investments		120,000	
Total	$762,000	$373,000	$ 45,000
Working capital was applied to:			
Dividends	$ 70,000	$ 70,000	
Intangible assets	10,000		
Long-term investments	70,000		125,000
Land, buildings, and equipment	390,000	15,000	110,000
Total	$540,000	$ 85,000	$ 235,000
Increase (decrease) in working capital	$222,000	$288,000	$(190,000)

Instructions:

(1) Prepare a comparative income statement for the three-year period, offering percentage analysis of component revenue and expense items in terms of net sales for each period.

(2) Prepare a comparative schedule of cost of goods manufactured for the three-year period in support of the comparative income statement, offering percentage analysis of component cost of goods manufactured items in terms of the total cost of goods manufactured for each year.

26-4. (1) From the data for the Baltzer Mfg. Co. given in Problem 26-3, develop a comparative statement of changes in financial position for the three-year period, showing dollar and percentage changes in terms of 1975, which is to be considered the base year.

(2) Prepare a comparative retained earnings statement for the three-year period, showing dollar and percentage changes in terms of 1975, which is to be considered the base year.

26-5. (1) From the data for the Baltzer Mfg. Co. given in Problem 26-3, prepare a condensed common-size balance sheet comparing financial structure percentages for the three-year period.

(2) What analytical conclusions can be drawn from this common-size statement?

26-6. (1) From the data for the Baltzer Mfg. Co. given in Problem 26-3, prepare a common-size income statement for each year.

(2) What analytical conclusions can be drawn from this common-size statement?

26-7. Balance sheet data for the Jackson Company and the Moris Company are given below and at the top of the next page.

	Jackson Company	Moris Company
Assets		
Current assets	$ 51,000	$ 24,000
Long-term investments	5,000	28,000
Land, buildings, and equipment (net)	48,000	52,000
Intangible assets	6,000	10,000
Other assets	5,000	6,000
Total assets	$115,000	$120,000

	Jackson Company	Moris Company
Liabilities		
Current liabilities	$ 15,000	$ 18,000
Long-term liabilities	25,000	30,000
Deferred revenues	5,000	7,000
Total liabilities	$ 45,000	$ 55,000
Stockholders' Equity		
Preferred stock	$ 5,000	$ 10,000
Common stock	30,000	20,000
Additional paid-in capital	25,000	18,500
Retained earnings	10,000	16,500
Total stockholders' equity	$ 70,000	$ 65,000
Total liabilities and stockholders' equity	$115,000	$120,000

Instructions:
(1) Prepare a common-size statement comparing balance sheet data for the year.
(2) What analytical conclusions can be drawn from this comparative common-size statement?

26-8. From the data for the Baltzer Mfg. Co. given in Problem 26-3, prepare statements accounting for the variation in net income (1) for 1977 as compared with 1975, and (2) for 1977 as compared with 1976.

26-9. Sales for Johnson Mfg. Co. and its chief competitor, the Phillips Company, and the sales index for the industry, are given below:

	1977	1976	1975	1974	1973
Sales of Johnson Mfg. Co. (in thousands of dollars)	$7,000	$7,280	$7,735	$8,450	$8,385
Sales of Phillips Company (in thousands of dollars)	$9,700	$9,690	$9,975	$9,785	$9,880
Industry sales index (1965 = 100)	140	154	161	147	133

Instructions:
(1) Convert the three series to index numbers using 1973 as the base year.
(2) Prepare a short report for the management of Johnson Mfg. Co. summarizing your findings.

26-10. The LaSalle Corp., which sells a single commodity, shows the following operating results for a three-year period.

	1977	1976	1975
Sales	$12,600,000	$9,000,000	$9,500,000
Cost of goods sold	7,056,000	5,000,000	5,700,000
Gross profit on sales	$ 5,544,000	$4,000,000	$3,800,000
Operating expenses	3,700,000	2,000,000	1,500,000
Net income	$ 1,844,000	$2,000,000	$2,300,000

Sales prices of the commodity sold were as follows: 1977, $2.50; 1976, $2.25; 1975, $2.00.

Instructions: Prepare statements for 1977 and 1976 analyzing the change in gross profit as compared with the year immediately preceding in terms of volume changes and price changes for both sales and costs.

26-11. Revenue and expense data of Simpson's, Inc., for 1977 and 1976 follow:

	1977	1976
Sales	$1,600,000	$1,000,000
Cost of goods sold	700,000	400,000
Gross profit on sales	$ 900,000	$ 600,000
Operating expenses	250,000	200,000
Net income	$ 650,000	$ 400,000

(continued)

Instructions: Prepare a statement analyzing the variation in gross profit, giving as much information as can be determined concerning factors responsible for the change, under each of the following independent assumptions:
(1) No data are available relative to price and volume changes.
(2) Sales prices in 1977 are 20% above sales prices in 1976.
(3) Total units sold in 1977 are 25% above total units sold in 1976.

26-12. The Dawn Mining Company mines selum, a commonly used mineral. Following is the company's report of operations:

	1977	1976	Increase (Decrease)
Net sales	$891,000	$ 840,000	$ 51,000
Cost of goods sold	688,500	945,000	(256,500)
Gross profit (loss)	$202,500	$(105,000)	$ 307,500

The following information pertains to the company's operations:
(a) The sales price of selum was increased from $8 per ton to $11 per ton on January 1, 1977.
(b) New mining machinery was placed in operation on January 1, 1977, reducing the cost of mining from $9 per ton to $8.50 per ton.
(c) There was no change in ending inventories which were valued on the lifo basis.

Instructions: Prepare an analysis accounting for the change in the gross profit of The Dawn Mining Company. The analysis should account for the effects of the changes in price, volume, and volume-price factors upon (1) sales and (2) cost of goods sold. (AICPA adapted)

26-13. The president of the Redbrick Tile Company is concerned because gross profit has decreased from $130,000 in 1976 to $87,960 in 1977. The president asks you to prepare an analysis of the causes of change.

You find that the company operates two plants, each as a separate unit. Investigation reveals the following information:

Plant No. 1 (makes a variety of products):

	1977	1976
Sales	$200,000	$300,000
Cost of sales	160,000	210,000
Gross profit	$ 40,000	$ 90,000

Plant No. 2 (makes only one product):

	1977		1976	
	Amount	Per Unit	Amount	Per Unit
Sales	$112,200	$10.20	$100,000	$10.00
Cost of sales	64,240	5.84	60,000	6.00
Gross profit	$ 47,960	$ 4.36	$ 40,000	$ 4.00

Instructions: Prepare a detailed analysis of the causes for the change in gross profit for each of the plants to the extent that the above data permit such an analysis. Critical comment on the analysis is not required. (AICPA adapted)

26-14. You are preparing your long-form report in connection with the audit of the City Gas Company at December 31, 1977. The report will include an explanation of the 1977 increase in operating revenues. The following information is available from the company records:

	1977	1976	Increase (Decrease)
Average number of customers	26,000	27,000	(1,000)
MCF sales	520,000	486,000	34,000
Revenue	$1,274,000	$1,215,000	$59,000

Instructions: To explain the 1977 increase in operating revenues, prepare an analysis accounting for the effect of changes in:
(1) Average number of customers.
(2) Average gas consumption per customer.
(3) Average rate per MCF sold (MCF = thousand cubic feet). (AICPA adapted)

Financial Statement Analysis — Special Measurements of Liquidity and Profitability

There are a great many special measurements that may be developed from financial statements and supplementary financial data. These measurements may be classified as: (1) those that analyze financial position or the *liquidity and stability* of a firm, and (2) those that analyze operations or the *profitability* of a firm. Some of these measurements have special significance to particular groups, while others may be of general interest to all groups. Creditors, for example, are concerned with the ability of a company to pay its current obligations and seek information about the relationship of current assets to current liabilities. Stockholders are concerned with dividends and seek information relating to the earnings per share that will form the basis for dividend declarations. Managements are concerned with the liquidity of the merchandise stock and seek information relating to the number of times goods have turned over during the period. All parties are vitally interested in the profitability of operations and wish to be informed about the relationship of earnings to both liabilities and owners' equities.

A number of measurements developed from the financial data for a single period will be described and illustrated in this chapter. These measurements represent extensions of the vertical analysis procedure. Measurements will also be provided in comparative form and will therefore represent further applications of the horizontal procedure. The analyses described and illustrated in this chapter should not be considered all-inclusive; other ratios and measurements may be useful to various groups, depending upon their particular needs. It should be emphasized again that sound conclusions cannot be reached from an individual ratio or measurement. But this information, together with adequate investigation and study, may lead to a satisfactory interpretation and evaluation of financial data. The analyses presented are based upon the financial statements given in the preceding chapter for the Chaparral Company for 1975, 1976, and 1977.

RATIOS AND MEASUREMENTS DEVELOPED
FROM BALANCE SHEET DATA

A number of special analyses may be developed from balance sheet data. Some of these are based upon current assets and current liabilities and have become generally accepted as measurements of the liquidity of a business unit. Other analyses are based upon noncurrent assets, noncurrent liabilities, and owners' equity, and offer measurements of certain significant relationships within these groups. Although many of the measurements are made directly from the balance sheet, some require the use of income statement data.

Current Ratio   The comparison of current assets with current liabilities is regarded as a fundamental measurement of a company's liquidity. Total current assets divided by total current liabilities gives the ratio of current assets to current liabilities, variously referred to as the *current ratio* or the *working capital ratio*.

The current ratio is a valuable measure of the ability of a business unit to meet its current obligations. Since it is a measure of liquidity, care must be taken to determine that proper items have been included in the current asset and current liability categories. In the past, a ratio of current assets to current liabilities of less than 2 to 1 for a trading or manufacturing unit has frequently been regarded as unsatisfactory. Because liquidity needs are different for different industries and companies, the recognition of any such arbitrary measure is now regarded as inappropriate. However, a comfortable margin of current assets over current liabilities does suggest that a company will be able to meet maturing obligations even in the event of an unfavorable turn in business conditions and losses in the realization of such assets as marketable securities, receivables, and inventories.

In considering current conditions, reference is frequently made to a company's *working capital*. In this text working capital is used to denote the excess of current assets over current liabilities. In some cases the term is used to indicate total current assets. When the term working capital is used to indicate total current assets, the term *net working capital* is used to indicate the excess of current assets over current liabilities. Because of the different uses of the term, the definition used for working capital should be ascertained in interpreting working capital analyses.

For the Chaparral Company, working capital totals and current ratios for 1977 and 1976 are developed as follows:[1]

	1977	1976
Current assets..	$855,000	$955,500
Current liabilities	410,000	546,000
Working capital...	$445,000	$409,500
Current ratio...	2.1:1	1.8:1

[1]Comparative data for more than two years are generally required in evaluating financial trends. Analyses for only two years are given in the examples in this chapter, since these are sufficient to illustrate the analytical procedures involved.

Ratio calculations are sometimes carried out to two or more decimal places; however, ratios do not need to be carried out beyond one place unless some particularly significant interpretative value is afforded by the more refined measurement. The current ratio just given, as well as the other ratios to be described, can be expressed in terms of percentages. The ratios just given are expressed as percentages as follows:

	1977	1976
Current ratio..	209%	175%

From the standpoint of liquidity it is more important to consider the ratio of current assets to current liabilities than the amount of working capital. For example, assume balance sheet data for Companies A and B as follows:

Company A: Current assets, $400,000; Current liabilities, $50,000
Company B: Current assets, $1,050,000; Current liabilities, $700,000

Both Company A and Company B have a working capital of $350,000, but Company A has a current ratio of 8:1 while Company B has a current ratio of 1.5:1. The short-term creditors of Company A are more certain of receiving prompt and full payment than those of Company B. On requests for short-term loans, bankers would probably be more favorable to Company A than to Company B.

It is possible, however, to overemphasize the importance of a high current ratio. Assume a company is normally able to carry on its operations with current assets of $200,000 and current liabilities of $100,000. If the company finds itself with current assets of $500,000, current liabilities remaining at $100,000, its current ratio has increased from 2:1 to 5:1. The company may now have considerably more working capital than it actually requires. It should also be observed that certain unfavorable conditions may be accompanied by an improving ratio. For example, with a slowdown in business and postponement of programs for advertising, research, and buildings and equipment repairs and replacements, a company's cash balance may rise. At the same time, slower customer collections may result in rising trade receivables, and reduced sales volume may result in rising inventories.

The amount of working capital required by a particular enterprise depends not only upon its size and its sales activity but also upon the character of its business. For example, a company that does business for cash and maintains a small inventory that turns over rapidly does not require as much working capital as a company with the same volume of business that sells goods on a credit basis and maintains a large inventory that turns over slowly. Working capital requirements may vary, too, depending upon the industry within which the enterprise is found. A construction company may require a large amount of working capital in financing construction activities; a public utility, on the other hand, may require only a small amount of working capital in its operations.

In analyzing working capital position, particular note should be taken of the valuation procedures used for the various assets and liabilities. Inventories reported on a last-in, first-out basis may be substantially below their market values during a period of rising prices; marketable securities reported at cost may be substantially below market; both receivables and payables reported at face or settlement amounts may be considerably above their present values. Special reference should also be made to estimated liabilities and to contingent liabilities in evaluating the effects of possible payment requirements that may differ from reported amounts.

Acid-Test Ratio

A test of a company's immediate liquidity is made by comparing the sum of cash, marketable securities, notes receivable, and accounts receivable, commonly referred to as the *quick assets*, with current liabilities. The total of the quick assets when divided by current liabilities gives the ratio of quick assets to current liabilities, known as the *acid-test ratio* or *quick ratio*. Considerable time may be required in the conversion of raw materials, goods in process, and finished goods into receivables and then receivables into cash. A company with a satisfactory current ratio may be in an unsatisfactory condition in terms of liquidity when inventories form a significant part of the current asset total. This is revealed by the acid-test ratio. In developing the ratio, close inspection must be given to the receivables and the securities included in the quick asset total. There may be instances where these items are actually less liquid than inventories.

Usually a ratio of quick assets to current liabilities of not less than 1 to 1 has been regarded as desirable. Again, however, special conditions applicable to the particular business must be evaluated. Questions such as the following should be considered: What is the composition of the quick assets? What special requirements are made by current activities upon these assets? How soon are the current payables due?

Acid-test ratios for the Chaparral Company are computed as follows:

	1977	1976
Quick assets:		
Cash	$ 60,000	$100,500
Marketable securities	150,000	150,000
Receivables (net)	420,000	375,000
Total quick assets	$630,000	$625,500
Total current liabilities	$410,000	$546,000
Acid-test ratio	1.5:1	1.1:1

Other Measurements of Working Capital Position

It may be desirable to develop other ratios in analyzing a company's working capital position. For example, it may be useful to show the relationship of total current assets to total assets, and of individual current assets, such as receivables and inventories to total current assets. In the case of liabilities, it may be useful to show the relationship of total current liabilities to total liabilities, and of individual current liabilities to total current liabilities. Vertical analysis, as applied to comparative statements in the previous chapter, provided these data and also reported the changes and the trends in these relationships over a period of years.

The foregoing comparisons may provide information concerning the relative liquidity of total assets and the maturity of total obligations as well as the structure of working capital and shifts within the working capital group. The latter data are significant, since all of the items within the current classification are not equally current. What may be considered reasonable relationships in the analysis of the working capital position will depend upon the particular enterprise.

Analysis of Receivables

There are special tests that may be applied in considering the liquidity of two significant working capital elements, receivables and inventories. In both cases, analysis is directed toward evaluation of both the amount and the quality of the assets.

Accounts Receivable Turnover. The amount of receivables usually bears a close relationship to the volume of credit sales. The receivable position and approximate collection time may be evaluated by computing the *accounts receivable turnover*. This rate is determined by dividing net credit sales for the period by the average notes and accounts receivable from trade debtors. In developing an average receivables amount, monthly balances should be used if available; the average is computed from thirteen monthly balances, those of January 1, January 31, February 28, and the last day of each of the remaining months of the year.

Assume in the case of the Chaparral Company that all sales are made on a credit basis, that receivables arise only from sales, and that receivable totals for only the beginning and the end of the year are available. Receivable turnover rates are computed as follows:

	1977	1976
Net credit sales	$1,425,000	$1,650,000
Net receivables:		
Beginning of year	$ 375,000	$ 333,500
End of year	$ 420,000	$ 375,000
Average receivables	$ 397,500	$ 354,250
Receivables turnover for year	3.6	4.7

Number of Days' Sales in Receivables. Average receivables are sometimes expressed in terms of the *number of days' sales in receivables*. The average time required to collect receivables is thus shown. For example, assume for convenience there are 360 days per year. Annual dollar sales are divided by 360 to find average daily sales. Average receivables divided by average daily sales then gives the number of days' sales in average receivables. The latter procedure for the Chaparral Company is illustrated at the top of the next page.

	1977	1976
Average receivables..	$ 397,500	$ 354,250
Net sales on account	$1,425,000	$1,650,000
Average daily sales on account (net sales on account ÷ 360)..	$ 3,958	$ 4,583
Number of days' sales in average receivables (average receivables ÷ average daily sales on account).............	100	77

The same measurements can be obtained by dividing the number of days representing the year by the receivable turnover rates. A comparable number of days for each year should be used in developing comparisons. Computations are generally based on the calendar year, consisting of 365 days, often rounded to 360 days, or a business year consisting of 300 days (365 days less Sundays and holidays). The calendar year basis, rounded to 360 days, is used in this chapter.

In certain instances, instead of developing the number of days' sales in average receivables, it may be considered more useful to report the number of days' credit sales in receivables at the end of the period. Data in this form would be of special significance in evaluating current position and particularly the receivable position as of a given date. This information for the Chaparral Company is presented below:

	1977	1976
Receivables at end of year..	$420,000	$375,000
Average daily credit sales	$ 3,958	$ 4,583
Number of days' credit sales in receivables at end of year...	106	82

What constitutes a reasonable number of days in receivables varies with the individual business. For example, if merchandise is sold on terms of net 60 days, 40 days' sales in receivables would not be unreasonable; but if terms are net 30 days, a receivable balance equal to 40 days' sales would indicate slow collections.

Sales activity just before the close of the period should be considered in interpreting the accounts receivable measurements. If sales are unusually light or heavy just before the end of the fiscal period, this affects total receivables as well as the measurements for which they are used. When such unevenness prevails, it may be better to analyze accounts receivable according to their due dates, as was illustrated in Chapter 6.

The problem of keeping accounts receivable at a minimum without losing desirable business is important. The company's investment in receivables usually does not provide revenue. The cost of carrying these accounts must be covered by the margin of profit made on sales. The longer the accounts are carried, the smaller will be the percentage return realized on invested capital. In addition, heavier bookkeeping and collection charges and increased bad debts must be considered.

To attract business, credit is frequently granted for relatively long periods. The element of cost involved in granting long-term credit should be recognized. Assume a business has an average daily credit sales volume of $5,000 and the average amount of accounts receivable is

$250,000. The latter figure represents the average daily credit business for 50 days. If collections and the credit period can be improved so that accounts receivable represent only 30 days' sales, then accounts receivable will be reduced to $150,000. Assuming a total cost of 10% to carry and service the accounts, the decrease in accounts of $100,000 would represent an annual savings of $10,000.

Analysis of Inventories   Procedures similar to those for evaluating receivables may be employed in evaluating inventory position. Both the number of times the average inventory has been replenished during a fiscal period, known as the *inventory turnover*, and the average time to dispose of an inventory, known as the *number of days' sales in inventories*, may be computed from inventory and cost of goods sold data.

Inventory Turnover. The amount of inventory carried in stock frequently bears a close relationship to the sales volume. The inventory position and the approximate disposal time may be evaluated by computing the inventory turnover. The inventory turnover is computed by dividing the cost of goods sold for the period by the average inventory. Whenever possible, monthly figures should be used in developing a representative average inventory balance.

Assume for the Chaparral Company that inventory balances for only the beginning and the end of the year are available. Inventory turnover rates are computed as follows:

	1977	1976
Cost of goods sold	$1,000,000	$1,200,000
Merchandise inventory:		
Beginning of year	$ 330,000	$ 125,000
End of year	$ 225,000	$ 330,000
Average merchandise inventory	$ 277,500	$ 227,500
Inventory turnover for year	3.6	5.3

Number of Days' Sales in Inventories. Average inventories are sometimes expressed in terms of the number of days' sales in inventories. Information is thus afforded concerning the average time it takes to dispose of the inventory. The number of days' sales in inventories is calculated by dividing the average inventory by the average daily cost of goods sold. When an inventory turnover rate has been computed, the number of days' sales can be obtained by dividing the number of days in the year by the turnover rate for the year. The latter procedure for the Chaparral Company is illustrated below:

	1977	1976
Inventory turnover for year	3.6	5.3
Number of days' sales in average inventory (assuming a year of 360 days)	100	68

In certain instances, instead of developing the number of days' sales in average inventories, it may be considered more useful to report the number of days' sales in inventories at the end of the period. The latter measurement is determined by dividing the ending inventory by the average daily cost of goods sold. This information would be helpful in evaluating the current asset position and particularly the inventory position as of a given date.

A company with departmental classifications for merchandise will find it desirable to support the inventory measurements for the company as a whole with individual measurements for each department since there may be considerable variation among departments. A company engaged in manufacturing may compute turnover rates for finished goods, goods in process, and raw materials. The finished goods turnover is computed by dividing the cost of goods sold by the average finished goods inventory. Goods in process turnover is computed by dividing the cost of goods manufactured by the average goods in process inventory. Raw materials turnover is computed by dividing the cost of raw materials used by the average raw materials inventory.

The same valuation methods must be employed for inventories in successive periods if measurements developed from inventory figures are to be comparable. Maximum accuracy in developing measurements is possible if information relating to inventories and cost of goods sold is available in terms of physical units rather than dollar costs.

The effect of seasonal factors on the size of inventories at the end of the period should be considered in the inventory analyses. Inventories may be abnormally high or low at the end of the period. Many companies adopt a fiscal year ending when operations are at their lowest point. This is referred to as a *natural business year*. Inventories will normally be at their lowest point at the end of such a period. The organization is able to take inventory and complete year-end closing most conveniently. Under these circumstances, monthly inventory balances should be calculated by the gross profit method as illustrated in Chapter 9 in arriving at a representative average inventory figure.

With an increased rate of turnover of the stock of merchandise, the amount of investment necessary for a given volume of business is smaller, and consequently the rate of return on invested capital is higher. This conclusion assumes an enterprise can acquire goods in smaller quantities sufficiently often at no price disadvantage. If merchandise must be bought in very large quantities in order to get favorable prices, then the savings on quantity purchases must be weighed against the additional investment and the increased costs of storage and other carrying charges.

The financial advantage of an increased turnover rate may be illustrated as follows. Assume the cost of goods sold for a year was $1,000,000, and the average inventory at cost was $250,000; the rate of turnover, then, was 4 times. Assume, further, that through careful buying the same volume of business can be maintained with turnover of 5 times, or an average inventory of only $200,000. If interest on the money invested in carrying the inventory is 10%, the savings on $50,000 will be $5,000 annually. The above does not include possible advantages gained from a decrease in merchandise spoilage and obsolescence, savings in storage costs, insurance, and taxes, and a reduction in the risk of losses from price declines.

Inventory investments and turnover rates vary among different businesses. The facts of each business unit must be judged in terms of the financial structure and the operations of the particular unit. Each business must plan an inventory policy that will avoid the extremes of a dangerously low stock, which may impair sales volume, and an overstocking of goods involving a heavy capital investment which is attended by dangers that the goods may become shopworn or obsolete, that prices may fall, and that difficulties may arise in meeting the obligations resulting from purchases.

Further Analysis of Current Assets and Current Liabilities

Turnover analysis applied to specific receivable and inventory items can be applied to total current assets and to working capital. Current asset turnover is calculated by dividing net sales by average current assets. Working capital turnover is calculated by dividing net sales by the average working capital. The turnover figures may be viewed as the number of times current assets or working capital is replenished, or alternatively, as the number of sales dollars emerging for every dollar invested in current assets or in working capital. Increases in the turnover rates would generally indicate more effective utilization of current assets or working capital.

Procedures similar to those used in analyzing specific assets may also be used in analyzing specific liabilities. An accounts payable turnover rate, for example, may be developed by dividing purchases by the average payables balance; the number of days' purchases in accounts payable may be developed by dividing accounts payable by the average daily purchases. Assuming all purchases of merchandise are made on a credit basis, all accounts payables arise only from purchases, and accounts payable totals are available only for the beginning and end of the year, the accounts payable turnover and the number of days' purchases in accounts payable for the Chaparral Company are computed as follows:

	1977	1976
Net purchases	$895,000	$1,405,000
Net accounts payable:		
Beginning of year	$546,000	$ 130,000
End of year	$410,000	$ 546,000
Average accounts payable	$478,000	$ 338,000
Accounts payable turnover for year	1.9	4.2

	1977	1976
Average payables	$478,000	$ 338,000
Net purchases	$895,000	$1,405,000
Average daily purchases (net purchases ÷ 360)	$ 2,486	$ 3,903
Number of days' purchases in accounts payable	192	87

Analysis of liabilities in terms of due dates may assist management in its cash planning activities. Useful relationships may also be obtained by comparing specific assets or liabilities with other assets or liabilities or with asset or liability totals. For example, data concerning the relationship of cash to accounts payable and of cash to total liabilities may be useful.

Ratio of Stockholders' Equity to Total Liabilities

Instead of expressing stockholders' and creditors' equities in terms of total assets, equities may also be expressed in terms of each other. For example, stockholders may have a 60% interest in total assets and creditors a 40% interest. Here one can say that the ratio of the stockholders' equity to the creditors' equity is 1.5 to 1, or that the stockholders' equity is 150% of the total liabilities of the business.

Comparative data reporting stockholders' and creditors' equities in assets and the relationships of these equities to each other show the changes taking place in the sources of business capital. As the stockholders' equity rises in relation to the total liabilities, the margin of protection to the creditor group goes up. From the stockholders' point of view, such as increase makes the organization less vulnerable to a decline in business and possible inability to meet obligations, and also serves to minimize the cost of carrying the debt.

However, it should not be overlooked that it is often advantageous to supplement funds invested by stockholders with a certain amount of funds provided by creditors. The use of borrowed funds is known as *trading on the equity* or *applying leverage*. It is assumed that the additional earnings accruing to the business through use of borrowed funds will exceed the interest charges for such use. When the rate earned on borrowed funds exceeds the rate paid on borrowings, the rate of return on the stockholders' equity rises and the stockholders realize a gain through trading on the equity; when the rate earned is less than that paid, the rate of return shrinks and the stockholders suffer a loss.

The effects of trading on the equity are illustrated in the following example. Assume a company with 10,000 shares of stock outstanding is able to borrow $1,000,000 at 10% interest. The company estimates that pretax earnings will be $80,000 if it operates without the borrowed capital. Income tax is estimated at 45% of earnings. The summary below reports the effects upon net income, assuming that borrowed capital earns (1) 20%, and (2) 8%.

	Results of Operations Without Borrowed Capital	Results of Operations If Borrowed Capital Earns 20%	Results of Operations If Borrowed Capital Earns 8%
Operating income...	$ 80,000	$280,000	$160,000
Interest expense		100,000	100,000
Income before income tax...	$ 80,000	$180,000	$ 60,000
Income tax at 45%..	36,000	81,000	27,000
Net income...	$ 44,000	$ 99,000	$ 33,000
Number of shares outstanding.................................	10,000	10,000	10,000
Earnings per share...	$4.40	$9.90	$3.30

For the Chaparral Company, relationships of the stockholders' equity to total liabilities are calculated as follows:

	1977	1976
Stockholders' equity	$1,468,000	$1,445,000
Total liabilities	$ 810,000	$ 946,000
Ratio of stockholders' equity to total liabilities	1.8:1	1.5:1

In analyzing the relationship of the stockholders' equity to total liabilities, particular note should be made of any lease arrangements representing primarily financing devices. Both the property rights provided under the leases and the liabilities accompanying such rights should be considered in arriving at a full evaluation of the status of equities, the relationships of equities, and changes in equities from period to period.

Ratio of Land, Buildings, and Equipment to Long-Term Liabilities

Comparisons may be made between land, buildings, and equipment and long-term liabilities. When property items are pledged on long-term obligations, this ratio indicates the protection afforded to the long-term creditor group as well as the possibility for the expansion of long-term indebtedness on the basis of available security.

In the development of the ratio of land, buildings, and equipment to long-term liabilities, current economic values of the property items instead of book values should be used whenever available, since the protection to creditors, as well as the ability of the business to borrow, is based on the present market values of the properties pledged. If a bond retirement fund is maintained consisting of a company's own obligations reacquired but not retired, this fund should be subtracted from the long-term liabilities in developing the ratio; a bond retirement fund consisting of other investments, however, would represent additional security on the indebtedness rather than a reduction in debt and should be added to land, buildings, and equipment for purposes of this ratio. Long-term creditors generally limit their loans to a certain percentage of the value of properties pledged, so there may be an adequate margin of safety in the event of business failure, presenting a need to apply the properties to the payment of the indebtedness.

For the Chaparral Company, ratios of land, buildings, and equipment to long-term liabilities are as follows:

	1977	1976
Land, buildings, and equipment (net)	$775,000	$875,000
Long-term liabilities	$400,000	$400,000
Ratio of land, buildings, and equipment to long-term liabilities	1.9:1	2.2:1

Ratio of Stockholders' Equity to Land, Buildings, and Equipment

The changes in the relationship of stockholders' equity to land, buildings, and equipment need to be considered in judging whether expansion is taking place through increases in the stockholders' equity or through borrowing. An increasing ratio indicates that property acquisitions are being financed through funds supplied by the sale of stock or the retention of earnings, and normally this would be looked upon favorably by the creditor group. A declining ratio indicates that the increase of properties has exceeded the expansion in stockholders' equity. This may suggest possible overexpansion, excessive use of credit, and greater vulnerability to financial difficulties in the event of a decline in business.

For the Chaparral Company, ratios of stockholders' equity to land, buildings, and equipment are as follows:

	1977	1976
Stockholders' equity	$1,468,000	$1,445,000
Land, buildings, and equipment (net)	$ 775,000	$ 875,000
Ratio of stockholders' equity to land, buildings, and equipment	1.9:1	1.7:1

Book Value per Share of Stock

An important measurement of the stockholders' equity is afforded by a determination of the *book value per share*. This is the recorded dollar equity related to each share. The calculation of share book value was described in Chapter 21. It was indicated there that, when there is only one class of stock, book value per share is calculated by dividing the total stockholders' equity by the number of shares outstanding. When both common and preferred shares are outstanding, it is necessary to allocate the total stockholders' equity to the two classes of stock. Redemption or liquidation values and cumulative features of the preferred issue must be considered in determining the portion of the stockholders' equity relating to preferred stock.

Both common and preferred stock of the Chaparral Company are $10 par. The preferred stock is cumulative and no dividends are in arrears. The preferred stock has a liquidation value equal to its par value. The book values per share for common and preferred stock are computed as follows:

	1977	1976
Total stockholders' equity	$1,468,000	$1,445,000
Equity related to preferred shares	350,000	350,000
Equity related to common shares	$1,118,000	$1,095,000
Number of shares outstanding: Preferred	35,000	35,000
Common	75,000	75,000
Book value per share: Preferred	$10.00	$10.00
Common	$14.91	$14.60

Retained earnings are sometimes reduced by the amount of intangible assets reported on the balance sheet for the purpose of share book value calculations. This procedure would be appropriate when intangible assets are of doubtful value. After the adjustment, the book value of the stock would offer a more conservative measure of the stockholders' equity.

Other Measurements of Financial Position

A number of measurements of financial position other than those already described may be developed in specific instances. Among these might be mentioned the ratio of individual noncurrent assets to total assets of the business or to total assets of the group, and individual noncurrent liabilities to total liabilities of the business or to total liabilities of the group. Relationships such as the foregoing may be presented directly on comparative statements by means of vertical analysis procedures.

RATIOS AND MEASUREMENTS DEVELOPED FROM INCOME STATEMENT DATA

A number of special analyses are developed from income statement data. Many of these provide indications of the profitability of operations. Others offer measurements of certain significant relationships relative to operating performance. Although some of these measurements are made directly from the income statement, others require the use of balance sheet data.

Ratio of Net Sales to Total Assets

Among the measurements developed from balance sheet and income statement data is the *ratio of net sales to total assets*, sometimes called the *assets turnover rate*. This ratio is calculated by dividing the net sales figure by the total assets producing the sales. The resulting figure indicates the contribution made by total assets to sales. With comparative data, judgments can be made concerning the relative effectiveness of asset utilization. A ratio increase may suggest the better utilization of assets, although a point may be reached where there is a strain on assets and a company is unable to achieve its full sales potential. An increase in total assets when accompanied by a ratio decrease may suggest the overinvestment in assets or their inefficient use.

In developing the ratio, long-term investments should be excluded from the asset total when these make no contribution to sales. On the other hand, leased properties should be added to the asset total to permit comparability between companies owning their properties and those that lease them. If monthly figures for assets are available, they may be used in developing a representative average for total assets employed during the year. Often the assets at the end of the year are used as a basis for the computation. When sales can be expressed in terms of units sold, ratios in terms of sales units to total assets offer more reliable guides to interpretation than sales dollars, since unit results are not affected by product sales prices.

Assume in the case of the Chaparral Company that only asset totals for the beginning and end of the year are available and that sales cannot be expressed in terms of units. Ratios of net sales to total assets are computed as follows:

	1977	1976
Net sales	$1,425,000	$1,650,000
Total assets (excluding long-term investments):		
Beginning of year	$1,991,000	$1,510,000
End of year	$1,778,000	$1,991,000
Average total assets	$1,884,500	$1,750,500
Ratio of net sales to average total assets	0.8:1	0.9:1

Ratio of Net Sales to Land, Buildings, and Equipment

Related to the ratio just described in the *ratio of net sales to land, buildings, and equipment*, sometimes referred to as the *property turnover* or the *fixed asset turnover*. Net sales, here, is divided by the investment in land, buildings, and equipment. The resulting measurement indicates how effectively these properties are utilized in terms of sales. With comparative data, judgments may be made concerning the relative efficiency of utilization of these assets and the effects on sales of increases or decreases in property totals. An increase in land, buildings, and equipment when accompanied by a ratio decrease may suggest overexpansion in property facilities.

Assume for the Chaparral Company that balances at the beginning and end of the year are used in measuring the average investment in land, buildings, and equipment. Ratios of net sales to land, buildings, and equipment are computed as follows:

	1977	1976
Net sales	$1,425,000	$1,650,000
Land, buildings, and equipment (net):		
Beginning of year	$ 875,000	$ 675,000
End of year	$ 775,000	$ 875,000
Average investment in land, buildings, and equipment...	$ 825,000	$ 775,000
Ratio of net sales to average land, buildings, and equipment	1.7:1	2.1:1

When intangible assets and leased assets contribute significantly to sales, these should be combined with land, buildings, and equipment in establishing the base for this measurement.

It may be pointed out that with increasing price levels and an unchanged sales volume in terms of units sold, the ratio of sales to land, buildings, and equipment may show regular improvement because sales prices are increasing while property costs remain unchanged. In order to obtain a more meaningful ratio, the fair market values of property items rather than historical book values may be used.

Rate Earned on Total Assets

The adequacy of earnings may be measured in terms of (1) the rate earned on sales, (2) the rate earned on total assets, and (3) the rate earned on the stockholders' equity. There should be an adequate rate of earnings in terms of each of the three standards if operating results are to be considered satisfactory. The rate earned on sales was measured in the preceding chapter where vertical analysis was applied to income statement data. The rate earned on total assets and on stockholders' equity are described in this and in the following section.

The *rate earned on total assets*, frequently referred to as the *asset productivity rate*, is found by dividing the net income for the year by the total assets employed in the production of net income. This rate measures the degree of efficiency in the use of the resources to generate net income. If total assets by months are available, they should be used in developing an average for the year. Frequently, however, the assets at the beginning of the year or the assets at the end of the year are used for the calculation. In some instances it may be desirable to limit net income to that resulting from trading operations by excluding revenue items arising from investments, such as interest, dividends, and rents. When this is the case, total assets should be reduced by the investments in developing the rate of earnings. Sometimes comparisons are developed for the rate of operating income to total assets or, perhaps, the rate of income before income tax to total assets, so that rates of earnings are not affected by financial management items or by changes in income tax rates.

Rates earned on total assets for the Chaparral Company are determined as follows:

	1977	1976
Net income	$ 70,000	$ 60,000
Total assets:		
Beginning of year	$2,391,000	$1,760,000
End of year	$2,278,000	$2,391,000
Average total assets	$2,334,500	$2,075,500
Rate earned on average total assets	3.0%	2.9%

Rate Earned on Stockholders' Equity

Net income may be expressed as the *rate earned on the stockholders' equity* by dividing net income by the stockholders' equity. By excluding liabilities, a rate is computed reflecting the use of leverage to generate net income. In the development of this rate, it is preferable to use the average stockholders' equity for a year calculated from monthly data, particularly when significant changes have occurred during the year as a result of the sale of additional stock, the retirement of stock, the payment of dividends, and the accumulation of earnings. Sometimes the beginning or the ending stockholders' equity is used for the measurement.

For the Chaparral Company, rates earned on the stockholders' equity are calculated as follows:

	1977	1976
Net income	$ 70,000	$ 60,000
Stockholders' equity:		
Beginning of year	$1,445,000	$1,330,000
End of year	$1,468,000	$1,445,000
Average stockholders' equity	$1,456,500	$1,387,500
Rate earned on average stockholders' equity	4.8%	4.3%

As a company's liabilities increase in relationship to the stockholders' equity, the spread between the rate earned on stockholders' equity and the rate earned on total assets rises. The rate earned on the stockholders' equity is of interest to the investor who must reconcile the risk of a highly leveraged company with the potentially greater profitability.

Rate Earned on Common Stockholders' Equity

Earnings may be measured in terms of the residual common stockholders' equity. The *rate earned on the common stockholders' equity* is computed by dividing the net income after preferred dividend requirements by the equity of the common stockholders. The average equity for common stockholders should be determined, although the rate is frequently based upon the beginning or ending common equity.

In the case of the Chaparral Company whose preferred stock is non-participating, preferred dividend requirements are limited to 6%. The rate earned on the common stockholders' equity, then, is calculated as follows:

	1977	1976
Net income..	$ 70,000	$ 60,000
Less dividend requirements on preferred stock...............	21,000	21,000
Net income related to common stockholders' equity......	$ 49,000	$ 39,000
Common stockholders' equity:		
Beginning of year...	$1,095,000	$1,080,000
End of year...	$1,118,000	$1,095,000
Average common stockholders' equity............................	$1,106,500	$1,087,500
Rate earned on average common stockholders' equity ..	4.4%	3.6%

Number of Times Bond Interest Requirements Were Earned

Earnings may also be measured in terms of (1) their relationship to bond interest requirements, (2) their relationship to preferred dividend requirements, and (3) their availability to common stockholders.

The number of times earnings cover the bond interest is calculated by dividing income before any charges for bond interest or income tax by the bond interest requirements for the period. The ability of the company to meet interest payments and the degree of safety afforded the bondholders are thus reported. The number of times interest charges were earned by the Chaparral Company follows:

	1977	1976
Income before income tax..	$100,000	$ 85,000
Add bond interest (8% of $400,000)...	32,000	32,000
Amount available in meeting bond interest requirements....	$132,000	$117,000
Number of times bond interest requirements were earned..	4.1	3.7

Income before income tax was used in the calculation above in view of the fact that income tax applies only after bond interest is deducted and it is pretax income that affords the protection to the bondholder group. However, the calculation is frequently made in terms of net income after income tax. The latter procedure is employed because it is easier to apply since it is based on the last figure on the income statement, it is consistent with other measurements employing net income, and it offers a more conservative approach in measuring the ability of the company to meet periodic interest requirements. For the Chaparral Company, net income balances after income tax were $70,000 for 1977 and $60,000 for 1976. These balances would be raised by interest requirements for each year of $32,000 and the sums divided by the periodic interest, resulting in times-interest-earned amounts for 1977 of 3.2 and for 1976 of 2.9.

In addition to calculations of interest coverage, calculations may be made of the number of times all fixed charges are covered in measuring a company's ability to meet its regularly recurring financial commitments, such as management salaries, rents, taxes, and interest.

Number of Times Preferred Dividend Requirements Were Earned

The number of times that earnings cover the preferred dividends is calculated by dividing net income for the year by the annual preferred dividend requirements. For the Chaparral Company, calculations are:

	1977	1976
Net income...	$70,000	$60,000
Preferred dividend requirements (6% of $350,000)...............	$21,000	$21,000
Number of times preferred dividend requirements were earned..	3.3	2.9

The relationship of earnings to preferred dividend requirements may also be indicated by dividing net income by the number of preferred shares outstanding. It should be recognized that this calculation does not show the amount of earnings to which preferred shares are entitled, but simply the amount of earnings available in meeting preferred dividend requirements.

For the Chaparral Company, earnings available in meeting preferred dividend requirements are calculated as follows:

	1977	1976
Net income...	$70,000	$60,000
Number of shares of preferred outstanding..........................	35,000	35,000
Income available in meeting preferred dividend requirements per share	$2.00	$1.71

Since preferred stock is 6%, $10 par, earnings required to cover preferred dividends are 60 cents per share.

Earnings Per Share on Common Stock

Earnings per share calculations were described in detail in Chapter 21. It will be recalled that the Accounting Principles Board in Opinion No. 15 indicated earnings per share data were of such importance to investors and others interested in the results of a company's operations that such data should be presented prominently on the periodic statements. In computing per share earnings on common stock, earnings are first reduced by the prior dividend rights of preferred stock. Computations are made in terms of the weighted average number of common shares and common share equivalents for each period presented. When net income on the income statement includes amounts for extraordinary items and for the cumulative changes in accounting principles, earnings per share amounts would be reported for each of these items as well as for the final net income balance. When the capital structure of a corporation includes no potentially dilutive convertible securities, options, warrants, or other rights, a single presentation of earnings per share is appropriate; when the capital structure includes potentially dilutive items, a dual presentation of earnings in the form of primary earnings per share and fully diluted earnings per share would be required.

In the case of the Chaparral Company, it is assumed that no potentially dilutive items are present and earnings per share on common stock call for simple computations as shown at the top of the next page.

	1977	1976
Net income	$70,000	$60,000
Less dividend requirements on preferred stock	21,000	21,000
Income related to common stockholders' equity	$49,000	$39,000
Number of shares of common stock outstanding	75,000	75,000
Earnings per share on common stock	$ .65	$ .52

Price-Earnings Ratio on Common Stock

The market price of common stock may be expressed as a multiple of its earnings to provide a means of evaluating the attractiveness of common stock as an investment. This measurement is referred to as the *price-earnings ratio* and is computed by dividing the market value per share of stock by the annual earnings per share. Instead of using the average market value of shares for the period covered by earnings, the latest market value is normally used. Assuming market values per common share of the Chaparral Company at the end of 1977 of $10 and at the end of 1976 of $6.50, price-earnings ratios would be computed as follows:

	1977	1976
Market value per common share at end of year	$10.00	$ 6.50
Earnings per share	$ .65	$ .52
Price-earnings ratio	15.4	12.5

As an alternative to the above, earnings per share can be presented as a percentage based on the market value of the stock. Care should be taken to indicate that the earnings rate thus computed is stated in terms of the increase in the stockholders' equity as a result of profitable operations and not in terms of dividends actually paid to stockholders.

Yield on Common Stock

A rate of return in terms of actual distributions to common stockholders may be provided. Such a rate, referred to as the *yield on common stock*, is found by dividing the annual dividends on a common share by the latest market value per common share. For the Chaparral Company, the yield on the common stock is computed as follows:

	1977	1976
Dividends for year per common share	$ .35	$ .32
Market value per common share at end of year	$10.00	$ 6.50
Yield on common stock	3.5%	4.9%

Distribution of Earnings to Creditor and Ownership Equities

Inasmuch as earnings are the ultimate source upon which the creditors and the owners of an enterprise must rely for a return of both principal and income, and because the different classes of security holders normally obtain different rates of return, a percentage analysis of the disposition of the earnings of a company may be of interest to all groups. In the case of the Chaparral Company, it is possible to prepare a summary of the distribution of earnings as shown at the top of the next page.

Other Measurements of Operations

A number of other measurements of operations that are significant in various instances can be developed. Among these may be mentioned such ratios as gross profit to sales, operating income to sales, net income to sales, individual manufacturing costs to cost of goods manufactured,

	Equity Totals[1]		Equity Percentage		Amount of Earnings Paid or Accruing* on Equities		Percentage Distribution of Total Earnings Paid or Accruing* on Equities		Percentage Paid or Accruing* on Equities	
	1977	1976	1977	1976	1977	1976	1977	1976	1977	1976
Bondholders' (8% long-term liability)..............	$ 400,000	$ 400,000	22%	22%	$ 32,000	$32,000	31%	35%	8.0%	8.0%
Preferred stockholders	350,000	350,000	19%	19%	21,000	21,000	21%	23%	6.0%	6.0%
Common stockholders.	1,106,500	1,087,500	59%	59%	{ 26,000	24,000	25%	26%	2.3%[2]	2.2%
					{ 23,000*	15,000*	23%*	16%*	2.1%*	1.4%*
Total............................	$1,856,500	$1,837,500	100%	100%	$102,000	$92,000	100%	100%	5.5%	5.0%

individual selling expenses and individual general and administrative expenses to the totals for these groups. These relationships are generally presented by means of comparative statements offering horizontal and vertical analyses of income statement data.

INTERPRETATION OF ANALYSES

Analyses offered in Chapter 26 and in this chapter are developed to help the analyst arrive at certain conclusions with regard to the business. It has already been stated that these are merely guides to the intelligent interpretation of financial data.

All of the ratios and measurements need not be used, but rather only those that will actually assist the analyst in arriving at informed conclusions with respect to questions raised. The measurements developed need to be interpreted in terms of the conditions relating to the particular enterprise, the conditions relating to the particular industry in which the enterprise is found, and the conditions relating to the general business and the economic environment within which the enterprise operates. If measurements are to be of maximum value, they need to be compared with similar data developed for the particular enterprise for past periods, with similar measurements for the industry as a whole that may be regarded as standard, and with pertinent data relating to general business conditions and business and price fluctuations as these affect the individual enterprise. Only through the intelligent use and integration of the foregoing sources of data can financial weaknesses and strengths be identified and reliable opinions be developed concerning business structure, operations, and growth.

---

[1]Average equities for the year are indicated in this illustration. It would be possible to base analyses on equities as of the beginning of the year or on equities as of the end of the year.

[2]This percentage, although stated in terms of the common stockholders' equity as reported by the books, could be stated in terms of the par or stated value of the common stock or in terms of market value of the stock.

QUESTIONS

1. Define *working capital* and appraise its significance.

2. Distinguish between the *current ratio* and the *acid-test ratio*.

3. Balance sheets for the Baxter Corporation and the Rogers Corporation each show a working capital total of $500,000. Does this indicate that the short-term liquidity of the Baxter Corporation is approximately equal to that of the Rogers Corporation? Explain.

4. Define (a) quick assets, (b) price-earnings ratio.

5. (a) How is the *accounts receivable turnover* computed? (b) How is the *number of days' purchases in accounts payable* computed?

6. (a) How is the *merchandise inventory turnover* computed? (b) What precautions are necessary in arriving at the basis for the turnover calculation? (c) How would you interpret a rising inventory turnover rate?

7. What is meant by a *natural business year*?

8. (a) What is meant by *trading on the equity*? (b) Give figures to illustrate a gain accruing to owners through this practice. (c) What are the disadvantages of "applying leverage"?

9. The ratio of stockholders' equity to total liabilities offers information about the long-term liquidity of a business unit. Explain.

10. Give rules for computing share book values when a company has both common and preferred stock outstanding.

11. State the significance of each of the following measurements: (a) the ratio of land, buildings, and equipment to long-term liabilities, (b) the ratio of stockholders' equity to land, buildings, and equipment, (c) the ratio of sales to total assets, and (d) the ratio of sales to land, buildings, and equipment.

12. (a) What is meant by the *asset productivity rate*? (b) How is it calculated?

13. Indicate how each of the following measurements is calculated and appraise its significance:

(a) The number of times bond interest requirements were earned.
(b) The number of times preferred dividend requirements were earned.
(c) The rate of earnings on the common stockholders' equity.
(d) The earnings per share on common stock.
(e) The price-earnings ratio on common stock.
(f) The yield on common stock.

14. On what basis are measurements selected for financial statement analyses? What key factors should be considered in interpreting the analyses conducted?

EXERCISES

1. The following data are taken from comparative balance sheets prepared for the Morrell Company:

	1977	1976
Cash	$ 20,000	$ 10,000
Marketable securities (net)	9,000	35,000
Trade receivables (net)	43,000	30,000
Inventories	65,000	50,000
Prepaid expenses	3,000	2,000
Land, buildings, and equipment (net)	79,000	75,000
Intangible assets	10,000	15,000
Other assets	7,000	8,000
	$236,000	$225,000
Current liabilities	$ 80,000	$ 60,000

(a) From the data given, compute for 1977 and for 1976: (1) the working capital, (2) the current ratio, (3) the acid-test ratio, (4) the ratio of current assets to total assets, (5) the ratio of cash to current liabilities.

(b) Evaluate each of the above changes.

2. Statements for the Millard Co. show the following balances:

	1977	1976	1975
Average receivables (net)	$ 50,000	$ 40,000	$ 30,000
Net sales	420,000	360,000	300,000

Give any significant measurements that may be developed in analyzing the foregoing, assuming a 360-day year and assuming approximately one third of the sales are for cash, the balance being on account. What conclusions may be made concerning the receivables if sales on account are made on a 2/30, n/60 basis?

3. Operating statements for the Molten Sales Co. show the following:

	1977	1976	1975
Sales	$105,000	$100,000	$ 75,000
Cost of goods sold:			
Beginning inventory	$ 30,000	$ 25,000	$ 5,000
Purchases	95,000	80,000	85,000
	$125,000	$105,000	$ 90,000
Ending inventory	50,000	30,000	25,000
	$ 75,000	$ 75,000	$ 65,000
Gross profit on sales	$ 30,000	$ 25,000	$ 10,000

Give whatever measurements may be developed in analyzing the inventory position at the end of each year. What conclusions would you make concerning the inventory trend?

4. The following data are taken from the Tyler Corporation records for the years ending December 31, 1977, 1976, and 1975:

	1977	1976	1975
Finished goods inventory	$ 60,000	$ 40,000	$ 30,000
Goods in process inventory	60,000	65,000	60,000
Raw materials inventory	60,000	40,000	35,000
Sales	400,000	340,000	300,000
Cost of goods sold	225,000	230,000	210,000
Cost of goods manufactured	260,000	250,000	200,000
Raw materials used in production	150,000	130,000	120,000

Compute turnover rates for 1977 and for 1976 for (a) finished goods, (b) goods in process, and (c) raw materials.

5. The total purchases of goods by Skip's Wholesale Company during 1977 were $360,000. All purchases were on a 2/10, n/30 basis. The average balance in the vouchers payable account was $33,000. Was the company prompt, slow, or average in paying for goods? How many days' average purchases were there in accounts payable, assuming a 360-day year?

6. The Hepburn Company estimates that pretax earnings for the year ended December 31, 1977, will be $70,000 if it operates without borrowed capital. Income tax is 45% of earnings. There are 15,000 shares of common stock outstanding for the entire year. Assuming that the company is able to borrow $800,000 at 10% interest, show the effects upon net income if borrowed capital earns (1) 20%, and (2) 8%.

7. The stockholders' equity of the Ryker Corporation on December 31, 1977, is as follows:

Preferred 6% stock, $25 par	$400,000
Common stock, $20 par	800,000
Additional paid-in capital	150,000
Retained earnings	150,000

Compute the book value per share of both preferred and common stocks, assuming each of the following conditions. (Assume dividends may legally be paid from additional paid-in capital.)

(a) Preferred stock is cumulative, with no dividends in arrears.
(b) Preferred stock is cumulative, and dividends are in arrears since January 1, 1976.

8. The balance sheets for the Adams Corp. showed long-term liabilities and stockholders' equity balances at the end of each year as given at the top of the next page.

	1977	1976
8% Bonds payable	$ 600,000	$600,000
Preferred 6% stock, $100 par	600,000	400,000
Common stock, $25 par	1,200,000	900,000
Additional paid-in capital	150,000	100,000
Retained earnings	300,000	100,000

Net income after income tax was: 1977, $110,000; 1976, $80,000. Using the foregoing data, compute for each year:

    (a) The rate of earnings on the total stockholders' equity at the end of the year.
    (b) The number of times bond interest requirements were earned (income after tax).
    (c) The number of times preferred dividend requirements were earned.
    (d) The rate earned on the common stockholders' equity.
    (e) The earnings per share on common stock.

PROBLEMS

27-1. The balance sheet data for the Montopoli Corp. on December 31, 1977, are given below:

Assets		Liabilities and Stockholders' Equity	
Cash	$ 100,000	Notes and accounts payable	$ 130,000
Marketable securities	25,000	Income tax payable	40,000
Notes and accounts receivable (net)	175,000	Wages and interest payable	10,000
Inventories	600,000	Dividends payable	25,000
Prepaid expenses	15,000	Bonds payable	450,000
Bond redemption fund (securities of		Deferred revenues	30,000
other companies)	400,000	Common stock, $20 par	1,200,000
Land, buildings, and equipment (net)	780,000	Preferred 6% stock, $20 par (noncumula-	
Intangible assets	420,000	tive, liquidating value at par)	200,000
Unamortized bond issue costs	20,000	Retained earnings appropriated for plant	
		expansion	200,000
		Retained earnings	250,000
	$2,535,000		$2,535,000

Instructions: From the balance sheet data, compute the following:
    (1) The amount of working capital.
    (2) The current ratio.
    (3) The acid-test ratio.
    (4) The ratio of current assets to total assets.
    (5) The ratio of stockholders' equity to total liabilities.
    (6) The ratio of land, buildings, and equipment to bonds payable.
    (7) The book value per share of preferred stock.
    (8) The book value per share of common stock.

27-2. Comparative data for Stevenson, Inc., for the three-year period 1975–1977 are presented below and on page 813.

Income Statement Data

	1977	1976	1975
Net sales	$1,200,000	$ 900,000	$1,100,000
Cost of goods sold	760,000	600,000	650,000
Gross profit on sales	$ 440,000	$ 300,000	$ 450,000
Selling, general, and other expenses	350,000	280,000	290,000
Operating income	$ 90,000	$ 20,000	$ 160,000
Income tax	40,500	9,000	72,000
Net income	$ 49,500	$ 11,000	$ 88,000
Dividends paid	35,000	30,000	30,000
Net increase (decrease) in retained earnings	$ 14,500	$ (19,000)	$ 58,000

Balance Sheet Data

Assets	1977	1976	1975
Cash	$ 60,000	$ 40,000	$ 75,000
Trade notes and accounts rec. (net)	300,000	320,000	300,000
Inventory (at cost)	380,000	420,000	350,000
Prepaid expenses	30,000	10,000	40,000
Land, buildings, and equipment (net)	760,000	600,000	690,000
Intangible assets	100,000	100,000	125,000
Other assets	70,000	10,000	20,000
	$1,700,000	$1,500,000	$1,600,000

Liabilities and Stockholders' Equity	1977	1976	1975
Trade notes and accounts payable	$ 120,000	$ 180,000	$ 170,000
Wages, interest, dividends payable	25,000	25,000	25,000
Income tax payable	39,500	10,000	80,000
Miscellaneous current liabilities	10,000	4,000	10,000
8% bonds payable	300,000	300,000	300,000
Deferred revenues	10,000	10,000	25,000
Preferred 6% stock, cumulative, $100 par and liquidating value	200,000	200,000	200,000
No-par common stock, $10 stated value	500,000	400,000	400,000
Additional paid-in capital	310,000	200,000	200,000
Retained earnings — appropriated	80,000	60,000	60,000
Retained earnings — unappropriated	105,500	111,000	130,000
	$1,700,000	$1,500,000	$1,600,000

Instructions:

(1) From the foregoing data, calculate comparative measurements for 1977 and 1976 as follows:
   (a) The amount of working capital.
   (b) The current ratio.
   (c) The acid-test ratio.
   (d) The trade receivables turnover rate for the year (all sales are on a credit basis).
   (e) The average days' sales in trade receivables at the end of the year (assume a 360-day year and all sales on a credit basis).
   (f) The trade payables turnover rate for the year.
   (g) The average days' purchases in trade payables at the end of the year.
   (h) The inventory turnover rate.
   (i) The number of days' sales in the inventory at the end of the year.
   (j) The ratio of stockholders' equity to total liabilities.
   (k) The ratio of land, buildings, and equipment to bonds payable.
   (l) The ratio of stockholders' equity to land, buildings, and equipment.
   (m) The book value per share of preferred stock (no dividends in arrears).
   (n) The book value per share of common stock.
(2) Based upon the measurements made in (1), evaluate the liquidity position of Stevenson, Inc., at the end of 1977 as compared with the end of 1976.

27-3. (1) Using the comparative data for Stevenson, Inc., as given in Problem 27-2, compute comparative measurements for 1977 and 1976 as follows:
   (a) The ratio of net sales to average total assets.
   (b) The ratio of net sales to average land, buildings, and equipment.
   (c) The rate earned on net sales.
   (d) The gross profit rate on net sales.
   (e) The rate earned on average total assets.
   (f) The rate earned on average stockholders' equity.
   (g) The number of times bond interest requirements were earned (before income tax).
   (h) The number of times preferred dividend requirements were earned.
   (i) The rate earned on average common stockholders' equity.
   (j) The earnings per share on common stock.

(2) Based upon the measurements made in (1), evaluate the profitability of Stevenson, Inc., for 1977 as compared with 1976.

27-4. Using the comparative data for Stevenson, Inc., as given in Problem 27-2, prepare a summary of the distribution of earnings for the three-year period similar to that illustrated on page 809. Measurements are to be based on equity totals as of the end of each year.

27-5. (1) Using the data for the Baltzer Mfg. Co. as given in Problem 26-3 on pages 786–788, compute comparative measurements for 1977 and 1976 as follows:

(a) The amount of working capital.
(b) The current ratio.
(c) The acid-test ratio.
(d) The current asset turnover rate.
(e) The finished goods inventory turnover rate.
(f) The raw materials inventory turnover rate.
(g) The number of days' sales in average finished goods inventory (assume a 360-day year).
(h) The number of days' raw materials requirements in average raw materials inventory.
(i) The ratio of stockholders' equity to total liabilities.
(j) The ratio of land, buildings, and equipment to long-term liabilities.
(k) The book value per share of the preferred stock.
(l) The book value per share of the common stock.

(2) Based upon the measurements made in (1), evaluate the liquidity position of Baltzer Mfg. Co. at the end of 1977 as compared with the end of 1976.

27-6. (1) Using the data for the Baltzer Mfg. Co. as given in Problem 26-3 on pages 786–788, compute comparative measurements for 1977 and 1976 as follows:

(a) The ratio of net sales to average total assets (excluding long-term investments).
(b) The ratio of net sales to average land, buildings, and equipment.
(c) The rate earned on net sales.
(d) The gross profit rate on net sales.
(e) The rate earned on average total assets.
(f) The rate earned on average stockholders' equity.
(g) The number of times long-term liabilities interest requirements were earned (before income tax).
(h) The number of times preferred dividend requirements were earned.
(i) The rate earned on average common stockholders' equity.
(j) The earnings per share on common stock.

(2) Based upon the measurements made in (1), evaluate the profitability of Baltzer Mfg. Co. for 1977 as compared with 1976.

27-7. Using the comparative data for the Baltzer Mfg. Co. as given in Problem 26-3 on pages 786–788, prepare a summary of the distribution of earnings for 1977 and 1976. Measurements are to be based on equity totals as of the end of each year.

27-8. Inventory and receivable balances and also gross profit data for Thomas, Inc., appear below:

	1977	1976	1975
Balance sheet data:			
Inventory, December 31	$100,000	$ 90,000	$ 80,000
Accounts receivable, December 31	60,000	40,000	20,000
Accounts payable, December 31	70,000	60,000	45,000
Net purchases	140,000	100,000	80,000
Income statement data:			
Net sales	$290,000	$270,000	$250,000
Cost of goods sold	210,000	200,000	180,000
Gross profit on sales	$ 80,000	$ 70,000	$ 70,000

Instructions: Assuming a 300-day business year and all sales on a credit basis, compute the following measurements for 1977 and 1976.
    (1) The receivables turnover rate.
    (2) The average days' sales in receivables at the end of the year.
    (3) The inventory turnover rate.
    (4) The number of days' sales in inventory at the end of the year.
    (5) The accounts payable turnover rate.
    (6) The number of days' purchases in accounts payable at the end of the year.

27-9. Stockholders' equities for the Beasley Corporation at the end of 1977 and 1976 were:

	1977	1976
Preferred 6% stock, $50 par and liquidating value	$100,000	$100,000
Common stock, $10 par	300,000	200,000
Additional paid-in capital	500,000	350,000
Retained earnings	90,000	150,000

Instructions: Compute the book value per share of both preferred stock and common stock at the end of 1977 and at the end of 1976, assuming the conditions stated in each case below. (Assume dividends may legally be paid from additional paid-in capital.)
    (1) Preferred is cumulative; dividend requirements on preferred stock have been met annually.
    (2) Preferred is cumulative; the last dividend on preferred stock was paid for the year 1974.

27-10. For each of the following numbered items, you are to select the letter items which indicate its effects on the corporation's statements. Indicate your choice by giving the letters identifying the effects which you select. If there is no appropriate response among the effects listed, leave the item blank. If more than one effect is applicable to a particular item, be sure to list *all* applicable letters. (Assume the state statutes do not permit declaration of nonliquidating dividends except from earnings.)

Item	Effect
(1) Declaration of a cash dividend due in one month on preferred stock.	A. Reduces working capital.
(2) Declaration and payment of an ordinary stock dividend.	B. Increases working capital.
	C. Reduces current ratio.
(3) Receipt of a cash dividend, not previously recorded, on stock of another corporation.	D. Increases current ratio.
	E. Reduces the dollar amount of total capital stock.
(4) Passing of a dividend on preferred stock.	F. Increases the dollar amount of total capital stock.
(5) Receipt of preferred shares as a dividend on stock held as a temporary investment. This was not a regularly recurring dividend.	G. Reduces total retained earnings.
	H. Increases total retained earnings.
	S. Reduces equity per share of common stock.
(6) Payment of dividend mentioned in (1).	T. Reduces equity of each common stockholder.
(7) Issue of new common shares in a 5-for-1 stock split.	

(AICPA adapted)

27-11. The following are partially condensed financial statements.

X Corporation
Balance Sheet
December 31, 1977

Assets	
Cash	$ 63,000
Trade receivables, less estimated uncollectibles of $12,000	238,000
Inventories	170,000
Prepaid expenses	7,000
Land, buildings, and equipment, cost less $182,000 charged to operations	390,000
Other assets	13,000
	$881,000

(continued)

Liabilities and Stockholders' Equity

Accounts and notes payable — trade	$ 98,000
Current liabilities payable	17,000
Income tax payable	18,000
First-mortgage, 7% bonds, due in 1987	150,000
$7 Preferred stock — no par value (entitled to $110 per share in liquidation); authorized 1,000 shares; in treasury 400 shares; outstanding 600 shares	108,000
Common stock — no par; authorized 100,000 shares, issued and outstanding 10,000 shares stated at a nominal value of $10 per share	100,000
Paid-in capital from sale of common stock at more than stated value	242,000
Retained earnings appropriated for plant expansion	50,000
Retained earnings appropriated for cost of treasury stock	47,000
Retained earnings	98,000
Cost of 400 shares of treasury stock	(47,000)
	$881,000

NOTES: (1) Working capital — 12/31/76 was $205,000. (2) Trade receivables — 12/31/76 were $220,000 gross, $206,000 net. (3) Dividends for 1977 have been declared and paid. (4) There has been no change in amount of bonds outstanding during 1977.

X Corporation
Income Statement
For Year Ended December 31, 1977

	Cash	Charge	Total
Gross sales	$116,000	$876,000	$992,000
Less: Sales discount	$ 3,000	$ 12,000	$ 15,000
Sales returns and allowances	1,000	6,000	7,000
	$ 4,000	$ 18,000	$ 22,000
Net sales	$112,000	$858,000	$970,000
Cost of sales:			
Inventory of finished goods, January 1		$ 92,000	
Cost of goods manufactured		680,000	
Inventory of finished goods, December 31		(100,000)	672,000
Gross profit on sales			$298,000
Selling expenses		$173,000	
General expenses		70,000	243,000
Income from operations			$ 55,000
Other additions and deductions (net)			3,000
Income before income tax			$ 58,000
Income tax (estimated)			18,000
Net income			$ 40,000

Instructions: For each item listed below select the best answer from the approximate answers. Indicate your choice by giving the appropriate letter for each. Give the calculations in support of each choice.

Items To Be Computed	Approximate Answers				
	(a)	(b)	(c)	(d)	(e)
(1) Acid test ratio	3.2:1	2.3:1	2.9:1	2.4:1	3.07:1
(2) Average number of days' charge sales uncollected	86	94	103	100	105
(3) Average finished goods turnover	7	10.1	10.3	9.7	6.7
(4) Number of times bond interest was earned (before tax)	4.81	6.83	6.52	10.3	5.92
(5) Number of times preferred dividend was earned	5.71	8.3	13.8	9.52	8.52
(6) Earnings per share of common stock	$4.00	$3.30	$3.58	$5.10	$5.38
(7) Book value per share of common stock	$33.80	$35.00	$49.80	$48.80	$53.20
(8) Current ratio	3.6:1	1:2.7	2.7:1	4.2:1	1:3.6
				(AICPA adapted)	

27-12. Derr Sales Corporation's management is concerned over the corporation's current financial position and return on investment. They request your assistance in analyzing their financial statements and furnish the following statements:

Derr Sales Corporation
Statement of Working Capital Deficit
December 31, 1977

Current liabilities..		$223,050
Less current assets:		
Cash...	$ 5,973	
Accounts receivable (net)	70,952	
Inventory..	113,125	190,050
Working capital deficit..		$ 33,000

Derr Sales Corporation
Income Statement
For Year Ended December 31, 1977

Sales (90,500 units)...	$760,200
Cost of goods sold...	452,500
Gross profit..	$307,700
Selling and general expenses, including depreciation of $22,980......................	155,660
Income before income tax	$152,040
Income tax	68,418
Net income	$ 83,622

Assets other than current assets consist of land, buildings, and equipment with a book value of $352,950 on December 31, 1977.

Sales of 100,000 units are forecasted for 1978. Within this relevant range of activity costs are estimated as follows (excluding income tax):

	Fixed Costs	Variable Costs per Unit
Cost of goods sold...		$4.90
Selling and general expenses, including depreciation of $15,450..	$129,720	1.10
Total..	$129,720	$6.00

The income tax rate is expected to be 45%. Past experience indicates that current assets vary in direct proportion to sales.

Instructions:

(1) Assuming Derr Sales Corporation operates 300 days per year, compute the following (show your computations):
(a) Number of days' sales uncollected.
(b) Inventory turnover.
(c) Number of days' operations to cover the working capital deficit.
(d) Return on total assets as a product of asset turnover and the net income ratio (sometimes called profit margin).
(2) Management feels that in 1978 the market will support a sales price of $8.30 at a sales volume of 100,000 units. Compute the rate of return on book value of total assets after income tax assuming management's expectations are realized.
(3) Assuming sales of 100,000 units at a price of $8.30 per unit in 1978, prepare an analysis of the variation in gross profit between 1977 and 1978. Your analysis should show the effects of changes in 1978 in sales volume, sales prices, and unit costs on gross profit. (AICPA adapted)

27-13. Near the close of your audit, the Treasurer of Ezy Corporation, your client, informs you that the company is planning to acquire the ATU Corporation and requests that you prepare certain statistics for 1977 and 1976 from the statements of ATU Corporation which appear on pages 818 and 819.

ATU Corporation
Balance Sheet
December 31, 1977 and 1976

Assets	1977	1976
Current assets:		
Cash	$ 1,610,000	$ 1,387,000
Marketable securities, at cost (market value $550,000)	510,000	
Accounts receivable, less allowance for doubtful accounts: 1977, $125,000; 1976, $110,000	4,075,000	3,669,000
Inventories, at lower of cost or market	7,250,000	7,050,000
Prepaid expenses	125,000	218,000
Total current assets	$13,570,000	$12,324,000
Land, buildings, and equipment, at cost:		
Land and buildings	$13,500,000	$13,500,000
Equipment	9,250,000	8,520,000
Total land, buildings, and equipment	$22,750,000	$22,020,000
Less accumulated depreciation	13,470,000	12,549,000
Total land, buildings, and equipment — net	$ 9,280,000	$ 9,471,000
Long-term receivables	$ 250,000	$ 250,000
Deferred charges	$ 25,000	$ 75,000
Total assets	$23,125,000	$22,120,000
Liabilities and Stockholders' Equity		
Current liabilities:		
Accounts payable	$ 2,950,000	$ 3,426,000
Miscellaneous expenses	1,575,000	1,644,000
Income tax payable	875,000	750,000
Current maturities on long-term liabilities	500,000	500,000
Total current liabilities	$ 5,900,000	$ 6,320,000
Other liabilities:		
7% Sinking fund debentures, due January 1, 1983 ($500,000 redeemable annually)	$ 5,000,000	$ 5,500,000
Deferred tax on income, related to depreciation	350,000	210,000
Total other liabilities	$ 5,350,000	$ 5,710,000
Total liabilities	$11,250,000	$12,030,000
Stockholders' equity:		
Capital stock:		
$1 Preferred stock, $20 par, preference on liquidation $100 per share (authorized: 100,000 shares; issued and outstanding: 50,000 shares)	$ 1,000,000	$ 1,000,000
Common stock, $1 par (authorized: 900,000 shares; issued and outstanding: 1977, 550,000 shares; 1976, 500,000 shares)	550,000	500,000
Premium on common stock	3,075,000	625,000
Retained earnings	7,250,000	7,965,000
Total stockholders' equity	$11,875,000	$10,090,000
Total liabilities and stockholders' equity	$23,125,000	$22,120,000

Additional information:

(a) The inventory at January 1, 1976, was $6,850,000.

(b) The market prices of the common stock at December 31, 1977 and 1976 were $73.50 and $47.75 respectively.

(c) The cash dividends for both preferred and common stock were declared and paid in June and December of each year. The stock dividend on common stock was declared and distributed in August, 1977.

(d) Building and equipment sales and retirements during 1977 and 1976 were $375,000 and $425,000 respectively. The related accumulated depreciation amounts were $215,000 in 1977 and $335,000 in 1976. At December 31, 1975, the building and equipment asset balance was $21,470,000 and the related accumulated depreciation was $11,650,000.

ATU Corporation
Statement of Income and Retained Earnings
For Years Ended December 31, 1977 and 1976

	1977	1976
Revenues:		
Net sales	$48,400,000	$41,700,000
Royalties	70,000	25,000
Interest	30,000	
Total	$48,500,000	$41,725,000
Costs and expenses:		
Cost of sales	$31,460,000	$29,190,000
Selling, general, and administrative expenses	12,090,000	8,785,000
Interest on 7% sinking fund debentures	385,000	420,000
Provision for income tax	2,205,000	1,575,000
Total	$46,140,000	$39,970,000
Net income	$ 2,360,000	$ 1,755,000
Retained earnings, beginning of year	7,965,000	6,760,000
Total	$10,325,000	$ 8,515,000
Dividends paid:		
Preferred stock, $1 per share in cash	$ 50,000	$ 50,000
Common stock:		
Cash — $1 per share	525,000	500,000
Stock — (10%) — 50,000 shares at market value of $50 per share	2,500,000	
Total	$ 3,075,000	$ 550,000
Retained earnings, end of year	$ 7,250,000	$ 7,965,000

Instructions: Prepare a schedule computing the following selected statistics for 1977 and 1976. The current equivalent number of shares outstanding as of the respective year-end dates should be utilized in computing per-share statistics. (The current equivalent shares means the number of shares outstanding in the prior period in terms of the present stock position.)
   (1) At December 31:
       (a) Current ratio.
       (b) Acid-test (quick) ratio.
       (c) Book value per common share.
   (2) Year ended December 31:
       (a) Gross profit rate.
       (b) Inventory turnover rate.
       (c) Times interest earned (before tax).
       (d) Earnings per common share.
       (e) Common stock price-earnings ratio (end of year value).
       (f) Gross capital expenditures. (AICPA adapted)

27-14. Ratio analysis is often applied to test the reasonableness of the relationships among current financial data against those of prior financial data. Given prior financial relationships and a few key amounts, a CPA could prepare estimates of current financial data to test the reasonableness of data furnished by a client.

Argo Sales Corporation has in recent prior years maintained the following relationships among the data on its financial statements:

Gross profit rate on net sales	40%
Net profit rate on net sales	10%
Rate of selling expenses to net sales	20%
Accounts receivable turnover	8 per year
Inventory turnover	6 per year
Acid-test ratio	2 to 1
Current ratio	3 to 1
Quick-asset composition: 8% cash, 32% marketable securities, 60% accounts receivable	
Asset turnover	2 per year
Ratio of total assets to intangible assets	20 to 1

(continued)

Ratio of accumulated depreciation to cost of fixed assets.................................. 1 to 3
Ratio of accounts receivable to accounts payable... 1.5 to 1
Ratio of working capital to stockholders' equity.. 1 to 1.6
Ratio of total liabilities to stockholders' equity .... 1 to 2

The corporation had a net income of $120,000 for 1977 which resulted in earnings of $5.20 per share of common stock. Additional information includes the following:

(a) Capital stock authorized, issued (all in 1969), and outstanding: Common, $10 per share par value, issued at 10% premium; 6% Preferred, $100 per share par value, issued at a 10% premium.

(b) Market value per share of common at December 31, 1977, $78.

(c) Preferred dividends paid in 1977, $3,000.

(d) Number of times interest earned in 1977, 21 (income after tax).

(e) The amounts of the following were the same at December 31, 1977 as at January 1, 1977. Inventory, accounts receivable, 8% bonds payable — due 1979, and total stockholders' equity.

(f) All purchases and sales were "on account."

Instructions:

(1) Prepare in good form: (a) the condensed balance sheet, and (b) the condensed income statement for the year ending December 31, 1977, presenting the amounts you would expect to appear on Argo's financial statements (ignoring income tax). Major captions appearing on Argo's balance sheet are: Current assets, Fixed assets, Intangible assets, Current liabilities, Long-term liabilities, and Stockholders' equity. In addition to the accounts divulged in the problem, you should include accounts for prepaid expenses, miscellaneous expenses payable, and administrative expenses. Supporting computations should be in good form.

(2) Compute the following for 1977 (show your computations):

(a) Rate of return on stockholders' equity.

(b) Price-earnings ratio for common stock.

(c) Dividends paid per share of common stock.

(d) Dividends paid per share of preferred stock.

(e) Yield on common stock. (AICPA adapted)

A

Future and Present Value: Concepts and Applications

A basic knowledge of future and present value concepts and techniques is becoming increasingly important for students of accounting. Presumably, most students have already become acquainted with these concepts in previous courses. However, because of limited or noncurrent exposure, some students may need to review future and present value concepts in connection with their study of intermediate accounting. To fulfill this need, the material in this appendix is intended to: (1) provide a brief review of the basic concepts and applications of interest; and (2) present some illustrations of business problems utilizing future and present value tables.

INTEREST DEFINED

In some respects money is like any other commodity. It is a scarce resource, and a payment is generally required for its use. This payment (cost) for the use of money is *interest*. For example, if $100 is borrowed, whether from an individual, a business, or a bank, and $110 is paid back, $10 interest has, in effect, been paid for the use of the $100. Thus, interest represents the excess cash paid over the amount of cash borrowed.

Generally interest is specified in terms of a percentage rate for a period of time, usually a year. For example, interest at 8% means the annual cost of borrowing an amount of money, called the *principal*, is equal to 8% of that amount. The interest rate and the time period are assumed to be stated in common units. To illustrate, if $100 is borrowed at 8% annual interest, the total to be repaid is $108 — the amount of the principal, $100, and the interest for a year, $8 ($100 × .08 × 1). Interest on a $1,000 note for 6 months at 8% is $40 ($1,000 × .08 × 6/12). Thus, the formula for computing *simple interest* is $i = p \times r \times t$, where:

i = Amount of simple interest
p = Principal amount
r = Interest rate (per period)
t = Time (number of periods)

The foregoing discussion relates to simple interest. Many transactions involve *compound interest*. This means the amount of interest earned for a certain period is added to the principal for the next period. Interest for the subsequent period is computed on the new amount, which includes both principal and interest. As an example, assume $100 is deposited in a bank and left for two years at 6% annual interest. At the end of the first year, the $100 has earned $6 interest ($100 × .06 × 1). At the end of the second year, $6 has been earned for the first year, plus another $6.36 interest (6% on the $106 balance at the beginning of the second year). Thus, the total interest earned is $12.36 rather than $12 because of the compounding effect. The table below, based on the foregoing example, illustrates the computation of simple and compound interest for four years. Formulas relative to common compound interest situations are provided in the next section of this appendix.

	Simple Interest			Compound Interest		
Year	Computation	Interest	Total	Computation	Interest	Total
1	($100 × .06)	$6	$106	($100.00 × .06)	$6.00	$106.00
2	(100 × .06)	6	112	(106.00 × .06)	6.36	112.36
3	(100 × .06)	6	118	(112.36 × .06)	6.74	119.10
4	(100 × .06)	6	124	(119.10 × .06)	7.15	126.25

Because of the compounding effect of interest, an adjustment of the stated annual rate of interest to its effective rate often must be made. This also requires adjusting the number of interest periods. To illustrate, 6% annual interest for 10 years compounded semianually would be converted to 3% for 20 periods; 12% for 6 years compounded quarterly would convert to 3% for 24 periods. A first step in working compound interest related problems is to adjust the stated interest rate to its effective interest rate for the appropriate number of periods.

FUTURE AND PRESENT VALUE COMPUTATIONS

Since money earns interest, $100 received today is more valuable than $100 received one year from today. Future and present value analysis is a method of comparing the value of money received or expected to be received at different time periods.

Analyses requiring alternative computations in terms of present dollars relative to future dollars may be viewed from one of two perspectives, the future or the present. If the future point in time is chosen, all cash flows must be *accumulated* to that future point. In this instance, the effect of interest is to increase the amounts or values over time. Examples of questions which might be answered by future value computations include:

How much will $500 deposited today at 6% annual interest amount to in 20 years?

How long would it take to accumulate a $10,000 down payment on a home if one saved $100 a month and received 5% per year on the savings?

What rate of return on an investment must be received for money to double in 20 years?

If, on the other hand, the present is chosen as the point in time at which to evaluate the alternatives, all cash flows must be *discounted* to the present. In this instance, the discounting effect reduces the amounts or values. Assuming a certain rate of interest, examples of questions using the present value approach include:

How much should be accepted today for an apartment house in lieu of rental income for the next 10 years?

How much is $5,000 due in 5 years worth today?

What lump-sum amount should be paid today for a series of equal payments of $100 a month, beginning now, for the next 5 years?

The future value and present value situations are essentially reciprocal relationships, and both are based on the concept of interest. Thus, if interest can be earned at 6% per year, the future worth of $100 one year from now is $106. Conversely, assuming the same rate of interest, the present value of a $106 payment due in one year is $100.

There are four common future and present value situations, each with a corresponding formula. Two of the situations deal with one-time, lump-sum payments or receipts[1] (either future or present values), and the other two involve annuities (either future or present values). An *annuity* consists of a series of equal payments over a specified number of periods.

Without going into the derivation of the formulas, these four situations are as follows:

1. *Future Value of a Lump-Sum Payment:* $FV = P(1 + i)^n$

   This may also be referred to as $FV = P(FVF_{\overline{n}|\,i})$ or simply $FV = P$(Table I value), where:

FV	= Future value
P	= Principal amount to be accumulated
i	= Interest rate per period
n	= Number of periods
$FVF_{\overline{n}|\,i}$	= Future value factor for a particular interest rate and for a certain number of periods from Table I

2. *Present Value of a Lump-Sum Payment:* $PV = A\left[\dfrac{1}{(1 + i)^n}\right]$

   This may also be referred to as $PV = A(PVF_{\overline{n}|\,i})$ or simply $PV = A$(Table II value), where:

PV	= Present value
A	= Accumulated amount to be discounted
i	= Interest rate per period
n	= Number of periods
$PVF_{\overline{n}|\,i}$	= Present value factor for a particular interest rate and for a certain number of periods from Table II

[1]Hereafter in this appendix, the terms *payments* and *receipts* will be used interchangeably. A payment by one party in a transaction becomes a receipt to the other party and vice versa. The term *rent* is used to designate either a receipt or a payment.

3. *Future Value of an Annuity:* $FV_n = R\left[\dfrac{(1 + i)^n - 1}{i}\right]$

This may also be referred to as $FV_n = R(FVAF_{\overline{n}|\,i})$ or simply $FV_n = R$(Table III value), where:

FV_n	= Future value of an annuity
R	= Annuity payment or periodic rent to be accumulated
i	= Interest rate per period
n	= Number of periods
$FVAF_{\overline{n}|\,i}$	= Future value annuity factor for a particular interest rate and for a certain number of periods from Table III

4. *Present Value of an Annuity:* $PV_n = R\left[\dfrac{1 - \dfrac{1}{(1 + i)^n}}{i}\right]$

This may also be referred to as $PV_n = R(PVAF_{\overline{n}|\,i})$ or simply $PV_n = R$(Table IV value), where:

PV_n	= Present value of an annuity
R	= Annuity payment or periodic rent to be discounted
i	= Interest rate per period
n	= Number of periods
$PVAF_{\overline{n}|\,i}$	= Present value annuity factor for a particular interest rate and for a certain number of periods from Table IV

Because using the formulas would be time-consuming, tables have been developed for each of the four situations. Such tables are provided at the end of this appendix, beginning on page 837. Each table is based upon computing the value of $1 for various interest rates and periods of time. Future and present value computations can be made by multiplying the appropriate table value factor for $1 by the lump-sum or annuity payment (rent) involved in the problem. To illustrate, consider the question described earlier: How much will $500 deposited today at 6% annual interest amount to in 20 years? This is an example of the first situation, the future value of a lump-sum payment, and involves Table I. The table value for $n = 20$ and $i = 6\%$ is 3.2071. This value times $500, the principal amount to be accumulated, is approximately $1,604. Thus, the future value of $500 deposited now, accumulating at 6% per year for 20 years, is about $1,604.

The following examples demonstrate the application of future and present value tables in solving business problems. At least one example is provided for each of the four situations just described. Note that business problems sometimes require solving for the number of periods, the interest rate, or the rental payment instead of the future or present value amounts. In each of the formulas there are four variables. If information is given about any three of the variables, the fourth (unknown value) can be determined.

Problem 1:

Joe loans his brother $5,000 for a new car. The debt is evidenced by a note due in 4 years with interest at 8% compounded semiannually. After 1 year, Joe runs out of cash and sells the note to a friend who discounts the note at 12% compounded quarterly. How much cash did Joe receive from his friend?

Solution to Problem 1:

This problem involves a lump-sum payment to be accumulated 4 years into the future at one interest rate, then discounted back 3 years at a different interest rate.

In many present and future value problems, a time line is helpful in visualizing the problem:

First, the $5,000 must be accumulated for 4 years at 8% compounded semiannually. Table I is used, and the applicable formula is:

$FV = P(FVF_{\overline{n}|\,i})$ where: FV = The future value of the lump sum
  P = $5,000
  n = 8 periods (4 years × 2)
  i = 4% effective interest rate per period (8% ÷ 2)

$FV = \$5,000\ (\text{Table I}_{\overline{8}|\,4\%})$

$FV = \$5,000\ (1.3686)$

$FV = \$6,843$

In 4 years, the holder of the note will receive $6,843. After Joe sells the note to his friend, the note will be worth $6,843 to the friend in 3 years. The opportunity cost of money to the friend is apparently 12% compounded quarterly. Therefore, the $6,843 must be discounted back 3 years at 12% to find the amount the friend is willing to pay Joe.

Table II is used, and the applicable formula is:

$PV = A(PVF_{\overline{n}|\,i})$ where: PV = The value of the future sum discounted back three years
  A = $6,843
  n = 12 periods (3 years × 4 quarters)
  i = 3% effective interest rate per period (12% ÷ 4 quarters)

$PV = \$6,843\ (\text{Table II}_{\overline{12}|\,3\%})$

$PV = \$6,843\ (.7014)$

$PV = \$4,800$

The friend will pay roughly $4,800. Thus, Joe is willing to give up $2,043 ($6,843 − $4,800) in order to collect the note at the end of 1 year.

Problem 2:

Miller Sporting Goods is contemplating an investment which will require $1,250,000 capital investment and which will provide these net receipts:

Year	Estimated Net Receipts
1	$195,000
2	457,000
3	593,000
4	421,000
5	95,000
6	5,000

Miller will accept the investment only if the rate of return is greater than 10%. Will Miller accept the investment?

Solution to Problem 2:

A series of unequal future receipts must be compared with a present lump-sum investment. For such a comparison to be made, all future cash flows must be discounted to the present.

If the rate of return on the amount invested is greater than 10%, then the total of all yearly net receipts discounted to the present at 10% will be greater than the amount invested. Since the receipts are unequal, each amount must be discounted individually. Table II is used, and the applicable formula is:

$$PV = A(PVF_{\overline{n}|\,i}) \quad \text{where:}$$

(1) Year = n	(2) A (Net Receipts)	(3) Table II$_{\overline{n}|\,10\%}$	(2) × (3) = (4) PV (Discounted Amount)
1	$195,000	.9091	$ 177,275
2	457,000	.8264	377,665
3	593,000	.7513	445,521
4	421,000	.6830	287,543
5	95,000	.6209	58,986
6	5,000	.5645	2,823
Total			$1,349,813

The total discounted receipts are greater than the investment; thus, the rate of return is more than 10%. Therefore, other things being equal, Miller will invest.

Problem 3:

Brothwell, Inc., owes an installment debt of $1,000 per quarter for 5 years. The creditor has indicated that he will accept an equivalent lump-sum payment at the end of the contract period instead of the series of payments. If money is worth 8% compounded quarterly and the first four payments have been made, what is the equivalent lump-sum payment?

Solution to Problem 3:

The equivalent lump-sum payment can be found by accumulating the quarterly $1,000 payments to the end of the contract period. Table III is used, and the applicable formula is:

$$FV_n = R(FVAF_{\overline{n}|\,i}) \quad \text{where:} \quad FV_n = \text{The unknown equivalent lump-sum payment}$$

R = $1,000 quarterly installment to be accumulated

n = 16 periods [(5 years × 4 quarters) − 4 quarters already paid]

i = 2% effective compound rate (8% ÷ 4 quarters)

$$FV_n = \$1,000(\text{Table III}_{\overline{16}|\,2\%})$$
$$FV_n = \$1,000(18.6393)$$
$$FV_n = \$18,639$$

$18,639 paid at the end of the 5 years is equivalent to the remaining 16 payments.

Problem 4:

Mr. Robinson, proprietor of Jefferson Davis Appliance, received two offers for his last deluxe-model refrigerator. Ms. Butler will pay $650 in cash. Mr.

McBride will pay $700 consisting of a down payment of $100 and 12 monthly payments of $50. If the installment interest rate is 24% compounded monthly, which offer should Robinson accept?

Solution to Problem 4:

In order to compare the two alternative methods of payment, all cash flows must be accumulated or discounted to one point in time. As illustrated by the time line, the present is selected as the point of comparison.

McBride $100 $50 $50 $50 $50 $50 $50 $50 $50 $50 $50 $50 $50

| 0 | 1 | 2 | 3 | 4 | 5 | 6 | 7 | 8 | 9 | 10 | 11 | 12 months |

Butler $650

Ms. Butler's offer is $650 today. The present value of $650 today is $650.

Mr. McBride's offer consists of an annuity of 12 payments, plus $100 due today which is not part of the annuity. The annuity may be discounted to the present by using Table IV and the applicable formula:

$$PV_n = R(PVAF_{\overline{n}|\,i}) \quad \text{where:} \quad \begin{aligned} PV_n &= \text{Unknown present value of 12 payments} \\ R &= \$50 \text{ monthly payment to be discounted} \\ n &= 12 \text{ periods} \\ i &= 2\% \text{ effective compound rate } (24\% \div 12 \\ &\quad \text{ periods per year}) \end{aligned}$$

$$PV_n = \$50(\text{Table IV}_{\overline{12}|\,2\%})$$
$$PV_n = \$50(10.5753)$$
$$PV_n = \$529$$

Present value of McBride's payments	$529
Present value of McBride's $100 down payment	100
Total present value of McBride's offer	$629

Therefore, Ms. Butler's offer of $650 cash is more desirable than Mr. McBride's offer.

Problem 5:

The Angelo Company is investigating the purchase of a block of bonds. Each $1,000 bond has a stated interest rate of 12% paid semiannually and is due in 10 years. The prevailing market rate for comparable bonds is 8%, also paid semiannually. How much should Angelo Company pay for each bond?

Solution to Problem 5:

This problem involves finding the present value of the cash flows resulting from the purchase of a bond. A bond pays both a series of equal interest payments and the principal amount when the bond matures. To ascertain the fair price of the bond, both the series of interest payments and the future payment of the principal must be discounted to the present at the going market rate of 8% compounded semiannually.

First the series of interest payments is discounted to the present using Table IV and the applicable formula:

$$PV_n = R(PVAF_{\overline{n}|\,i}) \quad \text{where:} \quad \begin{aligned} PV_n &= \text{Unknown present value} \\ R &= \$60 \text{ semiannual interest payment } (\$1,000 \\ &\quad \times .12 \times \tfrac{1}{2} \text{ year}) \\ n &= 20 \text{ periods } (10 \text{ years} \times 2 \text{ periods per} \\ &\quad \text{year}) \\ i &= 4\% \text{ effective compound rate } (8\% \div 2 \\ &\quad \text{ periods per year}) \end{aligned}$$

$$PV_n = \$60(\text{Table IV}_{\overline{20}|\,4\%})$$
$$PV_n = \$60(13.5903)$$
$$PV_n = \$815$$

Second, the future payment of principal is discounted to the present using Table II and the applicable formula:

$$PV = A(PVF_{\overline{n}|\,i})$$ where: PV = Unknown present value of the principal payment
                                           A   = \$1,000, the principal payment
                                           n   = 20 periods
                                           i   = 4% effective compound rate

$$PV = \$1,000(\text{Table II}_{\overline{20}|\,4\%})$$
$$PV = \$1,000(.4564)$$
$$PV = \$456$$

Therefore, the price Angelo Company should pay for each bond is $815 + $456, or $1,271.

INTERPOLATION

A difficulty in using future and present value tables arises when the exact factor does not appear in the table. One solution is to use the formula. Interpolation is another, often more practical, solution. Interpolation assumes the change between two values is linear. Although such an assumption is not correct, the margin of error is often insignificant, especially if the table value ranges are not too wide.

For example, determine the table value for the present value of $1 at $4\frac{1}{2}\%$ for 9 periods. The appropriate factor does not appear in Table II. However, the two closest values are Table $II_{\overline{9}|\,4\%} = .7026$ and Table $II_{\overline{9}|\,5\%} = .6446$. Interpolation relates the unknown value to the change in the known values. This relationship may be shown as a proportion:

$$\frac{y}{Y} = \frac{x}{X}$$

$$\frac{5 - 4\frac{1}{2}}{5 - 4} = \frac{x}{.7026 - .6446}$$

$$\frac{\frac{1}{2}}{1} = \frac{x}{.0580}$$

$$x = .0290$$

The .0290 is the difference between the value for 5% and the value for $4\frac{1}{2}\%$. Therefore, the value needed is $.0290 + .6446 = .6736$. Using the mathematical formula for Table II $\left\{ PV = A\left[\frac{1}{(1 + i)^n}\right]\right\}$, the present value of $1 at $4\frac{1}{2}\%$ interest for 9 periods is $.6729 \left\{ PV = 1\left[\frac{1}{(1 + .045)^9}\right]\right\}$. The difference $(.6736 - .6729 = .0007)$ is insignificant for many purposes.

Interpolation is useful in finding a particular unknown table value that lies between two given values. This procedure is also used in approximating the number of periods or unknown interest rates when the table value is known. The following problems illustrate the determination of these two variables.

Problem 6:

Ms. Novella leaves $600,000 to a university for a new building on the condition that construction will not begin until her bequest, invested at 5% per year, amounts to $1,500,000. How long before construction may begin?

Solution to Problem 6:

This problem involves finding the time (number of periods) required for a lump-sum payment to accumulate to a specified future amount. Table I is used and, the applicable formula is:

$$FV = P(FVF_{\overline{n}|i})$$

where:
FV = $1,500,000
P = $600,000
n = Unknown number of periods
i = 5% effective interest rate per year

$$\$1,500,000 = \$600,000(\text{Table } I_{\overline{n}|5\%})$$

$$\frac{\$1,500,000}{\$\ 600,000} = \text{Table } I_{\overline{n}|5\%}$$

$$2.5 = \text{Table } I_{\overline{n}|5\%}$$

Referring to Table I, reading down the i = 5% column:

n		Table Factor
18	=	2.4066
19	=	2.5270

Interpolating:

$$\frac{y}{Y} = \frac{x}{X}$$

2.4066   2.5000   2.5270 — y / Y

18   ?   19 — x / X

$$\frac{2.5270 - 2.5000}{2.5270 - 2.4066} = \frac{x}{19 - 18}$$

$$\frac{.0270}{.1204} = \frac{x}{1}$$

$$x = .2243$$

The .2243 is the difference between the number of periods at table factor 2.5270 and the number of periods at table factor 2.5000. Therefore, the number of periods needed is 19.0000 − .2243 = 18.7757. In other words, about 18¾ periods (in this case, years) are required for $600,000 to amount to $1,500,000 at 5% annual interest.

Problem 7:

The Newports have entered into an automobile lease-purchase arrangement. The fair market value of the leased automobile is $5,814, and the contract calls for quarterly payments of $570 due at the end of each quarter for 3 years. What is the implicit rate of interest on the lease arrangement?

Solution to Problem 7:

The implicit interest rate must be computed for the present value of an annuity. The present value is the fair market value of the automobile, and the payment is the lease payment. Table IV is used, and the appropriate formula is given at the top of the next page.

$PV_n = R(PVAF_{\overline{n}|\,i})$ where: PV_n = \$5,814
                                       R   = \$570
                                       n   = 12(3 years × 4 payments per year)
                                       i   = The unknown quarterly interest rate

$\$5,814 = \$570(\text{Table IV}_{\overline{12}|\,i})$

$\dfrac{\$5,814}{\$570} = \text{Table IV}_{\overline{12}|\,i}$

$10.20 = \text{Table IV}_{\overline{12}|\,i}$

Reading across the $n = 12$ row of Table IV:

i		Table Factor
2%	=	10.5753
3%	=	9.9540

Interpolating:

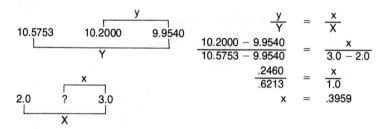

$$\frac{y}{Y} = \frac{x}{X}$$

$$\frac{10.2000 - 9.9540}{10.5753 - 9.9540} = \frac{x}{3.0 - 2.0}$$

$$\frac{.2460}{.6213} = \frac{x}{1.0}$$

$$x = .3959$$

The .3959 is the difference between the interest rate at the table factor 9.9540 and the interest rate at the table factor 10.2000. Therefore, the quarterly implicit interest rate is $3.0000 - .3959 = 2.6041\%$; and the annual implicit interest rate is 10.4164% (2.6041% × 4).

ORDINARY ANNUITY AND ANNUITY DUE

Annuities are of two types: ordinary annuities (annuities in arrears) and annuities due (annuities in advance). The periodic rents or payments for an *ordinary annuity* are made at the *end* of each period, and the last payment coincides with the end of the annuity term. The periodic rents or payments for an *annuity due* are made at the *beginning* of each period, and one period of the annuity term remains after the last payment. These differences are illustrated as follows:

Ordinary Annuity for 3 Years

1st payment	2nd payment	3rd payment

Beginning of annuity term   interest period   interest period   End of annuity term

Annuity Due for 3 Years

Most future and present value tables are computed for ordinary annuities; however, with slight adjustment, these same tables may be used in solving annuity due problems. To illustrate the conversion of an ordinary annuity table value to an annuity due value, consider the *future* amount of an ordinary annuity for three years (see the diagram at the bottom of page 830). This situation involves three payments (3p); but because the first payment is made at the end of the first period, interest is earned for only two periods (2i), or in total, 3p + 2i. On the other hand, the future amount of an annuity due for three years (the diagram above) involves three payments as well as interest for three periods because the first payment is made at the beginning of the first period (3p + 3i).

As shown below, an ordinary annuity involving four payments would earn interest for three periods (4p + 3i); thus, if the fourth payment were deducted, the value would be comparable to an annuity due of 3 periods [i.e., (4p + 3i) − 1p = 3p + 3i].

Ordinary Annuity for 4 Years

Annuity Due for 3 Years

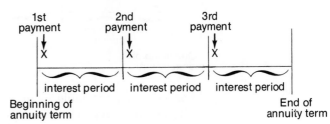

Therefore, to find the future value of an annuity due using ordinary annuity table values, simply select the appropriate table value for an ordinary annuity for one additional period (n + 1) and subtract the extra payment (which is 1.0000 in terms of the table value because the tables are computed for rents of $1.0000). The formula is $FV_n = R(FVAF_{\overline{n+1}|i} - 1)$.

For example, the table value (Table III) for the future amount of an annuity due for 3 periods at 8% is:

(1) Factor for future value of an ordinary annuity of $1 for 4 periods (n
    + 1) at 8%.. 4.5061
(2) Less one payment... 1.0000
(3) Factor for future value of an annuity due of $1 for 3 periods at 8%..... 3.5061

The situation and the underlying reasoning are reversed in converting a present value factor of an ordinary annuity to the present value factor of an annuity due. As shown in the diagrams below, the present value of an annuity due for three years involves three payments; but interest (discount) is only earned for two periods (3p + 2i). To obtain comparable interest (discount) periods, an ordinary annuity for two years is required (2p + 2i). However, one additional payment must be added to make the situations equivalent; i.e., (2p + 2i) + 1p = 3p + 2i. Consequently, to convert the present value of an ordinary annuity to the present value of an annuity due, look at the table factor for one less period (n − 1) and then add one payment (+1.0000). The formula is $PV_n = R(PVAF_{\overline{n-1}|i} + 1)$.

Ordinary Annuity for 2 Years

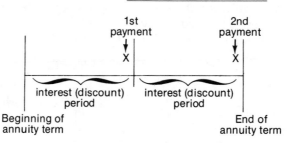

Annuity Due for 3 Years

For example, the table value (Table IV) for the present value of an annuity due for three periods at 8% is:

(1) Factor for present value of an ordinary annuity of $1 for two periods
    (n − 1) at 8%.. 1.7833
(2) Plus one payment 1.0000
(3) Factor for present value of an annuity due of $1 for 3 periods at 8% .. 2.7833

The following problems illustrate the application of converting from ordinary annuity table values to annuity due table values.

Problem 8:

The Sampson Corporation desires to accumulate funds to retire a $200,000 bond issue at the end of 15 years. Funds set aside for this purpose would be invested to yield 6%. What annual payment starting immediately would provide the needed funds?

Solution to Problem 8:

Annuity payments of an unknown amount are to be accumulated toward a specific dollar amount at a known interest rate. Therefore, Table III is used. Because the first payment is to be made immediately, all payments will fall due at the beginning of each period and an annuity due is used. The appropriate formula is:

$$FV_n = R(FVAF_{\overline{n+1}|\,i} - 1)$$

where:
FV_n = $200,000
R = Unknown annual payment
n = 15 periods
i = 6% annual interest

$$\$200,000 = R(\text{Table III}_{\overline{16}|\,6\%} - 1)$$

$$\$200,000 = R(24.6725)$$

$$\frac{\$200,000}{24.6725} = R$$

$$\$8,106 = R$$

Sampson Corporation must deposit $8,106 annually, starting immediately, to accumulate $200,000 in 15 years at 6% annual interest.

Problem 9:

Brigham Corporation has completed lease-purchase negotiations. The fair market value of the leased equipment is $45,897. The lease contract specifies semiannual payments of $3,775 for 10 years beginning immediately. At the end of the lease, Brigham Corporation may purchase the equipment for a nominal amount. What is the implicit annual rate of interest on the lease purchase?

Solution to Problem 9:

The implicit interest rate must be computed for the present value of an annuity due. The present value is the fair market value of the equipment, and the payment is the lease payment. Table IV is used, and the applicable formula is:

$$PV_n = R(PVAF_{\overline{n-1}|\,i} + 1)$$

where:
PV_n = $45,897
R = $3,775
n = 20 periods (10 years × 2 payments per year)
i = The unknown semiannual interest rate

$$\$45,897 = \$3,775 (\text{Table IV}_{\overline{19}|\,i} + 1)$$

$$\frac{\$45,897}{\$3,775} = 12.1581 = \text{Table IV}_{\overline{19}|\,i} + 1$$

$$11.1581 = \text{Table IV}_{\overline{19}|\,i}$$

Examination of Table IV for 19 periods and a factor of 11.1581 shows Table IV$_{\overline{19}|\,6\%}$ = 11.1581. Therefore, i = 6%. The implicit annual interest rate is twice the semiannual rate, or 2 × 6% = 12%.

Problem 10:

Three years remain on the lease of Nyland Food Service, Inc.'s building. The lease is non-cancelable and requires payments of $5,000 on March 1 and September 1. During February, Nyland located a new store building and asked the lessor of the old store to accept $25,000 now in full payment of the old lease. The building is very old and will not be used again. If the value of money to the lessor is 16% compounded semiannually, should she accept Nyland's offer?

Solution to Problem 10:

The lessor must compare the $25,000 now to the value of the six remaining lease payments. The lease payments must be discounted to the present for proper comparison. Because the next payment is due now, the lease payments are an annuity due. Table IV is adjusted to find the appropriate value. The formula is:

$$PV_n = R(PVAF_{\overline{n-1}|\,i} + 1)$$

where:
PV_n = Unknown present value of lease payments
R = $5,000 per period (6 months)
n = 6 periods (3 years $\times$ 2 periods per year)
i = 8% (16% $\div$ 2 periods per year)

$$PV_n = \$5,000(\text{Table IV}_{\overline{5}|\,8\%} + 1)$$
$$PV_n = \$5,000(3.9927 + 1)$$
$$PV_n = \$24,964$$

The offer of $25,000 now is greater than $24,964, the present value of the remaining lease payments. Therefore, the lessor should accept the offer.

EXERCISES

1. John borrowed $500 from his brother-in-law at 8% simple interest. The loan is to be repaid in 6 months. How much will John have to pay his brother-in-law to settle this obligation? How much of this payment will be interest? If John were to borrow the $500 from his credit union at 12% compounded quarterly, how much interest would he have to pay?

2. Indicate the *rate per period* and the *number of periods* for each of the following:
  - (a) 10% per annum, for 3 years, compounded annually.
  - (b) 10% per annum, for 3 years, compounded semiannually.
  - (c) 10% per annum, for 3 years, compounded quarterly.
  - (d) 10% per annum, for 3 years, compounded monthly.

3. What is the *future amount* for each of the following independent situations?
  - (a) The amount of $1,000 for 4 years at 8% compounded annually.
  - (b) The amount of $1,000 for 4 years at 8% compounded quarterly.
  - (c) The amount of $500 for 1 year at 24% compounded monthly.

4. What is the *present value* for each of the following independent situations?
  - (a) The present value of $1,000 due in 5 years at 10% compounded annually.
  - (b) The present value of $1,000 due in 5 years at 10% compounded semiannually.
  - (c) The present value of $25,000 due in 10 years at 8% compounded quarterly.

5. For each of the following, compute the *future amount* of an *ordinary annuity* (also known as an annuity in arrears).
  - (a) 12 payments of $100 at 6%.
  - (b) 8 payments of $500 at 10%.
  - (c) 19 payments of $125 at 12%.

6. What are the *future amounts* in Exercise 5 if the annuities are *annuities due* (also known as annuities in advance)?

7. For each of the following, compute the *present value* of an *ordinary annuity*.
  (a) $1,000 for 10 years at 8%.
  (b) $350 for 7 years at 5%.
  (c) $250 for 20 years at 10%.

8. What are the *present values* in Exercise 7 if the annuities are *annuities due*?

9. Mr. Baxter has $2,000 to invest. One alternative will yield 10% per year for 4 years. A second alternative is to deposit the $2,000 in a bank which will pay 8% per year, compounded quarterly. Which alternative should Mr. Baxter select?

10. RaNae Allen wishes to have $6,000 to buy a new car at the end of 5 years. How much must she invest today to accomplish her purpose if the interest rate she can earn on her investment is 6%?

11. The Nielsens plan to save $1,500 each year to apply as a down payment on a home. If their first deposit is made on January 1, 1978, and their last deposit is made on January 1, 1982, how much will the Nielsens have for their down payment by January 1, 1982? Assume an interest rate of 8%.

12. If Mike Knudsen invests $800 on July 1 of each year from 1975 to 1985, inclusive, how much will have accumulated on July 1, 1986, if the interest rate is 12%?

13. Professor Andersen is about to retire. He has $55,000 accumulated in his retirement fund and plans to invest that amount in an annuity on September 1, 1979. If Professor Andersen purchases an annuity of 20 annual payments, the first to be made on September 1, 1980, how much will he receive each year, assuming an interest rate of 8%?

14. Miss Doakes borrowed from a friend $4,000 which was due on August 1, 1976. On that date she was unable to pay the obligation but was able to arrange for Western Loan Company to pay her friend the $4,000. Miss Doakes agreed to pay Western Loan Company a series of 5 equal annual payments, such payments being in part a payment on the unpaid principal and in part a payment of interest at 12% per annum. What is the amount of Miss Doakes' payments if she makes her first payment on August 1, 1976?

15. An accounting student bought a calculator for $250 to assist in homework assignments. The student bought the calculator on time, agreeing to pay $23.64 at the end of each month for 12 months. What annual interest rate did the student pay?

16. Maria Garcia is about to purchase a new freezer. She can pay $375 cash or make 8 monthly payments of $51.75 each. If she chooses to buy the freezer over time, what approximate annual interest rate will she be paying?

17. The Johnsons are trying to accumulate $5,000 to buy some mountain property. They are able to deposit $1,200 a year into their savings account which earns 6% per year. In how many years can the Johnsons expect to buy their property?

18. K agrees to lease from L certain property for 10 years at the following annual rentals, payable in advance:

Years 1 and 2	$1,000 per annum
Years 3 to 6	$2,000 per annum
Years 7 to 10	$2,500 per annum

What single immediate sum will pay all of these rents if they are discounted at 6%? Prove by setting up a table showing the reduction of the leasehold.

19. Comment on the following statement issued by the president of a large corporation: "The directors have accepted a bid of $103.75 for $10,000,000, 20-year, first mortgage, 6½% bonds, thus securing $10,375,000 new capital. They gave serious consideration to a competing offer of par for 6% bonds. Although this would have meant an interest saving, the receipt of $375,000 additional capital at this time is of great advantage and offsets the interest saving under the lower coupon rate."

20. ABC Company is offered two alternative methods of purchasing a piece of equipment: (1) $20,000 cash or (2) $10,000 down plus $1,900 per year due at the end of each year for 6 years. Should the buyer accept the cash or the time-interest installment if money is worth 5% per annum?

21. An existing building is under consideration as an investment. Estimates of expected annual cash receipts for the next 20 years are $8,000 per year. Cash outlays will be $2,000 per year. (Assume cash flows at the end of the year.)

   (a) How much is the building worth to the buyer if 10% per annum is an appropriate rate of return?
   (b) If $30,000 is borrowed to finance purchase of the building and is to be repaid annually by means of 10 year-end payments at 6% interest, what will the annual payments be?

22. (a) Determine the price of a 5-year, $10,000, 6% bond, with semiannual coupons, bought to yield 8%. (b) What is the price if the above bond bears interest at 6% and is bought to yield 5%?

TABLE I
Amount of $1 Due in n Periods

$$FV = P(1 + i)^n = P(FVF_{\overline{n}|i})$$

n	2%	3%	4%	5%	6%	8%	10%	12%	16%	20%
1	1.0200	1.0300	1.0400	1.0500	1.0600	1.0800	1.1000	1.1200	1.1600	1.2000
2	1.0404	1.0609	1.0816	1.1025	1.1236	1.1664	1.2100	1.2544	1.3456	1.4400
3	1.0612	1.0927	1.1249	1.1576	1.1910	1.2597	1.3310	1.4049	1.5609	1.7280
4	1.0824	1.1255	1.1699	1.2155	1.2625	1.3605	1.4641	1.5735	1.8106	2.0736
5	1.1041	1.1593	1.2167	1.2763	1.3382	1.4693	1.6105	1.7623	2.1003	2.4883
6	1.1262	1.1941	1.2653	1.3401	1.4185	1.5869	1.7716	1.9738	2.4364	2.9860
7	1.1487	1.2299	1.3159	1.4071	1.5036	1.7138	1.9487	2.2107	2.8262	3.5832
8	1.1717	1.2668	1.3686	1.4775	1.5938	1.8509	2.1436	2.4760	3.2784	4.2998
9	1.1951	1.3048	1.4233	1.5513	1.6895	1.9990	2.3579	2.7731	3.8030	5.1598
10	1.2190	1.3439	1.4802	1.6289	1.7908	2.1589	2.5937	3.1058	4.4114	6.1917
11	1.2434	1.3842	1.5395	1.7103	1.8983	2.3316	2.8531	3.4785	5.1173	7.4301
12	1.2682	1.4258	1.6010	1.7959	2.0122	2.5182	3.1384	3.8960	5.9360	8.9161
13	1.2936	1.4685	1.6651	1.8856	2.1329	2.7196	3.4523	4.3635	6.8858	10.6993
14	1.3195	1.5126	1.7317	1.9799	2.2609	2.9372	3.7975	4.8871	7.9875	12.8392
15	1.3459	1.5580	1.8009	2.0789	2.3966	3.1722	4.1772	5.4736	9.2655	15.4070
16	1.3728	1.6047	1.8730	2.1829	2.5404	3.4259	4.5950	6.1304	10.7480	18.4884
17	1.4002	1.6528	1.9479	2.2920	2.6928	3.7000	5.0545	6.8660	12.4677	22.1861
18	1.4282	1.7024	2.0258	2.4066	2.8543	3.9960	5.5599	7.6900	14.4625	26.6233
19	1.4568	1.7535	2.1068	2.5270	3.0256	4.3157	6.1159	8.6128	16.7765	31.9480
20	1.4859	1.8061	2.1911	2.6533	3.2071	4.6610	6.7275	9.6463	19.4608	38.3376
25	1.6406	2.0938	2.6658	3.3864	4.2919	6.8485	10.8347	17.0001	40.8742	95.3962
30	1.8114	2.4273	3.2434	4.3219	5.7435	10.0627	17.4494	29.9599	85.8499	237.3763
40	2.2080	3.2620	4.8010	7.0400	10.2857	21.7245	45.2593	93.0509	378.7212	1469.7716
50	2.6916	4.3839	7.1067	11.4674	18.4202	46.9016	117.3909	289.0022	1670.7038	9100.4382

TABLE II

Present Value of $1 Due in n Periods

$$PV = A \left[\frac{1}{(1 + i)^n} \right] = A(PVF_{\overline{n}|\,i})$$

n	2%	3%	4%	5%	6%	8%	10%	12%	16%	20%
1	0.9804	0.9709	0.9615	0.9524	0.9434	0.9259	0.9091	0.8929	0.8621	0.8333
2	0.9612	0.9426	0.9246	0.9070	0.8900	0.8573	0.8264	0.7972	0.7432	0.6944
3	0.9423	0.9151	0.8890	0.8638	0.8396	0.7938	0.7513	0.7118	0.6407	0.5787
4	0.9238	0.8885	0.8548	0.8227	0.7921	0.7350	0.6830	0.6355	0.5523	0.4823
5	0.9057	0.8626	0.8219	0.7835	0.7473	0.6806	0.6209	0.5674	0.4761	0.4019
6	0.8880	0.8375	0.7903	0.7462	0.7050	0.6302	0.5645	0.5066	0.4104	0.3349
7	0.8706	0.8131	0.7599	0.7107	0.6651	0.5835	0.5132	0.4523	0.3538	0.2791
8	0.8535	0.7894	0.7307	0.6768	0.6274	0.5403	0.4665	0.4039	0.3050	0.2326
9	0.8368	0.7664	0.7026	0.6446	0.5919	0.5002	0.4241	0.3606	0.2630	0.1938
10	0.8203	0.7441	0.6756	0.6139	0.5584	0.4632	0.3855	0.3220	0.2267	0.1615
11	0.8043	0.7224	0.6496	0.5847	0.5268	0.4289	0.3505	0.2875	0.1954	0.1346
12	0.7885	0.7014	0.6246	0.5568	0.4970	0.3971	0.3186	0.2567	0.1685	0.1122
13	0.7730	0.6810	0.6006	0.5303	0.4688	0.3677	0.2897	0.2292	0.1452	0.0935
14	0.7579	0.6611	0.5775	0.5051	0.4423	0.3405	0.2633	0.2046	0.1252	0.0779
15	0.7430	0.6419	0.5553	0.4810	0.4173	0.3152	0.2394	0.1827	0.1079	0.0649
16	0.7284	0.6232	0.5339	0.4581	0.3936	0.2919	0.2176	0.1631	0.0930	0.0541
17	0.7142	0.6050	0.5134	0.4363	0.3714	0.2703	0.1978	0.1456	0.0802	0.0451
18	0.7002	0.5874	0.4936	0.4155	0.3503	0.2502	0.1799	0.1300	0.0691	0.0376
19	0.6864	0.5703	0.4746	0.3957	0.3305	0.2317	0.1635	0.1161	0.0596	0.0313
20	0.6730	0.5537	0.4564	0.3769	0.3118	0.2145	0.1486	0.1037	0.0514	0.0261
25	0.6095	0.4776	0.3751	0.2953	0.2330	0.1460	0.0923	0.0588	0.0245	0.0105
30	0.5521	0.4120	0.3083	0.2314	0.1741	0.0994	0.0573	0.0334	0.0116	0.0042
40	0.4529	0.3066	0.2083	0.1420	0.0972	0.0460	0.0221	0.0107	0.0026	0.0007
50	0.3715	0.2281	0.1407	0.0872	0.0543	0.0213	0.0085	0.0035	0.0006	0.0001

TABLE III

Amount of an Annuity of $1 per Period

$$FV_n = R\left[\frac{(1+i)^n - 1}{i}\right] = R(FVAF_{\overline{n}|i})$$

n	2%	3%	4%	5%	6%	8%	10%	12%	16%	20%
1	1.0000	1.0000	1.0000	1.0000	1.0000	1.0000	1.0000	1.0000	1.0000	1.0000
2	2.0200	2.0300	2.0400	2.0500	2.0600	2.0800	2.1000	2.1200	2.1600	2.2000
3	3.0604	3.0909	3.1216	3.1525	3.1836	3.2464	3.3100	3.3744	3.5056	3.6400
4	4.1216	4.1836	4.2465	4.3101	4.3746	4.5061	4.6410	4.7793	5.0665	5.3680
5	5.2040	5.3091	5.4163	5.5256	5.6371	5.8666	6.1051	6.3528	6.8771	7.4416
6	6.3081	6.4684	6.6330	6.8019	6.9753	7.3359	7.7156	8.1152	8.9775	9.9299
7	7.4343	7.6625	7.8983	8.1420	8.3938	8.9228	9.4872	10.0890	11.4139	12.9159
8	8.5830	8.8923	9.2142	9.5491	9.8975	10.6366	11.4359	12.2997	14.2401	16.4991
9	9.7546	10.1591	10.5828	11.0266	11.4913	12.4876	13.5795	14.7757	17.5185	20.7989
10	10.9497	11.4639	12.0061	12.5779	13.1808	14.4866	15.9374	17.5487	21.3215	25.9587
11	12.1687	12.8078	13.4864	14.2068	14.9716	16.6455	18.5312	20.6546	25.7329	32.1504
12	13.4121	14.1920	15.0258	15.9171	16.8699	18.9771	21.3843	24.1331	30.8502	39.5805
13	14.6803	15.6178	16.6268	17.7130	18.8821	21.4953	24.5227	28.0291	36.7862	48.4966
14	15.9739	17.0863	18.2919	19.5986	21.0151	24.2149	27.9750	32.3926	43.6720	59.1959
15	17.2934	18.5989	20.0236	21.5786	23.2760	27.1521	31.7725	37.2797	51.6595	72.0351
16	18.6393	20.1569	21.8245	23.6575	25.6725	30.3243	35.9497	42.7533	60.9250	87.4421
17	20.0121	21.7616	23.6975	25.8404	28.2129	33.7502	40.5447	48.8837	71.6730	105.9306
18	21.4123	23.4144	25.6454	28.1324	30.9057	37.4502	45.5992	55.7497	84.1407	128.1167
19	22.8406	25.1169	27.6712	30.5390	33.7600	41.4463	51.1591	63.4397	98.6032	154.7400
20	24.2974	26.8704	29.7781	33.0660	36.7856	45.7620	57.2750	72.0524	115.3797	186.6880
25	32.0303	36.4593	41.6459	47.7271	54.8645	73.1059	98.3471	133.3339	249.2140	471.9811
30	40.5681	47.5754	56.0849	66.4388	79.0582	113.2832	164.4940	241.3327	530.3117	1181.8816
40	60.4020	75.4013	95.0255	120.7998	154.7620	259.0565	442.5926	767.0914	2360.7572	7343.8578
50	84.5794	112.7969	152.6671	209.3480	290.3359	573.7702	1163.9085	2400.0182	10435.6488	45497.1908

TABLE IV

Present Value of an Annuity of $1 per Period

$$PV_n = R \left[\frac{1 - \frac{1}{(1+i)^n}}{i} \right] = R(PVAF_{\overline{n}|\,i})$$

n	2%	3%	4%	5%	6%	8%	10%	12%	16%	20%
1	0.9804	0.9709	0.9615	0.9524	0.9434	0.9259	0.9091	0.8929	0.8621	0.8333
2	1.9416	1.9135	1.8861	1.8594	1.8334	1.7833	1.7355	1.6901	1.6052	1.5278
3	2.8839	2.8286	2.7751	2.7232	2.6730	2.5771	2.4869	2.4018	2.2459	2.1065
4	3.8077	3.7171	3.6299	3.5460	3.4651	3.3121	3.1699	3.0373	2.7982	2.5887
5	4.7135	4.5797	4.4518	4.3295	4.2124	3.9927	3.7908	3.6048	3.2743	2.9906
6	5.6014	5.4172	5.2421	5.0757	4.9173	4.6229	4.3553	4.1114	3.6847	3.3255
7	6.4720	6.2303	6.0021	5.7864	5.5824	5.2064	4.8684	4.5638	4.0386	3.6016
8	7.3255	7.0197	6.7327	6.4632	6.2098	5.7466	5.3349	4.9676	4.3436	3.8372
9	8.1622	7.7861	7.4353	7.1078	6.8017	6.2469	5.7590	5.3282	4.6065	4.0310
10	8.9826	8.5302	8.1109	7.7217	7.3601	6.7101	6.1446	5.6502	4.8332	4.1925
11	9.7868	9.2526	8.7605	8.3064	7.8869	7.1390	6.4951	5.9377	5.0286	4.3271
12	10.5753	9.9540	9.3851	8.8633	8.3838	7.5361	6.8137	6.1944	5.1971	4.4392
13	11.3484	10.6350	9.9856	9.3936	8.8527	7.9038	7.1034	6.4235	5.3423	4.5327
14	12.1062	11.2961	10.5631	9.8986	9.2950	8.2442	7.3667	6.6282	5.4675	4.6106
15	12.8493	11.9379	11.1184	10.3797	9.7122	8.5595	7.6061	6.8109	5.5755	4.6755
16	13.5777	12.5611	11.6523	10.8378	10.1059	8.8514	7.8237	6.9740	5.6685	4.7296
17	14.2919	13.1661	12.1657	11.2741	10.4773	9.1216	8.0216	7.1196	5.7487	4.7746
18	14.9920	13.7535	12.6593	11.6896	10.8276	9.3719	8.2014	7.2497	5.8178	4.8122
19	15.6785	14.3238	13.1339	12.0853	11.1581	9.6036	8.3649	7.3658	5.8775	4.8435
20	16.3514	14.8775	13.5903	12.4622	11.4699	9.8181	8.5136	7.4694	5.9288	4.8696
25	19.5235	17.4131	15.6221	14.0939	12.7834	10.6748	9.0770	7.8431	6.0971	4.9476
30	22.3965	19.6004	17.2920	15.3725	13.7648	11.2578	9.4269	8.0552	6.1772	4.9789
40	27.3555	23.1148	19.7928	17.1591	15.0463	11.9246	9.7791	8.2438	6.2335	4.9966
50	31.4236	25.7298	21.4822	18.2559	15.7619	12.2335	9.9148	8.3045	6.2463	4.9995

Appendix

 B

Illustrative
Financial Statements

Consolidated Results of Operations

General Mills

GENERAL MILLS, INC., AND SUBSIDIARIES

	Fiscal Year Ended	
	May 30, 1976 (53 Weeks)	May 25, 1975 (52 Weeks)
	(in thousands)	
SALES	$2,644,952	$2,308,900
COSTS AND EXPENSES:		
Costs of sales, exclusive of items shown below	1,654,169	1,531,535
Depreciation expense (Note 1)	45,006	39,744
Amortization expense (Note 1)	1,701	2,043
Interest expense	29,400	36,219
Contributions to employees' retirement plans (Note 9)	17,903	11,465
Profit sharing distribution (Note 10)	3,527	3,129
Selling, general and administrative expenses	692,985	539,132
TOTAL	2,444,691	2,163,267
EARNINGS BEFORE TAXES ON INCOME and Other Items shown below	200,261	145,633
TAXES ON INCOME (Note 11)	(99,964)	(70,650)
OTHER ITEMS:		
Add share of net earnings of 20-50% owned companies	1,094	1,268
Less minority interests in net earnings of consolidated subsidiaries	(853)	(38)
NET EARNINGS	$ 100,538	$ 76,213
EARNINGS PER COMMON SHARE AND COMMON SHARE EQUIVALENT (Notes 1 and 7)	$ 2.04	$ 1.59
Average number of common shares and common share equivalents (Note 1)	49,203	47,845

Earnings Employed in the Business

	Fiscal Year Ended	
	May 30, 1976 (53 Weeks)	May 25, 1975 (52 Weeks)
	(in thousands)	
NET EARNINGS FOR THE YEAR	$ 100,538	$ 76,213
DIVIDENDS—Common stock ($0.66 per share—1976, and $0.58½ per share—1975) (Note 7)	(32,391)	(27,806)
NET EARNINGS AFTER DIVIDENDS	68,147	48,407
Other adjustments	(149)	—
NET INCREASE IN RETAINED EARNINGS	67,998	48,407
RETAINED EARNINGS AT BEGINNING OF YEAR	401,011	352,604
RETAINED EARNINGS AT END OF YEAR (Note 6)	$ 469,009	$ 401,011

See accompanying notes to consolidated financial statements.

Consolidated Balance Sheets

GENERAL MILLS, INC., AND SUBSIDIARIES

ASSETS

	May 30, 1976	May 25, 1975
CURRENT ASSETS:	*(in thousands)*	
Cash (Note 5)...	$ 4,478	$ 7,623
Marketable securities (at cost, approximates market value)...............	77,351	2,345
Receivables:		
Customers...	199,966	197,062
Miscellaneous..	22,425	22,525
	222,391	219,587
Less allowance for possible losses..............................	(6,428)	(6,006)
	215,963	213,581
Inventories (Notes 1 and 4).......................................	353,654	345,907
Prepaid expenses...	21,351	20,917
TOTAL CURRENT ASSETS.................................	672,797	590,373
OTHER ASSETS:		
Land, buildings and equipment (Note 1):		
Land...	41,806	39,577
Buildings...	256,570	232,862
Equipment..	393,265	365,377
Construction in progress....................................	47,621	47,423
	739,262	685,239
Less accumulated depreciation................................	(267,770)	(244,261)
	471,492	440,978
Miscellaneous assets:		
Investment in 20-50% owned companies (Note 1).................	11,339	12,289
Other...	23,071	15,780
	34,410	28,069
Intangible assets (Note 1):		
Excess of cost over net assets of acquired companies................	138,802	128,658
Patents, copyrights and other intangibles.......................	10,695	17,555
TOTAL OTHER ASSETS.................................	655,399	615,260
TOTAL ASSETS...	$1,328,196	$1,205,633

See accompanying notes to consolidated financial statements.

LIABILITIES AND STOCKHOLDERS' EQUITY

	May 30, 1976	May 25, 1975
CURRENT LIABILITIES:	*(in thousands)*	
Notes payable (Note 5)	$ 24,098	$ 55,048
Current portion of long-term debt.................................	4,405	3,637
Accounts payable and accrued expenses:		
Accounts payable—trade....................................	194,622	147,888
Accounts payable—miscellaneous.............................	46,671	27,284
Accrued payroll...	29,933	24,557
Accrued interest..	5,546	8,335
	276,772	208,064
Accrued taxes...	69,045	43,301
Thrift accounts of officers and employees..........................	3,363	3,484
TOTAL CURRENT LIABILITIES............................	377,683	313,534
OTHER LIABILITIES:		
Long-term debt, excluding current portion (Note 6)...................	281,763	304,912
Deferred Federal income taxes (Note 1)...........................	11,231	15,338
Deferred compensation..	6,442	6,346
Other liabilities and deferred credits.............................	5,773	1,895
	305,209	328,491
TOTAL LIABILITIES......................................	682,892	642,025
MINORITY INTERESTS..	5,059	3,119
STOCKHOLDERS' EQUITY:		
Common stock (Notes 7 and 8).................................	172,897	161,657
Retained earnings (Note 6)......................................	469,009	401,011
Less common stock in Treasury, at cost............................	(1,661)	(2,179)
TOTAL STOCKHOLDERS' EQUITY...........................	640,245	560,489
COMMITMENTS, LITIGATION AND CLAIMS (NOTES 12, 13 AND 14)		
TOTAL LIABILITIES AND STOCKHOLDERS' EQUITY..................	$1,328,196	$1,205,633

Consolidated Changes in Financial Position

General Mills

GENERAL MILLS, INC., AND SUBSIDIARIES

Fiscal Year Ended

	May 30, 1976 (53 Weeks)	May 25, 1975 (52 Weeks)
	(in thousands)	
WORKING CAPITAL PROVIDED BY:		
Net earnings....................................	$100,538	$ 76,213
Add non-cash items:		
Depreciation and amortization...............	46,707	41,787
Discontinued operations....................	6,494	(249)
Writeoffs of goodwill......................	2,476	145
Deferred Federal income taxes..............	(3,376)	4,651
Other......................................	361	1,363
Working capital provided from operations..	153,200	123,910
Proceeds from long-term debt issued.................	834	3,191
Common stock issued.............................	7,500	26,038
Sale of stock upon exercise of options................	3,788	2,367
Other sources...................................	4,577	1,821
TOTAL WORKING CAPITAL PROVIDED...	169,899	157,327
WORKING CAPITAL USED FOR:		
Gross additions to buildings and equipment............ $ 94,442		$ 99,832
Less proceeds from sales...................... (12,637)		(4,327)
Net additions to buildings and equipment..........	81,805	95,505
Purchase price of businesses........................ 10,789		29,891
Less working capital acquired.................. (2,683)		(16,207)
Balance.....................................	8,106	13,684
Consisting of—Fixed assets..................... 5,166		7,765
—Intangibles and miscellaneous assets.. 7,173		19,626
—Long-term debt.................. (3,032)		(13,782)
—Minority interest................. (1,075)		346
—Other........................ (126)		(271)
Dividends.......................................	32,391	27,806
Reductions of long-term debt......................	25,376	10,728
Other uses......................................	3,946	872
TOTAL WORKING CAPITAL USED........	151,624	148,595
NET INCREASE (DECREASE) IN WORKING CAPITAL...	18,275	8,732
Consisting of—Cash and marketable securities.......... 71,861		(9,918)
—Receivables......................... 2,382		27,110
—Inventories........................ 7,747		(7,404)
—Payables.......................... (64,149)		(1,104)
—Other............................ 434		48
WORKING CAPITAL AT BEGINNING OF YEAR........	276,839	268,107
WORKING CAPITAL AT END OF YEAR...............	$295,114	$276,839

See accompanying notes to consolidated financial statements.

Notes to
Consolidated Financial Statements
May 30, 1976, and May 25, 1975

1. SUMMARY OF SIGNIFICANT ACCOUNTING POLICIES

Significant accounting policies used to prepare the consolidated financial statements are summarized below.

A: CONSOLIDATION

The consolidated financial statements include the following domestic and foreign operations: (1) parent company operations and 100 per cent owned subsidiaries; (2) majority-owned subsidiaries; and (3) General Mills' investment in and share of net earnings or losses of 20-50% owned companies.

All significant intercompany items have been eliminated from the consolidated financial statements.

The fiscal years of foreign operations generally end in April.

B: LAND, BUILDINGS, EQUIPMENT AND DEPRECIATION

Land, buildings and equipment are stated substantially at cost.

Part of the cost of buildings and equipment is charged against earnings each year as depreciation expense. This amount is computed primarily by the straight-line method, which means that equal amounts of depreciation expense are charged against operations each year during the useful life of an item. For tax purposes, accelerated methods of depreciation are used which provide more depreciation expense in the early years than in the later years of the life of the item. The related tax effect for accelerated depreciation is reflected in "Deferred Federal income taxes."

The useful lives employed for computing depreciation on principal classes of buildings and equipment are:

Buildings..........................20-50 years
Machinery and equipment......... 5-25 years
Office furniture and equipment..... 5-10 years
Transportation equipment......... 3-12 years

General Mills' policy is to charge maintenance, repair and minor renewal expenses to earnings in the year incurred and to charge major improvements to buildings and equipment accounts. When major equipment items are sold or retired, the accounts are relieved of cost and the related accumulated depreciation. Gains and losses on assets sold or retired are credited or charged to results of operations.

C: INVENTORIES

Grain, family flour and bakery flour are valued at market and include adjustments for open cash trades and unfilled orders.

Raw materials, work-in-process and finished goods for a portion of the domestic food inventories, domestic crafts, games and toys inventories and certain other inventories are stated at the lower of cost, determined by the Last-in, First-out (LIFO) method, or market. Other inventories are generally stated at the cost of the most recently purchased materials (FIFO) reduced to market when lower.

D: AMORTIZATION OF INTANGIBLES

The costs of patents and copyrights are amortized evenly over their lives by charges against earnings. Most of these costs were incurred through purchases of businesses.

"Excess of cost over net assets of acquired companies" ("excess cost") is the difference between purchase prices and the values of assets of businesses acquired and accounted for under the purchase method of accounting. Any "excess cost" acquired after October, 1970, is amortized over not more than 40 years. Annually, the Audit Committee of the Board of Directors reviews these intangibles and balances are reduced if values have diminished. Because of low earnings to date and significant organizational changes in the company's travel venture, "excess cost" in the amount of $2,400,000 (both before and after taxes) was charged against earnings

Notes to Consolidated Financial Statements (continued)

General Mills

during the second quarter of fiscal 1976. At its meeting on May 24, 1976, the Board of Directors confirmed that the remaining amounts comprising the "excess cost" have continuing value.

E: RESEARCH AND DEVELOPMENT

All expenditures for research and development are charged against earnings in the year incurred. The charges for fiscal 1976 and 1975 were $25,700,000 and $22,900,000, respectively.

F: RETIREMENT EXPENSE

The company has numerous retirement plans, as described in Note 9. The annual retirement expense for the plans includes both (1) the current year's normal cost, and (2) certain prior-years costs. Prior-year costs include interest on unfunded balances, plus amortization of the unfunded balance over periods of up to 40 years.

The plans use different actuarial methods of estimating these costs. In addition, each plan's assumptions (such as turnover rates or future wage levels) may vary, according to the individual circumstances of the plan. Certain changes were made in these methods and assumptions in both fiscal 1976 and 1975. In addition, some benefit increases were made in both years, and adverse prior years' pension fund investment results were experienced. All of these factors influenced the amount of retirement expense charged to operations in each year, thereby affecting comparability. See Note 9 for additional details.

G: FOREIGN EXCHANGE

Foreign balance sheet accounts are translated into U.S. dollars at exchange rates in effect at fiscal year-end except for such accounts as land, buildings and equipment, accumulated depreciation and intangibles which are translated at exchange rates in effect when the assets were acquired. Income and expense accounts for each month are translated at the month-end exchange rates except for depreciation and amortization which are translated at the exchange rates in effect for the related assets.

Unrealized gains and losses resulting from translation procedures are credited or charged to the results of operations without deferral. The company accrues gains and losses on open forward exchange contracts based on forward contract market rates.

In fiscal 1977, the company will require only minor changes in foreign exchange accounting procedures, to conform to new rules in Standard #8 of the Financial Accounting Standards Board. Prior-year financial statements will not be restated, because the new rules do not have a material effect on such years.

H: INCOME TAXES

Investment tax credit is accounted for by the "flow-through" method; taxes on income are thus reduced by the amount of credit arising during the year.

Deferred income taxes result from timing differences between income for financial reporting purposes and tax purposes. These differences relate principally to depreciation, deferred compensation and discontinued operations.

The company's policy is to accrue appropriate U.S. income taxes on earnings of foreign subsidiary companies which are intended to be remitted to the parent company.

I: EARNINGS PER SHARE

The weighted average number of common shares outstanding and "common share equivalents" are totaled in determining "earnings per common share and common share equivalent." Common share equivalents represent potentially dilutive common shares (weighted average) as follows: (1) shares of common stock reserved for issuance upon exercise of outstanding stock options granted pursuant to company option plans (93,000 in 1976 and 81,782 in 1975); and (2) treasury shares purchased and reserved for issuance under a profit sharing plan (64,398 in 1976 and 64,296 in 1975). See Note 7 for a description of the October, 1975, stock-split, and restatement of fiscal 1975 data previously reported.

Notes to Consolidated Financial Statements (continued)

General Mills

2. ACQUISITIONS

The company made the following significant acquisitions during the past two fiscal years:

Fiscal Year 1976	Ownership	Date Acquired	Product or Major Product Group
Foot-Joy, Inc.	60%	July, 1975	Fashions
Clipper Games	100%	August, 1975	Toys
Saluto Foods Corp.	85%	March, 1976	Mixes, Family Flour, Seafoods & Other
Fiscal Year 1975			
Stevens Court, Inc.	65%	August, 1974	Corporate Unallocated
Bowers and Ruddy Galleries, Inc.	85%	October, 1974	Crafts, Games & Toys
Lord Jeff Knitting Co., Inc.	85%	December, 1974	Fashions
General Interiors	100%	April, 1975	Furniture

All of the above were accounted for by the "purchase" method. Following are the cash and common stock costs of these acquisitions, plus increased ownership in other partially owned companies and performance earnings agreements:

	Fiscal Year	
	1976	1975
Acquisitions—Cash	$2,111,000	$ 379,000
—Shares*	322,534 (a)	1,450,034 (b)
Increased ownership in partially owned companies and performance earnings agreements—Cash	$1,041,000	$3,194,000
—Shares*	13,709	—

*All share data reflect October, 1975, split.

(a) General Mills acquired 60% of the outstanding shares of Foot-Joy, Inc., in exchange for 140,680 shares of common stock and 85% of the outstanding shares oτ Saluto Foods Corp. for 181,854 shares of common stock. Clipper Games and all outstanding Red Lobster Restaurant franchises were purchased for cash.

(b) General Mills acquired substantially all of the assets and liabilities of General Interiors Corporation in exchange for 999,138 shares of General Mills' common stock. Two additional purchases for common stock were Bowers and Ruddy in exchange for 237,860 shares and Lord Jeff in exchange for 213,036 shares.

Sales, costs and earnings of businesses accounted for as purchases are included in results of operations from the dates of acquisition. In each of fiscal 1976 and 1975, the impact on the company's sales from these acquisitions in the year of acquisition was less than 1% of consolidated sales. Related earnings were not material.

3. FOREIGN OPERATIONS

Included in General Mills' consolidated financial statements are amounts for foreign (non-U.S.) operations, as follows:

	1976	1975
	(in thousands)	
Sales	$433,823	$386,299
Net earnings	14,991	13,462
Total assets	267,409	270,392
Net assets	135,503	131,707

The 1975 amounts have been restated from figures reported last year, in order to conform to the 1976 presentation.

Substantially all investments in 20-50% owned companies included in the consolidated balance sheets and net earnings of 20-50% owned companies included in the consolidated results of operations are for foreign operations. Significant foreign operations are primarily located in Canada and western Europe. Foreign exchange gains and losses were not material in either 1976 or 1975.

General Mills

4. INVENTORIES

Following is a comparison of year-end inventories:

	May 30, 1976	May 25, 1975
	(in thousands)	
Grain, family flour and bakery flour..............	$ 38,798	$ 29,442
Raw materials, work in process, finished goods and supplies as follows:		
Valued at LIFO..........	148,112	124,413
Valued primarily at FIFO..	166,744	192,052
Total Inventories............	$353,654	$345,907

If the FIFO method of inventory accounting had been used throughout by the company, inventories would have been $12,496,000 and $15,884,000 higher than reported at May 30, 1976, and May 25, 1975, respectively. See Note 1 for a description of inventory valuation policies. During fiscal 1976, the domestic inventories of the Gorton Division (a seafoods operation) were changed from FIFO to LIFO. In addition, certain inventories were reduced in 1976, resulting in a liquidation of some LIFO inventory quantities, carried at costs lower than 1976 purchases. Neither of these events had a material effect on earnings.

The amounts of opening and closing inventories as used in determining costs of sales are as follows (in thousands):

May 30, 1976..........................	$353,654
May 25, 1975..........................	345,907
May 26, 1974..........................	353,311

5. SHORT-TERM BORROWINGS

The components of "notes payable" are as follows:

May 30, 1976		May 25, 1975			12-MONTH WEIGHTED AVERAGES		
						Average Interest Rates	
Balance	Interest Rate	Balance	Interest Rate		Outstanding In Fiscal '76	Fiscal '76	Fiscal '75
$22,887,000	11.2%	$32,921,000	11.3%	.. Banks (foreign)........	$21,900,000	13.1%	12.8%
—	—	—	—	.. Commercial paper (U.S.).	9,700,000	6.6%	10.8%
—	—	20,978,000	5.6%	.. Master Notes (U.S.)....	16,500,000	6.4%	7.8%
1,211,000	5.9%	1,149,000	5.3%	.. Miscellaneous.........	1,300,000	6.5%	9.0%
$24,098,000		$55,048,000	....	Total..............	$49,400,000		

The maximum amount of notes payable outstanding at any month-end during fiscal 1976 was $118,345,000 on August 24, 1975.

The company maintains unsecured domestic credit lines to support its commercial paper, and to ensure the availability of extra funds if needed. At May 30, 1976, the company had $144,500,000 of such domestic lines available, $120,000,000 of which was paid for by fees and $24,500,000 of which was supported by 10% compensating balances (20% if the credit lines are used). The amount of the credit lines and the cost thereof are generally negotiated each year.

Notes to Consolidated Financial Statements (continued)

General Mills

6. LONG-TERM DEBT	May 30, 1976	May 25, 1975
	(in thousands)	
4⅝% sinking fund debentures, due August 1, 1990	$ 24,695	$ 24,699
8% sinking fund debentures, due February 15, 1999	98,528	98,465
8⅞% sinking fund debentures, due October 15, 1995	82,993	99,176
Three 25-year 4¼% promissory notes of $10,000,000 each, due May 1, 1982, May 1, 1983, and May 1, 1984	30,000	30,000
7% sinking fund Eurodollar debentures, due November 1, 1980	12,119	12,377
8% sinking fund Eurodollar debentures, due March 1, 1986	16,040	16,638
Miscellaneous debt	21,793	27,194
	286,168	308,549
Less amounts due within one year	4,405	3,637
	$281,763	$304,912

The above amounts are net of unamortized bond discount ($3,180,000 in 1976 and $3,545,000 in 1975).

The sinking fund and principal payments due on long-term debt are $4,405,000, $5,782,000, $9,973,000, $16,924,000 and $18,779,000 in fiscal years ending in 1977, 1978, 1979, 1980 and 1981, respectively.

The terms of the promissory note agreements place restrictions on the payment of dividends, capital stock purchases and redemptions. At May 30, 1976, $289,992,000 of retained earnings was free of such restrictions.

7. CHANGES IN CAPITAL STOCK

The following table describes changes in capital stock from May 26, 1974, to May 30, 1976:

	Common Stock			
	$0.75 Par Value		In Treasury	
(dollars in thousands)	Shares	Value	Shares	Value
Balance at May 26, 1974	47,301,404	$133,252	171,612	$2,418
Stock option and profit sharing plans	146,832	2,367	(18,768)	(239)
Shares issued—acquisitions	1,450,034	26,017	—	—
Other	1,062	21	—	—
Balance at May 25, 1975	48,899,332	$161,657	152,844	$2,179
Stock option and profit sharing plans	229,926	3,788	(22,618)	(321)
Shares issued—acquisitions	322,534	7,452	(13,709)	(197)
Balance at May 30, 1976	49,451,792	$172,897	116,517	$1,661

The shareholders also have authorized 5,000,000 shares of cumulative preference stock, no par value. None of these shares was outstanding during either fiscal 1976 or 1975. If issued, the Directors may specify a dividend rate, convertibility rights, liquidating value and voting rights at the time of issuance.

Notes to Consolidated Financial Statements (continued)

General Mills

Effective as of October 10, 1975, the shareholders voted to (1) increase the authorized common stock from 30,000,000 to 70,000,000 shares; (2) change each share of common stock, $1.50 par value, into two fully-paid and nonassessable shares of common stock, $.75 par value; and (3) eliminate the 1,000,000 shares of class B common stock previously authorized. None of the class B common was outstanding in either fiscal 1976 or 1975. Information throughout these financial statements is retroactively restated for the 2-for-1 split, to present all data on a consistent and comparable basis.

Some of the unissued shares of common stock are reserved for the following purposes:

	Number of Shares	
	May 30, 1976	May 25, 1975
Stock options outstanding.......	1,323,306	1,087,298
Stock options available for grant........	714,300	43,916

8. STOCK OPTIONS

In September, 1975, the shareholders of General Mills, Inc., approved a stock option plan under which options for the purchase of 1,200,000 shares, in the aggregate, of the company's common stock may be granted to officers and key employees. The plan expires on August 31, 1980. The options under the 1975 plan may be granted subject to approval of the Compensation Committee of the Board of Directors and at a price of not less than 100% of fair market value on the date the option is granted. Options outstanding include options granted under a previous stock option plan which has expired and under which no further options may be granted. Both plans provide for termination of options at either five or 10 years after date of grant with certain exceptions due to death, disability or retirement. Information on stock options is shown in the following table.

	Shares	Average Per Share		Total Fair Market Value
		Option Price	Fair Market Value	
Granted:				
1975...............................	105,000	$24.60	$24.60	$ 2,583,000 (a)
1976...............................	485,700	30.98	30.98	15,047,000 (a)
Became exercisable:				
1975...............................	250,396	27.81	21.66	5,422,000 (b)
1976...............................	218,667	28.20	29.74	6,504,000 (b)
Exercised:				
1975...............................	146,832	16.12	23.82	3,497,000 (c)
1976...............................	229,926	16.47	29.46	6,774,000 (c)
Expired and cancelled:				
1975...............................	23,096	23.42	23.42	541,000 (a)
1976...............................	19,766	28.88	28.88	571,000 (a)
Outstanding at end of year:				
1975—to 279 officers and employees.....	1,087,298	24.85	24.85	27,015,000 (a)
1976—to 355 officers and employees.....	1,323,306	28.49	28.49	37,704,000 (a)

(a) At date of grant.   (b) At date exercisable.   (c) At date exercised.

Notes to Consolidated Financial Statements (continued)

General Mills

9. RETIREMENT PLANS

The company and many of its subsidiaries have retirement plans covering most of their domestic employees and some foreign employees. In general, the plans provide for normal retirement at age 65 with benefits computed on the basis of length of service and employee earnings. Retirement plans are reviewed and company contributions are approved by the Board of Directors, upon recommendation of the five-member Benefit Finance Committee. Two committee members are General Mills officers. The remaining three are Directors, one of whom is a member of General Mills management.

In both fiscal 1975 and 1976, various plans improved their benefits, and changed certain actuarial methods and assumptions. These changes increased fiscal 1976 costs by $3,100,000 over fiscal 1975 costs. Also, the effect of adverse retirement fund investment performance in prior years caused fiscal 1976 costs to increase by an additional $2,400,000 over fiscal 1975 costs.

By policy, the company funds all retirement costs accrued. The company's policies for accruing costs are described in Note 1. As of the latest available actuarial estimates (December 31, 1975), vested benefits approximated $192,000,000 of which $28,000,000 was unfunded. The total unfunded accrued liability (including the unfunded vested benefits) approximated $41,000,000. The comparable unfunded amounts at December 31, 1974, were $50,000,000 and $67,000,000, respectively. The decrease in unfunded liabilities was caused both by improvement in current year retirement fund investment performance, and by certain actuarial and accounting changes.

Many of the changes in U.S. retirement plans that were required by the Employees Retirement Income Security Act of 1974 (ERISA) have now been implemented. The benefit and actuarial changes described in the above paragraphs were made for reasons other than compliance with ERISA. Remaining changes for compliance with ERISA are not expected to have a material effect on retirement expense.

10. PROFIT SHARING PLANS

General Mills and certain subsidiaries have profit sharing plans covering officers and key employees who have the greatest opportunities to contribute to current earnings and the future success of their operations. The amounts to be distributed under the plans are generally determined by the relationship of net profits to predetermined profit goals. Profit sharing plans and associated payments are approved by the Board of Directors upon recommendation of the Compensation Committee. This committee consists of Directors who are not members of General Mills' management.

11. TAXES ON INCOME

The provision for income taxes is made up of the following:

	Fiscal Year	
	1976	1975
	(in thousands)	
Federal taxes	$85,313	$52,702
Foreign taxes	10,755	9,097
State and local taxes	10,298	6,906
Deferred taxes	(3,376)	4,651
U.S. investment tax credit	(3,026)	(2,706)
Total taxes on income	$99,964	$70,650

Deferred taxes result from timing differences in the recognition of revenue and expense for tax and financial statement purposes. The tax effects of these differences are as follows:

	Fiscal Year	
	1976	1975
	(in thousands)	
Depreciation	$ 393	$ 6,333
Deferred compensation	(139)	(512)
Bad debts	(121)	(231)
Discontinued operations	(2,997)	(37)
Other	(512)	(902)
Total deferred taxes	$(3,376)	$ 4,651

Notes to Consolidated Financial Statements (continued)

General Mills

The effective tax rate is different from the statutory U.S. Federal income tax rate of 48% for the following reasons:

	Fiscal Year	
	1976	1975
U.S. statutory rate.............	48.0%	48.0%
State and local income taxes, net of Federal tax benefits....	2.7	2.4
Investment tax credit..........	(1.5)	(1.9)
Other......................	.7	—
Effective income tax rate.....	49.9%	48.5%

As of May 30, 1976, management has designated $56,917,000 of the undistributed earnings of foreign subsidiaries as permanently invested. Such earnings have already been taxed once by foreign governments. As a result, no extra U.S. taxes have been accrued on those earnings. However, extra U.S. taxes have been accrued on undistributed foreign earnings in excess of the $56,917,000, because of the policy stated in Note 1. The additional U.S. taxes so accrued were not material in either fiscal 1976 or 1975.

12. LEASE COMMITMENTS

Rent expense was $19,112,000 in fiscal 1976, and $16,523,000 in 1975. The company and its subsidiaries have a variety of noncancellable lease commitments, longer than one year in duration, for which minimum annual net rentals will total approximately $13,002,000 in fiscal 1977; $10,197,000 in 1978; $8,684,000 in 1979; $7,031,000 in 1980; $5,839,000 in 1981; $20,899,000 from 1982 to 1986; $11,015,000 from 1987 to 1991; $7,309,000 from 1992 to 1996; and $2,898,000 in all years after fiscal 1996. 92% of the commitments are for real estate. Certain leases require payment of property taxes, insurance and maintenance costs in addition to the rental payments. The company and its subsidiaries do not have any significant financing leases.

13. OTHER COMMITMENTS

At May 30, 1976, authorized but unexpended appropriations for property additions and improvements were $83,344,000.

In addition, there are options outstanding to purchase the remaining minority interests of some partially-owned companies. The options could have a maximum cost to General Mills of up to $63,000,000. In general, the option contracts provide that payments depend on actual earnings performance up to the exercise date, and would result in return on investment satisfactory to the company. The main option periods run from 1979 to 1986. The majority of such cost could be payable with shares of common stock.

14. LITIGATION AND CLAIMS

In management's opinion, all claims or litigation pending at May 30, 1976, which could have a significant effect on the consolidated financial position of General Mills, Inc., and its subsidiaries have been provided for in the accounts. The FTC complaint described below is discussed because of the significance of the company's cereals business.

In 1972 the Federal Trade Commission (FTC) issued a complaint against General Mills, Kellogg Co., General Foods Corporation and the Quaker Oats Company, alleging that the four companies share an illegal monopoly of the ready-to-eat cereal industry. The FTC seeks relief in the form of divestiture of certain cereal-producing assets, licensing of cereal brands and prohibitions of certain present practices and future acquisitions in the cereal industry. The four

Notes to Consolidated Financial Statements (continued)

General Mills

companies have denied the allegations. An FTC "Administrative Law Judge" started hearing testimony in April, 1976.

The hearing may take over a year to complete. The Judge's findings will then be subject to review by the FTC. Any adverse decision by the FTC will then be subject to further review in U.S. Federal courts. The company expects the matter to take several years and involve costly litigation. In the opinion of General Mills' General Counsel, the company's ready-to-eat cereal activities do not violate existing anti-trust laws. The company will continue to contest the complaint vigorously.

---

15. OTHER 1976 CHARGES (CREDIT)

During fiscal 1976, the company recorded the following unusual charges (credit) which were significant in total.

	Amount
Sale of Silna Division in second quarter...	$2,100,000
Write-off of a portion of goodwill in travel venture in second quarter (see Note 1-D)........	2,400,000
Gain from restructuring German toy operations in second quarter.......................	(2,200,000)
Charges of $750,000 in the second quarter and $2,750,000 in the fourth quarter for converting a protein plant to package foods production........................	3,500,000
Total net charge (after related income taxes).................................	$5,800,000

Accountants' Report

PEAT, MARWICK, MITCHELL & CO.

CERTIFIED PUBLIC ACCOUNTANTS

1700 IDS CENTER

MINNEAPOLIS, MINNESOTA 55402

The Stockholders and the Board of Directors
General Mills, Inc.:

July 23, 1976

We have examined the consolidated balance sheets of General Mills, Inc. and subsidiaries as of May 30, 1976 and May 25, 1975 and the related consolidated statements of results of operations, earnings employed in the business and changes in financial position for the fiscal years then ended. Our examination was made in accordance with generally accepted auditing standards, and accordingly included such tests of the accounting records and such other auditing procedures as we considered necessary in the circumstances.

In our opinion, the aforementioned consolidated financial statements present fairly the financial position of General Mills, Inc. and subsidiaries at May 30, 1976 and May 25, 1975 and the results of their operations and the changes in their financial position for the fiscal years then ended, in conformity with generally accepted accounting principles applied on a consistent basis.

Peat, Marwick, Mitchell & Co.

Index of References to APB and FASB Pronouncements

The following list of pronouncements by the Accounting Principles Board and the Financial Accounting Standards Board (as of January 1, 1977) is provided to give students an overview of the standards issued since 1962 and to reference these standards to the relevant chapters in this book. Earlier pronouncements by the Committee on Accounting Procedure of the AICPA have been largely superseded or amended. In those cases where no change has been made by subsequent standard-setting bodies, the earlier pronouncements are still accepted as official.

ACCOUNTING PRINCIPLES BOARD OPINIONS

Date Issued	Opinion Number	Title	Status	Chapter Number(s) in Which Reference Occurs
November, 1962	1	*New Depreciation Guidelines and Rules*	Unchanged	
December, 1962	2	*Accounting for the "Investment Credit"; addendum to Opinion No. 2 — Accounting Principles for Regulated Industries*	Amended	11
October, 1963	3	*The Statement of Source and Application of Funds*	Superseded	
March, 1964	4	*Accounting for the "Investment Credit"*	Unchanged	11
September, 1964	5	*Reporting of Leases in Financial Statements of Lessee*	Superseded	
October, 1965	6	*Status of Accounting Research Bulletins*	Amended	6, 19
May, 1966	7	*Accounting for Leases in Financial Statements of Lessors*	Superseded	
November, 1966	8	*Accounting for the Cost of Pension Plans*	Unchanged	17
December, 1966	9	*Reporting the Results of Operations*	Partially superseded	4

APB OPINIONS (continued)

Date Issued	Opinion Number	Title	Status	Chapter Number(s) in Which Reference Occurs
December, 1966	10	*Omnibus Opinion — 1966*	Amended and partially superseded	4, 16
December, 1967	11	*Accounting for Income Taxes*	Amended and partially superseded	16
December, 1967	12	*Omnibus Opinion — 1967*	Amended and partially superseded	12
March, 1969	13	*Amending Paragraph 6 of APB Opinion No. 9, Application to Commercial Banks*	Amended	
March, 1969	14	*Accounting for Convertible Debt and Debt Issued with Stock Purchase Warrants*	Unchanged	15, 19
May, 1969	15	*Earnings per Share*	Unchanged	4, 21, 27
August, 1970	16	*Business Combinations*	Amended	
August, 1970	17	*Intangible Assets*	Unchanged	13
March, 1971	18	*The Equity Method of Accounting for Investments in Common Stock*	Amended and partially superseded	14
March, 1971	19	*Reporting Changes in Financial Position*	Unchanged	24
July, 1971	20	*Accounting Changes*	Unchanged	4, 5, 21, 22, 26
August, 1971	21	*Interest on Receivables and Payables*	Unchanged	6, 11, 15
April, 1972	22	*Disclosure of Accounting Policies*	Unchanged	3, 9
April, 1972	23	*Accounting for Income Taxes — Special Areas*	Amended	
April, 1972	24	*Accounting for Income Taxes — Investments in Common Stock Accounted for by the Equity Method (Other than Subsidiaries and Corporate Joint Ventures)*	Unchanged	16
October, 1972	25	*Accounting for Stock Issued to Employees*	Unchanged	19
October, 1972	26	*Early Extinguishment of Debt*	Unchanged	15
November, 1972	27	*Accounting for Lease Transactions by Manufacturer or Dealer Lessors*	Superseded	
May, 1973	28	*Interim Financial Reporting*	Partially superseded	26
May, 1973	29	*Accounting for Nonmonetary Transactions*	Unchanged	11, 14, 15, 20
June, 1973	30	*Reporting the Results of Operations*	Unchanged	4, 11, 13, 16
June, 1973	31	*Disclosure of Lease Commitments by Lessees*	Superseded	

ACCOUNTING PRINCIPLES BOARD STATEMENTS

Date Issued	Statement Number	Title	Status	Chapter Number(s) in Which Reference Occurs
April, 1962	1	*Statement by the Accounting Principles Board* (on Accounting Research Studies Nos. 1 and 3)	Unchanged	
September, 1967	2	*Disclosure of Supplemental Financial Information by Diversified Companies*	Superseded	
June, 1969	3	*Financial Statements Restated for General Price-Level Changes*	Unchanged	25
October, 1970	4	*Basic Concepts and Accounting Principles Underlying Financial Statements of Business Enterprises*	Unchanged	1, 3, 4, 26

FINANCIAL ACCOUNTING STANDARDS BOARD STATEMENTS OF FINANCIAL ACCOUNTING STANDARDS

Date Issued	Statement Number	Title	Status	Chapter Number(s) in Which Reference Occurs
December, 1973	1	*Disclosure of Foreign Currency Translation Information*	Amended	
October, 1974	2	*Accounting for Research and Development Costs*	Unchanged	13, 22
December, 1974	3	*Reporting Accounting Changes in Interim Financial Statements*	Unchanged	26
March, 1975	4	*Reporting Gains and Losses from Extinguishment of Debt*	Unchanged	4, 15
March, 1975	5	*Accounting for Contingencies*	Amended	3, 5, 20, 22
May, 1975	6	*Classification of Short-Term Obligations Expected to be Refinanced*	Unchanged	3, 10, 15
June, 1975	7	*Accounting and Reporting by Development Stage Enterprises*	Unchanged	4, 11, 13
October, 1975	8	*Accounting for the Translation of Foreign Currency Transactions and Foreign Currency Financial Statements*	Unchanged	
October, 1975	9	*Accounting for Income Taxes — Oil and Gas Producing Companies*	Unchanged	
October, 1975	10	*Extension of "Grandfather" Provisions for Business Combinations*	Unchanged	
December, 1975	11	*Accounting for Contingencies — Transition Method*	Unchanged	22

FASB STATEMENTS (continued)

Date Issued	Statement Number	Title	Status	Chapter Number(s) in Which Reference Occurs
December, 1975	12	*Accounting for Certain Marketable Securities*	Unchanged	3, 5, 14
November, 1976	13	*Accounting for Leases*	Unchanged	17
December, 1976	14	*Financial Reporting for Segments of a Business Enterprise*	Unchanged	26

FINANCIAL ACCOUNTING STANDARDS BOARD EXPOSURE DRAFTS
(Proposed Statements)

Date Issued	Title	Chapter Number(s) in Which Reference Occurs
July, 1976	*Prior Period Adjustments*	4
October, 1976	*Accounting for Income Taxes in Interim Periods*	
December, 1976	*Accounting by Debtors and Creditors for Troubled Debt Restructurings*	15

FINANCIAL ACCOUNTING STANDARDS BOARD DISCUSSION MEMORANDUMS
UNDER STUDY AT JANUARY 1, 1977

Date Issued	Title	Chapter Number(s) in Which Reference Occurs
March, 1975	*Criteria for Determining Materiality*	1
October, 1975	*Accounting and Reporting for Employee Benefit Plans*	17
August, 1976	*Accounting for Business Combinations and Purchased Intangibles*	
December, 1976	*Conceptual Framework for Financial Accounting and Reporting: Elements of Financial Statements and Their Measurement*	1
December, 1976	*Financial Accounting and Reporting in the Extractive Industries*	12

Index

A